Alan Greenwood launched *Vintage Guitar* magazine in 1986. *Vintage Guitar* is the largest monthly publication for guitar collectors, enthusiasts, and dealers. He also publishes *Vintage Guitar*® Online at www.VintageGuitar.com, and *The Official Vintage Guitar Magazine Price Guide*. His collection includes several vintage instruments from the '20s to the '80s, as well as newer production and custom-made guitars, amps, effects, lap steels, and ukuleles. He lives in Bismarck, North Dakota.

Gil Hembree began collecting guitars in 1966 while working at Kitt's Music, in Washington, D.C. Familiarity with the professional musicians playing on Georgetown's M-Street allowed him to dabble in early buy-sell, but his academic interest in finance led to a corporate job in Michigan. Throughout his financial career he played in bands, and searched for original-owner vintage guitars in cities like Flint, Saginaw, Bay City, Port Huron, Pontiac, Battle Creek, and Kalamazoo. In 2000, freshly retired from corporate finance, he became the co-author of *the Official Vintage Guitar Price Guide*. In 2007, the Hal Leonard Corp released his biography of Ted McCarty: *Gibson Guitars: Ted McCarty's Golden Era: 1948-1966*. After residing in Michigan for 35 years, Hembree and his wife, Jane, relocated to Austin, Texas.

The Official Vintage Guitar® magazine Price Guide

By Alan Greenwood and Gil Hembree

Vintage Guitar Books
An imprint of Vintage Guitar Inc., PO Box 7301, Bismarck, ND 58507, (701) 255-1197, Fax (701) 255-0250, publishers of *Vintage Guitar*® magazine and Vintage Guitar® Online at www.VintageGuitar.com. Vintage Guitar is a registered trademark of Vintage Guitar, Inc.

ISBN: 978-1-884883-23-1

Cover photos: 1958 Gibson Les Paul Custom: VG Archive/Dave Rogers. 1952 Fender Telecaster: VG Archive/Alan Greenwood. 1955 Gretsch Round Up 6130: VG Archive/Dave Hinson. 1961 Fender Stratocaster: VG Archive/Dave Rogers. 1940 Gibson SJ-200: VG Archive. 1960s Vox Streamliner 1960s: VG Archive/Willie's American Guitars. 1958 Gibson Les Paul: VG Archive. **Back photos:** A 1969 Fender Telecaster and a 1963 Fender Deluxe Amp: VG Archive/Alan Greenwood/Ward Meeker.

Cover Design: Doug Yellow Bird/Vintage Guitar, Inc.

Printed in the United States of America

EXCLUSIVELY DISTRIBUTED BY
HAL•LEONARD® CORPORATION
7777 W. BLUEMOUND RD. P.O. BOX 13819
MILWAUKEE, WISCONSIN 53213

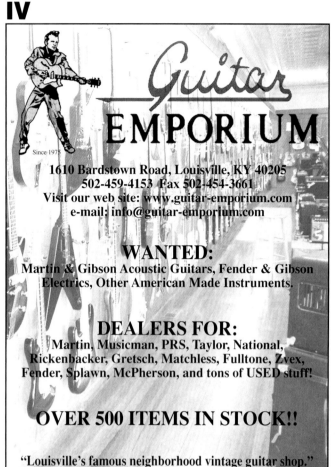
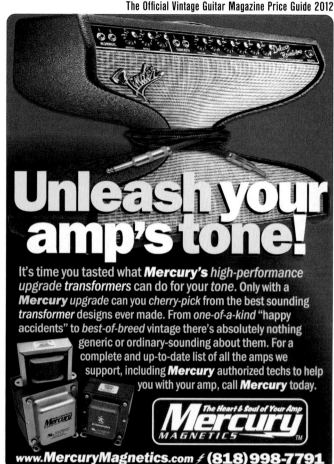

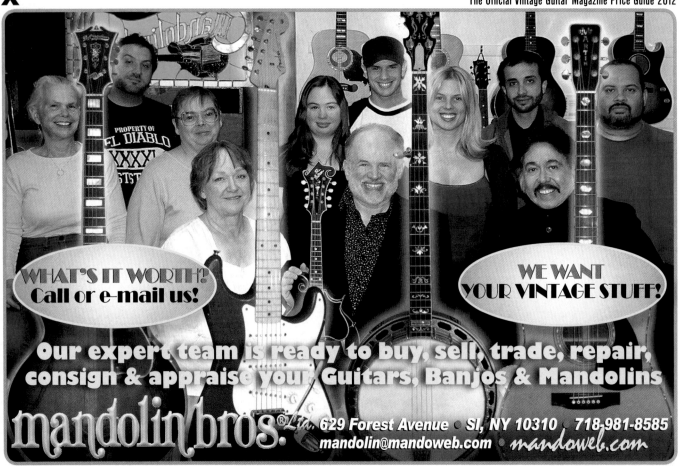

TABLE OF CONTENTS

Using the Price Guide XVI

Introduction XVIII

Guitars 1

Basses 309

Amps 363

Effects 459

Steels & Laps 505

Mandolins 519

Ukuleles 545

Banjo Ukuleles 557

Banjos 559

Bibliography 570

Dealer Directory 571

Manufacturer Directory 574

Tech/Repair 575

Index 576

1952 (LEFT) and 1953 Gibson Les Paul goldtops with a Gibson GA-400 amp. Photo: VG Archive.

USING THE GUIDE

Understanding the Values

The values presented in *The Official Vintage Guitar Price Guide* are for excellent-condition, all-original instruments. Our definition of excellent condition allows for some wear, but the instrument should be well-maintained, with no significant blemishes, wear, repairs, or damage. All-original means the instrument has the parts and finish it had when it left the factory. Replacement parts and refinishes can greatly affect value, as can the appropriate case (or cover) in excellent condition. In many instances, a "wrong" case will not greatly affect value, but with the top-dollar collectibles, it can.

We use a range of excellent-condition values, as there is seldom agreement on a single price point for vintage and used instruments. A tighter range suggests there is a general consensus, while a wide range means the market isn't in strict agreement. A mint-condition instrument can be worth more than the values listed here, and anything in less-than-excellent condition will have a reduced value. And, of course, when dealing with high-end collectibles, values can quickly change.

Repairs affect value differently. Some repair is necessary to keep an instrument in playable condition. The primary concern is the level of expertise displayed in the work and an amateurish repair will lower the value more than one that is obviously professional. A refinished guitar, regardless of the quality of the work, is generally worth 50% or less of the values shown in *The Guide*. A poorly executed neck repair or significant body repair can mean a 50% reduction in a guitar's value. A professional re-fret or minor, nearly invisible body repair will reduce a guitar's value by only 5%.

The values in the *The Guide* are for unfaded finishes. Slight color fade reduces the value by only 5%, but heavily faded examples can reduce the value by 25% to 50%.

Finding the Information

The table of contents shows the major sections and each is organized in alphabetical order by brand, then by model. In a few instances, there are separate sections for a company's most popular models, especially when there is a large variety of similar instruments. Examples include Fender's Stratocasters, Telecasters, Precision and Jazz basses, and Gibson's Les Pauls. The outer top corner of each page uses a dictionary-type header that tells the models or brands on that page. This provides a quick way to navigate each section. The index at the back shows the page numbers for each type of instrument, by brand, and is a great place to start when looking for a specific model or brand.

The Guide has excellent brand histories and in most cases the guitar section has the most detailed information for each brand. When possible, *The Guide* lists each model's years of availability and any design changes that affect values.

More information on many of the brands covered in *The Guide* is available in the pages of *Vintage Guitar* magazine and on the "Features" section of our website, www.VintageGuitar.com.

The authors of *The Guide* always appreciate your help, so if you find any errors, or have additional information on certain brands or models, we'd like to hear from you. We are especially looking for info on any brand not yet listed. Whatever you may have to contribute, feel free to drop us a line at Alan@VintageGuitar.com.

New Retail Pricing Information

The Guide continues to add information on individual luthiers and smaller shops. It's difficult to develop values on used instruments produced by these builders because much of their output is custom work, production is low, and/or they haven't been producing for a period of time sufficient to see their instruments enter the used/resale market. To give you an idea about their instruments, we've developed five grades of retail values for new instruments. These convey only the prices charged by the builder, and are not indicative of the quality of construction. *The Guide* applies this scale to all builders and manufacturers of new instruments.

The five retail-price grades are:
Budget - up to $250,
Intermediate - $251 to $1,000,
Professional - $1,001 to $3,000,
Premium - $3,001 to $10,000,
Presentation - more than $10,000.

The Guide uses the terms "production" and "custom" to differentiate between builders who do true custom work versus those who offer standard production models. "Production" means the company offers specific models, with no variations. "Custom" means they do only custom orders, and "production/custom" indicates they do both. Here's an example:

Greenwood Guitars

1990-present. Luthier Jack Greenwood builds premium-grade, custom, solidbody guitars in St. Paul, Minnesota. He also builds basses.

This tells who the builder is, the type of instruments they build, where they build them, how long they've been operating under that brand, that they do only custom work, and that they ask between $3,000 and $10,000 for their guitars (premium-grade).

We've applied the retail price grades and production and/or custom labels to most new-instrument manufacturers.

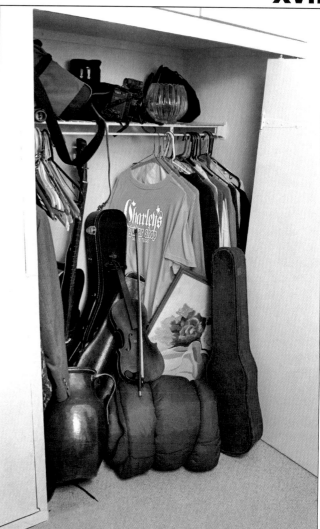

INTRODUCTION

The guitar has long been a dominant instrument in the music trades. According to the International Music Products Association (NAMM), in the last eight years, an average of nearly three million new guitars were sold annually. That's about 32 million instruments in that span alone, and when you consider the hundreds of thousands made during the guitar boom of the late '60s along with those made from '70 to '02 and toss onto the pile those made since the 1830s, there exists an enormous potential market for used, collectible, and vintage guitars.

That market has not always been important. In 1966, a used guitar or amp wasn't worth much to a traditional music store; often, they were deemed a nuisance, unable to generate profit, and thus were practically given away. However, by the '70s, a few stores had begun to focus on used gear, and the market began to evolve. In the '80s, guitar shows became successful. In the mid '90s, musical-instrument chain stores began to compete for used gear with independent shops, and by the late '90s, internet auctions became a major player.

Today, guitarists, collectors, independent shops, guitar-show promoters, music-industry corporations, auction houses, and internet businesses all compete for a share in a market that includes tens of millions of instruments.

What are these guitars worth? *The Official Vintage Guitar Price Guide* provides guidance pricing for everything from a $150 Bradford flat-top to a $400,000 Martin D-45, a $100 Teisco electric to a $325,000 Gibson Explorer, a $150 Fender Acoustasonic amp to a $45,000 Dumble Overdrive Special amp. *The Guide* covers instruments made from the 1830s through 2012. And this year, we've reintroduced the section on banjos!

Human nature is such that people are typically most curious about high-end vintage instruments. So, this introduction will focus on that segment. But, we want to stress that because this is a complex market and some high-end instruments show decreases in value from 2011 to 2012, there are many

THE 42 INDEX

FROM FENDER
1952 blond Precision Bass
1952 blond Esquire
1953 blond Telecaster
1956 sunburst Stratocaster
1958 sunburst Jazzmaster
1958 blond Telecaster
1960 sunburst Stratocaster
1961 sunburst, stack knob, Jazz Bass
1962 sunburst, 3-knob, Jazz Bass
1963 sunburst Telecaster Custom
1963 sunburst Esquire Custom
1964 Lake Placid Blue Jaguar
1964 sunburst Precision Bass
1966 Candy Apple Red Stratocaster

FROM GIBSON
1952 sunburst ES-5
1952 Les Paul Model
1954 Les Paul Jr.
1958 sunburst EB-2 Bass
1958 Les Paul Custom
1958 natural ES-335

1958 Super 400CES
1959 Les Paul Jr.
1959 J-160E
1961 sunburst ES-355
1961 Les Paul SG
1964 sunburst Thunderbird II Bass
1965 EB-3 Bass
1969 sunburst Citation

FROM MARTIN
1931 OM-28
1935 00-28
1935 D-18
1944 scalloped-brace 000-28
1944 D-28
1950 D-28
1958 000-18
1959 D-18
1959 D-28E
1962 D-28
1967 GT-75
1968 000-18
1969 N-20
1969 D-45

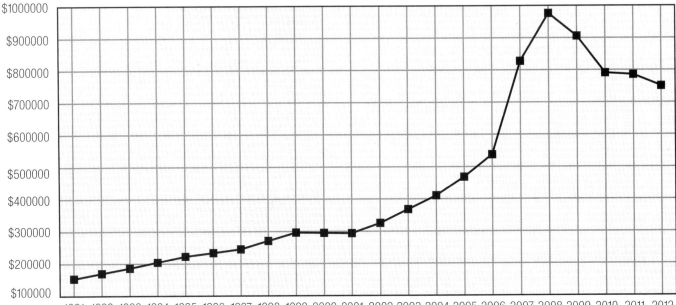

The 42 Guitar Index 1991 - 2012

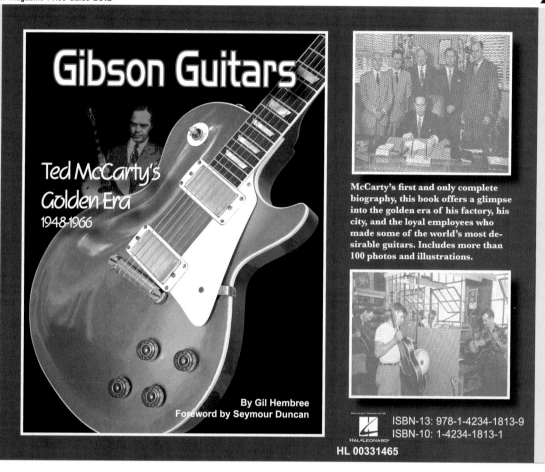

instruments and amplifier models selling at increased values. Additionally, there are variations in the prices dealers charge. For the sake of discussion, we categorize sellers in two ways – idealists and realists, and *The Guide* reconciles the two. Idealists are those who carry a lifetime of experience in vintage guitars, and have seen or studied every nuance of the instruments, and their chronology. They sell guitars for what they think they're worth. Realists, on the other hand, believe a guitar is only worth what someone is willing to pay for it. Realists drop their asking price when they have to.

An idealist thinks an all-original, "excellent-condition" (looks/sounds fantastic, plays well, no stories or excuses) 1957 Fender Stratocaster tremolo-equipped model with sunburst finish carries an ideal selling price of about $35,000. A realist thinks the same guitar is worth $25,000 to $32,000 if he can find a cash-paying buyer. Most guitars are in "very good" condition – not excellent, so an excellent-condition guitar is rare, which is one reason it will sell for a higher price.

Historically, idealists have been the backbone of the market, and the well-capitalized ones have a bias to excellent, all-original guitars, and they appreciate the quality and history of vintage guitars. They have long been willing to hold them in personal collections just as well as sell them. This type of market worked well for most of the last two and a half decades, but when the economy declined, consumer confidence followed, and the market became less than ideal.

The difference between idealists and realists in the guitar market has never been greater than it is today. Idealists, thanks to their tenure and associations, have "better" guitars and "better" customers (or at least some with more cash!), so they often sell instruments at higher prices. For several decades, if a group of idealists agreed that a certain guitar was worth a certain amount, that amount became the precedent value of the instrument.

Today, realists affect the market slightly more than idealists because they're more likely to reduce selling prices. Both contend with scarcity; we often think in terms of the number of original/excellent/rare guitars. But in today's market there is also a scarcity of buyers who are willing to pay $35,000 for a '57 Stratocaster.

In the '07 *Guide*, a '57 Strat was worth $50,000, and at the time, some idealists thought '50s Strats and '50s Gibson Les Paul goldtops were going to be the next quarter-million-dollar guitar (following in the footsteps of the '59 Gibson Les Paul Standard). The purpose of the *The Guide* is to offer pricing data and reconcile the views of the realist, idealist, and the speculator – someone who buys a guitar with the intent of making an outsized profit.

So, what is a '57 Strat worth? Having researched the market and listened to everyone including realists, idealists, speculators, auction houses, internet auctions, guitar show promoters, the Vintage Guitar survey team, and everyday customers, a '57 Stratocaster, in all-original/excellent condition has a 2012 precedent value of between $25,000 and $32,000. Some idealists disagree, but we feel a seller has a better chance of selling it within one year if his asking price is $25,000 to $32,000. Part of the reason we see it as being worth slightly less than the idealist is there are

GUITAR DEALER PARTICIPANTS

The information refined on these pages comes from several sources, including the input of many knowledgeable guitar dealers. Without the help of these individuals, it would be very hard for us to provide the information here and in each issue of *Vintage Guitar* magazine. We deeply appreciate the time and effort they provide.

Andy Eder
Andy's Guitars

Les Haynie & Tim Grear
Blue Moon Music

Bob Page & Tim Page
Buffalo Brothers

Dave Belzer & Drew Berlin
Burst Brothers

David Kalt
Chicago Music Exchange

Joe Gallenberger
Cream City Music

Dave Rogers
Dave's Guitar Shop

Andrew Winn
Drew's Vintage Guitars

Stan Werbin & S.J. "Frog" Forgey
Elderly Instruments

Richard Johnston
Gryphon Strings

Vallis Kolbeck
GuitarVille (Seattle)

Kennard Machol & Leonard Coulson
Intermountain Guitar & Banjo

Jim Singleton
Jim's Guitars

Kevin Borden & Ben Sopranzetti
Kebo's BassWorks

Dave Hinson
Killer Vintage

Timm Kummer
Kummer's Vintage Instruments

Buzzy Levine
Lark Street Music

Larry Wexer
Laurence Wexer, Ltd.

Bob November
McKenzie River Music

Lowell Levinger
Players Vintage Instruments

Howie Statland
Rivington Guitars

Mike Reeder
Mike's Music

Eliot Michael
Rumble Seat Music

Mike Rock
Sam Ash Music Stores

Eric Schoenberg
Schoenberg Guitars

Richard Friedman & David Davidson
We Buy Guitars

Nate Westgor
Willie's American Guitars

Stan Jay
Mandolin Brothers

*Alan Greenwood with his 1966 Gibson ES-335
(serial number 853677) in faded Pelham Blue.*

*Gil Hembree with his 1957 Fender
Stratocaster, serial number -19572.*

more '57 Strats for sale than there are people willing to buy them. Even idealists, who are unwilling to sell for $25,000, agree there are too many '57 Strats for sale, but they also feel the situation is temporary and their higher asking price is a reflection of the true long-term value of the guitar.

The '57 Strat as just one example, and that idealism applies just as well to '57 Silvertone Model 1382 Thin Twin guitar worth $1,100. Think about it. $1,100 for a Silvertone? Is this not a $100 guitar? Idealists who specialize in vintage Silvertones have shown this student-grade guitar has relative value, and nice original/excellent examples sell rather quickly.

The Guide uses The 42 Guitar Index to demonstrate how the values of expensive vintage guitars have changed since 1991. The average value of a guitar in the current Index is $17,876. Chart 1 shows that the index value has increased since 1991; the average annual increase from 1991 to 2012 is 8.9 percent. Focusing on the most recent year, 31 percent of the 42 guitars increased in value, 14 percent did not materially change, and 55 percent dropped in value. The 2012 Index value of $750,800 decreased by 4.4 percent

from the 2011 level.

Specifically, for the three brands in the Index, from 2011 to 2012, the value of the 14-guitar Fender group dropped by 3.7 percent, while the 14-guitar Gibson group value decreased by 6.1 percent and the 14-guitar Martin group value declined by 3.7 percent. But, keeping that in mind, the only way to truly find out what is happening is to check your favorite instrument or amplifier in the *2012 Guide*.

The Official Vintage Guitar Price Guide is published annually because our research suggests it takes about a year to establish a new precedent value, which represents the "new normal" in the market. The evolution to a new normal takes time, and only after multiple dealers adjust prices will it become a new precedent value. These guitar dealers are the realists that we referenced earlier; they alter prices in order to stimulate sales. But realists can also increase prices if they discover a shortage for a particular guitar. Even in this market, a new precedent price does not always mean a lower price.

We are careful when we analyze data. Over a 12-month pe-

BUILDER UPDATES AND CORRECTIONS

If you produce instruments for sale and would like to be included in the next *VG Price Guide*, send your infomation to alan@VintageGuitar.com. Include info on the types of instruments you build, model names and prices, yearly production, the year you started, where you are located and a short bio about yourself.

If you spot errors in the information about brands and models in this guide, or have information on a brand you'd like to see included, please contact us at the above email address. Your help is appreciated.

riod, quick-money sales, speculative purchases, and most importantly, multiple reasonable exchanges and rational bargains can be analyzed to discover new precedents. And, after our analysis is completed, we do not average the data and take a median or a mean. We select the "best data" in the population and use that to establish a new precedent value.

While the market has changed in the last year, underlying valuation principals remain. The primary reason vintage guitars are valuable is their relevance to contemporary music and the fact they are considered superior in terms of sound, build quality, and playability. Another factor is buyers' preferences for beauty, quality, history, and provenance. These attributes do not change.
- Gil Hembree

More Information

VintageGuitar.com, the official website of *Vintage Guitar* magazine, is updated continuously from the magazine's article archive. This ever-expanding resource includes interviews with noted guitarists, reviews of new gear and recordings, and historical information on many of the brands and models covered in this book. Of course, you can read more on classic guitars and your favorite players each month in *Vintage Guitar*.

If a model is missing from *The Guide*, or if you'd like something clarified, please drop a line to Gil@VintageGuitar.com. If you are a builder and would like to be included, want to correct your info, or have information on your favorite brand, drop a line to Alan@VintageGuitar.com.

Acknowledgements

The Guide is a massive undertaking. We use many sources to determine values, but the vintage instrument dealers who give their time and expertise to provide market information play an important role. Many provide info on brands and models, and they are acknowledged on page XX.

Randy Klimpert provided information and photos in the ukulele section. Several of the brand histories used in this edition are based on the work of longtime *VG* contributor Michael Wright. Stan Werbin, of Elderly Instruments, provided many new photos for the banjo section. Hundreds of readers and builders have contributed other photos.

Several people at *VG* played an important role, as well. Wanda Huether does an initial edit of text and enters the data. Doug Yellow Bird designs the cover and lays out pages. Jeanine Shea and Dawn Flanagin assist with proofreading, and Jeanine helps James Jiskra and Barbara Seerman compile ads and the dealer directory. Ward Meeker helps with editing. We thank all of them for their usual fine work.

We always welcome suggestions, criticisms, and ideas to improve future editions of *The Guide*. Contact us at *Vintage Guitar*, Inc., PO Box 7301, Bismarck, ND 58507, or by e-mail to Gil@VintageGuitar.com or Alan@VintageGuitar.com.

Thank you,

Alan Greenwood and Gil Hembree

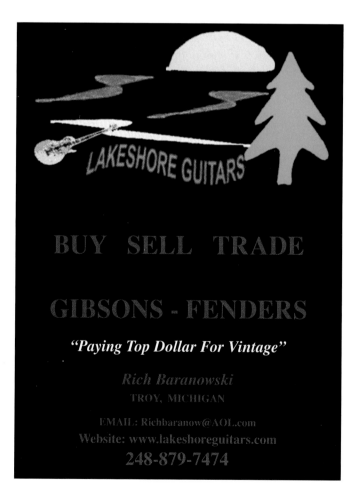

GUITARS

GUITARS

MODEL		EXC. COND.	
YEAR	FEATURES	LOW	HIGH

A Fuller Sound Steel String

Abyss NSII Archtop

17th Street Guitars
2004-2009. Founded by Dave Levine and Colin Liebich. Professional grade, production/custom, solidbody guitars built by luthier John Carruthers in Venice, California.

A Fuller Sound
1998-present. Professional and premium grade, custom nylon and steel-string flat-tops built by Luthier Warren Fuller in Oakland, California.

Abel
1994-present. Custom aircraft-grade aluminum body, wood neck, guitars built by twins Jim and Jeff Abel in Evanston, Wyoming. They offered the Abel Axe from '94-'96 and 2000-'01, and still do custom orders. They also made the Rogue Aluminator in the late '90s.

Axe
1994-1996. Offset double-cut aluminum body with dozens of holes in the body, wood neck, various colors by annodizing the aluminum body. Abel Axe logo on the headstock.

1994-1996	Non-trem or trem	$750	$950

Abilene
Budget and intermediate grade, production, acoustic and electric guitars imported by Samick.

Abyss
See listing under Pederson Custom Guitars.

Acme
1960s. Imported inexpensive copy electric guitar models for the student market.

Acoustic
Ca. 1965-ca. 1987, 2001-2005, 2008-present. Mainly known for solidstate amps, the Acoustic Control Corp. of Los Angeles, California, did offer guitars and basses from around '69 to late '74. The brand was revived by Samick on a line of amps.

Black Widow
1969-1970, 1972-1974. Both versions featured a unique black equal double-cut body with German carve, 2 pickups, a zero fret, and a protective spider design pad on back. The early version (called the AC500 Black Widow) had 22 frets, an ebonite 'board, and pickups with 1 row of adjustable polepieces. The later version was 24 frets, a rosewood 'board, and humbuckers with 2 rows of adjustable pole pieces (some '72s have the older style pickup). The jack and 4 control knobs were configured differently on the 2 versions, Acoustic outsourced the production of the guitars, possibly to Japan, but final 200 or so guitars produced by Semie Moseley. The AC700 Black Widow 12-string was also available for '69-'70.

1969-1970	2 pickups	$1,100	$1,375
1972-1974	1 pickup	$1,000	$1,225

Agile
1985-present. Budget grade, production, acoustic and electric guitars imported by Rondo Music of Union, New Jersey. They also offer mandolins.

Aims
Ca. 1972-ca. 1976. Aims (American International Music Sales, Inc.) instruments, distributed by Randall Instruments in the mid-'70s, were copies of classic American guitar and bass models. They also offered a line of Aims amps during the same time.

Airline
Ca. 1958-1968, 2004-present. Airline originally was a brand used by Montgomery Ward on acoustic, electric archtop and solidbody guitars and basses, amplifiers, steels, and possibly banjos and mandolins. Instruments manufactured by Kay, Harmony and Valco. In '04, the brand was revived on a line of imported intermediate grade, production, reissues from Eastwood guitars (see that listing for new info).

Acoustic Res-O-Glas Resonator
1964. Res-o-glas, coverplate with M-shaped holes, asymmetrical peghead.

1964		$725	$850

Amp-In-Case Model
1960s. Double-cut, single pickup, short scale guitar with amplifier built into the case, Airline on grille.

1960s		$450	$575

Archtop Acoustic
1950-1960s	Higher-end	$400	$500
1950-1960s	Lower-end	$125	$175

Electric Hollowbody
1950s	Kay Barney Kessel		
	Artist copy	$625	$750
1960s	ES-175 copy	$475	$575
1960s	Harmony H-54		
	Rocket II copy	$425	$525
1960s	Harmony H-75 copy	$475	$575
1960s	Harmony H-76		
	Rocket III, 3 pu	$575	$675

Electric Res-O-Glas
1960s. Res-o-glas is a form of fiberglass. The bodies and sometimes the necks were made of this material.

1960s	Jack White's		
	Red Jetson style	$2,000	$2,400
1960s	JB Hutto, red	$2,000	$2,400
1960s	Other styles, 1 pickup	$600	$700
1960s	Other styles, 2 pickups	$700	$900

Electric Res-O-Glas Resonator
1960s. Res-o-glas is a form of fiberglass. These models have resonator cones in the body.

1960s		$750	$900

Electric Solidbody (Standard Lower-End)
1960s		$150	$350

Electric Solidbody (Deluxe Higher-End)
1950s-1960s. Appointments may include multiple pickups, block inlays, additional logos, more binding.

1950s		$700	$900
1960s		$600	$750

MODEL YEAR	FEATURES	EXC. COND. LOW	HIGH
Flat-Top Acoustic			
1950-1960s	Higher-end, 14"-15" body	$425	$550
1950-1960s	Lower-end, 13" body	$125	$175

Alamo

1947-1982. Founded by Charles Eilenberg, Milton Fink, and Southern Music, San Antonio, Texas, and distributed by Bruno & Sons. Alamo started out making radios, phonographs, and instrument cases. In '49 they added amplifiers and lap steels. From '60 to '70, the company produced beginner-grade solidbody and hollow-core body electric Spanish guitars. The amps were all-tube until the '70s. Except for a few Valco-made examples, all instruments were built in San Antonio.

Electric Hollowbody			
1950-1970s	Higher-end	$500	$600
1950-1970s	Lower-end	$350	$425
Electric Solidbody			
1950-1970s	Higher-end	$500	$600
1950-1970s	Lower-end	$350	$425

Alamo Guitars

1999-2008. The Alamo brand was revived for a line of handcrafted, professional grade, production/custom, guitars by Alamo Music Products, which also offers Robin and Metropolitan brand guitars and Rio Grande pickups.

Tonemonger

2002-2005. Ash or African Fakimba offset double cut solidbody, 3 single coils, tremolo.

2002-2005		$750	$900

Alan Carruth

1970-present. Professional and premium grade, production/custom, classical and archtop guitars built by luthier Alan Carruth in Newport, New Hampshire. He also builds violins, harps and dulcimers. He started out building dulcimers and added guitars in '74.

Albanus

Late 1950s-1973. Luthier Carl Albanus Johnson built around 100 high quality archtop guitars in Chicago, Illinois. He died in '73. He also built violins.

Alberico, Fabrizio

1998-present. Luthier Fabrizio Alberico builds his premium grade, custom, flat-top and classical guitars in Cheltenham, Ontario.

Alden

2005-present. Located in Plympton, Massachusetts, owners Ian Campbell and David Nabreski import their intermediate grade, production, electric guitars from China.

Alden (Chicago)

1960s. Chicago's Alden was a department store and mail-order house offering instruments from Chicago builders such as Harmony.

H-45 Stratotone

1960s. Alden's version of the H45 Stratotone Mars model, single plain cover pickup.

1960s		$375	$450

Alembic

1969-present. Premium and presentation grade, production/custom, guitars, baritones, and 12-strings built in Santa Rosa, California. They also build basses. Established in San Francisco by Ron and Susan Wickersham, Alembic started out as a studio working with the Grateful Dead and other bands on a variety of sound gear. By '70 they were building custom basses, later adding guitars and cabinets. By '73, standardized models were being offered.

California Special

1988-2009. Double-cut neck-thru solidbody, six-on-a-side tuners, various colors.

1988-2009		$2,000	$2,500

Orion

1990-present. Offset double-cut glued neck solidbody, various colors.

1990-2010		$2,000	$2,500

Series I

Early-1970s-present. Neck-thru, double-cut solidbody, bookmatched koa, black walnut core, 3 pickups, optional body styles available, natural.

1970-1980s	12-string	$4,100	$5,200
1970-1980s	6-string	$3,900	$5,000

Alfieri Guitars

1990-present. Luthier Don Alfieri builds his premium and presentation grade, custom/production, acoustic and classical guitars in Long Island, New York.

Alhambra

1930s. The Alhambra brand was most likely used by a music studio (or distributor) on instruments made by others, including Regal-built resonator instruments.

Allen Guitars

1982-present. Premium grade, production resonators, steel-string flat-tops, and mandolins built by Luthier Randy Allen, Colfax, California.

Alleva-Coppolo Basses and Guitars

1995-present. Professional and premium grade, custom/production, solidbody electric guitars built by luthier Jimmy Coppolo in Dallas, Texas for '95-'97, in New York City for '98-2008, and since in Upland, California. He also builds basses.

Aloha

1935-1960s. Private branded by Aloha Publishing and Musical Instruments Company, Chicago, Illinois. Made by others. There was also the Aloha Manufacturing Company of Honolulu which made musical instruments from around 1911 to the late '20s.

2006 Agile Cool Cat Prestige
Jon Way

1959 Airline 7216
Zak Izbinsky

4   Alosa – American Conservatory

MODEL YEAR	FEATURES	EXC. COND. LOW	HIGH

Alternative Guitar and Amplifier Company Alien

Alosa
1947-1958. Luthier Alois Sandner built these acoustic archtop guitars in Germany.

Alpha
1970s-1980s. One of the brand names of guitars built in the Egmond plant in Holland. Sold by Martin for a while in the 1980s.

Alray
1967. Electrics and acoustics built by the Holman-Woodell guitar factory in Neodesha, Kansas, who also marketed similar models under the Holman brand.

Alternative Guitar and Amplifier Company
2006-present. Intermediate grade, custom/production, solidbody electric guitars made in Piru, California, by luthiers Mal Stich and Sal Gonzales and imported from Korea under the Alternative Guitar and Amplifier Company, and Mal n' Sal brands. They also build basses and have future plans for amps.

AlumiSonic
2006-present. Luthier Ray Matter builds his production/custom, professional grade, aluminum/wood hybrid electric guitars in Bohemia and West Islip, New York.

Alvarez
1965-present. Intermediate and professional grade, production, acoustic guitars imported by St. Louis Music. They also offer lap steels, banjos and mandolins. Initially high-quality handmade guitars Yairi made by K. (Kazuo) Yairi were exclusively distributed, followed by lower-priced Alvarez line. In '90 the Westone brand used on electric guitars and basses was replaced with the Alvarez name; these Alvarez electrics were offered until '02. Many Alvarez electric models designed by luthier Dana Sutcliffe; several models designed by Dan Armstrong.
Classic I, II, III
1994-1999. Designs based on classic solidbody American models.

1994-1999		$200	$250

Flat-Top (Lower-End)
1966-present. Beginner-grade instruments, solid or laminate tops, laminate back and sides, little or no extra appointments. Some are acoustic/electric.

1970s		$75	$100
1980s		$75	$100
1990s		$75	$100

Flat-Top (Mid-Level)
1966-present. Solid tops, laminated back and sides, lower appointments such as bound 'boards and headstocks, nickel hardware and pearl inlay.

1970s		$100	$200
1980s		$100	$200
1990s		$100	$200

1997 Alvarez Yairi DY90
Jon Way

Flat-Top (Mid-to-Higher-End)
1966-present. Solid spruce tops, solid mahogany or rosewood backs, laminated mahogany or rosewood sides, may have scalloped bracing, mid-level appointments like abalone headstock inlay, soundhole rosettes and herringbone body binding.

1970s		$200	$400
1980s		$200	$400
1990s		$200	$400

Flat-Top (Higher-End)
1966-present. Solid rosewood and/or mahogany backs and sides, solid spruce tops, may have dovetail neck joint, highest appointments like abalone inlay and real maple binding.

1980s		$400	$600
1990s		$400	$600

Alvarez Yairi
1966-present. Alvarez Yairi guitars are hand-crafted and imported by St. Louis Music.
Flat-Top (Mid-Level)
Solid top of cedar or spruce, depending on model, mid-level appointments.

1970s		$300	$375
1980s		$325	$400
1990s		$375	$475
2000s		$375	$475

Flat-Top (Higher-End)
Solid top of cedar or spruce, depending on model, higher-end appointments.

1970s		$600	$725
1980s		$625	$750
1990s		$700	$850
2000s		$750	$925

Alvarez, Juan
1952-present. Professional and premium grade, production/custom, classical and flamenco guitars made in Madrid, Spain, originally by luthier Juan Alvarez Gil and now by son Juan Miguel Alvarez.

American Acoustech
1993-2001. Production steel string flat-tops made by Tom Lockwood (former Guild plant manager) and Dave Stutzman (of Stutzman's Guitar Center) as ESVL Inc. in Rochester, New York.

American Archtop Guitars
1995-present. Premium and presentation grade, custom 6- and 7-string archtops by luthier Dale Unger, in Stroudsburg, Pennsylvania.

American Conservatory (Lyon & Healy)
Late-1800s-early-1900s. Guitars, mandolins and harp guitars built by Chicago's Lyon & Healy and sold mainly through various catalog retailers. Mid-level instruments above the quality of Lyon & Healy's Lakeside brand, and generally under their Washburn brand.

MODEL YEAR	FEATURES	EXC. COND. LOW	HIGH
Acoustic			
1920s	Spanish 6-string	$500	$575
1920s	Tenor 4-string	$500	$575

G2740 Monster Bass

Early-mid-1900s. Two 6-string neck (one fretless), acoustic flat-top harp guitar, spruce top, birch back and sides with rosewood stain, natural. Their catalog claimed it was "Indispensable to the up-to-date mandolin and guitar club."

1917		$3,000	$4,000

Style G Series Harp Guitar

Early-1900s. Two 6-string necks with standard tuners, 1 neck fretless, rosewood back and sides, spruce top, fancy rope colored wood inlay around soundhole, sides and down the back center seam.

1917	Natural	$3,000	$4,000

American Showster

1986-2004. Established by Bill Meeker and David Haines, Bayville, New Jersey, building guitars shaped like classic car tailfins or motorcycle gas tanks. The Custom Series was made in the U.S.A., while the Standard Series (introduced in '97) was made in Czechoslovakia. They also made a bass.

AS-57 Classic (Original '57)

1987-2004. Body styled like a '57 Chevy tail fin, basswood body, bolt-on neck, 1 humbucker or 3 single-coil pickups, various colors.

1987-2004		$1,650	$1,900

Ampeg

1949-present. Founded in '49 by Everett Hull as the Ampeg Bassamp Company in New York and has built amplifiers throughout its history. In '62 the company added instruments with the introduction of their Baby Bass and from '63 to '65, they carried a line of guitars and basses built by Burns of London and imported from England. In '66 the company introduced its own line of basses. In '67, Ampeg was acquired by Unimusic, Inc. From '69-'71 contracted with Dan Armstrong to produce lucite "see-through" guitars and basses with replaceable slide-in pickup design. In '71 the company merged with Magnavox. Beginning around '72 until '75, Ampeg imported the Stud Series copy guitars from Japan. Ampeg shut down production in the spring of '80. MTI bought the company and started importing amps. In '86 St. Louis Music purchased the company. In '97 Ampeg introduced new and reissue American-made guitar and bass models. They discontinued the guitar line in '01, but offered the Dan Armstrong plexi guitar again starting in '05, adding wood-bodied versions in '08. They also offer a bass. In '05 LOUD Technologies acquired SLM and the Ampeg brand.

AMG1

1999-2001. Dan Amstrong guitar features, but with mahogany body with quilted maple top, 2 P-90-style or humbucker-style pickups.

1999-2001	Humbuckers, gold hardware	$775	$900
1999-2001	Kent Armstrong pickups	$350	$425

MODEL YEAR	FEATURES	EXC. COND. LOW	HIGH
1999-2001	P-90s, standard hardware	$350	$425

Dan Armstrong Lucite Guitar

1969-1971. Clear plexiglas solidbody, with interchangable pickups, Dan Armstrong reports that around 9,000 guitars were produced, introduced in '69, but primary production was in '70-'71, reissued in '98.

1969-1971	Clear	$2,400	$2,900
1969-1971	Smoke	$3,000	$3,500

Dan Armstrong Plexi Guitar

1998-2001, 2006-2011. Reissue of Lucite guitar, produced by pickup designer Kent Armstrong (son of Dan Armstrong), offered in smoked (ADAG2) or clear (ADAG1). Latest version is Japanese-made ADA6.

1998-2011	Clear or smoke	$700	$900

Heavy Stud (GE-150/GEH-150)

1973-1975. Import from Japan, single-cut body, weight added for sustain, single-coils or humbuckers (GEH).

1973-1975		$450	$550

Sonic Six (By Burns)

1964-1965. Solidbody, 2 pickups, tremolo, cherry finish, same as the Burns Nu-Sonic guitar.

1964-1965		$475	$575

Stud (GE-100/GET-100)

1973-1975. Import from Japan, double-cut, inexpensive materials, weight added for sustain, GET-100 included tremolo.

1973-1975		$475	$575

Super Stud (GE-500)

1973-1975. Double-cut, weight added for sustain, top-of-the-line in Stud Series.

1973-1975		$450	$550

Thinline (By Burns)

1963-1964. Semi-hollowbody, 2 f-holes, 2 pickups, double-cut, tremolo, import by Burns of London, same as the Burns TR2 guitar.

1963-1964		$625	$750

Wild Dog (By Burns)

1963-1964. Solidbody, 3 pickups, shorter scale, tremolo, sunburst finish, import by Burns of London, same as the Burns Split Sound.

1963-1964		$675	$825

Wild Dog De Luxe (By Burns)

1963-1964. Solidbody, 3 pickups, bound neck, tremolo, sunburst finish, import by Burns of London, same as the Burns Split Sonic guitar.

1963-1964		$700	$850

Anderberg

2002-present. Professional and premium grade, production/custom, electric guitars built by luthier Michael Anderberg in Jacksonville, Florida. He also builds basses.

Andersen Stringed Instruments

1978-present. Luthier Steve Andersen builds premium and presentation grade, production/custom flat-tops and archtops in Seattle, Washington. He also builds mandolins.

American Archtop Guitars American Legend

1973 Ampeg Heavy Stud

MODEL YEAR	FEATURES	EXC. COND. LOW	HIGH

1977 Aria Pro II PE 1500

Aria Pro II RS-750

Andreas

1995-present. Luthier Andreas Pichler builds his aluminum-necked, solidbody guitars and basses in Dollach, Austria.

Andy Powers Musical Instrument Co.

1996-present. Luthier Andy Powers, builds his premium and presentation grade, custom, archtop, flat-top, and semi-hollow electric guitars in Oceanside, California. He also builds ukes and mandolins.

Angelica

Ca. 1967-1972. Entry-level guitars and basses imported from Japan.

Acoustic

1967-1972		$150	$175
1980-1990s		$100	$150

Electric Solidbodies

1967-1972		$200	$250

Angus

1976-present. Professional and premium grade, custom-made steel and nylon string flat-tops built by Mark Angus in Laguna Beach, California.

Antares

1980s-1990s. Korean-made budget electric and acoustic guitars imported by Vega Music International of Brea, California.

Double Neck 6/4

1990s. Cherry finish double-cut.

1990s		$400	$475

Solidbody

1980-1990s	Various models	$125	$175

Antique Acoustics

1970s-present. Luthier Rudolph Blazer builds production/custom flat-tops, 12 strings, and archtops in Tubingen, Germany.

Antonio Hermosa

2006-present. Imported budget grade, production, acoustic and acoustic/electric classical guitars from The Music Link.

Antonio Lorca

Intermediate and professional grade, production, classical guitars made in Valencia, Spain.

Apollo

Ca. 1967-1972. Entry-level guitars imported by St. Louis Music. They also offered basses and effects.

Electric

1967-1972. Japanese imports.

1967-1972	Advanced model, 4 pickups	$400	$450
1967-1972	Mid-range model	$225	$275
1967-1972	Standard model, less features	$175	$200

Applause

1976-present. Budget and intermediate grade, production, acoustic and acoustic/electric guitars. They also offer basses, mandolins and ukes. Kaman Music's entry-level Ovation-styled brand. The instruments were made in the U.S. until around '82, when production was moved to Korea. On the U.S.-made guitars, the back of the neck was molded Urelite, with a cast aluminum neck combining an I-beam neck reinforcement, fingerboard, and frets in one unit. The Korean models have traditional wood necks.

AA Models

1976-1990s. Acoustic, laminate top, plastic or composition body. Specs and features can vary on AA Models.

1976-1981	U.S.-made	$150	$175
1980s	Import	$100	$125
1990s	Import	$100	$125

AE Models

1976-2000s. Acoustic/electric, laminate top, plastic or composition body. Specs and features can vary on AE Models.

1976-1981	U.S.-made	$200	$225
1980s	Import	$125	$175
1990-2000s	Import	$125	$175

Applegate

2001-present. Premium grade, production/custom, acoustic and classical guitars built by luthier Brian Applegate in Minneapolis, Minnesota.

APS Custom

2005-present. Luthier Andy Speake builds his production/custom, professional and premium grade, solidbody guitars in Victoria, British Columbia.

Arbor

1983-present. Budget and intermediate grade, production, classical, acoustic, and solid and semi-hollow body electric guitars imported by Musicorp (MBT). They also offer basses.

Acoustic

1980s		$75	$100
1990s		$75	$100

Electric

1980s		$150	$175
1990s		$125	$150

Arch Kraft

1933-1934. Full-size acoustic archtop and flat-top guitars. Budget brand produced by the Kay Musical Instrument Company and sold through various distributors.

Acoustic (Archtop or Flat-Top)

1933-1934		$175	$250

Aria Diamond

1960s. Brand name used by Aria in the '60s.

MODEL YEAR	FEATURES	EXC. COND. LOW	HIGH

Electric
1960s. Various models and appointments in the '60s.

1960s		$400	$500

Aria/Aria Pro II

1960-present. Budget, intermediate nad professional grade, production, electric, acoustic, acoustic/electric, and classical guitars. They also make basses, mandolins, and banjos. Aria was established in Japan in '53 and started production of instruments in '60 using the Arai, Aria, Aria Diamond, and Diamond brands. The brand was renamed Aria Pro II in '75. Aria Pro II was used mainly on electric guitars, with Aria used on others. Over the years, they have produced acoustics, banjos, mandolins, electrics, basses, amplifiers, and effects. Around '87 production of cheaper models moved to Korea, reserving Japanese manufacturing for more expensive models. Around '95 some models were made in U.S., though most contemporary guitars sold in U.S. are Korean. In '01, the Pro II part of the name was dropped altogether.

Early Arias don't have serial numbers or pot codes. Serial numbers began to be used in the mid '70s. At least for Aria guitars made by Matsumoku, the serial number contains the year of manufacture in the first one or two digits (Y##### or YY####). Thus, a guitar from 1979 might begin with 79####. One from 1981 might begin with 1#####. The scheme becomes less sure after 1987. Some Korean- made guitars use a serial number with year and week indicated in the first four digits (YYWW####). Thus 9628#### would be from the 28th week of 1996. However, this is not the case on all guitars, and some have serial numbers which are not date-coded.

Models have been consolidated by sector unless specifically noted.

Acoustic Solid Wood Top
1960s-present. Steel string models, various appointments, generally mid-level imports.

1970-2010		$275	$300

Acoustic Veneer Wood Top
1960s-present. Steel string models, various appointments, generally entry-level imports.

1970-2010		$150	$175

Classical Solid Wood Top
1960s-present. Various models, various appointments, generally mid-level imports.

1970-2010		$225	$275

Classical Veneer Wood Top
1960s-present. Various models, various appointments, generally entry-level imports.

1970-2010		$125	$150

Fullerton Series
1995-2000. Various models with different appointments and configurations based on the classic offset double-cut solidbody.

1995-2000		$225	$275

Herb Ellis (PE-175/FA-DLX)
1978-1987 (Model PE-175) and 1988-1993 (Model FA-DLX). Archtop hollowbody, ebony 'board, 2 humbuckers.

1977-1987		$450	$550

Model 1702T
1970s. The same as the Univox Hi Flier Mosrite Ventures copy, 2 slanted single-coil pickups, Aria headstock logo, tremolo, dot markers.

1970s		$600	$700

Solidbody
1960s-present. Various models, various appointments, generally mid-level imports.

1980-1999		$325	$400

Titan Artist TA Series
1967-present. Double cut, semi-hollow bodies, 2 pickups, various models.

1967-2010		$500	$600

Aristides

2010-present. Dutch engineer Aristides Poort developed the material (arium) used to build production/custom, premium grade, solidbody electric guitars in the Netherlands. They also build basses.

ARK - New Era Guitars

2006-present. Luthier A. R. Klassen builds his professional and premium grade, production/custom, reproductions of vintage Larson Brothers instruments in Chesterton, Indiana.

Armstrong, Rob

1971-present. Custom steel- and nylon-string flat-tops, 12 strings, and parlor guitars made in Coventry, England by luthier Rob Armstrong. He also builds mandolins and basses.

Arpeggio Korina

1995-present. Professional, premium and presentation grade, production/custom, korina wood solidbody guitars built by luthier Ron Kayfield in Pennsylvania.

Art & Lutherie

Budget and intermediate grade, production, steel- and nylon-string acoustic and acoustic/electric guitars. Founded by luthier Robert Godin, who also has the Norman, Godin, Seagull, and Patrick & Simon brands of instruments.

Artesano

Intermediate and professional grade, production, classical guitars built in Valencia, Spain, and distributed by Juan Orozco. Orozco also made higher-end classical Orozco Models 8, 10 and 15.

Artinger Custom Guitars

1997-present. Luthier Matt Artinger builds his professional and premium grade, production/custom, hollow, semi-hollow, and chambered solidbody guitars in Emmaus, Pennsylvania. He also builds basses.

ARK - New Era Guitars Prairie State

Artinger Chambered Solidbody

Avante AV-2

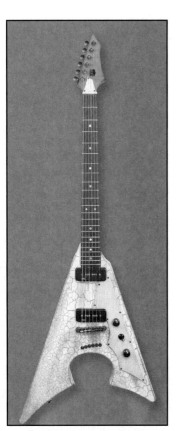

AXL Badwater Jackknife

MODEL YEAR	FEATURES	EXC. COND. LOW	HIGH

Artur Lang
1949-1975. German luthier Artur Lang is best known for his archtops, but did build classicals early on. His was a small shop and much of his output was custom ordered. The instruments were mostly unbranded, but some have L.A. engraved on the headstock.

Asama
1970s-1980s. Some models of this Japanese line of solidbody guitars featured built-in effects. They also offered basses, effects, drum machines and other music products.

Ashborn
1848-1864. James Ashborn, of Wolcottville, Connecticut, operated one of the largest guitar making factories of the mid-1800s. Models were small parlor-sized instruments with ladder bracing and gut strings. Most of these guitars will need repair. Often of more interest as historical artifacts or museum pieces versus guitar collections.

Model 2
1848-1864. Flat-top, plain appointments, no position markers on the neck, identified by Model number.

1855	Fully repaired	$500	$650

Model 5
1848-1864. Flat-top, higher appointments.

1855	Fully repaired	$1,300	$1,600

Asher
1982-present. Luthier Bill Asher builds his professional grade, production/custom, solidbody electric guitars in Venice, California. He also builds lap steels.

Ashland
Intermediate grade, production, acoustic and acoustic/electric guitars made by Korea's Crafter Guitars.

Astro
1963-1964. The Astro AS-51 was a 1 pickup kit guitar sold by Rickenbacker. German luthier Arthur Strohmer also built archtops bearing this name.

Asturias
Professional and premium grade, production, classical guitars built on Kyushu island, in Japan.

Atkin Guitars
1993-present. Luthier Alister Atkin builds his production/custom steel and nylon string flat-tops in Canterbury, England. He also builds mandolins.

Atlas
Archtop guitars, and possibly other types, built in East Germany and by Zero Sette of Italy.

Atomic
2006-present. Production/custom, intermediate and professional grade, solidbody electric guitars built by luthiers Tim Mulqueeny and Harry Howard in Peoria, Arizona. They also build basses.

MODEL YEAR	FEATURES	EXC. COND. LOW	HIGH

Audiovox
Ca. 1935-ca. 1950. Paul Tutmarc's Audiovox Manufacturing, of Seattle, Washington, was a pioneer in electric lap steels, basses, guitars and amps. Tutmarc was a talented Hawaiian steel guitarist and ran a music school.

Austin
1999-present. Budget and intermediate grade, production, acoustic, acoustic/electric, resonator, and electric guitars imported by St. Louis Music. They also offer basses, amps, mandolins, ukes and banjos.

Acoustic Flat-Top

1999-2010	Various models	$125	$150

Solidbody Electric

1999-2010	Various models	$150	$175

Austin Hatchet
Mid-1970s-mid-1980s. Trademark of distributor Targ and Dinner, Chicago, Illinois.

Hatchet
1981. Travel guitar.

1981		$350	$425

Solidbody Electric
1970s-1980s. Various classic designs.

1980s		$225	$250

Avalon
1920s. Instruments built by the Oscar Schmidt Co. and possibly others. Most likely a brand made for a distributor.

Avalon (Ireland)
2002-present. Luthiers Stevie Graham, Mark Lyttle, Ernie McMillan, Balazs Prohaszka and Robin Thompson build premium and presentation grade, production/custom, steel-string and classical, acoustic and electro-acoustic guitars in Northern Ireland. In '04-'05 their Silver series was imported from South Korea, and '05 the Gold series from Czech Republic.

Avante
1997-2007. Intermediate grade, production, imported sharp cutaway acoustic baritone guitars designed by Joe Veillette and Michael Tobias and offered by MusicYo. Originally higher priced instruments offered by Alvarez, there was the baritone, a 6-string and a bass.

AV-2 Baritone
1997-2007. Baritone guitar tuned B to B, solid spruce cutaway top, mahogany sides and back.

1997-2007		$275	$325

Avanti
1964-late 1960s. Italian-made guitar brand imported by European Crafts, of Los Angeles. Earlier models were plastic covered; later ones had paint finishes.

Electric Solidbody
1960s. Solidbody, 3 single-coils, dot markers.

1960s		$200	$250

MODEL YEAR	FEATURES	EXC. COND. LOW	HIGH

Avar

Late-1960s. Import copy models from Japan, not unlike Teisco, for the U.S. student market.

Solidbody Electric

1969		$225	$275

Aztec

1970s. Japanese-made copy guitars imported into Germany by Hopf.

b3 Guitars

2004-present. Premium grade, custom/production, solid, chambered and hollow-body guitars built by luthier Gene Baker in Arroyo Grande, California. He previously made Baker U.S.A. guitars.

Babicz

2004-present. Started by luthier Jeff Babicz and Jeff Carano, who worked together at Steinberger, the company offers intermediate, professional, and premium grade, production/custom, acoustic and acoustic/electric guitars made in Poughkeepsie, New York, and overseas.

Bacon & Day

Established in 1921 by David Day and Paul Bacon, primarily known for fine quality tenor and plectrum banjos in the '20s and '30s. Purchased by Gretsch ca. '40.

Belmont

1950s. Gretsch era, 2 DeArmond pickups, natural.

1950s		$1,300	$1,525

Flat-Top

1930s-1940s. Large B&D headstock logo.

1930s	Fancy appointments	$3,000	$3,500
1930s	Plain appointments	$2,400	$2,800
1940s	Fancy appointments	$2,700	$3,100
1940s	Plain appointments	$2,100	$2,400

Ramona Archtop

1938-1940. Sunburst.

1938-1940		$1,000	$1,175

Senorita Archtop

1940. Lower-end, sunburst, mahogany back and sides.

1940		$1,500	$1,725

Style B Guitar Banjo (Bacon)

1920s. 6-string guitar neck on a banjo-resonator body.

1920s	Fancy appointments	$2,300	$2,700
1920s	Plain appointments	$1,200	$1,400

Sultana I

1930s. Large 18 1/4" acoustic archtop, Sultana engraved on tailpiece, block markers, bound top and back, sunburst.

1938		$3,000	$3,500

MODEL YEAR	FEATURES	EXC. COND. LOW	HIGH

Baden

Founded in 2006, by T.J. Baden, a former vice president of sales and marketing at Taylor guitars, initial production based on six models built in Vietnam, intermediate retail-price grade.

Baker U.S.A.

1997-present. Professional and premium grade, production/custom, solidbody electric guitars. Established by master builder Gene Baker after working at the Custom Shops of Gibson and Fender, Baker produced solid- and hollowbody guitars in Santa Maria, California. They also built basses. Baker also produced the Mean Gene brand of guitars from '88-'90. In September '03, the company was liquidated and the Baker U.S.A. name was sold to Ed Roman. Gene Baker currently builds b3 Guitars.

B1/B1 Chambered/B1 Hollow

1997-present. Double-cut mahogany body, maple top, with a wide variety of options including chambered and hollowbody construction, set-neck. Gene Baker era USA-made until 2003, Ed Roman era import after.

1997-2003	USA	$2,300	$2,750
2004-2010	Import	$950	$1,150

BJ/BJ Hollow

1997-2003. Double-cut mahogany body, P-90-type pickups, several options available, set-neck.

1997-2003		$1,800	$2,200

BNT

1997-2000. Mahogany solidbody, maple top, neck-thru body, with various finishes and options.

1997-2000		$2,000	$2,500

Baldwin

1965-1970. Founded in 1862, in Cincinnati, when reed organ and violin teacher Dwight Hamilton Baldwin opened a music store that eventually became one of the largest piano retailers in the Midwest. By 1965, the Baldwin Piano and Organ company was ready to buy into the guitar market but was outbid by CBS for Fender. Baldwin did procure Burns of London in September '65, and sold the guitars in the U.S. under the Baldwin name. Baldwin purchased Gretsch in '67. English production of Baldwin guitars ends in '70, after which Baldwin concentrates on the Gretsch brand.

Baby Bison (Model 560 by Mid-1966)

1966-1970. Double-cut solidbody, V headstock, 2 pickups, shorter scale, tremolo, black, red or white finishes.

1965-1966		$775	$875
1966-1970	Model 560	$675	$775

Bison (Model 511 by Mid-1966)

1965-1970. Double-cut solidbody, scroll headstock, 3 pickups, tremolo, black or white finishes.

1965-1966		$1,125	$1,400
1966-1970	Model 511	$1,050	$1,300

Babicz Identity Spider

Baker U.S.A. B1

Ballurio Artist

Bazzolo Spruce Top Classical

MODEL YEAR	FEATURES	EXC. COND. LOW	HIGH

Double Six (Model 525 by Mid-1966)
1965-1970. Offset double-cut solidbody, 12 strings, 3 pickups, green or red sunburst.

1965-1966		$1,125	$1,400
1966-1970	Model 525	$1,050	$1,300

G.B. 65
1965-1966. Baldwin's first acoustic/electric, single-cut D-style flat-top, dual bar pickups.

1965-1966		$650	$800

G.B. 66 De Luxe
1965-1966. Same as Standard with added density control on treble horn, golden sunburst.

1965-1966		$750	$900

G.B. 66 Standard
1965-1966. Thinline Electric archtop, dual Ultra-Sonic pickups, offset cutaways, red sunburst.

1965-1966		$700	$850

Jazz Split Sound/Split Sound (Model 503 Mid-1966)
1965-1970. Offset double-cut solidbody, scroll headstock, 3 pickups, tremolo, red sunburst or solid colors.

1965-1966		$900	$1,100
1966-1970	Model 503	$750	$900

Marvin (Model 524 by Mid-1966)
1965-1970. Offset double-cut solidbody, scroll headstock, 3 pickups, tremolo, white or brown finish.

1965-1966		$1,100	$1,300
1966-1970	Model 524	$1,000	$1,200

Model 706
1967-1970. Double-cut semi-hollowbody, scroll headstock, 2 pickups, 2 f-holes, no vibrato, red or golden sunburst.

1967-1970		$675	$825

Model 706 V
1967-1970. Model 706 with vibrato.

1967-1970		$725	$875

Model 712 R Electric XII
1967-1970. Double-cut semi-hollow body with regular neck, red or gold sunburst.

1967-1970		$600	$700

Model 712 T Electric XII
1967-1970. Model 712 with thin neck, red or gold sunburst.

1967-1970		$600	$700

Model 801 CP Electric Classical
1968-1970. Grand concert-sized classical with transducer based pickup system, natural pumpkin finish.

1968-1970		$625	$725

Nu-Sonic
1965-1966. Solidbody electric student model, 6-on-a-side tuners, black or cherry finish.

1965-1966		$650	$750

Vibraslim (Model 548 by Late-1966)
1965-1970. Double-cut semi-hollowbody, 2 pickups, tremolo, 2 f-holes, red or golden sunburst. Notable spec changes with Model 548 in '66.

1965-1966		$900	$1,100
1966-1970	Model 548	$800	$1,000

Virginian (Model 550 by Mid-1966)
1965-1970. Single-cut flat-top, 2 pickups (1 on each side of soundhole), scroll headstock, tremolo, natural.

1965-1966		$800	$950
1966-1970	Model 550	$775	$925

Ballurio
2000-present. Luthier Keith Ballurio builds his intermediate, professional, and premium grade, production/custom, solidbody and chambered guitars in Manassas, Virginia.

Baltimore
2007-2008. Budget grade, production, solidbody electric guitars imported by The Music Link.

Baranik Guitars
1995-present. Premium grade, production/custom steel-string flat-tops made in Tempe, Arizona by luthier Mike Baranik.

Barclay
1960s. Thinline acoustic/electric archtops, solidbody electric guitars and basses imported from Japan. Generally shorter scale beginner guitars.
Electric Solidbody
1960s. Various models and colors.

1960s		$175	$200

Barcus-Berry
1964-present. Founded by John Berry and Les Barcus introducing the first piezo crystal transducer. Martin guitar/Barcus-Berry products were offered in the mid-'80s. They also offered a line of amps from around '76 to ca. '80.

Barrington
1988-1991. Imports offered by Barrington Guitar Werks, of Barrington, Illinois. Models included solidbody guitars and basses, archtop electrics, and acoustic flat-tops. Barrington Music Products is still in the music biz, offering LA saxophones and other products.
Acoustic/Electric
1988-1991. Acoustic/electric, flat-top single-cut with typical round soundhole, opaque white.

1988-1991		$150	$175

Solidbody
1988-ca 1991. Barrington's line of pointy headstock, double-cut solidbodies, black.

1988-1991		$125	$150

Bartell of California
1964-1969. Founded by Paul Barth (Magnatone) and Ted Peckels. Mosrite-inspired designs.
Double Neck

1967		$1,900	$2,200

Electric 12
1967. Mosrite-style body.

1967		$1,100	$1,250

MODEL		EXC. COND.	
YEAR	FEATURES	LOW	HIGH

Barth

1950s-1960s. Paul Barth was involved with many guitar companies including National, Rickenbacker, Magnatone and others. He also built instruments under his own brand in California, including guitars, lap steels and amps. Most will have either a Barth logo on plastic plate, or decal.

Mark VIII

1959. Double-cut solidbody, 2 pickups, dot markers, Barth headstock logo.

| 1959 | | $1,800 | $2,200 |

Bartolini

1960s. European-made (likely Italian) guitars made for the Bartolini Accordion Company. Similar to Gemelli guitars, so most likely from same manufacturer. Originally plastic covered, they switched to paint finishes by the mid '60s.

Solidbody

| 1960s | | $450 | $525 |

Bashkin Guitars

1998-present. Luthier Michael Bashkin builds his premium grade, custom, steel-string acoustics in Fort Collins, Colorado.

Basone Guitars

1999-present. Luthier Chris Basaraba builds his custom, professional grade, solid and hollowbody electric guitars in Vancouver, British Columbia. He also builds basses.

Bauer, George

1894-1911. Luthier George Bauer built guitars, mandolins, and banjos in Philadelphia, Pennsylvania. He also built instruments with Samuel S. Stewart (S.S. Stewart).

Baxendale & Baxendale

1975-present. Luthiers Scott Baxendale (father) and John Baxendale (son) build their professional and premium grade, custom, steel-string acoustic and solidbody electric guitars in Denver, Colorado. They were previously located in Tennessee and Texas.

Bay State

1865-ca.1910. Bay State was a trademark for Boston's John C. Haynes Co.

Parlor Guitar

1900s. Small parlor size, mahogany body with salt & pepper binding.

| 1865-1910 | | $800 | $950 |

Bazzolo Guitarworks

1983-present. Luthier Thomas Bazzolo began building his premium grade, production/custom, classical and flat-top guitars in Lebanon, Connecticut and since 2008 in Sullivan, Maine.

BC Kingston

1977-present. From 1977 to '96, luthier Brian Kingston built flat-top and semi-hollow acoustic guitars along with a few solidbodies. Presently he builds premium grade, production/custom, archtop jazz and semi-hollow guitars in Prince Edward Island, Canada.

BC Rich

Ca. 1966/67-present. Budget, intermediate, and premium grade, production/custom, import and U.S.-made, electric and acoustic guitars. They also offer basses. Founded by Bernardo Chavez Rico in Los Angeles, California. As a boy he worked for his guitar-maker father Bernardo Mason Rico (Valencian Guitar Shop, Casa Rico, Bernardo's Guitar Shop), building first koa ukes and later, guitars, steel guitars and Martin 12-string conversions. He started using the BC Rich name ca. '66-'67 and made about 300 acoustics until '68, when first solidbody electric made using a Fender neck.

Rich's early models were based on Gibson and Fender designs. First production instruments were in '69 with 10 fancy Gibson EB-3 bass and 10 matching Les Paul copies, all carved out of single block of mahogany. Early guitars with Gibson humbuckers, then Guild humbuckers, and, from '74-'86, DiMarzio humbuckers. Around 150 BC Rich Eagles were imported from Japan in '76. Ca. '76 or '77 some bolt-neck guitars with parts made by Wayne Charvel were offered. Acoustic production ended in '82 (acoustics were again offered in '95).

For '83-'86 the BC Rich N.J. Series (N.J. Nagoya, Japan) was built by Masan Tarada. U.S. Production Series (U.S.-assembled Korean kits) in '84. From '86 on, the N.J. Series was made by Cort in Korea. Korean Rave and Platinum series begin around '86. In '87, Rich agrees to let Class Axe of New Jersey market the Korean Rave, Platinum and N.J. Series. Class Axe (with Neal Moser) introduces Virgin in '87 and in '88 Rave and Platinum names are licensed to Class Axe. In '89, Rico licensed the BC Rich name to Class Axe. Both imported and American-made BC Riches are offered during Class Axe management. In 2000, BC Rich became a division of Hanser Music Group.

During '90-'91, Rico begins making his upscale Mason Bernard guitars (approx. 225 made). In '94, Rico resumes making BC Rich guitars in California. He died in 1999.

First 340-360 U.S.-built guitars were numbered sequentially beginning in '72. Beginning in '74, serial numbers change to YYZZZ pattern (year plus consecutive production). As production increased in the late-'70s, the year number began getting ahead of itself. By '80 it was 2 years ahead; by '81 as much as 4 years ahead. No serial number codes on imports.

The American B.C. Rich company was first and foremost a custom shop, therefore surprising variants are possible for the models described below, especially in the early years of the company. Many of the first models were offered as either a Standard (also called Deluxe) model or as an upgrade called

BC Kingston Fusion

2006 BC Rich NJC Series Eagle
Michael Korabek

1981 BC Rich Eagle

BC Rich Kerry King Warlock
Wartribe

the Supreme model.

The Deluxe or Standard model has diamond markers, unbound rosewood fretboard, three-on-a-side tuners, generally solid mahogany body, some rare examples with maple body or other woods, some with runners or stringers of alternate exotic wood.

The Supreme model has specific options including cloud markers, fully bound ebony fretboard and three-on-a-side headstock, various woods including solid koa, maple, highly-figured maple (birdseye, quilted, curly), other exotic woods offered, most models with runners or stringers of alternating exotic wood, also available as single solid wood, mid-1980s with original Kahler tremolo unit option, custom colors and sunburst finishes generally on a custom order basis, certain custom colors are worth more than the values shown, early models circa '75-'82 had a Leo Quan Badass bridge option and those models are highly favored by collectors, early style control knobs had silver metal inserts and full electronics with Varitone and PreAmp and Grover Imperial bullseye tuners, the earliest models had red head mini-switches (later became silver-chrome switches). Technically speaking the Supreme model only applied to the Mockingbird, Eagle, Bich, and Wave.

The prime collector's market for B.C. Rich is the '72-'85 era. The Seagull, Eagle, Mockingbird, Bich, and Wave models are the true vintage models from that epoch.

Pre-1985 BC Rich Standard Finishes were Natural, Gloss White, Black, Competition Red, Medium Blue, Metallic Red, and Cherry. Any other finish would be a Custom Color. Most custom colors started appearing in late 1978. Prior to '78, guitars had two tone transparent burst finishes, natural finishes and occasional one color paint schemes. Custom Color finishes are worth 10% more than standard finish colors. Special thanks to Matt Touchard for his help with specifications.

Assassin
1986-1998. Double-cut body, 2 humbuckers, maple thru-neck dot markers, various colors.

MODEL YEAR	FEATURES	EXC. COND. LOW	HIGH
1986-1989	1st Rico era	$625	$775
1989-1993	Class Axe era, neck-thru	$575	$725
1994-1998	2nd Rico era USA, neck-thru	$575	$725
2000s	Includes QX & PX	$250	$300

B-28 Acoustic
Ca.1967-1982. Acoustic flat-top, hand-built, solid spruce top, rosewood back and sides, herringbone trim, pearl R headstock logo.

1967-1982		$600	$750

B-30 Acoustic
Ca.1967-1982. Acoustic flat-top.

1967-1982		$650	$800

B-38 Acoustic
Ca.1967-1982. Acoustic flat-top, cocobolo back and sides, herringbone trim.

1967-1982		$675	$850

B-41 Acoustic
1970s. Brazilian rosewood.

1970s		$1,275	$1,575

B-45 Acoustic
Hand-built, D-style rosewood body.

1970s		$1,850	$2,300

Beast (U.S.A. Custom Shop)
1999-present. Exaggerated four point cutaway body, flamed or quilted top.

1999-2010		$1,025	$1,275

Bich (U.S.A. Assembly)
1978-1998. Four-point sleek body, came in Standard top or Supreme with highly figured maple body and active EQ.

MODEL YEAR	FEATURES	EXC. COND. LOW	HIGH
1978-1979	Standard Deluxe	$1,450	$1,800
1978-1979	Supreme	$1,925	$2,400
1980-1985	Standard Deluxe	$1,200	$1,500
1980-1985	Supreme	$1,675	$2,075
1986-1989		$1,200	$1,500
1989-1993	Class Axe era	$825	$1,025
1994-1998	2nd Rico era USA, bolt-on	$750	$950

Bich 10-String
1978-present. Doubles on 4 low strings.

1978-1982	Highly flamed	$3,600	$4,500
1978-1982	Koa	$2,900	$3,600
1978-1982	Koa and maple	$2,725	$3,400

Black Hole
1988. Bolt neck, rosewood 'board, integrated pickup design, Floyd Rose.

1988		$225	$275

Body Art Collection
2003-2006. Imports with different exotic graphics on different models issued each month from January '03 to March '04, 25th Anniversary model available into '06, headstock logo states Body Art Collection.

2003	Boris Beast	$200	$250
2003	Skull Pile	$225	$275
2003	Space Face Ironbird	$225	$275
2003	Spiro Light	$200	$250
2003	Torchy ASM	$200	$250
2004	40 Lashes Mockingbird	$225	$275
2004	Umethar Jr. V	$200	$250

Bronze Series
2001-2007. Made in China. Includes 2 models; Mockingbird and Warlock.

2001-2007		$60	$75

Doubleneck Models
1980-1988. Doublenecks were sporadically made and specs (and values) may vary.

1980-1988	Bich	$4,000	$5,000
1980-1988	Eagle	$4,500	$5,500
1980-1988	Iron Bird	$3,200	$4,000
1980-1988	Mockingbird	$4,500	$5,500
1980-1988	Seagull	$4,800	$6,000

Eagle
1975-1982, 2000-2004. Made in USA, often called the Eagle model, but also called Eagle Deluxe or Eagle Standard, features include diamond inlays, unbound rosewood fretboard, 3-on-a-side tuners, generally solid

MODEL		EXC. COND.	
YEAR	FEATURES	LOW	HIGH

mahogany body, some rare examples with maple body or other woods, some with runners or stringers of alternate exotic wood. (See additional notes in the Eagle Supreme listing.)

1975-1976	Custom Shop	$1,925	$2,400
1977		$1,925	$2,400
1978-1979		$1,675	$2,100
1980-1982		$1,525	$1,900

Eagle Special (U.S.A.)

1977-1982. A variant of the Eagle with even more switches and electronic options, the extra options are not particularly considered an advantage in the BC Rich collector community, therefore an Eagle Special is worth less than the Standard or Eagle Supreme.

| 1977-1982 | | $1,675 | $2,100 |

Eagle Supreme

1975-1982. Made in USA, Eagle body style with specific options including cloud inlays, fully bound ebony fretboard, 3-on-a-side headstock, various woods including solid koa, maple, highly-figured maple (birdseye, quilted, curly), other exotic woods offered, most with runners or stringers of alternating exotic wood, also available as single solid wood, mid-'80s with original Kahler tremolo unit option, custom colors and sunburst finishes generally on a custom order basis, certain custom colors are worth more than the values shown, early models ca. '75-'82 had a Leo Quan Badass bridge option and those models are highly favored by collectors, early style control knobs with silver metal inserts, full electronics with Varitone and PreAmp and Grover Imperial bullseye tuners, the earliest models had red head mini-switches (later became silver-chrome switches).

1975-1976	Custom Shop	$2,550	$3,200
1977		$2,550	$3,200
1978-1979		$2,325	$2,900
1980-1982		$2,150	$2,700
2000-2004		$2,100	$2,600

Eagle Supreme Condor

1983-1987. Less than 50 made, simplified electronics system based on customer's requests, features can include cloud inlays, fully bound ebony fretboard neck, bound 3-on-a-side headstock, bookmatched figured maple top over solid mahogany body with slight arch, no runners or stringers, basic electronics with master volume, master tone, and pickup switch, also commonly called Condor Supreme.

| 1983-1987 | Common color | $1,350 | $1,700 |
| 1983-1987 | Rare color, highly figured | $1,600 | $2,000 |

Elvira

2001. Elvira (the witch) photo on black Warlock body, came with Casecore coffin case.

| 2001 | | $450 | $500 |

Exclusive EM1

1996-2004. Offset double-cut, bound top, 2 humbuckers.

| 1996-2004 | | $150 | $175 |

Gunslinger

1987-1999. Inverted headstock, 1 (Gunslinger I) or 2 (Gunslinger II) humbuckers, recessed cutout behind Floyd Rose allows player to pull notes up 2 full steps.

| 1987-1989 | Standard finish | $600 | $700 |

1987-1989	Various graphic designs	$650	$750
1989-1993	Class Axe era	$550	$650
1994-1999	2nd Rico era, bolt-on	$550	$650
1994-1999	2nd Rico era, neck-thru	$550	$650

Ironbird

1983-2004. Pointy body and headstock.

| 1983-1989 | | $800 | $1,000 |

Kerry King Wartribe 1 Warlock

2004-present. Tribal Fire finish, 2 pickups.

| 2004-2010 | | $150 | $200 |

Mockingbird

1976-present. Made in USA, often called the Mockingbird model, but also called the Mockingbird Standard or Mockingbird Deluxe, features include diamond inlays, unbound rosewood fretboard, 3-on-a-side tuners, generally solid mahogany body, some rare examples with maple body or other woods, some with runners or stringers of alternate exotic wood. (See additional notes in the Mockingbird Supreme listing.)

1976		$2,250	$2,800
1977-1978	Short horn	$2,200	$2,750
1979-1983	Long horn	$2,150	$2,700
1984-1985		$1,600	$2,000
1986-1989	Last of 1st Rico era	$1,400	$1,800
1989-1993	Class Axe era	$1,300	$1,700
1994-1999	2nd Rico era, bolt-on	$1,200	$1,500

Mockingbird (Custom Shop)

2000-present. Comes with Certificate of Authenticity.

| 2000-2010 | | $2,000 | $2,300 |

Mockingbird Ice Acrylic

2004-2006. See-thru acrylic body.

| 2004-2006 | | $275 | $325 |

Mockingbird Supreme

1976-1989. Made in USA, Mockingbird body style with specific options including cloud inlays, fully bound ebony fretboard, 3-on-a-side headstock, various woods including solid koa, maple, highly-figured maple (birdseye, quilted, curly), other exotic woods offered, most with runners or stringers of alternating exotic wood, also available as single solid wood, mid-'80s with original Kahler tremolo unit option, custom colors and sunburst finishes generally on a custom order basis, certain custom colors are worth more than the values shown, early models ca. '76-'82 had a Leo Quan Badass bridge option and those models are highly favored by collectors, early style control knobs with silver metal inserts, full electronics with Varitone and PreAmp and Grover Imperial bullseye tuners, the earliest models had red head mini-switches (later became silver-chrome switches).

1976	Earlier short horn	$2,875	$3,600
1976-1978	Supreme short horn	$2,800	$3,500
1977-1978	Earlier short horn	$2,800	$3,500
1979	Later long horn	$2,600	$3,300
1980-1983		$2,325	$2,900
1984-1985		$2,000	$2,500
1986-1989		$1,600	$2,000

BC Rich Mockingbird

1970s BC Rich Mockingbird

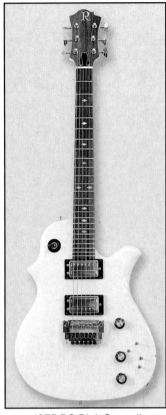

1975 BC Rich Seagull

2003 BC Rich MJ Series Warlock

MODEL YEAR	FEATURES	EXC. COND. LOW	HIGH
1989-1993	Class Axe era	$1,350	$1,700
1994-1999	2nd Rico era, bolt-on	$1,200	$1,500

Nighthawk
1978-ca.1982. Eagle-shaped body with bolt neck.

1978-1982		$575	$725

NJ Series/NJC Series
1983-2006. Earlier models made in Japan. Made in Korea '86 forward. All NJ models fall within the same price range. Models include; Assassin, Beast, Bich, Ironbird, Eagle, Mockingbird, Outlaw, ST III, Virgin, Warlock. C for Classic added in '06.

1983-1984	Early NJ Japan	$400	$700
1985-1986	Later Japan	$325	$500
1986-2006	Korea	$275	$375

Phoenix
1977-ca.1982. Mockingbird-shaped with bolt neck.

1977-1982		$575	$725

Platinum Series
1986-2006. Lower-priced import versions including Assassin, Beast, Bich, Ironbird, ST, Warlock.

1986-2006		$125	$275

Rave Series
1986-ca. 1990. Korean-made down-market versions of popular models.

1986-1990		$125	$150

Seagull
1972-1975. Single-cut solidbody, neck-thru, 2 humbuckers.

1972-1973	Earliest, 30 made	$2,950	$3,700
1973-1974		$2,800	$3,500
1975		$2,475	$3,100

Seagull II
1974-1977. Double-cut solidbody, neck-thru, 2 humbuckers. Transitional model in '75 between Seagull and Eagle, Seagull Jr. is used interchangable with Seagull II, the company made several variants during this period which some collectors consider to be Seagull Jr. while others consider to be Seagull II. The II/Jr. design finally was changed and called the Eagle.

1974	1st 50, Gibson pickups	$2,400	$3,000
1974	Moser, 16 made	$2,400	$3,000
1974	Other from '74	$2,350	$2,950
1976-1977		$2,325	$2,900

Seagull Jr./Seagull II
1975-1977. Another transitional model starting in '75, the model name Seagull Jr. is used interchangable with Seagull II, the company made several variants during this period which some collectors consider to be Seagull Jr. while others consider to be Seagull II. The design finally was changed and called the Eagle.

1975-1977	Jr. and II	$2,325	$2,900

Stealth I Series
1983-1989. Includes Standard (maple body, diamond inlays) and Series II (mahogany body, dot inlays), 2 pickups.

1983-1989	Series II	$1,400	$1,750
1983-1989	Standard	$1,400	$1,750

ST-III (U.S.A.)
1987-1998. Double-cut solidbody, hum/single/single or 2 humbucker pickups, Kahler tremolo.

1987-1989	Bolt-on	$550	$675
1987-1989	Neck-thru	$650	$800
1989-1993	Class Axe era	$525	$650
1994-1998	New Rico era, neck-thru & bolt-on	$525	$650

The Mag
2000. U.S. Handcrafted Series Mockingbird Acoustic Supreme, solid spruce top, quilt maple back and sides, pickup with preamp and EQ optional, dark sunburst.

2000		$675	$850

Warlock
1981-present. Made in USA, also called Warlock Standard, 4-point sleek body style with widow headstock.

1981-1985	Standard	$950	$1,200
1986-1989	Standard	$950	$1,200
1990-1999	2nd Rico era, bolt-on	$750	$950
1990-1999	2nd Rico era, neck-thru	$925	$1,150

Warlock Ice Acrylic
2004-2006. See-thru acrylic body.

2004-2006		$225	$275

Wave
1983. U.S.-made, very limited production based upon the Wave bass.

1983		$2,300	$2,700

Bear Creek Guitars
1995-present. Luthier Bill Hardin worked for OMI Dobro and Santa Cruz Guitar before introducing his own line of professional and premium grade, custom-made Weissenborn-style guitars, made in Kula, Hawaii. He also builds ukes.

Beardsell Guitars
1996-present. Production/custom flat-tops, classical and electric solidbody guitars built by luthier Allan Beardsell in Toronto, Ontario.

Beaulieu
2006-present. Luthier Hugues Beaulieu builds his production/custom, professional and premium grade, flat-top, flamenco and classical guitars in Pont-Rouge, Quebec.

Beauregard
1992-present. Luthier Mario Beauregard builds his premium and presentation grade, production/custom, flat-top, archtop and jazz guitars in Montreal, Quebec.

Bedell Guitars
1964-present. Intermediate and premium grade, production/custom, flat-top guitars built in Spirit Lake, Iowa and imported from China, designed by luthier Tom Bedell, Dan Mills and Sophia Yang. They also offer Great Divide Guitars and in 2010 acquired Breedlove.

MODEL YEAR	FEATURES	EXC. COND. LOW	HIGH

Behringer

1989-present. The German professional audio products company added budget, production, solid-body guitars in '03, sold in amp/guitar packages. They also offer effects and amps.

Beltona

1990-present. Production/custom metal body resonator guitars made in New Zealand by Steve Evans and Bill Johnson. Beltona was originally located in England. They also build mandolins and ukes.

Beltone

1920s-1930s. Acoustic and resonator guitars made by others for New York City distributor Perlberg & Halpin. Martin did make a small number of instruments for Beltone, but most were student-grade models most likely made by one of the big Chicago builders. They also made mandolins.

Archtop

1930s		$350	$400

Resonator Copy

1930s. Resonator copy but without a real resonator, rather just an aluminum plate on a wooden top, body mahogany plywood.

1938		$350	$400

Beltone (Import)

1950s-1960s. Japan's Teisco made a variety of brands for others, including the Beltone line of guitars, basses and amps. Carvin sold some of these models in the late 1960s. Italy's Welson guitars also marketed marble and glitter-finished guitars in the U.S. under this brand.

Electric Solidbody

1960s. Import from Japan during the import era of the '60s, large B headstock logo with Beltone block lettering on the large B, 4 pickups.

1960s		$175	$250

Benedetto

1968-present. Premium and presentation grade, production/custom archtop and chambered solid-body guitars, built by luthier Robert Benedetto. He has also built a few violins and solidbodies. He was located in East Stroudsburg, Pennsylvania, up to '99; in Riverview, Florida, for '00-'06; and in Savanah, Georgia, since '07. He is especially known for refining the 7-string guitar. From '99 to '06 he licensed the names of his standard models to Fender (see Benedetto FMIC); during that period, Benedetto only made special order instruments. In '06, Howard Paul joined Benedetto as President of the company to begin manufacturing a broader line of more affordable professional instruments.

Benny

1990s-present. Electric chambered single-cut mahogany body, carved spruce top, 2 humbuckers.

1990s		$2,700	$3,100

Benny Deluxe

1990s-2011. Deluxe version of the Benny.

1990s		$4,200	$4,800

Bravo Deluxe

2004-present. Electric 1 pickup archtop, laminated back and top, deluxe binding.

2004-2010		$3,000	$3,500

Cremona

1988-present. Acoustic/electric archtop, single-cut, 17" body, natural.

1988-1999		$11,000	$12,500

Fratello

1980-present. Electric archtop, single-cut, 17" body, blond or sunburst.

1980s		$7,500	$8,500
1990s		$7,500	$8,500
2000s		$7,500	$8,500

La Venezia

1990s-present. Acoustic archtop, single-cut, 17" body, sunburst.

1990s		$9,000	$10,500

Limelite Custom

1990s. Single-cut, neck pickup, select aged wood, blond.

1990s		$16,000	$19,000

Manhattan

1989-present. Archtop with 16" body, neck pickup, blond.

1989-1999		$7,500	$8,500

Manhattan Custom

1990s. Carved 17" body, blond.

1990s		$10,000	$11,500

Benedetto (FMIC)

1999-2006. Premium and presentation, production/custom, acoustic and electric archtops. From '99 to '06, Bob Benedetto had an agreement with Fender (FMIC) to build Benedetto guitars under his guidance and supervision. The guitars were originally built in the FMIC Guild Custom Shop in Nashville, and later in Fender's Corona, California, facility.

Benedict

1988-present. Founded by Roger Benedict. Professional and premium grade, production/custom, solid and semi-hollow body guitars built by luthier Bill Hager in Cedar, Minnesota. He also builds basses.

Beneteau

1974-present. Custom, premium grade, classical, baritone and steel string acoustic guitars built first in Ottawa, Ontario, and since 1986 in St. Thomas, Ontario by luthier Marc Beneteau. He also builds ukuleles.

Bennett Music Labs

1998-present. Custom guitars built by luthier Bruce Bennett, who helped design the first Warrior line of instruments with J.D. Lewis. He also built amps and Brown Sound effects.

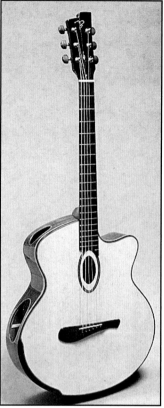

Beardsell 4G

Behringer iAXE629

*Bernie Rico Jr. Guitars
Custom Hellicon*

Blackbird Super OM

MODEL YEAR	FEATURES	EXC. COND. LOW	HIGH

Bently

ca.1985-1998. Student and intermediate grade copy style acoustic and electric guitars imported by St. Louis Music Supply. Includes the Series 10 electrics and the Songwriter acoustics (which have a double reversed B crown logo on the headstock). St. Louis Music replaced the Bently line with the Austin brand.

Berkowitz Guitars

1995-present. Luthier David D. Berkowitz builds his premium grade, custom/production, steel string and baritone guitars in Washington, DC. He also builds basses.

Bernie Rico Jr. Guitars

Professional and premium grade, production/custom, solidbody electrics built by luther Bernie Rico, Jr., the son of BC Rich founder, in Hesperia, California. He also makes basses.

Bertoncini Stringed Instruments

1995-present. Luthier Dave Bertoncini builds his premium grade, custom, flat-top guitars in Olympia, Washington. He has also built solidbody electrics, archtops, mandolins and ukes.

Beyond The Trees

1976-present. Luthier Fred Carlson offers a variety of innovative designs for his professional and presentation grade, production/custom 6- and 12-string flat-tops in Santa Cruz, California. He also produces the Sympitar (a 6-string with added sympathetic strings) and the Dreadnautilus (a unique shaped headless acoustic).

Big Lou Guitar

Mid-2010-present. Located in Perris, California, owner Louis Carroll imports his intermediate grade, production, electric guitars from China.

Big Tex Guitars

2000-present. Production/custom, professional grade, vintage-style replica guitars, built for owner Eric Danheim, by luthiers James Love, Mike Simon and Eddie Dale in Houston and Dripping Springs, Texas and Seattle, Washington.

Bigsby

1946-present. Pedal steel guitars, hollow-chambered electric Spanish guitars, electric mandolins, double-necks, replacement necks on acoustic guitars, hand vibratos, all handmade by Paul Arthur Bigsby, machinist and motorcycle enthusiast (designer of '30s Crocker motorcycles), in Downey, California. Initially built for special orders.

Bigsby was a pioneer in developing pedal steels. He designed a hand vibrato for Merle Travis. In '48, his neck-through hollow electrics (with Merle Travis) influenced Leo Fender, and Bigsby employed young Semie Moseley. In '56, he designed the Magnatone

Mark series guitars and 1 Hawaiian lap steel. He built guitars up to '63.

He built less than 50 Spanish guitars, 6 mandolins, 70 to 150 pedal steels and 12 or so neck replacements. SN was stamped on the end of fingerboard: MMD-DYY. In '65, the company was sold to Gibson president Ted McCarty who moved the tremolo/vibrato work to Kalamazoo. Bigsby died in '68. Fred Gretsch purchased the Bigsby company from Ted McCarty in '99. A solidbody guitar and a pedal steel based upon the original Paul Bigsby designs were introduced January, 2002. These were modeled on the 1963 Bigsby catalog, but look very similar to the typical Bigsby solidbodys made since the early 1950s. Early Bigsby guitars command high value on the collectible market.

Solidbody

Late-1940s-1950s, 2002. Solidbody, natural. Reissue offered in '02.

1948-1952		$25,000	$30,000
1953-1956		$25,000	$30,000
2002	Reissue	$3,000	$3,500

Bil Mitchell Guitars

1979-present. Luthier Bil Mitchell builds his professional and premium grade, production/custom, flat-top and archtop guitars originally in Wall, New Jersey, and since '02 in Riegelsville, Pennsylvania.

Bilt Guitars

2010-present. Professional grade, production/custom, solidbody and semi-hollowbody electric guitars built in Des Moines, Iowa by luthiers Bill Henss and Tim Thelen.

Birdsong Guitars

2001-present. Luthiers Scott Beckwith and Jamie Hornbuckle build their professional grade, production/custom, solidbody guitars in Wimberley, Texas. They also build basses.

Bischoff Guitars

1975-present. Professional and premium-grade, custom-made flat-tops built by luthier Gordy Bischoff in Eau Claire, Wisconsin.

Bishline

1985-present. Luthier Robert Bishline, of Tulsa, Oklahoma, mainly builds banjos, but did build flat-tops and resonators in the past, and still does occasionally.

Black Jack

1960s. Violin-body hollowbody electric guitars and basses, possibly others. Imported from Japan by unidentified distributor. Manufacturers unknown, but some may be Arai.

Blackbird

2006-present. Luthier Joe Luttwak builds his professional grade, production/custom, carbon fiber acoustic guitars in San Francisco, California. He also offers a uke.

MODEL		EXC. COND.	
YEAR	FEATURES	LOW	HIGH

Blackshear, Tom

1958-present. Premium and presentation grade, production, classical and flamenco guitars made by luthier Tom Blackshear in San Antonio, Texas.

Blade

1987-present. Intermediate and professional grade, production, solidbody guitars from luthier Gary Levinson and his Levinson Music Products Ltd. located in Switzerland. He also builds basses.

California Custom

1994-2010. California Standard with maple top and high-end appointments.

1994-2010		$700	$800

California Deluxe/Deluxe

1994-1995. Standard with mahogany body and maple top.

1994-1995		$525	$600

California Hybrid

1998-1999. Standard with piezo bridge pickup.

1998-1999		$425	$500

California Standard

1994-2007. Offset double-cut, swamp ash body, bolt neck, 5-way switch.

1994-2007		$300	$350

R 3

1988-1993. Offset double-cut maple solidbody, bolt maple neck, 3 single-coils or single/single/humbucker.

1988-1993		$525	$600

R 4

1988-1993. R 3 with ash body and see-thru color finishes.

1988-1992		$600	$700

Texas Series

2003-present. Includes Standard (3 single-coils) and Deluxe (gold hardware, single/single/hum pickups).

2003-2010	Deluxe	$400	$450
2003-2010	Special	$375	$425
2003-2010	Standard	$375	$425

Blanchard Guitars

1994-present. Luthier Mark Blanchard builds premium grade, custom steel-string and classical guitars originally in Mammoth Lakes, California, and since May '03, in northwest Montana.

Blindworm Guitars

2008-present. Luthiers Andrew J. Scott and Steven Sells build premium and presentation grade, production/custom, acoustic, electric and electric-acoustic guitars in Colorado Springs, Colorado. They also build basses, mandolins, banjos and others.

Blount

1985-present. Professional and premium grade, production/custom, acoustic flat-top guitars built by luthier Kenneth H. Blount Jr. in Sebring, Florida.

Blue Star

1984-present. Luthier Bruce Herron builds his production/custom guitars in Fennville, Michigan. He also builds mandolins, lap steels, dulcimers and ukes.

Bluebird

1920s-1930s. Private brand with Bluebird painted on headstock, built by the Oscar Schmidt Co. and possibly others. Most likely made for distributor.

13" Flat-Top

1930s		$125	$150

Blueridge

Early 1980s-present. Intermediate and professional grade, production, solid-top acoustic guitars distributed by Saga. In '00, the product line was redesigned with the input of luthier Greg Rich (Rich and Taylor guitars).

Bluesouth

1991-ca. 2006. Custom electric guitars built by luthier Ronnie Knight in Muscle Shoals, Alabama. He also built basses.

Boaz Elkayam Guitars

1985-present. Presentation grade, custom steel, nylon, and flamenco guitars made by luthier Boaz Elkayam in Chatsworth, California.

Boedigheimer Instruments

2000-present. Luthier Brian Boedigheimer builds his professional and premium grade, production/custom, semi-hollowbody electric guitars in Red Wing, Minnesota. He plans to add acoustic guitars in late 2011.

Bohmann

1878-ca. 1926. Acoustic flat-top guitars, harp guitars, mandolins, banjos, violins made in Chicago Illinois, by Joseph Bohmann (born 1848, in Czechoslovakia). Bohmann's American Musical Industry founded 1878. Guitar body widths are 12", 13", 14", 15". He had 13 grades of guitars by 1900 (Standard, Concert, Grand Concert sizes). Early American use of plywood. Some painted wood finishes. Special amber-oil varnishes. Tuner bushings. Early ovalled fingerboards. Patented tuner plates and bridge design. Steel engraved label inside. Probably succeeded by son Joseph Frederick Bohmann.

Ca. 1896 12" body faux rosewood, 13", 14" and 15" body faux rosewood birch, 12", 13", 14" and 15" body sunburst maple, 12", 13", 14" and 15" body rosewood. By 1900 Styles 0, 1, 2 and 3 Standard, Concert and Grand Concert maple, Styles 1, 2, 3, 4, 5, 6, 7, 8, 9, 10, 11 and 12 in Standard, Concert, and Grand Concert rosewood.

14 3/4" Flat-Top

Solid spruce top, veneered Brazilian rosewood back and sides, wood marquetry around top and soundhole, natural. Each Bohmann should be valued on a case-by-case basis.

1896-1900	Brazilian	$800	$1,000
1896-1900	Other woods	$300	$400

2007 Blade Texas Custom 20

Blueridge BR-40CE

*Boulder Creek
Solitaire Series R3N*

Borges Hayride

MODEL YEAR	FEATURES	EXC. COND. LOW	HIGH

Harp Guitar
1896-1899	All styles	$3,000	$3,500

Bolin
1978-present. Professional and premium grade, production/custom, solidbody guitars built by luthier John Bolin in Boise, Idaho. Bolin is well-known for his custom work. His Cobra guitars are promoted and distributed by Sanderson Sales and Marketing as part of the Icons of America Series. He also builds basses.

NS
1996-present. Slot-headstock, bolt-on neck, single-cut solidbody, Seymour Duncan passive pickups or EMG active, from '96 to the fall of 2001 custom-built serial numbers to 0050 then from the fall of '01 to the present production model build starting with SN 0051.
1996-2001	Custom-built	$1,400	$1,700
2001-2010	Standard production	$750	$900

Bolt
1988-1991. Founded by luthier Wayne Bolt and Jim Dala Pallu in Schnecksville, Pennsylvania, Bolt's first work was CNC machined OEM necks and bodies made for Kramer and BC Rich. In '90, they started building solidbody Bolt guitars, many with airbrushed graphics. Only about 100 to 125 were built, around 40 with graphics.

Bond
1984-1985. Andrew Bond made around 1,400 Electraglide guitars in Scotland. Logo says 'Bond Guitars, London'.

ElectraGlide
1984-1985. Black carbon graphite 1-piece body and neck, double-cut, 3 single-coils (2 humbuckers were also supposedly available), digital LED controls that required a separate transformer.
1984-1985		$900	$1,100

Borges Guitars
2000-present. Luthier Julius Borges builds his premium grade, production/custom, acoustic guitars in Groton, Massachusetts.

Boulder Creek Guitars
2007-present. Intermediate and professional grade, production, imported dreadnought, classical, and 12-string guitars distributed by Morgan Hill Music of Morgan Hill, California. They also offer basses and ukes.

Bourgeois
1993-1999, 2000-present. Luthier Dana Bourgeois builds his professional and premium grade, production/custom, acoustic and archtop guitars in Lewiston, Maine. Bourgeois co-founded Schoenberg guitars and built Schoenberg models from '86-'90. Bourgeois' 20th Anniversary model was issued in '97. Bourgeois Guitars, per se, went of business

at the end of '99. Patrick Theimer created Pantheon Guitars, which included 7 luthiers (including Bourgeois) working in an old 1840s textile mill in Lewiston, Maine and Bourgeois models continue to be made as part of the Pantheon organization.

Blues
1996. D-style, all koa.
1996		$3,200	$3,600

Country Boy
1990s-present. Pre-war D-style model designed for Ricky Skaggs with Sitka spruce top, select mahogany back and sides, Bourgeois script logo headstock inlay, individually labeled with a Ricky Skaggs label, natural.
1990-2010		$1,700	$2,200

Country Boy Deluxe
2000-present. Country Boy with Adirondack spruce top.
2000-2010		$2,100	$2,600

D - 20th Anniversary
1997. 20 made, bearclaw spruce top, rosewood back and sides, mother-of-pearl 'board, ornate abalone floral pattern inlay, abalone rosette and border, natural.
1997		$2,900	$3,300

Georgia Dreadnought
2003. Mahogany, Adirondack.
2003		$2,200	$2,600

JOM
1990s-present. Jumbo Orchestra Model flat-top, 15 5/8". Model includes one with cedar top, mahogany back and sides, and one with spruce top, Brazilian rosewood back and sides.
1990s	Brazilian rosewood	$3,200	$3,850
1990s	Indian rosewood	$1,800	$2,200
1990s	Mahogany	$1,150	$1,400

JOMC/OMC
1990s-present. JOM (jumbo) cutaway.
1995	OMC, figured mahogany	$2,400	$2,900
1995-2005	JOMC200, Indian rosewood	$2,300	$2,800

JR-A
1990s. Artisan Series, 15 5/8", spruce top, rosewood back and sides.
1990s		$1,000	$1,250

Martin Simpson
1997-2003. Grand auditorium with unusual cutaway that removes one-half of the upper treble bout, Englemann spruce top, Indian rosewood back and sides, natural.
1997-2003		$2,100	$2,500

OM Deluxe Artisan
2002. Indian rosewood, sitka.
2002		$1,700	$2,000

OM Soloist
1990s-present. Full-sized, soft cutaway flat-top, Adirondack spruce top, figured Brick Red Brazilian rosewood back and sides, natural.
1990s		$4,500	$5,000

MODEL YEAR	FEATURES	EXC. COND. LOW	HIGH

Ricky Skaggs Signature
1998. D-style, rosewood sides and back, spruce top.

1998		$2,300	$2,500

Slope D
1993-present. D-size, 16", spruce top, mahogany back and sides.

1993-2010		$1,950	$2,300

Vintage D
2000s. Adirondack spruce (Eastern red spruce) top, optional rosewood back and sides.

2000s	Brazilian rosewood	$3,700	$4,200
2000s	Indian rosewood	$1,900	$2,200

Vintage OM
2005. Madagascar rosewood and Italian spruce top.

2005		$3,000	$3,500

Bown Guitars
1981-present. Luthier Ralph Bown builds custom steel-string, nylon-string, baritone, and harp guitars in Walmgate, England.

Bozo
1964-present. Bozo (pronounced Bo-zho) Podunavac learned instrument building in his Yugoslavian homeland and arrived in the United States in '59. In '64 he opened his own shop and has built a variety of high-end, handmade, acoustic instruments, many being one-of-a-kind. He has built around 570 guitars over the years. There were several thousand Japanese-made (K. Yairi shop) Bell Western models bearing his name made from '79-'80; most of these were sold in Europe. He currently builds premium and presentation grade, production/custom guitars in East Englewood, Florida.

Acoustic 12-String
1970-1980s. Indian rosewood.

1970-1980s		$1,600	$1,900

Classical
1969. Limited production.

1969		$2,000	$2,300

Cutaway 12-String
1977-1998. Often old world Balkan ornamentation, generally Sitka spruce top, Indian rosewood back and sides, widow-style headstock, ornamentation can vary (standard or elaborate).

1977	Standard	$1,550	$1,800
1993	Elaborate	$3,200	$3,700
1998	Elaborate Custom	$4,000	$4,600

Bradford
Mid-1960s. Brand name used by the W.T. Grant Company, one of the old Five & Ten style retail stores similar to F.W. Woolworth and Kresge. Many of these guitars and basses were made in Japan by Guyatone.

Acoustic Flat-Top

1960s		$150	$175

Electric Solidbody

1960s	1 or 2 pickups	$175	$200
1960s	3 pickups	$200	$250
1960s	4 pickups	$300	$350

MODEL YEAR	FEATURES	EXC. COND. LOW	HIGH

Bradley
1970s. Budget Japanese copy models imported by Veneman's Music Emporium.

Brawley Basses
Headquartered in Temecula, California, and designed by Keith Brawley, offering solidbody guitars made in Korea. They also made basses.

Brazen
2005-present. Owner Steve Tsai, along with luthier Eddie Estrada, build professional and premium grade, production, electric guitars in Plainview, New York and assemble them in Covina, California. Steve also imports a line of intermediate grade guitars from China which are set up in Covina.

Breedlove
1990-present. Founded by Larry Breedlove and Steve Henderson. Intermediate, professional, premium, and presentation grade, production/custom, steel and nylon string flat-top built in Tumalo, Oregon and imported. They also build mandolins, basses, lapsteels and ukes. Several available custom options may add to the values listed here. They offered chambered electric guitars starting in 2008 but in January 2010, Breedlove discontinued all electric guitar production. Also in '10, they became part of Two Old Hippies.

AC Series
2004-present. Atlas series Concert guitars, imports.

2004-2009		$500	$575

AD Series
2004-present. Atlas series Dreadnought guitars, imports

2004-2010		$250	$350

Bossa Nova
2009-present. Nylon concert, soft cutaway, rosewood body, SN25 features.

2009-2010		$1,600	$2,000

C1 (C10)
1990-present. Shallow concert-sized flat-top, non-cut, solid spruce top, mahogany back and sides, natural.

1990-2010		$1,300	$1,600

C2 (C22)
1990-2004. Highly figured walnut body with sitka spruce top, large sloping cutaway.

1990-2004		$1,700	$2,100

C5/Northwest
1995-present. Grand concert with large soft cutaway, sitka spruce top, figured myrtlewood body.

2000-2010		$1,800	$2,200

C15/R
1990-2004. Concert-size C1 with soft rounded cutaway, and optional cedar top and rosewood back and sides, gold tuners.

1990-2004		$1,500	$1,900

C20
1990s-2004. Concert series, mahgoany back and sides, sitka spruce top.

2000-2004		$1,500	$1,900

Bourgeois Country Boy

Brazen Fantasy Series

GUITARS

Breedlove C25 Custom

Breedlove Ed Gerhard

MODEL YEAR	FEATURES	EXC. COND. LOW	HIGH

C20 Limited (Brazilian)
2007. Brazilian rosewood back and sides, spruce top, natural gloss finish.

2007		$2,900	$3,500

C25 Custom
1990s-present. Custom koa body, sitka spruce top.

2000-2010		$2,000	$2,500

CM
1990s-present. Unusual double-cut style, walnut body and top.

1990s		$3,000	$3,600

D20
2002-2010. Sitka spruce top, mahogany body, non cut.

2002-2010		$1,600	$2,000

D25/R
2002-present. Cutaway, sitka spruce top, Indian rosewood back and sides.

2002-2010		$1,700	$2,100

Ed Gerhard
1997-2010. Shallow jumbo, soft cut, Indian rosewood body.

1997-2010	Custom	$2,000	$2,500
1997-2010	Signature	$1,900	$2,300

J Series (Jumbo)
1990s-present. Spruce top, myrtlewood body.

2000-2010	J25	$2,100	$2,400

Mark IV Custom
2008-2010. Single-cut chambered body, 2 pickups.

2008-2010		$1,400	$1,750

Myrtlewood Limited 01
1990s-2003. Acoustic/electric, D-size, solid spruce top, solid myrtlewood back and sides.

1995-2003		$1,350	$1,700

N25E
2000-2004. Acoustic/electric version of N25.

2000-2004		$1,350	$1,700

N25R
2000-2004. Classical, Western red cedar top, solid Indian rosewood back and sides.

2000-2004		$1,450	$1,800

RD/R
1993. Solid spruce and rosewood.

1993		$1,100	$1,300

RD20 X/R
1999. Indian rosewood back and sides, sitka spruce top, winged bridge, abalone soundhole rosette.

1999		$1,400	$1,700

SC Series
1995-2007. S Series Concert size, made in U.S. but with less ornamentation then most premier models.

1990-2004	SC20, Brazilian	$2,000	$2,500
1990-2007	SC20, other	$1,300	$1,600
1990-2007	SC25, other	$1,500	$1,800
1998	SC25, Koa Adirondack LE	$2,000	$2,500
1999	SC20 -Z		
	Custom (Zircote)	$1,400	$1,700

MODEL YEAR	FEATURES	EXC. COND. LOW	HIGH

SJ Series
1995-2007. S Series Jumbo size, made in U.S. but with less ornamentation then most premier models.

1995-2007	SJ20-12 W	$1,400	$1,700
1997-2007	SJ25	$1,100	$1,400

Brentwood
1970s. Student models built by Kay for store or jobber.

K-100
1970s. 13" student flat-top, K-100 label inside back, K logo on 'guard.

1970s		$40	$50

Brian May Guitar Company
2006-present. Guitarist Brian May teamed up with Barry Moorhouse and Pete Malandrone to offer versions of his Red Special Guitar. They also offer a bass.

Brian May Special
2006-present. Mahogany solidbody, 3 pickups, various colors.

2006-2010		$400	$450

Brian Moore
1992-present. Founded by Patrick Cummings, Brian Moore and Kevin Kalagher in Brewster, New York; they introduced their first guitars in '94. Initially expensive custom shop guitars with carbon-resin bodies with highly figured wood tops; later went to all wood bodies cut on CNC machines. The intermediate and professional grade, production, iGuitar/i2000series was introduced in 2000 and made in Korea, but set up in the U.S. Currently the premium grade, production/custom, Custom Shop Series guitars are handcrafted in La Grange, New York. They also build basses and electric mandolins.

C-45
1999-2001. Solidbody, mahogany body, bolt neck, 2 P-90-type pickups, natural satin.

1999-2001		$750	$950

C-55/C-55P
1997-2004. Solidbody, burl maple body, bolt neck, currently produced as a limited edition. C-55P indicates Piezo option.

1997-2004		$750	$950

C-90/C-90P
1996-present. Solidbody, figured maple top, mahogany body, bolt neck, hum-single-hum pickups, red sunburst. C-90P has Piezo option.

1996-2010	USA	$800	$1,000

DC-1/DC-1P
1997-present. Quilted maple top, 2 humbuckers, single-cut, gold hardware. DC-1P has Piezo option.

1997-2010		$1,600	$2,000

iGuitar Series
2000-present.

2000-2010	2.13	$650	$800
2000-2010	2P	$600	$750
2000-2010	8.13 & 81.13	$400	$500
2000-2010	i1	$550	$675

MODEL		EXC. COND.	
YEAR	FEATURES	LOW	HIGH

MC1

1994-present. High-end model, quilted maple top, various pickup options including piezo and midi, gold hardware, currently a limited edition with only 12 produced each year. Should be evaluated on a case-by-case basis.

1994-2010		$1,500	$1,800

Brian Stone Classical Guitars

Luthier Brian Stone builds his classical guitars in Corvallis, Oregon.

Briggs

1999-present. Luthier Jack Briggs builds his professional and premium grade, production/custom, chambered and solidbody guitars in Raleigh, North Carolina.

Broman

1930s. The Broman brand was most likely used by a music studio (or distributor) on instruments made by others, including Regal-built resonator instruments.

Bronson

1930s-1950s. George Bronson was a steel guitar instructor in the Detroit area and his instruments were made by other companies. They were mainly lap steels, but some other types were also offered. Usually were sold with matching amp.

Honolulu Master Hawaiian

1938		$4,600	$5,700

Student Hawaiian

1930s	13" flat-top	$175	$225

Brook Guitars

1993-present. Simon Smidmore and Andy Petherick build their production/custom Brook steel-string, nylon-strings, and archtops in Dartmoor, England.

Brown's Guitar Factory

1982-present. Luthier John Brown builds professional and premium grade, production/custom, solidbody guitars in Inver Grove Heights, Minnesota. He also builds basses.

Bruné, R. E.

1966-present. Luthier Richard Bruné builds his premium and presentation grade, custom, classical and flamenco guitars in Evanston, Illinois. He also offers his professional and premium grade Model 20 and Model 30, which are handmade in a leading guitar workshop in Japan. Bruné's "Guitars with Guts" column appears quarterly in Vintage Guitar magazine.

Bruno and Sons

1834-present. Established in 1834 by Charles Bruno, primarily as a distributor, Bruno and Sons marketed a variety of brands, including their own. Later became part of Kaman Music.

MODEL		EXC. COND.	
YEAR	FEATURES	LOW	HIGH

Harp Guitar

1924		$2,000	$2,500

Hollowbody Electric

1960s-1970s. Various imported models.

1960s		$150	$550

Parlor Guitar

1880-1920. Various woods used on back and sides.

1880-1920	Birch	$375	$475
1880-1920	Brazilian rosewood	$1,000	$1,250
1880-1920	Mahogany	$475	$600

Buddy Blaze

1985-present. Professional and premium grade, custom/production, solidbody electric guitars built by luthier Buddy Blaze from '85 to '87 in Arlington, Texas, and presently in Kailua Kona, Hawaii. He also designs intermediate grade models which are imported.

Bunker

1961-present. Founded by guitarist Dave Bunker, who began building guitars with his father. He continued building custom guitars and basses while performing in Las Vegas in the '60s and developed a number of innovations. Around '92 Bunker began PBC Guitar Technology with John Pearse and Paul Chernay in Coopersburg, Pennsylvania, building instruments under the PBC brand and, from '94-'96, for Ibanez' USA Custom Series. PBC closed in '97 and Bunker moved back to Washington State to start Bunker Guitar Technology and resumed production of several Bunker models. In early 2002, Bunker Guitars became part of Maple Valley Tone Woods of Port Angeles, Washington. Currently Bunker offers intermediate, professional, and premium grade, production/custom, guitars and basses built in Port Angeles. Most early Bunker guitars were pretty much custom-made in low quantities.

Burly Guitars

2007-present. Luthier Jeff Ayers builds his professional and premium grade, custom, solid and semi-hollowbody guitars in Land O' Lakes, Wisconsin. He plans on adding basses.

Burns

1960-1970, 1974-1983, 1992-present. Intermediate and professional grade, production, electric guitars built in England and Korea. They also build basses. Jim Burns began building guitars in the late-'50s and established Burns London Ltd in '60. Baldwin Organ (see Baldwin listing) purchased the company in '65 and offered the instruments until '70. The Burns name was revived in '91 by Barry Gibson as Burns London, with Jim Burns' involvement, offering reproductions of some of the classic Burns models of the '60s. Jim Burns passed away in August '98.

Baby Bison

1965. Double-cut solidbody, scroll headstock, 2 pickups, shorter scale, tremolo.

1965		$825	$925

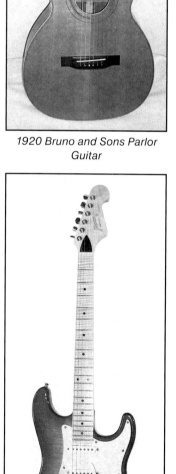

1920 Bruno and Sons Parlor Guitar

Bunker Classic 57

GUITARS

Burns Bison

Campellone Special

MODEL		EXC. COND.	
YEAR	FEATURES	LOW	HIGH

Bison
1964-1965, 2003-present. Double-cut solidbody, 3 pickups, tremolo, black or white, scroll-headstock, replaced flat headstock Black Bison. Has been reissued with both types of headstocks.
| 1964-1965 | | $1,200 | $1,500 |
| 2003-2010 Reissue | | $375 | $400 |

Black Bison
1961-1962. Double cut solid, large horns, 4 pickups, flat headstock. Replaced by scroll-headstock Bison.
| 1961-1962 | | $1,425 | $1,775 |

Brian May Signature - Red Special
2001-2006. Replica of May's original 'Red Special' but with added whammy-bar, red finish. Korean-made.
| 2001-2006 | | $650 | $850 |

Cobra
2004-present. Double-cut solid, 2 pickups.
| 2004-2010 | | $125 | $175 |

Double Six
1964-1965, 2003-present. Solidbody 12-string, double-cut, 3 pickups, greenburst. Has been reissued.
| 1964-1965 | | $1,200 | $1,500 |
| 2003-2009 | | $200 | $300 |

Flyte
1974-1977. Fighter jet-shaped solidbody, pointed headstock, 2 humbucking pickups, silver, has been reissued.
| 1974-1977 | | $700 | $850 |

GB 66 Deluxe
1965. Like 66 Standard, but with bar pickups and add Density control.
| 1965 | | $800 | $950 |

GB 66 Deluxe Standard
1965. Offset double-cut, f-holes, 2 Ultra-Sonic pickups.
| 1965 | | $750 | $900 |

Jazz
1962-1965. Offset double-cut solid, shorter scale, 2 pickups.
| 1962-1965 | | $850 | $1,050 |

Jazz Split Sound
1962-1965. Offset double-cut solid, 3 pickups, tremolo, red sunburst.
| 1962-1965 | | $1,000 | $1,200 |

Marquee
2000-present. Offset double-cut solid, 3 pickups, scroll headstock
| 2000-2010 | | $200 | $250 |

Marvin
1964-1965. Offset double-cut solidbody, scroll headstock, 3 pickups, tremolo, white.
| 1964-1965 | | $1,300 | $1,550 |

Nu-Sonic
1964-1965. Solidbody, 2 pickups, tremolo, white or cherry, has been reissued.
| 1964-1965 | | $725 | $900 |

Sonic
1960-1964. Double shallow cut solid, 2 pickups, cherry.
| 1960-1964 | | $600 | $725 |

Split Sonic
1962-1964. Solidbody, 3 pickups, bound neck, tremolo, red sunburst.
| 1962-1964 | | $900 | $1,100 |

Steer
2000-present. Semi-hollowbody, sound-hole, 2 pickups, non-cut and single-cut versions.
| 2000-2010 | | $325 | $375 |

TR-2
1963-1964. Semi-hollow, 2 pickups, red sunburst.
| 1963-1964 | | $900 | $1,075 |

Vibraslim
1964-1965. Double-cut, f-holes, 2 pickups, red sunburst.
| 1964-1965 | | $975 | $1,200 |

Virginian
1964-1965. Burns of London model, later offered as Baldwin Virginian in '65.
| 1964-1965 | | $850 | $1,000 |

Vista Sonic
1962-1964. Offset double-cut solid, 3 pickups, red sunburst.
| 1962-1964 | | $725 | $850 |

Burnside
1987-1988. Budget solidbody guitars imported by Guild.

Solidbody Electric/Blade
1987-1988. Solidbody, fat pointy headstock.
| 1987-1988 | | $150 | $200 |

Burns-Weill
1959. Jim Burns and Henry Weill teamed up to produce three solidbody electric and three solidbody bass models under this English brand. Models included the lower end Fenton, a small single-cutaway, 2 pickups and an elongated headstock and the bizarrely styled RP2G. Henry Weill continued to produce a slightly different RP line under the re-named Fenton-Weill brand.

Burny
1980s-1990s. Solidbody electric guitars from Fernandes and built in Japan, Korea or China.

Burrell
1984-2010. Luthier Leo Burrell built his professional grade, production/custom, acoustic, semi-hollow, and solidbody guitars in Huntington, West Virginia. He also built basses. Leo retired in '10.

Burton Guitars
1980-present. Custom classical guitars built by luthier Cynthia Burton in Portland, Oregon.

Buscarino Guitars
1981-present. Luthier John Buscarino builds his premium and presentation grade, custom archtops and steel-string and nylon-string flat-tops in Franklin, North Carolina.

MODEL YEAR	FEATURES	EXC. COND. LOW	HIGH

Byers, Gregory

1984-present. Premium grade, custom classical and Flamenco guitars built by luthier Gregory Byers in Willits, California.

Byrd

1998-present. Custom/production, professional and premium grade, V-shaped electric guitars, built by luthiers James Byrd and Joe Riggio, in Seattle and several other cities in the state of Washington.

C. Fox

1997-2002. Luthier Charles Fox built his premium grade, production/custom flat-tops in Healdsburg, California. In '02 he closed C. Fox Guitars and move to Portland, Oregon to build Charles Fox Guitars.

CA (Composite Acoustics)

1999-2010, 2011-present. Professional grade, production, carbon fiber composite guitars that were built in Lafayette, Louisiana. The company ceased production in February, '10. At the end of '10 CA was acquired by Peavey, which launched the new Meridian, Mississippi-based line in February, '10.

Califone

1966. Six and 12-string guitars and basses made by Murphy Music Industries (maker of the Murph guitars) for Rheem Califone-Roberts which manufactured tape recorders and related gear. Very few made.

Callaham

1989-present. Professional, production/custom, solidbody electric guitars built by luthier Bill Callaham in Winchester, Virginia. They also make tube amp heads.

Camelli

1960s. Line of solidbody electric guitars imported from Italy.

Solidbody Electric

1960s		$500	$600

Cameo

1960s-1970s. Japanese- and Korean-made electric and acoustic guitars. They also offered basses.

Electric

1960-1970s	Higher-end	$300	$350

Campbell American Guitars

2005-present. Luthier Dean Campbell builds his intermediate and professional grade, production/custom, solidbody guitars originally in Pawtucket, Rhode Island, and currently in Westwood, Massachusetts. From '02 to '05, he built guitars under the Greene & Campbell brand.

Campellone

1978-present. Luthier Mark Campellone builds his premium grade, custom archtops in Greenville, Rhode Island. He also made electrics and basses in the '70s and '80s, switching to archtops around '90.

Deluxe

1990-present. 16" to 18" archtop, middle of the company product line, blond or sunburst.

1990-2010		$4,200	$5,000

Special

1994-present. 16" to 18" archtop, top of the company product line, carved spruce top, carved flamed maple back, flamed maple sides, blond or sunburst.

1994-2010		$5,500	$6,500

Standard

2000-present. 16" to 18" archtop, lower of the 3 model lines offered.

2000-2010		$3,000	$3,500

Canvas

2004-present. Budget and intermediate grade, production, solid and semi-hollow body guitars imported from China by America Sejung Corp. They also offer basses.

Carbonaro

1974-present. Luthier Robert Carbonaro builds his premium grade, production/custom, archtop and flat-top guitars in Santa Fe, New Mexico.

Carl Fischer

1920s. Most likely a brand made for a distributor. Instruments built by the Oscar Schmidt Co. and possibly others.

Carlos

ca.1976-late 1980s. Imported copies of classic American acoustics distributed by Coast Wholesale Music.

Acoustic Flat-Top

1976-1980s	Various models	$50	$200

Carvin

1946-present. Intermediate and professional grade, production/custom, acoustic and electric guitars. They also offer basses and amps. Founded in Los Angeles by Hawaiian guitarist and recording artist Lowell C. Kiesel as the L.C. Kiesel Co. making pickups for guitars. Bakelite Kiesel-brand electric Hawaiian lap steels are introduced in early-'47. Small tube amps introduced ca. '47. By late-'49, the Carvin brand is introduced, combining parts of names of sons Carson and Gavin. Carvin acoustic and electric Spanish archtops are introduced in '54. Instruments are sold by mail-order only. The company relocated to Covina, California in '49 and to Escondido, California in '68. Two retail stores opened in Hollywood and Santa Ana, California in '91.

Approx. 2,000-4,000 guitars made prior to '70 with no serial number. First serial number appeared

Carbonaro Dreadnaught

1997 Carvin DC-127

Jon Way

1966 Carvin Doubleneck

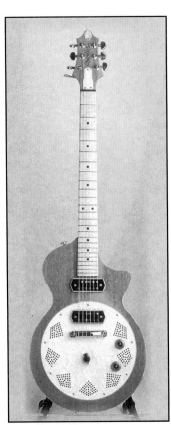

Chandler Lectra Slide

MODEL		EXC. COND.	
YEAR	FEATURES	LOW	HIGH

in '70, stamped on end of fingerboard, beginning with #5000. All are consecutive. Later SN on neck plates.

Approximate SN ranges include:
1970: First serial number #5000 to 10019 ('79).
'80-'83: 10768 to 15919.
'84-'87: 13666 to 25332.
'88-'90: 22731 to 25683.
'91-'94: 25359 to 42547.
'95-'99: 45879 to 81427.
'00-present: 56162 upward.

Casa Montalvo

1987-present. Intermediate and professional grade, production/custom flamenco and classical guitars made in Mexico for George Katechis of Berkeley Musical Instrument Exchange.

Casio

1987-1988. Line of digital guitars imported from Japan, sporting plastic bodies and synthesizer features.

DG1

1987		$50	$75

DG10
1987. Self-contained digital guitar.

1987		$150	$175

DG20
1987. Midi-capable digital guitar.

1987		$200	$250

PG-300
1987. Similar to PG-380, but with less features.

1987		$325	$375

PG-310
1987. Similar to PG-380, but with less features.

1987		$400	$475

PG-380
1987. Guitar synth, double-cut, over 80 built-in sounds, midi controller capable.

1987		$650	$800

Casper Guitar Technologies

2009-present. Professional grade, production/custom, solidbody electric guitars built by luthier Stephen Casper in Leisure City, Florida. He also builds basses.

Cat's Eyes

1980s. Made by Tokai, Cat's Eyes headstock logo, see Tokai guitar listings.

Champion

Ca. 1894-1897. Chicago's Robert Maurer built this brand of instruments before switching to the Maurer brand name around 1897.

Chandler

1984-present. Intermediate and professional grade, production/custom, solidbody electric guitars built by luthiers Paul and Adrian Chandler in Chico, California. They also build basses, lap steels

MODEL		EXC. COND.	
YEAR	FEATURES	LOW	HIGH

and pickups. Chandler started making pickguards and accessories in the '70s, adding electric guitars, basses, and effects in '84.

555 Model
1992-present. Sharp double-cut, 3 mini-humbuckers, TV Yellow.

1992-2010		$700	$875

Austin Special
1991-1999. Resembles futuristic Danelectro, lipstick pickups, available in 5-string version.

1991-1999		$625	$750

Austin Special Baritone
1994-1999. Nicknamed Elvis, gold metalflake finish, mother-of-toilet-seat binding, tremolo, baritone.

1994-1999		$625	$750

LectraSlide
2001-present. Single-cut, Rezo 'guard, 2 pickups.

2001-2010		$700	$850

Metro
1995-2000. Double-cut slab body, P-90 in neck position and humbucker in the bridge position.

1995-2000		$525	$650

Telepathic
1994-2000. Classic single-cut style, 3 models; Basic, Standard, Deluxe.

1994-2000	Basic	$450	$550
1994-2000	Deluxe 1122 Model	$600	$750
1994-2000	Standard	$550	$700

Chantus

1984-present. Premium grade, production/custom, classical and flamenco guitars built in Austin, Texas, by luthier William King. He also builds ukes.

Chapin

Professional and premium grade, production/custom, semi-hollow, solidbody, and acoustic electric guitars built by luthiers Bill Chapin and Fred Campbell in San Jose, California.

Chapman

1970-present. Made by Emmett Chapman, the Stick features 10 strings and is played by tapping both hands. The Grand Stick features 12 strings.

Stick
10 or 12 strings, touch-tap hybrid electric instrument.

1970-1999	10-string	$1,400	$1,700
1970-1999	12-string	$1,600	$2,000
2000-2003	10-string	$1,400	$1,700

Char

1985-present. Premium grade, custom, classical and steel string acoustic guitars built in Portland, Oregon by luthier Kerry Char. He also builds harp-guitars and ukuleles.

Charis Acoustic

1996-present. Premium grade, custom/production, steel-string guitars built by luthier Bill Wise in Bay City, Michigan.

MODEL YEAR	FEATURES	EXC. COND. LOW	HIGH

Charles Fox Guitars

1968-present. Luthier Charles Fox builds his premium and presentation grade, custom, steel and nylon string guitars in Portland, Oregon. He also produced GRD acoustic and electric guitars for '78-'82 and C. Fox acoustic guitars for '97-'02. He also operates The American School of Lutherie in Portland.

Charles Shifflett Acoustic Guitars

1990-present. Premium grade, custom, classical, flamenco, resonator, and harp guitars built by luthier Charles Shifflett in High River, Alberta. He also builds basses and banjos.

Charvel

1976 (1980)-present. Intermediate and professional grade, production, solidbody electric guitars. They also build basses. Founded by Wayne Charvel as Charvel Manufacturing in '76, making guitar parts in Asuza, California. Moved to San Dimas in '78. Also in '78 Grover Jackson bought out Charvel. In '79 or early '80 Charvel branded guitars are introduced. U.S.-made to '85, a combination of imports and U.S.-made post-'85. Charvel also manufactured the Jackson brand.

Charvel licensed its trademark to IMC (Hondo) in '85. IMC bought Charvel in '86 and moved the factory to Ontario, California. On October 25, 2002, Fender Musical Instruments Corp. (FMIC) took ownership of Jackson/Charvel Manufacturing Inc.

Pre-Pro (Pre-Production) Charvels began in November 1980 and ran until sometime in 1981. These are known as 'non-plated' indicating pre-production versus a production neck plate. Production serialized neck plates are considered to be San Dimas models which have a Charvel logo, serial number, and a PO Box San Dimas notation on the neck plate. These Serialized Plated Charvels came after Pre-Pros. Late '81 and '82 saw the early serialized guitars with 21-fret necks; these are more valuable. During '82 the 22-fret neck was introduced. The so-called Soft Strat-, Tele-, Flying V-, and Explorer-style headstocks are associated with the early San Dimas Charvel models. In late '82 the pointy headstock, called the Jackson style, was introduced. In '82 the Superstrat style with a neck plate was introduced. Superstrats with a Kahler tailpiece have a lower value than the Pre-Pro models (with Fender-style trem tailpiece).

Collectors of vintage Charvels look for the vintage Charvel 3-on-a-side logo. This is a defining feature and a cutoff point for valuations. Bogus builders are replicating early Charvels and attempting to sell them as originals so fakes can be a problem for Charvel collectors, so buyer beware.

Other electric guitar manufacturing info:
1986-1989 Japanese-made Models 1 through 8
1989-1991 Japanese-made 550 XL, 650 XL/ Custom, 750 XL (XL=neck-thru)
1989-1992 Japanese-made Models 275, 375, 475, 575

1990-1991 Korean-made Charvette models
1992-1994 Korean-made Models 325, 425

Early Charvel serial numbers (provided by former Jackson/Charvel associate Tim Wilson):
The first 500 to 750 guitars had no serial number, just marked "Made In U.S.A." on their neckplates. Five digit serial numbers were then used until November '81 when 4-digit number adopted, starting with #1001.
1981: 1001-1095
1982: 1096-1724
1983: 1725-2938
1984: 2939-4261
1985: 4262-5303
1986: 5304-5491

Pre-Pro

November 1980-1981. Pre-Pros came in different configurations of body styles, pickups, and finishes. There are five basic Pre-Pro formats: the Standard Body, the Bound Body, the Graphic Body, the Flamed Top, and the Matching Headstock. It is possible to have a combination, such as a Bound Body and Matching Headstock. Line items are based on body style and can feature any one of four neck/headstock-styles used: the so-called Tele-headstock, Strat-headstock, Flying V headstock, and Explorer headstock. Finishes included white, black, red, metallic Lake Placid Blue, and special graphics. All original parts adds considerable value and it is often difficult to determine what is original on these models, so expertise is required. An original Fender brass trem tailpiece, for example, adds considerable value. The Pre-Pro models were prone to modification such as added Kahler and Floyd Rose trems. Price ranges are wide because this is a relatively new market without mature pricing.

1980-1981	Bound body	$3,300	$4,200
1980-1981	Flamed top, stained body	$4,300	$5,500
1980-1981	Graphic body	$3,800	$4,800
1980-1981	Matching headstock & body	$4,800	$6,000
1980-1981	Standard body	$2,700	$3,500

275 Deluxe Dinky

1989-1991. Made in Japan, offset double-cut solidbody, 1 single-coil and 1 humbucker ('89), 3 stacked humbuckers ('90-'91), tremolo.

1989	1 single, 1 humbucker	$225	$275
1990-1991	Stacked humbuckers	$225	$275

325SL

1992-1994. Dot inlays.

1992-1994		$225	$275

325SLX

1992-1994. Surfcaster-like thinline acoustic/electric, dual cutaways, f-hole, on-board chorus, shark inlays, made in Korea.

1992-1994		$225	$275

375 Deluxe

1989-1992. Maple or rosewood 'board, dot inlays, single-single-humbucker.

1989-1992		$225	$275

Char AJ Model

Charis Acoustic

1986 Charvel Model 5

*Charvel So-Cal Series
Style 1 2H*

MODEL YEAR	FEATURES	EXC. COND. LOW	HIGH

475
1989-1992. Humbucker-single-single configuration, bolt-on neck, dot markers.

| 1989-1992 | | $225 | $275 |

475 Deluxe/Special
1989-1992. Introduced as Special, changed to Deluxe, bound rosewood board, shark tooth inlays, 2 oval stacked humbuckers and 1 bridge humbucker.

| 1989-1992 | | $225 | $275 |

525
1989-1994. Acoustic-electric, single-cut.

| 1989-1994 | | $225 | $275 |

550XL
1989-1990. Neck-thru (XL), dot markers, single rail humbucker and single bridge humbucker.

| 1989-1990 | | $325 | $400 |

625-C12
1993-2000. Acoustic-electric cutaway 12-string, spruce top.

| 1993-2000 | | $225 | $275 |

625F/625ACEL
1993-1995. Acoustic-electric cutaway, figured maple top.

| 1993-1995 | | $225 | $275 |

650XL/Custom
1989-1991. Introduced as neck-thru XL and discontinued as Custom, shark fin markers, 2 stacked oval humbuckers and 1 bridge humbucker, custom version of 550XL.

| 1989-1991 | | $700 | $850 |

750XL Soloist
1989-1990. Introduced as neck-thru XL, shark fin markers, carved alder archtop body, 2 humbuckers (1 neck/1 bridge), large Charvel logo.

| 1980s | | $1,000 | $1,250 |

Avenger
1990-1991. Randy Rhoads-style batwing-shaped solidbody, 3 stacked humbuckers, tremolo, made in Japan.

| 1990-1991 | | $300 | $375 |

Charvette
1989-1992. Charvette Series made in Korea, superstrat-style, model number series 100 through 300.

| 1990-1991 | | $175 | $225 |

CX Series
1991-1994. Imported offset double cut solidbodies, with body-mounted pickups – HS (192), HSS (292), SSS (392), HSS (692) or HSH (592) – or pickguard mounted pickups – HSS pickups (290, 390) or SSS (291, 391). All with standard tremolo except the 692, 592, 390, and 391 with deluxe locking trem.

| 1991-1994 | | $200 | $250 |

EVH Art Series
2004-2007. Offset double-cut solidbody, 1 humbucker, striped finish.

2004-2007	Black/white	$1,600	$2,000
2004-2007	White/black on red	$1,700	$2,500
2004-2007	Yellow/black	$1,600	$2,000

Fusion Deluxe
1989-1991. Double-cut solidbody, tremolo, 1 humbucker and 1 single-coil pickup, made in Japan.

| 1989-1991 | | $325 | $375 |

Fusion Standard/AS FX 1
1993-1996. Double-cut solidbody, tremolo, 1 regular and 2 mini humbuckers, made in Japan, also named AS FX1.

| 1993-1996 | | $275 | $325 |

Model 1/1A/1C
1986-1989. Offset double-cut solidbody, bolt-on maple neck, dot inlays, 1 humbucker, tremolo, made in Japan. Model 1A has 3 single-coils. Model 1C has 1 humbucker and 2 single-coils.

| 1986-1989 | | $350 | $450 |

Model 2
1986-1989. As Model 1, but with rosewood 'board.

| 1986-1989 | | $350 | $450 |

Model 3/3A/3DR/3L
1986-1989. As Model 2, but with 1 humbucker, 2 single coils. Model 3A has 2 humbuckers. Model 3DR has 1 humbucker and 1 single-coil.

| 1986-1989 | | $350 | $450 |

Model 4/4A
1986-1989. As Model 2, but with 1 regular humbucker and 2 stacked humbuckers mounted in the body (no pickguard), and with active electronics, shark-fin inlays. Model 4A has 2 regular humbuckers and dot markers.

| 1986-1989 | | $425 | $500 |

Model 5/5A
1986-1989. As Model 4A, but is neck-thru construction, with JE1000TG active elctronics. Model 5A is single humbucker and single knob version of Model 5, limited production, made in Japan.

| 1986-1989 | | $425 | $500 |

Model 6
1986-1989. As Model 4, but with shark's tooth 'board inlays, standard or various custom finishes.

| 1986-1989 | | $500 | $600 |

Model 7
1988-1989. Single-cut solidbody, bound top, reversed headstock, 2 single-coils, made in Japan.

| 1988-1989 | | $425 | $500 |

Model 88 LTD
1988. Double-cut solidbody, 1 slanted humbucker, shark fin inlay, 1000 built, made in Japan.

| 1988 | | $475 | $575 |

Predator
1989-1991. Offset double-cut, bridge humbucker, single-coil neck, bolt-on.

| 1989-1991 | | $300 | $375 |

San Dimas Serialized Plated
1981-1986, 1995-1997. U.S.-made with San Dimas neck plate, bolt neck, rounded headstock early production, pointy headstock later, reissued in mid-'90s.

1981-1982	Soft headstock	$2,600	$3,100
1982-1986	Pointy headstock	$1,700	$1,950
1995-1997	Soft headstock	$700	$900

San Dimas LTD 25th Anniversary
2006. About 100 made, 25th Anniversary logo on neck plate with production number, highly figured top, high-end appointments.

| 2006 | | $1,600 | $2,000 |

MODEL YEAR	FEATURES	EXC. COND. LOW	HIGH

San Dimas Reissue (FMIC)
2004-present. Alder body, bolt neck.
| 2004-2010 | | $700 | $1,000 |

So-Cal Series
2008-present. Offset double cut solidbody.
| 2008-2010 | Style 1 2H | $700 | $850 |

ST Custom
1990-1992. Offset double-cut ash solidbody, 2 single-coils and 1 humbucker, rosewood 'board, tremolo, made in Japan.
| 1990-1992 | | $325 | $375 |

ST Deluxe
1990-1992. Same as ST Custom but with maple 'board.
| 1990-1992 | | $300 | $350 |

Standard
2002-2003. Typical offset double-cut Charvel body, 2 Seymour Duncan humbucker pickups, various opaque colors.
| 2002-2003 | | $225 | $275 |

Star
1980-1981. The Star is considered by early-Charvel collectors to be Charvel's only original design with its unique four-point body.
| 1980-1981 | | $2,500 | $3,100 |

Surfcaster
1991-1994. Offset double-cut, f-hole, various pickup options, bound body, tremolo, made in Japan.
1991-1994	1 single-coil, 1 humbucker	$850	$1,025
1991-1994	2 single-coils, hardtail	$900	$1,075
1991-1994	2 single-coils, vibrato	$950	$1,125
1991-1994	3 single-coils	$925	$1,100
1991-1994	Optional custom color & features	$950	$1,125

Surfcaster 12
1991-1995. 12-string version of Surfcaster, no tremolo, made in Japan.
| 1991-1995 | | $950 | $1,125 |

Surfcaster Double Neck
1992. Very limited production, 6/12 double neck, Charvel logo on both necks, black.
| 1992 | | $1,700 | $2,100 |

Surfcaster HT (Model SC 1)
1992-1996. Made in Japan. Hard Tail (HT) non-tremolo version of Surfcaster, has single-coil and bridge humbucker.
| 1992-1996 | Custom color & features | $1,050 | $1,250 |
| 1992-1996 | Standard colors & features | $975 | $1,150 |

Chiquita

1979-present. Intermediate grade, production guitars made by Erlewine Guitars in Austin, Texas (see that listing). There was also a mini amp available.

Travel Guitar
1979-present. Developed by Mark Erlewine and ZZ Top's Billy Gibbons, 27" overall length solidbody, 1 or 2 pickups, various colors.
| 1980s | | $250 | $450 |

Chris George

1966-present. Professional and premium grade, custom, archtop, acoustic, electric and resonator guitars built by luthier Chris George in Tattershall Lincolnshire, UK.

Christopher Carrington

1988-present. Production/custom, premium grade, classical and flamenco acoustic guitars built by luthier Chris Carrington in Rockwall, Texas.

Chrysalis Guitars

1998-present. Luthier Tim White builds his premium grade, production/custom Chrysalis Guitar System, which includes interchangeable components that can be quickly assembled into a full-size electric/acoustic guitar, in New Boston, New Hampshire. A variety of instruments may be created, including 6- and 12-string electrics and acoustics, electric and acoustic mandocello and acoustic basses.

Cimar/Cimar by Ibanez

Early-1980s. Private brand of Hoshino Musical Instruments, Nagoya, Japan, who also branded Ibanez. Headstock with script Cimar logo or Cimar by Ibanez, copy models and Ibanez near-original models such as the star body.

Cimar
| 1982 | Double-cut solidbody | $175 | $200 |
| 1982 | Star body style | $175 | $200 |

Cimarron

1978-present. Luthiers John Walsh and Clayton Walsh build their professional grade, production/custom, flat top acoustic guitars in Ridgway, Colorado. Between '94 and '98 they also produced electric guitars.

Cipher

1960s. Solidbody electric guitars and basses imported from Japan by Inter-Mark. Generally strange-shaped bodies.

Electric Solidbody
1960s. For any student-grade import, a guitar with any missing part, such as a missing control knob or trem arm, is worth much less.
| 1960s | | $150 | $200 |

Citron

1995-present. Luthier Harvey Citron builds his professional and premium grade, production/custom solidbody guitars in Woodstock, New York. He also builds basses. In '75, Citron and Joe Veillette founded Veillette-Citron, which was known for handcrafted, neck-thru guitars and basses. That company closed in '83.

Clifford

Clifford was a brand manufactured by Kansas City, Missouri instrument wholesalers J.W. Jenkins & Sons. First introduced in 1895, the brand also offered mandolins.

1975 Cimar

Cimarron Model P

2008 Collings 000-2H

Collings D-1

Clovis

Mid-1960s. Private brand made by Kay.

Electric Solidbody

Mid-1960s. Kay slab solidbody, 2 pickups.

1965		$300	$350

Cole

1890-1919. W.A. Cole, after leaving Fairbanks & Cole, started his own line in 1890. He died in 1909 but the company continued until 1919. He also made banjos.

Parlor

1897. Small size, Brazilian rosewood sides and back, spruce top, ebony 'board, slotted headstock, dot markers.

1897		$550	$700

Coleman Guitars

1976-1983. Custom made presentation grade instruments made in Homosassa, Florida, by luthier Harry Coleman. No headstock logo, Coleman logo on inside center strip.

Collings

1986-present. Professional, premium, and presentation grade, production/custom, flat-top, archtop and electric guitars built in Austin, Texas. They also build mandolins and ukuleles. Bill Collings started with guitar repair and began custom building guitars around '73. In '80, he relocated his shop from Houston to Austin and started Collings Guitars in '86. In '06 they moved to a new plant in southwest Austin.

0-1

2008-present. Mother-of-pearl Collings logo, sitka spruce, Honduran mahogany neck, back & sides, ebony 'board and bridge, high gloss lacquer finish.

2008-2010		$2,000	$2,400

00-2H

1999-present. Indian rosewood.

1999-2010		$2,000	$2,500

00-41

2001. Premium Brazilian rosewood back and sides, Adirondack spruce top, abalone top purfling.

2001		$6,500	$8,000

000-1

1990s-present. Mahogany body, spruce top.

1990s	000-1	$2,600	$3,300
1990s	000-1A Adirondack	$2,800	$3,500
2000s	000-1A Adirondack	$2,800	$3,500

000-1Mh

2006. All mahogany body, 000 size.

2006		$2,500	$3,000

000-2H

1994-present. 15" 000-size, Indian rosewood back and sides, spruce top, slotted headstock, 12-fret neck, dot markers. AAA Koa back and sides in '96.

1994-1995	Indian rosewood	$2,200	$2,750
1996	AAA Koa	$2,500	$3,000
2007-2010	Indian rosewood	$2,200	$2,750

000-41

1999. Indian rosewood sides and back, Sitka spruce top, slotted headstock.

1999		$3,000	$3,700

290 Series

2004-present. Solid Honduran mahogany body, East Indian rosewood 'board, 2 P-90 style pickups, '50s style wiring, high gloss lacquer finish.

2004-2010	Deluxe	$1,600	$2,000

C-10

1994-present. 000-size, mahogany back and sides, spruce top, natural.

1994-2010		$2,600	$3,200

C-10 Custom

2007	Koa	$3,300	$4,000

C-10 Deluxe

1994-present. Indian rosewood or flamed maple back and sides, natural.

1994-2010	Flamed maple	$2,900	$3,500
1994-2010	Indian rosewood	$2,900	$3,500
1994-2010	Koa	$3,100	$3,600

C-100

1986-1995. Quadruple 0-size, mahogany back and sides, spruce top, natural, replaced by CJ Jumbo.

1986-1995		$2,100	$2,600

CJ Jumbo

1995-present. Quadruple 0-size, Indian rosewood back and sides, spruce top, natural.

1995-2010		$2,500	$2,900

CJ Koa ASB

2007. Adirondack spruce top, scalloped bracing ASB, flamed koa sides and back.

2007		$3,400	$3,900

CL Series

2004-present. City Limits series, fully carved flame maple top, solid Honduran mahogany body, East Indian rosewood 'board, high gloss lacquer finish.

2004-2010	Deluxe	$2,900	$3,500

CW Clarence White

2005	Indian rosewood	$2,900	$3,500

D-1 Gruhn

1989. Short run for Gruhn Guitars, Nashville, Gruhn script logo on the headstock instead of Collings, signed by Bill Collins, Indian rosewood back and sides, sitka spruce top.

1989		$3,000	$3,700

D-1/D-1SB/D-1A Custom

1992-present. D-size, 15 5/8", mahogany back and sides, spruce top, natural. D-1SB is sunburst option. D-1A Custom upgrades to Adirondack spruce top and higher appointments, natural.

1992-2003	D-1	$2,200	$2,700
1999-2002	D-1A Custom	$2,500	$3,000
2001	D-1SB	$2,200	$2,700

D-2

1986-1995. D-1 with Indian rosewood back and sides, natural.

1986-1995		$2,400	$2,800

MODEL YEAR	FEATURES	EXC. COND. LOW	HIGH

D-2H
1986-present. Dreadnought, same as D-2 with herringbone purfling around top edge.

1986-2010		$2,300	$2,700

D-2HA
2004. Indian rosewood back and sides, Adirondack spruce top, top herringbone trim, gloss natural finish.

2004		$2,900	$3,400

D-2HB
1994-2001. Grade AA Brazilian rosewood, spruce top.

1994-2001	Spruce	$5,200	$6,400
2008	Adirondack	$5,800	$6,800

D-2HV
1994. D-2H with V shaped neck.

1994		$2,300	$2,800

D-3
1990-present. Similar to D-2H but with abalone purfling/rosette.

1990-1999	Brazilian rosewood	$6,000	$7,000
2000-2010	Indian rosewood	$3,100	$3,600

D-42
2000s. Brazilian rosewood back and sides, fancy.

2000s		$6,200	$7,000

DS-1A
2004-present. D size, slope shoulders, 12 fret neck, slotted headstock, Adirondack.

2004-2010		$2,900	$3,500

DS-2H
1995-present. D size, slope shoulders, 12 fret neck, slotted headstock.

2000-2010		$3,300	$3,800

DS-41
1995-2007. Indian rosewood, abalone top trim, snowflake markers.

1995-2007		$3,800	$4,800

I-35 Deluxe
2007-present. Fully carved flame or quilted maple top, mahogany body, Brazilian or Madagascar rosewood 'board, high Gloss lacquer finish.

2007-2010		$3,300	$3,700

OM-1/OM-1A
1994-present. Grand concert, sitka spruce top, mahogany back and sides, natural. OM-1A includes Adirondack spruce upgrade.

1994-1999	OM-1	$2,400	$3,300
1994-1999	OM-1A	$2,800	$3,500
2000-2010	OM-1 Koa	$2,800	$3,500
2000-2010	OM-1 Mahogany	$2,600	$3,200
2007-2010	OM-1 Cutaway	$2,600	$3,200
2007-2010	OM-1A Cutaway	$2,800	$3,500

OM-2
2008. Indian rosewood back and sides.

2008	Cutaway	$2,600	$3,200

OM-2H
1990-present. Indian rosewood back and sides, herringbone binding.

1990-2010		$2,500	$3,000

OM-2H GSS
2008. Indian rosewood sides and back, German spruce top, herringbone trim top.

2008		$2,600	$3,200

OM-2HAV
1998. Adirondack spruce top, Brazilian rosewood back and sides, ivoroid-bound body.

1998		$6,000	$7,000

OM-3
1998-present. Brazilian rosewood back and sides, Adirondack spruce top, fancy rosette, later Indian rosewood and figured maple.

1998	Brazilian rosewood	$6,100	$7,300
2002-2010	Indian rosewood	$3,000	$3,700
2003	Figured maple	$3,300	$3,900
2008	Mahogany	$3,300	$3,900

OM-3HC
1986-1996. Single rounded cutaway, 15", Indian rosewood back and sides, spruce top, herringbone purfling.

1986-1996		$3,500	$4,000

OM-41BrzGCut
2007. Brazilian rosewood sides and back, German spruce top, rounded cutaway.

2007		$6,500	$8,000

OM-42B
2000. Brazilian rosewood back and sides, Adirondack spruce top, fancy rosette and binding.

2000		$6,500	$8,000

SJ
1986-present. Spruce top, quilted maple back and sides or Indian rosewood (earlier option).

1986-1999	Indian rosewood	$3,000	$3,500
2000-2010	Maple	$3,000	$3,500

SJ-41
1996. Brazilian rosewood back and sides, cedar top.

1996		$6,500	$8,000

Winfield
2004-2006. D-style, Brazilian rosewood back and sides, Adirondack spruce top, mahogany neck, ebony board.

2004	Winfield Rose, Indian rosewood	$3,500	$3,900
2005-2006	Brazilian rosewood	$5,500	$7,000

Columbia
Late 1800s-early 1900s. The Columbia brand name was used on acoustic guitars by New York's James H. Buckbee Co. until c.1987 and afterwards by Galveston's Thomas Goggan and Brothers.

Comins
1992-present. Premium and presentation grade, custom archtops built by luthier Bill Comins in Willow Grove, Pennsylvania. He also builds mandolins and offers a combo amp built in collaboration with George Alessandro.

Commander
Late 1950s-early 1960s. Archtop acoustic guitars made by Harmony for the Alden catalog company.

Concertone
Ca. 1914-1930s. Concertone was a brand made by Chicago's Slingerland and distributed by Montgomery Ward. The brand was also used on other instruments such as ukuleles.

Collings SOCO DLX

Comins Chester Avenue

2002 Cort Earth 900 Parlor
Bill Cherensky

Crafter USA D-6/N

MODEL YEAR	FEATURES	EXC. COND. LOW	HIGH

Conklin

1984-present. Intermediate, professional and premium grade, production/custom, 6-, 7-, 8-, and 12-string solid and hollowbody electrics, by luthier Bill Conklin. He also builds basses. Originally located in Lebanon, Missouri, in '88 the company moved to Springfield, Missouri. Conklin instruments are made in the U.S. and overseas.

Conn Guitars

Ca.1968-ca.1978. Student to mid-quality classical and acoustic guitars, some with bolt-on necks, also some electrics. Imported from Japan by band instrument manufacturer and distributor Conn/Continental Music Company, Elkhart, Indiana.

Acoustic
1968-1978. Various models.

1968-1978		$100	$175

Classical
1968-1978. Various student-level models.

1968-1978		$75	$125

Electric Solidbody
1970s. Various models.

1970-1978		$150	$175

Connor, Stephan

1995-present. Luthier Stephan Connor builds his premium grade, custom nylon-string guitars in Waltham, Massachusetts.

Conrad Guitars

Ca. 1968-1978. Mid- to better-quality copies of glued-neck Martin and Gibson acoustics and bolt-neck Gibson and Fender solidbodies. They also offered basses, mandolins and banjos. Imported from Japan by David Wexler and Company, Chicago, Illinois.

Acoustic 12-String
1970s. Dreadnought size.

1970s		$100	$125

Acoustical Slimline (40080/40085)
1970s. Rosewood 'board, 2 or 3 DeArmond-style pickups, block markers, sunburst.

1970s		$250	$300

Acoustical Slimline 12-String (40100)
1970s. Rosewood 'board, 2 DeArmond-style pickups, dot markers, sunburst.

1970s		$250	$300

Bison (40035/40030/40065/40005)
1970s. 1 thru 4 pickups available, rosewood 'board with dot markers, six-on-side headstock.

1970s		$250	$300

Bumper (40223)
1970s. Clear Lucite solidbody.

1970s		$350	$400

Classical Student (40150)

1970s		$90	$110

De Luxe Folk Guitar
1970s. Resonator acoustic, mahogany back, sides and neck, Japanese import.

1970s		$175	$225

MODEL YEAR	FEATURES	EXC. COND. LOW	HIGH

Master Size (40178)
1972-1977. Electric archtop, 2 pickups.

1972-1977		$225	$300

Resonator Acoustic
1970s. Flat-top with wood, metal resonator and 8 ports, round neck.

1970s		$350	$400

Violin-Shaped 12-String Electric (40176)
1970s. Scroll headstock, 2 pickups, 500/1 control panel, bass side dot markers, sunburst.

1970s		$325	$375

Violin-Shaped Electric (40175)
1970s. Scroll headstock, 2 pickups, 500/1 control panel, bass side dot markers, vibrato, sunburst.

1970s		$325	$375

White Styrene 1280
1970s. Solid maple body covered with white styrene, 2 pickups, tremolo, bass side dot markers, white.

1970s		$250	$300

Contessa

1960s. Acoustic, semi-hollow archtop, solidbody and bass guitars made in Italy and imported by Hohner. They also made banjos.

Electric Solidbody
1967. Various models.

1967		$300	$400

Contreras

See listing for Manuel Contreras and Manuel Contreras II.

Coral

1967-1969. In '66 MCA bought Danelectro and in '67 introduced the Coral brand of guitars, basses and amps.

Firefly
1967-1969. Double-cut, f-holes, 2 pickups, with or without vibrato.

1967-1969		$900	$1,100

Hornet 2
1967-1969. Solidbody, 2 pickups, with or without vibrato.

1967-1969		$900	$1,100

Hornet 3
1967. Solidbody, 3 pickups.

1967		$1,000	$1,200

Sitar
1967-1969. Six-string guitar with 13 drone strings and 3 pickups (2 under the 6 strings, 1 under the drones), kind of a USA-shaped body.

1967-1969		$2,000	$2,500

Córdoba

Line of classical guitars handmade in Portugal and imported by Guitar Salon International.

Classical

1999	1A India	$1,850	$2,100
2000s	Gipsy King	$850	$1,050
2000s	Higher-end	$600	$800
2000s	Mid-level	$375	$500
2000s	Student-level	$200	$275

MODEL YEAR	FEATURES	EXC. COND. LOW	HIGH

Cordova

1960s. Classical nylon string guitars imported by David Wexler of Chicago.

Grand Concert Model WC-026

1960s. Highest model offered by Cordova, 1-piece rosewood back, laminated rosewood sides, spruce top, natural.

1960s		$225	$300

Corey James Custom Guitars

2005-present. Luthier Corey James Moilanen builds his professional and premium grade, production/custom solidbody guitars in Davisburg, Michigan. He also builds basses.

Coriani, Paolo

1984-present. Production/custom nylon-string guitars and hurdy-gurdys built by luthier Paolo Coriani in Modeila, Italy.

Cort

1973-present. North Brook, Illinois-based Cort offers budget, intermediate and professional grade, production/custom, acoustic and solidbody, semi-hollow, hollow body electric guitars built in Korea. They also offer basses.

Cort was the second significant Korean private-label (Hondo brand was the first) to come out of Korea. Jack Westheimer, based upon the success of Tommy Moore and Hondo, entered into an agreement with Korea's Cort to do Cort-brand, private-label, and Epiphone-brand guitars.

CP Thornton Guitars

1985-present. Luthier Chuck Thornton builds professional and premium grade, production/custom, semi-hollow and solidbody electric guitars in Sumner, Maine. Up to '96 he also built basses.

Crafter

1986-present. Crafter offers budget and intermediate grade, production, classical, acoustic, acoustic/electric, and electric guitars made in Korea. They also build basses and amps. From '72 to '86 they made Sungeum classical guitars.

Crafters of Tennessee

See listing under Tennessee.

Cranium

1996-present. Professional grade, production/custom, hollow, semi-hollow, and solidbody electrics built by luthier Wayne O'Connor in Peterborough, Ontario.

Crescent Moon

1999-present. Professional grade, production/custom, solidbody guitars and basses built by luthier Craig Muller in Baltimore, Maryland.

Creston

2004-present. Professional grade, custom, solidbody electric guitars built by luthier Creston Lea in Burlington, Vermont. He also builds basses.

Crestwood

1970s. Copies of the popular classical guitars, flat-tops, electric solidbodies and basses of the era, imported by La Playa Distributing Company of Detroit.

Acoustic 12-String

1970s		$175	$225

Electric

1970s. Various models include near copies of the 335 (Crestwood model 2043, 2045 and 2047), Les Paul Custom (2020), Strat (2073), Jazzmaster (2078), Tele (2082), and the SG Custom (2084).

1970s		$225	$450

Crimson Guitars

2005-present. Luthiers Benjamin Crowe and Aki Atrill build professional and premium grade, custom, solidbody guitars in Somerset, United Kingdom. They also build basses.

Cromwell

1935-1939. Budget model brand built by Gibson and distributed by mail-order businesses like Grossman, Continental, Richter & Phillips, and Gretsch & Brenner.

Acoustic Archtop

1935-1939. Archtop acoustic, f-holes, pressed mahogany back and sides, carved and bound top, bound back, 'guard and 'board, no truss rod.

1935-1939		$1,000	$1,200
1935-1939	With '30s era pickup	$1,250	$1,500

Acoustic Flat-Top

1935-1939	G-2 (L-00)	$950	$1,150

Tenor Guitar (Flat-Top)

1935-1939	GT-2	$575	$700

Cromwell (Guild)

1963-1964. Guild imported these 2- or 3-pickup offset double cut solidbodies from Hagstrom. These were basically part of Hagstrom's Kent line with laminated bodies and birch necks. About 500 were imported into the U.S.

Crook Custom Guitars

1997-present. Professional grade, custom, solidbody electric guitars built in Moundsville, West Virginia by luthier Bill Crook. He also builds basses.

Crossley

2005-present. Professional grade, production/custom, solidbody and chambered electric guitars built in Melbourne, Victoria, Australia by luthier Peter Crossley.

Crimson Vee Mark II

Crossley Goldtop

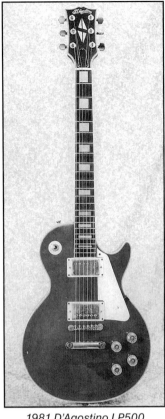

1981 D'Agostino LP500

Daion Headhunter S-555

MODEL YEAR	FEATURES	EXC. COND. LOW	HIGH

Crown

1960s. Violin-shaped hollowbody electrics, solidbody electric guitars and basses, possibly others. Imported from Japan.

Acoustic Flat-Top
1960s. 6-string and 12-string.

1960s		$100	$150

Electric Archtop
1960s. Double pointed cutaways, 2 humbucking pickups, laminated top, full-depth body.

1960s		$350	$450

Electric Solidbody/Semi-Hollow
1960s. Student-level Japanese import.

1960s	Copy models	$250	$350
1960s	Pointy violin-shaped body	$250	$350
1960s	Standard models	$150	$175

Crucianelli

Early 1960s. Italian guitars imported into the U.S. by Bennett Brothers of New York and Chicago around '63 to '64. Accordion builder Crucianelli also made Imperial, Elite, PANaramic, and Elli-Sound brand guitars.

Cruzer

Intermediate grade, production, solidbody electric guitars made by Korea's Crafter Guitars. They also build basses, amps and effects.

CSR

1996-present. Father and daughter luthiers Roger and Courtney Kitchens build their premium grade, production/custom, archtop guitars in Byron, Georgia. They also build basses.

Cumpiano

1974-present. Professional and premium grade, custom steel-string and nylon-string guitars, and acoustic basses built by luthier William Cumpiano in Northampton, Massachusetts.

Curbow String Instruments

1994-present. Premium grade, production/custom, solidbody guitars built by luthier Doug Somervell in Morganton, Georgia. Founded by Greg Curbow who passed away in '05. They also make basses.

Custom

1980s. Line of solidbody guitars and basses introduced in the early '80s by Charles Lawing and Chris Lovell, owners of Strings & Things in Memphis, Tennessee.

Custom Kraft

Late-1950s-1968. A house brand of St. Louis Music Supply, instruments built by Valco and others. They also offered basses and amps.

MODEL YEAR	FEATURES	EXC. COND. LOW	HIGH

Electric Solidbody
1950s-1960s. Entry-level import, 1or 2 pickups.

1950-1960s	1 pickup	$175	$225
1950-1960s	2 pickups	$225	$275

Sound Saturator
1960s	12-string	$350	$400

Super Zapp
1960s		$350	$400

Thin Twin Jimmy Reed (style)
Late-1950s-early-1960s. Single cut, 2 pickups, 4 knobs and toggle, dot markers.

1959	U.S.-made	$550	$700

D.J. Hodson

1994-2007. Luthier David J.Hodson built his professional and premium grade, production/custom, acoustic guitars in Loughborough, Leicestershire, England. He also built ukes. He passed away in '07.

Daddy Mojo String Instruments Inc.

2005-present. Luthiers Lenny Piroth-Robert and Luca Tripaldi build their intermediate and professional grade, production/custom, solidbody electric, resonator and cigar box guitars in Montreal, Quebec.

D'Agostino

1976-early 1990s. Acoustic and electric solidbody guitars and basses imported by PMS Music, founded in New York City by former Maestro executive Pat D'Agostino, his brother Steven D'Agostino, and Mike Confortti. First dreadnought acoustic guitars imported from Japan in '76. First solidbodies manufactured by the EKO custom shop beginning in '77. In '82 solidbody production moved to Japan. Beginning in '84, D'Agostinos were made in Korea. Overall, about 60% of guitars were Japanese, 40% Korean. They also had basses.

Acoustic Flat-Top
1976-1990. Early production in Japan, by mid-'80s, most production in Korea.

1976-1990		$150	$200

Electric Semi-Hollowbody
1981-early 1990s. Early production in Japan, later versions from Korea.

1981-1990		$250	$475

Electric Solidbody
1977-early 1990s. Early models made in Italy, later versions from Japan and Korea.

1981-1990		$250	$300

Daily Guitars

1976-present. Luthier David Daily builds his premium grade, production/custom classical guitars in Sparks, Nevada.

Daion

1978-1984. Mid- to higher-quality copies imported from Japan. Original designs introduced in the '80s. Only acoustics offered at first; in '81 they added acoustic/electric and solid and semi-hollow electrics. They also had basses.

MODEL YEAR	FEATURES	EXC. COND. LOW	HIGH

Acoustic

1978-1985. Various flat-top models.

| 1978-1985 | Higher-end | $500 | $1,000 |
| 1978-1985 | Lower-end | $300 | $400 |

Electric

1978-1985. Various solid and semi-hollow body guitars.

| 1978-1985 | Higher-end | $500 | $700 |
| 1978-1985 | Lower-end | $300 | $400 |

Daisy Rock

2001-present. Budget and intermediate grade, production, full-scale and 3/4 scale, solidbody, semi-hollow, acoustic, and acoustic/electric guitars. Founded by Tish Ciravolo as a Division of Schecter Guitars, the Daisy line is focused on female customers. Initial offerings included daisy and heart-shaped electric guitars and basses.

D'Ambrosio

2001-present. Luthier Otto D'Ambrosio builds his premium grade, custom/production, acoustic and electric archtop guitars in Providence, Rhode Island.

Dan Armstrong

Dan Armstrong started playing jazz in Cleveland in the late-'50s. He moved to New York and also started doing repairs, eventually opening his own store on 48th Street in '65. By the late-'60s he was designing his Lucite guitars for Ampeg (see Ampeg for those listings). He moved to England in '71, where he developed his line of colored stomp boxes. He returned to the States in '75. Armstrong died in '04.

Wood Body Guitar

1973-1975. Sliding pickup, wood body, brown.

| 1973-1975 | | $1,900 | $2,400 |

Dan Kellaway

1976-present. Production/custom, premium grade, classical and steel string guitars built by luthier Dan Kellaway in Singleton NSW, Australia. He also builds mandolins and lutes.

Danelectro

1946-1969, 1996-present. Founded in Red Bank, New Jersey, by Nathan I. (Nate or Nat) Daniel, an electronics enthusiast with amplifier experience. In 1933, Daniel built amps for Thor's Bargain Basement in New York. In '34 he was recruited by Epiphone's Herb Sunshine to build earliest Electar amps and pickup-making equipment. From '35 to '42, he operated Daniel Electric Laboratories in Manhattan, supplying Epiphone. He started Danelectro in '46 and made his first amps for Montgomery Ward in '47. Over the years, Danelectro made amplifiers, solidbody, semi-hollow and hollowbody electric guitars and basses, electric sitar, and the Bellzouki under the Danelectro, Silvertone, and Coral brands. In '48, began supplying Silvertone amps for Sears

(various coverings), with his own brand (brown leatherette) distributed by Targ and Dinner as Danelectro and S.S. Maxwell.

He developed an electronic vibrato in '48 on his Vibravox series amps. In '50 he developed a microphone with volume and tone controls and outboard Echo Box reverb unit. In the fall of '54, Danelectro replaced Harmony as provider of Silvertone solidbody guitars for Sears. Also in '54, the first Danelectro brand guitars appeared with tweed covering, bell headstock, and pickups under the pickguard. The Coke bottle headstock debuts as Silvertone Lightning Bolt in '54, and was used on Danelectros for '56 to '66. The company moved to Red Bank, New Jersey in '57, and in '58 relocated to Neptune, New Jersey. In '59, Harmony and Kay guitars replace all but 3 Danelectros in Sears catalog. In '66, MCA buys the company (Daniel remains with company), but by mid-'69, MCA halts production and closes the doors. Some leftover stock is sold to Dan Armstrong, who had a shop in New York at the time. Armstrong assembled several hundred Danelectro guitars as Dan Armstrong Modified with his own pickup design.

Rights to name acquired by Anthony Marc in late-'80s, who assembled a number of thinline hollowbody guitars, many with Longhorn shape, using Japanese-made bodies and original Danelectro necks and hardware. In '96, the Evets Corporation, of San Clemente, California, introduced a line of effects bearing the Danelectro brand. Amps and guitars, many of which were reissues of the earlier instruments, soon followed. In early 2003, Evets discontinued offering guitar and amps, but revived the guitar and bass line in '05.

MCA-Danelectro made guitars were called the Dane Series. Dane A model numbers start with an A (e.g. A2V), Dane B models start with a B (e.g. B3V), Dane C (e.g. C2N), and Dane D (e.g. D2N). The least expensive series was the A, going up to the most expensive D. All Dane Series instruments came with 1, 2 or 3 pickups and with hand vibrato options. The Dane Series were made from '67 to '69. MCA did carry over the Convertible, Guitarlin 4123, Long Horn Bass-4 and Bass-6 and Doubleneck 3923. MCA also offered the Bellzouki Double Pickup 7021. Each Dane Series includes an electric 12-string. Danelectro also built the Coral brand instruments (see Coral).

Baritone Model 1449

1963. Double-cut, baritone tuning, 3-on-a-side tuners, 2 lipstick pickups, Coke bottle headstock shape with large verticle Danelectro logo.

| 1963 | | $1,450 | $1,750 |

Baritone 6-String Reissue

1999-2003, 2008-2009. Single cutaway, 6-string baritone tuning.

| 1999-2003 | | $225 | $275 |
| 2008-2009 | '63 Baritone, 1449 reissue | $225 | $275 |

D'Ambrosio El Rey

Danelectro '63

Danelectro Convertible

1957 Danelectro U-1

MODEL YEAR	FEATURES	EXC. COND. LOW	HIGH

Bellzouki
1961-1969. 12-string electric, teardrop-shaped body, single pickup, sunburst. Vincent Bell model has modified teardrop shape with 2 body points on both treble and bass bouts and 2 pickups.

1960s	1 pickup	$800	$1,000
1960s	Vincent Bell, 2 pickups	$950	$1,200

Convertible
1959-1969. Acoustic/electric, double-cut, guitar was sold with or without the removable single pickup.

1950s	Pickup installed, natural	$425	$525
1960s	Acoustic, no pickup, natural	$350	$425
1960s	Pickup installed, natural	$425	$525
1960s	Pickup installed, rare color	$350	$425

Convertible Reissue
1999, 2000-2003. The Convertible Pro was offered '00-'03 with upgraded Gotoh tuners and metalflake and pearl finishes.

1999	Blond	$200	$250
1999	Green	$225	$275

Dane A Series
1967-1969. 1 and 2 pickup models, solid wood slab body, hard lacquer finish with 4 color options.

1967-1969		$425	$500

Dane B Series
1967-1969. 1 and 3 pickup models, semi-solid Durabody.

1967-1969		$475	$550

Dane C Series
1967-1969. 2 and 3 pickup models, semi-solid Durabody with 2-tone Gator finish.

1967-1969		$475	$550

Dane D Series
1967-1969. 2 and 3 pickup models, solid wood sculptured thinline body, 'floating adjustable pickguard-fingerguide', master volume with 4 switches.

1967-1969		$475	$550

Danoblaster Series
2000-2003. Offset double-cuts, 3 pickups, built-in effects – distortion on the Hearsay, distortion, chorus, trem and echo on Innuendo. Also in 12-string and baritone.

2000-2003		$125	$175

DC-12/Electric XII
1999-2003. 12-string version of 59-DC.

1999-2003		$325	$400

Deluxe Double Pickup (6026/6027/6028)
1960s. Double-cut, 2 pointer knobs, 2 pickups, standard-size pickguard, master control knob, white (6026), dark walnut (6027), honey walnut (6028).

1960s		$1,100	$1,400

Deluxe Triple Pickup (6036/6037/6038)
1960s. Double-cut, 3 pointer knobs, 3 pickups, standard-size pickguard, master control knob, white (6036), dark walnut (6037), honey walnut (6038).

1960s		$1,200	$1,500

MODEL YEAR	FEATURES	EXC. COND. LOW	HIGH

Doubleneck (3923)
1959-1969. A shorthorn double-cut, bass and 6-string necks, 1 pickup on each neck, Coke bottle headstocks, white sunburst.

1959-1969		$1,800	$2,300

Doubleneck Reissue
1999-2003. Baritone 6-string and standard 6-string double neck, shorthorn body style, or the 6-12 model with a 6-string and 12-string neck. Price includes $75 for a guitar case, but many sales do not seem to include a guitar case because of unusual body size.

1999-2003		$450	$575

Electric Sitar
1967-1969. Traditional looking, oval-bodied sitar, no drone strings as on the Coral Sitar of the same period.

1967-1969		$1,700	$1,900

Guitaralin (4123)
1963-1969. The Longhorn guitar, with 2 huge cutaways, 32-fret neck, and 2 pickups.

1963-1964		$2,100	$2,600
1965-1969		$2,000	$2,500

Hand Vibrato Double Pickup (4021)
1960s. Double-cut, 2 pickups, batwing headstock, simple design vibrato, black.

1960s		$900	$1,100

Hand Vibrato Single Pickup (4011)
1960s. Double-cut, 1 pickup, batwing headstock, simple design vibrato, black.

1960s		$800	$1,000

Model C
1955-ca.1958. Single-cut, 1 pickup.

1955-1958		$550	$750

Pro 1
1963-ca.1964. Odd-shaped double-cut electric with squared off corners, 1 pickup.

1963-1964		$600	$800

Pro Reissue
2007. Based on '60s Pro 1, but with 2 pickups.

2007		$250	$300

Standard Single Pickup
1958-1967. A Shorthorn double-cut, 1 pickup, 2 regular control knobs, seal-shaped pickguard, Coke bottle headstock.

1958-1967		$1,000	$1,200

Standard Double Pickup
1959-1967. A shorthorn double-cut, 2 pickups, 2 stacked, concentric volume/tone controls, seal-shaped 'guard, Coke bottle headstock, black version of this guitar is often referred to as the Jimmy Page model because he occasionally used one. Reissued in 1998 as 59-DC.

1959-1967		$1,250	$1,550

59-DC/'59 Dano (Standard Double Pickup Reissue)
1998-1999, 2007. Shorthorn double-cut, 2 pickups, seal-shaped pickguard, Coke bottle headstock, '07 version called '59 Dano.

1998-1999		$275	$325

U-1

1956-ca.1960. Single-cut, 1 pickup, Coke bottle headstock.

MODEL YEAR	FEATURES	EXC. COND. LOW	HIGH
1956-1960	Common color	$800	$950
1956-1960	Rare color	$1,000	$1,200

U-1 '56 Reissue

1998-1999. Single-cut semi-hollow, masonite top and bottom, bolt-on neck, reissue of '56 U-1, with single 'lipstick tube' pickup, various colors.

1998-1999		$175	$250

U-2

1956-1959. Single-cut, 2 pickups, stacked concentric volume/tone controls, Coke bottle headstock.

1956-1959	Common color	$850	$1,000
1956-1959	Rare color	$1,250	$1,500

U-2 '56 Reissue

1998-2003. 2 pickup U-1.

1998-2003		$200	$250

U-3

1957-1959. Single-cut, 3 pickups.

1957-1959		$1,050	$1,250

U-3 '56 Reissue

1999-2003. Single-cut reissue of '56 U-3 with 3 'lipstick tube' pickups, various colors.

1999-2003	Common color	$200	$275
1999-2003	Rare color	$225	$350

D'Angelico

John D'Angelico built his own line of archtop guitars, mandolins and violins from 1932 until his death in 1964. His instruments are some of the most sought-after by collectors.

D'Angelico (L-5 Snakehead)

1932-1935. D'Angelico's L-5-style with snakehead headstock, his first model, sunburst.

1932-1935		$11,000	$14,000

Excel/Exel (Cutaway)

1947-1964. Cutaway, 17" width, 1- and 3-ply bound f-hole, Larry Wexer noted from '50-'57, D'Angelico guitars suffer from severe binding problems and many have replaced bindings. Replaced bindings make the guitar non-original and these repaired guitars have lower values.

1947-1949	Natural, original binding	$32,000	$38,000
1947-1949	Sunburst, original binding	$31,000	$37,000
1950-1959	Natural, original binding	$31,000	$37,000
1950-1959	Sunburst, original binding	$28,000	$33,000
1960-1964	Natural	$31,000	$37,000
1960-1964	Sunburst	$27,000	$32,000

Excel/Exel (Non-Cutaway)

1936-1949. Non-cut, 17" width, 1- and 3-ply bound f-hole, natural finishes were typically not offered in the '30s, non-cut Excels were generally not offered after '49 in deference to the Excel cutaway.

1936-1939	Sunburst, straight f-hole	$15,000	$18,000
1938-1939	Sunburst, standard f-hole	$15,000	$18,000
1940-1949	Natural	$16,000	$19,000
1940-1949	Sunburst, standard f-hole	$16,000	$19,000

New Yorker (Cutaway)

1947-1964. Cutaway, 18" width, 5-ply-bound f-hole, New Yorker non-cut orders were overshadowed by the cut model orders starting in '47, all prices noted are for original bindings, non-original (replaced) bindings will reduce the value by 33%-50%.

1947-1949	Natural, 4 made	$51,000	$59,000
1947-1949	Sunburst	$43,000	$52,000
1950-1959	Natural	$48,000	$56,000
1950-1959	Sunburst	$43,000	$52,000
1960-1964	Natural	$48,000	$56,000
1960-1964	Sunburst	$43,000	$52,000

New Yorker (Non-Cutaway)

1936-1949. Non-cut, 18" width, 5-ply-bound f-hole, New Yorker non-cut orders were overshadowed by the cut model orders starting in '47, all prices noted are for original bindings, non-original (replaced) bindings will reduce the value by 33%-50%.

1936-1939	Sunburst	$21,000	$24,000
1940-1949	Natural	$26,000	$30,000
1940-1949	Sunburst	$24,000	$28,000

New Yorker Special

1947-1964. Also called Excel New Yorker or Excel Cutaway New YorkerCutaway, 17" width, New Yorker styling, prices are for original bindings, non-original (replaced) bindings reduce values by 33%-50%, not to be confused with D'Angelico Special (A and B style).

1947-1964	Natural	$32,000	$37,000
1947-1964	Sunburst	$32,000	$37,000

Special

1947-1964. Generally Style A and B-type instruments made for musicians on a budget, plain specs with little ornamentation, not to be confused with New Yorker Special.

1947-1964	Natural	$13,000	$15,000
1947-1964	Sunburst	$12,000	$14,000

Style A

1936-1945. Archtop, 17" width, unbound f-holes, block 'board inlays, multi-pointed headstock, nickel-plated metal parts.

1936-1939	Sunburst	$8,800	$10,000
1940-1945	Sunburst	$8,300	$9,500

Style A-1

1936-1945. Unbound f-holes, 17" width, arched headstock, nickel-plated metal parts.

1936-1939	Sunburst	$7,800	$9,000
1940-1945	Sunburst	$7,800	$9,000

Style B

1933-1948. Archtop 17" wide, unbound F-holes, block 'board inlays, gold-plated parts.

1936-1939	Sunburst	$12,000	$14,000
1940-1948	Sunburst	$9,000	$10,500

1947 D'Angelico New Yorker

D'Angelico New Yorker NYL-2

D'Aquisto New Yorker Classic

Dave King Louise

MODEL		EXC. COND.	
YEAR	FEATURES	LOW	HIGH

Style B Special
1933-1948. D'Angelico described variations from standard features with a 'Special' designation, Vintage dealers may also describe these instruments as 'Special'.

1936-1939	Sunburst	$14,000	$16,000
1940-1948	Sunburst	$13,000	$15,000

D'Angelico (D'Angelico Guitars of America)
1988-present. Intermediate and professional grade, production/custom, archtop, flat-top, and solidbody guitars made in South Korea and imported by D'Angelico Guitars of America, of Colts Neck, New Jersey. From 1988 to '04, they were premium and presentation grade instruments built in Japan by luthier Hidesato Shino and Vestax.

D'Angelico (Lewis)
1994-present. Luthier Michael Lewis builds presentation grade, custom/production, D'Angelico replica guitars in Grass Valley, California, under an agreement with the GHS String Company, which owns the name in the U.S. He also builds guitars and mandolins under the Lewis name.

D'Angelico II
Mid-1990s. Archtops built in the U.S. and distributed by Archtop Enterprises of Merrick, New York. Mainly presentation grade copies of Excel and New Yorker models, but also made lower cost similar models.

Jazz Classic
1990s. Electric archtop, cutaway, carved spruce top, figured maple back and sides, single neck pickup, transparent cherry.

1990s		$2,400	$2,800

Daniel Friederich
1955-present. Luthier Daniel Friederich builds his custom/production, classical guitars in Paris, France.

D'Aquisto
1965-1995. James D'Aquisto apprenticed under D'Angelico until the latter's death, at age 59, in '64. He started making his own brand instruments in '65 and built archtop and flat top acoustic guitars, solidbody and hollowbody electric guitars. He also designed guitars for Hagstrom and Fender. He died in '95, at age 59.

Avant Garde
1987-1994. 18" wide, non-traditional futuristic model, approximately 5 or 6 instruments were reportedly made, because of low production this pricing is for guidance only.

1990	Blond	$80,000	$95,000

Centura/Centura Deluxe
1994 only. 17" wide, non-traditional art deco futuristic archtop, approximately 10 made, the last guitars made by this luthier, due to the low production this pricing is for guidance only.

1994	Blond	$75,000	$90,000

MODEL		EXC. COND.	
YEAR	FEATURES	LOW	HIGH

Excel (Cutaway)
1965-1992. Archtop, 17" width, with modern thin-logo started in '81.

1965-1967	Blond	$35,000	$40,000
1965-1967	Sunburst	$32,000	$37,000
1968-1980	Blond	$32,000	$37,000
1968-1980	Sunburst	$31,000	$36,000
1981-1989	Blond	$37,000	$42,000
1981-1989	Sunburst	$34,000	$39,000
1990-1992	Blond	$35,000	$40,000
1990-1992	Sunburst	$32,000	$37,000

Excel (Flat-Top)
1970s-1980s. Flat-top, 16", flamed maple back and sides, Sitka spruce top, about 15 made, narrow Excel-style headstock, oval soundhole, D'Aquisto script logo on headstock.

1970-1980s		$18,000	$21,000

Hollow Electric
Early model with bar pickup, D'Aquisto headstock, '70s model with humbuckers.

1965	Sunburst	$14,000	$18,000
1972	Sunburst	$14,000	$18,000
1989		$14,000	$18,000

Jim Hall
Hollowbody electric, carved spruce top, 1 pickup.

1978	Solid top	$13,000	$15,000

New Yorker Classic (Archtop)
1986. Single-cut acoustic archtop with new modern design features such as large S-shaped soundholes.

1986		$44,000	$51,000

New Yorker Classic (Solidbody)
1980s. Only 2 were reported to be made, therefore this pricing is for guidance only.

1980s		$20,000	$23,000

New Yorker Deluxe (Cutaway)
1965-1992. Most are 18" wide.

1965-1967	Blond	$43,000	$50,000
1965-1967	Sunburst	$38,000	$45,000
1968-1979	Blond	$38,000	$45,000
1968-1979	Sunburst	$38,000	$45,000
1980-1989	Blond	$42,000	$49,000
1980-1989	Sunburst	$42,000	$49,000
1990-1992	Blond	$42,000	$49,000
1990-1992	Sunburst	$41,000	$48,000

New Yorker Special (7-String)
1980s. Limited production 7-string, single-cut.

1980s	Sunburst	$35,000	$41,000

New Yorker Special (Cutaway)
1966-1992. Most are 17" wide.

1966-1967	Blond	$35,000	$40,000
1966-1967	Sunburst	$33,000	$38,000
1968-1979	Blond	$33,000	$38,000
1968-1979	Sunburst	$33,000	$38,000
1980-1989	Blond	$35,000	$40,000
1980-1989	Sunburst	$33,000	$38,000
1990-1992	Blond	$36,000	$40,000
1990-1992	Sunburst	$32,000	$37,000

Solo/Solo Deluxe
1992-1993. 18" wide, non-traditional non-cut art deco model, only 2 reported made, because of low production this pricing is for guidance only.

1992-1993	Blond	$75,000	$90,000

| MODEL | | EXC. COND. | |
| YEAR | FEATURES | LOW | HIGH |

D'Aquisto (Aria)

May 2002-present. Premium grade, production, D'Aquisto designs licensed to Aria of Japan by D'Aquisto Strings, Inc., Deer Park, New York.

Various Models

| 2002-2010 | | $1,500 | $1,900 |

Dauphin

1970s-late 1990s. Classical and flamenco guitars imported from Spain and Japan by distributor George Dauphinais, located in Springfield, Illinois.

Dave King Acoustics

1980-present. Premium grade, custom/production, acoustic and resonator guitars built by luthier Dave King in Berkshire, U.K.

Dave Maize Acoustic Guitars

1991-present. Luthier Dave Maize builds his professional and premium grade, production/custom, flat-tops in Cave Junction, Oregon. He also builds basses.

David Rubio

1960s-2000. Luthier David Spink built his guitars, lutes, violins, violas, cellos and harpsichords first in New York, and after '67, in England. While playing in Spain, he acquired the nickname Rubio, after his red beard. He died in '00.

David Thomas McNaught

1989-present. Professional, premium, and presentation grade, custom, solidbody guitars built by luthier David Thomas McNaught and finished by Dave Mansel in Locust, North Carolina. In '97, they added the production/custom DTM line of guitars.

Davis, J. Thomas

1975-present. Premium and presentation grade, custom, steel-string flat-tops, 12-strings, classicals, archtops, Irish citterns and flat-top Irish bouzoukis made by luthier J. Thomas Davis in Columbus, Ohio.

Davoli

See Wandre listing.

DBZ

2008-present. Solidbody electric guitars from Dean B. Zelinsky, founder of Dean Guitars, and partners Jeff Diamant and Terry Martin.

de Jonge, Sergei

1972-present. Premium grade, production/custom classical and steel-string guitars built by luthier Sergei de Jonge originally in Oshawa, Ontario, and since '04 in Chelsea, Quebec.

| MODEL | | EXC. COND. | |
| YEAR | FEATURES | LOW | HIGH |

De Paule Stringed Instruments

1969-1980, 1993-present. Custom steel-string, nylon-string, archtop, resonator, and Hawaiian guitars built by luthier C. Andrew De Paule in Eugene, Oregon.

Dean

1976-present. Intermediate, professional and premium grade, production/custom, solidbody, hollowbody, acoustic, acoustic/electric, and resonator guitars made in the U.S., Korea, the Czech Republic and China. They also offer basses, banjos, mandolins, and amps. Founded in Evanston, Illinois, by Dean Zelinsky. Original models were upscale versions of Gibson designs with glued necks, fancy tops, DiMarzio pickups and distinctive winged headstocks (V, Z and ML), with production beginning in '77. In '80 the factory was relocated to Chicago. Dean's American manufacturing ends in '86 when all production shifts to Korea. In '91 Zelinsky sold the company to Tropical Music in Miami, Florida. For '93-'94 there was again limited U.S. (California) production of the E'Lite, Cadillac and ML models under the supervision of Zelinsky and Cory Wadley. Korean versions were also produced. In '95, Elliott Rubinson's Armadillo Enterprises, of Clearwater, Florida, bought the Dean brand. In '97 and '98, Dean offered higher-end USA Custom Shop models. In '98, they reintroduced acoustics. From 2000 to '08, Zelinsky was once again involved in the company.

Dating American models: first 2 digits are year of manufacture. Imports have no date codes.

Baby ML

1982-1986, 2000-present. Downsized version of ML model.

| 1980s | Import | $250 | $300 |
| 1980s | U.S.-made | $325 | $400 |

Baby V

1982-1986, 2000-present. Downsized version of the V model.

| 1980s | Import | $250 | $300 |
| 1980s | U.S.-made | $325 | $400 |

Baby Z

1982-1986, 2000-present. Downsized version of the Z model.

| 1980s | Import | $250 | $300 |
| 1980s | U.S.-made | $325 | $400 |

Bel Aire

1983-1984. Solidbody, possibly the first production guitar with humbucker/single/single pickup layout, U.S.-made, an import model was introduced in '87.

| 1980s | Import | $250 | $300 |
| 1983-1984 | U.S.-made | $325 | $400 |

Budweiser Guitar

Ca.1987. Shaped like Bud logo.

| 1987 | | $200 | $225 |

Cadillac (U.S.A.)

1979-1985. Single long treble horn on slab body.

| 1979-1985 | | $1,500 | $1,800 |

1982 Dean Baby V
Jeffrey Mallin

1983 Dean Bel-Air

1982 Dean V Standard

Jeffrey Mallin

DeArmond Starfire

MODEL YEAR	FEATURES	EXC. COND. LOW	HIGH

Cadillac 1980

2006-present. Block inlays, 2 humbuckers, gold hardware.

| 2006-2010 | | $350 | $425 |

Cadillac Deluxe (U.S.A.)

1993-1994, 1996-1997. Made in U.S., single longhorn shape, various colors.

| 1993-1994 | | $950 | $1,125 |
| 1996-1997 | | $950 | $1,125 |

Cadillac Reissue (Import)

1992-1994. Single longhorn shape, 2 humbuckers, various colors.

| 1992-1994 | | $275 | $325 |

Cadillac Select

2009-present. Made in Korea, figured maple top, mahogany, pearl block inlays.

| 2009-2010 | | $300 | $350 |

Cadillac Standard

1996-1997. Slab body version.

| 1996-1997 | | $1,200 | $1,400 |

Del Sol

2008. Import, small double-cut thinline semi-hollow, ES-335 style body, rising sun fretboard markers.

| 2008 | | $300 | $350 |

Dime O Flame (ML)

2005-present. ML-body, Dimebuckers, burning flames finish, Dime logo on headstock.

| 2005-2010 | | $350 | $400 |

Eighty-Eight (Import)

1987-1990. Offset double-cut solidbody, import.

| 1987-1990 | | $150 | $175 |

E'Lite

1978-1985, 1994-1996. Single-horn shape.

| 1978-1985 | | $1,000 | $1,200 |
| 1994-1996 | | $900 | $1,100 |

E'Lite Deluxe

1980s. Single-horn shape.

| 1980s | | $1,000 | $1,250 |

Golden E'Lite

1980. Single pointy treble cutaway, fork headstock, gold hardware, ebony 'board, sunburst.

| 1980 | | $1,000 | $1,250 |

Hollywood Z (Import)

1985-1986. Bolt-neck Japanese copy of Baby Z, Explorer shape.

| 1985-1986 | | $100 | $125 |

Jammer (Import)

1987-1989. Offset double-cut body, bolt-on neck, dot markers, six-on-a-side tuners, various colors offered.

| 1987-1989 | | $100 | $125 |

Leslie West

2008-present.

| 2008-2010 | Standard | $350 | $425 |

Mach I (Import)

1985-1986. Limited run from Korea, Mach V with six-on-a-side tunes, various colors.

| 1985-1986 | | $100 | $125 |

Mach V (Import)

1985-1986. Pointed solidbody, 2 humbucking pick-ups, maple neck, ebony 'board, locking trem, various colors, limited run from Korea.

| 1985-1986 | | $100 | $125 |

Mach VII (U.S.A.)

1985-1986. Mach I styling, made in America, offered in unusual finishes.

| 1985-1986 | | $1,000 | $1,200 |

ML (ML Standard/U.S.A.)

1977-1986. There is a flame model and a standard model.

1977-1981	Burst flamed top	$1,500	$1,800
1977-1981	Burst plain top	$1,300	$1,600
1977-1981	Common opaque finish	$1,000	$1,300
1977-1981	Less common finish	$1,500	$1,800
1982-1986	Burst flamed top	$1,200	$1,500
1982-1986	Burst plain top	$1,200	$1,500
1982-1986	Common opaque finish	$1,000	$1,300
1982-1986	Less common finish	$1,300	$1,600

ML (Import)

1983-1990. Korean-made.

| 1983-1990 | | $375 | $425 |

Soltero SL

2007-2010. Made in Japan, single-cut solidbody, 2 pickups, flame maple top.

| 2007-2010 | | $1,200 | $1,500 |

V Standard (U.S.A.)

1977-1986. V body, there is a standard and a flame model offered.

1977-1981	Burst flamed top	$1,500	$1,800
1977-1981	Burst plain top	$1,300	$1,600
1977-1981	Common opaque finish	$1,000	$1,300
1977-1981	Less common finish	$1,500	$1,800
1982-1986	Burst flamed top	$1,200	$1,500
1982-1986	Burst plain top	$1,200	$1,500
1982-1986	Common opaque finish	$1,000	$1,300
1982-1986	Less common finish	$1,300	$1,600

USA Time Capsule Exotic V

2005-present. Flying V style, solid mahogany body with exotic spalted and flamed maple top, Dean V neck profile (split V headstock).

| 2005-2010 | | $2,000 | $2,300 |

Z Standard (U.S.A.)

1977-1986. Long treble cutaway solidbody, 2 humbuckers.

| 1977-1983 | Common finish | $1,000 | $1,300 |
| 1977-1983 | Less common finish | $1,500 | $1,800 |

USA Time Capsule Z

2000-present. Explorer style body, figured maple top.

| 2000-2010 | | $1,700 | $1,900 |

Z Autograph (Import)

1985-1987. The first Dean import from Korea, offset double-cut, bolt neck, dot markers, offered in several standard colors.

| 1985-1987 | | $200 | $225 |

MODEL YEAR	FEATURES	EXC. COND. LOW	HIGH

Z Coupe/Z Deluxe (U.S.A. Custom Shop)
1997-1998. Mahogany body offered in several standard colors, Z Deluxe with Floyd Rose tremolo.

1997-1998		$900	$1,100

Z Korina (U.S.A. Custom Shop)
1997-1998. Z Coupe with korina body, various standard colors.

1997-1998		$1,100	$1,300

Z LTD (U.S.A. Custom Shop)
1997-1998. Z Coupe with bound neck and headstock, offered in several standard colors.

1997-1998		$1,100	$1,300

Dean Markley
The string and pickup manufacturer offered a limited line of guitars and basses for a time in the '80s. They were introduced in '84.

DeArmond Guitars
1999-2004. Solid, semi-hollow and hollow body guitars based on Guild models and imported from Korea by Fender. They also offered basses. The DeArmond brand was originally used on pickups, effects and amps built by Rowe Industries.

Electric
1999-2004. Various import models, some with USA electronic components.

1999-2000	Bajo Jet Baritone	$550	$650
1999-2001	S-65 (S-100)	$325	$375
1999-2004	Jet Star (Polara style)	$400	$500
1999-2004	M-75/M-75T (Bluesbird)	$400	$500
1999-2004	M-77T Duo Jet	$400	$500
1999-2004	Starfire (Double-cut)	$500	$600
1999-2004	Starfire Special (Single-cut)	$400	$500
1999-2004	X135 Duane Eddy	$500	$600
1999-2004	X155 (Duane Eddy style)	$550	$650
2000-2001	M-70 (Bluesbird)	$350	$400
2000-2001	M-72 (Bluesbird)	$400	$500

Dearstone
1993-present. Luthier Ray Dearstone builds his professional and premium grade, custom, archtop and acoustic/electric guitars in Blountville, Tennessee. He also builds mandolin family instruments and violins.

Decar
1950s. A private brand sold by Decautur, Illinois music store, Decar headstock logo.

Stratotone H44 Model
1956. Private branded Stratotone with maple neck and fretboard instead of the standard neck/fretboard, 1 pickup and other Harmony H44 Stratotone attributes, bolt-on neck.

1956		$500	$600

DeCava Guitars
1983-present. Professional and premium grade, production/custom, archtop and classical guitars built by luthier Jim DeCava in Stratford, Connecticut. He also builds ukes, banjos, and mandolins.

Decca
Mid-1960s. Acoustic, solid and hollow body guitars made in Japan by Teisco and imported by Decca Records, Decca headstock logo, student-level instruments. They also offered amps and a bass.

Acoustic Flat-Top
1960s. Decca label on the inside back.

1960s		$100	$150

Electric Solidbody
1960s. Teisco-made in Japan, 3 pickups, sunburst.

1960s		$250	$300

Defil
Based out of Lubin, Poland, Defil made solid and semi-hollowbdy electric guitars at least from the 1970s to the '90s.

DeGennaro
2003-present. Premium grade, custom/production, acoustic, archtop, semi-hollow and solidbody guitars built by luthier William DeGennaro in Grand Rapids, Michigan. He also builds basses and mandolins.

Del Pilar Guitars
1956-1986. Luthier William Del Pilar made his classical guitars in Brooklyn, New York.

Del Vecchio
1902-present. Casa Del Vecchio builds a variety of Spanish instruments including acoustic and resonator guitars in São Paulo, Brazil.

Delaney Guitars
2004-present. Luthier Mike Delaney builds his professional grade, production/custom, chambered, solidbody, and semi-hollowbody electric guitars in Atlanta, Georgia. Prior to 2008 he built in Florence, Montana. He also builds basses.

Delgado
1928-present. The Delgado business began in Torreon, Coahuila, Mexico, then moved to Juarez in the '30s with a second location in Tijuana. In '48 they moved to California and opened a shop in Los Angeles. Since 2005, Manuel A. Delgado, a third generation luthier, builds his premium and presentation grade, production/custom, classical, flamenco and steel string acoustic guitars in Nashville, Tennessee. He also builds basses, mandolins, ukuleles and banjos.

Defil Guitar

DeGennaro Dynasty

2006 Dillion Phoenix

Jon Way

DiPinto Belvedere Jr.

MODEL		EXC. COND.	
YEAR	FEATURES	LOW	HIGH

Delirium Custom Guitars

2008-present. Luthiers Patrick and Vincent Paul-Victor along with Gael Canonne build their professional and premium grade, production/custom, solidbody electric guitars in Paris and Toulouse, France.

Dell'Arte

1997-present. Production/custom Maccaferri-style guitars from John Kinnard and Alain Cola. In '96, luthier John Kinnard opened a small shop called Finegold Guitars and Mandolins. In '98 he met Alain Cola, a long time jazz guitarist who was selling Mexican-made copies of Selmer/Maccaferri guitars under the Dell'Arte brand. Cola wanted better workmanship for his guitars, and in October '98, Finegold and Dell'Arte merged. As of May '99 all production is in California.

Delta Guitars

2005-2010. Acoustic, acoustic/electric, and solidbody electric guitars from Musician's Wholesale America, Nashville, Tennessee.

Dennis Hill Guitars

1991-present. Premium and presentation grade, production/custom, classical and flamenco guitars built by luthier Dennis Hill in Panama City, Florida. He has also built dulcimers, mandolins, and violins.

Desmond Guitars

1991-present. Luthier Robert B. Desmond builds his premium grade, production/custom classical guitars in Orlando, Florida.

DeTemple

1995-present. Premium grade, production/custom, solidbody electric guitars built by luthier Michael DeTemple in Sherman Oaks, California. He also builds basses.

DeVoe Guitars

1975-present. Luthier Lester DeVoe builds his premium grade, production/custom flamenco and classical guitars in Nipomo, California.

Diamond

Ca. 1963-1964. Line of sparkle finish solidbody guitars made in Italy for the Diamond Accordion company.

Ranger

Ca. 1963-1964. Rangers came with 1, 2, 3, or 4 pickups, sparkle finish.

1960s		$500	$625

Dick, Edward Victor

1975-present. Luthier Edward Dick currently builds his premium grade, custom, classical guitars in Denver, Colorado (he lived in Peterborough and Ottawa, Ontario until '95). He also operates the Colorado School of Lutherie.

MODEL		EXC. COND.	
YEAR	FEATURES	LOW	HIGH

Dickerson

1937-1947. Founded by the Dickerson brothers in '37, primarily for electric lap steels and small amps. Instruments were also private branded for Cleveland's Oahu company, and for the Gourley brand. By '47, the company changed ownership and was renamed Magna Electronics (Magnatone).

Dillion

1996-present. Dillion, of Cary, North Carolina, offers intermediate grade, production, acoustic, acoustic/electric, hollow-body and solidbody guitars made in Korea and Vietnam. They also have basses and mandolins.

Dillon

1975-present. Professional and premium grade, custom, flat-tops built by luthier John Dillon originally in Taos, New Mexico ('75-'81), then in Bloomsburg, Pennsylvania ('81-'01), and since 2001 back in Taos. He also builds basses.

Dino's Guitars

1995-present. Custom, professional grade, electric solidbody guitars built by a social co-op company founded by Alessio Casati and Andy Bagnasco, in Albisola, Italy. It also builds effects.

DiPinto

1995-present. Intermediate and professional grade, production retro-vibe guitars from luthier Chris DiPinto of Philadelphia, Pennsylvania. He also builds basses. Until late '99, all instruments built in the U.S., since then all built in Korea.

Ditson

1835-1930. Started in Boston by music publisher Oliver Ditson, by the end of the 1800s, the company was one of the east coast's largest music businesses, operating in several cities and was also involved in distribution and manufacturing of a variety of instruments, including guitars and ukes. From 1916-1930 Ditson guitars were made by Martin. The majority of Martin production was from '16 to '22 with over 500 units sold in '21. Ditson also established Lyon and Healy in Chicago and the John Church Company in Cincinnati.

Concert Models

1916-1922. Similar in size to Martin size 0. Models include Style 1, Style 2 and Style 3.

1916-1922	Style 1	$3,700	$4,600
1916-1922	Style 2	$4,500	$5,600
1916-1922	Style 3	$5,000	$6,200

Standard Models

1916-1922. Small body similar to Martin size 3, plain styling. Models include Style 1, Style 2 and Style 3.

1916-1922	Style 1	$2,300	$2,800
1916-1922	Style 2	$2,800	$3,500
1916-1922	Style 3	$3,900	$4,800

MODEL		EXC. COND.	
YEAR	FEATURES	LOW	HIGH

Style 111 Dreadnought

1916-1930. Dreadnought-sized exceeding the Martin 000 size, initially intended to be a 6-string bass guitar, fan bracing (only 7 made) on the top generally requires extensive restoration, X bracing is Martin-made (19 made).

1916-1922	Fan bracing	$16,000	$20,000
1923-1930	X bracing		
	(Martin)	$50,000	$62,000

D'Leco Guitars

1991-2003. Guitarist Maurice Johnson and luthier James W. Dale built premium grade, production/ custom archtop guitars in Oklahoma City, Oklahoma.

DM Darling Guitars

2006-present. Luthier Denis Merrill builds his professional and premium grade, custom, acoustic, classical, resonator and solidbody guitars in Tacoma, Washington. From 1978 to '06 he built under his own name and Merrill Custom Shop. He also builds mandolin family instruments.

Dobro

1929-1942, ca. 1954-present. Currently, professional and premium grade, production, wood and metal body resophonic guitars offered by Gibson.

Founded 1929 in Los Angeles by John Dopyera, Rudy Dopyera, Ed Dopyera and Vic Smith (Dobro stands for Dopyera Brothers). Made instruments sold under the Dobro, Regal, Norwood Chimes, Angelus, Rex, Broman, Montgomery Ward, Penetro, Bruno, Alhambra, More Harmony, Orpheum, and Magn-o-tone brands.

Dobro instruments have a single cone facing outward with a spider bridge structure and competed with National products. Generally, model names are numbers referring to list price and therefore materials and workmanship (e.g., a No. 65 cost $65). Because of this, the same model number may apply to various different instruments. However, model numbers are never identified on instruments!

In '30, the company name was changed to Dobro Corporation, Ltd. In '32, Louis Dopyera buys Ted Kleinmeyer's share of National. Louis, Rudy and Ed now hold controlling interest in National, but in '32 John Dopyera left Dobro to pursue idea of metal resophonic violin. In December of '34 Ed Dopyera joins National's board of directors (he's also still on Dobro board), and by March of '35 Dobro and National have merged to become the National Dobro Corporation. Dobro moves into National's larger factory but continues to maintain separate production, sales and distribution until relocation to Chicago is complete. Beginning in early-'36 National Dobro starts relocating its offices to Chicago. L.A. production of Dobros continues until '37, after which some guitars continue to be assembled from parts until '39, when the L.A. operations were closed down.

All resonator production ended in '42. Victor Smith, Al Frost and Louis Dopyera buy the company and change the name to the Valco Manufacturing Company. The Dobro name does not appear when production resumes after World War II.

In mid-'50s - some sources say as early as '54 - Rudy and Ed Dopyera began assembling wood-bodied Dobros from old parts using the name DB Original. In about '59, some 12-fret DB Originals were made for Standel, carrying both DB Original and Standel logos. In around '61, production was moved to Gardena, California, and Louis Dopyera and Valco transferred the Dobro name to Rudy and Ed, who produce the so-called Gardena Dobros. At this time, the modern Dobro logo appeared with a lyre that looks like 2 back-to-back '6s'. Dobro Original debuts ca. '62. In late-'64 the Dobro name was licensed to Ed's son Emil (Ed, Jr.) Dopyera. Ed, Jr. designs a more rounded Dobro (very similar to later Mosrites) and has falling out with Rudy over it.

In '66 Semi Moseley acquires the rights to the Dobro brand, building some in Gardena, and later moving to Bakersfield, California. Moseley introduced Ed, Jr's design plus a thinline double-cutaway Dobro. Moseley Dobros use either Dobro or National cones. In '67 Ed, Sr., Rudy and Gabriella Lazar start the Original Music Instrument Company (OMI) and produce Hound Dog brand Dobros. In '68 Moseley goes bankrupt and in '70 OMI obtains the rights to the Dobro brand and begins production of OMI Dobros. In '75 Gabriella's son and daughter, Ron Lazar and Dee Garland, take over OMI. Rudy Dupyera makes and sells Safari brand resonator mandolins. Ed, Sr. dies in '77 and Rudy in '78. In '84 OMI was sold to Chester and Betty Lizak. Both wood and metal-bodied Dobros produced in Huntington Beach, California. Chester Lizak died in '92. Gibson purchased Dobro in '93 and now makes Dobros in Nashville, Tennessee.

Dobros generally feature a serial number which, combined with historical information, provides a clue to dating. For prewar L.A. guitars, see approximation chart below adapted from Gruhn and Carter's Gruhn's Guide to Vintage Guitars (Miller Freeman, 1991). No information exists on DB Originals.

Gardena Dobros had D prefix plus 3 digits beginning with 100 and going into the 500s (reportedly under 500 made). No information is available on Moseley Dobros.

OMI Dobros from '70-'79 have either D prefix for wood bodies or B prefix for metal bodies, plus 3 or 4 numbers for ranking, space, then a single digit for year (D XXXX Y or B XXX Y; e.g., D 172 8 would be wood body #172 from '78). For '80-'87 OMI Dobros, start with first number of year (decade) plus 3 or 4 ranking numbers, space, then year and either D for wood or B for metal bodies (8 XXXX YD or 8 XXX YB; e.g., 8 2006 5B would be metal body #2008 from '85). From '88-'92, at least, a letter and number indicate guitar style, plus 3 or 4 digits for ranking, letter for neck style, 2 digits for

DM Darling

1977 Dobro

Dobro Classic 60

Dobro Josh Graves

MODEL YEAR	FEATURES	EXC. COND. LOW	HIGH

year, and letter for body style (AX XXXX N YY D or AX XXX N YY B).

L.A. Guitars (approx. number ranges, not actual production totals)

1929-30	900-2999
1930-31	3000-3999
1931-32	BXXX (Cyclops models only)
1932-33	5000-5599
1934-36	5700-7699
1937-42	8000-9999

Angelus
1933-1937. Wood body, round or square neck, 2-tone walnut finish, continues as Model 19 in Regal-made guitars.

1933-1937	Round neck	$1,100	$1,300
1933-1937	Square neck	$1,200	$1,450

Artist M-16
1934-1935. German silver alloy body, engraved.

1934-1935	H square neck	$3,500	$3,900
1934-1935	M round neck	$5,500	$6,500

Columbia D-12
1967-1968. Acoustic 12-string, typical Dobro resonator with spider style bridge, made during Dobro-Moseley era.

1967-1968	$800	$1,000

Cyclops 45
1932-1933. Bound walnut body, 1 screen hole.

1932-1933	Round neck	$2,300	$2,800
1932-1933	Square neck	$2,300	$2,800

D-40 Texarkana
1965-1967. Mosrite-era (identified by C or D prefix), traditional Dobro style cone and coverplate, dot inlays, Dobro logo on headstock, sunburst wood body. Red and blue finishes available.

1965-1967	Sunburst, square neck	$1,000	$1,200

D-40E Texarkana
1965-1967. D-40 electric with single pickup and 2 knobs.

1965-1967	$1,200	$1,450

D-100 Californian Resonator
1965-1969. Dobro's version of Mosrite thinline double-cut, resonator, 2 small metal ports, 2 pickups, 2 knobs, sunburst.

1965-1969	$1,300	$1,600

DM-33 California Girl/DM-33H
1996-2006. Chrome-plated bell brass body, biscuit bridge, spider resonator, rosewood 'board. Girl or Hawaiian-scene (H) engraving.

1996-2006	$1,400	$1,700

DM-75 Lily of the Valley
1990-1997, 2002-2005. Chrome plated bell brass body resonator, round neck, Lily of the Valley engraving.

1990-1997	$2,200	$2,400

Dobro/Regal 46/47
1935-1938 Dobro/Regal 46, renamed 47 1939-1942. Made by Regal of Chicago, aluminum body, round neck, 14 frets, slotted peghead, silver finish. Degraded finish was a common problem with the Dobro/Regal 47.

1935-1938	Model 46	$1,300	$1,600
1939-1942	Model 47, original finish	$1,700	$2,100

MODEL YEAR	FEATURES	EXC. COND. LOW	HIGH

Dobro/Regal 62/65
1935-1938 Dobro/Regal 62, continued as Dobro/Regal 65 for 1939-1942. Nickel-plated brass body, Spanish dancer etching, round or square neck. Note: Dobro/Regal 65 should not be confused with Dobro Model 65 which discontinued earlier.

1935-1938	Model 62, round neck	$2,700	$3,300
1935-1938	Model 62, square neck	$3,000	$3,500
1939-1942	Model 65, round neck	$2,600	$3,200
1939-1942	Model 65, square neck	$2,800	$3,400

Dobro/Regal Tenor 27-1/2
1930. Tenor version of Model 27.

1930	$600	$750

Dobrolektric
1996-2005. Resonator guitar with single-coil neck pickup, single-cut.

1996-2005	$900	$1,100

DS-33/Steel 33
1995-2000. Steel body with light amber sunburst finish, resonator with coverplate, biscuit bridge.

1995-2000	$1,050	$1,200

DW-90C
2001-2006. Single sharp cutaway, wood body, metal resonator, f-hole upper bass bout.

2001-2006	$1,100	$1,300

F-60/F-60 S
1986-2005. Round neck (60, discontinued '00)) or square neck (60 S), f-holes, brown sunburst.

1986-2005	$1,200	$1,500

Hound Dog
2002-present. Built at the Opry Mill plant, entry level, laminated wood, 10 1/2" spider-bridge resonator. Square neck version discontinued '06.

2002-2006	Square neck	$475	$600

Hula Blues
1987-1999. Dark brown wood body (earlier models have much lighter finish), painted Hawaiian scenes, round neck.

1987-1999	$1,200	$1,500

Josh Graves
1996-2006. Single bound ample body, spider cone, nickel plated.

1996-2006	Unsigned	$1,400	$1,700

Leader 14M/14H
1934-1935. Nickel plated brass body, segmented f-holes.

1934-1935	H square neck	$2,100	$2,500
1934-1935	M round neck	$1,700	$2,100

Model 27 Cyclops
1932-1933.

1932-1933	Round neck	$1,900	$2,400
1932-1933	Square neck	$2,000	$2,500

Model 27/27G
1933-1937. Regal-made, wooden body.

1933-1937	Round neck	$1,300	$1,600
1933-1937	Square neck	$1,700	$2,000

MODEL YEAR	FEATURES	EXC. COND. LOW	HIGH

Model 27 (OMI)
1976-1994. Wood body, square neck.

1976-1994		$1,300	$1,600

Model 27 Deluxe
1995-2005. 27 with figured maple top, nicer appointments.

1995-2005		$1,700	$2,200

Model 32
1939-1941. Regal-made, wooden body.

1939-1941		$1,700	$1,900

Model 33 (Duolian)
1972. Only made in '72, becomes Model 90 in '73.

1972		$1,000	$1,250

Model 33 H
1973-1997 (OMI & Gibson). Same as 33 D, but with etched Hawaiian scenes, available as round or square neck.

1980s	Round neck	$1,300	$1,600
1980s	Square neck	$1,300	$1,600

Model 35 (32)
1935-1942. Metal body, called Model 32 (not to be confused with wood body 32) for '35-'38.

1935-1942		$1,700	$1,900

Model 36
1932-1937. Wood body with resonator, round or square neck.

1932-1937	Round neck	$1,200	$1,500
1932-1937	Square neck	$1,700	$2,100

Model 36/36 S
1970s-1997, 2002-2005. Chrome-plated brass body, round or square (S) neck, dot markers, engraved rose floral art.

1970-1997		$1,200	$1,500

Model 37
1933-1937. Regal-made wood body, mahogany, bound body and 'board, round or square 12-fret neck.

1933-1937	Round neck	$1,900	$2,300
1933-1937	Square neck	$2,400	$2,800

Model 37 Tenor
1933-1937 (Regal). Tenor version of No. 37.

1933-1937		$1,000	$1,200

Model 45
1934-1939. Regal-made wood body, round or square neck.

1934-1939	Square neck	$2,000	$2,500

Model 55/56 Standard
1929-1931 Model 55 Standard, renamed 56 Standard 1932-1934. Unbound wood body, metal resonator, bound neck, sunburst.

1929-1931	Model 55	$2,000	$2,500
1932-1934	Model 56	$2,000	$2,500

Model 60
1933-1936. Similar to Model 66/66B.

1933-1936	Round neck	$4,000	$5,000
1933-1936	Square neck	$5,000	$6,000

Model 60 Cyclops
1932-1933.

1932-1933		$3,800	$4,600

Model 60/60 D (OMI)/60 DS
1970-1993. Wood body (laminated maple) with Dobro resonator cone, model 60 until '73 when re-
named 60 D, and various 60 model features offered, post-'93 was Gibson-owned production.

1970-1993	Model 60 Series	$950	$1,200

Model 65/66/66 B
1929-1933. Wood body with sandblasted ornamental design top and back, metal resonator, sunburst. Model 66 B has bound top.

1929-1931	Model 65	$3,200	$4,000
1932-1933	Model 66	$3,200	$4,000
1932-1933	Model 66 B	$3,200	$4,000

Model 66/66 S
1972-1995. Wood body with sandblasted ornamental design top and back, metal resonator, sunburst, round or square (S) neck.

1972-1995		$1,300	$1,600

Model 85/86
1929-1934. Wood body, triple-bound, round or square neck, renamed 86 in '32.

1929-1934		$2,500	$3,000

Model 90 (Duolian) (OMI)
1972-1995. Chrome-plated, f-holes, etched Hawaiian scene.

1972-1995		$1,200	$1,500

Model 90 (Woodbody)/WB90 G/WB90 S
1991-2005. Maple body with upper bout f-holes or sound holes, round neck, metal resonator with spider bridge, sunburst.

1991-2005		$1,150	$1,450

Model 125 De Luxe
1929-1934. Black walnut body, round or square neck, Dobro De Luxe engraved, triple-bound top, back and 'board, nickel-plated hardware, natural.

1929-1934	Round neck	$7,000	$8,000
1929-1934	Square neck	$11,000	$14,000

Professional 15M/15H
1934-1935. Engraved nickel body, round (M) or square (H) neck, solid peghead.

1934-1935	H square neck	$2,600	$3,200
1934-1935	M round neck	$2,300	$2,800

Dodge
1996-present. Luthier Rick Dodge builds his intermediate and professional grade, production, solidbody guitars with changeable electronic modules in Tallahassee, Florida. He also builds basses.

Doitsch
1930s. Acoustic guitars made by Harmony most likely for a music store or studio.

Domino
Ca. 1967-1968. Solidbody and hollowbody electric guitars and basses imported from Japan by Maurice Lipsky Music Co. of New York, New York, previously responsible for marketing the Orpheum brand. Models are primarily near-copies of EKO, Vox, and Fender designs, plus some originals. Models were made by Arai or Kawai. Earlier models may have been imported, but this is not yet documented.

1930s Dobro Model 45

1931 Dobro Model 66

D'Pergo Aged Vintage Classic

2006 Duesenberg Double Cat

MODEL YEAR	FEATURES	EXC. COND. LOW	HIGH

Electric

1967-1968. Various models include the Baron, Californian, Californian Rebel, Dawson, and the Spartan.

1967-1968		$250	$375

Dommenget

1978-1985, 1988-present. Luthier Boris Dommenget (pronounced dommen-jay) builds his premium grade, custom/production, solidbody, flat-top, and archtop guitars in Balje, Germany. From '78 to '85 he was located in Wiesbaden, and from '88-'01 in Hamburg. He and wife Fiona also make

Don Musser Guitars

1976-present. Custom, classical and flat-top guitars built by luthier Don Musser in Cotopaxi, Colorado.

Doolin Guitars

1997-present. Luthier Mike Doolin builds his premium grade, production/custom acoustics featuring his unique double-cut in Portland, Oregon.

Dorado

Ca. 1972-1973. Six- and 12-string acoustic guitars, solidbody electrics and basses. Brand used briefly by Baldwin/Gretsch on line of Japanese imports.

Acoustic Flat-Top/Acoustic Dobro

1972-1973. Includes folk D, jumbo Western, and grand concert styles (with laminated rosewood back and sides), and Dobro-style.

1972-1973	Higher-end models	$200	$300
1972-1973	Lower-end models	$100	$125
1972-1973	Mid-level models	$125	$175

Solidbody Electric

1972-1973. Includes Model 5985, a double-cuty with 2 P-90-style pickups.

1972-1973		$175	$300

Douglas Ching

1976-present. Luthier Douglas J. Ching builds his premium grade, production/custom, classical, acoustic, and harp guitars currently in Chester, Virginia, and previously in Hawaii ('76-'89) and Michigan ('90-'93). He also builds ukes, lutes and violins.

D'Pergo Custom Guitars

2002-present. Professional, premium, and presentation grade, production/custom, solidbody guitars built in Windham, New Hampshire. Every component of the guitars is built by D'Pergo.

Dragge Guitars

1982-present. Luthier Peter Dragge builds his custom, steel-string and nylon-string guitars in Ojai, California,

Dragonfly Guitars

1994-present. Professional grade, production/custom, sloped cutaway flat-tops, semi-hollow body electrics, and dulcitars built by luthier Dan Richter in Roberts Creek, British Columbia. He also builds basses.

Drive

2000s-present. Budget grade, production, import solidbody electric guitars. They also offer solidstate amps.

DTM

1997-present. See David Thomas McNaught listing.

Duelin Guitars

1994-present. Professional grade, production/custom, 6 ½ string guitars designed by Don Scheib of Simi Valley and built by luthier Mike Lipe in Sun Valley, California.

Duesenberg

1995-present. Professional and premium grade, production/custom, solid and hollow body electric guitars built by luthier Dieter Goelsdorf in Hannover, Germany. They also build basses. Rockinger had a Duesenberg guitar in the 1980s.

Dunwell Guitars

1996-present. Professional and premium grade, custom, flat-tops built by luthier Alan Dunwell in Nederland, Colorado.

Dupont

Luthier Maurice Dupont builds his classical, archtop, Weissenborn-style and Selmer-style guitars in Cognac, France.

Dwight

See info under Epiphone Dwight guitar.

Dyer

1902-1939. The massive W. J. Dyer & Bro. store in St. Paul, Minnesota, sold a complete line of music related merchandise though they actually built nothing but a few organs. The Larson Brothers of Chicago were commissioned to build harp guitar and harp mandolin pieces for them somewhat following the harp guitar design of Chris Knutsen, until 1912 when the Knutsen patent expired. Although the body design somewhat copied the Knutsen patent the resulting instrument was in a class by itself in comparison. These harp guitars have become the standard by which all others are judged because of their ease of play and the tremendous, beautiful sound they produce. Many modern builders are using the body design and the same structural ideas evidenced in the Larson originals. They were built in Styles 4 (the plainest), 5, 6, 7 and 8. The ornamentation went from the no binding, dot inlay Style 4 to the full treatment, abalone trimmed, tree-of-life fingerboard of the Style 8. All had mahogany back and sides with ebony fingerboard and bridge. There are also a very few Style 3 models found of late that are smaller than the standard and have a lower bout body point. Other Dyer instruments were built by Knutsen. Dyer also carried Stetson brand instruments made by the Larson Brothers.

MODEL YEAR	FEATURES	EXC. COND. LOW	HIGH
Harp Guitar			
1920s	Style 4, no binding	$5,500	$7,000
1920s	Style 5, bound top	$9,500	$12,000
1920s	Style 6, bound top/bottom	$10,500	$13,000
1920s	Style 7, fancy inlays	$11,500	$14,000
1920s	Style 8, tree-of-life	$16,000	$20,000

Dynacord

1950-present. Dynacord is a German company that makes audio and pro sound amps, as well as other electronic equipment. In 1966-'67 they offered solidbody guitars and basses from the Welson Company of Italy. They also had the Cora guitar and bass which is the center part of a guitar body with a tube frame in a guitar outline. They also offered tape echo machines.

Dynelectron

1960s-late 1970s. This Italian builder offered a variety of guitars and basses, but is best known today for their almost exact copies of Danelectro Longhorns of the mid-'60s.

E L Welker

1984-present. Luthier Eugene L. Welker builds his premium and presentation grade, production/custom, leather-wrapped archtop guitars in Claremont, New Hampshire.

Earthwood

1972-1985. Acoustic designs by Ernie Ball with input from George Fullerton. One of the first to offer acoustic basses.

Eastman

1992-present. Intermediate and professional grade, production, archtop and flat-top guitars mainly built in China, with some from Germany and Romania. Beijing, China-based Eastman Strings started out building violins and cellos. They added guitars in '02 and mandolins in '04.

Eastwood

1997-present. Mike Robinson's company imports budget and intermediate grade, production, solid and semi-hollowbody guitars, many styled after 1960s models. They also offer basses and mandolins.

Eaton, William

1976-present. Luthier William Eaton builds custom specialty instruments such as vihuelas, harp guitars, and lyres in Phoenix, Arizona. He is also the Director of the Robetto-Venn School of Luthiery.

Ed Claxton Guitars

1972-present. Premium grade, custom flat-tops made by luthier Ed Claxton, first in Austin, Texas, and currently in Santa Cruz, California.

Eduardo Duran Ferrer

1987-present. Luthier Eduardo Duran Ferrer builds his premium grade, classical guitars in Granada, Spain.

Edward Klein

1998-present. Premium grade, custom, guitars built by luthier Edward Klein in Mississauga, Ontario.

EER Custom

2005-present. Professional and premium grade, custom, soldibody and semi-hollowbody electric guitars built by luthier Ernest E. Roesler in Forks, Washington.

Egmond

1935-1972. Founded by Ulke Egmond, building acoustic, archtop, semi-hollow and solidbody guitars originally in Eindhoven, later in Best Holland. They also made basses. Egmond also produced instruments under the Orpheum (imported into U.S.) Rosetti (England), Miller, Wilson and Lion brand names.

Electric

1960s. Solid or semi-hollow bodies.

1960s		$350	$425

2009 Eastman El Rey ER-1

Ehlers

1968-present. Luthier Rob Ehlers builds his premium grade, production/custom, flat-top acoustic guitars, originally in Oregon and since '06, in Veracruz, Mexico.

15 CRC

Cutaway, Western red cedar top, Indian rosewood back and sides.

1996		$1,900	$2,400

15 SRC

Cutaway, European spruce top, Indian rosewood back and sides.

1998		$1,900	$2,400

16 BTM

European spruce top, mahogany back and sides, Troubadour peghead, black lacquer finish.

1998		$2,000	$2,500

16 C

16" lower bout, cutaway, flamed maple sides and back, European spruce top.

1990		$2,000	$2,500

16 SK Concert

16" lower bout, relatively small upper bout, small waist, European spruce top, flamed koa back and sides, diamond markers, natural.

1993		$1,800	$2,200

16 SM

European spruce top, mahogany back and sides.

1999		$1,700	$2,100

16 SSC

Cutaway, European spruce top, English sycamore back and sides.

1996		$1,800	$2,300

Ed Claxton E/M

Eichelbaum Grand Concert

1960s EKO Manta

MODEL YEAR	FEATURES	EXC. COND. LOW	HIGH

25 C
Limited Edition Anniversary Model, European spruce top, Indian rosewood back and sides, abalone top border.

| 2001 | | $2,700 | $3,400 |

GJ (Gypsy Jazz)
| 2000s | D-style | $1,700 | $2,100 |

Eichelbaum Guitars
1994-present. Luthier David Eichelbaum builds his premium grade, custom, flat-tops in Santa Barbara, California.

EKO
1959-present. Originally acoustic, acoustic/electric, electric thinline and full-size archtop hollowbody, solidbody electric guitars and basses built by Oliviero Pigini and Company in Recanati, Italy, and imported by LoDuca Brothers, Milwaukee, Radio and Television Equipment Company in Santa Ana, California and others. First acoustic guitars followed by sparkle plastic-covered electrics by '62. Sparkle finishes are gone ca. '66. Pigini dies ca. '67. LoDuca Bros. phases out in early-'70s. By '75 EKO offers some copy guitars and they purchased a custom shop to make other brands by '78. In '85 they ceased production in Italy, continuing the brand for a few years with Asian imports, and continued to distribute other brands. By 2004, the Eko line of guitar was revived with budget and intermediate grade, production, classical, acoustic, acoustic/electric, solidbody, solidbody, and hollowbody guitars made in Asia. They also make basses and amps.

Barracuda VI
1966-ca.1978. Double-cut semi-hollow, 2 pickups, 6-string.

| 1966-1978 | | $475 | $575 |

Barracuda XII
1966-ca.1978. Double-cut semi-hollow, 2 pickups, 12-string.

| 1966-1978 | | $500 | $600 |

Cobra I/II/III/XII
1966-1978. Double-cut solidbody, 2 knobs. Cobra I has 1 pickup, II 2 pickups and III 3 pickups. 12-string Cobra XII offered '67-'69, has 2 pickups.

1966-1969	Cobra I	$375	$425
1966-1969	Cobra II	$425	$475
1966-1969	Cobra III	$450	$500
1966-1969	Cobra XII	$450	$500
1970-1978	Cobra I	$300	$350
1970-1978	Cobra II	$325	$375
1970-1978	Cobra III	$300	$450
1970-1978	Cobra XII	$400	$450

Commander
1965 Single-cut archtop electric, 1 pickup, 2 controls, EKO logo on upper bass bout, maple body in 'dura-glos' finish.

| 1965 | | $300 | $375 |

Condor
1966-ca.1969. Double-cut solidbody with 3 or 4 pickups.

| 1966-1969 | | $400 | $575 |

MODEL YEAR	FEATURES	EXC. COND. LOW	HIGH

Dragon
1967-ca.1969. Single-cut archtop, 2 f-holes, 3 pickups, tremolo.

| 1967-1969 | | $550 | $675 |

Flat-Top Acoustic
1960s. Various student-level flat-top acoustic models.

| 1960s | | $175 | $225 |

Florentine
1964-ca.1969. Double-cut archtop, 2 pickups.

| 1964-1969 | | $450 | $550 |

Kadett/Kadett XII
1967-ca.1978. Double-cut solidbody with point on lower bass side of body, 3 pickups, tremolo. 12-string Kadett XII offered '68-'69.

| 1967-1978 | Kadett | $450 | $550 |
| 1968-1969 | Kadett XII | $450 | $550 |

Lancer Stereo
1967-1969. Lancer VI with stereo output (route output to 2 amplifiers requires EKO stereo cable for stereo application).

| 1967-1969 | | $375 | $450 |

Lancer VI
1967-ca.1969. Double-cut solidbody, 2 pickups.

| 1967-1969 | | $275 | $325 |

Lancer XII
1967-1969. Double-cut solidbody electric, 12-string.

| 1967-1969 | | $300 | $350 |

Lark I/II
1970. Thin hollow cutaway, sunburst. Lark I has 1 pickup and Lark II 2.

| 1970 | Lark I | $350 | $425 |
| 1970 | Lark II | $350 | $425 |

Model 180
1960s. Cutaway acoustic archtop.

| 1960s | | $300 | $350 |

Model 285 Modello
1960s. Thinline single-cut, 1 pickup.

| 1962 | | $325 | $375 |

Model 300/375
1962. Copy of Hofner Club-style electric, single-cut, 2 pickups, set-neck.

| 1962 | | $650 | $800 |

Model 500/1 / 500/1V
1961-1965. Plastic covered solidbody, 1 pickup. 500/1 no vibrato, 1V with vibrato.

| 1961-1965 | 500/1 | $500 | $625 |
| 1961-1965 | 500/1V | $600 | $700 |

Model 500/2 / 500/3V
1961-1964. Plastic covered solidbody, plastic sparkle finish. 500/2 no vibrato, 2 pickups. 3V with vibrato, 3 pickups.

| 1961-1965 | 500/2 | $575 | $700 |
| 1961-1965 | 500/3V | $650 | $750 |

Model 500/4 / 500/4V
1961-1964. Plastic covered solidbody, 4 pickups. 500/4 no vibrato, 4V with vibrato.

| 1961-1965 | 500/4 | $675 | $825 |
| 1961-1965 | 500/4V | $725 | $875 |

Model 540 (Classical)
1960s. Nylon-string classical guitar.

| 1960s | | $150 | $200 |

MODEL YEAR	FEATURES	EXC. COND. LOW	HIGH

Model 700/3V
1961-1964. Map-shape/tulip-shape body, 3 pickups, vibrato, woodgrain plastic finish.

1961-1964		$900	$1,100

Model 700/4V
1961-1967. Map-shape/tulip-shape body, 4 pickups, multiple switches, vibrato.

1961-1967	Red, blue, silver sparkle	$1,150	$1,400
1961-1967	Standard finish	$900	$1,100

Ranger 6/12
1967-ca.1982. D-size flat-top acoustic, large 3-point 'guard, dot inlays, EKO Ranger label. Ranger 12 is 12-string.

1967-1982	Ranger 12	$325	$400
1967-1982	Ranger 6	$325	$400

Ranger 6/12 Electra
1967. Ranger 6/12 with on-board pickup and 2 controls, 6-string with dot markers, 12-string with block markers.

1967	12 Electra	$350	$425
1967	6 Electra	$350	$425

Rocket VI/XII (Rokes)
1967-ca.1969. Rocket-shape design, solidbody, 6-string, says Rokes on the headstock, Rokes were a popular English band that endorsed EKO guitars, marketed as the Rocket VI in the U.S.; and as the Rokes in Europe, often called the Rok. Rocket XII is 12-string.

1967-1969	Rocket VI	$650	$775
1967-1969	Rocket XII	$650	$775

El Degas
Early-1970s. Japanese-made copies of classic America electrics and acoustics, imported by Buegeleisen & Jacobson of New York, New York.

Solidbody
Early-1970s. Copies of classic American models, including the Let's Play model.

1970s		$250	$300

Eleca
2004-present. Student/budget level, production, acoustic and electric guitars, imported by Eleca International. They also offer amps, effects and mandolins.

Electar
See Epiphone listing.

Electra
1971-1984. Imported from Japan by St. Louis Music. Most instruments made by Matsumoku in Matsumoto, Japan. The Electra line replaced SLM's Japanese-made Apollo and U.S.-made Custom Kraft lines. First guitar, simply called The Electra, was a copy of the Ampeg Dan Armstrong lucite guitar and issued in '71, followed quickly by a variety of bolt-neck copies of other brands. In '75 the Tree-of-Life guitars debut with a leaf pattern carved into the top, and the Electra line expanded to 25 models. Open-book headstocks changed to wave or fan shape by '78. By around '81 ties with Matsumoku further solidified and decision eventually made to merge SLM's Electra brand with Matsumoku's Westone brand. Some Korean production begins in early-'80s. In the fall of '83, the Electra Brand becomes Electra Phoenix. By beginning of '84, the brand becomes Electra-Westone and by the end of '84 just Westone. Matsumoku-made guitars have serial number in which first 1 or 2 digits represent the year of manufacture. Thus a guitar with a serial number beginning in 0 or 80 would be from 1980.

Concert Professional
Late 1970s. Howard Roberts style, single-cut electric flat-top with oval sound hole, single humbucking pickup, fancy markers.

1977		$750	$850

Custom
1970s. Double-cut solidbody, 2 pickups, Custom logo on truss rod, cherry finish.

1970s		$475	$575

Elvin Bishop
1976-ca.1980. Double-cut semi-hollow body, tree-of-life inlay.

1976-1980		$750	$850

Flying Wedge
1970s. V body, six-on-a-side tuners.

1970s		$350	$450

MPC Outlaw
1976-1983. Has separate modules that plug in for different effects.

1976-1983		$550	$700
1976-1983	MPC plug in module	$80	$100

Omega
1976-ca. 1980. Single-cut solidbody, block inlays, Omega logo on truss rod, black with rosewood neck, or natural with figured top and maple neck.

1976-1980		$400	$450

Phoenix
1980-1984. Classic offset double-cut solidbody, Phoenix logo on headstock.

1980-1984		$300	$350

Rock
1971-1973. Single cut solidbody, becomes the Super Rock in '73.

1971-1973		$375	$475

Super Rock
1973-ca.1978. Renamed from Rock ('71-'73).

1973-1978		$450	$525

X135
1982. Offset double-cut solidbody, 2 humbucker pickups.

1982		$275	$325

X145 60th Anniversary
1982. Classic offset double-cut only made one year, Anniversary plate on back of headstock, single/single/hum pickups.

1982		$225	$300

X150
1975. Offset double-cut, 2 humbucker pickups.

1975		$400	$450

1960s EKO 500/4V

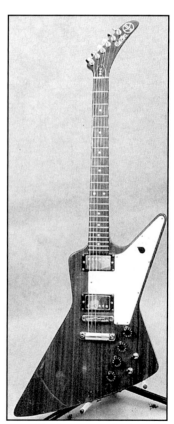

1981 Electra MPC X910

Elferink Excalibur

Engel 14"

MODEL		EXC. COND.	
YEAR	FEATURES	LOW	HIGH

X410

1975. Double-cut thinline acoustic archtop, 2 humbucker pickups, large split triangle markers, open-book style headstock shape.

| 1975 | | $900 | $1,100 |

X420

1978. Double-cut thinline acoustic archtop, 2 humbucker pickups, dot markers, wave-shape style headstock.

| 1978 | | $500 | $600 |

X935 Endorser

1983-1984. Double-cut solidbody, 2 humbuckers, tune-o-matic, dot markers.

| 1983-1984 | | $325 | $375 |

X960 Ultima

1978. Hybrid single-cut with additional soft bass bout cutaway, slab solidbody, dot markers, 2 humbucker pickups, wave-shape style headstock.

| 1978 | | $400 | $450 |

Electric Gypsy

See listing under Teye.

Electro

1964-1975. The Electro line was manufactured by Electro String Instruments and distributed by Radio-Tel. The Electro logo appeared on the headstock rather than Rickenbacker. Refer to the Rickenbacker section for models.

Electromuse

1940s-1950s. Mainly known for lap steels, Electromuse also offered acoustic and electric hollowbody guitars. They also had tube amps usually sold as a package with a lap steel.

Elferink

1993-present. Production/custom, premium grade, archtop guitars built in the Netherlands by luthier Frans Elferink.

Elite

1960s. Guitars made in Italy by the Crucianelli accordion company, which made several other brands.

Elk

Late-1960s. Japanese-made by Elk Gakki Co., Ltd. Many were copies of American designs. They also offered amps and effects.

Elliott Guitars

1966-present. Premium and presentation grade, custom, nylon-string classical and steel-string guitars built by luthier Jeffrey Elliott in Portland, Oregon.

Ellis

2000-present. Luthier Andrew Ellis builds his production/custom, premium grade, steel string acoustic and resophonic guitars in Perth, Western Australia. In 2008 he also added lap steels.

MODEL		EXC. COND.	
YEAR	FEATURES	LOW	HIGH

Elli-Sound

1960s. Guitars made in Italy by the Crucianelli accordion company, which made several other brands.

Ellsberry Archtop Guitars

2003-present. Premium and presentation grade, custom/production, acoustic and electric archtops built by luthier James Ellsberry originally in Torrance, California, and presently in Harbor City.

Emperador

1966-1992. Guitars and basses imported from Japan by Westheimer Musical Instruments. Early models appear to be made by either Teisco or Kawai; later models were made by Cort.

Acoustic

| 1960s | Archtop or flat-top | $125 | $150 |

Electric Solidbody

| 1960s | | $150 | $175 |

Empire

1997-present. Professional and premium grade, production/custom, solidbody guitars from Lee Garver's GMW Guitarworks of Glendora, California.

Encore

Ca. 1986-present. Budget grade, production, classical, acoustic, and electric guitars imported from China and Vietnam by John Hornby Skewes & Co. in the U.K. They also offer basses.

Engel Guitars

1990-present. Luthier Robert Engel builds his premium grade, production/custom, hollowbody and solidbody guitars in Stamford, Connecticut.

English Electronics

1960s. Lansing, Michigan, company named after owner, some private branded guitars and amps by Valco (Chicago), many models with large English Electronics vertical logo on headstock.

Tonemaster

1965. National Val-Pro 84 with neck pickup and bridge mounted pickup, black.

| 1965 | | $650 | $775 |

Epi

1970s. Typical Japanese copy-import, Epi logo on headstock with capital letter split-E logo, inside label says Norlin, thought to be for Japanese domestic market originally.

Acoustic Flat-Top

1970s. D-style, mahogany body.

| 1970s | | $140 | $160 |

Epiphone

Ca. 1873-present. Budget, intermediate, professional and premium grade, production, solidbody, archtop, acoustic, acoustic/electric, resonator, and

MODEL YEAR	FEATURES	EXC. COND. LOW	HIGH

classical guitars made in the U.S. and overseas. They also offer basses, amps, mandolins, ukes and banjos. Founded in Smyrna, Turkey, by Anastasios Stathopoulos and early instruments had his label. He emigrated to the U.S. in 1903 and changed the name to Stathoupoulo. Anastasios died in '15 and his son, Epaminondas ("Epi") took over. The name changed to House of Stathopoulo in '17 and the company incorporated in '23. In '24 the line of Epiphone Recording banjos debut and in '28 the company name was changed to the Epiphone Banjo Company. In '43 Epi Stathopoulo died and sons Orphie and Frixo took over. Labor trouble shut down the NYC factory in '51 and the company cut a deal with Conn/Continental and relocated to Philadelphia in '52. Frixo died in '57 and Gibson bought the company. Kalamazoo-made Gibson Epiphones debut in '58. In '69 American production ceased and Japanese imports began. Some Taiwanese guitars imported from '79-'81. Limited U.S. production resumed in '82 but sourcing shifted to Korea in '83. In '85 Norlin sold Gibson to Henry Juszkiewicz, Dave Barryman and Gary Zebrowski. In '92 Jim Rosenberg became president of the new Epiphone division.

AJ Masterbilt Series
2004-present. Sloped shoulder D size, solid spruce tops, solid rosewood or mahogany (M) back and sides.

2004-2010		$300	$450

Alleykat
2000-2010. Single cut small body archtop, 1 humbucker and 1 mini-humbucker.

2000-2010		$300	$375

B.B. King Lucille
1997-present. Laminated double-cut maple body, 2 humbuckers, Lucille on headstock.

1997-2010		$400	$500

Barcelona CE
1999-2000. Classical, solid spruce top, rosewood back and sides, EQ/preamp.

1999-2000		$300	$350

Barcelone (Classical)
1963-1968. Highest model of Epiphone '60s classical guitars, maple back and sides, gold hardware.

1963-1964		$800	$1,000
1965-1968		$700	$875

Bard 12-String
1962-1969. Flat-top, mahogany back and sides, natural or sunburst.

1962-1964		$1,500	$1,800
1965-1969		$1,150	$1,450

Beverly Tenor
1931-1936. Archtop, 4-string.

1931-1936		$800	$1,000

Biscuit
1997-2000, 2002-2010. Wood body resonator, biscuit bridge, round neck.

1997-2010		$225	$275

Blackstone
1931-1950. Acoustic archtop, f-holes, sunburst.

1933-1934	Masterbilt	$825	$1,000
1935-1937		$700	$850

1938-1939		$600	$725
1940-1941		$550	$675
1948-1950		$475	$575

Broadway (Acoustic)
1931-1958. Non-cut acoustic archtop.

1931-1938	Sunburst, walnut body	$1,950	$2,400
1939-1942	Sunburst, maple body	$2,100	$2,550
1946-1949	Natural	$1,900	$2,300
1946-1949	Sunburst	$1,700	$2,050
1950-1958	Sunburst	$1,600	$1,925

Broadway Regent (Acoustic Cutaway)
1950-1958. Single-cut acoustic archtop, sunburst.

1950-1958		$1,950	$2,400

Broadway (Electric)
1958-1969. Gibson-made electric archtop, single-cut, 2 New York pickups (mini-humbucking pickups by '61), Frequensator tailpiece, block inlays, sunburst or natural finish with cherry optional in '67 only.

1958-1959	Natural	$3,000	$3,700
1958-1959	Sunburst	$2,900	$3,600
1960-1964	Natural	$3,000	$3,700
1960-1964	Sunburst	$2,700	$3,400
1965	Natural	$2,600	$3,300
1965	Sunburst	$2,500	$3,100
1966-1967	Natural, cherry	$2,300	$2,800
1966-1967	Sunburst	$2,200	$2,800
1968-1969	Natural, cherry	$2,200	$2,800
1968-1969	Sunburst	$2,100	$2,700

Broadway Reissue
1997-present. Full depth acoustic-electric single cut archtop, 2 humbuckers.

1997-2010		$475	$575

Broadway Tenor
1937-1953. Acoustic archtop, sunburst.

1937-1949		$725	$875
1950-1953		$600	$725

Byron
1949-ca.1955. Acoustic archtop, mahogany back and sides, sunburst.

1949-1955		$300	$375

C Series Classical (Import)
1995-2006. Nylon-string classical guitars, including C-25 (mahogany back & sides), C-40 (cedar top, mahogany), C-70-CE (rosewood).

1998-2005	C-40	$140	$160

Caiola Custom
1963-1970. Introduced as Caiola, renamed Caiola Custom in '66, electric thinbody archtop, 2 mini-humbuckers, multi-bound top and back, block inlays, walnut or sunburst finish (walnut only by '68).

1963-1964		$3,500	$4,200
1965		$3,100	$3,800
1966-1967		$2,900	$3,600
1968-1970		$2,700	$3,400

Caiola Standard
1966-1970. Electric thinbody archtop, 2 P-90s, single-bound top and back, dot inlays, sunburst or cherry.

1966-1967		$2,500	$3,100
1968-1970		$2,300	$2,900

1964 English Electronics Tonemaster
Zak Izbinsky

Epiphone Broadway

1965 Epiphone Casino

Epiphone SQ-180 Don Everly

MODEL YEAR	FEATURES	EXC. COND. LOW	HIGH

Casino (1 Pickup)
1961-1970. Thinline hollowbody, double-cut, 1 P-90 pickup, various colors.

1961		$2,600	$3,200
1962-1964		$2,600	$3,200
1965-1966		$2,100	$2,500
1967-1968		$2,000	$2,400
1969-1970		$1,900	$2,300

Casino (2 Pickups)
1961-1970. Two pickup (P-90) version, various colors. '61-'63 known as Keith Richards model, '64-'65 known as Beatles model.

1961		$4,500	$5,500
1962-1964		$4,000	$5,000
1965-1966		$3,200	$4,000
1967-1970		$2,900	$3,700

Casino J.L. U.S.A. 1965
2003-2006. 1,965 made.

2003-2006		$1,700	$2,100

Casino Reissue
1995-present. Sunburst.

1995-2010		$450	$550

Casino Revolution
1999-2005. Limited production 1965 reissue model, sanded natural.

1999-2005		$1,900	$2,300

Century
1939-1970. Thinline archtop, non-cut, 1 pickup, trapeze tailpiece, walnut finish, sunburst finish available in '58, Royal Burgundy available '61 and only sunburst finish available by '68.

1939-1948	Oblong shape pickup	$1,100	$1,325
1949	Large rectangular pickup	$1,050	$1,275
1950	New York pickup	$1,000	$1,200
1951-1957	Sunburst	$975	$1,175
1958-1962	Sunburst, P-90 pickup, plate logo	$1,400	$1,800
1963-1964	Sunburst, P-90 pickup, no plate logo	$1,400	$1,800
1965-1967	Sunburst, cherry	$1,000	$1,300
1968-1970	Sunburst	$1,000	$1,300

Classic (Classical)
1963-1970.

1963-1964		$525	$650
1965-1970		$450	$550

Collegiate
2004-2005. Les Paul-style body, 1 humbucker, various college graphic decals on body.

2004-2005		$125	$175

Coronet (Electric Archtop)
1939-1949. Electric archtop, laminated mahogany body, 1 pickup, trapeze tailpiece, sunburst, name continued as an electric solidbody in '58.

1939-1949		$800	$975

Coronet (Solidbody)
1958-1969. Solidbody electric, 1 New York pickup ('58-'59), 1 P-90 ('59-'69), cherry or black finish, Silver Fox finish available by '63, reintroduced as Coronet

USA '90-'94, Korean-made '95-'98.

1958-1959		$3,600	$4,500
1960-1964	Various colors	$3,500	$4,400
1965	Custom color (3 options)	$3,900	$4,800
1965	Standard color	$1,850	$2,200
1966-1967	Various colors	$1,700	$2,100
1968-1969	Various colors	$1,500	$1,900

Coronet U.S.A.
1990-1994. Made in Nashville, reverse banana headstock, typical Coronet styled body, single-coil and humbucker.

1990-1994		$625	$775

Coronet (Import)
1995-1998. Import version.

1995-1998		$250	$300

Crestwood Custom
1958-1970. Solidbody, 2 New York pickups ('58-'60), 2 mini-humbuckers ('61-'70), symmetrical body and 3+3 tuners ('58-'62), asymmetrical and 1x6 tuners ('63-'70), slab body with no Gibson equivalent model.

1958-1960	Cherry, New York pickups, 3+3	$4,400	$5,400
1959-1960	Sunburst, New York pickups	$4,400	$5,400
1961-1962	Cherry, mini-humbuckers	$4,100	$5,100
1961-1962	White, mini-humbuckers	$5,000	$6,000
1963-1964	Cherry, 1x6	$3,100	$3,900
1963-1964	Custom color (3 options)	$5,500	$9,500
1965	Cherry	$2,900	$3,500
1965	Custom color (3 options)	$5,400	$7,000
1966-1967	Cherry	$2,700	$3,300
1966-1967	Custom color (3 options)	$3,500	$4,300
1968-1970	Cherry, white	$2,500	$3,100

Crestwood Deluxe
1963-1969. Solidbody with 3 mini-humbuckers, block inlay, cherry, white or Pacific Blue finish, 1x6 tuners.

1963-1964	Cherry	$4,400	$5,500
1963-1964	Custom color (3 options)	$6,000	$10,000
1965	Cherry	$4,000	$5,000
1965	Custom color (3 options)	$5,800	$9,500
1966-1967	Cherry	$3,000	$3,700
1966-1967	Custom color (3 options)	$3,800	$4,700
1968-1969	Cherry, white	$3,000	$3,700

De Luxe
1931-1957. Non-cut acoustic archtop, maple back and sides, trapeze tailpiece ('31-'37), frequensator tailpiece ('37-'57), gold-plated hardware, sunburst or natural finish.

1931-1934	Sunburst	$3,500	$4,200
1935-1938	Sunburst	$3,300	$4,000
1939-1944	Natural	$3,500	$4,200

MODEL YEAR	FEATURES	EXC. COND. LOW	HIGH
1939-1944	Sunburst	$3,000	$3,600
1945-1949	Natural	$3,000	$3,600
1945-1949	Sunburst	$2,600	$3,200
1950-1957	Natural	$2,600	$3,200
1950-1957	Sunburst	$2,300	$2,800

De Luxe Regent (Acoustic Archtop)
1948-1952. Acoustic cutaway archtop, high-end appointments, rounded cutaway, natural finish, renamed De Luxe Cutaway in '53.

1948-1952		$3,300	$4,000

De Luxe Cutaway/Deluxe Cutaway
1953-1970. Renamed from De Luxe Regent, cataloged Deluxe Cutaway by Gibson in '58, special order by '64 with limited production because acoustic archtops were pretty much replaced by electric archtops.

1953-1957	Epiphone NY-made	$3,000	$3,600
1958-1959		$4,500	$5,500
1960-1965	Gibson Kalamazoo, rounded cutaway	$4,500	$5,500
1965-1970	Special order only	$4,000	$5,000

De Luxe Electric (Archtop)
1954-1957. Single-cut electric archtop, 2 pickups, called the Zephyr De Luxe Regent from '48-'54. Produced with a variety of specs, maple or spruce tops, different inlays and pickup combinations.

1954-1957	Natural	$3,000	$3,600
1954-1957	Sunburst	$2,800	$3,400

Del Ray
1995-2000. Offset double-cut body, 2 blade humbuckers, dot markers, tune-o-matic, flamed maple top.

1995-2000		$300	$350

Devon
1949-1957. Acoustic archtop, non-cut, mahogany back and sides, sunburst finish, optional natural finish by '54.

1950-1953	Sunburst	$1,200	$1,500
1954-1957	Natural	$1,300	$1,600
1954-1957	Sunburst	$1,200	$1,500

Don Everly (SQ-180)
1997-2004. Jumbo acoustic reissue, large double 'guard, black gloss finish.

1997-2004		$450	$550

Dot (ES-335 Dot)/Dot Archtop
2000-present. Dot-neck ES-335.

2000-2010		$250	$275

Dot Studio
2004-present. Simplified Dot, 2 control knobs, black hardware.

2004-2010		$200	$225

Dove Limited Edition
2008. Dove Limited Edition logo on label, Dove script logo on truss rod cover, classic dove logo art on 'guard and dove inlay on bridge, cherry or ebony.

2008		$200	$225

Dwight
1963, 1967. Coronet labeled as Dwight and made for Sonny Shields Music of St. Louis, 75 made in '63 and 36 in '67, cherry. National-Supro made Dwight brand lap steels in the '50s.

1963		$2,500	$3,000
1967		$2,200	$2,700

EA/ET/ES Series (Japan)
1970-1979. Production of the Epiphone brand was moved to Japan in '70. Models included the EA (electric thinline) and ET (electric solidbody).

1970-1975	ET-270	$450	$550
1970-1975	ET-275	$375	$450
1970s	EA-250	$325	$400
1972	ES-255 Casino	$400	$500
1975-1979	ET-290 Crestwood	$375	$450

El Diablo
1994-1995. Offset double-cut acoustic/electric, onboard piezo and 3-band EQ, composite back and sides, spruce top, cherry sunburst.

1994-1995		$275	$325

Electar Model M
1935-1939. Epiphone's initial entry into the new electric guitar market of the mid-'30s, 14 3/4" laminate maple archtop, horseshoe pickup, trap door on back for electronics, Electar logo on headstock, oblong pickup replaces horseshoe in late-'37.

1935-1936	2 control knobs	$1,200	$1,500
1937-1939	3 control knobs	$1,200	$1,500

Electar Model M Tenor
1937-1939. 4-string electric tenor with Electar specs.

1937-1939	3 knobs, natural	$1,200	$1,500

Elitist Series
2003-2009. Made in Japan, higher-grade series, using finer woods and inlays and U.S.-made Gibson pickups.

2003-2004	J-200	$900	$1,100
2003-2004	L-00/VS	$900	$1,100
2003-2005	1961 SG Standard	$600	$700
2003-2008	1963 ES-335 Dot	$900	$1,100
2003-2008	Byrdland/L5	$900	$1,100
2003-2009	Broadway	$900	$1,100
2003-2009	Casino	$1,000	$1,200
2003-2009	Les Paul Custom	$700	$825
2003-2009	Les Paul Standard	$700	$825
2003-2009	Les Paul Standard '57 Goldtop	$700	$825
2003-2009	Les Paul Studio	$550	$675
2003-2009	Sheraton	$1,100	$1,400
2003-2009	Texan	$900	$1,100
2004-2005	Jim Croce L-00	$600	$700
2005	Chet Atkins Country Gentleman	$900	$1,100
2007-2009	Les Paul Plus	$700	$825

Emperor (Acoustic Archtop)
1935-1954. Acoustic archtop, non-cut, maple back and sides, multi-bound body, gold-plated hardware, sunburst, optional natural finish by '39.

1935-1938	Sunburst	$4,500	$5,300
1939-1949	Natural	$5,000	$5,800
1939-1949	Sunburst	$4,100	$4,800
1950-1954	Natural	$3,800	$4,500
1950-1954	Sunburst	$3,300	$4,000

Emperor Regent
1948-1953. Acoustic archtop with rounded cutaway, renamed Emperor Cutaway in '53.

1948-1953	Natural	$4,800	$5,700
1948-1953	Sunburst	$4,200	$5,200

Epiphone Dot Studio

Epiphone Elitist Series Casino

Epiphone 1958 Gothic Explorer

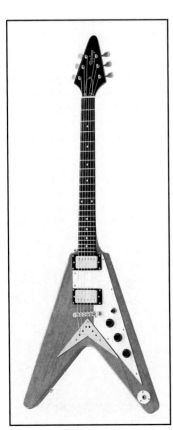

Epiphone 1958 Korina Flying V

MODEL YEAR	FEATURES	EXC. COND. LOW	HIGH

Emperor Cutaway
1953-1957. Renamed from Emperor Regent, acoustic archtop, single-cut, maple back and sides, multi-bound body, gold-plated hardware, sunburst or natural.

1953-1957	Natural	$4,800	$5,700
1953-1957	Sunburst	$4,200	$5,200

Emperor Electric
1953-1957. Archtop, single-cut, 3 pickups, multi-bound body, sunburst, called the Zephyr Emperor Regent in '50-'53.

1953-1957		$3,200	$3,900

Emperor (Thinline Electric)
1958-1969. Single-cut, thinline archtop, 3 New York pickups in '58-'60, 3 mini-humbuckers '61 on, multi-bound, gold-plated hardware, sunburst or natural finish until '65 when only sunburst was made.

1958-1969	Natural	$9,500	$11,500
1958-1969	Sunburst	$9,000	$11,000
1960-1962	Natural	$9,000	$11,000
1960-1962	Sunburst	$8,500	$10,500
1963-1964	Special order only	$8,500	$10,500
1965-1969	Special order only	$8,500	$10,500

Emperor/Emperor II
1982-1994. Single-cut archtop jazz guitar, 2 humbuckers, blocks, gold hardware. II added to name in '93, became Joe Pass Emperor II (see that listing) in '95, although his name was on the guitar as early as '91.

1982-1994		$475	$575

Entrada (Classical)
1963-1968. Classical, natural.

1963-1964		$550	$650
1965-1968		$475	$550

ES-295
1997-2001, 2003-present. Epi's version of classic Gibson goldtop.

1997-2001		$475	$575

Espana (Classical)
1962-1968. Classical, maple back and sides, U.S.-made, natural, imported in '69 from Japan.

1962-1964		$600	$700
1965-1968		$525	$625

Exellente
1963-1969, 1994-1995. Flat-top, rosewood back and sides, cloud inlays. Name revived on Gibson Montana insturment in '90s.

1963-1964		$5,700	$7,100
1965		$5,700	$7,100
1966-1967		$5,700	$7,100
1968-1969		$5,700	$7,100

1958 Korina Explorer
1998-present. Explorer with typical appointments, korina body. This guitar was produced with a variety of specs, ranging from maple tops to spruce tops, different inlay markers were also used, different pickup combinations have been seen, natural or sunburst finish.

1998-2010		$325	$400

1958 Gothic Explorer/Flying V
2002-present. Flat black finish. V ends in 2010.

2002-2010		$350	$400

Firebird
1995-2000. Two mini-humbuckers, Firebird Red, dot markers.

1995-2000		$325	$400

Firebird 300
1986-1988. Korean import, Firebird Red.

1986-1988		$325	$400

Firebird 500
1986-1988. Korean import, Firebird Red.

1986-1988		$375	$450

1963 Firebird VII/Firebird VII
2000-2005. Three mini-humbuckers, gold hardware, Maestro-style vibrato, block markers, Firebird Red, reverse body. 1963 added after first year.

2000-2005		$450	$550

Flamekat
1999-2005. Archtop, flame finish, double dice position markers, 2 mini-humbuckers, Epiphone Bigsby.

1999-2005		$375	$450

Flying V/'67 Flying V
1989-1998, 2003-2005. '67 or '58 specs, alder body, natural.

1989-1998	'67 specs	$300	$375
2003-2005	'58 specs	$300	$375

1958 Korina Flying V
1998-present. Typical Flying V configuration, korina body.

1998-2010		$325	$400

FT 30
1941-1949. Acoustic flat-top, brown stain, mahogany back and sides, reintroduced as Gibson-made FT 30 Caballero in '58.

1941-1949		$1,000	$1,250

FT 30 Caballero
1959-1970. Reintroduced from Epiphone-made FT 30, Gibson-made acoustic flat-top, natural, all mahogany body, dot inlay, tenor available '63-'68.

1959-1961		$950	$1,200
1962-1964		$700	$900
1965-1966		$600	$800
1967-1969		$600	$800
1970		$500	$600

FT 45
1941-1948. Acoustic flat-top, walnut back and sides, cherry neck, rosewood 'board, natural top, reintroduced as Gibson-made FT 45 Cortez in '58.

1941-1948		$1,250	$1,550

FT 45 Cortez
1958-1969. Reintroduced from Epiphone-made FT 45, Gibson-made acoustic flat-top, mahogany back and sides, sunburst or natural top (sunburst only in '59-'62).

1958-1959	Sunburst	$1,500	$1,800
1960-1964	Sunburst or natural	$1,400	$1,700
1965-1966	Sunburst or natural	$950	$1,200
1967-1969	Sunburst or natural	$775	$975

MODEL YEAR	FEATURES	EXC. COND. LOW	HIGH

FT 79

1941-1958. Acoustic 16" flat-top, square shoulder dreadnought, walnut back and sides until '49 and laminated maple back and sides '49 on, natural, renamed FT 79 Texan by Gibson in '58.

1941-1949	Walnut back & sides	$2,400	$3,000
1949-1958	Laminated pressed maple body	$2,200	$2,700

FT 79 Texan

1958-1970, 1993-1995. Renamed from Epiphone FT 79, Gibson-made acoustic flat-top, mahogany back and sides, sunburst or natural top, Gibson Montana made 170 in '93-'95.

1958-1959	$3,200	$4,000
1960-1964	$3,100	$3,900
1965	$2,700	$3,500
1966-1967	$2,500	$3,300
1968-1970	$2,200	$2,900

Paul McCartney 1964 Texan (U.S.A.)

2005. Reproduction of McCartney's '64 FT-79 Texan made in Gibson's Montana plant, two runs, one of 40 guitars, second of 250. First 40 were hand-aged and came with Sir Paul's autograph, display case and certificate.

2005	250 run	$5,000	$5,500

Paul McCartney 1964 Texan (Japan)

2006-2010. Limited run of 1,964 guitars.

2006-2010	$2,100	$2,500

FT 85 Serenader 12-String

1963-1969. 12 strings, mahogany back and sides, dot inlay, natural.

1963-1964	$1,100	$1,300
1965-1966	$850	$1,050
1967-1969	$675	$850

FT 90 El Dorado

1963-1970. Dreadnought flat-top acoustic, mahogany back and sides, multi-bound front and back, natural.

1963-1964	$2,400	$3,000
1965	$1,700	$2,200
1966-1967	$1,600	$2,100
1968-1970	$1,500	$2,000

FT 95 Folkster

1966-1969. 14" small body, mahogany back and sides, natural, double white 'guards.

1966-1967	$600	$800
1968-1969	$600	$800

FT 98 Troubadour

1963-1969. 16" square shouldered drednought, maple back and sides, gold-plated hardware, classical width 'board.

1963-1964	$2,500	$3,000
1965-1969	$2,000	$2,500

FT 110

1941-1958. Acoustic flat-top, natural, renamed the FT 110 Frontier by Gibson in '58.

1941-1949	Square shoulder	$2,500	$3,000
1949-1954	Round shoulder	$2,400	$2,900
1954-1958	Mahogany neck	$2,200	$2,700

FT 110 Frontier

1958-1970, 1994. Renamed from FT 110, acoustic flat-top, natural or sunburst, Gibson Montana made 30 in '94.

1958-1959		$3,100	$3,800
1960-1964		$3,000	$3,700
1965		$2,800	$3,500
1966-1967		$2,600	$3,300
1968-1970	Maple	$2,600	$3,300

FT Series (Flat-Tops Japan)

1970s. In '70 Epiphone moved production to Japan. Various models were made, nearly all with bolt necks and small rectangular blue labels on the inside back.

1970s	FT 120	$65	$75
1970s	FT 130, 132, 133, 140	$125	$150
1970s	FT 135	$200	$225
1970s	FT 145, 146, 147, 160 12-string, 160N	$175	$200
1970s	FT 150, 165 12-string	$200	$300
1970s	FT 155	$250	$325
1970s	FT 200 Monticello	$200	$250
1970s	FT 350 El Dorado, 565 12-string	$300	$350
1970s	FT 550	$300	$375
1970s	FT 570SB Super Jumbo	$350	$400

G 310

1989-present. SG-style model with large 'guard and gig bag.

1989-2010	$200	$225

G 400

1989-present. SG-style, 2 humbuckers, crown inlays.

1989-2010	$250	$300

G 400 Custom

1998-2000, 2003-present. 3 humbucker version, gold harware, block inlays.

1998-2010	$350	$425

G 400 Deluxe

1999-2007. Flame maple top version of 2 humbucker 400.

1999-2007	$300	$400

G 400 Limited Edition

2001-2002. 400 with Deluxe Maestro lyra vibrola, cherry red.

2001-2002	$275	$350

G 400 Tony Iommi

2003-present. SG-style model with cross 'board inlay markers, black finish.

2003-2010	$375	$425

G 1275 Custom Double Neck

1996-present. 6- & 12-string, SG-style alder body, maple top, mahogany neck, cherry red, set neck. Also offered as bolt-neck Standard for '96-'98.

1996-2010	$550	$650

Genesis

1979-1980. Double-cut solidbody, 2 humbuckers with coil-taps, carved top, red or black, available as Custom, Deluxe, and Standard models, Taiwan import.

1979-1980	$350	$425

Epiphone G 400 Tony Iommi

Epiphone G 1275

2003 Epiphone Les Paul Standard

Epiphone Slash Les Paul

MODEL YEAR	FEATURES	EXC. COND. LOW	HIGH
Granada (Non-cutaway Thinbody)			
1962-1969. Non-cut thinline archtop, 1 f-hole, 1 pickup, trapeze tailpiece, sunburst finish.			
1962-1965		$800	$1,000
1966-1969		$700	$900
Granada (Cutaway)			
1965-1970. Single-cut version.			
1965-1966		$800	$1,000
1967-1970		$700	$900
Howard Roberts Standard			
1964-1970. Single-cut acoustic archtop, bound front and back, cherry or sunburst finish, listed in catalog as acoustic but built as electric.			
1964		$2,600	$3,200
1965-1967		$2,100	$2,500
1968-1970		$1,700	$2,200
Howard Roberts Custom			
1965-1970. Single-cut archtop, bound front and back, 1 pickup, walnut finish (natural offered '66 only).			
1965-1967		$2,800	$3,300
1968-1970		$2,300	$2,800
Howard Roberts III			
1987-1991. Two pickups, various colors.			
1987-1991		$400	$500
Inspiration Style A Tenor			
1928-1929. Banjo resonator style body with round soundhole, A headstock logo, spruce top, walnut back, sides and neck.			
1928-1929		$2,100	$2,400
Joe Pass/Joe Pass Emperor II			
1995-present. Single-cut archtop jazz guitar, 2 humbuckers, blocks, gold hardware, renamed from Emperor II (see that listing).			
1995-2010		$425	$525
Les Paul '56 Goldtop			
1998-2010. Based on '56 specs with 2 P-90s.			
1998-2010		$375	$450
Les Paul Ace Frehley			
2001. Les Paul Custom 3-pickups, Ace's signature on 22nd fret, lightening bolt markers.			
2001		$600	$700
Les Paul Alabama Farewell Tour			
2003. Limited production, 1 pickup single-cut Jr., American flag and Alabama logo graphics and band signatures on body, Certificate of Authenticity.			
2003		$225	$400
Les Paul Black Beauty			
1997-present. Classic styling with three gold plated pickups, black finish, block markers.			
1997-2010		$450	$500
Les Paul Classic			
2003-2005. Classic Les Paul Standard specs, figured maple top, sunburst.			
2003-2005		$425	$475
Les Paul Custom			
1989-present. Various colors.			
1989-2010		$425	$475
Les Paul Custom Plus (Flame Top)			
1998-2010. Flamed maple top version of 2 pickup Custom, gold hardware, sunburst.			
1998-2010		$475	$550

MODEL YEAR	FEATURES	EXC. COND. LOW	HIGH
Les Paul Custom Silverburst			
2007-2008. 2 humbuckers, silverburst finish.			
2007-2008		$450	$550
Les Paul Dale Earnhardt			
2003. Dale Earnhardt graphics, 1 humbucker.			
2003		$225	$400
Les Paul Deluxe			
1998-2000. Typical mini-humbucker pickups.			
1998-2000		$350	$400
Les Paul ES Limited Edition			
1999-2000. Les Paul semi-hollow body with f-holes, carved maple top, gold hardware, cherry sunburst and other color options.			
1999-2000	Custom	$675	$775
1999-2000	Standard	$575	$675
Les Paul Jr. '57 Reissue			
2006. '57 Reissue on truss rod cover, logo and script Les Paul Junior stencil on headstock, lower back headstock states 'Epiphone Limited Edition Custom Shop'.			
2006		$450	$475
Les Paul LP-100			
1993-present. Affordable single-cut Les Paul, bolt-on neck.			
1993-2010		$200	$250
Les Paul Music Rising			
2006-2007. Music Rising (Katrina charity) graphic, 2 humbuckers.			
2006-2007		$225	$400
Les Paul Sparkle L.E.			
2001. Limited Edition LP Standard, silver, purple, red (and others) glitter finish, optional Bigsby.			
2001		$375	$450
Les Paul Special			
1994-2000. Double-cut, bolt neck.			
1994-2000		$200	$225
Les Paul Special II			
1996-present. Economical Les Paul, 2 pickups, single-cut, various colors.			
1996-2010	Guitar only	$85	$95
1996-2010	Player Pack with amp	$100	$110
Les Paul Special Limited Edition/TV Special			
2006. Copy of single-cut late '50s Les Paul Special with TV finish.			
2006		$425	$525
Les Paul Standard			
1989-present. Solid mahogany body, carved maple top, 2 humbuckers.			
1989-2010	Various colors	$300	$375
Les Paul Standard Baritone			
2004-2005. 27-3/4" long-scale baritone model.			
2004-2005		$325	$400
Les Paul Standard Plus FMT			
2003-present. LP Standard figured curly maple sunburst top.			
2003-2010		$400	$475
Les Paul Standard Ultra/Ultra II			
2005-present. LP Standard with chambered and contoured body, quilted maple top.			
2005-2010	Ultra	$400	$500
2005-2010	Ultra II	$475	$575

MODEL YEAR	FEATURES	EXC. COND. LOW	HIGH

Les Paul Studio

1995-present. Epiphone's version of Gibson LP Studio.

| 1995-2010 | | $325 | $375 |

Les Paul XII

1998-2000. 12-string solidbody, trapeze tailpiece, flamed maple sunburst, standard configuration.

| 1998-2000 | | $450 | $550 |

Slash Les Paul

1997-2000. Slash logo on body.

| 1997-2000 | | $550 | $675 |

Slash Les Paul Goldtop

2008-present. Limited Edition 2,000 made, goldtop finish, Seymour Duncan exposed humbuckers, Slash logo on truss rod cover, includes certificate of authenticity.

| 2008-2010 | With certificate | $800 | $875 |

Slash Les Paul Standard Plus-Top

2008-present. Figured top, exposed humbuckers, includes certificate of authenticity.

| 2008-2010 | With certificate | $850 | $975 |

Zakk Wylde Les Paul Custom

2002-present. Bull's-eye graphic, block markers, split diamond headstock inlay.

| 2002-2010 | | $450 | $525 |

Madrid (Classical)

1962-1969. Classical, natural.

| 1962-1964 | | $450 | $525 |
| 1965-1969 | | $400 | $475 |

MD-30

1993. D-size, round metal resonator, spruce top with dual screens.

| 1993 | | $327 | $375 |

Melody Tenor

1931-1937. 23" scale, bound body.

| 1931-1937 | Masterbilt | $1,000 | $1,200 |

Moderne

2000. Copy of '58 Gibson Moderne design, dot markers, Moderne script logo on 'guard, black.

| 2000 | | $500 | $650 |

Navarre

1931-1940. Flat-top, mahogany back and sides, bound top and back, dot inlay, brown finish.

| 1931-1937 | Hawaiian, Masterbilt label | $1,650 | $2,000 |
| 1938-1940 | Hawaiian, standard label | $1,450 | $1,800 |

Nighthawk Standard

1995-2000. Epiphone's version of the Gibson Nighthawk, single-cut, bolt neck, figured top.

| 1995-2000 | | $275 | $350 |

Noel Gallagher Union Jack/Super Nova

1997-2005. Limited edition, higher-end ES-335. Union Jack with British flag finish (introduced '99) or Supernova in solid blue.

| 1997-2005 | | $550 | $650 |

Olympic (Acoustic Archtop)

1931-1949. Mahogany back and sides.

| 1931-1939 | | $650 | $800 |
| 1940-1949 | | $600 | $700 |

Olympic Tenor (Acoustic Archtop)

1937-1949. 4-string version of the Olympic.

| 1937-1949 | | $650 | $800 |

Olympic Single (Solidbody)

1960-1970. Slab body, the same as the mid-'60s Coronet, Wilshire and Crestwood Series, single-cut '60-'62, asymmetrical double-cut '63-'70, 2 Melody maker single-coil pickups, vibrato optional in '64 and standard by '65.

1960-1962	Sunburst, single-cut	$1,100	$1,400
1963-1964	Sunburst, double-cut	$900	$1,300
1965-1970	Cherry or sunburst	$800	$1,200

Olympic Double (Solidbody)

1960-1969. Slab body, the same as the mid-'60s Coronet, Wilshire and Crestwood Series, single-cut '60-'62, asymmetrical-cut '63-'70, 2 Melody Maker single-coils, vibrato optional in '64 and standard by '65.

1960-1963	Sunburst, single-cut	$1,800	$2,200
1963-1964	Sunburst, double-cut	$1,400	$1,800
1965-1966	Cherry or sunburst	$1,100	$1,400
1967-1969	Cherry or sunburst	$1,000	$1,300

Olympic (3/4 Scale Solidbody)

1960-1963. 22" scale, sunburst.

| 1960-1963 | | $600 | $750 |

Olympic Special (Solidbody)

1962-1970. Short neck with neck body joint at the 16th fret (instead of the 22nd), single Melody Maker-style single-coil bridge pickup, small headstock, double-cut slab body, dot markers, Maestro or Epiphone vibrato optional '64-'65, slab body contour changes in '65 from symmetrical to asymmetrical with slightly longer bass horn, sunburst.

| 1962-1964 | Symmetrical | $550 | $700 |
| 1965-1970 | Asymmetrical | $500 | $650 |

PR-200 (EA-20)

1992-2000. Imported dreadnought, spruce top, satin finish, mahogany back and sides, natural.

| 1992-2000 | | $150 | $200 |

PR-350

1984-2000. Acoustic flat-top, mahogany body, also available with a pickup, 6- or 12-string.

| 1984-2000 | | $200 | $225 |

PR-350 CE

1989-2000. Cutaway 350, also available with a pickup.

| 1989-2000 | | $275 | $325 |

PR-600 ACS/ASB/N

1980-1985. Import 000-size flat-top, glued bridge, dot markers, sunburst.

| 1980-1985 | | $350 | $400 |

PR-755S

1980-1985. Flat-top, single-cut, solid spruce top, laminate rosewood body, set mahogany neck, block markers, gold hardware, natural.

| 1980-1985 | | $275 | $325 |

Pro 1

1989-1996. Solidbody, double-cut, 1 single-coil and 1 humbucking pickup, bolt-on neck, various colors.

| 1989-1996 | | $325 | $400 |

Epiphone Zakk Wylde Les Paul Custom

Epiphone Moderne

Epiphone SG Special

Epiphone Sheraton II (Reissue)

MODEL YEAR	FEATURES	EXC. COND. LOW	HIGH

Pro 2
1995-1998. Higher-end Pro I with Steinberger DB bridge, set-neck, 2 humbuckers, various colors.

1995-1998		$350	$400

Professional
1962-1967. Double-cut, thinline archtop, 1 pickup, mahogany finish. Values include matching Professional amp.

1962-1964	With matching amp	$2,000	$2,300
1965	With matching amp	$1,700	$2,000
1966-1967	With matching amp	$1,600	$1,900

Recording A
1928-1931. Asymmetrical body flat top with exaggerated treble bout cutaway, celluloid headstock veneer, dot inlays. All Recording models were offered in concert or auditorium body sizes.

1928-1931	Standard 6-string	$1,350	$1,650
1928-1931	Tenor 4-string	$1,250	$1,550

Recording B
1928-1931. As Recording A but with arched back, bound fingerboard, fancier body binding and zigzagging double slotted-diamond inlays.

1928-1931		$1,800	$2,200

Recording C
1928-1931. As Recording B but with arched top.

1928-1931		$2,200	$2,700

Recording D
1928-1931. As Recording C, but with large cross-hatched block inlays.

1928-1931		$2,600	$3,200

Recording E
1928-1931. As Recording D, but with large floral engraved block inlays.

1928-1931		$3,400	$4,100

Ritz
1940-1949. 15.5" acoustic archtop, large cello f-holes, dot inlays, no headstock ornamentation other than script Epiphone inlay, blond finish.

1940-1949		$775	$950

Riviera
1962-1970. Double-cut thinline archtop, 2 mini-humbuckers, Royal Tan standard finish changing to sunburst in '65, cherry optional by '66-'70, additional 250 were made in Nashville in '93-'94, a Riviera import was available in '82 and for '94-'06.

1962-1964	Tan or custom cherry	$3,800	$4,800
1965	Sunburst	$3,300	$4,000
1966-1967	Burgundy Mist	$3,100	$3,900
1966-1967	Sunburst or cherry	$2,900	$3,600
1967-1968	Walnut	$2,800	$3,400
1968-1970	Sunburst or cherry	$2,600	$3,200

Riviera (U.S.A.)
1993-1994. Made in U.S.A. on back of headstock.

1993-1994		$900	$1,100

Riviera Reissue (Korea)
1994-2006. Korean-made contemporary reissue, natural.

1994-2006		$475	$550

Riviera 12-String
1965-1970. Double-cut, 12 strings, thinline archtop, 2 mini-humbuckers, sunburst or cherry.

1965		$2,100	$2,600
1966-1967		$1,700	$2,100
1968-1970		$1,600	$2,000

Riviera 12-String Reissue (Korea)
1997-2000. Korean-made reissue, natural.

1997-2000		$475	$550

Royal
1931-1935. 15 1/2" acoustic archtop, mahogany back and sides, dot markers, sunburst, bound top, back and neck, Masterbilt headstock logo.

1931-1935		$1,700	$2,100

S-900
1986-1989. Neck-thru-body, locking Bender tremolo system, 2 pickups with individual switching and a coil-tap control.

1986-1989		$350	$425

SC350
1976-1979. Mahogany solidbody, scroll bass horn, rosewood 'board, dot inlays, bolt neck, 2 humbuckers, made in Japan.

1976-1979	Mahogany or Maple	$450	$550

SC550
1976-1979. Like SC450, but with gold hardware, block inlays, neck and body binding, and ebony 'board.

1976-1979	Maple, gold hardware	$550	$650

Seville EC-100 (Classical)
1938-1941, 1961-1969 (Gibson-made). Classical guitar, mahogany back and sides, natural, the '61-'63 version also available with a pickup.

1961-1964		$550	$650
1965-1969		$475	$550

SG Special
2000-present. SG body, dot markers, 2 open-coil humbuckers.

2000-2010	Guitar only	$85	$95
2000-2010	Player Pack with amp	$100	$110

Sheraton
1958-1970, 1993-1994. Double-cut thinline archtop, 2 New York pickups '58-'60, 2 mini-humbuckers '61 on, frequensator tailpiece, multi-bound, gold-plated hardware, sunburst or natural finish with cherry optional by '65.

1958-1959	Natural, New York pickups	$9,500	$11,500
1960	Natural, New York pickups	$9,500	$11,500
1961-1964	Natural, mini-humbuckers	$9,500	$11,500
1961-1964	Sunburst, mini-humbuckers	$8,700	$10,700
1965	Cherry	$7,600	$9,500
1965	Natural	$6,000	$7,400
1965	Sunburst	$5,500	$6,900
1966	Sunburst or cherry	$5,300	$6,600
1967	Sunburst or cherry	$4,900	$6,100
1968	Sunburst or cherry	$4,900	$6,100
1969-1970	Sunburst or cherry	$4,900	$6,100

MODEL YEAR	FEATURES	EXC. COND. LOW	HIGH

Sheraton (Japan)

1978-1983. Early reissue, not to be confused with Sheraton II issued in '90s, natural or sunburst.

1978-1983		$450	$550

Sheraton (Reissue U.S.A.)

1993-1994. An additional 250 American-made Sheratons were built from '93-'94.

1993-1994		$1,200	$1,500

Sheraton II (Reissue)

1994-present. Contemporary reissue, natural or sunburst.

1994-2010		$450	$550

Slasher

2001. Reverse offset double cut solidbody, bolt neck, six-on-a-side tuners, 2 pickups, dot markers.

2001		$225	$275

Sorrento (1 pickup)

1960-1970. Single-cut thinline archtop, 1 pickup in neck position, tune-o-matic bridge, nickel-plated hardware, sunburst, natural or Royal Olive finish, (cherry or sunburst by '68).

1960-1964		$1,700	$2,100
1965-1966		$1,500	$1,800
1967-1970		$1,400	$1,700

Sorrento (2 pickups)

1960-1970. Single-cut thinline archtop, 2 pickups, tune-o-matic bridge, nickel-plated hardware, sunburst, natural or Royal Olive finish, (cherry or sunburst by '68).

1960-1964		$2,400	$3,000
1965-1966		$2,100	$2,500
1967-1970		$2,000	$2,400

Sorrento (Reissue)

1994-2000. Reissue of 2 pickup model, import.

1994-2000		$425	$500

Spartan

1934-1949. Acoustic archtop, multi-bound, trapeze tailpiece, sunburst.

1934-1939		$500	$600
1940-1949		$400	$500

Special/SG Special (U.S.A.)

1979-1983. SG Special body style, dot markers, 2 exposed humbuckers, Special logo on truss rod cover.

1979-1983		$650	$800

Spider/The Spider

1997-2000. Wood body resonator, spider bridge, square neck.

1997-2000		$200	$250

Spirit

1979-1983. U.S.-made electric solidbody, Spirit logo on truss rod cover and new Epiphone U.S.A. designated script logo on headstock, double-cut, carved top with 2 humbuckers, various colors.

1979-1983		$550	$675

SST Classic

2007-present. Solidbody nylon-string classical acoustic/electric.

2007-2010		$175	$225

Paul McCartney 1964 Texan (U.S.A.)

2005. Reproduction of McCartney's '64 FT-79 Texan made in Gibson's Montana plant, two runs, one of 40

guitars, second of 250. First 40 were hand-aged and came with Sir Paul's autograph, display case and certificate.

2005	250 run	$5,000	$5,500

Paul McCartney 1964 Texan (Japan)

2006-2010. Limited run of 1,964 guitars.

2006-2010		$2,100	$2,500

Tom Delonge Signature ES-333

2008-present. One humbucker, dot inlays.

2008-2010		$300	$350

Trailer Park Troubadour Airscreamer

2003-2005. Airstream trailer-shaped body, identifying logo on headstock.

2003-2005		$400	$475

Triumph

1931-1957. 15 1/4" '31-'33, 16 3/8" '33-'36, 17 3/8" '36-'57, walnut back and sides until '33, laminated maple back and sides '33, solid maple back and sides '34, natural or sunburst.

1931-1932	Sunburst, laminated walnut body	$1,450	$1,800
1933	Sunburst, laminated maple body	$1,450	$1,800
1934-1935	Sunburst, solid maple body	$1,550	$1,900
1936-1940	Sunburst 17 3/8" body	$1,600	$2,000
1941-1949	Natural	$1,600	$2,000
1941-1949	Sunburst	$1,500	$1,850
1950-1957	Natural	$1,500	$1,850
1950-1957	Sunburst	$1,400	$1,700

Triumph Regent (Cutaway)

1948-1969. Acoustic archtop, single-cut, F-holes, renamed Triumph Cutaway in '53, then Gibson listed this model as just the Triumph from '58-'69.

1948-1952	Regent , natural	$2,400	$2,900
1948-1952	Regent , sunburst	$2,300	$2,800
1953-1957	Cutaway, natural	$2,400	$2,900
1953-1957	Cutaway, sunburst	$2,300	$2,800
1958-1959	Sunburst	$2,100	$2,600
1960-1964	Sunburst	$2,100	$2,600
1965	Sunburst	$2,100	$2,600
1966-1967	Sunburst	$2,100	$2,600
1968-1969	Sunburst	$2,100	$2,600

USA Map Guitar

1982-1983. U.S.-made promotional model, solidbody electric, mahogany body shaped like U.S. map, 2 pickups, natural.

1982-1983		$2,100	$2,600

USA Map Guitar Limited Edition

2007	Import		$450

Vee-Wee (Mini Flying V)

2003. Mini Flying V student guitar, Flying V shape with single bridge pickup, gig bag, solid opaque finish.

2003		$100	$125

Wildkat

2001-present. Thinline, single-cut, hollow-body, 2 P-90s, Bigsby tailpiece.

2001-2010		$350	$425

Epiphone Tom Delonge Signature ES-333

Epiphone SST Classic

Epiphone Zephyr Emperor Regent

Late '80s ESP

Wilshire

1959-1970. Double-cut solidbody, 2 pickups, tune-o-matic bridge, cherry.

MODEL YEAR	FEATURES	EXC. COND. LOW	HIGH
1959	Symmetrical body	$3,900	$4,900
1960-1962	Thinner-style body, P-90s	$3,300	$4,100
1962	Mini-humbuckers	$3,300	$4,100
1963-1964	Asymmetrical body	$2,600	$3,200
1965-1966	Custom color (3 options)	$3,500	$4,500
1965-1966	Standard color	$2,400	$2,900
1967-1970		$1,900	$2,300

Wilshire 12-String

1966-1968. Solidbody, 2 pickups, cherry.

MODEL YEAR	FEATURES	EXC. COND. LOW	HIGH
1966-1968		$2,300	$2,900

Wilshire II

1984-1985. Solidbody, maple body, neck and 'board, 2 humbuckers, 3-way switch, coil-tap, 1 tone and 1 volume control, various colors.

MODEL YEAR	FEATURES	EXC. COND. LOW	HIGH
1984-1985		$275	$300

Windsor (1 Pickup)

1959-1962. Archtop, 1 or 2 pickups, single-cut thinline, sunburst or natural finish.

MODEL YEAR	FEATURES	EXC. COND. LOW	HIGH
1959-1960	New York pickup, natural	$1,900	$2,400
1959-1960	New York pickup, sunburst	$1,800	$2,300
1961-1962	Mini-humbucker, natural	$1,900	$2,500
1961-1962	Mini-humbucker, sunburst	$1,800	$2,300

Windsor (2 Pickups)

1959-1962. Archtop, 1 or 2 pickups, single-cut thinline, sunburst or natural finish.

MODEL YEAR	FEATURES	EXC. COND. LOW	HIGH
1959-1960	New York pickup, natural	$2,600	$3,300
1959-1960	New York pickup, sunburst	$2,500	$3,200
1961-1962	Mini-humbucker, natural	$2,600	$3,300
1961-1962	Mini-humbucker, sunburst	$2,400	$3,100

X-1000

1986-1989. Electric solidbody, Korean-made, various colors.

MODEL YEAR	FEATURES	EXC. COND. LOW	HIGH
1986-1989		$250	$300

Zenith

1931-1969. Acoustic archtop, bound front and back, f-holes, sunburst.

MODEL YEAR	FEATURES	EXC. COND. LOW	HIGH
1931-1933		$900	$1,100
1934-1935	Larger 14 3/4" body	$900	$1,100
1936-1949	Still larger 16 3/8" body	$900	$1,100
1950-1957		$775	$950
1958-1959		$625	$775
1960-1969		$625	$775

Zephyr

1939-1957. Non-cut electric archtop, 1 pickup, bound front and back, blond or sunburst (first offered '53), called Zephyr Electric starting in '54.

MODEL YEAR	FEATURES	EXC. COND. LOW	HIGH
1939-1940	Natural, 16 3/8", metal handrest pickup	$1,050	$1,300
1941-1943	Natural, no metal handrest	$1,050	$1,300
1944-1946	Natural, top mounted pickup	$1,050	$1,300
1947-1948	17 3/8", metal covered pickup	$1,050	$1,300
1949-1952	Natural, New York pickup	$1,000	$1,200
1953-1957	Natural, New York pickup	$1,000	$1,200
1953-1957	Sunburst, New York pickup	$900	$1,100

Zephyr Regent

1950-1953. Single-cut electric archtop, 1 pickup, natural or sunburst, called Zephyr Cutaway for '54-'57.

MODEL YEAR	FEATURES	EXC. COND. LOW	HIGH
1950-1953	Natural	$1,300	$1,600
1950-1953	Sunburst	$1,200	$1,500

Zephyr Cutaway

1954-1957. Cutaway version of Zephyr Electric, called Zephyr Regent for 1950-'53.

MODEL YEAR	FEATURES	EXC. COND. LOW	HIGH
1954-1957	Natural	$2,200	$2,600
1954-1957	Sunburst	$2,000	$2,400

Zephyr Electric (Cutaway)

1958-1964. Gibson-made version, thinline archtop, single-cut, 2 pickups, natural or sunburst.

MODEL YEAR	FEATURES	EXC. COND. LOW	HIGH
1958-1959	Natural	$2,100	$2,600
1958-1959	Sunburst	$2,000	$2,500
1960-1964	Natural	$2,100	$2,600
1960-1964	Sunburst	$2,000	$2,500

Zephyr De Luxe (Non-cutaway)

1941-1954. Non-cut electric archtop, 1 or 2 pickups, multi-bound front and back, gold-plated hardware, natural or sunburst.

MODEL YEAR	FEATURES	EXC. COND. LOW	HIGH
1941-1942	Natural	$1,700	$2,100
1945-1949	Natural, 1 pickup	$1,900	$2,300
1945-1949	Natural, 2 pickups	$2,100	$2,500
1950-1954	Natural, 2 pickups	$2,100	$2,500
1950-1954	Sunburst, 2 pickups	$1,900	$2,300

Zephyr De Luxe Regent (Cutaway)

1948-1954. Single-cut electric archtop, 1 or 2 pickups until '50, then only 2, gold-plated hardware, sunburst or natural finish. Renamed Deluxe Electric in '54.

MODEL YEAR	FEATURES	EXC. COND. LOW	HIGH
1948-1949	Natural, 1 pickup	$2,600	$3,200
1948-1949	Natural, 2 pickups	$3,400	$4,100
1948-1949	Sunburst, 1 pickup	$2,200	$2,700
1948-1949	Sunburst, 2 pickups	$2,900	$3,600
1950-1954	Natural, 2 pickups	$2,900	$3,600
1950-1954	Sunburst, 2 pickups	$2,700	$3,400

Zephyr Emperor Regent

1950-1954. Archtop, single rounded cutaway, multi-bound body, 3 pickups, sunburst or natural finish, renamed Emperor Electric in '54.

MODEL YEAR	FEATURES	EXC. COND. LOW	HIGH
1950-1954	Natural	$4,200	$5,000
1950-1954	Sunburst	$3,900	$4,700

MODEL YEAR	FEATURES	EXC. COND. LOW	HIGH

Zephyr Tenor
1940. Natural, figured top.

| 1940 | | $1,050 | $1,300 |

Zephyr Blues Deluxe
1999-2005. Based on early Gibson ES-5, 3 P-90 pickups.

| 1999-2005 | | $575 | $700 |

Epoch

Economy level imports made by Gibson and sold through Target stores.

Equator Instruments

2006-present. Production/custom, professional and premium grade, solidbody, hollowbody, acoustic and classical guitars built in Chicago, Illinois by luthier David Coleman.

Erlewine

1979-present. Professional and premium grade, production/custom guitars built by luthier Mark Erlewine in Austin, Texas. Erlewine also produces the Chiquita brand travel guitar.

ESP

1983-present. Intermediate, professional, and premium grade, production/custom, Japanese-made solidbody guitars and basses. Hisatake Shibuya founded Electronic Sound Products (ESP), a chain of retail stores, in '75. They began to produce replacement parts for electric guitars in '83 and in '85 started to make custom-made guitars. In '87 a factory was opened in Tokyo. In '86 ESP opened a sales office in New York, selling custom guitars and production models. From around '98 to ca. '02 they operated their California-based USA custom shop. In '96, they introduced the Korean-made LTD brand and in '03 introduced the Xtone brand, which was folded into LTD in '10. Hisatake Shibuya also operated 48th Street Custom Guitars during the '90s but he closed that shop in 2003.

20th Anniversary
1995. Solidbody, double-cut, ESP95 inlaid at 12th fret, gold.

| 1995 | | $1,000 | $1,250 |

Eclipse Custom (U.S.A.)
1998-2002. U.S. Custom Shop-built, single-cut, mahogany body and maple top, various colors offered.

| 1998-2002 | | $625 | $775 |

Eclipse Custom/Custom T (Import)
1986-1988, 2003-2010. Single-cut mahogany solidbody, earliest model with bolt dot marker neck, 2nd version with neck-thru and blocks, the Custom T adds locking trem. Current has quilt maple top.

1986-1987	Bolt, dots	$525	$650
1987-1988	Neck-thru, blocks	$625	$700
1987-1988	Neck-thru, Custom T	$550	$675

Eclipse Deluxe
1986-1988. Single-cut solidbody, 1 single-coil and 1 humbucker, vibrato, black.

| 1986-1988 | | $525 | $650 |

Eclipse Series
1995-present. Recent Eclipse models.

| 1995-2000 | Eclipse (bolt
neck, mahogany) | $450 | $575 |
| 1996-2000 | Eclipse Archtop | $450 | $550 |

Horizon (Import)
1986, 1996-2001. Double-cut neck-thru, bound ebony 'board, 1 single-coil and 1 humbucker, buffer preamp, various colors, reintroduced '96-'01 with bolt neck, curved rounded point headstock.

| 1986 | | $525 | $625 |
| 1996-2001 | | $525 | $625 |

Horizon Classic (U.S.A.)
1993-1995. U.S.-made, carved mahogany body, set-neck, dot markers, various colors, optional mahogany body with figured maple top also offered.

| 1993-1995 | | $1,000 | $1,300 |

Horizon Custom (U.S.A.)
1998-2001. U.S. Custom Shop-made, mahogany body, figured maple top, bolt-on neck, mostly translucent finish in various colors.

| 1998-2001 | | $1,100 | $1,300 |

Horizon Deluxe (Import)
1989-1992. Horizon Custom with bolt-on neck, various colors.

| 1989-1992 | | $575 | $675 |

Hybrid I (Import)
1986 only. Offset double-cut body, bolt maple neck, dots, six-on-a-side tuners, vibrato, various colors.

| 1986 | | $300 | $375 |

Hybrid II (Import)
1980s. Offset double-cut, rosewood 'board on maple bolt neck, lipstick neck pickup, humbucker at bridge, Hybrid II headstock logo.

| 1980s | | $350 | $425 |

LTD EC-GTA Guitarsonist Model
2008. Flame graphic by Matt Touchard, 100 made.

| 2008 | | $1,000 | $1,200 |

LTD EC-SIN Sin City Model
2008. Vegas graphic by Matt Touchard, 100 made.

| 2008 | | $1,600 | $1,800 |

LTD Series
1998-present. Range of prices due to wide range of models.

| 1998-2010 | Various models | $100 | $600 |

Maverick/Maverick Deluxe
1989-1992. Offset double-cut, bolt maple or rosewood cap neck, dot markers, double locking vibrola, six-on-a-side tuners, various colors.

| 1989-1992 | | $325 | $400 |

Metal I
1986 only. Offset double-cut, bolt maple neck, rosewood cap, dots, various colors.

| 1986 | | $325 | $400 |

Metal II
1986 only. Single horn V body, bolt on maple neck with rosewood cap, dot markers, various colors.

| 1986 | | $350 | $425 |

Metal III
1986 only. Reverse offset body, bolt maple neck with maple cap, dot markers, gold hardware, various colors.

| 1986 | | $375 | $450 |

2008 ESP GL-56

ESP Eclipse

EVH Wolfgang Special

Exlusive Alien

MODEL YEAR	FEATURES	EXC. COND. LOW	HIGH

M-I Custom

1987-1994. Offset double-cut thru-neck body, offset block markers, various colors.

| 1987-1994 | | $575 | $700 |

M-I Deluxe

1987-1989. Double-cut solidbody, rosewood 'board, 2 single-coils and 1 humbucker, various colors.

| 1987-1989 | | $550 | $650 |

M-II

1989-1994, 1996-2000. Double-cut solidbody, reverse headstock, bolt-on maple or rosewood cap neck, dot markers, various colors.

| 1989-1994 | | $575 | $700 |

M-II Custom

1990-1994. Double-cut solidbody, reverse headstock, neck-thru maple neck, rosewood cap, dot markers, various colors.

| 1990-1994 | | $750 | $900 |

M-II Deluxe

1990-1994. Double-cut solidbody, reverse headstock, Custom with bolt-on neck, various colors.

| 1990-1994 | | $650 | $800 |

Mirage Custom

1986-1990. Double-cut neck-thru solidbody, 2-octave ebony 'board, block markers, 1 humbucker and 2 single-coil pickups, locking trem, various colors.

| 1986-1990 | | $650 | $800 |

Mirage Standard

1986 only. Single pickup version of Mirage Custom, various colors.

| 1986 | | $400 | $500 |

Phoenix

1987 only. Offset, narrow waist solidbody, thru-neck mahogany body, black hardware, dots.

| 1987 | | $550 | $650 |

Phoenix Contemporary

Late-1990s. 3 pickups vs. 2 on the earlier offering.

| 1998 | | $750 | $875 |

S-454/S-456

1986-1987. Offset double-cut, bolt maple or rosewood cap neck, dot markers, various colors.

| 1986-1987 | | $350 | $425 |

S-500

1991-1993. Double-cut figured ash body, bolt-on neck, six-on-a-side tuners, various colors.

| 1991-1993 | | $500 | $600 |

SV-II

2009-present. Neck-thru offset v-shaped solidbody, 2 pickups, dot inlays, part of Standard Series, made in Japan.

| 2009-2010 | | $1,400 | $1,700 |

Traditional

1989-1990. Double-cut, 3 pickups, tremolo, various colors.

| 1989-1990 | | $525 | $650 |

Vintage/Vintage Plus S

1995-1998. Offset double-cut, bolt maple or rosewood cap neck, dot markers, Floyd Rose or standard vibrato, various colors.

| 1995 | 20th Anniversary Edition, gold | $750 | $950 |
| 1995-1998 | | $700 | $850 |

Espana

1963-ca. 1973. Primarily acoustic guitars distributed by catalog wholesalers Bugeleisen & Jacobson. Built by Landola in Sweden.

Classical

1963-1973. Guitars with white spruce fan-braced tops with walnut, mahogany, or rosewood back and sides.

| 1963-1973 | | $150 | $200 |

EL (Electric) Series

1963-1973. Various double-cut models, 2 or 3 pickups, tremolo, '63-ca. '68 with nitro finish, ca. '69-'73 poly finish.

1963-1973	EL-30, 1 pickup	$200	$300
1963-1973	EL-31, 2 pickups	$250	$350
1963-1973	EL-32 (XII)	$200	$300
1963-1973	EL-36, 2 pickups	$250	$350

Jumbo Folk

1969-1973. Natural.

| 1969-1973 | | $150 | $300 |

Essex (SX)

1985-present. Budget grade, production, electric and acoustic guitars imported by Rondo Music of Union, New Jersey. They also offer basses.

Solidbody Electric

1980s-1990s. Copies of classic designs like the Les Paul and Telecaster.

| 1980s | | $100 | $125 |

Este

1909-1939. Luthier Felix Staerke's Este factory built classical and archtop guitars in Hamburg, Germany. They also built high-end banjos. The plant ceased instrument production in '39 and was destroyed in WW II.

Esteban

2002-present. Budget grade, production, acoustic and classical import guitars sold as packages with classical guitarist Esteban's (Stephen Paul) guitar lesson program, other miscellany and sometimes a small amp.

Steel or Nylon Acoustic

| 2002-2010 | | $40 | $80 |

EtaVonni

2008-present. Luthier Ben Williams builds premium grade, production/custom, carbon fiber and aluminum electric guitars in Kentwood, Michigan.

Euphonon

1930-1944. A Larson brothers brand, most Euphonons date from 1934-'44. Body sizes range from 13 ½" to the 19" and 21" super jumbos. The larger body 14-fret neck sizes have body woods of Brazilian rosewood, mahogany, or maple. Ornamentation and features are as important to value as rosewood vs. mahogany.

MODEL YEAR	FEATURES	EXC. COND. LOW	HIGH

Everett Guitars

1977-present. Luthier Kent Everett builds his premium and presentation grade, production/custom, steel-string and classical guitars in Atlanta, Georgia. From '01 to '03, his Laurel Series guitars were built in conjunction with Terada in Japan and set up in Atlanta. He has also built archtops, semi-hollow and solidbody electrics, resonators, and mandolins.

Evergreen Mountain

1971-present. Professional grade, custom, flat-top and tenor guitars built by luthier Jerry Nolte in Cove, Oregon. He also builds basses and mandolins and built over 100 dulcimers in the '70s.

Everly Guitars

1982-2001. Luthier Robert Steinegger built these premium grade, production/custom flat-tops in Portland, Oregon (also see Steinegger Guitars).

EVH

2007-present. Eddie Van Halen's line of professional and premium grade, production/custom, solidbody guitars built in the U.S. and Japan by Fender. They also build amps.

Excelsior

The Excelsior Company started offering accordions in 1924 and had a large factory in Italy by the late '40s. They started building guitars around '62, which were originally plastic covered, switching to paint finishes in the mid '60s. They also offered classicals, acoustics, archtops and amps. By the early '70s they were out of the guitar business.

Dyno and Malibu

1960s. Offset, double cut, 2 or 3 pickups, vibrato.

1960s	Dyno I	$175	$225
1960s	Dyno II	$200	$250
1960s	Malibu I	$200	$250
1960s	Malibu II	$250	$300

Exlusive

2008-present. Intermediate grade, production, electric guitars, imported from Asia and finished in Italy by luthier Galeazzo Frudua. He also offers basses.

Fairbuilt Guitar Co.

2000-present. Professional and premium grade, custom/production, archtop and flattop acoustic guitars built by luthiers Martin Fair and Stuart Orser in Loudoun County, Virginia. They also build mandolins and banjos.

Falk

1989-present. Professional and premium grade, production/custom archtop guitars built by luthier Dave Falk, originally in Independence, Missouri, and currently in Amarillo, Texas. He also builds mandolins and dulcimers.

Fano

1995-present. Professional grade, production/custom, solidbody electric guitars built by luthier Dennis Fano in Fleetwood, Pennsylvania. He also builds basses.

Farnell

1989-present. Luthier Al Farnell builds his professional grade, production, solidbody guitars in Ontario, California. He also offers his intermediate grade, production, C Series which is imported from China. He also builds basses.

Fat Cat Custom Guitars

2004-present. Intermediate to premium grade, production/custom, solidbody and chambered electric guitars built in Carpentersville, Illinois by luthier Scott Bond. He also builds basses.

Favilla

1890-1973. Founded by the Favilla family in New York, the company began to import guitars in 1970, but folded in '73. American-made models have the Favilla family crest on the headstock. Import models used a script logo on the headstock.

Acoustic Classical

1960s-1973. Various nylon-string classical models.

1960s-1969		$150	$400
1970-1973	Import	$150	$300

Acoustic Flat-Top

1960s-1973. Various flat-top models, 000 to D sizes, mahogany to spruce.

1960s-1969	U.S.-made, Crest logo	$150	$600
1970-1973	Import, Script logo	$150	$450

Fender

1946 (1945)-present. Budget, intermediate, professional and premium grade, production/custom, electric, acoustic, acoustic/electric, classical, and resonator guitars built in the U.S. and overseas. They also build amps, basses, mandolins, bouzoukis, banjos, lap steels, violins, and PA gear. Ca. 1939 Leo Fender opened a radio and record store called Fender Radio Service, where he met Clayton Orr 'Doc' Kauffman, and in '45 they started KF Company to build lap steels and amps. In '46 Kauffman left and Fender started the Fender Electric Instrument Company. By '50 Fender's products were distributed by F.C. Hall's Radio & Television Electronics Company (Radio-Tel, later owners of Rickenbacker). In '53 Radio-Tel is replaced by the Fender Sales Company which was ran by Don Randall.

In January '65 CBS purchased the company for $13 million and renamed it Fender Musical Instruments Corporation. The CBS takeover is synonymous with a decline in quality - whether true or not is still debated, but the perception persists among musicians and collectors, and Pre-CBS Fenders are more valuable. Fender experienced some quality

Falk Guitars Number One

Farnell GC-2

GUITARS

1964 Fender Jaguar

Tom Siska

Fender Avalon

problems in the late-'60s. Small headstock is enlarged in '65 and the 4-bolt neck is replaced by the 3-bolt in '71. With high value and relative scarcity of Pre-CBS Fenders, even CBS-era instruments are now sought by collectors. Leo Fender was kept on as consultant until '70 and went on to design guitars for Music Man and G&L.

Bill Schultz and Dan Smith were hired from Yamaha in '81. In '82 Fender Japan is established to produce licensed Fender copies for sale in Japan. Also in '82, the Fender Squier brand debuts on Japanese-made instruments for the European market and by '83 they were imported into U.S. In '85, the company was purchased by an investor group headed by Bill Schultz but the purchase does not include the Fullerton factory. While a new factory was being established at Corona, California, all Fender Contemporary Stratocasters and Telecasters were made either by Fender Japan or in Seoul, Korea. U.S. production resumes in '86 with American Standard Stratocaster. The Fender Custom Shop, run by Michael Stevens and John Page, opens in '87. The Mexican Fender factory is established in '90. In '95, Fender purchased the Guild guitar company. On January 3, 2002, Fender Musical Instruments Corporation (FMIC) recapitalized a minority portion of common stock, with partners including Roland Corporation U.S. and Weston Presidio, a private equity firm in San Francisco. As of January 1, 2003, Fred Gretsch Enterprises, Ltd granted Fender the exclusive rights to develop, produce, market and distribute Gretsch guitars worldwide. Around the same time, Fender also acquired the Jackson/Charvel Guitar Company. In October, '04, Fender acquired Tacoma Guitars. In April, '05, William Mendello succeeded Bill Schultz as CEO. On January 1, '08, Fender acquired Kaman Music Corporation and the Hamer, Ovation, and Genz Benz brands. The Groove Tubes brand was purchased by Fender in June, '08.

Dating older Fender guitars is an imprecise art form at best. While serial numbers were used, they were frequently not in sequence, although a lower number will frequently be older than a substantially higher number. Often necks were dated, but only with the date the neck was finished, not when the guitar was assembled. Generally, dating requires triangulating between serial numbers, neck dates, pot dates, construction details and model histories.

From '50 through roughly '65, guitars had more-or-less sequential numbers in either 4 or 5 digits, though some higher numbers may have an initial 0 or - prefix. These can range from 0001 to 99XXX.

From '63 into '65, some instruments had serial numbers beginning with an L prefix plus 5 digits (LXXXXX). Beginning in '65 with the CBS take-over into '76, 6-digit serial numbers were stamped on F neckplates roughly sequentially from 10XXXX to 71XXXX. In '76 the serial number was shifted to the headstock decal. From '76-'77, the serial number began with a bold-face 76 or S6 plus 5 digits (76XXXXX).

From '77 on, serial numbers consisted of a 2-place prefix plus 5 digits (sometimes 6 beginning in '91): '77 (S7, S8), '78 (S7, S8, S9), '79 (S9, E0), '80-'81 (S9, E0, E1), '82 (E1, E2, E3), '84-'85 (E4), '85-'86 (no U.S. production), '87 (E4), '88 (E4, E8), '89 (E8, E9), '90 (E9, N9, N0), '91 (N0), '92 (N2).

Serial numbers on guitars made by Fender Japan consist of either a 2-place prefix plus 5 digits or a single prefix letter plus 6 digits: '82-'84 (JV), '83-'84 (SQ), '84-'87 (E), '85-'86+ (A, B, C), '86-'87 (F), '87-'88+ (G), '88-'89 (H), '89-'90 (I, J), '90-'91 (K), '91-'92 (L), '92-'93 (M).

Factors affecting Fender values: The sale to CBS in '65 is a major point in Fender instrument values as CBS made many changes that collectors feel affected quality. The '70s introduced the 3-bolt neck and other design changes that aren't that popular with guitarists. Custom color instruments, especially Strats from the '50s and early-'60s, can be valued much more than the standard sunburst finishes. In '75 Fender dropped the optional custom colors and started issuing the guitars in a variety of standard colors. The various Telecaster and Stratocaster models are grouped under those general headings.

A custom color is worth more than a standard color. For a Stratocaster, Telecaster Custom and Esquire Custom the standard color is sunburst, while the Telecaster and Esquire standard color is blond. The first Precision Bass standard color was blond but changed to sunburst in the late 1950s. The Jazz Bass standard color is sunburst. The Telecaster Thinline standard color is natural. To understand a custom color, you need to know what the standard color is. Some custom colors are more rare than others. Below is a list of the custom colors offered in 1960 by Fender. They are sorted in ascending order with the most valuable color, Shell Pink, listed last. In this list, Black and Blond are the least valuable and Shell Pink is the most valuable. A Fiesta Red is typically worth 12% more than a Black or Blond. In the rare color group a Foam Green is normally worth 8% more than a Shoreline Gold. The two very rare colors are often worth 30% more than a Shoreline Gold. In our pricing information we will list the standard color, then the relative value of a common custom color, and then the value of a rare custom color. Remember that the amount of fade also affects the price.

These prices are for custom colors with slight or no fade. Fade implies a lighter color, but with custom colors a faded example can also be much darker in color. Blue can fade to dark green. White can fade to deep yellow.

The Price Guide lists the standard color, plus the value of a common color and the value of a rare color. The list below defines which group a color falls into for 1960, and again it is in ascending order so, for example, a Daphne Blue should be considered more valuable than a Lake Placid Blue, assuming they are in equal condition.

Common Color

Black, Blond, Olympic White, Lake Placid Blue, Dakota Red, Daphne Blue and Fiesta Red

The **Vintage Guitar Price Guide** shows low to high values for items in all-original excellent condition, and, where applicable, with original case or cover.

MODEL		EXC. COND.	
YEAR	FEATURES	LOW	HIGH

Rare Color
Shoreline Gold, Inca Silver, Burgundy Mist, Sherwood Green, Sonic Blue and Foam Green
Rare (Very Rare) Color
Surf Green and Shell Pink

Fender changed their color options in the 1960s. Below is a list of what was offered.

1960-1962
Black, Blond, Burgundy Mist, Dakota Red, Daphne Blue, Fiesta Red, Foam Green, Inca Silver, Lake Placid Blue, Olympic White, Shell Pink, Sherwood Green, Shoreline Gold, Sonic Blue, Sunburst and Surf Green
1963-1964
Black, Blond, Burgundy Mist, Candy Apple Red, Dakota Red, Daphne Blue, Fiesta Red, Foam Green, Inca Silver, Lake Placid Blue, Olympic White, Sherwood Green, Shoreline Gold, Sonic Blue, Sunburst and Surf Green
1965-1969
Black, Blond, Blue Ice, Candy Apple Red, Charcoal Frost, Dakota Red, Fiesta Red, Firemist Gold, Firemist Silver, Foam Green, Lake Placid Blue, Ocean Turquoise, Olympic White, Sonic Blue, Sunburst and Teal Green
1970-1971
Black, Blond, Candy Apple Red, Firemist Gold, Firemist Silver, Lake Placid Blue, Ocean Turquoise, Olympic White, Sonic Blue and Sunburst
1972
Black, Blond, Candy Apple Red, Lake Placid Blue, Olympic White, Sonic Blue and Sunburst
1973
Black, Blond, Candy Apple Red, Lake Placid Blue, Natural, Olympic White, Sunburst and Walnut
1974-1977
Black, Blond, Natural, Olympic White, Sunburst and Walnut
1978-1979
Antigua, Black, Blond, Natural, Olympic White, Sunburst, Walnut and Wine

Avalon
1984-1995. Acoustic, 6-on-a-side tuners, mahogany neck, back and sides (nato after '93), spruce top, various colors.

1984-1992		$175	$225

Broadcaster
Mid-1950-early-1951. For a short time in early-'51, before being renamed the Telecaster, models had no Broadcaster decal; these are called No-casters by collectors.

1950	Blond	$67,000	$83,000
1951	Clipped decal, "No Caster"	$49,000	$61,000

MODEL		EXC. COND.	
YEAR	FEATURES	LOW	HIGH

Broadcaster Leo Fender Custom Shop
1999 only. Leo Fender script logo signature replaces Fender logo on headstock, Custom Shop Certificate signed by Phyllis Fender, Fred Gretsch, and William Schultz, includes glass display case and poodle guitar case.

1999		$7,500	$9,000

'50s Relic/'51 NoCaster Custom Shop
1995-2009. Called the '50s Relic NoCaster for '96-'99, and '51 NoCaster in NOS, Relic, or Closet Classic versions 2000-'10, with the Relic Series being the highest offering. From June '95 to June '99 Relic work was done outside of Fender by Vince Cunetto and included a certificate noting model and year built, an instrument without the certificate is worth less than the value shown. Blonde or Honey Blonde finish. Also in '09, the Limited '51 NoCaster Relic was offered with Twisted Tele neck pickup, 50 each in 2-tone sunburst or Dakota Red.

1995-1999	1st Cunetto era	$2,500	$3,100
1997-1999	Cunetto era NOS & Closet Classic	$1,700	$1,900
1997-1999	Cunetto era Relic	$1,700	$1,900
2000-2009	NOS & Closet Classic	$1,700	$1,900
2000-2009	Relic	$1,750	$1,950

Bronco
1967-1980. Slab solidbody, 1 pickup, tremolo, red.

1967-1969	Nitro	$775	$1,000
1970-1980	Poly	$600	$775

Buddy Miller Signature
2007-2009. Flat-top, Fishman Ellipse Aura, 6-on-a-side tuner headstock.

2007-2009		$825	$925

Bullet/Bullet Deluxe
1981-1983. Solidbody, came in 2- and 3-pickup versions (single-coil and humbucker), and single- and double-cut models, various colors. Becomes Squire Bullet in '85.

1981-1983	Various models	$475	$550

California Series
2006-present. Acoustics, 6-on-a-side tuners, soft V neck, models include Kingman, Malibu, and Sonoran (flat-top, cutaway).

2008-2010	Sonoran	$200	$235

CG (Classical Guitar) Series
1995-2005. Various nylon-string classical acoustic and acoustic/electric models, label on the inside back clearly indicates the model number, back and sides of rosewood, mahogany or other woods.

1995-2005	Rosewood	$250	$325

Concert
1963-1970. Acoustic flat-top slightly shorter than King/Kingman, spruce body, mahogany back and sides (optional Brazilian or Indian rosewood, zebrawood or vermillion), natural, sunburst optional by '68.

1963-1965	Natural	$700	$800
1966-1968	Natural or sunburst	$600	$700
1969-1970	Natural or sunburst	$500	$600

Fender Buddy Miller Signature

1981 Fender Bullet Deluxe

1968 Fender Coronado XII

Fender Cyclone

MODEL YEAR	FEATURES	EXC. COND. LOW	HIGH

Concord
1987-1992. Dreadnought flat-top, 6-on-a-side headstock, natural.

1987-1992		$125	$150

Coronado I
1966-1969. Thinline semi-hollowbody, double-cut, tremolo, 1 pickup, single-bound, dot inlay.

1966-1967	Blue custom color	$1,225	$1,475
1966-1967	Cherry Red	$875	$1,050
1966-1967	Orange custom color	$1,225	$1,475
1966-1967	Sunburst	$975	$1,150
1966-1967	White (unfaded)	$1,150	$1,400
1968-1969	Sunburst	$775	$925

Coronado II
1966-1969 (Antigua finish offered until '70). Thinline semi-hollowbody, double-cut, tremolo optional, 2 pickups, single-bound, block inlay, available in standard finishes but special issues offered in Antigua and 6 different Wildwood finishes (labeled on the pickguard as Wildwood I through Wildwood VI to designate different colors). Wildwood finishes were achieved by injecting dye into growing trees.

1966-1967	Blue or orange custom colors	$1,500	$1,800
1966-1967	Cherry Red	$1,300	$1,600
1966-1967	Olympic White custom color	$1,350	$1,650
1966-1967	Silver custom color	$1,600	$1,900
1966-1967	Sunburst	$1,200	$1,500
1966-1967	Wildwood	$1,700	$2,100
1967-1969	Antigua	$1,700	$2,100
1968-1969	Cherry Red	$1,200	$1,400
1968-1969	Orange custom color	$1,350	$1,650
1968-1969	Sunburst	$1,250	$1,525
1968-1969	Wildwood	$1,600	$1,950
1970	Antigua	$1,600	$1,950
1970-1973	Cherry Red	$900	$1,100
1970-1973	Sunburst	$900	$1,100

Coronado XII
1966-1969 (Antigua finish offered until '70). Thinline semi-hollowbody, double-cut, 12 strings, 2 pickups, block inlay, standard, Antigua and Wildwood finishes available.

1966-1967	Blue or orange custom colors	$1,500	$1,800
1966-1967	Cherry Red	$1,300	$1,600
1966-1967	Sunburst	$1,300	$1,600
1966-1967	Wildwood	$1,700	$2,100
1968-1969	Antigua	$1,700	$2,100
1968-1969	Cherry Red	$1,200	$1,400
1968-1969	Orange custom color	$1,350	$1,650
1968-1969	Sunburst	$1,200	$1,400
1968-1969	Wildwood	$1,600	$1,950

Custom
1969-1971. Six-string solidbody that used up parts from discontinued Electric XII, asymmetrical-cut, long headstock, 2 split pickups, sunburst. Also marketed as the Maverick.

1969-1971		$2,500	$2,900

Cyclone
1998-2006. Mexican import, solidbody, contoured offset waist, poplar body, various colors.

1998-2006	Various options	$400	$500

D'Aquisto Elite
1984, 1989-1994, 1994-2002. Part of Fender's Master Series, archtop, single-cut, glued neck, 1 pickup, gold-plated hardware, made in Japan until '94, in '94 the Fender Custom Shop issued a version that retailed at $6,000, various colors.

1984		$1,800	$2,100
1989-1994		$1,500	$1,750

D'Aquisto Standard
1984 (Serial numbers could range from 1983-1985). Part of Fender's Master Series, archtop, single-cut, glued neck, 2 pickups, made in Japan, various colors.

1984		$1,575	$1,850

D'Aquisto Ultra
1994-2000. USA Custom Shop, made under the supervision of James D'Aquisto, flamed maple back and sides, spruce top, ebony tailpiece, bridge and 'guard, all hand carved.

1994-2000		$3,500	$4,500

DG (Dreadnought Guitar) Series
1995-1999, 2002-present. Made in China, various acoustic and acoustic/electric models.

1995-2010	Various lower-end	$75	$225

Duo-Sonic
1956-1969. Solidbody, 3/4-size, 2 pickups, Desert Sand ('56-'61), sunburst ('61-'63), blue, red or white after, short- and long-scale necks, short-scale necks listed here (see Duo-Sonic II for long-scale), reissued Mexican-made in '94.

1956-1959	Maple neck	$1,400	$1,700
1960-1965	Rosewood 'board	$1,300	$1,600
1966-1969		$950	$1,150

Duo-Sonic II
1965-1969. Solidbody, 2 pickups, blue, red or white, long-scale neck, though the long-scale neck Duo-Sonic was not known as the Duo-Sonic II until '65, we have lumped all long-scales under the II for the purposes of this Guide.

1965		$1,100	$1,400
1966-1969		$1,000	$1,250

Duo-Sonic Reissue
1993-1997. Made in Mexico, black, red or white.

1994-1997		$175	$225

Electracoustic
1993-1995, 2000-2005, 2007-present. Thin body acoustic-electric, available with Jazzmaster, Stratocaster and Telecaster body and neck shapes, spruce top, maple sides and back, Fishman Classic IV MB electronics with top-mounted pickup, sunburst and various color options.

2007-2010	JZM Deluxe	$375	$425
2007-2010	Stratacoustic Deluxe	$375	$425
2007-2010	Stratacoustic Standard	$200	$250
2007-2010	Telecoustic Deluxe	$375	$425
2007-2010	Telecoustic Standard	$200	$250

Electric XII

1965-1969. Solidbody, 12 strings, long headstock, 2 split pickups. Custom colors can fade or become darker; for example Lake Placid Blue changes to green. The price ranges below are for instruments that are relatively unfaded. Many older guitars have some color fade and minor fade is factored into these values. Each custom color should be evaluated on a case-by-case basis.

Custom color Fenders can be forged and bogus finishes have been a problem. As the value of custom color Fenders has increased, so has the problem of bogus non-original finishes. The prices in the Guide are for factory original finishes in excellent condition. The prices noted do not take into account market factors such as fake instruments, which can have the effect of lowering a guitar's market value unless the guitar's provenance can be validated. Please refer to the Fender Guitar Intro Section for details on Fender color options.

MODEL YEAR	FEATURES	EXC. COND. LOW	HIGH
1965-1966	Common colors	$3,000	$5,000
1965-1966	Rare colors	$5,000	$8,000
1965-1966	Sunburst, blocks	$2,400	$2,900
1965-1966	Sunburst, dots	$2,500	$3,000
1967-1969	Common colors	$3,000	$4,000
1967-1969	Rare colors	$4,000	$8,000
1967-1969	Sunburst	$2,400	$2,900

Ensenada Series

2005-2007. Made in Mexico acoustics, solid top, back and sides, A (grand auditorium), D (dreadnought), M (mini jumbo) and V (orchestra) sizes, E suffix denotes on-board electronics.

2005-2007	Various models	$375	$500

Esprit Elite

1983-1985. Part of the Master Series, made in Japan, double-cut, semi-hollow, carved maple top, 2 humbuckers, bound rosewood 'board, snowflake inlays, sunburst.

1983-1984		$1,400	$1,700

Esprit Standard

1983-1985. Part of the Master Series, made in Japan, double-cut, semi-hollow, carved maple top, 2 humbuckers, bound rosewood 'board, dot inlays, sunburst.

1983-1985		$1,300	$1,600

Esprit Ultra

1984. Part of the Master Series, made in Japan, double-cut, semi-hollow, carved spruce top, 2 humbuckers, bound rosewood 'board, split-block inlays, sunburst, gold hardware.

1984		$1,400	$1,700

Esquire

1950-1970. Ash body, single-cut, 1 pickup, maple neck, black 'guard '50-'54, white 'guard '54 on. Please refer to the Fender Guitar Intro Section for details on Fender color options.

MODEL YEAR	FEATURES	EXC. COND. LOW	HIGH
1950	Blond, black 'guard	$29,000	$35,000
1951	Blond, black 'guard	$25,000	$31,000
1952	Blond, black 'guard	$19,000	$24,000
1953	Blond, black 'guard	$19,000	$24,000

MODEL YEAR	FEATURES	EXC. COND. LOW	HIGH
1954	Blond, black 'guard	$18,000	$22,000
1954	Blond, white 'guard	$15,000	$18,000
1955	Blond, white 'guard	$15,000	$18,000
1956	Blond	$15,000	$18,000
1957	Blond	$15,000	$18,000
1958	Blond, backloader	$15,000	$18,000
1958	Blond, frontloader	$13,000	$16,000
1959	Blond, maple 'board	$13,000	$16,000
1959	Blond, rosewood 'board	$13,000	$16,000
1960	Blond	$11,000	$14,000
1960	Sunburst	$15,000	$18,000
1961	Blond	$10,500	$13,000
1961	Custom colors	$22,000	$35,000
1961	Sunburst	$14,500	$17,000
1962	Blond, curved 'board	$9,000	$12,000
1962	Blond, slab 'board	$10,000	$14,000
1962	Custom colors	$17,000	$35,000
1962	Sunburst, curved 'board	$10,500	$13,500
1962	Sunburst, slab 'board	$11,500	$15,500
1963	Blond	$8,000	$10,000
1963	Common colors	$14,000	$20,000
1963	Rare colors	$20,000	$30,000
1963	Sunburst	$10,500	$13,500
1964	Blond	$7,000	$8,000
1964	Common colors	$13,000	$19,000
1964	Rare colors	$19,000	$29,000
1964	Sunburst	$9,500	$12,500
1965	Blond	$7,000	$8,000
1965	Common colors	$9,000	$13,000
1965	Rare colors	$13,000	$19,000
1965	Sunburst	$7,200	$8,400
1966	Blond	$6,500	$7,500
1966	Common colors	$8,500	$12,500
1966	Rare colors	$12,500	$18,500
1966	Sunburst	$6,700	$7,900
1967	Blond	$6,500	$7,500
1967	Blond, smuggler cavity	$7,800	$8,800
1967	Common colors	$8,500	$12,500
1967	Rare colors	$12,500	$18,500
1967	Sunburst	$6,700	$7,900
1968	Blond	$6,000	$7,000
1968	Common colors	$7,500	$11,500
1968	Rare colors	$11,500	$17,500
1968	Sunburst	$6,200	$7,400
1969	Blond	$4,500	$6,000
1969	Common colors	$6,500	$8,500
1969	Rare colors	$8,500	$13,500
1969	Sunburst	$4,700	$6,400
1970	Blond	$4,000	$5,000
1970	Common colors	$5,500	$6,500
1970	Rare colors	$6,500	$9,000
1970	Sunburst	$4,200	$5,400

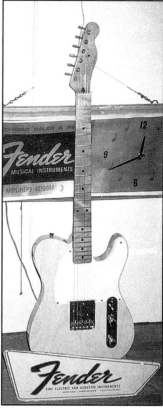

1955 Fender Esquire

1957 Fender Esquire

Fender Jag-Stang

1962 Fender Jazzmaster

Tom Siska

MODEL YEAR	FEATURES	EXC. COND. LOW	HIGH
Esquire (Japan)			
1985-1994. Made in Japan, '54 specs.			
1985-1986		$550	$625
1987-1994	'50s Esquire	$475	$525
'50s Esquire (Mexico)			
2005-2010. Maple neck, ash body.			
2005-2010		$325	$400
'59 Esquire			
2003-2007. Custom Shop model, Relic lasted to '07.			
2003-2006	Closet Classic	$1,650	$1,750
2003-2006	NOS	$1,650	$1,750
2003-2007	Relic	$1,900	$2,100
Esquire Custom			
1959-1970. Same as Esquire, but with bound alder sunburst body and rosewood 'board.			
1959	Sunburst	$18,000	$23,000
1960	Custom colors	$20,000	$45,000
1960	Sunburst	$14,000	$18,000
1961	Custom colors	$20,000	$45,000
1961	Sunburst	$14,000	$18,000
1962	Custom colors	$19,000	$40,000
1962	Sunburst	$13,000	$17,000
1963	Custom colors	$18,000	$39,000
1963	Sunburst	$13,000	$17,000
1964	Custom colors	$17,000	$35,000
1964	Sunburst	$12,500	$16,500
1965	Custom colors	$12,000	$24,000
1965	Sunburst	$8,500	$11,500
1966	Custom colors	$11,000	$20,000
1966	Sunburst	$7,500	$10,500
1967	Sunburst	$7,000	$10,000
1968	Sunburst	$6,500	$9,000
1969	Sunburst	$6,500	$9,000
1970	Sunburst	$5,000	$6,000
Esquire Custom (Import)			
1983. Made in Japan with all the classic bound Esquire features, sunburst.			
1983-1986		$525	$650
1987-1994		$525	$650
Esquire Custom GT/Celtic/Scorpion			
2003. Made in Korea, single-cut solidbody, 1 humbucker, 1 knob (volume), set-neck, solid colors.			
2003		$250	$300
Jeff Beck Tribute Esquire (Custom Shop)			
2006. Also called Beck Artist Esquire or Tribute Series Jeff Beck Esquire, specs include an extremely lightweight 2-piece offset ash body with Beck's original contours, distressed for an appearance like Beck's original Esquire that was used on many Yardbird records.			
2006		$7,000	$8,500
Flame Elite			
1984-1988. Part of the Master Series, made in Japan, neck-thru, offset double-cut, solidbody, 2 humbuckers, rosewood 'board, snowflake inlays.			
1984-1988		$1,550	$1,800
Flame Standard			
1984-1988. Part of the Master Series, made in Japan, neck-thru, offset double-cut, solidbody, 2 humbuckers, rosewood 'board, dot inlays.			
1984-1988		$1,400	$1,600

MODEL YEAR	FEATURES	EXC. COND. LOW	HIGH
Flame Ultra			
1984-1988. Part of the Master Series, made in Japan, neck-thru, double-cut, solidbody, 2 humbuckers, rosewood 'board, split block inlays (some with snowflakes), gold hardware.			
1984-1988		$1,650	$1,900
FR-48 Resonator			
2003-2009. Made in Korea, chromed steel body.			
2003-2009		$225	$400
F-Series Dreadnought Flat-Top			
1969-1981. The F-Series were Japanese-made flat-top acoustics, included were Concert- and Dreadnought-size instruments with features running from plain to bound necks and headstocks and fancy inlays, there was also a line of F-Series classical, nylon-string guitars. A label on the inside indicates the model. FC-20 is a classical with Brazilian rosewood. There was also an Asian (probably Korean) import Standard Series for '82-'90 where the models start with a F.			
1969-1981	Higher-end solid top	$125	$200
1969-1981	Lower-end laminated	$75	$125
1972-1981	FC-20 Classical	$150	$200
GC (Grand Concert) Series			
1997-2009. Various grand concert models, an oval label on the inside back clearly indicates the model number.			
1997-2009		$175	$225
Gemini Series			
1983-1990. Korean-made flat-tops, label on inside indicates model. I is classical nylon-string, II, III and IV are dreadnought steel-strings, there is also a 12-string and an IIE acoustic/electric.			
1983-1987	Gemini II	$150	$200
1983-1988	Gemini I	$125	$175
1987-1990	Gemini III/IV	$175	$250
GN (Grand Nylon) Series			
2001-2007. Various grand nylon acoustic models, an oval label on the inside back clearly indicates the model number.			
2001-2007		$375	$450
Harmony-Made Series			
1970-1973. Harmony-made with white stencil Fender logo, mahogany, natural or sunburst.			
1970-1973		$50	$100
Jag-Stang			
1996-2003. Japanese-made, designed by Curt Cobain, body similar to Jaguar, tremolo, 1 pickup, oversize Strat peghead, Fiesta Red or Sonic Blue.			
1996	1st issue, 50th Anniv. Label	$475	$575
1997-2003		$450	$550
Jaguar			
1962-1975. Reintroduced as Jaguar '62 in '95-'99. Custom colors can fade and often the faded color has very little similarity to the original color. The values below are for an instrument that is relatively unfaded. Each custom color should be evaluated on a case-by-case basis. As the value of custom color Fenders has increased, so has the problem of bogus non-original finishes. The prices in the Guide are for factory original finishes in excellent condition. Please refer to the Fender Guitar Intro Section for details on Fender color options.			

MODEL YEAR	FEATURES	EXC. COND. LOW	HIGH
1962	Common colors	$5,400	$6,500
1962	Rare colors	$6,500	$8,000
1962	Sunburst	$3,800	$4,800
1963	Common colors	$4,900	$5,800
1963	Rare colors	$5,800	$7,500
1963	Sunburst	$2,900	$3,600
1964	Common colors	$4,500	$5,500
1964	Rare colors	$5,500	$7,500
1964	Sunburst	$2,900	$3,600
1965	Common colors	$4,000	$5,000
1965	Rare colors	$5,000	$6,500
1965	Sunburst	$2,500	$3,100
1966	Common colors	$3,500	$4,500
1966	Rare colors	$4,500	$6,000
1966	Sunburst, block markers	$2,100	$2,600
1966	Sunburst, dot markers	$2,400	$2,900
1967-1970	Common colors	$3,500	$4,500
1967-1970	Rare colors	$4,500	$6,000
1967-1970	Sunburst	$2,200	$2,500
1971-1975	Custom colors	$2,500	$3,500
1971-1975	Sunburst	$1,900	$2,400

Jaguar '62

1994-present. Reintroduction of Jaguar, Japanese-made until '99, then U.S.-made, basswood body, rosewood 'board, various colors.

1994-1999	Import	$625	$750
1999-2010	U.S.A.	$925	$1,100

Jaguar Special Edition HH

2005-present. 2 humbuckers, matching headstock, no trem.

2005-2010		$425	$500

Jaguar Baritone Special Edition HH

2004-2009. Called Jaguar Baritone Custom for 2004. Baritone Special logo on matching headstock, 2 humbuckers, no trem, black.

2005-2009		$575	$625

Jaguar Classic Player Special

2008-present. Classic Player series, classic Jag look, trem, 2 single-coils.

2008-2010		$525	$600

Jaguar Classic Player Special HH

2008-present. Classic Player series. 2 humbucker version.

2008-2010		$525	$600

Jazzmaster

1958-1980. Contoured body, 2 pickups, rosewood 'board, clay dot inlay, reintroduced as Japanese-made Jazzmaster '62 in '96.

Custom color Fenders can be forged and bogus finishes have been a problem. As the value of custom color Fenders has increased, so has the problem of bogus non-original finishes. The prices in the Guide are for factory original finishes in excellent condition. Please refer to the Fender Guitar Intro Section for details on Fender color options.

1958	Sunburst	$6,600	$8,000
1958	Sunburst, rare maple 'board	$6,800	$8,200

MODEL YEAR	FEATURES	EXC. COND. LOW	HIGH
1959	Custom colors, includes rare	$9,000	$14,000
1959	Sunburst	$6,300	$7,700
1960	Common colors	$8,000	$10,000
1960	Rare colors	$10,000	$15,000
1960	Sunburst	$5,600	$7,000
1961	Common colors	$7,500	$9,000
1961	Rare colors	$9,000	$14,000
1961	Sunburst	$5,200	$6,500
1962	Common colors	$7,500	$9,000
1962	Rare colors	$9,000	$14,000
1962	Sunburst	$4,800	$6,000
1963	Common colors	$5,000	$7,000
1963	Rare colors	$7,000	$12,000
1963	Sunburst	$3,300	$4,100
1964	Common colors	$5,000	$7,000
1964	Rare colors	$7,000	$12,000
1964	Sunburst	$3,300	$4,100
1965	Common colors	$4,500	$6,500
1965	Rare colors	$6,500	$9,000
1965	Sunburst	$3,000	$3,700
1966	Common colors	$4,000	$6,500
1966	Rare colors	$6,000	$9,000
1966	Sunburst, block markers	$2,700	$3,400
1966	Sunburst, dot markers	$3,000	$3,700
1967-1969	Common colors	$3,500	$5,000
1967-1969	Rare colors	$5,000	$7,000
1967-1969	Sunburst	$2,700	$3,400
1970	Common colors	$3,400	$4,900
1970	Rare colors	$4,900	$6,900
1970-1974	Sunburst	$2,300	$2,900
1971-1975	Custom colors	$3,000	$4,000
1975-1977	Sunburst	$2,200	$2,800
1976-1980	Custom colors	$2,700	$3,300
1978-1980	Sunburst	$2,000	$2,500

Jazzmaster '62

1994-present. Japanese-made reintroduction of Jazzmaster, basswood body, rosewood 'board, U.S.-made from '99, various colors.

1994-1999	Import	$625	$750
2000-2010	Import	$550	$700
2000-2010	U.S.A.	$1,000	$1,200

Jazzmaster Elvis Costello (Artist Series)

2008-2010. Walnut stain, '70s neck, vintage style tremolo.

2008-2010		$1,000	$1,200

Jazzmaster J Mascis (Artist Series)

2007-2009. Purple sparkle finish, matching headstock, Adjusto-Matic bridge, reinforced tremolo arm.

2007-2009		$575	$700

Jazzmaster The Ventures Limited Edition

1996. Japanese-made, ash body, 2 pickups, block inlay, transparent purple/black.

1996		$900	$1,100

JZM Deluxe

2007-2010. Acoustic/electric, Jazzmaster/Jaguar body styling, Fishman and Tele pickups.

2007-2010		$325	$375

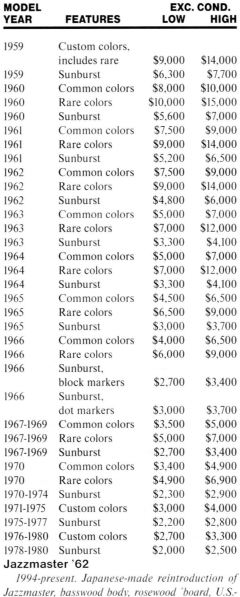

Fender Jaguar 1963

2009 Fender Jazzmaster Elvis Costello (Artist Series)

1965 Fender King

1964 Fender Musicmaster

MODEL YEAR	FEATURES	EXC. COND. LOW	HIGH

Katana
1985-1986. Japanese-made wedge-shaped body, 2 humbuckers, set neck, triangle inlays, black.

1985-1986		$300	$375

King
1963-1965. Full-size 15 5/8" wide acoustic, natural. Renamed Kingman in '65.

1963-1965		$900	$1,000

Kingman
1965-1971, 2006-present. Full-size 15 5/8" wide acoustic, slightly smaller by '70, offered in 3 Wildwood colors, referred to as the Wildwood acoustic which is a Kingman with dyed wood.

1965-1968		$850	$1,000
1969-1971		$750	$900

Lead I
1979-1982. Double-cut solidbody with 1 humbucker, maple or rosewood 'board, black or brown.

1979-1982		$600	$725

Lead II
1979-1982. Lead with 2 pickups, black or brown.

1979-1982		$700	$825

Lead III
1982. Lead with 2 split-coil humbuckers, 2 3-way switches, various colors.

1982		$725	$850

LTD
1969-1975. Archtop electric, single-cut, gold-plated hardware, carved top and back, 1 pickup, multi-bound, bolt-on neck, sunburst.

1969-1975		$3,300	$4,000

Malibu
1965-1971, 1983-1992. Flat top, spruce top, mahogany back and sides, black, mahogany or sunburst. Name used on Asian import model in '80s.

1965-1971		$450	$525

Malibu SCE
2006-present. Imported single-cut acoustic/electric, solid spruce top, laminated mahogany back and sides, block inlays.

2006-2010	Import	$350	$425

Marauder
1965 only. The Marauder has 3 pickups, and some have slanted frets, only 8 were made, thus it is very rare. 1st generation has hidden pickups, 2nd has exposed.

1965	1st generation	$8,500	$10,500
1965	2nd generation	$5,800	$7,200

Montara
1990-1994. Korean-made single-cut acoustic/electric flat-top.

1990-1994		$125	$150

Montego I/II
1968-1975. Electric archtop, single-cut, bolt-on neck, 1 pickup (I) or 2 pickups (II), chrome-plated hardware, sunburst.

1968-1975	I	$2,000	$2,500
1968-1975	II	$2,200	$2,700

Musiclander
1969-1972. Also called Swinger and Arrow, solidbody, 1 pickup, arrow-shaped headstock, no model name on peghead, red, white, and blue.

1969-1972		$1,300	$1,650

Musicmaster
1956-1980. Solidbody, 1 pickup, short-scale (3/4) neck, Desert Sand ('56-'61), sunburst ('61-'63), red, white or blue after. Regular-scale necks were optional and are called Musicmaster II from '64 to '69, after '69 II is dropped and Musicmaster continues with regular-scale neck.

1956-1959	Blond	$1,350	$1,550
1960-1964	Blond	$1,250	$1,450
1964-1969	Nitro, red, white, blue	$1,100	$1,250
1969-1972	Poly, red, white, blue	$800	$1,000
1973-1980	Red, white, blue	$800	$1,000

Musicmaster II
1964-1969. Solidbody, 1 pickup, long regular-scale neck version of Musicmaster, red, white, or blue.

1964-1969		$1,250	$1,425

Mustang
1964-1982, 1997-1998. Solidbody, 2 pickups. Reissued as '69 Mustang in 1990s, name changed back to Mustang '97-'98. Dakota Red, Daphne Blue and Olympic White with Competition Red, Blue and Orange finishes added ca. '69-'72. Competition finishes featured a racing stripe on the front of the body.

1964-1965	Red, white, or blue	$1,500	$1,850
1966-1969	Red, white, or blue	$1,400	$1,700
1969-1970	Competition colors	$1,600	$1,900
1970-1979	Various colors	$1,000	$1,250
1980-1982	Various colors	$900	$1,100

Mustang '65 Reissue
2006-present. Made in Japan.

2006-2010		$450	$550

Mustang '69 Reissue
1994-1998, 2005. Japanese-made, blue or white.

1994-1998		$525	$625

Newporter
1965-1971, 1983-1992. Acoustic flat-top, mahogany back and sides. Name used on Asian import model in '80s.

1965-1968	Spruce top	$325	$400
1968-1971	Mahogany top	$275	$325

Palomino
1968-1971. Acoustic flat-top, spruce top, mahogany back and sides, triple-bound, black or mahogany.

1968-1971		$500	$600

Performer
1985-1986. Imported Swinger-like body design, 2 slanted humbuckers.

1985-1986		$1,100	$1,300

Prodigy
1991-1993. Electric solidbody, double-cut, chrome-plated hardware, 2 single-coil and 1 humbucker pickups, blue or black.

1991-1993		$475	$575

MODEL YEAR	FEATURES	EXC. COND. LOW	HIGH

Redondo
1969-1971, 1983-1990. Mid-size flat-top, 14 3/8" wide, replaces Newport spruce top model. Name used on Asian import model in '80s.

1969-1971		$400	$500

Robben Ford
1989-1994. Symmetrical double-cut, 2 pickups, glued-in neck, solidbody with tone chambers, multi-bound, gold-plated hardware, sunburst. After '94 made in Fender Custom Shop.

1989-1994		$1,500	$1,800
1995	Custom Shop	$2,000	$2,500

Shenandoah 12-String
1965-1971. Acoustic flat-top, spruce top, mahogany back and sides.

1965-1968	Antigua	$800	$900
1965-1968	Blond	$650	$750
1969-1971	Antigua	$750	$850
1969-1971	Blond	$500	$600

Showmaster (Import)
2003-2007. Off-set double-cut solidbody, set neck, various models.

2003	Celtic, 1 bridge humbucker	$225	$275
2003-2007	HH, 2 humbuckers	$350	$425
2004-2006	3 single coils	$325	$400

Showmaster FMT (Custom Shop)
2000-2007. Bound figured maple top (FMT), 2 single-coil pickups and a bridge position humbucker, maple neck, Custom Shop certificate.

2000-2007		$1,300	$1,500

Squier Series
The following are all Squier Series instruments from Fender, listed alphabetically. Fender Japan was established in '82 with Squier production beginning in '83. Production was shifted to Korea in '87 and later allocated to China, India (Squier II '89-'90), Mexico and other countries.

Squier '51
2004-2006. Korean-made, Strat-style body with a Tele-style neck, various colors.

2004-2006		$75	$150

Squier Bullet
1985-1988, 2000-2006. Fender Japan was established in '82, Squier production began in '83, production was shifted to Korea in '87. Name revived in '06.

1985-1988	Sunburst, humbuckers	$175	$250
1985-1988	White	$175	$250
2000-2006	Revised	$50	$75

Squier Classic Vibe Stratocaster '50s
2009-present. Alder body, maple 'board, white pickguard, 2-tone sunburst, Lake Placid Blue or Oly White.

2009-2010		$200	$250

Squier Classic Vibe Stratocaster '60s
2009-present. As '50s Classic Vibe but with rose-wood 'board, tortoise pickguard, 3-tone sunburst or candy apple red.

2009-2010		$200	$250

Squier II Stratocaster
1989-1990. Import from India.

1989-1990		$100	$125

Squier Katana
1985-1986. Korean-made version, 1 humbucker, bolt neck, dot inlays, black.

1985-1986		$200	$250

Squier Showmaster
2002. 20th Anniversary (1982-2002), made in China.

2002		$75	$150

Squier Stagemaster HH
1999-2002. 2 humbuckers.

1999-2002		$125	$175

Squier Stratocaster Pro-Tone
1996-1998. Korean-made, higher-end Squier series with solid ash bodies, one-piece maple necks, alnico single-coils.

1996-1998		$350	$525

Squier Stratocaster Standard
1982-present. Initial production in Japan, shifted to Korea in '87 and later allocated to China, India and Mexico.

1983-1984	1st logo	$350	$450
1985-1989	2nd logo	$300	$350
1990-1999	Mexico	$175	$275
2000-2010	Indonesia	$85	$125

Squier Standard Fat Stratocaster
1998-2006. Hum/single/single pickups. Replaced by the HSS.

2000-2006		$95	$120

Squier Standard Double Fat Stratocaster
2000-2006. 2 humbucker pickups.

2000-2006		$95	$120

Squier Stratocaster Standard (Floyd Rose)
1995-1996. Floyd Rose tailpiece, fotoflame finish, large Fender script logo.

1995-1996		$175	$275

Squier Stratocaster Standard Affinity
1997-present. Made in China.

1997-2010		$60	$100

Squier Telecaster
1983-present. Initial production in Japan, shifted to Korea in '87 and later allocated to China, India and Mexico.

1983-1984	1st logo	$350	$450
1985-1989	2nd logo	$300	$350
1990-1999	Mexico	$175	$275
2000-2010	Indonesia	$85	$125

Squier Telecaster Affinity
1998-present. Made in China.

1998-2010		$60	$100

Squier Telecaster Custom
2003-present. Made in Indonesia.

2003-2010		$85	$125

Squier Telecaster Special Edition Affinity
2007-present. Made in China.

2007-2010		$125	$150

1964 Fender Mustang

Fender Squier '51

1955 Fender Stratocaster

1956 Fender Stratocaster

MODEL YEAR	FEATURES	EXC. COND. LOW	HIGH

Squier Thinline Telecaster
2004. Made in China, Thinline body with f-hole.

2004		$175	$250

Squier Tom Delonge Stratocaster
2001-2004. Hardtail, 1 humbucker.

2001-2004		$150	$175

Starcaster
1974-1980. Double-cut, thinline semi-hollowbody, 2 humbuckers, various colors. Fender currently uses the Starcaster name on a line of budget guitars sold through Costco stores.

1974-1980	Blond, highly flamed maple	$3,300	$4,100
1974-1980	Sunburst, moderate flame	$3,100	$3,900

Starcaster Acoustic
2000s. Acoustic flat-top with on-board electronics for student market.

2000s		$80	$110

Starcaster by Fender
2000s-present. Student economy pac guitar, Strat body with pointed-arrow headstock early, regular Fender one later. Sold in Costco and other discounters.

2000s	Guitar only	$70	$80
2000s	Pack with guitar, amp, stand	$85	$100

Stratocaster
The following are all variations of the Stratocaster. The first five listings are for the main American-made models and the '85 interim production Japanese model. All others are listed alphabetically after that in the following order:

Stratocaster
Standard Stratocaster (includes "Smith Strat")
American Standard Stratocaster
American Series Stratocaster
American Standard Series Stratocaster
25th Anniversary Stratocaster
30th Anniversary L.E. Guitar Center Strat
35th Anniversary Stratocaster
40th Anniv. Stratocaster Diamond Dealer
40th Anniversary American Standard Stratocaster
40th Anniversary Stratocaster (Japan)
'50s Stratocaster/Classic Series '50s Stratocaster
'50s Stratocaster Relic
Classic Player '50s Stratocaster
50th Anniversary 1954 Stratocaster
50th Anniversary American Deluxe Strat (USA)
50th Anniversary American Series Stratocaster
50th Anniversary Stratocaster
50th Anniversary Stratocaster (Matching Headstock)
50th Anniversary Stratocaster (Mexico)
50th Anniversary Stratocaster Relic
'54 Stratocaster
'54 Stratocaster FMT
'56 Stratocaster
'57 Special Stratocaster

'57 Stratocaster
George Fullerton 50th Ann. '57 Strat Ltd Ed. Set
'57 Stratocaster (USA)
American Vintage '57 Commemorative Stratocaster
'57 Vintage Stratocaster (Japan)
'58 Stratocaster
'58 Stratocaster (Dakota Red)
'60 FMT Stratocaster
'60 Stratocaster
'60s Stratocaster/Classic Series '60s Stratocaster
Classic Player '60s Stratocaster
'60s Stratocaster Relic
60th Diamond Anniversary Stratocaster
'61 Stratocaster
'62 Stratocaster (USA)
American Vintage '62 Commemorative Stratocaster
'62 Stratocaster ST62US Reissue
Deluxe Vintage Player '62 Stratocaster
'65 Stratocaster
'66 Stratocaster
'68 Reverse Strat Special (USA)
'68 Stratocaster
'68 Stratocaster (Japan)
'69 Stratocaster
'70s Stratocaster (Mexico)
'70s Stratocaster American Vintage
'72 Stratocaster (Japan)
Acoustasonic Stratocaster
Aerodyne Stratocaster
Aluminum Stratocaster
American Classic Holoflake Stratocaster
American Classic Stratocaster
American Deluxe Stratocaster
American Deluxe Fat Stratocaster
American Deluxe Stratocaster HSS
American Deluxe Stratocaster FMT HSS
American Series HSS/HH Stratocaster
American Standard Stratocaster HSS
American Standard Stratocaster Limited Edition
Antigua Stratocaster
Big Apple Stratocaster
Big Block Stratocaster
Bill Carson Stratocaster
Billy Corgan Stratocaster
Blackie Stratocaster
Blackie Stratocaster (Custom Shop 1987)
Blackie Stratocaster (Custom Shop)
Blue Flower Stratocaster
Bonnie Raitt Stratocaster
Bowling Ball/Marble Stratocaster
Buddy Guy Stratocaster (Mexico)
Buddy Guy Stratocaster (Signature)
California Fat Stratocaster
California Stratocaster
Classic Player Stratocaster
Collector's Edition Stratocaster ('62 Reissue)
Contemporary Stratocaster
Contemporary Stratocaster (Import)
Crash Stratocaster

The *Vintage Guitar Price Guide* shows low to high values for items in all-original excellent condition, and, where applicable, with original case or cover.

Custom 1960 Stratocaster
David Gilmour Signature Stratocaster
Deluxe Lone Star Stratocaster
Deluxe Players Special Edition Stratocaster
Deluxe Players Stratocaster
Deluxe Strat Plus
Dick Dale Stratocaster
Elite Stratocaster
Eric Clapton Gold Leaf Stratocaster
Eric Clapton Stratocaster
Eric Clapton Stratocaster (CS)
Eric Johnson Stratocaster
Floyd Rose Classic Relic Stratocaster
Floyd Rose Classic Stratocaster
Ford Shelby GT Stratocaster
Foto Flame Stratocaster
Freddy Tavares Aloha Stratocaster
Gold Stratocaster
Gold Elite Stratocaster
Gold Stratocaster (CS)
Hank Marvin Stratocaster
Hank Marvin 40th Anniversary Stratocaster
Harley-Davidson 90th Anniversary Stratocaster
Hellecaster Stratocaster
Highway One Stratocaster/HSS
HM Stratocaster (USA/Import)
Homer Haynes HLE Stratocaster
Hot Wheels Stratocaster
HRR Stratocaster
Ike Turner Tribute Stratocaster
Jeff Beck Stratocaster
Jeff Beck Signature Stratocaster (CS)
Jerry Donahue Hellecaster Stratocaster
Jimi Hendrix Monterey Pop Stratocaster
Jimi Hendrix Tribute Stratocaster
Jimi Hendrix Voodoo 29th Anniversary Strato-
    caster
Jimi Hendrix Voodoo Stratocaster
Jimmie Vaughan Tex-Mex Stratocaster
John Jorgenson Hellecaster Stratocaster
John Mayer Limited Edition Black1 Stratocaster
John Mayer Stratocaster
Koa Stratocaster
Kon Tiki Stratocaster
Lenny Stratocaster
Lone Star Stratocaster
Mark Knopfler Stratocaster
Milonga Deluxe Stratocaster
Moto Limited Edition Stratocaster
Moto Set Stratocaster
Paisley Stratocaster
Playboy 40th Anniversary Stratocaster
Powerhouse/Powerhouse Deluxe Stratocaster
Proud Stratocaster
Richie Sambora Stratocaster
Ritchie Blackmore Stratocaster
Roadhouse Stratocaster
Roadhouse Stratocaster (Mexico)
Robert Cray Signature Stratocaster
Robert Cray Stratocaster (Mexico)
Robin Trower Signature Stratocaster
Roland Ready Standard Stratocaster
Rory Gallagher Tribute Stratocaster

Set-Neck Stratocaster
Short-Scale (7/8) Stratocaster
So-Cal Speed Shop L.E. Stratocaster
Special Edition Stratocaster
Splatter Stratocaster
Standard Fat Stratocaster
Standard HH Stratocaster
Standard HSS Stratocaster
Standard Stratocaster (Japan)
Standard Stratocaster (Mexico)
Standard Stratocaster Satin Finish
Stevie Ray Vaughan Stratocaster
Stevie Ray Vaughan Tribute #1 Stratocaster
Strat Plus
Strat Pro Closet Classic
Stratocaster Junior
Stratocaster Special
Stratocaster XII
Strat-o-Sonic
Sub Sonic Stratocaster
Super Strat
Tanqurey Tonic Stratocaster
Texas Special Stratocaster
The Strat
Tie-Dye Stratocaster
Tom Delonge Stratocaster
Tree of Life Stratocaster
Turquoise Sparkle Stratocaster
U.S. Ultra / Ultra Plus Stratocaster
Ventures Limited Edition Stratocaster
VG Stratocaster
Vintage Hot Rod Stratocaster
Walnut Elite Stratocaster
Walnut Stratocaster
Western Stratocaster
Yngwie Malmsteen Stratocaster

Stratocaster

*1954-1981. Two-tone sunburst until '58, 3-tone after.
Custom color finishes were quite rare in the '50s and
early-'60s and are much more valuable than the standard sunburst finish. By the '70s, color finishes were
much more common and do not affect the value near
as much. In '75 Fender dropped the optional custom
colors and started issuing the guitars in a variety
of standard colors (sunburst, blond, white, natural,
walnut and black).*

*Custom color Fenders can be forged and bogus
finishes have been a problem. As the value of custom
color Fenders has increased, so has the problem of
bogus non-original finishes. The prices in the Guide
are for factory original finishes in excellent condition. One color, Shell Pink, is notable because many
vintage authorities wonder if a Shell Pink Strat even
exists? An ultra-rare custom color should have strong
documented provenance and be verifiable by at least
one (preferable two or more) well-known vintage
authorities. Please refer to the Fender Guitar Intro
Section for details on Fender color options.*

*Three-bolt neck '72-'81, otherwise 4-bolt. Unless
noted, all Stratocasters listed have the Fender tremolo
system. Non-tremolo models (aka hardtails) typically
sell for less. Many guitarists feel the tremolo block
helps produce a fuller range of sound. On average,*

1958 Fender Stratocaster

1959 Fender Stratocaster
Tom Siska

1965 Fender Stratocaster

1966 Fender Stratocaster

many more tremolo models were made. One year, '58, seems to be a year where a greater percentage of non-tremolo models were made. Tremolo vs. non-tremolo valuation should be taken on a brand-by-brand basis; for example, a pre-'65 Gibson ES-335 non-tremolo model is worth more than a tremolo equipped model.

From '63-'70, Fender offered both the standard Brazilian rosewood fretboard and an optional maple fretboard. Prices listed here, for those years, are for the rosewood 'board models. Currently, the market considers the maple 'board to be a premium, so guitars with maple, for those years, are worth 10% to 15% more than the values shown.

See Standard Stratocaster for '82-'84 (following listing), American Standard Stratocaster for '86-2000, and the American Series Stratocaster for 2000-'07. Currently called again the American Standard Stratocaster.

MODEL YEAR	FEATURES	EXC. COND. LOW	HIGH
1954	Early '54 production	$45,000	$56,000
1954	Sunburst, later production	$40,000	$50,000
1955	Blond, nickel hardware, late '55	$38,000	$46,000
1955	Sunburst	$29,000	$36,000
1956	Blond, nickel hardware	$38,000	$46,000
1956	Mary Kaye, gold hardware	$54,000	$66,000
1956	Sunburst, alder body	$27,000	$33,000
1956	Sunburst, ash body	$29,000	$35,000
1956	Sunburst, non-trem	$19,000	$23,000
1957	Blond, nickel hardware	$38,000	$46,000
1957	Mary Kaye, gold hardware	$54,000	$66,000
1957	Sunburst	$25,000	$32,000
1958	Blond, nickel hardware	$38,000	$46,000
1958	Mary Kaye, gold hardware	$54,000	$66,000
1958	Sunburst 2-tone	$25,000	$32,000
1958	Sunburst 2-tone, non-trem	$19,000	$24,000
1958	Sunburst 3-tone	$21,000	$26,000
1958	Sunburst 3-tone, non-trem	$16,000	$20,000
1959	Blond, nickel hardware	$37,000	$44,000
1959	Custom colors	$43,000	$65,000
1959	Mary Kaye, gold hardware, maple	$54,000	$66,000
1959	Mary Kaye, gold hardware, slab	$53,000	$65,000
1959	Sunburst, maple	$20,000	$24,000
1959	Sunburst, non-trem, slab	$13,500	$16,500
1959	Sunburst, slab	$18,000	$22,000
1960	Common colors	$25,000	$35,000

MODEL YEAR	FEATURES	EXC. COND. LOW	HIGH
1960	Rare colors	$35,000	$70,000
1960	Sunburst	$18,000	$22,000
1961	Common colors	$25,000	$35,000
1961	Rare colors	$35,000	$70,000
1961	Sunburst	$18,000	$22,000
1962	Common colors, curve	$21,000	$30,000
1962	Common colors, slab, 2 pat. Logo	$25,000	$35,000
1962	Common colors, slab, 3 pat. Logo	$23,000	$33,000
1962	Rare color, curve	$25,000	$35,000
1962	Rare color, slab, 2 pat. Logo	$35,000	$70,000
1962	Rare color, slab, 3 pat. Logo	$30,000	$65,000
1962	Sunburst, curve	$16,000	$20,000
1962	Sunburst, slab, 2 pat. Logo	$18,000	$22,000
1962	Sunburst, slab, 3 pat. Logo	$16,000	$20,000
1962	Sunburst, slab, tortoise 'guard	$18,000	$22,000
1963	Common colors	$21,000	$30,000
1963	Rare colors	$30,000	$45,000
1963	Sunburst	$16,000	$20,000
1964	Common colors	$19,000	$28,000
1964	Rare colors	$28,000	$42,000
1964	Sunburst, spaghetti logo	$16,000	$20,000
1964	Sunburst, transition logo	$13,000	$16,000
1965	Common colors	$15,000	$20,000
1965	Rare colors	$20,000	$38,000
1965	Sunburst, F-plate	$8,900	$11,100
1965	Sunburst, green 'guard	$12,000	$15,000
1965	Sunburst, white 'guard	$10,000	$12,500
1966	Common colors	$12,000	$15,000
1966	Rare colors	$15,000	$28,000
1966	Sunburst	$8,800	$11,000
1967	Common colors	$11,800	$14,800
1967	Rare colors	$14,800	$27,000
1967	Sunburst	$8,200	$10,500
1968	Common colors	$10,800	$13,800
1968	Rare colors	$13,800	$24,000
1968	Sunburst	$8,000	$10,000
1969	Common colors	$9,800	$12,800
1969	Rare colors	$12,800	$23,000
1969	Sunburst	$7,500	$9,500
1970	Common colors	$7,400	$9,600
1970	Rare colors	$9,600	$17,000
1970	Sunburst	$5,600	$7,100
1971	Common colors	$7,000	$9,000
1971	Rare colors	$9,000	$15,000
1971	Sunburst	$5,000	$6,200
1972	Common colors, 3-bolt	$4,500	$5,500
1972	Rare colors, 3-bolt	$5,500	$6,700
1972	Sunburst, 3-bolt	$3,600	$4,500

The *Vintage Guitar Price Guide* shows low to high values for items in all-original excellent condition, and, where applicable, with original case or cover.

MODEL YEAR	FEATURES	EXC. COND. LOW	HIGH
1973	Common colors	$4,000	$5,000
1973	Natural	$2,300	$2,900
1973	Rare colors	$5,000	$6,200
1973	Sunburst	$2,900	$3,600
1973	Walnut	$2,800	$3,500
1974	Black, blond, Olympic White	$3,300	$4,000
1974	Natural	$2,300	$2,900
1974	Sunburst	$2,400	$3,000
1974	Walnut	$2,400	$3,000
1975	Black, blond, Olympic White (black parts)	$2,200	$2,700
1975	Black, blond, Olympic White (white parts)	$2,600	$3,300
1975	Natural	$1,700	$2,200
1975	Sunburst, black parts	$1,900	$2,400
1975	Sunburst, white parts	$2,000	$2,500
1975	Walnut	$1,900	$2,400
1976	Black, blond, Olympic White	$2,000	$2,500
1976	Natural	$1,700	$2,200
1976	Sunburst	$1,700	$2,200
1976	Walnut	$1,700	$2,200
1977	Black, blond, Olympic White	$2,000	$2,500
1977	Natural	$1,600	$2,000
1977	Sunburst	$1,700	$2,200
1977	Walnut	$1,700	$2,200
1978	Antigua	$2,000	$2,500
1978	Black, blond, Olympic White, Wine	$1,800	$2,300
1978	Natural	$1,600	$2,000
1978	Sunburst	$1,700	$2,200
1978	Walnut	$1,700	$2,200
1979	Antigua	$2,000	$2,500
1979	Black, blond, Olympic White, Wine	$1,800	$2,300
1979	Natural	$1,600	$2,000
1979	Sunburst	$1,700	$2,200
1979	Walnut	$1,700	$2,200
1980	Antigua	$1,900	$2,300
1980	Black, Olympic White, Wine	$1,400	$1,700
1980	International colors	$2,000	$3,000
1980	Natural	$1,325	$1,675
1980	Sunburst	$1,425	$1,775
1981	Black, Olympic White, Wine	$1,400	$1,700
1981	International colors	$2,000	$3,000
1981	Sunburst	$1,225	$1,575

Standard Stratocaster (includes "Smith Strat")

1981-1984. Replaces the Stratocaster. Renamed the American Standard Stratocaster for '86-'00 (see next listing). Renamed American Series Stratocaster in '00.

From '81/'82 to mid-'83, 4 knobs same as regular Strat but with 4-bolt neck. In August '81, Dan Smith was hired by Bill Schultz and Fender produced an alder body, 4-bolt neck, 21-fret, small headstock Standard Stratocaster that has been nicknamed the Smith Strat (made from Dec. '81-'83). Mid-'83 to the end of '84 2 knobs and 'guard mounted input jack. Not to be confused with current Standard Stratocaster, which is made in Mexico.

1981	Smith Strat, 4-bolt, 3-knob	$1,600	$2,000
1982	Smith Strat, rare colors	$2,000	$2,500
1982	Smith Strat, various colors	$1,600	$2,000
1983	Smith Strat, various colors	$1,600	$2,000
1983	Stratoburst option	$1,700	$2,100
1983-1984	Sunburst, 2-knob	$1,500	$1,800
1983-1984	Various colors, 2-knob	$1,500	$1,800

American Standard Stratocaster

1986-2000. Fender's new name for the American-made Strat when reintroducing it after CBS sold the company. The only American-made Strats made in 1985 were the '57 and '62 models. See Stratocaster and Standard Stratocaster for earlier models, renamed American Series Stratocaster in 2000.

1986-1989	Various colors	$850	$1,050
1989	Mary Kaye Limited Edition	$900	$1,100
1990-1999	Various colors	$675	$850

American Series Stratocaster

2000-2007. Ash or alder body, rosewood or maple 'board, dot markers, 3 staggered single-coils, 5-way switch, hand polished fret edges. Renamed the American Standard Stratocaster again in '08.

2000-2007	Alder or ash body	$650	$800
2000-2007	Ash body, hardtail	$625	$750
2000-2007	Limited Edition colors	$725	$900
2000-2007	Limited Edition matching headstock	$750	$950
2006-2007	Non-veneer body, new routings	$650	$800

American Standard Series Stratocaster

2008-present. New bridge, neck and body finish, alder or ash body, rosewood or maple 'board, 3 single-coils.

2008-2010		$675	$850

25th Anniversary Stratocaster

1979-1980. Has ANNIVERSARY on upper body horn, silver metallic or white pearlescent finish.

1979	White, 1st issue	$2,000	$2,400
1979-1980	Silver, faded to gold	$1,500	$1,800
1979-1980	Silver, unfaded	$2,400	$2,800

30th Anniversary L.E. Guitar Center Strat

1994. Commemorates Guitar Center's opening in '64, 250 made, sunburst with tortoise guard, 30th Anniversary Limited Edition Guitar Center logo on neck plate.

1994		$950	$1,100

1977 Fender Stratocaster

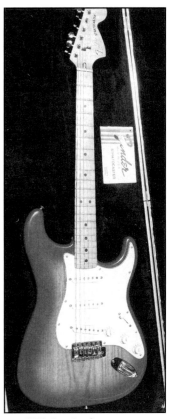

1979 Fender Stratocaster

GUITARS

2009 Fender '56 NOS Stratocaster

Philip Naessens

Fender American Vintage '57 Commemorative Stratocaster

Dan Drozdik

MODEL YEAR	FEATURES	EXC. COND. LOW	HIGH

35th Anniversary Stratocaster
1989-1991. Custom Shop model, 500 made, figured maple top, Lace Sensor pickups, Eric Clapton preamp circuit.

| 1989-1991 | | $2,400 | $2,900 |

40th Anniv. Stratocaster Diamond Dealer
1994 only. Custom Shop model, 150 made, 40th Anniversary headstock inlay, flamed maple top on ash body, '54-'94 inlay at 12th fret, gold etched 'guard, gold hardware, sunburst.

| 1994 | | $3,000 | $3,500 |

40th Anniversary American Standard Stratocaster
1994 only. US-made, American Standard model (not Custom Shop), plain top, appearance similar to a '54 maple-neck Strat, sunburst, 2 neck plates offered "40th Anniversary" and "40th Anniversary and still rockin'".

| 1994 | "40th Anniversary" neck plate | $925 | $1,100 |
| 1994 | "...and still rockin'" neck plate | $975 | $1,150 |

40th Anniversary Stratocaster (Japan)
1994 only. Made in Japan, '62 reissue specs.

| 1994 | | $575 | $675 |

'50s Stratocaster/Classic Series '50s Stratocaster
1985-present. Made in Japan (basswood body) until mid '99, then in Mexico with poplar or alder body. Foto-Flame finish offered in '92-'94 (see separate listing).

| 1985-1999 | Japan std colors | $475 | $525 |
| 1999-2010 | Mexico | $450 | $500 |

'50s Stratocaster Relic
1996-1999. Custom Shop model, reproduction of ca. '57 Strat with played-in feel, gold hardware is +$100, see-thru Mary Kaye ash body is +$100, replaced by '56 Strat.

| 1996-1999 | Various colors | $1,400 | $1,800 |

Classic Player '50s Stratocaster
2006-present. U.S.-made components but assembled in Mexico, alder body, maple neck and 'board, vintage-style pickups.

| 2006-2010 | | $500 | $700 |

50th Anniversary 1954 Stratocaster
2004-2005. Custom Shop, celebrates 50 years of the Strat, 1954 specs and materials, replica form-fit case, certificate, Fender took orders for these up to December 31, 2004.

| 2004-2005 | | $3,200 | $4,000 |

50th Anniversary American Deluxe Strat (USA)
2004. U.S.-made, Deluxe series features, engraved neck plate, tweed case.

| 2004 | | $1,100 | $1,275 |

50th Anniversary American Series Stratocaster
2004. U.S. made, '54 replica pickups, engraved neck plate, tweed case.

| 2004 | | $800 | $1,000 |

50th Anniversary Stratocaster
1995-1996. Custom Shop model, flame maple top, 3 vintage-style pickups, gold hardware, gold 50th Anniversary (of Fender) coin on back of the headstock, sunburst, 2500 made.

| 1995-1996 | | $1,450 | $1,600 |

50th Anniversary Stratocaster (Matching Headstock)
1994-1995. U.S.A. factory-special, limited edition, offered in several different custom colors.

| 1994-1995 | | $800 | $1,000 |

50th Anniversary Stratocaster (Mexico)
2004. Made in Mexico, Aztec gold finish, no logo on guitar to indicate 50th Anniv., CE on neck plate to indicate import.

| 2004 | | $525 | $625 |

50th Anniversary Stratocaster Relic
1995-1996. Custom Shop Relic model, aged played-in feel, diamond headstock inlay, Shoreline Gold finish, 200 units planned.

| 1995-1996 | | $2,700 | $3,300 |

'54 Stratocaster
1992-1998. Custom Shop Classic reissue, ash body, Custom '50s pickups, gold-plated hardware.

| 1992-1998 | Various options | $1,575 | $1,825 |

'54 Stratocaster FMT
1992-1998. Custom Classic reissue, Flame Maple Top, also comes in gold hardware edition.

| 1992-1998 | | $1,800 | $2,000 |
| 1992-1998 | Gold hardware option | $1,900 | $2,050 |

'56 Stratocaster
1996-present. Custom Shop model, most detailed replica (and most expensive to date) of '56 Strat, including electronics and pickups, offered with rosewood or maple 'board, gold hardware is +$100.

1996-1998	Cunetto built relic	$2,700	$3,300
1997-1998	Cunetto era (staff built)	$1,800	$2,200
1999-2010	Closet Classic	$1,700	$1,900
1999-2010	NOS	$1,600	$1,800
1999-2010	Relic	$1,900	$2,100

'57 Special Stratocaster
1992-1993. Custom Shop model, flamed maple top, birdseye maple neck, run of 60 made, sunburst.

| 1992-1993 | | $1,700 | $1,900 |

'57 Stratocaster
1994-1996. Custom Shop model, replaced by the more authentic, higher-detailed '56 Custom Shop Stratocaster by '99, Custom Shop models can be distinguished by the original certificate that comes with the guitar.

| 1994-1996 | Various colors | $1,300 | $1,600 |

George Fullerton 50th Ann. '57 Strat Ltd Ed. Sct
2007. 150 made, '57 Strat with matching relic Pro Junior tweed amp, certificates of authenticity signed by Fullerton, commemorative neck plate.

| 2007 | | $3,300 | $4,000 |

MODEL YEAR	FEATURES	EXC. COND. LOW	HIGH

'57 Stratocaster (USA)

1982-present. U.S.A.-made at the Fullerton, California plant ('82-'85) and at the Corona, California plant ('85-present).

1982-1984		$2,500	$3,000
1982-1984	Rare colors	$3,000	$3,500
1986-1989		$1,200	$1,500
1986-1989	Rare colors	$1,500	$1,800
1990-1999		$1,200	$1,500
1990-1999	Rare colors	$1,500	$1,700
2000-2010		$1,075	$1,300

American Vintage '57 Commemorative Stratocaster

2007. Limited production, part of American Vintage Series, 1957-2007 Commemorative logo neckplate.

2007		$1,150	$1,350

'57 Vintage Stratocaster (Japan)

1984-1985. Japanese-made, various colors.

1984-1985		$550	$675

'58 Stratocaster

1996-1999. Custom Shop model, ash body, Fat '50s pickups, chrome or gold hardware (gold is +$100.), Custom Shop models can be distinguished by the original certificate that comes with the guitar.

1996-1999	Various colors	$1,500	$1,800

'58 Stratocaster (Dakota Red)

1996. Custom Shop model, run of 30 made in Dakota Red with matching headstock, maple neck, Texas special pickups, gold hardware.

1996		$1,500	$1,800

'60 FMT Stratocaster

1997-1999. Custom Shop model, flame maple top.

1997-1999		$1,600	$1,800

'60 Stratocaster

1992-present. Custom Shop model, '92-'99 version with Texas Special pickups, later version is more detailed replica (and most expensive to date) of '60 Strat, including electronics and pickups, gold hardware is +$100. The price includes the original Certificate of Authenticity, which for the '92-'98 early models indicates the model as 1960 Stratocaster along with the year of manufacture, a guitar without the original certificate is worth less than the values shown.

1992-1998	1st issue	$1,500	$1,700
1996-1998	Cunetto built relic	$2,700	$3,300
1997-1998	Cunetto era (staff built)	$1,800	$2,200
1999-2010	Closet Classic	$1,700	$1,900
1999-2010	NOS	$1,600	$1,800
1999-2010	Relic	$1,900	$2,100
1999-2010	Various rare colors	$2,100	$2,400

'60s Stratocaster/Classic Series '60s Stratocaster

1985-present. Made in Japan (basswood body) until mid '99, then in Mexico with poplar or alder body. Foto-Flame finish offered in '92-'94 (see separate listing).

1985-1999	Japan std colors	$425	$525
1999-2010	Mexico	$400	$500

Classic Player '60s Stratocaster

2006-present. U.S.-made components but assembled in Mexico, alder body, maple neck, rosewood 'board, vintage-style pickups.

2006-2010		$500	$700

'60s Stratocaster Relic

1996-1999. Custom Shop model, reproduction of '60s Strat with played-in feel, gold hardware is +$100, see-thru Mary Kaye ash body is +$100, replaced by '60 Relic.

1996-1999	Various colors	$1,300	$1,800

60th Diamond Anniversary Stratocaster

2006. US-made, 'Sixty Years' decal logo on headstock, American Flag logo and black 'Diamond 1946-2006 60' logo on pickguard between neck and middle pickup, engraved neck plate, Z-series serial number, coin on back of headstock, paperwork.

2006		$900	$1,125

'61 Stratocaster

2001. Custom Shop model, Relic, white, Certificate of Authenticity.

2001		$1,900	$2,100

'62 Stratocaster (USA)

1982-present. Made at Fullerton plant ('82-'85) then at Corona plant ('86-present).

1982-1984		$2,500	$3,000
1982-1984	Rare colors	$3,000	$3,500
1986-1989		$1,200	$1,500
1986-1989	Rare colors	$1,500	$1,800
1990-1999		$1,200	$1,500
1990-1999	Rare colors	$1,500	$1,700
2000-2010		$1,075	$1,300

American Vintage '62 Commemorative Stratocaster

2007. Limited production, part of American Vintage Series, 1957-2007 Commemorative logo neckplate.

2007		$1,150	$1,350

'62 Stratocaster ST62US Reissue

2008-present. Made by Fender Japan for that market, US-made 'vintage' pickups.

2008-2010		$475	$600

Deluxe Vintage Player '62 Stratocaster

2005-2006. Design blends vintage and modern features based upon '62 specs including vintage style tuners, bridge and aged plastic parts. Updates include 3 Samarium Cobalt Noiseless pickups and Deluxe American Standard electronics, limited edition, Olympic White or Ice Blue Metallic.

2005-2006		$950	$1,100

'65 Stratocaster

1998-1999, 2003-2010. Custom Shop model, '65 small-headstock specs, rosewood or maple cap 'board, transition logo, offered in NOS, Relic, or Closet Classic versions.

1998-1999	NOS	$1,800	$2,000
2003-2010	Closet Classic	$1,700	$1,900
2003-2010	NOS	$1,600	$1,800
2003-2010	Relic	$1,900	$2,100

Fender American Vintage '62 Stratocaster

Fender '65 Closet Classic Stratocaster

GUITARS

Fender American Deluxe Stratocaster

Fender Big Block Stratocaster

MODEL YEAR	FEATURES	EXC. COND. LOW	HIGH

'66 Stratocaster
2004-2008. Custom Shop model, offered in Closet Classic, NOS or Relic versions.

2004-2008	Closet Classic	$1,700	$1,900
2004-2008	NOS	$1,600	$1,800
2004-2008	Relic	$1,900	$2,100

'68 Reverse Strat Special (USA)
2001-2002. With special reverse left-hand neck, large headstock (post-CBS style).

2001-2002		$900	$1,200

'68 Stratocaster
1990s. Custom Shop model, Jimi Hendrix-style, maple cap neck.

1990s		$1,600	$1,900

'68 Stratocaster (Japan)
1996-1999. '68 specs including large headstock, part of Collectables Series, sunburst, natural, Olympic White.

1996-1999		$600	$700

'69 Stratocaster
1997-2009. Custom Shop model, large headstock, U-shaped maple neck with rosewood or maple cap options, '69-style finish, gold hardware is +$100, since 2000, offered in NOS, Relic, or Closet Classic versions.

2000-2009	Closet Classic	$1,700	$1,900
2000-2009	NOS	$1,600	$1,800
2000-2009	Relic	$1,900	$2,100

'70s Stratocaster (Mexico)
1999-present. Large headstock, white pickups and knobs, rosewood 'board.

1999-2010		$450	$500

'70s Stratocaster American Vintage
2006-present. US-made, large '70s headstock, early '70s white pickups and knobs, 3-bolt neck.

2006-2010		$950	$1,100

'72 Stratocaster (Japan)
1985-1996. Basswood body, maple 'board, large headstock.

1985-1996		$550	$650

Acoustasonic Stratocaster
2003-2009. Hollowed out alder Strat body with braceless graphite top, 3 in-bridge Fishman piezo pickups, acoustic sound hole.

2003-2009		$500	$525

Aerodyne Stratocaster
2004-2009. Import Strat with Aerodyne body profile, bound body, black.

2004-2009		$450	$550

Aluminum Stratocaster
1994-1995. Aluminum-bodied American Standard with anodized finish in blue marble, purple marble or red, silver and blue stars and stripes. Some with 40th Anniversary designation. There is also a Custom Shop version.

1994-1995	Marble patterns	$2,000	$2,500
1994-1995	Red-silver-blue flag option	$2,500	$3,000

American Classic Holoflake Stratocaster
1992-1993. Custom Shop model, splatter/sparkle finish, pearloid 'guard.

1992-1993		$1,550	$1,900

MODEL YEAR	FEATURES	EXC. COND. LOW	HIGH

American Classic Stratocaster
1992-1999. Custom Shop version of American Standard, 3 pickups, tremolo, rosewood 'board, nickel or gold-plated hardware, various colors.

1992-1999	See-thru blond ash body	$1,200	$1,500
1992-1999	Various colors & options	$1,100	$1,400

American Deluxe Stratocaster
1998-2010. Made in USA, premium alder or ash body, noiseless pickups.

1998-2010		$775	$925

American Deluxe Fat Stratocaster
1998-2003. Made in USA, Fender DH-1 bridge humbucker for fat sound, premium alder or ash body.

1998-2003	Ash body, transparent finish	$800	$1,000
1998-2003	Various colors	$750	$950

American Deluxe Stratocaster HSS
2004-present. Deluxe features, hum/single/single pickups.

2004-2010		$775	$975

American Deluxe Stratocaster FMT HSS
2004-2009. Flame maple top version.

2004-2009		$900	$1,100

American Series HSS/HH Stratocaster
2003-2007. Made in U.S., HSS has humbucker/single/single, HH ('03-'05) 2 humbuckers. Renamed American Standard Strat HSS in '08.

2003-2007	Alder or ash body	$675	$825

American Standard Stratocaster HSS
2008-present. Renamed from American Series Stratocaster HSS.

2008-2010		$675	$825

American Standard Stratocaster Limited Edition
1995. 1950s style headstock decal, Ocean Turquoise or Candy Apple Red with matching headstock.

1995		$925	$1,150

Antigua Stratocaster
2004. Made in Japan, limited-edition reissue, '70s features and antigua finish.

2004		$550	$675

Big Apple Stratocaster
1997-2000. Two humbucking pickups, 5-way switch, rosewood 'board or maple neck, non-tremolo optional.

1997-2000	Various colors	$675	$825

Big Block Stratocaster
2005-2006. Pearloid block markers, black with matching headstock, 2 single coils (neck, middle) 1 humbucker (bridge), vintage style tremolo.

2005-2006		$600	$700

Bill Carson Stratocaster
1992. Based on the '57 Strat, birdseye maple neck, Cimarron Red finish, 1 left-handed and 100 right-handed produced, serial numbers MT000-MT100, made in Fender Custom Shop, and initiated by The Music Trader (MT) in Florida.

1992		$1,700	$2,000

MODEL YEAR	FEATURES	EXC. COND. LOW	HIGH

Billy Corgan Stratocaster

2008-present. US-made, 3 DiMarzio pickups, string-thru hardtail bridge.

2008-2010		$900	$1,050

Blackie Stratocaster

1989-2005. Production model, Blackie decal and Eric Clapton's signature decal on headstock.

| 1989-2000 | Lace pickups | $975 | $1,175 |
| 2001-2005 | Standard pickups | $1,025 | $1,225 |

Blackie Stratocaster (Custom Shop 1987)

1987. 12 made, includes Certificate of Authenticity.

1987		$2,000	$2,500

Blackie Stratocaster (Custom Shop)

November 2006. 185 instruments for U.S. market, 90 made for export, original retail price $24,000.

2006		$15,000	$18,000

Blue Flower Stratocaster

1988-1993, 2003-2004. Made in Japan, '72 Strat reissue with a reissue '68 Tele Blue Floral finish.

| 1988-1993 | 1st issue | $800 | $1,000 |
| 2003-2004 | 2nd issue | $500 | $600 |

Bonnie Raitt Stratocaster

1995-2000. Alder body, often in blueburst, Bonnie Raitt's signature on headstock.

1995-2000		$1,050	$1,250

Bowling Ball/Marble Stratocaster

1983-1984. Standard Strat with 1 tone and 1 volume control, jack on 'guard, called Bowling Ball Strat due to the swirling, colored finish.

1983-1984		$2,400	$3,000

Buddy Guy Stratocaster (Mexico)

1996-present. Maple neck, polka-dot finish.

1996-2010		$475	$575

Buddy Guy Stratocaster (Signature)

1995-2009. Maple neck, 3 Gold Lace Sensor pickups, ash body, signature model, blond or sunburst.

1995-2009		$1,000	$1,100

California Fat Stratocaster

1997-1998. Humbucker pickup in bridge position.

1997-1998		$500	$600

California Stratocaster

1997-1999. Made in the U.S., painted in Mexico, 2 pickups, various colors.

1997-1999		$500	$600

Classic Player Stratocaster

2000. Custom Shop model, Standard Stratocaster with useful 'player-friendly features' such as noiseless stacked single-coil pickups and factory Sperzel locking tuners, made in the Custom Shop, black, gold anodized 'guard.

2000		$1,300	$1,550

Collector's Edition Stratocaster ('62 Reissue)

1997. Pearl inlaid '97 on 12th fret, rosewood 'board, alder body, gold hardware, tortoise 'guard, nitro finish, sunburst, 1997 made.

1997		$925	$1,075

Contemporary Stratocaster

1989-1998. Custom Shop model, 7/8 scale body, hum/single/single pickups, various colors.

1989-1998		$1,150	$1,400

Contemporary Stratocaster (Import)

1985-1987. Import model used while the new Fender reorganized, black headstock with silver-white logo, black or white 'guard, 2 humbucker pickups or single-coil and humbucker, 2 knobs and slider switch.

1985-1987		$350	$425

Crash Stratocaster

2005. Master Built Custom Shop model, hand painted by John Crash Matos, approximately 50, comes with certificate, the original certificate adds value, the prices shown include the certificate.

2005		$6,000	$7,500

Custom 1960 Stratocaster

1994. Short run of 20 custom ordered and specified instruments that have 1960 specs along with other specs such as a pearloid 'guard, came with Certificate of Authenticity, matching headstock color.

1994		$2,900	$3,500

David Gilmour Signature Stratocaster

2008. Based on Gilmour's '70 black Stratocaster.

2008		$2,300	$2,900

Deluxe Lone Star Stratocaster

2007-present. Reissue of Lone Star Strat, made in Mexico, 1 humbucker and 2 single-coils, rosewood 'board.

2007-2010		$375	$450

Deluxe Players Special Edition Stratocaster

2007. Made in Mexico, Special Edition Fender oval sticker on back of headstock along with 60th Anniversary badge.

2007		$375	$450

Deluxe Players Stratocaster

2004-present. Made in Mexico, 3 noiseless single-coils, push-button switching system.

2004-2010		$350	$425

Deluxe Strat Plus

1987-1998. Three Lace Sensor pickups, Floyd Rose, alder (poplar available earlier) body with ash veneer on front and back, various colors, also see Strat Plus.

1987-1998		$950	$1,050

Dick Dale Stratocaster

1994-present. Custom Shop signature model, alder body, reverse headstock, sparkle finish.

1994-2010		$1,550	$1,800

Elite Stratocaster

1983-1984. The Elite Series feature active electronics and noise-cancelling pickups, push buttons instead of 3-way switch, Elite script logo on 4-bolt neck plate, various colors. Also see Gold Elite Stratocaster and Walnut Elite Stratocaster.

| 1983-1984 | Standard colors | $1,150 | $1,400 |
| 1983-1984 | Stratoburst option(s) | $1,150 | $1,400 |

Eric Clapton Gold Leaf Stratocaster

2004. Custom Shop model, special build for Guitar Center, 50 made, 23k gold leaf finish/covering.

2004		$4,250	$5,250

2008 Billy Corgan Stratocaster

Fender Crash Stratocaster

GUITARS

*1991 Fender Eric Clapton
Stratocaster*

Fender John Mayer Stratocaster

MODEL		EXC. COND.	
YEAR	FEATURES	LOW	HIGH

Eric Clapton Stratocaster
1988-present. U.S.-made, '57 reissue features, had Lace Sensor pickups until '01, when switched to Vintage. Black became an option in '91 and says Blackie on headstock.

| 1988-1989 | | $1,000 | $1,200 |
| 1990-2010 | | $1,000 | $1,200 |

Eric Clapton Stratocaster (CS)
2004-present. Custom Shop model, standard non-active single-coil pickups, black or blue finish.

| 2004-2007 | | $2,000 | $2,500 |
| 2008-2010 | | $1,900 | $2,300 |

Eric Johnson Stratocaster
2005-present. '57 spec body and soft-v-neck, maple or, since '09, rosewood 'board, special design pickups, vintage tremolo with 4 springs, EJ initials and guitar-player figure engraved neck plate..

| 2005-2010 | | $1,100 | $1,400 |

Floyd Rose Classic Relic Stratocaster
1998-1999. Custom Shop model, late '60s large headstock, 1 humbucker and 1 Strat pickup.

| 1998-1999 | | $1,600 | $1,800 |

Floyd Rose Classic Stratocaster
1992-1997. Two single-coils, bridge humbucker, Floyd Rose tremolo, various colors.

| 1992-1997 | | $800 | $1,000 |

Ford Shelby GT Stratocaster
2007. 200 made, black with silver Shelby GT racing stripe.

| 2007 | 200 made | $2,000 | $2,400 |

Foto Flame Stratocaster
1994-1996, 2000. Japanese-made Collectables model, alder and basswood body with Foto Flame (simulated woodgrain) finish on top cap and back of neck.

| 1994-1996 | | $450 | $550 |
| 2000 | | $450 | $550 |

Freddy Tavares Aloha Stratocaster
1993-1994. Custom Shop model, hollow aluminum body with hand engraved Hawaiian scenes, custom inlay on neck, 153 made.

| 1993-1994 | | $5,000 | $6,000 |

Gold Stratocaster
1981-1983. Gold metallic finish, gold-plated brass hardware, 4-bolt neck, maple 'board, skunk strip, trem.

| 1981-1983 | | $1,400 | $1,700 |

Gold Elite Stratocaster
1983-1984. The Elite series feature active electronics and noise-cancelling pickups, the Gold Elite has gold hardware and pearloid tuner buttons, also see Elite Stratocaster and Walnut Elite Stratocaster.

| 1983-1984 | | $1,400 | $1,700 |

Gold Stratocaster (CS)
1989. Custom Shop model, 500 made, gold finish with gold anodized and white 'guards included.

| 1989 | | $1,700 | $2,100 |

MODEL		EXC. COND.	
YEAR	FEATURES	LOW	HIGH

Hank Marvin Stratocaster
1995-1996. Custom Shop model, Feista Red.

| 1995-1996 | | $1,600 | $1,900 |

Hank Marvin 40th Anniversary Stratocaster
1998. Custom Shop logo with '40 Years 1958-1998' marked on back of headstock, Fiesta Red, only 40 made, Custom Shop certificate.

| 1998 | | $5,900 | $7,300 |

Harley-Davidson 90th Anniversary Stratocaster
1993. Custom Shop, 109 total made, Harley-Davidson and Custom Shop V logo on headstock (Diamond Edition, 40 units), 9 units produced for the Harley-Davidson company without diamond logo, 60 units were not Diamond Edition, chrome-plated engraved metal body, engraved 'guard, Custom Shop Certificate important attribute.

| 1993 | | $7,500 | $9,500 |

Hellecaster Stratocaster
1997. Custom Shop model, gold sparkle 'guard, gold hardware, split single-coils, rosewood 'board.

| 1997 | | $1,400 | $1,600 |

Highway One Stratocaster/HSS
2002-present. U.S.-made, alder body, satin lacquer finish, HSS version has humbucker/single/single pickups.

| 2002-2010 | | $575 | $650 |

HM Stratocaster (USA/Import)
1988-1992 ('88 Japanese-made, '89-'90 U.S.- and Japanese-made, '91-'92 U.S.-made). Heavy Metal Strat, Floyd Rose, regular or pointy headstock, black hardware, 1 or 2 humbuckers, 1 single-coil and 1 humbucker, or 2 single-coils and 1 humbucker. Later models have choice of 2 humbuckers and 1 single-coil or 2 single-coils and 1 humbucker.

1988-1990	Bud Dry logo finish	$275	$325
1988-1990	Import	$300	$350
1989-1992	U.S.A.	$425	$525

Homer Haynes HLE Stratocaster
1988-1989. Custom Shop model, '59 Strat basics with gold finish, gold anodized guard, and gold hardware, limited edition of 500.

| 1988-1989 | | $1,600 | $2,000 |

Hot Wheels Stratocaster
2003. Custom Shop model commissioned by Hot Wheels, 16 made, orange flames over blue background, large Hot Wheels logo.

| 2003 | | $2,500 | $3,000 |

HRR Stratocaster
1990-1995. Japanese-made, hot-rodded vintage-style Strat, Floyd Rose tremolo system, 3 pickups, maple neck, Foto Flame, black, Olympic White or sunburst.

| 1990-1995 | | $400 | $450 |

Ike Turner Tribute Stratocaster
2005. Custom Shop model, 100 made, replica of Ike Turner's Sonic Blue Strat.

| 2005 | | $1,850 | $2,000 |

MODEL YEAR	FEATURES	EXC. COND. LOW	HIGH

Jeff Beck Stratocaster

1994-present. Alder body, originally 4 Lace Sensors (H/S/S) changing to 3 Noiseless dual-coils in '03, rosewood 'board, Oly White and Surf Green (Midnight Purple until '02).

| 1994-2002 | Rarer Midnight Purple | $1,100 | $1,300 |
| 1994-2010 | White, Surf Green | $1,000 | $1,100 |

Jeff Beck Signature Stratocaster (CS)

2004-present. Custom Shop, 3 Noiseless dual-coils, Oly White or Surf Green.

| 2004-2010 | | $1,600 | $1,900 |

Jerry Donahue Hellecaster Stratocaster

1997. Made in the Fender Japan Custom Shop as one part of the 3-part Hellecasters Series, limited edition, Seymour Duncan pickups, maple, blue with blue sparkle guard.

| 1997 | | $950 | $1,150 |

Jimi Hendrix Monterey Pop Stratocaster

1997-1998. Custom Shop model, near replica of Monterey Pop Festival sacrifice guitar, red psychedelic-style finish.

| 1997-1998 | | $8,500 | $10,500 |

Jimi Hendrix Tribute Stratocaster

1997-2000. Left-handed guitar strung right-handed, maple cap neck, Olympic White finish. Fender headstock logo positioned upside down, made for right-handed player to look as if they are playing a left-handed guitar flipped over.

| 1997-2000 | | $1,450 | $1,800 |

Jimi Hendrix Voodoo 29th Anniversary Stratocaster

1993. Fender Custom Shop made only 35 for Guitar Center, large 'Guitar Center 29th Anniversary' logo on neckplate, right-handed body with reverse left-handed headstock and reversed Fender headstock logo, purple sparkle finish.

| 1993 | | $2,000 | $2,500 |

Jimi Hendrix Voodoo Stratocaster

1997-2002. Right-handed body with reverse peghead, maple neck, sunburst, Olympic White, or black.

| 1997-1998 | 1st year | $1,600 | $2,000 |
| 1999-2002 | | $1,400 | $1,600 |

Jimmie Vaughan Tex-Mex Stratocaster

1997-present. Poplar body, maple 'board, signature on headstock, 3 Tex-Mex pickups, various colors.

| 1997-2010 | | $400 | $500 |

John Jorgenson Hellecaster Stratocaster

1997. Made in the Fender Japan Custom Shop as one part of the 3-part Hellecasters Series, limited edition, special Seymour Duncan pickups, gold sparkle 'guard, gold hardware, split single-coils, rosewood 'board.

| 1997 | | $1,400 | $1,600 |

John Mayer Limited Edition Black1 Stratocaster

2010. Custom Shop, 83 made, black finish extreme relic, JC serial number, includes personal letter from John Mayer.

| 2010 | | $11,000 | $12,500 |

John Mayer Stratocaster

2005-2010. Custom Shop model alder body, special scooped mid-range pickups, vintage tremolo, special design gigbag with pocket for laptop computer.

| 2005-2010 | | $1,000 | $1,250 |

Koa Stratocaster

2006-2008. Made in Korea, Special Edition series, sunburst over koa veneer top, plain script Fender logo, serial number on back of headstock with.

| 2006-2008 | | $450 | $500 |

Kon Tiki Stratocaster

2003. Custom Shop model, limited run of 25, Tiki Green including Tiki 3-color art work on headstock.

| 2003 | | $1,350 | $1,500 |

Lenny Stratocaster

Introduced Dec. 12, 2007 by Guitar Center stores, Custom Shop model, 185 guitars made, initial product offering price was 17K.

| 2007 | | $8,000 | $9,000 |

Lone Star Stratocaster

1996-2001. Alder body, 1 humbucker and 2 single-coil pickups, rosewood 'board or maple neck, various colors.

| 1996 | 50th Anniv. Badge | $625 | $775 |
| 1997-2001 | | $625 | $775 |

Mark Knopfler Stratocaster

2003-present. '57 body with '62 maple neck.

| 2003-2010 | | $1,200 | $1,400 |

Milonga Deluxe Stratocaster

2005. Special Edition made in Mexico, Vintage Noiseless pickups, rosewood 'board, Olympic White, gold hardware.

| 2005 | | $400 | $425 |

Moto Limited Edition Stratocaster

1990s. Custom Shop model, pearloid cover in various colors, includes Certificate of Authenticity, not to be confused with white pearloid Moto Strat which is part of a guitar and amp set (as listed below).

| 1990s | | $1,500 | $1,700 |

Moto Set Stratocaster

1995-1996. Custom Shop set including guitar, case, amp and amp stand, white pearloid finish.

| 1995-1996 | Red (few made) | $3,900 | $4,100 |
| 1995-1996 | White | $3,600 | $3,900 |

Paisley Stratocaster

1988-1995, 2003-2004, 2008. Japanese-made '72 Strat reissue with a reissue '68 Tele Pink Paisley finish.

| 1988-1995 | 1st issue | $925 | $1,125 |
| 2008 | 200 made | $500 | $550 |

Playboy 40th Anniversary Stratocaster

1994. Custom Shop model, nude Marilyn Monroe graphic on body.

| 1994 | | $7,000 | $8,500 |

Powerhouse/Powerhouse Deluxe Stratocaster

1997-2010. Made in Mexico, Standard Strat configuration with pearloid 'guard, various colors.

| 1997-2010 | | $400 | $500 |
| 2005 | Powerbridge, TRS stereo | $450 | $550 |

Fender Lenny Stratocaster

Fender Mark Knopfler Stratocaster

GUITARS

Fender Ritchie Blackmore Stratocaster

Fender SRV Tribute #1 Stratocaster

MODEL YEAR	FEATURES	EXC. COND. LOW	HIGH

Proud Stratocaster
2003. Custom Shop model, only 3 made to commemorate a United Way and Rock & Roll Hall of Fame project, with only 3 made the value becomes more subjective and collector value may far exceed intrinsic value of similar Custom Shop instruments, the body was painted in detail by Fender's artist.

2003		$3,000	$3,500

Richie Sambora Stratocaster
1993-2002. Alder body, Floyd Rose tremolo, maple neck, sunburst. There was also a cheaper Richie Sambora Standard Stratocaster in blue or white.

1993-2002	USA	$1,700	$1,950
1994-2002	Import	$350	$450

Ritchie Blackmore Stratocaster
2009-present. Based on Blackmore's '70s large headstock model, scalloped rosewood 'board, Duncan Quarter Pound Flat pickups, Olympic White.

2009-2010		$825	$925

Roadhouse Stratocaster
1997-2000. U.S.-made, poplar body, tortoise shell 'guard, maple 'board, 3 Texas Special pickups, various colors.

1997-2000		$800	$900

Roadhouse Stratocaster (Mexico)
2008-present. Deluxe series reissue, Texas Special pickups.

2008-2010		$325	$400

Robert Cray Signature Stratocaster
1991-present. Custom Shop Artist model, rosewood 'board, chunky neck, lighter weight, non-trem, alder body, gold-plated hardware, various colors.

1991-2010		$1,100	$1,250

Robert Cray Stratocaster (Mexico)
1996-present. Artist series, chrome hardware.

1996-2010		$550	$625

Robin Trower Signature Stratocaster
2004-2006. Custom Shop model, 100 made, large headstock (post '65-era styling), with '70s logo styling, post '71 3-bolt neck, bullet truss rod, white.

2004-2006		$1,600	$2,000

Roland Ready Standard Stratocaster
1998-present. Made in Mexico, single synth pickup and 3 single-coils.

1998-2010		$375	$450

Rory Gallagher Tribute Stratocaster
2005. Custom Shop model, heavily distressed '61 model based on Gallagher's guitar, price includes the original Custom Shop certificate, a model without the certificate is worth less, Rory Gallagher logo signature on back of headstock.

2005	With certificate	$2,200	$2,600

Set-Neck Stratocaster
1992-1999. Custom Shop model, mahogany body and figured maple top, 4 pickups, glued-in neck, active electronics, by '96 ash body.

1992-1999		$1,200	$1,500

Short-Scale (7/8) Stratocaster
1989-1995. Similar to Standard Strat, but with 2 control knobs and switch, 24" scale vs. 25" scale, sometimes called a mini-Strat, Japanese import, various colors.

1989-1995		$500	$600

So-Cal Speed Shop L.E. Stratocaster
2005-2006. Limited edition for Musician's Friend, custom red, white, and black So-Cal paint job over basswood body and rosewood 'board, 1 humbucker, So-Cal Speed Shop decal.

2005-2006		$500	$625

Special Edition Stratocaster
2004-2009. Special Edition oval logo on back of headstock, import model, various styles offered, '50s or '60s vintage copy specs, maple fretboard, ash or koa body, see-thru or opaque finish.

2004-2009		$400	$475

Splatter Stratocaster
2003. Made in Mexico, splatter paint job, various color combinations, with gig bag.

2003		$375	$450

Standard Fat Stratocaster
2000-2006. Made in Mexico (vs. California Fat Strat).

2000-2006		$300	$350

Standard HH Stratocaster
2006. Tex Mex Fat Strat humbucker pickups, 1 volume and 2 tone control knobs.

2006		$250	$300

Standard HSS Stratocaster
2006-present. Made in Mexico, humbucker and 2 singles, Floyd Rose tremolo bridge.

2006-2010		$300	$375

Standard Stratocaster (Japan)
1985-1989. Interim production in Japan while the new Fender reorganized, standard pickup configuration and tremolo system, 3 knobs with switch, traditional style input jack, traditional shaped headstock, offered in black, red or white.

1985	Japan on headstock	$500	$700
1986-1989	Japan on back lower neck	$400	$600

Standard Stratocaster (Mexico)
1990-present. Fender Mexico started guitar production in '90. Not to be confused with the American-made Standard Stratocaster of '81-'84. High end of range includes a hard guitar case, while the low end of the range includes only a gig bag, various colors.

1990-1999		$300	$350
2000-2005		$300	$350
2006-2010	Thicker bridge block	$275	$325

Standard Stratocaster Satin Finish
2003-2006. Basically Mexico-made Standard with satin finish.

2003-2006		$200	$275

Stevie Ray Vaughan Stratocaster
1992-present. U.S.-made, alder body, sunburst, gold hardware, SRV 'guard, lefty tremolo, Brazilian rosewood 'board (pau ferro by '93).

1992-2010		$1,000	$1,250

Stevie Ray Vaughan Tribute #1 Stratocaster
2004. Custom Shop model limited edition recreation of SRV's #1 made by Master Builder John Cruz in the Custom Shop, 100 made, $10,000 MSRP,

MODEL YEAR	FEATURES	EXC. COND. LOW	HIGH

includes flight case stenciled "SRV - Number One," and other goodies.

| 2004 | | $16,000 | $20,000 |

Strat Plus

1987-1999. Three Lace Sensor pickups, alder (poplar available earlier) body, tremolo, rosewood 'board or maple neck, various colors. See Deluxe Strat Plus for ash veneer version.

1987-1989	Common colors	$750	$950
1987-1989	Rare colors	$1,000	$1,250
1990-1999	Common colors	$700	$900
1990-1999	Rare colors	$900	$1,100

Strat Pro Closet Classic

2007. Hand written 'Custom Shop' and 'Pro Model' on headstock back.

| 2007 | | $1,475 | $1,675 |

Stratocaster Junior

2004-2006. Import, short 22.7" scale, Alder body, non-trem hardtail bridge.

| 2004-2006 | | $250 | $275 |

Stratocaster Special

1993-1995. Made in Mexico, a humbucker and a single-coil pickup, 1 volume, 1 tone.

| 1993-1995 | | $275 | $300 |

Stratocaster XII

1988-1995. Alder body, maple neck, 21-fret rosewood 'board, 3 vintage Strat pickups, Japanese-made, various colors.

| 1988-1995 | | $575 | $725 |

Strat-o-Sonic

2003-2006. American Special Series, Stratocaster-style chambered body, includes Strat-o-Sonic Dove I (1 pickup, '03 only), Dove II/DV II (2 black P-90s, '03-'06) and HH (2 humbuckers, '05-'06).

2003	Dove I	$625	$725
2003-2006	Dove II/DV II	$1,000	$1,150
2003-2006	HH	$1,000	$1,150

Sub Sonic Stratocaster

2000-2001. Baritone model tuned B-E-A-D-G-B, single-single-hum pickup configuration, Strat-styling.

| 2000-2001 | | $750 | $950 |

Super Strat

1998-2003. Made in Mexico, 3 Super Fat single-coils, Super Switching gives 2 extra pickup options, gold trem.

| 1998-2003 | | $400 | $500 |

Tanqurey Tonic Stratocaster

1988. Made for a Tanqurey Tonic liquor ad campaign giveaway in '88; many were given to winners around the country, ads said that they could also be purchased through Tanqurey, but that apparently didn't happen.

| 1988 | Tanqurey
Tonic Green | $750 | $925 |

Texas Special Stratocaster

1991-1992. Custom Shop model, 50 made, state of Texas map stamped on neck plate, Texas Special pickups, maple fretboard, sunburst.

| 1991-1992 | | $1,700 | $1,900 |

The Strat

1980-1983. Alder body, 4-bolt neck, large STRAT on painted peghead, gold-plated brass hardware, various colors.

| 1980-1983 | Common colors | $950 | $1,050 |
| 1980-1983 | Rare colors | $1,100 | $1,400 |

Tie-Dye Stratocaster

2004-2005. Single-coil neck and humbucker bridge pickups, Band of Gypsies or Hippie Blue tie-dye pattern poly finish.

| 2004-2005 | Band of Gypsies | $275 | $325 |

Tom Delonge Stratocaster

2001-2004. 1 humbucker, rosewood back and sides. Also in Squier version.

| 2001-2004 | | $325 | $425 |

Tree of Life Stratocaster

1993. Custom Shop model, 29 made, tree of life fretboard inlay, 1-piece quilted maple body.

| 1993 | | $6,500 | $8,000 |

Turquoise Sparkle Stratocaster

2001. Custom Shop model, limited run of 75 for Mars Music, turquoise sparkle finish.

| 2001 | | $1,150 | $1,400 |

U.S. Ultra / Ultra Plus Stratocaster

1990-1997. Alder body with figured maple veneer on front and back, single Lace Sensor pickups in neck and middle, double Sensor at bridge, ebony 'board, sunburst.

| 1990-1997 | | $1,200 | $1,500 |

Ventures Limited Edition Stratocaster

1996. Japanese-made tribute model, matches Jazzmaster equivalent, black.

| 1996 | | $950 | $1,050 |

VG Stratocaster

2007-2009. Modeling technology using Fender's classic Strat design and Roland VG circuitry, 5 guitar tone banks deliver 16 sounds.

| 2007-2009 | | $950 | $1,050 |

Vintage Hot Rod Stratocaster

2007-present. Vintage styling with modern features.

| 2007-2010 | '57 Strat | $1,000 | $1,150 |
| 2007-2010 | '62 Strat | $1,000 | $1,150 |

Walnut Elite Stratocaster

1983-1984. The Elite Series features active electronics and noise-cancelling pickups, Walnut Elite has a walnut body and neck, gold-plated hardware and pearloid tuner buttons. Also see Elite Stratocaster and Gold Elite Stratocaster.

| 1983-1984 | | $1,800 | $2,100 |

Walnut Stratocaster

1981-1983. American black walnut body and 1-piece neck and 'board.

| 1981-1983 | | $1,700 | $2,000 |

Western Stratocaster

1995. Custom Shop model, only 5 made, featured in Fender Custom Shop book from the 1990s.

| 1995 | | $9,000 | $11,000 |

Yngwie Malmsteen Stratocaster

1988-present. U.S.-made, maple neck, scalloped 'board, 3 single-coil pickups, blue, red, white.

| 1988-2010 | | $1,100 | $1,400 |

Fender VG Stratocaster

Fender Vintage Hot Rod Stratocaster

GUITARS

1954 Fender Telecaster

Tom Siska

1956 Fender Telecaster

MODEL YEAR	FEATURES	EXC. COND. LOW	HIGH

TC-90/TC-90 Thinline
2004. Made in Korea, semi-hollow thinline, double-cut, Duncan SP-90 pickups stop bar and tune-o-matic tailpiece.

2004		$425	$500

Telecaster
The following are all variations of the Telecaster. The first five listings are for the main American-made models and the '85 interim production Japanese model. All others are listed alphabetically after that in the following order. Broadcaster and Nocaster models are under Broadcaster.

Telecaster
Standard Telecaster
Standard Telecaster (Japan)
American Standard Telecaster
American Series Telecaster
40th Anniversary Telecaster
'50 Custom Telecaster
'50s Telecaster/Classic Series '50s Telecaster
50th Anniversary Spanish Guitar Set Custom Shop
50th Anniversary Telecaster
'52 Telecaster
'60s Telecaster Custom
'60s Telecaster/Classic Series '60s Telecaster
'60 Telecaster Custom
60th Anniversary Telecaster
60th Diamond Anniversary Telecaster
'62 Custom Telecaster (Import)
'62 Custom Telecaster (USA)
'62 Telecaster Reissue (Japan)
'63 Custom Telecaster Relic LTD
'63 Telecaster
'67 Telecaster (CS)
'69 Tele/Telecaster Thinline (Import)
'69 Telecaster Thinline (Custom Shop)
'72 Telecaster Custom (Import)
'72 Telecaster Reissue (Japan)
'72 Telecaster Thinline (Import)
1998 Collectors Edition Telecaster
'90s Tele Thinline
'90s Telecaster Deluxe (Foto-Flame)
Aerodyne Telecaster
Albert Collins Telecaster
Aluminum Telecaster
American Classic Holoflake Telecaster
American Classic Telecaster
American Deluxe HH Telecaster
American Deluxe Power Telecaster
American Deluxe Telecaster
Antigua Telecaster
Big Block Telecaster
Bigsby Telecaster
Black and Gold Telecaster
Blue Flower Telecaster
Buck Owens Limited Edition Telecaster
California Fat Telecaster
California Telecaster
Chambered Mahogany Telecaster

Classic Player Baja Telecaster
Collector's Edition Telecaster
Contemporary Telecaster (Import)
Danny Gatton Telecaster
Deluxe Nashville Telecaster (Mexico)
Deluxe Nashville Power Telecaster
Deluxe Telecaster (USA)
Elite Telecaster
Fat Telecaster
Foto Flame Telecaster
G.E. Smith Telecaster
Highway One Telecaster/Texas Telecaster
HMT Telecaster (Import)
J5 Triple Telecaster Deluxe
James Burton Telecaster
Jerry Donahue JD Telecaster
Jerry Donahue Telecaster
Jim Root Telecaster
Jimmy Bryant Tribute Telecaster
Joe Strummer Telecaster
John Jorgenson Telecaster
Jr. Telecaster
Koa Telecaster
Matched Set Telecaster
Moto Limited Edition Telecaster
Muddy Waters Telecaster
Nashville Telecaster
NHL Premier Edition Telecaster
Nokie Edwards Telecaster
Paisley Telecaster
Plus/Plus Deluxe Telecaster
Rosewood Telecaster
Rosewood Telecaster (Japan)
Set-Neck Telecaster
Sparkle Telecaster
Special Telecaster/Telecaster Special
Standard Telecaster (Mexico)
Telecaster Custom
Telecaster Custom (2nd Edition)
Telecaster Custom (Japan)
Telecaster Custom HH FMT (Korea)
Telecaster Stratocaster Hybrid
Telecaster Thinline (Custom Shop)
Telecaster Thinline/Thinline II
Tele-Sonic
Texas Special Telecaster
Twisted Telecaster Limited Edition
Vintage Hot Rod '52 Telecaster
Will Ray Jazz-A-Caster
Will Ray Mojo Telecaster

Telecaster
1951-1982. See Standard Telecaster (following listing) for '82-'85, American Standard Telecaster for '88-2000 and American Series Telecaster for 2000-'07. Renamed American Standard Telecaster again in '08. In the late '60s and early '70s Fender began to increase their use of vibrato tailpieces. A vibrato tailpiece for this period is generally worth about 13% less than the values shown. Please refer to the Fender Guitar Intro Section for details on Fender color options.

From '63-'70, Fender offered both the standard Brazilian rosewood fretboard and an optional maple fretboard. Prices listed here, for those years, are for the rosewood 'board models. Currently, the market considers the maple 'board to be a premium, so guitars with maple, for those years, are worth 10% to 15% more than the values shown.

MODEL YEAR	FEATURES	EXC. COND. LOW	HIGH
1951	Blond, black 'guard	$30,000	$38,000
1952	Blond, black 'guard	$28,000	$35,000
1953	Blond, black 'guard	$25,000	$32,000
1954	Blond, black 'guard	$25,000	$32,000
1954	Blond, white 'guard	$22,000	$28,000
1955	Blond, white 'guard	$21,000	$26,000
1956	Blond	$20,000	$25,000
1957	Blond	$20,000	$25,000
1958	Blond, backloader	$18,000	$23,000
1958	Blond, top loader	$15,000	$20,000
1958	Sunburst, backloader	$21,000	$26,000
1958	Sunburst, top loader	$18,000	$22,000
1959	Blond, maple	$15,000	$20,000
1959	Blond, slab	$15,000	$20,000
1959	Custom colors	$32,000	$52,000
1959	Sunburst, maple	$17,000	$21,000
1959	Sunburst, slab	$17,000	$21,000
1960	Blond	$15,000	$20,000
1960	Common colors	$20,000	$30,000
1960	Rare colors	$30,000	$50,000
1960	Sunburst	$17,000	$21,000
1961	Blond	$13,000	$16,000
1961	Common colors	$20,000	$30,000
1961	Rare colors	$30,000	$50,000
1961	Sunburst	$16,000	$20,000
1962	Blond, curved	$12,000	$15,000
1962	Blond, slab	$12,000	$15,000
1962	Common colors	$20,000	$30,000
1962	Rare colors	$30,000	$50,000
1962	Sunburst, curved	$15,000	$19,000
1962	Sunburst, slab	$15,000	$19,000
1963	Blond	$11,000	$14,000
1963	Common colors	$18,000	$25,000
1963	Rare colors	$25,000	$40,000
1963	Sunburst	$14,000	$17,000
1964	Blond	$10,000	$13,000
1964	Common colors	$18,000	$25,000
1964	Rare colors	$25,000	$40,000
1964	Sunburst	$13,000	$16,000
1965	Blond	$8,000	$10,000
1965	Common colors	$9,000	$15,000
1965	Rare colors	$15,000	$25,000
1965	Sunburst	$9,000	$11,000
1966	Blond	$7,000	$8,500
1966	Common colors	$11,000	$14,000
1966	Rare colors	$14,000	$21,000
1966	Sunburst	$7,500	$9,000
1967	Blond	$7,000	$8,500
1967	Blond, smuggler	$11,000	$14,000

MODEL YEAR	FEATURES	EXC. COND. LOW	HIGH
1967	Common colors	$11,000	$14,000
1967	Rare colors	$14,000	$21,000
1967	Sunburst	$7,500	$9,000
1968	Blond	$7,000	$8,500
1968	Blue Floral	$10,000	$12,500
1968	Common colors	$10,000	$13,000
1968	Pink Paisley	$10,000	$12,500
1968	Rare colors	$13,000	$20,000
1968	Sunburst	$7,000	$8,500
1969	Blond	$6,000	$7,500
1969	Blue Floral	$10,000	$12,500
1969	Common colors	$10,000	$13,000
1969	Pink Paisley	$10,000	$12,500
1969	Rare colors	$13,000	$18,000
1969	Sunburst	$6,000	$7,500
1970	Blond	$4,500	$5,600
1970	Common colors	$7,500	$9,000
1970	Rare colors	$9,000	$13,000
1970	Sunburst	$4,500	$5,600
1971	Blond	$3,800	$4,500
1971	Common colors	$5,500	$6,500
1971	Rare colors	$6,500	$10,000
1971	Sunburst	$3,800	$4,500
1972	Blond	$2,900	$3,600
1972	Common colors	$3,500	$4,500
1972	Rare colors	$4,500	$6,500
1972	Sunburst	$3,000	$3,500
1973	Black, blond, Lake Placid Blue, Olympic White	$3,000	$3,500
1973	Natural	$2,300	$2,900
1973	Sunburst	$2,900	$3,600
1973	Walnut	$2,800	$3,500
1974	Black, blond, Olympic White	$3,300	$4,000
1974	Natural	$2,300	$2,900
1974	Sunburst	$2,400	$3,000
1974	Walnut	$2,400	$3,000
1975	Black, blond, Olympic White	$2,200	$2,700
1975	Natural	$1,800	$2,500
1975	Sunburst	$1,900	$2,400
1975	Walnut	$1,900	$2,400
1976	Black, blond, Olympic White	$2,000	$2,500
1976	Natural	$1,700	$2,200
1976	Sunburst	$1,700	$2,200
1976	Walnut	$1,700	$2,200
1977	Black, blond, Olympic White, Antigua	$2,000	$2,500
1977	Natural	$1,600	$2,000
1977	Sunburst	$1,700	$2,200
1977	Walnut	$1,700	$2,200
1978	Antigua	$2,000	$2,500
1978	Black, blond, Olympic White, Wine	$2,000	$2,500
1978	Natural	$1,600	$2,000
1978	Sunburst	$1,700	$2,200
1978	Walnut	$1,700	$2,200

1957 Fender Telecaster

Tom Siska

1964 Fender Telecaster

To get the most from this book, be sure to read "Using *The Guide*" in the introduction.

Fender '52 Telecaster

Fender '60 Telecaster Custom

MODEL YEAR	FEATURES	EXC. COND. LOW	HIGH
1979	Antigua	$2,000	$2,500
1979	Black, blond, Olympic White, Wine	$2,000	$2,500
1979	Natural	$1,600	$2,000
1979	Sunburst	$1,700	$2,200
1979	Walnut	$1,700	$2,200
1980	Antigua	$1,900	$2,300
1980	Black, blond, Olympic White, Wine	$1,400	$1,700
1980	International colors	$2,000	$3,000
1980	Natural	$1,325	$1,675
1980	Sunburst	$1,425	$1,775
1981	Black, blond, Olympic White, Wine	$1,400	$1,700
1981	International colors	$2,000	$3,000
1981	Sunburst	$1,225	$1,575

Standard Telecaster

1982-1984. See Telecaster for '51-'82, and American Standard Telecaster (following listing) for '88-2000. Not to be confused with the current Standard Tele-caster, which is made in Mexico.

1982-1984	Blond, sunburst	$1,200	$1,500

Standard Telecaster (Japan)

1985. Interim production in Japan while the new Fender reorganized.

1985		$550	$625

American Standard Telecaster

1988-2000, 2008-present. Name used when Fender re-issued the standard American-made Tele after CBS sold the company. The only American-made Tele available for '86 and '87 was the '52 Telecaster. See Telecaster for '51-'81, and Standard Telecaster for '82-'84. All '94 models have a metal 40th Anniversary pin on the headstock, but should not be confused with the actual 40th Anniversary Telecaster model (see separate listing), all standard col-ors. Renamed the American Series Telecaster in 2000, then back to American Standard Telecaster in '08.

1988-1989		$800	$1,000
1990-2000		$675	$825
2008-2010		$725	$825

American Series Telecaster

2000-2007. See Telecaster for '51-'81, Standard Telecaster for '82-'84, and American Standard for '88-'99. Renamed American Standard again in '08.

2000-2007		$650	$800

40th Anniversary Telecaster

1988, 1999. Custom Shop model limited edition run of 300, 2-piece flamed maple top, gold hardware ('88), flamed maple top over ash body, gold hardware ('99).

1988	1st run, higher-end	$2,200	$2,500
1999	2nd run, plain top	$1,600	$1,800

'50 Custom Telecaster

1997. Custom Shop model, limited run of 10, hum-bucker neck pickup, standard unbound body, highly figured maple neck, blackguard specs.

1997		$1,800	$2,100

'50s Telecaster/Classic Series '50s Telecaster

1990-present. Made in Japan (basswood body) until mid '99, then in Mexico with ash body. Foto-Flame finish offered in '94 (see separate listing).

1990-1999	Japan	$500	$600
1999-2010	Mexico	$475	$525

50th Anniversary Spanish Guitar Set Custom Shop

1996. 50 sets made, Tele Prototype reproduction with similar era copy of woodie amp.

1996		$5,000	$5,500

50th Anniversary Telecaster

1995-1996. Custom Shop model, flame maple top, 2 vintage-style pickups, gold hardware, sunburst, gold 50th Anniversary coin on back of the headstock, 1250 made.

1995-1996		$1,450	$1,600

'52 Telecaster

1982-present. Ash body, maple neck or rosewood 'board, blond.

1982-1984		$2,500	$3,000
1986-1989		$1,200	$1,500
1990-1999		$1,200	$1,500
1990-1999	Copper (limited number)	$1,000	$1,250
2000-2010		$1,075	$1,300

'60s Telecaster Custom

1997-1998. U.S. Custom Shop model, bound alder body, black or custom colors.

1997-1998		$1,500	$1,700

'60s Telecaster/Classic Series '60s Telecaster

1992-present. Made in Japan (basswood body) until mid '99, then in Mexico with ash body. Foto-Flame finish offered in '94 (see separate listing).

1992-1999	Japan	$500	$600
1999-2010	Mexico	$475	$525

'60 Telecaster Custom

2003-2004. Custom Shop model, alder body, offered in NOS, Closet Classic and Relic versions.

2003-2004	Relic	$1,500	$1,800

60th Anniversary Telecaster

2006. Special Edition commemorating Fender's 60th year with banner 60th logo on headstock, neck plate reads Diamond Anniversary 1946-2006, made in U.S.A., sunburst.

2006		$900	$1,000

60th Diamond Anniversary Telecaster

2006. Limited Edition of 1,000, 60 Diamond An-niversary 1946-2006 logo engraved in neck plate, American Flag logo on pickguard, '51 NoCaster pickup layout, 60 wood inlay on the face below bridge, clear nitro finish on natural ash body, silver guitar case with Fender 60 logo on inside lid.

2006		$900	$1,125

'62 Custom Telecaster (Import)

1984-1999. Made in Japan, bound top and back, rosewood 'board, sunburst or red.

1984-1999		$550	$675

MODEL YEAR	FEATURES	EXC. COND. LOW	HIGH

'62 Custom Telecaster (USA)
1999-present. American Vintage Series, rosewood board.

| 1999-2010 | Standard colors | $1,200 | $1,400 |

'62 Telecaster Reissue (Japan)
1989-1990, 2006. Made by Fender Japan.

| 1989-1990 | | $525 | $650 |
| 2006 | | $525 | $650 |

'63 Custom Telecaster Relic LTD
2006. Custom Shop model, Limited Edition.

| 2006 | | $1,900 | $2,100 |

'63 Telecaster
1999-present. Custom Shop model, alder body (or blond on ash), original spec pickups, C-shaped neck, rosewood 'board.

1999-2010	Closet Classic	$1,500	$1,900
1999-2010	NOS	$1,400	$1,800
2007	Relic	$1,600	$2,000

'67 Telecaster (CS)
2005-2008, 2010-present. Custom Shop, alder body, rosewood or maple 'board, Relic, NOS or Closet Classic, 2010 and later is rosewood 'board, Relic or NOS.

| 2005-2008 | Relic | $1,500 | $1,900 |

'69 Tele/Telecaster Thinline (Import)
1986-present. Import, Classic Series, 2 Tele pickups, natural.

| 1986-2010 | | $450 | $550 |

'69 Telecaster Thinline (Custom Shop)
2005-2006. Semi-hollow mahoganhy body, maple neck with maple 'board.

| 2005-2006 | | $1,650 | $2,000 |

'72 Telecaster Custom (Import)
1986-present. Import, Classic Series, 1 humbucker and 1 single-coil, 2 humbuckers after '99.

| 1986-1999 | Japan | $300 | $350 |
| 2000-2010 | Mexico | $300 | $350 |

'72 Telecaster Reissue (Japan)
1994. Made by Fender Japan.

| 1994 | | $550 | $650 |

'72 Telecaster Thinline (Import)
1988-present. Import, Classic Series, 2 humbuckers, f-hole.

| 1988-2010 | | $550 | $650 |

1998 Collectors Edition Telecaster
1998. 1,998 made, 1998 logo inlay on 'board, maple, gold hardware.

| 1998 | | $1,150 | $1,300 |

'90s Tele Thinline
1997-2000. Bound semi-hollow ash body, f-hole, 2 single-coils.

| 1997-2000 | | $750 | $900 |

'90s Telecaster Deluxe (Foto-Flame)
1995-1998. Import, 1 Tele-style bridge pickup and 2 Strat-style pickups, rosewood 'board, Foto Flame '95-'97 and standard finishes '97-'98.

| 1995-1997 | Foto-Flame | $575 | $700 |
| 1997-1998 | Standard finish | $600 | $750 |

Aerodyne Telecaster
2004-2009. Imported Tele with Aerodyne body profile, bound body, black.

| 2004-2009 | | $450 | $550 |

Albert Collins Telecaster
1990-present. U.S.-made Custom Shop signature model, bound swamp ash body, humbucker pickup in neck position.

| 1990-2010 | Natural | $1,250 | $1,350 |
| 1995 | Silver sparkle | $1,350 | $1,450 |

Aluminum Telecaster
1994-1995. Aluminum-bodied American Standard with anodized finish in blue marble, purple marble or red, silver and blue stars and stripes.

| 1994-1995 | Marble patterns | $1,900 | $2,400 |
| 1994-1995 | Red-silver-blue flag option | $2,300 | $2,800 |

American Classic Holoflake Telecaster
1996-1999. Custom Shop model, splatter/sparkle finish, pearloid 'guard.

| 1996-1999 | | $1,550 | $1,900 |

American Classic Telecaster
1996-1999. Custom Shop model, handcrafted version of American Standard, thin lacquer-finished ash body, maple or rosewood 'board, various options and colors, earlier versions had gold hardware and custom-color options.

| 1996-1999 | | $1,100 | $1,350 |

American Deluxe HH Telecaster
2004-2006. Rosewood, maple top, 2 humbucker pickups.

| 2004-2006 | | $800 | $900 |

American Deluxe Power Telecaster
1999-2001. Made in USA, with Fishman power bridge piezo pickups.

| 1999-2001 | | $1,300 | $1,400 |

American Deluxe Telecaster
1998-present. Premium ash or alder body with see-thru finishes.

| 1998-2010 | | $775 | $925 |

Antigua Telecaster
2004. Made in Japan, limited edition (400 made) reissue, '70s features and antigua finish.

| 2004 | | $500 | $600 |

Big Block Telecaster
2005-2006. Pearloid block markers, black with matching headstock, 3 single-coils with center pickup reverse wound.

| 2005-2006 | | $600 | $675 |

Bigsby Telecaster
2003. Made in Mexico, standard Tele specs with original Fender-logo Bigsby tailpiece.

| 2003 | | $500 | $600 |

Black and Gold Telecaster
1981-1982. Black finish, gold-plated brass hardware.

| 1981-1982 | | $1,000 | $1,200 |

Blue Flower Telecaster
1986-1993, 2003-2004. Import, Blue Flower finish.

| 1986-1993 | 1st issue | $900 | $1,100 |
| 2003-2004 | 2nd issue | $500 | $550 |

Buck Owens Limited Edition Telecaster
1998. Red, white and blue sparkle finish, gold hardware, gold 'guard, rosewood 'board.

| 1998-2002 | | $1,200 | $1,350 |

Fender '62 Custom Telecaster

Fender Albert Collins Telecaster

GUITARS

Fender Danny Gatton Telecaster

Fender James Burton Telecaster

MODEL YEAR	FEATURES	EXC. COND. LOW	HIGH

California Fat Telecaster
1997-1998. Alder body, maple fretboard, Tex-Mex humbucker and Tele pickup configuration.

1997-1998		$500	$600

California Telecaster
1997-1998. Alder body, maple fretboard, sunburst, Tex-Mex Strat and Tele pickup configuration.

1997-1998		$500	$600

Chambered Mahogany Telecaster
2006. U.S.-made, chambered mahogany body, Delta Tone System.

2006		$975	$1,050

Classic Player Baja Telecaster
2007-present. Made in Mexico, Custom Shop designed neck plate logo, thin gloss poly blond finish.

2007-2010		$525	$600

Collector's Edition Telecaster
1998. Mid-1955 specs including white 'guard, offered in sunburst with gold hardware (which was an option in '55), 1,998 made.

1998		$1,300	$1,600

Contemporary Telecaster (Import)
1985-1987. Japanese-made while the new Fender reorganized, 2 or 3 pickups, vibrato, black chrome hardware, rosewood 'board.

1985-1987		$300	$375

Danny Gatton Telecaster
1990-present. Custom Shop model, like '53 Telecaster, maple neck, 2 humbuckers.

1990-1999	Frost Gold	$1,900	$2,300

Deluxe Nashville Telecaster (Mexico)
1997-present. Made in Mexico, Tex-Mex Strat and Tele pickup configuration, various colors.

1997-2010		$525	$575

Deluxe Nashville Power Telecaster
1999-present. Like Deluxe Nashville, but with piezo transducer in each saddle.

1999-present		$475	$550

Deluxe Telecaster (USA)
1972-1981. Two humbuckers, various colors. Mexican-made version offered starting in 2004.

1972		$2,700	$3,200
1973		$2,700	$3,200
1974		$2,700	$3,200
1975		$2,200	$2,700
1976		$2,200	$2,700
1977		$2,200	$2,700
1978		$2,200	$2,700
1978-1979	Antigua	$2,500	$3,000
1979-1981		$1,700	$2,100

Elite Telecaster
1983-1985. Two active humbucker pickups, 3-way switch, 2 volume knobs, 1 presence and filter controls, chrome hardware, various colors.

1983-1985		$1,150	$1,400

Fat Telecaster
1999-2001. Humbucker pickup in neck, Tele bridge pickup.

1999-2001		$700	$800

Foto Flame Telecaster
1994-1996. Import, sunburst or transparent.

1994-1996		$450	$550

G.E. Smith Telecaster
2007-present. Swamp ash body, vintage style hardware, U-shaped neck, oval and diamond inlays.

2007-2010		$1,200	$1,500

Highway One Telecaster/Texas Telecaster
2003-present. U.S.-made, alder body, satin lacquer finish, Texas version (introduced in '04) has ash body and Hot Vintage pickups.

2003-2010		$700	$900

HMT Telecaster (Import)
1990-1993. Japanese-made Metal-Rock Tele, available with or without Floyd Rose tremolo, 1 Fender Lace Sensor pickup and 1 DiMarzio bridge humbucker pickup, black.

1990-1993		$275	$325

J5 Triple Telecaster Deluxe
2007-present. John 5 model, made in Mexico, 3 humbuckers, medium jumbo frets.

2007-2010		$650	$775

James Burton Telecaster
1990-present. Ash body, 3 Fender Lace pickups, available in black with Gold Paisley, black with Candy Red Paisley, Pearl White, and Frost Red until '05. In '06 in black with red or blue flame-shaped paisley, or Pearl White.

1990-2005	Black & gold paisley, gold hardware	$1,125	$1,300
1990-2005	Black & red paisley, black hardware	$1,225	$1,400
1990-2010	Frost Red or Pearl White	$825	$900
2006-2010	Paisley flames	$1,050	$1,150

Jerry Donahue JD Telecaster
1993-1999. Made in Japan, Custom Strat neck pickup and Custom Tele bridge pickup, basswood body, special "V" shaped maple neck.

1993-1999		$675	$800

Jerry Donahue Telecaster
1992-2001. Custom Shop model designed by Donahue, Tele bridge pickup and Strat neck pickup, birdseye maple neck, top and back, gold hardware, passive circuitry, there was also a Japanese JD Telecaster.

1992-1999	Sunburst	$1,400	$1,600
1992-1999	Transparent Crimson or Sapphire Blue	$1,600	$1,800

Jim Root Telecaster
2007-present. Made in Mexico, black hardware, mahogany body, goes to 11.

2007-2010		$625	$750

Jimmy Bryant Tribute Telecaster
2004-2005. Custom Shop model, hand-tooled leather 'guard overlay with JB initials.

2004-2005		$1,900	$2,100

Joe Strummer Telecaster
Released July 2007-2009. Limited edition, heavily factory-distressed model based on the '66 Tele he used

MODEL YEAR	FEATURES	EXC. COND. LOW	HIGH

with his band The Clash, 'Rock Revolution' engraved neckplate, Fender also offered a unique limited edition art customization kit as part of the product package.

| 2007-2009 | | $600 | $750 |

John Jorgenson Telecaster

1998-2001. Custom Shop model, double-coil stacked pickups, sparkle or black finish, korina body.

| 1998-2001 | Sparkle | $1,600 | $1,900 |

Jr. Telecaster

1994, 1997-2000. Custom Shop model, transparent blond ash body, 2 P-90-style pickups, set neck, 11 tone chambers, 100 made in '94, reintroduced in '97.

| 1994 | | $1,600 | $1,900 |
| 1997-2000 | | $1,600 | $1,900 |

Koa Telecaster

2006-2008. Made in Korea, Special Edition series, standard Tele specs, koa veneer top over basswood body, pearloid 'guard, sunburst.

| 2006-2008 | | $400 | $475 |

Matched Set Telecaster

1994. Matching Tele and Strat Custom Shop models, model name on certificate is "Matched Set Telecaster", 3 sets were built, each set has serial number 1, 2, or 3.

| 1994 | | $3,000 | $3,500 |

Moto Limited Edition Telecaster

1990s. Custom Shop model, pearloid cover in various colors. There were also Strat and Jag versions.

| 1990s | | $1,500 | $1,700 |

Muddy Waters Telecaster

2001-2009. Made in Mexico, MZ serial number, Fender amp control knobs, Telecaster Custom on headstock, Muddy Waters signature logo on neck plate, Candy Apple Red.

| 2001-2009 | | $425 | $500 |

Nashville Telecaster

1995. Custom Shop model, 3 pickups.

| 1995 | | $1,700 | $1,900 |

NHL Premier Edition Telecaster

1999-2000. Limited edition of 100 guitars with NHL hockey art logo on the top.

| 1999-2000 | | $1,300 | $1,600 |

Nokie Edwards Telecaster

1996. Made in Japan, limited edition, book matched flamed top, multi-lam neck, Seymour Duncan pickups, gold hardware, zero fret, tilted headstock.

| 1996 | | $1,700 | $2,000 |

Paisley Telecaster

1986-1998, 2003-2004, 2008. Import, Pink Paisley finish.

1986-1989		$925	$1,125
1990-1998		$900	$1,100
2003-2004		$500	$550
2008	600 made	$500	$550

Plus/Plus Deluxe Telecaster

1990-1997. Tele with Strat 3-pickup combination, Deluxe has added Strat-style tremolo system, various colors.

| 1990-1997 | 2 pickups | $1,200 | $1,500 |
| 1990-1997 | 3 pickups | $900 | $1,100 |

Rosewood Telecaster

1969-1972. Rosewood body and neck.

| 1969-1972 | | $10,000 | $12,000 |

Rosewood Telecaster (Japan)

1986-1996. Japanese-made reissue, rosewood body and neck.

| 1986-1996 | | $1,550 | $1,850 |

Set-Neck Telecaster

1990-1996. Glued-in neck, Custom Shop, 2 humbucking pickups, Set-Neck CA (Country Artist) has 1 humbucker and 1 Tele pickup, various colors.

| 1990-1996 | | $1,200 | $1,500 |

Sparkle Telecaster

1993-1995. Custom Shop model, poplar body, white 'guard, sparkle finish: champagne, gold, silver.

| 1993-1995 | | $1,400 | $1,600 |

Special Telecaster/Telecaster Special

2004. Made in Mexico, Special Edition logo with star logo sticker on back of headstock, special features like 6-way bridge and modern tuners.

| 2004 | | $425 | $475 |

Standard Telecaster (Mexico)

1990-present. Guitar production at the Mexico facility started in '91. High end of range includes a hard guitar case, while the low end of the range includes only a gig bag, various colors.

| 1990-1999 | | $300 | $350 |
| 2000-2010 | | $300 | $350 |

Telecaster Custom

1959-1972. Body bound top and back, rosewood 'board, 2 Tele pickups, see Telecaster Custom (2nd Edition) for the 1 Tele/1 humbucker version. Please refer to the Fender Guitar Intro Section for details on Fender color options.

1959	Sunburst, maple	$20,000	$24,000
1960	Custom colors	$25,000	$70,000
1960	Sunburst	$18,000	$22,000
1961	Custom colors	$25,000	$70,000
1961	Sunburst	$18,000	$22,000
1962	Custom colors	$21,000	$45,000
1962	Sunburst	$16,000	$20,000
1963	Custom colors	$21,000	$45,000
1963	Sunburst	$16,000	$20,000
1964	Custom colors	$19,000	$42,000
1964	Sunburst	$13,000	$20,000
1965	Custom colors	$15,000	$38,000
1965	Sunburst	$8,900	$15,000
1966	Custom colors	$12,000	$28,000
1966	Sunburst	$8,800	$11,000
1967	Custom colors	$11,800	$27,000
1967	Sunburst	$8,200	$10,500
1968	Custom colors	$10,800	$24,000
1968	Sunburst	$8,000	$10,000
1969	Custom colors	$9,800	$23,000
1969	Sunburst	$7,500	$9,500
1970	Custom colors	$7,400	$17,000
1970	Sunburst	$5,600	$7,100
1971	Custom colors, 3-bolt	$4,500	$6,700
1971	Custom colors, 4-bolt	$7,000	$15,000

Fender Joe Strummer Telecaster

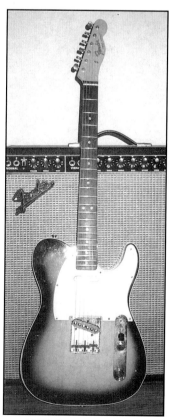

1967 Fender Telecaster Custom

1972 Fender Telecaster Thinline

*Fender Vintage Hot Rod '52
Telecaster*

MODEL YEAR	FEATURES	EXC. COND. LOW	HIGH
1971	Sunburst, 3-bolt	$3,600	$4,500
1971	Sunburst, 4-bolt	$5,000	$6,200
1972	Custom colors, 3-bolt	$4,500	$6,700
1972	Sunburst, 3-bolt	$3,000	$3,700

Telecaster Custom (2nd Edition)
1972-1981. One humbucking and 1 Tele pickup, standard colors, see above for 2 Tele pickup version. Also called Custom Telecaster.

1972-1974		$2,800	$3,500
1975-1979		$2,600	$3,200
1980		$2,400	$3,000
1981		$2,200	$2,800

Telecaster Custom (Japan)
1985. Made in Japan during the period when Fender suspended all USA manufacturing in '85, Tele Custom specs including bound body.

| 1985 | | $550 | $625 |

Telecaster Custom HH FMT (Korea)
2003-present. Part of Special Edition, Korean-made, flamed maple top, 2 humbuckers.

| 2003-2010 | | $350 | $450 |

Telecaster Stratocaster Hybrid
2006. Custom Shop model, Tele body shape, Strat pickup system and wiring, Strat headstock shape, dot markers on rosewood board, reissue tremolo, includes Custom Shop Certificate that reads "Telecaster Stratocaster Hybrid".

| 2006 | | $2,300 | $2,500 |

Telecaster Thinline (Custom Shop)
1990s. Custom Shop version.

| 1990s | | $1,200 | $1,500 |

Telecaster Thinline/Thinline II
1968-1980. Semi-hollowbody, 1 f-hole, 2 Tele pickups, ash or mahogany body, in late-'71 the tilt neck was added and the 2 Tele pickups were switched to 2 humbuckers. Please refer to the Fender Guitar Intro Section for details on Fender color options.

1968	Common colors	$9,000	$11,000
1968	Natural ash	$6,000	$7,500
1968	Natural mahogany	$6,000	$7,500
1968	Rare colors	$11,000	$18,000
1968	Sunburst	$6,000	$7,500
1969	Common colors	$8,500	$10,500
1969	Natural ash	$6,000	$7,500
1969	Natural mahogany	$6,000	$7,500
1969	Rare colors	$10,500	$17,000
1969	Sunburst	$6,000	$7,500
1970	Common colors	$5,000	$7,000
1970	Natural ash	$3,500	$4,200
1970	Natural mahogany	$3,500	$4,200
1970	Rare colors	$7,000	$11,000
1970	Sunburst	$5,000	$6,000
1971	Color option, 3-bolt	$4,500	$6,000
1971	Color option, 4-bolt	$5,000	$11,000
1971	Natural ash, 3-bolt	$3,300	$3,800
1971	Natural ash, 4-bolt	$3,500	$4,200
1971	Natural mahogany, 3-bolt	$3,300	$3,800
1971	Natural mahogany, 4-bolt	$3,500	$4,200

MODEL YEAR	FEATURES	EXC. COND. LOW	HIGH
1971	Sunburst, 3-bolt	$3,800	$4,700
1971	Sunburst, 4-bolt	$5,000	$6,000
1972-1974	Color option	$3,000	$3,500
1972-1974	Mahogany, humbuckers	$2,600	$3,200
1972-1974	Natural ash, humbuckers	$2,600	$3,200
1972-1974	Sunburst, humbuckers	$2,600	$3,200
1975	Color option	$3,000	$3,500
1975	Natural ash, humbuckers	$2,600	$3,200
1975	Sunburst, humbuckers	$2,600	$3,200
1976-1978	Color option	$3,000	$3,500
1976-1978	Natural ash, humbuckers	$2,600	$3,200
1976-1978	Sunburst, humbuckers	$2,600	$3,200

Tele-Sonic
1998-2000. U.S.A., chambered Telecaster body, 2 DeArmond pickups, dot markers, upper bass bout 3-way toggle switch.

| 1998-2000 | | $750 | $850 |

Texas Special Telecaster
1991. Custom Shop model, 60 made, state of Texas outline on the 'guard, ash body with Texas Orange transparent finish, large profile maple neck.

| 1991 | | $1,700 | $1,900 |

Twisted Telecaster Limited Edition
2005. Custom Shop, 50 built by Master Builder Yuriy Shishkov, 100 built by the Custom Shop team, top loaded Bigsby.

| 2005 | Shishkov built | $3,500 | $3,800 |
| 2005 | Team built | $2,500 | $2,800 |

Vintage Hot Rod '52 Telecaster
2007-present. '52 Tele Reissue with spec changes to neck, '07-'08 in blond only, '09 added black finish with white guard.

| 2007-2010 | | $1,000 | $1,150 |

Will Ray Jazz-A-Caster
1997. Made in Fender Japan Custom Shop as one part of the three part Hellecasters Series, Strat neck on a Tele body with 2 soap-bar Seymour Duncan Jazzmaster-style pickups, gold leaf finish, limited edition.

| 1997 | | $975 | $1,200 |

Will Ray Mojo Telecaster
1998-2001. Custom Shop, ash body, flamed maple Strat neck, locking tuners, rosewood 'board, skull inlays, double coil pickups, optional Hipshot B bender.

| 1998-2001 | | $3,000 | $3,300 |

Toronado/Toronado Deluxe
1999-2006. Contoured offset-waist body.

1999-2001	Atomic humbuckers	$400	$500
1999-2001	DE-9000 P-90s	$400	$475
2002-2006	GT with racing stripes, humbuckers	$400	$500

Villager 12-String
1965-1969, 2011-present. Acoustic flat-top, spruce top, mahogany back and sides, 12 strings, natural.

The *Vintage Guitar Price Guide* shows low to high values for items in all-original excellent condition, and, where applicable, with original case or cover.

MODEL YEAR	FEATURES	EXC. COND. LOW	HIGH

Reintroduced in '11 with on-board Fishman System, made in China.

1965-1969		$500	$600
2011	Reintroduced	$300	$350

Violin - Electric

1958-1976. Sunburst is the standard finish.

1958-1959		$1,600	$1,900
1960-1969		$1,500	$1,800
1970-1976		$1,400	$1,700

Wildwood

1963-1971. Acoustic flat-top with Wildwood dyed top.

1966-1971	Various (unfaded)	$1,200	$1,500

Fenton-Weill

See info under Burns-Weill.

Fernandes

1969-present. Established in Tokyo. Early efforts were classical guitars, but they now offer a variety of intermediate grade, production, imported guitars and basses.

Nomad Travel/Nomad Deluxe

1998-present. Unusual body style, extra large banana headstock, built-in effects, amp and speaker. Deluxe models have added features..

1998-2010	Standard	$175	$225
2000-2009	Deluxe	$500	$600
2010	Deluxe, Digitech FX	$650	$800

Fina

Production classical and steel-string guitars built at the Kwo Hsiao Music Wooden Factory in Huiyang City, Guang Dong, mainland China. They also build acoustic basses.

Finck, David

1986-present. Luthier David Finck builds his production/custom, professional and premium grade, acoustic guitars, presently in Valle Crucis, North Carolina. In the past, he has built in Pittsburg, Kansas and Reader, West Virginia.

Fine Resophonic

1988-present. Professional and premium grade, production/custom, wood and metal-bodied resophonic guitars (including reso-electrics) built by luthiers Mike Lewis and Pierre Avocat in Vitry Sur Seine, France. They also build ukes and mandolins.

First Act

1995-present. Budget and professional grade, production/custom, acoustic, solid and semi-hollow body guitars built in China and in their Custom Shop in Boston. They also make basses, violins, and other instruments.

Firth Pond & Company

1822-1867. Firth and Pond was an east coast retail distributor that had Martin Guitars and Ashborn Guitars private brand instruments. The company operated as Firth and Hall from 1822-1841, also known as Firth, Hall & Pond, the company operated in New York City and Litchfield, Connecticut. Most instruments were small parlor size (11" lower bout) guitars, as was the case for most builders of this era. Brazilian rosewood sides and back instruments fetch considerably more than most of the other tone woods and value can vary considerably based on condition. Guitars from the 1800s are sometimes valued more as antiques than working vintage guitars. In 1867 Firth & Sons sold out to Oliver Ditson, a company which went on to become an important progressive force in the guitar distributor retailer business. Sometimes the inside back center seam will be branded Firth & Pond.

Flammang Guitars

1990-present. Premium grade, custom/production, steel string guitars built by luthier David Flammang in Greene, Iowa and previously in East Hampton and Higganum, Connecticut.

Flaxwood

2004-present. Professional grade, production/custom, solid and semi-hollow body guitars built in Finland, with bodies of natural fiber composites.

Fleishman Instruments

1974-present. Premium and presentation grade, custom flat-tops made by luthier Harry Fleishman in Sebastopol, California. He also offers basses and electric uprights. Fleishman is the director of Luthiers School International.

Fletcher Brock Stringed Instruments

1992-present. Custom flat-tops and archtops made by luthier Fletcher Brock originally in Ketchum, Idaho, and currently in Seattle, Washington. He also builds mandolin family instruments.

Flowers Guitars

1993-present. Premium grade, custom, archtop guitars built by luthier Gary Flowers in Baltimore, Maryland.

Floyd Rose

2004-2006. Floyd Rose, inventor of the Floyd Rose Locking Tremolo, produced a line of intermediate and professional grade, production, solidbody guitars from '04 to '06. They continue to offer bridges and other accessories.

Foggy Mountain

2005-present. Intermediate grade, production, steel and nylon string acoustic and acoustic/electric guitars imported from China.

Fontanilla Guitars

1987-present. Luthier Allan Fontanilla builds his premium grade, production/custom, classical guitars in San Francisco, California.

2005 First Act Volkwagen Ragemaster

Fontanilla Classical

GUITARS

Framus Strato de Luxe

Fraulini Leadbelly 12-string Reproduction

MODEL YEAR	FEATURES	EXC. COND. LOW	HIGH

Fouilleul

1978-present. Production/custom, classical guitars made by luthier Jean-Marie Fouilleul in Cuguen, France.

Fox or Rocking F

1983-present. Premium grade, custom, steel string acoustic guitars built in Seattle, Washington by luthier Cat Fox.

Foxxe

1990-1991. Short-lived brand of solidbodies offered by the same company that produced Barrington guitars, Korean-made.

Frame Works

1995-present. Professional grade, production/custom, steel- and nylon-string guitars built by luthier Frank Krocker in Burghausen, Germany. The instruments feature a neck mounted on a guitar-shaped frame. Krocker has also built traditional archtops, flat-tops, and classicals.

Framus

1946-1977, 1996-present. Professional and premium grade, production/custom, guitars made in Markneukirchen, Germany. They also build basses, amps, mandolins and banjos. Frankische Musikindustrie (Framus) founded in Erlangen, Germany by Fred Wilfer, relocated to Bubenreuth in '54, and to Pretzfeld in '67. Begun as an acoustic instrument manufacturer, Framus added electrics in the mid-'50s. Earliest electrics were mostly acoustics with pickups attached. Electric designs begin in early-'60s. Unique feature was a laminated maple neck with many thin plies. By around '64-'65 upscale models featured the organtone, often called a spigot, a spring-loaded volume control that allowed you to simulate a Leslie speaker effect. Better models often had mutes and lots of switches.

In the '60s, Framus instruments were imported into the U.S. by Philadelphia Music Company. Resurgence of interest in ca. '74 with the Jan Akkermann hollowbody followed by original mid-'70s design called the Nashville, the product of an alliance with some American financing.

The brand was revived in '96 by Hans Peter Wilfer, the president of Warwick, with production in Warwick's factory in Germany.

Amateur

Early 1960s to mid-1970s. Model 5/1, small flat-top, early without pickguard, plain, dot markers.

1960s-70s		$200	$250

Atilla Zoller AZ-10

Early-1960s-early-1980s. Single-cut archtop, 2 pickups, neck glued-in until the '70s, bolt-on after, sunburst. Model 5/65 (rounded cutaway, made until late '60s) and Model 5/67 (sharp cutaway).

1960s	Model 5/65	$600	$700
1960s-70s	Model 5/67	$600	$700

Atlantic

Ca. 1965-ca. 1970. Model 5/110, single-cut thin body electric archtop, 2 pickups, tremolo optional.

1965-1970		$475	$600

Atlantic (08000) Elec-12

Mid to late 1960s. Model 5/011 and 5/013, double cut semi-hollow, 2 pickups, 12-string.

1960s	Model 5/013	$475	$600

Big 18 Doubleneck

Late 1960s. Model 5/200 is a solidbody and Model 5/220 is acoustic.

1960s	Model 5/200	$650	$750
1960s	Model 5/220	$650	$750

Caravelle

Ca.1965-ca. 1975. Model 5/117-52 2 pickups and 5/117-54 3 pickups, double-cut archtop, tremolo.

1965-1975		$550	$675

Gaucho

Late 1960s-mid 1970s. Model 5/194, lower grade flat-top, concert size, spruce top, mahogany sides and back, rosewood bridge and 'board, sunburst or natural finish.

1970s		$250	$300

Jan Akkerman

1974-1977. Single-cut semi-hollowbody, 2 pickups, gold hardware.

1974-1977		$325	$375

Jumbo

1963-late 1970s. Models earlier 5/97, later 5/197, jumbo flat-top, mahogany or maple sides and back.

1963-70s		$350	$400

Jumbo 12-String

Late 1960s-mid 1970s. Model 5/297, 12-string version.

1960s-70s		$375	$450

Missouri (E Framus Missouri)

Ca.1955-ca. 1975. Originally non-cut acoustic archtop until early '60s when single-cut archtop with 1 or 2 pickups added.

1960s	Model 5/60	$325	$400

New Sound Series

Late 1950s to mid-1960s. Model 5/116-52 2 pickups and Model 5/116-54 has 3, double-cut thin line.

1960s	Model 5/115-54	$650	$800
1960s	Model 5/116-52	$600	$750

Sorella Series

Ca.1955-mid 1970s. Single-cut, Model 5/59 is acoustic archtop (with or without single pickup), 5/59-50 is 1-pickup electric archtop, 5/59-52 is electric 2-pickup.

1955-1975	Model 5/59	$500	$600
1965-1972	Model 5/59-50	$550	$675
1965-1972	Model 5/59-52	$575	$700

Sorento

Ca.1963-ca. 1970. Model 5/112, thinline archtop, single-cut, 2 pickups, organ effect, f-holes.

1963-1970		$550	$675

Sorento 12

Ca.1963-ca. 1970. Model 5/012, 12-string version.

1963-1970		$600	$750

Sport

Early 1950s-mid-1970s. Model 50/1, small beginner flat-top, plain appointments, dot markers.

1950s-70s		$175	$225

MODEL YEAR	FEATURES	EXC. COND. LOW	HIGH

Strato de Luxe Series

Ca.1964-ca. 1970. 1, 2 (5/155, 5/167-52, 5/168-52) or 3 (5/167-54, 5/168-54) pickups, some models have gold hardware.

1960s	2 pickups	$525	$625
1960s	3 pickups	$625	$750

Strato de Luxe 12 String

Ca. 1963-ca. 1970. Model 5/067(metal pickguard) and 5/068 (wood grain pickguard and large gold cover plates), 2 pickups, tremolo.

1963-1970	Model 5/068	$625	$750

Strato Super

Early to late 1960s. Model 5/155-52, offset double-cut, 2 pickups.

1960s		$625	$750

Studio Series

Late 1950s-mid 1970s. Model 5/51 (a.k.a. 030) is non-cut acoustic archtop (some with pickup - 5/51E), 5/108 is electric archtop, 1 pickup.

1960s	Model 5/51, E	$200	$275
1960s	Model 5/108	$275	$350

Television Series

Early to late 1960s. Model 5/118-52 2 pickups and 5/118-54 3 pickups, offset double-cut thinline hollowbody.

1960s	Model 5/118-52	$550	$650
1960s	Model 5/118-54	$650	$750

Texan Series

Late 1960s-early 1980s. Model 5/196, 5/196E (with pickup) and 5/296 12-string flat-top, mahogany back and sides. 6-string ends in late '70s.

1960s-80s	12-string	$250	$325
1960s-70s	6-string	$250	$325

Western

1960s. Model 5/195, grand concert size, lower grade flat-top, spruce top, maple sides and back.

1960s		$275	$325

Fraulini

2001-present. Luthier Todd Cambio builds his professional and premium grade, primarily custom, early 20th century style guitars, in Madison, Wisconsin.

FreeNote

Intermediate to professional grade, the innovative FreeNote 12-Tone Ultra Plus provides two frets for every traditional fret placement which provides an unlimited number of playable notes.

Fresher

1973-1985. The Japanese-made Fresher brand models were mainly copies of popular brands and were not imported into the U.S., but they do show up at guitar shows. They also made basses.

Solidbody Electric

1970s. Import from Japan.

1970s		$225	$300

Fret-King

2008-present. Luthier Trev Wilkinson builds professional and premium grade, production, solidbody and semi-hollow electric guitars in Yorkshire, U.K., and also offers a line imported from Korea. He also builds basses.

Fritz Brothers

1988-present. Premium grade, production/custom, acoustic, semi-hollow, and solidbody guitars built by luthier Roger Fritz, originally in Mobile, Alabama, currently in Mendocino, California. He also builds basses.

Froggy Bottom Guitars

1970-present. Luthier Michael Millard builds his premium and presentation grade, production/custom flat-tops in Newfane, Vermont (until '84 production was in Richmond, New Hampshire).

Frudua Guitar Works

1988-present. Luthier Galeazzo Frudua builds his intermediate to premium grade, production/custom, electric guitars in Imola, Italy. He also builds basses and amps.

Fukuoka Musical Instruments

1993-present. Custom steel- and nylon-string flat-tops and archtops built in Japan.

Furch

See listing for Stonebridge.

Furnace Mountain Guitar Works

1995-1999. Instruments built by luthier Martin Fair in New Mexico. He currently builds under the Fairbuilt Guitar Co. brand.

Fury

1962-present. Founded by Glenn McDougall in Saskatoon, Saskatchewan, Fury currently offers production, solidbody electrics. They also build basses. They have built hollow and semi-hollow body guitars in the past.

Futurama

1957-mid to late 1960s. Futurama was a brand name used by Selmer in the United Kingdom. Early instruments made by the Drevokov Cooperative in Czechoslovakia, models for '63-'64 made by Sweden's Hagstrom company. Some later '60s instruments may have been made in Japan. Hobbyists will recognize the brand name as Beatle George Harrison's first electric.

Futurama/Futurama II

1960s. Offset double-cut, 2- or 3-pickup versions available, large Futurama logo on headstock with the reverse capital letter F.

1960s		$400	$500

Fylde Guitars

1973-present. Luthier Roger Bucknall builds his professional and premium grade, production/custom acoustic guitars in Penrith, Cumbria, United Kingdom. He also builds basses, mandolins, mandolas, bouzoukis, and citterns.

Fret-King Blue Label Esprit 3

Fukuoka FN Standard

G & L ASAT Classic

G & L Classic Blues Boy

MODEL YEAR	FEATURES	EXC. COND. LOW	HIGH

G & L

1980-present. Intermediate and professional grade, production/custom, solidbody and semi-hollowbody electric guitars made in the U.S. and overseas. They also make basses. Founded by Leo Fender and George Fullerton following the severance of ties between Fender's CLF Research and Music Man. Company sold to John MacLaren and BBE Sound, when Leo Fender died in '91. In '98 they added their Custom Creations Department. In '03 G & L introduced the Korean-made G & L Tribute Series. George Fullerton died in July, '09.

ASAT
1986-1998. Called the Broadcaster in '85. Two or 3 single-coil or 2 single-coil/1 humbucker pickup configurations until early-'90s, 2 single-coils after.

1986		$1,000	$1,200
1987	Leo sig. on headstock	$1,200	$1,400
1988-1991	Leo sig. on body	$1,100	$1,300
1992-1998	BBE era	$775	$925

ASAT 20th Anniversary
2000. Limited Edition of 50, ash body, tinted birdseye maple neck, 2-tone sunburst.

2000		$1,100	$1,300

ASAT '50
1999. Limited edition of 10.

1999		$1,200	$1,500

ASAT Bluesboy Limited Edition
1999. Limited edition of 20.

1999		$1,100	$1,400

ASAT Bluesboy Semi-Hollow Limited Edition
1999. Limited edition of 12, thin semi-hollow.

1999		$1,200	$1,500

ASAT Classic
1990-present. Two single-coil pickups, individually adjustable bridge saddles, neck-tilt adjustment and tapered string posts.

1990-1991	Leo sig. on body	$1,100	$1,300
1992-1997	3-bolt neck	$775	$950
1997-2010	4-bolt neck	$675	$850

ASAT Classic B-Bender
1997. 12 made with factory-original B-Bender.

1997		$1,200	$1,500

ASAT Classic Bluesboy
2001-present. Humbucker neck pickup, single-coil at bridge.

2001-2010		$875	$975

ASAT Classic Bluesboy Rustic
2010-present. Classic Bluesboy configuration including nitrocellulous lacquer finish, Rustic refinement includes boxed steel bridge with individual brass saddles for each string and Rustic aging for broke-in feel.

2010		$1,300	$1,500

ASAT Classic Bluesboy Semi-Hollow
1997-present. Chambered Classic with f-hole.

1997-2010		$900	$1,000

MODEL YEAR	FEATURES	EXC. COND. LOW	HIGH

ASAT Classic Commemorative
1991-1992. Leo Fender signature and birth/death dating.

1991-1992	Australian lacewood, 6 made	$4,000	$5,000
1991-1992	Cherryburst, 350 made	$875	$975

ASAT Classic Custom
1996-1997, 2002-present. Large rectangular neck pickup, single-coil bridge pickup.

1996-1997	1st version	$700	$850
2002-2010	2nd version, 4-bolt neck	$750	$900

ASAT Classic Custom Semi-Hollow
2002-present. Custom with f-hole.

2002-2010		$750	$900

ASAT Classic S
2007. Limited run of 50, certificate, swamp ash body, 3 single-coil pickups, Nashville pickup configuration.

2007		$850	$925

ASAT Classic Semi-Hollow
1997-present. With f-hole.

1997-2010		$850	$925

ASAT Classic Three
1998. Limited Edition of 100 units.

1998		$1,200	$1,500

ASAT Custom
1996. No pickguard, 25 to 30 made.

1996		$800	$900

ASAT Deluxe
1997-present. Two humbuckers, flamed maple top, bound body.

1997	3-bolt neck, less than 100 made	$1,050	$1,200
1997-2010	4-bolt neck	$900	$1,050

ASAT Deluxe Semi-Hollow
1997-present. Two humbuckers.

1997-2010		$1,075	$1,250

ASAT III
1988-1991, 1996-1998. Single-cut body, 3 single-coil pickups.

1988-1991	1st version, Leo era, 150 made	$1,000	$1,200
1996-1998	Post Leo era	$700	$900

ASAT JD-5
2004-2007. Jerry Donahue model, single-cut, 2 single-coils, special wired 5-way switch.

2004-2007		$1,250	$1,500

ASAT Junior Limited Edition
1998-1999. Single-cut semi-hollowbody, 2 single-coils, run of 250 units.

1998-1999		$1,000	$1,200

ASAT S-3
1998-2000. Three soap bar single coil pickups, limited production.

1998-2000		$900	$1,000

ASAT Special
1992-present. Like ASAT, but with 2 larger P-90-type pickups, chrome hardware, various colors.

1992-1997	3-bolt neck	$800	$900

MODEL YEAR	FEATURES	EXC. COND. LOW	HIGH
1997-1999	4-bolt neck	$800	$900
2000-2010	4-bolt neck	$800	$900

ASAT Special Semi-Hollow

1997-present. Semi-hollow version of ASAT Special.

1997-2010		$900	$1,000

ASAT Special Deluxe

2001-present. No 'guard version of the Special with figured maple top.

2001-2010		$950	$1,050

ASAT Z-2 Limited Edition

1999. Limited edition of 10 instruments, semi-hollow construction, natural ash, tortoise bound, engraved neckplate.

1999		$1,100	$1,200

ASAT Z-3

1998-present. Three offset-style Z-3 high output pickups, sunburst.

1998-2010		$850	$950

ASAT Z-3 Semi-Hollow

1998-present. F-hole version of Z-3.

1998-2010		$850	$950

Broadcaster

1985-1986. Solidbody, 2 single-coils with adjustable polepieces act in humbucking mode with selector switch in the center position, black parts and finish, name changed to ASAT in early-'86.

1985-1986	Kahler	$800	$900
1985-1986	Signed by Leo, ebony board	$1,900	$2,000
1985-1986	Signed by Leo, maple board	$1,900	$2,000

Cavalier

1983-1986. Offset double-cut, 2 humbuckers, 700 made, sunburst.

1983-1986		$850	$900

Climax

1992-1996. Offset double-cut, bolt maple neck, six-on-a-side tuners, double locking vibrato, blue.

1992-1996		$800	$850

Climax Plus

1992-1996. Two humbuckers replace single-coils of the Climax, plus 1 single-coil.

1992-1996		$800	$850

Climax XL

1992-1996. Two humbuckers only.

1992-1996		$800	$850

Comanche V

1988-1991. Solidbody, 3 Z-shaped single-coil humbuckers, maple neck in choice of 3 radii, rosewood 'board, vibrato, fine tuners, Leo Fender's signature on the body, sunburst.

1988-1991		$1,300	$1,500

Comanche VI

1990-1991. Leo Fender's signature on the body, 6 mini-toggles.

1990-1991		$1,500	$1,700

Comanche (Reintroduced)

1998-present. Reissue with either swamp ash or alder body, bolt-on maple neck, 3 Z-coil pickups, standard or premium finish options.

1998-2010	Standard finish	$900	$950

MODEL YEAR	FEATURES	EXC. COND. LOW	HIGH
1998-2010	Premium finish, flame top	$1,000	$1,100

Commemorative

1992-1997. About 350 made, Leo Fender signature on upper bass bout.

1991	Cherryburst	$2,000	$2,500
1992-1997	Sunburst	$1,800	$2,000

F-100 (Model I and II)

1980-1986. Offset double-cut solidbody, 2 humbuckers, natural. Came in a I and II model - only difference is the radius of the 'board.

1980-1986		$800	$1,000

F-100 E (Model I and II)

1980-1982. Offset double-cut solidbody, 2 humbuckers, active electronics, pre-amp, natural. Came in a I and II model - only difference is the radius of the 'board.

1980-1982		$850	$1,050

G-200

1981-1982. Mahogany solidbody, maple neck, ebony 'board, 2 humbucking pickups, coil-split switches, natural or sunburst, 209 made.

1981-1982		$1,700	$2,100

GBL-LE (Guitars by Leo Limited Edition)

1999. Limited edition of 25, semi-hollowbody, 3 pickups.

1999		$1,000	$1,200

George Fullerton Signature

1995-2007. Double-cut solidbody, sunburst.

1995-1997	3-bolt neck	$1,000	$1,200
1997-2007	4-bolt neck	$900	$1,000

HG-1

1982-1983. Offset double-cut, 1 humbucker, dot inlays. Very rare as most were made into HG-2s.

1982-1983		$1,500	$1,800

HG-2

1982-1984. 2-humbucker HG, body changes to classic offset double-cut in '84.

1982-1983	Mustang-body	$1,200	$1,500
1984	S-body	$1,200	$1,500

Interceptor

1983-1991. To '86 an X-shaped solidbody, either 3 single-coils, 2 humbuckers, or 1 humbucker and 2 single-coils, '87-'89 was an offset double-cut solidbody.

1983-1985	1st X-body, 70 made	$2,000	$2,300
1985-1986	2nd X-body, 12 made	$2,000	$2,300
1987-1991	Double-cut	$1,400	$1,600

Invader

1984-1991, 1998-present. Double-cut solidbody, 2 single-coil and 1 humbucker pickups.

1984-1991	1st version	$800	$900
1998-2010	2nd version	$800	$900

Invader Plus

1998-present. Two humbuckers and single blade pickup in the middle position.

1998-2010		$750	$850

John Jorgenson Signature Model ASAT

1995. About 190 made, Silver Metalflake finish.

1995		$900	$1,000

1981 G & L F-100 Model 1

G & L Invader Plus

2008 G & L Legacy Semi-Hollow

1986 G & L S-500

MODEL YEAR	FEATURES	EXC. COND. LOW	HIGH
Legacy			
1992-present. Classic double-cut configuration, various colors.			
1992-1994	3-bolt neck, Duncan SSLs	$650	$850
1995-1997	3-bolt neck, Alnicos	$600	$800
1998-2006	4-bolt neck, Alnicos	$600	$800
2007-2010		$550	$750
Legacy 2HB			
2001-present. Two humbucker pickups.			
2001-2010		$650	$800
Legacy Deluxe			
2001-present. No 'guard, figured maple top.			
2001-2010		$750	$900
Legacy HB			
2001-present. One humbucker pickup at bridge position plus 2 single-coil pickups.			
2001-2010		$750	$900
Legacy Special			
1993-present. Legacy with 3 humbuckers, various colors.			
1992-1997	3-bolt neck	$700	$850
1998-2010	4-bolt neck	$650	$800
25th Anniversary Limited Edition			
2006. G&L Custom Creations, 250 made, combines appearance of '81 F-100 with contours and control layout of ASAT Super, single-cut mahogany body, 2 custom wound MFD humbuckes, custom blend 'root beer' finish.			
2006		$950	$1,200
Nighthawk			
1983. Offset double-cut solidbody, 3 single-coil pickups, 269 made, sunburst, name changed to Skyhawk in '84.			
1983		$700	$850
Rampage			
1984-1991. Offset double-cut solidbody, hard rock maple neck, ebony 'board, 1 bridge-position humbucker pickup, sunburst. Currently available as Jerry Cantrell Signature Model.			
1984-1991	Common color	$1,000	$1,250
1984-1991	Rare color	$1,600	$2,000
Rampage (Reissue)			
2000. Limited Edition of 70 units, supplied with gig bag and not hard case, ivory finish.			
2000		$750	$900
S-500			
1982-present. Double-cut mahogany or ash solidbody, maple neck, ebony or maple 'board, 3 single-coil pickups, vibrato.			
1982-1987		$950	$1,200
1988-1991	Mini-toggle, Leo sig. on body	$900	$1,150
1992-1997	3-bolt neck	$800	$1,000
1997-2010	4-bolt neck	$700	$900
S-500 Deluxe			
2001-present. Deluxe Series features, including no 'guard and flamed maple top, natural.			
2001-2010	Flame & solid tops	$800	$1,000

MODEL YEAR	FEATURES	EXC. COND. LOW	HIGH
SC-1			
1982-1983. Offset double-cut solidbody, 1 single-coil pickup, tremolo, sunburst, 250 made.			
1981-1982		$775	$975
SC-2			
1982-1983, 2010-present. Offset double-cut solidbody, 2 MFD soapbar pickups, about 600 made in original run.			
1982-1983	Shallow cutaway	$950	$1,200
1983	Deeper, pointed cutaway	$750	$900
SC-3			
1982-1991. Offset double-cut solidbody, 3 single-coil pickups, tremolo.			
1982-1983	Shallow cutaway	$875	$1,075
1984-1987	Deeper cutaway, no 'guard	$900	$1,100
1988-1991	Deeper cutaway, 'guard	$800	$1,000
Skyhawk			
1984-1991. Renamed from Nighthawk, offset double-cut, 3 single-coils, signature on headstock '84-'87, then on body '88-'91.			
1984-1987	Dual-Fulcrum or saddle lock	$750	$950
1984-1987	Kahler	$575	$700
1988-1991	Dual-Fulcrum or saddle lock	$750	$950
1988-1991	Kahler	$575	$700
Superhawk			
1984-1987. Offset double-cut, maple neck, ebony 'board, G&L or Kahler tremolos, 2 humbuckers, signature on headstock.			
1984-1987		$700	$900
Will Ray Signature Model			
2002-present. Will Ray signature on headstock, 3 Z-coil pickups, Hipshot B-Bender.			
2002-2010		$750	$950

G.L. Stiles

1960-1994. Built by Gilbert Lee Stiles (b. October 2, 1914, Independence, West Virginia; d. 1994) primarily in the Miami, Florida area. First solidbody, including pickups and all hardware, built by hand in his garage. Stiles favored scrolls, fancy carving and walnut fingerboards. His later instruments were considerably more fancy and refined. He moved to Hialeah, Florida by '63 and began making acoustic guitars and other instruments. His acoustics featured double stressed (bent) backs for increased tension. He later taught for the Augusta Heritage Program and Davis and Elkins College in Elkins, West Virginia. Only his solidbodies had consecutive serial numbers. Stiles made approximately 1000 solidbodies and 500 acoustics.

Gabriel's Guitar Workshop

1979-present. Production/custom steel- and nylon-stringed guitars built by luthier Gabriel Ochoteco in Germany until '84 and in Brisbane, Australia since.

MODEL YEAR	FEATURES	EXC. COND. LOW	HIGH

Gadotti Guitars

1997-present. Luthier Jeanfranco Biava Gadotti builds his premium grade, custom/production, nylon- and steel-string, carved, chambered solidbodies in Orlando, Florida.

Gadow Guitars

2002-present. Luthier Ryan Gadow builds his professional and premium grade, custom/production, solid and semi-hollow body guitars in Durham, North Carolina. He also builds basses.

Gagnon

1998-present. Luthier Bill Gagnon builds his premium and presentation grade, production/custom, archtop guitars in Beaverton, Oregon.

Galanti

Ca.1962-ca.1967. Electric guitars offered by the longtime Italian accordion maker. They may have also offered acoustics.

Electric

1962-1967. Solidbody or hollowbody.

1962-1967	Fancy features	$600	$750
1962-1967	Plain features	$250	$575

Galiano

New Yorkers Antonio Cerrito and Raphael Ciani offered guitars under the Galiano brand during the early part of the last century. They used the brand both on guitars built by them and others, including The Oscar Schmidt Company. They also offered mandolins.

Gallagher

1965-present. Professional and premium grade, production/custom, flat-top guitars built in Wartrace, Tennessee. J.W. Gallagher started building Shelby brand guitars in the Slingerland Drum factory in Shelbyville, Tennessee in '63. In '65 he and his son Don made the first Gallagher guitar, the G-50. Doc Watson began using Gallagher guitars in '68. In '76, Don assumed operation of the business when J. W. semi-retired. J. W. died in '79.

71 Special

1970-present. Rosewood back and sides, spruce top, herringbone trim, bound ebony 'board, natural.

1970s		$1,700	$2,000

A-70 Ragtime Special

1978-present. Smaller auditorium/00 size, spruce top, mahogany back and sides, G logo, natural.

1980s		$1,200	$1,500

Custom 12-String

Introduced in 1965. Mahogany, 12-fret neck, natural.

1965		$1,200	$1,500

Doc Watson

1974-present. Spruce top, mahogany back and sides, scalloped bracing, ebony 'board, herringbone trim, natural.

1974-1979		$1,800	$2,100

MODEL YEAR	FEATURES	EXC. COND. LOW	HIGH
1980-1989		$1,500	$1,800
1990-1999		$1,400	$1,700
2000-2010		$1,200	$1,600

Doc Watson (Cutaway)

1975-present. Spruce top, mahogany back and sides, scalloped bracing, ebony 'board, herringbone trim, natural.

1980s		$1,800	$2,100

Doc Watson 12-String

1995-2000. Natural.

1995-2000		$1,400	$1,700

Doc Watson Signature

2000-present. Signature inlay 12th fret.

2000-2010		$1,800	$2,100

G-45

1970-2008. Mahogany back and sides, spruce top, ebony 'board, natural.

1980s		$900	$1,100

G-50

1980s-present. Mahogany back and sides, spruce top, ebony 'board, natural.

1980s		$1,300	$1,600

G-65

1980s-present. Rosewood back and sides, spruce top, ebony 'board, natural.

1980s		$1,500	$1,800

G-70

1978-present. Rosewood back and sides, herringbone purfling on top and soundhole, mother-of-pearl diamond 'board inlays, bound headstock, natural.

1980s		$1,600	$1,900

G-71

1970s. Indian rosewood, gold tuners.

1970s		$1,700	$2,000

Gallagher, Kevin

1996. Kevin Gallagher, luthier, changed name brand to Omega to avoid confusion with J.W. Gallagher. See Omega listing.

Gallotone

1950s-1960s. Low-end foreign brand similar to 1950s Stellas, the Gallotone Champion, a 3/4 size student flat top, is associated with John Lennon as his early guitar.

Galloup Guitars

1994-present. Luthier Bryan Galloup builds his professional and premium grade, production/custom flat-tops in Big Rapids, Michigan. He also operates the Galloup School of Lutherie and The Guitar Hospital repair and restoration business.

Galveston

Budget and intermediate grade, production, imported acoustic, acoustic/electric, resonator and solidbody guitars. They also offer basses and mandolins.

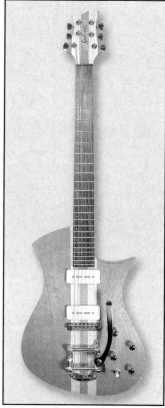

Gadotti Electroking

Gallagher A-70

Ganz Classical

Gauge DC

MODEL YEAR	FEATURES	EXC. COND. LOW	HIGH

Gamble & O'Toole

1978-present. Premium grade, custom classical and steel string guitars built by luthier Arnie Gamble in Sacramento, California, with design input and inlay work from his wife Erin O'Toole.

Ganz Guitars

1995-present. Luthier Steve Ganz builds his professional grade, production/custom classical guitars in Bellingham, Washington.

Garcia

Made by luthier Federico Garcia in Spain until late-1960s or very early-'70s when production moved to Japan.

Classical

1960s-1970s. Mid-level, '60s model is solid spruce top with solid mahogany, rosewood or walnut back and sides, '70s model is Spanish pine top with walnut back and sides.

1960s	Mahogany	$200	$300
1960s	Rosewood	$400	$500
1960s	Walnut	$200	$300
1970s	Spanish pine/ Brazilian rosewood	$500	$700
1970s	Spanish pine/walnut	$200	$300

Garrison

2000-present. Intermediate and professional grade, production, acoustic and acoustic/electric guitars designed by luthier Chris Griffiths using his Active Bracing System (a single integrated glass-fiber bracing system inside a solid wood body). He started Griffiths Guitar Works in 1993 in St. John's, Newfoundland, and introduced Garrison guitars in 2000. In '07, Garrison was acquired by Gibson.

Gary Kramer

2005-present. Gary Kramer, the founder of the original Kramer brand, started a new business in 2005. The initial line was based upon a half-moon shaped model called the USA Delta Wing. Later import models were added.

Gauge Guitars

2002-present. Luthier Aaron Solomon builds custom, professional and premium grade, solidbody and semi-solid electric guitars in New Jersey.

Gemelli

Early 1960s-ca. 1966. European-made (likely Italian) guitars. Similar to Bartolini guitars, so most likely from same manufacturer. Originally plastic covered, they switched to paint finishes by around '65.

Gemunder

1870s-1910s. New York shop that specialized in reproduction-aged violins, but also made parlor-sized guitars that were similar to Martin guitars of the era. An original label on the inside back identifies August Gemunder and Sons, New York.

MODEL YEAR	FEATURES	EXC. COND. LOW	HIGH

Parlor

1870s-1910s. Style 28 appointments, rosewood body, spruce top.

1870-1910s		$1,200	$1,500

George

See listing under Chris George.

German Guitars

2001-present. Luthier Greg German builds his premium grade, custom/production, acoustic archtop guitars in Broomfield, Colorado.

Giannini

1900-present. Classical, acoustic, and acoustic/ electric guitars built in Salto, SP, Brazil near Sao Paolo. They also build violas, cavaquinhos and mandolins. Founded by guitar-builder Tranquillo Giannini, an Italian who traveled to Brazil in 1890 and discovered the exotic woods of Brazil. The company was producing 30,000 instruments a year by '30. They began exporting their acoustic instruments to the U.S. in '63. They added electric guitars in '60, but these weren't imported as much, if at all. Gianninis from this era used much Brazilian Rosewood.

Classical

Early-1970s. Nylon string import, small body.

1970s	Brazilian rosewood	$400	$500
1970s	Pau ferro, mahogany	$200	$250

CraViolia

1970s. Kidney bean-shaped rosewood body, acoustic, natural, line included a classical, a steel string, and a 12-string.

1972-1974		$400	$500

CraViolia 12-String

1972-1974, 2004-present. Kidney bean-shaped body, 12 strings.

1972-1974		$400	$500
2004-2010		$175	$225

Gibson

1890s (1902)-present. Intermediate, professional, and premium grade, production/custom, acoustic and electric guitars made in the U.S. They also build basses, mandolins, amps, and banjos under the Gibson name. Gibson also offers instruments under the Epiphone, Kramer, Steinberger, Dobro, Tobias, Valley Arts, Garrison, Slingerland (drums), Baldwin (pianos), Trace Elliot, Electar (amps), Maestro, Gibson Labs, Oberheim, and Echoplex brands.

Founded in Kalamazoo, Michigan by Orville Gibson, a musician and luthier who developed instruments with tops, sides and backs carved out of solid pieces of wood. Early instruments included mandolins, archtop guitars and harp guitars. By 1896 Gibson had opened a shop. In 1902 Gibson was bought out by a group of investors who incorporated the business as Gibson Mandolin-Guitar Manufacturing Company, Limited. The company was purchased by Chicago Musical Instrument Company (CMI) in '44. In '57 CMI also purchased

MODEL		EXC. COND.	
YEAR	FEATURES	LOW	HIGH

the Epiphone guitar company, transferring production from Philadelphia to the Gibson plant in Kalamazoo. Gibson was purchased by Norlin in late-'69 and a new factory was opened in Nashville, Tennessee in '74. The Kalamazoo factory ceased production in '84. In '85, Gibson was sold to a group headed by Henry Juskewiscz. Gibson purchased the Flatiron Company in '87 and built a new factory in '89, moving acoustic instrument production to Bozeman, Montana.

The various models of Firebirds, Flying Vs, Les Pauls, SGs, and Super 400s are grouped together under those general headings. Custom Shop and Historic instruments are listed with their respective main model (for example, the '39 Super 400 Historical Collection model is listed with the Super 400s).

335 S Custom
1980-1981. Solidbody, 335-shaped, mahogany body, unbound rosewood 'board, 2 exposed Dirty Finger humbuckers, coil-tap, TP-6 tailpiece. Also available in natural finish, branded headstock Firebrand version.

1980-1981	Firebrand	$725	$850
1980-1981	Sunburst	$975	$1,150

335 S Deluxe
1980-1982. Same as 335 S Custom but with bound ebony 'board, brass nut.

1980-1982	Cherry	$1,050	$1,200
1980-1982	Silverburst	$1,200	$1,350
1980-1982	Sunburst	$1,100	$1,250

335 S Standard
1980-1981. Solidbody, 335-shaped, maple body and neck, 2 exposed split-coil humbuckers, stop tailpiece, no coil-tap, unbound 'board. Also available in natural finish, branded headstock Firebrand version.

1980-1981	Sunburst	$850	$1,000

Advanced Jumbo
1936-1940. Dreadnought, 16" wide, round shoulders, Brazilian rosewood back and sides, sunburst, reintroduced '90-'97.

1936		$53,000	$66,000
1937		$51,000	$64,000
1938		$50,000	$62,000
1939		$48,000	$60,000
1940		$47,000	$59,000

Advanced Jumbo (Reissue)
1990-1999, 2002-present. Issued as a standard production model, but soon available only as a special order for most of the '90s; currently offered as standard production. Renamed 1936 Advanced Jumbo for '97-'98. There were also some limited-edition AJs offered during the '90s.

1990-1999	Reissue	$1,500	$1,900
1990-1999	Special Ed., flamed maple	$2,400	$3,000
1994	Machiche, Mexican rosewood	$2,900	$3,600
2002-2010	Reintroduced	$1,500	$1,900

Advanced Jumbo Koa (Custom Shop)
2006. Custom Shop model, koa back and sides, Adirondack top.

2006		$2,300	$2,800

Advanced Jumbo Luthier's Choice (CS)
2000-2005, 2008. Custom Shop model.

2000-2005	Brazilian	$4,000	$5,000
2008	Cocobolo	$3,800	$4,800

Advanced Jumbo Supreme (CS)
2007. Custom Shop model, Madagascar rosewood back and sides, Adirondack spruce top.

2007		$2,500	$3,000

All American II
1996. Solidbody electric with vague double-cut Melody Maker body style, 2 pickups.

1996		$375	$475

B.B. King Custom
1980-1988. Lucille on peghead, 2 pickups, multi-bound, gold-plated parts, Vari-tone, cherry or ebony, renamed B.B. King Lucille in '88.

1980-1988		$1,500	$1,900

B.B. King Lucille
1988-present. Introduced as B.B. King Custom, renamed B.B. King Lucille. Lucille on peghead, 2 pickups, multi-bound, gold-plated parts, Vari-tone, cherry or ebony.

1988-1999		$1,700	$2,200
2000-2010		$1,700	$2,200

B.B. King Standard
1980-1985. Like B.B. King Custom, but with stereo electronics and chrome-plated parts, cherry or ebony.

1980-1985		$1,600	$2,000

B.B. King Commemorative ES-355 Lucille
2006. Limited edition of 80 guitars, price includes matching serial number/certificate number, matching B.B. King script logo case.

2006		$4,200	$5,100

B-15
1967-1971. Mahogany, spruce top, student model, natural finish.

1967-1969		$475	$575
1970-1971		$400	$475

B-20
1971-1972. 14.5" flat-top, mahogany back and sides, dot markers, decal logo, strip in-line tuners with small buttons.

1971-1972		$425	$525

B-25
1962-1977. Flat-top, mahogany, bound body, cherry sunburst (natural finish is the B-25 N).

1962-1964		$1,375	$1,700
1965		$1,200	$1,400
1966		$1,075	$1,250
1967-1969		$1,225	$1,500
1970-1977		$1,000	$1,250

B-25 3/4
1962-1968. Short-scale version, flat-top, mahogany body, cherry sunburst (natural finish is the B-25 3/4 N).

1962-1964		$1,000	$1,200
1965-1968		$850	$1,000

B-25 N
1962-1977. Flat-top, mahogany, bound body, natural (cherry sunburst finish is the B-25).

1962-1964		$1,400	$1,700
1965		$1,300	$1,600
1966-1968		$1,150	$1,425
1969-1977		$1,000	$1,225

German Archtop

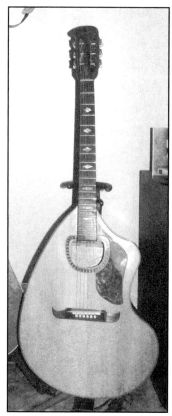

1969 Giannini CraViolia

Late '60s Gibson B-45-12

Gibson Challenger III

MODEL YEAR	FEATURES	EXC. COND. LOW	HIGH
B-25 N 3/4			
1966-1968. Short-scale version, flat-top, mahogany body, natural (cherry sunburst finish is the B-25 3/4).			
1966-1968		$850	$1,000
B-25-12			
1962-1970. Flat-top 12-string version, mahogany, bound body, cherry sunburst (natural finish is the B-25-12 N).			
1962-1964		$1,300	$1,600
1965-1968		$1,100	$1,400
1969-1970		$900	$1,100
B-25-12 N			
1962-1977. Flat-top 12-string version, mahogany, bound body, natural (cherry sunburst is the B-25-12).			
1962-1964		$1,300	$1,600
1965-1968		$1,100	$1,400
1969-1977		$900	$1,100
B-45-12			
1961-1979. Flat-top 12-string, mahogany, round shoulders for '61, square after, sunburst (natural finish is the B-45-12 N).			
1961-1962	Round shoulder	$1,700	$2,000
1962-1964	Square shoulder	$1,500	$1,800
1965-1968		$1,150	$1,450
1969-1979		$875	$1,100
B-45-12 N			
1962-1979. Flat-top 12-string, mahogany, natural (cherry sunburst finish is the B-45-12).			
1962	Round shoulder	$1,700	$2,000
1962-1964	Square shoulder	$1,500	$1,800
1965-1968		$1,200	$1,500
1969-1979		$900	$1,100
B-45-12 Limited Edition			
1991-1992. Limited edition reissue with rosewood back and sides, natural.			
1991-1992		$950	$1,150
Barney Kessel Custom			
1961-1973. Double-cut archtop, 2 humbuckers, gold hardware, cherry sunburst.			
1961-1964		$3,600	$4,400
1962	Black finish	$3,600	$4,400
1965-1969		$3,100	$3,800
1970-1973		$2,500	$3,000
Barney Kessel Regular			
1961-1974. Double-cut archtop, 2 humbuckers, nickel hardware, cherry sunburst.			
1961		$3,500	$4,000
1962		$3,400	$3,900
1963		$3,200	$3,800
1964		$3,000	$3,500
1965		$2,500	$2,900
1966-1967		$2,400	$2,800
1968		$2,400	$2,700
1969		$2,200	$2,600
1970-1973		$2,100	$2,500
Blue Ridge			
1968-1979, 1989-1990. Flat-top, dreadnought, laminated rosewood back and sides, natural finish, reintroduced for '89-'90.			
1968-1969		$1,000	$1,200
1970-1979		$800	$1,000

MODEL YEAR	FEATURES	EXC. COND. LOW	HIGH
Blue Ridge 12			
1970-1978. Flat-top, 12 strings, laminated rosewood back and sides, natural finish.			
1970-1978		$800	$1,000
Blueshawk			
1996-2006. Small single-cut, f-holes, 2 single-coil hum cancelling Blues 90 pickups, 6-way Varitone dial, gold hardware, Maestro Tremolo (Bigsby) option starts '98.			
1996-2006		$700	$850
B-SJ Blue Ridge			
1989. Model name on label is B-SJ, truss rod covers logo is Blue Ridge, SJ appointments but with narrow peghead shape.			
1989		$1,400	$1,700
Byrdland			
1955-1992. Thinline archtop, single-cut (rounded until late-'60, pointed '60-late-'69, rounded after '69, rounded or pointed '98-present), 2 pickups, now part of the Historic Collection.			
1956-1957	Natural, Alnicos	$7,000	$9,000
1956-1957	Sunburst, Alnicos	$6,000	$7,500
1958-1959	Natural, PAFs	$10,900	$13,500
1958-1959	Sunburst, PAFs	$9,400	$11,500
1960-1962	Natural, PAFs	$8,900	$11,000
1960-1962	Sunburst, PAFs	$7,600	$9,200
1963-1964	Natural, pat. #	$6,500	$8,000
1963-1964	Sunburst, pat. #	$5,500	$7,000
1965-1966	Natural	$5,600	$7,000
1965-1966	Sunburst	$5,000	$6,000
1967-1969	Natural	$5,600	$7,000
1967-1969	Sunburst	$5,000	$6,000
1970-1992	Various colors	$4,200	$5,000
Byrdland Historic Collection			
1993-present. Various colors.			
1993-2002	Various colors	$3,600	$4,400
2003-2010	Natural	$4,300	$5,300
C-0 Classical			
1962-1971. Spruce top, mahogany back and sides, bound top, natural.			
1962-1964		$575	$700
1965		$500	$600
1966-1971		$450	$550
C-1 Classical			
1957-1971. Spruce top, mahogany back and sides, bound body, natural.			
1957-1964		$650	$800
1965		$550	$650
1966-1971		$500	$600
C-1 D Laredo			
1963-1971. Natural spruce top, mahogany sides and back, upgrade to standard C-1.			
1963-1964		$700	$850
1965		$600	$700
C-1 E Classical Electric			
1960-1967. C-1 with ceramic bridge pickup, catalog notes special matched amplifier that filters out fingering noises.			
1960-1964		$700	$850
1965		$600	$700
1966-1967		$550	$650

MODEL YEAR	FEATURES	EXC. COND. LOW	HIGH

C-1 S Petite Classical
1961-1966. Petite 13 1/4" body, natural spruce top, mahogany back and sides.
1961-1964		$575	$700
1965		$500	$600
1966-1967		$450	$550

C-2 Classical
1960-1971. Maple back and sides, bound body, natural.
1960-1964		$725	$925
1965		$650	$750
1966-1971		$575	$675

C-4 Classical
1962-1968. Maple back and sides, natural.
1962-1964		$800	$1,000
1965		$750	$925
1966-1968		$700	$875

C-5 Classical
1957-1960. Rosewood back and sides, previously named GS-5 Classical in '54-'56.
| 1957-1960 | | $900 | $1,100 |

C-6 Classical
1958-1971. Rosewood back and sides, gold hardware, natural.
1958-1964		$1,100	$1,400
1965		$1,050	$1,300
1966-1971		$1,000	$1,250

C-8 Classical
1962-1969. Rosewood back and sides, natural.
1962-1964		$1,500	$1,800
1965		$1,300	$1,500
1966-1969		$1,250	$1,450

C-100 Classical
1971-1972. Slotted peghead, spruce top, mahogany back and sides, ebony 'board, Gibson Master Model label, non-gloss finish.
| 1971-1972 | | $325 | $400 |

C-200 Classical
1971-1972. C-100 with gloss finish.
| 1971-1972 | | $475 | $550 |

C-300 Classical
1971-1972. Similar to C-100, but with rosewood 'board, wood binding, wider soundhole ring.
| 1971-1972 | | $525 | $600 |

C-400 Classical
1971-1972. Rosewood sides and back, spruce top, high-end appointments, chrome hardware.
| 1971-1972 | | $825 | $950 |

C-500 Classical
1971-1972. C-400 with gold hardware.
| 1971-1972 | | $925 | $1,100 |

CF-100
1950-1958. Flat-top, pointed cutaway, mahogany back and sides, bound body, sunburst finish.
| 1950-1958 | | $3,200 | $3,750 |

CF-100 E
1951-1958, 2009. CF-100 with a single-coil pickup. Also offered in '94 1950 CF-100 E limited edition and in '07 as a Custom Shop model.
| 1950-1958 | | $3,700 | $4,600 |

Challenger I
1983-1985. Single-cut Les Paul-shaped solidbody, 1 humbucker, bolt-on maple neck, rosewood 'board, dot markers, silver finish standard.
| 1983-1985 | | $400 | $500 |

Challenger II
1983-1985. 2 humbucker version.
| 1983-1985 | | $450 | $550 |

Challenger III
1984. 3 single-coil version, never cataloged so could be very limited.
| 1984 | | $475 | $575 |

Chet Atkins CE
1981-2005. CE stands for Classical Electric, single-cut, multi-bound body, rosewood 'board until '95, then ebony, standard width nut, gold hardware, various colors.
| 1981-1999 | | $1,100 | $1,400 |
| 2000-2005 | | $1,000 | $1,300 |

Chet Atkins CEC
1981-2005. Same as CE but with ebony 'board and 2" classical width nut, black or natural.
| 1981-1999 | | $1,100 | $1,400 |
| 2000-2005 | | $1,000 | $1,300 |

Chet Atkins Country Gentleman
1987-2005. Thinline archtop, single rounded cutaway, 2 humbuckers, multi-bound, gold hardware, Bigsby. Part of Gibson's Custom line.
| 1987-2005 | | $1,900 | $2,400 |

Chet Atkins SST
1987-2006. Steel string acoustic/electric solidbody, single-cut, bridge transducer pickup, active bass and treble controls, gold hardware.
| 1986-1999 | | $1,100 | $1,400 |
| 2000-2006 | | $1,000 | $1,300 |

Chet Atkins SST-12
1990-1994. 12-string model similar to 6-string, mahogany/spruce body, preamp circuit controls single transducer pickup, natural or ebony finish.
| 1990-1994 | | $1,100 | $1,400 |

Chet Atkins Tennessean
1990-2005. Single rounded cutaway archtop, 2 humbuckers, f-holes, bound body. Part of Gibson's Custom line.
| 1990-2005 | | $1,300 | $1,600 |

Chicago 35
1994-1995. Flat-top dreadnought, round shoulders, mahogany back and sides, prewar script logo.
| 1994-1995 | Factory electronics | $900 | $1,050 |

Citation
1969-1971. 17" full-depth body, single-cut archtop, 1 or 2 floating pickups, fancy inlay, natural or sunburst. Only 8 shipped for '69-'71, reissued the first time '79-'83 and as part of the Historic Collection in '93.
| 1969-1971 | Sunburst, natural | $10,000 | $12,500 |

Citation (1st Reissue)
1979-1983. Reissue of '69-'71 model, reintroduced in '93 as part of Gibson's Historic Collection.
| 1979-1983 | Sunburst, natural | $9,500 | $12,000 |

1987 Gibson Chet Atkins Country Gentleman

Brett Ivers

Gibson Citation

Gibson CJ-165 Rosewood

1974 Gibson Dove

MODEL YEAR	FEATURES	EXC. COND. LOW	HIGH
Citation (2nd Reissue)			
1993-present. Limited production via Gibson's Historic Collection, natural or sunburst.			
1994-2010	Various colors	$8,000	$10,000
CJ-165 Maple			
2006-2008. Classic small body non-cutaway flat top, solid spruce top, maple back and sides.			
2006-2008		$1,400	$1,800
CJ-165 Rosewood			
2007-2008. Scaled down jumbo non-cutaway flat top, solid spruce top, Indian rosewood back and sides.			
2007-2008		$1,400	$1,800
CJ-165 EC Rosewood			
2007-2009. Jumbo, single-cut, Indian rosewood back and sides.			
2007-2009		$1,500	$1,900
CL-20/CL-20+			
1997-1998. Flat-top, laminated back and sides, 4-ply binding with tortoiseshell appointments, abalone diamond inlays.			
1997-1998		$900	$1,100
CL-30 Deluxe			
1997-1998. J-50 style dreadnought, solid spruce top, bubinga back and sides, factory electronics.			
1997-1998		$1,000	$1,200
CL-35 Deluxe			
1997-1998. Single cutaway CL-30.			
1997-1998		$1,000	$1,200
CL-45 Artist			
1997-1998. Cutaway flat-top, gold hardware, rosewood back and sides.			
1997-1998		$1,400	$1,600
CL-50			
1999. Custom Shop model, D-style body, higher-end appointments, offered with Brazilian rosewood.			
1999	Brazilian rosewood	$2,800	$3,500
Corvus I			
1982-1984. Odd-shaped solidbody with offset V-type cut, bolt maple neck, rosewood 'board, 1 humbucker, standard finish was silver gloss, but others available at an additional cost.			
1982-1984		$525	$650
Corvus II			
1982-1984. Same as Corvus I, but with 2 humbuckers, 2 volume controls, 1 master tone control.			
1982-1984		$600	$750
Corvus III			
1982-1984. Same as Corvus I, but with 3 single-coil pickups, master volume and tone control, 5-way switch.			
1982-1984		$700	$875
Crest Gold			
1969-1971. Double-cut thinline archtop, Brazilian rosewood body, 2 mini-humbuckers, bound top and headstock, bound f-holes, gold-plated parts.			
1969-1971		$4,400	$5,500
Crest Silver			
1969-1972. Silver-plated parts version of Crest.			
1969-1972		$3,900	$4,800

MODEL YEAR	FEATURES	EXC. COND. LOW	HIGH
CS Series			
2002-present. Scaled down ES-335 body style, made in Custom Shop.			
2002-2003	CS-356 (plain top)	$1,700	$2,100
2002-2008	CS-356F (figured top)	$2,200	$2,700
2002-2010	CS-336 (plain top)	$1,600	$2,000
2002-2010	CS-336F (figured top)	$1,800	$2,200
Dove			
1962-1996, 1999-present. Flat-top acoustic, maple back and sides, square shoulders.			
1962-1964	Natural	$5,000	$5,700
1962-1964	Sunburst	$4,500	$5,200
1965	Natural, sunburst	$3,700	$4,400
1966-1968	Natural, sunburst	$3,200	$3,700
1969	Natural, sunburst	$2,300	$2,800
1970-1979	Various colors	$2,200	$2,600
1980-1989	Various colors	$1,900	$2,300
1990-1996	Various colors	$1,675	$2,100
1999-2010	Reissue model	$1,675	$2,100
'60s Dove			
1997-2004. Spruce top, maple back and sides, Dove appointments.			
1997-2004		$1,625	$2,000
Dove Commemorative			
1994-1996. Heritage or Antique Cherry finish.			
1994-1996		$1,800	$2,200
Dove In Flight Limited Edition (Custom Shop)			
1996. 250 made, figured maple sides and back, Adirondack spruce top, Certificate of Authenticity, dove inlays on headstock, Custom logo on truss rod cover, Custom Shop logo on back of headstock.			
1996		$3,400	$4,200
Doves In Flight (Production Model)			
1996-present. Gibson Custom model, maple back and sides, doves in flight inlays.			
1996-2010		$2,600	$3,200
Dove Elvis Presley Signature			
2008-2010. Artist Series, Certificate of Authenticity, black.			
2008-2010		$2,500	$3,000
EAS Deluxe			
1992-1994. Single-cut flat-top acoustic/electric, solid flamed maple top, bound rosewood 'board, trapezoid inlays, 3-band EQ, Vintage Cherry Sunburst.			
1992-1994		$675	$850
EAS Standard/Classic			
1992-1995. Like EAS Deluxe, but with spruce top, unbound top, dot inlays, called EAS Classic for '92.			
1992-1995		$775	$950
EBS(F)-1250 Double Bass			
1962-1970. Double-cut SG-type solidbody, double-neck with bass and 6-string, originally introduced as the EBSF-1250 because of a built-in fuzztone, which was later deleted, only 22 made.			
1962-1964		$7,200	$9,000
1965		$6,500	$8,000
1966-1970		$6,000	$7,500

The *Vintage Guitar Price Guide* shows low to high values for items in all-original excellent condition, and, where applicable, with original case or cover.

MODEL		EXC. COND.	
YEAR	FEATURES	LOW	HIGH

EC-10 Standard
1997-1998. Jumbo single-cut, on-board electronics, solid spruce top, maple back and sides.

1997-1998		$750	$950

EC-20 Starburst
1997-1998. Jumbo single-cut, on-board electronics, solid spruce top, maple back and sides, renamed J-185 EC in '99.

1997-1998		$1,450	$1,750

EC-30 Blues King Electro (BKE)
1997-1998. Jumbo single-cut, on-board electronics, solid spruce top, figured maple back and sides, renamed J-185 EC in '99.

1997-1998		$1,600	$1,825

EDS-1275 Double 12
1958-1968, 1977-1991, 1995-present. Double-cut doubleneck with one 12- and one 6-string, thinline hollowbody until late-'62, SG-style solidbody '62 on.

1958-1959	Black, cherry, sunburst, white	$13,500	$16,500
1960-1964	Black, cherry, sunburst, white	$12,500	$15,500
1965	Black, cherry, sunburst, white	$9,000	$11,000
1968	Black, cherry, white	$8,000	$10,000
1977-1979	Various colors	$2,500	$3,100
1977-1979	White	$2,700	$3,400
1980-1991	Various colors	$2,300	$2,800
1995-2010	Various colors	$2,200	$2,700

EDS-1275 Double 12 (Historic Collection)
1991-1994. Historic Collection reissue.

1991-1994	White	$2,200	$2,700

EDS-1275 Double 12 Centennial
1994. Guitar of the Month (May), gold medallion on back of headstock, gold hardware.

1994	Cherry	$2,200	$2,700

EDS-1275 Double 12 Jimmy Page VOS Signature
2008. Custom Shop model with Certificate of Authenticity, 250 made.

2008		$5,700	$7,000

EMS-1235 Double Mandolin
1958-1968. Double-cut, doubleneck with 1 regular 6-string and 1 short 6-string (the mandolin neck), thinline hollowbody until late-1962, SG-style solidbody '62-'68, black, sunburst or white, total of 61 shipped.

1958-1959		$13,500	$16,500
1960-1962		$12,500	$15,500
1963		$12,500	$14,500
1964		$12,500	$15,500
1965		$9,000	$11,000
1966-1968		$8,000	$10,000

ES-5
1949-1955. Single-cut archtop, 3 P-90 pickups, renamed ES-5 Switchmaster in '55.

1949-1955	Natural	$5,900	$7,100
1949-1955	Sunburst	$5,500	$7,000

ES-5 Switchmaster
1956-1962. Renamed from ES-5, single-cut (rounded until late-'60, pointed after) archtop, 3 P-90s until end of '57, humbuckers after, switchmaster control. The

PAF pickups in this model are worth as much as the rest of the guitar. We have listed a non-original '58 with replaced pickups to demonstrate how value is reduced when the original PAFs are removed.

1956-1957	Natural, P-90s	$6,400	$8,000
1956-1957	Sunburst, P-90s	$5,900	$7,300
1957-1960	Natural, humbuckers	$10,000	$12,500
1957-1960	Sunburst, humbuckers	$9,000	$11,500
1960-1962	Pointed Florentine cutaway	$9,000	$11,500

ES-5/ES-5 Switchmaster Custom Shop Historic
1995-2006.

1995-2002	ES-5, sunburst, P-90s	$2,500	$3,100
1995-2002	Switchmaster, sunburst, humbuckers	$2,600	$3,200
1995-2002	Switchmaster, Wine Red, humbuckers	$2,300	$2,800
1995-2006	Switchmaster, natural option, humbuckers	$2,900	$3,500

ES-100
1938-1941. Archtop, 1 pickup, bound body, sunburst, renamed ES-125 in '41.

1938-1941		$1,400	$1,700

ES-120 T
1962-1970. Archtop, thinline, 1 f-hole, bound body, 1 pickup, sunburst.

1962-1964		$900	$1,150
1965		$800	$1,000
1966-1970		$750	$950

ES-125
1941-1943, 1946-1970. Archtop, non-cut, 1 pickup, sunburst, renamed from ES-100.

1941-1943	Blade pickup	$1,400	$1,700
1947-1949	1st non-adj., P-90s	$1,400	$1,700
1950	1st non-adj., P-90s	$1,225	$1,525
1951-1959	Adj. P-90s with poles	$1,225	$1,525
1960-1964		$1,175	$1,500
1965		$1,050	$1,250
1966-1969		$1,000	$1,200
1970		$900	$1,100

ES-125 C
1966-1970. Wide body archtop, single pointed cutaway, 1 pickup, sunburst.

1965		$1,200	$1,450
1966-1970		$1,100	$1,350

ES-125 CD
1966-1970. Wide body archtop, single-cut, 2 pickups, sunburst.

1965		$1,400	$1,800
1966-1970		$1,300	$1,700

*1959 Gibson
EDS-1275 Double 12*

*1957 Gibson ES-5
Switchmaster*

1964 Gibson ES-125 TDC

Matthew Leo

Gibson ES-135 (Thinline)

MODEL YEAR	FEATURES	EXC. COND. LOW	HIGH
ES-125 D			
1957. Limited production (not mentioned in catalog), 2 pickup version of thick body ES-125, sunburst.			
1957		$1,500	$1,900
ES-125 T			
1956-1969. Archtop thinline, non-cut, 1 pickup, bound body, sunburst.			
1956-1964		$1,400	$1,800
1965		$1,100	$1,400
1966-1969		$1,000	$1,300
ES-125 T 3/4			
1957-1970. Archtop thinline, short-scale, non-cut, 1 pickup, sunburst.			
1957-1964		$1,100	$1,400
1965		$1,000	$1,200
1966-1970		$900	$1,100
ES-125 TC			
1960-1970. Archtop thinline, single pointed cutaway, bound body, 1 P-90 pickup, sunburst.			
1960-1964		$1,700	$2,100
1965		$1,500	$1,800
1966-1970		$1,400	$1,700
ES-125 TD			
1957-1963. Archtop thinline, non-cut, 2 pickups, sunburst.			
1957-1963		$2,000	$2,500
ES-125 TDC or ES-125 TCD			
1960-1971. Archtop thinline, single pointed cutaway, 2 P-90 pickups, sunburst.			
1960-1964		$2,600	$3,200
1965		$2,300	$2,900
1966-1969		$2,200	$2,700
1970-1971		$2,100	$2,600
ES-130			
1954-1956. Archtop, non-cut, 1 pickup, bound body, sunburst, renamed ES-135 in '56.			
1954-1956		$1,400	$1,600
ES-135			
1956-1958. Renamed from ES-130, non-cut archtop, 1 pickup, sunburst, name reused on a thin body in the '90s.			
1957-1959		$1,200	$1,400
ES-135 (Thinline)			
1991-2003. Single-cut archtop, laminated maple body, 2 humbuckers or 2 P-90s, chrome or gold hardware, sunburst.			
1991-2003	Stop tail	$1,100	$1,250
1991-2003	Trapeze	$1,100	$1,250
ES-137 Classic			
2002-present. Thin-body electric single cut, trapezoid inlays, 2 humbuckers, f-holes, gold hardware.			
2002-2010		$1,100	$1,350
ES-137 Custom			
2002-2006. Like Classic, but with split-diamond inlays and varitone.			
2002-2006		$1,200	$1,450
ES-137 P			
2002-2005. Like Classic, but with exposed humbuckers, chrome hardware and very small trapezoid inlays.			
2002-2005		$800	$1,000

MODEL YEAR	FEATURES	EXC. COND. LOW	HIGH
ES-140 (3/4)			
1950-1956. Archtop, single-cut, 1 pickup, bound body, short-scale, sunburst or natural option (140N).			
1950-1956	Natural option	$1,550	$1,900
1950-1956	Sunburst	$1,450	$1,800
ES-140 3/4 T			
1957-1968. Archtop thinline, single-cut, bound body, 1 pickup, short-scale, sunburst.			
1956-1964		$1,450	$1,800
1965		$1,250	$1,600
1966-1968		$1,150	$1,450
ES-140N (3/4) T			
1956-1958. Natural finish option, low run production, 57 made.			
1956-1958		$1,700	$2,100
ES-150			
1936-1942, 1946-1956. Historically important archtop, non-cut, bound body, Charlie Christian bar pickup from '36-'39, various metal covered pickups starting in '40, sunburst.			
1936-1939	Charlie Christian pickup	$4,500	$5,600
1940-1942	Metal covered pickup	$3,000	$3,500
1946-1956	P-90 pickup	$2,000	$2,500
ES-150 DC			
1969-1975. Archtop, double rounded cutaway, 2 humbuckers, multi-bound.			
1969-1975	Cherry or walnut	$2,000	$2,300
1969-1975	Natural	$2,100	$2,600
ES-165 Herb Ellis Model			
1991-present. Single pointed cut hollowbody, 1 humbucker, gold hardware.			
1991-2005		$1,600	$2,000
2006-2007		$1,500	$1,900
2008		$1,450	$1,800
2009		$1,400	$1,700
2010		$1,300	$1,600
ES-175/ES-175N			
1949-1971. Archtop, single pointed cutaway, 1 pickup (P-90 from '49-early-'57, humbucker early-'57-'71), multi-bound, sunburst or natural option (175N).			
1949-1956	Natural, P90	$3,800	$4,800
1949-1956	Sunburst, P-90	$3,300	$4,200
1957-1959	Natural, humbucker	$6,500	$8,000
1957-1959	Sunburst, humbucker	$5,500	$6,800
1960	Sunburst	$5,000	$6,100
1961	Sunburst	$4,300	$5,300
1962	Sunburst	$4,100	$5,100
1963	Sunburst	$3,900	$4,900
1964	Sunburst	$3,500	$4,400
1965	Sunburst	$3,100	$3,800
1966-1969	Sunburst	$2,900	$3,600
1967-1969	Black	$3,200	$4,000
1970-1971	Various colors	$2,200	$2,700
ES-175 D/ES-175N D			
1952-present. Archtop, single-cut, 2 pickups (P-90s from '53-early-'57, humbuckers early-'57 on), sunburst or natural option (175N D). Humbucker pickups were			

MODEL YEAR	FEATURES	EXC. COND. LOW	HIGH

converted from PAF-stickers to Pat. No.-stickers in '62. Different models were converted at different times. An ES-175 model, made during the transitional time, with PAFs, will fetch more. In some of the electric-archtop models, the transition period may have been later than '62. Cataloged as the ES-175 Reissue in the '90s, Currently as the ES-175 under Gibson Custom.

1952-1956	Natural, P-90s	$4,000	$5,000
1952-1956	Sunburst, P-90s	$4,500	$5,500
1957-1959	Natural, humbuckers	$10,200	$12,800
1957-1959	Sunburst, humbuckers	$8,000	$10,000
1960	Natural	$9,000	$11,000
1960	Sunburst	$6,800	$8,000
1961	Natural	$7,000	$8,500
1961	Sunburst	$5,200	$6,000
1962	Natural	$6,000	$7,500
1962	Sunburst	$4,800	$5,600
1963	Natural	$5,500	$6,800
1963	Sunburst	$4,400	$5,500
1964	Natural	$5,500	$6,800
1964	Sunburst	$4,400	$5,500
1965	Natural	$5,000	$6,100
1965	Sunburst	$4,000	$4,900
1966	Natural	$4,500	$5,600
1966	Sunburst	$3,500	$4,400
1967-1969	Black	$3,600	$4,500
1967-1969	Various colors	$3,500	$4,400
1970-1971	Various colors	$2,500	$3,000
1972-1979	Various colors	$2,200	$2,700
1980-1999	Various colors	$1,900	$2,400
2000-2010	Various colors	$1,900	$2,400

ES-175 CC
1978-1979. 1 Charlie Christian pickup, sunburst or walnut.

1978-1979		$2,000	$2,500

ES-175 T
1976-1980. Archtop thinline, single pointed cutaway, 2 humbuckers, various colors.

1976-1980		$2,200	$2,700

ES-175AN D
1999-2000. P-90s, Antique Natural finish.

1999-2000		$2,200	$2,700

ES-175 Steve Howe
2001-2007. Maple laminate body, multi-bound top, sunburst.

2001-2007		$2,200	$2,500

ES-225 T
1955-1959. Thinline, single pointed cutaway, 1 P-90 pickup, bound body and neck, sunburst or natural.

1955-1959	Natural	$2,000	$2,400
1955-1959	Sunburst	$1,800	$2,200

ES-225 TD
1956-1959. Thinline, single-cut, 2 P-90s, bound body and neck.

1956-1959	Natural	$2,900	$3,600
1956-1959	Sunburst	$2,700	$3,400

ES-250
1939-1940. Archtop, carved top, special Christian pickup, multi-bound, high-end appointments.

1939-1940	Natural	$13,000	$17,000
1939-1940	Sunburst	$11,500	$15,000

ES-295
1952-1958. Single pointed cutaway archtop, 2 pickups (P-90s from '52-late-'57, humbuckers after), gold finish, gold-plated hardware.

1952-1957	P-90s	$5,700	$7,100
1957-1958	Humbuckers	$16,000	$20,000

ES-295 Reissue
1990-1993. Gold finish, 2 P-90 pickups, Bigsby.

1990-1993		$1,900	$2,400

ES-295 '52 Historic Collection
1990-2000. Higher-end reissue, Antique Gold finish, 2 P-90 pickups, Bigsby.

1990-2000		$2,600	$3,300

ES-300/ES-300N
1940-1942, 1945-1953. Archtop, non-cut, f-holes, had 4 pickup configurations during its run, sunburst or natural (300N).

1940	Natural, oblong diagonal pickup	$3,500	$4,400
1940	Sunburst, oblong diagonal pickup	$3,100	$3,900
1941-1942	Natural, 1 pickup	$3,100	$3,900
1941-1942	Sunburst, 1 pickup	$2,800	$3,500
1945	Black, 1 pickup	$3,000	$3,700
1945-1949	Sunburst, 1 pickup	$2,500	$3,100
1949-1953	Natural, 2 pickups	$3,400	$4,300
1949-1953	Sunburst, 2 pickups	$3,000	$3,700

ES-320 TD
1971-1974. Thinline archtop, double-cut, 2 single-coil pickups, bound body, cherry, natural, or walnut.

1971-1974		$1,000	$1,200

ES-325 TD
1972-1978. Thinline archtop, double-cut, 2 mini-humbuckers, 1 f-hole, bound body, top mounted control panel, cherry or walnut.

1972-1978		$1,400	$1,700

ES-330 T
1959-1963. Double rounded cutaway, thinline, 1 pickup, bound body and neck, in the '60s came with either an original semi-hard case (better than chip board) or a hardshell case. Prices quoted are for hardshell case; approximately $100 should be deducted for the semi-hard case.

1959-1961	Natural	$7,000	$9,000
1959-1961	Sunburst	$3,600	$4,500
1961	Cherry	$3,600	$4,500
1962	Cherry	$3,500	$4,400
1962-1963	Sunburst	$3,500	$4,400

ES-330 TD
1959-1972. Double rounded cutaway, thinline, 2 pickups, bound body and neck, in the '60s came with either an original semi-hard case (better than chip board) or a hardshell case. Prices noted for the hardshell case; approximately $100 should be deducted for the semi-hard case.

1959	Natural	$8,000	$10,000
1959-1960	Sunburst	$4,600	$5,500
1960	Natural	$7,000	$9,000

1956 Gibson ES-140

Tom Siska

Gibson ES-175 Steve Howe

1964 Gibson ES-330 TD

Luis Barrios

1963 Gibson ES-335 Block

MODEL YEAR	FEATURES	EXC. COND. LOW	HIGH
1960-1961	Cherry	$4,500	$5,400
1961	Sunburst	$4,600	$5,500
1962-1964	Sunburst or Cherry	$4,500	$5,400
1965	Sunburst or Cherry	$3,800	$4,700
1966-1968	Sunburst or Cherry	$3,000	$3,800
1967-1968	Burgundy Metallic (unfaded)	$3,100	$3,900
1968	Walnut option	$2,600	$3,300
1969-1972	Various colors, long neck	$2,600	$3,300

ES-330 TDC
1999. Custom Shop model, block markers.

1999		$2,000	$2,500

ES-333
2002-2005. Economy ES-335, no 'guard, no headstock inlay, exposed coils, stencil logo, satin finish.

2002-2005		$1,050	$1,300

ES-335/ES-335 TD
1958-1981. The original design ES-335 has dot 'board inlays and a stop tailpiece. Block inlays replaced dots in mid-'62, in late-'64 the stop tailpiece was replaced with a trapeze tailpiece. Replaced by the ES-335 DOT in '81.

MODEL YEAR	FEATURES	EXC. COND. LOW	HIGH
1958	Natural, unbound neck	$56,000	$69,000
1958	Natural, unbound neck, Bigsby	$39,000	$48,000
1958	Sunburst, bound neck	$33,000	$41,000
1958	Sunburst, bound neck, Bigsby	$23,000	$29,000
1958	Sunburst, unbound neck	$30,000	$37,000
1958	Sunburst, unbound neck, Bigsby	$22,000	$28,000
1959	Natural, bound neck	$68,000	$82,000
1959	Natural, bound neck, Bigsby	$51,000	$62,000
1959	Sunburst	$40,000	$50,000
1959	Sunburst, factory Bigsby	$30,000	$38,000
1960	Cherry, factory Bigsby	$19,000	$23,000
1960	Cherry, factory stop tail	$25,000	$30,000
1960	Natural, factory Bigsby	$26,000	$33,000
1960	Natural, factory stop tail	$35,000	$44,000
1960	Sunburst, factory Bigsby	$19,000	$23,000
1960	Sunburst, factory stop tail	$25,000	$30,000
1961	Cherry, factory Bigsby	$17,000	$20,000
1961	Cherry, factory stop tail	$23,000	$27,000
1961	Sunburst, factory Bigsby	$17,000	$20,000

MODEL YEAR	FEATURES	EXC. COND. LOW	HIGH
1961	Sunburst, factory stop tail	$23,000	$27,000
1962	Cherry, blocks, PAFs	$18,000	$22,000
1962	Cherry, blocks, pat. #	$17,000	$21,000
1962	Cherry, dots, PAFs	$18,000	$22,000
1962	Cherry, vibrola tail	$12,000	$15,000
1962	Sunburst, blocks, PAFs	$18,000	$22,000
1962	Sunburst, blocks, pat. #	$17,000	$21,000
1962	Sunburst, dots, PAFs	$18,000	$22,000
1962	Sunburst, dots, pat. #	$17,000	$21,000
1962	Sunburst, vibrola tail	$12,000	$15,000
1963-1964	Cherry, factory Bigsby	$11,000	$14,500
1963-1964	Cherry, factory Maestro	$11,000	$14,500
1963-1964	Cherry, factory stop tail	$14,800	$19,300
1963-1964	Sunburst, factory Bigsby	$11,000	$14,500
1963-1964	Sunburst, factory Maestro	$11,000	$14,500
1963-1964	Sunburst, factory stop tail	$14,800	$19,300
1965	Early '65, wide neck, trapeze or tremolo	$8,000	$10,000
1965	Mid '65, narrow neck, trapeze or tremolo	$6,000	$7,500
1966	Burgundy Metallic (unfaded)	$6,500	$8,500
1966	Cherry or sunburst, trapeze or tremolo	$4,800	$6,000
1966	Pelham Blue (unfaded)	$7,500	$9,500
1967	Black	$5,500	$6,700
1967	Burgundy Metallic (unfaded)	$6,500	$8,500
1967	Cherry or sunburst, trapeze or tremolo	$4,400	$5,400
1967	Pelham Blue (unfaded)	$7,500	$9,500
1968	Burgundy Metallic (unfaded)	$6,000	$8,000
1968	Cherry or sunburst, trapeze or tremolo	$4,400	$5,400
1968	Pelham Blue (unfaded)	$7,000	$9,000
1969	Cherry or sunburst, trapeze or tremolo	$3,600	$4,500
1969	Walnut finish option	$3,200	$4,000

The *Vintage Guitar Price Guide* shows low to high values for items in all-original excellent condition, and, where applicable, with original case or cover.

MODEL YEAR	FEATURES	EXC. COND. LOW	HIGH
1970	Cherry or sunburst, trapeze or tremolo	$3,500	$4,200
1970	Walnut finish option	$2,900	$3,600
1971-1976	Cherry or sunburst, trapeze or tremolo	$2,900	$3,600
1971-1976	Walnut finish option	$2,900	$3,600
1977-1979	Various colors, coil tap	$2,900	$3,600
1980-1981	Various colors	$1,900	$2,400

ES-335 TD CRR

1979. Country Rock Regular, 2 stereo pickups, coil-tap, sunburst.

1979		$2,500	$3,100

ES-335 Dot

1981-1990. Reissue of 1960 ES-335 and replaces ES-335 TD. Name changed to ES-335 Reissue. Various color options including highly figured wood.

1981-1990	Cherry or sunburst	$1,600	$2,000
1981-1990	Natural	$2,600	$3,200

ES-335 Dot CMT (Custom Shop)

1983-1985. Custom Shop ES-335 Dot with curly maple top and back, full-length center block, gold hardware, various colors.

1983-1985		$2,200	$2,700

ES-335 Reissue/ES-335 '59 Dot Reissue/ ES-335

1991-present. Replaced the ES-335 DOT, dot inlays, various color options including highly figured wood. Renamed the 1959 ES-335 Dot Reissue in '98 and currently just ES-335 followed by options - Dot, Block (added in '98), Fat Neck (added in '08), Figured (added in '06), Plain, Satin ('06-'10).

1991-2010	Cherry or sunburst	$1,600	$2,000
1991-2010	Natural	$1,850	$2,250
2006-2010	Satin finish	$1,500	$1,850

ES-335 Dot P-90

2007. Custom Shop limited edition with black dog-ear P-90s, stop tailpiece.

2007		$2,000	$2,500

ES-335-12

1965-1971. 12-string version of the 335.

1965-1968		$2,200	$2,600

ES-335 '59 Dot Historic Collection (CS)

1999-2000, 2002-present. Custom Shop model, Historical Series based upon 1959 ES-335 dot neck, figured maple top on early series, plain on later, nickel hardware.

1999-2000	Figured top	$2,800	$3,500
2002-2010	Figured top	$2,800	$3,500
2002-2010	Plain top	$2,400	$2,900

1959 ES-335 Dot Reissue Limited Edition

2009-present. Custom Shop, plain laminated maple top/back/sides, rounded '59 neck profile, '57 Classic humbuckers, Certificate of Authenticity, 250 each to be made in Antique Vintage Sunburst or Antique Natural (standard gloss or V.O.S. treatments).

2009-2010		$2,800	$3,000

ES-335 '60s Block Inlay

2004-2007. Made in Memphis facility, plain maple top, small block markers.

2004-2007		$2,000	$2,400

50th Anniversary 1960 ES-335TD (Custom Shop)

2010-present. Dot markers, double-ring vintage-style tuners, Antique Faded Cherry, Antique Vintage Sunburst, or Antique Natural.

2010	Natural	$3,000	$3,200

ES-335 '63 Block Historic Collection (CS)

1998-2000, 2002-present. Custom Shop model, Historical Series based upon 1963 ES-335 with small block markers, figured maple top on early series, plain on later, nickel hardware.

1998-2000	Figured top	$2,800	$3,500
2002-2010	Figured top	$2,800	$3,500
2002-2010	Plain top	$2,400	$2,900

ES-335 Alvin Lee

2006-2007. Custom Division Nashville, 50 made, features reflect Alvin Lee's Big Red ES-335 complete with decal art, cherry red, includes certificate of authenticity (if missing value is reduced). There is also an unlimited version without certificate.

2006-2007	With certificate	$2,800	$3,500

ES-335 Artist

1981. Off-set dot markers, large headstock logo, metal truss rod plate, gold hardware, 3 control knobs with unusual toggles and input specification.

1981		$2,200	$2,800

ES-335 Centennial

1994. Centennial edition, gold medallion in head-stock, diamond inlay in tailpiece, cherry.

1994		$4,300	$5,200

ES-335 Diamond Edition

2006. Trini Lopez style diamond f-holes, Bigsby tailpiece option, gold hardware, Pelham Blue, pearl white or black pearl.

2006		$2,000	$2,500

ES-335 Eric Clapton Crossroads '64 Reissue

2005. Reissue of EC's, with certificate

2005		$8,000	$10,000

ES-335 Jimmy Wallace Reissue

Special order by Texas Gibson dealer Jimmy Wallace.

1980	Blond	$2,600	$3,300

ES-335 King of the Blues

2006. Offered through Guitar Center, 150 made, based on B.B.'s Lucille.

2006		$2,200	$2,600

ES-335 Larry Carlton

2002-present. Mr. 335 logo on truss rod cover, block neck like Larry's guitar, vintage (faded) sunburst.

2002-2010		$2,000	$2,500

ES-335 Limited Edition

2001. ES-335 style crown inlay on headstock, P-90 pickups.

2001	P-90s	$2,000	$2,500

1996 Gibson ES-335 Custom Shop

2007 Gibson ES-335 Reissue

2007 Gibson ES-339

Rob Bernstein

Gibson ES-345 Reissue

MODEL YEAR	FEATURES	EXC. COND. LOW	HIGH

ES-335 Nashville
1994. All serial numbers begin with 94, first year Custom Shop run (not the Centennial).

1994		$2,500	$2,900

ES-335 Pro
1979-1981. Two humbucking pickups with exposed coils, bound 'board, cherry or sunburst.

1979-1981		$1,600	$2,000

ES-335 Roy Orbison
2006. About 70 made, RO serial number, black finish.

2006		$2,400	$3,000

ES-335 Showcase Edition
1988. Guitar of the Month series, limited production, transparent white/beige finish, black gothic-style hardware, EMG pickups.

1988		$2,100	$2,600

ES-335 Studio
1986-1991. No f-holes, 2 Dirty Finger humbuckers, bound body, cherry or ebony.

1986-1991		$1,100	$1,400

ES-336
1996-1998. Custom Shop smaller sized ES-335 with smaller headstock, dot markers.

1996-1998	All options	$1,600	$2,000

ES-339
2007-present. Smaller-sized double-cut semi-hollowbody, 2 humbuckers, 2 neck options; the 30/60 slim-wide profile and the '59 rounder-fuller profile, cherry sunburst, tobacco sunburst, cherry.

2007-2010		$1,450	$1,700

ES-340 TD
1968-1973. The 335 with a laminated maple neck, master volume and mixer controls, various colors.

1968-1973		$2,700	$3,300

ES-345 TD/ES-345 TDSV
1959-1983. The 335 with Vari-tone, stereo, 2 humbuckers, gold hardware, double parallelogram inlays, stop tailpiece '59-'64 and '82-'83, trapeze tailpiece '65-'82. Cataloged as ES-345 TDSV by '80.

1959	Cherry, Bigsby	$8,500	$10,400
1959	Cherry, stud tail	$11,000	$13,800
1959	Natural, Bigsby	$18,000	$22,000
1959	Natural, stud tail	$24,000	$30,000
1959	Sunburst, Bigsby	$8,500	$10,400
1959	Sunburst, stud tail	$11,000	$13,800
1960	Cherry, Bigsby	$8,300	$10,300
1960	Cherry, stud tail	$11,000	$13,800
1960	Natural, Bigsby	$18,000	$22,000
1960	Natural, stud tail	$24,000	$30,000
1960	Sunburst, Bigsby	$8,300	$10,300
1960	Sunburst, stud tail	$11,000	$13,800
1961	Cherry, Bigsby	$7,800	$9,700
1961	Cherry, stud tail	$10,400	$13,000
1961	Sunburst, Bigsby	$7,800	$9,700
1961	Sunburst, stud tail	$10,400	$13,000
1962-1964	Bigsby	$7,000	$8,800
1962-1964	Stud tail	$9,500	$11,700
1965	Various colors	$3,900	$4,700
1966-1968	Various colors	$3,700	$4,400
1969	Various colors	$3,000	$3,800

MODEL YEAR	FEATURES	EXC. COND. LOW	HIGH
1970-1979	Various colors	$2,900	$3,600
1980-1983	TDSV, Various colors	$1,900	$2,400

ES-345 Historic Collection
1998-1999. Custom shop, stopbar, Bigsby or Maestro tailpiece, Viceroy Brown, Vintage Sunburst, Faded Cherry or natural.

1998-1999	Natural	$2,400	$2,900

ES-345 Reissue
2003-2007. ES-345 features with 6-position Varitone selector, gold hardware, stop tailpiece, various colors.

2003-2007		$1,800	$2,300

ES-347 TD/ES-347 S
1978-1985, 1987-1993. 335-style with gold hardware, tune-o-matic bridge, 2 Spotlight double-coil pickups, coil-tap, bound body and neck, S added to name in '87.

1978-1985	TD	$2,500	$3,000
1987-1993	S	$2,500	$3,000

ES-350
1947-1956. Originally the ES-350 Premier, full body archtop, single-cut, 1 P-90 pickup until end of '48, 2 afterwards.

1947-1948	Natural, 1 pickup	$6,500	$8,000
1947-1948	Sunburst, 1 pickup	$5,500	$7,000
1949-1956	Natural, 2 pickups	$7,000	$8,500
1949-1956	Sunburst, 2 pickups	$6,000	$7,500

ES-350 Centennial
1994. ES-350 with all the Centennial Custom Shop appointments.

1994		$3,300	$4,100

ES-350 T
1955-1963. McCarty era, called the ES-350 TD in early-'60s, thinline archtop, single-cut (round '55-'60 and '77-'81, pointed '61-'63), 2 P-90 pickups '55-'56, humbuckers after, gold hardware.

1956	Natural, P-90s	$6,500	$8,000
1956	Sunburst, P-90s	$4,600	$5,800
1957-1959	Natural, humbuckers	$8,500	$11,000
1957-1959	Sunburst, humbuckers	$7,200	$9,300
1960-1963	Natural	$7,200	$9,300
1960-1963	Sunburst	$5,500	$7,000

ES-350 T (2nd Issue)
1977-1981. Norlin era, second issue of ES-350 T.

1977-1981	Natural	$2,800	$3,300
1977-1981	Sunburst	$2,600	$3,100

ES-350 T Limited Edition Reissue
1990s. Special medallion on back of headstock.

1990s		$2,800	$3,500

ES-355 TD
1958-1970. A 335-style with large block inlays, multi-bound body and headstock, 2 humbuckers, the 355 model was standard with a Bigsby, sideways or Maestro vibrato, non-vibrato models were an option. The prices shown assume a vibrato tailpiece, a factory stop tailpiece was considered an advantage and will fetch more. Early examples have factory Bigsby vibratos, early '60s have sideways vibratos, and late '60s have Maestro vibratos, cherry finish was the standard finish.

1958-1962	Cherry, PAFs, stop tail	$13,000	$16,000

MODEL YEAR	FEATURES	EXC. COND. LOW	HIGH
1958-1962	Cherry, PAFs, vibrato	$11,500	$14,200
1963-1964	Cherry, pat. #, vibrato	$9,500	$11,700
1965	Burgundy Metallic (unfaded)	$6,500	$8,200
1965	Cherry or sunburst	$5,500	$6,900
1966	Burgundy Metallic (unfaded)	$6,500	$8,200
1966	Cherry or sunburst	$5,500	$6,900
1967	Burgundy Metallic (unfaded)	$6,500	$8,200
1967	Cherry or sunburst	$5,500	$6,900
1968	Various colors	$5,000	$6,200
1969-1970		$3,800	$4,700

ES-355/ES-355 TD Custom Shop
1994, 1997, 2006-2007. Mono, Bigsby or stop tail.

1994		$3,400	$4,100
1997		$3,400	$4,100
2006-2007		$3,400	$4,100

ES-355 Centennial
1994. Custom Shop Guitar of the Month in June '94, high-end custom appointments, gold-plated hardware, sunburst.

1994		$4,300	$5,200

ES-355 TDSV
1959-1982. Stereo version of ES-355 with Vari-tone switch, a mono version was available but few were made, the 355 model was standard with a Bigsby, sideways or Maestro vibrato, non-vibrato models were an option. The prices shown assume a vibrato tailpiece. A factory stop tailpiece was considered an advantage and will fetch more, early examples have factory Bigsby vibratos, early-'60s have sideways vibratos and late-'60s have Maestro vibratos, cherry finish was standard, walnut became available in '69.

1959-1960	Bigsby	$12,000	$15,000
1961-1962	Sideways, late PAFs	$12,000	$15,000
1962	Maestro, late PAFs	$12,000	$15,000
1963-1964	Maestro, pat. #	$8,000	$10,000
1965	Burgundy Metallic (unfaded), Maestro	$6,500	$8,200
1965	Cherry or sunburst, Maestro	$5,500	$6,900
1966	Burgundy Metallic (unfaded) Maestro	$6,500	$8,200
1966-1967	Cherry or sunburst, Maestro	$5,500	$6,900
1968	Various colors, Maestro	$5,000	$6,200
1969	Various colors, Bigsby	$3,800	$4,700
1970-1979	Various colors, Bigsby	$3,300	$4,000
1980-1982	Various colors, Bigsby	$2,800	$3,500

ES-355 TDSV/79
1980. Offered with stereo or monaural circuitry and dual output jacks.

1980		$3,200	$3,900

ES-369
1981-1982. A 335-style with 2 exposed humbucker pickups, coil-tap, sunburst.

1981-1982		$1,800	$2,200

ES-446
1999-2003. Single cut semi-hollow, 2 humbuckers, Bigsby, Custom Shop.

1999-2003	Various colors	$1,900	$2,300

ES-775
1990-1993. Single-cut hollowbody, 2 humbuckers, gold hardware, ebony, natural or sunburst.

1990-1993		$2,200	$2,700

ES-Artist
1979-1985. Double-cut thinline, semi-hollowbody, no f-holes, 2 humbuckers, active electronics, gold hardware, ebony, fireburst or sunburst. Moog electronics includes 3 mini-switches for compressor, expander and bright boost.

1979-1985		$2,500	$3,000

EST-150 (Tenor)
1937-1939. Tenor version of ES-150, renamed ETG-150 in '40, sunburst.

1937-1939		$2,500	$3,100

ETG-150 (Tenor)
1940-1942, 1947-1971. Renamed from EST-150, tenor version of ES-150, 1 pickup, sunburst.

1940-1942		$2,500	$3,100
1947-1959		$1,750	$2,200
1960-1971		$1,650	$2,000

Everly Brothers
1962-1972. Jumbo flat-top, huge double 'guard, star inlays, natural is optional in '63 and becomes the standard color in '68, reintroduced as the J-180 Everly Brothers in '86.

1962	Black	$10,200	$11,800
1963	Natural option	$9,800	$11,500
1963-1964	Black	$9,800	$11,500
1965	Black	$8,500	$9,900
1966-1967	Black	$7,850	$9,200
1968-1969	Natural replaces black	$4,800	$5,700
1970-1972	Natural	$3,800	$4,500

Explorer
1958-1959, 1963. Some '58s shipped in '63, korina body, 2 humbuckers. The Explorer market is a very specialized and very small market, with few genuine examples available and a limited number of high-end buyers. The slightest change to the original specifications can mean a significant drop in value. The narrow price ranges noted are for all original examples that have the original guitar case.

1958-1959		$265,000	$325,000
1963		$170,000	$210,000

Explorer (Mahogany)
1976-1980. Mahogany body, 2 humbucking pickups.

1976-1979		$2,100	$2,600
1980-1982		$1,900	$2,300

Explorer I
1981-1982. Replaces Explorer (Mahogany), 2 Dirty Finger humbuckers, stoptail or Kahler vibrato, becomes Explorer 83 in '83.

1981-1982		$700	$850

1961 Gibson ETG-150

1959 Gibson Explorer

Gibson Explorer Shred X

1964 Gibson Firebird I

MODEL YEAR	FEATURES	EXC. COND. LOW	HIGH

Explorer 83/Explorer (Alder)
1983-1989. Renamed Explorer 83 from Explorer I, changed to Explorer in '84, alder body, 2 humbuckers, maple neck, ebony 'board, dot inlays, triangle knob pattern.

1983-1984		$1,500	$1,800
1984-1989	Custom colors, limited run	$1,100	$1,400
1984-1989	Standard finishes	$900	$1,100

Explorer II (E/2)
1979-1983. Five-piece maple and walnut laminate body sculptured like V II, ebony 'board with dot inlays, 2 humbuckers, gold-plated hardware, natural finish.

1979-1983	Figured maple top option	$1,400	$1,750
1979-1983	Natural top	$1,700	$2,100

Explorer III
1984-1985. Alder body, 3 P-90 pickups, 2 control knobs.

1984-1985	Chrome hardware	$950	$1,200
1984-1985	Chrome hardware, locking trem	$950	$1,200
1985	Black hardware, Kahler	$950	$1,200

Explorer 90 Double
1989-1990. Mahogany body and neck, 1 single-coil and 1 humbucker, strings-thru-body.

1989-1990		$900	$1,100

Explorer '76/X-plorer/Explorer
1990-present. Mahogany body and neck, rosewood 'board, dot inlays, 2 humbucking pickups, name changed to X-plorer in 2002 and to Explorer in '09.

1990-1999	Standard finish	$650	$800
1998	Sunburst or natural, limited run	$900	$1,100
2000-2001	Various colors	$650	$800
2002-2010	X-plorer/Explorer	$900	$1,100

Explorer Centennial
1994 only. Les Paul Gold finish, 100 year banner inlay at 12th fret, diamonds in headstock and gold-plated knobs, Gibson coin in rear of headstock, only 100 made.

1994		$4,300	$5,200

Explorer CMT/The Explorer
1981-1984. Flamed maple body, bound top, exposed-coil pickups, TP-6 tailpiece.

1981-1984		$1,450	$1,800

Explorer Custom Shop
2003. Custom Shop model with Certificate of Authenticity, Korina body, gold hardware.

2003		$3,600	$4,400

Explorer Designer Series
1983-1984. Custom paint finish.

1983-1984		$800	$1,000

Explorer Gothic
1998-2003. Gothic Series with black finish and hardware.

1998-2003		$575	$750

Explorer Heritage
1983. Reissue of '58 Explorer, korina body, gold hardware, inked serial number, limited edition.

1983	Black	$3,000	$3,700

1983	Natural	$3,500	$4,500
1983	White	$3,000	$3,700

Explorer (Limited Edition Korina)
1976. Limited edition korina body replaces standard mahogany body, natural.

1976		$4,300	$5,300

Explorer Korina
1982-1984. Korina body and neck, 2 humbucking pickups, gold hardware, standard 8-digit serial (versus the inked serial number on the Heritage Explorer of the same era).

1982-1984		$4,000	$4,500

Explorer Pro
2002-2005, 2007-2008. Explorer model updated with smaller, lighter weight mahogany body, 2 humbuckers, ebony or natural.

2002-2008		$800	$1,000

Explorer Voodoo
2002-2004. Juju finish, red and black pickup coils.

2002-2004		$825	$1,000

Reverse Explorer
2008. Guitar of the Month Sept. '08, 1,000 made, Antique Walnut finish, includes custom guitar case.

2008		$1,150	$1,400

Robot Explorer
2008-present. Announced Sept. '08, Robot Tuning System, trapezoid markers, 2 exposed humbuckers, red finish.

2008-2010		$950	$1,150

Shred X Explorer
2008. Guitar of the Month June '08, 1,000 made, mahogany body with ebony finish, black hardware, 2 EMG 85 pickups, Kahler 2215K tremolo system.

2008		$900	$1,100

X-Plorer/X-Plorer V New Century
2006-2007. Full-body mirror 'guard, mahogany body and neck, 2 humbuckers, mirror truss rod cover.

2006-2007		$625	$725

Firebird I
1963-1969. Reverse body and 1 humbucker '63-mid-'65, non-reversed body and 2 P-90s mid-'65-'69.

1963	Sunburst, reverse, hardtail	$15,000	$18,500
1963	Sunburst, reverse, tremolo	$7,000	$8,500
1964	Cardinal Red, reverse	$15,000	$18,500
1964	Sunburst, reverse, hardtail	$12,000	$15,000
1964	Sunburst, reverse, tremolo	$7,000	$8,500
1965	Cardinal Red, reverse	$13,000	$17,000
1965	Custom colors, non-reverse	$9,500	$12,500
1965	Sunburst, non-reverse, 2 P-90s	$3,300	$3,900
1965	Sunburst, reverse	$6,500	$7,500
1966	Custom colors, non-reverse	$7,000	$9,000
1966	Sunburst, non-reverse	$3,000	$3,700

MODEL YEAR	FEATURES	EXC. COND. LOW	HIGH
1967	Custom colors, non-reverse	$7,000	$9,500
1967	Sunburst, non-reverse	$3,000	$3,700
1968-1969	Sunburst, non-reverse	$2,800	$3,400

Firebird I 1963 Reissue Historic Collection
2000-2006. Neck-thru, reverse body, Firebird logo on 'guard, various colors including sunburst and Frost Blue.

2000-2006		$1,900	$2,500

Firebird I Custom Shop
1991-1992. Limited run from Custom Shop, reverse body, 1 pickup, gold-plated, sunburst.

1991-1992		$2,100	$2,500

Firebird 76
1976-1978. Reverse body, gold hardware, 2 pickups.

1976	Bicentennial, red/white/blue Firebird logo	$2,700	$3,200
1977-1978		$2,000	$2,600

Firebird I/ Firebird 76
1980-1982. Reintroduced Firebird 76 but renamed Firebird I.

1980-1982		$2,400	$2,700

Firebird II/Firebird 2
1981-1982. Maple body with figured maple top, 2 full size active humbuckers, TP-6 tailpiece.

1981-1982		$1,500	$1,900

Firebird III
1963-1969. Reverse body and 2 humbuckers '63-mid-'65, non-reversed body and 3 P-90s mid-'65-'69.

1963	Cardinal Red	$15,000	$19,000
1963	Golden Mist	$15,000	$19,000
1963	Polaris White	$14,000	$18,000
1963	Sunburst	$10,000	$12,000
1964	Cardinal Red, reverse	$14,000	$18,500
1964	Golden Mist, reverse	$14,000	$18,500
1964	Pelham Blue	$14,000	$18,500
1964	Polaris White, reverse	$13,000	$17,000
1964	Sunburst, reverse	$10,000	$12,000
1965	Cherry, non-reverse, 3 P90s	$5,500	$7,000
1965	Cherry, reverse	$8,500	$10,000
1965	Frost Blue, non-reverse	$9,500	$12,500
1965	Frost Blue, reverse	$12,500	$16,000
1965	Inverness Green, non-reverse	$9,500	$12,500
1965	Iverness Green, reverse	$12,500	$16,000
1965	Sunburst, non-reverse, 3 P-90s	$4,000	$5,000
1965	Sunburst, reverse, 2 P-90s (trans. model)	$4,300	$5,200
1965	Sunburst, reverse, mini humbuckers	$9,000	$11,000

MODEL YEAR	FEATURES	EXC. COND. LOW	HIGH
1966	Polaris White	$8,000	$10,000
1966-1967	Frost Blue	$9,000	$12,000
1966-1967	Pelham Blue	$9,000	$12,000
1966-1967	Sunburst	$3,000	$3,500
1967	Cherry	$5,500	$7,000
1968	Pelham Blue	$6,500	$8,500
1968	Sunburst	$3,000	$3,500
1969	Pelham Blue	$6,000	$7,500
1969	Sunburst	$3,000	$3,500

Firebird III 1964 Reissue (Custom Shop)
2000-present. Maestro, mini-humbuckers, sunburst or color option.

2000-2010		$1,800	$2,200

Firebird Non-Reverse Reissue
2002. Non-reverse body, 2 humbucker pickups.

2002		$1,300	$1,600

Firebird Studio/Firebird III Studio
2004-2010. Two humbuckers, dot markers, tune-o-matic and bar stoptail, reverse body, dark cherry finish.

2004-2010		$700	$875

Firebird V
1963-1969. Two humbuckers, reverse body '63-mid-'65, non-reversed body mid-'65-'69.

1963	Pelham Blue	$21,000	$27,000
1963	Sunburst	$13,000	$17,000
1964	Cardinal Red, reverse	$21,000	$26,000
1964	Sunburst, reverse	$12,000	$16,000
1965	Cardinal Red, reverse	$18,000	$22,000
1965	Sunburst, non-reverse	$4,000	$5,500
1965	Sunburst, reverse	$9,000	$11,000
1966-1967	Cardinal Red, non-reverse	$11,000	$14,000
1966-1967	Sunburst, non-reverse	$3,900	$5,400
1968-1969	Sunburst	$3,900	$5,400

Firebird V (Reissue)
1986-1987, 1990-present. Reverse body, 2 humbuckers or mini-humbuckers.

1990-1999	Various colors	$1,500	$1,900
2000-2010		$1,200	$1,500

Firebird V 1965 Reissue (Custom Shop)
2000-present. Reverse body, 2 mini-humbuckers, Maestro tremolo, certificate, sunburst or colors.

2000-2010		$2,600	$3,000

Firebird V Celebrity Series
1990-1993. Reverse body, gold hardware, 2 humbuckers, various colors.

1990-1993		$1,250	$1,600

Firebird V Guitar Trader Reissue
1982. Guitar Trader commissioned Firebird reissue, only 15 made, sunburst or white.

1982		$2,500	$2,900

Firebird V Limited Edition Zebrawood
2007. Limited edition from Gibson USA, 400 made, zebrawood reverse body.

2007		$1,250	$1,450

1965 Gibson Firebird III

1964 Gibson Firebird V

1972 Gibson Firebird V Medallion

Tom Mazz

1968 Gibson Flying V

MODEL YEAR	FEATURES	EXC. COND. LOW	HIGH
Firebird V Medallion			
1972-1973. Reverse body, 2 humbuckers, Limited Edition medallion mounted on body.			
1972-1973		$6,000	$7,500
Firebird V-12			
1966-1967. Non-reverse Firebird V-style body with standard six-on-a-side headstock and split diamond headstock inlay (like ES-335-12 inlay), dot markers, special twin humbucking pickups (like mini-humbuckers).			
1966-1967	Custom colors	$9,000	$12,000
1966-1967	Sunburst	$3,900	$5,400
Firebird VII			
1963-1969. Three humbuckers, reverse body '63-mid-'65, non-reversed body mid-'65-'69, sunburst standard.			
1963	Sunburst	$17,000	$22,000
1964	Sunburst	$16,000	$21,000
1965	Custom colors	$16,000	$21,000
1965	Sunburst, non-reverse	$7,200	$8,700
1965	Sunburst, reverse	$14,000	$17,000
1966-1967	Sunburst, non-reverse	$7,000	$8,500
1968	Custom colors	$9,000	$12,000
1968	Sunburst, non-reverse	$7,000	$8,500
1969	Sunburst, non-reverse	$7,000	$8,500
Firebird VII 1965 Reissue (Historic/ Custom Shop)			
2000-present. Historic Collection, 3 mini-humbuckers, Vintage Sunburst or solid colors.			
1997-2004	Various colors	$2,500	$3,000
Firebird VII Centennial			
1994 only. Headstock medallion, sunburst.			
1994		$4,300	$5,200
Firebird VII Reissue			
2003-2004. Reverse body, 3 mini-pickups, block markers, vibrola, matching headstock finish.			
2003-2004	Various colors	$1,300	$1,600
Flamenco 2			
1963-1967. Natural spruce top, 14 3/4", cypress back and sides, slotted headstock, zero fret.			
1963-1964		$1,600	$2,000
1965-1967		$1,400	$1,800
Flying V			
1958-1959, 1962-1963. Only 81 shipped in '58 and 17 in '59, guitars made from leftover parts and sold in '62-'63, natural korina body, string-thru-body design.			
As with any ultra high-end instrument, each instrument should be evaluated on a case-by-case basis. The Flying V market is a very specialized market, with few untouched examples available, and a limited number of high-end buyers. The price ranges noted are for all-original, excellent condition guitars with the original Flying V case. The slightest change to the original specifications can mean a significant drop in value.			
1958-1959		$180,000	$220,000

MODEL YEAR	FEATURES	EXC. COND. LOW	HIGH
Flying V (Mahogany)			
1966-1970, 1975-1980. Mahogany body, around 200 were shipped for '66-'70. Gibson greatly increased production of Flying Vs in '75. See separate listing for the '71 Medallion V version.			
1966	Cherry, sunburst	$15,000	$18,000
1967-1970	Cherry, sunburst	$13,000	$16,000
1975-1978	Various colors	$3,500	$4,250
1979	Silverburst	$3,800	$4,600
1979	Various colors	$3,500	$4,250
1980	Various colors	$3,000	$3,700
1981	Silverburst	$3,700	$4,400
Flying V (Mahogany string-through-body)			
1981-1982. Mahogany body, string-thru-body design, only 100 made, most in white, some red or black possible.			
1981	Silverburst	$3,700	$4,400
1981-1982	Black, red, white	$2,400	$2,800
Flying V Heritage			
1981-1982. Limited edition based on '58 specs, korina body, 4 colors available.			
1981-1982	Natural	$3,500	$4,500
1981-1982	Various colors	$3,000	$3,700
Flying V (Korina)			
1983. Name changed from Flying V Heritage, korina body, various colors.			
1983		$3,500	$4,500
Flying V I/V '83/Flying V (no pickguard)			
1981-1988. Introduced as Flying V I, then renamed Flying V '83 in 1983, called Flying V from '84 on. Alder body, 2 exposed humbuckers, maple neck, ebony 'board, dot inlays, black rings, no 'guard, ebony or ivory finish, designed for lower-end market.			
1981-1988		$1,500	$1,800
Flying V (Reissue)			
1990-present. Mahogany body, called Flying V Reissue first year, then '67 Flying V '91-'02, V Factor X '03-'08, Flying V '09-present.			
1990-2008	Rare colors	$900	$1,100
1990-2008	Standard colors	$650	$900
Flying V II			
1979-1982. Five-piece maple and walnut laminate sculptured body (1980 catalog states top is either walnut or maple), ebony 'board with dot inlays, 2 V-shaped pickups (2 Dirty Fingers humbuckers towards end of run), gold-plated hardware, natural.			
1979-1982		$1,700	$2,100
Flying V '58 (Historic/Custom Shop)			
1991-present. Historic Collection, based on '58/'59 Flying V, gold hardware, natural korina.			
1991-2010		$4,000	$5,000
Flying V '67 (Historic/Custom Shop)			
1997-2004. Historic Collection, '67 Flying V specs, korina body, natural or opaque colors.			
1997-2004		$2,500	$3,100
Flying V 50th Anniversary			
2008. Built as replica of '58 square shoulder V, 100 made, natural finish on korina body and neck, rosewood 'board, 8-series serial number, price includes original certificate.			
2008		$4,800	$6,000

The *Vintage Guitar Price Guide* shows low to high values for items in all-original excellent condition and, where applicable, with original case or cover.

MODEL YEAR	FEATURES	EXC. COND. LOW	HIGH

Flying V 50-Year Commemorative Brimstone

2008. Guitar of the Month March '08, 1,000 made, AA flamed maple top, higher-end appointments, 50th logo on truss rod cover, Brimstone Burst finish.

2008		$1,100	$1,350

Flying V '90 Double

1989-1990. Mahogany body, stud tailpiece, 1 single-coil and 1 double-coil humbucker, Floyd Rose tremolo, ebony, silver or white.

1989-1990		$900	$1,100

Flying V '98

1998. Mahogany body, '58 style controls, gold or chrome hardware.

1998		$900	$1,100

Flying V Centennial

1994 only. 100th Anniversary Series, all gold, gold medalion, other special appointments.

1994		$4,300	$5,200

Flying V CMT/The V

1981-1985. Maple body with a curly maple top, 2 pickups, stud tailpiece, natural or sunburst.

1981-1985		$1,450	$1,800

Flying V Custom (Limited Edition)

2002. Appointments similar to Les Paul Custom, including black finish, only 40 made.

2002		$3,500	$4,500

Flying V Designer Series

1983-1984. Custom paint finish.

1983-1984		$800	$1,000

Flying V Faded

2002-present. Worn cherry finish.

2002-2010		$550	$675

Flying V Gothic/'98 Gothic

1998-2003. Satin black finish, black hardware, moon and star markers.

1998-2003		$575	$750

Flying V Hendrix Hall of Fame

Late-1991-1993. Limited Edition (400 made), numbered, black.

1991-1993		$2,000	$2,500

Flying V Hendrix Psychedelic

2006. Hand-painted 1967 Flying V replica, 300 made, includes certificate, instruments without the certificate are worth less than the amount shown.

2006		$4,500	$5,500

Flying V Lenny Kravitz

2002. Custom Shop, 125 made.

2002		$2,500	$3,100

Flying V Lonnie Mack

1993-1994. Mahogany body with Lonnie Mack-style Bigsby vibrato, cherry.

1993-1994		$3,100	$3,800

Flying V Medallion

1971. Mahogany body, stud tailpiece, numbered Limited Edition medalion on bass side of V, 350 made in '71 (3 more were shipped in '73-'74).

1971-1974		$8,000	$10,000

Flying V New Century

2006-2007. Full-body mirror 'guard, mahogany body and neck, 2 humbuckers, Flying V style neck profile, mirror truss rod cover.

2006-2007		$625	$725

Flying V Primavera

1994. Primavera (light yellow/white mahogany) body, gold-plated hardware.

1994	Natural yellow/ white	$1,600	$2,000
1994	Various special colors	$1,500	$1,900

Flying V Voodoo

2002-2003. Black finish, red pickups.

2002-2003		$825	$1,000

Reverse Flying V

2006-2008. Introduced as part of Guitar of the Week program, reintroduced by popular demand in a '07 limited run, light colored solid mahogany body gives a natural Korina appearance or opaque white or black, V-shaped reverse body, traditional Flying V neck profile.

2006	1st run	$1,100	$1,300
2007	2nd run	$1,000	$1,200
2008	400 made, Guitar of the Week	$900	$1,100

Robot Flying V

2008-present. Robot Tuning System.

2008-2010		$950	$1,150

Rudolph Schenker Flying V

1993. Only 103 made, black and white body and headstock, signature on 'guard.

1993		$2,200	$2,600

Shred V

2008. Guitar of the Month, 1000 made, EMG humbuckers, Kahler, black.

2008		$900	$1,100

Tribal V

2009-present. Part of Gibson USA Limited Run Series, 350 made, white with black tribal art pattern, black hardware.

2009-2010		$575	$700

F-25 Folksinger

1963-1971. 14-1/2" flat-top, mahogany body, most have double white 'guard, natural.

1963-1964		$1,300	$1,500
1965-1969		$1,000	$1,200
1970-1971		$950	$1,100

Folk Singer Jumbo (FJN)

1963-1967. Square shoulders, jumbo flat-top, natural finish with deep red on back and sides.

1963		$3,400	$4,200
1964		$3,300	$4,100
1965		$2,700	$3,200
1966		$2,400	$3,000
1967		$2,200	$2,700

Futura

1982-1984. Deep cutout solidbody, 2 humbucker pickups, gold hardware, black, white or purple.

1982-1984		$1,100	$1,350

1983 Gibson Flying V (Korina)
Tom Siska

Gibson Flying V 50-Year Commemorative Brimstone

1970s Gibson Heritage

1974 Gibson Howard Roberts

MODEL YEAR	FEATURES	EXC. COND. LOW	HIGH

GB-1
1922-1940. Guitar-banjo, 6-string neck, walnut, renamed GB-5 in '23.

| 1922-1940 | Diamond flange | $1,900 | $2,400 |
| 1922-1940 | Thick rim (Mastertone-style) | $1,900 | $2,400 |

GB-3
1923-1931. Style 4 appointments, maple.

| 1917-1931 | Archtop (Mastertone-style) | $2,400 | $2,900 |
| 1923-1931 | Two-piece flange | $2,400 | $2,900 |

GB-4
1923-1931. Style 4 appointments, 14" rim.

| 1918-1931 | | $3,900 | $4,800 |

GB-6/GB-6 Custom
1922-1934. Special order availability.

| 1922-1934 | Standard or Custom | $4,800 | $5,900 |

GGC-700
1981-1982. Slab single-cut body, beveled bass edge, 2 exposed humbuckers, top mounted controls and pickups, dot markers, set-neck, ebony or transparent brown finish.

| 1981-1982 | | $600 | $700 |

Gospel
1973-1979. Flat-top, square shoulders, laminated maple back and sides, arched back, Dove of Peace headstock inlay, natural.

| 1973-1979 | | $775 | $900 |

Gospel Reissue
1992-1997. Flat-top, laminated mahogany back and sides and arched back, natural or sunburst.

| 1992-1997 | | $1,100 | $1,250 |

GS-1 Classical
1950-1956. Mahogany back and sides.

| 1950-1956 | | $1,000 | $1,250 |

GS-2 Classical
1950-1956. Maple back and sides.

| 1950-1959 | | $1,000 | $1,250 |

GS-5 Classical
1954-1956. Rosewood back and sides, renamed C-5 Classical in '57.

| 1954-1959 | | $1,600 | $2,000 |

GS-35 Classical/Gut String 35
1939-1942. Spruce top, mahogany back and sides, only 39 made.

| 1939-1942 | | $2,300 | $2,900 |

GS-85 Classical/Gut String 85
1939-1942. Rosewood back and sides.

| 1939-1942 | | $3,800 | $4,700 |

GY (Army-Navy)
1918-1921. Slightly arched top and back, low-end budget model, Sheraton Brown.

| 1918-1921 | | $750 | $925 |

Harley Davidson Limited Edition
1994-1995. Body 16" wide, flat-top, Harley Davidson in script and logo, black, 1500 sold through Harley dealers to celebrate 100th Anniversary of Harley.

| 1994-1995 | | $1,200 | $1,500 |

Heritage
1965-1982. Flat-top dreadnought, square shoulders, rosewood back and sides (Brazilian until '67, Indian '68 on), bound top and back, natural finish.

1965	Brazilian rosewood	$1,400	$1,700
1966-1969	Brazilian rosewood	$1,300	$1,600
1970-1982	Indian rosewood	$1,000	$1,250

Heritage-12
1968-1971. Flat-top dreadnought, 12 strings, Indian rosewood back and sides, bound top and back, natural finish.

| 1968 | Brazilian rosewood (1st run) | $1,300 | $1,600 |
| 1969-1971 | Indian rosewood | $1,000 | $1,250 |

HG-00 (Hawaiian)
1932-1942. Hawaiian version of L-00, 14 3/4" flat-top, mahogany back and sides, bound top, natural.

| 1932-1947 | | $3,100 | $3,900 |

HG-20 (Hawaiian)
1929-1933. Hawaiian, 14 1/2" dreadnought-shaped, maple back and sides, round soundhole and 4 f-holes.

| 1929-1933 | | $3,100 | $3,900 |

HG-22 (Hawaiian)
1929-1932. Dreadnought, 14", Hawaiian, round soundhole and 4 f-holes, white paint logo, very small number produced.

| 1929-1932 | | $3,500 | $4,500 |

HG-24 (Hawaiian)
1929-1932. 16" Hawaiian, rosewood back and sides, round soundhole plus 4 f-holes, small number produced.

| 1929-1932 | | $7,000 | $9,000 |

HG-Century (Hawaiian)
1937-1938. Hawaiian, 14 3/4" L-C Century of Progress.

| 1937-1938 | | $3,300 | $4,100 |

Howard Roberts Artist
1976-1980. Full body single-cut archtop, soundhole, 1 humbucking pickup, gold hardware, ebony 'board, various colors.

| 1976-1980 | | $2,300 | $2,900 |

Howard Roberts Artist Double Pickup
1979-1980. Two pickup version of HR Artist.

| 1979-1980 | | $2,500 | $3,100 |

Howard Roberts Custom
1974-1981. Full body single-cut archtop, soundhole, 1 humbucking pickup, chrome hardware, rosewood 'board, various colors.

| 1974-1981 | | $1,800 | $2,200 |

Howard Roberts Fusion/Fusion II/Fusion III
1979-2009. Single-cut, semi-hollowbody, 2 humbucking pickups, chrome hardware, ebony 'board, TP-6 tailpiece, various colors, renamed Howard Roberts Fusion II in late-'88, and Howard Roberts Fusion III in '91.

1979-1988	Fusion	$1,600	$2,000
1988-1990	Fusion II	$1,500	$1,850
1991-2009	Fusion III	$1,400	$1,750

Hummingbird

1960-present. Flat-top acoustic, square shoulders, mahogany back and sides, bound body and neck.

MODEL YEAR	FEATURES	EXC. COND. LOW	HIGH
1960	Cherry Sunburst	$3,700	$4,500
1961-1962	Cherry Sunburst	$3,300	$4,100
1962-1963	Cherry Sunburst, maple option	$3,300	$4,100
1963-1964	Cherry Sunburst	$3,300	$4,100
1965	Cherry Sunburst	$2,700	$3,300
1966	Cherry Sunburst or natural	$2,500	$3,100
1967-1968	Screwed 'guard	$2,500	$3,100
1969	Natural or sunburst	$2,500	$3,100
1970-1971	Natural or sunburst	$2,100	$2,600
1972-1979	Double X, block markers	$2,000	$2,400
1980-1985	Double X, block markers	$1,900	$2,300
1985-1988	Single X	$1,100	$1,400
1989-1999	25 1/2" scale	$1,300	$1,600
1994	100 Years 1894-1994 label	$1,300	$1,600
2000-2010		$1,400	$1,700

Hummingbird Custom

2001. Highly flamed koa back and sides, spruce top, gloss finish.

2001		$3,400	$4,200

Hummingbird 12 (Custom Shop)

2006. 12-string, vintage sunburst.

2006		$1,600	$2,100

Hummingbird Custom Shop Quilt Series

2007. Quilted maple, gold tuners, cherry sunburst.

2007		$2,500	$2,900

Hummingbird Limited Edition

1993-1994. Only 30 made, quilted maple top and back.

1993-1994		$2,700	$3,100

Invader

1983-1988. Single cutaway solid mahogany body, two humbucker pickups, four knobs with three-way selector switch, stop tailpiece, bolt-on maple neck.

1983-1988	Black, red, white	$450	$575
1983-1988	Silverburst	$600	$750

J-25

1983-1985. Flat-top, laminated spruce top, synthetic semi-round back, ebony 'board, natural or sunburst.

1983-1985		$400	$500

J-30

1985-1993. Dreadnought-size flat-top acoustic, mahogany back and sides, sunburst, renamed J-30 Montana in '94.

1985-1993		$850	$1,050

J-30 Cutaway

1990-1995. Cutaway version of J-30, transducer pickup.

1990-1995		$900	$1,100

J-30 Montana

1994-1997. Renamed from J-30, dreadnought-size flat-top acoustic, mahogany back and sides, sunburst.

1994-1997		$850	$1,050

J-30 RCA Limited Edition

1991. Limited edition for RCA Nashville, RCA logo on headstock.

1991		$1,200	$1,500

J-40

1971-1982. Dreadnought flat-top, mahogany back and sides, economy satin finish.

1971-1982	Natural satin finish	$900	$1,100

J-45

1942-1982, 1984-1993, 1999-present. Dreadnought flat-top, mahogany back and sides, round shoulders until '68 and '84 on, square shoulders '69-'82, sunburst finish (see J-50 for natural version) then natural finish also available in '90s, renamed J-45 Western in '94, renamed Early J-45 in '97 then renamed J-45 in '99. The prices noted are for all-original crack free instruments. A single professionally repaired minor crack that is nearly invisible will reduce the value only slightly. Two or more, or unsightly repaired cracks will devalue an otherwise excellent original acoustic instrument. Repaired cracks should be evaluated on a case-by-case basis.

MODEL YEAR	FEATURES	EXC. COND. LOW	HIGH
1942-1946	Sunburst, banner logo	$6,500	$7,700
1947-1949	Sunburst	$5,300	$6,500
1950-1956	Sunburst	$4,300	$5,300
1957	Sunburst	$4,000	$5,000
1958	Sunburst	$3,800	$4,800
1959	Sunburst	$3,700	$4,600
1960	Sunburst	$3,500	$4,300
1961	Sunburst	$3,200	$3,900
1962	Sunburst	$3,000	$3,700
1963	Sunburst	$2,600	$3,300
1964	Sunburst	$2,400	$3,000
1965	Sunburst	$2,100	$2,600
1966-1967	Sunburst	$1,900	$2,300
1968	Black, round shoulders	$3,000	$3,700
1968	Cherry, round shoulders	$1,825	$2,200
1968	Sunburst, Gibson 'guard	$1,825	$2,200
1969	Sunburst, round shoulders	$1,825	$2,200
1969	Sunburst, square shoulders	$1,500	$1,850
1970	Sunburst, square shoulders	$1,200	$1,500
1971-1972	Sunburst	$1,200	$1,500
1973-1979	Sunburst	$1,100	$1,400
1980-1982	Sunburst	$1,200	$1,500
1984-1993	Various colors	$1,200	$1,500
1999-2010	Sunburst	$1,200	$1,500

J-45/Early J-45

1997-1998. J-45 model name for '97 and '98.

1997-1998		$1,350	$1,700

J-45 1968 Reissue

2004. Special run using '68 specs including Gibson logo 'guard, black finish.

2004		$1,400	$1,700

1968 Gibson Hummingbird

1967 Gibson J-45

1956 Gibson J-50

1987 Gibson J-180

MODEL YEAR	FEATURES	EXC. COND. LOW	HIGH

J-45 Buddy Holly Limited Edition
1995-1996. 250 made.

1995-1996		$1,700	$2,100

J-45 Celebrity
1985. Acoustic introduced for Gibson's 90th anniversary, spruce top, rosewood back and sides, ebony 'board, binding on body and 'board, only 90 made.

1985		$1,700	$2,100

J-45 Custom
2001. Custom Shop decal, double bound slope shoulder, solid spruce top, figured maple sides and back.

2001		$1,500	$1,900

J-45 Custom Shop
2006. Figured mahogany, Adirondack.

2006		$1,700	$1,900

J-45 Historic
2005. Limited edition, 670 made, Historic Collection logo rear headstock, sunburst.

2005		$1,450	$1,750

J-45 Rosewood
1999-2005. Indian rosewood body, spruce top.

1999-2005		$1,425	$1,775

J-45 True Vintage
2007-present. Part of Vintage Series.

2007-2010		$1,650	$2,000

J-45 Vine
2003. Custom Shop model, D-size with sloped shoulders, Indian rosewood sides and back, fancy pearl and abalone vine inlay in ebony 'board, pearl Gibson logo and crown, natural gloss finish.

2003		$2,600	$3,200

J-45 Western
1994-1997. Previously called J-45, name changed to Early J-45 in '97.

1994-1997		$1,400	$1,700

Working Man 45 (J-45)
1998-2005. Soft shoulder J-45 style, gloss finish spruce top, satin finish mahogany back and sides, dot markers, natural.

1998-2005		$1,000	$1,175

J-50
1942, 1945-1981, 1990-1995, 1998-2008. Dreadnought flat-top, mahogany back and sides, round shoulders until '68, square shoulders after, natural finish (see J-45 for sunburst version).

1945-1946		$6,500	$7,700
1947-1949		$5,300	$6,500
1950-1955		$4,300	$5,300
1956		$4,400	$5,100
1957		$4,000	$5,000
1958		$3,800	$4,800
1959		$3,700	$4,600
1960		$3,500	$4,300
1961		$3,200	$3,900
1962		$3,000	$3,700
1963		$2,600	$3,300
1964		$2,400	$3,000
1965		$2,100	$2,600
1966-1967		$1,900	$2,300
1968	Black, round shoulders	$3,000	$3,700

MODEL YEAR	FEATURES	EXC. COND. LOW	HIGH
1968	Sunburst, Gibson 'guard	$1,825	$2,200
1969	Round shoulders	$1,825	$2,200
1969	Square shoulders	$1,500	$1,850
1970-1972	Square shoulders	$1,200	$1,500
1973-1979		$1,100	$1,400
1980-1981		$1,200	$1,500
1990-1995		$1,200	$1,500
1998-2008		$1,200	$1,500

J-55 (Jumbo 55) Limited Edition
1994 only. 16" flat-top, spruce top, mahogany back and sides, 100 made, sunburst.

1994		$1,400	$1,700

J-55 (Reintroduced)
1973-1982. Flat-top, laminated mahogany back and sides, arched back, square shoulders, sunburst. See Jumbo 55 listing for '39-'43 version.

1973-1982		$950	$1,200

J-60
1992-1999. Solid spruce top dreadnought, square shoulders, Indian rosewood back and sides, multiple bindings, natural or sunburst.

1992-1999		$1,200	$1,500

J-60 Curly Maple
1993 and 1996. Curly maple back and sides, limited edition from Montana shop, natural.

1993		$1,450	$1,800
1996		$1,450	$1,800

J-100/J-100 Custom
1970-1974, 1985-1997. Flat-top jumbo, multi-bound top and back, black 'guard, dot inlays, mahogany back and sides, '80s version has maple back and sides, dot inlays and tortoise shell 'guard, '90s model has maple back and sides, no 'guard, and J-200 style block inlays.

1970-1974	Mahogany	$1,350	$1,650
1985-1989	Maple	$1,350	$1,650
1990-1997		$1,350	$1,650

J-100 Xtra

1991-2004		$1,200	$1,500

J-150
1999-2005. Super jumbo body, solid spruce top, figured maple back and sides (later rosewood), MOP crown inlays, moustache bridge with transducer.

1999-2005		$1,500	$1,900

J-160E
1954-1979. Flat-top jumbo acoustic, 1 bridge P-90 pickup, tone and volume controls on front, sunburst finish, reintroduced as J-160 in '90.

1954	19 frets, large bridge dots	$4,300	$5,300
1955	20 frets	$4,000	$5,000
1956-1959		$4,000	$5,000
1960-1961		$3,400	$4,200
1962	Beatles' vintage June '62	$3,800	$4,500
1963		$3,400	$4,200
1964	Lennon's 2nd model	$3,800	$4,500
1965		$3,200	$3,700
1966-1969		$2,700	$3,300
1970-1979		$1,550	$1,850

MODEL YEAR	FEATURES	EXC. COND. LOW	HIGH

J-160E Reissue/Peace/John Lennon Peace

1991-1997, 2003-present. Reintroduced J-160E with solid spruce top, solid mahogany back and sides.

1991-1997		$1,350	$1,650
2003-2010		$1,350	$1,650

J-180/Everly Brothers/The Everly Brothers

1986-2005. Reissue of the '62-'72 Everly Brothers model, renamed The Everly Brothers ('92-'94), then The Everly ('94-'96), then back to J-180, black.

1986-2005		$1,500	$1,800

J-180 Special Edition

1993. Gibson Bozeman, only 36 made, Everly Brother specs, large double white pearloid 'guard.

1993		$2,400	$2,900

J-185/J-185N

1951-1959. Flat-top jumbo, figured maple back and sides, bound body and neck, sunburst (185) or natural (185N).

1951-1959	Natural	$16,000	$20,000
1951-1959	Sunburst	$11,500	$14,500

J-185 Reissue

1990-1995, 1999-present. Flat-top jumbo, figured maple back and sides, bound body and neck, natural or sunburst, limited run of 100 between '91-'92.

1990-1995		$1,600	$2,000
1999-2010		$1,500	$1,900

J-185 EC (Blues King)

1999-present. Acoustic/electric, rounded cutaway, flamed maple back and sides, sunburst or natural.

1999-2010		$1,500	$1,800

J-185 EC Custom

2005. Limited Edition, 200 made, spruce top, figured maple sides and back, pearl double parallelogram markers, Fishman Prefix Plus on-board electronics.

2005		$1,600	$2,000

J-185 EC Rosewood

2006-present. Acoustic/electric, rounded cutaway, Indian rosewood back and sides.

2006-2010		$1,500	$1,900

J-185 Vine

2005-2006. 185 with vine fretboard inlay.

2005-2006		$2,500	$3,100

J-185-12

2001-2004. 12-string J-185, flamed maple sides and back.

2001-2004		$1,600	$2,000

J-190 EC Super Fusion

2001-2004. Jumbo single cut acoustic/electric, spruce top, curly maple back and sides, neck pickup and Fishman Piezo.

2001-2004		$1,400	$1,700

J-200/SJ-200/J-200N/SJ-200N

1946-present. Labeled SJ-200 until ca.'54. Super Jumbo flat-top, maple back and sides, see Super Jumbo 200 for '38-'42 rosewood back and sides model, called J-200 Artist for a time in the mid-'70s, renamed '50s Super Jumbo 200 in '97 and again renamed SJ-200 Reissue in '99. Currently again called the SJ-200. 200N indicates natural option.

1946-1949	Natural option	$15,000	$18,500
1946-1949	Sunburst	$14,000	$17,000
1950-1952	Natural option	$13,000	$16,000
1950-1952	Sunburst	$11,000	$14,000
1953-1955	Natural option	$11,000	$14,000
1953-1955	Sunburst	$9,000	$12,000
1956-1959	Natural option	$10,000	$12,500
1956-1959	Sunburst	$8,000	$10,000
1960	Natural option	$9,000	$11,000
1960	Sunburst	$8,000	$10,000
1961	Natural option	$8,000	$10,000
1961	Sunburst	$7,000	$9,000
1962	Natural option	$8,000	$10,000
1962	Sunburst	$7,000	$9,000
1963	Natural option	$7,000	$9,000
1963	Sunburst	$6,100	$7,500
1964	Natural option	$7,100	$8,500
1964	Sunburst	$6,100	$7,500
1965	Natural or sunburst	$5,000	$6,000
1966	Natural or sunburst	$4,000	$5,000
1967-1969	Natural or sunburst	$3,500	$4,200
1970-1979	Natural or sunburst	$2,000	$2,500
1980-1989	Natural or sunburst	$2,100	$2,600
1990-1999	Natural or sunburst	$2,000	$2,500
2000-2010	Natural or sunburst	$1,900	$2,400

J-200 Celebrity

1985-1987. Acoustic introduced for Gibson's 90th anniversary, spruce top, rosewood back, sides and 'board, binding on body and 'board, sunburst, only 90 made.

1985-1987		$2,600	$3,200

J-200 Elvis Presley Signature

2002. 250 made, large block letter Elvis Presley name on 'board, figured maple sides and back, gloss natural spruce top, black and white custom designed 'guard after one of Presley's personal guitars.

2002		$2,500	$3,100

J-200 Koa

1994. Figured Hawaiian Koa back and sides, spruce top, natural.

1994		$2,400	$3,000

J-200 Western Classic Prewar 200 Brazilian

2003. Based on Ray Whitley's 1937 J-200, Custom Shop, limited production, Brazilian rosewood back and sides.

2002		$5,000	$6,200

J-250 R

1972-1973, 1976-1978. A J-200 with rosewood back and sides, sunburst, only 20 shipped from Gibson.

1972-1973		$2,400	$2,900
1976-1978		$2,400	$2,900

J-1000/SJ-1000

1992-1994. Jumbo cutaway, spruce top, rosewood back and sides, on-board electronics, diamond-shape markers and headstock inlay.

1992-1994		$1,600	$2,000

J-1500

1992. Jumbo cutaway flat-top, higher-end appointments including Nick Lucas-style position markers, sunburst.

1992		$1,675	$2,100

2007 Gibson J-185 Reissue

Gibson J-200

GUITARS

1965 Gibson Johnny Smith Double

1929 Gibson L-1

MODEL YEAR	FEATURES	EXC. COND. LOW	HIGH

J-2000/J-2000 Custom/J-2000 R

1986, 1992-1999. Cutaway acoustic, rosewood back and sides (a few had Brazilian rosewood or maple bodies), ebony 'board and bridge, Sitka spruce top, multiple bindings, sunburst or natural. Name changed to J-2000 Custom in '93 when it became available only on a custom-order basis.

1986	J-2000 R, rosewood	$2,600	$3,300
1986	J-2000, maple	$2,600	$3,300
1992	Rosewood	$2,600	$3,300
1993-1996	J-2000 Custom	$2,600	$3,300
1999	J-2000 Custom Cutaway	$2,800	$3,500

JG-0

1970-1972. Economy square shouldered jumbo, follows Jubilee model in '70.

1970-1972		$750	$900

JG-12

1970. Economy square shouldered jumbo 12-string, follows Jubilee-12 model in '70.

1970		$750	$900

Johnny A Signature Series

2004-present. Thinline semi-hollow, sharp double-cut, flamed maple top, humbucking pickups, Johnny A truss rod cover, gold plated hardware, Bigsby vibrato (part of his signature style), sunburst, includes certificate of authenticity.

2004-2010	Includes rare color option	$2,200	$2,700

Johnny Smith

1961-1989. Single-cut archtop, 1 humbucking pickup, gold hardware, multiple binding front and back, natural or sunburst. By '80 cataloged as JS model.

1961-1969		$7,000	$8,700
1970-1979		$5,600	$7,000
1980-1989		$5,600	$7,000

Johnny Smith Double

1963-1989. Single-cut archtop, 2 humbucking pickups, gold hardware, multiple binding front and back, natural or sunburst. By '80 cataloged as JSD model.

1961-1969		$7,500	$9,300
1970-1979		$6,000	$7,500
1980-1989		$6,000	$7,500

Jubilee

1969-1970. Flat-top, laminated mahogany back and sides, single bound body, natural with black back and sides.

1969-1970		$750	$900

Jubilee Deluxe

1970-1971. Flat-top, laminated rosewood back and sides, multi-bound body, natural finish.

1970-1971		$1,000	$1,200

Jubilee-12

1969-1970. Flat-top, 12 strings, laminated mahogany back and sides, multi-bound, natural.

1969-1970		$1,000	$1,200

Jumbo

1934-1936. Gibson's first Jumbo flat-top, mahogany back and sides, round shoulders, bound top and back, sunburst, becomes the 16" Jumbo 35 in late-'36.

1934-1936		$20,000	$25,000

Jumbo 35/J-35

1936-1942. Jumbo flat-top, mahogany back and sides, silkscreen logo, sunburst, reintroduced as J-35, square-shouldered dreadnought, in '83.

1936-1942		$12,000	$15,000

Jumbo 55/J-55

1939-1943. Flat-top dreadnought, round shoulders, mahogany back and sides, pearl inlaid logo, sunburst, reintroduced in '73 as J-55.

1939-1943		$14,000	$18,000

Jumbo Centennial Special

1994. Reissue of 1934 Jumbo, natural, 100 made.

1994		$2,000	$2,400

Junior Pro

1987-1989. Single-cut, mahogany body, KB-X tremolo system 1 humbucker pickup, black chrome hardware, various colors.

1987-1989		$400	$500

Kalamazoo Award Model

1978-1981. Single-cut archtop, bound f-holes, multi-bound top and back, 1 mini-humbucker, gold-plated hardware, woodgrain 'guard with bird and branch abalone inlay, highly figured natural or sunburst.

1978-1981	Natural	$9,500	$12,000
1978-1981	Sunburst	$8,500	$11,000

Keb' Mo' Signature Bluesmaster

2010. Limited run of 300, small-bodied flat-top acoustic, Baggs pickup, soundhole-mounted volume control, vintage sunburst or antique natural finish.

2010		$1,900	$2,300

Kiefer Sutherland KS-336

2007. Custom Shop model inspired by Artist Series.

2007		$2,000	$2,500

KZ II

1980-1981. Double-cut solidbody, 2 humbuckers, 4 knob and toggle controls, tune-o-matic, dot markers, stencil Gibson logo on headstock, walnut stain.

1980		$900	$1,100

L-0

1926-1933, 1937-1942. Acoustic flat-top, maple back and sides '26-'27, mahogany after.

1926-1928	13.5", maple	$4,000	$5,000
1928-1930	13.5", mahogany	$3,400	$4,200
1931-1933	14.75"	$3,900	$4,700
1937-1942	Reissue, spruce top	$3,500	$4,300

L-00

1932-1946. Acoustic flat-top, mahogany back and sides, bound top to '36 and bound top and back '37 on.

1932-1946		$4,400	$5,500

L-00 1937 Legend

2006-present. Part of the Vintage Series.

2006-2010		$3,000	$3,700

L-00/Blues King

1991-1997, 1999-present. Reintroduced as L-00, called Blues King L-00 for '94-'97, back as L-00 for '99-'02, called Blues King '03-present.

1991-1997	L-00/Blues King	$1,075	$1,300
2003-2010	Blues King	$1,300	$1,575

MODEL YEAR	FEATURES	EXC. COND. LOW	HIGH

L-1 (Archtop)

1902-1925. Acoustic archtop, single-bound top, back and soundhole, name continued on flat-top model in '26.

1902-1907	12.5", round hole	$1,500	$1,900
1908-1925	13.5", round hole	$1,600	$2,000

L-1 (Flat-Top)

1926-1937. Acoustic flat-top, maple back and sides '26-'27, mahogany after.

1926-1929	13.5", 12-fret	$4,400	$5,500
1930-1931	14.75", 13-fret	$4,400	$5,500
1932-1937	14-fret	$4,200	$5,200

L-1 Robert Johnson

2007-present. 1926 specs, Robert Johnson inlay at end of 'board.

2007-2010		$1,200	$1,500

L-2 (Archtop)

1902-1926. Round soundhole archtop, pearl inlay on peghead, 1902-'07 available in 3 body sizes: 12.5" to 16", '24-'26 13.5" body width.

1902-1907	12.5", round hole	$1,600	$2,000
1924-1926	13.5", round hole	$1,700	$2,100

L-2 (Flat-Top)

1929-1935. Acoustic flat-top, rosewood back and sides except for mahogany in '31, triple-bound top and back, limited edition model in '94.

1929-1933	12-fret, rosewood	$6,000	$7,000
1934-1935	14-fret	$7,000	$8,000

L-2 1929 Reissue

1994 only. Spruce top, Indian rosewood back and sides, raised 'guard.

1994		$1,800	$2,200

L-3 (Archtop)

1902-1933. Acoustic archtop, available in 3 sizes: 12.5", 13.5", 16".

1902-1907		$1,700	$2,100
1908-1926		$1,800	$2,200
1927-1933		$2,000	$2,500

L-4

1912-1956. Acoustic archtop, 16" wide.

1912-1922	Oval hole	$2,600	$3,200
1923-1924	Loar era, oval hole	$2,600	$3,200
1925-1927	Oval hole	$2,600	$3,200
1928-1934	Round hole	$2,600	$3,200
1935-1946	F-holes, fleur-de-lis	$2,600	$3,200
1947-1956	Crown peghead inlay, triple bound	$2,600	$3,200

L-4 A

2003-2005. 15 3/4" lower bout, mid-size jumbo, rounded cutaway, factory electronics with preamp.

2003-2005		$1,100	$1,350

L-4 C/L-4 CN

1949-1971. Single-cut acoustic archtop.

1949-1959	Natural	$3,300	$3,800
1949-1959	Sunburst	$2,900	$3,400
1960-1964	Natural	$2,500	$3,000
1960-1964	Sunburst	$2,300	$2,800
1965	Natural, sunburst	$2,100	$2,600
1966-1971	Natural, sunburst	$2,000	$2,500

L-4 CES/L-4 CES Mahogany

1958, 1969, 1986-present. Single pointed cutaway archtop, 2 humbuckers, gold parts, natural or sunburst, maple back and sides '58 and '69, mahogany laminate back and sides for '86-'93, became part of Gibson's Historic Collection with laminated maple back and sides for '94, renamed L-4 CES Mahogany with solid mahogany back and sides in '04, Custom Shop model.

1958	Natural, PAF humbuckers	$10,200	$12,800
1958	Sunburst, PAF humbuckers	$8,000	$10,000
1969	Natural	$3,500	$4,400
1969	Sunburst	$3,500	$4,400
1986-1993	Laminate mahogany	$2,600	$3,200
1994-2003	Laminate maple	$2,600	$3,200
2004-2010	Solid mahogany	$2,600	$3,200

L-4 Special Tenor/Plectrum

Late-1920s. Limited edition 4-string flat-top.

1929		$2,300	$2,800

L-5

1923-1958. Acoustic archtop, non-cut, multiple bindings, Lloyd Loar label until '24, 17" body by '35, Master Model label until '27, sunburst with natural option later.

1923-1924	Lloyd Loar era	$40,000	$50,000
1925-1927	Master Model label	$24,000	$30,000
1928	Carter, banjo tuners	$30,000	$37,000
1928	Non-Carter, no banjo tuners	$13,000	$17,000
1929	Early 1929	$10,000	$12,500
1929-1930	Block markers	$8,500	$10,600
1931-1932	Kaufman vibrola	$8,000	$10,000
1931-1932	Standard trapeze	$8,000	$10,000
1933-1939	16" body	$7,500	$9,500
1935-1940	17" body	$7,000	$8,700
1939-1940	Natural option	$8,000	$9,700
1946-1949	Natural option	$6,700	$8,300
1946-1949	Sunburst	$5,500	$6,800
1950-1958	Natural	$5,400	$6,600
1950-1958	Sunburst	$4,900	$6,100

L-5 '34 Non-Cutaway Historic

1994. 1934 specs including block pearl inlays, bound snakehead peghead, close grained solid spruce top, figured solid maple sides and back, Cremona Brown sunburst finish, replica Grover open back tuners.

1994		$4,000	$5,000

L-5 Premier/L-5 P

1939-1943. Introduced as L-5 Premier (L-5 P) and renamed L-5 C in '48, single rounded cutaway acoustic archtop.

1939-1943	Natural option	$15,000	$18,000
1939-1943	Sunburst	$12,000	$15,000

L-5 C

1948-1982. Renamed from L-5 Premier (L-5 P), single rounded cutaway acoustic archtop, sunburst.

1948-1949	Natural	$12,000	$15,000

Gibson L-4 CES

1933 Gibson L-5

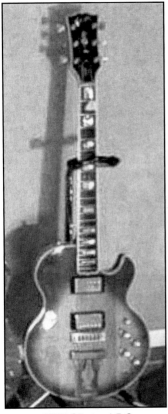

1977 Gibson L5-S

Roland Gonzales

1952 Gibson L-7

MODEL YEAR	FEATURES	EXC. COND. LOW	EXC. COND. HIGH
1948-1949	Sunburst	$11,000	$14,000
1950-1955	Natural	$11,000	$13,500
1950-1955	Sunburst	$9,000	$11,500
1956-1959	Natural	$10,000	$12,500
1956-1959	Sunburst	$9,500	$10,500
1960-1964	Natural	$8,000	$9,800
1960-1964	Sunburst	$7,500	$9,300
1965	Natural	$7,200	$8,800
1965	Sunburst	$6,200	$7,800
1966	Natural	$6,500	$8,000
1966	Sunburst	$5,400	$6,500
1967-1969	Natural	$5,400	$6,500
1967-1969	Sunburst	$5,400	$6,500
1970-1972	Natural	$4,800	$5,800
1970-1972	Sunburst	$4,800	$5,800
1973-1982	Natural, sunburst	$4,800	$5,800

L-5 CES/L-5 CESN

1951-present. Electric version of L-5 C, single round cutaway (pointed mid-'60-'69), archtop, 2 pickups (P-90s '51-'53, Alnico Vs '54-mid-'57, humbuckers after), now part of Gibson's Historic Collection.

MODEL YEAR	FEATURES	EXC. COND. LOW	EXC. COND. HIGH
1951-1957	Natural, single coils	$13,000	$16,000
1951-1957	Sunburst, single coils	$12,000	$15,000
1958-1959	Natural, PAFs	$20,000	$25,000
1958-1959	Sunburst, PAFs	$17,000	$21,000
1960-1962	Natural, PAFs	$20,000	$25,000
1960-1962	Sunburst, PAFs	$16,000	$20,000
1963-1964	Natural, pat. #	$16,000	$20,000
1963-1964	Sunburst, pat. #	$13,000	$17,000
1965-1966	Natural	$9,200	$11,000
1965-1966	Sunburst	$6,500	$8,000
1966	Natural	$7,200	$8,700
1967-1969	Natural	$7,200	$8,700
1967-1969	Sunburst	$6,500	$7,500
1970-1972	Natural	$6,500	$7,200
1970-1972	Sunburst	$4,500	$5,600
1973-1975	Natural	$4,500	$5,600
1973-1975	Sunburst	$4,500	$5,600
1976-1979	Natural, sunburst	$4,500	$5,600
1980-1984	Kalamazoo made	$4,300	$5,300
1985-1992	Nashville made	$4,300	$5,300

L-5 CES Custom Shop Historic Collection

1994-1997. Historic Collection Series, sunburst or natural.

MODEL YEAR	FEATURES	EXC. COND. LOW	EXC. COND. HIGH
1994	100th Anniv., black	$5,400	$6,500
1994-1996	Natural, highly figured back	$5,900	$7,100
1994-1996	Sunburst	$5,400	$6,500
1997	Wine Red	$5,000	$6,000

L-5 CT (George Gobel)

1959-1961. Single-cut, thinline archtop acoustic, some were built with pickups, cherry.

MODEL YEAR	FEATURES	EXC. COND. LOW	EXC. COND. HIGH
1959-1961		$15,000	$19,000

L-5 CT Reissue

1998-2007. Historic Collection, acoustic and electric versions, natural, sunburst, cherry.

MODEL YEAR	FEATURES	EXC. COND. LOW	EXC. COND. HIGH
1998-2007		$5,000	$6,000

L-5 S

1972-1985, 2004-2005. Single-cut solidbody, multi-bound body and neck, gold hardware, 2 pickups (low impedence '72-'74, humbuckers '75 on), offered in natural, cherry sunburst or vintage sunburst. 1 humbucker version issued in '04 from Gibson's Custom, Art & Historic division.

MODEL YEAR	FEATURES	EXC. COND. LOW	EXC. COND. HIGH
1972-1974	Natural, gold hardware, low impedence pickups	$3,700	$4,800
1972-1974	Sunburst, low impedence pickups	$3,500	$4,500
1975-1980	Natural, gold hardware, humbuckers	$3,700	$4,800
1975-1980	Natural, sunburst, humbuckers	$3,500	$4,500

L-5 Studio

1996-2000. Normal L-5 dual pickup features, marble-style 'guard, translucent finish, dot markers.

MODEL YEAR	FEATURES	EXC. COND. LOW	EXC. COND. HIGH
1996-2000		$1,900	$2,300

L-5 Wes Montgomery Custom Shop

1993-present. Various colors.

MODEL YEAR	FEATURES	EXC. COND. LOW	EXC. COND. HIGH
1993-2010		$4,800	$6,100

L-6 S

1973-1975. Single-cut solidbody, 2 humbucking pickups, 6 position rotary switch, stop tailpiece, cherry or natural, renamed L-6 S Custom in '75.

MODEL YEAR	FEATURES	EXC. COND. LOW	EXC. COND. HIGH
1973-1975	Cherry	$950	$1,150
1973-1975	Natural	$900	$1,100

L-6 S Custom

1975-1980. Renamed from the L-6 S, 2 humbucking pickups, stop tailpiece, cherry or natural.

MODEL YEAR	FEATURES	EXC. COND. LOW	EXC. COND. HIGH
1975-1980	Cherry, natural	$1,300	$1,600
1978-1979	Silverburst option	$1,400	$1,700

L-6 S Deluxe

1975-1981. Single-cut solidbody, 2 humbucking pickups, no rotary switch, strings-thru-body design, cherry or natural.

MODEL YEAR	FEATURES	EXC. COND. LOW	EXC. COND. HIGH
1975-1981		$1,400	$1,700

L-7

1932-1956. Acoustic archtop, bound body and neck, fleur-de-lis peghead inlay, 16" body '32-'34, 17" body X-braced top late-'34.

MODEL YEAR	FEATURES	EXC. COND. LOW	EXC. COND. HIGH
1932-1934	16" body	$3,200	$4,000
1935-1939	17" body, X-braced	$3,200	$4,000
1940-1950	Natural	$2,800	$3,400
1940-1950	Sunburst	$2,500	$3,100
1951-1956	Natural	$2,800	$3,400
1951-1956	Sunburst	$2,500	$3,100

L-7 C

1948-1972, 2002-present. Single-cut acoustic archtop, triple-bound top, sunburst or natural finish. Gibson revived the L-7 C name for a new acoustic archtop in 2002.

MODEL YEAR	FEATURES	EXC. COND. LOW	EXC. COND. HIGH
1948-1949	Natural	$4,500	$5,600
1948-1949	Sunburst	$4,500	$5,600
1950-1959	Natural	$4,500	$5,600
1950-1959	Sunburst	$4,000	$5,000
1960-1962	Natural	$3,700	$4,500
1960-1962	Sunburst	$3,500	$4,300

MODEL YEAR	FEATURES	EXC. COND. LOW	HIGH
1963-1964	Natural	$3,700	$4,500
1963-1964	Sunburst	$3,500	$4,300
1965	Natural	$3,400	$4,200
1965	Sunburst	$3,400	$4,200
1966	Natural	$3,300	$4,100
1966	Sunburst	$3,300	$4,100
1967-1969	Natural	$3,300	$4,100
1967-1969	Sunburst	$3,300	$4,100
1970-1972	Natural, sunburst	$3,300	$4,100

L-7 Custom Electric
1936. L-7 with factory Christian-style pickup, limited production, often custom ordered.

1936		$4,000	$5,000

L-7 C Custom Shop
2006. Custom Shop logo, Certificate of Authenticity.

2006		$2,700	$3,200

L-10
1923-1939. Acoustic archtop, single-bound body and 'board.

1923-1934	Black, 16", F-holes	$3,500	$4,300
1935-1939	Black, sunburst, 17", X-braced	$3,500	$4,300

L-12
1930-1955. Acoustic archtop, single-bound body, 'guard, neck and headstock, gold-plated hardware, sunburst.

1930-1934	16"	$4,000	$4,800
1935-1939	17", X-braced	$4,000	$4,800
1940-1941	Parallel top braced	$3,800	$4,600
1946-1949	Post-war	$3,100	$3,900
1950-1955		$2,700	$3,400

L-12 Premier/L-12 P
1947-1950. L-12 with rounded cutaway, sunburst.

1947-1950		$4,000	$5,000

L-20 Special/L-20 K International Special
1993-1994. Rosewood back and sides (koa on the K), ebony 'board, block inlays, gold tuners, multi-bound.

1993-1994	L-20, mahogany	$1,100	$1,300
1993-1994	L-20K, koa	$1,350	$1,600

L-30
1935-1943. Acoustic archtop, single-bound body, black or sunburst.

1935-1943		$1,300	$1,600

L-37
1937-1941. 14-3/4" acoustic archtop, flat back, single-bound body and 'guard, sunburst.

1937-1941		$1,400	$1,700

L-48
1946-1971. 16" acoustic archtop, single-bound body, mahogany sides, sunburst.

1946-1949		$1,300	$1,600
1950-1959		$1,100	$1,400
1960-1964		$1,000	$1,200
1965		$900	$1,100
1966-1969		$850	$1,050
1970-1971		$800	$1,000

L-50
1932-1971. 14.75" acoustic archtop, flat or arched back, round soundhole or f-holes, pearl logo pre-war, decal logo post-war, maple sides, sunburst, 16" body late-'34.

1932-1934	14.75" body	$1,400	$1,700
1934-1949	16" body	$1,600	$1,900
1950-1959		$1,400	$1,700
1960-1964		$1,200	$1,500
1965		$1,100	$1,400
1966-1969		$1,000	$1,200
1970-1971		$950	$1,050

L-75
1932-1939. 14.75" archtop with round soundhole and flat back, size increased to 16" with arched back in '35, small button tuners, dot markers, lower-end style trapeze tailpiece, pearl script logo, sunburst.

1932	14.75", dot neck	$1,600	$2,000
1933-1934	14.75", pearloid	$1,800	$2,200
1935-1939	16" body	$1,900	$2,300

L-130
1999-2005. 14 7/8" lower bout, small jumbo, solid spruce top, solid bubinga back and sides, rosewood 'board, factory electronics with preamp.

1999-2005		$1,000	$1,200

L-140
1999-2005. Like L-130 but with rosewood back and sides, ebony 'board.

1999-2005		$1,100	$1,300

L-200 Emmylou Harris
2002-present. SJ-200/J-200 reissue, L-series smaller and thinner than standard jumbo body, solid Sitka spruce top, flamed maple sides and back, gold hardware, crest markers, natural or sunburst.

2002-2010		$1,800	$2,100

L-C Century
1933-1941. Curly maple back and sides, bound body, white pearloid 'board and peghead (all years) and headstock (until '38), sunburst.

1933-1941		$4,900	$6,100

L-C Reissue
1994. Pearloid headstock and 'board.

1994		$2,100	$2,500

LC-1 Cascade
2002-2006. LC-Series acoustic/electric, advanced L-00-style, solid quilted maple back and sides.

2002-2006		$1,275	$1,600

LC-2 Sonoma
2002-2006. Released November '02, LC-Series acoustic/electric, advanced L-00-style, solid walnut back and sides.

2002-2006		$1,125	$1,400

LC-3 Caldera
2003-2004. 14 3/4" flat-top, soft cutaway, solid cedar top, solid flamed Koa back and sides, fancy appointments.

2003-2004		$1,650	$2,000

Le Grande
1993-2008. Electric archtop, 17", formerly called Johnny Smith.

1993-2008		$4,700	$5,900

1946 Gibson L-50
Robbie Keene

Gibson L-C Century of Progress

GUITARS

1957 Gibson Les Paul Model

1989 Gibson Les Paul Custom

Les Paul

Following are models bearing the Les Paul name, beginning with the original Les Paul Model. All others are then listed alphabetically as follows:

Les Paul Model
'52 Les Paul Goldtop
'54 Les Paul Goldtop
'56 Les Paul Goldtop
'57 Les Paul Goldtop
'57 Les Paul Goldtop (R-7 wrap-around)
1957 Les Paul Junior Single Cut (VOS)
'58 Les Paul Figured Top
'58 Les Paul Plaintop (VOS)
1958 Les Paul Junior Double Cut (VOS)
'59 Les Paul Flametop/Reissue/Standard
'60 Les Paul Corvette
'60 Les Paul Flametop/Standard
'60 Les Paul Junior
'60 Les Paul Special
Les Paul (All Maple)
Les Paul 25/50 Anniversary
Les Paul 25th Silver Anniversary (Guitar Center)
Les Paul 30th Anniversary
Les Paul 40th Anniversary (from 1952)
Les Paul 40th Anniversary (from 1959)
Les Paul 50th Anniversary 1960 Les Paul Standard
Les Paul 50th Anniversary '56 Les Paul Standard
Les Paul 50th Anniversary '59 Les Paul Standard
Les Paul 50th Anniversary Korina Tribute
Les Paul 55
Les Paul 295
Les Paul Ace Frehley Signature
Les Paul Artisan and Artisan/3
Les Paul Artist/L.P. Artist/Les Paul Active
Les Paul BFG
Les Paul Bird's-Eye Standard
Les Paul Carved Series
Les Paul Centennial ('56 LP Standard Goldtop)
Les Paul Centennial ('59 LP Special)
Les Paul Class 5
Les Paul Classic
Les Paul Classic Antique Mahogany
Les Paul Classic Custom
Les Paul Classic H-90
Les Paul Classic Limited Edition
Les Paul Classic Mark III/MIII
Les Paul Classic Plus
Les Paul Classic Premium Plus
Les Paul Classic Tom Morgan Limited Edition
Les Paul Cloud 9 Series
Les Paul Custom
Les Paul Custom (Custom Shop)
Les Paul Custom 20th Anniversary
Les Paul Custom 35th Anniversary
Les Paul Custom '54
Les Paul Custom Historic '54
Les Paul Custom Historic '57 Black Beauty
Les Paul Custom Historic '68

Les Paul Custom Lite
Les Paul Custom Lite (Show Case Ed.)
Les Paul Custom Mick Ronson '68
Les Paul Custom Music Machine
Les Paul Custom Peter Frampton Signature
Les Paul Custom Plus
Les Paul Custom Showcase Edition
Les Paul Dale Earnhardt
Les Paul Dale Earnhardt Intimidator
Les Paul DC AA
Les Paul DC Classic
Les Paul DC Pro
Les Paul DC Standard (Plus)
Les Paul DC Studio
Les Paul Deluxe
Les Paul Deluxe 30th Anniversary
Les Paul Deluxe '69 Reissue
Les Paul Deluxe Hall of Fame
Les Paul Deluxe Limited Edition
Les Paul Dickey Betts Goldtop
Les Paul Dickey Betts Red Top
Les Paul Dusk Tiger
Les Paul Elegant
Les Paul Eric Clapton 1960
Les Paul Florentine Plus
Les Paul Gary Moore BFG
Les Paul Gary Moore Signature
Les Paul Gary Rossington Signature
Les Paul Goddess
Les Paul GT
Les Paul Guitar Trader Reissue
Les Paul HD.6-X Pro Digital
Les Paul Heritage 80
Les Paul Heritage 80 Award
Les Paul Heritage 80 Elite
Les Paul Heritage 80/Standard 80
Les Paul Indian Motorcycle
Les Paul Jim Beam
Les Paul Jimmy Page (Custom Authentic)
Les Paul Jimmy Page Signature
Les Paul Jimmy Page Signature Custom Shop
Les Paul Jimmy Wallace Reissue
Les Paul Joe Perry Signature
Les Paul Jumbo
Les Paul Junior
Les Paul Junior 3/4
Les Paul Junior Billie Joe Armstrong Signature
Les Paul Junior DC Hall of Fame
Les Paul Junior Double Cutaway
Les Paul Junior John Lennon LTD
Les Paul Junior Lite
Les Paul Junior Special
Les Paul Junior Tenor/Plectrum
Les Paul Katrina
Les Paul KM (Kalamazoo Model)
Les Paul Leo's Reissue
Les Paul Limited Edition (3-tone)
Les Paul LP295 Goldtop
Les Paul Melody Maker
Les Paul Menace
Les Paul Music Machine 25th Anniversary
Les Paul Music Machine Brazilian Stinger
Les Paul Old Hickory

The *Vintage Guitar Price Guide* shows low to high values for items in all-original excellent condition, and, where applicable, with original case or cover.

Les Paul Pee Wee
Les Paul Personal
Les Paul Pro Deluxe
Les Paul Pro Showcase Edition
Les Paul Professional
Les Paul Recording
Les Paul Reissue Flametop
Les Paul Reissue Goldtop
Les Paul Richard Petty LTD
Les Paul SG '61 Reissue
Les Paul SG Standard Authentic
Les Paul SG Standard Reissue
Les Paul Signature/L.P. Signature
Les Paul Slash Signature
Les Paul SmartWood Exotic
Les Paul SmartWood Standard
Les Paul SmartWood Studio
Les Paul Special
Les Paul Special (Reissue)
Les Paul Special 3/4
Les Paul Special Centennial
Les Paul Special Custom Shop
Les Paul Special Double Cutaway
Les Paul Special Faded
Les Paul Special New Century
Les Paul Special Tenor
Les Paul Special Worn Cherry
Les Paul Spider-Man
Les Paul Spotlight Special
Les Paul Standard (Sunburst)
Les Paul Standard (SG body)
Les Paul Standard (reintroduced)
Les Paul Standard 2008
Les Paul Standard '82
Les Paul Standard Billy Gibbons 'Pearly Gates'
Les Paul Standard Lite
Les Paul Standard Plus
Les Paul Standard Premium Plus
Les Paul Standard Sparkle
Les Paul Strings and Things Standard
Les Paul Studio
Les Paul Studio Baritone
Les Paul Studio BFD
Les Paul Studio Custom
Les Paul Studio Faded
Les Paul Studio Gem
Les Paul Studio Gothic
Les Paul Studio Limited Edition
Les Paul Studio Lite
Les Paul Studio MLB Baseball
Les Paul Studio Plus
Les Paul Studio Premium Plus
Les Paul Studio Robot
Les Paul Studio Swamp Ash/Swamp Ash
   Studio
Les Paul Supreme
Les Paul Tie Dye (St. Pierre)
Les Paul Tie Dye Custom Shop
Les Paul Traditional
Les Paul TV
Les Paul TV 3/4
Les Paul Ultima
Les Paul Vixen

Les Paul Voodoo/Voodoo Les Paul
Les Paul XR-I/XR-II/XR-III
Les Paul Zakk Wylde Signature
The Les Paul
The Paul
The Paul Firebrand Deluxe
The Paul II

Les Paul Model

1952-1958. The Goldtop, 2 P-90 pickups until mid-'57, humbuckers after, trapeze tailpiece until late-'53, stud tailpiece/bridge '53-mid-'55, Tune-o-matic bridge '55-'58, renamed Les Paul Standard in '58. All gold option add +10% if the neck retains 90% of the gold paint. All gold option with ugly green wear on the neck is equal to or below the value of a standard paint job. Some instruments had all mahogany bodies which did not have the maple cap. These instruments are of lower value than the standard maple on mahogany bodies. The all mahogany version, although more rare, has a 10% lower value. A factory installed Bigsby tailpiece will reduce value by 30%. A non-factory installed Bigsby will reduce value up to 50%.

MODEL YEAR	FEATURES	EXC. COND. LOW	HIGH
1952	1st made, unbound neck	$14,000	$17,000
1952	5/8" knobs, bound neck	$11,500	$14,500
1953	1/2" knobs, late-'53 stud tailpiece	$18,000	$22,000
1953	1/2" knobs, trapeze tailpiece	$11,000	$14,000
1954	Stud tailpiece, wrap-around	$19,000	$24,000
1955	Stud tailpiece, wrap-around, early-'55	$21,000	$26,000
1955	Tune-o-matic tailpiece, late-'55	$31,000	$38,000
1956	Tune-o-matic tailpiece	$27,000	$34,000
1957	P-90s, early-'57	$27,000	$34,000
1957	PAF humbuckers, black plastic	$71,000	$90,000
1957	PAF humbuckers, white plastic	$77,000	$95,000
1958	PAF humbuckers	$80,000	$100,000

'52 Les Paul Goldtop

1997-2002. Goldtop finish, 2 P-90s, '52-style trapeze tailpiece/bridge.

1997-2002		$1,900	$2,200
1997-2002	Murphy aged	$2,200	$2,700

'54 Les Paul Goldtop

1996-present. Goldtop finish, 2 P-90s, '53-'54 stud tailpiece/bridge.

1996-2000		$1,800	$2,100
2001-2003	R-4 (very accurate)	$1,800	$2,100
2003	Brazilian rosewood, with certificate	$2,700	$3,400
2004-2006	VOS	$1,800	$2,100
2007	R-4, limited, 1/4 sawn fleck	$2,400	$2,600
2007-2010	VOS	$1,800	$2,100

1957 Gibson Les Paul Model

Gibson '54 Les Paul Goldtop

Gibson '56 Les Paul Goldtop

Gibson 1957 Les Paul Junior (Reissue)

MODEL YEAR	FEATURES	EXC. COND. LOW	HIGH

'56 Les Paul Goldtop

1991-present. Renamed from Les Paul Reissue Gold-top. Goldtop finish, 2 P-90 pickups, Tune-o-matic, now part of Gibson's Historic Collection, Custom Authentic aging optional from '01, Vintage Original Specs aging optional from '06.

1991-2005		$1,800	$2,100
2003	Brazilian rosewood, with certificate	$2,700	$3,400
2006-2010	VOS	$1,800	$2,100

'57 Les Paul Goldtop

1993-present. Goldtop finish, 2 humbuckers, now part of Gibson's Historic Collection.

1993-1999		$1,900	$2,300
2000-2005	With certificate	$1,900	$2,300
2003	Brazilian rosewood, with certificate	$2,800	$3,400
2006-2010	VOS	$1,900	$2,300

'57 Les Paul Goldtop (R-7 wrap-around)

2007. Special run with wrap-around bar tailpiece/bridge similar to tailpiece on an original '54 Les Paul Goldtop.

2007		$1,900	$2,300

1957 Les Paul Junior Single Cut (VOS)

1998-present. Custom Shop, certificate of authenticity, nickel-plated hardware, Vintage Original Spec aging optional from '06.

1998-2010		$1,300	$1,600

'58 Les Paul Figured Top

1996-1999, 2001-2003. Less top figure than '59 Reissue, Custom Shop, sunburst.

1996-2003		$2,700	$3,300
2003	Brazilian rosewood, with certificate	$4,000	$5,000

'58 Les Paul Plaintop (VOS)

1994-1999, 2003-present. Custom Shop model, plain maple top version of '58 Standard reissue, sunburst, VOS model starts in '04.

1994-1999		$1,900	$2,300
2003		$1,900	$2,300
2004-2010	VOS, non-chambered	$1,900	$2,300
2006-2010	VOS, chambered	$2,400	$2,900

1958 Les Paul Junior Double Cut (VOS)

1998-present. Custom Shop, nickel plated hardware, Vintage Original Spec aging optional from '06.

1998-2010		$1,400	$1,700

'59 Les Paul Flametop/Reissue/Standard

1991-present. Renamed from Les Paul Reissue Flametop, for 2000-'05 called the 1959 Les Paul Reissue, in '06 this model became part of Gibson's Vintage Original Spec series and is called the '59 Les Paul Standard VOS. Flame maple top, 2 humbuckers, thick '59-style neck, sunburst finish, part of Gibson's Historic Collection, the original certificate authenticity adds value, an instrument without the matching certificate has less value. By '98 Gibson guaranteed only AAA Premium grade maple tops would be used.

1991-2003	R-9	$3,300	$4,000
1994	Murphy aged	$3,700	$4,500
1999-2000	Murphy aged, highly flamed	$4,000	$5,000

MODEL YEAR	FEATURES	EXC. COND. LOW	HIGH
2003	Brazilian rosewood, figured top	$6,200	$7,700
2003	Brazilian rosewood, Murphy aged	$6,200	$7,700
2003	Brazilian rosewood, plain top	$4,600	$5,700
2004	Limited run transparent color, certificate	$3,200	$3,900
2004-2005	Figured top	$3,500	$4,300
2004-2009	R-9, Murphy aged	$3,600	$4,500
2006-2010	VOS Series	$3,200	$3,900
2008	Korina, figured, natural	$3,600	$4,500

'60 Les Paul Corvette

1995-1997. Custom Shop Les Paul, distinctive Chevrolet Corvette styling from '60, offered in 6 colors.

1995-1997		$4,400	$5,500

'60 Les Paul Flametop/Standard

1991-present. Renamed from Les Paul Reissue Flametop, flame maple top, 2 humbuckers, thinner neck, sunburst finish, part of Gibson's Historic Collection, in '06 this model became part of Gibson's Vintage Original Spec series and is called the '60 Les Paul Standard VOS.

1991-2005		$3,300	$4,000
2003	Brazilian rosewood, figured top	$6,200	$7,700
2003	Brazilian rosewood, Murphy aged	$6,200	$7,700
2004-2005	R-9, Murphy aged	$3,600	$4,500
2006-2010	VOS	$3,200	$3,900

'60 Les Paul Plaintop (VOS)

2006-2010. Plain maple top version of '60 Standard reissue.

2006-2010		$2,000	$2,500

'60 Les Paul Junior

1992-2003. Historic Collection reissue.

1992-2003		$1,300	$1,600

'60 Les Paul Special

1998-present. Historic Collection reissue, single-cut or double-cut.

1998-2010		$1,550	$1,900
2007	Murphy-aged, limited	$1,800	$2,200

Les Paul (All Maple)

1984. Limited run, all maple body, Super 400-style inlay, gold hardware.

1984		$2,900	$3,400

Les Paul 25/50 Anniversary

1978-1979. Regular model with 25/50 inlay on headstock, sunburst.

1978-1979	Moderate flame	$2,500	$2,900
1978-1979	Premium flame	$3,100	$3,600

Les Paul 25th Silver Anniversary (Guitar Center)

1978. Special order of 50 Les Paul Customs with metallic silver top, back, sides and neck, commissioned by Guitar Center of California, most have 25th Anniversary etched in tailpiece.

1978		$2,400	$2,800

MODEL YEAR	FEATURES	EXC. COND. LOW	HIGH

Les Paul 30th Anniversary

1982-1984. Features of a 1958 Les Paul Goldtop, 2 humbuckers, 30th Anniversary inlay on 19th fret.

1982-1984		$2,400	$2,800

Les Paul 40th Anniversary (from 1952)

1991-1992. Black finish, 2 soapbar P-100 pickups, gold hardware, stop tailpiece, 40th Anniversary inlay at 12th fret.

1991-1992		$2,300	$2,700

Les Paul 40th Anniversary (from 1959)

1999. Reissue Historic, humbuckers, highly figured top, price includes 40th Anniversary Edition Certificate of Authenticity with matching serial number, a guitar without the certificate is worth less.

1999		$3,600	$4,200

Les Paul 50th Anniversary 1960 Les Paul Standard

Jan. 2010-present. Custom Shop, Limited Edition, promoted as "The original Standard, in period-correct detail", offered in Heritage Cherry Sunburst, Heritage Dark Burst, Sunset Tea Burst and Cherry Burst.

2010		$3,700	$4,600

Les Paul 50th Anniversary '56 Les Paul Standard

2006. Custom Shop, '56 tune-o-matic P-90 specs.

2006		$2,000	$2,500

Les Paul 50th Anniversary '59 Les Paul Standard

2009-present. Custom Shop, highly figured top, Certificate of Authenticity.

2009-2010		$3,700	$4,600

Les Paul 50th Anniversary Korina Tribute

2009. Custom Shop model, 100 made, single-cut Korina natural finish body, 3 pickups, dot markers, V-shaped Futura headstock, Custom logo on truss rod cover, slanted raised Gibson logo on headstock.

2009		$3,800	$4,700

Les Paul 55

1974, 1976-1981. Single-cut Special reissue, 2 pickups. By '78 the catalog name is Les Paul 55/78.

1974	Sunburst	$1,500	$1,800
1974	TV limed yellow	$1,700	$2,000
1976-1981	Sunburst	$1,500	$1,800
1976-1981	Wine Red	$1,400	$1,700

Les Paul 295

2008. Guitar of the Month, Les Paul Goldtop with ES295 appointments.

2008		$1,600	$2,000

Les Paul Ace Frehley Signature

1997-2001. Ace's signature inlay at 15th fret, 3 humbuckers, sunburst.

1997	1st year	$3,200	$3,900
1998-2001		$2,700	$3,300

Les Paul Artisan and Artisan/3

1976-1982. Carved maple top, 2 or 3 humbuckers, gold hardware, hearts and flowers inlays on 'board and headstock, ebony, sunburst or walnut.

1976-1982	2 pickups	$2,700	$3,300
1976-1982	3 pickups	$2,800	$3,500

Les Paul Artist/L.P. Artist/Les Paul Active

1979-1982. Two humbuckers (3 optional), active electronics, gold hardware, 3 mini-switches, multibound, Fireburst, ebony or sunburst.

1979-1982		$2,100	$2,600

Les Paul BFG

2006-2008. Les Paul body with Burstbucker 3 humbucker pickup at bridge and 1 P-90 at neck, 2 volume and 1 tone knobs, kill switch toggle in traditional location, mini-toggle for pickup selection, '60s slim taper neck profile, rosewood 'board, figured maple top over mahogany body.

2006-2008		$700	$850
2008	Silverburst	$700	$850

Les Paul Bird's-Eye Standard

1999. Birdseye top, gold hardware, 2 humbucking pickups, transparent amber.

1999		$1,800	$2,200

Les Paul Carved Series

2003-2005. Custom Shop Standards with relief-carved tops, one in diamond pattern, one with flame pattern.

2003-2005	Carved Diamond (top)	$2,000	$2,400

Les Paul Centennial ('56 LP Standard Goldtop)

1994. Part of the Guitar of the Month program commemorating Gibson's 100th year, limited edition of 100, Goldtop Les Paul mahogany body with '56-style configuration, gold hardware, gold truss rod plate, gold medallion, engraved light-gold 'guard, with certificate of authenticity.

1994		$4,300	$5,200

Les Paul Centennial ('59 LP Special)

1994. Part of the Guitar of the Month program commemorating Gibson's 100th year, limited edition of 100, slab body Les Paul Special-style configuration, gold hardware, P-90 pickups, gold medallion, commemorative engraving in 'guard, cherry, with certificate of authenticity.

1994		$3,600	$4,400

Les Paul Class 5

2001-2006. Custom Shop, highly flamed or quilt top, or special finish, 1960 profile neck, weight relieved body, Burst Bucker humbucking pickups, several color options.

2001-2006		$2,400	$3,000
2001-2006	Stars and Stripes, 50 made	$2,900	$3,600

Les Paul Classic

1990-1998, 2001-2008. Early models have 1960 on pickguard, 2 exposed humbucker pickups, Les Paul Model on peghead until '93, Les Paul Classic afterwards.

1990	1st year, all gold neck & body	$1,700	$1,950
1990	1st year, various colors, plain top	$1,400	$1,750
1991-1998	Goldtop, all gold	$1,550	$1,850
1991-1998	Various colors, plain top	$1,250	$1,550
2001-2008	Various colors, plain top	$1,175	$1,450

Gibson '58 Les Paul Junior

2004 Gibson Les Paul 1959 Reissue

Rob Bernstein

1961 Gibson Les Paul Custom

Tom Siska

1971 Gibson Les Paul Custom

Les Paul Classic Antique Mahogany

2007. Antiqued binding, crown headstock inlay, all mahogany body, exposed humbuckers, Guitar of the Week, limited run of 400.

2007		$1,100	$1,350

Les Paul Classic Custom

2007-2008. Custom with two exposed pickups, black finish, gold hardware.

2007-2008		$1,800	$2,200

Les Paul Classic H-90

2008. Guitar of the Week, 400 made, gold hardware, H-90 soapbar pickups.

2008		$1,150	$1,425

Les Paul Classic Limited Edition

2000. Limited Edition logo on back of headstock, Les Paul Classic stencil logo, 3 exposed humbuckers, gold hardware, black finish.

2000		$1,500	$1,800

Les Paul Classic Mark III/MIII

1991-1993. Les Paul Classic features, no 'guard, exposed-coil humbuckers at neck and bridge and single-coil at middle position, 5-way switch, coil-tap.

1991-1993		$1,450	$1,750

Les Paul Classic Plus

1991-1996, 1999-2003. Les Paul Classic with fancier maple top, 2 exposed humbucker pickups. Price depends on top figure.

1991-2003		$1,600	$1,900

Les Paul Classic Premium Plus

1993-1996, 2001-2002. Les Paul Classic with AAA-grade flame maple top, 2 exposed humbucker pickups. Price depends on top figure.

1993-1996		$1,900	$2,300

Les Paul Classic Tom Morgan Limited Edition

2007. 400 made, custom finish top, black finish back/sides, Classic logo on truss rod cover.

2007		$1,650	$1,850

Les Paul Cloud 9 Series

2003-2006. Special lightweight Les Paul series run for three dealers, Music Machine, Dave's Guitar Shop, and Wildwood Guitars, '59 Les Paul body specs, CR serial series number, '59 or '60 neck profile options, various colors, other reissue models available.

2003	'59 or '60 models	$3,000	$3,600
2003-2004	'52, '54, '56, '57, '58 models	$2,600	$3,100

Les Paul Custom

1953-1963 (renamed SG Custom late-1963), 1968-present. Les Paul body shape except for SG body '61-'63, 2 pickups (3 humbuckers mid-'57-'63 and '68-'70, 3 pickups were optional various years after), '75 Price List shows a Les Paul Custom (B) model which is equipped with a Bigsby tailpiece versus a wraparound. By '80 offered as Les Paul Custom/Gold Parts and /Nickel Parts, because gold plating wears more quickly and is therefore less attractive there is no difference in price between an '80s Gold Parts and Nickel Parts instrument.

1954-1957	Single coils	$20,000	$25,000
1954-1957	Single coils, factory Bigsby	$15,000	$19,000
1957-1960	2 Humbuckers	$63,000	$77,000

MODEL YEAR	FEATURES	EXC. COND. LOW	HIGH
1957-1960	2 Humbuckers, factory Bigsby	$47,000	$58,000
1957-1960	3 Humbuckers	$42,000	$52,000
1957-1960	3 Humbuckers, factory Bigsby	$31,000	$38,000
1961	Early '61, 3 PAFs, single-cut	$42,000	$52,000
1961-1963	Black option, SG body, factory stop tail	$17,000	$21,000
1961-1963	Black option, SG body, side-pull vibrato	$12,500	$15,500
1961-1963	White, SG body, Maestro vibrola	$12,500	$15,500
1961-1963	White, SG body, Maestro, ebony block	$12,500	$15,500
1961-1963	White, SG body, side-pull vibrato	$12,500	$15,500
1962-1963	White, SG body, factory stop tail	$17,000	$21,000
1968-1969	Black, 1-piece body	$11,000	$14,000
1968-1969	Black, 3-piece body	$8,500	$10,500
1970-1974	Volute, 2 pickups	$3,800	$4,800
1970-1974	Volute, 3 pickups	$4,000	$5,000
1975	Maple fretboard, 2 pickups	$2,600	$3,300
1975	Maple fretboard, 3 pickups	$2,600	$3,300
1975	Volute, 2 pickups	$2,400	$3,000
1975	Volute, 3 pickups	$2,400	$3,000
1976	Maple fretboard, 2 pickups	$2,200	$2,700
1976	Maple fretboard, 3 pickups	$2,200	$2,700
1976	Volute, 2 pickups	$2,200	$2,700
1976	Volute, 3 pickups	$2,200	$2,700
1977-1978	Maple fretboard, 2 pickups, blond	$2,400	$2,900
1977-1978	Volute, 2 pickups	$2,200	$2,700
1977-1978	Volute, 3 pickups	$2,200	$2,700
1979-1982	2 pickups	$2,200	$2,700
1979-1982	3 pickups	$2,300	$2,800
1979-1982	Volute, 2 pickups, silverburst	$2,800	$3,400
1983-1985	2 pickups	$2,100	$2,600
1983-1985	3 pickups	$2,200	$2,700
1986	2 pickups	$1,900	$2,400
1986	3 pickups	$2,000	$2,500
1987-1989	Various colors	$1,900	$2,400
1990-1999	Limited Edition color series	$2,200	$2,700
1990-1999	Various colors	$1,900	$2,400
2000	Silverburst, 300 made	$1,700	$2,100
2000-2010	Various colors	$1,600	$2,000
2003	Silverburst	$1,700	$2,100
2007	Silverburst reissue, certificate	$1,700	$2,100
2008-2010	Black	$1,600	$2,000

The *Vintage Guitar Price Guide* shows low to high values for items in all-original excellent condition, and, where applicable, with original case or cover.

MODEL YEAR	FEATURES	EXC. COND. LOW	HIGH

Les Paul Custom (Custom Shop)
2004-present. Made by Custom Shop but not part of a specified series, Certificate of Authenticity, colors can vary.

2004-2010	Various colors	$2,400	$2,800
2009-2010	Silverburst	$2,600	$3,200

Les Paul Custom 20th Anniversary
1974. Regular 2-pickup Custom, with 20th Anniversary inlay at 15th fret, black or white.

1974		$2,700	$3,100

Les Paul Custom 35th Anniversary
1989. Gold hardware, 3 pickups, carved, solid mahogany body and neck, 35th Anniversary inlay on headstock, black.

1989		$2,800	$3,500

Les Paul Custom '54
1972-1973. Reissue of 1954 Custom, black finish, Alnico V and P-90 pickups.

1972-1973		$4,800	$5,900

Les Paul Custom Historic '54
1991-present. Historic Collection, 1954 appointments and pickup configuration, black, gold hardware.

1991-2010		$2,400	$2,800

Les Paul Custom Historic '57 Black Beauty
1991-present. Black finish, gold hardware, 2 or 3 humbucker pickups, part of Gibson's Historic Collection.

1991-1999	3 pickups	$2,600	$3,000
1991-2010	2 pickups	$2,400	$2,800
2000-2010	3 pickups	$2,700	$3,100
2007	3 pickups, goldtop	$2,700	$3,100

Les Paul Custom Historic '68
2003-2008. Historic Collection, ebony block marked fretboard, gold hardware, flamed maple top available, 2 pickups.

2003-2007		$2,300	$2,700
2008	Custom F Chambered, sunburst	$2,300	$2,700

Les Paul Custom Lite
1987-1990. Carved maple top, ebony 'board, pearl block inlays, gold hardware, PAF pickups, bound neck, headstock and body.

1987-1990		$1,800	$2,200
1987-1990	Floyd Rose	$1,800	$2,200

Les Paul Custom Lite (Show Case Ed.)
1988. Showcase Edition, only 200 made, gold top.

1988		$2,000	$2,500

Les Paul Custom Mick Ronson '68
2007. Custom Shop, includes certificate and other authentication material.

2007		$3,300	$4,000

Les Paul Custom Music Machine
2003. Custom run for dealer Music Machine with special serial number series, chambered body style for reduced body weight, quilt tops.

2003		$3,100	$3,800

Les Paul Custom Peter Frampton Signature
2008. Limited Edition 3-pickup version of Frampton's LP Custom, PF serial number series, black.

2008		$2,900	$3,500

Les Paul Custom Plus
1991-1998. Regular Custom with figured maple top, sunburst finish or colors.

1991-1998		$2,200	$2,700

Les Paul Custom Showcase Edition
1988. Showcase Edition logo on back of headstock, goldtop, black hardware.

1988		$2,000	$2,500

Les Paul Dale Earnhardt
1999. 333 made, Dale's image and large number 3 on the front and headstock, Dale Earnhardt signature script on fretboard, chrome hardware, several pieces of literature and an original certificate are part of the overall package, lack of an original matching serial number certificate will reduce the value, a lower serial number may add value.

1999		$3,100	$3,800

Les Paul Dale Earnhardt Intimidator
2000. 333 made, Dale's 'Goodwrench' car on the front of the body, The Intimidator inlay on the fretboard, includes certificate, chrome hardware.

2000		$3,100	$3,800

Les Paul DC AA
2007. Double A flamed top.

2007		$1,700	$2,100

Les Paul DC Classic
1992-1993. Gold finish.

1992-1993		$1,500	$1,850

Les Paul DC Pro
1997-1998, 2006-2007. Custom Shop, body like a '59 Les Paul Junior, carved highly figured maple top, various options. Name revived in '06 but not a Custom Shop model.

1997-1998		$1,700	$2,100
2006-2007		$1,200	$1,500

Les Paul DC Standard (Plus)
1998-1999, 2001-2006. Offset double-cut, highly flamed maple top, translucent lacquer finishes in various colors, typical Les Paul Model stencil logo on headstock and 'Standard' notation on truss rod cover, reintroduced as Standard Lite in '99 but without Les Paul designation on headstock or truss rod cover.

1998-1999		$1,100	$1,350
2001-2006		$1,100	$1,350

Les Paul DC Studio
1997-1999. DC Series double-cut like late '50s models, carved maple top, 2 humbucker pickups, various colors.

1997-1999		$750	$925

Les Paul Deluxe
1969-1985. In 1969, the Goldtop Les Paul Standard was renamed the Deluxe. Two mini-humbuckers (regular humbuckers optional in mid-'70s). Mid-'70s sparkle tops, made at the request of the Sam Ash chain, are worth more than standard finishes. The market slightly favors the Goldtop finish, but practically speaking condition is more important than finish, such that all finishes fetch about the same amount (with the exception of the sparkle finish). Initially, the Deluxe was offered only as a Goldtop and the first year models are more highly prized than the others.

2004 Gibson Les Paul Custom Historic '68
Robbie Keene

Gibson Les Paul Dale Earnhardt

1971 Gibson Les Paul Deluxe

Tom Siska

Gibson Les Paul Goddess

MODEL YEAR	FEATURES	EXC. COND. LOW	HIGH

Cherry sunburst was offered in '71, cherry in '71-'75, walnut in '71-'72, brown sunburst in '72-'79, natural in '75, red sparkle in '75 only, blue sparkle in '75-'77, wine red/see-thru red offered '75-'85. In '99, the Deluxe was reissued for its 30th anniversary.

1969	Goldtop	$4,100	$5,000
1970	Goldtop	$3,600	$4,400
1971-1975	Goldtop	$2,900	$3,600
1971-1975	Natural	$1,800	$2,200
1971-1975	Red (solid)	$1,900	$2,300
1971-1975	Sunburst	$2,300	$2,900
1971-1975	Wine	$1,800	$2,200
1975	Red sparkle, fewer made	$3,200	$3,900
1975-1977	Blue sparkle, more made	$2,500	$3,100
1976-1979	Goldtop	$2,300	$2,900
1976-1985	Various colors	$2,000	$2,500

Les Paul Deluxe 30th Anniversary
1999. 30th Anniversary of the 1969 introduction of the Les Paul Deluxe, Limited Edition logo on the lower back of the headstock neck, Deluxe logo on truss rod cover, Wine Red.

1999		$1,600	$2,000

Les Paul Deluxe '69 Reissue
2000-2005. Mini-humbuckers, gold top

2000-2005		$1,300	$1,600

Les Paul Deluxe Hall of Fame
1991. All gold finish.

1991		$1,700	$2,100

Les Paul Deluxe Limited Edition
1999-2002. Limited edition reissue with Les Paul Standard features and Deluxe mini-humbuckers, black.

1999-2002		$1,700	$2,100

Les Paul Dickey Betts Goldtop
2001-2003. Aged gold top.

2001-2003		$5,200	$6,300

Les Paul Dickey Betts Red Top
2003. Transparent red, gold hardware.

2003		$3,600	$4,500

Les Paul Dusk Tiger
Late-2009-present. Limited edition, 1000 to be made, features Gibson's Robot Technology, Burst-bucker bridge, P-90H neck and 6 Piezo pickups.

2009-2010		$2,500	$3,000

Les Paul Elegant
1996-2004. Custom Shop, highly flamed maple top, abalone crown markers and Custom Shop headstock inlay.

1996-2004		$2,100	$2,500

Les Paul Eric Clapton 1960
2011-present. '60 thinner 'Clapton' neck profile, Custom Bucker pickups, nickel-plated Grover kidney button tuners, lightly figured maple cap, traditional 17 degree angled headstock, total of 500 made; 55 Murphy Aged and signed by Clapton, 95 unsigned Murphy Aged, 350 finished with Gibson's VOS treatment.

2011	Aged	$9,400	$10,600
2011	Aged and signed	$19,000	$21,000
2011	VOS	$5,500	$6,500

Les Paul Florentine Plus
1997-2001. Custom Shop model, hollowbody with f-holes, higher-end appointments.

1997-2001		$3,000	$3,800

Les Paul Gary Moore BFG
2009-present. Plain appointment BFG specs, P-90 neck pickup and Burstbucker 3 bridge pickup.

2009-2010		$725	$875

Les Paul Gary Moore Signature
2000-2002. Signature Series model, Gary Moore script logo on truss rod cover, flamed maple top.

2000-2002		$2,100	$2,600

Les Paul Gary Rossington Signature
2002. GR serial number series, replica of his '59 LP Standard, built and aged by Custom Shop Art and Historic division, 250 made, includes display case with backdrop photo of Rossington, price includes certificate with matching serial number.

2002	With certificate	$5,500	$6,700

Les Paul Goddess
2006-2007. Maple carved top, trapezoid inlays, smaller body, 2 humbuckers, 2 controls, tune-a-matic bridge.

2007		$1,100	$1,350

Les Paul GT
2007. Includes over/under dual truss rods, GT logo on truss rod cover, several specs designed to add durability during heavy professional use.

2007		$1,500	$1,800

Les Paul Guitar Trader Reissue
1982-1983. Special order flametop Les Paul by the Guitar Trader Company, Redbank, New Jersey. Approximately 47 were built, the first 15 guitars ordered received original PAFs, all were double black bobbins (except 1 Zebra and 1 double white), 3 of the guitars were made in the '60-style. The PAF equipped models were based on order date and not build date. The serial number series started with 9 1001 and a second serial number was put in the control cavity based upon the standard Gibson serial number system, which allowed for exact build date identification. Gibson's pickup designer in the early-'80s was Tim Shaw and the pickups used for the last 32 guitars have been nicknamed Shaw PAFs. After Gibson's short run for Guitar Trader, 10 non-Gibson replica Les Pauls were made. These guitars have a poorly done Gibson logo and other telltale issues.

1982-1983	Actual PAFs installed	$8,000	$10,000
1982-1983	Shaw PAFs, highly flamed	$4,000	$4,900
1982-1983	Shaw PAFs, low flame	$3,500	$4,300

Les Paul HD.6-X Pro Digital
2008-2009. Digital sound system, hex pickups.

2008-2009		$2,200	$2,700

Les Paul Heritage 80
1980-1982. Copy of '59 Les Paul Standard, curly maple top, mahogany body, rosewood 'board, nickel hardware, sunburst. In '80 cataloged as Les Paul

MODEL YEAR	FEATURES	EXC. COND. LOW	HIGH

Standard-80 without reference to Heritage, the catalog notes that the guitar has Heritage Series truss rod cover.

| 1980-1982 | Figuring can vary | $3,000 | $3,700 |
| 1980-1982 | Plain top | $2,400 | $3,000 |

Les Paul Heritage 80 Award
1982. Ebony 'board, 1-piece mahogany neck, gold-plated hardware, sunburst.

| 1982 | Figuring can vary | $3,700 | $4,600 |

Les Paul Heritage 80 Elite
1980-1982. Copy of '59 Les Paul Standard, quilted maple top, mahogany body and neck, ebony 'board, chrome hardware, sunburst. In '80 cataloged as Les Paul Standard-80 Elite without reference to Heritage, the catalog notes that the guitar has the distinctive Heritage Series truss rod cover.

| 1980-1982 | Quilting can vary | $3,700 | $4,600 |

Les Paul Heritage 80/Standard 80
1982. Based on '57 Les Paul Standard Goldtop, Heritage Series Standard 80 logo on truss rod cover.

| 1982 | | $2,800 | $3,400 |

Les Paul Indian Motorcycle
2002. 100 made, has Indian script logo on fretboard and chrome cast war bonnet on the body, crimson red and cream white.

| 2002 | | $3,000 | $3,700 |

Les Paul Jim Beam
2000. Custom Shop, JBLP serial number series, Jim Beam logo art on top of guitar, award-ribbon-style B Bean logo on headstock, white background with logo.

| 2000 | | $1,000 | $1,250 |

Les Paul Jimmy Page (Custom Authentic)
2004-2006. Custom Shop, includes certificate.

| 2004-2006 | | $6,800 | $8,500 |

Les Paul Jimmy Page Signature
1995-1999. Jimmy Page signature on 'guard, mid-grade figured top, push-pull knobs for phasing and coil-tapping, Grover tuners, gold-plated hardware. This is not the '04 Custom Shop Jimmy Page Signature Series Les Paul (see separate listing).

1995	Highly figured, 1st year	$4,000	$5,000
1995	Low to moderate figure, 1st year	$3,300	$4,100
1996-1999	Highly figured	$3,800	$4,700
1996-1999	Low to moderate figure	$3,000	$3,700

Les Paul Jimmy Page Signature Custom Shop
2004. Introduced at the January '04 NAMM Show, 175 planned production, the first 25 were personally inspected, played-in, and autographed by Jimmy Page. Initial retail price for first 25 was $25,000, the remaining 150 instruments had an initial retail price of $16,400. Cosmetically aged by Tom Murphy to resemble Page's No. 1 Les Paul in color fade, weight, top flame, slab cut attribution on the edges, neck size and profile.

| 2004 | 1st 25 made | $17,000 | $21,000 |
| 2004 | Factory order 25-150 | $14,000 | $17,000 |

Les Paul Jimmy Wallace Reissue
1978-1997. Les Paul Standard '59 reissue with Jimmy Wallace on truss rod cover, special order by dealer Jimmy Wallace, figured maple top, sunburst.

1978-1983	Kalamazoo-made, highly flamed	$3,600	$4,400
1978-1983	Kalamazoo-made, low flame	$3,000	$3,600
1983-1989	Nashville-made	$3,200	$3,900
1990-1997		$3,200	$3,900

Les Paul Joe Perry Signature
1997-2001. Unbound slab body with push-pull knobs and Joe Perry signature below bridge, Bone-Yard logo model with typical Les Paul Standard bound body, configuration and appointments.

| 1997-2001 | Bone-Yard option with logo | $2,000 | $2,500 |
| 1997-2001 | Unbound standard model | $1,600 | $2,000 |

Les Paul Jumbo
1969-1970. Single rounded cutaway, flat-top dreadnought acoustic/electric, 1 pickup, rosewood back and sides, natural.

| 1969-1970 | | $2,000 | $2,400 |

Les Paul Junior
1954-1963, 1986-1992, 2001-2002, 2005-present. One P-90 pickup, single-cut solidbody '54-mid-'58, double-cut '58-early-'61, SG body '61-'63, renamed SG Jr. in '63, reintroduced as single-cut for '86-'92, reissued as the 1957 Les Paul Jr. Single Cutaway in '98. Current version from Musician's Friend. Headstock repair reduces the value by 40% - 50%. Reinstalled tuners reduces the value by 5% to 10%. Replaced tuner buttons reduces the value by 5% to 10%.

1954	Sunburst, single-cut	$5,000	$6,000
1955	Sunburst, single-cut	$4,900	$5,900
1956-1958	Sunburst, single-cut	$4,900	$5,900
1958	Cherry, early double-cut	$4,800	$5,800
1959-1961	Cherry, double-cut	$4,800	$5,800
1961-1963	Cherry, SG body	$3,400	$4,100
1986-1992	Sunburst, single-cut, Tune-o-matic	$700	$850
1998-2010	Sunburst, single-cut, stop tail	$500	$600

Les Paul Junior 3/4
1956-1961. One P-90 pickup, short-scale, single-cut solidbody '54-mid-'58, double-cut '58-early-'61.

| 1956-1958 | Sunburst, single-cut | $2,500 | $3,100 |
| 1958-1961 | Cherry, double-cut | $2,500 | $3,100 |

Les Paul Junior Billie Joe Armstrong Signature
2006-present. 1956 LP Jr. Specs.

| 2006-2010 | | $950 | $1,150 |

1959 Gibson Les Paul Junior

Gibson Les Paul Junior Billie Joe Armstrong

*Gibson Les Paul Slash
Signature*

*1956 Gibson
Les Paul Special*

MODEL		EXC. COND.	
YEAR	FEATURES	LOW	HIGH

Les Paul Junior DC Hall of Fame
1990-1992. Part of Hall of Fame Series, limited run of LP Junior Double Cutaway but with P-100 pickup.
1990-1992		$775	$950

Les Paul Junior Double Cutaway
1986-1992, 1995-1996. Copy of '50s double-cut Jr., cherry or sunburst, reissued as the 1958 Les Paul Jr. Double Cutaway in '98.
1986-1989		$775	$950

Les Paul Junior John Lennon LTD
2008. Custom Shop, 300 made, Charlie Christian neck pickup and P-90 bridge as per Lennon's modified Junior, aged-relic finish, certificate, book and New York t-shirt.
2008		$2,800	$3,400

Les Paul Junior Lite
1999-2002. Double-cut, Tune-o-matic, 2 P-100 pickups, stop tail, mini-trapezoid markers, burnt cherry gloss finish.
1999-2002		$450	$550

Les Paul Junior Special
1999-2004. LP Jr. single-cut slab body with 2 P-90s (making it a Special) instead of the standard single P-90, double pickup controls, cherry, tinted natural or sunburst.
1999-2004		$675	$825

Les Paul Junior Tenor/Plectrum
Late-1950s. Four string neck on Junior body, cherry.
1959		$3,200	$3,900

Les Paul Katrina
2005. 300 made in cooperation with Music Rising Foundation and the Edge U2.
2005		$2,500	$3,000

Les Paul KM (Kalamazoo Model)
1979. Regular Les Paul Standard with 2 exposed humbuckers, KM on headstock, sunburst, approximately 1500 were made in the Kalamazoo plant.
1979		$2,200	$2,700

Les Paul Leo's Reissue
1980-1985. Special order from Gibson's Nashville facility for Leo's Music, Oakland, California. Identified by serial number with L at the beginning, flamed maple top. About 800 guitars were made, with about 400 being exported to Japan. Kalamazoo-made Leo's have a 2nd serial number in the control cavity, Nashville-made Leo's do not have a 2nd serial number.
1980-1983	Kalamazoo-made, highly flamed	$3,600	$4,400
1980-1983	Kalamazoo-made, lower-level flame	$3,000	$3,600
1983-1985	Nashville-made	$3,200	$3,900

Les Paul Limited Edition (3-tone)
1997. Limited Edition stamped on the back of the headstock, Les Paul Standard configuration with cloud inlay markers, 2-piece 3-tone sunburst finish over non-figured maple top.
1997		$1,900	$2,300

Les Paul LP295 Goldtop
2008. Guitar of the Month (April, '08), limited run of 1000, Les Paul body style, goldtop, 2 humbuckers, ES-295 appointments such as 'guard and fretboard markers, Bigsby tailpiece option.
2008		$1,900	$2,300

MODEL		EXC. COND.	
YEAR	FEATURES	LOW	HIGH

Les Paul Melody Maker
2003-present. Slab body single-cut solidbody, P-90, dot markers, cherry finish.
2003-2006		$375	$450
2007-2010	Revised specs	$350	$425

Les Paul Menace
2006-2007. Carved mahogany body, 2 humbucker pickups.
2006-2007		$600	$725

Les Paul Music Machine 25th Anniversary
2002. Custom run for dealer Music Machine with special serial number series, 14 flame top and 14 quilt top instruments were produced, Music Machine 25th Anniversary logo on truss rod cover, special cherry sunburst finish.
2002	Flame top	$3,400	$4,200
2002	Quilt top	$3,400	$4,200

Les Paul Music Machine Brazilian Stinger
2003. Custom run for dealer Music Machine with special serial number series, Brazilian rosewood 'board, black stinger paint on back of neck-headstock, '59 or '60 reissue body and neck profile options, highly figured flame or quilt top options, other reissue options available.
2003	'54, '56 or '58, figured flame or quilt	$3,700	$4,600
2003	'54, '56 or '58, goldtop	$2,700	$3,400
2003	'59 or '60, figured flame or quilt	$6,200	$7,700
2003	'59 or '60, plain top	$3,700	$4,600

Les Paul Old Hickory
1998 only. Limited run of 200, tulip poplar body wood from The Hermitage, Custom-style trim.
1998		$3,000	$3,700

Les Paul Pee Wee
1999. 3/4" sized Les Paul Jr. style guitar, included battery-powered amp.
1999		$400	$475

Les Paul Personal
1969-1972. Two angled, low impedence pickups, phase switch, gold parts, walnut finish.
1969-1972		$2,000	$2,500

Les Paul Pro Deluxe
1978-1982. Chrome-plated hardware, Pro engraved on truss rod cover, 2 P-90 pickups, various colors.
1978-1982		$1,550	$1,900

Les Paul Pro Showcase Edition
1988. Goldtop 1956 specs, Showcase Edition decal, 200 made.
1988		$2,100	$2,600

Les Paul Professional
1969-1971, 1977-1979. Single-cut, 2 angled, low impedence pickups, carved top, walnut finish.
1969-1971		$1,900	$2,400

Les Paul Recording
1971-1980. Two angled, low impedence pickups, high/low impedence selector switch, various colors.
1971-1980		$1,900	$2,400

MODEL YEAR	FEATURES	EXC. COND. LOW	HIGH

Les Paul Reissue Flametop
1983-1990. Flame maple top, 2 humbuckers, thicker '59-style neck, sunburst finish, renamed '59 Les Paul Flametop in '91.

1983-1990	Highly figured	$2,900	$3,600

Les Paul Reissue Goldtop
1983-1991. Goldtop finish, 2 P-100 pickups, renamed '56 Les Paul Goldtop in '91.

1983-1991		$1,800	$2,200

Les Paul Richard Petty LTD
2003. Richard Petty's image on front and back, 'The King' inlay on fretboard.

2003		$3,000	$3,700

Les Paul SG '61 Reissue
1993-2003. Renamed the Les Paul SG '61 Reissue from SG '62 Reissue, early '60s Les Paul Standard SG specs with small guard, trapezoid markers, heritage cherry finish, by 2003 the Les Paul script marking was not on the truss rod cover, renamed to SG '61 Reissue.

1993-2003	Stud tail	$1,250	$1,550

Les Paul SG Standard Authentic
2005. SG '61 specs, small guard, Les Paul truss rod logo, stud tailpiece.

2005		$1,650	$1,950

Les Paul SG Standard Reissue
2000-2004. Reissue of early-'60s specs including Deluxe Maestro vibrato with lyre tailpiece and Les Paul script truss rod logo, small pickguard, holly head veneer, rosewood 'board with tapezoid markers, available with stop bar tailpiece, extra slim low action '60 profile neck, small neck to body heel, standard color faded cherry, available in Classic White or TV Yellow, becomes the SG Standard Reissue by '05.

2000-2004	Maestro	$1,650	$1,950

Les Paul Signature/L.P. Signature
1973-1978. Thin semi-hollowbody, double-cut, 2 low impedence pickups, f-holes, various colors. The Price List refers to as L.P. Signature.

1973-1978		$2,200	$2,700

Les Paul Slash Signature
2007. Slash logo on truss rod, SL serial number series.

2007		$2,600	$3,100

Les Paul SmartWood Exotic
1998-2001. Full-depth Les Paul-style built with eco-friendly woods, Muiracatiara (or Muir) top, mahogany back, Preciosa 'board, pearloid dots.

1998-2001		$800	$975

Les Paul SmartWood Standard
1996-2002. Smartwood Series, figured maple top, mahogany body, Smartwood on truss rod cover, antique natural.

1996-2002		$675	$850

Les Paul SmartWood Studio
2002-2006. Muiracatiara (Muir) top and mahogany back, Preciosa (Prec) 'board, Studio appointments including pearl-style dot markers.

2002-2006		$675	$850

Les Paul Special
1955-1959. Slab solidbody, 2 pickups (P-90s in '50s, P-100 stacked humbuckers on later version), single-cut until end of '58, double in '59, the '89 reissue is a single-cut, renamed SG Special in late-'59.

1955-1959	TV Yellow	$8,900	$11,000
1959	Cherry (mid- to late-'59)	$6,300	$7,900

Les Paul Special (Reissue)
1989-1999, 2001-2005. Briefly introduced as Les Paul Junior II but name changed to Special in the first year, single-cut, 2 P-100 stacked humbucking pickups, tune-o-matic bridge, TV Yellow, in '90 there was a run of 300 with LE serial number, renamed Special SL in '98.

1989-1998	490R and 496T humbuckers	$600	$750
1989-1999	2 P-100 stacked humbuckers	$675	$850
2001-2005	Humbuckers	$600	$750

Les Paul Special 3/4
1959. Slab solidbody, 2 P-90 pickups, double-cut, short-scale, cherry finish, renamed SG Special 3/4 in late-'59.

1959		$4,500	$5,500

Les Paul Special Centennial
1994 only. 100 made, double-cut, cherry, 100 year banner at the 12th fret, diamonds in headstock and in gold-plated knobs, gold-plated Gibson coin in back of headstock.

1994		$3,000	$3,700

Les Paul Special Custom Shop
1999-2008. 1960 Special, offered in single- or double-cut version. Currently a VOS model.

1999-2005		$1,500	$1,800
2006-2008	VOS	$1,500	$1,800

Les Paul Special Double Cutaway
1976-1979, 1993-1998. Double-cut, 2 pickups (P-90s in '70s, P-100 stacked humbuckers in later version), various colors.

1976-1979	P-90s	$1,100	$1,350
1993-1998	P-100s	$1,000	$1,250

Les Paul Special Faded
2005-2007. Faded TV limed mahogany finish, double-cut, dot markers, 2 P-90 pickups, stop tail with Nashville Tune-o-matic bridge, script Special logo on truss rod cover.

2005-2007		$600	$725

Les Paul Special New Century
2006-2008. Full-body mirror 'guard, 490R and 498T humbucker pickups, classic '60s neck profile, mirror truss rod cover.

2006-2008		$625	$725

Les Paul Special Tenor
1959. Four-string electric tenor, LP Special body, TV Yellow.

1959		$4,400	$5,100

Les Paul Special Worn Cherry
2003-2006. Single-cut, non-bound LP Special with 2 humbuckers.

2003-2006		$550	$675

1958 Gibson Les Paul Special
Tom Siska

1959 Gibson
Les Paul Special 3/4

1960 Gibson
Les Paul Standard

1991 Gibson Les Paul Standard

MODEL		EXC. COND.	
YEAR	FEATURES	LOW	HIGH

Les Paul Spider-Man

Released December 3, 2002. Custom Art & Historic division's rendering with the superhero depicted on the body, red spider logo, gold hardware, Standard appointments. 15 guitars were produced as a Gibson/Columbia TriStar Home Entertainment/Tower Records promotion, while a larger batch was sold at retail.

2002		$2,900	$3,500

Les Paul Spotlight Special

1983-1984. Curly maple and walnut top, 2 humbuckers, gold hardware, multi-bound top, Custom Shop Edition logo, natural or sunburst.

1983-1984		$3,400	$4,300

Les Paul Standard (Sunburst)

1958-1960, special order 1972-1975. Les Paul Sunbursts from '58-'60 should be individually valued based on originality, color and the amount and type of figure in the maple top, changed tuners or a Bigsby removal will drop the value. Approximately 15% came with the Bigsby tailpiece. The noted price ranges are guidance valuations. Each '58-'60 Les Paul Standard should be evaluated on a case-by-case basis. As is always the case, the low and high ranges are for an all original, excellent condition, undamaged guitar. About 70% of the '58-'60 Les Paul Standards have relatively plain maple tops. The majority of '58-'60 Les Paul Standards have moderate or extreme color fade.

Wider fret wire was introduced in early-'59. White bobbins were introduced in early- to mid-'59. Double ring Kluson Deluxe tuners were introduced in late-'60. It has been suggested that all '58-'60 models have 2-piece centerseam tops. This implies that 1-piece tops, 3-piece tops and off-centerseam tops do not exist.

The terminology of the 'Burst includes: arching medullary grain, swirling medullary grain, ribbon-curl, chevrons, Honey-Amber, receding red aniline, pinstripe, bookmatched, double-white bobbins, zebra bobbins, black bobbins, fiddleback maple, sunburst finish, Honeyburst, lemon drop, quarter sawn, blistered figure, width of gradation, flat sawn, Teaburst, Bigsby-shadow, rift sawn, heel size, aged clear lacquer, 3-dimensional figure, intense fine flame, tag-shadow, red pore filler, Eastern maple fleck, medium-thick flame, shrunk tuners, wave and flame, flitch-matched, elbow discoloration, ambered top coat, natural gradation, grain orientation, script oxidation, asymmetrical figure Tangerineburst, Greenburst, and birdseye.

The bobbins used for the pickup winding were either black or white. The market has determined that white bobbin PAFs are the most highly regarded. Generally speaking, in '58 bobbins were black, in '59 the bobbin component transitioned to white and some guitars have 1 white and 1 black bobbin (aka zebra). In '60, there were zebras and double blacks returned.

Rather than listing separate line items for fade and wood, the Guide lists discounts and premiums as follows. The price ranges shown below are for instruments with excellent color, excellent wood, with the original guitar case. The following discounts and

MODEL		EXC. COND.	
YEAR	FEATURES	LOW	HIGH

premiums should be considered.

An instrument with moderate or total color fade should be discounted about 10%.

One with a factory Bigsby should be discounted about 10%-15%.

Original jumbo frets are preferred over original small frets and are worth +10%.

1958	Figured top	$260,000	$325,000
1958	Minor figured top	$180,000	$230,000
1958	Plain top, no figuring	$140,000	$170,000
1959	Figured top	$270,000	$340,000
1959	Minor figured top	$200,000	$250,000
1959	Plain top, no figuring	$150,000	$180,000
1960	Figured top	$210,000	$260,000
1960	Minor figured top	$160,000	$200,000
1960	Plain top, no figuring	$125,000	$160,000

Les Paul Standard (SG body)

1961-1963 (SG body those years). Renamed SG Standard in late-'63.

1961-1963	Cherry, side vibrola, PAFs	$9,500	$12,000
1962-1963	Cherry, side vibrola, pat. #	$9,500	$12,000
1962-1963	Ebony block, SG, PAFs, deluxe vibrola	$10,500	$13,000
1962-1963	Ebony block, SG, pat. #, deluxe vibrola	$10,000	$12,500

Les Paul Standard (reintroduced then renamed)

1968-1969. Comes back as a goldtop with P-90s for '68-'69 (renamed Les Paul Deluxe, '69), available as special order Deluxe '72-'76.

1968	P-90s, small headstock	$11,500	$14,000
1968-1969	P-90s, large headstock	$11,500	$14,000

Les Paul Standard (reintroduced)

1976-July 2008. Available as special order Deluxe '72-'76, reintroduced with 2 humbuckers '76-present. The '75 Price List shows a Les Paul Standard (B) model which is equipped with a Bigsby tailpiece versus a wraparound, also shows a Les Paul Standard (B) with palm pedal. Renamed Les Paul Standard 2008 in August '08.

1971	Early special order goldtop, P-90s	$3,500	$4,300
1972-1974	Special order goldtop, P-90s	$2,400	$3,000
1972-1974	Special order sunburst, P-90s	$2,400	$3,000
1974-1975	Special order sunburst, humbuckers	$2,400	$3,000

MODEL YEAR	FEATURES	EXC. COND. LOW	HIGH
1976	Sunburst, 4-piece pancake body	$2,200	$2,700
1976	Wine Red or natural	$2,200	$2,700
1977	Sunburst	$2,200	$2,700
1977	Various colors	$2,200	$2,700
1978	Natural	$2,200	$2,700
1978	Sunburst	$2,200	$2,700
1978	Various colors	$2,200	$2,700
1979	Brown Sunburst	$2,200	$2,700
1979	Cherry Sunburst	$2,200	$2,700
1979	Goldtop	$2,200	$2,700
1979	Natural	$2,200	$2,700
1979	Wine Red	$2,200	$2,700
1980	Black	$2,200	$2,700
1980	Natural	$2,200	$2,700
1980	Sunburst	$2,200	$2,700
1980	Sunburst, mild flame	$2,200	$2,700
1980	Wine Red	$2,200	$2,700
1981	Goldtop	$2,200	$2,700
1981	Sunburst	$2,200	$2,700
1981	Wine Red	$2,200	$2,700
1982	Black	$2,200	$2,700
1982	Brown Sunburst	$2,200	$2,700
1982	Candy Apple Red, gold hardware, LD	$2,200	$2,700
1982	Cherry Sunburst	$2,200	$2,700
1982	Goldtop	$2,200	$2,700
1982	Natural	$2,200	$2,700
1982	Wine Red	$2,200	$2,700
1983	Black	$2,100	$2,600
1983	Natural	$2,100	$2,600
1983	Sunburst	$2,100	$2,600
1984	Sunburst	$2,100	$2,600
1985	Black	$2,100	$2,600
1985	Cherry sunburst, highly figured top	$3,000	$3,700
1985	Sunburst, plain top	$2,100	$2,600
1985	Wine Red	$2,100	$2,600
1986	Sunburst	$2,000	$2,400
1987	Various colors	$2,000	$2,400
1988	Highly figured flame	$3,000	$3,700
1988	Various colors	$2,000	$2,400
1989	Various colors	$2,000	$2,400
1990-1993	Limited Edition colors with sticker	$2,200	$2,700
1990-1995	Various colors	$1,700	$2,100
1996-1999	Various colors	$1,700	$2,100
2000-2007	Various colors, plain top	$1,500	$1,850
2008	End old specs, Jan.-July	$1,500	$1,850

Les Paul Standard 2008

August 2008-present. 2008 added to name, chambered mahogany body, locking grovers, plain or flamed maple top, Ebony, Gold top, various sunbursts.

2008-2010	Figured top	$1,700	$2,100
2008-2010	Gold top	$1,450	$1,800
2008-2010	Plain top	$1,500	$1,850

Les Paul Standard '82

1982. Standard 82 on truss rod cover, made in Kalamazoo, Made in USA stamp on back of the headstock, generally quilted maple tops.

1982		$2,200	$2,700

Les Paul Standard Billy Gibbons 'Pearly Gates'

Introduced July 2009-present. Three variants; Aged - 50 made, Aged and signed - 50 made, V.O.S. - 250 made.

2009-2010	VOS	$6,400	$7,800

Les Paul Standard Lite

1999-2001. A member of DC body-style, renamed from DC Standard in '99, reintroduced as Les Paul Standard DC Plus in 2001, various translucent finishes, available in 2004 under this name also.

1999-2001		$1,100	$1,375

Les Paul Standard Plus

1995-1997, 2001-2008. Cherry sunburst standard with mid-level flame.

2001-2008		$1,625	$2,000

Les Paul Standard Premium Plus

2002-2008. Premium plus flamed maple top.

2002-2008		$1,800	$2,200

Les Paul Standard Sparkle

2001. Sparkle holoflake top, reflective back, Standard logo on truss rod.

2001		$1,700	$2,100

Les Paul Strings and Things Standard

1975-1978. Special order flamed maple top Les Paul Standard model, built for Chris Lovell, owner of Strings and Things, a Gibson dealer in Memphis, approximately 28 were built, authentication of a Strings and Things Les Paul is difficult due to no diffinitive attributes, valuation should be on a case-by-case basis, sunburst.

1975	2-piece top	$4,800	$6,000
1975	3-piece top	$3,500	$4,300
1976	2-piece top	$4,700	$5,900
1976	3-piece top	$3,000	$3,600
1977	2-piece top	$4,600	$5,800
1977	3-piece top	$2,700	$3,200
1978	2-piece top	$4,500	$5,700
1978	3-piece top	$2,500	$3,000

Les Paul Studio

1983-present. Alder body, 2 humbuckers, various colors.

1983-1999		$775	$975
2000-2010		$750	$950
2009-2010	Silverburst	$850	$1,050

Les Paul Studio Baritone

2004-2006. 28" baritone scale.

2004-2006		$725	$900

Les Paul Studio BFD

2007. Studio specs but with BFD electronics.

2007		$550	$650

Les Paul Studio Custom

1984-1985. Alder body, 2 humbucking pickups, multi-bound top, gold-plated hardware, various colors.

1984-1985		$800	$1,000

2005 Gibson Les Paul Standard

Dan Drozdik

1983 Gibson Les Paul Studio

Gibson Les Paul Supreme

Gibson Les Paul Zakk Wylde Signature

MODEL YEAR	FEATURES	EXC. COND. LOW	HIGH

Les Paul Studio Faded
2005-present. Faded sunburst tops.

2005-2010		$525	$625

Les Paul Studio Gem
1996-1998. Limited edition with Les Paul Studio features, but using P-90 pickups instead of humbucker pickups, plus trapezoid markers and gold hardware.

1996-1998		$750	$925

Les Paul Studio Gothic
2000-2001. Orville Gibson image on back of headstock, single Gibson crescent and star neck marker, Gothic Black with black hardware.

2000-2001		$575	$750

Les Paul Studio Limited Edition
1997. P-100 pickups, black.

1997		$650	$775

Les Paul Studio Lite
1987-1998. Carved maple top, mahogany back and neck, 2 humbucker pickups, various colors.

1987-1998		$725	$900

Les Paul Studio MLB Baseball
2008. Major League Baseball graphics on body, only 30 made, satin finish, dot markers.

2008		$1,400	$1,700

Les Paul Studio Plus
2002-2007. Two-piece AA flamed unbound top, gold hardware, Desert Burst or see-thru black.

2002-2007		$900	$1,100

Les Paul Studio Premium Plus
2006-2008. AAA flamed-maple top.

2006-2008		$1,075	$1,325

Les Paul Studio Robot
2008-present. Robot tuning, trapezoid inlays.

2008-2010		$950	$1,150

Les Paul Studio Swamp Ash/Swamp Ash Studio
2004-present. Studio model with swamp ash body.

2004-2010		$725	$850

Les Paul Supreme
2003-present. Highly figured AAAA maple top and back on translucent finishes only, custom binding, deluxe split style pearl inlay markers, chambered mahogany body, globe logo on headstock, solid colors available by '06.

2003-2010	AAAA top	$2,300	$2,700
2003-2010	Various colors	$2,200	$2,600

Les Paul Tie Dye (St. Pierre)
1996-1997. Hand colored by George St. Pierre, just over 100 made.

1996-1997		$2,200	$2,700

Les Paul Tie Dye Custom Shop
2002. Limited series of one-off colorful finishes, Custom Shop logo.

2002		$1,600	$1,900

Les Paul Traditional
2008-present. Traditional on truss rod, '80s Les Paul styling with weight-relief holes in an unchambered body, Les Paul Standard appointments, figured maple options, goldtop, black.

2008-2009	Black or Goldtop	$1,200	$1,500

Les Paul TV
1954-1959. Les Paul Jr. with limed mahogany (TV Yellow) finish, single-cut until mid-'58, double-cut after, renamed SG TV in late-'59.

1955-1958	Single-cut	$6,900	$8,600
1958-1959	Double-cut	$6,900	$8,600

Les Paul TV 3/4
1954-1957. Limed mahogany (TV Yellow) Les Paul Jr. 3/4, short-scale, single-cut.

1954-1957		$3,500	$4,300

Les Paul Ultima
1996-2007. Custom Shop model, flame or quilted sunburst top, fancy abalone and mother-of-pearl tree of life, harp, or flame fingerboard inlay, multi abalone bound body.

1996-2007		$5,500	$6,600

Les Paul Vixen
2006-2007. Les Paul Special single-cut slab body, dot markers, 2 humbuckers, 2 controls, wrap-around bridge.

2006-2007		$575	$700

Les Paul Voodoo/Voodoo Les Paul
2004-2005. Single-cut, swamp ash body, 2 exposed humbuckers, black satin finish.

2004-2005		$825	$1,000

Les Paul XR-I/XR-II/XR-III
1981-1983. No frills model with Dirty Finger pickups, dot markers, Les Paul stencil logo on headstock, goldburst, silverburst and cherryburst finishes.

1981-1983	XR-I, goldburst	$675	$825
1981-1983	XR-II	$675	$825
1981-1983	XR-III	$675	$825

Les Paul Zakk Wylde Signature
2003-present. Custom shop, black and antique-white bullseye graphic finish.

1999	Black/white bullseye	$2,800	$3,500
2003-2010	Black/white bullseye	$2,200	$2,700
2003-2010	Green Camo bullseye option	$2,200	$2,700

The Les Paul
1976-1980. Figured maple top, 2 humbuckers, gold hardware, rosewood binding, 'guard, 'board, knobs, cover plates, etc., natural or rosewood finishing, natural only by '79.

1976-1980	Natural or rosewood	$9,000	$11,500

The Paul
1978-1982. Offered as The Paul Standard with solid walnut body and The Paul Deluxe with solid mahogany body, 2 exposed humbuckers.

1978-1982	Walnut or mahogany	$900	$1,100

The Paul Firebrand Deluxe
1980-1982. Single-cut mahogany solidbody, rough natural finish, Gibson branded in headstock, 2 exposed humbuckers.

1980-1982	Black	$600	$750
1980-1982	Pelham Blue	$700	$875
1980-1982	Rough natural	$600	$750

MODEL YEAR	FEATURES	EXC. COND. LOW	HIGH

The Paul II

1996-1998. Mahogany body, 2 humbucking pickups, rosewood dot neck, renamed The Paul SL in '98.

| 1996-1998 | | $425 | $525 |

LG-0

1958-1974. Flat-top acoustic, mahogany, bound body, rosewood bridge '58-'61 and '68-'74, plastic bridge '62-'67, natural.

1958-1961	Rosewood bridge	$950	$1,200
1962-1964	Plastic bridge	$700	$900
1965	Plastic bridge	$650	$850
1966	Plastic bridge	$600	$800
1967-1969	Rosewood bridge	$600	$800
1970-1974		$500	$600

LG-1

1943-1968. Flat-top acoustic, spruce top, mahogany back and sides, bound body, rosewood bridge '43-'61, plastic bridge after, examples seen to '74, sunburst.

1943-1949		$1,500	$1,800
1950-1961	Rosewood bridge	$1,400	$1,700
1962-1964	Plastic bridge	$1,300	$1,600
1965		$1,000	$1,200
1966-1968		$875	$1,100

LG-2

1942-1962. Flat-top acoustic, spruce top, mahogany back and sides (some with maple '43-'46), banner headstock '42-'46, bound body, X-bracing, sunburst finish, replaced by B-25 in '62.

1942-1945		$3,000	$3,700
1946		$2,800	$3,400
1947		$2,700	$3,200
1948-1949		$2,500	$3,000
1950-1957		$2,100	$2,600
1958		$1,900	$2,400
1959-1961	Rosewood bridge (last)	$1,800	$2,200
1962	Ajustable bridge	$1,400	$1,700

LG-2 3/4

1949-1962. Short-scale version of LG-2 flat-top, wood bridge, sunburst.

1949-1957		$1,700	$2,000
1958		$1,500	$1,800
1959-1961	Rosewood bridge (last)	$1,400	$1,700
1962	Ajustable bridge	$1,200	$1,500

LG-2 3/4 Arlo Guthrie

2003, 2005-present. Vintage replica finish.

| 2003-2010 | | $1,300 | $1,625 |

LG-2 H

1945-1955. Flat-top, Hawaiian, natural or sunburst.

1944-1945		$3,000	$3,700
1946		$2,800	$3,400
1947		$2,700	$3,200
1948-1949		$2,500	$3,000
1950-1955		$2,100	$2,600

LG-3

1942-1964. Flat-top acoustic, spruce top, mahogany back and sides, natural finish, replaced by B-25 N.

| 1942 | | $3,400 | $4,000 |
| 1943 | | $3,300 | $3,900 |

MODEL YEAR	FEATURES	EXC. COND. LOW	HIGH
1944		$3,200	$3,800
1945		$3,100	$3,700
1946		$3,000	$3,600
1947		$2,900	$3,500
1948		$2,800	$3,400
1949		$2,700	$3,300
1950-1957		$2,400	$3,000
1958		$2,200	$2,800
1959-1962	Early-'62 last wood bridge	$2,100	$2,700
1962-1964	Late-'62 1st plastic bridge	$1,700	$2,200

LG-12 (12-string)

1967-1974. 14-1/8" wide, mahogany back and sides, bound top, natural.

| 1967-1969 | Adjustable saddle | $875 | $1,100 |
| 1970-1974 | Set saddle | $775 | $975 |

Longhorn Double Cutaway

2008. Guitar of the Month for July '08, DC body style with longer slightly pointy curved horns, AA figured maple top over mahogany body, 2 EMG 85 active pickups (without poles), L.R. Baggs piezo pickup underneath tune-o-matic bridge, 3 control knobs with toggle switch, small-block inlays, higher-end Flowerpot headstock inlay, sunburst or transparent finishes.

| 2008 | | $1,300 | $1,600 |

M III Series

1991-1996. Double-cut solidbody with extra long bass horn, six-on-a-side tuners on a reverse pointy headstock, dot markers, reverse Gibson decal logo.

| 1991-1992 | Deluxe | $1,500 | $1,800 |
| 1991-1996 | Standard | $800 | $1,000 |

Mach II

1990-1991. Renamed from U-2, offset double-cut, 2 single coils and 1 humbucking pickup.

| 1990-1991 | | $725 | $875 |

Map Guitar

1983, 1985. Body cutout like lower 48, 2 humbuckers, limited run promotion, '83 version in natural mahogany or red, white and blue, '85 version red, white and blue stars and stripes on a white background. This model can often be found in better than excellent condition because the instrument is as much a show piece as it is a player guitar, and the price range reflects that.

| 1983 | Natural | $2,300 | $2,800 |
| 1983 | Red, white & blue | $2,600 | $3,200 |

Marauder

1975-1980. Single-cut solidbody, pointed headstock, 2 pickups, bolt-on neck, various colors.

| 1975-1980 | | $700 | $850 |

Marauder Custom

1976-1977. Marauder with 3-way selector switch, bound 'board, block markers, bolt-on neck, Marauder logo on truss rod cover, sunburst.

| 1976-1977 | | $900 | $1,100 |

Melody Maker

1959-1971. Slab solidbody, 1 pickup, single-cut until '61, double '61-'66, SG body '66-'71, reintroduced as single-cut in '86-'93. A single-cut Les Paul Melody Maker was offered from '03-'06.

| 1959-1960 | Sunburst, single-cut | $1,500 | $1,800 |

2008 Gibson Longhorn Double Cutaway

1985 Gibson Map

Gibson Melody Maker 3/4

Gibson Melody Maker
Single Coil

MODEL YEAR	FEATURES	EXC. COND. LOW	HIGH
1961	Sunburst, single-cut	$1,200	$1,500
1962	Sunburst or cherry, double-cut	$1,200	$1,500
1963	Sunburst or cherry, double-cut	$1,100	$1,400
1964	Cherry, double-cut	$1,100	$1,400
1965	Cherry, double cut	$900	$1,200
1966	Cherry, double cut	$800	$1,100
1966-1969	Blue, burgundy or red, SG body	$1,100	$1,400
1968-1971	Walnut, SG body	$900	$1,200

Melody Maker 3/4
1959-1970. Short-scale version.

1959-1961	Single-cut	$750	$900
1961-1962	Double-cut	$600	$750
1963-1966	Double-cut	$550	$700
1966-1970	SG body	$600	$700

Melody Maker D
1960-1970. Two pickup version of Melody Maker, reintroduced as Melody Maker Double in '77.

1960-1961	Sunburst, single-cut	$1,900	$2,350
1961-1962	Sunburst or cherry, double-cut	$1,600	$1,900
1963-1964	Sunburst or cherry, double-cut	$1,500	$1,900
1965-1966	Sunburst or cherry, double-cut	$1,200	$1,500
1966	Blue, SG body	$1,600	$1,950
1966	Burgundy or red, SG body	$1,600	$1,950
1967-1969	Blue, SG body	$1,500	$1,850
1967-1969	Burgundy or red, SG body	$1,500	$1,850
1968-1970	Walnut, SG body	$1,300	$1,650

Melody Maker Double
1977-1983. Reintroduction of Melody Maker D, double-cut solidbody, 2 pickups, cherry or sunburst.

1977-1983		$825	$1,050

Melody Maker III
1967-1971. SG-style double-cut solidbody, 3 pickups, various colors.

1967-1969		$1,750	$2,150
1970-1971		$1,550	$1,900

Melody Maker 12
1967-1971. SG-style solidbody, 12 strings, 2 pickups, red, white or Pelham Blue.

1967-1971		$1,450	$1,800

Melody Maker Faded
2003. Les Paul Jr. styling, single-cut, 1 P-90 style pickup, Nashville tune-o-matic bridge, black satin finish.

2003		$325	$400

Melody Maker (Single Coil)
2007-present. US-made, Les Paul Jr. styling, single special design bridge single-coil pickup, or 2 pickup option (available until '08).

2007-2008	2 pickup option	$300	$350
2007-2010	1 pickup	$225	$275

MODEL YEAR	FEATURES	EXC. COND. LOW	HIGH

MK-35
1975-1978. Mark Series flat-top acoustic, mahogany back and sides, black-bound body, natural or sunburst, 5226 made.

1975-1978		$700	$850

MK-53
1975-1978. Mark Series flat-top acoustic, maple back and sides, multi-bound body, natural or sunburst, 1424 made.

1975-1978		$750	$900

MK-72
1975-1978. Mark Series flat-top acoustic, rosewood back and sides, black-bound body, chrome tuners, natural or sunburst, 1229 made.

1975-1978		$775	$925

MK-81
1975-1978. Mark Series flat-top acoustic, rosewood back and sides, multi-bound body, gold tuners, high-end appointments, natural or sunburst, 431 made.

1975-1978		$800	$950

Moderne Heritage
1981-1983. Limited edition, korina body, 2 humbucking pickups, gold hardware.

1981-1983	Black or white	$3,200	$3,900
1981-1983	Natural	$4,200	$5,000

Nick Lucas
1928-1938. Flat-top acoustic, multi-bound body and neck, sunburst, reintroduced in '91 and '99. Also known as Nick Lucas Special and Gibson Special.

1927-1928	Mahogany, 12-fret, 13 1/3"	$11,000	$14,000
1927-1928	Rosewood, 12-fret, 13 1/2"	$20,000	$25,000
1929	Rosewood, 13-fret, 14 3/4"	$25,000	$31,000
1930-1933	Rosewood, 13-fret, 14 3/4", pin bridge	$23,000	$29,000
1930-1933	Rosewood, 13-fret, 14 3/4", trapeze	$21,000	$29,000
1934-1938	Maple, 14-fret, 14 3/4"	$29,000	$37,000
1934-1938	Maple, tenor 4-string	$5,500	$7,000

Nick Lucas Reissue
1991-1992, 1999-2004. Limited edition flat-top acoustic, sunburst.

1991-1992		$1,700	$2,000
1999-2004		$1,600	$1,900

Nick Lucas Elite
2003-2005. Ebony 'board, abalone inlay, gold tuners.

2003-2005		$2,500	$3,000

Nighthawk Custom
1993-1998. Flame maple top, ebony 'board, gold hardware, fireburst, single/double/mini pickups.

1993-1998		$1,400	$1,700

Nighthawk Special
1993-1998. Single-cut solidbody, figured maple top, double-coil and mini-pickup or with additional single-coil options, dot marker inlay, cherry, ebony or sunburst.

1993-1998		$750	$900

MODEL YEAR FEATURES	EXC. COND. LOW	HIGH

Nighthawk Standard

1993-1998. Single-cut solidbody, figured maple top, 2 or 3 pickups, double-parallelogram inlay, amber, fireburst or sunburst.

| 1993-1998 | $1,150 | $1,400 |

Nouveau NV6T-M

1986-1987. A line of Gibson flat-tops with imported parts assembled and finished in the U.S., acoustic dreadnought, bound maple body, natural.

| 1986-1987 | $450 | $525 |

Original Jumbo (Custom Shop)

2003. 16" jumbo body, Adirondack (red) spruce top, mahogany sides and back, Gotoh vintage-style tuners with butterbean buttons, deep sunburst finish on complete body, Custom Art Historic.

| 2003 | $2,000 | $2,400 |

Pat Martino Custom/Signature

1999-2006. Sharp single-cut thinline, f-holes, 2 humbuckers, flamed cherry sunburst maple top, small snakehead style headstock, Pat Martino logo on truss rod cover.

| 1999-2006 | $1,900 | $2,300 |

PG-00

1932-1937. Plectrum neck, flat-top.

| 1932-1937 | $2,300 | $2,800 |

PG-1

1928-1938. Plectrum neck, flat-top.

| 1928-1938 | $2,400 | $3,000 |

PG-175

1950. Acoustic/electric with ES-175 bobdy and 4-string plectrum neck, bow-tie markers, sunburst.

| 1950 | $4,000 | $5,000 |

Q-100

1985-1986. Offset double-cut solidbody, Kahler trem, 6-on-a-side tuners, 1 humbucker, black hardware.

| 1985-1986 | $475 | $575 |

Q-200/Q2000

1985-1986. Like Q-100, but with 1 single-coil and 1 humbucker, black or chrome hardware.

| 1985-1986 | $525 | $650 |

Q-300/Q3000

1985-1986. Like Q-100, but with 3 single-coils, black or chrome hardware.

| 1985-1986 | $550 | $675 |

Q-400/Q4000

Late-1985-1987. Limited custom production, very few made, like Q-100, but with 2 single-coils and 1 humbucker, black hardware, Ferrari red or Pink Panther finish.

| 1985-1987 | $1,200 | $1,500 |

Q3000 Custom Shop

1985. 3 single-coil pickups.

| 1985 | $1,200 | $1,500 |

Randy Scruggs Advanced Jumbo Limited Edition

2010-present. Sitka spruce top, East Indian rosewood body, king's crown logo on headstock, crown position markers, Fishman Matrix VT pickup, vintage sunburst.

| 2010 | $1,800 | $2,200 |

RD Artist/77

1980. The 77 model has a 25.5" scale versus 24.75".

| 1980 | $1,100 | $1,350 |

RD Artist/79

1978-1982. Double-cut solidbody, 2 humbuckers, TP-6 tailpiece, active electronics, ebony 'board, block inlays, gold-plated parts, various colors, called just RD (no Artist) in '81 and '82.

| 1978-1982 | $1,250 | $1,550 |

RD Custom

1977-1979. Double-cut solidbody, 2 humbuckers, stop tailpiece, active electronics, dot inlays, maple 'board, chrome parts, natural or walnut.

| 1977-1979 | $1,300 | $1,650 |

RD Standard

1977-1979. Double-cut solidbody, 2 humbuckers, stop tailpiece, rosewood 'board, dot inlays, chrome parts, natural, sunburst or walnut.

| 1977-1979 | $1,000 | $1,250 |

RD Standard Reissue

2007. 400 made, Silverburst.

| 2007 | $875 | $1,100 |

Roy Smeck Radio Grande Hawaiian

1934-1939. Dreadnought acoustic flat-top, rosewood back and sides, bound body and neck, natural.

| 1934-1939 | $12,000 | $15,000 |

Roy Smeck Radio Grande Hawaiian Reissue

1996. Part of SmartWood Series, Grenadillo back and sides.

| 1996 | $2,100 | $2,500 |

Roy Smeck Radio Grande Hawaiian Limited

1994. Centennial Guitar of the Month in '94, 100 made, Indian rosewood.

| 1994 | $2,100 | $2,500 |

Roy Smeck Stage Deluxe Hawaiian

1934-1942. Dreadnought acoustic flat-top, mahogany back and sides, bound body, natural.

| 1934-1942 | $6,000 | $7,400 |

S-1

1976-1980. Single-cut solidbody, pointed headstock, 3 single-coil pickups, similar to the Marauder, various colors.

| 1976-1980 | $600 | $750 |

SG

Following are models, listed alphabetically, bearing the SG name.

SG I

1972-1977. Double-cut, mahogany body, 1 mini-humbucker (some with SG Jr. P-90), cherry or walnut.

| 1972-1977 | $700 | $875 |

SG II

1972-1976. 2 mini-humbuckers (some in '75 had regular humbuckers), cherry or walnut.

| 1972-1976 | $875 | $1,100 |

SG III

1972-1974. The sunburst version of the II, some shipped as late as '79.

| 1972-1974 | $900 | $1,150 |

Gibson Randy Scruggs Advanced Jumbo Limited Edition

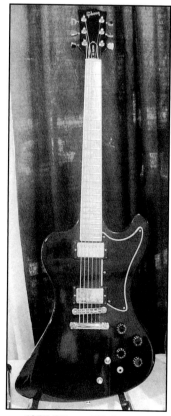

1977 Gibson RD Custom

GUITARS

Gibson SG '61 Reissue

Gibson SG Diablo

MODEL YEAR	FEATURES	EXC. COND. LOW	HIGH

SG-3
2007-2008. SG styling, SG Standard appointments, 3 gold humbuckers or 3 single coils, 1 rotor switch, 2 knobs, stop tail.

2007-2008	3 humbuckers	$950	$1,200
2007-2008	3 single coils	$600	$800

SG '61 Reissue
2003-present. Renamed from Les Paul SG '61 Reissue, no Les Paul script on truss rod, small 'guard, stop bar tailpiece (no Deluxe Maestro vibrato), '60 slim-taper neck profile.

2003-2010		$1,100	$1,400

SG '62 Reissue/SG Reissue
1986-1991. Trapezoid markers, stop bar, 2 humbuckers, called SG Reissue '86-'87, SG '62 Reissue '88-'91. Reintroduced as Les Paul SG '61 Reissue for '93-'03 and SG '61 Reissue '03-present, cherry.

1986-1991		$1,100	$1,400

SG '62 Reissue Showcase Edition
1988. Guitar of the Month, bright blue opaque finish, 200 made.

1988		$1,150	$1,450

Les Paul '63 Corvette Sting Ray
1995-1997. Custom Shop SG-style body carved to simulate split rear window on '63 Corvette, Sting Ray inlay, 150 instruments built, offered in black, white, silver or red.

1995-1997		$3,400	$4,200

SG-90 Double
1988-1990. SG body, updated electronics, graphite reinforced neck, 2 pickups, cherry, turquoise or white.

1988-1990		$575	$700

SG-90 Single
1988-1990. SG body, updated electronics, graphite reinforced neck, 1 humbucker pickup, cherry, turquoise or white.

1988-1990		$550	$675

SG-100
1971-1972. Double-cut solidbody, 1 pickup, cherry or walnut.

1971-1972	Melody Maker pickup	$625	$750
1971-1972	P-90 pickup option	$625	$750
1971-1972	Sam Ash model	$625	$750

SG-200
1971-1972. Two pickup version of SG-100 in black, cherry or walnut finish, replaced by SG II.

1971-1972	Melody Maker pickups	$550	$675

SG-250
1971-1972. Two-pickup version of SG-100 in cherry sunburst, replaced by SG III.

1971-1972	Melody Maker pickups	$625	$750

SG-400/SG Special 400
1985-1987. SG body with 3 toggles, 2 knobs (master volume, master tone), single-single-humbucker pickups, available with uncommon opaque finishes.

1985-1987		$700	$860

SG Classic
1999-2001, 2003-present. Late '60s SG Special style, Classic on truss rod cover, large 'guard, black soapbar single-coil P-90s, dot markers, stop bar tailpiece, cherry or ebony stain. Offered by Musician's Friend since '03.

1999-2001		$650	$800
2003-2010		$650	$800

SG Custom
1963-1980. Renamed from Les Paul Custom, 3 humbuckers, vibrato, made with Les Paul Custom plate from '61-'63 (see Les Paul Custom), white finish until '68, walnut and others after.

1963	White, pat. #	$12,000	$15,000
1964	White	$12,000	$15,000
1965	White	$11,500	$14,000
1966-1968	White	$6,000	$8,000
1969	Walnut or white, Lyre	$4,000	$6,000
1970	Walnut or white, Lyre	$3,500	$4,500
1970-1973	Walnut	$3,000	$3,700
1970-1973	White option	$3,000	$3,700
1974-1976	Various colors	$2,400	$2,900
1977-1980	Various colors	$2,200	$2,700

SG Custom 30th Anniversary
1991. Custom Shop, block inlay, 3 57 Classic humbuckers, engraved 30th Anniversary headstock logo, gold hardware, darker TV yellow.

1991		$2,000	$2,500

SG Custom '67 Reissue/Les Paul SG '67 Custom
1991-1993. The SG Custom '67 Reissue has a wine red finish, the Les Paul SG '67 Custom ('92-'93) has a wine red or white finish.

1991-1993		$1,650	$2,000

SG Custom Elliot Easton Signature
2006-2007. Custom Shop, SG Custom specs, Maestro deluxe vibrola, Pelham Blue or white, includes Certificate of Authenticity.

2006-2007		$3,200	$4,000

SG Deluxe
1971-1972, 1981-1985, 1998-1999. The '70s models were offered in natural, cherry or walnut finishes, reintroduced in '98 with 3 Firebird mini-humbucker-style pickups in black, Ice Blue or red finishes.

1971-1972	Cherry	$1,300	$1,600
1971-1972	Natural or walnut	$1,300	$1,600
1981-1985	Various colors	$975	$1,200
1998-1999	Various colors	$975	$1,200

SG Diablo
2008. Guitar of the Month for Dec. '08, 1,000 made, based on vintage '61 SG Standard, metallic silver finish with matching headstock, new control configuration, 1 volume, 1 tone knob, 3-way toggle switch, 24.74" scale with 24 frets (2 more than standard).

2008		$1,325	$1,575

SG Elegant
2004-present. Custom Shop, quilt maple top, gold hardware, Blue Burst, Firemist and Iguana Burst finishes.

2004-2010		$2,100	$2,600

The *Vintage Guitar Price Guide* shows low to high values for items in all-original excellent condition, and, where applicable, with original case or cover.

MODEL YEAR	FEATURES	EXC. COND. LOW	HIGH

SG Exclusive

1979. SG with humbuckers, coil-tap and rotary control knob, block inlay, pearl logo (not decal), black/ebony finish.

1979		$1,700	$2,100

SG Firebrand

1980-1982. Double-cut mahogany solidbody, rough natural finish, Gibson branded in headstock, 2 exposed humbuckers, Firebrand logo on The SG (Standard) model.

1980-1982		$700	$850

SG Goddess

2007. SG Goddess logo on truss rod cover, only 2 control knobs versus standard 4, exposed humbuckers.

2007		$875	$1,050

SG Gothic

2000-2003. SG Special with satin black finish, moon and star marker on 12th fret, black hardware.

2000-2003		$575	$750

SG GT

2006-2007. '61 SG Standard reissue specs with racing stripes paint job and removable tailpiece hood scoop, locking tuners, dual truss rod system, Candy Apple Red, Daytona Blue, or Phantom Black.

2006-2007		$1,150	$1,450

SG Judas Priest Signature

2003. Custom Shop, 30 made, dot markers, exposed '57 classic humbucker and EMG58 pickups, black, large chrome metal 'guard, also sold as a set with Flying V Judas Priest, includes Certificate of Authenticity.

2003		$1,700	$2,000

SG Junior

1963-1971, 1991-1994. One pickup, solidbody. Prices are for an unfaded finish, cherry finish faded to brown reduces the value by 30%.

1963	Cherry	$2,700	$3,200
1963	White	$3,300	$4,100
1964	Cherry	$2,700	$3,200
1964	White	$3,300	$4,100
1965	Early-'65 cherry	$2,500	$3,000
1965	Late-'65 cherry	$2,000	$2,500
1965	Pelham Blue	$3,800	$4,700
1965	White	$2,700	$3,200
1966	Cherry	$1,800	$2,200
1966	White	$2,500	$3,000
1967	Cherry	$1,800	$2,200
1967	White	$2,500	$3,000
1968	Cherry	$1,800	$2,200
1968	White	$2,500	$3,000
1969	Cherry	$1,700	$2,000
1970	Cherry	$1,600	$2,000
1971	Cherry or walnut	$1,400	$1,700
1991-1994	Various colors	$625	$750

SG Junior P-90

2007. Single P-90 pickup, large 'guard, stop tail, cherry finish.

2007		$475	$575

SG Les Paul '61 Custom Reissue

1997-2005. 1961 specs, SG body style, 3 humbuckers, Deluxe Maestro vibrato or stud with tune-o-matic bridge, white or silver option.

1997-2005	White or silver	$1,800	$2,200

SG Les Paul '62 Custom

1986-1990. 1962 specs, 3 humbuckers.

1986-1990		$1,700	$2,100

SG Les Paul '90 Custom

1990-1992. 1962 specs, 3 humbuckers.

1990-1992		$1,700	$2,100

SG Les Paul Custom 30th Anniversary

1991. SG body, 3 humbuckers, gold hardware, TV Yellow finish, 30th Anniversary on peghead.

1991		$1,900	$2,300

SG Menace

2006-2007. Carved mahogany body, 2 exposed humbuckers, flat black finish, black hardware, single brass knuckle position marker, gig bag.

2006-2007		$525	$650

SG Music Machine Stinger

2003. Custom run for dealer Music Machine, special serial number series, SG Custom with 2 pickups and SG Standard models available, black stinger paint job on neck/headstock, various colors.

2003	SG Custom	$2,600	$3,100
2003	SG Standard	$2,200	$2,700

SG Pete Townshend Signature (Historic/Custom Shop)

2000-2003. SG Special with '70 specs, large 'guard, 2 cases, cherry red.

2000-2003	Includes certificate	$1,800	$2,200

SG Platinum

2005. A mix of SG Special and SG Standard specs, platinum paint on the body, back of neck, and headstock, no crown inlay, Gibson stencil logo, exposed humbucker pickups, large plantium-finish 'guard, special plantinum colored Gibson logo guitar case.

2005		$650	$800

SG Pro

1971-1973. Two P-90 pickups, tune-o-matic bridge, vibrato, cherry, mahogany or walnut.

1971-1973	Cherry	$1,100	$1,375
1971-1973	Mahogany or walnut	$1,000	$1,250

SG Reissue

1986-1987. Standard early to mid-'60s small guard SG specs, stop tailpiece with tune-o-matic bridge, no designation on truss rod cover, cherry finish, renamed SG '62 Reissue in '88.

1986-1987		$1,100	$1,400

SG Robot Special

2008-present. Dot markers, robot tuning.

2008-2010		$950	$1,150

SG Robot Special Ltd

2008. Trapezoid markers, robot tuning.

2008		$950	$1,150

SG Robot Special Ltd Silverburst

2008. 400 made.

2008		$1,000	$1,200

SG Select

2007. Made in Nashville, TN, carved solid book-matched AAA flame maple, 3-piece flamed maple neck, described as the most exquisite SG offered to date, 2 humbuckers, gold hardware.

2007		$1,900	$2,400

1965 Gibson SG Junior
David Daviee

Gibson SG Select

GUITARS

1969 Gibson SG Standard

Gibson SG Standard
Angus Young Signature

MODEL YEAR	FEATURES	EXC. COND. LOW	HIGH

SG Silverburst Limited
2010. 400 made, standard tuners.

2010		$1,300	$1,600

SG Special
1959-1978, 1985-present. Rounded double-cut for '59-'60, switched to SG body early-'61, 2 P-90s '59-'71, 2 mini-humbuckers '72-'78, 2 regular humbuckers on current version, reintroduced in '85. Prices are for an unfaded finish, cherry finish faded to brown reduces the value by 20%-30%. Instruments with stop tailpieces vs. Maestro tailpiece have the same value.

1959	Cherry, slab, high neck pickup	$5,300	$6,600
1960	Cherry, slab, lower neck pickup	$5,300	$6,600
1961	Cherry, SG body	$4,500	$5,600
1962	Cherry	$4,200	$5,200
1962	White	$5,200	$6,300
1963	Cherry	$4,200	$5,200
1963	White	$5,200	$6,300
1964	Cherry	$4,200	$5,200
1964	White	$5,200	$6,300
1965	Cherry	$3,600	$4,500
1965	White	$4,100	$5,100
1966	Cherry, large 'guard	$2,800	$3,500
1966	Cherry, small 'guard	$3,000	$3,700
1966	White, large 'guard	$3,500	$4,200
1966	White, small 'guard	$3,900	$4,900
1967	Cherry	$2,800	$3,500
1967	White	$3,500	$4,200
1968-1969	Cherry	$2,800	$3,500
1970-1971	Cherry	$2,500	$3,100
1972-1975	Cherry or walnut	$1,350	$1,600
1976-1978	Cherry or walnut	$1,175	$1,400

SG Special (redesigned)
1985-1996. In mid-'85 Gibson introduced a redesigned SG Special model with 2 control knobs (1 pickup) or 3 control knobs (2 pickups) versus the previously used 4-knob layout.

1985-1986	1 pickup, 2 knobs	$500	$600
1985-1996	2 pickups, 3 knobs	$550	$675

SG Special (reintroduced)
1996-2007. In '96 Gibson reintroduced the original 4-knob layout, 2 humbucker pickups, dot markers.

1996-2007		$550	$675
2007	Trapezoids, stoptail	$550	$675

SG Special 3/4
1961. Only 61 shipped.

1961		$3,000	$3,700

SG Special '60s Tribute
2011-present. '60s specs including small guard, dot markers, 2 P-90s, Slim Taper '60s neck profile, 4 worn-finish options.

2011		$525	$650

SG Special Faded (3 pickups)
2007. Made in Nashville, TN, 3 exposed 490 humbuckers, dot markers, stop tail, SG initials on truss rod cover, 2 knobs and 6-position selector switch, hand-worn satin finish.

2007		$425	$525

SG Special Faded/Faded SG Special
2002-present. Aged worn cherry finish.

2002-2005	Half moon markers	$550	$675
2003-2010	Dot markers	$500	$625

SG Special I
1983-1985. Typical SG Special features including dot markers, 1 exposed-coil humbucker pickup, called by various names including Gibson Special ('83), Special I, and SG Special I.

1983-1985		$550	$675

SG Special II
1983-1985. Typical SG Special features including dot markers, 2 exposed-coil humbucker pickups, called by various names including Gibson Special ('83), Special II, SG Special II.

1983-1985		$550	$675

SG Special II EMG
2007. EMG humbucker pickups, no position markers, standard 4-knob and 3-way toggle switch SG format, black satin finish over entire guitar, black hardware.

2007		$750	$900

SG Special New Century
2006-2008. Dramatic full-body mirror 'guard, mahogany body and neck, 490R and 498T humbuckers, classic '60s neck profile, mirror truss rod cover, dot markers.

2006-2008		$625	$725

SG Standard
1963-1981, 1983-present. Les Paul Standard changes to SG body, 2 humbuckers, some very early models have optional factory Bigsby. Prices are for an unfaded finish, a cherry finish faded to brown reduces the value by 30% or more.

1963-1964	Cherry, small 'guard, deluxe vibrato	$9,500	$12,000
1964	Pelham Blue, small 'guard, deluxe vibrato	$16,000	$20,000
1965	Cherry, small 'guard, deluxe vibrato	$9,000	$11,000
1965	Pelham Blue, small 'guard, deluxe vibrato	$15,000	$18,000
1966	Cherry, large 'guard	$5,000	$6,000
1966	Cherry, small 'guard, deluxe vibrato	$7,500	$9,000
1967	Burgundy Metallic	$5,500	$6,700
1967	Cherry	$4,500	$5,500
1967	White	$5,500	$6,700

MODEL YEAR	FEATURES	EXC. COND. LOW	HIGH
1968	Cherry, engraved lyre	$4,500	$5,500
1969	Engraved lyre, 1-piece neck	$4,000	$5,000
1969	Engraved lyre, 3-piece neck	$3,000	$3,700
1970	Cherry, non-lyre tailpiece	$2,300	$2,800
1970	Engraved lyre, 3-piece neck	$2,500	$3,100
1970	Walnut, non-lyre tailpiece	$2,000	$2,500
1971	Cherry, non-lyre tailpiece	$2,000	$2,500
1971	Engraved lyre, 3-piece neck	$2,500	$3,100
1971-1975	New specs, block markers	$1,700	$2,100
1976-1981	New color line-up	$1,600	$2,000
1983-1987		$1,300	$1,600
1988-1999	New specs	$800	$1,000
2000-2010	Standard colors, large 'guard, stoptail	$775	$975
2006-2007	Silverburst, 400 made	$1,200	$1,500

SG Standard '61 Reissue

2004-2008. Small 'guard, stop tail, Nashville tune-o-matic bridge, Gibson Deluxe Keystone tuners, standard Gibson logo and crown inlay, no Les Paul logo, Vintage Original Spec aging optional from '06.

2007-2008		$1,250	$1,550

SG Standard Angus Young Signature

2000-present. Late-'60s specs with large 'guard, Deluxe Maestro lyre vibrato with Angus logo, late-'60s style knobs, Angus logo on headstock, aged cherry finish.

2000-2010		$1,450	$1,750

SG Standard Celebrity Series

1991-1992. SG Standard with large 'guard, gold hardware, black finish.

1991-1992		$1,350	$1,650

SG Standard Gary Rossington Signature

2004. '63-'64 SG Standard specs with Deluxe Maestro vibrola, '60 slim taper neck, limited edition, faded cherry aged by Tom Murphy.

2004		$2,600	$3,100

SG Standard Korina

1993-1994. Korina version of SG Standard, limited run, natural.

1993-1994		$1,800	$2,200

SG Standard Limited Edition

2000. Limited Edition logo back of headstock, 2 humbuckers, large pearloid guard, gold hardware, dark opaque finish.

2000		$950	$1,150

SG Standard Reissue

2004-present. Reissue of near '63-'64 specs with Deluxe Maestro lyre vibrato and small 'guard, also offered with stop bar tailpiece, cherry finish, '60 slim taper neck, smooth neck heel joint, trapezoid markers, unmarked truss rod cover without Les Paul designa-

tion, formerly called Les Paul SG Standard Reissue, by 2005 part of Gibson's 'Vintage Original Spec' Custom Shop series.

2004-2010		$1,800	$2,200

SG Supreme

2004-2007. '57 humbuckers, flamed maple top, split-diamond markers, various colors.

2004-2007		$1,300	$1,600

SG Tommy Iommi Signature (Historic/Custom Shop)

2001-2003. Custom Shop higher-end, signature humbuckers without poles, cross inlays, ebony or Wine Red.

2001-2003		$4,400	$5,500

SG Tommy Iommi Signature (Production)

2002-2003. Standard production model.

2002-2008		$1,150	$1,400

SG TV

1959-1968. Les Paul TV changed to SG body, double rounded cutaway solidbody for '59-'60, SG body '61-'68, 1 pickup, limed mahogany (TV yellow) finish. Prices are for unfaded finish, a faded finish reduces the value by 20%-30%.

1959-1961	TV Yellow, slab body	$5,900	$7,400
1961	White, SG body	$3,900	$4,800
1962	White, SG body	$3,700	$4,600
1963	White, SG body	$3,500	$4,300

SG Voodoo/Voodoo SG

2002-2004. Carved top, black hardware, voodoo doll inlay at 5th fret, Juju finish (black with red wood filler).

2002-2004		$800	$975

SG-R1/SG Artist

1980-1982. Active RD-era electronics. SG style but thicker body, no 'guard, ebony 'board, black finish, dot markers, renamed SG Artist in '81.

1980	SG-R1	$775	$950
1981-1982	SG Artist	$725	$900

SG-X (All American I)

1995-2000. Renamed the SG-X in '98, previously part of the All American series, SG body with single bridge humbucker, various colors.

1995-1999		$625	$750

SG-X Tommy Hilfiger

1998. Large Tommy Hilfiger colored logo on front of guitar below tailpiece, dot markers, plain headstock like a SG Special, dark blue finish, 100 made.

1998		$450	$550

The SG

1979-1983. Offered as The SG Standard with solid walnut body and The SG Deluxe with solid mahogany body, normal SG specs, ebony 'board, 2 humbuckers, model name logo on truss rod.

1979-1983	Walnut or mahogany	$675	$825

Sheryl Crow Signature

2001-present. Based on Sheryl Crow's 1962 Country and Western with Hummingbird influences.

2001-2010		$1,350	$1,650

Gibson SG Special Faded

Gibson Sheryl Crow

1966 Gibson SJ

Carl Pepka

Gibson SJ-100

SJ (Southern Jumbo)

1942-1969, 1991-1996. Flat-top, sunburst standard, natural optional starting in '54 (natural finish version called Country-Western starting in '56), round shoulders (changed to square in '62), catalog name changed to SJ Deluxe in '70, refer to that listing.

Model Year	Features	Low	High
1942-1944		$10,200	$11,800
1948-1953		$5,800	$7,000
1954-1955	Sunburst	$5,600	$6,800
1954-1956	Natural option	$6,400	$7,800
1956	Sunburst	$5,500	$6,700
1957		$5,400	$6,600
1958		$5,300	$6,500
1959		$5,200	$6,500
1960		$5,000	$6,300
1961		$4,700	$5,800
1962	Round shoulder (last year)	$4,500	$5,500
1962	Square shoulder (1st year)	$3,500	$4,000
1963-1964	Square shoulder	$3,500	$4,000
1965		$2,800	$3,300
1966		$2,500	$3,000
1967-1968		$2,375	$2,850
1969	Below belly bridge	$2,150	$2,550

SJ Deluxe (Southern Jumbo)

1970-1978. SJ name changed to SJ Deluxe in catalog, along with a series of engineering changes.

Model Year	Features	Low	High
1970-1971	Non-adj. saddle	$1,700	$2,100
1972-1973	Unbound 'board	$1,600	$2,000
1974-1978	4-ply to binding	$1,500	$1,900

SJN (Country-Western)

1956-1969. Flat-top, natural finish version of SJ, round shoulders '56-'62, square shoulders after, called the SJN in '60 and '61, the SJN Country Western after that, catalog name changed to SJN Deluxe in '70, refer to that listing.

Model Year	Features	Low	High
1956		$5,000	$6,300
1957-1959		$4,500	$5,500
1960-1961		$4,100	$4,900
1962	Round shoulders (last year)	$4,100	$4,900
1962	Square shoulder (1st year)	$3,500	$4,000
1963-1964		$3,500	$4,000
1965		$2,800	$3,300
1966		$2,500	$3,000
1967-1968		$2,375	$2,850
1969	Below belly bridge, SJN logo	$2,150	$2,550

SJN Deluxe (Country-Western Jumbo)

1970-1978. SJN name changed to SJN Deluxe in catalog, along with a series of engineering changes.

Model Year	Features	Low	High
1970-1971	Non-adj. saddle	$1,675	$1,925
1972-1973	Unbound 'board	$1,500	$1,750
1974-1978	4-ply to binding	$1,450	$1,700

SJ 1942 Reissue (Southern Jumbo)

2000. Custom Shop, mahogany back and sides, '42 SJ appointments, 'Only A Gibson is Good Enough' banner logo.

Model Year	Features	Low	High
2000		$2,100	$2,600

SJ Reissue (Southern Jumbo)

2003-2007. Sunburst.

Model Year	Features	Low	High
2003-2007		$1,350	$1,650

SJ Hank Williams Jr. Hall of Fame (Southern Jumbo)

1997. Custom Shop, mahogany back and sides, SJ appointments.

Model Year	Features	Low	High
1997		$2,000	$2,400

SJ Woody Guthrie (Southern Jumbo)

2003-present. Single-bound round shoulder body, mahogany back and sides, parallelogram inlays.

Model Year	Features	Low	High
2003-2010		$1,700	$2,000

SJ-100

2008. Jumbo body, dot markers, crown headstock inlay, inlaid Gibson logo, natural.

Model Year	Features	Low	High
2008		$975	$1,200

SJ-100 1939 Centennial

1994. Acoustic flat-top, limited edition, sunburst.

Model Year	Features	Low	High
1994		$1,850	$2,200

SJ-200 Centennial Limited Edition

1994. Made in Bozeman, Montana, 100 made, includes Certificate of Authenticity, 'guard specs based on '38 design.

Model Year	Features	Low	High
1994		$2,800	$3,400

SJ-200 Elite

1998-2007. Gibson Custom Shop Bozeman, maple sides and back.

Model Year	Features	Low	High
1998-2007		$2,250	$2,700

SJ-200 Ray Whitley/J-200 Custom Club

1994-1995. Based on Ray Whitley's late-1930s J-200, including engraved inlays and initials on the truss rod cover, only 37 made, one of the limited edition models the Montana division released to celebrate Gibson's 100th anniversary.

Model Year	Features	Low	High
1994-1995		$7,300	$8,600

SJ-200 Ron Wood

1997. Based on a '57 SG-200 with Wood's oversized double 'guard on either side of the sound hole, flame-pattern fretboard inlays, script signature inlay on headstock, natural.

Model Year	Features	Low	High
1997		$1,650	$2,000

SJ-200 Summer Jam Koa

2006. Custom Shop, only 6 made, offered to attendees of Gibson Guitar Summer Jam, highly figured koa back/sides.

Model Year	Features	Low	High
2006		$4,300	$5,200

SJ-200 Vine

2002. Custom Shop, Sitka spruce top, Eastern curly maple back/sides, abalone vine inlay in 'board, abalone body trim.

Model Year	Features	Low	High
2002		$5,700	$7,000

SJ-300

2007-2010. Super Jumbo with Indian rosewood back and sides, ebony 'board, abalone crown inlays and rosette, gold imperial tuners, active transducer.

Model Year	Features	Low	High
2007-2010		$2,700	$3,300

Sonex-180 Custom

1980-1982. Two Super humbuckers, coil-tap, maple neck, ebony 'board, single-cut, body of Multi-Phonic synthetic material, black or white.

Model Year	Features	Low	High
1980-1982		$500	$600

MODEL YEAR	FEATURES	EXC. COND. LOW	HIGH

Sonex-180 Deluxe
1980-1984. Hardwood neck, rosewood 'board, single-cut, body of Multi-Phonic synthetic material, 2 pickups, no coil-tap, various colors.

1980-1984	Ebony	$550	$675
1982-1984	Red or Fireburst	$600	$725
1982-1984	Silverburst	$600	$725

Sonex-180 Standard
1980. Dirty-fingers pickups, rosewood 'board, ebony finish.

1980		$625	$775

Songbird Deluxe
1999-2003. Square shoulder flat top, Indian rosewood back and sides and 'board, on-board electronics.

1999-2003		$975	$1,200

Songwriter Deluxe
2003-present. Square shoulder flat top, Indian rosewood back and sides, on-board electronics.

2003-2010	Cutaway	$1,000	$1,200
2003-2010	Non-cutaway	$1,000	$1,200

Special 400
1985. Special designation, dot markers, single headstock logo, double-cut SG body, exposed humbucker bridge, 2 single-coils in the neck and middle, Kahler locking tremolo, mini-switches, push-pull knobs, coil tap.

1985		$500	$625

Spirit I
1982-1988. Double rounded cutaway, 1 pickup, chrome hardware, various colors.

1982-1988		$525	$675

Spirit II XPL
1985-1987. Double-cut solidbody, Kahler tremolo, 2 pickups, various colors.

1985-1987		$575	$725

SR-71
1987-1989. Floyd Rose tremolo, 1 humbucker, 2 single-coil pickups, various colors, Wayne Charvel designed.

1987-1989		$575	$725

Star
1992. Star logo on headstock, star position markers, single sharp cutaway flat-top, sunburst.

1991-1992		$1,175	$1,425

Starburst Standard/Flame
1992-1994. Single-cut acoustic/electric, star inlays, figured maple back and sides.

1992-1994		$1,050	$1,225

Style O
1902-1925. Acoustic archtop, oval soundhole, bound top, neck and headstock, various colors.

1902-1906	Paddle headstock	$5,000	$6,000
1902-1906	Paddle headstock, fancy	$7,000	$8,000
1906	Slotted headstock	$5,000	$6,000
1907-1908	Slotted headstock	$6,000	$7,000
1908-1913	Solid headstock	$6,000	$7,000
1914-1921	Scroll variation	$5,000	$6,000
1922-1924	Loar era	$5,500	$6,500
1925	Scroll, truss rod	$6,000	$7,000

Style O-1
1902. Acoustic archtop, celluloid binding.

1902		$7,000	$9,000

Style O-2
1902. Acoustic archtop, pearl/ebony binding.

1902		$7,000	$9,000

Style O-3
1902. Acoustic archtop, green/white binding.

1902		$7,000	$9,000

Style U Harp Guitar
1902-1939. Acoustic 6-string, with 10 or 12 sub-bass strings, maple back and sides, bound soundhole, black.

1915-1919		$7,000	$8,700

Super 300
1948-1955. Acoustic archtop, non-cut, bound body, neck and headstock, sunburst.

1948		$4,200	$4,900
1949		$4,100	$4,800
1950		$4,000	$4,700
1951		$3,900	$4,600
1952		$3,800	$4,500
1953		$3,700	$4,400
1954		$3,700	$4,300
1955		$3,700	$4,300

Super 300 C
1954-1958. Acoustic archtop, rounded cutaway, bound body, neck and headstock, sunburst with natural option.

1954-1958	Sunburst	$5,100	$5,900

Super 400
1935-1941, 1947-1955. Acoustic archtop, non-cut, multi-bound, f-holes, sunburst (see Super 400 N for natural version).

1935	Early '35 Super L-5 Deluxe (Intro. Model)	$16,000	$19,000
1935	Later '35 Super 400	$12,000	$15,000
1936-1941		$10,000	$13,000
1947-1949		$7,000	$9,000
1950-1955		$6,000	$8,000

Super 400 N
1940, 1948-1955. Natural finish version of Super 400, non-cut, acoustic archtop.

1940		$11,000	$14,000
1948		$11,000	$14,000
1949		$11,000	$14,000
1950-1955		$7,000	$9,000

Super 400 P (Premier)
1939-1941. Acoustic archtop, single rounded cutaway, '39 model 'board rests on top, sunburst finish.

1939-1941		$17,000	$21,000

Super 400 PN (Premier Natural)
1939-1940. Rounded cutaway, '39 'board rests on top, natural finish.

1939-1940		$29,000	$36,000

Super 400 C
1948-1982. Introduced as Super 400 Premier, acoustic archtop, single-cut, sunburst finish (natural is called Super 400 CN).

1948-1949		$12,000	$15,000

Gibson SJ-300

Gibson Songwriter Deluxe

1962 Gibson Tal Farlow

Gibson Trini Lopez Standard

MODEL YEAR	FEATURES	EXC. COND. LOW	HIGH
1950-1959		$10,800	$13,500
1960-1964		$9,700	$12,000
1965		$6,400	$8,000
1966-1969		$5,900	$7,000
1970-1975		$4,900	$6,000
1976-1980		$4,900	$5,500
1981-1982		$4,900	$5,000

Super 400 CN
1950-1987. Natural finish version of Super 400 C.

1950-1959		$11,800	$14,500
1960-1964		$10,700	$13,000
1965		$8,000	$9,800
1966-1969		$7,000	$8,000

Super 400 CES
1951-present. Electric version of Super 400 C, archtop, single-cut (round '51-'60 and '69-present, pointed '60-'69), 2 pickups (P-90s '51-'54, Alnico Vs '54-'57, humbuckers '57 on), sunburst (natural version called Super 400 CESN), now part of Gibson's Historic Collection.

1951-1953	P-90s	$11,000	$14,000
1954-1957	Alnico Vs	$11,000	$14,000
1957-1959	PAFs	$14,500	$18,000
1960	PAFs	$13,500	$17,000
1961-1962	PAFs, sharp cut intro.	$10,500	$12,500
1963-1964	Pat. #	$10,500	$12,500
1965		$7,000	$8,700
1966-1969		$5,500	$7,000
1970-1987		$5,000	$6,500

Super 400 CESN
1952-present. Natural version of Super 400 CES, now part of Gibson's Historic Collection.

1952-1953	P-90s	$13,000	$16,000
1954-1956	Alnico Vs	$13,000	$16,000
1957-1960	PAFs	$18,000	$23,000
1961-1962	PAFs, sharp cut intro.	$14,500	$18,000
1963-1964	Pat. #	$11,500	$14,000
1965		$8,000	$9,700
1966-1969		$6,500	$8,000
1970-1987		$6,000	$7,500
1990-2010		$6,000	$7,500

'39 Super 400
1993-1997. Part of Historic Collection, reissue of non-cut '39 version, various colors.

1993-1997		$6,300	$7,800

Super Jumbo 100
1939-1943. Jumbo flat-top, mahogany back and sides, bound body and neck, sunburst, reintroduced as J-100 with different specs in '84.

1939-1941	Stairstep peghead	$27,000	$33,000
1941-1943	Standard peghead	$25,000	$30,000

Super Jumbo/Super Jumbo 200
1938-1942. Initially called Super Jumbo in '38 and named Super Jumbo 200 in '39. Name then changed to J-200 (see that listing) by '47 (with maple back and sides) and SJ-200 by the '50s. Named for super large jumbo 16 7/8" flat-top body, double braced with rosewood back and sides, sunburst finish.

1938-1941	Stairstep peghead	$100,000	$125,000
1941-1942	Standard peghead	$75,000	$95,000

MODEL YEAR	FEATURES	EXC. COND. LOW	HIGH

Super V CES
1978-1993. Archtop, L-5 with a Super 400 neck, 2 humbucker pickups, natural or sunburst.

1978-1993		$5,600	$6,700

Super V BJB
1978-1983. A Super V CES but with a single floating pickup.

1978-1983		$5,600	$6,700

Tal Farlow
1962-1971, 1993-2006. Full body, single-cut archtop, 2 humbuckers, triple-bound top, reintroduced '93, now part of Gibson's Historic Collection.

1962-1964	Viceroy Brown	$5,800	$7,000
1965-1966	Viceroy Brown	$5,300	$6,500
1967-1969	Viceroy Brown	$4,900	$6,000
1970-1971	Viceroy Brown	$3,700	$4,500
1993-2006	Natural, figured wood	$2,400	$3,000
1993-2006	Various colors	$2,300	$2,800

TG-0 (L-0 based)
1927-1933. Acoustic tenor based on L-0, mahogany body, light amber.

1927-1933		$1,700	$2,100

TG-0 (LG-0 based)
1960-1974. Acoustic tenor based on LG-0, mahogany body, natural.

1960-1964		$850	$1,050
1965		$675	$800
1966-1969		$575	$675
1970-1974		$450	$550

TG-00 (L-00 based)
1932-1943. Tenor flat-top based on L-00.

1932-1943		$1,500	$1,800

TG-1/L-1 Tenor/L-4 Tenor (and Plectrum)
1927-1937. Acoustic flat-top, tenor or plectrum guitar based on L-1, mahogany back and sides, bound body, sunburst.

1927-1937		$1,700	$2,100

TG-7
1934-1940. Tenor based on the L-7, sunburst.

1934-1940		$3,200	$4,000

TG-25/TG-25 N
1962-1970. Acoustic flat-top, tenor guitar based on B-25, mahogany back and sides, sunburst or natural (25 N).

1962-1964		$750	$950
1965-1966		$650	$800
1967-1970		$550	$700

TG-50
1934-1958. Acoustic archtop, tenor guitar based on L-50, mahogany back and sides, sunburst.

1934-1940		$1,450	$1,800
1947-1959		$1,200	$1,500
1960-1963		$1,200	$1,500

Traveling Songwriter EC
2005-present. Solid spruce top, solid mahogany sides and back, soft cutaway, on-board electronics and EQ.

2005-2010		$1,400	$1,750

MODEL YEAR	FEATURES	EXC. COND. LOW	HIGH

Trini Lopez Standard

1964-1970. Double rounded cutaway, thinline archtop, 2 humbuckers, tune-o-matic bridge, trapeze tailpiece, single-bound, cherry, sparkling burgundy and Pelham Blue finishes.

1964	Cherry	$5,000	$6,000
1965	Cherry	$4,300	$5,300
1965	Pelham Blue	$5,300	$6,300
1965-1966	Sparkling Burgundy	$4,500	$5,500
1966	Cherry	$4,000	$5,000
1966	Pelham Blue	$5,000	$6,000
1967-1969	Cherry	$3,800	$4,800
1967-1969	Sparkling Burgundy, Pelham Blue	$3,900	$4,900
1970	Cherry	$3,200	$4,000
1970	Sparkling Burgundy, Pelham Blue	$3,300	$4,100

Trini Lopez Standard (Custom Shop)

2010-present. Custom Shop reissue of thinline Trini Lopez Standard, diamond f-holes, 6-on-a-side tuners, trapeze tailpiece, Certificate of Authenticity, cherry red.

2010		$1,600	$2,000

Trini Lopez Deluxe

1964-1970. Double pointed cutaway, thinline archtop, 2 humbuckers, triple-bound, sunburst.

1964		$4,800	$6,000
1965		$4,600	$5,800
1966-1970		$2,650	$3,100

U-2

1987-1989. Double-cut, 1 humbucker and 2 single-coil pickups, ebony or red, renamed Mach II in '90-'91.

1987-1991		$600	$750

U-2 Showcase Edition

1988. November 1988 Guitar of the Month series, 250 made.

1988		$700	$800

US-1/US-3

1986-1991. Double-cut maple top with mahogany back, 3 humbucker pickups (US-1), or 3 P-90s (US-3), standard production and Custom Shop.

1986-1991		$550	$700

Vegas Standard

2006-2007. Flat top semi-hollowbody thinline, slim neck, 2 humbuckers, f-holes, split diamond inlays.

2006-2007		$1,100	$1,325

Vegas High Roller

2006-2007. Upgraded version, AAA maple top, gold hardware and frets, block inlays.

2006-2007		$1,150	$1,400

Victory MV II (MV 2)

1981-1984. Asymetrical double-cut with long horn, 3-way slider, maple body and neck, rosewood 'board, 2 pickups.

1981-1984		$750	$1,000

Victory MV X (MV 10)

1981-1984. 3 humbuckers, 5-way switch, various colors.

1981-1984		$900	$1,100

MODEL YEAR	FEATURES	EXC. COND. LOW	HIGH

XPL Custom

1985-1986. Explorer-like shape, exposed humbuckers, locking tremolo, bound maple top, sunburst or white.

1985-1986		$975	$1,200

Giffin

1977-1988, 1997-present. Professional and premium grade, production/custom, hollow-, semi-hollow-, and solidbody guitars built by luthier Roger Giffin in West San Fernando Valley, California. For '77-'88, Giffin's shop was in London. From '88 to '93, he worked for the Gibson Custom Shop in California as a Master Luthier. In '97, Giffin set up shop in Sweden for a year, moving back to California in the Spring of '98. He also built small numbers of instruments during '67-'76 and '94-'96 (when he had a repair business).

Gigliotti

2000-present. Premium grade, production/custom, electric guitars with a metal plate top and tone chambers and designed by Patrick Gigliotti in Tacoma, Washington.

Gila Eban Guitars

1979-present. Premium grade, custom, classical guitars built by luthier Gila Eban in Riverside, Connecticut.

Gilbert Guitars

1965-present. Custom classical guitars by luthiers John Gilbert and William Gilbert in Paso Robles, California. Son William has handled all production since 1991.

Gilet Guitars

1976-present. Luthier Gerard Gilet builds production/custom, premium grade, acoustic, classical, flamenco, and wooden bodied resonator guitars in Botany, Sydney, New South Wales, Australia. He also builds lap steels.

Girl Brand Guitars

1996-present. Premium-grade, production/custom, guitars built by luthier Chris Larsen in Tucson, Arizona.

Gitane

2003-present. Intermediate and professional grade, production, classic Selmer-Maccaferri style jazz guitars made in China for Saga.

Gittler

1974-ca.1985. Minimalistic electric guitar designed by Allan Gittler, consisting basically of a thin rod with frets welded to it. A total of 560 were built, with Gittler making the first 60 in the U.S. from '74 to the early '80s. The remainder were made around '85 in Israel by the Astron corporation under a licensing agreement. Three Gittler basses were

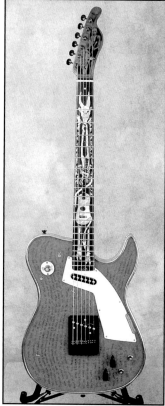

Girl Brand Crossroads Girl

Gitane D-500

Godin Montreal

Gold Tone PBS8

also built. Gittler emigrated to Israel in the early '80s and changed his name to Avraham Bar Rashi. He died in 2002. A U.S.-made Gittler is the only musical instrument in the Museum of Modern Art in New York.

Metal Skeleton
1971-1999.

MODEL YEAR	FEATURES	EXC. COND. LOW	HIGH
1971-1982		$2,100	$2,400
1982-1999		$1,700	$2,000

Glendale
2004-present. Professional grade, production/custom, solidbody guitars built by luthier Dale Clark in Arlington, Texas.

GLF
1991-1997. Solidbody electric guitars built by luthier Kevin Smith in Minnesota. In '97 he started building his ToneSmith line of guitars.

Glick Guitars
1996-present. Premium grade, production/custom, acoustic and electric archtop, and acoustic guitars built in Santa Barbara, California by luthier Mike Glick.

Global
Late-1960s-1970s. Budget copy models, not unlike Teisco, imported from Asia for the student market. They also offered amps.

Electric Solidbody
Late-1960s-1970s.

MODEL YEAR	FEATURES	EXC. COND. LOW	HIGH
1968		$75	$175

GMP
1990-2005. Professional and premium grade solidbody electric guitars built by GM Precision Products, Inc. of San Dimas, California. Original owners were Gary and Cameron Moline, Dave Pearson and Glenn Matejzel. Many guitars featured fancy tops or custom graphics. They also made basses. Overall production is estimated at 1120 guitars and basses. GMP reopened in '10 under new ownership (see following).

GMP (Genuine Musical Products)
2010-present. The GMP brand was acquired by Dan and Kim Lawrence in '08. Since '10, Dan along with fellow luthiers Glenn Matejzel and William Stempke build professional and premium grade, production/custom, electric guitars in San Dimas, California. They also build basses.

GMW
1998-present. Professional grade, production/custom, solidbody guitars from Lee Garver's GMW Guitarworks of Glendora, California.

Godin
1987-present. Intermediate and professional grade, production, solidbody electrics and nylon and steel string acoustic/electrics from luthier Robert Godin. They also build basses and mandolins. Necks and bodies are made in La Patrie, Quebec with final assembly in Berlin, New Hampshire. Godin is also involved in the Seagull, Norman, Richmond, Art & Lutherie, and Patrick & Simon brand of guitars. SA on Godin models stands for Synth Access.

A Series
1990s-present. Multiac-style body.

MODEL YEAR	FEATURES	EXC. COND. LOW	HIGH
1990s-2010	A-12, 12-string	$400	$475
1990s-2010	A-6, 6-string	$375	$450

Acousticaster (6)
1987-present. Thin line single-cut chambered maple body, acoustic/electric, maple neck, 6-on-a-side tuners, spruce top.

1987-2010		$400	$500

Acousticaster 6 Deluxe
1994-2008. Acousticaster 6 with mahogany body.

1994-2008		$450	$550

Artisan ST I/ST I
1992-1998. Offset double-cut solidbody, birdseye maple top, 3 pickups.

1992-1998		$300	$400

Flat Five X
2002-2004. Single-cut, semi-hollow with f-holes, 3-way pickup system (magnetic to transducer).

2002-2004		$650	$800

Freeway Classic/Freeway Classic SA
2004-present. Offset double-cut solidbody, birdseye maple top on translucent finishes, hum-single-hum pickups.

2004-2010		$400	$500

G-1000/G-2000/G-3000
1993-1996. Offset double-cut solidbody, extra large bass horn, various pickup options.

1993-1996		$200	$300

Glissentar A11
2000-present. Electric/acoustic nylon 11-string, solid cedar top, chambered maple body, fretless, natural.

2000-2010		$475	$575

Jeff Cook Signature
1994-1995. Quilted maple top, light maple back, 2 twin rail and 1 humbucker pickups.

1994-1995		$525	$650

L.R. Baggs Signature
1990s. Single-cut chambered thinline electric, spruce top, mahogany body, EQ.

1990s		$400	$475

LG/LGT
1995-present. Single-cut carved slab mahogany body, 2 Tetrad Combo pickups ('95-'97) or 2 Duncan SP-90 pickups ('98-present), various colors, satin lacquer finish. LGT with tremolo.

1995-2010		$275	$350

MODEL YEAR	FEATURES	EXC. COND. LOW	HIGH

LGX/LGXT/LGX-SA

1996-present. Single-cut maple-top carved solid-body, 2 Duncan humbuckers, various quality tops offered. LGXT with tremolo.

1996-2010	Standard top	$600	$700
1997-2010	SA synth access	$800	$1,000
1998-2010	AA top	$800	$1,000
1998-2010	AAA top	$900	$1,100

Montreal

2004-present. Chambered body carved from solid mahogany, f-holes, 2 humbuckers, saddle transducer, stereo mixing output.

2004-2010		$700	$900

Multiac Series

1994-present. Single-cut, thinline electric with solid spruce top, RMC Sensor System electronics, available in either nylon string or steel string versions, built-in EQ, program up/down buttons.

1994-2010	Duet Nylon, classical	$650	$800
1994-2010	Steel string	$725	$925
2000-2010	ACS-SA Nylon	$750	$900
2000-2010	Grand Concert SA	$725	$925
2000-2010	Jazz SA	$800	$1,000
2008-2010	Spectrum SA	$800	$1,000

Radiator

1999-present. Single-cut, dual pickup, pearloid top, dot markers.

1999-2010		$200	$250

Solidac - Two Voice

2000-2009. Single-cut, 2-voice technology for electric or acoustic sound.

2000-2009		$300	$350

TC Signature

1987-1999. Single-cut, quilted maple top, 2 Tetrad Combo pickups.

1987-1999		$500	$600

Gold Tone

1993-present. Wayne and Robyn Rogers build their intermediate and professional grade, production/custom guitars in Titusville, Florida. They also build basses, lap steels, mandolins, ukuleles, banjos and banjitars.

Goldbug Guitars

1997-present. Presentation grade, production/custom, acoustic and electric guitars built by luthier Sandy Winters in Delavan, Wisconsin.

Golden Hawaiian

1920s-1930s. Private branded lap guitar most likely made by one of the many Chicago makers for a small retailer, publisher, cataloger, or teaching studio.

Guitars

1920-1930s	Sunburst	$400	$500

Goldentone

1960s. Guitars made by Ibanez most likely in the mid to late '60s. Often have a stylized I (for Ibanez) on the tailpiece or an Ibanez logo on the headstock.

MODEL YEAR	FEATURES	EXC. COND. LOW	HIGH

Goldon

German manufacturer of high-quality archtops and other guitars before and shortly after WW II. After the war, they were located in East Germany and by the late 1940s were only making musical toys.

Goodall

1972-present. Premium grade, custom flat-tops and nylon-strings, built by luthier James Goodall originally in California and, since '92, in Kailua-Kona, Hawaii.

Classical

1986. Brazilian and cedar.

1986	BC425	$5,500	$7,000

Concert Jumbo

2007-present. Red cedar and Indian rosewood.

2007-2010		$2,500	$3,100

Concert Jumbo Cutaway

2004-present. Rosewood.

2004-2010		$2,800	$3,400

Jumbo KJ

1995-present. Sitka, koa.

1995-2010		$2,100	$2,500

RS Rosewood Standard

1989-1997. Indian rosewood back and sides.

1989-1997		$2,100	$2,500

Standard

1980s-present. Jumbo-style with wide waist, mahogany back and sides, sitka spruce top.

1980-2010		$1,800	$2,200

Goodman Guitars

1975-present. Premium grade, custom/production, archtop, flat top, classical, and electric guitars built by luthier Brad Goodman in Brewster, New York. He also builds mandolins.

Gordon-Smith

1979-present. Intermediate and professional grade, production/custom, semi-hollow and solidbody guitars built by luthier John Smith in Partington, England.

Gower

1955-1960s. Built in Nashville by Jay Gower, later joined by his son Randy. Gower is also associated with Billy Grammer and Grammer guitars.

G-55-2 Flat-Top

1960s. Square shoulder-style flat-top, triple abalone rosette, abalone fretboard trim, small block markers, natural.

1960s		$700	$850

G-65 Flat-Top

1960s. Square shoulder-style flat-top, lower belly bridge with pearl dots on bridge, dot markers, sunburst.

1960s		$500	$600

G-100 Flat-Top

1960s	Brazilian rosewood	$750	$900

Goodall Concert Jumbo

2007 Gordon Smith GS-1

Jon Way

Granata SJ-C

1960 Greco

Solidbody Electric
1960s. Mosrite influenced odd-shaped body, 2 single-coils, bolt neck, Bigsby bridge.

1960s		$500	$600

Goya
1952-1996. Brand initially used by Hershman Musical Instrument Company of New York City, New York, in mid-'50s for acoustic guitars made in Sweden by Levin, particularly known for its classicals. From '58 to '61 they imported Hagstrom- and Galanti-made electrics labeled as Goya; in '62 they offered electrics made by Valco. In '67 they again offered electrics, this time made by Zero Sette in Castelfidardo, Italy. By '63 the company had become the Goya Musical Instrument Corporation, marketing primarily Goya acoustics. Goya was purchased by Avnet, Inc., prior to '66, when Avnet purchased Guild Guitars. In '69, Goya was purchased by Kustom which offered the instruments until '71. Probably some '70s guitars were made in Japan. The brand name was purchased by C.F. Martin in '76, with Japanese-made acoustic guitars, solidbody electric guitars and basses, banjos and mandolins imported in around '78 and continuing into the '90s.

Model 80/Model 90
1959-1962. Single-cut body, replaceable modular pickup assembly, sparkle top.

1959-1962		$1,000	$1,250

Panther S-3
1967-1968. Double-cut solidbody, 3 pickups, Panther S-3 Goya logo, volume and tone knobs with 6 upper bass bout switches, bolt-on neck.

1967-1968		$1,000	$1,250

Rangemaster
1967-1968. Wide variety of models.

1967-1968		$800	$1,000

Graf
See listing under Oskar Graf Guitars.

Grammer
1965-1971. Acoustic guitars built in Nashville. Founded by country guitarist Bill Grammer, music store owner Clyde Reid and luthier J.W. Gower (who also built his own line). Grammer sold the company to Ampeg in '68 who sold it again in '71, but it quickly creased business. Originally the Grammer headstock logo had an upper-case G, Ampeg-made instruments have a lower-case one.

G-10
1965-1970. Solid Brazilian rosewood back and sides, solid spruce top, large crown-shaped bridge, pearl dot markers, natural.

1965-1967	Grammer era	$1,700	$2,100
1968-1970	Ampeg era	$1,500	$1,900

G-20
1965-1970. Natural.

1965-1967	Grammer era	$1,700	$2,100
1968-1970	Ampeg era	$1,500	$1,900

G-30
1965-1970. Natural.

1965-1967	Grammer era	$1,700	$2,100
1968-1970	Ampeg era	$1,500	$1,900

G-50
1965-1970. Top-of-the-line Grammer, Brazilian rosewood back and sides, Adirondack spruce top.

1965-1967	Grammer era	$2,100	$2,500
1968-1970	Ampeg era	$1,900	$2,200

S-30
1965-1970. Solid spruce top, solid ribbon mahogany back and sides.

1965-1967	Grammer era	$1,600	$2,000
1968-1970	Ampeg era	$1,400	$1,800

Granada
1970s-1980s. Japanese-made acoustic, electric solid, semi-hollow and hollowbody guitars, many copies of classic American models. They also offered basses.

Acoustic
1970s. Import from Japan, various copy models.

1970s		$100	$150

Electric
1970s. Import from Japan, various copy models.

1970s		$150	$200

Granata Guitars
1989-present. Luthier Peter Granata builds his professional grade, custom, flat-top and resonator guitars in Oak Ridge, New Jersey.

Graveel
Production/custom, solidbody guitars built by luthier Dean Graveel in Indianapolis, Indiana.

Grazioso
1950s. Grazioso was a brand name used by Selmer in England on instruments made in Czechoslovakia. They replaced the brand with their Futurama line of guitars.

GRD
1978-1982. High-end acoustic and electric guitars produced in Charles Fox's Guitar Research & Design Center in Vermont. GRD introduced the original thin-line acoustic-electric guitar to the world at the '78 Winter NAMM show.

Great Divide Guitars
2009-present. Budget and intermediate grade, production, flat-top guitars imported from China, designed by luthier Tom Bedell, Dan Mills and Sophia Yang. They also offer Bedell Guitars.

Greco
1960s-present. Brand name used in Japan by Fuji Gen Gakki, maker of many Hoshino/Ibanez guitars; thus often Greco guitars are similar to Ibanez. During the '70s the company sold many high-quality copies of American designs, though

MODEL YEAR	FEATURES	EXC. COND. LOW	HIGH

by '75 they offered many weird-shaped original designs, including the Iceman and carved people shapes. By the late-'70s they were offering neck-through-body guitars. Currently owned by Kanda Shokai and offering solidbody, hollowbody and acoustic guitars, including models licensed by Zemaitis.

Green, Aaron

1990-present. Premium and presentation grade, custom, classical and flamenco guitars built by luthier Aaron Green in Waltham, Massachusetts.

Greene & Campbell

2002-2005. Luthier Dean Campbell builds his intermediate and professional grade, production/custom, solidbody guitars in Westwood, Massachusetts. Founding partner Jeffrey Greene left the company in '04; Greene earlier built guitars under his own name. In '05, Campbell changed the name to Campbell American Guitars.

Greene, Jeffrey

2000-2002. Professional grade, production/custom, electric solidbody guitars built by luthier Jeffrey Greene in West Kingston, Rhode Island. He went to work with Dean Campbell building the Greene & Campbell line of guitars.

Greenfield Guitars

1996-present. Luthier Michael Greenfield builds his production/custom, presentation grade, acoustic steel string, concert classical and archtop guitars in Montreal, Quebec.

Gretsch

1883-present. Currently Gretsch offers intermediate, professional, and premium grade, production, acoustic, solidbody, hollowbody, double neck, resonator and Hawaiian guitars. They also offer basses, amps and lap steels.

Previous brands included Gretsch, Rex, 20th Century, Recording King (for Montgomery Ward), Dorado (Japanese imports). Founded by Friedrich Gretsch in Brooklyn, New York, making drums, banjos, tambourines, and toy instruments which were sold to large distributors including C. Bruno and Wurlitzer. Upon early death of Friedrich, son Fred Gretsch, Sr. took over business at age 15. By the turn of the century the company was also making mandolins. In the '20s, they were distributing Rex and 20th Century brands, some made by Gretsch, some by others such as Kay. Charles "Duke" Kramer joined Gretsch in '35. In '40 Gretsch purchased Bacon & Day banjos. Fred Gretsch, Sr. retired in '42 and was replaced by sons Fred, Jr. and Bill. Fred departs for Navy and Bill runs company until his death in '48, when Fred resumes control. After the war the decision was made to promote the Gretsch brand rather than selling to distributors, though some jobbing continues.

MODEL YEAR	FEATURES	EXC. COND. LOW	HIGH

Kramer becomes Chicago branch manager in '48.

In '67 Baldwin of Cincinnati buys Gretsch. During '70-'72 the factory relocates from Brooklyn to Booneville, Arkansas and company headquarters moves to Cincinnati. A '72 factory fire drastically reduces production for next two years. In '78 Baldwin buys Kustom amps and sells Gretsch to Kustom's Charlie Roy, and headquarters are moved to Chanute, Kansas. Duke Kramer retires in '80. Guitar production ends '80-'81. Ca. '83 ownership reverts back to Baldwin and Kramer was asked to arrange the sale of the company. In '84 Fred Gretsch III was contacted and in '85 Gretsch guitars came back to the Gretsch family and Fred Gretsch Enterprises, Ltd (FGE). Initial Gretsch Enterprise models were imports made by Japan's Terada Company. In '95, some U.S.-made models were introduced.

As of January 1, 2003, Fred Gretsch Enterprises, Ltd granted Fender Musical Instruments Corporation the exclusive rights to develop, produce, market and distribute Gretsch guitars worldwide where FMIC is responsible for all aspects of the Gretsch stringed instrument product lines and brands, including development of new products. Fred Gretsch consulted during the changeover and on product development and quality control.

12-String Electric Archtop (6075/6076)
1967-1972. 16" double-cut, 2 Super Tron pickups, 17" body option available, sunburst (6075) or natural (6076).

1967-1972	Natural	$2,000	$2,500
1967-1972	Sunburst	$1,900	$2,400

12-String Flat-Top (6020)
1969-1972. 15 1/5" body, mahogany back and sides, spruce top, slotted headstock, dot markers.

1969-1972		$800	$950

Anniversary (6124/6125)
1958-1971, 1993-1999. Single-cut hollowbody archtop, 1 pickup (Filtron '58-'60, Hi-Lo Tron '61 on), bound body, named for Gretsch's 75th anniversary. 6124 is 2-tone green with 2-tone option, 6125 sunburst. Model numbers revived in '90s.

1958-1959	Green 2-tone	$2,600	$3,200
1958-1959	Sunburst	$1,600	$2,000
1960-1961	2-tone green or tan	$2,600	$3,200
1960-1961	Sunburst	$1,600	$2,000
1962-1964	2-tone green or tan	$2,000	$2,500
1962-1964	Sunburst	$1,400	$1,750
1965-1966	Various colors	$1,200	$1,500
1967-1969	Various colors	$1,100	$1,400
1970-1971	Various colors	$1,000	$1,250

Anniversary (6117/6118)
1993-present. 2 pickup like Double Anniversary, 6118 in 2-tone green with (T) or without Bigsby, 6117 is sunburst.

1993-2010	Various colors	$1,000	$1,200

Astro-Jet (6126)
1965-1967. Solidbody electric, double-cut, 2 pickups, vibrato, 4/2 tuner arrangement, red top with black back and sides.

1965-1967		$2,000	$2,500

1979 Greco EG800
Jon Way

1966 Gretsch Astro-Jet

MODEL YEAR	FEATURES	EXC. COND. LOW	HIGH

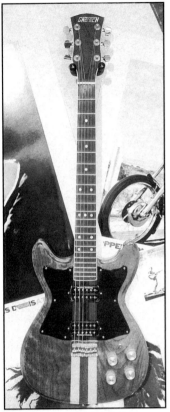

Gretsch BST 2000 Beast

Atkins Axe (7685/7686)
1976-1980. Solidbody electric, single pointed cutaway, 2 pickups, ebony stain (7685) or red rosewood stain (7686), called the Super Axe with added on-board effects.

1976-1980		$1,000	$1,250

Atkins Super Axe (7680/7681)
1976-1981. Single pointed cutaway solidbody with built-in phaser and sustain, five knobs, three switches, Red Rosewood (7680) or Ebony (7681) stains.

1976-1981		$1,900	$2,300

Bikini (6023/6024/6025)
1961-1962. Solidbody electric, separate 6-string and bass neck-body units that slide into 1 of 3 body butterflies - 1 for the 6-string only (6023), 1 for bass only (6024), 1 for double neck (6 and bass - 6025). Components could be purchased separately.

1961-1962	6023/6024, single neck	$800	$1,000
1961-1962	6025, double neck	$1,600	$2,000

Billy-Bo Jupiter Thunderbird (G6199)
2005-present. Billy Gibbons and Bo Diddley influenced, chambered mahogany body, laminate maple top, 2 pickups.

2005-2010		$1,500	$1,900

Black Falcon (6136BK/TBK/DSBK)
1992-1997, 2003-present. Black version of Falcon, single-cut, 2.75" body, oversize f-holes, G tailpiece, DSBK with DynaSonic pickups replaces Filter'Tron BK in '06. Had the Limited Edition 1955 designation for '96-'97. Bigsby-equipped TBK offered '04-present.

1992-1997		$1,800	$2,100

Black Falcon (7594BK)
1992-1998. Black version of G7594 Falcon, double-cut, 2" thick body, Bigsby.

1992-1998		$1,800	$2,100

Black Falcon I (7593BK)
1993-1998, 2003-2005. G63136BK with Bigsby and standard f-holes. Came back in '03 as Black Falcon I with wire handle Gretsch Bigsby tailpiece.

1993-1998		$1,800	$2,100

Black Hawk (6100/6101)
1967-1972. Hollowbody archtop, double-cut, 2 pickups, G tailpiece or Bigsby vibrato, bound body and neck, sunburst (6100) or black (6101).

1967-1969	6100, sunburst	$1,600	$1,800
1967-1969	6101, black	$1,600	$1,800
1970-1972	6100, sunburst	$1,500	$1,700
1970-1972	6101, black	$1,500	$1,700

Black Penguin (G6134B)
2003-present. Jet black version.

2003-2010		$1,800	$2,100

Bo Diddley (G1810/G5810)
2000-present. Korean-made version.

2000-2010		$175	$225

Bo Diddley (G6138)
1999-present. Reproduction of rectangle-shaped, semi-hollow guitar originally made for Diddley by Gretsch, Firebird Red.

1999-2010		$1,300	$1,600

1960 Gretsch Chet Atkins Country Gentleman 6122

Brian Setzer Hot Rod (6120SHx)
1999-present. Like SSL, but with only pickup switch and 1 master volume control, Hot Rod red.

1999-2010		$1,500	$1,800

Brian Setzer Nashville (6120SSL, etc.)
1993-present. Hollowbody electric, double-cut, 2 Alnico PAF Filtertron pickups, based on the classic Gretsch 6120.

1993-2010	Western Orange	$2,000	$2,300

Broadkaster (Hollowbody)
1975-1980. Double-cut archtop, hollowbody, 2 pickups, natural or sunburst.

1975-1977	7603, Bigsby, natural	$825	$975
1975-1977	7604, Bigsby, sunburst	$825	$975
1975-1977	7607, G tailpiece, natural	$775	$925
1975-1977	7608, G tailpiece, sunburst	$725	$875
1977-1980	7609, red	$725	$875

Broadkaster (Solidbody)
1975-1979. Double-cut, maple body, 2 pickups, bolt-on neck, natural (7600) or sunburst (7601).

1975-1979		$675	$825

BST 1000 Beast
1979-1980. Single-cut solidbody, bolt-on neck, mahogany body, available with 1 pickup in walnut stain (8210) or red stain (8216) or 2 pickups in walnut (7617, 8215, 8217) or red stain (8211).

1979-1980		$550	$700

BST 2000 Beast
1979. Symmetrical double-cut solidbody of mahogany, 2 humbucking pickups, bolt-on neck, walnut stain (7620 or 8220) or red stain (8221).

1979		$600	$750

BST 5000 Beast
1979-1980. Asymmetrical double-cut solidbody, neck-thru, walnut and maple construction, 2 humbucker pickups, stud tailpiece, natural walnut/maple (8250).

1979-1980		$650	$800

Burl Ives (6004)
1949-1955. Flat-top acoustic, mahogany back and sides, bound body, natural top (6004).

1949-1955		$450	$550

Chet Atkins Country Gentleman (6122/7670)
1957-1981. Hollowbody, single-cut to late-'62 and double after, 2 pickups, painted f-holes until '72, real after, mahogany finish (6122). Model number changes to 7670 in '71. Guitars made during and after '64 might have replaced body binding which reduces the value shown by about 10% or more.

1957-1959		$6,000	$7,500
1960		$5,500	$6,800
1961		$5,000	$6,300
1962-1963	George Harrison specs	$3,700	$4,400
1964		$3,400	$4,000
1965		$3,400	$4,000
1966		$2,300	$2,800
1967-1970		$1,900	$2,350
1971-1981	7670	$1,900	$2,350

MODEL YEAR	FEATURES	EXC. COND. LOW	HIGH

Chet Atkins Country Gentleman (6122-1958)
2007-present. Single-cut reissue of '58.

2007-2010		$1,300	$1,600

Chet Atkins Country Gentleman (6122-1962)
2007-present. Double-cut reissue of '62, double muffler (mutes) system, Filter'Trons.

2007-2010		$1,300	$1,600

Chet Atkins Hollowbody (6120)
1954-1966, 2007-present. Archtop electric, single-cut to '61, double after, 2 pickups, vibrato, f-holes (real to '61 and fake after), G brand on top '54-'56, orange finish (6120). Renamed Chet Atkins Nashville in '67.

1954-1955	G brand	$10,500	$13,000
1955-1956	No G brand	$7,000	$8,700
1957-1959	No G brand	$6,800	$8,500
1960		$5,500	$6,800
1961	Double-cut	$3,000	$3,700
1961	Single-cut	$5,000	$6,300
1962	Double-cut	$2,900	$3,600
1963	Double-cut	$2,900	$3,600
1964-1965	Double-cut	$2,600	$3,300
1966	Double-cut	$2,000	$2,500
2007-2010	Single-cut	$1,300	$1,600

Chet Atkins Junior
1970. Archtop, single-cut, 1 pickup, vibrato, open f-holes, double-bound body, orange stain.

1970		$1,000	$1,250

Chet Atkins Nashville (6120/7660)
1967-1980. Replaced Chet Atkins Hollowbody (6120), electric archtop, double-cut, 2 pickups, amber red (orange). Renumbered 7660 in '72, reissued in '90 as the Nashville 6120.

1967-1971	6120	$1,700	$2,100
1972-1980	7660	$1,400	$1,700

Chet Atkins Solidbody (6121)
1955-1963. Solidbody electric, single-cut, maple or knotty pine top, 2 pickups, Bigsby vibrato, G brand until '57, multi-bound top, brown mahogany, orange finish (6121).

1955-1956		$10,500	$13,000
1957	G brand	$8,500	$10,500
1957	No G brand	$7,500	$9,500
1958-1959		$5,500	$7,000
1960		$5,200	$6,500
1961-1963		$4,800	$6,000

Chet Atkins Tennessean (6119/7655)
1958-1980. Archtop electric, single-cut, 1 pickup until '61 and 2 after, vibrato. Renumbered as the 7655 in '71.

1958		$2,500	$3,100
1959		$2,400	$3,000
1960-1961	1 pickup	$2,300	$2,900
1961-1964	2 pickups	$2,500	$3,100
1965		$2,300	$2,800
1966-1967		$2,200	$2,700
1968-1970		$1,900	$2,300
1971-1980	7655	$1,700	$2,100

MODEL YEAR	FEATURES	EXC. COND. LOW	HIGH

Chet Atkins Tennessee Rose (G6119-1959, 1962)
1995-present. Import, 16" maple body, maple neck, dual FilterTron pickups.

1995-2010		$1,250	$1,500

Clipper (6185/6186/6187/7555)
1958-1975. Archtop electric, single-cut, sunburst, 1 pickup (6186) until '72 and 2 pickups (6185) from '72-'75, also available in 1 pickup natural (6187) from '59-'61.

1958-1961	6186	$800	$1,000
1959-1961	6187	$900	$1,100
1962-1967	6186	$800	$1,000
1968-1971	6186	$700	$900
1972-1975	7555	$800	$1,000

Committee (7628)
1977-1980. Neck-thru electric solidbody, double-cut, walnut and maple body, 2 pickups, 4 knobs, natural.

1977-1980		$600	$750

Constellation
1955-1960. Renamed from Synchromatic 6030 and 6031, archtop acoustic, single-cut, G tailpiece, humped block inlay.

1955-1956		$1,600	$2,000
1957-1958		$1,500	$1,900
1959-1960		$1,400	$1,700

Convertible (6199)
1955-1958. Archtop electric, single-cut, 1 pickup, multi-bound body, G tailpiece, renamed Sal Salvadore in '58.

1955-1958		$2,100	$2,600

Corsair
1955-1960. Renamed from Synchromatic 100, archtop acoustic, bound body and headstock, G tailpiece, available in sunburst (6014), natural (6015) or burgundy (6016).

1955-1959		$900	$1,100
1960-1965		$800	$1,000

Corvette (Hollowbody)
1955-1959. Renamed from Electromatic Spanish, archtop electric, 1 pickup, f-holes, bound body, Electromatic on headstock, non-cut, sunburst (6182), natural or Jaguar Tan (6184), and ivory with rounded cutaway (6187).

1955-1959	6182, sunburst	$900	$1,100
1955-1959	6184, Jaguar Tan	$1,100	$1,400
1955-1959	6184, natural	$1,100	$1,400
1957-1959	6187, ivory	$1,100	$1,400

Corvette (Solidbody)
1961-1972, 1976-1978. Double-cut slab solidbody. Mahogany 6132 and cherry 6134 1 pickup for '61-'68. 2 pickup mahogany 6135 and cherry 7623 available by '63-'72 and '76-'78. From late-'61 through '63 a Twist option was offered featuring a red candy stripe 'guard. Platinum Gray 6133 available for '61-'63 and the Gold Duke and Silver Duke sparkle finishes were offered in '66.

1961-1962	Mahogany, cherry	$750	$950
1961-1963	Platinum Gray	$1,100	$1,400
1961-1963	Twist 'guard	$1,300	$1,600
1963-1965	Custom color	$900	$1,100

1967 Gretsch Chet Atkins 6120

1967 Chet Atkins Tennessean

1959 Gretsch Double Anniversary

1998 Gretsch Duo Jet Reissue 6128 T

MODEL YEAR	FEATURES	EXC. COND. LOW	HIGH
1963-1965	Mahogany, cherry, 1 pickup	$725	$900
1963-1965	Mahogany, cherry, 2 pickups	$850	$1,050
1966	Gold Duke	$1,100	$1,400
1966	Silver Duke	$1,100	$1,400
1966-1968	Mahogany, cherry, 1 pickup	$650	$800
1966-1968	Mahogany, cherry, 2 pickups	$850	$1,050
1969-1972	Mahogany, cherry, 2 pickups	$800	$1,000
1976-1978	7623, 2 pickups	$650	$800

Country Classic I/II (6122 Reissue)

1989-2006. Country Gentleman reissue in '58 (I) and '62 (II) specs. Also cataloged as G6122-1958 and G6122-1962 Country Classic.

1989-2006	'58, single-cut	$1,200	$1,500
1989-2006	'62, double-cut	$1,200	$1,500

Country Classic II Custom Edition (6122)

2005. Reissue of George Harrison's 2nd 6122 Country Gentleman, the Custom Edition has TV Jones Filtertron pickups.

2005		$1,300	$1,600

Country Club

1954-1981. Renamed from Electro II Cutaway, archtop electric, single-cut, 2 pickups (Filter Trons after '57), G tailpiece, multi-bound, various colors.

1954-1956	Cadillac Green or natural	$3,400	$4,200
1954-1956	Sunburst	$3,100	$3,900
1957-1958	Cadillac Green	$3,400	$4,200
1957-1958	Natural	$3,200	$3,800
1957-1958	Sunburst	$2,900	$3,500
1959	Cadillac Green	$2,900	$3,500
1959	Natural	$2,700	$3,400
1959	Sunburst	$2,400	$3,000
1960	Cadillac Green	$2,800	$3,300
1960	Sunburst	$2,200	$2,800
1961	Cadillac Green	$2,500	$3,100
1961	Natural	$2,300	$2,800
1961	Sunburst	$2,000	$2,400
1962	Cadillac Green	$2,100	$2,600
1962	Natural	$2,000	$2,500
1962-1963	Sunburst	$1,800	$2,300
1964	Cadillac Green	$1,900	$2,400
1964	Sunburst	$1,700	$2,100
1965-1969	Sunburst or walnut	$1,650	$2,050
1970-1972	Various colors	$1,600	$2,000
1973-1981	Various colors	$1,500	$1,900

Country Club 1955 Reissue (6196-1955) (FGE)

1995-1999. U.S.-made reissue of Country Club, single-cut, 2 DeArmond pickups, hand-rubbed lacquer finish.

1995-1999		$1,400	$1,700

Country Club (G6196, etc.)

2001-present. Includes Cadillac Green (G6196, '01-present), sunburst (G6192, '03-'08), amber natural (G6193, '03-'08), bamboo yellow (G6196TSP-BY, '09-present), and smoky gray and violet 2-tone

(G6196TSP-2G, '09-present) T means Bigsby.

2001-2010	Cadillac green	$1,500	$1,800
2009-2010	Bamboo yellow	$1,400	$1,700

Country Roc (7620)

1974-1978. Single-cut solidbody, 2 pickups, belt buckle tailpiece, western scene fretboard inlays, G brand, tooled leather side trim.

1974-1978		$1,500	$1,700

Custom (6117)

1964-1968. Limited production, smaller thinner version of Double Anniversary model, 2 pickups, cat's eye soundholes, red or black finish.

1964-1968		$2,100	$2,600

Deluxe Chet (7680/7681)

1972-1974. Electric archtop with rounded cutaway, Autumn Red (7680) or brown walnut (7681) finishes.

1972-1974		$2,400	$2,900

Deluxe Flat-Top (7535)

1972-1978. 16" redwood top, mahogany back and sides.

1972-1978		$1,600	$2,000

Double Anniversary Mono (6117/6118)

1958-1976. Archtop electric, single-cut, 2 pickups, stereo optional until '63, sunburst (6117) or green 2-tone (6118). Reissued in '93 as the Anniversary 6117 and 6118.

1958-1959	Green 2-tone	$2,800	$3,400
1958-1959	Sunburst	$2,100	$2,600
1960-1961	Green 2-tone	$2,800	$3,400
1960-1961	Sunburst	$2,100	$2,600
1962-1964	Green 2-tone	$2,400	$2,900
1962-1964	Sunburst	$1,700	$2,100
1963	Tan 2-tone	$2,400	$2,900
1965-1966	Various colors	$1,750	$2,100
1967-1969	Various colors	$1,500	$1,900
1970-1974	Various colors	$1,400	$1,750
1975-1976	Various colors	$1,300	$1,600

Double Anniversary Stereo (6111/6112)

1961-1963. One stereo channel/signal per pickup, sunburst (6111) or green (6112).

1961-1963	Green	$2,600	$3,200
1961-1963	Sunburst	$2,300	$2,800

Duane Eddy (6210DE)

1997-2002. Import, 6120 style, 2 DeArmond single coils, Bigsby, orange.

1997-1998		$1,700	$2,100

Duo-Jet (6128)

1953-1971. Solidbody electric, single-cut until '61, double after, 2 pickups. black (6128) with a few special ordered in green, sparkle finishes were offered '63-'66, reissued in '90.

1953-1956	Black	$5,000	$6,100
1956-1957	Cadillac Green	$7,500	$9,300
1957	Black	$5,000	$6,100
1958-1960	Black	$5,000	$6,100
1961-1964	Black	$4,500	$5,500
1963-1966	Sparkle-gold, champagne, burgundy or tangerine	$5,000	$6,100
1964-1966	Silver sparkle	$5,000	$6,100

MODEL YEAR	FEATURES	EXC. COND. LOW	HIGH
1965-1967	Black	$2,800	$3,500
1968-1971	Black	$2,600	$3,200

Duo-Jet Reissue (6128/6128T)

1990-present. Reissue of the '50s solidbody, black, optional Bigsby (G6128T).

1990-2010		$1,400	$1,700

Duo-Jet Tenor

1959-1960. Electric tenor, 4 strings, block inlays, black.

1959-1960		$2,600	$3,300

Eldorado (6040/6041)

1955-1970, 1991-1997. This is the larger 18" version, renamed from Synchromatic 400, archtop acoustic, single-cut, triple-bound fretboard and peghead, sunburst (6040) or natural (6041). Reintroduced in '91, made by Heritage in Kalamazoo, as the G410 Synchromatic Eldorado in sunburst or natural (G410M).

1955-1959	Natural	$2,500	$2,900
1955-1959	Sunburst	$2,200	$2,600
1960-1963	Natural	$2,100	$2,500
1960-1963	Sunburst	$1,800	$2,200
1964-1965	Natural	$1,800	$2,200
1964-1965	Sunburst	$1,600	$2,000
1966-1967	Natural	$1,700	$2,100
1966-1967	Sunburst	$1,500	$1,900
1968-1969	Sunburst	$1,400	$1,900
1991-1997	Natural	$1,600	$2,000
1991-1997	Sunburst	$1,300	$1,700

Eldorado (6038/6039)

1959-1968. The smaller 17" version, named Fleetwood from '55 to '58, sunburst (6038) or natural (6039), also available as a full body non-cutaway.

1959-1963	Natural	$1,500	$1,900
1959-1963	Sunburst	$1,400	$1,700
1964-1965	Natural	$1,300	$1,600
1964-1965	Sunburst	$1,100	$1,400
1966-1968	Natural	$1,200	$1,500
1966-1968	Sunburst	$1,100	$1,400

Electro Classic (6006/6495)

1969-1973. Classical flat-top with piezo pickup.

1969-1970	6006	$600	$750
1971-1973	6495	$500	$625

Electro II Cutaway (6192/6193)

1951-1954. Archtop electric, single-cut, Melita bridge by '53, 2 pickups, f-holes, sunburst (6192) or natural (6193). Renamed Country Club in '54.

1951-1954	Natural	$2,900	$3,600
1951-1954	Sunburst	$2,500	$3,100

Electro II Non-Cutaway (6187/6188)

1951-1954. 16" electric archtop, 2 DeArmonds, large f-holes, block markers, 6187 sunburst, 6188 natural, label is Model 6187-8, verticle Electromatic logo on headstock.

1951-1954	Natural	$900	$1,100
1951-1954	Sunburst	$800	$1,000

Electromatic Spanish (6185/6185N)

1940-1955. Hollowbody, 17" wide, 1 pickup, sunburst (6185) or natural (6185N). Renamed Corvette (hollowbody) in '55.

1940-1949	Sunburst	$1,050	$1,200
1950-1955	Natural	$1,200	$1,400
1950-1955	Sunburst	$1,050	$1,200

MODEL YEAR	FEATURES	EXC. COND. LOW	HIGH

Fleetwood (6038/6039)

1955-1958. Named Synchromatic prior to '55, single-cut, sunburst (6038) or natural (6039). Renamed Eldorado in '59, available by custom order.

1955-1958		$2,200	$2,800

Folk/Folk Singing (6003/7505/7506)

1963-1975. Lower-model of Gretsch flat-tops, 14 1/4", mahogany back and sides. Renamed from Jimmie Rodgers model, renamed Folk Singing in '63.

1963-1965		$525	$650
1966-1969		$425	$525
1970-1975		$375	$475

Golden Classic (Hauser Model/Model 6000)

1961-1969. Grand Concert body size, nylon-string classical, 14 1/4" spruce top, mahogany back and sides, multiple inlaid sound hole purfling, inlaid headstock.

1961-1969		$425	$525

Grand Concert (6003)

1955-1959. Lower-model of Gretsch flat-tops, 14 1/4", mahogany back and sides. Renamed from Model 6003 and renamed Jimmie Rodgers in '59.

1955-1959		$525	$650

Guitar-Banjo

1920s. 6-string guitar neck on banjo body, slotted headstock, open back.

1920s		$500	$600

Jet 21

Late-1940s. 16" acoustic archtop, Jet 21 engraved logo on headstock, bound top and back, white 'guard, jet black finish.

1947-1948		$450	$550

Jet Firebird (6131)

1955-1971. Solidbody electric, single-cut until '61, double '61-'71, 2 pickups, black body with red top.

1955-1956		$3,600	$4,500
1957		$3,500	$4,300
1958-1960		$3,400	$4,200
1961-1964		$3,000	$3,700
1965-1967		$2,600	$3,300
1968-1971	Super Trons	$2,200	$2,700

Jet Firebird Reissue (6131/6131T)

1989-1997, 2003-present. Based on single-cut '58 specs, red top, 2 FilterTrons, thumbprint markers, gold hardware for '91-'05, currently chrome. Bigsby available (T). Non-Bigsby 6131 ends in '05. DynaSonic-equipped TDS starts in '05.

2003-2010		$1,000	$1,200

Jimmie Rodgers (6003)

1959-1962. 14" flat-top with round hole, mahogany back and sides, renamed from Grand Concert and renamed Folk Singing in '63.

1959-1962		$500	$650

Jumbo Synchromatic (125F)

1947-1955. 17" flat-top, triangular soundhole, bound top and back, metal bridge anchor plate, adjustable wood bridge, natural top with sunburst back and sides or optional translucent white-blond top and sides.

1947-1955	Natural	$1,800	$2,200
1947-1955	White-blond	$2,000	$2,400

1954 Gretsch Electro-II

Gretsch Jet Firebird Reissue

Gretsch Monkees

Gretsch Rancher

MODEL YEAR	FEATURES	EXC. COND. LOW	HIGH

Keith Scott Nashville (G6120KS)
1999-present. Hump-back inlays, gold hardware, metallic gold finish.

1999-2010		$1,200	$1,500

Model 25 (Acoustic)
1933-1939. 16" archtop, no binding on top or back, dot markers, sunburst.

1933-1939		$500	$600

Model 30 (Acoustic)
1939-1949. 16" archtop, top binding, dot markers, sunburst.

1939-1949		$550	$650

Model 35 (Acoustic)
1933-1949. 16" archtop, single-bound top and back, dot markers, sunburst.

1933-1949		$650	$750

Model 40 Hawaiian (Acoustic)
1936-1949. Flat top, bound top and neck, diamond inlays.

1936-1949		$800	$900

Model 50/50R (Acoustic)
1936-1949. Acoustic archtop, f-holes. Model 50R (1936-'39) has round soundhole.

1936-1949	50/50R	$750	$850
1936-1939	TG-50 Tenor	$500	$600

Model 65 (Acoustic)
1933-1939. Archtop acoustic, bound body, amber.

1933-1939		$800	$900

Model 75 Tenor (Acoustic)

1933-1939		$500	$600

Model 6003
1951-1955. 14 1/4", mahogany back and sides, renamed Grand Concert in '55.

1951-1954		$600	$700

Monkees
1966-1969. Hollowbody electric, double-cut, 2 pickups, Monkees logo on 'guard, bound top, f-holes and neck, vibrato, red.

1966-1969		$2,600	$3,000

New Yorker
Ca.1949-1970. Archtop acoustic, f-holes, sunburst.

1949-1951		$550	$650
1952-1954		$500	$600
1955-1959		$450	$550
1960-1965		$450	$550
1966-1970		$400	$500

Ozark/Ozark Soft String (6005)
1965-1968. 16" classical, rosewood back and sides.

1965-1968		$500	$650

Princess (6106)
1963. Corvette-type solidbody double-cut, 1 pickup, vibrato, gold parts, colors available were white/grape, blue/white, pink/white, or white/gold, often sold with the Princess amp.

1963		$1,800	$2,200

Rally (6104/6105)
1967-1969. Archtop, double-cut, 2 pickups, vibrato, racing stripe on truss rod cover and pickguard, green or yellow.

1967-1969		$1,550	$1,950

MODEL YEAR	FEATURES	EXC. COND. LOW	HIGH

Rambler (6115)
1957-1961. Small body electric archtop, single-cut, 1 pickup, G tailpiece, bound body and headstock.

1957-1961		$1,100	$1,300

Rancher
1954-1980. Flat-top acoustic, triangle soundhole, Western theme inlay, G brand until '61 and '75 and after, Golden Red (orange), reissued in '90.

1954-1955	G brand	$3,500	$4,300
1956-1957	G brand	$3,200	$3,800
1958-1961	G brand	$2,700	$3,300
1962-1964	No G brand	$2,300	$2,800
1965-1966	No G brand	$2,100	$2,600
1967-1969	No G brand	$2,000	$2,500
1970-1974	No G brand	$1,800	$2,200
1975-1980	G brand	$1,500	$1,800

Roc I/Roc II (7635/7621)
1974-1976. Electric solidbody, mahogany, single-cut, Duo-Jet-style body, 1 pickup (7635) or 2 pickups (7621), bound body and neck.

1974-1976	Roc I	$1,000	$1,200
1974-1977	Roc II	$1,200	$1,400

Roc Jet
1969-1980. Electric solidbody, single-cut, 2 pickups, adjustamatic bridge, black, cherry, pumpkin or walnut.

1970-1972		$1,800	$2,200
1973-1976		$1,500	$1,800
1977-1980		$1,200	$1,500

Round-Up (6130)
1954-1960. Electric solidbody, single-cut, 2 pickups, G brand, belt buckle tailpiece, maple, pine, knotty pine or orange. Reissued in '90.

1954-1956	Knotty pine (2 knots)	$15,000	$18,000
1954-1956	Knotty pine (4 knots)	$17,000	$21,000
1954-1956	Mahogany (few made)	$11,000	$13,000
1954-1956	Maple	$11,000	$13,000
1954-1956	Pine	$13,000	$15,000
1957-1960	Orange	$11,000	$13,000

Round-Up Reissue (6121/6121W)
1989-1995, 2003-2006. Based on the '50s model, Bigsby, Western Orange, G brand sticker.

1989-2006		$1,250	$1,550

Sal Fabraio (6117)
1964-1968. Double-cut thin electric archtop, distinctive cats-eye f-holes, 2 pickups, sunburst, ordered for resale by guitar teacher Sal Fabraio.

1964-1968		$1,750	$2,000

Sal Salvador (6199)
1958-1968. Electric archtop, single-cut, 1 pickup, triple-bound neck and headstock, sunburst.

1958-1959		$2,600	$3,000
1960-1962		$2,100	$2,500
1963-1964		$1,700	$2,000
1965-1966		$1,600	$1,900
1967-1968		$1,400	$1,700

MODEL YEAR	FEATURES	EXC. COND. LOW	HIGH

Sho Bro (Hawaiian/Spanish)
1969-1978. Flat-top acoustic, multi-bound, resonator, lucite fretboard, Hawaiian version non-cut, square neck and Spanish version non- or single-cut, round neck.

1969-1978	Hawaiian	$800	$975
1969-1978	Spanish	$800	$975

Silver Classic (Hauser Model/Model 6001)
1961-1969. Grand Concert body size, nylon-string classical. Similar to Golden Classic but with less fancy appointments.

1961-1969		$300	$400

Silver Falcon (6136SL) (1955) (T)
1995-1999, 2003-2005. Black finish, silver features, single cut, G tailpiece available until '05, T for Bigsby available starting 2'05. Had the 1955 designation in the '90s.

1995-1999		$1,800	$2,100

Silver Falcon (7594SL)
1995-1999. Black finish and silver features, double-cut, 2" thick body.

1995-1999		$1,800	$2,100

Silver Jet (6129)
1954-1963. Solidbody electric, single-cut until '61, double '61-'63, 2 pickups, Duo-Jet with silver sparkle top, reissued in '90. Optional sparkle colors were offered but were not given their own model numbers; refer to Duo-Jet listing for optional colors.

1954-1956		$7,500	$9,400
1957		$6,500	$7,500
1958-1960		$6,000	$7,000
1961-1963	Double-cut	$5,500	$6,500

Silver Jet 1957 Reissue (6129-1957)
1990-present. Reissue of single-cut '50s Silver Jet, silver sparkle.

1990-2010		$1,200	$1,500

Silver Jet 1962 Reissue (6129-1962)
Ca. 2000-2009. Reissue of double-cut Silver Jet, silver sparkle.

2000-2009		$1,200	$1,500

Songbird (Sam Goody 711)
1967-1968. Standard body thinline double cutaway with G soundholes, offered by Sam Goody of New York.

1967-1968		$2,000	$2,400

Southern Belle (7176)
1983. Electric archtop, walnut, parts from the late-'70s assembled in Mexico and U.S., 5 made with all original parts, several others without pickguard and case.

1983		$925	$1,150

Sparkle Jet (6129/6129T)
1994-present. Electric solidbody, single-cut, 2 pickups, Duo-Jet with sparkle finish.

1994-2010		$1,100	$1,400

Streamliner Single Cutaway (6189/6190/6191)
1955-1959. Electric archtop, single-cut, maple top, G tailpiece, 1 pickup, multi-bound, Bamboo Yellow (6189), sunburst (6190), or natural (6191), name reintroduced as a double-cut in '68.

1955-1959		$1,700	$2,100

Streamliner Double Cutaway (6102/6103)
1968-1973. Reintroduced from single-cut model, electric archtop, double-cut, 2 pickups, G tailpiece, cherry or sunburst.

1968-1969		$1,450	$1,800
1970-1973		$1,350	$1,700

Sun Valley (6010/7515/7514)
1959-1977. Flat-top acoustic, laminated Brazilian rosewood back and sides, multi-bound top, natural or sunburst.

1959-1964		$750	$850
1965-1969		$650	$750
1970-1977		$550	$650

Super Chet (7690/7690-B/7691/7691-B)
1972-1980. Electric archtop, single rounded cutaway, 2 pickups, gold hardware, mini control knobs along edge of 'guard, Autumn Red or walnut.

1972-1976		$1,900	$2,300
1977-1980		$1,800	$2,200

Supreme (7545)
1972-1978. Flat-top 16", spruce top, mahogany or rosewood body options, gold hardware.

1972-1978	Mahogany	$1,000	$1,250
1972-1979	Rosewood	$1,250	$1,500

Synchromatic (6030/6031)
1951-1955. 17" acoustic archtop, becomes Constellation in '55.

1951-1955		$1,400	$1,800

Synchromatic (6038/6039)
1951-1955. 17" acoustic archtop, single-cut, G tailpiece, multi-bound, sunburst (6038) or natural (6039), renamed Fleetwood in '55.

1951-1955	Sunburst	$1,650	$2,100

Synchromatic 75
1939-1949. Acoustic archtop, f-holes, multi-bound, large floral peghead inlay.

1939-1949		$1,100	$1,300

Synchromatic 100 (6014/6015)
1939-1955. Renamed from No. 100F, acoustic archtop, double-bound body, amber, sunburst (6014) or natural (6015), renamed Corsair in '55.

1939-1949	Natural	$1,000	$1,250
1939-1949	Sunburst	$900	$1,100
1950-1955	Natural	$850	$1,050

Synchromatic 160 (6028/6029)
1939-1943, 1947-1951. Acoustic archtop, cats-eye soundholes, maple back and sides, triple-bound, natural or sunburst.

1939-1943	Sunburst	$1,500	$1,800
1947-1951	Sunburst	$1,400	$1,700
1948-1951	Natural	$1,300	$1,600

Synchromatic 200
1939-1949. Acoustic archtop, cats-eye soundholes, maple back and sides, multi-bound, gold-plated hardware, amber or natural.

1939-1949		$1,700	$2,100

Synchromatic 300
1939-1955. Acoustic archtop, cats-eye soundholes until '51 and f-holes after, multi-bound, natural or sunburst.

1939-1949	Natural	$2,500	$3,100

1954 Gretsch Silver Jet

1972 Gretsch Super Chet

Gretsch White Falcon I

Gretsch White Penguin

MODEL YEAR	FEATURES	EXC. COND. LOW	EXC. COND. HIGH
1939-1949	Sunburst	$2,100	$2,600
1950-1955	Natural	$2,100	$2,600
1950-1955	Sunburst	$1,900	$2,400

Synchromatic 400
1940-1955. Acoustic archtop, cats-eye soundholes until '51 and f-holes after, multi-bound, gold hardware, natural or sunburst.

1940-1949	Natural	$5,500	$6,500
1940-1949	Sunburst	$5,000	$6,000
1950-1955	Natural	$5,000	$6,000
1950-1955	Sunburst	$4,500	$5,500

Synchromatic 400F/6042 Flat Top
1947-1955. 18" flat top, renamed 6042 in the late '40s.

1947-1948	400F	$4,000	$5,000
1949-1955	6042	$3,500	$4,500

Synchromatic G400C
1990-2008. Acoustic archtop, full-body, single-cut (round), sunburst.

1990-2008		$900	$1,100

Synchromatic Limited (450/450M)
1997. Acoustic archtop, hand carved spruce (G450) or maple (G450M) top, floating pickup, sunburst, only 50 were to be made.

1997	Maple	$1,000	$1,200
1997	Spruce	$900	$1,100

Synchromatic Sierra
1949-1955. Renamed from Synchromatic X75F (see below), acoustic flat-top, maple back and sides, triangular soundhole, sunburst.

1949-1955		$1,250	$1,500

Synchromatic X75F
1947-1949. Acoustic flat-top, maple back and sides, triangular soundhole, sunburst, renamed Synchromatic Sierra in '49.

1947-1949		$1,250	$1,500

TK 300 (7624/7625)
1977-1981. Double-cut maple solidbody, 1 humbucker, bolt-on neck, six-on-a-side tuners, hockey stick headstock, Autumn Red or natural.

1977-1981		$550	$650

Town and Country (6021)
1954-1959. Renamed from Jumbo Synchromatic 125 F, flat-top acoustic, maple back and sides, triangular soundhole, multi-bound.

1954-1959		$1,450	$1,800

Traveling Wilburys (TW300T)
1988-1990. Promotional guitar, solidbody electric, single-cut, 1 and 2 pickups, 6 variations, graphics.

1988-1990		$325	$400

Van Eps 6-String (6081/6082)
1968-1971. Electric archtop, single-cut, 2 pickups, 6 strings.

1968-1971		$2,800	$3,500

Van Eps 7-String (6079/6080)
1968-1978. Electric archtop, single-cut, 2 pickups, 7 strings, sunburst or walnut.

1968-1978		$2,400	$3,000

Viking (6187/6188/6189)
1964-1975. Electric archtop, double-cut, 2 pickups, vibrato, sunburst (6187), natural (6188) or Cadillac Green (6189).

1964-1967	Cadillac Green	$3,200	$4,000

MODEL YEAR	FEATURES	EXC. COND. LOW	EXC. COND. HIGH
1964-1967	Natural	$2,800	$3,500
1964-1967	Sunburst	$2,000	$2,500
1968-1970	Cadillac Green	$2,500	$3,000
1968-1970	Natural	$2,300	$2,800
1968-1970	Sunburst	$1,800	$2,200
1971-1972	Various colors	$1,600	$2,000
1973-1975	Various colors	$1,500	$1,900

Wayfarer Jumbo (6008)
1969-1971. Flat-top acoustic dreadnought, non-cut, maple back and sides, multi-bound.

1969-1971		$750	$950

White Falcon Mono (6136/7594)
1955-1981. Includes the single-cut 6136 of '55-'61, the double-cut 6136 of '62-'70, and the double-cut 7594 of '71-'81.

1955	Single-cut 6136	$18,000	$21,000
1956		$18,000	$21,000
1957		$18,000	$21,000
1958		$18,000	$21,000
1959-1961		$18,000	$21,000
1962-1963	Double-cut 6136	$8,000	$10,000
1964		$7,000	$9,000
1965		$6,000	$7,000
1966		$5,500	$6,700
1967-1969		$5,000	$6,200
1970		$4,500	$5,500
1971-1972	7594	$4,200	$5,200
1973-1979		$3,500	$4,300
1980-1981		$3,100	$3,800

White Falcon Stereo (6137/7595)
1958-1981. Features Project-O-Sonic Stereo, includes Includes the single-cut 6137 of '58-'61, the double-cut 6137 of '62-'70, and the double-cut 7595 of '71-'81.

1958-1961	Single-cut 6137	$18,000	$21,000
1962-1963	Double-cut 6137	$8,000	$10,000
1964		$7,000	$9,000
1965		$6,000	$7,000
1966		$5,500	$6,700
1967-1969		$5,000	$6,200
1970		$4,500	$5,500
1971-1972	7595	$4,200	$5,200
1973-1979		$3,500	$4,300
1980-1981		$3,100	$3,800

White Falcon (6136) (T) (DS)
1989-present. Single-cut, white, 2.75" thick body, thumbnail fret markers, Cadillac G tailpiece standard through '05, Bigsby (T) optional starting '04, standard in starting '06. DynaSonic (DS) model starting '06. See Black and Silver Falcons under those listings.

1989-2010		$1,800	$2,200

White Falcon (6136T-LTV)
2007-present. 6136 with TV Jones Classic pickups, Grovers.

2007-2010		$2,200	$2,700

White Falcon (7593) (I)
1989-present. Similar to 6136, but with block inlays, Bigsby. Called the White Falcon I for '91-'92, the G7593 for '93-ca. '02, and White Falcon I G7593 after.

1989-2010		$1,800	$2,200

The *Vintage Guitar Price Guide* shows low to high values for items in all-original excellent condition, and, where applicable, with original case or cover.

MODEL YEAR	FEATURES	EXC. COND. LOW	HIGH

White Falcon (7594) (II)
1989-2006. Double-cut, block inlays, white, 2" thick body, Bigsby. Called the White Falcon II for '91-'92, the G7594 for '93-ca. '02, and White Falcon II G7594 after.

1989-2006		$1,800	$2,200

White Falcon Custom U.S.A. (6136-1955)
1995-1999. U.S.-made, single-cut, DynaSonic pickups, gold sparkle appointments, rhinestone embedded knobs, white. In '04, Current U.S. model called G6136CST is released. The import White Falcon has sometimes been listed with the 1955 designation and is not included here.

1995-1999		$3,200	$4,000

White Penguin (6134)
1955-1964. Electric solidbody, single-cut until '62, double '62-'64, 2 pickups (DeArmond until '58 then Filter Tron), fewer than 100 made, white, gold sparkle bound, gold-plated parts. More than any other model, there seems a higher concern regarding forgery.

1956-1958		$65,000	$78,000
1959-1960		$52,000	$64,000
1961-1962		$50,000	$62,000
1962-1964		$38,000	$47,000

White Penguin (G6134)
1993, 2003-present. White, single-cut, metalflake binding, gold hardware, jeweled knobs, Cadillac G tailpiece.

2003-2010		$1,550	$1,900

Greven
1969, 1975-present. Luthier John Greven builds his premium grade, production/custom, acoustic guitars in Portland, Oregon.

Griffin String Instruments
1976-present. Luthier Kim Griffin builds his professional and premium grade, production/custom, parlor, steel-string, and classical guitars in Greenwich, New York.

Grimes Guitars
1972-present. Premium and presentation grade, custom, flat-tops, nylon-strings, archtops, semi-hollow electrics made by luthier Steve Grimes originally in Port Townsend, Washington, and since '82 in Kula, Hawaii. He also made mandolins early on.

Grinnell
Late 1930s-early 1940s. Private brand made by Gibson for Grinnell Music of Detroit and Southeast Michigan, which at the time, was the largest music chain in the Detroit area.

KG-14
1940. Gibson-made L-0/L-00 style with maple sides and back, tortoise-style binding on top and back, ladder bracing.

1940		$850	$1,050

Groehsl
1890-1921. Chicago's Groehsl Company made guitars for Wards and other mass-marketers. In 1921 the company became Stromberg-Voisinet, which in turn became the Kay Musical Instrument Company.

Groove Tools
2002-2004. Korean-made, production, intermediate grade, 7-string guitars that were offered by Conklin Guitars of Springfield, Missouri. They also offered basses.

Grosh
1993-present. Professional and premium grade, production/custom, solid and semi-hollow body guitars built by luthier Don Grosh originally in Santa Clarita, California and, since '05 in Broomfield, Colorado. He also builds basses. Grosh worked in production for Valley Arts from '84-'92. Guitars generally with bolt necks until '03 when set-necks were added to the line.

Classical Electric
1990s. Single-cut solidbody with nylon strings and piezo-style hidden pickup, highly figured top.

1990s		$1,300	$1,600

Custom S Bent Top
2003-present. Offset double-cut, figured maple carved top, 2 pickups.

2003-2010		$1,350	$1,650

Custom T Carve Top
2003-present. Single-cut, figured maple carved top, 2 pickups.

2003-2010		$1,350	$1,650

ElectraJet Custom
2009-present. Modified offset double-cut, 2 P-90s, 2 hums, or single-single-hum pickups.

2009-2010		$1,300	$1,600

Retro Classic
1993-present. Offset double-cut, 3 pickups.

1993-2010		$1,300	$1,600

Retro Classic Vintage T
1993-present. Single-cut, black 'guard.

1993-2010		$1,300	$1,600

Gruen Acoustic Guitars
1999-present. Luthier Paul Gruen builds his professional grade, custom steel-string guitars in Chapel Hill, North Carolina. His speciality is his E.Q. model, which features 5 soundholes, 4 of which can be plugged with wooden stoppers to give different tonal balances.

Gruggett
Mid 1960s-present. In the 1960s, luthier Bill Gruggett worked with Mosrite and Hallmark guitars as well as building electric guitars under his own name in Bakersfield, California. He still makes his Stradette model for Hallmark guitars.

Grimes Kula Rose

Don Grosh Retro Classic

1981 Guild D-55
Robbie Keene

1957 Guild Aristocrat M-75

MODEL YEAR	FEATURES	EXC. COND. LOW	HIGH

Guernsey Resophonic Guitars

1989-present. Production/custom, resonator guitars built by luthier Ivan Guernsey in Marysville, Indiana.

Guild

1952-present. Professional and premium grade, production/custom, acoustic and acoustic/electric guitars. They have built solid, hollow and semi-hollowbody guitars in the past. Founded in New York City by jazz guitarist Alfred Dronge, employing many ex-Epiphone workers. The company was purchased by Avnet, Inc., in '66 and the Westerly, Rhode Island factory was opened in '68. Hoboken factory closed in '71 and headquarters moved to Elizabeth, New Jersey. Company was Guild Musical Instrument Corporation in '86 but was in bankruptcy in '88. Purchased by Faas Corporation, New Berlin, Wisconsin, which became the U.S. Musical Corporation. The brand was purchased by Fender Musical Instrument Corporation in '95 and production was moved from Westerly to the Fender plant in Corona, California in 2001. In '05, Fender moved Guild production to their newly-acquired Tacoma plant in Washington. In '08, production moved to the Ovation/Hamer plant in New Hartford, Connecticut.

With the 2001 move to the Fender Corona plant, Bob Benedetto and Fender veteran Tim Shaw (who previously ran the Nashville-based custom shop) created a line of Guild acoustic guitars that were primarily based on vintage Guild Hoboken designs.

Designs of Tacoma-built Guild product were nothing like Tacoma guitars. The new Guilds were dovetail neck based with nitrocellulose finishes. Later, FMIC Guild introduced the Contemporary Series giving the Tacoma factory another line in addition to the vintage-based F and D model Traditional Series.

A-50

1994-1996. Original A-50 models can be found under the Cordoba A-50 listing, the new model drops the Cordoba name, size 000 flat top, spruce top, Indian rosewood body.

1994-1996		$925	$1,075

Aragon F-30

1954-1986. Acoustic flat-top, spruce top, laminated maple arched back (mahogany back and sides by '59), reintroduced as just F-30 in '98.

1954-1959		$1,900	$2,200
1960-1969		$1,800	$2,100
1970-1986		$1,300	$1,800

Aragon F-30 NT

1959-1985. Natural finish version of F-30.

1959-1969		$1,800	$2,100
1970-1985		$1,300	$1,800

Aragon F-30 R

1973-1995. Rosewood back and sides version of F-30, sunburst.

1973-1979		$1,500	$1,800

MODEL YEAR	FEATURES	EXC. COND. LOW	HIGH

Aristocrat M-75

1954-1963. Electric archtop, routed semi-hollow single-cut body, 2 pickups, sunburst, natural (added '59) or cherry (added '61), reintroduced as Bluesbird M-75 in '67.

1954-1959		$3,300	$4,100
1960-1963		$2,700	$3,300

Aristocrat M-75 Tenor

Mid-late 1950s. Tenor version of 6-string Aristocrat electric, dual soapbar pickups, 4 knobs.

1950s		$2,600	$3,200

Artist Award

1961-1999. Renamed from Johnny Smith Award, single-cut electric archtop, floating DeArmond pickup (changed to humbucker in '80), multi-bound, gold hardware, sunburst or natural.

1961-1969		$4,500	$5,300
1970-1979		$4,000	$4,700
1980-1989		$3,600	$4,300
1990-1999		$3,500	$4,200

Artist F-312 12-String

1963-1973. Flat-top, rosewood back and sides, spruce top, no board inlay (but some in '72 may have dots).

1964-1968	Brazilian rosewood	$3,200	$4,000
1969-1973	Indian rosewood	$2,000	$2,500

Bluegrass D-25/D-25 M

1968-1999. Flat-top, mahogany top until '76, spruce after, mahogany back and sides, various colors, called Bluegrass D-25 M in late-'70s and '80s, listed as D-25 in '90s.

1968-1979		$675	$850
1980-1989		$575	$725
1990-1999		$550	$700

Bluegrass D-25-12

1987-1992, 1996-1999. 12-string version of D-25.

1987-1992		$675	$850
1996-1999		$675	$850

Bluegrass D-35

1966-1988. Acoustic flat-top, spruce top and mahogany back and sides, rosewood 'board and bridge, natural.

1966-1969		$775	$975
1970-1979		$775	$975
1980-1988		$775	$975

Bluegrass F-40

1954-1963, 1973-1983. Acoustic flat-top, spruce top, maple back and sides, rosewood 'board and bridge, natural or sunburst.

1954-1956	F-40	$1,900	$2,300
1957-1963	F-40	$1,700	$2,100
1973-1983	Bluegrass F-40	$900	$1,100

Bluegrass F-47

1963-1976. 16" narrow-waist style, mahogany sides and back, acoustic flat-top, spruce top, mahogany back and sides, bound rosewood 'board and bridge, natural.

1963-1969		$1,900	$2,300
1970-1976		$1,800	$2,200

MODEL YEAR	FEATURES	EXC. COND. LOW	HIGH

Bluegrass Jubilee D-40
1963-1992. Acoustic flat-top, spruce top, mahogany back and sides, rosewood 'board and bridge, natural. Has been reissued.

1963-1969		$1,250	$1,550
1970-1979		$1,100	$1,400
1980-1992		$1,000	$1,250

Bluegrass Jubilee D-40 C
1975-1991. Acoustic flat-top, single Florentine cutaway, mahogany back and sides, rosewood 'board and bridge, natural.

1975-1979		$900	$1,100
1980-1991		$800	$1,000

Bluegrass Jubilee D-44
1965-1972. Acoustic flat-top, spruce top, pearwood back and sides, ebony 'board, rosewood bridge.

1965-1969		$1,000	$1,200
1970-1972		$900	$1,100

Bluegrass Jubilee D-44 M
1971-1985. Acoustic flat top, spruce top, maple back & sides, ebony fingerboard, rosewood bridge.

1971-1979		$1,000	$1,200
1980-1985		$900	$1,100

Bluegrass Special D-50
1963-1993. Acoustic flat-top, spruce top, rosewood back and sides, ebony fretboard, multi-bound.

1963-1968	Brazilian rosewood	$2,000	$2,400
1969-1979	Indian rosewood	$1,000	$1,200
1980-1993	Indian rosewood	$900	$1,150

Bluegrass Special D-50 (Reissue)/D-50
2003-present. Also available with pickup system, initially listed as D-50.

2003-2010		$1,000	$1,250

Blues 90
2000-2002. Bluesbird single-cut, chambered body, unbound rosewood board, dots, 2 Duncan 2 P-90s.

2000-2002		$750	$925

Bluesbird M-75 (Hollowbody)
1967-1970. Reintroduced from Aristocrat M-75, thinbody electric archtop of maple, spruce ('67) or mahogany, single-cut, 2 pickups, Deluxe has gold hardware, Standard chrome. A solidbody Bluesbird was also introduced in '70.

1967-1970		$1,750	$2,200

Bluesbird M-75 (Solidbody)
1970-1978. Solidbody version of Bluesbird M-75, mahogany body, rounded cutaway, 2 pickups.

1970-1978	CS, plain top, chrome hardware	$1,575	$2,000
1970-1978	GS, flamed top, gold hardware	$1,750	$2,200

Bluesbird M-75 (Solidbody) Reintroduced
1984-1988.

1984-1985	3 single-coil pickups	$800	$1,000
1986	EMG pickups	$800	$1,000
1987-1988	DiMarzio pickups	$800	$1,000

Bluesbird (Reintroduced)
1997-2003. Single-cut chambered solidbody, 2 humbuckers, block inlays, available with AAA flamed top.

1997-2001	Goldtop	$1,050	$1,300
1998-2001	AAA maple	$1,100	$1,350

MODEL YEAR	FEATURES	EXC. COND. LOW	HIGH
2001	Fender Custom Shop	$2,000	$2,300
2002-2003		$1,100	$1,350

Brian May BHM-1
1984-1987. Electric solidbody, double-cut, vibrato, 3 pickups, bound top and back, red or green, Brian May Pro, Special and Standard introduced in '94.

1984-1987		$2,600	$3,200

Brian May Pro
1994-1995. Electric solidbody, double-cut, vibrato, 3 pickups, bound top and back, various colors.

1994-1995		$2,100	$2,400

Brian May Signature Red Special
1994. Produced only 1 year, signature initials on truss rod cover, script signature on back of headstock, BM serial number series, dot markers, custom Seymour Duncan pickups, custom vibrola, red special finish.

1994		$2,100	$2,400

CA-100 Capri
1956-1973. Acoustic archtop version of CE-100, sharp Florentine cutaway, solid spruce top, laminated maple back and sides, rosewood 'board and bridge, nickel-plated metal parts, natural or sunburst.

1956-1959		$1,250	$1,550
1960-1969		$1,100	$1,350
1970-1973		$1,075	$1,325

Capri CE-100
1956-1985. Electric archtop, single Florentine cutaway, 1 pickup (2 pickups by '83), maple body, Waverly tailpiece, sunburst, in '59-'82 CE-100 D listed with 2 pickups.

1956-1959		$1,250	$1,550
1960-1969		$1,100	$1,350
1970-1979		$1,075	$1,325
1980-1985		$900	$1,100

Capri CE-100 D
1956-1982. Electric archtop, single Florentine cutaway, 2 pickups, maple body, sunburst, Waverly tailpiece (D dropped, became the Capri CE-100 in '83).

1956-1959		$1,900	$2,300
1960-1969		$1,800	$2,200
1970-1979		$1,700	$2,100
1980-1982		$1,600	$2,000

Capri CE-100 T Tenor
1950s. Electric-archtop Capri 4-string tenor guitar, sunburst.

1956		$850	$1,050

CO Series
2007. F-30 style, 000-size, cedar top, mahogany sides and back, gloss natural finish, the '07 made in Tacoma.

2007	CO-1	$750	$925
2007	CO-2	$850	$1,025
2007	CO-2C	$950	$1,125

Cordoba A-50
1961-1972. Acoustic archtop, lowest-end in the Guild archtop line, named Granda A-50 prior to '61.

1961-1965		$800	$1,000
1966-1972		$800	$1,000

1997 Guild Bluesbird

Guild Capri CE-100D

Guild D-25 M

1968 Guild D-35

MODEL YEAR	FEATURES	EXC. COND. LOW	HIGH
Cordoba T-50 Slim			
1961-1973. Thinbody version of Cordoba X-50.			
1961-1964		$800	$1,000
1965-1973		$800	$1,000
Cordoba X-50			
1961-1970. Electric archtop non-cut, laminated maple body, rosewood 'board, 1 pickup, nickel-plated parts.			
1961-1970		$800	$1,000
Cromwell			
1963-1964. Solidbody guitars imported by Guild from Hagstrom and sold under the Cromwell brand.			
1963-1964		$800	$1,000
CR-1 Crossroads Single E/Double E			
1993-2000. Single-cut solidbody acoustic, hum-bucker (S2 in '93) neck pickup and Piezo bridge, Crossroads logo on truss rod, 97 single necks (Single E, '93-'97) and very few 6/12 double necks (Double E) made by Guild custom shop.			
1993-2000	Double neck	$2,700	$3,200
1993-1997	Single neck	$1,300	$1,600
Custom F-412 12-String			
1968-1986. Special order only from '68-'74, then regular production, 17" wide body 12-string version of F-50 flat-top, spruce top, maple back and sides, arched back, 2-tone block inlays, gold hardware, natural finish.			
1968-1969		$1,700	$2,000
1970-1979		$1,600	$1,900
1980-1986		$1,500	$1,800
Custom F-512 12-String			
1968-1986, 1990. Rosewood back and sides version of F-412. See F-512 for reissue.			
1968-1969		$1,700	$2,000
1970-1979		$1,600	$1,900
1980-1986		$1,500	$1,800
Custom F-612 12-String			
1972-1973. Acoustic 12-string, similar to Custom F-512, but with 18" body, fancy mother-of-pearl inlays, and black/white marquee body, neck and headstock binding.			
1972-1973	Brazilian rosewood	$3,000	$3,700
1972-1973	Indian rosewood	$1,700	$2,000
Custom Shop 45th Anniversary			
1997. Built in Guild's Nashville Custom Shop, all solid wood, spruce top, maple back and sides, with high-end appointments.			
1997	Natural, gold hardware	$1,900	$2,400
CV-1C			
2007. Contemporary Vintage series, F-40 style, solid spruce top, solid Indian rosewood sides and back, sharp cutaway, sunburst lacquer finish.			
2007		$800	$1,000
D-4 Series			
1991-2002. Dreadnought flat-top, mahogany sides, dot markers.			
1991-2002	6-String	$425	$525
1992-1999	12-String	$425	$525

MODEL YEAR	FEATURES	EXC. COND. LOW	HIGH
D-6 (D-6 E/D-6 HG/D-6 HE)			
1992-1995. Flat-top, 15 3/4", mahogany back and sides, natural satin non-gloss finish, options available.			
1992-1995		$450	$550
D-15 Mahogany Rush			
1983-1988. Dreadnought flat-top, mahogany body and neck, rosewood 'board, dot inlays, stain finish.			
1983-1988		$475	$600
D-15 12-String			
1983-1985. 12-string version of Mahogany Rush D-15.			
1983-1985		$475	$600
D-16 Mahogany Rush			
1984-1986. Like D-15, but with gloss finish.			
1984-1986		$475	$600
D-17 Mahogany Rush			
1984-1988. Like D-15, but with gloss finish and bound body.			
1984-1988		$550	$675
D-25/D25 M/GAD-25			
2003, 2006-present. Solid mahogany body. Refer to Bluegrass D-25 for earlier models. Reintroduced in '06 as GAD-25.			
2003		$475	$600
D-30			
1987-1999. Acoustic flat top, spruce-top, laminated maple back and solid maple sides, rosewood 'board, multi-bound, various colors.			
1987-1989		$700	$850
1990-1999		$600	$750
D-40			
1999-2007. Solid spruce top, mahogany back and sides, rosewood 'board. See earlier models under Bluegrass Jubilee D-40.			
1999-2007		$1,000	$1,300
D-40C NT			
1975-1991. Pointed cutaway version.			
1975-1991		$1,100	$1,375
D-40 Bluegrass Jubilee			
2009-present. Dreadnought, Indian rosewood, solid red spruce top, mahogany back and sides, 3-piece neck (mahogany/walnut/mahogany), high gloss finish.			
2009-2010	No pickup	$1,000	$1,300
2009-2010	With Seymour Duncan D-TAR	$1,100	$1,400
D-40 Richie Havens			
2003-present. Richie Havens signature logo on truss rod cover, solid mahogany sides and back, solid spruce top, factory Fishman Matrix Natural electronics.			
2003-2010		$1,000	$1,250
D-46			
1980-1985. Dreadnought acoustic, ash back, sides, neck, spruce top, ebony 'board, ivoroid body binding.			
1980-1985		$625	$775
D-55			
1968-1987, 1990-present (Special Order 1968-1973, regular production after). Dreadnought-size acoustic, spruce top, rosewood back and sides, scalloped bracing, gold-plated tuners, called the TV Model in earlier years, sunburst or natural.			
1990-2010		$1,600	$2,000

MODEL		EXC. COND.	
YEAR	FEATURES	LOW	HIGH

D-60
1987-1990, 1998-2000. Renamed from D-66, rosewood back and sides, 15 3/4", scalloped bracing, multi-bound top, slotted diamond inlay, G shield logo.
| 1987-1990 | | $1,600 | $2,000 |
| 1998-2000 | | $1,500 | $1,900 |

D-64
1984-1986. Maple back and side, multi-bound body, notched diamond inlays, limited production.
| 1984-1986 | | $1,500 | $1,900 |

D-66
1984-1987. Amber, rosewood back and sides, 15 3/4", scalloped bracing, renamed D-60 in '87.
| 1984-1987 | | $1,500 | $1,900 |

D-70
1981-1985. Dreadnought acoustic, spruce top, Indian rosewood back and sides, multi-bound, ebony 'board with mother-of-pearl inlays.
| 1981-1985 | | $1,500 | $1,900 |

D-100
1999. Top-of-the-line dreadnought-size acoustic, spruce top, rosewood back and sides, scalloped bracing.
| 1999 | | $1,800 | $2,200 |

D-212 12-String
1981-1983. 12-string version of D-25, laminated mahogany back and sides, natural, sunburst or black, renamed D-25-12 in '87, reintroduced as D-212 '96-present.
| 1981-1983 | | $700 | $875 |

D-412 12-String
1990-1997. Dreadnought, 12 strings, mahogany sides and arched back, satin finished, natural.
| 1990-1997 | | $800 | $975 |

DC-130
1994-1995. US-made, limited run, D-style cutaway, flamed maple top/back/sides.
| 1994-1995 | | $2,000 | $2,400 |

DCE True American
1993-2000. Cutaway flat-top acoustic/electric, 1 with mahogany back and sides, 5 with rosewood.
| 1993-2000 | DCE1 | $575 | $725 |
| 1994-2000 | DCE5 | $625 | $775 |

Del Rio M-30
1959-1964. Flat-top, 15", all mahogany body, satin non-gloss finish.
| 1959-1964 | | $1,100 | $1,350 |

Detonator
1987-1990. Electric solidbody, double-cut, 3 pickups, bolt-on neck, Guild/Mueller tremolo system, black hardware.
| 1987-1990 | | $525 | $650 |

Duane Eddy Deluxe DE-500
1962-1974, 1984-1987. Electric archtop, single rounded cutaway, 2 pickups (early years and '80s version have DeArmonds), Bigsby, master volume, spruce top with maple back and sides, available in blond (BL) or sunburst (SB).
1962	Natural	$4,700	$5,900
1962	Sunburst	$3,900	$4,900
1963	Natural	$4,600	$5,700
1963	Sunburst	$3,800	$4,700
1964	Natural	$4,400	$5,500
1964	Sunburst	$3,500	$4,400
1965	Natural	$3,900	$4,900
1965	Sunburst	$3,400	$4,200
1966	Natural	$3,500	$4,400
1966	Sunburst	$3,200	$3,900
1967-1969	Various colors	$3,100	$3,800
1970-1974	Various colors	$2,700	$3,400
1984-1987	Various colors	$2,300	$2,900

Duane Eddy Standard DE-400
1963-1974. Electric archtop, single rounded cutaway, 2 pickups, vibrato, natural or sunburst, less appointments than DE-500 Deluxe.
1963	Natural	$3,300	$4,100
1963	Sunburst	$2,800	$3,500
1964	Natural	$3,100	$3,800
1964	Sunburst	$2,500	$3,100
1965	Natural	$2,800	$3,500
1965	Sunburst	$2,300	$2,900
1966	Natural	$2,500	$3,100
1966	Sunburst	$2,100	$2,600
1967-1969	Various colors	$2,000	$2,500
1970-1974	Various colors	$1,700	$2,100

DV Series
1992-1999, 2007-present. Acoustic flat-top, spruce top, solid mahogany or rosewood back and sides, ebony or rosewood 'board and bridge, mahogany neck, satin or gloss finish.
| 1996-2010 | | $500 | $2,200 |

Economy M-20
1958-1965, 1969-1973. Mahogany body, acoustic flat-top, natural or sunburst satin finish.
1958		$1,550	$1,900
1959-1965		$1,550	$1,900
1969-1973		$1,350	$1,650

F-4 CEHG
1992-2002. High Gloss finish, single-cut flat-top, acoustic/electric.
| 1992-2002 | | $550 | $700 |

F-5 CE
1992-2001. Acoustic/electric, single cutaway, rosewood back and sides, dot inlays, chrome tuners.
| 1992-2001 | | $575 | $700 |

F-30
1998-1999. Made in Westerly, Rhode Island.
| 1998-1999 | | $750 | $925 |

F-30 R-LS
1990s. Custom Shop model, other F-30 models are listed under Aragon F-30 listing, rosewood sides and back, bearclaw spruce top, limited production.
| 1990s | | $850 | $1,050 |

F-45 CE
1983-1992. Acoustic/electric, single pointed cutaway, active EQ, preamp, spruce top, mahogany back and sides, rosewood 'board, natural finish.
| 1983-1992 | | $700 | $875 |

F-46 NT
1984. Jumbo body style flat-top, designed for Guild by George Gruhn.
| 1984 | | $1,550 | $1,900 |

Guild Duane Eddy Deluxe DE-500

1968 Guild F-30

Guild F-47MC

Guild F-50 R

MODEL YEAR	FEATURES	EXC. COND. LOW	HIGH
F-47 M/F-47 MC			
2007-present. Made in USA, solid flamed maple sides and back, MC with cutaway.			
2007-2010	F-47M	$1,400	$1,600
2007-2010	F-47MC	$1,500	$1,700
F-47 RCE Grand Auditorium			
1999-2003. Cutaway acoustic/electric, solid spruce top, solid maple back and sides, block inlays.			
1999-2003		$1,100	$1,350
F-50			
2002-present. Jumbo, solid spruce top, solid maple sides, arched laminated maple back, abalone rosette. See Navarre F-50/F-50 for earlier models.			
2002-2010	Maple	$1,100	$1,300
2002-2010	Rosewood	$1,300	$1,500
F-65 CE			
1992-2001. Acoustic/electric, single cutaway, rosewood back and sides, block inlay, gold tuners.			
1992-2001		$1,300	$1,500
F-212 12-String			
1964-1982. Acoustic flat-top jumbo, 12 strings, spruce top, mahogany back and sides, 16" body.			
1964-1969		$1,400	$1,700
1970-1979		$1,000	$1,250
1980-1982		$900	$1,150
F-212 XL 12-String			
1966-1986, 1998-2000. Acoustic flat-top, 17" body, 12 strings, spruce top, mahogany back and sides, ebony fingerboard.			
1966-1969		$1,400	$1,700
1970-1979		$1,000	$1,250
1980-1986		$900	$1,150
1998-2000		$750	$950
F-412			
2002-present. Solid spruce top, solid maple back and sides, block inlays, 12-string. See Custom F-412 for earlier models.			
2002-2010		$1,200	$1,500
F-512			
2002-present. Solid spruce top, rosewood back and sides, 12-string. See Custom F-512 for earlier models.			
2002-2010		$1,400	$1,700
Freshman M-65			
1958-1973. Electric archtop, single-cut, mahogany back and sides, f-holes, 1 single-coil (some with 2), sunburst or natural top.			
1958-1959		$1,200	$1,500
1960-1969		$1,100	$1,300
1970-1973		$1,000	$1,200
Freshman M-65 3/4			
1958-1973. Short-scale version of M-65, 1 pickup.			
1958-1959	Natural or sunburst	$900	$1,100
1960-1969	Cherry, natural or sunburst	$800	$1,000
1970-1973	Cherry or sunburst	$750	$950
FS-20 CE			
1986-1987. Solidbody acoustic, routed mahogany body.			
1986-1987		$650	$800

MODEL YEAR	FEATURES	EXC. COND. LOW	HIGH
FS-46 CE			
1983-1986. Flat-top acoustic/electric, pointed cutaway, mahogany, black, natural or sunburst.			
1983-1986		$750	$900
G-5 P			
1988-ca.1989. Handmade in Spain, cedar top, gold-plated hardware.			
1988-1989		$650	$825
G-37			
1973-1986. Acoustic flat-top, spruce top, laminated maple back and sides, rosewood 'board and bridge, sunburst or natural top.			
1973-1986		$600	$775
G-41			
1974-1978. Acoustic flat-top, spruce top, mahogany back and sides, rosewood 'board and bridge, 20 frets.			
1975-1978		$950	$1,175
G-75			
1975-1977. Acoustic flat-top, 3/4-size version of D-50, spruce top, rosewood back and sides, mahogany neck, ebony 'board and bridge.			
1975-1977		$950	$1,175
G-212 12-String			
1974-1983. Acoustic flat-top 12-string version of D-40, spruce top, mahogany back and sides, natural or sunburst.			
1974-1983		$950	$1,175
G-212 XL 12-String			
1974-1983. Acoustic flat-top, 12 strings, 17" version of G-212.			
1974-1983		$950	$1,175
G-312 12-String			
1974-1987. Acoustic flat-top 12-string version of the D-50, spruce top, rosewood back and sides.			
1974-1987		$1,100	$1,400
GAD (Guild Acoustic Design) Series			
2004-present. Made in China.			
2004-2010		$400	$750
George Barnes AcoustiLectric			
1962-1972. Electric archtop, single-cut, solid spruce top, curly maple back and sides, multi-bound, 2 humbuckers, gold-plated hardware, sunburst or natural finish.			
1962-1972		$2,500	$3,100
GF-25			
1987-1992. Acoustic flat-top, mahogany back and sides.			
1987-1992		$675	$775
GF-30			
1987-1991. Acoustic flat-top, maple back/sides/neck, multi-bound.			
1987-1991		$800	$1,000
GF-40			
1987-1991. Mahogany back and sides, multi-bound.			
1987-1991		$800	$1,000
GF-50			
1987-1991. Acoustic flat-top, rosewood back and sides, mahogany neck, multi-bound.			
1987-1991		$800	$1,000

The *Vintage Guitar Price Guide* shows low to high values for items in all-original excellent condition, and, where applicable, with original case or cover.

GF-60

1987-1989. Jumbo size, rosewood or maple sides and back, diamond markers.

1987-1989	GF-60M, maple	$900	$1,125
1987-1989	GF-60R, rosewood	$900	$1,125

Granda A-50 (Acoustic Archtop)

1956-1960. Lowest-end acoustic archtop in the Guild line, renamed Cordoba A-50 in '61.

1956-1960	$800	$1,000

Granda X-50

1954-1961. Electric archtop, non-cut, laminated all maple body, rosewood 'board and bridge, nickel-plated metal parts, 1 pickup, sunburst. Renamed Cordoba X-50 in '61.

1955-1959	$950	$1,200
1960-1961	$950	$1,200

GV Series

1993-1995. Flat-top, rosewood back and sides, various enhancements.

1993-1995	GV-52, jumbo, gloss	$875	$1,075
1993-1995	GV-52, jumbo, satin	$875	$1,075
1993-1995	GV-70, abalone, gloss	$925	$1,125
1993-1995	GV-72, herringbone, gloss	$925	$1,125

Jet Star S-50

1963-1970. Electric solidbody, double-cut, mahogany or alder body, 1 pickup, vibrato optional by '65, asymmetrical headstock until '65, reintroduced as S-50 in '72-'78 with body redesign.

1963-1965	3-on-side tuners, single-coil	$1,200	$1,450
1966-1970	6-in-line tuners, single-coil	$1,150	$1,400

JF-30

1987-2004. Jumbo 6-string acoustic, spruce top, laminated maple back, solid maple sides, multi-bound.

1987-1999	$800	$1,000
2000-2004	$800	$1,000

JF-30 E

1994-2004. Acoustic/electric version.

1994-2004	$875	$1,075

JF-30-12

1987-2004. 12-string version of the JF-30.

1987-2004	$925	$1,125

JF-50 R

1987-1988. Jumbo 6-string acoustic, rosewood back and sides, multi-bound.

1987-1988	$1,250	$1,550

JF-55

1989-2000. Jumbo flat-top, spruce top, rosewood body.

1989-2000	$1,600	$1,900

JF-55-12

1991-2000. 12-string JF-55.

1991-2000	$1,600	$1,900

JF-65

1987-1994. Renamed from Navarre F-50, Jumbo flat-top acoustic, spruce top, R has rosewood back and sides and M has maple.

1987-1994	JF-65M, maple	$1,400	$1,700
1987-1994	JF-65R, rosewood	$1,400	$1,700

JF-65-12

1987-2001. 12-string, version of JF-65.

1987-2001	JF-65M-12, maple	$1,400	$1,700
1987-2001	JF-65R-12, rosewood	$1,400	$1,700

Johnny Smith Award

1956-1961. Single-cut electric archtop, floating DeArmond pickup, multi-bound, gold hardware, sunburst or natural, renamed Artist Award in '61.

1956-1961	$7,500	$9,000

Johnny Smith Award Benedetto

2004-2006. 18 custom made instruments under the supervision of Bob Benedetto, signed by Johnny Smith, with certificate of authenticity signed by Smith and Benedetto.

2004-2006 18 made	$4,500	$5,500

Liberator Elite

1988. Limited Edition, top-of-the-line, set-neck, offset double-cut solidbody, 2-piece figured maple top, mahogany body, rising-sun inlays, 3 active Bartolini pickups, 2 knobs and 4 toggles, last of the Guild solidbodies.

1988	$800	$975

M-80 CS

1975-1984. Solidbody, double-cut, 2 pickups, has M-80 on truss rod cover, called just M-80 from '80-'84.

1975-1984	$750	$850

Manhattan X-170 (Mini-Manhattan X-170)

1985-2002. Called Mini-Manhattan X-170 in '85-'86, electric archtop hollowbody, single rounded cutaway, maple body, f-holes, 2 humbuckers, block inlays, gold hardware, natural or sunburst.

1985-1989	$1,500	$1,800
1990-2002	$1,200	$1,500

Manhattan X-175 (Sunburst)

1954-1985. Electric archtop, single rounded cutaway, laminated spruce top, laminated maple back and sides, 2 pickups, chrome hardware, sunburst. Reissued as X-160 Savoy.

1954-1959	$1,800	$2,200
1960-1969	$1,600	$2,000
1970-1985	$1,400	$1,800

Manhattan X-175 B (Natural)

1954-1976. Natural finish X-175.

1954-1959	$2,200	$2,500
1960-1969	$2,100	$2,400
1970-1976	$1,700	$2,000

Mark I

1961-1972. Classical, Honduras mahogany body, rosewood 'board, slotted headstock.

1961-1969	$475	$550
1970-1973	$400	$475

Mark II

1961-1987. Like Mark I, but with spruce top and body binding.

1961-1969	$500	$575
1970-1979	$475	$500
1980-1987	$350	$450

Mark III

1961-1987. Like Mark II, but with Peruvian mahogany back and sides and floral soundhole design.

1961-1969	$550	$650
1970-1979	$450	$550
1980-1987	$375	$450

1968 Guild F-212 12-String

1988 Guild Liberator Elite

1976 Guild S-100

Guild Savoy X-150

Mark IV

1961-1985. Like Mark III, but with flamed pearwood back and sides (rosewood offered in '61, maple in '62).

		LOW	HIGH
1961-1969	Pearwood	$650	$800
1970-1979	Pearwood	$550	$700
1980-1985	Pearwood	$500	$650

Mark V

1961-1987. Like Mark III, but with rosewood back and sides (maple available for '61-'64).

1961-1968	Brazilian rosewood	$2,000	$2,500
1969-1979	Indian rosewood	$1,200	$1,500
1980-1987	Indian rosewood	$800	$1,000

Mark VI

1962-1973. Rosewood back and sides, spruce top, wood binding.

1962-1968	Brazilian rosewood	$2,200	$2,700
1969-1973	Indian rosewood	$1,300	$1,600

Mark VII Custom

1968-1973. Special order only, spruce top, premium rosewood back and sides, inlaid rosewood bridge, engraved gold tuners.

1962-1968	Brazilian rosewood	$2,400	$2,900
1969-1973	Indian rosewood	$1,400	$1,700

Navarre F-48

1972-1975. 17", mahogany, block markers.

1972-1975		$1,100	$1,350

Navarre F-50/F-50

1954-1986, 1994-1995, 2002-present. Acoustic flat-top, spruce top, curly maple back and sides, rosewood 'board and bridge, 17" rounded lower bout, laminated arched maple back, renamed JF-65 M in '87. Reissued in '94 and in '02.

1954-1956		$3,400	$4,000
1957-1962	Pearl block markers added	$2,700	$3,300
1963-1969	Ebony 'board added	$2,500	$3,100
1970-1975		$2,000	$2,500
1976-1979		$1,900	$2,300
1980-1986		$1,800	$2,200
1994-1995		$1,400	$1,700

Navarre F-50 R/F-50 R

1965-1987, 2002-present. Rosewood back and side version of F-50, renamed JF-65 R in '87. Reissued in '02.

1965-1968	Brazilian rosewood	$3,400	$4,300
1969-1975	Indian rosewood	$2,000	$2,500
1976-1979		$1,900	$2,300
1980-1987		$1,800	$2,200

Nightbird

1985-1987. Electric solidbody, single sharp cutaway, tone chambers, 2 pickups, multi-bound, black or gold hardware, renamed Nightbird II in '87.

1985-1987		$1,900	$2,200

Nightbird I

1987-1988. Like Nightbird but with chrome hardware, less binding and appointments, 2 pickups, coil-tap, phaser switch.

1987-1988		$1,700	$2,000

Nightbird II

1987-1992. Renamed from Nightbird, electric solidbody, single sharp cut, tone chambers, 2 pickups, multi-bound, black hardware, renamed Nightbird X-2000 in '92.

1987-1992		$2,000	$2,300

Nightbird X-2000

1992-1996. Renamed from Nightbird II.

1992-1996		$1,700	$2,000

Park Ave X-180

2005. Cutaway acoustic archtop, 2 pickups, block markers.

2005		$1,500	$1,875

Polara S-100

1963-1970. Electric solidbody, double-cut, mahogany or alder body, rosewood 'board, 2 single coil pickups, built-in stand until '70, asymmetrical headstock, in '70 Polara dropped from title (see S-100), renamed back to Polara S-100 in '97.

1963-1964	2 pickups	$1,300	$1,600
1965-1970	3 pickups	$1,300	$1,600

Roy Buchanan T-200

1986. Single-cut solidbody, 2 pickups, pointed six-on-a-side headstock, poplar body, bolt-on neck, gold and brass hardware.

1986		$550	$675

S-50

1972-1978. Double cut solidbody, 1 single-coil (switched to humbucker in '74), dot inlay.

1972-1973	Single-coil	$700	$875
1974-1978	Humbucker	$650	$825

S-60/S-60 D

1976-1981. Double-cut solidbody, 1 pickup, all mahogany body, rosewood 'board. Renamed S-60 D in '77 with 2 DiMarzio pickups.

1976-1980	S-60, 1 humbucker	$650	$800
1977-1981	S-60D, 2 single-coil	$700	$850

S-65 D

1980-1981. Electric solidbody, double-cut, 3 DiMarzio pickups, rosewood 'board.

1980-1981		$700	$850

S-70 D/S-70 AD

1979-1981. Solidbody (mahogany D, ash AD), rosewood 'board, 3 single-coils.

1979-1981	D-70AD, ash	$750	$900
1979-1981	S-70D, mahogany	$700	$850

S-90

1972-1977. Double-cut SG-like body, 2 humbuckers, dot inlay, chrome hardware.

1972-1977		$775	$900

S-100

1970-1978, 1994-1996. S-100 Standard is double-cut solidbody, 2 humbuckers, block inlays. Deluxe of '72-'75 had added Bigsby. Standard Carved of '74-'77 has acorns and oakleaves carved in the top.

1970-1978	Standard	$1,100	$1,400
1972-1975	Deluxe	$1,100	$1,400
1974-1977	Standard Carved	$1,200	$1,500

S-100 Reissue

1994-1997. Renamed Polara in '97.

1994-1997		$825	$975

The *Vintage Guitar Price Guide* shows low to high values for items in all-original excellent condition, and, where applicable, with original case or cover.

MODEL YEAR	FEATURES	EXC. COND. LOW	HIGH

S-250
1981-1983. Double-cut solidbody, 2 humbuckers.

| 1981-1983 | | $600 | $750 |

S-261
Ca.1985. Double-cut, maple body, black Kahler tremolo, 1 humbucker and 2 single-coil pickups, rosewood 'board.

| 1985 | | $500 | $600 |

S-270 Runaway
1985. Offset double-cut solidbody, 1 humbucker, Kahler.

| 1985 | | $500 | $600 |

S-271 Sprint
1986. Replaced the S-270.

| 1986 | | $500 | $600 |

S-275
1982-1983. Offset double-cut body, 2 humbuckers, bound figured maple top, sunburst or natural.

| 1982-1983 | | $500 | $600 |

S-280 Flyer
1983-1984. Double-cut poplar body, 2 humbuckers or 3 single-coils, maple or rosewood neck, dot markers.

| 1983-1984 | | $500 | $600 |

S-281 Flyer
1983-1988. Double-cut poplar body S-280 with locking vibrato, optional pickups available.

| 1983-1988 | | $500 | $600 |

S-284 Starling/Aviator
1984-1988. Starling (early-'84) and Aviator (late-'84-'88), double-cut, 3 pickups.

| 1984 | Starling | $500 | $600 |
| 1984-1988 | Aviator | $500 | $600 |

S-285 Aviator
1986. Deluxe Aviator, bound 'board, fancy inlays.

| 1986 | | $500 | $600 |

S-300 Series
1976-1983. Double-cut mahogany solidbody with larger bass horn and rounded bottom, 2 humbuckers. S-300 A has ash body, D has exposed DiMarzio humbuckers.

1976-1983	S-300	$800	$1,000
1977-1982	S-300D	$800	$1,000
1977-1983	S-300A	$800	$1,000

S-400/S-400 A
1980-1981. Double-cut mahogany (400) or ash (400 A) solidbody, 2 humbuckers.

| 1980-1981 | | $1,100 | $1,300 |

Savoy A-150
1958-1973. Acoustic archtop version of X-150, available with floating pickup, natural or sunburst finish.

| 1958-1961 | Natural | $1,700 | $2,100 |
| 1958-1961 | Sunburst | $1,600 | $2,000 |

Savoy X-150
1954-1965, 1998-2005. Electric archtop, single rounded cutaway, spruce top, maple back and sides, rosewood 'board and bridge, 1 single-coil pickup, sunburst, blond or sparkling gold finish.

1954	Sunburst	$1,900	$2,300
1955-1959	Sunburst	$1,800	$2,200
1960-1961	Sunburst	$1,600	$2,000

Slim Jim T-100
1958-1973. Electric archtop thinline, single-cut, laminated all-maple body, rosewood 'board and bridge, Waverly tailpiece, 1 pickup, natural or sunburst.

1958-1960		$1,300	$1,600
1961-1964		$1,200	$1,500
1965-1969		$1,100	$1,400
1970-1973		$1,000	$1,200

Slim Jim T-100 D
1958-1973. Semi-hollowbody electric, single Florentine cutaway, thinline, 2-pickup version of the T-100, natural or sunburst.

1958-1960		$1,600	$2,000
1961-1964		$1,500	$1,900
1965-1969		$1,400	$1,800
1970-1973		$1,200	$1,600

Songbird S Series
1984-1991. Designed by George Gruhn, flat-top, mahogany back, spruce top, single pointed cutaway, pickup with preamp, multi-bound top, black, natural or white. Renamed S-4 later in run.

| 1984-1991 | | $800 | $1,000 |

Standard F-112 12-String
1968-1982. Acoustic flat-top, spruce top, mahogany back, sides and neck.

1968-1969		$800	$950
1970-1979		$800	$950
1980-1982		$750	$900

Starfire I
1960-1964. Electric archtop, single-cut thinline, laminated maple or mahogany body, bound body and neck, 1 pickup.

| 1960-1961 | Starfire Red | $1,400 | $1,750 |
| 1962-1964 | | $1,300 | $1,650 |

Starfire II
1960-1976, 1997-2001. Electric archtop, single-cut thinline, laminated maple or mahogany body, bound body and rosewood neck, 2 pickups.

1960-1961	Sunburst	$1,900	$2,300
1962	Emerald Green	$2,000	$2,400
1962-1966	Special color options	$2,100	$2,500
1962-1966	Sunburst, Starfire Red	$1,800	$2,200
1967-1969	Sunburst, Starfire Red	$1,600	$2,000
1970-1975	Sunburst, Starfire Red	$1,500	$1,900
1997-2001	Reissue model	$1,250	$1,550

Starfire III
1960-1974, 1997-2005. Electric archtop, single-cut thinline, laminated maple or mahogany body, bound body and rosewood neck, 2 pickups, Guild or Bigsby vibrato, Starfire Red.

1960-1961		$1,900	$2,300
1962-1966		$1,800	$2,200
1967-1969		$1,600	$2,000
1970-1974		$1,500	$1,900
1997-2005	Reissue model	$1,250	$1,550

1965 Guild Starfire II
Bob "Willard" Henke

Guild Starfire III

1969 Guild Stuart X-500

1966 Guild Thunderbird S-200

MODEL YEAR	FEATURES	EXC. COND. LOW	HIGH

Starfire IV
1963-1987, 1991-2005. Thinline, double-cut semi-hollowbody, laminated maple or mahogany body, f-holes, 2 humbuckers, rosewood 'board, cherry or sunburst.

1963-1966		$2,000	$2,500
1967-1969		$1,800	$2,300
1970-1975		$1,700	$2,200
1976-1979		$1,600	$2,100
1980-1987		$1,400	$1,800
1991-2005	Reissue model	$1,250	$1,550

Starfire IV Special (Custom Shop)
2001-2002. Nashville Custom Shop.

2001-2002		$1,800	$2,200

Starfire V
1963-1973, 1999-2001. Same as Starfire IV but with block markers, Bigsby and master volume, natural or sunburst finish, reissued in '99.

1963-1966		$2,100	$2,400
1967-1969		$1,900	$2,400
1970-1973		$1,800	$2,300
1999-2001	Reissue model	$1,400	$1,800

Starfire VI
1964-1979. Same as Starfire IV but with higher appointments such as ebony 'board, pearl inlays, Guild/Bigsby vibrato, natural or sunburst.

1964-1966		$2,600	$3,100
1967-1969		$2,400	$2,900
1970-1975	Sunburst or natural	$2,300	$2,800
1976-1979		$2,200	$2,700

Starfire XII
1966-1973. Electric archtop, 12-string, double-cut, maple or mahogany body, set-in neck, 2 humbuckers, harp tailpiece.

1966-1967		$1,900	$2,300
1968-1969		$1,800	$2,200
1970-1973		$1,600	$2,000

Stratford A-350
1956-1973. Acoustic archtop, single rounded cutaway, solid spruce top with solid curly maple back and sides, rosewood 'board and bridge (changed to ebony by '60), sunburst.

1956-1959		$2,000	$2,400
1960-1965		$1,900	$2,300
1966-1969		$1,800	$2,200
1970-1973		$1,700	$2,100

Stratford A-350 B
1956-1973. A-350 in blond/natural finish option.

1956-1959		$2,200	$2,600
1960-1965		$2,100	$2,500
1966-1969		$2,000	$2,400
1970-1973		$1,900	$2,300

Stratford X-350
1954-1965. Electric archtop, single rounded cutaway, laminated spruce top with laminated maple back and sides, rosewood 'board, 6 push-button pickup selectors, sunburst finish (natural finish is X-375).

1954-1959		$2,200	$2,700
1960-1965		$2,100	$2,600

Stratford X-375/X-350 B
1953-1965. Natural finish version of X-350, renamed X-350 B in '58.

1953-1958	X-375	$2,500	$3,000
1959-1965	X-350B	$2,300	$2,800

Stuart A-500
1956-1969. Acoustic archtop single-cut, 17" body, A-500 sunburst, available with Guild logo, floating DeArmond pickup.

1956-1959		$2,100	$2,600
1960-1965		$2,000	$2,500
1966-1969		$1,900	$2,400

Stuart A-550/A-500 B
1956-1969. Natural blond finish version of Stuart A-500, renamed A-500 B in '60.

1956-1959		$2,400	$2,900
1960-1965		$2,300	$2,800
1966-1969		$2,200	$2,700

Stuart X-500
1953-1995. Electric archtop, single-cut, laminated spruce top, laminated curly maple back and sides, 2 pickups, sunburst.

1953-1959		$2,600	$3,200
1960-1964		$2,400	$3,000
1965-1969		$2,200	$2,700
1970-1979		$2,100	$2,600
1980-1995		$2,000	$2,500

Stuart X-550/X-500 B
1953-1995. Natural blond finish Stuart X-500, renamed X-500 B in '60.

1953-1959		$2,800	$3,400
1960-1964		$2,600	$3,200
1965-1969		$2,400	$3,000
1970-1979		$2,200	$2,700
1980-1995		$2,100	$2,500

Studio 301/ST301
1968-1970. Thinline, semi-hollow archtop Starfire-style but with sharp horns, 1 pickup, dot inlays, cherry or sunburst.

1968-1969	Single-coil	$900	$1,100
1970	Humbucker	$1,000	$1,200

Studio 302/ST302
1968-1970. Like Studio 301, but with 2 pickups.

1968-1969	Single-coils	$1,200	$1,500
1970	Humbuckers	$1,300	$1,600

Studio 303/ST303
1968-1970. Like Studio 301, but with 2 pickups and Guild/Bigsby.

1968-1969	Single-coils	$1,300	$1,600
1970	Humbuckers	$1,400	$1,700

Studio 402/ST402
1969-1970. Inch thicker body than other Studios, 2 pickups, block inlays.

1969-1970	Humbuckers	$1,600	$2,000
1969-1970	Single-coils	$1,500	$1,900

T-250
1986-1988. Single-cut body and pickup configuration with banana-style headstock.

1986-1988		$550	$675

The *Vintage Guitar Price Guide* shows low to high values for items in all-original excellent condition, and, where applicable, with original case or cover.

MODEL YEAR	FEATURES	EXC. COND. LOW	HIGH

Thunderbird S-200

1963-1968. Electric solidbody, offset double-cut, built-in rear guitar stand, AdjustoMatic bridge and vibrato tailpiece, 2 humbucker pickups until changed to single-coils in '66.

1963-1965	Humbuckers	$3,700	$4,500
1966-1968	Single-coils	$3,200	$4,000

Troubadour F-20

1956-1987. Acoustic flat-top, spruce top with maple back and sides (mahogany '59 and after), rosewood 'board and bridge, natural or sunburst.

1956-1959		$1,500	$1,900
1960-1964		$1,400	$1,800
1965-1969		$1,400	$1,800
1970-1979		$1,200	$1,500
1980-1987		$900	$1,100

TV Model D-55/D-65/D-55

1968-1987, 1990-present (special order only for 1968-1973). Dreadnought acoustic, spruce top, rosewood back and sides, scalloped bracing, gold-plated tuners, renamed D-65 in '87. Reintroduced as D-55 in '90.

1968-1969		$2,000	$2,400
1970-1975		$1,900	$2,300
1976-1979		$1,700	$2,100
1980-1987		$1,600	$2,000
1988-1989	D-65	$1,500	$1,900
1990-1999		$1,300	$1,600

Willy Porter Signature

2007. Production started in '07 in FMIC's Guild Tacoma facility, based on acoustic stylist Willy Porter's guitar, AAA sitka spruce top, solid flamed maple sides and back, special appointments, Fishman Ellipse Matrix Blend pickup system.

2007		$1,100	$1,400

X-79 Skyhawk

1981-1986. Four-point solidbody, 2 pickups, coil-tap or phase switch, various colors.

1981-1986		$700	$875

X-80 Skylark/Swan

1982-1985. Solidbody with 2 deep cutaways, banana-style 6-on-a-side headstock, renamed Swan in '85.

1982-1985		$700	$875

X-82 Nova/Starfighter

1981-1986. Solidbody, XR-7 humbuckerss, also available with 3 single-coil pickups, Quick Change SP-6 tailpiece, Adjusto-Matic bridge, Deluxe tuning machine.

1981-1983	Nova	$700	$875
1984-1986	Starfighter	$675	$850

X-88 D Star

1984-1987. 2 humbucker version X-88.

1984-1987		$700	$875

X-88 Flying Star Motley Crue

1984-1986. Pointy 4-point star body, rocketship meets spearhead headstock on bolt neck, 1 pickup, optional vibrato.

1984-1986		$700	$875

X-92 Citron

1984. Electric solidbody, detachable body section, 3 pickups.

1984		$575	$725

X-100/X-110

1953-1954. Guild was founded in 1952, so this is a very early model, 17" non-cut, single-coil soapbar neck pickup, X-100 sunburst, X-110 natural blond.

1953-1954	X-100	$1,100	$1,350
1953-1954	X-110	$1,200	$1,450

X-150 D Savoy

1998-2005. Reissue of Manhattan X-175, 2 humbuckers.

1998-2005		$1,000	$1,250

X-160 Savoy

1989-1993. No Bigsby, black or sunburst.

1989-1993		$1,150	$1,400

X-161/X-160B Savoy

1989-1994. X-160 Savoy with Bigsby, black or sunburst.

1989-1994		$1,150	$1,400

X-200/X-220

1953-1954. Electric archtop, spruce top, laminated maple body, rosewood 'board, non-cut, 2 pickups. X-200 is sunburst and X-220 blond.

1953-1954	X-200	$1,300	$1,700
1953-1954	X-220	$1,500	$1,900

X-300/X-330

1953-1954. No model name, non-cut, 2 pickups, X-300 is sunburst and X-330 blond. Becomes Savoy X-150 in '54.

1953-1954	X-300	$1,300	$1,700
1953-1954	X-330	$1,500	$1,900

X-400/X-440

1953-1954. Electric archtop, single-cut, spruce top, laminated maple body, rosewood 'board, 2 pickups, X-400 in sunburst and X-440 in blond. Becomes Manhattan X-175 in '54.

1953-1954	X-400	$1,800	$2,200
1953-1954	X-440	$2,000	$2,400

X-600/X-660

1953. No model name, single-cut, 3 pickups, X-600 in sunburst and X-660 in blond. Becomes Statford X-350 in '54.

1953	X-600	$2,800	$3,100
1953	X-660	$3,000	$3,300

X-700

1994-1999. Rounded cutaway, 17", solid spruce top, laminated maple back and sides, gold hardware, natural or sunburst.

1994-1999		$2,000	$2,500

Guillermo Roberto Guitars

2000-present. Professional grade, solidbody electric bajo quintos made in San Fernando, California.

Guitar Company of America

1971-present. Professional grade, production, acoustic guitars built by luthier Dixie Michell. Originally built in Tennessee, then Missouri; currently being made in Tulsa, Oklahoma. She also offers mandolins.

Guild Willy Porter Signature

Guitar Company of America

1966 Guyatone Lafayette

Hagstrom HJ-600

MODEL YEAR	FEATURES	EXC. COND. LOW	HIGH

Guitar Mill

2006-2001. Luthier Mario Martin builds his production/custom, professional grade, semi-hollow and solidbody guitars in Murfreesboro, Tennessee. He also builds basses. In '11, he started branding his guitars as Mario Martin.

Gurian

1965-1981. Luthier Michael Gurian started making classical guitars on a special order basis, in New York City. In '69, he started building steel-string guitars as well. 1971 brought a move to Hinsdale, Vermont, and with it increased production. In February, '79 a fire destroyed his factory, stock, and tools. He reopened in West Swanzey, New Hampshire, but closed the doors in '81. Around 2,000 Gurian instruments were built. Dealers have reported that '70s models sometimes have notable wood cracks which require repair.

CL Series

1970s. Classical Series, mahogany (M), Indian rosewood (R), or Brazilian rosewood (B).

1970s	CLB, Brazilian rosewood	$2,500	$3,100
1970s	CLM, mahogany	$1,100	$1,400
1970s	CLR, Indian rosewood	$1,300	$1,600

FLC

1970s. Flamenco guitar, yellow cedar back and sides, friction tuning pegs.

1970s		$1,200	$1,500

JB3H

1970s	Brazilian rosewood	$1,500	$1,900

JM/JMR

1970s. Jumbo body, mahogany (JM) or Indian rosewood (JMR), relatively wide waist (versus D-style or SJ-style).

1970s	JM	$1,100	$1,400
1970s	JMR	$1,300	$1,600

JR3H

1970s. Jumbo, Indian rosewood sides and back, 3-piece back, herringbone trim.

1970s		$1,400	$1,800

S2B3H

1970s	Brazilian rosewood	$2,500	$3,100

S2M

1970s. Size 2 guitar with mahogany back and sides.

1970s		$1,000	$1,200

S2R/S2R3H

1970s. Size 2 with Indian rosewood sides and back, R3H has 3-piece back and herringbone trim.

1970s	S2R	$1,100	$1,400
1970s	S2R3H	$1,400	$1,700

S3B3H

1981	Brazilian rosewood	$2,500	$3,100

S3M

1970s	Mahogany	$1,100	$1,400

S3R/S3R3H

1970s. Size 3 with Indian Rosewood, S3R3H has has 3-piece back and herringbone trim.

1970s	S3R	$1,200	$1,500
1970s	S3R3H	$1,500	$1,800

Guyatone

1933-present. Made in Tokyo by Matsuki Seisakujo, founded by Hawaiian guitarists Mitsuo Matsuki and Atsuo Kaneko (later of Teisco). Guya brand Rickenbacker lap copies in '30s. After a hiatus for the war ('40-'48), Seisakujo resumes production of laps and amps as Matsuki Denki Onkyo Kenkyujo. In '51 the Guyatone brand is first used on guitars, and in '52 they changed the company name to Tokyo Sound Company. Guyatones are among the earliest U.S. imports, branded as Marco Polo, Winston, Kingston and Kent. Other brand names included LaFayette and Bradford. Production and exports slowed after '68.

Hagenlocher, Henner

1996-present. Luthier Henner Hagenlocher builds his premium grade, custom, nylon-string guitars in Granada, Spain.

Hagstrom

1958-1983, 2004-present. Intermediate, professional, and premium grade, production/custom, solidbody, semi-hollowbody and acoustic guitars made in the U.S. and imported. Founded by Albin Hagström of Älvdalen, Sweden, who began importing accordions in 1921 and incorporated in '25. The name of the company was changed to A.B. Hagström, Inc. in '38, and an American sales office was established in '40. Electric guitar and bass production began in '58 with plastic-covered hollowbody De Luxe and Standard models. The guitars were imported into the U.S. by Hershman Music of New York as Goya 90 and 80 from '58-'61. Bass versions were imported in '61. Following a year in the U.S., Albin's son Karl-Erik Hagström took over the company as exclusive distributor of Fender in Scandinavia; he changed the U.S. importer to Merson Musical Instruments of New York (later Unicord in '65), and redesigned the line. The company closed its doors in '83. In 2004 American Music & Sound started manufacturing and distributing the Hagstrom brand under license from A.B. Albin Hagstrom.

Corvette/Condor

1963-1967. Offset double-cut solidbody, 3 single-coils, multiple push-button switches, spring vibrato, called the Condor on U.S. imports.

1963-1967		$1,050	$1,275

D'Aquisto Jimmy

1969-1975, 1976-1979. Designed by James D'Aquisto, electric archtop, f-holes, 2 pickups, sunburst, natural, cherry or white. The '69 had dot inlays, the later version had blocks. From '77 to '79, another version with an oval soundhole (no f-holes) was also available.

1969-1975	1st design	$950	$1,200
1976-1979	2nd design	$950	$1,200

Deluxe (D-2H)

2004-2008. Carved single-cut mahogany body, set-neck, 2 humbuckers, sparkle tops or sunburst.

2004-2008		$175	$225

MODEL YEAR	FEATURES	EXC. COND. LOW	HIGH

F Series (China)
2004-2008. Offset double-cut basswood body.

2004-2008	F-20	$150	$175
2004-2008	F-200	$100	$125
2004-2008	F-300	$125	$150
2004-2008	F-301	$125	$150

H-12 Electric/Viking XII
1965-1967. Double-cut, 2 pickups, 12 strings.

1965-1967	$575	$675

H-22 Folk
1965-1967. Flat-top acoustic.

1965-1967	$375	$450

Impala
1963-1967. Two-pickup version of the Corvette, sunburst.

1963-1967	$750	$900

Kent
1962-1967. Offset double-cut solidbody, 2 pickups.

1962-1967	$625	$725

Model I
1965-1971. Small double-cut solidbody, 2 single-coils, early models have plastic top.

1965-1971	Rare finish	$700	$875
1965-1971	Standard finish	$550	$675

Model II/F-200 Futura/H II
1965-1972, 1975-1976. Offset double-cut slab body with beveled edge, 2 pickups, called F-200 Futura in U.S., Model II elsewhere, '75-'76 called H II. F-200 reissued in 2004.

1965-1970	Rare finish, 6-on-a-side	$700	$875
1965-1970	Standard finish, 6-on-a-side	$550	$675
1970-1972	3-on-a-side	$500	$625

Model III/F-300 Futura/H III
1965-1972, 1977. Offset double-cut slab body with beveled edge, 3 pickups, called F-300 Futura in U.S., Model III elsewhere, '77 called H III.

1965-1972		$725	$900
1977		$425	$550

Swede
1970-1982, 2004-present. Bolt-on neck, single-cut solidbody, black, cherry or natural, '04 version is set-neck.

1979-1982	$800	$975

Super Swede
1979-1983, 2004-present. Glued-in neck upgrade of Swede, '04 version is maple top upgrade of Swede.

1979-1983		$925	$1,150
1979-1983	Custom color, blue	$1,400	$1,800
2004-2010	Reissue	$350	$400

Viking/V1
1965-1975, 1978-1979, 2004-present. Double-cut thinline, 2 f-holes, 2 pickups, chrome hardware, dot inlays, also advertised as the V-1. '60s had 6-on-side headstock, '70s was 3-and-3, latest version back to 6-on-side.

1965-1969	$900	$1,100
1970-1975	$800	$1,000
2004-2010 Reissue	$275	$325

Viking Deluxe/V2
1967-1968, 2004-present. Upscale version, gold hardware, block inlays, bound headstock and f-holes. Current version upgrades are blocks and flame maple.

1967-1968		$1,000	$1,250
2004-2010	Reissue	$300	$350

Hahn
2007-present. Professional and premium grade, custom electric guitars built by luthier Chihoe Hahn in Garnervile, New York.

Haight
1989-present. Premium and presentation grade, production/custom, acoustic (steel and classical) guitars built in Scottsdale, Arizona by luthier Norman Haight. He also builds mandolins.

Halfling Guitars and Basses
2003-present. Luthier Tom Ribbecke builds premium grade, production/custom, pin bridge, thinline and jazz guitars in Healdsburg, California. He also builds basses.

Hallmark
1965-1967, 2004-present. Imported and U.S.-made, intermediate and premium grade, production/custom, guitars from luthiers Bob Shade and Bill Gruggett, and located in Greenbelt, Maryland. They also make basses. The brand was originally founded by Joe Hall in Arvin, California, in '65. Hall had worked for Semie Moseley (Mosrite) and had also designed guitars for Standel in the mid-'60s. Bill Gruggett, who also built his own line of guitars, was the company's production manager. Joe Hall estimates that less than 1000 original Hallmark guitars were built. The brand was revived by Shade in '04.

Sweptwing
1965-1967. Pointed body, sorta like a backwards Flying V.

1965-1967	$1,800	$2,100

Hamblin Guitars
1996-present. Luthier Kent Hamblin built his premium grade, production/custom, flat-top acoustic guitars in Phoenix, Arizona and Telluride, Colorado, and presently builds in Colorado Springs.

Hamer
1974-present. Intermediate, professional and premium grade, production/custom, electric guitars made in the U.S. and overseas. Hamer also makes basses and the Slammer line of instruments. Founded in Arlington Heights, Illinois, by Paul Hamer and Jol Dantzig. Prototype guitars built in early-'70s were on Gibson lines, with first production guitar, the Standard (Explorer shape), introduced in '75. Hamer was puchased by Kaman Corporation (Ovation) in '88. The Illinois factory was closed and the operations were moved to the

1965 Hagstrom Model II
Bill Cherensky

2004 Hamer Studio Custom
Rob Bernstein

GUITARS

Hamer Duo-Tone Custom

Hamer Monaco Elite

Ovation factory in Connecticut in '97. On January 1, '08, Fender a--cquired Kaman Music Corporation and the Hamer brand. In '90, they started the Korean-import Hamer Slammer series which in '97 became Hamer Import Series (no Slammer on headstock). In '05 production was moved to China and name changed to XT Series (in '07 production moved to Indonesia). The U.S.-made ones have U.S.A. on the headstock. The less expensive import Slammer brand (not to be confused with the earlier Slammer Series) was introduced in '99 (see that listing).

Artist/Archtop Artist/Artist Custom
1995-present. U.S.-made, similar to Sunburst Archtop with semi-solid, f-hole design, sunburst, named Archtop Artist, then renamed Artist (with stop tailpiece)/Artist Custom in '97.

Year	Features	Low	High
1995-2010	Higher-end specs	$1,000	$1,250
1995-2010	Standard specs	$800	$1,000

Artist 25th Anniversary Edition
1998. Made in USA, 25th Anniversary Edition script logo on headstock.

1998		$750	$950

Blitz
1982-1984 (1st version), 1984-1990 (2nd version). Explorer-style body, 2 humbuckers, three-on-a-side peghead, dot inlays, choice of tremolo or fixed bridge, second version same except has angled six-on-a-side peghead and Floyd Rose tremolo.

Year	Features	Low	High
1982-1984	3-on-a-side peghead	$750	$900
1984-1990	6-on-a-side peghead	$700	$825

Californian
1987-1997. Solidbody double cut, bolt neck, 1 humbucker and 1 single-coil, Floyd Rose tremolo.

1987-1989		$750	$900
1990-1997		$700	$825

Californian Custom
1987-1997. Downsized contoured body, offset double-cut, neck-thru-body, optional figured maple body, Duncan Trembucker and Trem-single pickups.

1987-1989		$750	$900
1990-1997		$700	$825

Californian Elite
1987-1997. Downsized contoured body, offset double-cut, optional figured maple body, bolt-on neck, Duncan Trembucker and Trem-single pickups.

1987-1989		$900	$1,100
1990-1997		$875	$1,050

Centaura
1989-1995. Contoured body of alder or swamp ash, offset double-cut, bolt-on neck, 1 humbucker and 2 single-coil pickups, Floyd Rose tremolo, sunburst.

1989-1995		$600	$750

Chaparral
1985-1987 (1st version), 1987-1994 (2nd version). Contoured body, offset double-cut, glued maple neck, angled peghead, 1 humbucker and 2 single-coils, tremolo, second version has bolt neck with a modified peghead.

Year	Features	Low	High
1985-1987	Set-neck	$800	$950
1987-1994	Bolt-on neck	$750	$850

Daytona
1993-1997. Contoured body, offset double-cut, bolt maple neck, dot inlay, 3 single-coils, Wilkinson VSV tremolo.

1993-1997		$700	$825

Diablo
1992-1997. Contoured alder body, offset double-cut, bolt maple neck, rosewood 'board, dot inlays, reversed peghead '92-'94, 2 pickups, tremolo.

1992-1997		$575	$675

DuoTone
1993-2003. Semi-hollowbody, double-cut, bound top, glued-in neck, rosewood 'board, 2 humbuckers, EQ.

1993-2003		$550	$625

Eclipse
1994-2003. Asymmetrical double-cut slab mahogany body, glued neck, three-on-a-side peghead, rosewood 'board, dot inlays, 2 Duncan Mini-Humbuckers, cherry.

1994-2003		$650	$800

FB I
1986-1987. Reverse Firebird-style body, glued-in neck, reverse headstock, 1 pickup, rosewood 'board with dot inlays, also available in non-reverse body.

1986-1987		$500	$600

FB II
1986-1987. Reverse Firebird-style, glued-in neck, ebony 'board with boomerang inlays, angled headstock, 2 humbuckers, Floyd Rose tremolo, also available as a 12-string.

1986-1987		$600	$675

Korina Standard
1995-1996. Limited run, Korina Explorer-type body, glued-in neck, angled peghead, 2 humbuckers.

1995-1996		$1,100	$1,300

Maestro
1990. Offset double-cut, 7 strings, tremolo, bolt-on maple neck, 3 Seymour Duncan rail pickups.

1990		$750	$925

Mirage
1994-1998. Double-cut carved figured koa wood top, transparent flamed top, initially with 3 single-coil pickups, dual humbucker option in '95.

1994-1998		$725	$900

Monaco Elite
2003-present. Single-cut solidbody, 2 humbuckers, 3-in-a-line control knobs, tune-o-matic-style bridge, mother-of-pearl inlaid 'victory' position markers, carved flamed maple cap over mahogany body, flamed maple sunburst.

2003-2010		$900	$1,100

Newport Series
1999-present. Made in USA, Newport logo on truss rod cover, double-cut thinline with solid center block and 2 f-holes, 2 humbucker pickups (Newport 90 has P-90s), wraparound bridge tailpiece.

Year	Features	Low	High
1999-2010	Newport	$1,000	$1,250
1999-2010	Newport Pro	$1,100	$1,325

Phantom A5
1982-1884, 1985-1986 (2nd version). Contoured offset double-cut, glued neck, 3-on-a-side peghead, 1

MODEL YEAR	FEATURES	EXC. COND. LOW	HIGH

triple-coil and 1 single-coil pickup, second version same but with 6-on-a-side peghead and Kahler tremolo.

| 1982-1984 | | $650 | $750 |

Phantom GT
1984-1986. Contoured body, offset double-cut, glued-in fixed neck, six-on-a-side peghead, 1 humbucker, single volume control.

| 1984-1986 | | $575 | $700 |

Prototype
1981-1985. Contoured mahogany body, double-cut with 1 splitable triple-coil pickup, fixed bridge, three-on-a-side peghead, Prototype II has extra pickup and tremolo.

| 1981-1985 | | $825 | $925 |

Scarab I
1984-1986. Multiple cutaway body, six-on-a-side peghead, 1 humbucker, tremolo, rosewood or ebony 'board, dot inlays.

| 1984-1986 | | $550 | $650 |

Scarab II
1984-1986. Two humbucker version of the Scarab.

| 1984-1986 | | $575 | $725 |

Scepter
1986-1990. Futuristic-type body, ebony 'board with boomerang inlays, angled six-on-a-side peghead, Floyd Rose tremolo.

| 1986-1990 | | $900 | $1,100 |

Slammer Series
1990-1997. Various models imported from Korea, not to be confused with Hamer's current Slammer budget line started in '98.

| 1990-1997 | | $300 | $400 |

Special
1980-1983 (1st version), 1984-1985 (Floyd Rose version), 1992-1997 (2nd version). Double-cut solidbody, flame maple top, glued neck, 3-on-a-side peghead, 2 humbuckers, Rose version has mahogany body with ebony 'board, the second version is all mahogany and has tune-o-matic bridge, stop tailpiece and Duncan P-90s, cherry red.

1980-1983	1st version	$850	$1,000
1984-1985	With Floyd Rose	$825	$975
1992-1997	2nd version	$800	$900

Special FM
1993-1997. Special with flamed maple top, 2 humbuckers, renamed the Special Custom in '97.

| 1993-1999 | | $950 | $1,050 |

Standard
1974-1985, 1995-1999. Futuristic body, maple top, bound or unbound body, glued neck, angled headstock, either unbound neck with dot inlays or bound neck with crown inlays, 2 humbuckers. Reissued in '95 with same specs but unbound mahogany body after '97. Higher dollar Standard Custom still available.

1974-1975	Pre-production, about 20 made	$6,200	$7,500
1975-1977	Production, about 50 made, PAFs	$6,200	$7,500
1977-1979	Dimarzio PAF-copies	$3,100	$3,600
1980-1985		$2,100	$2,600
1995-1999		$1,400	$1,700

Stellar 1
1999-2000. Korean import, double-cut, 2 humbuckers.

| 1999-2000 | | $125 | $150 |

Steve Stevens I
1984-1992. Introduced as Prototype SS, changed to Steve Stevens I in '86, contoured double-cut, six-on-a-side headstock, dot or crown inlays, 1 humbucker and 2 single-coil pickups.

| 1984-1992 | | $950 | $1,175 |

Steve Stevens II
1986-1987. One humbucker and 1 single-coil version.

| 1986-1987 | | $1,050 | $1,275 |

Studio
1993-present. Double-cut, flamed maple top on mahogany body, 2 humbuckers, cherry or natural.

| 1993-2010 | | $775 | $950 |

Sunburst
1977-1983, 1990-1992. Double-cut bound solidbody, flamed maple top, glue-in neck, bound neck and crown inlays optional, 3-on-a-side headstock, 2 humbuckers.

1977-1979		$1,725	$2,150
1980-1983	Arlington Heights built	$1,500	$1,800
1990-1992		$1,200	$1,400

Sunburst (Import)
1997-present. Import version of Sunburst, flat-top or archtop, 2 pickups.

| 1997-2010 | | $200 | $250 |

Sunburst Archtop
1991-present. Sunburst model with figured maple carved top, 2 humbuckers, offered under various names:

> *Standard - unbound neck and dot inlays, tune-o-matic and stop tailpiece '91-'93.*
> *Custom - a Standard with bound neck and crown inlays '91-'93.*
> *Archtop - bound neck with crown inlays '94-'97.*
> *Studio Custom - bound neck with crown inlays '97-present.*
> *Studio - unbound body, by '95 stud wrap-around tailpiece '93-present.*
> *Archtop GT - Gold top with P-90 soapbar-style pickups '93-'97.*

| 1991-1997 | | $950 | $1,150 |

T-51
1993-1997. Classic single-cut southern ash body, 2 single-coils.

| 1993-1997 | | $700 | $850 |

T-62
1991-1995. Classic offset double-cut solidbody, tremolo, pau ferro 'board, Lubritrak nut, locking tuners, 3-band active EQ, various colors.

| 1991-1995 | | $750 | $900 |

TLE
1986-1992. Single-cut mahogany body, maple top, glued neck, 6-on-a-side headstock, rosewood 'board, dot inlays, 3 pickups.

| 1986-1992 | | $850 | $1,050 |

Hamer Scarab

1993 Hamer Special
Rob Bernstein

To get the most from this book, be sure to read "Using *The Guide*" in the introduction.

GUITARS

Harmony Broadway

Harmony H62

MODEL YEAR	FEATURES	EXC. COND. LOW	HIGH

TLE Custom
1986-1992. Bound, single-cut solidbody with maple top, glued-in neck, angled headstock, ebony 'board with boomerang inlays, 3 pickups.

1986-1992		$850	$1,050

Vector
1982-1985. V-style body (optional flame maple top), 3-on-a-side peghead, rosewood 'board, 2 humbuckers, Sustain Block fixed bridge (Kahler or Floyd Rose tremolos may also be used).

1982-1985	Maple top	$925	$1,125
1982-1985	Regular top	$875	$1,075

Vector Limited Edition Korina
1997. 72 built in Hamer's Arlington Heights, Illinois shop, price includes original Hamer Certificate of Authenticity with matching serial number, Flying-V Vector style body, gold hardware, natural finish.

1997		$2,100	$2,500

Hanson
2009-present. Founders John and Bo Pirruccello import intermediate grade, electric guitars which are set up in Chicago, Illinois.

Harden Engineering
1999-present. Professional grade, custom, solidbody guitars built by luthier William Harden in Chicago, Illinois. He also builds effects pedals.

Harmony
1892-1976, late 1970s-present. Huge, Chicago-based manufacturer of fretted instruments, mainly budget models under the Harmony name or for many other American brands and mass marketers. Harmony was at one time the largest guitar builder in the world. In its glory days, Harmony made over one-half of the guitars built in the U.S., with '65 being their peak year. But by the early-'70s, the crash of the '60s guitar boom and increasing foreign competition brought an end to the company. The Harmony brand appeared on Asian-built instruments starting in the late '70s to the '90s with sales mainly is mass-retail stores. In 2000, the Harmony brand was distributed by MBT International. In '02, former MBT International marketing director Alison Gillette announced the launch of Harmony Classic Reissue Guitars and Basses.

Many Harmony guitars have a factory order number on the inside back of the guitar which often contains the serial number. Most older Harmony acoustics and hollowbodies have a date ink-stamped inside the body. DeArmond made most of the electronic assemblies used on older Harmony electrics, and they often have a date stamped on the underside.

Amplifying Resonator Model 27
1930s. Dobro-licensed with Dobro metal resonator, wood body.

1930s		$600	$700

Archtone H1215/H1215 Tenor
1950s. Lower-end archtop, sunburst.

1950-1960s	4-string tenor	$250	$325
1950-1960s	6-string	$225	$275

Bob Kat H14/H15
1968. Replaces Silhouette solidbody, H14 has single pickup and 2 knobs, H15 has 2 pickups. When vibrato is added it becomes the H16 model.

1968	H14	$250	$300
1968	H15	$400	$500

Brilliant Cutaway H1310/H1311
1962-1965. 16 1/2" body (Grand Auditorium), acoustic archtop cutaway, block markers, sunburst.

1962-1965		$600	$750

Broadway H954
1930s-1971. 15-3/4" body, acoustic archtop, dot markers, sunburst.

1960s		$225	$275

Buck Owens
1969. Acoustic flat-top, red, white and blue.

1969		$850	$1,100

Cremona
1930s-1952. Full-size archtop line, Harmony and Cremona logo on headstock, natural. Cutaways became available in '53.

1940s		$300	$375

D Series (Electric)
Late-1980s-Early-1990s. Electric copy models, including offset double- and single-cut solidbody and double-cut thin hollowbody (D720), 1 to 3 pickups. All models begin with D, some models part of Harmony Electric series and others the Harmony Igniter series.

1980-1990s	Various models	$80	$100

Espanada H63
1950s-1965. Thick body, single-cut, jazz-style double pickups, black finish with white appointments, by early '60s 'Espanada' logo on lower bass bout.

1950s		$1,300	$1,600
1960-1965		$1,300	$1,600

Grand Concert H165
1960s. Flat-top, all mahogany body.

1960s		$200	$250

H/HG Series (Electric)
Late-1980s-Early-1990s. Classic electric copy models including offset double-cut, single-cut and double-cut semi-hollow, 1 to 3 pickups, with or without tremolo. All models begin with H or HG, some models part of Harmony Electric series and others the Harmony Igniter series.

1980-1990s	Various models	$50	$100

H60 Double Cutaway Hollowbody
1970. Thinline double-cut, 2 pickups, trapeze tailpiece, sunburst.

1970		$750	$950

H62 Blond
1950s-1965. Thin body, dual pickup archtop, curly maple back and sides, spruce top, block markers, blond.

1950s		$1,200	$1,500
1960-1965		$1,200	$1,500

MODEL		EXC. COND.	
YEAR	FEATURES	LOW	HIGH

H62VS (Reissue)
2000s. H62 with sunburst finish.
| 2000s | | $800 | $900 |

H64 Double Cutaway Electric
1968-1970. Factory Bigsby, dot markers, sunburst.
| 1968-1970 | | $650 | $800 |

H72/H72V Double Cutaway Hollowbody
1966-1971. Multiple bindings, 2 pickups, cherry red, H72V has Bigsby.
| 1966-1971 | | $550 | $700 |

H73 Double Cutaway Hollowbody
1960s. Double cutaway, 2 pickups.
| 1960s | | $550 | $700 |

H74 Thinline
1964. Thinline, partial cutaway on bass bout, full cutaway on treble bout, 2 pickups.
| 1964 | | $650 | $775 |

H75 Double Cutaway Hollowbody
1963-1970. Three pickups, multi-bound body, 3-part f-holes, block inlays, bolt neck, brown sunburst.
| 1963-1970 | | $700 | $875 |

H76 Double Cutaway Hollowbody
1960-1962. H75 with Bigsby.
| 1960-1962 | | $700 | $875 |

H77 Double Cutaway Hollowbody
1964-1970. Same as H75, but in cherry sunburst.
| 1964-1970 | | $775 | $975 |

H78 Double Cutaway Hollowbody
Late-1960s. H78 with Bigsby.
| 1960s | | $775 | $975 |

H79 Double Cutaway Hollowbody 12-String
1966-1970. Unique slotted headstock, cherry finish.
| 1966-1970 | | $775 | $975 |

H910 Classical
1970s. Beginner guitar, natural.
| 1970s | | $75 | $150 |

H1200 Auditorium Series
1960-1965. Moderately-priced acoustic archtop, treble-cleff artwork on headstock, 3 models; 1213 & 1215 (shaded brown) and 1214 (blond ivory).
| 1960-1965 | H1213, H1215 | $250 | $300 |
| 1960-1965 | H1214 | $375 | $450 |

H1270 12-String Flat-Top
1965. 16" deluxe acoustic 12-string flat-top, spruce top, mahogany sides and back, dot markers.
| 1965 | | $500 | $600 |

H4101 Flat-Top Tenor
1972-1976. Mahogany body, 4-string.
| 1972-1976 | | $350 | $400 |

Holiday Rocket
Mid-1960s. Similar to H59 Rocket III but with push-button controls instead of rotary selector switch, 3 Goldentone pickups, pickup trim rings, Holiday logo on 'guard, higher model than standard Rocket.
| 1960s | | $1,000 | $1,250 |

Hollywood H37
1960-1961. Electric archtop, auditorium size 15.75" body, 1 pickup, 2-tone gold metallic finish, block markers.
| 1960-1961 | | $650 | $800 |

Hollywood H39
1960-1965. Like H37 but with sunburst.
| 1960-1965 | | $500 | $625 |

Hollywood H41
1960-1965. Like H37 but with 2 pickups, sunburst.
| 1960-1965 | | $550 | $675 |

Igniter Series (D/H/HG)
Late-1980s-Early-1990s. Pointy-headstock electric copy models, offset double-cut, all models begin with D, H, or HG.
| 1980-1990s | Various models | $80 | $100 |

Lone Ranger
1950-1951. Lone Ranger headstock stencil, Lone Ranger and Tonto stencil on brown body. This model was first introduced in 1936 as the Supertone Lone Ranger with same stencil on a black body.
| 1950-1951 | | $275 | $350 |

Master H945
1965-1966. 15" (Auditorium) acoustic archtop, block markers, music note painted logo on headstock, sunburst.
| 1965-1966 | | $300 | $350 |

Meteor H70/H71
1958-1966. Single rounded cutaway 2" thin body, 2 pickups, 3-part f-holes, block inlays, bolt neck, H70 sunburst, H71 natural (ended '65), lefty offered '65-'66, reintroduced as H661 and H671 (without Meteor name) in '72-'74.
| 1958-1965 | H71 | $775 | $950 |
| 1958-1966 | H70 | $775 | $950 |

Meteor Single Cutaway
1959. Two pickups, natural.
| 1959 | | $950 | $1,200 |

Monterey H950/H952/H1325/H1456/H1457/H6450
1930s-1974. Line of Auditorium and Grand Auditorium acoustic archtop models.
1950s	H952 Colorama	$350	$450
1950s	Other models	$225	$300
1960s		$225	$300
1970s	H6450	$150	$200

Patrician
1932-1973. Model line mostly with mahogany bodies and alternating single/double dot markers (later models with single dots), introduced as flat-top, changed to archtop in '34. In '37 line expanded to 9 archtops (some with blocks) and 1 flat-top. Flat-tops disappeared in the '40s, with various archtops offered up to '73.
| 1940s-1973 | | $350 | $425 |

Professional H1252 Hawaiian
1940. Hawaiian acoustic jumbo, high-end appointments, vertical Professional logo on front of headstock, figured koa or mahogany back and sides, spruce top, Brazilian rosewood fretboard, various-shaped fretboard markers.
| 1940 | | $2,300 | $2,800 |

Rebel H81
1968-1971. Single pickup version of Rebel, brown sunburst.
| 1968-1971 | | $275 | $350 |

Harmony H75

1966 Harmony Meteor H70

1970 Harmony Sovereign

'50s Harmony Stratotone

MODEL YEAR	FEATURES	EXC. COND. LOW	HIGH

Rebel H82/H82G
Listed as a new model in 1971. Thin body, hollow tone chamber, double-cut, 2 pickups, H82 sunburst, H82G greenburst avacado shading (renumbered as H682 and H683 in '72).

1970s	H82	$450	$550
1970s	H82G	$500	$600

Rocket H53/H54/H56/H59
1959-1973. Single-cut, f-holes, dot inlays, 2-tone brown sunburst ('59-'62) or red sunburst ('63 on), came with 1 pickup (Rocket I H53 '59-'71), 2 pickups (Rocket II H54), Rocket III H59 has 3 pickups, Rocket VII H56 has 2 pickups and vibrato.

1959-1969	1 pickup	$425	$500
1959-1969	2 pickups	$650	$900
1959-1969	3 pickups	$900	$1,150
1970-1973	1 pickup	$300	$400
1970-1973	2 pickups	$400	$600
1970-1973	3 pickups	$650	$800

Roy Rogers H600
1954-1958. 3/4 size, stencil, sold through Sears.

1954-1958		$250	$325

Roy Smeck
1963-1964. Electric hollowbody archtop, Roy Smeck logo on headstock or upper bass bout, single neck position silver bar-style pickup or 2 Harmony pickups, standard 4 knobs and toggle, pickup without poles.

1963-1964		$700	$850

Roy Smeck Artiste
1930s-1940s. Large-body acoustic archtop, old style Harmony script logo on headstock, block letter Roy Smeck Artiste logo on headstock, split rectangle markers, small button tuners, black finish with white guard.

1930-1940s		$550	$675

Silhouette De Luxe Double H19
1965-1969. Double-cut solidbody, deluxe pickups, block markers, advanced vibrato, sunburst.

1965-1969		$400	$500

Silhouette H14/H15/H17
1964-1967. Double-cut solidbody, H14 single pickup, H15 dual pickup, H17 dual with vibrato (offered until '66).

1965-1966	H17	$375	$450
1965-1967	H14	$250	$300
1965-1967	H15	$350	$425

Singing Cowboys H1057
1950s. Western chuck-wagon scene stencil top, Singing Cowboys stenciled on either side of upper bouts, brown background versus earlier Supertone version that had black background.

1950s		$275	$350

Sovereign Jumbo Deluxe H1266
1960s-1970s. Jumbo nearly D-style, 16" wide body with out-size 'guard, natural.

1960s		$500	$575
1970s		$475	$550

Sovereign Jumbo H1260
1960s-1970s. Jumbo shape, 16" wide body, natural.

1960s		$475	$575
1970s		$425	$500

Sovereign Western Special Jumbo H1203
1960s-1970s. 15" wide body, 000-style.

1960s		$525	$600

Stratotone Deluxe Jupiter H49
1958-1965. Single-cut, tone chamber construction, 2 pickups, bound spruce top, curly maple back and 6 control knobs, blond finish.

1958-1965		$800	$1,000

Stratotone H44
1954-1957. First edition models had small bodies and rounded cutaway, 1 pickup with plain cover using 2 mounting rivets, sometimes called Hershey Bar pickup, '60s models had slightly larger bodies and sharp cutaways, some with headstock logo Harmony Stratotone with atomic note graphic.

1954-1957		$1,000	$1,200

Stratotone H88
1954-1957. Small body, 2 pickups.

1954-1957		$1,200	$1,400

Stratotone Mars Electric H45/H46
1958-1968. Single-cut, tone chamber construction, sunburst finish, H45 with 1 pickup, H46 with 2 pickups.

1960s	H45	$425	$525
1960s	H46	$450	$550

Stratotone Mercury Electric H47/H48
1958-1968. Single-cut, tone chamber construction, H47 with 1 pickup, block inlay and curly maple sunburst top, H48 is the same with a blond top.

1960s	H47	$600	$750
1960s	H48	$650	$800

TG1201 Tenor
1950s. Spruce top, two-on-a-side tuners, Sovereign model tenor, natural.

1950s		$300	$350

Vibra-Jet H66
1962-1966. Thinline single-cut, 2 pickups, built-in tremolo circuit and control panel knobs and selection dial, sunburst.

1962-1966		$650	$800

Harptone
1893-ca. 1975. The Harptone Manufacturing Corporation was located in Newark, New Jersey. They made musical instrument cases and accessories and got into instrument production from 1934 to '42, making guitars, banjos, mandolins, and tiples. In '66 they got back into guitar production, making the Standel line from '67 to '69. Harptone offered flat-tops and archtops under their own brand until the mid-'70s when the name was sold to the Diamond S company, which owned Micro-Frets.

Acoustic
1966-mid-1970s. Various models.

1966-1970s	Common models	$1,050	$1,300
1966-1970s	Fancy models	$1,500	$1,800

Electric
1966-mid-1970s. Various models.

1966-1970s		$1,400	$1,750

MODEL		EXC. COND.	
YEAR	FEATURES	LOW	HIGH

Harrison Guitars

1992-present. Luthier Douglas Harrison builds premium grade, production/custom, archtop and semi-hollowbody jazz guitars in Toronto, Ontario.

Harwood

Harwood was a brand introduced in 1885 by Kansas City, Missouri instrument wholesalers J.W. Jenkins & Sons (though some guitars marked Harwood, New York). May have been built by Jenkins until circa 1905, but work was later contracted out to Harmony.

Parlor

1890s. Slotted headstocks, most had mahogany bodies, some with Brazilian rosewood body, considered to be well made.

1890s	Brazilian rosewood	$1,000	$1,250
1890s	Mahogany	$500	$625

Hascal Haile

Late 1960s-1986. Luthier Hascal Haile started building acoustic, classical and solidbody guitars in Tompkinsville, Kentucky, after retiring from furniture making. He died in '86.

Hauver Guitar

2001-present. Professional and premium grade, custom, acoustic guitars, built in Sharpsburg, Maryland by luthier Michael S. Hauver.

Hayes Guitars

1993-present. Professional and premium grade, production/custom, steel and nylon string guitars made by luthier Louis Hayes in Paonia, Colorado.

Hayman

1970-1973. Solid and semi-hollowbody guitars and basses developed by Jim Burns and Bob Pearson for Ivor Arbiter of the Dallas Arbiter Company and built by Shergold in England.

Haynes

1865-early 1900s. The John C. Haynes Co. of Boston also made the Bay State brand.

Heartfield

1989-1994. Founded as a joint venture between Fender Musical Instrument Corporation (U.S.A.) and Fender Japan (partnership between Fender and distributors Kanda Shokai and Yamano Music) to build and market more advanced designs (built by Fuji Gen-Gakki). First RR and EX guitar series and DR Bass series debut in '90. Talon and Elan guitar series and Prophecy bass series introduced in '91. The brand was dead by '94.

Elan

1989-1994. Carved-style bound double-cut body, flamed top, 2 humbuckers, offset headstock.

1989-1994		$450	$550

EX/EX II

1990-1994. 3 single-coils, Floyd Rose tremolo.

1990-1994		$450	$550

Talon

1989-1994. Offset double-cut, wedge-triangle headstock, dot markers, hum/single/hum pickups.

1989-1994	I, II, III	$300	$450
1989-1994	IV	$450	$550

Heiden Stringed Instruments

1974-present. Luthier Michael Heiden builds his premium grade, production/custom, flat-top guitars in Chilliwack, British Columbia. He also builds mandolins.

Heit Deluxe

Ca. 1967-1970. Imported from Japan by unidentified New York distributor. Many were made by Teisco, the most famous being the Teisco V-2 Mosrite copy. They also had basses.

Acoustic Archtop

1967-1970. Various models.

1967-1970		$125	$200

Electric Solidbody

1967-1970. Various models.

1967-1970		$150	$350

Electric Thinline Hollowbody

1967-1970. Various models.

1967-1970		$200	$350

Hembry Guitars

2002-present. Professional grade, production/custom, solidbody electric guitars built by luthier Scott Hembry in Shelton, Washington. He also builds basses.

Hemken, Michael

1993-present. Luthier Michael Hemken builds his premium grade, custom, archtops in St. Helena, California.

HenBev

2005-present. Premium grade, production, solid and hollow body electric guitars built by luthier Scotty Bevilacqua in Oceanside, California. He also builds basses.

Henman Guitars

2010-present. Owners Graham and Paris Henman offer premium grade, production/custom, solidbody and chambered electric guitars built by luthier Rick Turner in Santa Cruz, California. They also offer basses.

Heritage

1985-present. Professional, premium, and presentation grade, production/custom, hollow, semi-hollow, and solidbody guitars built in Kalamazoo, Michigan. They have also made banjos, mandolins, flat-tops, and basses in the past.

Founded by Jim Deurloo, Marvin Lamb, J.P. Moats, Bill Paige and Mike Korpak, all former Gibson employees who did not go to Nashville

Ca. 1971 Harptone E-6N Eagle

HenBev S2

Heritage H-140

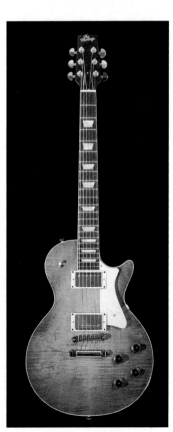

Heritage H-150

MODEL YEAR	FEATURES	EXC. COND. LOW	HIGH

when Norlin closed the original Gibson factory in '84. In 2007, Vince Margol bought out Paige.

Eagle
1986-2009. Single rounded cut semi-hollowbody, mahogany body and neck, bound body, 1 jazz pickup, f-holes, sunburst or natural.

1986-1999		$1,600	$1,900
2000-2009		$1,600	$1,900

Eagle Classic
1992-present. Eagle with maple body and neck, bound neck and headstock, gold hardware.

1993		$2,100	$2,500

Gary Moore Model
1989-1991. Single-cut solidbody, 2 pickups, chrome hardware, sunburst.

1989-1991		$1,500	$1,800

Golden Eagle
1985-present. Single-cut hollowbody, back inlaid with mother-of-pearl eagle and registration number, multi-bound ebony 'board with mother-of-pearl cloud inlays, bound f-holes, gold-plated parts, ebony bridge inlaid with mother-of-pearl, mother-of-pearl truss rod cover engraved with owner's name, 1 Heritage jazz pickup, multi-bound curly maple 'guard.

1985-1999		$2,400	$2,900
2000-2010		$2,600	$3,100

H-137
1980s-present. Single-cut solidbody, 2 P-90s, sunburst.

1980s-10	Sunburst	$800	$1,000
2008	Natural Lime	$900	$1,100

H-140/H-140 CM
1985-2005, 2007-present. Single pointed cutaway solidbody, bound curly maple ('85-'04) or solid gold top ('94-'05), 2 humbuckers, chrome parts.

1985-1904	CM, curly maple	$900	$1,100
1994-1905	Goldtop	$900	$1,100
2001	Black	$800	$900
2001	CM, flamed maple	$900	$1,100
2007-2010	2nd edition, goldtop	$900	$1,100

H-147
1990-1991. Single-cut solidbody, 2 humbuckers, mahogany body, mother-of-pearl block inlays, black with black or gold hardware.

1990-1991		$625	$800

H-150 C/H-150 CM
1985-present. Single rounded cutaway solidbody, curly maple top, 2 pickups, chrome parts, cherry sunburst.

1985-2010		$1,000	$1,250
1985-2010	Goldtop	$1,200	$1,500
1985-2010	Highly flamed	$1,300	$1,600

H-150 Deluxe Limited Edition
1992. 300 made.

1992		$1,300	$1,550

H-157 Ultra
1993-1994. Single-cut solidbody, large block markers, highly figured maple top.

1993-1994		$1,000	$1,250

MODEL YEAR	FEATURES	EXC. COND. LOW	HIGH

H-160
1986, 2007. Limited production.

1986		$700	$900
2007	2nd Edition	$800	$1,000

H-170
1980s. Double-cut solidbody, 2 humbuckers, bound carved top, was also a later curly maple top version (H-170CM).

1980s		$900	$1,000

H-204 DD
1986-1989. Single-cut solidbody of mahogany, curly maple top, 1-piece mahogany neck, 22-fret rosewood 'board.

1986-1989		$500	$625

H-207 DD
1986-1989. Double-cut solidbody of mahogany, curly maple top, 1-piece mahogany neck, 22-fret rosewood 'board.

1986-1989		$500	$625

H-357
1989-1994. Asymmetrical solidbody, neck-thru.

1989-1994		$1,750	$2,100

H-535
1987-present. Double-cut semi-hollowbody archtop, rosewood 'board, 2 humbucker pickups.

1987-1999		$1,300	$1,500
1987-1999	Flamed maple top	$1,300	$1,500
2000-2010		$1,300	$1,500

H-537
1990. Single-cut, thinline, dots.

1990		$1,150	$1,400

H-550
1990-present. Single-cut hollowbody, laminated maple top and back, multiple bound top, white bound 'guard, f-holes, 2 humbuckers.

1990-2010		$1,500	$1,825

H-555
1989-present. Like 535, but with maple neck, ebony 'board, pearl and abalone inlays, gold hardware.

1989-2010		$1,650	$2,000

H-575
1987-present. Single sharp cut hollowbody, solid maple top and back, cream bound top and back, wood 'guard, f-holes, 2 humbuckers.

1987-1989		$1,500	$1,850
1990-1999		$1,500	$1,850
2000-2010		$1,500	$1,850

H-576
1990-2004. Single rounded cut hollowbody, laminated maple top and back, multiple bound top, single bound back and f-holes and wood 'guard, 2 humbuckers.

1990-2004		$1,100	$1,375

Henry Johnson Signature
2005-present. Pointed single cut curly maple back and sides hollowbody, 2 humbuckers, block inlays, multi-bound.

2005-2010		$1,275	$1,600

HFT-445
1987-2000. Flat-top acoustic, mahogany back and sides, spruce top, maple neck, rosewood 'board.

1987-2000		$650	$775

MODEL		EXC. COND.	
YEAR	FEATURES	LOW	HIGH

Johnny Smith

1989-2001. Custom hand-carved 17" hollowbody, single-cut, f-holes, 1 pickup.

1989-2001	Optional colors	$2,500	$3,100
1989-2001	Sunburst	$2,300	$2,800

Kenny Burrell KB Groovemaster

2004-present. Single-cut 16" hollow body, 1 humbucker, gold hardware, block inlays.

2004-2010		$1,600	$2,000

Millennium Eagle 2000

2000-2009. Single-cut semi-solidbody, multiple bound curly maple top, single-bound curly maple back, f-holes, 2 humbuckers, block inlays.

2000-2009		$1,600	$2,000

Millennium Eagle Custom

2000-2009. Like ME 2000 but with curlier maple, multiple bound neck, split block inlays.

2000-2009		$2,000	$2,500

Millennium SAE

2000-2009. Single-cut semi-solidbody, laminated arch top, single cream bound top and back, f-holes, 2 humbuckers.

2000-2009		$1,000	$1,250

Millennium Standard Ultra

2004-present. Single-cut, ultra curly maple top, mahogany back and sides, 1-piece mahogany neck, f-holes, mother of pearl block inlays.

2004-2010		$1,300	$1,600

Parsons Street

1989-1992. Offset double-cut, curly maple top on mahogany body, single/single/hum pickups, pearl block markers, sunburst or natural.

1989-1992		$750	$900

Roy Clark

1992-present. Thinline, single-cut semi-hollow archtop, gold hardware, 2 humbuckers, block markers, cherry sunburst.

1992-2010		$1,500	$1,800

SAE Custom

1992-2000. Single-cut maple semi-hollowbody, f-holes, 2 humbuckers and 1 bridge pickup.

1992-2000		$1,000	$1,200

Super Eagle

1988-present. 18" body, single-cut electric archtop, 2 humbuckers.

1989-2010		$2,700	$3,300

Sweet 16

1987-present. Single-cut maple semi-hollowbody, spruce top, 2 pickups, pearl inlays.

1987-2010		$2,000	$2,500

Hermann Hauser

Born in 1882, Hauser started out building zithers and at age 23 added classical guitars and lutes, most built in his shop in Munich, Germany. He died in 1952. His son and grandson and great-granddaughter, Hermann II and III and Kathrin, continued the tradition. The Hermann Hauser's legacy is based on his innovative approach to bracing and top thickness which gave his instruments their own voice. Hermann I Era instruments are linked with

Andres Segovia who used them. Hermann II Era instruments are linked with modern players like Julian Bream. Hermann III builds Segovia style and custom-made instruments. Kathrin Hauser, daughter of Hermann III, is a fourth generation builder. The original Hauser shop in Munich was destroyed by Allied bombing in 1946 and was moved to Reisbach in the Bavaria region, where the shop remains. Hauser instruments used paper labels on the inside back. The labels often stipulate the city of construction as well as the Hermann Hauser name. Labels are easily removed and changed, and an original instrument should be authenticated. Beautiful violin-like clear varnish finish ends in '52, approximately 400 instruments were made by Hermann I. Under Hermann II, nitrocellulose lacquer spray replaces varnish in '52, bracing patterns change in the '60s, which was a welcome change for modern players. Instruments should be evaluated on a case by case basis.

Hermann Hauser II

1952-1988. Born in 1911 and the son of Hermann Hauser I, he built between 500 and 600 classical guitars in Germany during his career. He died in 1988.

Hermann Hauser III

1988-present. Hermann III started build guitars in '74, and took over the family business upon the death of his father in '88. He continues to build Segovia style and custom-made classical guitars in Munich, Germany.

Hess

1872-ca. 1940. Located in Klingenthal, Germany, Hess built acoustic and harp guitars, as well as other stringed instruments and accordians.

Hewett Guitars

1994-present. Luthier James Hewett builds his professional and premium grade, custom/production, steel string, archtop jazz, solidbody and harp guitars in Panorama Village, Texas.

Hill Guitar Company

1972-1980, 1990-present. Luthier Kenny Hill builds his professional and premium grade production/custom, classical and flamenco guitars in Felton, California and Michoacan, Mexico.

Hirade Classical

1968-present. Professional grade, production, solid top, classical guitars built in Japan by Takamine. The late Mass Hirade was the founder of the Takamine workshop. He learned his craft from master luthier Masare Kohno. Hirade represents Takamine's finest craftsmanship and material.

HML Guitars

1997-present. Howard Leese custom-designs premium grade, electric guitars, which are built by luthier Jack Pimentel in Puyallup, Washington.

2009 Heritage HJ Henry Johnson Signature

HML Guitars

To get the most from this book, be sure to read "Using *The Guide*" in the introduction.

GUITARS

Hoffman Jumbo

Höfner Verythin

MODEL YEAR	FEATURES	EXC. COND. LOW	HIGH

Hoffman Guitars

1971-present. Premium grade, custom flat-tops and harp guitars built by luthier Charles Hoffman in Minneapolis, Minnesota.

Höfner

1887-present. Budget, intermediate, professional and premium grade, production, solidbody, semi-hollow, archtop, acoustic, and classical guitars built in Germany and the Far East. They also produce basses and bowed-instruments. Founded by Karl Höfner in Schonbach, Germany. The company was already producing guitars when sons Josef and Walter joined the company in 1919 and '21 and expanded the market worldwide. They moved the company to Bavaria in '50 and to Hagenau in '97.

Beatle Electric Model 459TZ
1966-1967. Violin-shaped 500/1 body, block-stripe position markers, transistor-powered flip-fuzz and treble boost, sunburst.

1966-1967		$1,700	$2,100

Beatle Electric Model 459VTZ
1966-1967. Same as Model 459TZ except with vibrato tailpiece, brown (standard) or blond option.

1966-1967	Blond option	$2,000	$2,500
1966-1967	Brown	$1,800	$2,200

Beatle Electric Model G459TZ Super
1966-1967. Deluxe version of Model 459TZ, flamed maple sides, narrow grain spruce top, gold hardware, elaborate inlays and binding, natural blond.

1966-1967		$1,800	$2,200

Beatle Electric Model G459VTZ Super
1966-1967. Same as G459TZ Super but with vibrato tailpiece.

1966-1967		$1,800	$2,300

Club Model 50
1959-1962. Mid-level of the late '50s 'Club Series', single-cut, 2 pickups, sunburst.

1959-1962		$1,500	$1,900

Club Model 60
1959. Highest model of late '50s 'Club Series', single-cut, 2 black bar pickups, 2 knobs and 2 slider switches on control panel, highest-end split-diamond style markers, natural blond finish.

1959		$1,700	$2,100

Club Model 126
1954-1970. Mid-sized single-cut solidbody, dot markers, flamed maple back and sides, spruce top, sunburst. Listed with Hofner Professional Electric Series.

1954-1958		$825	$950

Committee Model 4680 Thin Electric
1961-1968. Thinline single-cut archtop, 2 pickups, split-arrowhead markers, no vibrato, sunburst.

1961-1968		$1,200	$1,500

Deluxe Model 176
1964-1983. Double-cut, 3 pickups, polyester varnished sunburst finish, vibrola tailpiece, similar to Model 175 polyester varnished red and gold version.

1964-1969		$550	$700
1970-1983		$450	$575

Galaxy Model 175
1963-1966. Double-cut, 3 pickups, red and gold vinyl covering, fancy red-patch 'guard, vibrola, similar to Model 176 polyester varnished sunburst version.

1963-1966	Red & gold vinyl	$900	$1,100
1963-1966	Sunburst	$800	$1,000

Golden Hofner
1959-1963. Single-cut archtop, blond, 2 pickups, f-holes.

1959-1963		$7,000	$8,500

Jazzica Custom
2000-2010. Full body, single soft cutaway, acoustic/electric archtop, carved German spruce top, sunburst.

2000-2010		$1,600	$1,900

Model 165
1975-1976. Offset double-cut, S-style body, 2 single-coil pickups, bolt-on neck.

1975-1976		$500	$625

Model 171
1975-1976. Copy of Tele-Thinline.

1975-1976		$325	$400

Model 172 II (R) (S) (I)
1962-1963. Double-cut body, polyester varnished wood (S) or scuff-proof red (R) or white (I) vinyl, 2 pickups, vibrato.

1962-1963		$400	$500

Model 173 II (S) (I)
1962-1963. Double-cut body, polyester varnished wood (S) or scuffproof vinyl (I), 3 pickups, vibrato.

1962-1963	Gold foil vinyl	$550	$675
1962-1963	White vinyl	$550	$675

Model 178
1967-ca. 1969. Offset double-cut solidbody, 2 pickups with an array of switches and push button controls, fancy position markers, vibrola, sunburst. 178 used on different design in the '70s.

1967-1969		$550	$675

Model 180 Shorty Standard
1982. Small-bodied travel guitar, single-cut, solidbody, 1 pickup, travel, the Shorty Super had a built-in amp and speaker.

1982		$300	$350

Model 450S Acoustic Archtop
Mid-1960s. Economy single-cut acoustic archtop in Hofner line, dot markers, Hofner logo on 'guard, sunburst.

1960s		$500	$625

Model 455/S
1950s-1970. Archtop, single-cut, block markers.

1959		$650	$800

Model 456 Acoustic Archtop
1950s. Full body acoustic archtop, f-holes, laminated maple top, sides, back, large pearloid blocks, two color pearloid headstock laminate.

1950s		$675	$825

Model 457 President
1959-1972. Single-cut thinline archtop, 2 pickups, non-vibrato.

1959-1972		$700	$1,000

MODEL		EXC. COND.	
YEAR	FEATURES	LOW	HIGH

Model 457/12 12-String Electric
1969-1970. Comfort-thin cutaway archtop, shaded brown.
1969-1970 | $575 | $700

Model 462S Acoustic Archtop
1950s. Similar to Model 456 except cutaway, natural, 1, 2 or 3 pickups.
1950s | $550 | $675

Model 463
1950s. Archtop electric, 2 or 3 pickups.
1950s | $1,000 | $1,250

Model 470SE2 Electric Archtop
1961-1994. Large single rounded cutaway electric archtop on Hofner's higher-end they call "superbly flamed maple (back and sides), carved top of best spruce," 2 pickups, 3 control knobs, gold hardware, pearl inlay, natural finish only.
1961-1994 | $900 | $1,100

Model 471SE2 Electric Archtop
1969-1977. Large single pointed cutaway electric archtop, flamed maple back and sides, spruce top, black celluloid binding, ebony 'board, pearl inlays, sunburst version of the 470SE2.
1969-1977 | $900 | $1,100

Model 490 Acoustic
Late 1960s. 16" body, 12-string, spruce top, maple back and sides, dot markers, natural.
1960s | $250 | $300

Model 490E Acoustic Electric
Late 1960s. Flat-top 12-string with on-board pickup and 2 control knobs.
1960s | $350 | $425

Model 491 Flat-Top
1960s-1970s. Slope shoulder body style, spruce top, mahogany back and sides, shaded sunburst.
1970s | $350 | $425

Model 492 Acoustic
Late 1960s. 16" body, 12-string, spruce top, mahogany back and sides, dot markers.
1960s | $325 | $375

Model 492E Acoustic Electric
Late 1960s. Flat-top 12-string with on-board pickup and 2 control knobs.
1960s | $325 | $375

Model 496 Jumbo Flat-Top
1960s. Jumbo-style body, selected spruce top, flamed maple back and sides, gold-plated hardware, vine pattern 'guard, sunburst.
1960s | $800 | $1,000

Model 514-H Classical Concert
1960s. Concert model, lower-end of the Hofner classical line, natural.
1960s | $150 | $225

Model 4500 Thin Electric
Late-1960s-early-1970s. Thinline archtop, single-cut, 3 options, laminated maple top and back, dot markers, top mounted controls, brown sunburst.
1960-1970s E1, 1 pickup | $600 | $700
1960-1970s E2, 2 pickups | $750 | $850
1960-1970s V2, 2 pickups, vibrato | $775 | $875

Model 4560 Thin Electric
Late-1960s-early-1970s. Thinline archtop, single-cut, 2 options, laminated maple top and back, 2-color headstock, large block markers, top mounted controls, brown sunburst.
1960-1970s E2 | $800 | $900
1960-1970s V2, vibrato | $825 | $925

Model 4574VTZ Extra Thin
Late-1960s-early-1970s. Extra thinline acoustic, 2 pickups.
1960-1970s | $825 | $925

Model 4575VTZ Extra Thin
Late-1960s-early-1970s. Extra-thinline acoustic, double-cut with shallow rounded horns, 3 pickups, vibrato arm, treble boost and flip-fuzz, straight-line markers.
1960-1970s | $900 | $1,025

Model 4578TZ President
1959-1970. Double-cut archtop. 'President' dropped from name by late-'60s and renamed Model 4578 Dual Cutaway, also added sharp horns.
1959-1965 | $850 | $1,000
1966-1970 | $750 | $900

Model 4600 Thin Electric
Late-1960s-early-1970s. Thinline acoustic, double-cut, 2 pickups, dot markers, sunburst, V2 with vibrato.
1960-1970s E2 | $750 | $850
1960-1970s V2, vibrato | $775 | $875

Model 4680 Thin Electric
Late-1960s-early-1970s. Single-cut thinline electric, 2 pickups, 3-in-a-line control knobs, ornate inlays, spruce top, brown sunburst, V2 with vibrato.
1960-1970s E2 | $1,100 | $1,350
1960-1970s V2, vibrato | $1,200 | $1,450

Model 4700 Thin Electric
Late-1960s-early-1970s. Deluxe version of Model 4680, gold plated appointments and natural finish, V2 with vibrato.
1960-1970s E2 | $1,300 | $1,600
1960-1970s V2, vibrato | $1,400 | $1,700

Senator Acoustic Archtop
1958-1960s. Floating pickup option available, full body archtop, f-holes, made for Selmer, London.
1958-1960 | $500 | $600

Senator E1
1961. Senator full body archtop with single top mounted pickup and controls.
1961 | $750 | $900

Verythin Standard
2001-2008. Update of the 1960s Verythin line, 2 humbuckers, f-holes, dot inlays.
2001-2008 | $900 | $1,050

Hohner

1857-present. Budget and intermediate grade, production, acoustic and electric guitars. They also have basses, mandolins, banjos and ukuleles. Matthias Hohner, a clockmaker in Trossingen, Germany, founded Hohner in 1857, making harmonicas. Hohner has been offering guitars and basses at least since the early '70s. HSS was founded in 1986 as a

Höfner Verythin Custom

Hohner G 3T Headless

1980s Hohner GT 76

Hopkins Marquis

MODEL YEAR	FEATURES	EXC. COND. LOW	HIGH

distributor of guitars and other musical products. By 2000, Hohner was also offering the Crafter brands of guitars.

Alpha Standard
1987. Designed by Klaus Scholler, solidbody, stereo outputs, Flytune tremolo.

1987		$175	$200

G 2T/G 3T Series
1980s-1990s. Steinberger-style body, 6-string, neck-thru, locking tremolo.

| 1980-1990s | | $200 | $300 |

Jacaranda Rosewood Dreadnought
1978. Flat-top acoustic.

| 1978 | | $150 | $200 |

Jack
1987-1990s. Mate for Jack Bass. Headless, tone circuit, tremolo, 2 single-coils and 1 humbucker.

| 1987-1992 | | $175 | $200 |

L 59/L 75 Series
Late-1970s-1980s. Classic single-cut solidbody, 2 humbuckers, glued neck, sunburst, 59 has upgrade maple body with maple veneer top.

| 1970s | | $250 | $275 |

Miller Beer Guitar
1985. Solidbody, shaped like Miller beer logo.

| 1985 | | $250 | $275 |

Professional
1980s. Single-cut solidbody, maple neck, extra large 'guard, natural.

| 1980s | | $225 | $250 |

Professional Series - TE Custom
1980s-1990s. Single-cut solidbody, bolt neck.

| 1980-1990s | | $700 | $850 |

Professional Series - TE Prinz
Late 1980s-early 1990s. Based on Prince's No. 1 guitar, 2 single-coils, bolt neck, Professional The Prinz headstock logo, natural.

| 1989-1990 | | $700 | $850 |

SE 35
1989-mid-1990s. Semi-hollow thinline, 2 humbuckers, natural.

| 1989 | | $300 | $375 |

SG Lion
1980s-1990s. Offset double-cut, pointy headstock, glued neck.

| 1980-1990s | | $200 | $225 |

ST Series
1986-1990s. Includes the bolt neck ST 57, ST Special, ST Special S, Viper I, Viper II (snakeskin finish option), ST Victory, ST Metal S, and the ST Custom.

| 1986-1992 | | $150 | $200 |

Standard Series - EX Artist
1970s-1980s. Solidbody, 2 humbuckers, gold hardware, neck-thru, solid maple body, rosewood 'board, tremolo.

| 1970-1980s | | $200 | $225 |

Standard Series - RR Custom
1970s-1980s. Randy Rhoads V body, 2 humbuckers, chrome hardware, glued neck, mahogany body, rosewood 'board, tremolo.

| 1970-1980s | | $200 | $225 |

Standard Series - SR Heavy
1970s-1980s. Hybrid body, 2 humbuckers, neck-thru, solid maple body, rosewood 'board, tremolo.

| 1970-1980s | | $200 | $225 |

Holiday
1960s. Student-level, private-branded similar to Stella but may have solid tops.

Silhouette Bobcat
1964-1967. Private branded solidbody electric made by Harmony, similar to Harmony Silhouette, offset double-cut, 2 pickups, toggle switch, 4-in-a-row control knobs, 6-on-a-side tuner.

| 1964-1967 | | $350 | $400 |

Hollenbeck Guitars
1970-2008. Luthier Bill Hollenbeck built his premium grade, production/custom, hollow and semi-hollow body acoustics and electric guitars in Lincoln, Illinois. Bill passed away in '08.

Hollingworth Guitars
1995-present. Luthier Graham Hollingworth builds his production/custom, premium grade, electric, acoustic and archtop guitars in Mermaid Beach, Gold Coast, Queensland, Australia. He also builds lap steels.

Holman
1966-1968. Built by the Holman-Woodell guitar factory in Neodesha, Kansas. The factory was started to build guitars for Wurlitzer, but that fell through by '67.

Holst
1984-present. Premium grade, custom, archtop, flat top, semi-hollow, and classical guitars built in Creswell, Oregon by luthier Stephen Holst. He also builds mandolins. Until '01 he was located in Eugene, Oregon.

Hondo
1969-1987, 1991-2005. Budget grade, production, imported acoustic, classical and electric guitars. They also offered basses, banjos and mandolins. Originally imported by International Music Corporation (IMC) of Fort Worth, Texas, founded by Jerry Freed and Tommy Moore and named after a small town near San Antonio, Texas. Early pioneers of Korean guitarmaking, primarily targeted at beginner market. Introduced their first electrics in '72. Changed brand to Hondo II in '74. Some better Hondos made in Japan '74-'82/'83. In '85 IMC purchases major interest in Jackson/Charvel, and the Hondo line was supplanted by Charvels. 1987 was the last catalog before hiatus. In '88 IMC was sold and Freed began Jerry Freed International and in '91 he revived the Hondo name. Acquired by MBT International in '95, currently part of Musicorp.

MODEL YEAR	FEATURES	EXC. COND. LOW	HIGH

Acoustic Flat-Top
1969-1987, 1991-present.
| 1970s | | $50 | $125 |

Electric Hollowbody
1969-1987, 1991-present.
| 1980s | | $150 | $550 |

Electric Solidbody
1969-1987, 1991-present.
1969-1987		$150	$550
1991-1999		$150	$250
2000-2010		$50	$150

Longhorn 6/12 Doubleneck Copy
1970s-1980s. Copy of Danelectro Longhorn 6/12 Doubleneck guitar, Dano coke bottle-style headstock, white sunburst.
| 1980s | | $700 | $875 |

Longhorn Copy
Ca. 1978-1980s. Copy of Danelectro Long Horn guitar, Dano Coke bottle-style headstock, brown-copper.
| 1970s | | $475 | $575 |

M 16 Rambo-Machine Gun
1970s-1980s. Machine gun body-style, matching machine gun-shaped guitar case, black or red. Price includes original case which is long and slender and has form-fit interior, an instrument without the case is worth as much as 40% less.
| 1970-1980s | | $375 | $450 |

Hopf
1906-present. Intermediate, professional, premium, and presentation grade, production/custom, classical guitars made in Germany. They also make basses, mandolins and flutes.

The Hopf family of Germany has a tradition of instrument building going back to 1669, but the modern company was founded in 1906. Hopf started making electric guitars in the mid-'50s. Some Hopf models were made by others for the company. By the late-'70s, Hopf had discontinued making electrics, concentrating on classicals.

Explorer Standard
1960s. Double-cut semi-hollow, sharp horns, center block, 2 mini-humbuckers.
| 1960s | | $475 | $600 |

Saturn Archtop
1960s. Offset cutaway, archtop-style soundholes, 2 pickups, white, says Saturn on headstock.
| 1960s | | $600 | $750 |

Super Deluxe Archtop
1960s. Archtop, 16 3/4", catseye soundholes, carved spruce top, flamed maple back and sides, sunburst.
| 1960s | | $625 | $775 |

Hopkins
1998-present. Luthier Peter Hopkins builds his presentation grade, custom, hand-carved archtop guitars in British Columbia.

Horabe
Classical and Espana models made in Japan.

Classical
| 1960-1980s Various models | | $250 | $600 |

Hottie
2005-present. In '09, amp builders Jean-Claude Escudie and Mike Bernards added production/custom, professional and premium grade, solid-body electric guitars built by luthier Saul Koll in Portland, Oregon.

House Guitars
2004-present. Luthier Joshua House builds his production/custom, premium grade, acoustic guitars and guitar-bouzoukis in Goderich, Ontario.

Howe-Orme
1897-ca. 1910. Elias Howe and George Orme's Boston-based publishing and distribution buisness offered a variety of mandolin family instruments and guitars and received many patents for their designs. Many of their guitars featured detachable necks.

Hoyer
1874-present. Intermediate grade, production, flat-top, classical, electric, and resonator guitars. They also build basses. Founded by Franz Hoyer, building classical guitars and other instruments. His son, Arnold, added archtops in the late-1940s, and solidbodies in the '60s. In '67, Arnold's son, Walter, took over, leaving the company in '77. The company changed hands a few times over the following years. Walter started building guitars again in '84 under the W.A. Hoyer brand, which is not associated with Hoyer.

Acoustic
1960s. Acoustic archtop or flat-top.
| 1960s | | $200 | $300 |

Junior
Early-1960s. Solidbody with unusual sharp horn cutaway, single neck pickup, bolt-on neck, dot markers, Arnold Hoyer logo on headstock, shaded sunburst.
| 1960s | | $400 | $500 |

Soloist Electric
1960-1962. Single-cut archtop, 2 pickups, teardrop f-holes, sunburst.
| 1960-1962 | | $500 | $625 |

Huerga
1995-present. Professional to presentation grade, production/custom, archtop, flat-top, and metal-front solidbody electric guitars built by luthier Diego Huerga in Buenos Aires, Argentina.

Humming Bird
1947-ca.1968. Japanese manufacturer. By 1968 making pointy Mosrite inspirations. Probably not imported into the U.S.

Electric Solidbody
| 1950s | | $125 | $225 |

Hottie 454

Huerga Belleza

GUITARS

Huss and Dalton 00

Ibanez AEL50SERLV

MODEL YEAR	FEATURES	EXC. COND. LOW	HIGH

Humphrey, Thomas

1970-2008. Premium and presentation grade, custom, nylon-string guitars built by luthier Thomas Humphrey in Gardiner, New York. In 1996 Humphrey began collaborating with Martin Guitars, resulting in the Martin C-TSH and C-1R. Often the inside back label will indicate the year of manufacture. Humphrey died in April, 2008.

Classical

1976-1984. Brazilian or Indian rosewood back and sides, spruce top, traditionally-based designs evolved over time with Millenium becoming a benchmark design in 1985, values can increase with new designs. Valuations depend on each specific instrument and year and type of construction, price ranges are guidance only; each instrument should be evaluated on a case-by-case basis.

1976-1984		$5,700	$6,800

Millennium (Classical)

1985-2008. Professional performance-grade high-end classical guitar with innovative taper body design and elevated 'board, tops are generally spruce (versus cedar) with rosewood back and sides.

1995-2008		$9,700	$11,700

Steel String

1974. D-style, only 4 made.

1974		$3,500	$4,000

Huss and Dalton Guitar Company

1995-present. Luthiers Jeff Huss and Mark Dalton build their professional and premium grade flat-tops and banjos in Staunton, Virginia.

Hutchins

2006-present. Gary Hutchins in Sussex, U.K. imports intermediate and professional grade, production, acoustic and electric guitars from China, Germany and Korea. He also offers basses.

Ian A. Guitars

1991-present. In the early 1990s luthier Ian Anderson built guitars under his name, in 2005 he began using the Ian A. brand. He builds premium grade, production/custom, solidbody electric guitars in Poway, California.

Ian Anderson Guitars

See listing under Ian A. Guitars.

Ibanez

1932-present. Budget, intermediate, and professional grade, production/custom, acoustic and electric guitars. They also make basses, amps, mandolins, and effects.

Founded in Nagoya, Japan, by Matsujiro Hoshino as book and stationary supply, started retailing musical instruments in 1909. He began importing instruments in '21. His son Yoshitaro became president in '27 and began exporting. Manufacturing of Ibanez instruments began in '32. The company's

factories were destroyed during World War II, but the business was revived in '50. Junpei Hoshino, grandson of founder, became president in '60; a new factory opened called Tama Seisakusho (Tama Industries). Brand names by '64 included Ibanez, Star, King's Stone, Jamboree and Goldentone, supplied by 85 factories serving global markets. Sold acoustic guitars to Harry Rosenblum of Elger Guitars ('59-ca.'65) in Ardmore, Pennsylvania, in early-'60s. Around '62 Hoshino purchased 50% interest in Elger Guitars, and ca. '65 changed the name to Ibanez.

Jeff Hasselberger headed the American guitar side beginning '73-'74, and the company headquarters were moved to Cornwells Heights, Pennsylvania in '74. By '75 the instruments are being distributed by Chesbro Music Company in Idaho Falls, Idaho, and Harry Rosenblum sells his interest to Hoshino shortly thereafter. Ca. '81, the Elger Company becomes Hoshino U.S.A. An U.S. Custom Shop was opened in '88.

Most glued-neck guitars from '70s are fairly rare.

Dating: copy guitars begin ca. '71. Serial numbers begin '75 with letter (A-L for month) followed by 6 digits, the first 2 indicating year, last 4 sequential (MYYXXXX). By '88 the month letter drops off. Dating code stops early-'90s; by '94 letter preface either F for Fuji or C for Cort (Korean) manufacturer followed by number for year and consecutive numbers (F4XXXX=Fuji, C4XXXX=Cort, 1994).

AE (Acoustic Electric) Series

1983-present. Models include AE, AEF, AEL flat-tops (no archtops).

1983-2010	Various models	$100	$400

AH10 (Allan Holdsworth)

1985-1987. Offset double-cut solidbody, bolt neck, bridge humbucker, dots, various colors.

1985-1987		$350	$400

AH20 (Allan Holdsworth)

1986. As AH10 but with 2 humbuckers.

1986		$375	$425

AM Series

1985-1991. Small body archtops, models include AM70, 75, 75T, 100, 225. Becomes Artstar in '92.

1985-1991	Various models	$500	$800

AM Stagemaster Series

1983-1984, 1989-1990. Made in Japan, small double-cut semi-hollow body, 2 humbuckers, models include AM50, 100, 205, 255. Model name used again, without Stagemaster in '89-'90.

1983-1984		$600	$750

AR50 "Jr. Artist"

1979-1983. Double-cut solidbody, dot markers, 2 humbuckers.

1979-1983		$450	$550

AR100 Artist

1979-1984. Double-cut solidbody, set neck, maple top, 2 humbuckers.

1979-1984		$650	$800

MODEL YEAR	FEATURES	EXC. COND. LOW	HIGH

AR300 Artist
1979-1982. Symmetrical double-cut, carved maple top.
| 1979-1982 | | $650 | $800 |

AR500 Artist
1979-1982. 2 humbuckers, EQ.
| 1979-1982 | | $800 | $1,000 |

Artcore Series
2002-present. Made in China, hollowbody electric, models include AF, AG, AK, AM, AS and TM.
| 2002-2010 | Various models | $200 | $550 |

AS50 Artist
1980-1981. Made in Japan, semi-acoustic.
| 1980-1981 | | $600 | $700 |

AS50 Artstar
1998-1999. Laminated maple body, bound rosewood 'board, dot inlays, 2 humbuckers.
| 1998-1999 | | $500 | $625 |

AS80 Artstar
1994-2002. Made in Korea, double cut semi-hollow body, dots, 2 humbuckers.
| 1994-2002 | | $500 | $625 |

AS100 Artist
1979-1981. Set neck, gold hardware.
| 1979-1981 | | $1,000 | $1,200 |

AS180 Artstar
1997-1999. Double cut semi-hollow body, plain top, dots, 2 humbuckers.
| 1997-1999 | | $900 | $1,100 |

AS200 Artist
1979-1981. Double-cut semi-acoustic, flamed maple, block markers, gold hardware, 2 humbuckers, replaced Artist 2630. Artist dropped from name when model becomes hollowbody archtop in '82.
| 1979-1981 | | $1,300 | $1,600 |

AS200 Artstar
1992-2000. Flame maple top, gold hardware, 2 humbuckers, block inlays.
| 1992-2000 | | $1,100 | $1,400 |

AW Artwood Series
1979-present. Electric/acoustics, various models.
| 1979-2010 | Various models | $150 | $500 |

BL Blazer Series
1980-1982, 1997-1998. Offset double-cut, 10 similar models in the '80s with different body woods and electronic configurations. Series name returns on 3 models in late '90s.
| 1980-1982 | Various models | $300 | $350 |
| 1997-1998 | Various models | $250 | $300 |

Bob Weir Model 2681
1975-1980, 1995. Double-cut solidbody of carved solid ash, maple neck, ebony 'board with tree-of-life inlay, gold-plated Super 70 pickups, produced in limited numbers. Reintroduced as a limited run in '95.
| 1975-1980 | | $1,800 | $2,100 |

Bob Weir Standard Model 2680
1976-1980. Double-cut solidbody of carved solid ash, maple neck, ebony 'board, dot markers, gold-plated Super 70 pickups, production model.
| 1976-1980 | | $1,200 | $1,500 |

Bob Weir Model One BWM1 (Cowboy Fancy)
2005. Double-cut swamp ash solidbody, ebony 'board, pearl vine inlay down neck and part way around body, 30 made.
| 2005 | | $2,800 | $3,500 |

Challenger 2552ASH
1977-1978. T-style ash solidbody.
| 1977-1978 | | $350 | $425 |

CN100 Concert Standard
1978-1979. Double-cut solidbody, set neck, 2 humbuckers, chrome hardware, dot markers.
| 1978-1979 | | $250 | $300 |

CN200 Concert Custom
1978-1979. Carved maple top, mahogany body, 7 layer black/white binding, bolt-on neck, gold hardware, block inlays, 2 Super 80 pickups.
| 1978-1979 | | $400 | $500 |

CN250 Concert
1978-1979. Like CN200 but with vine inlay.
| 1978-1979 | | $575 | $700 |

Concord Series
1974-1978. D-size flat-top.
| 1974-1978 | Various models | $400 | $500 |

DG350 Destroyer II
1986-1987. X Series, flamed maple.
| 1986-1987 | | $375 | $475 |

DT50 Destroyer II
1980-1982. Bolt neck, 1 humbucker, thick paint.
| 1980-1982 | | $500 | $600 |

DT150 Destroyer II
1982-1984. Birch/basswood, 1 humbucker, bolt neck.
| 1982-1984 | | $500 | $600 |

DT155 Destroyer II
1982-1984. Like DT150 but with 3 humbuckers.
| 1982-1984 | | $800 | $1,000 |

DT350 Destroyer II
1984-1985. X Series, opaque finish.
| 1984-1985 | | $275 | $375 |

DT400 Destroyer II
1980-1982. Basswood body, set-neck, 2 pickups, cherry sunburst. Model changed to DT500 in '82.
| 1980-1982 | | $400 | $500 |

DT500 Destroyer II
1982-1984. Replaced the DT400.
| 1982-1984 | | $400 | $500 |

DT555 Destroyer II Phil Collen
1983-1987. Bound basswood solidbody, 3 humbuckers, vibrato, black.
| 1983-1987 | | $1,900 | $2,100 |

DTX120 Destroyer
2000-2004. X Series, known as the Millennium Destroyer, 2 humbuckers.
| 2000-2004 | | $225 | $275 |

EX Series
1988-1993. Double-cut solidbodies with long thin horns.
| 1988-1993 | Various models | $150 | $300 |

2005 Ibanez Bob Weir Model One BWM1

1977 Ibanez Concord 673
Mark Menna

To get the most from this book, be sure to read "Using *The Guide*" in the introduction.

GUITARS

Ibanez George Benson GB10

1979 Ibanez Iceman PS10

MODEL YEAR	FEATURES	EXC. COND. LOW	HIGH
FA (Full Acoustic) Series			
1978-1982. Single-cut full body jazz-style.			
1978-1982		$1,000	$1,225
FG-100			
1982-1987. Single-cut archtop, maple top, 2 humbuckers.			
1982-1987		$1,000	$1,225
GAX Series			
1998-2009. Symmetrical double-cut (Gibson SG style) with 2 humbuckers, lower cost of the AX line.			
1998-2009		$90	$175
George Benson GB10			
1977-present. Single-cut, laminated spruce top, flame maple back and sides, 2 humbuckers, 3-piece set-in maple neck, ebony 'board.			
1977-1979	Blond	$1,900	$2,200
1977-1979	Sunburst	$1,800	$2,100
1980-1989	Blond	$1,800	$2,100
1980-1989	Sunburst	$1,600	$1,900
1990-1999	Blond	$1,600	$1,900
1990-1999	Sunburst	$1,500	$1,800
2001	Sunburst	$1,400	$1,700
2004	Blond	$1,400	$1,700
2007	Sunburst	$1,400	$1,700
George Benson GB15			
2006-2010. Like GB10, but with 1 humbucker.			
2006-2010		$1,900	$2,200
George Benson GB20			
1978-1982. Larger than GB10, laminated spruce top, flame maple back and sides.			
1978-1982		$2,000	$2,300
George Benson GB100 Deluxe			
1993-1996. GB-10 with flamed maple top, pearl binding, sunburst finish 'guard, pearl vine inlay tailpiece, gold hardware.			
1993-1996		$2,400	$2,800
GSA Series			
2000-present. Offset double-cut body.			
2000-2010	GSA20/GSA60	$75	$125
Iceman 2663/2663 TC/2663 SL			
1975-1978. The original Iceman Series models, called the Flash I, II and III respectively, I has 2 humbuckers, II (TC) and III (SL) have 1 triple-coil pickup.			
1975-1978		$750	$900
Iceman PS10 Paul Stanley			
1978-1981. Limited edition Paul Stanley model, abalone trim, Stanley's name engraved at 21st fret, reissued in '95 with upgraded model names.			
1978-1981	Korina finish	$2,700	$3,300
1978-1981	Sunburst or black	$2,700	$3,300
Iceman PS10 II Paul Stanley			
1995-1996. Reissue of original PS-10.			
1995-1996	Black	$1,400	$1,700
Iceman PS10 LTD Paul Stanley			
1995-1996. Limited edition, gold mirror appointments, gold hardware, black pearl metalflake finish.			
1995-1996		$3,000	$3,700
Iceman Series			
1975-2010. Ibanez unique body styles with hooked lower treble horn body.			
1978	IC210	$1,000	$1,150

MODEL YEAR	FEATURES	EXC. COND. LOW	HIGH
1978-1979	IC250	$950	$1,100
1978-1979	IC300 (Korina)	$750	$900
1978-1982	IC400	$850	$1,025
1978-1990	IC200	$750	$900
1981	IC400 CS	$950	$1,100
1994	IC500	$900	$1,000
1994-2003	IC300	$325	$400
1995-1996	IC350	$325	$400
IMG-2010 Guitar Controller MIDI			
1985-1987. Similar to Roland GR-707, slim triangle-wedge body with treble horn.			
1985-1987	Guitar only	$500	$625
JEM 7 Series			
1988-2010. Basswood or alder body, various models, alder 7V offered until '10.			
1988-2010	Various colors	$1,350	$1,750
JEM 77 Series			
1988-1999, 2003-2010. Basswood body, monkey grip handle, 3 pickups, 'board with tree of life or pyramids inlay, finishes include floral pattern or multicolor swirl. Current version has dot inlays and solid finish. The JEM 77BRMR Bad Horsie was introduced in '05 with a mirror finish.			
1980-2010	Various colors	$1,400	$3,000
JEM 555			
1994-2000. Basswood, dots and vine inlay, 3 pickups.			
1994-2000		$550	$650
JEM 777 Series			
1987-1996. Basswood body, monkey grip 3 pickups, pyramids or vine inlay.			
1987-1996	Various colors	$1,400	$3,000
JEM 10th Anniversary			
1996. Limited Edition signature Steve Vai model, bolt neck, vine metal 'guard, vine neck inlays and headstock art.			
1996		$4,000	$4,600
JEM 20th Anniversary			
2007. Steve Vai 20th Anniversary JEM model, green acrylic illuminating body, celebrates the 20th year (1987-2007) of the Ibanez JEM series, limited edition.			
2007		$4,000	$4,600
JEM 90th Anniversary			
1997. Limited Edition signature Steve Vai model, textured silver finish, chrome 'guard.			
1997		$1,400	$1,700
JEM Y2KDNA (Limited Edition)			
2000. Red Swirl marble finish using Steve Vai's blood in the paint.			
2000		$3,300	$4,000
Joe Pass JP20			
1981-1990. Full body, single-cut, 1 pickup, abalone and pearl split block inlay, JP inlay on headstock.			
1981-1990	Sunburst	$1,700	$2,100
Joe Satriani JS6			
1993. Limited production, lightweight mahogany body, non-gloss finish, JS Series headstock logo.			
1993		$1,200	$1,500

MODEL YEAR	FEATURES	EXC. COND. LOW	HIGH

Joe Satriani JS100

1994-present. Offset double cut basswood body, 2 humbuckers, vibrato, red, black, white or custom finish.

1994-2010	Custom finish	$425	$525
1994-2010	Standard finish	$350	$425

Joe Satriani JS1000

1994-1996, 1998-present. 2 DiMarzio humbuckers, lightweight body.

1994-2010	Various colors	$750	$1,000

Joe Satriani JS1200

2004-present. Candy Apple Red.

2004-2010		$875	$1,100

Joe Satriani JS 10th Anniversary

1998. Chrome-metal body, Satriani Anniversary script on back cover plate.

1998		$2,300	$2,900

Joe Satriani JS 20th Anniversary

2008. Opaque finish with alien surfer graphic.

2008		$2,300	$2,900

Joe Satriani Y2K

2000. Clear see-thru plexi-style body.

2000		$1,800	$2,300

John Petrucci JPM100 P2

1996. Offset double-cut solidbody, 2 pickups, multi-color graphic.

1996		$1,700	$2,000

John Petrucci JPM100 P3

1997. As P2 but with same graphic in black and white.

1997		$1,700	$2,000

John Petrucci JPM100 P4

1998. As P2 but with same graphic in camo colors.

1998		$1,700	$2,000

John Scofield JSM100

2001-present. Double-cut semi hollow body, 2 humbuckers, ebony 'board, gold hardware.

2001-2010		$1,500	$1,800

Lee Ritenour LR10

1981-1987. Flame maple body, bound set neck, Quick Change tailpiece, 2 pickups, dark red sunburst, foam-filled body to limit feedback.

1981-1987		$1,400	$1,600

M340

1978-1979. Flat-top, spruce top, flamed maple back and sides, maple 'board.

1978-1979		$275	$350

Maxxas

1987-1988. Solidbody (MX2) or with internal sound chambers (MX3, '88 only), 2 pickups, all-access neck joint system.

1987-1988	MX2	$1,100	$1,350
1988	MX3	$1,300	$1,600

MC Musician Series

1978-1982. Solidbodies, various models.

1978-1980	MC500, carved top	$1,200	$1,500
1978-1980	Neck-thru body	$725	$900
1978-1982	Bolt neck	$625	$775

Mick Thompson MTM-1

2006. Seven logo on fretboard, MTM1 logo on back of headstock.

2006		$675	$800

Model 600 Series

1974-1978. Copy era acoustic flat-tops with model numbers in the 600 Series, basically copies of classic American square shoulder dreadnoughts. Includes the 683, 684, 693, and the six-on-a-side 647; there were 12-string copies as well.

1974-1978		$375	$450

Model 700 Series

1974-1977. Upgraded flat-top models such as the Brazilian Scent 750, with more original design content than 600 Series.

1974-1977		$375	$450

Model 900 Series

1963-1964. Offset double-cut solidbody with sharp curving horns, Burns Bison copy.

1963-1964	901, 1 pickup	$175	$225
1963-1964	992, 2 pickups	$200	$250

Model 1453

1971-1973. Copy of classic single-cut hollowbody, replaced by Model 2355 in '73.

1971-1973		$1,300	$1,600

Model 1800 Series

1962-1963. Offset double-cut solidbody (Jazzmaster-style), models came with bar (stud) or vibrato tailpiece, and 2, 3 or 4 pickups.

1962-1963	1830, 2 pickups, bar	$200	$225
1962-1963	1850, 3 pickups, bar	$225	$250
1962-1963	1860, 2 pickups, vibrato	$200	$225
1962-1963	1880, 3 pickups, vibrato	$225	$250

Model 1912

1971-1973. Double-cut semi-hollow body, sunburst finish.

1971-1973		$1,000	$1,200

Model 2020

1970. Initial offering of the copy era, offset double-cut, 2 unusual rectangular pickups, block markers, raised nailed-on headstock logo, sunburst.

1970		$550	$700

Model 2240M

Early 1970s. Thick hollowbody electric copy, single pointed cutaway, double-parallelogram markers, 2 humbuckers, natural finish.

1971-1973		$1,200	$1,400

Model 2336 Les Jr.

1974-1976. Copy of classic slab solidbody, TV Lime.

1974-1976		$500	$625

Model 2340 Deluxe '59er

1974-1977. Copy of classic single-cut solidbody, Hi-Power humbuckers, opaque or flametop.

1974-1977		$650	$800

Model 2341 Les Custom

1974-1977. Copy of classic single-cut solidbody.

1974-1977		$650	$800

Model 2342 Les Moonlight/Sunlight Special

1974-1977. Copy of classic slab solidbody, black (Moonlight) or ivory (Sunlight).

1974-1977		$550	$675

Ibanez Joe Satriani JS100

1988 Ibanez Maxxas

GUITARS

Ibanez Model 2020

Ibanez Model 2384

MODEL YEAR	FEATURES	EXC. COND. LOW	HIGH

Model 2343 FM Jr.
1974-1976. Copy of LP Jr.

1974-1976		$500	$625

Model 2344
1974-1976. Copy of classic double-cut solidbody.

1974-1976		$400	$500

Model 2345
1974-1976. Copy of classic sharp double-cut solidbody, set neck, walnut or white, vibrato, 3 pickups.

1974-1976		$600	$750

Model 2346
1974. Copy of classic sharp double-cut solidbody, vibrato, set neck, 2 pickups.

1974		$600	$725

Model 2347
1974-1976. Copy of classic sharp double-cut solidbody, set-neck, 1 pickup.

1974-1976		$500	$600

Model 2348 Firebrand
1974-1977. Copy of classic reverse solidbody, mahogany body, bolt neck, 2 pickups.

1974-1977		$650	$800

Model 2350 Les
1971-1977. Copy of classic single-cut solidbody, bolt neck, black, gold hardware, goldtop version (2350G Les) also available. A cherry sunburst finish (2350 Les Custom) was offered by '74.

1971-1977		$600	$725

Model 2351
1974-1977. Copy of classic single-cut solidbody, gold top, 2 pickups.

1974-1977		$600	$725

Model 2351DX
1974-1977. Copy of classic single-cut solidbody, gold top, 2 mini-humbuckers.

1974-1977		$600	$725

Model 2352 Telly
1974-1978. Copy of early classic single-cut solidbody, 1 bridge pickup, white finish.

1974-1978		$600	$725

Model 2352CT
1974-1978. Copy of classic single-cut solidbody, single-coil bridge and humbucker neck pickup.

1974-1978		$550	$675

Model 2352DX Telly
1974-1978. Copy of classic single-cut solidbody, 2 humbuckers.

1974-1978		$550	$675

Model 2354
1974-1977. Copy of classic sharp double-cut solidbody, 2 humbuckers, vibrato.

1974-1977		$550	$675

Model 2354S
1972-1977. Stop tailpiece version of 2354.

1972-1977		$550	$675

Model 2355/2355M
1973-1977. Copy of classic single-cut hollowbody, sunburst or natural maple (M).

1973-1977		$1,300	$1,600

Model 2356
1973-1975. Copy of classic double pointed cutaway hollowbody, bowtie markers, sunburst. There was another Model 2356 in '74, a copy of a different hollowbody.

1973-1975		$850	$1,050

Model 2363R
1973-1974. Cherry finish copy of classic varitone double-cut semi-hollow body.

1973-1974		$900	$1,100

Model 2364 Ibanex
1971-1973. Dan Armstrong see-thru Lucite copy, 2 mounted humbuckers.

1971-1973		$700	$850

Model 2368 Telly
1973-1978. Copy of classic single-cut thinline, chambered f-hole body, single coil pickup, mahogany body.

1973-1978		$550	$675

Model 2368F
1973-1974. Classic single-cut black 'guard copy.

1973-1974		$550	$700

Model 2370
1972-1977. Sunburst version of Model 2363R.

1972-1977		$900	$1,100

Model 2372 Les Pro/2372DX Les Pro
1972-1977. Copy of classic single-cut solidbody, bolt neck, low impedance pickups, DX with gold hardware available for '73-'74.

1972-1977		$600	$750

Model 2374 Crest
1974-1976. Copy of classic double-cut semi-hollow body, walnut finish.

1974-1976		$900	$1,100

Model 2375 Strato
1971-1978. Copy of classic offset double-cut solidbody, 3 single-coils, sunburst.

1971-1978		$500	$625

Model 2375ASH Strato
1974-1978. 2375 with ash body.

1974-1978		$550	$700

Model 2375WH/N/BK Strato
1974-1978. 2375 in white (WH), natural (N), and black (BK) finishes.

1974-1978		$500	$625

Model 2377
1974-1975. Copy of classic double sharp-cut solidbody, short production run, dot markers.

1974-1975		$450	$550

Model 2380
1973-1977. Copy of LP Recording, single-cut solidbody, low impedence pickups, small block markers.

1973-1977		$600	$750

Model 2383
1974-1976. Copy of classic double sharp cut solidbody, white or walnut, 3 humbuckers, gold hardware.

1974-1976	Walnut	$500	$700
1974-1976	White	$650	$750

Model 2384 Telly
1974-1976. Copy of classic single-cut, f-holes, 2 humbuckers, ash body.

1974-1976		$500	$700

MODEL YEAR	FEATURES	EXC. COND. LOW	HIGH

Model 2387 Rocket Roll/Rocket Roll Sr.
1975-1977. Copy of classic v-shaped solidbody, set-neck, dot markers, gold-covered pickups.

| 1975-1977 | | $1,000 | $1,250 |

Model 2390
1974-1976. Copy of classic double-cut semi-hollow body, maple 'board, walnut finish.

| 1974-1976 | | $800 | $1,000 |

Model 2394
Ca. 1974-ca. 1976. SG style, 2 humbuckers, maple 'board, black block inlays.

| 1974-1976 | | $650 | $800 |

Model 2395
1974-1976. Natural finished 2390.

| 1974-1976 | | $800 | $1,000 |

Model 2397
1974-1976. Double-cut semi-hollow body, low impedance electronics, trapezoid markers, goldtop.

| 1974-1976 | | $800 | $1,000 |

Model 2399DX Jazz Solid
1974-1976. Single-cut solidbody, sunburst, set-neck, gold hardware.

| 1974-1976 | | $750 | $900 |

Model 2401 Signature
1974-1976. Double-cut semi-hollow archtop, gold top, bolt neck.

| 1974-1976 | | $800 | $1,000 |

Model 2402/2402DX Double Axe
1974-1977. Double sharp cut solidbody 6/12 double-neck, cherry or walnut, DX model has gold hardware and white finish.

| 1974-1977 | | $1,200 | $1,500 |

Model 2404 Double Axe
1974-1977. Double sharp cut solidbody guitar/bass doubleneck copy, walnut, white available '75 only.

| 1974-1977 | | $1,200 | $1,500 |

Model 2405 Custom Agent
1974-1977. Single-cut solidbody, set neck, scroll headstock, pearl body inlay, 2 humbuckers.

| 1974-1977 | | $1,200 | $1,500 |

Model 2406 Double Axe
1974-1977. Double sharp cut solidbody doubleneck, two 6-strings, cherry or wlanut.

| 1974-1977 | | $1,200 | $1,500 |

Model 2407 Strato Jazz
1974-1976. Offset double-cut solidbody doubleneck.

| 1974-1976 | | $1,100 | $1,400 |

Model 2451
1974-1977. Single-cut solidbody, maple 'board, black or natural, set neck.

| 1974-1977 | | $725 | $900 |

Model 2453 Howie Roberts
1974-1977. Single-cut archtop, round soundhole, maple body, set neck, rosewood 'board, block markers, 1 pickup, gold hardware, burgundy or sunburst.

| 1974-1977 | | $1,200 | $1,500 |

Model 2454
1974-1977. Copy of classic double-cut semi-hollow body, set-neck, small block markers, cherry finish over ash.

| 1974-1977 | | $800 | $1,000 |

Model 2455
1974-1977. Copy of classic single-cut archtop, 2 pickups, natural.

| 1974-1977 | | $1,300 | $1,700 |

Model 2459 Destroyer
1975-1977. Korina finished mahogany body.

| 1975-1977 | | $1,500 | $1,800 |

Model 2460
1975-1977. Copy of classic single-cut archtop, natural.

| 1975-1977 | | $1,300 | $1,600 |

Model 2461
1975-1977. Copy of classic single-cut archtop, laminated spruce top, curly maple body, set-neck, ebony 'board, pearl blocks, 2 pickups, gold hardware, sunburst or natural.

| 1975-1977 | | $1,400 | $1,800 |

Model 2464
1975-1977. Copy of classic single-cut thinline archtop, natural.

| 1975-1977 | | $1,300 | $1,600 |

Model 2469 Futura
1976-1977. Korina finished furturistic model copy.

| 1976-1977 | | $1,300 | $1,600 |

Model 2601 Artist
1976-1978. D-style flat-top with fancy appointments.

| 1976-1978 | | $200 | $250 |

Model 2612 Artist
1974-1975. Rounded double-cut solidbody, black finish, birch top, gold hardware, bound rosewood 'board, 2 humbuckers, fleur-de-lis inlay.

| 1974-1975 | | $800 | $1,000 |

Model 2613 Artist
1974-1975. Natural version of 2612.

| 1974-1975 | | $800 | $1,000 |

Model 2616 Jazz Artist
1974-1975. Single-cut hollow body, curly maple, 2 humbuckers.

| 1974-1975 | | $1,350 | $1,650 |

Model 2617 Artist
1976-1980. Pointed double-cut natural ash solidbody, set-neck, German carved top, spilt block inlays, bound ebony 'board, 2 humbuckers, later would evolve into the Professional model.

| 1976-1980 | | $1,000 | $1,200 |

Model 2618 Artist
1976-1979. Like 2617, but with maple and mahogany body and dot markers. Becomes AR200 in '79.

| 1976-1979 | | $800 | $1,000 |

Model 2619 Artist
1976-1979. Like 2618, but with split block markers. Becomes AR300 in '79.

| 1976-1979 | | $800 | $1,000 |

Model 2622 Artist EQ
1977-1979. EQ, Steve Miller model. Becomes AR500 in '79.

| 1977-1979 | | $800 | $1,000 |

Model 2630 Artist Deluxe
1976-1979. Double cut semi-hollow body, sunburst, name changed to AS200 in '79.

| 1976-1979 | | $1,075 | $1,325 |

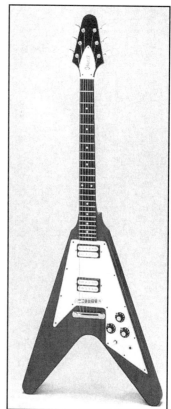

1976 Ibanez Model 2348 Firebrand

Ibanez Model 2387 Rocket Roll

Ibanez Pat Metheny PM120

Ibanez PGM Paul Gilbert

MODEL YEAR	FEATURES	EXC. COND. LOW	HIGH

Model 2640 Artist/AR1200 Doubleneck
1977-1984. Double-cut solidbody, set 6/12 necks, 4 humbuckers, gold hardware. Called 2640 until '79 when changed to AR1200.

1977-1984		$1,100	$1,350

Model 2800 Andorra Series
1974-1979. Classical nylon-string guitars, part of Ibanez Andorra Series, all with 2800-2899 model numbers.

1974-1979		$150	$400

Model 2900 Andorra Professional Series
1974-1979. Steel-string dreadnought models with solid spruce tops, all with 2909-2912 model numbers.

1974-1979		$150	$400

Pat Metheny PM
1996-present. Acoustic-electric archtops, single or single/half cutaway, 1 or 2 humbuckers.

1996-2010	PM100	$1,100	$1,300
1997-1999	PM20	$900	$1,100
2000-2010	PM120	$1,400	$1,600

Paul Gilbert PGM
1992-present. Superstrat body style, painted f-holes, appointments vary with model numbers.

1997-2010	PGM300 WH		
	(white)	$1,150	$1,400
1998	PGM 90th	$1,350	$1,650
1998	PGM200 FB	$1,350	$1,650

PF Performer Series Acoustics
1987-present. Mostly dreadnought size flat-tops, various models.

1987-2010	Various models	$75	$225

PF100 Performer Standard
1978-1979. Single-cut solidbody, plain birch top, mahogany body, bolt neck, dot inlays, 2 humbuckers.

1978-1979		$350	$450

PF200 Performer Custom
1978-1979. Maple top PF100.

1978-1979		$375	$475

PF300 Performer
1978-1980. Single-cut solidbody, maple top, mahogany body, set neck, 2 humbuckers, Tri-Sound.

1978-1980		$500	$600

PF400 Performer
1978-1979. Single cut solidbody, flame maple top, alder body, set neck, block inlays, 2 humbuckers, Tri-Sound.

1978-1979		$500	$650

PL Pro Line Series
1985-1987. Pro Line models begin with PL or PR.

1985-1987	Various models	$275	$450

PR Pro Line Series
1985-1987. Pro Line models begin with PL or PR.

1985-1987	Various models	$250	$425

RBM1 Reb Beach Voyager
1991-1996. Unusual cutaway lower bout, extreme upper bout cutaways, RBM Series logo on headstock.

1991-1996		$975	$1,200

RG/RS Roadstar Series
1992-present. A large family of guitars whose model identification starts with RG or RS prefix, includes the Roadstar Standard and Roadstar Deluxe models.

1992-2010	Higher-range	$500	$600

MODEL YEAR	FEATURES	EXC. COND. LOW	HIGH
1992-2010	Highest-range	$700	$1,500
1992-2010	Low to mid-range	$250	$350
1992-2010	Lower-range	$150	$250
1992-2010	Mid-range	$400	$500

Rocket Roll II RR550
1982-1984. Flying V body, six-on-side headstock, pearloid blocks, cherry sunburst, maple top, set neck.

1982-1984		$875	$1,075

RT Series
1992-1993. Offset double-cut, bolt neck, rosewood 'board, dot markers, various models.

1992-1993	Various models	$275	$425

RX Series
1994-1997. Offset double-cut, solidbodies, various models.

1994-1997	Various models	$75	$150

S Models
1987-present. In '87 Ibanez introduced a new line of highly tapered, ultra-thin body, offset double-cut guitars that were grouped together as the S Models. Intially the S Models were going to be called the Sabre models but that name was trademarked by Music Man and could not be used. The S models will carry an S suffix or S prefix in the model name.

1987-2010	Various models	$250	$550

ST Studio Series
1978-1982. Double-cut solidbodies, lots of natural finishes, various models, even a doubleneck.

1978-1982	Various models	$275	$525

STW Double
1999. Double neck with 7-string and 6-string neck, limited edition.

1999		$1,700	$1,900

TC/TV Talman Series
1994-1998. Softer double-cut solidbodies, various models.

1994-1998	Various models	$275	$450

Universe UV7/UV7P/UV77 Series
1990-1997. Basswood 7-strings, hum/single/hum pickups. The '90-'93 white 7P and multi-colored 77 have pyramid inlays, the black '90-'97 7 has dots.

1990-1997	Various models	$1,200	$3,500

Universe UV777 Series
1991-present. Basswood 7-string, pyramid inlays, maple 'board, hum/single/hum pickups.

1991-2010	Various models	$1,200	$2,000

USRG U.S.A. Custom Series
1994-1995. RG style guitars built in the U.S. by PBC Guitar Technology.

1994-1996	Various models	$1,000	$1,300

USRG-10 (U.S.A.)
1994-1995. RG style guitars built in the U.S. by PBC Guitar Technology.

1994-1995		$1,000	$1,100

V300 Vintage Series
1978-1991. Vintage Series acoustic dreadnought, spruce top, mahogany back and sides, sunburst or various colors.

1978-1991		$150	$200

GUITARS

MODEL YEAR	FEATURES	EXC. COND. LOW	HIGH

XV500

1985-1987. Sharply pointed X-body with scalloped bottom.

1985-1987 ... $300 ... $400

Ibanez, Salvador

1875-1920. Salvador Ibanez was a Spanish luthier who operated a small guitar-building workshop. In the early 1900s he founded Spain's largest guitar factory. In 1929 Japan's Hoshino family began importing Salvador Ibanez guitars. Demand for the Salvador Ibanez guitars became so great that the Hoshino family began building their own guitars, which ultimately became known as the Ibanez brand. Guitars from 1875-1920 were mostly classical style and often can be identified by a label on the inside back which stipulates Salvador Ibanez.

Ignacio Fleta

1970s. Classical guitar builder from Barcelona, Spain.

Classical

1971. Higher-end guitar.

1971 ... $18,000 ... $22,000

Ignacio Rozas

1987-present. Luthier Ignacio M. Rozas builds his classical and flamenco guitars in Madrid, Spain. He also offers factory-made guitars built to his specifications.

Illusion Guitars

1992-present. Luthier Jeff Scott builds his premium grade, production/custom, solidbody guitars in Fallbrook, California.

Imperial

Ca.1963-ca.1970. Imported by the Imperial Accordion Company of Chicago, Illinois. Early guitars made in Italy by accordion builder Crucianelli. By ca. '66 switched to Japanese guitars. They also made basses.

Electric Solidbody

1963-1968. Italian-made until '66, then Japanese-made, includes the Tonemaster line.

1963-1968 ... $200 ... $250

Imperial (Japan)

1957-1960. Early, budget grade, Japanese imports from the Hoshino company which was later renamed Ibanez.

Infeld

2003-2005. Solidbody guitars and basses offered by string-maker Thomastik-Infeld of Vienna.

Infinox

1980s. Infinox by JTG, of Nashville, offered a line of 'the classic shapes of yesterday and the hi tech chic of today'. Classic shapes included copies of many classic American solidbody designs with the block letter Infinox by JTG logo on headstock, special metallic grafteq paint finish, space-age faux graphite-feel neck, Gotoh tuning machines, Gotoh locking nut tremolo with fine tuners, all models with 1 or 2 humbucker pickups.

Interdonati

1930s. Guitars built by luthier Philip Interdonati, of Staten Island, New York, originally professional grade, luthier's label is on the inside back.

Size 000 Flat-Top

1920s-1930s.

1920-1930s ... $4,500 ... $5,500

Italia

1999-present. Intermediate grade, production, solid, semi-solid, and hollow body guitars designed by Trevor Wilkinson and made in Korea. They also build basses.

J Backlund Design

2008-present. Luthier Bruce Bennett builds professional and premium grade, production/custom, electric guitars designed by J. Backlund in Chattanooga, Tennessee. He also offers basses.

J Burda Guitars

Flat-top guitars built by luthier Jan Burda in Berrien Springs, Michigan.

J. Frog Guitars

1978-present. Professional and premium grade, production/custom, solidbody guitars made in Las Vegas, Nevada by Ed Roman.

J.B. Player

1980s-present. Budget and intermediate grade, production, imported acoustic, acoustic/electric, and solidbody guitars. They also offer basses, banjos and mandolins. Founded in United States. Moved production of guitars to Korea but maintained a U.S. Custom Shop. MBT International/Musicorp took over manufacture and distribution in '89.

J.R. Zeidler Guitars

1977-2002. Luthier John Zeidler built premium and presentation grade, custom, flat-top, 12-string, and archtop guitars in Wallingford, Pennsylvania. He also built mandolins. He died in '02 at age 44.

J.S. Bogdanovich

1996-present. Production/custom, premium grade, classical and steel string guitars built by luthier John S. Bogdanovich in Swannanoa, North Carolina.

J.T. Hargreaves Basses & Guitars

1995-present. Luthier Jay Hargreaves builds his premium grade, production/custom, classical and steel string guitars in Seattle, Washington. He also builds basses.

Ibanez S420

Illusion '59 Caddy

Jackson JS32 Rhoads

Jackson Phil Collen PC1 (U.S.A.)

MODEL YEAR	FEATURES	EXC. COND. LOW	HIGH

Jack Daniel's

2004-present. Acoustic and electric guitar models, some with custom Jack Daniel's artwork on the body and headstock, built by Peavey for the Jack Daniel's Distillery. There is also an amp model and a bass.

Jackson

1980-present. Currently Jackson offers intermediate, professional, and premium grade, production, electric guitars. They also offer basses. In '78 Grover Jackson bought out Charvel Guitars and moved it to San Dimas. Jackson made custom-built bolt-on Charvels. In '82 the pointy, tilt-back Jackson headstock became standard. The Jackson logo was born in '80 and used on a guitar designed as Randy Rhoad's first flying V. Jacksons were neck-through construction. The Charvel trademark was licensed to IMC in '85. IMC moved the Jackson factory to Ontario, California in '86. Grover Jackson stayed with Jackson/Charvel until '89 (see Charvel). On October 25, 2002, Fender Musical Instruments Corp (FMIC) took ownership of Jackson/Charvel Manufacturing Inc.

Dinky Reverse

1991	Import	$350	$400

DR2

1996-1998. U.S.-made offset double-cut solidbody, 2 Duncan humbuckers, ebony 'board.

1996-1998	U.S.-made	$650	$800

DR3

1996-2001. Dinky Reverse, double-cut solidbody, reverse headstock, triangle markers, 2 humbuckers, locking vibrato, made in Japan, flamed maple top available.

1996-2001		$250	$300

DR5

1996 only. Offset double-cut solidbody, 2 Kent Armstrong humbuckers, rosewood 'board, dot markers.

1996		$250	$300

DX Series

2000-2007. Standard offset double-cut body, reverse headstock.

2000-2007		$175	$200

Fusion Pro

Late 1980s-early 1990s. Import from Japan.

1990s		$450	$550

Fusion U.S.A.

1992-1994. Jackson with Made In USA logo on headstock, graphics.

1992-1994		$750	$900

Jenna II RX10D Rhoads

2009. Limited production, Rhoads body style, named after performer Jenna Jameson.

2009		$450	$550

JSX94

1994-1995. Offset double-cut solidbody, single/single/hum, rosewood 'board, dot markers.

1994-1995		$225	$275

MODEL YEAR	FEATURES	EXC. COND. LOW	HIGH

JTX

1993-1995. Partial offset double-cut, single-coil neck pickup, humbucker bridge pickup, Jackson-Rose double lock vibrato, bolt-on neck, dot markers on maple fretboard, JTX truss rod cover logo.

1993-1995		$300	$350

Kelly Custom

1984-early 1990s. Solidbody, Kahler tremolo, 2 humbuckers, ebony 'board with shark's tooth inlays, bound neck and headstock.

1984-1985		$1,200	$1,500
1986-1993		$1,100	$1,400

Kelly Pro

1994-1995. Pointy-cut solidbody, neck-thru, 2 humbuckers, bound ebony 'board, sharkfin inlays.

1994-1995		$500	$600

Kelly Standard

1993-1995. Pointy cutaway solidbody, bolt neck, 2 humbuckers, dot markers.

1993-1995		$375	$475

Kelly U.S.A. (KE2)

1998-present. Alder solidbody, flame maple top, neck-thru.

1998-2010		$800	$1,000

Kelly XL

1994-1995. Pointy cutaway solidbody, bolt neck, 2 humbuckers, bound rosewood 'board, sharkfin inlays.

1994-1995		$500	$600

King V (KV2)

2003-present. King V Pro reissue, neck-thru, sharkfin markers, Floyd Rose, U.S.-made.

2003-2010		$600	$750

King V Pro

1993-1995. Soft V-shaped neck-thru solidbody, sharkfin markers, 2 humbuckers.

1993-1995		$400	$500

King V STD

1993-1995. Bolt neck version of King V.

1993-1995		$250	$300

Phil Collen

1989-1991, 1993-1995. Offset double-cut maple neck-thru solidbody, six-on-a-side tuners, 1 volume, bound ebony 'board, U.S.-made, early version has poplar body, 1 humbucker; later version with basswood body, 1 single-coil and 1 humbucker.

1993-1995		$1,000	$1,300

Phil Collen PC1 (U.S.A.)

1996-present. Quilt maple top, bolt-on maple neck, maple board, koa body '96-'00, mahogany body '01-present, 1 humbucker and 1 single coil '96-'97, humbucker, stacked humbucker, and single coil '98-present.

1996-2010		$1,100	$1,400

Phil Collen PC3 (Import)

1996-2001. Downscale version of Collen model, poplar body, bolt neck, humbucker\single\single.

1996-2001		$400	$475

PS Performers Series

1994-2003. Some with PS model number on truss rod cover.

1994-1999	PS3 Rhoads body h/h	$250	$325
1994-2000	PS1 Dinky body h/s/h	$250	$325

GUITARS

MODEL YEAR	FEATURES	EXC. COND. LOW	HIGH
1994-2003	PS2 Dinky body s/s/h	$250	$325
1995-2001	PS4 Dinky body h/s/h	$250	$325
1995-2001	PS7 h/s/s	$250	$325
1997-2001	PS6/PS6T Kelly body	$250	$325

Randy Rhoads (Import)
1992-present. Bolt neck import version.

1992-2010		$250	$300

Randy Rhoads (Japan)
1995-present.

1995-2010	RR3, bolt-on	$225	$275
2001-2010	RR5, neck-thru	$375	$425

Randy Rhoads (U.S.A.)
1983-present. V-shaped neck-thru solidbody, 2 humbuckers, originally made at San Dimas plant, serial numbers RR 0001 to RR 1929, production moved to the Ontario plant by '87, serial numbers RR 1930 to present in sequential order.

1983	Early serial #, no trem	$2,700	$3,400
1983-1986	Kahler trem	$1,700	$2,000
1983-1986	Rose trem or string-thru	$2,000	$2,300
1987-1989	Early Ontario-built	$1,700	$2,000
1990-1992	Early '90s vintage	$1,600	$1,900
1993-1999		$1,500	$1,800
2002-2005	RR5	$725	$875
2002-2010	RR1	$1,500	$1,800

Randy Rhoads Limited Edition
1992 only. Shark fin-style maple neck-thru body, gold hardware, white with black pinstriping, block inlays, six-on-a-side tuners, U.S.-made, only 200 built.

1992		$5,000	$6,000

Randy Rhoads Relic Tribute
2010-2011. Custom Shop limited edition to celebrate the 30th anniversary of the Randy Rhoads Concorde, 60 made, exacting dimension and design of Rhoads' original custom-made Concorde guitar, relic-treatment to mimic the original.

2010-2011		$5,400	$6,400

RX Series
2000s-present. Bolt-on, shark fin inlays.

2007-2010	RX10D Rhoads	$225	$275

San Dimas Serialized Plated
1980-1982. Various custom-built solidbody models, values vary depending on each individual instrument. The values are true for so-called "Serialized Plated" with Jackson neck plate, Jackson logo and serial number.

1980-1982		$3,200	$4,000

Soloist
1984-1990. U.S.-made, double-cut, neck-thru, string-thru solidbody, 2 humbuckers, bound rosewood 'board, standard vibrato system on Soloist is Floyd Rose locking vibrato, a guitar with Kahler vibrato is worth less. Replaced by the Soloist USA in '90.

1984-1986	Custom order features	$1,500	$1,800
1984-1986	San Dimas-built	$1,300	$1,600
1986-1990	Custom order features	$1,400	$1,700
1986-1990	Ontario-built	$1,100	$1,400

Soloist Custom
1993-1995. Double-cut, neck-thru solidbody, 1 humbucker and 2 single-coils, bound ebony 'board, shark's tooth inlays, U.S.-made.

1993-1995		$1,000	$1,250

Soloist Shannon Model
1998. Shark fin inlays, single-single-hum pickups, Rose, signed by Mike Shannon.

1998		$1,500	$1,750

Soloist Student J1 (U.S.A.)
1984-1999. Double-cut neck-thru solidbody, Seymour Duncan single-single-hum pickups, rosewood 'board, dot inlays, no binding.

1984-1986	San Dimas-built	$850	$1,050
1986-1999	Ontario-built	$800	$1,000

Soloist U.S.A./SL Series
1990-present. Replaces Soloist, sharkfin markers.

1990-1999	Various models	$1,000	$1,250
2006	SL1, h/s/s, flamed	$1,300	$1,550
2006	SL1, h/s/s, graphic	$1,400	$1,650
2006	SL1, h/s/s, opaque	$900	$1,075
2006-2007	SL2H, h/h	$1,100	$1,250

Stealth EX
1992-late 1990s. Offset double-cut, pointed headstock, H/S/S pickups, offset dot markers, tremolo, Jackson Professional logo.

1990s		$275	$325

Stealth HX
1992-1995. 3 humbucker version of Stealth, string-thru body.

1992-1995		$400	$500

Stealth XL
1993. Stealth XL truss rod cover logo, 1 humbucker, 2 single-coils, left edge dot markers.

1993		$400	$500

Surfcaster SC1
1998-2001. Jackson logo on headstock, Charvel Surfcaster styling.

1998-2001		$800	$1,000

Warrior Pro (Import)
1990-1992. Japanese version.

1990-1992		$275	$325

Warrior U.S.A.
1990-1992. Four point neck-thru solidbody, 1 humbucker and 1 single-coil, triangle markers, active electronics, U.S.-made, the Warrior Pro was Japanese version.

1990-1992	Red	$800	$1,000

Y2KV Dave Mustaine Signature
2000-2002. V-shaped body, shark tooth markers, neck-thru, 2 humbuckers.

2000-2002		$1,800	$2,200

Jackson-Guldan/Jay G Guitars

1920s-1960s. The Jackson-Guldan Violin Company, of Columbus, Ohio, mainly built inexpensive violins, violas, cellos, etc. but also offered acoustic guitars in the 1950s and early '60s, some of which were distributed by Wards. Their sales flyers from that era state - Made in America by Jackson-Guldan

Jackson Randy Rhoads RR1 (U.S.A.)

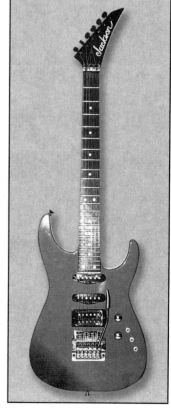

Jackson Soloist

MODEL		EXC. COND.	
YEAR	FEATURES	LOW	HIGH

James Trussart Deluxe Steelcaster
Stephen Rabinowitz

James Tyler Studio Elite

Craftsman. Very similar to small (13"-14") Stella economy flat-tops. Jay G name with quarter-note logo is sometimes on the headstock. They also offered lap steels and small tube amps early on.

Jacobacci

1930s-1994. Founded in France by Italian Vincent Jacobacci and originally building basso-guitars, banjos, and mandolins. Sons Roger and Andre joined the company and encouraged pop to add lapsteels and electric and regular acoustic guitars around '52. The guitars are sometimes labeled as Jaco and, from ca. '54 to ca. '66, as Jaco Major. In '58 the company introduced aluminum neck models, and in '59 their first solidbodies. In the '60s they also made instruments branded Royal, Texas, Ohio, Star and made instruments for Major Conn and other companies. By the mid '60s, they were producing mainly jazz style guitars.

Jamboree

1960s. Guitar brand exported by Japan's Hoshino (Ibanez).

James Einolf Guitars

1964-present. Production/custom, professional grade, flat-top guitars built in Denver, Colorado by luthier James Einolf.

James R. Baker Guitars

1996-present. Luthier James R. Baker builds his premium grade, custom, archtops in Shoreham, New York.

James Trussart

1980-present. Luthier James Trussart builds his premium grade, custom/production, solid and semi-hollow body electric guitars in Los Angeles, California. He also builds basses.

James Tyler

Early 1980s-present. Luthier James Tyler builds his professional and premium grade, custom/production, solidbody guitars in Van Nuys, California, and also has a model built in Japan. He also builds basses.

Janofsky Guitars

1978-present. Production classical and flamenco guitars built by luthier Stephen Janofsky in Amherst, Massachusetts.

Jaros

1995-present. Professional and premium grade, production/custom, solidbody and acoustic/electric guitars originally built by father and son luthiers Harry and Jim Jaros in Rochester, Pennsylvania. In '01 Ed Roman in Las Vegas, bought the brand. He sold it in '04 to Dave Weiler in Nashville. Serial numbers under 1000 were made by the Jaros', numbers 1001-2000 were made by Ed Roman, over 2000 made by Dave Weiler.

Jasmine

1994-present. Budget and intermediate grade, production, steel and classical guitars offered by Takamine Jasmine or Jasmine by Takamine. Student level instruments.

Jason Z. Schroeder Guitars

1994-present. Luthier Jason Schroeder builds premium grade, production/custom, electric guitars in Redding, California.

Jay Turser

1997-present. Budget and intermediate grade, production, imported acoustic, acoustic/electric, electric and resonator guitars. They also offer basses and amps. Designed and developed by Tommy Rizzi for Music Industries Corp.

JD Bluesville

2005-present. John Schappell and luthier Davis Millard build their professional grade, custom/production, solidbody electric guitars in Allentown, Pennsylvania.

Jeff Traugott Guitars

1991-present. Premium and presentation grade, custom, flat-top, nylon-string, and acoustic/electric guitars built by luthier Jeff Traugott, in Santa Cruz, California.

Jeremy Locke Guitars

1985-present. Premium grade, production/custom, classical and flamenco guitars built by luthier Jeremy Locke in Coomera, South East Queensland, Australia.

Jeronimo Pena Fernandez

1967-present. Luthier Jeronimo Pena Fernandez started building classical guitars in Marmolejo, Spain, in the '50s. In '67, he went full-time and soon became well-known for his fine work. He is now retired, but still builds a few guitars a year.

Classical

Late 1960s-1990s. Brazilian rosewood back and sides, cedar top, full-size classical guitar, higher-end luthier. Prices can vary depending on model specs, each instrument should be evaluated on a case-by-case basis.

1960-1990s		$5,000	$6,000

Jerry Jones

1981-2011. Intermediate grade, production, semi-hollowbody electric guitars and sitars from luthier Jerry Jones, built in Nashville, Tennessee. They also build basses. Jones started building custom guitars in '81, and launched his Danelectro-inspired line in '87. He retired in 2011.

Electric Models

Various models include Baritone 6-string ('89-'11); Electric Sitar ('90-'11) with buzz-bar sitar bridge, individual pickup for sympathetic strings and custom

MODEL		EXC. COND.	
YEAR	FEATURES	LOW	HIGH

color gator finish; Longhorn Guitarlin ('89-'00, '05-'11) with large cutaway Guitarlin-style body, 24 frets in '89 and 31 after;and the Neptune 12-string ('81-'11) single-cut with 3 pickups.

1981-2011	Neptune Electric 12-string	$525	$625
1989-2011	Baritone 6-string	$525	$625
1989-2011	Longhorn Guitarlin	$550	$650
1990-2011	Baby Sitar	$550	$650
1990-2011	Electric Sitar	$550	$650
1990-2011	Shorthorn	$525	$625

Jersey Girl

1991-present. Premium grade, production/custom, solidbody guitars made in Japan. They also build effects.

JET

1998-present. Premium grade, custom/production, chambered solidbody electric guitars built by luthier Jeffrey Earle Terwilliger in Raleigh, North Carolina.

Jewel

1920s. Instruments built by the Oscar Schmidt Co. and possibly others. Most likely a brand made for a distributor.

JG Guitars

1991-present. Luthier Johan Gustavsson builds his premium and presentation grade, production/custom, solidbody electric guitars in Malmö, Sweden.

Jim Dyson

1972-present. Intermediate, professional and premium grade, production/custom electric guitars built by luthier Jim Dyson in Torquay, Southern Victoria, Australia. He also builds basses and lap steels.

Jim Redgate Guitars

1992-present. Luthier Jim Redgate builds his premium grade, custom, nylon-string classical guitars in Belair, Adelaide, South Australia.

John Le Voi Guitars

1970-present. Production/custom, gypsy jazz, flat-top, and archtop guitars built by luthier John Le Voi in Lincolnshire, United Kingdom. He also builds mandolin family instruments.

John Page Guitars

2006-present. Luthier John Page builds his custom, premium grade, chambered and solidbody electric guitars in Sunny Valley, Oregon.

John Price Guitars

1984-present. Custom classical and flamenco guitars built by luthier John Price in Australia.

Johnson

Mid-1990s-present. Budget, intermediate and professional grade, production, acoustic, classical, acoustic/electric, resonator and solidbody guitars imported by Music Link, Brisbane, California. Johnson also offers basses, amps, mandolins, ukuleles and effects.

Jon Kammerer Guitars

1997-present. Luthier Jon Kammerer builds his professional and premium grade, custom/production, solidbody, chambered, hollow-body, and acoustic guitars in Keokuk, Iowa. He also builds basses.

Jones

See TV Jones listing.

Jordan

1981-present. Professional and premium grade, custom, flat-top and archtop guitars built by luthier John Jordan in Concord, California. He also builds electric violins and cellos.

Jose Oribe

1962-present. Presentation grade, production, classical, flamenco, and steel-string acoustic guitars built by luthier Jose Oribe in Vista, California.

Jose Ramirez

See listing under Ramirez, Jose.

JY Jeffrey Yong Guitars

2003-present. Professional and premium grade, production/custom, classical, acoustic and electric guitars and harpguitars built by Jeffrey Yong in Kuala Lumpur, Malaysia. He also builds basses.

K & S

1992-1998. Hawaiian-style and classical guitars distributed by George Katechis and Marc Silber and handmade in Paracho, Mexico. A few 16" wide Leadbelly Model 12-strings were made in Oakland, California by luthier Stewart Port. K & S also offered mandolins, mandolas and ukes. In '98, Silber started marketing guitars under the Marc Silber Guitar Company brand and Katechis continued to offer instruments under the Casa Montalvo brand.

Kakos, Stephen

1972-present. Luthier Stephen Kakos builds his premium grade, production/custom, classical guitars in Mound, Minnesota.

Kalamazoo

1933-1942, 1965-1970. Budget brand built by Gibson. Made flat-tops, solidbodies, mandolins, lap steels, banjos and amps. Name revived for a line of amps, solidbodies and basses in '65-'67.

JET Earlwood Plus

Jon Kammerer Glitter Rose Series

GUITARS

1968 Kalamazoo KG-1

Karol Dragonfly

MODEL YEAR	FEATURES	EXC. COND. LOW	HIGH

KG-1/KG-1 A
1965-1969. Offset double-cut (initial issue) or SG-shape (second issue), 1 pickup, Model 1 A with spring vibrato, red, blue or white.

| 1965-1969 | Early Mustang body | $225 | $325 |
| 1965-1969 | Later SG body | $275 | $375 |

KG-2/KG-2 A
1965-1970. Offset double-cut (initial shape) or SG-shape, 2 pickups, Model 2 A with spring vibrato, red, blue or white.

| 1965-1970 | Early Mustang body | $350 | $450 |
| 1965-1970 | Later SG body | $400 | $500 |

KG-11
1933-1941. Flat-top, all mahogany, 14" with no 'guard, sunburst.

| 1933-1941 | | $600 | $800 |

KTG-11 Tenor
1936-1940. Tenor version of 11.

| 1936-1940 | | $450 | $550 |

KG-14
1936-1940. Flat-top L-0-size, mahogany back and sides, with 'guard, sunburst.

| 1936-1940 | | $900 | $1,100 |

KTG-14 Tenor
1936-1940. Tenor version of 14.

| 1936-1940 | | $500 | $600 |

KG-16
1939-1940. Gibson-made archtop, small body, f-hole.

| 1939-1940 | | $450 | $600 |

KG-21
1936-1941. Early model 15" archtop (bent, not curved), dot markers, bound top, sunburst.

| 1936-1941 | | $450 | $600 |

KTG-21 Tenor
1935-1939. Tenor version of 21.

| 1935-1939 | | $600 | $725 |

KG-22
1940-1942. Early model 16" archtop.

| 1940-1942 | | $675 | $775 |

KG-31
1935-1940. Archtop L-50-size, 16" body, non-carved spruce top, mahogany back and sides.

| 1935-1940 | | $675 | $775 |

KG-32
1939-1942. Archtop, 16" body.

| 1939-1942 | | $675 | $775 |

KGN-32 Oriole
1940. 16" acoustic archtop, Kalamazoo brand logo, stencil Oriole-bird picture on headstock, natural.

| 1940 | | $1,200 | $1,500 |

KHG Series
1936-1941. Acoustic Hawaiian guitar (HG), some converted to Spanish set-up.

| 1936-1940 | KHG-11 | $600 | $800 |
| 1936-1941 | KHG-14 | $900 | $1,100 |

Kamico
1947-1951. Flat-top acoustic guitars. Low-end budget brand made by Kay Musical Instrument Company and sold through various distributors. They also offered lap steel and amp sets.

MODEL YEAR	FEATURES	EXC. COND. LOW	HIGH

K Stratotone Thin Single
1950s. Similar to Kay Stratotone-style neck-thru solidbody, single slim-tube pickup.

| 1950s | | $1,100 | $1,350 |

Kapa
Ca. 1962-1970. Begun by Dutch immigrant and music store owner Koob Veneman in Hyattsville, Maryland whose father had made Amka guitars in Holland. Kapa is from K for Koob, A for son Albert, P for daughter Patricia, and A for wife Adeline. Crown shield logo from Amka guitars. The brand included some Hofner and Italian imports in '60. Ca. '66 Kapa started offering thinner bodies. Some German Pix pickups ca. '66. Thinlines and Japanese bodies in '69. Kapa closed shop in '70 and the parts and equipment were sold to Micro-Frets and Mosrite. Later Veneman was involved with Bradley copy guitars imported from Japan. Approximately 120,000 Kapa guitars and basses were made.

Electric
1962-1970. Various models include Challenger with 3-way toggle from '62-'66/'67 and 2 on/off switches after; Cobra with 1 pickup; Continental and Continental 12-string; Minstrel and Minstrel 12-string with teardrop shape, 3 pickups; and the Wildcat, mini offset double-cut, 3 pickups and mute.

| 1962-1970 | Various models | $200 | $500 |

Karol Guitars
2001-present. Luthier Tony Karol builds his custom, premium grade, acoustic and electric guitars in Mississauga, Ontario.

Kasha
1967-1997. Innovative classical guitars built by luthier Richard Schneider in collaboration with Dr. Michael Kasha. Schneider also consulted for Gibson and Gretsch. Schneider died in '97.

Kathy Wingert Guitars
1996-present. Luthier Kathy Wingert builds her premium grade, production/custom, flat-tops in Rancho Palos Verdes, California.

Kawai
1927-present. Kawai is a Japanese piano and guitar maker. They started offering guitars around '56 and they were imported into the U.S. carrying many different brand names, including Kimberly and Teisco. In '67 Kawai purchased Teisco. Odd-shaped guitars were offered from late-'60s through the mid-'70s. Few imports carrying the Kawai brand until the late-'70s; best known for high quality basses. By '90s they were making plexiglass replicas of Teisco Spectrum 5 and Kawai moon-shaped guitar. Kawai quit offering guitars and basses around 2002.

Acoustic

| 1956-2002 | | $200 | $350 |

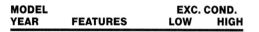

MODEL YEAR	FEATURES	EXC. COND. LOW	HIGH
Electric			
1956-2002	Common model	$200	$450
1956-2002	Rare model	$500	$750

Kay

Ca. 1931 (1890)-present. Originally founded in Chicago, Illinois as Groehsl Company (or Groehsel) in 1890, making bowl-backed mandolins. Offered Groehsl, Stromberg, Kay Kraft, Kay, Arch Kraft brand names, plus made guitars for S.S.Maxwell, Old Kraftsman (Spiegel), Recording King (Wards), Supertone (Sears), Silvertone (Sears), National, Dobro, Custom Kraft (St.Louis Music), Hollywood (Shireson Bros.), Oahu and others.

In 1921 the name was changed to Stromberg-Voisinet Company. Henry Kay "Hank" Kuhrmeyer joined the company in '23 and was secretary by '25. By the mid-'20s the company was making many better Montgomery Ward guitars, banjos and mandolins, often with lots of pearloid. First production electric guitars and amps are introduced with big fanfare in '28; perhaps only 200 or so made. Last Stromberg instruments seen in '32. Kuhrmeyer becomes president and the Kay Kraft brand was introduced in '31, probably named for Kuhrmeyer's middle name, though S-V had used Kay brand on German Kreuzinger violins '28-'36. By '34, if not earlier, the company is changed to the Kay Musical Instrument Company. A new factory was built at 1640 West Walnut Street in '35. The Kay Kraft brand ends in '37 and the Kay brand is introduced in late-'36 or '37.

Violin Style Guitars and upright acoustic basses debut in '38. In '40 the first guitars for Sears, carrying the new Silvertone brand, are offered. Kamico budget line introduced in '47 and Rex flat-tops and archtops sold through Gretsch in late-'40s. Kuhrmeyer retires in '55 dies a year later. New gigantic factory in Elk Grove Village, Illinois opens in '64. Seeburg purchased Kay in '66 and sold it to Valco in '67. Valco/Kay went out of business in '68 and its assets were auctioned in '69. The Kay name went to Sol Weindling and Barry Hornstein of W.M.I. (Teisco Del Rey) who began putting Kay name on Teisco guitars. By '73 most Teisco guitars are called Kay. Tony Blair, president of Indianapolis-based A.R. Musical Enterprises Inc. (founded in '73) purchased the Kay nameplate in '79 and currently distributes Kay in the U.S. Currently Kay offers budget and intermediate grade, production, acoustic, semi-hollow body, solidbody, and resonator guitars. They also make amps, basses, banjos, mandolins, ukes, and violins.

K20
1939-1942. 16" archtop, solid spruce top, maple back and sides, sunburst.

1939-1942		$250	$325

K20T
1970s. Japanese-made solidbody, 2 pickups, tremolo, model number on neck plate, circle-capital K logo on headstock.

1970s		$125	$150

K22
1947-1956. Flat-top similar to Gibson J-100 17", spruce top, mahogany back and sides.

1947-1956		$600	$750

K26
1947-1951. Flat-top, block markers, natural.

1947-1951		$650	$800

K27
1952-1956. 17" Jumbo, fancy appointments.

1952-1956		$1,000	$1,250

K37T Spanish Tenor
1952-1956. Mahogany bodied archtop, tenor.

1952-1956		$200	$250

K44
1947-1951. Non-cut archtop, solid spruce top, 17" curly maple veneered body, block markers, sunburst.

1947-1951		$450	$550

K45
1952-1954. Non-cut archtop, 17" body, engraved tortoiseshell-celluloid headstock, large block markers, natural.

1952-1954		$550	$675

K45 Travel Guitar
1981. Made in Korea, known as the 'rifle guitar', 'travel guitar', or 'Austin-Hatchet copy', circle K logo.

1981		$325	$400

K46
1947-1951. Non-cut archtop, solid spruce top, 17" curly maple-veneered body, double-eighth note headstock inlay, sunburst.

1947-1951		$475	$600

K48 Artist
1947-1951. Non-cut archtop, 17" solid spruce top with figured maple back and sides, split block inlays, sunburst or black.

1947-1951		$850	$1,100

K48/K21 Jazz Special
Late-1960s. Slim solidbody with 3 reflective pickups, garden spade headstock, fancy position Circle K headstock logo, white.

1968		$450	$550

K100 Vanguard
1961-1966. Offset double-cut slab solidbody, genuine maple veneered top and back over hardwood body, sunburst.

1961-1966		$225	$275

K102 Vanguard
1961-1966. Double pickup version of the K100, sunburst.

1961-1966		$275	$325

K136 (aka Stratotone)
1955-1957. Small single-cut slab solidbody electric, similar to Harmony Stratotone style, set neck, 1 pickup, trapeze tailpiece, triangle paint graphic in Spring Green and White Mist, matching green headstock, attractive finish adds value to this otherwise lower-end student model.

1955-1957		$1,300	$1,600

Kathy Wingert Flat-Top

Kay Square Neck

1960 Kay K775 Jazz II
Art Vogue

1960 Kay K8995 Upbeat

MODEL YEAR	FEATURES	EXC. COND. LOW	HIGH

K142 (aka Stratotone)
1955-1957. Small slab solidbody, introduced in '55 along with the K136, offered with 1 pickup or 2 pickups (more rare), trapeze tailpiece, copper finish.

| 1955-1957 | 1 pickup | $1,000 | $1,250 |
| 1955-1957 | 2 pickups | $1,200 | $1,500 |

K161 Thin Twin/Jimmy Reed
1952-1958. Single-cut semi-hollow body, 2 pickups.

| 1952-1958 | | $1,400 | $1,800 |

K300 Double Cutaway Solid Electric
1962-1966. Two single-coils, block inlays, some with curly maple top and some with plain maple top, natural.

| 1962-1966 | | $425 | $525 |

K535
1961-1965. Thinline double-cut, 2 pickups, vibrato, sunburst.

| 1961-1965 | | $500 | $650 |

K550 Dove
1970s. Square shoulder D-style, 2 Dove-style 'guards, capital K logo.

| 1970s | | $100 | $125 |

K571/K572/K573 Speed Demon
1961-1965. Thinline semi-acoustic/electric, single pointed cutaway, some with Bigsby vibrato, with 1 (K571), 2 (K572) or 3 (K573) pickups. There was also a Speed Demon solidbody.

1961-1965	571, 1 pickup	$400	$525
1961-1965	572, 2 pickups	$475	$575
1961-1965	573, 3 pickups	$550	$675

K580 Galaxy
1963. Thinline, single-cut, 1 pickup.

| 1963 | | $425 | $525 |

K592 Double Cutaway Thinline
1962-1966. Thinline semi-acoustic/electric, double Florentine cut, 2 or 3 pickups, Bigsby vibrato, pie-slice inlays, cherry.

| 1962-1966 | | $500 | $625 |

K672/K673 Swingmaster
1961-1965. Single rounded cutaway semi-hollowbody, with 2 (K672) or 3 (K673) pickups.

| 1961-1965 | 672, 2 pickups | $1,000 | $1,250 |
| 1961-1965 | 673, 3 pickups | $1,200 | $1,450 |

K775/K776 Jazz II
1961-1966. Electric thinline archtop, double-cut, standard Bigsby vibrato, 2 Gold K pickups, 4 knobs with toggle controls. Replaces Barney Kessel series as top-of-the-line model.

| 1961-1966 | 775, shaded | $1,400 | $1,700 |
| 1961-1966 | 776, blond | $1,400 | $1,700 |

K797 Acoustic Archtop
1930s. Full size student-intermediate acoustic archtop, 3-on-a-strip tuners, dot markers, sunburst.

| 1935-1937 | | $250 | $325 |

K1160 Standard
1957-1964. Small 13" (standard) flat-top, laminated construction.

| 1957-1964 | | $50 | $65 |

K1452 Aristocrat
1952. Acoustic-electric archtop, 2 pickups, sunburst.

| 1952 | | $800 | $1,000 |

K1700/K1701 Barney Kessel Pro
1957-1960. 13" hollowbody, single-cut, Kelvinator headstock, ebony 'board with pearl inlays, white binding, 1 (K1701) or 2 (K1700) pickups, sunburst.

| 1957-1960 | 1700, 2 pickups | $2,500 | $3,000 |
| 1957-1960 | 1701, 1 pickup | $2,200 | $2,700 |

K1961/K1962/K1963 Value Leader
1960-1965. Part of Value Leader line, thinline single-cut, hollowbody, identified by single chrome-plated checkered, body-length guard on treble side, laminated maple body, maple neck, dot markers, sunburst, with 1 (K1961), 2 (K1962) or 3 (K1963) pickups.

1960-1965	1961, 1 pickup	$425	$525
1960-1965	1962, 2 pickups	$525	$625
1960-1965	1963, 3 pickups	$575	$675

K1982/K1983 Style Leader/Jimmy Reed
1960-1965. Part of the Style Leader mid-level Kay line. Sometimes dubbed Jimmy Reed of 1960s. Easily identified by the long brushed copper dual guardplates on either side of the strings. Brown or gleaming golden blond (natural) finish, laminated curly maple body, simple script Kay logo, with 2 (K1982) or 3 (K1983) pickups.

| 1960-1965 | 1982, 2 pickups | $575 | $700 |
| 1960-1965 | 1983, 3 pickups | $650 | $800 |

K3500 Studio Concert
1966-1968. 14 1/2" flat-top, solid spruce top, laminated maple back and sides.

| 1966-1968 | | $75 | $95 |

K5113 Plains Special
1968. Flat-top, solid spruce top, laminated mahogany back and sides.

| 1968 | | $125 | $175 |

K5160 Auditorium
1957-1965. Flat-top 15" auditorium-size, laminated construction.

| 1957-1965 | | $125 | $175 |

K6100 Country
1950s-1960s. Jumbo flat-top, spruce x-braced top, mahogany back and sides, natural.

| 1957-1962 | | $350 | $450 |

K6116 Super Auditorium
1957-1965. Super Auditorium-size flat-top, laminated figured maple back and sides, solid spruce top.

| 1957-1965 | | $200 | $250 |

K6120 Western
1960s. Jumbo flat-top, laminated maple body, pinless bridge, sunburst.

| 1962 | | $175 | $225 |

K6130 Calypso
1960-1965. 15 1/2" flat-top with narrow waist, slotted headstock, natural.

| 1960-1965 | | $250 | $300 |

K6533/K6535 Value Leader
1961-1965. Value Leader was the budget line of Kay, full body archtop, with 1 (K6533) or 2 (K6535) pickups, sunburst.

| 1961-1965 | 6533, 1 pickup | $300 | $375 |
| 1961-1965 | 6535, 2 pickups | $350 | $400 |

MODEL YEAR	FEATURES	EXC. COND. LOW	HIGH

K6700/K6701 Barney Kessel Artist
1956-1960. Single-cut, 15 1/2" body, 1 (K6701) or 2 (K6700) pickups, Kelvinator headstock, sunburst or blond.

1956-1960	6700, 2 pickups	$2,500	$3,000
1956-1960	6701, 1 pickup	$2,200	$2,700

K7000 Artist
1960-1965. Highest-end of Kay classical series, fan bracing, spruce top, maple back and sides.

1960-1965		$375	$450

K7010 Concerto
1960-1965. Entry level of Kay classical series.

1960-1965		$75	$100

K7010 Maestro
1960-1965. Middle level of Kay classical series.

1960-1965		$200	$275

K8110 Master
1957-1960. 17" master-size flat-top which was largest of the series, laminated construction.

1957-1960		$150	$200

K8127 Solo Special
1957-1965. Kay's professional grade flat-top, narrow waist jumbo, block markers.

1957-1965		$425	$550

K8700/K8701 Barney Kessel Jazz Special
1956-1960. Part of the "Gold K Line", top-of-the-line model, 17" single-cut archtop, 1 (K8701) or 2 (K8700) pickups, 4 controls and toggle, distinctive Kelvinator headstock with white background, natural or shaded sunburst, Barney Kessel signature logo on acrylic scalloped 'guard, no signature logo on '60 model.

1956-1960	8700, 2 pickups	$2,500	$3,000
1956-1960	8701, 1 pickup	$2,200	$2,700

K8990/K8995 Upbeat
1956/1958-1960. Less expensive alternative to Barney Kessel Jazz Special, 2 (K8990) or 3 (K8995) pickups, sunburst.

1956-1960	8990, 2 pickups	$1,500	$2,000
1958-1960	8995, 3 pickups	$1,700	$2,200

Wood Amplifying Guitar
1934. Engineered after Dobro/National metal resonator models except the resonator and chamber on this model are made of wood, small production.

1934		$2,400	$3,000

Kay Kraft
1927-1937. First brand name of the Kay Musical Instrument Company as it began its transition from Stromberg-Voisinet Company to Kay (see Kay for more info).

Recording King

1931-1937		$500	$625

Venetian Archtop
1930s. Unique Venetian cutaway body style, acoustic with round soundhole, flower-vine decal art on low bout.

1930s		$800	$1,000

KB
1989-present. Luthier Ken Bebensee builds his premium grade, custom, acoustic and electric gui-

tars in North San Juan, California. He was located in San Luis Obispo from '89-'01. He also builds basses and mandolins.

Kel Kroydon (by Gibson)
1930-1933. Private branded budget level instruments made by Gibson. They also had mandolins and banjos. The name has been revived on a line of banjos by Tom Mirisola and made in Nashville.

KK-1
1930-1933. 14 3/4" L-0 sytle body, colorful parrot stencils on body.

1930-1933		$2,900	$3,500

Keller Custom Guitars
1994-present. Professional grade, production/custom, solidbody guitars built by luthier Randall Keller in Mandan, North Dakota.

Keller Guitars
1975-present. Premium grade, production/custom, flat-tops made by luthier Michael L. Keller in Rochester, Minnesota.

Kelly Guitars
1968-present. Luthier Rick Kelly builds professional grade, custom, solidbody electric guitars in New York, New York.

Ken Franklin
2003-present. Luthier Ken Franklin builds his premium grade, production/custom, acoustic guitars in Ukiah, California.

Kendrick
1989-present. Premium grade, production/custom, solidbody guitars built in Texas. Founded by Gerald Weber in Pflugerville, Texas and currently located in Kempner, Texas. Mainly known for their handmade tube amps, Kendrick added guitars in '94 and also offers speakers and effects.

Kent
1961-1969. Imported from Japan by Buegeleisen and Jacobson of New York, New York. Manufacturers unknown but many early guitars and basses were made by Guyatone and Teisco.

Acoustic Flat-Top
1962-1969. Various models.

1962-1969		$125	$150

Acoustic/Electric
1962-1969. Various models.

1962-1969		$150	$175

Electric 12-String
1965-1969. Thinline electric, double pointy cutaways, 12 strings, slanted dual pickup, sunburst.

1965-1969		$250	$350

Semi-Hollow Electric
1962-1969. Thinline electric, offset double pointy cutaways, slanted dual pickups, various colors.

1962-1969		$250	$350

1933 Kay Kraft Style A

Ken Franklin Merlin

GUITARS

Kevin Ryan Rosewood

Kingslight Jumbo Cutaway

MODEL YEAR	FEATURES	EXC. COND. LOW	HIGH

Solidbody Electric
1962-1969. Models include Polaris I, II and III, Lido, Copa and Videocaster.

1962-1969	Common model	$125	$250
1962-1969	Rare model	$250	$350

Kevin Ryan Guitars
1989-present. Premium grade, custom, flat-tops built by luthier Kevin Ryan in Westminster, California.

Kiesel
See Carvin.

Kimberly
Late-1960s-early-1970s. Private branded import made in the same Japanese factory as Teisco. They also made basses.

May Queen
1960s. Same as Teisco May Queen with Kimberly script logo on headstock and May Queen Teisco on the 'guard.

1960s		$500	$625

Kinal
1969-present. Production/custom, professional and premium grade, solid body electric and archtop guitars built and imported by luthier Michael Kinal in Vancouver, British Columbia. He also builds basses.

King's Stone
1960s. Guitar brand exported by Japan's Hoshino (Ibanez).

Kingsley
1960s. Early Japanese imports, Teisco-made.

Soldibody Electric
1960s. Four pickups with tremolo.

1960s		$275	$350

Kingslight Guitars
1980-present. Luthier John Kingslight builds his premium grade, custom/production, steel string guitars in Portage, Michigan (in Taos, New Mexico for '80-'83). He also builds basses.

Kingston
Ca. 1958-1967. Guitars and basses imported from Japan by Jack Westheimer and Westheimer Importing Corporation of Chicago, Illinois. Early examples made by Guyatone and Teisco. They also offered mandolins.

Electric
1958-1967. Various models include: B-1, soldibody, 1 pickup; B-2T/B-3T/B-4T, solidbodies, 2/3/4 pickups and tremolo; SA-27, thin hollowbody, 2 pickups, tremolo.

1958-1967	Common model	$125	$250
1958-1967	Rare model	$250	$350

Kinscherff Guitars
1990-present. Luthier Jamie Kinscherff builds his premium grade, production/custom, flat-top guitars in Austin, Texas.

Kleartone
1930s. Private brand made by Regal and/or Gibson.

Small Flat-Top

1930s		$500	$650

Klein Acoustic Guitars
1972-present. Luthiers Steve Klein and Steven Kauffman build their production/custom, premium and presentation grade flat-tops in Sonoma, California. They also build basses.

Klein Electric Guitars
1988-2007. Steve Klein added electrics to his line in '88. In '95, he sold the electric part of his business to Lorenzo German, who continued to produce professional grade, production/custom, solidbody guitars in Linden, California. He also built basses.

K-Line Guitars
2005-present. Professional grade, production/custom, T-style and S-style guitars built by luthier Chris Kroenlein in St. Louis, Missouri. He also builds basses.

Klira
1887-1980s. Founded by Johannes Klira in Schoenbach, Germany, mainly made violins, but added guitars in the 1950s. The guitars of the '50s and '60s were original designs, but by the '70s most models were similar to popular American models. The guitars of the '50s and '60s were aimed at the budget market, but workmanship improved with the '70s models. They also made basses.

Electric

1960s	Common model	$300	$400
1960s	Rare model	$400	$650

Knox
Early-mid-1960s. Budget grade guitars imported from Japan, script Knox logo on headstock.

Electric Solidbody
1960s. Student models, 2 pickups, push buttons.

1960s		$100	$150

Knutsen
1890s-1920s. Luthier Chris J. Knutsen of Tacoma and Seattle, Washington, experimented with and perfected Hawaiian and harp guitar models. He moved to Los Angeles, California around 1916, where he also made steels and ukes. Dealers state the glue used on Knutsen instruments is prone to fail and instruments may need repair.

MODEL		EXC. COND.	
YEAR	FEATURES	LOW	HIGH

Convertible

1909-1914. Flat-top model with adjustable neck angle that allowed for a convertible Hawaiian or Spanish setup.

| 1909-1914 | | $3,100 | $3,600 |

Harp Guitar

1900s. Normally 11 strings with fancy purfling and trim.

| 1900-1910 | | $2,400 | $3,100 |

Knutson Luthiery

1981-present. Professional and premium grade, custom, archtop and flat-top guitars built by luthier John Knutson in Forestville, California. He also builds basses, lap steels and mandolins.

Kohno

1960-present. Luthier Masaru Kohno built his classical guitars in Tokyo, Japan. When he died in '98, production was taken over by his nephew, Masaki Sakurai.

Koll

1990-present. Professional and premium grade, custom/production, solidbody, chambered, and archtop guitars built by luthier Saul Koll, originally in Long Beach, California, and since '93, in Portland, Oregon. He also builds basses.

Kona

1910s-1920s, 2001-present. Acoustic Hawaiian guitars sold by C.S. Delano and others, with later models made by the Herman Weissenborn Co. Weissenborn appointments are in line with style number, with thicker body and solid neck construction. Since '01, the Kona name is now used on an import line of budget grade, production, acoustic and electric guitars and basses. They also offer banjos and amps.

Style 2

| 1927-1928 | | $2,800 | $3,400 |

Style 3

| 1920s | Koa | $3,500 | $4,100 |

Style 4

| 1920s | Brown koa | $4,000 | $4,700 |

Kona Guitar Company

2000-present. Located in Fort Worth, Texas, Kona imports budget and intermediate grade, production, nylon and steel string acoustic and solid and semi-hollow body electric guitars. They also offer basses, amps, mandolins and ukes.

Koontz

1970-late 1980s. Luthier Sam Koontz started building custom guitars in the late '50s. Starting in '66 Koontz, who was associated with Harptone guitars, built guitars for Standel. In '70, he opened his own shop in Linden, New Jersey, building a variety of custom guitars. Koontz died in the late '80s. His guitars varied greatly and should be valued on a case-by-case basis.

Kopp String Instruments

2000-present. Located in Republic, Ohio from 2000-2004, luthier Denny Kopp presently builds his professional and premium grade, production/custom, semi-hollow archtop electric and hand-carved archtop jazz guitars in Catawba Island, Ohio.

Kopy Kat

1970s. Budget copy-era solidbody, semi-hollow body and acoustic guitars imported from Japan, Kopy Kat logo on headstock or on inside label. They also made basses and mandolins.

Acoustic

| 1970s | J-200 copy | $125 | $175 |

Kragenbrink

2001-present. Premium grade, production/custom, steel string acoustic guitars built by luthier Lance Kragenbrink in Vandercook Lake, Michigan.

Kramer

1976-1990, 1995-present. Currently Kramer offers budget and intermediate grade, production, imported acoustic, acoustic/electric, semi-hollow and solidbody guitars. They also offer basses, amps and effects.

Founded by New York music retailer Dennis Berardi, ex-Travis Bean partner Gary Kramer and ex-Norlin executive Peter LaPlaca. Initial financing provided by real estate developer Henry Vaccaro. Parent company named BKL Corporation (Berardi, Kramer, LaPlaca), located in Neptune City, New Jersey. The first guitars were designed by Berardi and luthier Phil Petillo and featured aluminum necks with wooden inserts on back to give them a wooden feel. Guitar production commenced in late-'76. Control passed to Guitar Center of Los Angeles for '79-'82, which recommended a switch to more economical wood necks. Aluminum necks were phased out during the early-'80s, and were last produced in '85. In '84 they added their first import models, the Japanese-made Focus line, followed by the Korean-made Striker line. By 1986 Kramer was the top American electric guitarmaker. In '89, a new investment group was brought in with James Liati as president, hoping for access to Russian market, but the company went of business in late-'90. In '95 Henry Vaccaro and new partners revived the company and designed a number of new guitars in conjunction with Phil Petillo. However, in '97 the Kramer brand was sold to Gibson. In '98, Henry Vaccaro released his new line of aluminum-core neck, split headstock guitars under the Vacarro brand. From the late 1990s to the late 2000s, Kramer distribution was limited and done only through Gibson's MusicYo website. By the late 2000s, Gibson began to distribute the brand through traditional music retail channels with new issues and 1980s legacy models.

Non-U.S.-made models include the following lines: Aerostar, Ferrington, Focus, Hundred (post-

1960s Kingston Swinger
Bill Cherensky

Kohno Professional-J

Kramer Baretta

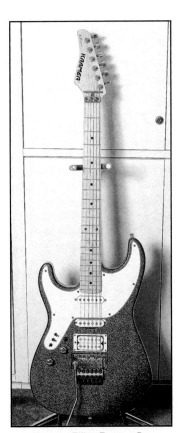

Kramer Eliot Easton Pro

MODEL YEAR	FEATURES	EXC. COND. LOW	HIGH

'85 made with 3 digits in the 100-900), Showster, Striker, Thousand (post-'85 made with 4 digits in the 1000-9000), XL (except XL-5 made in '80s).

Serial numbers for import models include:

Two alpha followed by 4 numbers: for example AA2341 with any assortment of letters and numbers.

One alpha followed by 5 numbers: for example B23412.

Five numbers: for example 23412.

Model number preceding numbers: for example XL1-03205.

The notation "Kramer, Neptune, NJ" does indicate U.S.A.-made production.

Most post-'85 Kramers were ESP Japanese-made guitars. American Series were ESP Japanese components that were assembled in the U.S.

The vintage/used market makes value distinctions between U.S.-made and import models.

Headstock and logo shape can help identify U.S. versus imports as follows:

Traditional or Classic headstock with capital K as Kramer: U.S.A. '81-'84.

Banana (soft edges) headstock with all caps KRAMER: U.S.A. American Series '84-'86.

Pointy (sharp cut) headstock with all caps KRAMER: U.S.A. American Series '86-'87.

Pointy (sharp cut) headstock with down-sized letters Kramer plus American decal: U.S.A. American Series '87-'94.

Pointy (sharp cut) headstock with down-sized letters Kramer but without American decal, is an import.

1984 Reissue
2003-2007. Made in the U.S., based on EVH's Kramer, single Gibson humbucker, Rose tremolo, various colors.

2003-2007		$500	$600

250-G Special
1977-1979. Offset double-cut, tropical woods, aluminum neck, dot markers, 2 pickups.

1977-1979		$700	$850

350-G Standard
1976-1979. Offset double-cut, tropical woods, aluminum neck, tuning fork headstock, ebonol 'board, zero fret, 2 single coils, dot inlays. The 350 and 450 were Kramer's first models.

1976-1979		$900	$1,050

450-G Deluxe
1976-1980. Like 350-G, but with block inlays, 2 humbuckers. Became the 450G Deluxe in late '77 with dot inlays.

1976-1980		$1,000	$1,150

650-G Artist
1977-1980. Aluminum neck, ebonol 'board, double-cut solidbody, 2 humbuckers.

1977-1980		$1,400	$1,700

MODEL YEAR	FEATURES	EXC. COND. LOW	HIGH

Baretta
1984-1990. Offset double-cut, banana six-on-a-side headstock, 1 pickup, Floyd Rose tremolo, black hardware, U.S.A.-made.

1984	1st style, larger headstock	$1,250	$1,550
1984-1985	2nd style, angled headstock	$775	$975
1985-1987	3rd style, ESP neck	$425	$525
1985-1987	With graphics	$475	$600
1988-1990	Standard opaque	$500	$625
1988-1990	With graphics	$625	$725
1990	Baretta III hybrid	$425	$525

Baretta '85 Reissue
2006. Made in the U.S., based on 1985 banana headstock model, Rose tremolo.

2006		$500	$700

Baretta II/Soloist
1986-1990. Soloist sleek body with pointed cutaway horns.

1986-1990		$375	$450

Classic Series
1986-1987. Solidbody copies of the famous Southern California builder, including offset contoured double-cut (Classic I) and slab body single-cut designs (Classic II and Classic III).

1986-1987	Classic I	$425	$525
1986-1987	Classic II	$400	$500
1986-1987	Classic III	$400	$500

Condor
1985-1986. Futuristic 4-point body with large upper bass horn and lower treble horn.

1985-1986		$400	$500

DMZ Custom Series
1978-1981. Solidbody double-cut with larger upper horn, bolt-on aluminum T-neck, slot headstock, models include the 1000 (super distortion humbuckers), 2000 (dual-sound humbuckers), 3000 (3 SDS single-coils), 6000 (dual-sound humbuckers, active DBL).

1978-1981	DMZ-1000	$850	$1,050
1978-1981	DMZ-2000	$875	$1,075
1978-1981	DMZ-3000	$1,000	$1,200
1978-1981	DMZ-6000	$1,100	$1,300

Duke Custom/Standard
1981-1982. Headless aluminum neck, 22-fret neck, 1 pickup, Floyd Rose tremolo.

1981-1982		$350	$450

Duke Special
1982-1985. Headless aluminum neck, two pickups, tuners on body.

1982-1985		$400	$500

Eliot Easton Pro I
1987-1988. Designed by Eliot Easton, offset double-cut, six-on-a-side headstock, Floyd Rose tremolo, 2 single-coils and 1 humbucker.

1987-1988		$600	$725

Eliot Easton Pro II
1987-1988. Same as Pro I, but with fixed-bridge tailpiece, 2 single-coils.

1987-1988		$500	$600

MODEL YEAR	FEATURES	EXC. COND. LOW	HIGH

Ferrington

1985-1990. Acoustic-electric, offered in single- and double-cut, bolt-on electric-style neck, transducers, made in Korea.

1985-1990		$275	$350

Floyd Rose Signature Edition

1983-1984. Four pointed-bout body with deep cutaway below tremolo assembly, Floyd Rose vibrato system.

1983-1984		$575	$625

Focus/F Series (Import)

1983-1989. Kramer introduced the Focus series as import copies of their American-made models like the Pacer, Baretta, Vanguard (Rhoads-V), and Voyager (star body). Model numbers were 1000-6000, plus the Focus Classic I, II, and III. Most models were offset, double-cut solidbodies. In '87 the Focus line was renamed the F-Series. In '88 a neck-through body design, which is noted as NT, was introduced for a short time. The Classic series was offered with over a dozen color options.

YEAR	FEATURES	LOW	HIGH
1983	Focus 4000, Pacer	$225	$300
1983-1984	Focus 1000, Pacer Special	$175	$225
1983-1987	Focus 2000, Pacer Imperial	$175	$225
1983-1987	Focus 3000, Pacer Deluxe	$225	$300
1983-1987	Focus 6000, Pacer Custom	$225	$300
1984-1986	Focus 1000, Baretta	$275	$350
1984-1986	Focus 4000, Vanguard	$225	$300
1986-1987	Focus 5000, Voyager	$225	$300
1987-1989	Focus 1000/F1000	$250	$300
1987-1989	Focus Classic I, 3 pickups	$225	$300
1987-1989	Focus Classic II	$225	$300
1987-1989	Focus Classic III	$225	$300
1988	Focus 1000/F1000 NT	$325	$400
1988	Focus 2000/F2000 NT	$225	$300
1988-1989	Focus 2000/F2000	$150	$200
1988-1989	Focus 3000/F3000	$225	$300
1988-1989	Focus 6000/F6000	$225	$300
1989	Focus 1000/F1000	$250	$300

Gene Simmons Axe

1980-1981. Axe-shaped guitar, aluminum neck, 1 humbucker, slot headstock, stop tailpiece, 25 were made.

1980-1981		$2,500	$3,000

Gorky Park (Import)

1986-1989. Triangular balalaika, bolt-on maple neck, pointy droopy six-on-a-side headstock, 1 pickup, Floyd Rose tremolo, red with iron sickle graphics, tribute to Russian rock, reissued in late-'90s.

1986-1989		$175	$225

Hundred Series

1988-1990. Import budget line, most with offset double-cut 7/8th solidbody.

1988-1989	615, bound 610	$250	$275

MODEL YEAR	FEATURES	EXC. COND. LOW	HIGH
1988-1990	110, 1 pickup	$175	$200
1988-1990	120	$225	$250
1988-1990	210, 2 pickups	$200	$225
1988-1990	220	$225	$250
1988-1990	310, 3 pickups	$200	$225
1988-1990	410	$200	$225
1988-1990	420, V-body	$250	$275
1988-1990	610, sleek body, 3 pickups	$225	$250
1988-1990	620	$225	$250
1989-1990	111, 2 pickups	$200	$225
1989-1990	112, carved 111	$225	$250
1989-1990	612	$225	$250
1989-1990	710	$225	$250
1989-1990	720, revised 710	$225	$250

Jersey Star

2004-2007. A reissue of the Richie Sambora model.

2004-2007		$675	$800

Liberty '86 Series

1986-1987. Offset double cut arched-top solidbody, pointy head, 2 humbuckers, black, white or flame-maple bound body.

1986-1987	Black or white	$550	$650
1986-1987	Flame maple	$600	$725

Metalist/Showster Series

1989-1990. Korean-made offset double-cut solidbody, metal trim in body design, pointy droopy six-on-a-side headstock, various pickup options, Floyd Rose.

1989-1990		$350	$400

Night Rider

2000-2007. Inexpensive import double-cut semi-hollow, 2 humbuckers.

2000-2007		$75	$125

Nightswan

1987-1990. Offset double-cut, six-on-a-side headstock, 2 Duncan humbuckers, Floyd Rose tremolo, blue metallic.

1987-1990		$900	$1,125
1987-1990	Custom color or finish	$1,050	$1,200

Pacer Series

1981-1987. Offset double-cut, six-on-a-side headstock, various pickup options, bolt-on maple neck.

1981-1982	Pacer, 2 pickups, soft headstock	$950	$1,150
1982	Imperial, soft headstock	$525	$650
1982	Special, 1 pickup	$500	$625
1982-1984	Carerra, 2 pickups, classic headstock	$575	$725
1982-1984	Pacer, 2 pickups, classic headstock	$550	$700
1983-1984	Custom, classic headstock	$575	$725
1983-1984	Deluxe, classic headstock	$550	$675
1983-1984	Imperial, classic headstock	$525	$650
1984	Pacer, 2 pickups, banana headstock	$550	$700

Kramer Focus

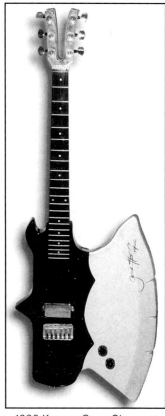

1980 Kramer Gene Simmons Axe

Kramer Vanguard

Lacey Arch Nouveau

MODEL YEAR	FEATURES	EXC. COND. LOW	HIGH
1985	Carerra USA, 2 pickups, banana headstock	$575	$725
1985	Custom USA, banana headstock	$575	$725
1985	Deluxe USA, banana headstock	$550	$675
1985	Imperial USA, banana headstock	$525	$650
1986	Carerra Japan, 2 pickups, pointy headstock	$575	$725
1986-1987	Custom Japan, pointy headstock	$575	$725
1986-1987	Deluxe USA/Japan, pointy headstock	$550	$675
1986-1987	Imperial USA/ Japan, pointy headstock	$525	$650
1987	Custom II	$575	$725

Paul Dean

1986-1988. Offset double cut, neck-thru, hum/single/single pickups, droopy pointy head.

1986-1988		$600	$750

ProAxe (U.S.A.)

1989-1990. U.S.A.-made, offset double-cut, sharp pointy headstock, dot markers, 2 or 3 pickups, smaller 7/8ths size body, 3 models offered with slightly different pickup options. The model was discontinued when Kramer went out of business in 1990.

1989-1990	Deluxe	$650	$800
1989-1990	Special	$625	$775
1989-1990	Standard	$600	$750

Richie Sambora

1987-1989. Designed by Sambora, mahogany offset double-cut, maple neck, pointy droopy 6-on-a-side headstock, gold hardware, Floyd Rose, 3 pickups, 2 coil-taps.

1987-1989		$925	$1,175

Ripley Series

1984-1987. Offset double-cut, banana six-on-a-side headstock, 22 frets, hexophonic humbucking pickups, panpots, dual volume, Floyd Rose tremolo, black hardware, stereo output, pointy droopy headstock in '87.

1984-1987		$800	$1,000

Savant/Showster Series

1989-1990. Offset double-cut solidbody, pointy headstock, various pickup options.

1989-1990		$250	$300

Stagemaster Deluxe (U.S.A.)

1981. U.S.-made version.

1981		$1,200	$1,500

Stagemaster Series (Import)

1983-1987. Offset double-cut neck-thru solidbody models, smaller 7/8th body, built by ESP in Japan.

1983-1987	Custom/Custom I	$600	$700
1983-1987	Deluxe/Deluxe I	$575	$675
1983-1987	Imperial	$550	$650
1983-1987	Special	$500	$600
1983-1987	Standard/Standard I	$550	$650
1987	Deluxe II	$475	$575

Striker Series (Import)

1984-1989. Korean imports, offset double-cut, various pickup options, series included Striker 100, 200, 300, 400, 600 and 700 Bass.

1984-1989	100ST, 1 pickup	$200	$250
1984-1989	200ST, 2 pickups	$225	$275
1984-1989	300ST, 3 pickups	$250	$300
1985-1989	400ST, Rhoads-body	$250	$300
1985-1989	500ST, Star-body	$275	$325
1986-1989	600ST, 3 pickups	$275	$325
1988-1989	605ST, 3 pickups, bound	$300	$350

Sustainer

1989. Offset double-cut solidbody, reverse pointy headstock, Floyd Rose tremolo.

1989		$625	$750

Vanguard Series

1981-1986, 1999-present. U.S.-made or American Series (assembled in U.S.). V shape, 1 humbucker, aluminum (Special '81-'83) or wood (Custom '81-'83) neck. Added for '83-'84 were the Imperial (wood neck, 2 humbuckers) and the Headless (alum neck, 1 humbucker). For '85-'86, the body was modified to a Jackson Randy Rhoads style V body, with a banana headstock and 2 humbuckers. In '99 this last design was revived as an import.

1981-1983	Custom	$500	$600
1981-1983	Special	$475	$575
1983-1984	Imperial, wood neck	$475	$575
1985-1986	Rhoads V-body	$500	$600

Vanguard (Reissue)

1999-present. 2 humbuckers, pointy headstock, licensed Floyd Rose.

1999-2010		$200	$250

Voyager

1982-1985. Wood neck, classic headstock, rosewood 'board, 1 pickup (2 optional), Floyd Rose tremolo, black.

1982-1985	Imperial	$450	$550

XKG-10

1980-1981. Aluminum neck, V-shaped body.

1980-1981		$575	$725

XKG-20

1980-1981. More traditional double-cut body with small horns.

1980-1981		$475	$575

XL Series

1980-1981, 1987-1990. The early-'80s U.S.-made models had aluminum necks were completely different than the late-'80s wood neck models, which were inexpensive imports.

1980-1981	XL-5, 2 humbuckers	$700	$850
1987-1990	XL-1, 2 pickups	$100	$150
1987-1990	XL-6, 3 pickups	$100	$150
1989	XL-2, 2 humbuckers	$100	$150
1989	XL-3, 3 pickups	$100	$150

ZX Aero Star Series (Import)

1986-1989. Offset double-cut solidbodies, pointy six-on-a-side headstock. Models include the 1 humbucker ZX-10, 2 humbucker ZX-20, 3 single coil ZX-30, and hum/single/single ZX-30H.

1986-1989		$150	$200

MODEL YEAR	FEATURES	EXC. COND. LOW	HIGH

Kramer-Harrison, William

1977-present. Luthier William Kramer-Harrison builds his premium grade, custom, classical and flat-top guitars in Kingston, New York.

KSM

1988-present. Luthier Kevin S. Moore builds his premium grade, custom/production, solidbody electric guitars in Logan, Utah.

Kubicki

1973-present. Kubicki is best known for their Factor basses, but did offer a few guitar models in the early '80s. See Bass section for more company info.

Kustom

1968-present. Founded by Bud Ross in Chanute, Kansas, and best known for the tuck-and-roll amps, Kustom also offered guitars from '68 to '69. See Amp section for more company info.

Electric Hollowbody
1968-1969. Hollowed-out 2-part bodies; includes the K200A (humbucker, Bigsby), the K200B (single-coils, trapeze tailpiece), and the K200C (less fancy tuners), various colors.

1960s		$800	$1,000

Kwasnycia Guitars

1997-present. Production/custom, premium grade, acoustic guitars built by luthier Dennis Kwasnycia in Chatham, Ontario.

Kyle, Doug

1990-present. Premium grade, custom, Selmer-style guitars made by luthier Doug Kyle in England.

L Benito

2001-present. Professional grade, steel and nylon string acoustics from luthier Lito Benito and built in Chile.

La Baye

1967. Designed by Dan Helland in Green Bay, Wisconsin and built by the Holman-Woodell factory in Neodesha, Kansas. Introduced at NAMM and folded when no orders came in. Only 45 prototypes made. A few may have been sold later as 21st Century. They also had basses.

2x4 6-String
1967. Narrow plank body, controls on top, 2 pickups, tremolo, 12-string version was also made.

1967		$1,100	$1,400

La Mancha

1996-present. Professional and premium grade, production/custom, classical guitars made in Mexico under the supervision of Kenny Hill and Gil Carnal and distributed by Jerry Roberts of Nashville, Tennessee.

La Patrie

Production, classical guitars. Founded by luthier Robert Godin, who also has the Norman, Godin, Seagull, and Patrick & Simon brands of instruments.

La Scala

Ca. 1920s-1930s. La Scala was another brand of the Oscar Schmidt Company of New Jersey, and was used on guitars, banjos, and mandolins. These were often the fanciest of the Schmidt instruments. Schmidt made the guitars and mandolins; the banjos were made by Rettberg & Lang.

Lace Music Products

1979-present. Intermediate and professional, production, electric guitars from Lace Music Products, a division of Actodyne General Inc. which was founded by Don Lace Sr., inventor of the Lace Sensor Pickup. In '96 Lace added amplifiers and in 2001 they added guitars. In '02, they also started offering the Rat Fink brand of guitars.

Lacey Guitars

1974-present. Luthier Mark Lacey builds his premium and presentation archtops and flat-tops in Nashville, Tennessee.

Lado

1973-present. Founded by Joe Kovacic, Lado builds professional and premium grade, production/custom, solidbody guitars in Lindsay, Ontario. Some model lines are branded J. K. Lado. They also build basses.

Lafayette

Ca. 1963-1967. Sold through Lafayette Electronics catalogs. Early Japanese-made guitars and basses from pre-copy era, generally shorter scale beginner instruments. Many made by Guyatone, some possibly by Teisco.

Acoustic Thinline Archtop
1963-1967. Various models.

1963-1967		$300	$400

Laguna

2008-present. Guitar Center private label, budget and intermediate grade, production, imported electric and acoustic guitars price range.

Lakeside (Lyon & Healy)

Early-1900s. Mainly catalog sales of guitars and mandolins from the Chicago maker. Marketed as a less expensive alternative to the Lyon & Healy Washburn product line.

Harp Guitar
Early-1900s. Spruce top, rosewood finished birch back and sides, two 6-string necks with standard tuners, 1 neck is fretless without dot markers, rectangular bridge.

1900s	Various models	$2,000	$2,500

Lado Rocker 902 Custom CU-P

Laguna LG300CE

Lakewood M-14

Larrivee D-09

Lakewood

1986-present. Luthier Martin Seeliger builds his professional and premium grade, production/custom, steel and nylon string guitars in Giessen, Germany. He has also built mandolins.

Langdon Guitars

1997-present. Luthier Jeff Langdon builds his professional and premium grade, production/custom, flat top, archtop, and solidbody guitars in Eureka, California.

Langejans Guitars

1971-present. Premium grade, production/custom, flat-top, 12-string, and classical guitars built by luthier Delwyn Langejans in Holland, Michigan.

Larrivee

1968-present. Professional and premium grade, production/custom, acoustic, acoustic/electric, and classical guitars built in Vancouver, British Columbia and, since '01, in Oxnard, California. Founded by Jean Larrivee, who apprenticed under Edgar Monch in Toronto. He built classical guitars in his home from '68-'70 and built his first steel string guitar in '71. Moved company to Victoria, BC in '77 and to Vancouver in '82. In '83, he began building solidbody electric guitars until '89, when focus again returned to acoustics.

Up to 2002, Larrivee used the following model designations: 05 Mahogany Standard, 09 Rosewood Standard, 10 Deluxe, 19 Special, 50 & 60 Standard (unique inlay), 70 Deluxe, and 72 Presentation. Starting in '03 designations used are: 01 Parlor, 03 Standard, 05 Select Mahogany, 09 Rosewood Artist, 10 Rosewood Deluxe, 19 California Anniv. Special Edition Series, 50 Traditional Series, 60 Traditional Series, E = Electric, R = Rosewood.

C-10 Deluxe
Late-1980s-1990s. Sitka spruce top, Indian rosewood back and sides, sharp cutaway, fancy binding.

1980s		$1,600	$2,000

C-72 Presentation
1990s. Spruce top, Indian rosewood back and sides, non-cut Style D, ultra-fancy abalone and pearl hand-engraved headstock.

1990s	Jester headstock	$2,000	$2,500

C-72 Presentation Cutaway
1990s. Spruce top, Indian rosewood back and sides, sharp cutaway, ultra-fancy abalone and pearl hand-engraved headstock.

1990s	Mermaid headstock	$2,500	$3,000

D-03E
2008-present. Solid mahogany back and sides, spruce top, satin finish.

2008-2010		$700	$850

D-03R
2002-2010. Rosewood.

2002-2010		$775	$900

MODEL YEAR	FEATURES	EXC. COND. LOW	HIGH
D-05-12E			
2008-present. 12 strings.			
2008-2010		$1,500	$1,800
D-09			
2001-present. Rosewood, spruce top, gloss finish.			
2001-2010	Brazilian	$1,900	$2,300
2001-2010	Indian	$1,200	$1,500
D-10 Deluxe			
1990s-present. Spruce top, rosewood rims, abalone top and soundhole trim.			
1995-2010		$1,600	$1,900
D-70 Deluxe			
1992		$1,600	$1,900
D-Style Classical			
1970s. Rosewood body, unicorn inlays.			
1970s		$1,500	$1,800
DV Series			
2000s	DV-03K, koa	$1,200	$1,500
J-05-12			
2000s. Jumbo acoustic-electric 12-string, spruce top, mahogany back and sides.			
2000s		$1,100	$1,400
J-09			
2008-2009		$1,300	$1,600
J-09-12K			
2008-2009		$1,600	$1,900
J-70			
1990s. Jumbo, sitka spruce top, solid Indian rosewood back and sides, presentation grade fancy appointments, limited production.			
1994		$1,700	$2,100
JV-05 Mahogany Standard			
2000s		$1,000	$1,250
L Series			
1990s	L-50	$1,500	$1,800
1990s	L-72 Presentation Custom	$3,000	$3,600
L-0 Standard Series			
1980s-present. Models include L-03 (satin finish), L-05 (mahogany) and L-09 (Indian rosewood).			
1980s-2010	L-05	$1,000	$1,200
1983-2010	L-09	$1,200	$1,400
1990s-2010	L-03	$600	$700
2008-2010	L-03R, rosewood	$700	$750
2008-2010	L-03RE	$800	$1,000
LJ Series			
1991	LJ-72 Presentation	$1,600	$1,900
LV Series			
2002-present.			
1990s-2010	LV-05, LV-05E	$1,100	$1,350
1990s-2010	LV-09	$1,000	$1,250
2002	LV-19 Special Vine	$2,700	$3,300
2007-2010	LV-03, LV-03E	$800	$1,000
2007-2010	LV-10, LV-10E	$1,700	$2,100
OM Series			
1990s-present.			
1990s-2000	OM-02	$475	$600
1990s-2010	OM-03, mahogany, satin	$700	$800
1990s-2010	OM-10 Custom, rosewood	$1,700	$2,000

MODEL YEAR	FEATURES	EXC. COND. LOW	HIGH
1999-2010	OM-05, mahogany	$1,000	$1,200
2000-2010	OM-03R, rosewood	$800	$900
2000-2010	OM-50, mahogany	$1,600	$1,900
2000s	OM-09K	$1,500	$1,800
2008-2010	OM-60 Bluegrass, rosewood	$1,700	$2,000
OMV Series			
2000s	OMV-50	$1,500	$1,800
2009	OMV-60	$1,500	$1,800
OO-09			
2000s		$1,100	$1,400
OO-10			

2000s. OO-size 14" lower bout, spruce top, rosewood back and sides, gloss finish.

2000s		$1,400	$1,700
OOO-50			

2008-present. Mahogany back and sides.

2008-2010		$1,500	$1,800
OOO-60			

2006-present. Indian rosewood.

2006-2010		$1,500	$1,800
Parlor Walnut			

Early 2000s. Spruce top, solid walnut back and sides.

2002		$575	$650
PV Series			

2007-present.

2007-2010	PV-09 Parlor, Brazilian	$1,900	$2,300
2007-2010	PV-09 Parlor, maple	$1,200	$1,500
RS-2			
2010		$750	$950
RS-4 CM Carved Top			

1988-1989. Carved top solidbody, curly maple top, single-single-humbucker pickups, sunburst or translucent finishes.

1988-1989		$1,200	$1,500

Larson Brothers

1900-1944. Chicago's Carl and August Larson bought Maurer & Company in 1900 where they built guitars and mandolin family instruments until 1944. Their house brands were Maurer, Prairie State and Euphonon and they also built for catalog companies Wm. C. Stahl and W. J. Dyer & Bro., adding brands like Stetson, a house brand of Dyer. See brand listings for more information.

Laskin

1973-present. Luthier William "Grit" Laskin builds his premium and presentation grade, custom, steel-string, classical, and flamenco guitars in Toronto, Ontario. Many of his instruments feature extensive inlay work.

Laurie Williams Guitars

1983-present. Luthier Laurie Williams builds his premium and presentation grade, custom/production, steel string, classical and archtop guitars on the North Island of New Zealand. He also builds mandolins.

Leach Guitars

1980-present. Luthier Harvey Leach builds his professional and premium grade, custom, flat-tops, archtops, and solidbody electrics and travel guitars in Cedar Ridge, California. He also builds basses.

Lehmann Stringed Instruments

1971-present. Luthier Bernard Lehmann builds his professional and premium grade, production/custom, flat-top, archtop, classical and Gypsy guitars in Rochester, New York. He also builds lutes, vielles and rebecs.

Lehtela

1993-present. Professional and premium grade, custom/production, acoustic, acoustic/electric, archtop, and solidbody guitars built by luthier Ari Lehtela in Newell, North Carolina. He also builds basses.

Lentz

1975-present. Luthier Scott Lentz builds his professional, premium, and presentation grade, custom/production, solidbody electric guitars in San Marcos, California.

Les Stansell Guitars

1980-present. Luthier Les Stansell builds his premium grade, custom, nylon-string guitars in Pistol River, Oregon.

Levin

1900-1973. Founded by Herman Carlson Levin and located in Gothenburg, Sweden, Levin was best known for their classical guitars, which they also built for other brands, most notably Goya from ca. 1955 to the mid '70s. They also built mandolins and ukes.

Levy-Page Special

1930s. Acoustic guitars likely built by Gibson, having many features of Kalamzoo guitars of the era. Possibly made for a distributor.

Lewis

1981-present. Luthier Michael Lewis builds his premium and presentation grade, custom/production, archtop guitars in Grass Valley, California. He also builds mandolins. Since '94 he has also built guitars under the D'Angelico name.

Linc Luthier

1991-present. Professional and premium grade, custom/production, electric and acoustic guitars built by luthier Linc Luthier in Upland, California. He also builds basses and double-necks.

Lindberg

Ca. 1950s. Line of guitars produced by Hoyer for Germany's Lindberg music store.

Larrivee LV-03E

Leach Franconia

Line 6 Variax 600

Liscombe KL74

MODEL YEAR	FEATURES	EXC. COND. LOW	HIGH

Lindert

1986-present. Luthier Chuck Lindert makes his intermediate and professional grade, production/custom, Art Deco-vibe electric guitars in Chelan, Washington.

Line 6

1996-present. Professional grade, production, imported solidbody and acoustic modeling guitars able to replicate the tones of a variety of instruments. Line 6 also builds effects and amps.

Lion

1960s. One of the brand names of guitars built for others by Egmond in Holland.

Lipe Guitars USA

1983-1989, 2000-present. Custom, professional grade, guitars built in Sun Valley, California by luthier Michael Lipe. He also builds basses.

Liscombe

1992-present. Professional grade, production and limited custom, chambered electric guitars built by luthier Ken Liscombe in Burlington, Ontario.

Loar (The)

2005-present. Professional grade, production, imported archtop acoustic guitars designed by Greg Rich for The Music Link, which also has Johnson and other brands of instruments.

Lollar

1979-present. Luthier Jason Lollar builds his premium grade, production/custom, solidbody and archtop guitars in Vashon, Washington.

Lopez, Abel Garcia

1985-present. Luthier Abel Garcia Lopez builds his premium grade, custom, classical guitars in Mexico.

Loprinzi

1972-present. Professional and premium grade, production/custom, classical and steel-string guitars built in Clearwater, Florida. They also build ukes. Founded by Augustino LoPrinzi and his brother Thomas in New Jersey. The guitar operations were taken over by AMF/Maark Corp. in '73. LoPrinzi left the company and again started producing his own Augustino Guitars, moving his operations to Florida in '78. AMF ceased production in '80, and a few years later, LoPrinzi got his trademarked name back.

Classical

1970s. Various models.

1970s	Brazilian rosewood	$1,500	$1,800
1970s	Indian rosewood	$850	$1,000
1970s	Mahogany	$800	$950

MODEL YEAR	FEATURES	EXC. COND. LOW	HIGH

Lord

Mid-1960s. Acoustic and solidbody electric guitars imported by Halifax.

Acoustic or Electric Solidbody

1960s	Various models	$75	$150

Lotus

Late-1970s-2004. Budget grade acoustic and electric guitars imported originally by Midco International, of Effingham, Illinois, and most recently by Musicorp. They also made basses, banjos and mandolins.

Louis Panormo

Early to mid-1800s. Spanish guitars made in London, England by luthier Louis (Luis) Panormo. He was born in Paris in 1784, and died in 1862.

Lowden

1973-present. Luthier George Lowden builds his premium and presentation grade, production/custom, steel and nylon string guitars in Downpatrick, Northern Ireland. From '80 to '85, he had some models made in Japan.

Flat-Tops

1980s-2000s. Standard models include D, F, O, and S sizes and models 10 thru 32.

1980-1990s	Premium 6-string	$2,200	$2,600
2000s	12-string	$1,700	$2,300
2000s	Premium 6-string	$2,500	$3,000
2000s	Standard 6-string	$1,700	$2,300

LSL Instruments

2008-present. Luthier Lance Lerman builds his production, professional grade, solidbody electric guitars in Los Angeles, California.

LSR Headless Instruments

1988-present. Professional and premium grade, production/custom, solidbody headless guitars made in Las Vegas, Nevada by Ed Roman. They also make basses.

LTD

1995-present. Intermediate grade, production, Korean-made solidbody guitars offered by ESP. They also offer basses.

Lucas Custom Instruments

1989-present. Premium and presentation grade, production/custom, flat-tops built by luthier Randy Lucas in Columbus, Indiana.

Lucas, A. J.

1990-present. Luthier A. J. Lucas builds his production/custom, classical and steel string guitars in Lincolnshire, England.

MODEL YEAR	FEATURES	EXC. COND. LOW	HIGH

Luis Feu de Mesquita

2000-present. Professional and premium grade, custom, acoustic and flat top guitars including Spanish, classical and flamenco built in Toronto, Ontario by luthier Luis Feu de Mesquita.

Luna Guitars

2005-present. Located in Tampa, Florida, Yvonne de Villiers imports her budget to professional grade, production, acoustic and electric guitars from Japan, Korea and China. She also imports basses, added ukuleles in '09 and amps in '10.

Lyle

Ca. 1969-1980. Imported by distributor L.D. Heater of Portland, Oregon. Generally higher quality Japanese-made copies of American designs by unknown manufacturers, but some early ones, at least, were made by Arai and Company. They also had basses and mandolins.

Lyon & Healy

In the 1930s, Lyon & Healy was an industry giant. It operated a chain of music stores, and manufactured harps (their only remaining product), pianos, Washburn guitars and a line of brass and wind instruments. See Washburn, American Conservatory, Lakeside, and College brands.

Lyon by Washburn

1990s-present. Budget grade, production, solid-body guitars sold by mass merchandisers such as Target. They also offer basses.

Lyra

1920s. Instruments built by the Oscar Schmidt Co. and possibly others. Most likely a brand made for a distributor.

Lyric

1996-present. Luthier John Southern builds his professional and premium grade, custom, semi-hollow and solidbody guitars in Tulsa, Oklahoma. He also builds basses.

M. Campellone Guitars

See listing under Campellone Guitars

Maccaferri

1923-1990. Built by luthier and classical guitarist Mario Maccaferri (b. May 20, 1900, Cento, Italy; d. 1993, New York) in Cento, Italy; Paris, France; New York, New York; and Mount Vernon, New York. Maccaferri was a student of Luigi Mozzani from '11 to '28. His first catalog was in '23, and included a cutaway guitar. He designed Selmer guitars in '31. Maccaferri invented the plastic clothespin during World War II and used that technology to produce plastic ukes starting in '49 and Dow Styron plastic guitars in '53. He made several experimental plastic electrics in the '60s and plastic violins in the late-'80s.

MODEL YEAR	FEATURES	EXC. COND. LOW	HIGH

Plastic (Dow Styron)

1950s. Plastic construction, models include Deluxe (archtop, crown logo), Islander (Islander logo), TV Pal (4-string cutaway) and Showtime (Showtime logo).

1950s	Deluxe	$250	$300
1950s	Islander	$225	$275
1950s	Romancer	$225	$275
1950s	Showtime	$225	$275
1950s	TV Pal	$175	$225

Madeira

Late-1970s. Imports serviced and distributed exclusively by Guild Guitars, budget to low-intermediate grade.

Maestro

1950s-1970s, 2001-present. Maestro is a brand name Gibson first used on 1950s accordian amplifiers. The first Maestro effects were introduced in the early-'60s and they used the name until the late-'70s. In 2001, Gibson revived the name for a line of effects, banjos and mandolins. Those were dropped in '09, when imported budget and intermediate, production, acoustic and electric guitars and amps were added.

Electric

2009-present. Various student models, Maestro headstock logo, 'By Gibson' logo on truss rod cover.

| 2009-2010 | | $50 | $100 |

Magnatone

Ca. 1937-1971. Founded as Dickerson Brothers in Los Angeles, California and known as Magna Electronics from '47, with Art Duhamell president. Brands include Dickerson, Oahu (not all), Gourley, Natural Music Guild, Magnatone. In '59 Magna and Estey merged and in '66 the company relocated to Pennsylvania. In '71, the brand was taken over by a toy company. Between 1957 and '67, the company produced four different model lines of Spanish electrics.

Cyclops

1930s. Dobro-made resonator guitar.

| 1930s | Round neck | $1,300 | $1,700 |
| 1930s | Square neck | $1,500 | $1,900 |

Mark Artist Series

| 1959-1961 | | $2,700 | $3,300 |

Mark Series

1955-1960. Solidbody series made by Paul Bigsby in small quantities, then taken over by Paul Barth at Magnatone in '59.

| 1955-1959 | Mark IV | $3,200 | $3,800 |
| 1955-1959 | Mark V | $3,200 | $3,800 |

Model Series

1962	Model 100	$350	$400
1962	Model 150	$350	$400
1962	Model 200, 2 pickups	$350	$400

Tornado X-15

1965-1966. Offset double-cut body, 3 DeArmond pickups, vibrato.

| 1965-1966 | | $600 | $850 |

1915 Lyon & Healy

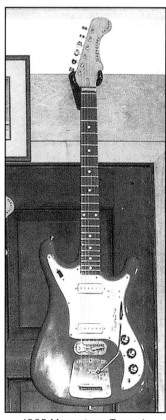

1965 Magnatone Tornado
Tom Roberts

1965 Magnatone Typhoon X-20
Tom Roberts

Manne Raven

MODEL YEAR	FEATURES	EXC. COND. LOW	HIGH

Typhoon X-20
1965-1966. Double-cut solidbody, 3 DeArmond pickups, vibrato.

1965-1966		$600	$850

Zephyr X-5
1965-1966. Double-cut with 2 DeArmond single-coil pickups, metallic finish, vibrato.

1965-1966		$600	$850

Magno-Tone
1930s. Brand most likely used by a music studio (or distributor) on instruments made by others, including Regal-built resonator instruments.

Mai Kai
1910s. Line of Hawaiian guitars built in Los Angeles, California by the Shireson Brothers.

Mako
1985-1989. Line of budget to lower-intermediate solidbody guitars from Kaman (Ovation, Hamer). They also offered basses and amps.

Solidbody

1985-1989	Various models	$75	$200

Mal n' Sal
See listing for Alternative Guitar and Amplifier Company.

Malden
Introduced ca. 2004. Import.

Malinoski
1986-present. Luthier Peter Malinoski builds his production/custom, professional and premium grade, solidbody electric guitars in Hyattsville, Maryland. He also builds basses.

MalinoskiArt Guitars
1986-present. Luthier Peter Malinoski builds his professional and premium grade, production/custom, solidbody electric guitars in Hyattsville, Maryland. He also builds basses.

Manne
1987-present. Professional and premium grade, production/custom, semi-acoustic and electric guitars built by luthier Andrea Ballarin in Italy. He also builds basses.

Manuel & Patterson
1993-present. Luthiers Joe Manuel and Phil Patterson build professional, premium and presentation grade, production/custom, flat-top, archtop and solidbody electric guitars in Abita Springs, Louisiana. They also offer mandolins.

Manuel Contreras
1962-1994. Luthier Manuel Gonzalez Contreras worked with José Ramirez III, before opening his own shop in Madrid, Spain, in '62.

MODEL YEAR	FEATURES	EXC. COND. LOW	HIGH

Manuel Contreras II
1986-present. Professional grade, production/custom, nylon-string guitars made in Madrid, Spain, by luthier Pablo Contreras, son of Manuel.

Manuel Ramirez
See listing under Ramirez, Manuel.

Manuel Rodriguez and Sons, S.L.
1905-present. Professional, premium, and presentation grade, custom flat-top and nylon-string guitars from Madrid, Spain.

Manuel Velázquez
1933-present. Luthier Manuel Velázquez has built his classical guitars in Puerto Rico ('72-'82), New York City, Virginia, and Florida. His son and daughter now build guitars with him.

Manzanita Guitars
1993-present. Custom, steel-string, Hawaiian, and resonator guitars built by luthiers Manfred Pietrzok and Moritz Sattler in Rosdorf, Germany.

Manzer Guitars
1976-present. Luthier Linda Manzer builds her premium and presentation grade, custom, steel-string, nylon-string, and archtop guitars in Toronto, Ontario.

Maple Lake
2003-present. Intermediate grade, production, flat-top and acoustic/electric imported guitars from luthier Abe Wechter. Wechter also builds guitars under his own name.

Mapson
1995-present. Luthier James L. Mapson builds his premium and presentation grade, production/custom, archtops in Santa Ana, California.

Marc Silber Guitar Company
1998-present. Intermediate and professional grade, production, flat-top, nylon-string, and Hawaiian guitars designed by Marc Silber and made in Mexico. These were offered under the K & S Guitars and/or Silber brands for 1992-'98. Silber also has ukuleles.

Marchione Guitars
1993-present. Premium and presentation grade, custom, archtops and solidbodies built by Stephen Marchione originally in New York City, but currently in Houston, Texas.

Marcia
1920s. Instruments built by the Oscar Schmidt Co. and possibly others. Most likely a brand made for a distributor.

MODEL YEAR	FEATURES	EXC. COND. LOW	HIGH

Marco Polo

1960-ca. 1964. Imported from Japan by Harry Stewart and the Marco Polo Company of Santa Ana, California. One of the first American distributors to advertise inexpensive Japanese guitars and basses. Manufacturers unknown, but some acoustics by Suzuki, some electrics by Guyatone.

Acoustic Hollowbody

1960-1964	Various models	$75	$200

Mario Martin Guitars

2011-present. Luthier Mario Martin builds his production/custom, professional grade, semi-hollow and solidbody guitars in Murfreesboro, Tennessee. He also builds basses. From 2006 to '11, he built guitars under the Guitar Mill brand name.

Mark Wescott Guitars

1980-present. Premium grade, custom, flat-tops, built by luthier Mark Wescott in Somers Point, New Jersey.

Marling

Ca. 1975. Budget line guitars and basses marketed by EKO of Recanati, Italy; probably made by them, although possibly imported.

Acoustic

1975. Includes the steel-string S.110, and the dreadnoughts W.354 Western, and W.356 Western.

1975		$75	$125

Electric Soldibody

1975. Includes the E.400 (semi-acoustic/electric), E.490 (solidbody), E.480 (single-cut-style), and the 460 (Manta-style).

1975		$125	$175

Martelle

1934. Private brand attributed to Gibson and some to Kay.

De Luxe

1934. Gibson 12-fret round shoulder Jumbo construction, mahogany back and sides, sunburst, Hawaiian or Spanish option.

1934		$9,000	$11,000

Martin

1833-present. Intermediate, professional, premium, and presentation grade, production/custom, acoustic, acoustic/electric, archtop and resonator guitars. Founded in New York City by Christian Frederick Martin, former employee of J. Staufer in Vienna, Austria. Moved to Nazareth, Pennsylvania in 1839. Early guitars were made in the European style, many made with partners John Coupa, Charles Bruno and Henry Schatz. Scalloped X-bracing was introduced in the late-1840s. The dreadnought was introduced in 1916 for the Oliver Ditson Company, Boston; and Martin introduced their own versions in 1931.

Martin model size and shape are indicated by the letter prefix (e.g., 0, 00, 000, D, etc.); materials and ornamentation are indicated by number, with the higher the number, the fancier the instrument (e.g., 18, 28, 35, etc.). Martin offered electric thinline guitars from '61-'68 and electric solidbodies from '78-'82. The Martin Shenandoah was made in Asia and assembled in U.S. Japanese Martin Sigma ('72-'73) and Korean Martin Stinger ('85 on) imported solidbodies.

Most Martin flat-top guitars, particularly Style 18 and above, came with a standard natural finish, therefore Martin guitar finish coloring is generally not mentioned because it is assumed to be see-through natural. Conversely, Gibson's standard finish for their flat-tops during their Golden Era was sunburst. Martin introduced their shaded (sunburst) finish as an option on their Style 18 in 1934 and their Style 28 in 1931. An original Martin shaded factory (sunburst) finish from the 1930's is worth 40% more than the value shown in the Price Guide. A shaded finish option in the 1940s adds 30%, in the 1950s it adds 20%, and in the 1960s it adds 20%. A refinished guitar with a sunburst finish is not included in this analysis, in fact a refinished guitar is generally worth less than one-half that of an original finish guitar. In particular, a refinished sunburst guitar would be worth one-half the value of an original natural finish guitar. The amount of added value associated with a shaded (sunburst) finish for a guitar made between the 1930s and the 1960s also depends on the model. A Style 18 model shaded finish option is more common than some of the other styles, and D-body, OM-body, and 000-body styles can have different premiums for a shaded finish. Braced for steel strings specifications described under certain models are based on current consensus information and data provided by the late Martin employee-historian Mike Longworth, and is for guidance only. Variations from these specs have been found, so "bracing" should be considered on a case-by-case basis.

0-15

1935, 1940-1943, 1948-1961. All mahogany, unbound rosewood 'board, slotted peghead and 12-fret neck until '34, solid peghead and 14-fret neck thereafter, natural mahogany.

1935	2 made	$2,100	$2,600
1940-1943		$1,800	$2,200
1948-1949		$1,600	$2,000
1950-1959		$1,500	$1,800
1960-1961		$1,400	$1,700

0-15 T

1960-1963. Tenor with Style 15 appointments, natural mahogany.

1960-1963		$1,000	$1,200

0-16

1961 only. Six made.

1961		$1,650	$2,000

0-16 NY

1961-1995. Mahogany back and sides, 12 frets, slotted peghead, unbound extra-wide rosewood 'board, natural.

1961-1969		$1,550	$1,900

*Manuel & Patterson
Old Time Special*

Manzer Studio

1936 Martin 0-17

Martin 0-28 Ian Anderson

MODEL YEAR	FEATURES	EXC. COND. LOW	HIGH
1970-1979		$1,400	$1,750
1980-1989		$1,300	$1,600
1990-1995		$1,300	$1,600

0-17

1906-1917, 1929-1948, 1966-1968. First version has mahogany back and sides, 3 black soundhole rings, rosewood bound back, unbound ebony 'board, 12 frets, slotted peghead. Second version ('29 and on) is all mahogany, 3 white-black-white soundhole rings, top bound until '30, thin black backstripe, 12 frets and slotted peghead until '34, solid peghead and 14 frets thereafter, natural mahogany.

MODEL YEAR	FEATURES	EXC. COND. LOW	HIGH
1906-1917	Gut	$1,900	$2,200
1929-1933	12 fret, steel	$2,200	$2,700
1934	Flat natural finish, 14 fret	$2,800	$3,500
1934-1938	Gloss dark finish, 14 fret	$2,800	$3,500
1939	Early '39, 1.75 neck	$2,800	$3,500
1939	Later '39, 1.68 neck	$2,300	$2,800
1940-1945		$2,000	$2,500
1946-1948		$1,800	$2,300
1966-1968		$1,600	$2,000

0-17 H

1930, 1935-1941. Hawaiian, mahogany back and sides, 12 frets clear of body, natural.

MODEL YEAR	FEATURES	EXC. COND. LOW	HIGH
1930	60 made	$2,700	$3,400
1935-1941		$2,700	$3,400

0-17 S

Early 1930s. Limited production style 17 with spruce top, unique 'guard.

MODEL YEAR	FEATURES	EXC. COND. LOW	HIGH
1931		$3,800	$4,500

0-17 T

1932-1960. Mahogany back and sides, tenor, natural.

MODEL YEAR	FEATURES	EXC. COND. LOW	HIGH
1932-1949		$1,200	$1,500
1950-1960	Mahogany	$1,200	$1,500

0-18

1898-1996. Rosewood back and sides until 1917, mahogany back and sides after, Adirondack spruce top until 1946, slotted peghead and 12 frets until 1934, solid peghead and 14 frets after 1934, improved neck in late-1934, non-scalloped braces appear late-'44, natural.

MODEL YEAR	FEATURES	EXC. COND. LOW	HIGH
1898-1917	Brazilian rosewood	$3,400	$3,900
1918-1922	Mahogany	$2,400	$2,900
1923-1928	12 fret, steel strings	$3,700	$4,300
1929-1933		$3,700	$4,300
1934-1937		$3,800	$4,400
1938-1939	Early '39, 1.75 neck	$3,800	$4,400
1939-1941	Later '39, 1.68 neck	$3,800	$4,400
1942-1944		$3,500	$4,100
1945-1949		$3,200	$3,800
1950-1959		$2,200	$3,000
1960-1969		$1,900	$2,700
1970-1979		$1,400	$1,800
1980-1996		$1,100	$1,600

0-18 G

1960s. Special order classical nylon-string model, natural.

MODEL YEAR	FEATURES	EXC. COND. LOW	HIGH
1961		$1,200	$1,400

0-18 K

1918-1935. Hawaiian, all koa wood, T-frets and steel T-bar neck in late-1934, natural.

MODEL YEAR	FEATURES	EXC. COND. LOW	HIGH
1918-1922		$3,400	$3,900
1923-1927		$3,500	$4,000
1928-1935		$3,700	$4,200

0-18 KH

1927-1928. Hawaiian, koa.

MODEL YEAR	FEATURES	EXC. COND. LOW	HIGH
1927-1928		$2,800	$3,200

0-18 T

1929-1995. Mahogany body, spruce top, tenor, natural.

MODEL YEAR	FEATURES	EXC. COND. LOW	HIGH
1929-1939		$1,900	$2,400
1940-1959		$1,800	$2,200
1960-1964		$1,700	$2,100
1965-1969		$1,300	$1,500
1970-1979		$1,100	$1,300
1980-1989		$1,000	$1,200
1990-1995		$900	$1,100

0-21

1898-1948. Rosewood back and sides, Adirondack spruce top until 1946, 12 frets, T-frets and steel T-bar neck in late-1934, non-scalloped braces in late-1944, natural.

MODEL YEAR	FEATURES	EXC. COND. LOW	HIGH
1898-1922		$3,600	$4,600
1923-1926		$3,600	$4,600
1927-1939	1.75 neck, steel braces	$5,200	$6,600
1939-1943	1.68 neck, scalloped braces	$5,200	$6,600
1944-1948	Non-scalloped	$4,300	$5,400

0-26

1850-1890. Rosewood back and sides, ivory-bound top, rope-style purfling.

MODEL YEAR	FEATURES	EXC. COND. LOW	HIGH
1850-1890		$5,000	$6,000

0-27

1850-1898. Rosewood back and sides, ivory-bound top.

MODEL YEAR	FEATURES	EXC. COND. LOW	HIGH
1850-1859	Antique market value	$8,000	$9,200
1890-1898		$5,500	$6,500

0-28

1870s-1931, 1937 (6 made), 1969 (1 made). Brazilian rosewood back and sides, herringbone binding until 1937, natural.

MODEL YEAR	FEATURES	EXC. COND. LOW	HIGH
1870-1898		$5,500	$6,500
1899-1919		$5,300	$6,200
1920-1922	Gut & some steel	$5,700	$6,700
1923-1924	Gut & some steel	$6,500	$7,500
1925-1927	Steel	$7,500	$9,000
1928-1929		$8,000	$10,000
1930-1931		$9,000	$11,000

0-28 Ian Anderson

2004. Adirondack spruce top, scalloped bracing, Indian rosewood sides and back, slotted headstock, gloss natural finish, limited edition 87 made.

MODEL YEAR	FEATURES	EXC. COND. LOW	HIGH
2004		$2,700	$3,200

0-28 K

1917-1931, 1935. Hawaiian, all koa wood, braced for steel strings in '23, natural.

MODEL YEAR	FEATURES	EXC. COND. LOW	HIGH
1917	Spruce top option	$6,300	$7,100
1917-1924	Figured koa	$6,300	$7,100
1925-1931	Steel braces	$6,500	$7,500

MODEL YEAR	FEATURES	EXC. COND. LOW	HIGH
0-28 T			
1930-1931. Tenor neck.			
1930-1931		$3,300	$3,800
0-28 VS			
2009-present. Rosewood back and sides, slotted head, 12 fret neck.			
2009-2010		$2,400	$2,800
0-30			
1899-1921. Brazilian rosewood back and sides, ivory-bound body, neck and headstock.			
1899-1921		$7,000	$9,000
0-34			
1880s. Brazilian rosewood.			
1880s		$7,100	$9,100
0-42			
1870s-1942. Brazilian rosewood back and sides, 12 frets, natural.			
1890-1926	Gut braces	$12,500	$15,500
1927-1930	Steel braces	$15,500	$19,000
0-45			
1904-1939. Brazilian rosewood back and sides, natural, special order only for '31-'39.			
1904-1927	Gut braces	$25,000	$31,000
1927-1930	Steel braces	$39,000	$48,000
0-45 S Stephen Stills			
2007. 91 made, Madagascar rosewood sides and back, Adirondack spruce top.			
2007		$7,000	$8,000
00-15			
2005-2010.			
2005-2010		$575	$650
00-15 M			
2009-present. All mahogany.			
2009-2010		$575	$650
00-16 C			
1962-1977, 1980-1981. Classical, mahogany back and sides, 5-ply bound top, satin finish, 12 frets, slotted peghead, natural.			
1962-1969		$975	$1,225
1970-1977		$950	$1,150
1980-1981	2 made	$850	$1,050
00-16 DB Women and Music Series			
1998, 2000, 2006. Limited editions, 00 size, various body materials.			
1998	R, rosewood	$1,100	$1,300
2000	M, all mahogany	$800	$1,000
2006	FM, flamed maple	$900	$1,075
00-17			
1908-1917, 1930-1960, 1982-1988, 2000-2003. Mahogany back and sides, 12 frets and slotted headstock until '34, solid headstock and 14 frets after '34, natural mahogany, reissued in 2000 with a high gloss finish.			
1908-1917	Gut	$2,500	$2,900
1930-1933	Steel, 12-fret	$2,700	$3,300
1934	14-fret, flat natural finish	$3,100	$3,600
1935-1938	14-fret, gloss dark finish	$3,100	$3,600
1939	Early '39, 1.75 neck	$3,100	$3,600
1939	Later '39, 1.68 neck	$2,700	$3,300
1940-1944		$2,600	$3,100

MODEL YEAR	FEATURES	EXC. COND. LOW	HIGH
1945-1949		$2,400	$2,900
1950-1960		$1,800	$2,200
2000-2003	Reissue model	$950	$1,200
00-17 H			
1934-1935. Hawaiian set-up, mahogany body, no binding.			
1934-1935		$2,900	$3,500
00-17 SO Sing Out!			
2000. Limited edition, commemorates the 50th anniversary of Sing Out Magazine, folk era logo inlays including Liberty Bell, folk hammer, and SING OUT inlay on 20th fret, mahogany body, natural gloss finish over mahogany top.			
2000		$1,200	$1,500
00-18			
1898-1995. Rosewood back and sides until 1917, mahogany after, braced for steel strings in 1923, improved neck in late-1934, war-time design changes 1942-1946, non-scalloped braces in late-1944, Adirondack spruce top until 1946, natural.			
1898-1917	Brazilian rosewood	$4,500	$5,500
1918-1922	Mahogany	$4,000	$4,900
1923-1931	Steel strings, 12-fret	$4,300	$5,300
1932-1933	12-fret option	$4,300	$5,300
1932-1933	14-fret option	$5,000	$6,200
1934-1937	14-fret	$5,000	$6,200
1938-1939	Early '39, 1.75 neck	$5,000	$6,200
1939-1941	Later '39, 1.68 neck	$4,300	$5,300
1942-1944	Scalloped braces	$4,200	$5,200
1944-1946	Non-scalloped	$3,700	$4,800
1947-1949		$3,200	$4,000
1950-1952		$2,700	$3,300
1953-1959		$2,500	$3,200
1960-1962		$2,400	$3,100
1963-1965		$2,300	$2,800
1966	Tortoise guard	$2,300	$2,800
1966	Black guard	$2,200	$2,700
1967		$2,200	$2,700
1968		$2,200	$2,700
1969		$2,100	$2,500
1970-1979		$1,900	$2,300
1980-1989		$1,400	$1,700
1990-1995		$1,250	$1,450
00-18 C			
1962-1995. Renamed from 00-18 G in '62, mahogany back and sides, classical, 12 frets, slotted headstock, natural.			
1962-1969		$1,300	$1,500
1970-1979		$1,100	$1,300
00-18 CTN Elizabeth Cotton			
2001. Commemorative Edition, 76 made.			
2001		$2,000	$2,500
00-18 E			
1959-1964. Flat top Style 18, single neck pickup and 2 knobs, heavier bracing, natural.			
1959-1964		$3,000	$3,700
00-18 G			
1936-1962. Mahogany back and sides, classical, natural, renamed 00-18 C in '62.			
1936-1939		$1,800	$2,200
1940-1949		$1,500	$1,800
1950-1962		$1,250	$1,550

1920 Martin 0-42

1936 Martin 00-18

To get the most from this book, be sure to read "Using *The Guide*" in the introduction.

Martin 0-28 VS

Martin 00-28 VS

MODEL		EXC. COND.	
YEAR	FEATURES	LOW	HIGH

00-18 Gruhn Limited Edition
1995. Sitka spruce top, C-shaped neck profile, 25 made.

1995		$1,700	$2,100

00-18 H
1935-1941. Hawaiian, mahogany back amd sides, 12 frets clear of body, natural. The Price Guide is generally for all original instruments. The H conversion is an exception, because converting from H (Hawaiian-style) to 00-18 specs is considered by some to be a favorable improvement and something that adds value.

1935-1941		$6,600	$8,400

00-18 H Geoff Muldaur
2006-present. Solid Adirondack spruce top, solid mahogany sides and back, sunburst.

2006-2010		$2,100	$2,600

00-18 K
1917-1925. All koa wood.

1917-1925	Gut	$6,000	$7,500
1923-1925	Steel	$6,000	$7,500

00-18 SH Steve Howe
1999-2000. Limited edition run of 250.

1999-2000		$1,800	$2,200

00-18 V
1984, 2003-present. Mahogany back and sides, spruce top, Vintage Series.

1984	9 made	$1,700	$2,000
2003-2010		$1,600	$1,850

00-21
1898-1996. Brazilian rosewood back and sides, changed to Indian rosewood in 1970, dark outer binding, unbound ebony 'board until 1947, rosewood from 1947, slotted diamond inlays until '44, dot after, natural.

1898-1926		$5,500	$6,900
1927-1931	Steel bracing	$6,600	$8,200
1932-1937	Natural	$7,500	$9,200
1938-1939	Early '39, 1.75 neck	$7,500	$9,200
1939-1941	Later '39, 1.68 neck	$7,000	$8,400
1942-1944	Scalloped braces	$11,000	$13,200
1944-1946	Non-scalloped	$8,000	$10,000
1947-1949		$6,500	$7,000
1950-1952		$5,500	$6,500
1953-1959		$5,200	$6,500
1960-1965		$5,200	$6,500
1966-1969	Brazilian rosewood	$5,200	$6,500
1970-1996	Indian rosewood	$2,600	$3,200

00-21 Custom
2005-2006. Custom order size 00 style 21, Brazilian rosewood sides and back.

2005-2006		$3,000	$3,700

00-21 Golden Era
1998. Limited edition, Adirondack spruce top, scalloped braces, rosewood back and sides.

1998		$2,100	$2,700

00-21 H
Special order limited production Hawaiian.

1914	1 made	$7,200	$9,200
1952	1 made	$5,000	$6,000
1955	1 made	$5,000	$6,000

MODEL		EXC. COND.	
YEAR	FEATURES	LOW	HIGH

00-21 Kingston Trio LTD
2008-2009. Celebrating the 50th Anniversary of the Kingston Trio, inspired by founder Dave Guard's 00-21, 100 made, 12-fret body, Indian rosewood body, Italian spruce top, inside label with picture of Kingston Trio and notation "In Memory of Dave Guard 1934-1991".

2008-2009		$2,700	$3,300

00-21 LE
1987. Guitar of the Month, 19 made.

1987		$2,300	$2,800

00-21 NY
1961-1965. Brazilian rosewood back and sides, no inlay, natural.

1961-1965		$3,600	$4,500

00-21 S
1968. Slotted headstock, Brazilian rosewood sides and back.

1968		$5,700	$7,100

00-25 K
1980-1988. Spruce top, koa back and sides.

1980-1988		$1,600	$1,900

00-258 K2
1980-1989. Koa top, back and sides.

1980-1989		$1,800	$2,200

00-28
1898-1941, 1958 (1 made), 1977 (1 made), 1984 (2 made). Brazilian rosewood back and sides, changed to Indian rosewood in 1977, herringbone purfling through 1941, white binding and unbound 'board after 1941, no inlays before 1901, diamond inlays from 1901-41, dot after, natural.

1898-1924	Gut braces	$9,000	$10,000
1925-1931	Steel bracing	$17,000	$21,000
1934	5 made	$18,000	$22,000
1936	6 made	$16,000	$20,000
1939	1 made	$16,000	$20,000
1940	2 made	$16,000	$20,000
1941	1 made	$16,000	$20,000
1958	Special order	$3,200	$3,900

00-28 C
1966-1995. Renamed from 00-28 G, Brazilian rosewood back and sides, changed to Indian rosewood in '70, classical, 12 frets, natural.

1966-1969	Brazilian rosewood	$2,700	$3,400
1970-1979	Indian rosewood	$1,400	$1,700

00-28 G
1936-1962. Brazilian rosewood back and sides, classical, natural, reintroduced as 00-28 C in '66.

1936-1939		$5,000	$6,000
1940-1949		$3,900	$5,000
1951-1962		$3,100	$3,800

00-28 K Hawaiian
1919-1921, 1926-1933. Koa back and sides, Hawaiian set-up.

1919-1921	34 made	$7,000	$8,800
1926-1933	1 made per year	$9,200	$11,400

00-28 VS
2008-present.

2008-2010		$2,100	$2,400

00-30
1890s-1921.

1903		$7,000	$9,000

MODEL YEAR	FEATURES	EXC. COND. LOW	HIGH

00-37 K2 Steve Miller
2001. All koa 12-fret style 00. The 00-37K SM has a spruce top. 68 made of each version.

| 2001 | | $4,000 | $5,000 |

00-40 H
1928-1939. Hawaiian, Brazilian rosewood back and sides, 12 frets clear of body, natural. H models are sometimes converted to standard Spanish setup, in higher-end models this can make the instrument more valuable to some people.

| 1928-1929 | Pyramid bridge | $21,000 | $25,000 |
| 1930-1939 | Belly bridge | $17,000 | $21,000 |

00-40 K
Few were made (only 6), figured koa, natural.

| 1918 | 1 made | $22,000 | $26,000 |
| 1930 | 5 made | $18,000 | $22,000 |

00-40 Martin Stauffer
1997. Rosewood/spruce, 35 made.

| 1997 | | $5,500 | $6,500 |

00-41 Custom Shop
2005. Custom Shop model.

| 2005 | | $3,500 | $4,200 |

00-42
1898-1942, 1973 (one made), 1994-1996. Brazilian rosewood back and sides, Indian rosewood in 1973, pearl top borders, 12 frets, ivory bound peghead until 1918, ivoroid binding after 1918, natural.

1898-1926	Pyramid bridge	$20,000	$25,000
1927-1942	Belly bridge, 12-fret	$27,000	$33,000
1930-1936	14-fret	$29,000	$35,000
1938	1 made	$22,000	$27,000
1939	Early '39, 1.75 neck	$22,000	$27,000
1939	Later '39, 1.68 neck	$20,000	$25,000
1940	12 made	$20,000	$25,000
1942	6 made	$20,000	$25,000
1973	1 made	$2,900	$3,600
1994-1996		$2,500	$3,100

00-42 G
1936-1939. Gut string slotted headstock classical, only 3 made.

| 1936-1939 | 3 made | $10,000 | $12,500 |

00-42 K
1919. Koa body, only 1 made.

| 1919 | 1 made | $25,000 | $31,000 |

00-42 K2 Robbie Robertson
2008-2009. Limited Edition, all koa body (K2), 00-12 fret style, high-end appointments.

| 2008-2009 | | $3,600 | $4,300 |

00-42 Linda Ronstadt Limited Edition
2009-2010. Madagascar rosewood, slotted headstock.

| 2009-2010 | | $5,800 | $7,100 |

00-44 Soloist/Olcott-Bickford Artist Model
1913-1939. Custom-made in small quantities, Brazilian rosewood, ivory or faux-ivory-bound ebony 'board.

| 1913-1939 | 6 made | $26,000 | $35,000 |

00-45
1904-1929, 1936-1938, 1970-1995. Brazilian rosewood back and sides, changed to Indian rosewood

in '70, 12 frets and slotted headstock until '34 and from '70 on 14 frets, and solid headstock from '34-'70, natural.

1904-1927	Gut braces	$28,000	$35,000
1927-1929	Steel braces	$45,000	$60,000
1936-1938	3 made	$45,000	$60,000
1970-1979	Reintroduced	$3,100	$3,800
1980-1989		$2,600	$3,200
1990-1995		$2,400	$3,000

00-45 K
1919. Koa body, 1 made.

| 1919 | | $45,000 | $60,000 |

00-45 S
1970. Slotted headstock.

| 1970 | | $3,400 | $4,200 |

00-45 S Limited Edition
2002. 1902 vintage-pattern with fancy inlays, 00 size style 45, 50 made.

| 2002 | | $10,000 | $12,500 |

00-45 Stauffer Commemorative Limited Edition
1997. Stauffer six-on-a-side headstock, 45-style appointments, 00-size body, Sitka spruce top, Brazilian rosewood back and sides.

| 1997 | 25 made | $10,000 | $12,500 |

00C-16 DBRE
2005-2009. Rounded cutaway, rosewood back and sides, abalone dot inlays and rosette, Fishman.

| 2007 | | $1,450 | $1,700 |

00CXAE
2000-present. Single-cut acoustic-electric flat-top, composite laminate back and sides, made in U.S.

| 2000-2010 | | $325 | $400 |

000-1 Series
1995-2005. Solid spruce top with laminated mahogany (000-1) or Indian rosewood (000-1R) sides.

| 1995-2002 | Indian rosewood | $600 | $750 |
| 1996-2005 | Mahogany | $475 | $700 |

000-15 Auditorium
1997-2010. All solid wood mahogany body, dot markers, natural.

| 1997-2010 | | $525 | $625 |

000-15 M
2010-present. All mahogany.

| 2010 | | $750 | $875 |

000-15/000-15 S
1998-2009. Headstock is slotted (15 S, 2000-present) or solid (15).

| 1998-2010 | | $750 | $875 |

000-16 Series
1989-present. Acoustic, mahogany back and sides, diamonds and squares inlaid, sunburst, name changed to 000-16 T Auditorium with higher appointments in '96, in 2000-2005 slotted (000-16 S) and gloss finish (000-16 SGT) were offered.

| 1989-2010 | | $800 | $1,450 |

000-17 S
2002-2003. All mahogany, slotted headstock, 12 fret neck.

| 2002-2003 | | $1,050 | $1,300 |

1929 Martin 00-40 H

Martin 000-1 Series

1956 Martin 000-21

1927 Martin 000-28

MODEL YEAR	FEATURES	EXC. COND. LOW	HIGH

000-18

1911-present (none in 1932-1933). Rosewood back and sides until '17, mahogany back and sides from '17, longer scale in '24-'34, 12 frets clear of body until '33, changed to 14 frets in '34. Improved neck late-'34, war-time changes '41-'46, non-scalloped braces in late-'44, switched from Adirondack spruce to Sitka spruce top in '46 (though some Adirondack tops in '50s and '60s), natural. Now called the 000-18 Auditorium.

Year	Features	Low	High
1924-1928		$12,000	$15,000
1929-1931		$13,000	$16,000
1934	Early '34, long scale	$15,000	$19,000
1934-1937	14-fret	$15,000	$19,000
1938-1939	Early '39 1.75 neck	$15,000	$19,000
1939-1941	Late '39, 1.68 neck	$9,000	$11,000
1942-1944	Scalloped braces	$7,400	$7,200
1944-1946	Non-scalloped	$5,800	$7,300
1947-1949	Natural	$5,000	$6,200
1950-1952		$4,000	$5,000
1953-1959		$3,600	$4,500
1960-1962		$3,000	$3,700
1963-1965		$2,900	$3,600
1966	Black guard	$2,700	$3,300
1966	Tortoise guard	$2,800	$3,400
1967		$2,700	$3,300
1968		$2,600	$3,200
1969		$2,400	$3,000
1970-1974		$1,500	$1,900
1975-1979		$1,400	$1,800
1980-1989		$1,300	$1,600
1990-1999		$1,200	$1,500
2000-2010		$1,200	$1,500

000-18 Golden Era 1937

2006-present.

Year		Low	High
2006-2010		$2,000	$2,500

000-18 Golden Era Sunburst

2006-present.

Year		Low	High
2006-2010		$2,100	$2,400

000-18 Kenny Sultan

2007-2009. Flamed mahogany sides, diamond and squares inlays, label signed by Sultan.

Year		Low	High
2007-2009		$2,300	$2,800

000-18 WG Woody Guthrie

1999. Signed label including artwork and model identification.

Year		Low	High
1999		$2,000	$2,500

000-21

1902-1923 (22 made over that time), 1931(2), 1938-1959, 1965 (1), 1979 (12). Brazilian rosewood back and sides, changed to Indian rosewood in '70, natural.

Year	Features	Low	High
1902-1913		$13,000	$16,000
1918-1923		$14,000	$17,000
1931	12-fret, 2 made	$15,000	$18,000
1938-1939	Early '39, 1.75 neck	$20,000	$25,000
1939-1941	Late '39, 1.68 neck	$14,000	$17,000
1942-1944		$11,000	$13,000
1944-1946		$8,500	$10,500
1947-1949		$6,500	$8,000
1950-1952		$6,000	$7,500

MODEL YEAR	FEATURES	EXC. COND. LOW	HIGH
1953-1959		$5,500	$7,000
1965	1 made	$5,000	$6,000
1979	12 made	$2,300	$2,900

000-28

1902-present. Brazilian rosewood back and sides, changed to Indian rosewood in '70, herringbone purfling through '41, white binding and unbound 'board after '41, no inlays before '01, slotted diamond inlays from '01-'44, dot after, 12 frets until '32, 14 frets '31 on (both 12 and 14 frets were made during '31-'32), natural.

Year	Features	Low	High
1902-1924	Gut (standard)	$20,000	$25,000
1924-1927	Steel (mostly)	$35,000	$43,000
1928	12-fret	$35,000	$43,000
1929	Pyramid bridge, 12-fret	$35,000	$43,000
1930	Belly bridge, 12-fret	$35,000	$43,000
1931-1933	12 fret	$35,000	$43,000
1934	Early '34 long scale	$40,000	$49,000
1934-1937	14-fret	$40,000	$49,000
1938		$31,000	$38,000
1939	Early '39, 1.75 neck	$31,000	$38,000
1939	Late '39, 1.68 neck	$26,000	$32,000
1940-1941		$25,000	$31,000
1942-1944	Scalloped braces	$27,000	$32,000
1945-1946	Herringbone, non-scalloped	$20,000	$24,000
1947-1949	'47 start of non-herringbone	$11,000	$13,500
1950-1952		$10,000	$12,500
1953-1958	Early '58, last of Kluson	$8,500	$10,500
1958-1959	Late '58, Grover tuners	$7,600	$9,500
1960-1962		$6,200	$7,500
1963-1965		$5,500	$6,700
1966	Early '66, Tortoise guard	$5,500	$6,700
1966	Late '66, black guard	$5,000	$6,200
1967		$5,000	$6,200
1968		$5,000	$6,200
1969	Last of Brazilian rosewood	$5,000	$6,200
1970-1979	Indian rosewood	$1,900	$2,400
1980-1989	Indian rosewood	$1,700	$2,100
1990-1999	Indian rosewood	$1,400	$1,800
2000-2010		$1,300	$1,650

000-28 C

1962-1969. Brazilian rosewood back and sides, classical, slotted peghead, natural.

Year		Low	High
1962-1969		$3,400	$4,300

000-28 EC Eric Clapton Signature

1996-present. Sitka spruce top, Indian rosewood back and sides, herringbone trim, natural.

Year		Low	High
1996-2010		$1,800	$2,250

000-28 ECB Eric Clapton

2003. Limited edition, 2nd edition of EC Signature Series with Brazilian rosewood.

Year		Low	High
2003		$5,500	$6,500

The *Vintage Guitar Price Guide* shows low to high values for items in all-original excellent condition, and, where applicable, with original case or cover.

MODEL YEAR	FEATURES	EXC. COND. LOW	HIGH

000-28 ECSB Eric Clapton
2005-present. Sunburst version of 000-28 EC.

| 2005-2010 | Sunburst | $1,800 | $2,250 |

000-28 G
1937-1955. Special order classical guitar, very limited production.

1937-1940	3 made	$7,500	$9,500
1946-1949	10 made	$4,900	$6,100
1950-1955	4 made	$4,100	$5,000

000-28 Golden Era
1996 only. Sitka spruce top, rosewood back and sides, scalloped braces, herringbone trim, 12-fret model, natural.

| 1996 | | $3,000 | $3,700 |

000-28 H
2000-2001. Herringbone top trim.

| 2000-2001 | | $1,500 | $1,850 |

000-28 HB Brazilian 1937 Reissue
1997. Pre-war specs including scalloped bracing, Brazilian rosewood.

| 1997 | | $4,900 | $6,100 |

000-28 K
1921. Non-catalog special order model, only 2 known to exist, koa top, back and sides.

| 1921 | | $28,000 | $35,000 |

000-28 LSH/LSH Custom
2008. Large sound hole (LSH), high-end style 28 appointments, Adirondack spruce top, wild grain East Indian sides and back, 000-14 fret specs.

| 2008 | | $2,900 | $3,600 |

000-28 VS
2006-present. VS Vintage Series, spruce top with aging toner and scalloped bracing, rosewood (not Brazilian) sides and back, slotted diamond markers, ebony pyramid bridge, herringbone top trim, nickel Waverly butterbean tuners.

| 2006-2010 | | $2,100 | $2,500 |

000-28(B) Norman Blake Signature Edition
2004. 12-fret neck on 14-fret body, B version is Brazilian rosewood.

| 2004 | Brazilian rosewood | $5,000 | $6,200 |
| 2004 | Indian rosewood | $2,500 | $3,100 |

000-40
1909. Ivoroid bound top and back, snowflake inlay, 1 made.

| 1909 | | $34,000 | $40,000 |

000-40 PR Peter Rowan
2001. Mahogany back and sides, slotted headstock, 12-fret, phases of the moon inlays.

| 2001 | | $2,500 | $3,000 |

000-40 Q2GN Graham Nash
2003. Limited edition of 147 guitars, quilted mahogany top/back/sides, flying-heart logo on headstock, Graham Nash signature on frets 18-20.

| 2003 | | $2,700 | $3,300 |

000-41
1996. Custom shop style 000-41.

| 1996 | | $3,000 | $3,500 |

000-42
1918, 1921-1922, 1925, 1930, 1934, 1938-1943, 2003-present. Brazilian rosewood back and sides, natural. The 1918-1934 price range is wide due to the variety of specifications.

1918-1925	Limited production	$40,000	$50,000
1930	1 made, 14-fret	$55,000	$65,000
1934	1 made	$55,000	$65,000
1938	27 made	$68,000	$82,000
1939	Early '39, 1.75 neck	$66,000	$80,000
1939	Later '39, 1.68 neck	$55,000	$67,000
1940	12 made	$55,000	$67,000
1941	24 made	$55,000	$67,000
1942	12 made	$55,000	$67,000
1943	6 made, last pearl border	$55,000	$67,000
2003-2010	Indian rosewood, 12-fret	$2,800	$3,500

000-42 EC Eric Clapton
1995. Style 45 pearl-inlaid headplate, ivoroid bindings, Eric Clapton signature, 24.9" scale, flat top, sunburst top price is $8320 ('95 price), only 461 made; 433 natural, 28 sunburst.

| 1995 | Natural | $5,800 | $7,300 |
| 1995 | Sunburst | $6,000 | $7,500 |

000-42 ECB Eric Clapton
2000. With Brazilian rosewood, 200 made.

| 2000 | | $12,000 | $15,000 |

000-42 M Eric Clapton L.E.
2008. Limited Edition, 250 made, Madagascar rosewood sides and back, Carpathian spruce top.

| 2008 | | $5,400 | $6,700 |

000-42 Marquis
2007-2009. Indian rosewood.

| 2007-2009 | | $2,500 | $3,000 |

000-42 SB
2004. 1935 style with sunburst finish, Indian rosewood back and sides.

| 2004 | | $3,000 | $3,800 |

000-45
1906, 1911-1914, 1917-1919, 1922-1929, 1934-1942, 1971-1993. Brazilian rosewood back and sides, changed to Indian rosewood in '70, 12-fret neck and slotted headstock until '34 (but 7 were made in '70 and 1 in '75), 14-fret neck and solid headstock after '34, natural.

1906-1919		$42,000	$50,000
1922-1927	Gut	$50,000	$60,000
1928-1929	Steel	$86,000	$102,000
1934-1936	14-fret, C.F.M. inlaid	$135,000	$160,000
1937		$135,000	$160,000
1938	Early '38	$130,000	$155,000
1938	Late '38	$125,000	$155,000
1939	Early '39, 1.75 neck	$125,000	$155,000
1939	Late '39, 1.68 neck	$104,000	$130,000
1940-1942		$80,000	$100,000

000-45 Custom
| 2002 | | $13,000 | $16,000 |

2006 Martin 000-40-S Mark Knopfler

1928 Martin 000-45

1928 Martin 000-45 S Stephen Stills

Martin 000CXE

MODEL YEAR	FEATURES	EXC. COND. LOW	HIGH

000-45 JR Jimmie Rodgers Golden Era
1997. Adirondack spruce top, Brazilian rosewood back and sides, scalloped high X-braces, abalone trim, natural, 100 made.

| 1997 | | $10,000 | $12,500 |

000-45 S Stephen Stills
2005. Only 91 made.

| 2005 | | $7,000 | $7,500 |

000C David Gray Custom
2005-2006. Custom Artist Edition, 000-size cutaway, Italian spruce top, mahogany back and sides, interior label signed by David Gray.

| 2005-2006 | | $1,800 | $2,200 |

000C DB Dion The Wanderer
2002. Only 57 made, cutaway acoustic/electric, gloss black finish, Sitka spruce top, scalloped bracing, mahogony sides and back, slotted diamond and square markers, Dion logo on headstock.

| 2002 | | $2,800 | $3,500 |

000C Series
1990-2010. French-style small soft cutaway (like vintage Selmer), models include; 000C-1E (mahogany body) and 000C-16RGTE (premium, rosewood body).

1990-1995	000C-16	$900	$1,200
1996-2000	000C-1E	$900	$1,200
2001-2006	000C-16 RGTE	$900	$1,200
2003	000C-16 SGTNE	$1,200	$1,450
2004	000C-16 SRNE	$1,200	$1,450

000C Steve Miller Pegasus
2005-2006. Cutaway, mahogany back and sides, Pegasus logo.

| 2005-2006 | | $2,800 | $3,400 |

000CXE
2002-present. Acoustic-electric, rounded cutaway, high pressure laminated body, black finish.

| 2002-2010 | | $425 | $525 |

000-ECHF Bellezza Bianca
2006. Adirondack spruce top, big-lead flamed maple back/sides, model name logo on 20th fret, white finish, all-white case, 410 made.

| 2006 | | $4,100 | $4,700 |

000-ECHF Bellezza Nera
2005-2006. Limited edition Eric Clapton and Hiroshi Fujiwara Black Beauty Model, 476 made, Italian Alpine spruce top, Indian rosewood sides and back, black finish, white/blond option.

| 2005-2006 | Black | $3,900 | $4,500 |
| 2005-2006 | White/blond option | $3,900 | $4,500 |

000-JBP Jimmy Buffett Pollywog
2003. Model name and number on label inside back, 168 made.

| 2003 | | $2,800 | $3,500 |

000-M Mahogany Auditorium
2004-2006. Auditorium 000-size, mahogany sides and back.

| 2004-2006 | | $500 | $575 |

000X Hippie
2007. Limited Edition of 200, celebrates the 40th Anniversary of the 'Summer of Love'.

| 2007 | | $1,100 | $1,400 |

MODEL YEAR	FEATURES	EXC. COND. LOW	HIGH

0000-18 Custom/Custom 0000-18
2005-2009. 16" lower bout, spruce top with high X-brace, mahogany sides and back, gloss finish, commissioned for Gruhn Guitars 35th Anniversary and first year models have signed Anniversary labels.

| 2005-2009 | | $1,900 | $2,300 |

0000-28 Series
1997-2000. Several models, jumbo-size 0000 cutaway body, models include; H (herringbone trim), Custom (Indian rosewood, sitka spruce top), H-AG (Arlo Guthrie 30th anniversary, Indian rosewood back and sides, only 30 made), H Custom Shop (herringbone).

1997-2000	0000-28 H	$1,700	$2,100
1998	0000-28 Custom	$2,000	$2,500
1999	0000-28 H-AG	$2,900	$3,500

0000-38 (M-38)
1997-1998. Called M-38 in '77-'97 and '07-present (see that listing), 0000-size, Indian rosewood back and sides, multi-bound.

| 1997-1998 | | $1,800 | $2,300 |

1/4 - 28
1973, 1979. 14 made.

| 1973-1979 | | $3,000 | $3,600 |

1-17
1906-1917 (1st version), 1931-1934 (2nd version). First version has spruce top, mahogany back and sides, second version has all mahogany with flat natural finish.

| 1906-1917 | | $1,700 | $2,100 |
| 1930-1934 | | $2,100 | $2,600 |

1-17 P
1928-1931. Mahogany back and sides, plectrum neck, 272 made.

| 1928-1931 | | $1,750 | $2,150 |

1-18
1899-1927. Brazilian rosewood or mahogany back and sides.

1899-1917	Brazilian rosewood	$2,400	$3,000
1918-1922	Mahogany	$2,100	$2,600
1923-1927	Steel braces, 12-fret	$2,200	$2,700

1-20
| 1867 | | $6,000 | $7,500 |

1-21
1860-1926. Initially offered in size 1 in the 1860s, ornate soundhole rings.

1860	Antique market value	$4,000	$5,000
1890-1898		$3,000	$3,700
1900-1926		$3,000	$3,700

1-22
1850s.

| 1855 | Antique market value | $5,000 | $6,000 |

1-26
1850-1890. Rosewood back and sides, ivory-bound top, rope-style purfling.

| 1855 | Antique market value | $5000 | $6,000 |
| 1890 | | $4,000 | $5,000 |

MODEL YEAR	FEATURES	EXC. COND. LOW	HIGH
1-27			
1880s-1907.			
1880-1907		$4,000	$5,000
1-28			
1880-1923. Style 28 appointments including Brazilian rosewood back and sides.			
1880	Antique market value	$5,000	$6,000
1890		$4,000	$5,000
1-30			
1860s. Size 1 Style 30 with pearl soundhole trim, cedar neck.			
1860s	Antique market value	$6,000	$7,500
1-42			
1858-1919. Rosewood back and sides, ivory-bound top and 'board.			
1858-1919		$11,000	$14,000
1-45			
1904-1919. Only 6 made, slotted headstock and Style 45 appointments.			
1904-1919		$24,000	$29,000
2-15			
1939-1964. All mahogany body, dot markers.			
1939	Special order	$1,700	$2,100
1951		$1,200	$1,500
2-17			
1910, 1922-1938. 1910 version has spruce top, mahogany back and sides. '22 on, all mahogany body, no body binding after '30.			
1910	6 made	$1,500	$1,800
1922-1930		$2,000	$2,500
2-17 H			
1927-1931. Hawaiian, all mahogany, 12 frets clear of body.			
1927-1931		$2,000	$2,500
2-20			
1855-1899. Rare style only offered in size 2.			
1855-1899		$2,600	$3,200
2-21			
1885-1929. Rosewood back and sides, herringbone soundhole ring.			
1890		$2,900	$3,600
1920		$2,500	$3,100
2-22			
1870s-1890s. Gut string instrument.			
1870-1890s		$4,000	$5,000
2-24			
1857-1898.			
1850s	Antique market value	$5,300	$6,500
1890s		$4,000	$5,000
2-27			
1857-1907. Brazilian rosewood back and sides, pearl ring, zigzag back stripe, ivory bound ebony 'board and peghead.			
1857-1860s	Antique market value	$6,000	$7,500
1890s		$4,000	$5,000
1900-1907		$3,500	$4,500

MODEL YEAR	FEATURES	EXC. COND. LOW	HIGH
2-28			
1880		$4,000	$5,000
2-28 T			
1929-1930. Tenor neck, Brazilian rosewood back and sides, herringbone top purfling.			
1929-1930		$2,300	$2,800
2-30			
1902-1921. Similar to 2-27, only 7 made.			
1902-1921		$5,000	$6,000
2-34			
1870-1898. Similar to 2-30.			
1880s		$6,000	$7,000
2-40			
1850s-1898, 1909.			
1877		$8,000	$10,000
2-44			
1940. Style 44, Olcott-Bickford Soloist custom order, only 4 made.			
1940		$20,000	$25,000
2 1/2-17			
1856-1897, 1909-1914. The first Style 17s were small size 2 1/2 and 3, these early models use Brazilian rosewood.			
1850s	Antique market value	$2,400	$3,000
1890s		$2,100	$2,600
1909-1914		$1,600	$2,000
2 1/2-18			
1865-1923. Parlor-size body with Style 18 appointments.			
1865-1898	Antique market value	$2,400	$3,000
1901-1917	Brazilian rosewood	$2,100	$2,600
1918-1923	Mahogany	$1,600	$2,000
2 1/2-42			
1880s. Style 42 size 2 1/2 with Brazilian rosewood.			
1880s		$10,000	$12,000
3-17			
1856-1897, 1908 (1 made). The first Style 17s were small size 2 1/2 and 3. The early models use Brazilian rosewood, spruce top, bound back, unbound ebony 'board.			
1856-1889	Brazilian rosewood	$2,500	$3,000
1890-1897		$2,200	$2,700
1908	1 made	$1,700	$2,100
3-24/3-34			
1860. Brazilian rosewood.			
1860		$5,000	$6,000
5-15			
2005-2007. Sapele or mahogany body, shorter scale.			
2003-2007		$800	$1,000
5-15 T			
1949-1963. All mahogany, non-gloss finish, tenor neck.			
1949-1963		$900	$1,100
5-16			
1962-1963. Mahogany back and sides, unbound rosewood 'board.			
1962-1963		$1,600	$2,000
5-17 T			
1927-1949. All mahogany, tenor neck.			
1927-1949		$1,000	$1,250

Martin 000CX1E

1927 Martin 2-17
Tom Siska

Martin 5-28

Martin Alternative II Resophonic

MODEL YEAR	FEATURES	EXC. COND. LOW	HIGH
5-18			
1898-1989. Rosewood back and sides (changed to mahogany from 1917 on), 12 frets, slotted headstock.			
1918-1922	Gut braces, mahogany	$2,200	$2,700
1923-1939	Steel braces in '23	$2,800	$3,200
1940-1944		$2,700	$3,100
1945-1949		$2,400	$3,000
1950-1959		$1,600	$2,000
1960-1969		$1,400	$1,700
1970-1989		$1,200	$1,500
5-21			
1890s, 1902, 1912-1920, 1927, 1977. Rosewood back and sides.			
1890s		$2,600	$3,200
5-21 T			
1926-1928. Tenor guitar with 21-styling.			
1926-1928		$2,000	$2,500
5-28			
2001-2002. Special edition, 1/2-size parlor guitar size 15 with Terz tuning, Indian rosewood back and sides.			
2001-2002		$1,600	$2,000
7-28			
1980-1995, 1997-2002. 7/8-body-size of a D-model, Style 28 appointments.			
1980-1995		$1,600	$2,000
1997-2002		$1,600	$2,000
7-37 K			
1980-1987. 7/8-size baby dreadnought acoustic, koa back and sides, spruce top, oval soundhole.			
1980-1987		$2,200	$2,700
Alternative II Resophonic			
2004-2007. Textured aluminum top, matching headstock overlay, high pressure laminate sides and back, spun aluminum cone resonator, Fishman pickup.			
2004-2007		$650	$800
Alternative X			
2001-present. OO-Grand Concert body shape, textured aluminum top, matching headstock overlay, spun aluminum cone resonator, Fishman pickup.			
2001-2009		$550	$700
Alternative X Midi			
2003-2004. Roland GK Midi pickup with 13-pin output, additional Fishman Prefix Pro pickup and preamp system, requires Roland GA-20 interface.			
2003-2004		$700	$850
Alternative XT			
2002-2005. Alternative with DiMarzio humbucker, volume & tone controls, coil tap, Bigsby.			
2003-2005		$700	$850
America's Guitar 175th Anniversary			
2008. D-style, 14-fret, Adirondack spruce top, Madagascar rosewood sides and back, 175 made, 'America's Guitar' headstock inlay, '175th Anniversary 1833-2008'.			
2008		$3,500	$4,300
ASD-41 Australian Series			
2005. Tasmanian Blackwood sides and back, Sitka spruce top, Australian theme appointments and label.			
2005		$4,200	$5,100

MODEL YEAR	FEATURES	EXC. COND. LOW	HIGH
Backpacker			
1994-present. Small-bodied travel guitar, nylon or steel strings.			
1994-2010		$120	$150
BC-15E			
2004. Natural mahogany top/back/sides, single-cut, on-board electronics.			
2004		$900	$1,100
C-1			
1931-1942. Acoustic archtop, mahogany back and sides, spruce top, round hole until '33, f-holes appear in '32, bound body, sunburst.			
1931-1933	Round, 449 made	$2,400	$3,000
1932-1942	F-hole, 786 made	$2,400	$3,000
C-1 R Humphrey			
1997-2000. Solid cedar top, laminated rosewood back and sides, satin finish.			
1997-2000		$900	$1,100
C-2			
1931-1942. Acoustic archtop, Brazilian rosewood back and sides, carved spruce top, round hole until '33, f-holes appear in '32, zigzag back stripe, multi-bound body, slotted-diamond inlay, sunburst.			
1931-1933	Round, 269 made	$4,000	$5,000
1932-1942	F-hole, 439 made	$4,000	$5,000
C-3			
1931-1934. Archtop, Brazilian rosewood back and sides, round soundhole until early '33, f-holes after.			
1931-1933	Round, 53 made	$5,500	$6,700
1933-1934	F-hole, 58 made	$5,500	$6,700
CEO Series			
1997-2006. Chief Executive Officer C.F. Martin IV special editions.			
1998	CEO-2, Iam Mac, ebony	$1,400	$1,700
2000-2001	CEO-4R, rosewood	$1,500	$1,800
2000-2003	CEO-4, mahogany	$1,200	$1,500
2001-2004	CEO-5, bearclaw top	$1,600	$1,900
CF-1 American Archtop			
2005. 17" body, laminated arched spruce top, X-braced, solid maple sides, laminated arched maple back, maple neck, ebony 'board, dot markers, floating pickup, gold decal.			
2005		$2,000	$2,500
Concept III			
2003. U.S.-made, solid spruce top, solid mahogany back and sides, cutaway, on-board electronics, sparkle-mist finish.			
2003		$1,400	$1,700
Cowboy Series			
2000-2009. Inside label identifies model number. Models include Cowboy X (2000, 250 made), Cowboy II ('01, 500 made), Cowboy III ('03, 750 made), and Cowboy IV ('05-'06, 250 made), Cowboy V ('06-'09, 500 made).			
2001-2009		$500	$550
CSN Crosby Stills & Nash			
2007-2009. CSN logo on headstock, Crosby Stills & Nash on label, D-style, high-end appointments, Englemann spruce top, East Indian rosewood sides and back.			
2007-2009		$2,500	$3,000

The *Vintage Guitar Price Guide* shows low to high values for items in all-original excellent condition, and, where applicable, with original case or cover.

MODEL YEAR	FEATURES	EXC. COND. LOW	HIGH

C-TSH (Humphrey/Martin)
Late-1990s. Designed by high-end classical guitar luthier Thomas Humphrey for Martin, based on his Millenium model, arched Englemann spruce top, rosewood back and sides.

| 1998 | | $2,000 | $2,500 |

Custom 15
1991-1994. Renamed HD-28V Custom 15 in ca. 2001.

| 1991-1994 | | $1,900 | $2,400 |

Custom Ne Plus Ultra
2005. Very fancy appointments, 0000 M-size body, rhinestone on pearloid peghead.

| 2005 | | $4,000 | $4,900 |

D-1
1992-2005. Name first used for the prototype of the D-18, made in 1931, revived for current model with mahogany body, A-frame bracing, available as an acoustic/electric.

| 1992-2005 | | $650 | $800 |

D-1 R
1994-1999. Laminated rosewood back and sides, solid spruce top, mahogany neck, optional MEQ-932, Martin Porta Com, and Fishman AGP-2 preamps.

| 1994-1999 | | $575 | $675 |

D-2 R
1996-2002. D-size, Style 28 appointments, laminated rosewood back/sides, solid spruce top, natural satin finish.

| 1996-2002 | | $675 | $800 |

D-3-18
1991. Sitka spruce top, 3-piece mahogany back, 80-piece limited edition.

| 1991 | | $1,550 | $1,850 |

D-12 Custom
1987-present. Custom Shop.

| 1987-2010 | | $800 | $1,000 |

D12-1
1996-2001. Mahogany, satin finish, 12-string.

| 1996-2001 | | $500 | $625 |

D12-18
1973-1995. Mahogany back and sides, 12 strings, 14 frets clear of body, solid headstock.

1973-1979		$1,200	$1,500
1980-1989		$1,100	$1,400
1990-1995		$1,000	$1,250

D12-20
1964-1991. Mahogany back and sides, 12 strings, 12 frets clear of body, slotted headstock.

1964-1969		$1,500	$1,900
1970-1979		$1,400	$1,700
1980-1991		$1,300	$1,600

D12-28
1970-present. Indian rosewood back and sides, 12 strings, 14 frets clear of body, solid headstock.

1970-1979		$1,500	$1,800
1980-1989		$1,400	$1,700
1990-1999		$1,300	$1,600
2000-2010		$1,300	$1,600

D12-35
1965-1995. Brazilian rosewood back and sides, changed to Indian rosewood in '70, 12 strings, 12 frets

clear of body, slotted headstock.

1965-1969	Brazilian rosewood	$3,700	$4,500
1970-1979	Indian rosewood	$1,500	$1,900
1980-1989		$1,500	$1,900
1990-1995		$1,400	$1,800

D12-45
1970s. Special order instrument, not a standard catalog item, with D-45 appointments, Indian rosewood.

| 1970-1979 | | $5,700 | $7,000 |

D12X1
2008-present. 12-string.

| 2008-2010 | | $425 | $525 |

D12XM
1999-2000. 12-string version of the DXM.

| 1999-2000 | | $375 | $475 |

D-15
1970-present. All mahogany body.

| 1970-2010 | | $625 | $750 |

D-15 S
2006-2009. Slotted headstock, top, back and sides can be solid sapele or mahogany.

| 2006-2009 | Mahogany | $675 | $825 |

D-16 A
1987-1990. North American ash back and sides, solid spruce top, scalloped bracing, rosewood 'board and bridge, solid mahogany neck.

| 1987-1990 | | $1,050 | $1,300 |

D-16 GT/GTE/D-16 RGT
1999-present. D-16 T specs, GT with gloss top and mahogany back and sides, RGT with gloss top and rosewood back and sides.

| 1999-2010 | GTE, factory pickup | $750 | $900 |
| 1999-2010 | Mahogany, gloss | $650 | $800 |

D-16 H
1991-1995. Full-size dreadnought, mahogany back and sides with satin finish, herringbone marquetry, vintage X-bracing, scalloped braces, optional acoustic pickup or active preamp system, replaced by D-16 T in '96.

| 1991-1995 | | $900 | $1,100 |

D-16 Lyptus
2003-2005. Lyptus sides and back.

| 2003-2005 | | $900 | $1,100 |

D-16 M
1986, 1988-1990. Mahogany back and sides, non-gloss satin finish.

| 1988-1990 | | $850 | $1,050 |

D-16 R
2006-2009. All solid wood, Indian rosewood sides and back, spruce top.

| 2006-2009 | | $1,100 | $1,300 |

D-16 T
1995-2002. Solid spruce top, solid mahogany back and sides, scalloped braces, satin finish.

| 1995-2002 | | $850 | $1,050 |

D-16 TR
1995-2002. Indian rosewood version of 16 T.

| 1995-2002 | | $1,100 | $1,300 |

2005 Martin CF-1 American Archtop

Martin D-16 GT

1957 Martin D-18

Robbie Keene

Martin D-25 K2

MODEL YEAR	FEATURES	EXC. COND. LOW	HIGH

D-17
2000-2005. All solid mahogany back, sides and top, natural brown mahogany finish.

2000-2005		$825	$975

D-18
1932-present. Mahogany back and sides, spruce top, black back stripe, 12-fret neck, changed to 14 frets in '34.

Year	Features	Low	High
1932	12-fret	$55,000	$68,000
1933-1934	12-fret	$55,000	$68,000
1934-1936	14-fret	$47,000	$57,000
1937		$40,000	$48,000
1938	Early '38, Advanced X	$36,000	$44,000
1938	Late '38, Rear X	$32,000	$39,000
1939	Early '39, 1.75 neck	$28,000	$35,000
1939	Late '39, 1.68 neck	$26,000	$32,000
1940-1941		$25,000	$30,000
1942-1944	Scalloped braces	$22,000	$28,000
1944-1946	Non-scalloped	$12,000	$15,000
1947-1949		$7,500	$9,300
1950-1952		$5,200	$6,400
1953-1959		$4,700	$5,800
1960-1962		$3,400	$4,300
1963-1965		$3,200	$4,000
1966	Early '66, Tortoise 'guard	$3,200	$4,000
1966	Late '66, black 'guard	$3,000	$3,800
1967	Last of maple bridgeplate	$2,700	$3,300
1968	Rosewood bridgeplate	$2,500	$3,000
1969		$2,500	$3,000
1970-1974		$1,500	$1,900
1975-1979		$1,400	$1,800
1980-1989		$1,300	$1,600
1983	50th Ann. 1833-1983	$1,500	$1,900
1990-1999		$1,200	$1,500
2000-2010		$1,200	$1,500

D-18 75th Anniversary Edition
2009. Limited edition only available in '09, '75th Anniversary Edition 1934-2009' noted on label and headstock stencil.

2009		$3,000	$3,700

D-18 Andy Griffith
2003. D-18 specs with bear claw spruce top, Andy's script signature on 18th fret.

2003		$1,900	$2,400

D-18 Authentic 1937
2006-present. The most authentic pre-war recreation to date including original specs using 'Hide Glue' and gloss lacquer. Adirondack spruce top with forward X-brace and scalloped Adirondack bracing, 14-fret neck.

2006-2010		$3,800	$4,400

D-18 DC David Crosby
2002. David Crosby signature at 20th fret, Engelmann spruce top, quilted mahogany back and sides, 250 made.

2002		$2,000	$2,500

D-18 E
1958-1959. D-18 factory built with DeArmond pickups which required ladder bracing (reducing acoustic volume and quality).

1958-1959		$4,300	$5,300

D-18 GE Golden Era
1995, 1999-present. 1995 version is a copy of a '37 D-18, 272 made. The current model is based on 1934 model.

1995	Natural, 272 sold	$1,900	$2,300
1995	Sunburst, 48 sold	$2,000	$2,400
1999-2010		$2,000	$2,500

D-18 Golden Era
2006. Natural or sunburst.

2006	Special Edition	$1,900	$2,300

D-18 LE
1986-1987. Limited Edition, quilted or flamed mahogany back and sides, scalloped braces, gold tuners with ebony buttons.

1986-1987		$1,700	$2,100

D-18 MB
1990. Limited Edition Guitar of the Month, flame maple binding, Engelmann spruce top signed by shop foremen, X-brace, total of 99 sold.

1990		$1,900	$2,300

D-18 S
1967-1993. Mahogany back and sides, 12-fret neck, slotted headstock, majority of production before '77, infrequent after that.

1967		$3,200	$4,000
1968		$2,700	$3,400
1969		$2,600	$3,300
1970-1979		$1,700	$2,100
1980-1993		$1,500	$1,900

D-18 Special
1989. Guitar of the Month, 28 made, first Martin to use rosewood for binding, heel cap and endpiece since 1932, scalloped top, mahogany back and sides, slotted-diamond markers.

1989		$1,900	$2,200

D-18 V (Vintage)
1985, 1992. Low-profile neck, scalloped braces, bound, total of 218 sold, Guitar of the Month in '85, Vintage Series in '92.

1985		$1,750	$2,050
1992		$1,900	$2,300

D-18 V/D-18 VS
1983-present. Vintage Series, 12-fret, V was Guitar of the Month in '85, mahogany back and sides, tortoise binding, V-neck, VS is slotted headstock version.

1983-2010		$1,600	$2,000

D-18 VE
2004-2007. D-18 V with Fishman Ellipse.

2004-2007		$1,600	$2,000

D-18 VM/D-18 VMS
1996-1999. Vintage Series, 14-fret, mahogany body, VMS is slotted headstock version.

1996-1999		$1,600	$2,000

The *Vintage Guitar Price Guide* shows low to high values for items in all-original excellent condition, and, where applicable, with original case or cover.

D-19

1977-1988. Deluxe mahogany dreadnought, optional mahogany top, multi-bound but unbound rosewood 'board.

1977-1988		$1,600	$2,000

D-21

1955-1969. Brazilian rosewood back and sides, rosewood 'board, chrome tuners.

1955-1958	Klusons to early '58	$6,500	$8,000
1958-1959	Grover tuners late '58	$6,000	$7,500
1960-1962		$5,700	$7,000
1963-1965		$5,300	$6,500
1966-1967		$4,800	$6,000
1968		$4,700	$5,800
1969		$4,500	$5,500

D-21 JCB Jim Croce Limited Edition

2001. Limited run of 73 instruments, Jim Croce signature inlay on neck, Brazilian rosewood back and sides.

2001		$5,200	$6,500

D-21 LE

1985. Limited Edition, 75 made.

1985		$1,800	$2,100

D-21 Special

2008-present. Sitka spruce top, East Indian rosewood back and sides, slotted diamond markers, rectangular pyramid-end bridge, herringbone soundhole rosette and backstripe.

2008-2010		$1,800	$2,100

D-25 K

1980-1989. Dreadnought-size, koa back and sides, spruce top.

1980-1989		$1,600	$1,900

D-25 K2

1980-1989. Same as D-25K, but with koa top and black 'guard.

1980-1989		$2,100	$2,500

D-28

1931-present. Brazilian rosewood back and sides (changed to Indian rosewood in '70), '36 was the last year for the 12-fret model, '44 was the last year for scalloped bracing, '47 was the last year herringbone trim was offered, natural. Ultra high-end D-28 Martin guitar (pre-'47) valuations are very sensitive to structural and cosmetic condition. Finish wear and body cracks for ultra high-end Martin flat tops should be evaluated on a case-by-case basis. Small variances within the 'excellent condition' category can lead to notable valuation differences.

1931	12-fret, 1 made	$145,000	$180,000
1932	12-fret, 4 made	$145,000	$180,000
1933	12-fret, 12 made	$145,000	$180,000
1934	12-fret	$145,000	$180,000
1934	14-fret	$115,000	$135,000
1935-1936	12-fret	$140,000	$175,000
1935-1936	14-fret	$115,000	$135,000
1937		$85,000	$105,000
1938	Early '38, Advanced X	$83,000	$103,000

1938	Late '38, Rear X	$73,000	$90,000
1939	Early '39, 1.75 neck	$64,000	$80,000
1939	Late '39, 1.68 neck	$60,000	$75,000
1940-1941		$58,000	$72,000
1942-1944	Scalloped braces, metal rod	$45,000	$57,000
1942-1944	Scalloped braces, wood rod	$44,000	$56,000
1944-1945	Herringbone, non-scalloped	$27,000	$34,000
1946	Herringbone, non-scalloped	$22,000	$27,000
1947-1949	Non-herringbone starting '47	$12,000	$15,000
1950-1952		$10,500	$13,000
1953-1958	Klusons to early '58	$9,500	$12,000
1958-1959	Grover tuners late '58	$8,000	$10,000
1960-1962		$6,800	$8,500
1963		$6,000	$7,500
1964		$5,700	$7,100
1965		$5,400	$6,700
1966	Early '66, Tortoise guard	$5,300	$6,600
1966	Late '66, black guard	$5,200	$6,500
1967	Last of maple bridgeplate	$5,200	$6,500
1968	Rosewood bridgeplate	$5,200	$6,500
1969	Last of Brazilian rosewood	$5,200	$6,500
1970-1979	Indian rosewood	$1,900	$2,400
1980-1989		$1,700	$2,100
1990-1999		$1,400	$1,800
2000-2010		$1,300	$1,650

D-28 (1935 Special)

1993. Guitar of the Month, 1935 features, Indian rosewood back and sides, peghead with Brazilian rosewood veneer.

1993		$1,900	$2,400

D-28 50th Anniversary

1983. Stamped inside '1833-1983 150th Anniversary', Indian rosewood back and sides.

1983		$2,100	$2,600

D-28 75th Anniversary

2009 only. Limited production celebrating 1934 to 2009, Madagascar rosewood back and sides, Adirondack spruce top.

2009		$4,500	$5,100

D-28 150th Anniversary

1983-1985. Limited production of 268, only '83 vintage have the anniversary stamp, Brazilian rosewood sides and back.

1983	150th stamp	$6,000	$7,500
1984-1985	No stamp	$5,800	$7,200

1939 Martin D-28

1940 Martin D-28

GUITARS

1990 Martin D-28 P

Martin D-35 Ernest Tubb

MODEL YEAR	FEATURES	EXC. COND. LOW	HIGH

D-28 Authentic 1937
2006-2009. Based on 1937 D-28, 25 made, Brazilian rosewood sides and back, Adirondack spruce top, forward scalloped bracing, fine pattern herringbone inlay.

| 2006-2009 | | $14,000 | $17,500 |

D-28 Custom
1984. Guitar of the Month Nov. '84, double bound D-body, multi-ring rosette, rosewood back/sides, spruce top, 43 made.

| 1984 | | $2,100 | $2,600 |

D-28 CW Commemorative
2005-2008. Special Edition copy of Clarence White's modified D-28, Adirondack spruce top, scalloped Adirondack forward shifted X-brace, rosewood sides and back, 'dalmatian' pickguard.

| 2005-2008 | | $2,700 | $3,200 |

D-28 CW/CWB Clarence White
2002-present. CW has Indian rosewood back and sides, the CWB Brazilian, only 150 CWBs were to be built.

| 2002-2004 CWB | | $4,800 | $6,000 |
| 2002-2010 CW | | $2,400 | $3,000 |

D-28 Dan Tyminski Custom
2010. Custom Artist limited edition, Indian rosewood back and sides, Adirondack spruce top, other bracing specs.

| 2010 | | $2,300 | $2,600 |

D-28 DM Del McCourey Signature
2003. Limited edition of 115 instruments, natural.

| 2003 | | $2,400 | $2,900 |

D-28 E
1959-1964. Electric, Brazilian rosewood back and sides, 2 DeArmond pickups, natural.

| 1959-1964 | | $5,000 | $6,200 |

D-28 GE Golden Era
1999-2002. GE Golden Era, Brazilian rosewood, herringbone trim.

| 1999-2002 | | $7,000 | $8,000 |

D-28 HW Hank Williams Limited Edition
1998. Replica of Hank Williams' 1944 D-28, Brazilian rosewood sides and back, scalloped braces, herringbone, 150 made.

| 1998 | | $8,000 | $10,000 |

D-28 LF Lester Flatt
1998. Only 2 made, 1 for Lester Flatt and 1 for Martin collection.

| 1998 | | $15,000 | $18,000 |

D-28 LSH
1991. Guitar of the Month, Indian rosewood back and sides, herringbone trim, snowflake inlay, zigzag back stripe.

| 1991 | | $2,500 | $3,100 |

D-28 LSV
1998. Large soundhole model.

| 1998 | | $2,000 | $2,500 |

D-28 M Elvis Presley Commemorative LE
2009. Limited Edition, 175 made, Madagascar rosewood sides and back, Adirondack spruce top, tooled leather guitar cover.

| 2009 | | $4,500 | $5,200 |

D-28 M Merle Travis
2008-2010. Travis photo label inside, only 100 made, Adirondack spruce top, Madagascar rosewood back and sides, custom curly maple neck, replica 6-on-a-side Bigsby guitar-style headstock, heart-diamond-spade-club inlay markers.

| 2008-2010 | | $4,400 | $5,100 |

D-28 Marquis
2004-present. D-28 reissue with specs designed to be close to the original, natural or sunburst.

| 2004-2010 | | $2,700 | $3,400 |

D-28 P
1988-1990. P stands for low-profile neck, Indian rosewood back and sides.

| 1988-1990 | | $1,200 | $1,500 |

D-28 S
1954-1993. Rosewood back and sides, 12-fret neck.

1960-1962	Special order	$7,500	$9,300
1963-1965	Special order	$7,000	$8,500
1966-1969	Brazilian rosewood	$5,300	$6,600
1970-1979	Indian rosewood	$2,300	$2,900
1980-1993	Indian rosewood	$2,100	$2,600

D-28 V
1983-1985. Brazilian rosewood back and sides, Limited Edition, herringbone trim, slotted diamond inlay.

| 1983-1985 | | $4,500 | $5,500 |

D-35
1965-present. Brazilian rosewood sides and 3-piece back, changed to Brazilian wings and Indian center in '70, then all Indian rosewood in '71, natural with sunburst option.

1965		$5,400	$6,700
1966-1970	Brazilian rosewood	$5,200	$6,500
1970-1979	Indian rosewood	$1,900	$2,400
1980-1989		$1,700	$2,100
1983	150th center strip	$1,700	$2,100
1990-1999		$1,400	$1,800
2000-2010		$1,300	$1,650

D-35 30th Anniversery Limited Edition
1995. D-35 with '1965-1995' inlay on 20th fret, gold hardware, limited edition of 207 instruments.

| 1995 | | $1,600 | $2,000 |

D-35 Ernest Tubb
2003. Indian rosewood back and sides, special inlays, 90 built.

| 2003 | | $2,900 | $3,600 |

D-35 JC Johnny Cash
2006-present. Rosewood back and sides.

| 2006-2010 | | $2,500 | $3,000 |

D-35 P
1986-1990. P indicates low-profile neck.

| 1986-1990 | | $1,300 | $1,600 |

D-35 S
1966-1993. Brazilian rosewood back and sides, changed to Indian rosewood in '70, 12-fret neck, slotted peghead.

1966-1969	Brazilian rosewood	$5,300	$6,600
1970-1979	Indian rosewood	$2,300	$2,900
1980-1993		$2,100	$2,600

MODEL YEAR	FEATURES	EXC. COND. LOW	HIGH

D-35 V Brazilian Rosewood
1984. 10 made.

1984		$4,200	$5,100

D-37 K
1980-1995. Dreadnought-size, koa back and sides, spruce top.

1980-1995		$2,400	$3,000

D-37 K2
1980-1995. Same as D-37 K, but has a koa top and black 'guard.

1980-1995		$2,700	$3,300

D-37 W Lucinda Williams
2003. Only 4 made, never put into production, Aztec pearl inlay favored by Lucinda Williams, quilted mahogany sides and back.

2003		$3,400	$4,200

D-40
1997-2005. Rosewood back and sides, hexagon inlays.

1997-2005		$1,900	$2,175

D-40 BLE
1990. Limited Edition Guitar of the Month, Brazilian rosewood back and sides, pearl top border except around 'board.

1990		$6,000	$7,000

D-40 FW Figured Walnut
1996. Limited edition, 148 made, figured claro walnut back and sides.

1996		$3,300	$4,000

D-40 DM Don McLean
1998. Only 50 made, Englemann spruce top.

1998		$6,000	$7,500

D-40 FMG
1995. Figured mahogany back and sides, 150 made.

1995		$5,000	$6,200

D-40 FW Limited Edition
1996. Figured walnut sides and back, 'Limited Edition D-40 FW' label, 150 made.

1996		$1,850	$2,300

D-40 QM Limited Edition
1996. Limited Edition, 200 made, quilted maple body.

1996		$2,200	$2,700

D-41
1969-present. Brazilian rosewood back and sides for the first ones in '69 then Indian rosewood, bound body, scalloped braces, natural.

1969	Brazilian rosewood	$18,000	$22,000
1970-1979	Indian rosewood	$3,200	$3,700
1980-1989		$2,900	$3,400
1990-1999		$2,900	$3,400
1990-1999	Sunburst option	$3,000	$3,500
2000-2010		$2,900	$3,400
2000-2010	Sunburst option	$2,600	$3,000

D-41 BLE
1989. Limited Edition Guitar of the Month, Brazilian rosewood back and sides, pearl top border except around 'board.

1989		$5,000	$6,000

MODEL YEAR	FEATURES	EXC. COND. LOW	HIGH

D-41 DF Dan Fogelberg
2001. 141 made, East Indian rosewood back and sides, hexagon 'board inlays, pearl snowflakes inlaid on bridge.

2001		$4,100	$4,700

D-41 GJ George Jones
2001. Style 41 appointments, limited edition of 100, label signed by the Opossum.

2001		$3,000	$3,800

D-41 Porter Wagoner
2008-present. Custom Artist series, Indian rosewood back and sides.

2008-2010		$2,700	$3,200

D-41 Special
2006-present.

2006-2010		$2,700	$3,200

D-42/D-42 E
1996-present. Dreadnought, Indian rosewood back and sides, spruce top, pearl rosette and inlays, snowflake 'board inlays, gold tuners, gloss finish.

1996-2004	D-42	$3,300	$4,100
1996-2004	D-42 E	$3,400	$4,200
2005-2010	D-42	$3,100	$3,900

D-42 AR (Amazon Rosewood)
2002-2003. 30 made, Amazon rosewood body which is similar to Brazilian rosewood but a different species and not restricted.

2002-2003		$4,000	$5,000

D-42 JC Johnny Cash
1997. Rosewood back and sides, gloss black lacquer on body and neck, Cash signature inlaid at 19th fret, have label signed by Cash and C.F. Martin IV, 80 sold.

1997		$4,600	$5,700

D-42 K Limited Edition
1998. Limited Edition, 150 made, highly flamed koa sides and back, sitka spruce top with aging toner, high X-brace design, 45-style abalone snowflake inlays.

1998		$3,500	$4,300

D-42 K/D-42 K2
2000-2008. K has koa back and sides, the all koa body K2 was discontinued in '05.

2000-2005	D-42 K2	$3,600	$4,400
2000-2008	D-42 K	$3,200	$4,000

D-42 LE
1988 only. Limited Edition (75 sold), D-42-style, scalloped braces, low profile neck.

1988		$2,800	$3,400

D-42 Peter Frampton
2006-2007. Indian rosewood back and sides, Style 45 features.

2006-2007		$4,000	$5,000

D-42 SB
2007. Sunburst finish, sitka spruce top, 45-style appointments.

2006-2007		$3,000	$3,700

D-42 V
1985. Vintage Series, 12 made, Brazilian rosewood, scalloped braces.

1985		$7,500	$9,500

1973 Martin D-41

2003 Martin D-41

1942 Martin D-45

Martin D-45 Mike Longworth

| MODEL | | EXC. COND. | |
YEAR	FEATURES	LOW	HIGH

D-45

1933-1942 (96 made), 1968-present. Brazilian rosewood back and sides, changed to Indian rosewood during '69. The pre-WWII D-45 is one of the holy grails. A pre-war D-45 should be evaluated on a case-by-case basis. The price ranges are for all-original guitars in excellent condition and are guidance pricing only. These ranges are for a crack-free guitar. Unfortunately, many older acoustics have a crack or two and this can make ultra-expensive acoustics more difficult to evaluate than ultra-expensive solidbody electrics. Technically, a repaired body crack makes a guitar non-original, but the vintage market generally considers a professionally repaired crack to be original. Crack width, length and depth can vary, therefore extra attention is suggested.

1936	2 made	$330,000	$400,000
1937	2 made	$330,000	$400,000
1938	9 made	$330,000	$400,000
1939	Early, wide neck	$300,000	$360,000
1939	Late, thin neck	$270,000	$330,000
1940	19 made	$250,000	$300,000
1941	24 made	$240,000	$290,000
1942	18 made	$240,000	$290,000
1968		$33,000	$41,000
1969	Brazilian rosewood	$30,000	$37,000
1970-1979		$6,000	$7,300
1980-1989		$4,900	$6,000
1990-1999		$4,500	$5,600
2000-2010		$4,100	$5,400

D-45 (1939 Reissue)

1992. High-grade spruce top, figured Brazilian rosewood back and sides, high X and scalloped braces, abalone trim, natural, gold tuners.

1992		$12,000	$14,000

D-45 100th Anniversary LE

1996. Limited edition, '1896-1996 C.F. Martin Commemorative Anniversary Model' label.

1996		$5,600	$6,800

D-45 150th Anniversary

1983. Brazilian rosewood back and sides, sitka spruce top, '150th' logo stamp.

1983		$14,000	$17,000

D-45 200th Anniversary (C.F. Martin Sr. Deluxe)

1996 only. Commemorative model for C.F. Martin Sr.'s birth in 1796, Brazilian Deluxe Edition, natural.

1996		$11,000	$14,000

D-45 Brazilian

1994. Brazilian rosewood.

1994		$11,000	$14,000

D-45 Celtic Knot

2006. Brazilian rosewood.

2006		$14,000	$17,000

D-45 Custom Shop

1984, 1991-1992. Various options and models, Indian rosewood back and sides in '84, then Brazilian rosewood.

1984	Indian rosewood	$5,400	$6,700
1991-1992	Brazilian rosewood	$11,000	$14,000

D-45 Deluxe

1993 only. Guitar of the Month, Brazilian rosewood back and sides, figured spruce top, inlay in bridge and 'guard, tree-of-life inlay on 'board, pearl borders and back stripe, gold tuners with large gold buttons, total of 60 sold.

1993		$17,000	$21,000

D-45 GE Golden Era

2001-2004. 167 made, '37 specs, Brazilian rosewood.

2001-2004		$14,000	$18,000

D-45 Gene Autry

1994 only. Gene Autry inlay (2 options available), natural.

1994	Gene Autry 'board	$14,000	$18,000
1994	Snowflake 'board option	$20,000	$25,000

D-45 KLE

1991. Limited Edition koa, Engelmann, 54 made.

1991		$7,000	$8,500

D-45 Koa

2006-2008. Flamed koa back and sides.

2006-2008		$4,400	$5,500

D-45 LE

1987. Limited Edition, 44 made, Guitar of the Month, September '87.

1987		$14,000	$18,000

D-45 Marquis

2006-2008. Rosewood back and sides.

2006-2008		$6,400	$7,700

D-45 Mike Longworth Commemorative Edition

2005-2006. East Indian rosewood back and sides, Adirondack spruce top, 91 made, label signed by Mike's wife Sue and C.F. Martin IV.

2005-2006		$5,500	$7,000

D-45 S

1969-1993. Brazilian rosewood back and sides in '69, Indian rosewood after, 12-fret neck, S means slotted peghead, only 50 made.

1969	Brazilian	$33,000	$41,000
1970-1979		$6,200	$7,700
1980-1989		$5,400	$6,700
1990-1993		$5,000	$6,300

D-45 S Deluxe

1992. Limited Edition, 50 made, Indian rosewood, spruce top, high-end appointments.

1992		$7,900	$9,800

D-45 SS Steven Stills

1998. Brazilian rosewood back and sides, 91 made.

1998		$15,000	$18,000

D-45 V

1983-1985. Brazilian rosewood back and sides, scalloped braces, snowflake inlay, natural.

1983-1985		$11,000	$14,000

D-45 VR/D-45 V

1997-present. Vintage specs, Indian rosewood back and sides, vintage aging toner, snowflake inlay. Name changed to D-45 V in '99 (not to be confused with Brazilian rosewood D-45 V of the '80s).

1997-1998	VR	$5,000	$6,200

MODEL YEAR	FEATURES	EXC. COND. LOW	HIGH

D-50/D-50 K/D-50 K2
2003-2006. Ultra high-end D-style solid Koa top, back and side, ultra fancy appointments, 5 made.

2003-2006	D-50	$18,000	$23,000
2003-2006	D-50 K	$15,000	$20,000
2003-2006	D-50 K2	$13,000	$18,000

D-50 DX
2001. Deluxe limited edition, 50 made, one of the most ornate Martin models ever made, Brazilian rosewood back and sides, highly ornate pearl inlay.

2001		$26,000	$33,000

D-62
1989-1995. Dreadnought, flamed maple back and sides, spruce top, chrome-plated enclosed Schaller tuners.

1989-1995		$1,500	$1,800

D-62 LE
1986. Limited Edition, Guitar of the Month October '86, flamed maple back and sides, spruce top, snowflake inlays, natural.

1986		$1,700	$2,100

D-76 Bicentennial Limited Edition
1975-1976. Limited Edition, 200 made in '75 and 1,976 made in '76, Indian rosewood back and sides, 3-piece back, herringbone back stripe, pearl stars on 'board, eagle on peghead.

1976		$3,100	$3,800

D-93
1993. Mahogany, spruce, 93 pertains to the year, not a style number.

1993		$2,800	$3,200

D-100 Deluxe
2004-present. Guitars have the first 50 sequential serial numbers following the millionth Martin guitar (1,000,001 to 1,000,050), fancy inlay work in pearl on back, 'guard, headstock, 'board and bridge. Herringbone top and rosette inlay, Adirondack spruce top, Brazilian rosewood back and sides.

2004-2010		$29,000	$36,000

DC Series
1980s-present. Cutaway versions, E models have electronics.

1981-1996	DC-28	$1,550	$1,900
1997	DCM	$650	$775
1997-2010	DC-1E/DC-1M	$550	$675
1998-2010	DC-15E	$750	$900
2000-2010	DCX-1E	$425	$525
2003-2006	DCME	$800	$950
2003-2010	DC-16GTE Premium	$800	$1,000
2005	DC-16RGTE	$1,050	$1,350
2005-2007	DC-16E Koa	$1,050	$1,350
2005-2010	DC-Aura	$1,750	$2,100
2006-2010	DC-28E	$1,650	$2,000

Ditson Dreadnaught 111
2006-2009. Special Edition by Martin based on their first model made for Ditson in 1916, Adirondack spruce top with aging toner, scalloped braces with forward shifted X-brace, mahogany back and sides, slotted headstock, 12-fret neck, abalone dot inlays.

2006-2009		$2,600	$3,300

DM
1990-2009. Solid sitka spruce top, laminated mahogany back and sides, dot markers, natural satin.

1990-2009		$450	$550

DM-12
1996-2009. 12-string DM.

1996-2009		$550	$700

Doobie-42 Tom Johnston Signature Edition
2007. D-42 style, 35 made, solid Indian rosewood sides and back, abalone and catseye markers, other special appointments.

2007		$3,000	$3,500

DVM Veterans
2002-2008. D-style, spruce top, rosewood back and sides, special veterans ornamentation.

2002-2008		$1,800	$2,200

DX 175th Anniversary Limited Edition
2008. D-style with custom legacy art on top, Indian rosewood laminate sides and back, Founders picture on top.

2008		$400	$500

DXM
1998-present. Wood composite mahogany laminate D body, solid wood neck, decal rosette, screened headstock logo, unique DX bracing.

1998-2010		$325	$400

E-18
1979-1983. Offset double-cut, maple and rosewood laminate solidbody, 2 DiMarzio pickups, phase switch, natural.

1979-1983		$775	$950

E-28
1980-1983. Double-cut electric solidbody, carved top, ebony 'board, 2 humbuckers.

1980-1983		$900	$1,075

EM-18
1979-1983. Offset double-cut, maple and rosewood laminate solidbody, 2 exposed-coil humbucking pickups, coil split switch.

1979-1983		$775	$925

EMP-1
1998-1999. Employee series designed by Martin employee team, cutaway solid spruce top, ovangkol wood back and sides with rosewood middle insert (D-35-style insert), on-board pickup.

1998-1999		$1,700	$2,100

F-1
1940-1942. Mahogany back and sides, carved spruce top, multi-bound, f-holes, sunburst.

1940-1942	91 made	$1,700	$2,100

F-2
1940-1942. Rosewood back and sides, carved spruce top, multi-bound, f-holes.

1940-1942	46 made	$2,200	$2,800

F-7
1935-1942. Brazilian rosewood back and sides, f-holes, carved top, back arched by braces, multi-bound, sunburst top finish.

1935-1942		$6,100	$7,600

Martin D-100 Deluxe

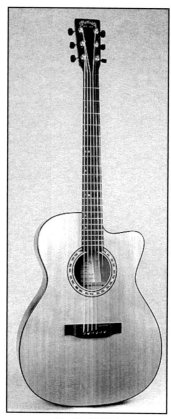

Martin EMP-1

GUITARS

1939 Martin F-9

1995 Martin HD-28

MODEL YEAR	FEATURES	EXC. COND. LOW	HIGH

F-9
1935-1941. Highest-end archtop, Brazilian rosewood, Martin inlaid vertically on headstock, 7-ply top binding, 45-style back strip, sunburst.

| 1935-1941 | | $10,000 | $12,500 |

F-50
1961-1965. Single-cut thinline archtop with laminated maple body, 1 pickup.

| 1961-1965 | | $1,100 | $1,350 |

F-55
1961-1965. Single-cut thinline archtop with laminated maple body, 2 pickups.

| 1961-1965 | | $1,400 | $1,800 |

F-65
1961-1965. Electric archtop, double-cut, f-holes, 2 pickups, square-cornered peghead, Bigsby, sunburst.

| 1961-1965 | | $1,600 | $2,000 |

Felix The Cat
2004-2010. Felix the Cat logo art, Don Oriolo logo, red body, Felix gig bag.

2004	Felix I, 756 made	$450	$550
2005-2006	Felix II, 625 made	$450	$550
2007-2010	Felix III, 1000 made	$450	$550

GCD-16 CP (Guitar Center)
1998. 15 5/8" Style D.

| 1998 | | $1,600 | $2,000 |

Grand Ole Opry 75th Anniversary/HDO/WSM
2000. 650 made, 'Grand Ole Opry 75th Anniversary' on neck block, WSM logo on ivory-style fretboard, sitka spruce top, East Indian rosewood back and sides.

| 2000 | | $2,200 | $2,600 |

GT-70
1966-1968. Electric archtop, bound body, f-holes, single-cut, 2 pickups, tremolo, burgundy or black finish.

| 1966-1968 | | $1,800 | $2,300 |

GT-75
1966-1968. Electric archtop, bound body, f-holes, double-cut, 2 pickups, tremolo, burgundy or black finish. There is also a 12-string version.

| 1966-1968 | | $1,500 | $1,900 |

Hawaiian X
2002-2004. Hawaiian scene painted on top, similar to the Cowboy guitar model, limited edition of 500.

| 2002-2004 | | $550 | $700 |

HD-16 R LSH
2007-present. Indian rosewood (R), large sound hole (LSH).

| 2007-2010 | | $1,350 | $1,650 |

HD-18 JB Jimmy Buffett
1998. 424 made, solid mahogany back and sides, herringbone trim, palm tree headstock logo, Style 42 markers, Buffett pearl signature.

| 1998 | | $3,000 | $4,000 |

HD-18 LE
1987. Indian rosewood.

| 1987 | | $2,200 | $2,400 |

HD-28 1935 Special
1993. 'HD-28 1935 Special' model name on label.

| 1993 | | $1,800 | $2,200 |

HD-28 2R
1992-1997. 2R specification for 2 herringbone soundhole rings, larger soundhole.

| 1992-1997 | | $1,900 | $2,300 |

HD-28 BLE
1990. Guitar of the Month, 100 made, Brazilian rosewood back and sides, herringbone soundhole ring, low profile neck (LE), chrome tuners, aging toner finish.

| 1990 | | $4,900 | $6,100 |

HD-28 BSE
1987. Brazilian rosewood, 93 made.

| 1987 | | $5,000 | $6,000 |

HD-28 CTB
1992. Guitar of the Month, mahogany back and sides, slotted peghead, herringbone back stripe, gold tuners, custom tortoise bound.

| 1992 | | $2,500 | $3,000 |

HD-28 Custom 150th Anniversary
1983. 150th Anniversary, Martin Custom Shop, Indian rosewood sides and back, '1833-1983 150th Year' stamped on inside backstrip.

| 1983 | | $2,100 | $2,600 |

HD-28 E/HD-28 VE
2005-2007. HD-28 V specs with onboard Fishman Ellipse Blend system.

| 2005-2007 | | $2,100 | $2,500 |

HD-28 GM
1989. Grand Marquis, Guitar of the Month, scalloped braced Sitka spruce top with 1930s-era bracing pattern that replaced the X-brace below the soundhole, herringbone top purfling, soundhole ring and back stripe, gold tuners.

| 1989 | | $3,000 | $3,500 |

HD-28 GM LSH
1994. Grand Marquis, Guitar of the Month, rosewood back and sides, large soundhole with double herringbone rings, snowflake inlay in bridge, natural (115 made) or sunburst (36 made).

| 1994 | | $2,500 | $3,100 |

HD-28 KM Keb Mo Signature Edition
2001-2002. Hawaiian Koa back and sides, 252 made.

| 2001-2002 | | $2,200 | $2,700 |

HD-28 LE
1985. Limited Edition, Guitar of the Month, rosewood back and sides, scalloped bracing, herringbone top purfling, diamonds and squares 'board inlay, V-neck.

| 1985 | | $2,400 | $2,900 |

HD-28 LSV
1999-2005. Vintage Series, large Soundhole Vintage, patterned after Clarence White's modified '35 D-28.

| 1999-2005 | | $2,200 | $2,800 |

HD-28 M
1988. Standard profile.

| 1988 | | $2,000 | $2,300 |

HD-28 MP
1990. Bolivian rosewood back and sides, scalloped braces, herringbone top purfling, zipper back stripe, low profile neck.

| 1990 | | $1,500 | $1,900 |

MODEL YEAR	FEATURES	EXC. COND. LOW	HIGH

HD-28 P
1987-1989. Rosewood back and sides, scalloped braces, herringbone, low profile neck (P), zigzag back stripe.

1987-1989		$1,500	$1,900

HD-28 PSE
1988. Signature Edition, Guitar of the Month, rosewood back and sides, signed by C.F. Martin IV and foremen, scalloped braces, herringbone top purfling, low profile neck, squared peghead, ebony tuner buttons.

1988		$2,500	$3,000

HD-28 S Custom
1995. Slotted headstock.

1995		$2,200	$2,700

HD-28 SE
1986. Signature Edition, Guitar of the Month, rosewood back and sides, signed by Martins and foremen, herringbone top purfling, V-neck, ebony tuner buttons.

1986		$2,200	$2,400

HD-28 SO Sing Out!
1996. Limited edition, 45 made, Indian rosewood back and sides.

1996		$2,400	$3,000

HD-28 Standard Series
1976-present. Indian rosewood back and sides, scalloped bracing, herringbone purfling.

1976-1979		$2,000	$2,500
1980-1989		$1,800	$2,200
1990-1999		$1,600	$2,000
2000-2010		$1,500	$1,850

HD-28 V/HD-28 VR
1996-present. 14-fret vintage series, Indian rosewood body, R dropped from name in '99.

1996-1999		$1,950	$2,400
2000-2010		$1,950	$2,400

HD-28 VS
1996-present. Slotted headstock, Indian rosewood sides and back.

1996-1999		$2,100	$2,500
2000-2010		$2,100	$2,500

HD-35
1978-present. Indian rosewood back and sides, herringbone top trim, zipper back stripe.

1978-1979		$2,100	$2,600
1980-1989		$2,000	$2,500
1990-1999		$1,500	$1,900
2000-2010		$1,400	$1,750

HD-35 Custom
2009. Custom Designed on neck block, Adirondack spruce top, East Indian rosewood sides and back.

2009		$2,100	$2,600

HD-35 Nancy Wilson
2006-2007. Englemann spruce top, 3-piece back with bubinga center wedge, 101 made.

2006-2007		$2,400	$2,900

HD-35 P
1987-1989. HD-35 with low profile neck.

1987-1989		$1,400	$1,700

HD-35 SJC Judy Collins
2002. 50 made, Collins signature headstock logo, wildflower headstock inlay, East Indian rosewood, 3-piece back with figured maple center.

2002		$2,300	$2,800

HD-40 MK Mark Knopfler Edition
2001-2002. Limited edition of 251 made, Mark Knopfler signature inlay 20th fret, herringbone trim, fancy marquetry soundhole rings.

2001-2002		$3,000	$3,800

HD-40 MS Marty Stuart
1996. Indian rosewood, 250 made, pearl/abalone inlay.

1996		$2,900	$3,700

HD-40 Tom Petty SE
2004-2006. Indian rosewood sides and back, high-end appointments, 274 made, inside label with signature.

2004-2006		$3,500	$4,000

HD-282 R
1992-1996. Large soundhole with 2 herringbone rings, zigzag backstripe.

1992-1996		$1,500	$1,850

HD Elliot Easton Custom Signature
2006-2008. Limited Edition, Adirondack spruce top with aging tone, Fishman Ellipse Aura pickup available on HDE.

2006-2008		$2,400	$2,800

HDN Negative L.E.
2003. 135 made, unusual appointments include pearloid headstock and black finish, HDN Negative Limited Edition notation on the inside label.

2003		$2,300	$2,800

HDO Grand Ole Opry
2000. 650 made, 'Grand Ole Opry 75th Anniversary' on neck block, WSM microphone headstock logo, off-white Micarta fingerboard, sitka spruce top, East Indian rosewood back and sides.

2000		$2,200	$2,600

HJ-28
1992, 1996-2000. Guitar of the Month in '92, regular production started in '96. Jumbo, non-cut, spruce top, Indian rosewood sides and back, herringbone top purfling, with or without on-board electronics.

1992	69 made	$2,900	$3,300
1996-2000		$1,800	$2,300

HJ-28 M
1994. Mahogany/spruce, herringbone top purfling, Guitar of the Month, 72 made.

1994		$3,500	$4,000

HJ-38 Stefan Grossman
2008-present. Madagascar rosewood back and sides.

2008-2010		$2,500	$3,000

HM Ben Harper
2008-2009. Special Edition, M-style width, 000-style depth, solid Adirondack spruce top, solid East Indian rosewood sides and back, onboard Fishman Ellipse Matrix Blend.

2008-2009		$2,800	$3,500

Martin HD-35

Martin HM Ben Harper

Martin J-41 Special

Martin M-21 Steve Earl

MODEL		EXC. COND.	
YEAR	FEATURES	LOW	HIGH

HOM-35
1989. Herringbone Orchestra Model, Guitar of the Month, scalloped braces, 3-piece Brazilian rosewood back, bookmatched sides, 14-fret neck, only 60 built.

1989		$4,500	$5,000

HPD-41
1999-2001. Like D-41, but with herringbone rosette, binding.

1999-2001		$2,500	$3,100

HTA Kitty Wells 'Honky Tonk Angel'
2002. D-size with 000-size depth, Indian rosewood back and sides, Queen of Country Music inlay logo on headstock (no Martin headstock logo).

2002		$1,800	$2,200

J-1 Jumbo
1997-2002. Jumbo body with mahogany back and sides.

1997-2002		$700	$875

J12-16 GT
2000-present. 16" jumbo 12-string, satin solid mahogany back and sides, gloss solid spruce top.

2000-2010		$850	$1,050

J12-40/J12-40 M
1985-1996. Called J12-40M from '85-'90, rosewood back and sides, 12 strings, 16" jumbo size, 14-fret neck, solid peghead, gold tuners.

1985-1990	J12-40M	$2,000	$2,500
1991-1996	J12-40	$2,000	$2,500

J12-65
1985-1995. Called J12-65M for '84-'90, Jumbo style 65 12-string, spruce top, figured maple back and sides, gold tuning machines, scalloped bracing, ebony 'board, tortoise shell-style binding, natural.

1985-1995		$2,000	$2,500

J-15
1999-2010. Jumbo 16" narrow-waist body, solid mahogany top, sides, and back satin finish.

1999-2010		$575	$725

J-18/J-18 M
1987-1996. J-size body with Style 18 appointments, natural, called J-18M for '87-'89.

1987-1996		$1,200	$1,475

J-21 MC
1986. J cutaway, oval soundhole.

1986		$1,700	$2,000

J-21/J-21 M
1985-1996. Called J-21M prior to '90, Indian rosewood back and sides, black binding, rosewood 'board, chrome tuners.

1985-1990	J-21 M	$1,900	$2,300
1991-1996	J-21	$1,900	$2,300

J-40
1990-present. Called J-40 M from '85-'89, Jumbo, Indian rosewood back and sides, triple-bound 'board, hexagonal inlays.

1990-1999		$1,900	$2,300
2000-2010		$1,800	$2,200

J-40 Custom
1993-1996. J-40 with upgrades including abalone top trim and rosette.

1993-1996		$2,400	$3,000

MODEL		EXC. COND.	
YEAR	FEATURES	LOW	HIGH

J-40 M/J-40 MBK
1985-1989. Jumbo, Indian rosewood back and sides, triple-bound 'board, hexagonal inlays, MBK indicates black, name changed to J-40 in '90.

1985-1989	J-40 M	$1,900	$2,400
1985-1989	J-40 MBK, black	$1,800	$2,300

J-40 MBLE
1987. Brazilian rosewood, Style 45 snowflakes, 17 made.

1987		$4,400	$5,100

J-41 Special
2004-2007. East Indian rosewood back and sides, Style 45 snowflake inlays.

2004-2007		$2,000	$2,500

J-45 M Deluxe
1986. Guitar of the Month, East Indian rosewood back and sides, tortoise-colored binding, mother-of-pearl and abalone, gold tuners with ebony buttons.

1986		$4,500	$5,200

J-65/J-65 E/J-65 M
1985-1995. Jumbo acoustic featuring maple back and sides, gold-plated tuners, scalloped bracing, ebony 'board, tortoise shell-style binding.

1985-1995		$1,800	$2,200

JC Buddy Guy
2006-2007. Only 36 made, rosewood back and sides.

2006-2007		$2,300	$2,800

JC-16 GTE
2000-2003. Cutaway, mahogany back and sides, Fishman.

2000-2003		$1,000	$1,200

JC-16 KWS Kenny Wayne Shepherd Signature
2001-2002. Cutaway, blue lacquer top, back and sides in gloss black, on-board electronics, 198 made.

2001-2002	198 made	$1,350	$1,650

JC-16 ME Aura
2006-2009. Jumbo size, solid European flamed maple back and sides, solid spruce top, tortoise 'guard, Aura Sound Imaging System.

2006-2009		$1,400	$1,700

JC-16 RE Aura
2006-2009. Like ME, but with rosewood back and sides.

2006-2009		$1,400	$1,700

JC-16 WE
2002. Jumbo cutaway, solid walnut sides and back, solid sitka spruce top.

2002		$1,000	$1,200

LXM Series
2003-present. Little Martin Series travel guitars, gig bag.

2003-2010		$175	$225

M2C-28
1988. Double-cut, Guitar of the Month, 22 made.

1988		$2,600	$3,000

M-3 H Cathy Fink
2005. Cathy Fink signature model, 0000 (M) size, gloss finish, Adirondack spruce top, rosewood sides, 3-piece back with flamed koa center panel, abalone rosette, torch headstock inlay, herringbone top trim, no Martin logo on headstock.

2005		$2,100	$2,500

MODEL YEAR	FEATURES	EXC. COND. LOW	HIGH

M-3 M George Martin
2005-2006. M Model, Style 40 appointments with Style 42 snowflake inlays, 127 made.

2005-2006		$3,200	$3,800

M-3 SC Shawn Colvin
2002-2003. 120 made, M (0000) size, mahogany sides, 3-piece mahogany/rosewood back, Fishman, Shawn Colvin & C.F.M. III signed label.

2002-2003		$1,500	$1,900

M-21 Custom
December 1984. Guitar of the Month, low profile neck M-Series, Indian rosewood back and sides, special ornamentation.

1984		$1,400	$1,800

M-21 Steve Earl
2008-present. East Indian rosewood back and sides, Italian Alpine spruce top.

2008-2010		$1,800	$2,200

M-28 Custom

2006		$2,400	$3,000

M-35/M-36
1978-1997, 2007-present. First 26 labeled as M-35, Indian rosewood back and sides, bound 'board, low profile neck, multi-bound, white-black-white back stripes.

1978	M-35, 26 made	$1,375	$1,700
1978-1997		$1,375	$1,700
2007-2010		$1,375	$1,700
2008	175th Anniversary	$1,375	$1,700

M-38 (0000-38)
1977-1997, 2007-present. Called 0000-38 (see that listing) in '97-'98, 0000-size, Indian rosewood back and sides, multi-bound.

1977-1979		$2,300	$2,900
1980-1989		$2,200	$2,700
1990-1997		$1,850	$2,300
2007-2010		$1,850	$2,300

M-42 David Bromberg
2006. 0000-14 body, rosewood back and sides, snowflakes.

2006	83 made	$3,700	$4,500

MC12-41 Richie Sambora
2006. 12-string version of OMC-41 Richie Sambora, planned 200 made combined models.

2006		$3,300	$4,100

MC-16 GTE
2002-2004. Acoustic/electric, M-size single cut, gloss finish solid spruce top, satin finish solid mahogany sides and back.

2002-2004		$825	$1,000

MC-28
1981-1996. Rosewood back and sides, single-cut acoustic, oval soundhole, scalloped braces, natural.

1981-1996		$1,650	$2,000

MC-68
1985-1995. Auditorium-size acoustic, rounded cutaway, maple back and sides, gold tuners, scalloped bracing, ebony 'board, tortoise shell-style binding, natural or sunburst.

1985-1995		$1,900	$2,300

MTV-1 Unplugged Edition
1996. Body is 1/2 rosewood and 1/2 mahogany, scalloped bracing, MTV logo on headstock, gloss (588 sold) or satin (73 sold) finish.

1996	Gloss finish	$1,400	$1,750
1996	Satin finish	$1,200	$1,550

MTV-2 Unplugged Edition
2003-2004. Body is 1/2 rosewood and 1/2 maple, scalloped bracing, MTV logo on headstock.

2003-2004		$900	$1,100

N-10
1968-1995. Classical, mahogany back and sides, fan bracing, wood marquetry soundhole ring, unbound rosewood 'board, 12-fret neck and slotted peghead from '70.

1968-1969	Short-scale	$1,425	$1,750
1970-1979	Long-scale	$1,350	$1,650
1980-1989	Long-scale	$1,250	$1,550
1990-1995	Long-scale	$1,250	$1,550

N-20
1968-1995. Classical, Brazilian rosewood back and sides (changed to Indian rosewood in '69), multi-bound, 12-fret neck, solid headstock (changed to slotted in '70), natural.

1968-1969	Brazilian, short-scale	$3,300	$4,100
1970-1979	Indian, long-scale	$1,600	$2,000
1980-1989	Long-scale	$1,500	$1,900
1990-1995	Long-scale	$1,500	$1,900

OM-18
1930-1934. Orchestra Model, mahogany back and sides, 14-fret neck, solid peghead, banjo tuners (changed to right-angle in '31).

1930	Banjo tuners, small 'guard	$23,000	$28,000
1931	Banjo tuners, small 'guard	$22,000	$26,000
1932-1933	Standard appointments, full 'guard	$20,000	$25,000

OM-18 GE Golden Era 1930/Special Edition GE
2003-2009. Mahogany back and sides, Brazilian rosewood purfling and binding.

2003-2009		$2,200	$2,700

OM-18 V
1999-2009. Vintage features.

1999-2009		$1,600	$2,000

OM-18 VLJ/OMC-18 VLJ
2002. 133 made.

2002		$2,300	$2,850

OM-21
1992-present. Indian rosewood back & sides, herringbone back stripe & soundhole ring, 14-fret neck, chrome tuners.

1992-2010		$1,300	$1,600

OM-21 Special
1991, 2007-present. Upgrade to ebony 'board, rosewood bindings.

1991	36 made	$3,300	$4,000
2007-2010		$2,000	$2,400

Martin OM-18 Golden Era

1996 Martin OM-21 Custom

Martin OM-42

1999 Martin OM-42

MODEL YEAR	FEATURES	EXC. COND. LOW	HIGH

OM-28
1929-1933. Orchestra Model, Brazilian rosewood back and sides, 14-fret neck, solid peghead, banjo tuners (changed to right-angle in '31), reintroduced with Indian rosewood in '90.

1929	Banjo pegs, small 'guard, pyramid end bridge	$80,000	$98,000
1930	Banjo tuners, small 'guard, standard bridge	$70,000	$87,000
1931	Early '31 Banjo tuners, small 'guard, standard bridge	$68,000	$84,000
1931	Mid '31 Banjo tuners, small 'guard, standard bridge	$58,000	$72,000
1931	Late '31 Standard tuners, full-size 'guard	$56,000	$69,000
1932-1933	Standard tuners, full-size 'guard	$56,000	$69,000

OM-28 Golden Era
2003-2004. Brazilian rosewood back and sides, Adirondack spruce top.

2003-2004		$7,000	$8,500

OM-28 JM John Mayer
2003. Limited Edition, 404 made.

2003		$3,500	$4,400

OM-28 LE
1985. Limited Edition only 40 made, Guitar of the Month, Indian rosewood back and sides, herringbone top binding, V-neck.

1985		$2,400	$2,900

OM-28 M Roseanne Cash
2008. Signature Edition, 100 made, Madagascar rosewood back and sides.

2008		$3,400	$4,200

OM-28 Marquis
2005-present. Orchestra Model, pre-war appointments, Adirondack red spruce top, ebony 'board and bridge, East Indian rosewood back, sides and headplate.

2005-2010		$3,000	$3,700

OM-28 Marquis Madagascar
2007-2008. Madagascar rosewood.

2007-2008		$3,400	$3,900

OM-28 PB Perry Bechtel
1993. Guitar of the Month, signed by Perry Bechtel's widow Ina, spruce top, Indian rosewood back and sides, zigzag back stripe, chrome tuners, V-neck, only 50 made.

1993		$4,000	$4,800

OM-28 Reissue
1990-1997. Indian rosewood back and sides.

1990-1997		$1,450	$1,800

OM-28 SO Sing Out!
1985. For Sing Out! Magazine's 35, label signed by Pete Seeger.

1985		$2,500	$3,000

OM-28 VR/OM-28 V
1984-1990, 1996-present. VR suffix until '99, then just V (Vintage Series), rosewood back and sides.

1984-1990	VR	$1,950	$2,400
1996-2010	V (Vintage Series)	$1,950	$2,400

OM-35
2003-2007. 000-size body, Indian rosewood sides and 3-piece back, spruce top, gloss natural finish.

2003-2007		$1,400	$1,750

OM-40 LE
1994. Limited Edition, Guitar of the Month, Indian rosewood back and sides, double pearl borders, snowflake inlay on 'board, gold tuners, natural (57 sold) or sunburst (29 sold).

1994	Natural	$3,700	$4,500
1994	Sunburst	$4,200	$5,200

OM-40 Rory Block
2004. Limited Edition, 38 made, 000-size, Indian rosewood back and sides, Englemann spruce top, 'the road' inlay markers, vintage-auto inlay on headstock.

2004		$2,400	$2,900

OM-41 Special
2005-2006. Rosewood back and sides, Style 45 snowflake inlays.

2005-2006		$2,400	$2,900

OM-42
1999-present. Indian rosewood back and sides, Style 45 snowflake inlays, there were 2 guitars labeled OM-42 built in 1930.

1999-2010		$3,100	$3,600

OM-42 Custom
1979. Built by Custom Shop, each guitar should be evaluated on an individual basis.

1979		$5,200	$6,500

OM-42 Koa
2005-2008. Koa sides and back.

2006-2008		$3,200	$4,000

OM-42 PS Paul Simon
1997. Bookmatched sitka spruce top, Indian rosewood back and sides, 42- and 45-style features, low profile PS neck, 500 planned but only 223 made.

1997		$3,500	$4,400

OM-45
1930-1933. OM-style, 45 level appointments. Condition is critically important on this or any ultra high-end instrument, minor flaws are critical to value.

1930	Banjo pegs, 19 made	$200,000	$250,000
1931	10 made	$200,000	$250,000
1932	5 made	$200,000	$250,000
1933	6 made	$200,000	$250,000

OM-45 Custom
1979, 1997, 2007. High grade appointments, spruce top, Indian rosewood.

1979		$5,400	$6,700
1997		$4,100	$5,100
2007		$4,600	$5,900

OM-45 Custom Deluxe
1998-1999. Limited custom shop run of 14, Adirondack spruce and typical Style 45 appointments.

1998-1999		$12,000	$14,000

MODEL YEAR	FEATURES	EXC. COND. LOW	HIGH

OM-45 Deluxe
1930. Only 14 made, OM-style, 45 level appointments with Brazilian rosewood back and sides, zipper pattern back stripe, pearl inlay in 'guard and bridge. Condition is critically important on this or any ultra high-end instrument, minor flaws are critical to value.

1930		$280,000	$350,000

OM-45 Deluxe (Special)
1999. 4 made on special order, highly figured Brazilian rosewood.

1999		$14,000	$16,000

OM-45 GE Golden Era
1999, 2001-2005. Red spruce top, Brazilian rosewood.

1999-2005		$11,000	$13,000

OM-45 Marquis
2005-2008. Pre-war appointments based on 1933 OM, spruce top, ebony 'board and bridge, East Indian rosewood back, sides and headplate.

2005-2008		$4,200	$5,300

OM-45 Roy Rogers
2006. Limited Edition, based on Roy's 1930 OM-45 Deluxe, Indian rosewood (84 made) or Brazilian rosewood (14 made).

2006	Brazilian rosewood	$13,000	$16,000
2006	Indian rosewood	$6,100	$7,600

OM-45 Tasmanian Blackwood
2005. Limited Edition, 29 made, Tasmanian Blackwood (koa-family) back and sides with curly grain, 000-size, OM and 45 style appointments.

2005		$7,500	$8,000

OM 1833 Custom Shop Limited Edition
2006. Italian alpine spruce top, flamed claro walnut back and sides, 000-size, low profile 14-fret neck, fancy inlay and appointments, natural gloss finish.

2006		$3,200	$4,000

OMC Fingerstyle 1
2005-2009. Rounded cutaway, Adirondack spruce top, Spanish cedar back and sides, satin finished 14-fret neck, gloss natural finish, on-board Fishman Ellipse Blend system.

2005-2009		$1,900	$2,250

OMC Cherry
2008-present. Sustainable wood program, solid cherry back and sides, solid rescued spruce top, 000 body, cutaway, Fishman.

2008-2010		$1,600	$1,900

OMC-1 E
Introduced April 2009. OM body with Style 28 appointments, cutaway, onboard Fishman.

2009		$625	$750

OMC-15 E
2001-2007. Acoustic-electric, 000-size body, rounded cutaway, all solid mahogany body.

2001-2007		$900	$1,100

OMC-16 E Koa
2005-2009. Koa back and sides, on-board electronics.

2005-2009		$1,600	$1,800

OMC-16 E/E Premium
2003-2007. Sapele back and sides, on-board electronics.

2003-2007		$1,400	$1,600

OMC-16 RE/RE Premium
2003. Solid rosewood back and sides, on-board electronics.

2003		$1,400	$1,600

OMC-16 WE
2002-2003. Walnut back and sides.

2002-2003		$1,400	$1,600

OMC-28
1990. Guitar of the Month, rounded cutaway, Indian rosewood, gold tuners, low profile neck, pearl Martin script logo in headstock, label signed by C.F. Martin IV.

1990		$2,500	$3,000

OMC-28 E
2006-2009. OMC-28 with Fishman Ellipse.

2006-2009		$1,800	$2,200

OMC-28 Laurence Juber
2004. 133 made, cutaway.

2004		$2,600	$3,100

OMC-41 Richie Sambora
2006-2009. Madagascar rosewood sides and back, combination Style 45 and 41 appointments, 12-string is MC12-41 Richie Sambora, planned 200 made combined models.

2006-2009		$3,600	$4,300

OMCRE
2008-2009. 000-size, 14-fret, solid Carpathian spruce top, solid East Indian rosewood sides and back, single-cut, Jeff Babicz adjustable neck joint, Fishman Aura Pro electronics, gloss finish.

2008-2009		$1,800	$2,150

OMJM John Mayer
2003-present. Indian rosewood sides and back.

2003-2010		$1,850	$2,300

POW MIA
2006-2010. POW MIA logo position marker lettering on fretboard, D-style body, dark finish.

2006-2010		$2,400	$2,900

PS2 Paul Simon Signature
2003. Paul Simon signature logo at bottom of fretboard, 200 made.

2003		$2,200	$2,800

R-17
1934-1942. All mahogany, arched top and back, 3-segment f-holes (changed to 1-segment in '37).

1934-1942	940 made	$1,400	$1,700

R-18
1933-1942. Spruce arched top (carved top by 1937), mahogany back and sides, bound top, sunburst.

1933-1942	1,928 made	$2,000	$2,400

R-18 T
1934-1941. Tenor archtop, 14 3/8" lower bout, 2 f-holes, dot markers, sunburst.

1934-1941		$1,400	$1,700

Martin OM-45 GE Golden Era
Tom Siska

Martin OMC-16E

Maton MS500/12 - Mastersound

McCollum Dreadnaught

MODEL YEAR	FEATURES	EXC. COND. LOW	HIGH
Shenandoah Series			
1983-1993.			
1983-1992	D12-2832	$650	$825
1984-1992	D-1832	$550	$700
1984-1992	D-1932	$550	$700
1984-1992	D-2832	$650	$825
1984-1992	HD-2832	$675	$850
1984-1993	D-3532	$650	$825
1984-1993	D-4132	$700	$900
SP000 Series			
1997-2000. Special Edition 000-size, spruce top with aging toner, scalloped bracing, rosewood or mahogany body.			
1997	16T, mahogany	$1,000	$1,200
1997	C-16TR	$1,000	$1,200
1998-1999	16R, rosewood	$1,000	$1,200
SPD12-16R			
1997-2004. 12-string, solid rosewood body, abalone soundhole ring, Style-45 backstripe.			
1999-2000		$1,000	$1,200
SPD-16 Series			
1997-2004. D-16 Series Special models.			
1997-1998	16R/TR, rosewood	$1,250	$1,500
1997-1998	16T	$1,250	$1,500
1998	16 Special Edition, mahogany	$1,250	$1,500
1999-2001	16M, flamed maple	$1,250	$1,500
2000-2004	16K/K2, koa	$1,250	$1,500
SPDC-16 Series			
1997-2001. Cutaway version of SPD-16.			
1997-2000	16R/16RE, rosewood	$1,250	$1,500
1997-2001	16T/TR, rosewood	$1,250	$1,500
SPJC-16RE			
2000-2003. Single-cut, East Indian rosewood body, 000-size, on-board electronics.			
2000-2003		$1,250	$1,500
Stauffer			
1830s-ca.1850s. One of C.F. Martin's earliest models, distinguished by the scrolled, six-on-a-side headstock, ornamentation varies from guitar to guitar.			
1830s	Plain, no ivory	$9,000	$15,000
1830s	Very fancy, ivory	$15,000	$35,000
Sting Mini			
2006. Limited Edition, 100 made, label reads 'Sting Mini', Size 5, Western red cedar top, Solomon padauk body.			
2005-2006		$2,000	$2,400
Stinger			
1980s-1990s. Import copy offset S-style electric solidbody.			
1980-1990s		$175	$225
SW00-D8 Machiche			
2006-2007. Smartwood Limited Edition, 125 made, rescued solid spruce top, sustainable machiche sides and back.			
2006-2007		$1,400	$1,650
SWC			
1998. Smartwood 'The Sting Signature Classical Model', machiche wood body.			
1998		$1,300	$1,600

MODEL YEAR	FEATURES	EXC. COND. LOW	HIGH
SWD			
1998-1999. Smartwood D-size, built from wood material certified by the Forest Stewardship Council, sitka top, cherry back and sides, natural satin finish.			
1998-1999		$775	$950
SWDTG			
2000-2007. Smartwood-certified, cherry back and sides, gloss finish.			
2000-2007		$675	$850
SWOMGT			
2000-2007. Smartwood-certified, 000-style body, SWOMGT model on neck block, rescued solid sitka spruce top, sustainable cherry sides and back, gloss finish.			
2000-2007		$750	$925
Yuengling 180th Anniversary Custom			
2008. Celebrating 180th company anniversary, limited production, large company logo on top of body, fancy D-41 style appointments, certificate.			
2008		$3,000	$3,500

Maruha

1960s-1970s. Japanese-made acoustic, classical, archtop and solidbody guitars, often copies of American brands. Probably not imported into the U.S.

Marvel

1950s-mid-1960s. Brand name used for budget guitars and basses marketed by Peter Sorkin Company in New York, New York. Sorkin manufactured and distributed Premier guitars and amplifiers made by its Multivox subsidiary. Marvel instruments were primarily beginner-grade. Brand disappears by mid-'60s. The name was also used on archtop guitars made by Regal and marketed by the Slingerland drum company in the 1930s to early 1940s.

Electric

1940s-1950s. Various models.

1940-1950s		$200	$600

Marveltone by Regal

1925-1930. Private branded by Regal, Marveltone pearl style logo on headstock.

Guitar

1925-1930. 14" Brazilian.

1925-1930		$3,200	$3,800

Masaki Sakurai

See Kohno brand.

Mason

1936-1939. Henry L. Mason on headstock, wholesale distribution, similar to Gibson/Cromwell, pressed wood back and sides.

Student/Intermediate Student

1936-1939. Various flat-top and archtop student/budget models.

1936-1939		$300	$800

MODEL		EXC. COND.	
YEAR	FEATURES	LOW	HIGH

MODEL		EXC. COND.	
YEAR	FEATURES	LOW	HIGH

Mason Bernard

1990-1991. Founded by Bernie Rico (BC Rich founder). During this period BC Rich guitars were liscensed and controlled by Randy Waltuch and Class Axe. Most Mason models were designs similar to the BC Rich Assassin, according to Bernie Rico only the very best materials were used, large MB logo on headstock. Around 225 guitars were built bearing this brand.

Maton

1946-present. Intermediate and professional grade, production/custom, acoustic, acoustic/electric, hollowbody and solidbody guitars built in Box Hill, Victoria, Australia. Founded by Bill May and his brother Reg and still run by the family. Only available in USA since '82.

Matsuda Guitars

See listing for Michihiro Matsuda.

Matsuoka

1970s. Ryoji Matsuoka from Japan built intermediate grade M series classical guitars that often featured solid tops and laminated sides and back.

Mauel Guitars

1995-present. Luthier Hank Mauel builds his premium grade, custom, flat-tops in Auburn, California.

Maurer

Late 1880s-1944. Robert Maurer built guitars and mandolins in the late 1880s under the Maurer and Champion brands in his Chicago shop. Carl and August Larson bought the company in 1900 and retained the Maurer name. The Larsons also built under the Prairie State, Euphonon, W. J. Dyer and Wm. C. Stahl brands.

Max B

2000-present. Luthier Sebastien Sulser builds professional grade, production/custom, electric guitars in Kirby, Vermont. He also builds basses.

May Bell

Late 1920s-1940s. Brand of flat top guitars, some with fake resonators, marketed by the Slingerland drum copy. Most were made by Regal.

McAlister Guitars

1997-present. Premium grade, custom, flat-tops built by luthier Roy McAlister in Watsonville, California.

McCollum Guitars

1994-2009. Luthier Lance McCollum builds his premium grade, custom, flat-top and harp guitars in Colfax, California. McCollum died in 2009.

McCurdy Guitars

1983-present. Premium grade, production/custom, archtops built by luthier Ric McCurdy originally in Santa Barbara, California and, since '91, New York, New York.

McElroy

1995-present. Premium grade, custom, classical and flat-top steel string acoustic guitars built by luthier Brent McElroy in Seattle, Washington.

McGill Guitars

1976-present. Luthier Paul McGill builds his premium grade, production/custom, classical, resonator, and acoustic/electric guitars in Nashville, Tennessee.

McGlynn Guitars

2005-2007. Luthier Michael J. McGlynn built his premium and presentation grade, custom, solidbody guitars in Henderson, Nevada. McGlynn died in '07.

McGowan Guitars

2004-present. Luthier Brian McGowan builds his production/custom, premium grade, steel-string acoustic guitars in Hampton, Virginia.

MCI, Inc

1967-1988. MusiConics International (MCI), of Waco, Texas, introduced the world to the Guitorgan, invented by Bob Murrell. Later, they also offered effects and a steel guitar. In the '80s, a MIDI version was offered. MCI was also involved with the Daion line of guitars in the late '70s and early '80s.

GuitOrgan B-35
1970s (ca. 1976-1978?). Duplicated the sounds of an organ and more. MCI bought double-cut semi-hollow body guitars from others and outfitted them with lots of switches and buttons. Each fret has 6 segments that correspond to an organ tone. There was also a B-300 and B-30 version, and the earlier M-300 and 340.

1970s		$600	$750

McInturff

1996-present. Professional and premium grade, production/custom, solidbody guitars built by luthier Terry C. McInturff originally in Holly Springs, North Carolina, and since '04, in Moncure, North Carolina. McInturff spent 17 years doing guitar repair and custom work before starting his own guitar line.

McCurdy

McInturff Forum

Megas Athena Solidbody

Mesrobian Session

MODEL YEAR	FEATURES	EXC. COND. LOW	HIGH

Monarch
2000-present. Offset double-cut contoured mahogany solidbody, set-neck, single-single-hum pickups, transparent cherry.

2000-2010		$1,200	$1,500

Taurus Custom
2000-present. Flame maple top, chambered mahogany body, matching flamed maple headstock, abalone slash inlays, gold hardware.

2000-2010		$2,000	$2,500

Taurus Standard
2000-present. Single-cut, carved flamed maple top on chambered mahogany body, dual humbucker pickups, gold hardware, sunburst.

2000-2010		$1,600	$2,000

McKnight Guitars
1992-present. Luthier Tim McKnight builds his custom, premium grade, acoustic steel string guitars in Morral, Ohio.

McPherson Guitars
1981-present. Premium grade, production, flat-tops built by luthier Mander McPherson in Sparta, Wisconsin.

Mean Gene
1988-1990. Heavy metal style solidbodies made by Gene Baker, who started Baker U.S.A. guitars in '97, and Eric Zoellner in Santa Maria, California. They built around 30 custom guitars. Baker currently builds b3 guitars.

Megas Guitars
1989-present. Luthier Ted Megas builds his premium grade, custom, archtop and solidbody guitars, originally in San Franciso, and currently in Portland, Oregon.

Melancon
Professional and premium grade, custom/production, solid and semi-hollow body guitars built by luthier Gerard Melancon in Thibodaux, Louisiana. They also build basses.

Mello, John F.
1973-present. Premium grade, production/custom, classical and flat-top guitars built by luthier John Mello in Kensington, California.

Melophonic
1960s. Brand built by the Valco Company of Chicago, Illinois.

Resonator Guitar
Valco-made.

1965		$700	$875

Melville Guitars
1988-present. Luthier Christopher Melville builds his premium grade, custom, flat-tops in Milton, Queensland, Australia.

Mercurio
2002-2005. Luthier Peter Mercurio built his custom/production solidbody guitars, featuring his interchangeable PickupPak system to swap pickups, in Chanhassen, Minnesota.

Mermer Guitars
1983-present. Luthier Richard Mermer builds his premium grade, production/custom, steel-string, nylon-string, and Hawaiian guitars in Sebastian, Florida.

Merrill Brothers
1998-present. Premium grade, production/custom, steel-string and harp guitars built by luthiers Jim and Dave Merrill in Williamsburg, Virginia.

Mesrobian
1995-present. Luthier Carl Mesrobian builds his professional and premium grade, custom, archtop guitars in Salem, Massachusetts.

Messenger
1967-1968. Built by Musicraft, Inc., originally of 156 Montgomery Street, San Francisco, California. The distinguishing feature of the Messengers is a metal alloy neck which extended through the body to the tailblock, plus mono or stereo outputs. Sometime before March '68 the company relocated to Astoria, Oregon. Press touted "improved" magnesium neck, though it's not clear if this constituted a change from '67. Brand disappears after '68. They also made basses.

Electric Hollowbody Archtop
1967-1968. Symmetrical double-cut body shape, metal neck with rosewood 'boards, stereo.

1967-1968	Rojo Red	$2,000	$2,500

Metropolitan
1995-2008. Professional and premium grade, production/custom, retro-styled solidbodies designed by David Wintz reminiscent of the '50s National Res-o-glas and wood body guitars. They featured full-scale set-neck construction and a wood body instead of Res-o-glas. Wintz also makes Robin and Alamo brand instruments.

Meyers Custom Guitars
2005-present. Founded by Donald Meyers in Houma, Louisiana, promoted as 100% on a custom order basis, professional grade classic body style electric models.

MODEL		EXC. COND.	
YEAR	FEATURES	LOW	HIGH

Miami

1920s. Instruments built by the Oscar Schmidt Co. and possibly others. Most likely a brand made for a distributor.

Michael Collins Custom Guitars

1975-present. Premium grade, custom/production, classical, flamenco and steel string guitars built in Argyle, New York, by luthier Michael Collins.

Michael Collins Guitars

2002-present. Luthier Michael Collins builds his professional and premium grade, custom, Selmer style, archtop and flat top guitars in Keswick, Ontario. He also builds mandolins.

Michael Cone

1968-present. Presentation grade, production/custom, classical guitars built previously in California and currently in Kihei Maui, Hawaii by luthier Michael Cone. He also builds ukuleles.

Michael Dunn Guitars

1968-present. Luthier Michael Dunn builds his production/custom Maccaferri-style guitars in New Westminster, British Columbia. He also offers a harp uke and a Weissenborn- or Knutsen-style Hawaiian guitar, and has built archtops.

Michael Kelly

2000-present. Intermediate and professional grade, production, acoustic, solidbody and archtop guitars imported by Elite Music Brands of Clearwater, Florida. Hanser Music Group purchased the Michael Kelly brand in 2004. They also offer mandolins and basses.

Michael Lewis Instruments

1992-present. Luthier Michael Lewis builds his premium and presentation grade, custom, archtop guitars in Grass Valley, California. He also builds mandolins.

Michael Menkevich

1970-present. Luthier Michael Menkevich builds his professional and premium grade, production/custom, flamenco and classical guitars in Elkins Park, Pennsylvania.

Michael Silvey Custom Guitars

2003-present. Solidbody electric guitars built by Michael Silvey in North Canton, Ohio.

MODEL		EXC. COND.	
YEAR	FEATURES	LOW	HIGH

Michael Thames

1972-present. Luthier Michael Thames builds his premium grade, custom/production, classical guitars in Taos, New Mexico.

Michael Tuttle

2003-present. Professional and premium grade, custom, solid and hollowbody guitars built by luthier Michael Tuttle in Saugus, California. He also builds basses.

Michihiro Matsuda

1997-present. Presentation grade, production/custom, steel and nylon string acoustic guitars built by luthier Michihiro Matsuda in Oakland, California. He also builds harp guitars.

Microfrets

1967-1975, 2004-2005. Professional grade, production, electric guitars built in Myersville, Maryland. They also built basses. Founded by Ralph S. Jones, Sr. in Frederick, Microfrets offered over 20 models of guitars that sported innovative designs and features, with pickups designed by Bill Lawrence. The brand was revived, again in Frederick, by Will Meadors and Paul Rose in '04.

Serial numbers run from about 1000 to about 3800. Not all instruments have serial numbers, particularly ones produced in '75. Serial numbers do not appear to be correlated to a model type, but are sequential by the general date of production.

Instruments can be identified by body styles as follows; Styles 1, 1.5, 2, and 3. An instrument may be described as a Model Name and Style Number (for example, Covington Style 1). Style 1 has a wavey-shaped pickguard with control knobs mounted below the guard and the 2-piece guitar body has a particle board side gasket. Style 1.5 has the same guard and knobs, but no side body gasket. Style 2 has an oblong pickguard with top mounted control knobs and a pancake style seam between the top and lower part of the body. Style 3 has a seamless 2-piece body and a Speedline neck.

Baritone Signature
1971. Baritone version of Signature Guitar, sharply pointed double-cut, with or without f-holes, single- or double-dot inlays.

1971		$750	$950

Baritone Stage II
1971-ca. 1975. Double-cut, 2 pickups.

1971-1975		$750	$950

Calibra I
1969-1975. Double-cut, 2 pickups, f-hole.

1969-1975		$600	$750

Covington
1967-1969. Offset double-cut, 2 pickups, f-hole.

1967-1969		$1,100	$1,400

Golden Comet
1969-1971. Double-cut, 2 pickups, f-hole.

1969-1971		$750	$950

Michael Thames Luis Panormo

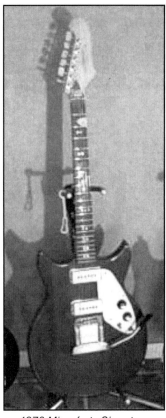

1970 Microfrets Signature
Roland Gonzales

Mirabella Trap Door

Mitre Cobra

MODEL YEAR FEATURES	EXC. COND. LOW	HIGH

Golden Melody

1969-1971, 2004-2005. Offset double-cut, 2 pickups, f-hole, M-shaped metal design behind tailpiece.

| 1969-1971 | $1,100 | $1,400 |

Huntington

1969-1975. Double-cut, 2 pickups.

| 1969-1975 | $1,100 | $1,400 |

Orbiter

1967-1969. Odd triple cutaway body, thumbwheel controls on bottom edge of 'guard.

| 1967-1969 | $1,100 | $1,400 |

Plainsman

1967-1969. Offset double-cut, 2 pickups, f-hole, thumbwheel controls on bottom edge of 'guard.

| 1967-1969 | $1,350 | $1,700 |

Signature

1967-1969. Double-cut, 2 pickups.

| 1967-1969 | $1,100 | $1,400 |

Spacetone

1969-1971, 2004-2005. Double-cut semi-hollow body, 2 pickups.

| 1969-1971 | $1,100 | $1,400 |

Stage II

1969-1975. Offset double-cut, 2 pickups.

| 1969-1975 | $1,000 | $1,250 |

Swinger

1971-1975. Offset double-cut, 2 pickups.

| 1971-1975 | $1,100 | $1,400 |

Voyager/The Voyager

1967-1968. Early model, less than a dozen made, Voyager headstock logo (no Microfrets logo), 2 DeArmond-style single-coils, offset double-cut body, FM transmitter on upper bass bout facilitates wireless transmission to Microfrets receiver or FM radio.

| 1967-1968 | $2,200 | $2,700 |

Wanderer

1969. Double-cut, 2 pickups.

| 1969 | $900 | $1,100 |

Mike Lull Custom Guitars

1995-present. Professional and premium grade, production/custom, guitars built by luthier Mike Lull in Bellevue, Washington. He also builds basses.

Milburn Guitars

1990-present. Luthiers Orville and Robert Milburn build their premium grade, custom, classical guitars in Sweet Home, Oregon.

Miller

1960s. One of the brand names of guitars built for others by Egmond in Holland.

Minarik

Luthier M.E. Minarik builds his professional and premium grade, custom/production, solid and chambered body guitars in Van Nuys, California.

Minerva

1930s. Resonator and archtop guitars sold through catalog stores, likely made by one of the big Chicago builders of the era.

Mirabella

1997-present. Professional and premium grade, custom archtops, flat-tops, hollowbody, and solidbody guitars built by luthier Cristian Mirabella in Babylon, New York. He also builds basses, mandolins and ukes.

Miranda Guitars

2002-present. Owner Phil Green uses components made by various shops in California to assemble and set-up, professional grade, full-size travel/silent-practice guitars in Palo Alto, California.

Mitre

1983-1985. Bolt neck, solidbody guitars made in Aldenville (or East Longmeadow), Massachusetts, featuring pointy body shapes, 2 humbuckers, active or passive electronics and with or without trems. They also offered a bass.

MJ Guitar Engineering

1993-present. Professional and premium grade, production/custom, hollowbody, chambered and solidbody guitars built by luthier Mark Johnson in Rohnert Park, California. He also builds basses.

Mobius Megatar

2000-present. Professional grade, production, hybrid guitars designed for two-handed tapping, built in Mount Shasta, California. Founded by Reg Thompson, Henri Dupont, and Traktor Topaz in '97, they released their first guitars in '00.

Modulus

1978-present. Founded by Geoff Gould in the San Francisco area, currently built in Novato, California. Modulus currently offers only basses but did build professional grade, production/custom, solidbody electric guitars up to '05.

Genesis 2/2T

1996-2005. Double-cut, long extended bass horn alder body, bolt-on carbon fiber/red cedar neck, hum-single-single pickups, locking vibrato (2T model).

| 1996-2005 | $900 | $1,100 |

Moll Custom Instruments

1996-present. Luthier Bill Moll builds his professional and premium grade, archtops in Springfield, Missouri. He has also built violins, violas and cellos.

Monrad, Eric

1993-present. Premium, custom, flamenco and classical guitars built by luthier Eric Monrad in Healdsburg, California.

MODEL YEAR	FEATURES	EXC. COND. LOW	HIGH

Monroe Guitars

2004-present. Luthier Matt Handley builds his custom, professional grade, solidbody electric guitars in State Center, Iowa. He also builds basses.

Montalvo

See listing under Casa Montalvo.

Montaya

Late 1970s-1980s. Montaya Hyosung 'America' Inc., Korean acoustic and electric import copies.

Monteleone

1976-present. Presentation grade, production/custom, archtop guitars built by Luthier John Monteleone in Islip, New York. He also builds mandolins.

Eclipse

1991-present. 17" electric archtop, natural orange.

1991-2010		$14,500	$16,500

OM-42

Mid-1970s-1985. Styled like an old Martin OM, spruce top, Brazilian rosewood back.

1975-1985		$10,000	$11,500

Radio City

1990s-present. 18" acoustic archtop cutaway, art deco fretboard inlays, golden blond.

1990s-2010		$19,000	$22,000

Montgomery Ward

The mail-order and retail giant offered a variety of instruments and amps from several different U.S. and overseas manufacturers.

Model 8379/H44 Stratotone

Mid-1950s. Private branded Harmony Stratotone, some without logo but with crown-style stencil/painted logo on headstock, many with gold-copper finish, 1 pickup.

1957		$800	$1,000

Monty

1980-present. Luthier Brian Monty builds his professional, premium and presentation grade, production/custom, archtop, semi-hollow, solidbody, and chambered electric guitars originally in Lennoxville, Quebec, and currently in Anne de Prescott, Ontario.

Moog

1964-present. Moog introduced its premium grade, production, Harmonic Control System solidbody guitar in 2008. They also offer guitar effects.

Moon (Japan)

1979-present. Professional and premium grade, production/custom, guitars made in Japan. They also build basses.

Moon (Scotland)

1979-present. Intermediate, professional and premium grade, production/custom, acoustic and electric guitars built by luthier Jimmy Moon in Glasgow, Scotland. They also build mandolin family instruments.

Moonstone

1972-present. Professional, premium, and presentation grade production/custom flat-top, solid and semi-hollow electric guitars, built by luthier Steve Helgeson in Eureka, California. He also builds basses. Higher unit sales in the early-'80s. Some models have an optional graphite composite neck built by Modulus.

Eclipse Standard

1979-1983. Figured wood body, offset double-cut, neck-thru, dot markers, standard maple neck, natural finish.

1979-1983		$1,300	$1,600
1979-1983	XII	$1,300	$1,600

Exploder

1980-1983. Figured wood solidbody, neck-thru, standard maple neck, natural finish.

1980-1983		$1,500	$1,900

Flaming V

1980-1984. Figured wood body, V-shaped, neck-thru, standard maple neck, natural finish.

1980-1984		$1,300	$1,600

M-80

1980-1984. Figured wood double-cut semi-hollow body, standard maple or optional graphite neck, natural finish.

1980s	Optional graphite neck	$2,200	$2,800
1980s	Standard maple neck	$1,900	$2,600

Vulcan Deluxe

1979-1983. Figured maple carved-top body, offset double-cut, diamond markers, standard maple neck, natural finish.

1979-1983		$1,900	$2,400
1979-1983	Optional graphite neck	$2,100	$2,600

Vulcan Standard

1979-1983. Mahogany carved-top body, offset double-cutaway, dot markers, standard maple neck, natural finish.

1979-1983		$1,600	$1,950
1979-1983	Optional graphite neck	$1,900	$2,300

Morales

Ca.1967-1968. Guitars and basses made in Japan by Zen-On, not heavily imported into the U.S., if at all.

Solidbody Electric

1967-1968	Various models	$125	$225

Moll Custom SJ

Moonstone M-80

GUITARS

Morgaine Mintage '61

*1968 Mosrite Joe Maphis
Mark 1*

MODEL YEAR	FEATURES	EXC. COND. LOW	HIGH

More Harmony

1930s. Private branded by Dobro for Dailey's More Harmony Music Studio. Private branding for catalog companies, teaching studios, publishers, and music stores was common for the Chicago makers. More Harmony silk-screen logo on the headstock.

Dobro
1930s. 14" wood body with upper bout f-holes and metal resonator, sunburst.

1930s		$1,100	$1,400

Morgaine Guitars

1994-present. Luthier Jorg Tandler builds his professional and premium grade, production/custom electrics in Germany.

Morgan Monroe

1999-present. Intermediate grade, production, acoustic, acoustic/electric and resonator guitars made in Korea and distributed by SHS International of Indianapolis, Indiana. They also offer basses, mandolins, banjos, and fiddles.

Morris

1967-present. Intermediate, professional and premium grade, production, acoustic guitars imported by Moridaira of Japan. Morris guitars were first imported into the U.S. from the early '70s to around '90. They are again being imported into the U.S. starting in 2001. They also offered mandolins in the '70s.

000 Copy
1970s. Brazilian rosewood laminate body.

1970s		$275	$350

Acoustic-Electric Archtop
1970s. Various models.

1970s		$400	$500

D-45 Copy
1970s. Brazilian laminate body.

1970s		$375	$475

Mortoro Guitars

1992-present. Luthier Gary Mortoro builds his premium grade, custom, archtop guitars in Miami, Florida.

Mosrite

The history of Mosrite has more ups and downs than just about any other guitar company. Founder Semie Moseley had several innovative designs and had his first success in 1954, at age 19, building doubleneck guitars for super picker Joe Maphis and protégé Larry Collins. Next came the Ventures, who launched the brand nationally by playing Mosrites and featuring them on album covers. At its '60s peak, the company was turning out around 1,000 guitars a month. The company ceased production in '69, and Moseley went back to playing gospel concerts and built a few custom instruments during the '70s.

In the early-'80s, Mosrite again set up shop in Jonas Ridge, North Carolina, but the plant burned down in November '83, taking about 300 guitars with it. In early-'92, Mosrite relocated to Booneville, Arkansas, producing a new line of Mosrites, of which 96% were exported to Japan, where the Ventures and Mosrite have always been popular. Semie Moseley died, at age 57, on August 7, '92 and the business carried on until finally closing its doors in '93. The Mosrite line has again been revived, offering intermediate and premium grade, production, reissues.

Throughout much of the history of Mosrite, production numbers were small and model features often changed. As a result, exact production dates are difficult to determine.

Brass Rail
1970s. Double-cut solidbody, has a brass plate running the length of the 'board.

1970s		$900	$1,100

Celebrity 1
Late-1960s-1970s. Thick hollowbody, 2 pickups, sunburst.

1970s		$950	$1,200

Celebrity 2 Standard
Late-1960s-1970s. Thin hollowbody, 2 pickups, in the '70s, it came in a Standard and a Deluxe version.

1970s		$950	$1,200

Celebrity 3
Late-1960s. Thin hollowbody, double-cut, 2 pickups, f-holes.

1960s		$950	$1,200

Combo Mark 1
1966-1968. Bound body, 1 f-hole.

1966-1968		$1,400	$1,700

Custom-Built
1952-1962. Pre-production custom instruments hand-built by Semie Moseley, guidance pricing only, each instrument will vary. A wide variety of instruments were made during this period. Some were outstanding, but others, especially those made around '60, could be very basic and of much lower quality. Logos would vary widely and some '60 logos looked especially homemade.

1952-1959	Rare, higher-end	$11,000	$14,000
1960-1962	Common, lower-end	$1,500	$1,800

D-40 Resonator Guitar
1960s. Symmetrical double-cut thinline archtop-style body with metal resonator in center of body, 2 pickups, 2 control knobs and toggle switch.

1960s		$1,300	$1,600

D-100 Californian
1960s. Double-cut, resonator guitar with 2 pickups.

1967		$1,300	$1,600

MODEL YEAR	FEATURES	EXC. COND. LOW	HIGH

Gospel
1967. Thinline double-cut, f-hole, 2 pickups, vibrato, Gospel logo on headstock.

| 1967 | Sunburst | $1,700 | $2,100 |
| 1967 | White | $2,400 | $2,900 |

Joe Maphis Doubleneck
1963-1968. Limited Edition reissue of the guitar Semie Moseley made for Maphis, with the smaller octave neck, sunburst.

| 1963-1968 | Production starts | $4,500 | $5,600 |

Joe Maphis Mark 1
1959-1972. Semi-hollow double-cut, 2 single-coils, spruce top, walnut back, rosewood 'board, natural.

| 1959-1972 | | $2,000 | $2,500 |

Joe Maphis Mark XVIII
1960s. 6/12 doubleneck, double-cut, 2 pickups on each neck, Moseley tremolo on 6-string.

| 1960s | | $3,300 | $4,000 |

Mosrite 1988
1988-early-1990s. Has traditional Mosrite body styling, Mosrite pickups and bridge.

| 1988 | | $675 | $825 |

Octave Guitar
1963-1965. 14" scale, 1 pickup, Ventures Mosrite body style, single neck pickup, very few made.

| 1963-1965 | | $5,600 | $7,000 |

Stereo 350
1974-1975. Single-cut solidbody, 2 outputs, 2 pickups, 4 knobs, slider and toggle, black.

| 1974-1975 | | $1,300 | $1,600 |

Ventures Model
1963-1967. Double-cut solidbody, triple-bound body '63, no binding after, Vibramute for '63-'64, Moseley tailpiece '65-'67.

1963	Blue or red, bound	$6,800	$8,100
1963	Sunburst, bound	$5,700	$6,800
1964	Blue or red, Vibramute	$5,100	$6,000
1964	Sunburst, Vibramute	$4,600	$5,500
1965	Moseley (2 screws)	$3,500	$4,300
1965	Vibramute, (3 screws)	$4,500	$5,400
1966	Moseley	$3,300	$4,000
1967	Moseley	$3,100	$3,700

Ventures (Jonas Ridge/Boonville)
1982-1993. Made in Jonas Ridge, NC or Booneville, AR, classic Ventures styling.

| 1982-1993 | | $1,500 | $1,900 |

Ventures Mark V
1963-1967. Double-cut solidbody.

| 1963-1967 | | $1,500 | $1,900 |

Ventures Mark XII (12-String)
1966-1967. Double-cut solidbody, 12 strings.

| 1966-1967 | | $2,900 | $3,600 |

Mossman
1965-present. Professional and premium grade, production/custom, flat-top guitars built in Sulphur Springs, Texas. They have also built acoustic basses. Founded by Stuart L. Mossman in Winfield, Kansas. In '75, fire destroyed one company building, including the complete supply of Brazilian rosewood. They entered into an agreement with C.G. Conn Co. to distribute guitars by '77. 1200 Mossman guitars in a Conn warehouse in Nevada were ruined by being heated during the day and frozen during the night. A disagreement about who was responsible resulted in cash flow problems for Mossman. Production fell to a few guitars per month until the company was sold in '86 to Scott Baxendale. Baxendale sold the company to John Kinsey and Bob Casey in Sulphur Springs in '89.

Flint Hills
1970-mid-1980s. Flat-top acoustic, Indian rosewood back and sides.

| 1970-1979 | | $1,600 | $1,900 |

Golden Era
1976-1977. D-style, vine inlay and other high-end appointments, Indian rosewood sides and back.

| 1976-1977 | | $3,000 | $3,500 |

Great Plains
1970-mid-1980s. Flat-top, Indian rosewood, herringbone trim.

| 1970-1979 | | $1,400 | $1,700 |

Southwind
1976-ca. 1986, mid-1990s-2002. Flat-top, abalone trim top.

| 1976-1979 | | $1,700 | $2,100 |

Tennessee
1975-1979. D-style, spruce top, mahogany back and sides, rope marquetry purfling, rope binding.

| 1975-1979 | | $1,000 | $1,250 |

Tennessee 12-String

| 1975-1979 | | $1,000 | $1,250 |

Timber Creek
1980. D-style, rosewood back and sides, spruce top.

| 1980 | | $1,300 | $1,600 |

Winter Wheat
1976-1979, mid-1990s-present. Flat-top, abalone trim, natural finish.

| 1976-1979 | | $1,700 | $2,100 |

Winter Wheat 12-String
1976-1979. 12-string version of Winter Wheat, natural.

| 1976-1979 | | $1,700 | $2,100 |

MotorAve Guitars
2002-present. Luthier Mark Fuqua builds his professional and premium grade, production, electric guitars originally in Los Angeles, California, and currently in Durham, North Carolina.

Mountain/C.F. Mountain
1970s-early 1980s. Japanese copy acoustics made by Hayashi Musical Instrument Ltd with headstock logo that looks very much like that of a certain classic American guitar company and made by Hayashi musical instrument Ltd .

Acoustic

| 1970s-80s | | $50 | $75 |

Mosrite Stereo 350

1963 Mosrite Ventures Model

Music Man Axis

1980 Music Man Sabre II

MODEL YEAR	FEATURES	EXC. COND. LOW	HIGH

Mouradian

1983-present. Luthiers Jim and Jon Mouradian build their professional and premium grade, production/custom, electric guitars in Winchester, Massachusetts. They also build basses.

Mozart

1930s. Private brand made by Kay.

Hawaiian (Square Neck)

1930s. Spruce top, solid mahogany sides and back, pealoid overlay on peghead with large Mozart inscribed logo, small jumbo 15 1/2" body.

1935-1939		$800	$975

Mozzani

Built in shops of Luigi Mozzani (b. March 9, 1869, Faenza, Italy; d. 1943) who opened lutherie schools in Bologna, Cento and Rovereto in 1890s. By 1926 No. 1 and 2 Original Mozzani Model Mandolin (flat back), No. 3 Mandola (flat back), No. 4 6-String Guitar, No. 5 7-, 8-, and 9-String Guitars, No. 6 Lyre-Guitar.

Muiderman Guitars

1997-present. Custom, premium grade, steel string and classical guitars built by luthier Kevin Muiderman currently in Grand Forks, North Dakota, and previously in Beverly Hills, Michigan, 1997-2001, and Neenah, Wisconsin, '01-'07. He also builds mandolins.

Murph

1965-1967. Mid-level electric semi-hollow and solidbody guitars built by Pat Murphy in San Fernado, California. Murph logo on headstock. They also offered basses and amps.

Electric Solidbody

1965-1967		$675	$825

Electric XII

1965-1967		$675	$825

Music Man

1972-present. Professional grade, production, solidbody guitars built in San Luis Obispo, California. They also build basses. Founded by ex-Fender executives Forrest White and Tom Walker in Orange County, California. Music Man originally produced guitar and bass amps based on early Fender ideas using many former Fender employees. They contracted with Leo Fender's CLF Research to design and produce a line of solidbody guitars and basses. Leo Fender began G & L Guitars with George Fullerton in '82. In '84, Music Man was purchased by Ernie Ball and production was moved to San Luis Obispo.

Albert Lee Signature

1993-present.

1993-1996	Pinkburst	$1,100	$1,300
1996-2010	Tremolo option	$1,100	$1,300

MODEL YEAR	FEATURES	EXC. COND. LOW	HIGH

Axis

1996-present. Offset double-cut solidbody, figured maple top, basswood body, 2 humbucker pickups, Floyd Rose.

1996-2010		$1,100	$1,300

Axis Sport

1996-2002. Two P-90s.

1996-2002		$900	$1,100

Axis Super Sport

2003-present. Figured top.

2003-2010		$850	$1,050

Edward Van Halen

1991-1995. Basswood solidbody, figured maple top, bolt-on maple neck, maple 'board, binding, 2 humbuckers, named changed to Axis.

1991-1995		$1,800	$2,200

John Petrucci 6

2008-present. Standard model.

2008-2010		$1,000	$1,250

S.U.B 1

2004-2006. Offset double-cut solidbody.

2004-2006		$375	$475

Sabre I

1978-1982. Offset double-cut solidbody, maple neck, 2 pickups, Sabre I comes with a flat 'board with jumbo frets.

1978-1982		$1,200	$1,500

Sabre II

1978-1982. Same as Sabre I, but with an oval 7 1/2" radius 'board.

1978-1982		$1,300	$1,600

Silhouette

1986-present. Offset double-cut, contoured beveled solidbody, various pickup configurations.

1986-2010		$800	$1,000
2006	20th Anniversary	$900	$1,100

Steve Morse

1987-present. Solidbody, 4 pickups, humbuckers in the neck and bridge positions, 2 single-coils in the middle, special pickup switching, 6-bolt neck mounting, maple neck.

1987-2010		$1,200	$1,500

Stingray I

1976-1982. Offset double-cut solidbody, flat 'board radius.

1976-1982		$800	$1,000

Stingray II

1976-1982. Offset double-cut solidbody, rounder 'board radius.

1976-1982		$1,000	$1,200

Musicvox

1996-2001, 2011-present. Intermediate grade, production, imported retro-vibe guitars and basses from Matt Eichen of Cherry Hill, New Jersey.

Myka

2003-present. Luthier David Myka builds his professional and premium grade, custom/production, solidbody, semi-hollowbody, hollowbody, archtop, and flat top guitars in Seattle, Washington. Until '07 he was located in Orchard Park, New York.

MODEL		EXC. COND.	
YEAR	FEATURES	LOW	HIGH

Nady

1976-present. Wireless sound company Nady Systems offered guitars and basses with built-in wireless systems for 1985-'87. Made by Fernandes in Japan until '86, then by Cort in Korea.

Lightning/Lightning I

1985-1987. Double-cut, neck-thru, solidbody, 24 frets, built-in wireless, labeled as just Lightning until cheaper second version came out in '86.

1985	Fernandes	$500	$600
1986-1987	Cort	$450	$550

Lightning/Lightning II

1986-1987. Cheaper, bolt-neck version of the Lightning I.

1986-1987	Cort	$275	$350

Napolitano Guitars

1993-present. Luthier Arthur Napolitano builds his professional and premium grade, custom, archtop guitars in Allentown, New Jersey.

NashGuitars

2001-present. Luthier Bill Nash builds his professional grade, production/custom, aged solidbody replica electric guitars in Olympia, Washington. He also builds basses.

Nashville Guitar Company

1985-present. Professional and premium grade, custom, flat-top guitars built by luthier Marty Lanham in Nashville, Tennessee. He has also built banjos.

National

Ca. 1927-present. Founded in Los Angeles, California as the National String Instrument Corporation by John Dopyera, George Beauchamp, Ted Kleinmeyer and Paul Barth. In '29 Dopyera left to start the Dobro Manufacturing Company with Rudy and Ed Dopyera and Vic Smith. The Dobro company competed with National until the companies reunited. Beauchamp and Barth then left National to found Ro-Pat-In with Adolph Rickenbacker and C.L. Farr (later becoming Electro String Instrument Corporation, then Rickenbacher). In '32 Dopyera returns to National and National and Dobro start their merger in late-'33, finalizing it by mid-'34. Throughout the '30s, National and Dobro maintained separate production, sales and distribution. National Dobro moved to Chicago, Illinois in '36. In Chicago, archtop and flat top bodies are built primarily by Regal and Kay; after '37 all National resonator guitar bodies made by Kay. L.A. production is maintained until around '37, although some assembly of Dobros continued in L.A. (primarily for export) until '39 when the L.A. offices are finally closed. By ca. '39 the Dobro brand disappears.

In '42, the company's resonator production ceased and Victor Smith, Al Frost and Louis Dopyera buy the company and change name to Valco Manufacturing Company. Post-war production resumes in '46. Valco is purchased by treasurer Robert Engelhardt

in '64. In '67, Valco bought Kay, but in '68 the new Valco/Kay company went out of business. In the Summer of '69 the assets, including brand names, were auctioned off and the National and Supro names were purchased by Chicago-area distributor/ importer Strum 'N Drum (Noble, Norma brands). The National brand is used on copies in early- to mid-'70s, and the brand went into hiatus by the '80s.

In '88 National Resophonic Guitars is founded in San Luis Obispo, California, by Don Young, with production of National-style resonator guitars beginning in '89 (see following). In the '90s, the National brand also resurfaces on inexpensive Asian imports.

National Resonator guitars are categorized by materials and decoration (from plain to fancy): Duolian, Triolian, Style 0, Style 1, Style 2, Style 3, Style 4, Don #1, Style 97, Don #2, Don #3, Style 35.

National guitars all have serial numbers which provide clues to date of production. This is a complex issue. This list combines information included in George Gruhn and Walter Carter's Gruhn's Guide to Vintage Guitars, which was originally provided by Bob Brozman and Mike Newton, with new information provided by Mike Newton.

Pre Chicago numbers

A101-A450	1935-1936

Chicago numbers

A prefix (some may not have the prefix)	1936-mid-1997
B prefix	Mid-1937-1938
C prefix	Late-1938-1940
G prefix up to 200	Ea. 1941-ea. 1942
G suffix under 2000	Ea. 1941-ea. 1942
G suffix 2000-3000s (probably old parts)	1943-1945
G suffix 4000s (old parts)	Late 1945-mid-1947
V100-V7500	1947
V7500-V15000	1948
V15000-V25000	1949
V25000-V35000	1950
V35000-V38000	1951
X100-X7000	1951
X7000-X17000	1952
X17000-X30000	1953
X30000-X43000	1954
X43000-X57000	1955
X57000-X71000	1956
X71000-X85000	1957
X85000-X99000	1958
T100-T5000	1958
T5000-T25000	1959
T25000-T50000	1960
T50000-T75000	1961
T75000-T90000	1962
G100-G5000	1962
T90000-T99000	1963
G5000-G15000	1963
G15000-G40000	1964
1 prefix	1965-ea. 1968
2 prefix	Mid-1968

Napolitano Primavera

Early 1960s National Westwood 75
Marco Parmiggiani

GUITARS

1949 National California

1931 National Duolian

MODEL YEAR	FEATURES	EXC. COND. LOW	HIGH

Aragon De Luxe
1939-1942. Archtop with resonator (the only archtop resonator offered), spruce top and maple back and sides, light brown.

1939-1942		$7,000	$8,500

Aristocrat 1110/1111
1948-1955. Electric archtop, full body non-cutaway, single neck pickup, 2 knobs, sunburst, early model with triple backslash markers, later with block markers, National-crest headstock inlaid logo, shaded finish (1110) and natural (1111).

1948-1955	1110, shaded	$800	$1,000
1948-1955	1111, natural	$1,000	$1,200

Avalon 1124/1124B
1954-1957. Small wood solidbody, 2 pickups, 4 control knobs and switch on top-mounted 'guard, block markers, short trapeze bridge, sunburst (1124) or blond (1124B).

1954-1957	1124, sunburst	$1,000	$1,200
1954-1957	1124B, blond	$1,100	$1,300

Bel-Aire 1109/1198
1953-1960. Single pointed cut archtop, 2 (1109) pickups until '57, 3 (1198) after, master tone knob and jack, bound body, sunburst.

1953-1957	1109, 2 pickups	$900	$1,100
1958-1960	1198, 3 pickups	$1,000	$1,200

Big Daddy LP-457-2
1970s. Strum & Drum import, single-cut, LP-style, 2 pickups, gold hardware, black.

1970s		$225	$275

Bluegrass 35
1963-1965. Acoustic, non-cut single-cone resonator, Res-O-Glas body in Arctic White.

1963-1965		$900	$1,100

Bobbie Thomas
Ca.1967-1968. Double-cut thinline hollowbody, bat-shaped f-holes, 2 pickups, Bobbie Thomas on 'guard, vibrato.

1967-1968		$400	$500

Bolero 1123
1954-1957. Les Paul-shape, control knobs mounted on 'guard, single pickup, trapeze tailpiece, sunburst.

1954-1957		$800	$1,000

California 1100
1949-1955. Electric hollowbody archtop, multi-bound, f-holes, trapeze tailpiece, 1 pickup, natural.

1949-1955		$800	$1,000

Cameo
1957-1958. Renamed from Model 1140 in '57, full-body acoustic archtop with carved top.

1957-1958		$600	$800

Club Combo 1170
1952-1955, 1959-1961. Electric hollowbody archtop, 2 pickups, rounded cutaway.

1952-1961		$900	$1,100

Collegian
1942-1943. Metal body resonator similar to Duolian, 14-fret round or square neck, yellow.

1942-1943		$1,400	$1,700

Cosmopolitan 1122
1954-1957. Small wood non-cutaway solidbody, dot markers, 1 pickup, 2 knobs on mounted 'guard.

1954-1957		$600	$800

Debonaire 1107
1953-1960. Single rounded-cutaway full-depth 16" electric archtop, single neck pickup, Debonaire logo on 'guard (for most models), large raised National script logo on headstock, sunburst.

1953-1960		$700	$900

Don Style 1
1934-1936. Plain body with engraved borders, pearl dot inlay, 14 frets, single-cone, silver (nickel-plated).

1934-1936		$5,500	$7,000

Don Style 2
1934-1936. Geometric Art Deco body engraving, 14 frets, single-cone, fancy square pearl inlays and pearloid headstock overlay, silver (nickel-plated).

1934-1936		$7,500	$9,000

Don Style 3
1934-1936. Same as Style 2 but more elaborate floral engravings, fancy pearl diamond inlays, 14 frets, single-cone, silver (nickel-plated), only a very few made.

1934-1936		$12,000	$15,000

Duolian
1930-1939. Acoustic steel body, frosted paint finish until '36, mahogany-grain paint finish '37-'39, round neck, square neck available in '33, 12-fret neck until '34 then 14-fret.

1930-1934	Round neck, 12 frets	$2,900	$3,300
1935-1939	Round neck, 14 frets	$2,800	$3,200

Dynamic 1125
1951-1959. Full body 15.5" acoustic-electric archtop, sunburst version of New Yorker 1120 with some appointments slightly below the New Yorker, dot markers, 1 pickup, sunburst.

1951-1959		$600	$800

EG 685 Hollow Body Electric
1970s. Strum & Drum distributed, double-cut hollowbody copy, 2 pickups.

1970s		$250	$300

El Trovador
1933 only. Wood body, 12 frets.

1933		$2,500	$3,100

Electric Spanish
1935-1938. 15 1/2" archtop with Pat. Appl. For bridge pickup, National crest logo, fancy N-logo 'guard, black and white art deco, sunburst, becomes New Yorker Spanish '39-'58.

1935-1938		$600	$800

Estralita
1934-1942. Acoustic with single-cone resonator, f-holes, multi-bound, 14-fret, mahogany top and back, shaded brown.

1934-1942		$1,000	$1,200

Glenwood 95
1962-1964. Glenwood 98 without third bridge-mount pickup.

1962-1964	Vermillion Red/ Flame Red	$2,900	$3,400

MODEL YEAR	FEATURES	EXC. COND. LOW	HIGH

Glenwood 98
1964-1965. USA map-shaped solidbody of molded Res-O-Glas, 2 regular and 1 bridge pickup, vibrato, pearl white finish.

| 1964-1965 | Pearl White | $3,100 | $3,800 |

Glenwood 99
1962-1965. USA map-shaped solidbody of molded Res-O-Glas, 2 regular and 1 bridge pickups, butterfly inlay.

| 1962-1963 | Snow White | $3,500 | $4,200 |
| 1964-1965 | Sea Foam Green | $4,000 | $4,800 |

Glenwood 1105
1954-1958. Les Paul-shaped solidbody, wood body, not fiberglass, single-cut, multi-bound, 2 pickups, natural, renamed Glenwood Deluxe with Bigsby in '59.

| 1954-1958 | | $1,500 | $1,800 |

Glenwood Deluxe
1959-1961. Renamed from Glenwood 1105, Les Paul-shaped solidbody, wood body, not fiberglass, multi-bound, 2 pickups, factory Bigsby, vibrato, natural.

| 1959-1961 | | $1,700 | $2,100 |

Havana
1938-1942. Natural spruce top, sunburst back and sides.

| 1938-1942 | Round neck | $1,000 | $1,200 |
| 1938-1942 | Square neck | $650 | $800 |

Model 1135 Acoustic Archtop
1948-1954. 17.25" full body acoustic archtop, carved top, split pearl markers.

| 1948-1954 | | $1,000 | $1,200 |

Model 1140 Acoustic Archtop
1948-1957. 15.5" full body acoustic archtop, carved top, dot markers.

| 1948-1957 | | $500 | $700 |

Model 1150 Flat-Top Auditorium
1951-1958. Auditorium-size flat-top, 14.25" narrow-waist, dot markers.

| 1951-1958 | | $450 | $550 |

Model 1155 Jumbo
1948-1961. Flat-top acoustic with Gibson Jumbo body, mahogany back and sides, bolt-on neck.

| 1948-1961 | | $1,600 | $1,900 |

N600 Series
1968. Offset double-cut solidbody, 1, 2, and 3 pickup models, with and without vibrato.

1968	N624, 1 pickup	$400	$500
1968	N634, 2 pickups, vibrato	$525	$650
1968	N644, 3 pickups, vibrato	$650	$800
1968	N654, 12-string	$525	$650

N700 Series
1968. Flat-top, 700/710 dreadnoughts, 720/730 jumbos.

1968	N700 Western	$650	$800
1968	N710	$325	$400
1968	N720 Western	$400	$475
1968	N730 Deluxe	$600	$700

N800 Series
1968. Double-cut semi-hollow body, various models with or without Bigsby.

| 1968 | No Bigsby | $575 | $650 |
| 1968 | With Bigsby | $675 | $750 |

New Yorker 1120
1954-1958. Renamed from New Yorker Spanish, 16.25" electric archtop, 1 pickup on floating 'guard, dot markers, blond.

| 1954-1958 | | $700 | $900 |

New Yorker Spanish
1939-1953. Electric archtop, 15.5" body until '47 then 16.25", 1 neck pickup, dot-diamond markers, sunburst or natural. Renamed New Yorker 1120 in '54.

| 1939-1946 | 15.5" | $600 | $800 |
| 1947-1953 | 16.25" | $600 | $800 |

Newport 82
1963-1965. Renamed from Val-Pro 82, USA map-shaped Res-O-Glas, 1 pickup, red finish.

| 1963-1965 | Pepper Red | $1,600 | $1,900 |

Newport 84
1963-1965. Renamed from Val-Pro 84, USA map-shaped Res-O-Glas, 1 regular and 1 bridge pickup, Sea Foam Green finish.

| 1963-1965 | Sea Foam Green | $2,300 | $2,800 |

Newport 88
1963-1965. Renamed from Val-Pro 88, USA map-shaped Res-O-Glas, 2 regular and 1 bridge pickup, black finish.

| 1963-1965 | Raven Black | $2,000 | $2,400 |

Reso-phonic
1956-1964. Pearloid-covered, single-cut semi-solidbody acoustic, single resonator, maroon or white, also a non-cut, square neck version was offered, which is included in these values.

| 1956-1964 | Round neck | $1,600 | $2,000 |
| 1956-1964 | Square neck | $1,500 | $1,900 |

Rosita
1933-1939. Plywood body by Harmony, plain metal resonator, plain appointments.

| 1933-1939 | | $800 | $1,000 |

Silvo (Electric Hawaiian)
1937-1941. Nickel-plated metal body flat-top, small upper bout, f-holes, square neck, multiple straight line body art over dark background, Roman numeral parallelogram markers, National badge headstock logo, Silvo name on coverplate.

| 1937-1941 | Silver | $3,000 | $3,600 |

Studio 66
1961-1964. Electric solidbody of Res-O-Glas, single-cut, 1 pickup, renamed Varsity 66 in '65.

| 1961-1962 | Sand Buff, bridge pickup | $1,100 | $1,400 |
| 1963-1964 | Jet Black, neck pickup | $1,100 | $1,400 |

Style O
1930-1942. Acoustic single-cone brass body (early models had a steel body), Hawaiian scene etching, 12-fret neck '30-'34, 14-fret neck '35 on, round (all years) or square ('33 on) neck.

| 1930-1934 | Round neck, 12-fret | $2,700 | $3,300 |

1932 National Duolian

1934 National Style O

1962 National Westwood 75

Zak Izbinsky

*National Reso-Phonic
Single-Biscuit Electric*

MODEL YEAR	FEATURES	EXC. COND. LOW	HIGH
1933-1942	Square neck	$2,400	$3,000
1935-1942	Round neck, 14-fret	$2,600	$3,200

Style O Tenor
1929-1930. Tenor, 4 strings, single-cone brass body, Hawaiian scene etching.

1929-1930		$1,200	$1,500

Style 1 Tricone
1927-1943. German silver body tricone resonator, ebony 'board, mahogany square (Hawaiian) or round (Spanish) neck, plain body, 12-fret neck until '34, 14-fret after.

1927-1943	Round neck	$5,000	$6,000
1928-1943	Square neck	$2,500	$3,100

Style 1 Tricone Plectrum
1928-1935. 26" scale versus the 23" scale of the tenor.

1928-1935		$1,900	$2,300

Style 1 Tricone Tenor
1928-1935. Tenor, 4 strings, 23" scale, square neck is Hawaiian, round neck is Spanish.

1928-1935		$1,900	$2,300

Style 1.5 Tricone
1930s. A "1/2" style like the 1.5 represents a different engraving pattern.

1930s		$3,600	$4,200

Style 2 Tricone
1927-1942. German silver body tricone resonator, wild rose engraving, square (Hawaiian) or round (Spanish) neck, 12-fret neck until '34, 14-fret after.

1930s	Round neck	$7,000	$8,700
1930s	Square neck	$3,500	$4,300

Style 2 Tricone Plectrum
1928-1935. 26" scale versus the 23" scale of the tenor.

1928-1935		$2,000	$2,500

Style 2 Tricone Tenor
1928-1935. Tenor.

1928-1935		$2,000	$2,500

Style 3 Tricone
1928-1941. German silver body tricone resonator, lily-of-the-valley engraving, square (Hawaiian) or round (Spanish) neck, 12-fret neck until '34, 14-fret after, reintroduced with a nickel-plated brass body in '94.

1930s	Round neck	$12,000	$15,000
1930s	Square neck	$6,000	$7,500
1940-1941	Square neck	$5,500	$7,000

Style 3 Tricone Plectrum
1928-1935. 26" scale versus the 23" scale of the tenor.

1928-1935		$3,500	$4,300

Style 3 Tricone Tenor
1928-1939. Tenor version.

1928-1939		$3,500	$4,300

Style 4 Tricone
1928-1940. German silver body tricone resonator, chrysanthemum etching, 12-fret neck until '34, 14-fret after, reissued in '95 with same specs.

1930s	Round neck	$14,000	$17,000
1930s	Square neck	$7,000	$8,500

Style 35
1936-1942. Brass body tricone resonator, sandblasted minstrel and trees scene, 12 frets, square (Hawaiian) or round (Spanish) neck.

1936-1942	Round neck	$17,000	$21,000
1936-1942	Square neck	$9,000	$11,000

Style 97
1936-1940. Nickel-plated brass body tricone resonator, sandblasted scene of female surfrider and palm trees, 12 frets, slotted peghead.

1930s	Round neck	$10,000	$12,000
1930s	Square neck	$5,000	$6,000

Style N
1930-1931. Nickel-plated brass body single-cone resonator, plain finish, 12 frets.

1930-1931		$4,700	$5,800

Town and Country 1104
1954-1958. Model just below Glenwood 1105, dots, 2 or 3 pickups, plastic overlay on back, natural finish.

1954-1958	2 pickups	$1,300	$1,600
1954-1958	3 pickups	$1,400	$1,700

Triolian
1928-1941. Single-cone resonator, wood body replaced by metal body in '29, 12-fret neck and slotted headstock '28-'34, changed to 14-fret neck in '35 and solid headstock in '36, round or square ('33 on) neck available.

1928-1936	Various colors	$2,900	$3,500
1936-1937	Fake rosewood grain finish	$2,200	$2,800

Triolian Tenor
1928-1936. Tenor, metal body.

1928-1936		$1,100	$1,400

Trojan
1934-1942. Single-cone resonator wood body, f-holes, bound top, 14-fret round neck.

1934-1942		$1,000	$1,300

Val-Pro 82
1962-1963. USA map-shaped Res-O-Glas, 1 pickup, Vermillion Red finish, renamed Newport 82 in '63.

1962-1963		$1,500	$1,700

Val-Pro 84
1962-1963. USA map-shaped Res-O-Glas, 1 regular and 1 bridge pickup, snow white finish, renamed Newport 84 in '63.

1962-1963		$1,600	$1,850

Val-Pro 88
1962-1963. USA map-shaped Res-O-Glas, 2 regular and 1 bridge pickup, black finish, renamed Newport 88 in '63.

1962-1963		$2,400	$2,900

Varsity 66
1964-1965. Renamed from Studio 66 in '64, molded Res-O-Glas, 1 pickup, 2 knobs, beige finish.

1964-1965		$1,300	$1,600

Westwood 72
1962-1964. USA map-shaped solid hardwood body (not fiberglass), 1 pickup, Cherry Red.

1962-1964		$1,700	$2,100

MODEL YEAR	FEATURES	EXC. COND. LOW	HIGH

Westwood 75

1962-1964. USA map-shaped solid hardwood body (not fiberglass), 1 regular and 1 bridge pickup, cherry-to-black sunburst finish.

| 1962-1964 | | $1,900 | $2,300 |

Westwood 77

1962-1965. USA map-shaped solid hardwood body (not fiberglass), 2 regular and 1 bridge pickup.

| 1962-1965 | Blond-Ivory | $1,900 | $2,300 |

National Reso-Phonic

1988-present. Professional and premium grade, production/custom, single cone, acoustic-electric, and tricone guitars (all with resonators), built in San Luis Obispo, California. They also build basses, mandolins and ukuleles. McGregor Gaines and Don Young formed the National Reso-Phonic Guitar Company with the objective of building instruments based upon the original National designs. Replicon is the aging process to capture the appearance and sound of a vintage National.

Collegian

2010-present. Thin gauge steel body, 9.5" cone, biscuit bridge, aged ivory finish.

| 2010 | | $1,300 | $1,500 |

Delphi/National Delphi

1996-2010. Single cone, satin nickel plating on steel body.

| 1996-2010 | Delphi | $1,100 | $1,300 |
| 2007 | Delphi, Brass | $1,500 | $1,800 |

El Trovador

2010-present. Wood body Dobro-style, single cone, biscuit bridge.

| 2010 | | $1,900 | $2,250 |

Estralita Deluxe

2006-present. Single cone, walnut body, figured maple top.

| 2006-2010 | | $1,300 | $1,500 |

Resoelectric Jr. II

2008-2010. Thin single-cut electric, pickup mounted round resonator.

| 2008-2010 | | $700 | $850 |

Resophonic

1992, 2009. Electric resonator, single biscuit, single-cut, dot markers, 1 'tube' pickup, badge Reso-National-Phonic decal logo on headstock.

| 1992 | | $1,450 | $1,800 |
| 2009 | | $1,350 | $1,600 |

ResoRocket N

2008-present.

| 2008-2010 | | $2,000 | $2,300 |

Style 1 Tricone

1994-present. Nickel-plated brass body, bound ebony 'board.

| 1994-2010 | | $1,900 | $2,200 |
| 2007 | Replicon | $1,900 | $2,200 |

Style N

1993-2005. Nickel-plated brass body single-cone resonator, plain mirror finish, 12 fret neck.

| 1993-2005 | | $1,500 | $1,900 |

MODEL YEAR	FEATURES	EXC. COND. LOW	HIGH

ResoRocket N

2008-present.

| 2008-2010 | | $2,000 | $2,300 |

Style O

1992-present.

| 1992-2009 | | $1,800 | $2,100 |

Navarro Custom

1986-present. Professional and premium grade, production/custom, electric guitars built in San Juan, Puerto Rico by luthier Mike Navarro. He also builds basses.

Neubauer

1966-1990s. Luthier Helmut Neubauer built his acoustic and electric archtop guitars in Bubenreuth, Germany.

New Era Guitars

See listing under ARK - New Era Guitars.

New Orleans Guitar Company

1992-present. Luthier Vincent Guidroz builds his premium grade, production/custom, solid and semi-hollow body guitars in New Orleans, Louisiana.

Nickerson Guitars

1983-present. Luthier Brad Nickerson builds his professional and premium grade, production/custom, archtop and flat-top guitars in Northampton, Massachusetts.

Nielsen

2004-present. Premium grade, custom/production, archtop guitars built by luthier Dale Nielsen in Duluth, Minnesota.

Nik Huber Guitars

1997-present. Premium grade, production/custom, electric guitars built in Rodgau, Germany by luthier Nik Huber.

Nioma

1930s. Brand most likely used by a music studio (or distributor) on instruments made by others, including Regal-built resonator instruments.

Noble

Ca. 1950-ca. 1969. Instruments made by others and distributed by Don Noble and Company of Chicago. Plastic-covered guitars made by EKO debut in '62. Aluminum-necked Wandré guitars added to the line in early-'63. By ca. '65-'66 the brand is owned by Chicago-area importer and distributor Strum 'N Drum and used mainly on Japanese-made solidbodies. Strum 'N Drum bought the National brand name in '69 and imported Japanese copies of American designs under the National brand and Japanese original designs under Norma through the early '70s. The Noble brand disappears at least by

Nickerson Virtuoso

Nik Huber Dolphin

Nordy Vs

1964 Oahu

MODEL YEAR	FEATURES	EXC. COND. LOW	HIGH

the advent of the Japanese National brand, if not before. They also offered amps and basses.

Nordy (Nordstrand Guitars)

2003-present. Professional and premium grade, production/custom, electric guitars built by luthier Carey Nordstrand in Yucaipa, California. He also builds basses.

Norma

Ca.1965-1970. Imported from Japan by Strum 'N Drum, Inc. of Chicago (see Noble brand info). Early examples were built by Tombo, most notably sparkle plastic covered guitars and basses.

Electric Solidbody

1965-1970s. Type of finish has affect on value. Various models include; EG-350 (student double-cut, 1 pickup), EG-403 (unique pointy cutaway, 2 pickups), EG-400 (double-cut, 2 pickups), EG-450 (double-cut, 2 split-coil pickups), EG-421 (double-cut, 4 pickups), EG-412-12 (double-cut, 12-string).

1965-1968	Blue, red, gold sparkle	$300	$400
1965-1970s	Non-sparkle	$150	$200

Norman

1972-present. Intermediate grade, production, acoustic and acoustic/electric guitars built in LaPatrie, Quebec. Norman was the first guitar production venture luthier Robert Godin was involved with. He has since added the Seagull, Godin, and Patrick & Simon brands of instruments.

Normandy Guitars

2008-present. Jim Normandy builds professional grade, production, aluminum archtop and electric guitars in Salem, Oregon. He also builds basses.

Northworthy Guitars

1987-present. Professional and premium grade, production/custom, flat-top and electric guitars built by luthier Alan Marshall in Ashbourne, Derbyshire, England. He also builds basses and mandolins.

Norwood

1960s. Budget guitars imported most likely from Japan.

Electric Solidbody

1960s. Offset double-cut body, 3 soapbar-style pickups, Norwood label on headstock.

1960s		$150	$200

Novax Guitars

1989-present. Luthier Ralph Novak builds his fanned-fret professional and premium grade, production/custom, solidbody and acoustic guitars in San Leandro, California. He also builds basses.

MODEL YEAR	FEATURES	EXC. COND. LOW	HIGH

Noyce

1974-present. Luthier Ian Noyce builds his production/custom, professional and premium grade, acoustic and electric guitars in Ballarat, Victoria, Australia. He also builds basses.

Nyberg Instruments

1993-present. Professional grade, custom, flat-top and Maccaferri-style guitars built by luthier Lawrence Nyberg in Hornby Island, British Columbia. He also builds mandolins, mandolas, bouzoukis and citterns.

Oahu

1926-1985, present. The Oahu Publishing Company and Honolulu Conservatory, based in Cleveland, Ohio was active in the sheet music and student instrument business in the '30s. An instrument, set of instructional sheet music, and lessons were offered as a complete package. Lessons were often given to large groups of students. Instruments, lessons, and sheet music could also be purchased by mail order. The Oahu Publishing Co. advertised itself as The World's Largest Guitar Dealer. Most '30s Oahu guitars were made by Kay with smaller numbers from the Oscar Schmidt Company.

Guitar Models from the Mid-'30s include: 71K (jumbo square neck), 72K (jumbo roundneck), 68B (jumbo, vine body decoration), 68K (deluxe jumbo square neck), 69K (deluxe jumbo roundneck), 65K and 66K (mahogany, square neck), 64K and 67K (mahogany, roundneck), 65M (standard-size, checker binding, mahogany), 53K (roundneck, mahogany), 51 (black, Hawaiian scene, pearlette 'board), 51K (black, pond scene decoration), 52K (black, Hawaiian scene decoration), 50 and 50K (student guitar, brown). The brand has been revived on a line of tube amps.

Graphic Body

1930s. 13" painted artwork bodies, includes Styles 51 and 52 Hawaiian scene.

1930s	Floral, higher appointments	$325	$400
1930s	Hawaiian scene	$325	$400

Round Neck 14" Flat-Top

1930s. Spruce top, figured maple back and sides, thin logo.

1932		$850	$1,100

Style 50K Student

1930s. Student-size guitar, brown finish.

1935		$200	$250

Style 52K

1930s. 13" with fancy Hawaiian stencil, slotted headstock.

1930s		$300	$350

Style 65M

1933-1935. Standard-size mahogany body, checker binding, natural brown.

1933-1935		$450	$550

MODEL YEAR	FEATURES	EXC. COND. LOW	HIGH

Style 68K De Luxe Jumbo
1930s. Hawaiian, 15.5" wide, square neck, Brazilian back and sides, spruce top, fancy pearl vine inlay, abalone trim on top and soundhole, rosewood pyramid bridge, fancy pearl headstock inlay, butterbean tuners, ladder-braced, natural. High-end model made for Oahu by Kay.

1935		$3,000	$3,600

Odessa
1981-1990s. Budget guitars imported by Davitt & Hanser (BC Rich). Mainly acoustics in the '90s, but some electrics early on.

O'Hagan
1979-1983. Designed by clarinetist and importer Jerol O'Hagan in St. Louis Park, Minnesota. Primarily neck-thru construction, most with German-carved bodies. In '81 became Jemar Corporation and in '83 it was closed by the I.R.S., a victim of recession.

SN=YYM(M)NN (e.g., 80905, September '80, 5th guitar); or MYMNNN (e.g., A34006, April 1983, 6th guitar). Approximately 3000 total instruments were made with the majority being Night-Watches (approx. 200 Twenty Twos, 100-150 Sharks, 100 Lasers; about 25 with birdseye maple bodies).

Electric
1979-1983. Models include; Laser (solidbody, double-cut, maple or walnut body, set-thru neck, 3 single-coil Schaller pickups), Shark (Explorer-looking solidbody) and Twenty Two (V, 2 humbuckers).

1979-1983		$650	$800

Ohio
1959-ca. 1965. Line of electric solidbodies and basses made by France's Jacobacci company, which also built under its own brand. Sparkle finish, bolt-on aluminum necks, strings-thru-body design.

Old Kraftsman
Ca. 1930s-ca. 1960s. Brandname used by the Spiegel catalog company for instruments made by other American manufacturers, including Regal, Kay and even Gibson. The instruments were of mixed quality, but some better grade instruments were comparable to those offered by Wards.

Archtop
1930s-1960s. Various models.

1930s	17", Stauffer-style headstock	$325	$425
1950s		$225	$300
1960s		$225	$300

Flat-Top
1930s-1960s. Various models.

1950s	Prairie Ramblers (stencil)	$250	$300

Jazz II K775
1960-1963. Kay 775 with Old Kraftsman logo on large headstock, small double-cut thinline, 2 pickups, Bigsby, natural.

1960-1963		$725	$900

MODEL YEAR	FEATURES	EXC. COND. LOW	HIGH

Sizzler K4140
1959. Single-cut, single neck pickup, Sizzler logo on body with other art images.

1959		$400	$500

Thin Twin Jimmy Reed
1952-1958		$800	$1,000

Value Leader
1961-1965. Electric single-cut semi-solid, 1 pickup, Kay Value Leader series.

1961-1965		$400	$500

OLP (Officially Licensed Product)
2001-2009. Intermediate grade, production, imported guitars based on higher dollar guitar models officially licensed from the original manufacturer. OLP logo on headstock. They also offered basses.

Olson Guitars
1977-present. Luthier James A. Olson builds his presentation grade, custom, flat-tops in Circle Pines, Minnesota.

Olympia by Tacoma
1997-present. Import acoustic guitars and mandolins from Tacoma Guitars.

OD Series
2000s	Various models	$75	$300

Omega
1996-present. Luthier Kevin Gallagher builds his premium grade, custom/production acoustic guitars in East Saylorsburg, Pennsylvania.

Oncor Sound
1980-ca. 1981. This Salt Lake City, Utah-based company made both a guitar and a bass synthesizer.

Optek
1980s-present. Intermediate grade, production, imported Fretlight acoustic/electric and electric guitars. Located in Reno, Nevada.

Fretlight
1989-present. Double-cut, 126 LED lights in fretboard controlled by a scale/chord selector.

1989-2010		$300	$400

Opus
1972-Mid 1970s. Acoustic and classical guitars, imported from Japan by Ampeg/Selmer. In '75-'76, Harmony made a line of acoustics with the Opus model name.

Original Senn
2004-present. Luthier Jeff Senn builds his professional and premium grade, production/custom, solidbody electric guitars in Nashville, Tennessee. He also builds basses.

Olson 12-String

Original Senn Pomona

Oskar Graf Parlour

Otwin Deluxe

MODEL YEAR	FEATURES	EXC. COND. LOW	HIGH

Ormsby Guitars

2003-present. Luthier Perry Ormsby builds his custom, professional and premium grade, solid and chambered electric guitars in Perth, Western Australia.

Orpheum

1897-1942, 1944-late 1960s, 2001-2006. Intermediate grade, production, acoustic and resonator guitars. They also offered mandolins. Orpheum originally was a brand of Rettberg and Lange, who made instruments for other companies as well. William Rettberg and William Lange bought the facilities of New York banjo maker James H. Buckbee in 1897. Lange went out on his own in '21 to start the Paramount brand. He apparently continued using the Orpheum brand as well. He went out of business in '42. In '44 the brand was acquired by New York's Maurice Lipsky Music Co. who used it primarily on beginner to medium grade instruments, which were manufactured by Regal, Kay, and United Guitar (and maybe others). In the early '60s Lipsky applied the brand to Japanese and European (by Egmond) imports. Lipsky dropped the name in the early '70s. The brand was revived for '01 to '06 by Tacoma Guitars.

Auditorium Archtop 835/837

1950s. Acoustic archtop, auditorium size, dot markers, Orpheum shell headpiece, white celluloid 'guard, model 835 with spruce top/back/sides, 837 with mahogany.

1950s		$225	$275

Orpheum Special (Regal-made)

1930s. Slot head, Dobro-style wood body, metal resonator, sunburst.

1930s		$850	$975

President

1940s. 18" pro-level acoustic archtop, Orpheum block logo and President script logo on headstock, large split-block markers, sunburst.

1940s		$1,500	$1,900

Thin Twin Jimmy Reed 865E

1950s. Model 865E is the Orpheum version of the generically named Thin Twin Jimmy Reed style electric Spanish cutaway thin solidbody, hand engraved shell celluloid Orpheum headpiece, described as #865E Cutaway Thin Electric Guitar in catalog.

1950s		$800	$1,000

Ultra Deluxe Professional 899

1950s. 17" cutaway, 2 pickups, 2 knobs, maple back and sides, top material varies, dot markers, finishes as follows: E-C copper, E-G gold, E-G-B gold-black sunburst, E-B blond curly maple, E-S golden orange sunburst.

1950s	All finishes	$1,200	$1,500

Orville

1984-1993. Orville by Gibson and Orville guitars were made by Japan's Fuji Gen Gakki for Gibson. See following listing for details. Guitars listed here state only Orville (no By Gibson) on the headstock.

MODEL YEAR	FEATURES	EXC. COND. LOW	HIGH

Electric

1990s	CE Atkins	$700	$800
1990s	ES-335	$1,000	$1,250
1990s	Les Paul Custom	$700	$800
1990s	Les Paul Standard	$700	$800

Orville by Gibson

1984-1993. Orville by Gibson and Orville guitars were made by Japan's Fuji Gen Gakki for Gibson. Basically the same models except the Orville by Gibson guitars had real Gibson USA PAF '57 Classic pickups and a true nitrocellulose lacquer finish. The Orville models used Japanese electronics and a poly finish. Some Orvilles were made in Korea and are of a lower quality. These Korean guitars had the serial number printed on a sticker. Prices here are for the Orville by Gibson models.

Electric

1990-1994	Les Paul Standard	$1,100	$1,300
1990s	Explorer	$1,100	$1,300
1990s	Les Paul Jr., double-cut	$500	$600
1990s	Les Paul Studio J.P.	$900	$1,100
1990s	MM/Les Paul Jr., single-cut	$400	$500
1990s	SG Les Paul Standard	$650	$800
1993	ES-175	$1,100	$1,300
1993	ES-335	$1,300	$1,600
1995	Flying V	$1,100	$1,300
1995-1998	Les Paul Custom	$1,100	$1,300

Osborne Sound Laboratories

Late 1970s. Founded by Ralph Scaffidi and wife guitarist Mary Osborne; originally building guitar amps, they did also offer solidbody guitars.

Oscar Schmidt

1879-1938, 1979-present. Budget and intermediate grade, production, acoustic, acoustic/electric, and electric guitars distributed by U.S. Music Corp. (Washburn, Randall, etc.). They also offer basses, mandolins, banjos, ukuleles and the famous Oscar Schmidt autoharp.

The original Oscar Schmidt Company, Jersey City, New Jersey, offered banjo mandolins, tenor banjos, guitar banjos, ukuleles, mandolins and guitars under their own brand and others (including Sovereign and Stella). By the early 1900s, the company had factories in the U.S. and Europe producing instruments producing instruments under their own brand as well as other brands for mailorder and other distributors. Oscar Schmidt was also an early contributor to innovative mandolin designs and the company participated in the '00-'30 mandolin boom. The company hit hard times during the Depression and was sold to Harmony by the end of the '30s. In '79, Washburn acquired the brand and it is now part of U.S. Music.

MODEL YEAR	FEATURES	EXC. COND. LOW	HIGH

Oskar Graf Guitars

1970-present. Premium and presentation grade, custom, archtop, acoustic and classical guitars built in Clarendon, Ontario, by luthier Oskar Graf. He also builds basses and lutes.

Otwin

1950s-1960s. A brand used on electric guitars made by the Musima company of East Germany. Musima also produced guitars under their own brand.

Outbound Instruments

1990-2002. Intermediate grade, production, travel-size acoustics from the Boulder, Colorado-based company.

Ovation

1966-present. Intermediate and professional grade, production, acoustic and acoustic/electric guitars built in the U.S. They also build basses and mandolins.

Ovation's parent company, helicopter manufacturer Kaman Corporation, was founded in 1945 by jazz guitarist and aeronautical engineer Charles Huron Kaman in Bloomfield, Connecticut. In the '60s, after losing a government contract, Kaman began looking to diversify. When offers to buy Martin and Harmony were rejected, Kaman decided to use their helicopter expertise (working with synthetic materials, spruce, high tolerances) and designed, with the help of employee and violin restorer John Ringso, the first fiberglass-backed (Lyracord) acoustic guitars in '65. Production began in '66 and the music factory moved to New Hartford, Connecticut, in '67. Early input was provided by fingerstyle jazz guitarist Charlie Byrd, who gave Kaman the idea for the name Ovation. C. William Kaman II became president of the company in '85. Kaman Music purchased Hamer Guitars in '88, and Trace Elliot amplifiers (U.K.) in '90. On January 1, '08, Fender acquired Kaman Music Corporation and the Ovation brand.

Adamas 1581-KK Kaki King

2011-present. Classic deep bowl cutaway, 5-piece mahogany/maple neck, rosewood 'board, 12th-fret crown inlay, OP-Pro preamp, Kaki personally signs the label on each guitar.

2011		$2,400	$2,800

Adamas 1587

1979-1998. Carbon top, walnut, single-cut, bowl back, binding, mini-soundholes.

1979-1998	Black Sparkle	$1,200	$1,500

Adamas 1597

1998-1999. Carbon birch composite top, on-board electronics.

1998-1999	Black	$550	$700

Adamas 1598-MEII Melissa Etheridge

2001-present. Classic mid-depth cutaway, ebony 'board and bridge, custom 'ME' maple symbol at 12th fret, OP-Pro preamp, Melissa personally signs the label on each guitar.

2001-2010	12-string	$1,200	$1,400

Adamas 1687

1977-1998. Acoustic/electric, carbon top, non-cut, bowl back, mini-soundholes.

1977-1998	Sunburst	$1,200	$1,500

Adamas CVT W591

2000. Crossweave fiber top, mid-depth body, on-board electronics.

2000		$850	$1,050

Adamas II 1881 NB-2

1993-1998. Acoustic/electric, single-cut, shallow bowl.

1993-1998	Brown	$1,100	$1,400

Adamas Millenium

2000	Cobalt Blue	$1,900	$2,200

Anniversary Electric 1657

1978. Deep bowl, acoustic/electric, abalone inlays, gold-plated parts, carved bridge, for Ovation's 10th anniversary. They also offered an acoustic Anniversary.

1978		$300	$400

Balladeer 1111

1968-1983, 1993-2000. Acoustic, non-cut with deep bowl, bound body, natural top, later called the Standard Balladeer.

1976-1983	Natural	$225	$300

Balladeer Artist 1121

1968-1990. Acoustic, non-cut with shallow bowl, bound body.

1968-1969	Early production	$300	$400
1970-1990		$225	$300

Balladeer Classic 1122

1970s. Classical shallow-bowl version of Concert Classic, nylon strings, slotted headstock.

1970s		$200	$275

Balladeer Custom 1112

1976-1990. Acoustic, deep bowl, diamond inlays.

1976-1990	Natural	$275	$375

Balladeer Custom 12-String Electric 1655/1755

1982-1994. 12-string version of Balladeer Custom Electric.

1982-1994	Sunburst	$275	$375

Balladeer Custom Electric 1612/1712

1976-1990. Acoustic/electric version of Balladeer Custom, deep bowl.

1976-1990	Natural	$325	$425

Balladeer Standard 1561/1661/1761/1861

1982-2000. Acoustic/electric, deep bowl, rounded cutaway.

1982-2000		$350	$450

Balladeer Standard 1771 LX

2008-2010. Acoustic/electric, mid-depth bowl, rosewood, sitka spruce top.

2008-2010		$400	$500

Balladeer Standard 12-String 6751 LX

2008-2010. Acoustic/electric, 12 strings, rosewood, spruce top.

2008-2010		$475	$575

Breadwinner 1251

1971-1983. Axe-like shaped single-cut solidbody, 2 pickups, textured finish, black, blue, tan or white.

1971-1983		$650	$800

1994 Ovation Adamas 1687

Ovation Balladeer Standard 1771 LX

Ovation Celebrity CC-48

*Ovation Collectors Series
2007-BCS*

MODEL YEAR	FEATURES	EXC. COND. LOW	HIGH

Celebrity CC-48
2007-present. Acoustic/electric, super shallow, laminated spruce top, white bound rosewood 'board with abalone dot inlays.

| 2007-2010 | | $200 | $250 |

Celebrity CC-57
1990-1996. Laminated spruce top, shallow bowl, mahogany neck.

| 1990-1996 | Black | $200 | $250 |

Celebrity CK-057
2002-2004. Acoustic/electric rounded cutaway, shallow back.

| 2002-2004 | | $275 | $325 |

Celebrity CS-257
1992-2005. Made in Korea, super shallow bowl back body, single-cut, Adamas soundholes, alternating dot and diamond markers.

| 1992-2005 | Celebrity | $250 | $300 |
| 2010 | Celebrity Deluxe | $350 | $425 |

Classic 1613/1713
1971-1993. Acoustic/electric, non-cut, deep bowl, no inlay, slotted headstock, gold tuners.

| 1971-1993 | Natural | $400 | $500 |

Classic 1663/1763
1982-1998. Acoustic/electric, single-cut, deep bowl, cedar top, EQ, no inlay, slotted headstock, gold tuners.

| 1982-1998 | | $475 | $575 |

Classic 1863
1989-1998. Acoustic/electric, single-cut, shallow bowl, no inlay, cedar top, EQ, slotted headstock, gold tuners.

| 1989-1998 | | $400 | $500 |

Collectors Series
1982-present. Limited edition, different model featured each year and production limited to that year only, the year designation is marked at the 12th fret, various colors (each year different).

| 1982-2010 | Common models | $425 | $500 |
| 1982-2010 | Rare models | $600 | $1,200 |

Concert Classic 1116
1974-1990. Deep-bowl nylon string classical, slotted headstock.

| 1974-1990 | | $225 | $275 |

Contemporary Folk Classic Electric 1616
1974-1990. Acoustic/electric, no inlay, slotted headstock, natural or sunburst.

| 1974-1990 | Natural | $200 | $300 |

Country Artist Classic Electric 1624
1971-1990. Nylon strings, slotted headstock, standard steel-string sized neck to simulate a folk guitar, on-board electronics.

| 1971-1990 | | $350 | $400 |

Country Artist Classic Electric 6773
1995-present. Classic electric, soft-cut, solid spruce top, slotted headstock, Ovation pickup system.

| 1995-2010 | | $350 | $400 |

Custom Ballader 1762
1992. Rounded cutaway, higher-end specs.

| 1992 | | $600 | $675 |

MODEL YEAR	FEATURES	EXC. COND. LOW	HIGH

Custom Legend 1117
1970s. Non-electrical 2nd generation Ovation, higher-end with abalone inlays and gold hardware, open V-bracing pattern. Model 1117-4, natural.

| 1970s | | $450 | $550 |

Custom Legend 1569
1980s. Rounded cutaway acoustic/electric, super shallow bowl, gloss black finish.

| 1980s | | $475 | $600 |

Custom Legend 1619/1719
1970s. Acoustic/electric 2nd generation Ovation, electric version of model 1117, higher-end with abalone inlays and gold hardware, open V-bracing pattern.

| 1970s | | $475 | $600 |

Custom Legend 1759
1984-2004. Single-cut acoustic/electric.

| 1990s | | $650 | $775 |

Custom Legend 1769
1982, 1993, 1996-1999. Single-cut acoustic/electric.

| 1990s | | $800 | $900 |

Custom Legend 1869
1994, 2003. Acoustic/electric, cutaway, super shallow bowl.

| 1994 | Natural | $600 | $750 |
| 2003 | | $600 | $750 |

Deacon 1252
1973-1980. Axe-shaped solidbody electric, active electronics, diamond fret markers.

| 1973-1980 | Sunburst | $600 | $750 |

Deacon 12-String 1253
1975. Axe-shaped solidbody, diamond inlay, 2 pickups. only a few made.

| 1975 | | $600 | $750 |

Eclipse
1971-1973. Thinline double cut acoustic-electric archtop, 2 pickups.

| 1971-1973 | | $600 | $750 |

Elite 1718
1982-1997. Acoustic/electric, non-cut, deep bowl, solid spruce top, Adamas-type soundhole, volume and tone controls, stereo output.

| 1982-1997 | Sunburst | $600 | $700 |

Elite 1758
1990-1998. Acoustic/electric, non-cut, deep bowl.

| 1990-1998 | | $625 | $750 |

Elite 1768
1990-1998. Acoustic/electric, cutaway, deep bowl.

| 1990-1998 | Natural | $575 | $700 |

Elite 1858 12-String
1993-2004. 12-string acoustic/electric, ebony 'board and bridge.

| 1993-2004 | | $700 | $850 |

Elite 1868
1983-2004. Acoustic/electric, cutaway, shallow bowl.

| 1983-2004 | Sunburst | $550 | $650 |

Elite 5858
1991. Super shallow bowl, single cutaway, Adamas-style soundhole, gold hardware, on-board factory OP24 pickup.

| 1991 | | $575 | $675 |

MODEL YEAR FEATURES	EXC. COND. LOW	HIGH
Elite Doubleneck		
1989-1990s. Six- and 12-string necks, can be ordered with a variety of custom options.		
1989	$750	$900
Elite Standard 6868		
1997	$550	$650
Folklore 1614		
1972-1983. Acoustic/electric, 12-fret neck on full-size body, wide neck, on-board electronics.		
1972-1983	$425	$525
GCXT		
2008. Acoustic-electric, single-cut, flamed paint graphic, made for Guitar Center.		
2008	$425	$525
Glen Campbell 12-String 1118 (K-1118)		
1968-1982. Acoustic, 12 strings, shallow bowl version of Legend, gold tuners, diamond inlay.		
1968-1982	$425	$525
Glen Campbell Artist 1627		
2006. Glen Campbell 40th Anniversary model, diamond inlay, gold tuners.		
2006	$850	$1,050
Glen Campbell Artist Balladeer 1127		
1968-1990. Acoustic, shallow bowl, diamond inlay, gold tuners.		
1968-1990 Natural	$425	$525
Hurricane 12-String K-1120		
1968-1969. ES-335-style electric semi-hollowbody, double-cut, 12 strings, f-holes, 2 pickups.		
1968-1969	$575	$700
Josh White 1114		
1967-1970, 1972-1983. Designed by and for folk and blues singer Josh White, has wide 12-fret to the body neck, dot markers, classical-style tuners.		
1967-1970	$475	$575
1972-1983	$400	$500
Legend 1117		
1972-1999. Deep bowl acoustic, 5-ply top binding, gold tuners, various colors (most natural).		
1972-1999	$400	$500
Legend 1567/1867		
1984-2004. Acoustic/electric, shallow bowl, single-cut, gold tuners.		
1984-2004	$475	$575
Legend 12-String 1866		
1989-2007. Acoustic/electric, cutaway, 12 strings, shallow bowl, 5-ply top binding.		
1989-2007 Black	$475	$575
Legend 1717		
1990-2008. Acoustic/electric, 5-ply top binding, various colors.		
1990-2008	$450	$525
Legend 1767		
1990s. Acoustic/electric, deep bowl, single-cut, black.		
1990s	$450	$525
Legend Cutaway 1667		
1982-1996. Acoustic/electric, cutaway, deep bowl, abalone, gold tuners.		
1982-1996	$500	$600

MODEL YEAR FEATURES	EXC. COND. LOW	HIGH
Legend Electric 1617		
1972-1998. Acoustic/electric, deep bowl, abalone, gold tuners, various colors.		
1972-1998	$325	$400
Pacemaker 12-String 1115/1615		
1968-1982. Originally called the K-1115 12-string, Renamed Pacemaker in '72.		
1968-1982	$425	$525
Patriot Bicentennial		
*1976. Limited run of 1776 guitars, Legend Custom model with drum and flag decal and 1776*1976 decal on lower bout.*		
1976	$700	$875
Pinnacle		
1990-1992. Spruce or sycamore top, broad leaf pattern rosette, mahogany neck, piezo bridge pickup.		
1990-1992 Sunburst	$375	$475
Pinnacle Shallow Cutaway		
1990-1994. Pinnacle with shallow bowl body and single-cut.		
1990-1994 Sunburst	$375	$475
Preacher 1281		
1975-1982. Solidbody, mahogany body, double-cut, 2 pickups.		
1975-1982	$525	$650
Preacher Deluxe 1282		
1975-1982. Double-cut solidbody, 2 pickups with series/parallel pickup switch and mid-range control.		
1975-1982	$475	$575
Preacher 12-String 1285		
1975-1983. Double-cut solidbody, 12 strings, 2 pickups.		
1975-1983	$525	$650
Thunderhead 1460		
1968-1972. Double-cut, 2 pickups, gold hardware, phase switch, master volume, separate tone controls, pickup balance/blend control, vibrato.		
1968-1972 Natural or rare color	$950	$1,150
1968-1972 Sunburst	$775	$950
Tornado 1260		
1968-1973. Same as Thunderhead without phase switch, with chrome hardware.		
1968-1973	$600	$700
UK II 1291		
1980-1982. Single-cut solidbody, 2 pickups, body made of Urelite on aluminum frame, bolt-on neck, gold hardware.		
1980-1982	$700	$875
Ultra GS/GP Series		
1984. Korean solidbodies and necks assembled in U.S., DiMarzio pickups, offset double-cut (GS) with 1 hum, or hum/single/single or LP style (GP) with 2 humbuckers. There was also a bass.		
1984	$325	$400
Ultra Series		
1970-2000s. Various Ultra model acoustic/electrics.		
1970-2000s	$150	$600
Viper 1271		
1975-1982. Single-cut, 2 single-coil pickups.		
1975-1982	$550	$700

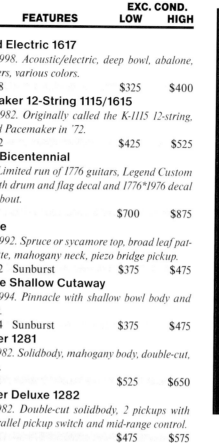

1980 Ovation Deacon
Jon Way

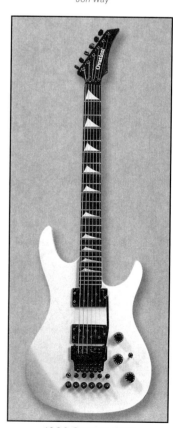

1986 Ovation G2S

Ovation Viper III 1273

Overture Relic

MODEL YEAR	FEATURES	EXC. COND. LOW	HIGH

Viper EA 68
1994-2008. Thin acoustic/electric, single-cut mahogany body, spruce top over sound chamber with multiple upper bout soundholes, black.

| 1994-2008 | | $550 | $700 |

Viper III 1273
1975-1982. Single-cut, 3 single-coil pickups.

| 1975-1982 | | $550 | $700 |

VXT Hybrid
2007-2009. Single-cut solidbody, 2 Seymour Duncan '59 humbuckers, Fishman Power Bridge.

| 2007-2009 | | $625 | $775 |

Overture Guitars
2008-present. Luthier Justin Hoffman builds professional to presentation grade, custom/production, solidbody guitars in Morton, Illinois. He also builds basses.

P. W. Crump Company
1975-present. Luthier Phil Crump builds his custom flat-top guitars in Arcata, California. He also builds mandolin-family instruments.

Pagan
Guitars made in Germany and imported into the U.S. by a guitar shop.

Palen
1998-present. Premium grade, production/custom, archtop guitars built by luthier Nelson Palen in Beloit, Kansas.

Palmer
Early 1970s-present. Budget and intermediate grade, production acoustic, acoustic/electric and classical guitars imported from Europe and Asia. They also have offered electrics.

Panache
2004-present. Budget grade, production, solidbody electric and acoustic guitars imported from China.

PANaramic
1961-1963. Guitars and basses made in Italy by the Crucianelli accordion company and imported by PANaramic accordion. They also offered amps made by Magnatone.

Acoustic-Electric Archtop
1961-1963. Full body cutaway, 2 pickups.

| 1961-1963 | | $1,100 | $1,400 |

Pantheon Guitars
2000-present. Patrick Theimer created Pantheon which offers premium grade, production/custom, flat-tops built by seven luthiers (including Dana Bourgeois) working in an old 1840s textile mill in Lewiston, Maine.

Paolo Soprani
Early 1960s. Italian plastic covered guitars with pushbutton controls made by the Polverini Brothers.

Paramount
1920s-1942, Late 1940s. The William L. Lange Company began selling Paramount banjos, guitar banjos and mandolin banjos in the early 1920s, and added archtop guitars in '34. The guitars were made by Martin and possibly others. Lange went out of business by '42; Gretsch picked up the Paramount name and used it on acoustics and electrics for a time in the late '40s.

GB
1920s-1930s. Guitar banjo.

| 1920s | | $1,200 | $1,500 |

Style C
1930s. 16" acoustic archtop, maple back and sides.

| 1930s | | $450 | $550 |

Style L
1930s. Small body with resonator, limited production to about 36 instruments.

| 1930s | Spanish 6-string | $3,200 | $4,000 |
| 1930s | Tenor 4-string | $2,800 | $3,500 |

Parker
1992-present. U.S.-made and imported intermediate, professional, and premium grade, production/custom, solidbody guitars featuring a thin skin of carbon and glass fibers bonded to a wooden guitar body. In '05, they added wood body acoustic/electrics. They also build basses. Originally located northwest of Boston, Parker was founded by Ken Parker and Larry Fishman (Fishman Transducers). Korg USA committed money to get the Fly Deluxe model into production in July '93. Parker added a Custom Shop in '03 to produce special build instruments and non-core higher-end models that were no longer available as a standard product offering. In early '04, Parker was acquired by U.S. Music Corp. and moved USA production from the Boston area to Chicago.

Concert
1997 only. Solid sitka spruce top, only piezo system pickup, no magnetic pickups, transparent butterscotch.

| 1997 | | $1,200 | $1,450 |

Fly
1993-1994. There are many Parker Fly models, the model simply called Fly is similar to the more common Fly Deluxe, except it does not have the Fishman piezo pickup system.

| 1993-1994 | | $1,100 | $1,350 |

Fly Artist
1998-1999. Solid sitka spruce top, vibrato, Deluxe-style electronics, transparent blond finish.

| 1998-1999 | | $1,500 | $1,750 |

Fly Classic
1996-1998, 2000-present. One-piece Honduras mahogany body, basswood neck, electronics same as Fly Deluxe.

| 1996-2010 | | $1,200 | $1,450 |

MODEL YEAR	FEATURES	EXC. COND. LOW	HIGH

Fly Classic Maple
2000. Classic with maple body (vs. mahogany), transparent butterscotch.

2000		$1,200	$1,450

Fly Deluxe
1993-present. Poplar body, basswood neck, 2 pickups, Fishman bridge transducer, '93-'96 models were offered with or without vibrato, then non-vibrato discontinued. The Deluxe normally came with a gig bag, but also offered with a hardshell case, which would add about $50 to the values listed.

1993-2010		$1,100	$1,350

Fly Supreme
1996-1999. One-piece flame maple body, electronics same as the Fly Deluxe, highly flamed butterscotch, includes hard molded case.

1996-1999		$1,800	$2,200

Mojo
2003-2010. Fly double-cut.

2003-2010		$1,600	$1,900

NiteFly/NiteFly NFV1/NFV3/NFV5
1996-1999. Three single-coil pickup NiteFly, Fishman piezo system, bolt neck, maple body for '96-'98, ash for '99. Called the NiteFly in '96, NiteFly NFV1 ('97-'98), NiteFly NFV3 ('98), NiteFly NFV5 ('99).

1996-1999		$575	$700

NiteFly/NiteFly NFV2/NFV4/NFV6/SA
1996-2009. Two single-coil and 1 humbucker pickup NiteFly, Fishman piezo system, bolt neck, maple body for '96-'98, ash for '99-present. Called the NiteFly in '96, NiteFly NFV2 ('97-'98), NiteFly NFV4 ('98), NiteFly NFV6 ('99), NiteFly SA ('00-present).

1996-2009		$525	$650

P Series
2000-2009. Various models include P-38 (ash body, bolt maple neck, rosewood 'board, vibrato, piezo bridge pickup and active Parker Alnico humbucker and 2 single-coils, gig bag); P-40 (as P-38, but with pickups mounted on body, no 'guard); P-44 (mahogany body, flamed maple top, piezo bridge pickup and 2 special Parker humbuckers).

2000-2009		$250	$450

Tulipwood Limited Edition
1998. Limited build of 35 guitars, standard Deluxe features with tulipwood body.

1998		$1,200	$1,450

Patrick Eggle Guitars
1991-present. Founded by Patrick Eggle and others in Birmingham, England, building solid and semi-solidbody electric guitars. They also build basses. In '95, Eggle left the company to build acoustics.

Patrick James Eggle
2001-present. Eggle co-founded the Patrick Eggle Guitar company in '91 building solidbodies. In '95, he left to do repairs and custom work. In '01 he opened a new workshop in Bedforshire, England, building professional and premium grade, production/custom, archtop and flatop guitars. He has since relocated to Hendersonville, North Carolina.

MODEL YEAR	FEATURES	EXC. COND. LOW	HIGH

Paul Berger
1972-present. Acoustic guitars built by luthier Paul Berger originally in Apopka, Florida, and currently in Nazareth, Pennsylvania.

Paul H. Jacobson
1974-present. Premium grade, production/custom, classical guitars built by luthier Paul H. Jacobson in Cleveland, Missouri.

Paul Reed Smith
1985-present. Intermediate, professional and premium grade, production/custom, solid, semi-hollow body, and acoustic guitars made in the U.S. and imported. They also build basses. Paul Reed Smith built his first guitar in '75 as an independent study project in college and refined his design over the next 10 years building custom guitars. After building two prototypes and getting several orders from East Coast guitar dealers, Smith was able to secure the support necessary to start PRS in a factory on Virginia Avenue in Annapolis, Maryland. On '95, they moved to their current location on Kent Island in Stevensville. In 2001 PRS introduced the Korean-made SE Series. Acoustics were added in '08.

10th Anniversary
1995. Only 200 made, offset double-cut, carved maple figured top, mahogany body, ebony 'board, mother-of-pearl inlays, abalone purfling, gold McCarty pickups, either 22-fret wide-fat or wide-thin mahogany neck, 10th Anniversary logo, price includes Certificate of Authenticity.

1995	With certificate	$4,500	$5,500

513 Rosewood
Dec. 2003-2006. Brazilian rosewood neck, newly developed PRS pickup system with 13 sound settings, hum-single-hum pickups.

2003-2006		$2,800	$3,400

513 25th Anniversary
2010. Carved figured maple top, 25th Anniversary shadow birds inlay.

2010		$2,400	$2,900

Artist/Artist I/Artist 24
1991-1994. Carved maple top, offset double-cut mahogany body, 24-fret neck, bird markers, less than 500 made. A different Custom 24 Artist package was subsequently offered in the 2000s.

1991-1994		$3,400	$4,200

Artist II/Artist 22
1993-1995. Curly maple top, mahogany body and neck, maple purfling on rosewood 'board, inlaid maple bound headstock, abalone birds, 22 frets, gold hardware, short run of less than 500 instruments.

1993-1995		$2,300	$2,800

Artist III
1996-1997. Continuation of the 22-fret neck with some changes in materials and specs, figured maple tops, short run of less than 500 instruments.

1996-1997		$2,700	$3,300

Pantheon Vintage Dreadnought

PRS 513 Rosewood

PRS CE 22

PRS Custom 22

Artist IV

1996. Continuation of the 22-fret neck with some upgrades in materials and specs, short run of less than 70 instruments.

1996		$3,700	$4,500

Artist Limited

1994-1995. Like the Artist II with 14-carat gold bird inlays, abalone purfling on neck, headstock and truss rod cover, Brazilian rosewood 'board, 165 made.

1994-1995		$3,700	$4,500

CE 22

1994-2000, 2005-2008. Double-cut carved alder body (1995), mahogany '96-'00 and '05-'07, back to alder in '08, bolt-on maple neck with rosewood 'board, dot inlays, 2 humbuckers, chrome hardware, translucent colors, options include vibrato and gold hardware and custom colors.

1994-1995	Alder	$1,100	$1,300
1996-2000	Mahogany	$1,100	$1,300
2005-2008	Reintroduced	$1,100	$1,300

CE 22 Maple Top

1994-2008. CE 22 with figured maple top, upgrade options included gold hardware, custom colors or 10 top.

1994-1995		$1,200	$1,400
1996-1999		$1,200	$1,400
2000-2004		$1,200	$1,400
2005-2008		$1,200	$1,400

CE 24 (Classic Electric, CE)

1988-2000, 2005-2008. Double-cut, alder body to '95, mahogany '96-'00 and '05-'07, back to alder in '08, carved top, 24-fret bolt-on maple neck, 2 humbuckers, dot inlays, upgrade options included gold hardware, custom colors or 10 top.

1988-1991	Rosewood 'board	$1,400	$1,600
1992-1995	Alder	$1,400	$1,600
1996-2000	Mahogany	$1,200	$1,400
2005-2007	Mahogany	$1,200	$1,400

CE 24 Maple Top (CE Maple Top)

1989-2008. CE 24 with figured maple top, upgrade options may include any or all the following: gold hardware, custom colors or 10 top.

1988-1991		$1,500	$1,800
1992-1995		$1,500	$1,800
1996-1999		$1,300	$1,600
2000-2008		$1,300	$1,600

Chris Henderson Model

2007-present. Single-cut, 3 exposed humbucker pickups, carved flame maple top on mahogany body, wide flat neck profile, 22 frets.

2007-2010		$1,500	$1,800

Corvette

2005-2006. Custom 22 with Velcity Yellow finish, Standard 22 red finish, Z06 inlays, Corvette logo on body.

2005	Custom 22, yellow	$1,250	$1,550
2006	Standard 22, red	$1,250	$1,550

Custom (Custom 24/PRS Custom)

1985-present. Double-cut solidbody, curly maple top, mahogany back and neck, pearl and abalone moon inlays, 24 frets, 2 humbuckers, tremolo, options include quilted or 10 Top, bird inlays, and gold hardware.

1985		$5,000	$5,800

MODEL YEAR	FEATURES	EXC. COND. LOW	HIGH
1985	Premium top	$5,800	$7,100
1986		$4,800	$5,600
1986	Premium top	$5,600	$7,000
1987		$3,800	$4,400
1987	Premium top	$4,400	$5,600
1988		$3,300	$4,000
1988	Premium top	$4,000	$5,000
1989		$2,800	$3,800
1989	Premium top	$3,800	$4,800
1990-1995		$1,900	$2,400
1996-2004		$1,750	$2,200
1996-2004	Custom 24 Artist	$1,900	$2,400
2005-2010		$1,700	$2,200
2005-2010	Custom 24 Artist	$1,900	$2,400

Custom 22

1993-2009. Custom 22 with flamed or quilted maple top on mahogany body, 22-fret set-neck, upgrade option is gold hardware, normally the quilt top is higher than flamed top.

1993-1995		$1,600	$2,000
1996-1999		$1,600	$2,000
2000-2005	Custom 22 Artist, bird markers	$1,800	$2,200
2000-2005	Dot marker	$1,600	$2,000
2006-2009		$1,800	$2,200

Custom 22 (Brazilian)

2003-2004. Limited run of 500 with Brazilian rosewood 'board, figured 10 top, pearl bird inlays.

2003-2004		$3,300	$4,100

Custom 22 20th Anniversary

2005. Abalone 20th Anniversary birds inlay, 20th engraved on truss rod cover.

2005		$2,200	$2,600

Custom 22 Soapbar

1998-2002. 3 Seymour Duncan soapbar single-coils.

1998-2002		$1,700	$2,100

Custom 22/12

December 2003-2009. 12-string version, flame or quilt maple top, hum/single/hum pickups.

2003-2009		$2,300	$2,900

Custom 24 (Brazilian)

2003-2004. Limited run with Brazilian rosewood 'board, figured 10 top, pearl bird inlays.

2003-2004		$3,400	$4,000

Custom 24 (Walnut)

1992. Seamless matched walnut over mahogany, 3 made.

1992		$3,400	$4,000

Custom 24 20th Anniversary

2005. Abalone 20th Anniversary birds inlay, 20th engraved on truss rod cover.

2005		$1,500	$1,800

Custom 24 25th Anniversary

2010. Carved figured maple top, 25th Anniversary shadow birds inlay.

2010		$1,900	$2,400

Dave Navarro Signature

2005-present. Carved maple top, bird inlays, tremolo, white.

2005-2010		$1,450	$1,800

The *Vintage Guitar Price Guide* shows low to high values for items in all-original excellent condition, and, where applicable, with original case or cover.

MODEL YEAR	FEATURES	EXC. COND. LOW	HIGH

DGT David Grissom Tremolo

2007-present. Based on the McCarty Tremolo model with an added volume control, a nitro topcoat, vintage colors, large frets designed for .011 gauge strings.

| 2007-2010 | | $1,700 | $2,100 |

Dragon I

1992. 22 frets, PRS Dragon pickups, wide-fat neck, gold hardware, 'board inlay of a dragon made of 201 pieces of abalone, turquoise and mother-of-pearl, limited production of 50 guitars.

| 1992 | | $17,000 | $20,000 |

Dragon II

1993. 22 frets, PRS Dragon pickups, wide-fat neck, gold hardware, 'board inlay of a dragon made of 218 pieces of gold, coral, abalone, malachite, onyx and mother-of-pearl, limited production of 100 guitars.

| 1993 | | $11,000 | $13,000 |

Dragon III

1994. Carved maple top, mahogany back, 22 frets, PRS Dragon pickups, wide-fat neck, gold hardware, 'board inlay of a dragon made of 438 pieces of gold, red and green abalone, mother-of-pearl, mammoth ivory, and stone, limited production of 100 guitars.

| 1994 | | $11,000 | $13,000 |

Dragon 2000

1999-2000. Three-D dragon inlay in body versus neck inlay of previous models, limited production of 50 guitars.

| 1999-2000 | | $10,500 | $12,000 |

Dragon 2002

2002. Limited edition of 100 guitars, ultra-inlay work depicting dragon head on the guitar body.

| 2002 | | $10,500 | $12,000 |

Dragon 25th Anniversary

Late 2009-Early 2010. 60 made, carved maple Private Stock top and African striped mahogany back, 59/09 pickups, multi-material dragon fingerboard inlay, green ripple abalone Modern Eagle headstock, body shape and electronics are modeled after an early company PRS guitar.

| 2009-2010 | | $12,000 | $14,000 |

Dragon Doubleneck

2005. Limited edition 20th Anniversary model, about 50 made.

| 2005 | | $13,000 | $15,000 |

EG II

1991-1995. Double-cut solidbody, bolt-on neck, 3 single-coils, single-single-hum, or hum-single-hum pickup options, opaque finish.

| 1991-1995 | | $1,000 | $1,200 |

EG II Maple Top

1991-1995. EG II with flamed maple top, chrome hardware.

| 1991-1995 | | $1,300 | $1,600 |

EG 3

1990-1991. Double-cut solidbody, bolt-on 22-fret neck, 3 single-coil pickups.

1990-1991	Flamed 10 top	$1,300	$1,600
1990-1991	Opaque finish	$1,100	$1,300
1990-1991	Plain top, sunburst	$1,100	$1,300

EG 4

1990-1991. Similar to EG 3 with single-single-hum pickup configuration, opaque finish.

| 1990-1991 | | $1,100 | $1,300 |

Golden Eagle

1997-1998. Very limited production, eagle head and shoulders carved into lower bouts, varied high-end appointments.

| 1997-1998 | | $14,500 | $17,000 |

Johnny Hiland

2006-2007. Maple fretboard.

| 2006-2007 | | $1,400 | $1,750 |

KQ-24 Custom 24 (Killer Quilt)

2009. Limited Edition of 120, quilted maple top over korina body, 24 frets.

| 2009 | | $2,000 | $2,300 |

Limited Edition

1989-1991, 2000. Double-cut, semi-hollow mahogany body, figured cedar top, gold hardware, less than 300 made. In '00, single-cut, short run of 5 antique white and 5 black offered via Garrett Park Guitars.

| 1989-1991 | Various colors, tune-o-matic | $4,000 | $4,500 |
| 2000 | Various colors | $4,000 | $4,500 |

Limited Edition Howard Leese Golden Eagle

2009. Private Stock, curly maple top, old style mother of pearl birds, 100 made.

| 2009 | | $4,500 | $5,600 |

LTD Experience (Limited Experience)

2007. 200 built to commemorate PRS 2007 Experience Open House, 24 frets, matching headstock, maple top with mahogany body.

| 2007 | | $2,000 | $2,500 |

McCarty Model

1994-2007. Mahogany body with figured maple top, upgrade options may include a 10 top, gold hardware, bird inlays. Replaced by McCarty II.

1994-1995		$1,600	$2,000
1996-1999		$1,500	$1,900
2000-2005	Factory tremolo, low prod.	$1,400	$1,700
2000-2010		$1,400	$1,700

McCarty II

2008-2009. Replaced the McCarty, featured new MVC (Mastering Voice Control) circuitry for switching between a single-coil voice to a heavy-metal voice, opaque finish.

| 2008-2009 | | $1,400 | $1,700 |

McCarty Archtop (Spruce)

1998-2000. Deep mahogany body, archtop, spruce top, 22-fret set-neck.

| 1998-2000 | | $2,100 | $2,600 |

McCarty Archtop Artist

1998-2002. Highest grade figured maple top and highest appointments, gold hardware.

| 1998-2002 | | $3,600 | $4,400 |

McCarty Archtop II (Maple)

1998-2000. Like Archtop but with figured maple top.

| 1998-2000 | Flamed 10 top | $2,500 | $3,100 |
| 1998-2000 | Quilted 10 top | $2,500 | $3,100 |

2003 PRS Custom 24 (Brazilian)

2007 PRS DGT David Grissom Tremolo

GUITARS

PRS McCarty Soapbar

PRS Mira

MODEL YEAR	FEATURES	EXC. COND. LOW	HIGH

McCarty Hollowbody I/Hollowbody I
1998-2009. Medium deep mahogany hollowbody, maple top, 22-fret set-neck, chrome hardware. McCarty dropped from name in '06.

1998-2009		$2,100	$2,600
2000-2009	Baggs Piezo option	$2,200	$2,700

McCarty Hollowbody II/Hollowbody II
1998-present. Like Hollowbody I but with figured maple top and back. McCarty dropped from name in '06.

1998-2010		$2,600	$3,300

McCarty Hollowbody/Hollowbody Spruce
2000-2009. Similar to Hollowbody I with less appointmentsm spruce top. McCarty dropped from name in '06.

2000-2009		$2,500	$3,100

McCarty Model/McCarty Brazilian
2003-2004. Limited run of 250, Brazilian rosewood 'board, Brazilian is printed on headstock just below the PRS script logo.

1999		$3,400	$4,000
2003-2004		$3,000	$3,600

McCarty Rosewood
2004-2005. PRS-22 fret with Indian rosewood neck.

2004-2005		$2,000	$2,500

McCarty Soapbar (Korina)
2008-2009. Korina body, 2 Duncan soapbar pickups.

2008-2009		$1,500	$1,900

McCarty Soapbar (Maple)
1998-2007. Soapbar with figured maple top option, nickel hardware.

1998-2007		$1,500	$1,900

McCarty Soapbar/Soapbar Standard
1998-2009. Solid mahogany body, P-90-style soapbar pickups, 22-fret set-neck, nickel-plated hardware, upgrade options may include gold hardware and bird inlays.

1998-2009		$1,400	$1,700

McCarty Standard
1994-2006. McCarty Model with carved mahogany body but without maple top, nickel-plated hardware, upgrade options may include gold hardware and bird inlays.

1994-2006		$1,400	$1,700

Metal
1985-1986. Solid mahogany body with custom 2-color striped body finish and graphics, 24-fret set-neck, nickel hardware, 2 humbuckers.

1985-1986		$6,000	$7,000

Metal '85 Reissue (Private Stock)
2008. With Certificate of Authenticity.

2008		$5,300	$6,100

Mira
2007-present. US-made, 24 fret neck, regular or wide-thin neck profiles, non-adjustable stoptail, 2 exposed-coil humbuckers, abalone moon inlays, East Indian rosewood 'board, solid mahogany body and neck, various opaque finish options.

2007-2010	Korina, natural	$800	$1,000
2007-2010	Mahogany	$800	$1,000

Modern Eagle
2004-2007. Higher-end model based on Private Stock innovations, satin nitrocellulose finish, Brazilian rosewood neck.

2004-2007		$3,700	$4,500

Modern Eagle II/MEII
2008-2009. Curly maple top, black rosewood neck and 'board.

2008-2009		$3,100	$3,800

Modern Eagle Quatro/ME Quatro
2010-present. Updated version of Modern Eagle, 53/10 humbucker pickups, select upgraded woods.

2010		$2,700	$3,300

Private Stock Program
April 1996-present. One-off custom instruments based around existing designs such as the McCarty Model. Values may be somewhat near production equivalents or they may be higher. The Private Stock option was reintroduced by 2003 and a '03 typical offering might retail at about $7,500, but a '03 Santana I Private Stock might retail at over $15,000, so each guitar should be evaluated on a case-by-case basis.

1996-2010	Normal specs	$6,000	$7,500

PRS Guitar
1984-1986. Set-neck, solid mahogany body, 24-fret 'board, 2 humbuckers, chrome hardware, renamed Standard from '87-'98 then Standard 24 from '98. The wide range for PRS preproduction guitars is due to the fact each instruments needs to be valued on case by case basis.

1984-1985	Preproduction with provenance	$9,000	$35,000
1985-1986		$5,000	$8,000

Rosewood Limited
1996. Mahogany body with figured maple top, 1-piece rosewood neck with ultra-deluxe tree-of-life neck inlay, gold hardware.

1996		$8,000	$10,000

Santana
1995-1998. Mahogany body, slightly wider lower bout than other models, figured maple top, 24-fret set-neck, symmetric Santana headstock, unique body purfling, chrome and nickel-plated hardware, limited production special order.

1995-1998		$4,200	$5,200

Santana II
1998-2007. Three-way toggle replaces former dual mini-switches, special order.

1998-2007		$3,200	$3,900

Santana III
2001-2006. Less ornate version of Santana II.

2001-2006		$1,700	$2,100

Santana (Brazilian)
2003. Quilted maple top on mahogany body, Brazilian rosewood neck and fretboard, eagle inlay on headstock, Santana fretwire, Santana Brazilian logo on back cover plate, 200 made.

2003		$4,000	$5,000

SC 245
2008-2009. Single-cut 22-fret, 2 humbuckers, bird markers, SC 245 logo on truss rod cover.

2007-2009		$1,550	$1,800

The *Vintage Guitar Price Guide* shows low to high values for items in all-original excellent condition, and, where applicable, with original case or cover.

MODEL YEAR	FEATURES	EXC. COND. LOW	HIGH

SC 250

2007-2010. Figured maple top, 2 humbuckers, 25" scale and locking tuners.

| 2007-2010 | | $2,000 | $2,400 |

SC-J Thinline

2008. Large full-scale single-cut hollowbody, originally part of Private Stock program until made in limited run of 300, select grade maple top and back over a mahogany middle body section, SC-J logo on truss rod cover.

| 2008 | | $4,000 | $5,000 |

SE Series

2001-present. PRS import line.

| 2001-2010 | | $225 | $425 |

Signature/PRS Signature

1987-1991. Solid mahogany body, figured maple top, set-neck, 24 frets, hand-signed signature on headstock, limited run of 1,000.

| 1987-1991 | | $4,500 | $5,500 |

Signature (Private Stock)

2011-present. Limited run by Private Stock, 100 made, 408 humbucker pickups (8 tonal configurations), special signature headstock and fretboard inlays.

| 2011 | | $6,500 | $8,000 |

Singlecut

2000-2004, 2005-early 2007. Single-cut mahogany body, maple top, 22-fret 'board, upgrade options include 10 top flamed maple, gold hardware, bird inlays. Replaced by SC 245 and SC 250.

2000-2004	1st edition	$1,500	$1,900
2000-2004	Artist, maple top	$1,700	$2,100
2001	Brazilian neck/'board	$2,700	$3,300
2005-2007	2nd issue	$1,400	$1,800
2006	Artist 20th Anniv., Brazilian	$2,700	$3,300
2006	Standard 20th Anniv., Indian	$1,750	$1,950
2006-2007	Artist package	$1,600	$2,000
2007-2008	Ltd. Ed., Indian	$1,900	$2,200

Singlecut Standard Satin

2006-2007. Thinner solid mahogany body, thin nitro cellulose finish, humbuckers or soapbars.

| 2006-2007 | | $1,300 | $1,600 |

Special

1987-1990, 1991-1993. Similar to Standard with upgrades, wide-thin neck, 2 HFS humbuckers. From '91-'93, a special option package was offered featuring a wide-thin neck and high output humbuckers.

| 1987-1990 | Solid color finish | $2,500 | $3,000 |
| 1991-1993 | Special order only | $2,800 | $3,400 |

Standard

1987-1998. Set-neck, solid mahogany body, 24-fret 'board, 2 humbuckers, chrome hardware. Originally called the PRS Guitar from '85-'86 (see that listing), renamed Standard 24 from '98.

| 1987-1989 | Sunburst & optional colors | $2,700 | $3,200 |
| 1990-1991 | Last Brazilian 'board | $2,200 | $2,800 |

| 1992-1995 | | $1,200 | $1,500 |
| 1995-1998 | Stevensville | $1,100 | $1,400 |

Standard 22

1994-2009. 22-fret Standard.

1994-1995		$1,200	$1,500
1995-1999	Stevensville	$1,100	$1,400
2000-2009		$1,100	$1,400

Standard 24

1998-2009. Renamed from Standard, solid mahogany body, 24-fret set-neck.

| 1998-1999 | | $1,100 | $1,400 |
| 2000-2009 | | $1,100 | $1,400 |

Starla

2008-present. Single-cut solidbody with retro-vibe, glued neck, 2 chrome humbuckers.

| 2008-2010 | | $1,300 | $1,500 |

Studio

1988-1991. Standard model variant, solid mahogany body, 24-fret set-neck, chrome and nickel hardware, single-single-hum pickups, special Studio package offered '91-'96.

| 1988-1991 | | $1,600 | $1,900 |

Studio Maple Top

1990-1991. Mahogany solidbody, bird 'board inlays, 2 single-coils and 1 humbucker, tremolo, transparent finish.

| 1990-1991 | | $1,800 | $2,100 |

Swamp Ash Special

1996-2009. Solid swamp ash body, 22-fret bolt-on maple neck, 3 pickups, upgrade options available.

| 1996-2009 | | $1,300 | $1,600 |

Tonare Grand

2009-present. Full-body flat-top, European/German spruce top, rosewood back and sides, optional Adirondack red spruce top or AAAA grade top, onboard Acoustic Pickup System.

| 2009-2010 | | $3,200 | $3,700 |

Tremonti Signature (U.S.A.)

2001-present. Single-cut, contoured mahogany body, 2 humbuckers.

| 2001-2010 | Various options | $1,500 | $1,900 |
| 2004 | Tribal finish, about 60 made | $1,900 | $2,400 |

West Street/1980 West Street Limited

2008. 180 made for US market, 120 made for export market, faithful replica of the model made in the original West Street shop, Sapele top.

| 2008 | | $2,900 | $3,500 |

Pawar

1999-present. Founded by Jay Pawar, Jeff Johnston and Kevin Johnston in Willoughby Hills, Ohio, Pawar builds professional and premium grade, production/custom, solidbody guitars that feature the Pawar Positive Tone System with over 20 single coil and humbucker tones.

PBC Guitar Technology

See Bunker Guitars for more info.

2001 PRS Santana III

2009 PRS Starla X
Luke Single

GUITARS

Peavey Cropper Classic

Peavey Rotor EXP

MODEL YEAR	FEATURES	EXC. COND. LOW	HIGH

Peavey

1965-present. Headquartered in Meridan, Mississippi, Peavey builds budget, intermediate, professional, and premium grade, production/custom, acoustic and electric guitars. They also build basses, amps, PA gear, effects and drums. Hartley Peavey's first products were guitar amps. He added guitars to the mix in '78.

Axcelerator/AX
1994-1998. Offset double-cut swamp ash or poplar body, bolt-on maple neck, dot markers, AX with locking vibrato, various colors.

1994-1998		$325	$400

Cropper Classic
1995-2005. Single-cut solidbody, 1 humbucker and 1 single coil, figured maple top over thin mahogany body, transparent Onion Green.

1995-2005		$325	$400

Defender
1994-1995. Double-cut, solid poplar body, 2 humbuckers and 1 single-coil pickup, locking Floyd Rose tremolo, metallic or pearl finish.

1994-1995		$150	$200

Destiny
1989-1992. Double-cut, mahogany body, maple top, neck-thru-bridge, maple neck, 3 integrated pickups, double locking tremolo.

1989-1992		$250	$300

Destiny Custom
1989-1992. Destiny with figured wood and higher-end appointments, various colors.

1989-1992		$350	$425

Detonator AX
1995-1998. Double-cut, maple neck, rosewood 'board, dot markers, hum/single/hum pickups, black.

1995-1998		$175	$200

EVH Wolfgang
1996-2004. Offset double-cut, arched top, bolt neck, stop tailpiece or Floyd Rose vibrato, quilted or flamed maple top upgrade option.

1996	Pat. pending early production	$1,700	$2,100
1997-1998	Pat. pending	$1,300	$1,700
1999-2004	Flamed maple top	$1,100	$1,400
1999-2004	Standard top	$750	$950

EVH Wolfgang Special
1997-2004. Offset double-cut lower-end Wolfgang model, various opaque finishes, flamed top optional.

1996-2004	Standard top, D-Tuna	$750	$925
1997-2004	Flamed maple top	$750	$925
1997-2004	Standard basswood finish	$600	$725

Falcon/Falcon Active/Falcon Custom
1987-1992. Double-cut, 3 pickups, passive or active electronics, Kahler locking vibrato.

1987-1992	Custom color	$300	$350
1987-1992	Standard color	$200	$250

Firenza
1994-1999. Offset double-cut, bolt-on neck, single-coil pickups.

1994-1999		$275	$325

Firenza AX
1994-1999. Upscale Firenza Impact with humbucking pickups.

1994-1999		$300	$375

Generation Custom EX
2006-2008. Single-cut solidbody, 2 humbuckers, 5-way switch.

2006-2008		$125	$175

Generation S-1/S-2/S-3
1988-1994. Single-cut, maple cap on mahogany body, bolt-on maple neck, six-on-a-side tuners, active single/hum pickups, S-2 with locking vibrato system.

1988-1994		$125	$175

Horizon/Horizon II
1983-1985. Extended pointy horns, angled lower bout, maple body, rear routing for electronics, 2 humbucking pickups. Horizon II has added blade pickup.

1983-1985		$150	$175

HP Special USA
2008-present. Offset cutaway, 2 humbuckers.

2008-2010		$675	$800

Hydra Doubleneck
1985-1989. Available as a custom order, 6/12-string necks each with 2 humbuckers, 3-way pickup select.

1985-1989		$150	$175

Impact 1/Impact 2
1985-1987. Offset double-cut, Impact 1 has higher-end synthetic 'board, Impact 2 with conventional rosewood 'board.

1985-1987		$175	$225

Mantis
1984-1989. Hybrid X-shaped solidbody, 1 humbucking pickup, tremolo, laminated maple neck.

1984-1989		$200	$250

Milestone 12-String
1985-1986. Offset double-cut, 12 strings.

1985-1986		$150	$225

Milestone/Milestone Custom
1983-1986. Offset double-cut solidbody.

1983-1986		$100	$150

Mystic
1983-1989. Double-cut, 2 pickups, stop tailpiece initially, later Power Bend vibrato, maple body and neck.

1983-1989		$150	$225

Nitro I Active
1988-1990. Active electronics.

1988-1990		$200	$250

Nitro I/II/III
1986-1989. Offset double-cut, banana-style headstock, 1 humbucker (I), 2 humbuckers (II), or single/single/hum pickups (III).

1986-1989	Nitro I	$125	$150
1986-1989	Nitro II	$150	$200
1986-1989	Nitro III	$175	$250

Odyssey
1990-1994. Single-cut, figured carved maple top on mahogany body, humbuckers.

1990-1994		$400	$500

Odyssey 25th Anniversary
1990. Single-cut body, limited production.

1990		$525	$650

MODEL YEAR	FEATURES	EXC. COND. LOW	HIGH

Omniac JD USA

2005-2010. Jerry Donahue-designed single-cut solidbody, 2 single-coils.

2005-2010		$650	$775

Patriot

1983-1987. Double-cut, single bridge humbucker.

1983-1987		$140	$175

Patriot Plus

1983-1987. Double-cut, 2 humbucker pickups, bi-laminated maple neck.

1983-1987		$175	$200

Patriot Tremolo

1986-1990. Double-cut, single bridge humbucker, tremolo, replaced the standard Patriot.

1986-1990		$175	$200

Predator Plus 7ST

2008-2010. 7-string.

2008-2010		$225	$275

Predator Series

1985-1988, 1990-present. Double-cut poplar body, 2 pickups until '87, 3 after, vibrato.

1985-1988		$100	$125
1990-2010		$100	$125

Raptor Series

1997-present. Offset double-cut solidbody, 3 pickups.

1997-2010		$50	$75

Razer

1983-1989. Double-cut with arrowhead point for lower bout, 2 pickups, 1 volume and 2 tone controls, stop tailpiece or vibrato.

1983-1989		$300	$375

Reactor

1993-1999. Classic single-cut style, 2 single-coils.

1993-1999		$275	$300

Rockmaster II Stage Pack

2000s. Student solidbody Rockmaster electric guitar and GT-5 amp pack.

2000		$40	$50

Rotor Series

2004-2010. Classic futuristic body, elongated upper treble bout/lower bass bout, 2 humbuckers.

2004-2008	Rotor EXP	$225	$275
2004-2010	Rotor EX	$200	$225

T-15

1981-1983. Offset double-cut, bolt-on neck, dual ferrite blade single-coil pickups, natural.

1981-1983		$150	$175

T-15 Amp-In-Case

1981-1983. Amplifier built into guitar case and T-15 guitar.

1981-1983		$175	$250

T-25

1979-1985. Synthetic polymer body, 2 pickups, cream 'guard, sunburst finish.

1979-1985		$275	$300

T-25 Special

1979-1985. Same as T-25, but with super high output pickups, phenolic 'board, black/white/black 'guard, ebony black finish.

1979-1985		$275	$300

T-26

1982-1986. Same as T-25, but with 3 single-coil pickups and 5-way switch.

1982-1986		$275	$300

T-27

1981-1983. Offset double-cut, bolt-on neck, dual ferrite blade single-coil pickups.

1981-1983		$300	$325

T-30

1982-1985. Short-scale, 3 single-coil pickups, 5-way select, by '83 amp-in-case available.

1982-1985	Guitar only	$200	$250
1983-1985	Amp-in-case	$250	$300

T-60

1978-1988. Contoured offset double-cut, ash body, six-in-line tuners, 2 humbuckers, thru-body strings, by '87 maple bodies, various finishes.

1978-1988		$350	$425

T-1000 LT

1992-1994. Double-cut, 2 single-coils and humbucker with coil-tap.

1992-1994		$225	$275

Tracer Custom

1989-1990. Tracer with 2 single humbuckers and extras.

1989-1990		$175	$200

Tracer/Tracer II

1987-1994. Offset scooped double-cut with extended pointy horns, poplar body, 1 pickup, Floyd Rose.

1987-1994		$175	$200

Vandenberg Quilt Top

1989-1992. Vandenberg Custom with quilted maple top, 2 humbuckers, glued-in neck, quilted maple top, mahogany body and neck.

1989-1992		$1,100	$1,200

Vandenberg Signature

1988-1992. Double-cut, reverse headstock, bolt-on neck, locking vibrato, various colors.

1988-1992		$500	$525

Vortex I/Vortex II

1986. Streamlined Mantis with 2 pickups, 3-way, Kahler locking vibrato. Vortex II has Randy Rhoads Sharkfin V.

1986		$275	$325

V-Type Series

2004-2007. Offset double-cut solidbody, pointed reverse 6-on-a-side headstock, 2 humbuckers.

2004-2007		$250	$300

Pederson Custom Guitars

2009-present. Luthier Kevin Pederson builds his premium grade, production/custom, hollowbody and solidbody guitars in Forest City, Iowa. From 1997-2009 he produced guitars under the Abyss brand name.

Pedro de Miguel

1991-present. Luthiers Pedro Pérez and Miguel Rodriguez build their professional and premium grade, custom/production, classical guitars in Madrid, Spain. They also offer factory-made instruments built to their specifications.

1981 Peavey T-60

Pedro de Miguel Classical

MODEL		EXC. COND.	
YEAR	FEATURES	LOW	HIGH

Pedulla

1975-present. Know for basses, Pedulla did offer a few solidbody guitar models into the early 1980s

MVP

1980s. Double-cut solidbody, 2 humbuckers, dot markers, 4 knobs with main toggle and 3 mini-toggle switches, stencil Pedulla logo, MVP serial number series.

1980s		$800	$1,025

Peekamoose

1983-present. Production/custom, premium grade, solidbody, chambered, and archtop electric guitars built in New York City, New York by luthier Paul Schwartz.

Pegasus Guitars and Ukuleles

1977-present. Premium grade, custom steel-string guitars built by luthier Bob Gleason in Kurtistown, Hawaii, who also builds ukulele family instruments.

Penco

Ca. 1974-1978. Generally high quality Japanese-made copies of classic American acoustic, electric and bass guitars. Imported by Philadelphia Music Company of Limerick, Pennsylvania during the copy era. Includes dreadnought acoustics with laminated woods, bolt-neck solidbody electric guitars and basses, mandolins and banjos.

Acoustic Flat-Top

1974-1978. Various models.

1974-1978		$100	$125

Electric

1974-1978. Various copies.

1974-1978	Solidbody	$150	$250
1974-1978	Thinline Archtop	$150	$250

Penn

1950s. Archtop and acoustic guitars built by made by United Guitar Corporation in Jersey City, New Jersey, which also made Premier acoustics. Penn was located in L.A.

Pensa (Pensa-Suhr)

1982-present. Premium grade, production/custom, solidbody guitars built in the U.S. They also build basses. Rudy Pensa, of Rudy's Music Stop, New York City, New York, started building Pensa guitars in '82. In '85 he teamed up with John Suhr to build Pensa-Suhr instruments. Name changed back to Pensa in '96.

Classic

1992-Ca. 1998. Offest double-cut, 3 single-coils, gold hardware.

1992-1998		$1,400	$1,800

MK 1 (Mark Knopfler)

1985-present. Offset double-cut solidbody, carved flamed maple bound top, 3 pickups, gold hardware, dot markers, bolt-on neck.

1985-2010		$1,500	$1,900

Perlman Classical

Pheo Airline

MODEL		EXC. COND.	
YEAR	FEATURES	LOW	HIGH

Suhr Custom

1985-1989. Two-piece maple body, bolt-on maple neck with rosewood 'board, custom order basis with a variety of woods and options available.

1985-1989		$1,500	$1,900

Suhr Standard

1985-1991. Double-cut, single/single/hum pickup configuration, opaque solid finish normally, dot markers.

1985-1991		$1,400	$1,800

Perlman Guitars

1976-present. Luthier Alan Perlman builds his premium grade, custom, steel-string and classical guitars in San Francisco, California.

Perry Guitars

1982-present. Premium grade, production/custom, classical guitars built by luthier Daryl Perry in Winnipeg, Manitoba. He also builds lutes.

Petillo Masterpiece Guitars

1965-present. Father and son luthiers Phillip J. and David Petillo build their intermediate, professional and premium grade, custom, steel-string, nylon-string, 12-string, resonator, archtop, and Hawaiian guitars in Ocean, New Jersey. Phillip died in August, 2010.

Petros Guitars

1992-present. Premium grade, production/custom, flat-top, 12-string, and nylon-string guitars built by father and son luthiers Bruce and Matthew Petros in Kaukauna, Wisconsin.

Phantom Guitar Works

1992-present. Intermediate grade, production/custom, classic Phantom, and Teardrop shaped solid and hollowbody guitars assembled in Clatskanie, Oregon. They also offer basses and the MandoGuitar. Phantom was established by Jack Charles, former lead guitarist of the band Quarterflash. Some earlier guitars were built overseas.

Pheo

1996-present. Luthier Phil Sylvester builds his unique premium grade, production/custom, electric and acoustic guitars in Portland, Oregon.

Phoenix Guitar Company

1994-present. Luthiers George Leach and Diana Huber build their premium grade, production/custom, archtop and classical guitars in Scottsdale, Arizona.

Pieper

2005-present. Premium grade, custom, solidbody guitars built by luthier Robert Pieper in New Haven, Connecticut. He also builds basses.

MODEL YEAR	FEATURES	EXC. COND. LOW	HIGH

Pignose

1972-present. The original portable amp company also offers intermediate grade, procudtion, dreadnaught and amplified electric guitars. They also offer effects. Refer to Amps section for more company info.

Pimentel and Sons

1951-present. Luthiers Lorenzo Pimentel and sons build their professional, premium and presentation grade, flat-top, jazz, cutaway electric, and classical guitars in Albuquerque, New Mexico.

Player

1984-1985. Player guitars featured interchangable pickup modules that mounted through the back of the guitar. They offered a double-cut solidbody with various options and the pickup modules were sold separately. The company was located in Scarsdale, New York.

Pleasant

Late 1940s-ca.1966. Solidbody electric guitars, obviously others, Japanese manufacturer, probably not imported into the U.S.

Electric Solidbody

1940s-1966. Various models.

1940s-1966		$125	$200

Potvin

2003-present. Production/custom, professional and premium grade, chambered, hollowbody and solidbody electric guitars built by luthier Mike Potvin in Ontario.

Prairie State

1927-ca. 1940. A Larson Brothers brand, basically a derivative of Maurer & Company. The Prairie State models were slightly more expensive than the equivalent Maurer models. They featured a patented steel rod mechanism to strengthen the body, which ran from the end block to the neck block. The model usually had Brazilian rosewood back and sides, laminated necks and X-bracing. Some later models were built with figured maple.

1932 Prairie State Catalog Models - description and prices:

Style 225 Concert $65.00
Style 425 Auditorium $70.00
Style 426 Style 425 Steel $70.00
Style 427 Reinforced Neck $75.00
Style 428 Style 427 Steel $75.00
Style 235 Concert with trim $80.00
Style 335 Grand Concert + trim $83.00
Style 435 Auditorium with trim $85.00
Style 340 Grand Concert fancy $90.00
Style 350 Grand Concert fancy $97.00
Style 440 Auditorium fancy trim $93.00
Style 450 Auditorium fancy trim $100.00

Prairiewood

2005-present. Luthier Robert Dixon of Fargo, North Dakota builds professional grade, production/custom, hollowbody archtop and solidbody guitars.

Premier

Ca.1938-ca.1975, 1990s-2010. Brands originally offered by Premier include Premier, Multivox, Marvel, Belltone and Strad-O-Lin. Produced by Peter Sorkin Music Company in Manhattan, New York City, New York, who began in Philadelphia, relocating to NYC in '35. First radio-sized amplifiers and stick-on pickups for acoustic archtops were introduced by '38. After World War II, they set up the Multivox subsidiary to manufacture amplifiers ca. '46. First flat-top with pickup appeared in '46.

Most acoustic instruments made by United Guitar Corporation in Jersey City, New Jersey. Ca. '57 Multivox acquires Strad-O-Lin. Ca.'64-'65 their Custom line guitars are assembled with probably Italian bodies and hardware, Japanese electronics, possibly Egmond necks from Holland. By ca. '74-'75, there were a few Japanese-made guitars, then Premier brand goes into hiatus.

The rights to the Premier brand are held by Entertainment Music Marketing Corporation in New York. The Premier brand reappears on some Asian-made budget and intermediate grade, production, solidbody guitars and basses beginning in the '90s.

Bantam Custom

1950s-1960s. Model below Special, single-cut archtop, dot markers, early models with white potted pickups, then metal-covered pickups, and finally Japanese-made pickups (least valued).

1950-1960s		$625	$750

Bantam Deluxe

1950s-1960s. Single-cut archtop, fully bound, sparkle knobs, early models with white potted pickups, then metal-covered pickups, and finally Japanese-made pickups (least valued), block markers, single or double pickups (deduct $100 for single pickup instrument).

1950-1960s Blond		$1,300	$1,525
1950-1960s Sunburst		$1,200	$1,425

Bantam Special

1950s-1960s. Model below Deluxe, single-cut archtop, dot markers, early models with white potted pickups, then metal-covered pickups, and finally Japanese-made pickups (least valued), single or double pickup models offered (deduct $100 for single pickup instrument).

1950-1960s		$625	$775

Custom Solidbody

1958-1970. Notable solidbody bass scroll cutaway, various models with various components used, finally import components only.

1958-1970	1 pickup	$425	$525
1958-1970	2 pickups	$500	$600
1958-1970	3 pickups	$675	$775

Potvin El Camino - Korina

Prairiewood Fox

GUITARS

Prenkert Western Red

Jose Ramirez SI Classical

MODEL YEAR	FEATURES	EXC. COND. LOW	HIGH

Deluxe Archtop
1950s-1960s. Full body 17 1/4" archtop, square block markers, single-cut, early models with white potted pickups, later '60s models with metal pickups.

1950-1960s	Blond	$1,250	$1,550
1950-1960s	Sunburst	$1,250	$1,550

E-727
1958-1962. E-scroll style solidbody with scroll bass bout, 3 single-coil pickups, Premier headstock logo, made by the Multivox factory in New York.

1958-1962		$650	$775

Semi-Pro 16" Archtop
1950s-early-1960s. Thinline electric 16" archtop with 2 1/4" deep body, acoustic or electric.

1950-1960s	Acoustic	$650	$800
1950-1960s	Electric	$750	$900

Semi-Pro Bantam Series
1960s. Thinline electric archtop with 2 3/4" deep body, offered in cutaway and non-cut models.

1960s		$300	$375

Special Archtop
1950s-1960s. Full body 17 1/4" archtop, less fancy than Deluxe, single-cut, early models with white potted pickups, '60s models with metal pickups.

1950-1960s		$825	$975

Studio Six Archtop
1950s-early-1960s. 16" wide archtop, single pickup, early pickups white potted, changed later to metal top.

1950-1960s		$475	$600

Prenkert Guitars
1980-present. Premium and presentation grade, production/custom, classical and flamenco guitars built in Sebastopol, California by luthier Richard Prenkert.

Prestige
Intermediate, professional, and premium grade, production/custom, acoustic, solidbody and hollowbody guitars from Vancouver, British Columbia. They also offer basses.

Queen Shoals Stringed Instruments
1972-present. Luthier Larry Cadle builds his production/custom, flat-top, 12-string, and nylon-string guitars in Clendenin, West Virginia.

Queguiner, Alain
1982-present. Custom flat-tops, 12 strings, and nylon strings built by luthier Alain Queguiner in Paris, France.

R.C. Allen
1951-present. Luthier R. C. "Dick" Allen builds professional and premium grade, custom hollowbody and semi-hollowbody guitars in El Monte, California. He has also built solidbody guitars.

MODEL YEAR	FEATURES	EXC. COND. LOW	HIGH

Rahan
1999-present. Professional grade, production/custom, solidbody guitars built by luthiers Mike Curd and Rick Cantu in Houston, Texas.

Rahbek Guitars
2000-present. Professional and premium grade, production/custom, solidbody electrics built by luthier Peter Rahbek in Copenhagen, Denmark.

Raimundo
1970s-present. Intermediate, professional and premium grade flamenco and classical guitars made in Valencia, Spain, by luthiers Antonio Aparicio and Manual Raimundo.

RainSong
1991-present. Professional grade, production, all-graphite and graphite and wood acoustic guitars built in Woodinville, Washington. The guitars were developed after years of research by luthier engineer John Decker with help from luthier Lorenzo Pimentel, engineer Chris Halford, and sailboard builder George Clayton. The company was started in Maui, but has since moved to Woodinville.

RAM Guitars
2007-present. Luthier Rob Mielzynski builds his professional grade, production/custom, solidbody, chambered and archtop electric guitars in Fox River Grove, Illinois.

Rambler
See Strobel Guitars listing.

Ramirez, Jose
1882-present. Professional, premium, and presentation grade, custom/production, classical guitars built in Madrid, Spain. The company was founded by Jose Ramirez (1858-1923) who was originally a twelve year old apprentice at the shop of Francisco Gonzales. Jose eventually opened his own workshop in 1882 where he introduced his younger brother Manuel to the business. Manuel split with Jose and opened his own, competing workshop. Jose's business was continued by Jose's son Jose Ramirez II (1885-1957), grandson Jose III (1922-1995), and great grandchildren Jose IV (1953-2000) and Amalia Ramirez. From 1882 various techniques and methods were used including centuries-old traditions and new significant departures from old methods. In the 1930's a larger body instrument with improved fan bracing was developed to meet the needs for more power and volume. Other refinements were developed and the Ramirez 1A Tradicional was soon introduced which found favor with Andres Segovia. The Ramirez company has produced both student and professional instruments, but in the classical guitar field, like the old-master violin business, a student model is often a very fine instrument that is now valued at $2,000

MODEL		EXC. COND.	
YEAR	FEATURES	LOW	HIGH

or more. A student Ramirez instrument is not the same as a student-grade instrument such as a birch body 13" Stella flat top. By the 1980s the Ramirez factory was building as many as 1,000 guitars a year. In the 1980s Ramirez offered the E Series student guitar line that was built for, but not by, Ramirez. In 1991 the company offered the even more affordable R Series which was offered for about $1,300. The A, E, and R Series became the major product offerings but the company also continued to offer a limited number of very high-end instruments that were hand built in the company's shop. In the 1990s the company returned to their 1960s roots and offered the 1A Especial model. In the early 2000s Amalia Ramirez offered a third product line, the SP Series, selling for about $5,800, which was designed as a semi-professional instrument that would fit between the company's concert series and student series instruments. By 2005 the company offered the E, R, and SP lines, in addition to annually making several dozen highest-end master-grade instruments in their old workshop on General Margallo Street. As is typically the case, Ramirez classical guitars do not have a name-logo on the headstock. The brand is identified by a Ramirez label on the inside back which also may have the model number listed.

A/1A
1960s-2000s. Classical.

1960s		$2,000	$4,000
1970s		$2,000	$4,000
1980s		$2,000	$4,000
1990s		$2,000	$4,000
2000s		$2,000	$4,000

A/2A
1970-1980s		$2,200	$2,700

AE Estucio
2004		$1,800	$2,100

De Camera
1980s. Classical, cedar top, Brazilian rosewood back and sides.

1980s		$3,000	$3,500

E/1E/Estudio
Intermediate level.

1990s		$1,000	$1,250

E/2E
Red cedar top, Indian rosewood back and sides, Spanish cedar neck, ebony 'board.

2000s		$1,200	$1,500

E/3E Estudio
Cedar, rosewood.

1990s		$1,400	$1,800

E/4E
Top of the E Series line, solid red cedar top, solid Indian rosewood back and sides.

2000s		$1,700	$2,100

Flamenco
1920s-1979. European spruce top, cyprus back and sides.

1920s		$4,000	$5,000
1960-1969		$3,000	$4,000
1970-1979		$3,000	$4,000

MODEL		EXC. COND.	
YEAR	FEATURES	LOW	HIGH

R1
1991-present. Red cedar top, mahogany sides and back, Spanish cedar neck, ebony 'board.

1991-2010		$575	$700

R2
1991-present. Red cedar top, Indian rosewood back and sides, cedar neck, ebony 'board.

1991-2010		$675	$825

R4 Classical
1995-present. All solid wood, Western red cedar top, rosewood back and sides.

1995-2002		$1,025	$1,275

S/S1
2005-2007. Solid German spruce top, African mahogany sides and back, most affordable in Estudio line.

2005-2007		$625	$775

SP Series
2002-present. Semi-professional level designed to be between the company's 'concert/professional' series and 'student' series.

2002-2010		$5,000	$6,000

Ramirez, Manuel
1890-1916. Brother of Jose Ramirez, and a respected professional classical guitar builder from Madrid, Spain. His small shop left no heirs so the business was not continued after Manuel's death in 1916. Manuel was generally considered to be more famous during his lifetime than his brother Jose, and while his business did not continue, Manuel trained many well known Spanish classical guitar luthiers who prospered with their own businesses. During Manuel's era his shop produced at least 48 different models, with prices ranging from 10 to 1,000 pesetas, therefore vintage prices can vary widely. Guitars made prior to 1912 have a label with a street address of Arlaban 10, in 1912 the shop moved to Arlaban 11.

Randy Reynolds Guitars
1996-present. Luthier Randy Reynolds builds his premium grade, production/custom classical and flamenco guitars in Colorado Springs, Colorado.

Randy Wood Guitars
1968-present. Premium grade, custom/production, archtop, flat-top, and resonator guitars built by luthier Randy Wood in Bloomingdale, Georgia. He also builds mandolins.

Rarebird Guitars
1978-present. Luthier Bruce Clay builds his professional and premium grade, production/custom, guitars, originally in Arvada, Colorado, and currently in Woodstock, Georgia. He also builds basses.

Rat Fink
2002-present. Lace Music Products, the makers of the Lace Sensor pickup, offered the intermediate

Randy Reynolds Concert Grand

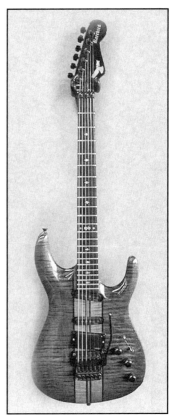

Rarebird Sparrow Hawk

Rayco D-Model

Recording King (TML) Century

grade, production, guitars and basses, featuring the artwork of Ed "Big Daddy" Roth until '05. They continue to offer amps.

Rayco

2002-present. Professional and premium grade, custom, resonator and Hawaiian-style acoustic guitars built in British Columbia, by luthiers Mark Thibeault and Jason Friesen.

Recco

1960s. Electric guitar imports made by Teisco, pricing similar to Teisco models, Recco logo on headstock, upscale solidbodies can have four pickups with several knobs and four switches.

Electric Solidbody

MODEL YEAR	FEATURES	EXC. COND. LOW	HIGH
1960s	4 pickups	$350	$450

Recording King

1929-1943. Brand name used by Montgomery Ward for instruments made by various American manufacturers, including Kay, Gibson and Gretsch. Generally mid-grade instruments. M Series are Gibson-made archtops.

Carson Robison/Model K

1933-1940. Flat-top, 14 3/4", mahogany back and sides, renamed Model K in early-'38.

1933-1940		$1,300	$1,500

Kay 17" flat top.

1940-1941. Large jumbo, 17" lower bout, pearloid veneer peghead, large Recording King logo.

1940-1941		$750	$900

M-2

1936-1941. Gibson-made archtop with carved top and f-holes, maple back and sides.

1936-1941		$650	$775

M-3

1936-1941. Gibson-made archtop, f-holes, maple back and sides, carved top.

1936-1941		$800	$950

M-4

1937-1940. Gibson-made archtop, f-holes, maple back and sides, rope-checkered binding, flying bat wing markers.

1937-1940		$1,000	$1,200

M-5

1936-1941. Gibson-made archtop with f-holes, maple back and sides, trapeze tailpiece, checkered top binding.

1936-1938	16" body	$1,200	$1,500
1939-1941	17" body	$1,300	$1,600

M-6

1938-1939. M-5 with upgraded gold hardware.

1938-1939		$1,300	$1,600

Model 1124

1937. 16" acoustic archtop, body by Gibson, attractive higher-end appointments, block-dot markers, sunburst.

1937		$1,700	$1,900

Ray Whitley

1939-1940. High-quality model made by Gibson, round shoulder flat-top, mahogany (Model 1028) or Brazilian rosewood (Model 1027) back and sides, 5-piece maple neck, Ray Whitley stencil script peghead logo, pearl crown inlay on peghead, fancy inlaid markers.

1939-1940	Brazilian	$19,000	$24,000
1939-1940	Mahogany	$8,500	$10,000

Roy Smeck

1938-1940. 16.25" electric archtop, large Recording King badge logo, Roy Smeck stencil logo, bar pickup, 2 control knobs on upper bass bout, dot markers.

1938-1940		$900	$1,200

Recording King (TML)

2005-present. Budget grade, production, acoustic cowboy stenciled guitars designed by Greg Rich for The Music Link, which also offers Johnson and other brand instruments. They also have banjos and ukes.

Redentore

2007-present. Luthier Mark Piper builds professional and premium grade, production/custom, archtop jazz, acoustic flat-top, carve-top and semi-hollow electric guitars in Columbia, Tennessee.

RedLine Acoustics and RedLine Resophonics

2007-present. Professional and premium grade, production, acoustic and resophonic guitars built in Hendersonville, Tennessee by luthiers Steve Smith, Jason Denton, Christian McAdams and Ryan Futch. They also build mandolins and plan to add lap steels.

Regal

Ca. 1884-1966, 1987-present. Intermediate and professional grade, production, acoustic and wood and metal body resonator guitars. They also build basses.

Originally a mass manufacturer founded in Indianapolis, Indiana, the Regal brand was first used by Emil Wulschner & Son. In 1901 new owners changed the company name to The Regal Manufacturing Company. The company was moved to Chicago in '08 and renamed the Regal Musical Instrument Company. Regal made brands for distributors and mass merchandisers as well as marketing its own Regal brand. Regal purchased the Lyon & Healy factory in '28. Regal was licensed to co-manufacture Dobros in '32 and became the sole manufacturer of them in '37 (see Dobro for those instruments). Most Regal instruments were beginner-grade; however, some very fancy archtops were made during the '30s. The company was purchased by Harmony in '54 and absorbed. From '59 to '66, Harmony made acoustics under the Regal name for Fender. In '87 the Regal name was revived on a line of resonator instruments by Saga.

MODEL YEAR	FEATURES	EXC. COND. LOW	HIGH

Acoustic Hawaiian
1930s. Student model, small 13" body, square neck, glued or trapeze bridge.

1930s	Faux grain painted finish	$325	$400
1930s	Plain sunburst, birch, trapeze	$200	$300

Concert Folk H6382
1960s. Regal by Harmony, solid spruce top, mahogany back and sides, dot markers, natural.

1960s		$225	$300

Deluxe Dreadnought H6600
1960s. Regal by Harmony, solid spruce top, mahogany back and sides, bound top and back, rosewood 'board, dot markers, natural.

1960s		$225	$325

Dreadnought 12-String H1269
1960s. Regal by Harmony, solid spruce top, 12-string version of Deluxe, natural.

1960s		$225	$325

Esquire
1940s. 15 1/2" acoustic archtop, higher-end appointments, fancy logo art and script pearl Esquire headstock logo and Regal logo, natural.

1940s		$1,000	$1,250

Meteor
1960s. Single-cut acoustic-electric archtop, 2 pickups.

1960s		$775	$950

Model 27
1933-1942. Birch wood body, mahogany or maple, 2-tone walnut finish, single-bound top, round or square neck.

1933-1942		$900	$1,100

Model 45
1933-1937. Spruce top and mahogany back and sides, bound body, square neck.

1933-1937		$1,300	$1,600

Model 46
1933-1937. Round neck.

1933-1937		$1,300	$1,600

Model 55 Standard
1933-1934. Regal's version of Dobro Model 55 which was discontinued in '33.

1933-1934		$900	$1,100

Model 75
1939-1940. Metal body, square neck.

1939-1940		$1,600	$2,000

Model TG 60 Resonator Tenor
1930s. Wood body, large single cone biscuit bridge resonator, 2 upper bout metal ports, 4-string tenor.

1930s		$1,300	$1,600

Parlor
1920s. Small body, slotted headstock, birch sides and back, spruce top.

1920s		$200	$325

Prince
1930s. High-end 18" acoustic archtop, fancy appointments, Prince name inlaid in headstock along with Regal script logo and strolling guitarist art.

1930s		$1,400	$1,700

RD-45
1994-2006. Standard style Dobro model with wood body, metal resonator, dual screen holes.

1994-2006		$175	$225

Spirit Of '76
1976. Red-white-blue, flat-top.

1976		$400	$500

Reliance
1920s. Instruments built by the Oscar Schmidt Co. and possibly others. Most likely a brand made for a distributor.

Relixx
2001-present. Intermediate and professional grade, production/custom, aged vintage-style solidbody guitars built in Sanborn, New York by luthier Nick Hazlett.

Renaissance
1978-1980. Plexiglass solidbody electric guitars and basses. Founded in Malvern, Pennsylvania, by John Marshall (designer), Phil Goldberg and Daniel Lamb. Original partners gradually leave and John Dragonetti takes over by late-'79. The line is redesigned with passive electronics on guitars, exotic shapes, but when deal with Sunn amplifiers falls through, company closes. Brandname currently used on a line of guitars and basses made by Rick Turner in Santa Cruz, California.

Fewer than 300 of first series made, plus a few prototypes and several wooden versions; six or so prototypes of second series made. SN=M(M)YYXXXX: month, year, consecutive number.

Electric Plexiglas Solidbody
1978-1980. Models include the SPG ('78-'79, DiMarzio pickups, active electronics), T-200G ('80, Bich-style with 2 passive DiMarzio pickups), and the S-200G ('80, double-cut, 2 DiMarzio pickups, passive electronics).

1978-1980		$650	$750

Renaissance Guitars
1994-present. Professional grade, custom, semi-acoustic flat-top, nylon-string and solidbody guitars built by luthier Rick Turner in Santa Cruz, California. He also builds basses and ukes.

Republic Guitars
2006-present. Intermediate grade, production, reso-phonic and Weissenborn-style guitars imported by American Folklore, Inc. of Rowlett, Texas. They also offer mandolins and ukes.

Reuter Guitars
1984-present. Professional and premium grade, custom, flat-top, 12-string, resonator, and Hawaiian guitars built by luthier John Reuter, the Director of Training at the Roberto-Venn School of Luthiery, in Tempe, Arizona.

Republic Bell Brass Body

Reuter Wolfcaster

Reverend Warhawk II HB

1959 Rex Solidbody

MODEL YEAR	FEATURES	EXC. COND. LOW	HIGH

Reverend

1996-present. Intermediate grade, production, guitars from luthier Joe Naylor, built first in Warren, and since '10 in Livonia, Michigan and in Korea. Naylor also founded Naylor Amps. Reverend also built basses, amps and effects in the past.

Rex

1920s-1940s, 1950s-1960s. Generally beginner-grade guitars made by Kay and sold through Fred Gretsch distributors. In the '50s and '60s, there were European-made electrics bearing the Rex brand that were not distributed by Gretsch. They also had amps.

Ribbecke Guitars

1973-present. Premium and presentation grade, custom thinline, flat-top, and archtop guitars built by luthier Tom Ribbecke in Healdsburg, California.

Rice Custom Guitars

1998-present. Father and son luthiers, Richard Rice and Christopher Rice, build professional and premium grade, custom, solidbody, semi-hollow and hollowbody electric guitars in Arlington Heights, Illinois. They also build basses.

Rich and Taylor

1993-1996. Custom acoustic and electric guitars and banjos from luthiers Greg Rich and Mark Taylor (Crafters of Tennessee).

Richard Schneider

1960s-1997. Luthier Richard Schneider built his acoustic guitars in Washington state. Over the years, he collaborated with Dr. Michael A. Kasha on many guitar designs and innovations. Originally from Michigan, he also was involved in designing guitars for Gretsch and Gibson. He died in early '97.

Richmond

2008-present. Luthiers Robert Godin (Godin Guitars) and Daniel Fiocco build intermediate and professional grade, production, chambered and solidbody electric guitars in Richmond, Quebec.

Richter Mfg.

1930s. One of many Chicago makers of the era, the company allegedly bought already-made guitars from other manufacturers, painted and decorated them to their liking and resold them.

Small 13"

1930s. Typical small 13" lower bout body, slotted headstock, decalmania art over black finish, single dot markers.

1930s		$300	$400

Rick Turner

1979-1981, 1990-present. Rick Turner has a long career as a luthier, electronics designer and innovator. He also makes the Renaissance line of guitars in

his shop in Santa Cruz, California. The guitars and basses built in 1979-'81 were numbered sequentially in the order they were completed and shipped with the second part of the serial number indicating the year the instrument was built. Turner estimates that approximately 200 instruments were made during that period.

Rickenbacker

1931-present. Professional and premium grade, production/custom, acoustic and electric guitars built in California. They also build basses. Founded in Los Angeles as Ro-Pat-In by ex-National executives George Beauchamp, Paul Barth and National's resonator cone supplier Adolph Rickenbacher. Rickenbacher was born in Basel, Switzerland in 1886, emigrated to the U.S. and moved to Los Angeles in 1918, opening a tool and die business in '20. In the mid-'20s, Rickenbacher began providing resonator cones and other metal parts to George Beauchamp and Louis Dopyera of National String Instrument Corporation and became a shareholder in National. Beauchamp, Barth and Harry Watson came up with wooden "frying pan" electric Hawaiian lap steel for National in '31; National was not interested, so Beauchamp and Barth joined with Rickenbacher as Ro-Pat-In (probably for ElectRO-PATent-INstruments) to produce Electro guitars. Cast aluminum frying pans were introduced in '32. Some Spanish guitars (flat-top, F-holes) with Electro pickups were produced beginning in '32. Ro-Pat-In changes their name to Electro String Instrument Corporation in '34, and brand becomes Rickenbacher Electro, soon changed to Rickenbacker, with a "k." Beauchamp retires in '40. There was a production hiatus during World War II. In '53, Electro was purchased by Francis Cary Hall (born 1908), owner of Radio and Television Equipment Company (Radio-Tel) in Santa Ana, California (founded in '20s as Hall's Radio Service, which began distributing Fender instruments in '46). The factory was relocated to Santa Ana in '62 and the sales/distribution company's name is changed from Radio-Tel to Rickenbacker Inc. in '65.

1950s serial numbers have from 4 to 7 letters and numbers, with the number following the letter indicating the '50s year (e.g., NNL8NN would be from '58). From '61 to '86 serial numbers indicate month and year of production with initial letter A-Z for the year A=1961, Z=1986) followed by letter for the month A-M (A=January) plus numbers as before followed by a number 0-9 for the year (0=1987; 9=1996). To avoid confusion, we have listed all instruments by model number. For example, the Combo 400 is listed as Model 400/Combo 400. OS and NS stands for Old Style and New Style. On the 360, for example, Ric changed the design in 1964 to their New Style with more rounded body horns and rounded top edges and other changes. But they still offered the Old Style with more pointed horns and top binding until the late 1960s. Ric still sometimes uses the two designations on some of their vintage reissues.

MODEL		EXC. COND.	
YEAR	FEATURES	LOW	HIGH

Electro ES-16
1964-1971. Double-cut, set neck, solidbody, 3/4 size, 1 pickup. The Electro line was manufactured by Rickenbacker and distributed by Radio-Tel. The Electro logo appears on the headstock.
| 1964-1971 | | $900 | $1,100 |

Electro ES-17
1964-1975. Cutaway, set neck, solidbody, 1 pickup.
| 1964-1969 | | $1,000 | $1,200 |
| 1970-1975 | | $850 | $1,050 |

Electro Spanish (Model B Spanish)
1935-1943. Small guitar with a lap steel appearance played Spanish-style, hollow black bakelite body augmented with 5 chrome plates (white enamel in '40), 1 octagon knob (2 round-ridged in '38), called the Model B ca. '40.
1935-1937	Chrome, 1 knob	$4,500	$5,200
1935-1937	Tenor 4-string, 1 knob	$3,200	$4,000
1938-1939	Chrome, 2 knobs	$4,300	$5,000
1940-1943	White, 2 knobs	$4,100	$4,800

Model 220 Hamburg
1992-1997. Solidbody.
| 1992-1997 | | $750 | $900 |

Model 230 GF Glenn Frey
1992-1997. Glenn Frey Limited Edition, solidbody, 2 high output humbuckers, black hardware, chrome 'guard.
| 1992-1997 | | $1,500 | $1,850 |

Model 230 Hamburg
1983-1991. Solidbody, offset double-cut, 2 pickups, dot inlay, rosewood 'board, chrome-plated hardware.
| 1983-1991 | | $750 | $900 |

Model 250 El Dorado
1983-1991. Deluxe version of Hamburg, gold hardware, white binding.
| 1983-1991 | | $600 | $750 |

Model 260 El Dorado
1992-1997. Replaces 250.
| 1992-1997 | | $700 | $850 |

Model 310
1958-1970, 1981-1985. Two-pickup version of Model 320.
1958-1960	Capri, thick body	$10,000	$12,500
1961-1969	Thinner body	$5,800	$7,200
1981-1985	Reintroduced	$1,500	$1,800

Model 315
1958-1974. Two-pickup version of Model 325.
1958-1960	Capri, thick body	$10,000	$12,500
1960-1969	Thinner body	$5,800	$7,200
1970-1973		$3,400	$4,000
1974		$3,100	$3,700

Model 320
1958-1992. Short-scale hollowbody, 3 pickups, f-holes optional in '61 and standard in '64 and optional again in '79.
1958-1960	Capri, thick body	$12,000	$15,000
1960-1969		$8,000	$10,000
1970-1973		$3,400	$4,000
1974-1979		$3,100	$3,700
1980-1992		$1,900	$2,400

Model 320/12V63
1986. Short run for Japanese market.
| 1986 | | $2,500 | $3,100 |

Model 325
1958-1975, 1985-1992. This was a low production model, with some years having no production. In the mid-'60s, the 325 was unofficially known as the John Lennon Model due to his guitar's high exposure on the Ed Sullivan Show and in the Saturday Evening Post.
1958	John Lennon specs, 8 made	$36,000	$45,000
1959-1960		$18,000	$23,000
1961-1963		$15,000	$19,000
1964-1966	Fireglo or black	$9,000	$11,000
1966	Mapleglo	$9,000	$11,000
1967-1969		$9,000	$11,000
1970-1973		$3,400	$4,000
1974		$3,100	$3,700

Model 325 B
1983-1984. Reissue of early '60s model.
| 1983-1984 | | $1,900 | $2,400 |

Model 325 JL
1989-1993. John Lennon Limited Edition, 3 vintage Ric pickups, vintage vibrato, maple body; 3/4-size rosewood neck, a 12-string and a full-scale version are also available.
| 1989-1993 | | $2,400 | $2,800 |

Model 325 S
1964-1967. F-holes.
| 1964-1967 | | $9,000 | $11,000 |

Model 325/12
1984-1985, 1999. Based on John Lennon's one-of-a-kind '64 325/12.
| 1985-1986 | | $2,500 | $3,100 |
| 1999 | | $2,500 | $3,100 |

Model 325C58
2002-present. Copy of the '58 model that John Lennon saw in Germany.
| 2002-2004 | | $2,500 | $3,100 |
| 2005-2010 | Hamburg | $2,500 | $3,100 |

Model 325C64
2002-present. Copy of the famous '64 model.
| 2002-2010 | | $2,500 | $3,100 |

Model 325V59
1984-2001. Reissue of John Lennon's modified '59 325, 3 pickups, short-scale.
| 1984-2001 | | $2,500 | $3,100 |

Model 325V63
1984-2001. Reissue of John Lennon's '63 325.
| 1987-2001 | | $2,500 | $3,100 |

Model 330
1958-present. Thinline hollowbody, 2 pickups, slash soundhole, natural or sunburst.
1958-1960	Capri, thick body	$8,000	$10,000
1961-1969	Thinner body	$4,000	$5,000
1970-1973		$3,400	$4,000
1974-1979		$3,100	$3,700
1980-1999		$1,500	$1,800
2000-2010		$1,350	$1,650

Rick Turner Model One

Rickenbacker Model 325C58

GUITARS

1960 Rickenbacker
Model 360 F

1971 Rickenbacker
Model 360/12

MODEL YEAR	FEATURES	EXC. COND. LOW	HIGH
Model 330 F			
1958-1969. F-style.			
1958-1960	Thick version	$8,000	$10,000
1961-1969	Thin version	$4,000	$5,000
Model 330/12			
1965-present. Thinline, 2 pickups, 12-string version of Model 300.			
1964	Only 1 made	$4,000	$5,200
1965-1969	330-style body	$4,000	$5,200
1970-1979		$2,000	$4,000
1980-1989		$1,600	$2,000
1990-1999		$1,300	$1,600
2000-2010		$1,300	$1,600
Model 330S/12			
1964 (1 made)-1965 (2 made).			
1964-1965		$4,000	$5,200
Model 331 Light Show			
1970-1975. Model 330 with translucent top with lights in body that lit up when played, needed external transformer. The first offering's design, noted as Type 1, had heat problems and a fully original one is difficult to find. The 2nd offering's design, noted as Type 2, was a more stable design and is more highly valued in the market.			
1970-1971	Type 1 1st edition	$9,000	$11,500
1972-1975	Type 2 2nd edition	$11,000	$13,500
Model 335			
1961-1977. Thinline, 330-style body, 2 pickups, vibrato, Fireglo. Called the 330VB from '85-'97.			
1958-1960	Capri, thick body	$8,000	$10,000
1961-1969	Thinner body	$4,000	$5,000
1970-1973		$3,400	$4,000
1974-1977		$3,100	$3,700
Model 335 F			
1958-1969. F-style.			
1958-1961	Thick version	$8,000	$10,000
1961-1969	Thin version	$4,000	$5,000
Model 336/12			
1966-1974. Like 300-12, but with 6-12 converter comb, 330-style body.			
1966-1969		$3,500	$4,500
1970-1974		$2,000	$3,000
Model 340			
1958-present. Thin semi-hollowbody, thru-body maple neck, 2 single-coil pickups, sharp point horns, very limited production '58-'65, with first notable volume of 45 units starting in '66.			
1958-1960	Capri, thick body	$8,000	$10,000
1961-1969	Thinner body	$4,000	$5,000
1970-1973		$3,400	$4,000
1974-1979		$3,100	$3,700
1980-1999		$1,500	$1,800
2000-2010		$1,350	$1,650
Model 340 F			
1958-1969. F-style.			
1958-1960	Thick version	$8,000	$10,000
1961-1969	Thin version	$4,000	$5,000
Model 340/12			
1980-present. 12-string version, 330-style body.			
1980-1999		$1,800	$2,200
2000-2010		$1,800	$2,200

MODEL YEAR	FEATURES	EXC. COND. LOW	HIGH
Model 345			
1961-1974. Thinline 330-345 series, version with 3 pickups and vibrato tailpiece.			
1958-1960	Capri, thick body	$8,000	$10,000
1961-1969	Thinner body	$4,000	$5,000
1970-1973	2 humbuckers, slant frets	$3,400	$4,000
1974		$3,100	$3,700
Model 345 F			
1958-1969. F-style.			
1958-1960	Thick version	$8,000	$10,000
1961-1969	Thin version	$4,000	$5,000
Model 345 Reissue			
2002. Low production, 3 pickups.			
2002		$2,000	$2,300
Model 350 Liverpool			
1983-1997. Thinline, 3 pickups, vibrato, no soundhole.			
1983-1997		$1,800	$2,200
Model 350 SH			
1988-1990. Susanna Hoffs Limited Edition.			
1988-1990		$2,800	$3,400
Model 350/12V63 Liverpool			
1994-present. Vintage Series, 12-string 350V63.			
1994-2010		$2,000	$2,400
Model 350V59			
1988. Very low production.			
1988		$1,700	$2,000
Model 350V63 Liverpool			
1994-present. Vintage Series, like 355 JL, but without signature.			
1994-2010		$2,000	$2,400
Model 355 JL			
1989-1993. John Lennon model, signature and drawing on 'guard.			
1989-1993		$2,500	$3,100
Model 355/12 JL			
1989-1993. 12-string 355 JL, limited production.			
1989-1993		$2,500	$3,100
Model 360/360 VB			
1958-1991, 2000-present. Deluxe thinline, 2 pickups, slash soundhole, bound body until '64.			
1958-1960	Capri, thick body	$8,000	$10,000
1961-1969		$4,000	$5,000
1970-1973	360, no vibrato	$3,400	$4,000
1974-1979	360 VB, vibrato	$3,100	$3,700
1980-1989	360 VB, vibrato	$1,500	$1,800
1990-1999		$1,450	$1,850
2000-2010		$1,450	$1,850
Model 360V64			
1991-2003. Reissue of '64 Model 360 old style body without vibrola, has binding with full length inlays.			
1991-2003		$2,500	$3,000
Model 360 CW			
2000. Carl Wilson Limited Edition, 6-string, includes certificate, 500 made.			
2000		$2,700	$3,200
Model 360 DCM 75th Anniversary			
2006. 360 with 75th Anniversary dark cherry metallic finish, 75 made.			
2006		$2,400	$2,900

⊛ Gretschworld ⊛ Cream City Music ⊛ Brookfield, Wisconsin ⊛

MODEL YEAR	FEATURES	EXC. COND. LOW	HIGH
Model 360 F			
1959-1972. F-style.			
1959-1960	Thick version	$6,800	$8,300
1961-1969	Thin version	$3,900	$4,700
1970-1972	Thin version	$3,400	$4,000
Model 360 Tuxedo			
1987 only. Tuxedo option included white body, white painted fretboard, and black hardware.			
1987		$2,000	$2,500
Model 360 WB			
1984-1998. Double bound body, 2 pickups, vibrato optional (VB).			
1984-1990		$2,200	$2,700
1991-1998	WB, no vibrato	$2,000	$2,500
1991-1998	WBVB, vibrato	$2,000	$2,500
Model 360/12			
1964-present. Deluxe thinline, 2 pickups, 12-string version of Model 360, Rick-O-Sound stereo.			
1964-1969		$5,000	$6,200
1966	Harrison specs	$9,000	$13,000
1970-1973		$4,000	$5,000
1974-1977		$2,900	$3,400
1978-1979		$2,300	$2,800
1980-2010		$1,800	$2,200
Model 360/12 CW			
2000. Carl Wilson, 12-string version of 360 CW.			
2000		$2,700	$3,200
Model 360/12 Tuxedo			
1987 only. 12-string version of 360 Tuxedo.			
1987		$2,200	$2,700
Model 360/12 VP			
2004. VP is vintage pickup.			
2004		$2,200	$2,700
Model 360/12 WB			
1984-1998. 12-string version of 360 WB.			
1984-1998		$2,200	$2,700
Model 360/12C63			
2004-present. More exact replica of the Harrison model.			
2004-2010		$2,600	$3,200
Model 360/12V64			
1985-2003. Deluxe thinline with '64 features, 2 pickups, 12 strings, slanted plate tailpiece.			
1985-1999		$2,500	$3,000
2000-2003		$2,500	$3,000
Model 362/12			
1975-1992. Doubleneck 6 & 12, 360 features.			
1975-1980		$2,500	$3,500
1981-1992		$2,000	$3,000
Model 365			
1958-1974. Deluxe thinline, 2 pickups, vibrato, called Model 360 WBVB from '84-'98.			
1958-1960	Capri, thick body	$8,000	$10,000
1961-1969		$4,000	$5,000
1970-1973		$3,400	$4,000
1974		$3,100	$3,700
Model 365 F			
1959-1972. Thin full-body (F designation), 2 pickups, Deluxe features.			
1959-1960	Thick version	$8,000	$10,000
1961-1969	Thin version	$4,000	$5,000
1970-1972		$3,400	$4,000

MODEL YEAR	FEATURES	EXC. COND. LOW	HIGH
Model 366/12 Convertible			
1966-1974. Two pickups, 12 strings, comb-like device that converts it to a 6-string, production only noted in '68, perhaps available on custom order basis.			
1966-1968	OS	$4,000	$5,000
Model 370			
1958-1990, 1994-present. Deluxe thinline, 3 pickups. Could be considered to be a dealer special order item from '58-'67 with limited production ('58=0, '59=4, '60=0, '61=3, '62-'67=0, then started more regularly in '68).			
1958-1960	Capri, thick body	$8,000	$10,000
1961-1969	Thin version	$4,000	$5,000
1970-1973		$3,400	$4,000
1974-1979		$3,100	$3,700
1980-1990		$1,500	$1,800
1994-2010		$1,350	$1,650
Model 370 F			
1959-1972. F-style, 3 pickups, Deluxe features.			
1959-1961	Thick version	$8,000	$10,000
1961-1969	Thin version	$4,000	$5,000
1970-1972		$3,400	$4,000
Model 370 WB			
1984-1998. Double bound body, 3 pickups, vibrato optional (VB).			
1984-1998		$1,600	$1,900
1990-1998		$1,600	$1,900
Model 370/12			
1965-1990, 1994-present. Not regular production until '80, deluxe thinline, 3 pickups, 12 strings. Could be considered to be a dealer special order item in the '60s and '70s with limited production.			
1965-1979	Roger McGuinn	$9,000	$13,000
1980-1990		$1,800	$2,200
1994-2010		$1,800	$2,000
Model 370/12 RM			
1988. Limited Edition Roger McGuinn model, 1000 made, higher-quality appointments.			
1988		$4,100	$5,200
Model 375			
1958-1974. Deluxe thinline, 3 pickups, vibrato, called Model 370 WBVB from '84-'98.			
1958-1960	Capri, thick body	$8,000	$10,000
1961-1969	Thin version	$4,000	$5,000
1970-1973		$3,400	$4,000
1974		$3,100	$3,700
Model 375 F			
1959-1972. F-style, 2 pickups.			
1959-1960	Thick version	$6,800	$8,300
1961-1969	Thin version	$3,900	$4,700
1970-1972		$3,400	$4,000
Model 380 L Laguna			
1996-2005. Semi-hollow, oil-finished walnut body, Maple neck and 'board, 2 humbuckers, PZ saddle pickups optional.			
1996-2005		$2,000	$2,500
1996-2005	PZ option	$2,000	$2,500

Rickenbacker Model 362/12

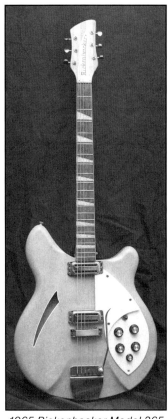

1965 Rickenbacker Model 365

Tom Siska

To get the most from this book, be sure to read "Using *The Guide*" in the introduction.

1975 Rickenbacker Model 481

1995 Rickenbacker Model 610

MODEL YEAR	FEATURES	EXC. COND. LOW	HIGH

Model 381

1958-1963, 1969-1974. Double-cut archtop, 2 pickups, slash soundhole, solid 'guard, reintroduced in '69 with double split-level 'guard.

1958-1963	Light sporadic production	$4,500	$10,000
1969-1974	Various colors, some rare	$3,300	$4,500

Model 381 JK

1988-1997. John Kay Limited Edition model, 2 humbucking pickups, active electronics, stereo and mono outputs.

1988-1997		$2,600	$3,200

Model 381/12V69

1987-present. Reissue of 381/12, deep double-cut body, sound body cavity, catseye soundhole, triangle inlays, bridge with 12 individual saddles. Finishes include Fireglo, Mapleglo and Jetglo.

1987-1999		$2,600	$3,200
2000-2010		$2,600	$3,200

Model 381V69

1991-present. Reissue of vintage 381.

1987-1999		$2,600	$3,200
2000-2010		$2,600	$3,200

Model 382

1958-1963, 1969-1974. 381 with vibrato unit. Very light production.

1958-1963	Light sporadic production	$4,500	$10,000
1969-1974	Various colors, some rare	$3,300	$4,500

Model 383

1958-1963, 1969-1974. 381 with 3 pickups. Very light production.

1958-1963	Light sporadic production	$4,500	$10,000
1969-1974	Various colors, some rare	$3,300	$4,500

Model 384

1958-1963, 1969-1974. 381 with 3 pickups and vibrato unit. Very light production.

1958-1963	Light sporadic production	$4,500	$10,000
1969-1974	Various colors, some rare	$3,300	$4,500

Model 400/Combo 400

1956-1958. Double-cut tulip body, neck-thru, 1 pickup, gold anodized 'guard, 21 frets, replaced by Model 425 in '58. Available in black (216 made), blue turquoise (53), Cloverfield Green (53), Montezuma Brown (41), and 4 in other custom colors.

1956-1958		$2,700	$3,300

Model 420

1965-1983. Non-vibrato version of Model 425, single pickup.

1965-1968		$1,200	$1,500
1969-1983		$1,100	$1,350

Model 425/Combo 425

1958-1973. Double-cut solidbody, 1 pickup, sunburst.

1958-1959	425 Cresting Wave	$2,700	$3,300
1960		$2,000	$2,500

MODEL YEAR	FEATURES	EXC. COND. LOW	HIGH
1961-1964		$1,900	$2,400
1965-1968		$1,400	$1,700
1969-1973		$1,300	$1,600

Model 425/12V63

1999-2000. 136 made.

1999-2000		$1,400	$1,700

Model 425V63

1999-2000. Beatles associated model, 145 JG black made, 116 BG burgundy transparent made, originally custom ordered by Rickenbacker collectors and they were not part of Rickenbacker's sales literature in the late '90s.

1999-2000		$1,400	$1,700

Model 430

1971-1982. Style 200 body, natural.

1971-1982		$750	$900

Model 450/Combo 450

1957-1984. Replaces Combo 450, 2 pickups (3 optional '62-'77), tulip body shape '57-'59, cresting wave body shape after.

1957-1958	450 Tulip body (Combo)	$3,200	$4,000
1958-1959	450 Cresting Wave	$2,800	$3,400
1960	Cresting Wave, flat body	$2,100	$2,600
1961-1966	Cresting Wave, super slim	$2,000	$2,500
1970-1979	Includes rare color	$1,600	$2,000
1980-1984		$1,200	$1,500

Model 450/12

1964-1985. Double-cut solidbody, 12-string version of Model 450, 2 pickups.

1964-1966		$2,000	$2,500
1967-1969		$1,800	$2,200
1970-1979	Includes rare color	$1,600	$2,000
1980-1985		$1,200	$1,500

Model 450V63

1999-2001. Reissue of '63 450.

1999-2001		$1,300	$1,600

Model 456/12 Convertible

1968-1978. Double-cut solidbody, 2 pickups, comb-like device to convert it to 6-string.

1968-1969		$2,500	$3,100
1970-1978		$2,000	$2,500

Model 460

1961-1985. Double-cut solidbody, 2 pickups, neck-thru-body, deluxe trim.

1961-1965		$2,500	$3,100
1966-1969		$2,200	$2,300
1970-1979	Includes rare color	$2,000	$2,500
1980-1985		$1,400	$1,700

Model 480

1973-1984. Double-cut solidbody with long thin bass horn in 4001 bass series style, 2 pickups, cresting wave body and headstock, bolt-on neck.

1973-1979		$2,500	$3,000
1980-1984		$2,000	$2,500

Model 481

1973-1983. Cresting wave body with longer bass horn, 2 humbuckers (3 optional), angled frets.

1973-1979		$2,600	$3,100
1980-1983		$2,100	$2,600

MODEL YEAR	FEATURES	EXC. COND. LOW	HIGH

Model 483

1973-1983. Cresting wave body with longer bass horn, 3 humbuckers.

1973-1979		$2,700	$3,200
1980-1983		$2,200	$2,700

Model 600/Combo 600

1954-1966. Modified double-cut.

1954-1957	Blond/white	$3,800	$4,800
1956-1959	OT/Blue Turquoise	$3,800	$4,800
1962-1966		$2,800	$3,500

Model 610

1985-1991. Cresting-wave cutaway solidbody, 2 pickups, trapeze R-tailpiece, Jetglo.

1985-1991		$900	$1,100

Model 610/12

1988-1997. 12-string version of Model 610.

1988-1997		$900	$1,100

Model 615

1962-1966, 1969-1977. Double-cut solidbody, 2 pickups, vibrato.

1962-1965		$2,000	$2,500
1966-1969		$1,800	$2,200
1970-1977		$1,600	$2,000

Model 620

1974-present. Double-cut solidbody, deluxe binding, 2 pickups, neck-thru-body.

1974-1979		$1,700	$2,100
1980-1989		$1,300	$1,600
1990-1999		$1,200	$1,500
2000-2010		$1,200	$1,500

Model 620/12

1981-present. Double-cut solidbody, 2 pickups, 12 strings, standard trim.

1981-1989		$1,300	$1,600
1990-2010		$1,200	$1,500

Model 625

1962-1977. Double-cut solidbody, deluxe trim, 2 pickups, vibrato.

1962-1965		$4,000	$5,000
1966-1969		$2,800	$3,500
1970-1977		$2,200	$2,700

Model 650/Combo 650

1957-1959. Standard color, 1 pickup.

1957-1959		$3,800	$4,800

Model 650 A Atlantis

1991-2004. Cresting wave solidbody, neck-thru, 2 pickups, chrome hardware, turquoise.

1991-2004		$1,000	$1,200

Model 650 C Colorado

1993-present. Maple neck and body, neck-thru, 2 pickups.

1993-2010		$1,000	$1,200

Model 650 D Dakota

1993-present. Tulip-shaped neck-thru solidbody, single pickup, chrome hardware, walnut oil-satin finish.

1993-2010		$1,000	$1,200

Model 650 E Excalibur/F Frisco

1991-2003. African Vermilion, gold hardware, gloss finish. Name changed to Frisco in '95.

1991-2003		$1,000	$1,200

Model 650 S Sierra

1993-present. Tulip-shaped neck-thru solidbody, single pickup, gold hardware, walnut oil-satin finish.

1993-2010		$1,000	$1,200

Model 660

1998-present. Cresting wave maple body, triangle inlays, 2 pickups.

1998-2010		$1,800	$2,100

Model 660 DCM 75th Anniversary

2006-2007. 75th 1931-2006 Anniversary pickguard logo.

2006-2007		$2,100	$2,600

Model 660/12

1998-present. 12-string 660.

1998-2010		$2,000	$2,500

Model 660/12 TP

1991-1998. Tom Petty model, 12 strings, cresting wave body, 2 pickups, deluxe trim, limited run of 1000.

1991-1998	With certificate	$3,000	$3,700

Model 800/Combo 800

1954-1966. Offset double-cut, 1 horseshoe pickup until late-'57, second bar type after, called the Model 800 in the '60s.

1954-1957	Blond/white, 1 pickup	$4,000	$5,000
1954-1957	Blue or green, 1 pickup	$4,000	$5,000
1957-1959	Blond/white, 2 pickups	$4,000	$5,000
1957-1959	Blue or green, 2 pickups	$4,000	$5,000
1962-1966		$3,000	$3,700

Model 850/Combo 850

1957-1959. Extreme double-cut, 1 pickup until '58, 2 after, various colors, called Model 850 in the '60s.

1957-1959		$4,000	$5,000

Model 900

1957-1980. Double-cut tulip body shape, 3/4 size, 1 pickup. Body changes to cresting wave shape in '69.

1957-1966		$1,500	$1,900

Model 950/Combo 950

1957-1980. Like Model 900, but with 2 pickups, 21 frets. Body changes to cresting wave shape in '69.

1957-1964		$1,800	$2,200
1965-1980		$1,700	$2,100

Model 1000

1957-1970. Like Model 900, but with 18 frets. Body does not change to cresting wave shape.

1956-1966		$1,400	$1,700
1967-1970		$1,300	$1,600

Model 1993/12 RM

1964-1967. Export 'slim-line' 12-string model made for English distributor Rose-Morris of London, built along the lines of the U.S. Model 360/12 but with small differences that are considered important in the vintage guitar market.

1964	Flat tailpiece	$5,000	$6,200
1965-1967	R tailpiece	$5,000	$6,200

Model 1996 RM

1964-1967. Rose-Morris import, 3/4 size built similiarly to the U.S. Model 325.

1964-1967		$9,000	$11,000

Rickenbacker Model 625

Rickenbacker Model 660

*1995 Rickenbacker Model 1997
RM Reissue*

Art Vogue

Rigaud Acoustic

MODEL YEAR	FEATURES	EXC. COND. LOW	HIGH

Model 1996 RM Reissue
2006. Reissue of the Rose-Morris version of Model 325, this reissue available on special order in 2006.

| 2006 | | $2,500 | $2,900 |

Model 1997 PT
1987-1988. Pete Townsend Signature Model, semi-hollowbody, single F-hole, maple neck, 21-fret rosewood 'board, 3 pickups, Firemist finish, limited to 250 total production.

| 1987-1988 | | $3,100 | $3,800 |

Model 1997 RM
1964-1967. Export 'slim-line' model made for English distributor Rose-Morris of London, built along the lines of the U.S. Model 335, but with small differences that are considered important in the vintage guitar market, 2 pickups, vibrola tailpiece. Rose-Morris export models sent to the USA generally had a red-lined guitar case vs. the USA domestic blue-lined guitar case.

| 1964-1967 | | $4,000 | $5,000 |

Model 1997 RM Reissue
1987-1995. Reissue of '60s Rose-Morris model, but with vibrola (VB) or without.

| 1987-1995 | | $1,800 | $2,200 |

Model 1997 SPC
1993-2002. 3 pickup version of reissue.

| 1993-2002 | | $1,500 | $1,900 |

Model 1998 RM
1964-1967. Export 'slim-line' model made for English distributor Rose-Morris of London, built along the lines of a U.S. Model 345 but with small differences that are considered important in the vintage guitar market, 3 pickups, vibrola tailpiece.

| 1964-1967 | | $4,000 | $5,000 |

Rickenbacker Spanish/Spanish/SP
1946-1949. Block markers.

| 1946-1949 | | $1,800 | $2,300 |

S-59
1940-1942. Arch top body built by Kay, horseshoe magnet pickup.

| 1940-1942 | | $1,600 | $2,100 |

Rigaud Guitars
1978-present. Luthier Robert Rigaud builds his premium grade, custom/production, flat top guitars in Greensboro, North Carolina. He also builds bowed psalterys and harps.

Ritz
1989. Solidbody electric guitars and basses produced in Calimesa, California, by Wayne Charvel, Eric Galletta and Brad Becnel, many of which featured cracked shell mosiac finishes.

RKS
2003-present. Professional and premium grade, production/custom, electric hollowbody and solidbody guitars designed by Ravi Sawhney and guitarist Dave Mason and built in Thousand Oaks, California. They also build basses.

MODEL YEAR	FEATURES	EXC. COND. LOW	HIGH

Robert Cefalu
1998-present. Luthier Robert Cefalu builds his professional grade, production/custom, acoustic guitars in Buffalo, New York. The guitars have an RC on the headstock.

Robert Guitars
1981-present. Luthier Mikhail Robert builds his premium grade, production/custom, classical guitars in Summerland, British Columbia.

Robertson Guitars
1995-present. Luthier Jeff Robertson builds his premium grade, production/custom flat-top guitars in South New Berlin, New York.

Robin
1982-2010. Professional and premium grade, production/custom, guitars from luthier David Wintz and built in Houston, Texas. Most guitars were Japanese-made until '87; American production began in '88. Most Japanese Robins were pretty consistent in features, but the American ones were often custom-made, so many variations in models exist. They also made Metropolitan ('96-'08) and Alamo ('00-'08) brand guitars.

Avalon Classic
1994-2010. Single-cut, figured maple top, 2 humbuckers.

| 1994-2010 | | $1,100 | $1,350 |

Medley Pro
1990s. Solidbody with 2 extreme cutaway horns, hum-single-single.

| 1990s | U.S.-made | $750 | $900 |

Medley Special
1992-1995. Ash body, maple neck, rosewood 'board, 24 frets, various pickup options.

| 1992-1995 | | $500 | $625 |

Medley Standard
1985-2010. Offset double-cut swamp ash solidbody, bolt neck, originally with hum-single-single pickups, but now also available with 2 humbuckers.

| 1985-1987 | Japan-made | $400 | $500 |
| 1988-2010 | U.S.-made | $750 | $900 |

Octave
1982-1990s. Tuned an octave above standard tuning, full body size with 15 1/2" short-scale bolt maple neck. Japanese-made production model until '87, U.S.-made custom shop after.

| 1990s | With original case | $650 | $800 |

Raider I/Raider II/Raider III
1985-1991. Double-cut solidbody, 1 humbucker pickup (Raider I), 2 humbuckers (Raider II), or 3 single-coils (Raider III), maple neck, either maple or rosewood 'board, sunburst.

1985-1991	1 pickup	$400	$475
1985-1991	2 pickups	$425	$525
1985-1991	3 pickups	$450	$550

MODEL YEAR	FEATURES	EXC. COND. LOW	HIGH

Ranger
1982. First production model with 2 single-coil pickups in middle and neck position, reverse headstock, dot markers.

1982		$775	$975

Ranger Custom
1982-1986, 1988-2010. Swamp ash bound body, bolt-on maple neck, rosewood or maple 'board, 2 single coils and 1 humbucker, orange, made in Japan until '86, U.S.-made after.

1982-1986	Japan-made	$400	$500
1988-2010	U.S.-made	$650	$800

RDN-Doubleneck Octave/Six
1982-1985. Six-string standard neck with 3 pickups, 6-string octave neck with 1 pickup, double-cut solidbody.

1982-1985	With original case	$750	$950

Savoy Deluxe/Standard
1995-2010. Semi-hollow thinline single cut archtop, 2 pickups, set neck.

1996-2010		$1,300	$1,600

Soloist/Artisan
1982-1986. Mahogany double-cut solidbody, carved bound maple top, set neck, 2 humbuckers. Renamed Artisan in '85. Only about 125 made in Japan.

1982-1986		$575	$725

Wedge
1985-ca. 1988. Triangle-shaped body, 2 humbuckers, Custom with set neck and triangle inlays, Standard with bolt neck and dots, about 200 made.

1985-1988		$575	$700

Wrangler
1995-2002. Classic '50s single-cut slab body, 3 Rio Grande pickups, opaque finish.

1995-2002		$575	$700

Robinson Guitars
2002-present. Premium and presentation grade, custom/production, steel string guitars built by luthier Jake Robinson in Kalamazoo, Michigan.

RockBeach Guitars
2005-present. Luthier Greg Bogoshian builds his custom, professional grade, chambered electric guitars in Rochester, New York. He also builds basses.

Rockinbetter
2011-present. Intermediate grade, production electric guitars, copies of Rickenbacker models, made in China. They also offer basses.

Rocking F
See listing under Fox.

Rockit Guitar
2006-present. Luthier Rod MacKenzie builds his premium grade, custom, electric guitars in Everett, Washington. He also builds basses.

Rogands
Late 1960s. Produced by France's Jacobacci company and named after brothers Roger and Andre. Short-lived brand; the brothers made instruments under several other brands as well.

Roger
Guitars built in Germany by luthier Wenzel Rossmeisl and named for his son Roger. Roger Rossmeisl would go on to work at Rickenbacker and Fender.

Rogue
2001-present. Budget and intermediate grade, production, acoustic, resonator, electric and sitar guitars. They also offer mandolins, banjos, ukuleles, lap steels and basses. They previously offered effects and amps.

Roland
Best known for keyboards, effects, and amps, Roland offered synthesizer-based guitars and basses from 1977 to '86.

GR-707 Synth Guitar
1983-1986. Slab-wedge asymmetrical body, bass bout to headstock support arm, 2 humbucker pickups, multi-controls.

1983-1986	Silver	$1,100	$1,300

GS-500 Synth Guitar/Module
1977-1986. Snyth functions in a single-cut solidbody guitar. The GS-300 was the same electronics in a classic offset double-cut body.

1977-1986	Sunburst	$900	$1,050

Rolando
1916-ca. 1919. Private branded instruments made for the Southern California Music Company of Los Angeles, by Martin. There were three models.

00-28K/1500
1916		$4,500	$5,500

Rolf Spuler
1981-present. Presentation grade, custom, hybrid electric-acoustic guitars, built by luthier Rolf Spuler in Gebenstorf, Switzerland. He also builds basses.

Roman & Lipman Guitars
1989-2000. Production/custom, solidbody guitars made in Danbury, Connecticut by Ed Roman. They also made basses.

Roman Abstract Guitars
1989-present. Professional and premium grade, production/custom, solidbody guitars made in Las Vegas, Nevada by Ed Roman.

Roman Centurion Guitars
2001-present. Premium and presentation grade, custom guitars made in Las Vegas, Nevada by Ed Roman.

Robin Wrangler Supreme

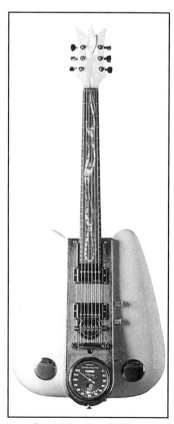
Rockit Limited Edition

Running Dog Concert

Sadowsky Vintage Style

MODEL YEAR	FEATURES	EXC. COND. LOW	HIGH

Roman Pearlcaster Guitars

1999-present. Professional and premium grade, production/custom, solidbody guitars made in Las Vegas, Nevada by Ed Roman.

Roman Quicksilver Guitars

1997-present. Professional and premium grade, production/custom, solid and hollow-body guitars made in Las Vegas, Nevada by Ed Roman.

Roman Vampire Guitars

2004-present. Professional and premium grade, production/custom, solidbody guitars made in Las Vegas, Nevada by Ed Roman.

Rono

1967-present. Luthier Ron Oates builds his professional and premium grade, production/custom, flat-top, jazz, Wiesenborn-style, and resonator guitars in Boulder, Colorado. He also builds basses and mandolins.

Ro-Pat-In

See Rickenbacker.

Rosetti

1950s-1960s. Guitars imported into England by distributor Rosetti, made by Holland's Egmond, maybe others.

Solid 7

1960. Symmetrical cutaway electric solidbody, large 'guard with top-mounted dual pickups, 4 control knobs, value is associated with Paul McCartney's use in '60, value dependent on completely original McCartney specs.

1960		$400	$500

Roudhloff

1810s-1840s. Luthier Francois Roudhloff built his instruments in France. Labels could state F. Roudhloff-Mauchand or Roudhloff Brothers. Valuation depends strongly on condition and repair. His sons built guitars under the D & A Roudhloff label.

Rowan

1997-present. Professional and premium grade, production/custom, solidbody and acoustic/electric guitars built by luthier Michael Rowan in Garland, Texas.

Royal

ca. 1954-ca. 1965. Line of jazz style guitars made by France's Jacobacci company, which also built under its own brand.

Royal (Japan)

1957-1960s. Early budget level instruments made by Tokyo Sound Company and Gakki and exported by Japan's Hoshino (Ibanez).

Royden Guitars

1996-present. Professional grade, production/custom, flat-tops and solidbody electrics built by luthier Royden Moran in Peterborough, Ontario.

RS Guitarworks

1994-present. Professional grade, production/custom, solid and hollowbody guitars built by luthier Roy Bowen in Winchester, Kentucky.

Rubio, German Vasquez

1993-present. Luthier German Vasquez Rubio builds his professional and premium grade, production/custom classical and flamenco guitars in Los Angeles, California.

Ruck, Robert

1966-present. Premium grade, custom classical and flamenco guitars built by luthier Robert Ruck originally in Kalaheo, Hawaii, and currently in Eugene, Oregon.

Running Dog Guitars

1994-present. Luthier Rick Davis builds his professional and premium grade, custom flat-tops in Seattle, Washington. He was originally located in Richmond, Vermont.

Ruokangas

1995-present. Luthier Juha Ruokangas builds his premium and presentation grade, production/custom, solidbody and semi-acoustic electric guitars in Hyvinkaa, Finland.

Rustler

1993-ca. 1998. Solidbody electrics with hand-tooled leather bound and studded sides and a R branded into the top, built by luthier Charles Caponi in Mason City, Iowa.

RVC Guitars

1999-present. Professional and premium grade, production/custom, solidbody guitars made in Las Vegas, Nevada by Ed Roman.

RWK

1991-present. Luthier Bob Karger builds his intermediate grade, production/custom, solidbody electrics and travel guitars in Highland Park, Illinois.

Ryder

1963. Made by Rickenbacker, the one guitar with this brand was the same as their solidbody Model 425.

S. B. Brown Guitars

1994-present. Custom flat-tops made by luthier Steve Brown in Fullerton, California.

MODEL		EXC. COND.	
YEAR	FEATURES	LOW	HIGH

S. B. MacDonald Custom Instruments

1988-present. Professional and premium grade, custom/production, flat-top, resonator, and solidbody guitars built by luthier Scott B. MacDonald in Huntington, New York.

S. Walker Custom Guitars

2002-present. Luthier Scott Walker builds his premium grade, production/custom, solid and semi hollow body electric guitars in Santa Cruz, California.

S. Yairi

Ca. 1960-1980s. Steel string folk guitars and classical nylon string guitars by master Japanese luthier Sadao Yairi, imported by Philadelphia Music Company of Limerick, Pennsylvania. Early sales literature called the brand Syairi. Most steel string models have dreadnought bodies and nylon-string classical guitars are mostly standard grand concert size. All models are handmade. Steel string Jumbos and dreadnoughts have Syairi logo on the headstock, nylon-classical models have no logo. The Model 900 has a solid wood body, others assumed to have laminate bodies.

S.D. Curlee

1975-1982. Founded in Matteson, Illinois by music store owner Randy Curlee, after an unsuccessful attempt to recruit builder Dan Armstrong. S.D. Curlee guitars were made in Illinois, while S.D. Curlee International instruments were made by Matsumoku in Japan. The guitars featured mostly Watco oil finishes, often with exotic hardwoods, and unique neck-thru-bridge construction on American and Japanese instruments. These were the first production guitars to use a single-coil pickup at the bridge with a humbucker at the neck, and a square brass nut. DiMarzio pickups. Offered in a variety of shapes, later some copies. Approximately 12,000 American-made basses and 3,000 guitars were made, most of which were sold overseas. Two hundred were made in '75-'76; first production guitar numbered 518.

Electric Solidbody

1975-1982. Models include the '75-'81 Standard I, II and III, '76-'81 International C-10 and C-11, '80-'81 Yanke, Liberty, Butcher, Curbeck, Summit, Special, and the '81-'82 Destroyer, Flying V.
1975-1982 $350 $400

S.L. Smith Guitars

2007-present. Professional grade, production/custom, acoustic guitars built by Steven Smith in Brant Lake, New York.

S.S. Stewart

The original S.S. Stewart Company (1878-1904), of Philadelphia, Pennsylvania is considered to be one of the most important banjo manufacturers of

MODEL		EXC. COND.	
YEAR	FEATURES	LOW	HIGH

the late 19th century. Samuel Swaim Stewart died in 1988 and his family was out of the company by the early 1900s, and the brand was soon acquired by Bugellsein & Jacobsen of New York. The brand name was used on guitars into the 1960s.

S101

2002-present. Budget and intermediate grade, production, classical, acoustic, resonator, solid and semi-hollow body guitars imported from China by America Sejung Corp. They also offer basses, mandolins, and banjos.

Sadowsky

1980-present. Professional and premium grade, production/custom, solidbody, semi-hollowbody, archtop, and electric nylon-string guitars built by luthier Roger Sadowsky in Brooklyn, New York. He also builds basses and amps. In '96, luthier Yoshi Kikuchi started building Sadowsky Tokyo instruments in Japan.

Saga

Saga Musical Instruments, of San Francisco, California distributes a wide variety of instruments and brands, occasionally including their own line of solidbody guitars called the Saga Gladiator Series (1987-'88, '94-'95). In the 2000s, Saga also offered component kits ($90-$130) that allowed for complete assembly in white wood.

Sahlin Guitars

1975-present. Luthier Eric Sahlin builds his premium grade, custom, classical and flamenco guitars in Spokane, Washington.

Samick

1958-2001, 2002-present. Budget, intermediate and professional grade, production, imported acoustic and electric guitars. They also offer basses, mandolins, ukes and banjos. Samick also distributes Abilene and Silvertone brand instruments.

Samick started out producing pianos, adding guitars in '65 under other brands. In '88 Samick greatly increased their guitar production. The Samick line of 350 models was totally closed out in 2001. A totally new line of 250 models was introduced January 2002 at NAMM. All 2002 models have the new compact smaller headstock and highly styled S logo.

Sammo

1920s. Labels in these instruments state they were made by the Osborne Mfg. Co. with an address of Masonic Temple, Chicago, Illinois. High quality and often with a high degree of ornamentation. They also made ukes and mandolins.

Sand Guitars

1979-present. Luthier Kirk Sand opened the Guitar Shoppe in Laguna Beach, California in 1972

S.L. Smith Guitars

Sahlin Guitars

Santa Cruz D

*1986 Schecter
Yngwie Malmsteen*

MODEL YEAR	FEATURES	EXC. COND. LOW	HIGH

with James Matthews. By '79, he started producing his own line of premium grade, production/custom-made flat-tops.

Sandoval Engineering

1979-present. Luthier Karl Sandoval builds his premium grade, custom, solidbody guitars in Santa Fe Springs, California.

Sano

1944-ca. 1970. Sano was a New Jersey-based accordion company that imported Italian-made solid and semi-hollow body guitars for a few years, starting in 1966; some, if not all, made by Zero Sette. They also built their own amps and reverb units.

Santa Cruz

1976-present. Professional, premium and presentation grade, production/custom, flat-top, 12-string, and archtop guitars from luthier Richard Hoover in Santa Cruz, California. They also build a mandocello and ukuleles. Founded by Hoover, Bruce Ross and William Davis. Hoover became sole owner in '89. Custom ordered instruments with special upgrades may have higher values than the ranges listed here.

Archtop
Early 1980s-present. Originally called the FJZ, but by mid-'90s, called the Archtop, offering 16", 17" and 18" cutaway acoustic/electric models, often special order. Spruce top, curly maple body, ebony 'board, floating pickup, f-holes, sunburst or natural. Many custom options available.
1980-1990s		$3,800	$4,700

D 12-Fret
1994-present. 15 1/2" scale, 12-fret neck, slotted headstock, round shoulders, spruce top, mahogany back and sides, notch diamond markers, herringbone trim and rosette, natural. Special order models will vary in value and could exceed the posted range.
| 1994-2010 | | $1,900 | $2,200 |

D Koa
1980s-1990s. Style D with koa back and sides.
| 1990s | | $1,900 | $2,200 |

D/HR (Richard Hoover)
| 2000 | Indian rosewood | $2,100 | $2,500 |

D/PW Pre-War
2001-present. Pre-war D-style.
| 2001-2010 | | $1,800 | $2,100 |

F
1976-present. 15 7/8" scale with narrow waist, sitka spruce top, Indian rosewood back and sides, natural.
| 1976-2010 | | $3,100 | $3,800 |

F46R
1980s. Brazilian rosewood, single-cut.
| 1980s | | $3,700 | $4,500 |

Firefly
2009-present. Premium quality travel/parlor guitar, cedar top, flamed maple sides and back.
| 2009 | | $2,300 | $2,800 |

FS (Finger Style)
1988-present. Single-cut, cedar top, Indian rosewood back and sides, mahogany neck, modified X-bracing.
| 1988-2010 | | $3,000 | $3,300 |

H/H13
1976-present. Parlor size acoustic, offered in cutaway and non-cut versions, and options included koa, rosewood or maple, special inlays, slotted headstock, and shallow or deep bodies.
| 1976-1999 | | $2,200 | $2,700 |
| 2000-2010 | | $2,200 | $2,700 |

H91
1990. 14 5/8", flamed koa.
| 1990 | | $2,400 | $3,000 |

OM (Orchestra Model)
1987-present. Orchestra model acoustic, sitka spruce top, Indian rosewood (Brazilian optional) back and sides, herringbone rosette, scalloped braces.
1987-2010	Brazilian rosewood	$4,800	$6,000
1987-2010	Indian rosewood	$2,400	$3,000
1995	Koa	$3,400	$4,100

OM/PW Pre-War
2000s. Indian rosewood.
| 2000s | | $1,800 | $2,200 |

Tony Rice
1976-present. Dreadnought, Indian rosewood body (Brazilian optional until Tony Rice Professional model available), sitka spruce top, solid peghead, zigzag back stripe, pickup optional.
| 1976-1999 | | $2,800 | $3,200 |
| 2000-2010 | | $2,800 | $3,200 |

Tony Rice Professional
1997-present. Brazilian rosewood back and sides, carved German spruce top, zigzag back stripe, solid peghead.
| 1997-2010 | | $5,500 | $6,300 |

Vintage Artist
1992-present. Mahogany body, sitka spruce top, zigzag back stripe, solid peghead, scalloped X-bracing, pickup optional.
| 1992-2010 | | $2,400 | $2,700 |

Vintage Artist Custom
1992-2004. Martin D-42 style, mahogany body, Indian rosewood back and sides, sitka spruce top, zigzag back stripe, solid peghead, scalloped X-bracing, pickup optional.
| 1992-2004 | | $2,600 | $3,200 |

VJ (Vintage Jumbo)
2000-present. 16" scale, round shouldered body, sitka spruce, figured mahogany back and sides, natural.
| 2000-2010 | | $2,200 | $2,700 |

Santos Martinez
Ca. 1997-present. Intermediate grade, production, acoustic and electro-acoustic classical guitars, imported from China by John Hornby Skewes & Co. in the U.K.

MODEL		EXC. COND.	
YEAR	FEATURES	LOW	HIGH

Saturn

1960s-1970s. Imported, most likely from Japan, solid and semi-hollow body electric guitars and basses. Large S logo with Saturn name inside the S. Many sold through Eaton's in Canada.

Saturn
1960s-1970. Solidbody, 4 pickups.
1960s-1970 $300 $400

Sawchyn Guitars

1972-present. Professional and premium grade, production/custom, flat-top and flamenco guitars and mandolins built by luthier Peter Sawchyn in Regina, Saskatchewan.

Schaefer

1997-present. Premium grade, production, electric archtops handcrafted by luthier Edward A. Schaefer, who was located in Fort Worth, Texas, until '03, then in Duluth, Minnesota until '07, then Bastrop, Texas, and currently in Austin.

Schecter

1976-present. Intermediate, professional and premium grade, production/custom, acoustic and electric guitars. They also offer basses. Guitar component manufacturer founded in California by four partners (David Schecter's name sounded the best), started offering complete instruments in '79. The company was bought out and moved to Dallas, Texas in the early '80s. By '88 the company was back in California and in '89 was purchased by Hisatake Shibuya. Schecter Custom Shop guitars are made in Burbank, California and their intermediate grade Diamond Series is made in South Korea.

Scheerhorn

1989-present. Professional and premium grade, custom, resonator and Hawaiian guitars built by luthier Tim Scheerhorn in Kentwood, Michigan.

Schoenberg

1986-present. Premium grade, production/custom, flat-tops offered by Eric Schoenberg of Tiburon, California. From '86-'94 guitars made to Schoenberg's specifications by Martin. From '86-'90 constructed by Schoenberg's luthier and from '90-'94 assembled by Martin but voiced and inlaid in the Schoenberg shop. Current models made to Schoenberg specs by various smaller shops.

Schon

1986-1991. Designed by guitarist Neal Schon, early production by Charvel/Jackson building about 200 in the San Dimas factory. The final 500 were built by Larrivee in Canada. Leo Knapp also built custom Schon guitars from '85-'87, and '90s custom-made Schon guitars were also available.

Standard (Canadian-made)
1987-1991. Made in Canada on headstock.
1987-1991 $425 $575

MODEL		EXC. COND.	
YEAR	FEATURES	LOW	HIGH

Standard (U.S.A.-made)
1986 only. San Dimas/Jackson model, single-cut, pointy headstock shape, Made in U.S.A. on headstock.
1986 $1,300 $1,600

Schramm Guitars

1990-present. Premium grade, production/custom, classical and flamenco guitars built by luthier David Schramm in Clovis, California.

Schroder Guitars

1993-present. Luthier Timothy Schroeder (he drops the first e in his name on the guitars) builds his premium grade, production/custom, archtops in Northbrook, Illinois.

Schulte

1950s-2000. Luthier C. Eric Schulte made solidbody, semi-hollow body, hollow body and acoustic guitars, both original designs and copies, covering a range of prices, in the Philadelphia area.

Custom Copy
1982. Single-cut solidbody, figured maple top.
1982 $800 $900

Schwartz Guitars

1992-present. Premium grade, custom, flat-top guitars built by luthier Sheldon Schwartz in Concord, Ontario.

ScoGo

2001-present. Professional and premium grade, production/custom, solidbody guitars built by luthier Scott Gordon in Parkesburg, Pennsylvania.

Scorpion Guitars

1998-present. Professional and premium grade, custom, solidbody guitars made in Las Vegas, Nevada by Ed Roman.

Scott French

2004-present. Professional grade, custom, electric guitars built by luthier Scott French in Auburn, California. He also builds basses.

Scott Walker Custom Guitars

Refer to S. Walker Custom Guitars.

Seagull

1982-present. Intermediate grade, production, acoustic and acoustic/electric guitars built in Canada. Seagull was founded by luthier Robert Godin, who also has the Norman, Godin, and Patrick & Simon brands of instruments.

Sebring

1980s-mid-1990s. Entry level Korean imports distributed by V.M.I. Industries.

Scorpion Neck-Thru

2007 Seagull Maritime

MODEL YEAR	FEATURES	EXC. COND. LOW	HIGH

1937 Selmer Orchestre

Seiwa

Early 1980s. Entry-level to mid-level Japanese electric guitars and basses, logo may indicate Since 1956.

Sekova

Mid-1960s-mid-1970s. Entry level instruments imported by the U.S. Musical Merchandise Corporation of New York.

Selmer

1932-1952. France-based Selmer & Cie was primarily a maker of wind instruments when they asked Mario Maccaferri to design a line of guitars for them. The guitars, with an internal sound chamber for increased volume, were built in Mantes-la-Ville. Both gut and steel string models were offered. Maccaferri left Selmer in '33, but guitar production continued, and the original models are gradually phased out. In '36, only the 14 fret oval model is built. Production is stopped for WWII and resumes in '46, finally stopping in '52. Less than 900 guitars are built in total.

Classique

1942. Solid Rosewood back and sides, no cutaway, solid spruce top, round soundhole, classical guitar size, possibly only 2 built.

| 1942 | | $6,000 | $7,000 |

Concert

1932-1933. For gut strings, cutaway, laminated Indian rosewood back and sides, internal resonator, spruce top with D hole, wide walnut neck, ebony 'board, only a few dozen built.

| 1932-1933 | | $17,000 | $20,000 |

Eddie Freeman Special

1933. For steel strings, 4 strings, laminated Indian rosewood back and sides, cutaway, no internal resonator, solid spruce top, D hole, black and white rosette inlays, walnut 12 fret neck, ebony 'board, 640mm scale, approx. 100 made.

| 1933 | | $6,000 | $7,000 |

Espagnol

1932. For gut strings, laminated Indian rosewood back and sides, no cutaway, internal resonator, solid spruce top, round soundhole, wide walnut neck, ebony 'board, only a few made.

| 1932 | | $8,500 | $10,000 |

Grand Modele 4 Cordes

1932-1933. For steel strings, 4 string model, laminated back and sides, cutaway, internal resonator, solid spruce top, D hole, walnut neck, ebony 'board, 12 fret, 640mm scale, 2 or 3 dozen made.

| 1932-1933 | | $10,000 | $12,000 |

Harp Guitar

1933. For gut strings, solid mahogany body, extended horn holding 3 sub bass strings, 3 screw adjustable neck, wide walnut neck, ebony 'board, only about 12 built.

| 1933 | | $14,000 | $16,000 |

Sheppard Minstral Grand Concert

MODEL YEAR	FEATURES	EXC. COND. LOW	HIGH

Hawaienne

1932-1934. For steel strings, 6 or 7 strings, laminated back and sides, no cutaway, internal resonator, solid spruce top, D hole, wide walnut neck, ebony 'board, 2 or 3 dozen built.

| 1932-1934 | | $22,000 | $25,000 |

Jazz

| 1936-1952 | | $25,000 | $29,000 |

Modeles de Transition

1934-1936. Transition models appearing before 14 fret oval hole model, some in solid maple with solid headstock, some with round soundhole and cutaway, some 12 fret models with oval hole.

| 1934-1936 | | $16,000 | $19,000 |

Orchestre

1932-1934. For steel strings, laminated back and sides, cutaway, internal resonator, solid spruce top, D hole, walnut neck, ebony 'board, about 100 made.

| 1932-1934 | | $29,000 | $34,000 |

Tenor

1932-1933. For steel strings, 4 strings, laminated back and sides, internal resonator, solid spruce top, D hole, walnut neck, ebony 'board, 12 fret, 570mm scale, 2 or 3 dozen built.

| 1932-1933 | | $5,500 | $6,500 |

Serenghetti

Late-2007-present. Luthier Ray Patterson builds his professional and premium grade, production/custom, 1-piece and neck-thru guitars in Ocala, Florida. He also builds basses.

Serge Guitars

1995-present. Luthier Serge Michaud builds his production/custom, classical, steel-string, resophonic and archtop guitars in Breakeyville, Quebec.

Sexauer Guitars

1967-present. Premium and presentation grade, custom, steel-string, 12-string, nylon-string, and archtop guitars built by luthier Bruce Sexauer in Petaluma, California.

Shadow

1990s. Made in Europe, copy models such as the classic offset double cutaway solidbody, large Shadow logo on headstock, Shadow logo on pickup cover, student to intermediate grade.

Shanti Guitars

1985-present. Premium and presentation grade, custom, steel-string, 12-string, nylon-string and archtop guitars built by luthier Michael Hornick in Avery, California.

Shelley D. Park Guitars

1991-present. Luthier Shelley D. Park builds her professional grade, custom, nylon- and steel-string guitars in Vancouver, British Columbia.

MODEL YEAR	FEATURES	EXC. COND. LOW	HIGH

Shelton-Farretta

1967-present. Premium grade, production/custom, flamenco and classical guitars built by luthiers John Shelton and Susan Farretta originally in Portland, Oregon, and since '05 in Alsea, Oregon.

Sheppard Guitars

1993-present. Luthier Gerald Sheppard builds his premium grade, production/custom, steel-string guitars in Kingsport, Tennessee.

Shergold

1968-1992. Founded by Jack Golder and Norman Houlder, Shergold originally made guitars for other brands like Hayman and Barnes and Mullins. In '75, they started building guitars and basses under their own name. By '82, general guitar production was halted but custom orders were filled through '90. In '91, general production was again started but ended in '92 when Golder died.

Sherwood

Late 1940s-early 1950s. Archtop and lap steel guitars made for Montgomery Ward made by Chicago manufacturers such as Kay. There were also Sherwood amps made by Danelectro. Value ranges are about the same as Kay model equivalent.

Shifflett

1990-present. Luthier Charles Shifflett builds his premium grade, production/custom, flat-top, classical, flamenco, resophonic, and harp guitars in High River, Alberta. He also builds basses and banjos.

Sho-Bro

1969-1978. Spanish and Hawaiian style resonator guitars made by Sho-Bud in Nashville, Tennessee and distributed by Gretsch. Designed Shot Jackson and Buddy Emmons.

Grand Slam

1978. Acoustic, spruce top, mahogany neck, jacaranda sides and back, and mother-of-pearl inlays, abalone soundhole purfling.

1970s		$450	$550

Resonator

1972-1978. Flat-top style guitar with metal resonator with 2 small circular grilled soundholes.

1972-1978		$750	$900

Siegmund Guitars & Amplifiers

1993-present. Luthier Chris Siegmund builds his professional, premium, and presentation grade, custom/production, archtop, solidbody, and resonator guitars in Los Angeles, California. He founded the company in Seattle, moving it to Austin, Texas for '95-'97. He also builds effects pedals and amps.

MODEL YEAR	FEATURES	EXC. COND. LOW	HIGH

Sierra

2006-present. Budget level imports by Musicorp. There is an unrelated brand of Sierra steels and lap steels.

Sigma

1970-2007. Budget and intermediate grade, production, import acoustic guitars distributed by C.F. Martin Company. They also offered basses, mandolins and banjos.

D-10 Anniversary

1980		$475	$600

DM Series

1987-1988	Various models	$150	$400

DR Series

1970-2003. Various dreadnought models.

1970-2003		$200	$650

DT Series

1980s	Various models	$175	$425

GCS Series

1994. Grand concert semi-narrow waist body, laminated spruce top, mahogany back and sides, natural.

1994		$150	$275

TB Series

2000s	Various models	$150	$275

Signet

1972-Mid 1970s. Acoustic flat-top guitars, imported from Japan by Ampeg/Selmer.

Silber

1992-1998. Solid wood, steel-string guitars designed by Marc Silber, made in Paracho, Mexico, and distributed by K & S Music. Silber continues to offer the same models under the Marc Silber Music brand.

Silver Street

1979-1986. Founded by brothers Bruce and Craig Hardy, production of solidbody electric guitars built in Elkhart, Indiana and later in Shelby, Michigan. Pre-production prototypes were built by luthier Richard Schneider. Suggested list prices ranged from $449 to $889.

Silvertone

1941-ca. 1970, present. Brand of Sears instruments which replaced their Supertone brand in '41. The Silvertone name was used on Sears phonographs, records and radios as early as the 'teens, and on occasional guitar models. When Sears divested itself of the Harmony guitar subsidiary in '40 it turned to other suppliers including Kay. In '40 Kay-made archtops and Hawaiian electric lap steels appeared in the catalog bearing the Silvertone brand, and after '41-'42, all guitars, regardless of manufacturer, were called Silvertone.

Sears offered Danelectro-made solidbodies in the fall of '54. Danelectro hollowbodies appeared in '56.

By '65, the Silvertones were Teisco-made guitars from W.M.I., but never sold through the catalog. First imports shown in catalog were in '69.

Sherwood Deluxe

1958 Silvertone 1303
Dave Kyle

1962 Silvertone Amp-in-Case Model 1448

James Goode

1959 Silvertone Model 1419

MODEL YEAR	FEATURES	EXC. COND. LOW	HIGH

By '70, most guitars sold by Sears were imports and did not carry the Silvertone name.

Currently, Samick offers a line of acoustic and electric guitars, basses and amps under the Silvertone name.

Special thanks to Brian Conner for providing Silvertone specifications.

Amp-In-Case
1962-1968. The 1-pickup guitar, introduced in '62, came with a smaller wattage amp without tremolo. The 2-pickup model, introduced in '63, came with a higher-watt amp with tremolo and better quality Jensen speaker. Gray tolex covered the guitar-amp case. In '67 the guitar body style changed from the sharp pointed cutaway horn to a more relaxed softer cutaway horn.

1962-1966	1448, 1 pickup	$450	$575
1963-1966	1449, 2 pickups	$550	$700
1967-1968	1451, 1 pickup	$450	$575
1967-1968	1452, 2 pickups	$550	$700

Belmont
1958. Single-cut solidbody, 2 pickups, black.

1958		$700	$850

Black Beauty Model 1384L
1956-1958. Called 'The Black Beauty' in Sears catalog, large body acoustic-electric archtop, cutaway model, 2 pickups, block position markers, white binding, spruce top, mahogany sides and back, black lacquer finish, Silvertone logo on headstock.

1956-1958		$1,300	$1,600

Black Beauty Model 1385
1957. Basically the same as 1384L.

1957		$1,300	$1,600

Espanada
1960s. Bigsby, 2 pickups, black.

1960s		$1,100	$1,400

Estrelita
1960s. Semi-hollowbody archtop, 2 pickups, black, Harmony-made.

1960s		$1,100	$1,400

F-66
1964. Similar to Harmony Rocket III, single-cut, thinline electric, 3 pickups, Bigsby.

1964		$1,000	$1,150

Gene Autry Melody Ranch
1941-1955. 13" Harmony-made acoustic, Gene Autry signature on belly, cowboy roundup stencil, same as earlier Supertone Gene Autry Roundup.

1941-1955		$275	$350

H-1214
1951. Full-size acoustic archtop, script Silvertone headstock logo, dot markers, blond with simulated grain finish.

1951		$350	$425

H-1260 Sovereigh Jumbo
1968. Silvertone's version of Harmony's Sovereigh jumbo flat-top, dot markers, sunburst.

1968		$500	$600

H-1434 Rocket
1965. Similar to Harmony Rocket H59, sold by Sears, 3 pickups, Bigsby vibrato.

1965		$1,000	$1,150

MODEL YEAR	FEATURES	EXC. COND. LOW	HIGH

Meteor
1955. Single-cut, 1 pickup, sunburst.

1955		$500	$600

Model 623
Late-1950s. Large-body acoustic archtop, white script Silvertone headstock logo, white dot markers, white 'guard, black finish, painted white binding to give a black and white attractive appearance.

1950s		$175	$225

Model 1381/Model 1382
1955-1957. Introduced in '54, made by Kay (note: many '50s Silvertones were made by Danelectro), slim-style electric similar to Thin Twin/Jimmy Reed, 2 lipstick-style pickups, 4 knobs, toggle switch, crown-crest logo on 'guard under strings, bolt-on neck, 3-on-a-side tuners, script Silvertone logo on headstock, block markers, sunburst finish, sold without a case (Model 1381) and with case (Model 1382).

1955-1957		$1,000	$1,200

Model 1415/Model 1416
1959-1962. Four-on-a-side headstock replaces the prior year U-1 coke-bottle headstock, 1 pickup on single-cut U-1 style body, bronze finish (1415) or black (1416).

1959-1962		$700	$850

Model 1420
1959-1963. Single-cut extra thin solidbody, bolt-on neck, 2 rectangular pickups, 3-way switch, script Silvertone headstock logo, natural shaded or black finish.

1959-1963		$350	$450

Model 1429L
1962-1963. Harmony-made and similar to Harmony's H-75, single-cut thinline electric, 3 pickups, trapeze tailpiece, 3 toggles, 6 knobs, block marker, sunburst.

1962-1963		$700	$875

Model 1446
1962-1966. Single-cut thin acoustic archtop, 2 special-design pickups, original factory Bigsby tailpiece, black lacquer finish with white 'guard.

1962-1966		$1,300	$1,600

Model 1454
1962-1966. Single-cut thin acoustic archtop, 3 pickups, original factory Bigsby tailpiece, red lacquer finish.

1962-1966		$1,000	$1,250

Model 1478
1964-1967. Offset double-cut, 2 rectangular pickups, tremolo, block markers, sunburst.

1964-1967		$275	$325

Model S1353
1955. Full body, single-cut, electric hollowbody, 1 pickup, 2 controls.

1955		$500	$625

Model S1453 Rebel
1968. Two sharp cutaway, single f-hole, 2 pickups, vibrato.

1968		$450	$550

Silhouette
1964-1967	1 pickup	$250	$300
1964-1967	2 pickups	$350	$425
1964-1967	3 pickups	$375	$450

The *Vintage Guitar Price Guide* shows low to high values for items in all-original excellent condition, and, where applicable, with original case or cover.

MODEL YEAR	FEATURES	EXC. COND. LOW	HIGH

Student-level 13" Flat-Top
1960s. Harmony-made, 13" lower bout.
| 1960s | | $40 | $50 |

Student-level 15.5" Flat-Top
| 1960s | Model S621 | $150 | $225 |

U-1
1957-1959. Danelectro-made, single pickup, Coke bottle headstock, bronze color.
| 1957-1959 | | $700 | $850 |

U-2
1957-1959. 2 pickups.
| 1957-1959 | | $800 | $950 |

U-3
1957-1959. Danoelectro-made, 3 pickups, single-cut.
| 1957-1959 | | $1,200 | $1,450 |

Ultra Thin Professional
1960s. Harmony-made, thin hollow cutaway, 3 pickups, Bigsby tailpiece.
| 1960s | | $700 | $850 |

Simon & Patrick

1985-present. Intermediate and professional grade, production, acoustic and acoustic/electric guitars built in Canada. Founded by luthier Robert Godin and named after his sons. He also produces the Seagull, Godin, and Norman brands of instruments.

Sims Custom Shop

2007-present. Custom, professional and premium grade, electric guitars built in Chattanooga, Tennessee by luthier Patrick Sims.

Singletouch

Luthier Mark Singleton builds his professional and premium grade, custom/production, solid and semi-hollow body guitars in Phillips Ranch, California. He also builds basses.

Skylark

1981. Solidbody guitars made in Japan and distributed by JC Penney. Two set-neck models and one bolt-neck model were offered. Most likely a one-time deal as brand quickly disappeared.

Slammer

1998-present. Budget and intermediate grade, production, guitars imported from Indonesia by Hamer. They also offer basses. Not to be confused with Hamer's Korean-made series of guitars from 1990-'97 called Hamer Slammer.

Slammer Series (Import)
| 1998-2009 | Various models | $125 | $200 |

Slingerland

Late 1920s-mid-1940s. The parent company was Slingerland Banjo and Drums, Chicago, Illinois. The company offered other stringed instruments into the '40s. They also marketed the May Bell brand. The guitars were made by other companies, mainly including Regal. Slingerland Drums is now owned by Gibson.

MODEL YEAR	FEATURES	EXC. COND. LOW	HIGH

Nitehawk
1930s. 16" archtop, Nitehawk logo on headstock, fancy position neck markers.
| 1930s | | $550 | $700 |

Songster Archtop/Flat-Top
| 1930s | Archtop | $450 | $550 |
| 1930s | Flat-Top | $825 | $1,000 |

Smart Musical Instruments

1986-present. Luthier A. Lawrence Smart builds his professional and premium grade, custom, flat-top guitars in McCall, Idaho. He also builds mandolin-family instruments.

Smith, George

1959-present. Custom classical and flamenco guitars built by luthier George Smith in Portland, Oregon.

Smith, Lawrence K.

1989-present. Luthier Lawrence Smith builds his professional and premium grade, production/custom, flat-top, nylon-string, and archtop guitars in Thirrow, New South Wales, Australia. He also builds mandolins.

SMK Music Works

2002-present. Luthier Scott Kenerson builds production/custom, professional grade, solidbody electric guitars in Waterford, Michigan. He also builds basses.

Smooth Stone Guitar

2007-present. Luthier R. Dale Humphries builds his professional and premium grade, production/custom, acoustic and electric guitars in Pocatello, Idaho. He also offers basses.

Solomon Guitars

1995-present. Luthier Erich Solomon builds his premium and presentation grade, production/custom, archtop, flat-top, classical and electric guitars in Epping, New Hampshire. Prior to '99 he was located in Anchorage, Alaska.

Somervell

1979-present. Luthier Douglas P. Somervell builds his premium and presentation grade, production/custom, classical and flamenco guitars in Brasstown, North Carolina.

Somogyi, Ervin

1971-present. Luthier Ervin Somogyi builds his presentation grade, production/custom, flat-top, flamenco, and classical guitars in Oakland, California.

Sonata

1960s. Private brand Harmony-made, Sonata brand logo on headstock and pickguard.

Simon & Patrick Songsmith

Lawrence K. Smith Archtop

Southwell A Series

1968 St. Moritz Stereo

MODEL YEAR	FEATURES	EXC. COND. LOW	HIGH

Superior
1965. Grand Auditorium acoustic archtop, block markers, celluloid bound edges, similar to Harmony 1456, Superior logo on headstock.
| 1965 | | $375 | $475 |

SonFather Guitars
1994-present. Luthier David A. Cassotta builds his production/custom, flat-top, 12-string, nylon-string and electric guitars in Rocklin, California.

Sorrentino
1930s. Private brand made by Epiphone and distributed by C.M.I. Quality close to similar Epiphone models.

Arcadia
1930s. Lower-end f-hole acoustic archtop similar to Epiphone Blackstone.
| 1930s | | $475 | $600 |

Sorrento
1960s. Electric guitar imports made by Teisco, pricing similar to Teisco models, Sorrento logo on headstock, upscale solidbodies can have four pickups with five knobs and four switches.

Electric Solidbody
| 1960s | 4 pickups | $275 | $350 |

Southwell Guitars
1983-present. Premium grade, custom, nylon-string guitars built by luthier Gary Southwell in Nottingham, England.

Sovereign
Ca. 1899-1938. Sovereign was originally a brand of The Oscar Schmidt Company of Jersey City, New Jersey, and used on guitars, banjos and mandolins starting in the very late 1800s. In the late '30s, Harmony purchased several trade names from the Schmidt Company, including Sovereign and Stella. Sovereign then ceased as a brand, but Harmony continued using it on a model line of Harmony guitars.

Spaltinstruments
2002-present. Luthier Michael Spalt builds his professional and premium grade, production/custom, electric solidbody and hollowbody guitars in Los Angeles, California. He also builds basses.

Sparrow Guitars
2004-present. Guitars manufactured in China are dismantled and "overhauled" in Vancouver, British Columbia. From these imports, luthier Billy Bones builds his intermediate and professional grade, production/custom solidbody and hollowbody electric guitars.

Specht Guitars
1991-present. Premium grade, production/custom, acoustic, baritone, parlor, jazz and classical guitars built by luthier Oliver Specht in Vancouver, British Columbia. He also builds basses.

Specimen Products
1984-present. Luthier Ian Schneller builds his professional and premium grade, production/custom, aluminum and wood body guitars in Chicago, Illinois. He also builds basses, ukes, amps and speaker cabs.

Spector/Stuart Spector Design
1975-1990 (Spector), 1991-1998 (SSD), 1998-present (Spector SSD). Known mainly for basses, Spector offered U.S.-made guitars during '75-'90 and '96-'99, and imports for '87-'90 and '96-'99. Since 2003, they again offer U.S.-professional grade, production, solidbody guitars. See Bass Section for more company info.

SPG
2006-2009. Originally professional grade, custom, solidbody and chambered guitars built by luthier Rick Welch in Farmingdale, Maine and Hanson, Massachusetts. He also built lapsteels. Currently brand is used on imported line.

Squier
See models listed under Squire in Fender section.

St. Blues
1980-1989, 2005-present. Intermediate and professional grade, production/custom, solidbody guitars imported and set up in Memphis, Tennessee. They also build basses. The original '80s line was designed by Tom Keckler and Charles Lawing at Memphis' Strings & Things.

St. George
Mid to late 1960s. Early Japanese brand imported possibly by Buegeleisen & Jacobson of New York, New York.

St. Moritz
1960s. Guitars and basses imported from Japan by unidentified distributor. Manufacturer unknown, but appears to be Fuji Gen Gakki. Generally shorter scale beginner guitars, some with interesting pickup configurations.

Stahl
1900-1941. William C. Stahl, of Milwaukee, Wisconsin, ran a publishing company, taught stringed instrument classes and sold instruments to his students as well as by mail order across America. His label claimed that he was the maker but most of his products were built by the Larson brothers of Maurer & Co. of Chicago, with the balance mostly from Washburn. The most commonly found Larson-built models are the Style 6 and 7 as seen in the ca. 1912 Stahl catalog. Jimi Hendrix was the

MODEL		EXC. COND.	
YEAR	FEATURES	LOW	HIGH

proud owner of a Style 8. The Style 6 is a moderately trimmed 15" Brazilian rosewood beauty that is much like the highly sought Maurer Style 551. The Style 7 and 8 are pearl trimmed 13 ½" concert size Brazilians comparable to the Maurer Style 562 ½. The 1912 Stahl catalog Styles 4, 5 and 9 were built by Washburn.

Stambaugh

1995-present. Luthier Chris Stambaugh builds his professional grade, custom/production, solidbody guitars in Stratham, New Hampshire. He also builds basses.

Standel

1952-1974, 1997-present. Amp builder Bob Crooks offered instruments under his Standel brand 3 different times during the '60s. In '61 Semie Moseley, later of Mosrite fame, made 2 guitar models and 1 bass for Standel, in limited numbers. Also in '61, Standel began distributing Sierra steels and Dobro resonators, sometimes under the Standel name. In '65 and '66 Standel offered a guitar and a bass made by Joe Hall, who also made the Hallmark guitars. In '66 Standel connected with Sam Koontz, who designed and produced the most numerous Standel models (but still in relatively small numbers) in Newark, New Jersey. These models hit the market in '67 and were handled by Harptone, which was associated with Koontz. By '70 Standel was out of the guitar biz. See Amp section for more company info.

Custom 420S
1967-1968. 2 pickups.

1967-1968		$1,125	$1,300

Custom Deluxe Solidbody 101/101X
1967-1968. Custom with better electronics, 101X has no vibrato, sunburst, black, pearl white and metallic red.

1967-1968		$1,125	$1,300

Custom Deluxe Thin Body 102/102X
1967-1968. Custom with better electronics, 102X has no vibrato, offered in sunburst and 5 solid color options.

1967-1968		$1,125	$1,300

Custom Solidbody 201/201X
1967-1968. Solidbody, 2 pickups, vibrola, 2 pointed cutaways, headstock similar to that on Fender XII, 201X has no vibrato, sunburst, black, pearl white and metallic red.

1967-1968		$725	$825

Custom Thin Body 202/202X
1967-1968. Thin body, headstock similar to that on Fender XII, 202X has no vibrato, offered in sunburst and 5 solid color options.

1967-1968		$725	$825

Star

1957-1960s. Early budget level instruments made by Tokyo Sound Company and Gakki and exported by Japan's Hoshino (translates to 'Star') company which also has Ibanez.

Starcaster

Early 2000s-present. Budget brand from Fender that has been used on acoustic, electric and bass guitars, effects, amps and drums and sold through mass retailers such as Costco, Target and others. See Fender listing for guitar values.

Starfield

1992-1993. Solidbody guitars from Hoshino (Ibanez) made in the U.S. and Japan. U.S. guitars are identified as American models; Japanese ones as SJ models. Hoshino also used the Star Field name on a line of Japanese guitars in the late '70s. These Star Fields had nothing to do with the '90s versions and were not sold in the U.S.

Starforce

Ca. 1989. Import copies from Starforce Music/Starforce USA.

Stars

Intermediate grade, production, solidbody guitars made in Korea.

Status Graphite

Professional grade, production/custom, solidbody guitars built in Colchester, Essex, England. They also build basses. Status was the first English company to produce a carbon fiber instrument.

Stauffer

1800s. Old World violin and guitar maker, Georg Stauffer. Valid attributions include signed or labeled by the maker indicating the guitar was actually made by Stauffer, as opposed to attributed to Stauffer or one of his contemporaries. See Martin for listing.

Stefan Sobell Musical Instruments

1982-present. Premium grade, production/custom, flat-top, 12-string, and archtop guitars built by luthier Stefan Sobell in Hetham, Northumberland, England. He also builds mandolins, citterns and bouzoukis.

Steinberger

1979-present. Currently Steinberger offers budget, intermediate, and professional grade, production, electric guitars. They also offer basses. Founded by Ned Steinberger, who started designing NS Models for Stuart Spector in '76. In '79, he designed the L-2 headless bass. In '80, the Steinberger Sound Corp. was founded. Steinberger Sound was purchased by the Gibson Guitar Corp. in '87, and in '92, Steinberger relocated to Nashville, Tennessee.

Headless model codes for '85-'93 are:
First letter is X for bass or G for guitar.
Second letter is for body shape: M is regular offset double-cut guitar body; L is rectangle body; P is mini V shaped body.

Stefan Sobell New World

Steinberger ZT3 Custom

1968 Stella/Harmony

Stratosphere Doubleneck

MODEL		EXC. COND.	
YEAR	FEATURES	LOW	HIGH

Number is pickup designation: 2 = 2 humbuckers, 3 = 3 single coils, 4 = single/single/humbucker.
Last letter is type of tremolo: S = S-Trem tremolo; T = Trans-Trem which cost more on original retail.

Steinegger
1976-present. Premium grade, custom steel-string flat-top guitars built by luthier Robert Steinegger in Portland, Oregon.

Stella
Ca. 1899-1974, 2000s. Stella was a brand of the Oscar Schmidt Company which started using the brand on low-mid to mid-level instruments in the very late 1800s. Oscar Schmidt produced all types of stringed instruments and was very successful in the 1920s. Company salesmen reached many rural areas and Stella instruments were available in general stores, furniture stores, and dry goods stores, ending up in the hands of musicians such as Leadbelly and Charlie Patton. Harmony acquired the Stella brand in '39 and built thousands of instruments with that name in the '50s and '60s. Harmony dissolved in '74. The Stella brand was reintroduced in the 2000s by MBT International.

00 Style
1900-1930. Oak body flat-top.

1900-1930		$450	$550

Flat-Top 15" 12-String
1920s-1930s. Associated with early blues and folk musicians, top of the line for Stella.

1920-1930s		$4,000	$5,000

Flat-Top by Harmony
1950s-1960s. The low end of the Harmony-built models, US-made until the end of the '60s, student level, Stella logo on headstock, playing action can often be very high which makes them difficult to play.

1950-1960s	13"	$50	$125
1950-1960s	14", 12-string	$100	$150
1950-1960s	Sundale (colors)	$400	$500
1950-1960s	Tenor 4-string	$225	$250

Harp Guitar
Early-1900s.

1915		$2,000	$2,500

Singing Cowboy
Late-1990s. Copy of Supertone (black background)/Silvertone/Harmony Singing Cowboy, import with laminated wood construction and ladder bracing.

2000	Stencil over black	$45	$55

Stetson
1884-ca. 1924. Stetson was a house brand of William John Dyer's St. Paul, Minnesota, music store. They started advertising this brand as early as 1894, but those built by the Larson brothers of Maurer & Co. date from ca. 1904-c. 1924. Most Stetsons were made by the Larsons. Others were built by Harmony (early ones), Washburn and three are credited to the Martin Co.

MODEL		EXC. COND.	
YEAR	FEATURES	LOW	HIGH

Stevenson
1999-present. Professional grade, production/custom, solidbody electric guitars built by luthier Ted Stevenson in Lachine, Quebec. He also builds basses and amps.

Stiehler
2005-present. Production/custom, professional and premium grade, acoustic electric and electric solidbody guitars built in Wellington, Nevada by luthier Bob Stiehler. He also builds basses.

Stonebridge
1981-present. Czech Republic luthier Frantisek Furch builds professional and premium grade, production/custom, acoustic guitars. He also builds mandolins.

Stonetree Custom Guitars
1996-present. Luthier Scott Platts builds his professional and premium grade, custom/production, solidbody and chambered electric guitars in Saratoga, Wyoming. He also builds basses.

Strad-O-Lin
Ca.1920s-ca.1960s. The Strad-O-Lin company was operated by the Hominic brothers in New York, primarily making mandolins for wholesalers. Around '57 Multivox/Premier bought the company and also used the name on guitars, making both electrics and acoustics. Premier also marketed student level guitars under the U.S. Strad brand.

Stratosphere
1954-1958. Solidbody electrics made in Springfield, Missouri by brothers Claude and Russ Deaver, some featuring fanned frets. They also made an odd double neck called the Stratosphere Twin with a regular 6-string neck and a 12-string tuned in minor and major thirds. The brothers likely made less than 200 instruments.

Electric Guitar

1954-1958		$800	$1,000

Strobel Guitars
2003-present. Luthier Russ Strobel builds custom, professional grade, electric travel guitars in Boca Raton, Florida. He also builds basses and offers a production, intermediate grade, travel guitar built in Korea.

Stromberg
1906-1955, 2001-present. Intermediate and professional grade, production, archtop guitars imported by Larry Davis.

Founded in Boston by master luthier Charles Stromberg, a Swedish immigrant, building banjos and drums. Son Harry joined the company in 1907and stayed until '27. Son Elmer started in 1910 at age 15. The shop was well known for tenor banjos, but when the banjo's popularity declined, they be-

MODEL YEAR	FEATURES	EXC. COND. LOW	HIGH

gan building archtop orchestra model guitars. The shop moved to Hanover Street in Boston in '27 and began producing custom order archtop guitars, in particular the 16" G-series and the Deluxe. As styles changed the G-series was increased to 17 3/8" and the 19" Master 400 model was introduced in '37. Stromberg designs radically changed around '40, most likely when Elmer took over guitar production. Both Charles and Elmer died within a few months of each other in '55.

Larry Davis of WD Music Products revived the Stromberg name and introduced a series of moderately priced jazz guitars in June, 2001. The models are crafted by a small Korean shop with component parts supplied by WD.

Deluxe
1927-1955. Non-cut, 16" body to '34, 17 3/8" body after '35, also sometimes labeled Delux.

1927-1930		$7,500	$9,500
1931-1955		$8,000	$10,000

G-1
1927-1955. Non-cut, 16" body to '35, 17 3/8" body after '35, sunburst.

1927-1955		$7,500	$9,500

G-3
Early 1930s. Archtop, 16 3/8", 3 segment F-holes, ladder bracing, gold hardware, engraved tailpiece, 8-ply 'guard, 5-ply body binding, laminate maple back, fancy engraved headstock with Stromberg name, less total refinement than higher-end Stromberg models.

1927-1935		$8,000	$10,000

Master 300
1937-1955. 19" non-cut.

1937-1955	Natural	$23,000	$30,000
1937-1955	Sunburst	$20,000	$25,000

Master 400
1937-1955. 19" top-of-the-line non-cut, the most common of Stromberg's models.

1937-1955	Natural	$28,000	$35,000
1937-1955	Sunburst	$23,000	$30,000

Master 400 Cutaway
1949. Only 7 cutaway Strombergs are known to exist.

1949	Natural	$37,000	$47,000

Stromberg-Voisinet
1921-ca.1932. Marketed Stromberg (not to be confused with Charles Stromberg of Boston) and Kay Kraft brands, plus guitars of other distributors and retailers. Stromberg was the successor to the Groehsl Company (or Groehsel) founded in Chicago, Illinois in 1890; and the predecessor to the Kay Musical Instrument Company. In 1921, the name was changed to Stromberg-Voisinet Company. Henry Kay "Hank" Kuhrmeyer joined the company in '23 and was secretary by '25. By the mid-'20s, the company was making many better Montgomery Ward guitars, banjos and mandolins, often with lots of pearloid.

Joseph Zorzi, Philip Gabriel and John Abbott left Lyon & Healy for S-V in '26 or '27, developing

2-point Venetian shape, which was offered in '27. The first production of electric guitars and amps was introduced with big fanfare in '28; perhaps only 200 or so made. The last Stromberg acoustic instruments were seen in '32. The Kay Kraft brand was introduced by Kuhrmeyer in '31 as the company made its transition to Kay (see Kay).

Archtop Deluxe
1920s-1930s. Venetian cutaways, oval soundhole, decalomania art on top, trapeze tailpiece, light sunburst. Later offered under the Kay-Kraft brand.

1930s		$350	$425

Archtop Standard
1920s-1930s. Venetian cutaways, oval soundhole, no decalomania art, plain top, trapeze tailpiece, light sunburst. Later offered under the Kay-Kraft brand.

1930s		$300	$375

Stroup
2003-present. Luthier Gary D. Stroup builds his intermediate and professional grade, production/custom, archtop and flat-top guitars in Eckley, Colorado.

Stuart Custom Guitars
2004-present. Professional and premium grade, production/custom, solid and semi-hollow body guitars built by luthier Fred Stuart in Riverside, California. Stuart was a Senior Master Builder at Fender. He also builds pickups.

Suhr Guitars
1997-present. Luthier John Suhr builds his professional and premium grade, production/custom, solidbody electrics in Lake Elsinore, California. He also builds basses and amps. He previously built Pensa-Suhr guitars with Rudy Pensa in New York.

Sunset
2010-present. Luthier Leon White builds professional and premium grade, production/custom, electric solidbody, chambered and hollowbody guitars in Los Angeles, California.

Superior Guitars
1987-present. Intermediate grade, production/custom Hawaiian, flamenco and classical guitars made in Mexico for George Katechis Montalvo of Berkeley Musical Instrument Exchange. They also offer lap steels and mandolin-family instruments.

Supersound
1952-1974. Founded by England's Alan Wootton, building custom amps and radios. In 1958-'59 he worked with Jim Burns to produce about 20 short scale, single-cut solidbodies bearing this name. They also built a bass model. The firm continued to build amps and effects into the early '60s.

Strobel Rambler Custom

Superior Hawaiian Spruce Top

1961 Supro

Supro Folk Star

MODEL		EXC. COND.	
YEAR	FEATURES	LOW	HIGH

Supertone

1914-1941. Brand used by Sears, Roebuck and Company for instruments made by various American manufacturers, including especially its own subsidiary Harmony (which it purchased in 1916). When Sears divested itself of Harmony in '40, instruments began making a transition to the Silvertone brand. By '41 the Supertone name was gone.

Acoustic Flat-Top (High-End Appointments)

1920s	Pearl trim 00-42 likeness	$1,300	$1,600
1920s	Pearl trim, Lindbergh model	$1,300	$1,600

Acoustic Flat-Top 13"

1920-1930s	Non-stencil, plain top	$150	$175
1920-1930s	Stencil top	$200	$225

Gene Autry Roundup

1932-1939. Harmony made acoustic, Gene Autry signature on belly, cowboy roundup stencil, 13" body until '35, then 14".

1932-1939		$300	$350

Lone Ranger

1936-1941. Black with red and silver Lone Ranger and Tonto stencil, silver-painted fretboard, 13 1/2" wide. "Hi-Yo Silver" added in '37, changed to "Hi-Ho Silver" in '38.

1936-1941		$300	$350

Robin Hood

1930s. 13" flat-top similar to Singing Cowboys, but with green and white art showing Robin Hood and his men against a black background.

1933		$350	$400

Singing Cowboys

1938-1943. Stencil of guitar strumming cowboys around chuck wagon and campfire, branded Silvertone after '41.

1938-1943		$300	$350

Supertone Wedge

1930s. Triangle-shaped wedge body, laminate construction, blue-silver Supertone label inside sound chamber, art decals on body.

1930s		$250	$300

Supro

1935-1968, 2004-present. Budget brand of National Dobro Company and Valco. Some Supro models also sold under the Airline brand for Montgomery Ward. In '42 Victor Smith, Al Frost and Louis Dopyera bought National and changed the name to Valco Manufacturing Company. Valco Manufacturing Company name changed to Valco Guitars, Inc., in '62. Company treasurer Robert Engelhardt bought Valco in '64. In '67 Valco bought Kay and in '68 Valco/Kay went out of business. In the summer of '69, Valco/Kay brands and assets were sold at auction and the Supro and National names purchased by Chicago-area importer and distributor Strum N' Drum (Norma, Noble). TIn the early-'80s, ownership of the Supro name was

MODEL		EXC. COND.	
YEAR	FEATURES	LOW	HIGH

transferred to Archer's Music, Fresno, California. Some Supros assembled from new-old-stock parts.

Amp builder Bruce Zinky revived the Supro name for a line of guitars built in the U.S. by luthier John Bolin and others. He also offers amps.

Belmont

1955-1964. For '55-'60, 12" wide, single-cut, 1 neck pickup, 2 knobs treble side in 'guard, reverse-stairs tailpiece, No-Mar plastic maroon-colored covering. For '60, size increased to 13 1/2" wide. For '62-'64, Res-o-glas fiberglass was used for the body, a slight cutaway on bass side, 1 bridge pickup, 2 knobs on opposite sides. Polar White.

1955-1962	Black or white No-Mar	$800	$1,000
1961-1964	Polar White Res-o-glas	$1,100	$1,400

Bermuda

1962 only. Slab body (not beveled), double pickups, dot markers, cherry glass-fiber finish.

1962		$1,200	$1,500

Collegian Spanish

1939-1942. Metal body, 12 frets. Moved to National line in '42.

1939-1942		$1,400	$1,700

Coronado/Coronado II

1961-1967. Listed as II in '62 15 1/2" scale, single-cut thinline, 2 pickups with 4 knobs and slider, natural blond spruce top. Changed to slight cutaway on bass side in '62 when renamed II.

1961-1962	Blond, natural spruce top	$1,400	$1,700
1963-1967	Black fiberglass	$1,700	$2,100

Dual-Tone

1954-1966, 2004-present. The Dual Tone had several body style changes, all instruments had dual pickups. '54, 11 1/4" body, No Mar Arctic White plastic body ('54-'62). '55, 12" body. '58, 13" body. '60, 13 1/2" body. '62, Res-o-glas Ermine White body, light cutaway on bass side.

1954-1961	Arctic White No-Mar	$1,100	$1,400
1962-1964	Ermine White Res-o-glas	$1,200	$1,500

Folk Star/Vagabond

1964-1967. Molded Res-o-glas body, single-cone resonator, dot inlays, Fire Engine Red. Name changed to Vagabond in '66.

1964-1967		$850	$1,050

Kingston

1962-1963. Double-cut slab body, bridge pickup, glass-fiber sand finish, similar to same vintage Ozark.

1962-1963		$800	$975

Lexington

1967. Double-cut, wood body, 1 pickup.

1967		$375	$450

Martinique (Val-Trol)

1962-1967. Single-cut, 13 1/2" wide, 2 standard and 1 bridge pickups, 6 knobs on bass side, 1 knob and slider on treble side, block markers, Val-Trol script on 'guard, Bigsby, blue or Ermine White Polyester Glas.

MODEL YEAR	FEATURES	EXC. COND. LOW	HIGH

Collectors sometimes call this Val-Trol, referring to the 6 mini tone and volume controls. Not to be confused with Silverwood model which also has 6 mini-knobs.

| 1962-1967 | | $2,000 | $2,500 |

N800 Thinline Electric
1967-1968. Thin body, symmetrical double-cut, 2 pickups, copy model, similar to National N800 series models.

| 1967-1968 | | $450 | $575 |

Ozark
1952-1954, 1958-1967, 2004-present. Non-cut, 1 pickup, dot inlay, white pearloid body, name reintroduced in '58 as a continuation of model Sixty with single-cut, Dobro tailpiece.

1952-1954	White pearloid	$800	$975
1958-1961	Red	$800	$975
1962-1967	Jet Black or Fire Bronze	$800	$975

Ranchero
1948-1960. Full body electric archtop, neck pickup, dot markers, bound body, sunburst.

| 1948-1960 | | $725 | $850 |

Rhythm Master (Val-Trol)
1959. Val-Trol 'guard.

| 1959 | | $1,900 | $2,300 |

S710 Flat-Top
1967-1968. Jumbo-style 15.5" flat-top, block markers, asymmetrical headstock, natural.

| 1967-1968 | | $350 | $425 |

Sahara/Sahara 70
1960-1967. 13 1/2" body-style similar to Dual-Tone, single pickup, 2 knobs, Sand-Buff or Wedgewood Blue, Sahara until '63, Sahara 70 after.

| 1960-1967 | | $1,100 | $1,400 |

Silverwood (Val-Trol)
1960-1962. Single-cut, 13 1/2" wide, 2 standard and 1 bridge pickups, 6 knobs on bass side, 1 knob and slider on treble side, block markers, natural blond, Val-Trol script on 'guard, renamed Martinique in '62. Collectors sometimes call this Val-Trol, referring to the guitar's 6 mini tone and volume controls. The Martinique also has the Val-Trol system but the knobs are not in a straight line like on the Silverwood.

| 1960-1962 | | $1,900 | $2,300 |

Sixty
1955-1958. Single-cut, single pickup, white No-Mar, becomes Ozark in '58.

| 1955-1958 | | $700 | $900 |

Special 12
1958-1960. Single-cut, replaces Supro Sixty, neck pickup 'guard mounted.

| 1958-1960 | | $700 | $900 |

Strum 'N' Drum Solidbody
1970s. Student-level import, 1 pickup, large Supro logo on headstock.

| 1970s | Higher-end | $425 | $550 |
| 1970s | Lower-end | $325 | $425 |

Super
1958-1964. 12" wide single-cut body style like mid-'50s models, single bridge pickup, short-scale, ivory.

| 1958-1964 | | $500 | $625 |

Super Seven
1965-1967. Offset double-cut solidbody, short scale, middle pickup, Calypso Blue.

| 1965-1967 | | $450 | $575 |

Suprosonic 30
1963-1967. Introduced as Suprosonic, renamed Suprosonic 30 in '64, double-cut, single neck pickup, vibrato tailpiece, more of a student model, Holly Red.

| 1963-1967 | | $475 | $600 |

Tremo-Lectric
1965. Fiberglas hollowbody, 2 pickups, unique built-in electric tremolo (not mechanical), Wedgewood Blue finish, multiple controls associated with electric tremolo.

| 1965 | | $1,600 | $2,000 |

White Holiday/Holiday
1963-1967. Introduced as Holiday, renamed White Holiday in '64, fiberglas double-cut, vibrato tailpiece, single bridge pickup, Dawn White.

| 1963-1967 | | $1,000 | $1,300 |

Suzuki Takeharu
See listing for Takeharu.

SX
See listing for Essex.

T.D. Hibbs
2005-present. Production/custom, professional grade, steel string and classical guitars built in Cambridge, Ontario by luthier Trevor Hibbs.

T.H. Davis
1976-present. Professional and premium grade, custom, steel string and classical guitars built by luthier Ted Davis in Loudon, Tennessee. He also builds mandolins.

Tacoma
1995-present. Intermediate, and professional grade, production, acoustic guitars produced in Tacoma, Washington and New Hartford, Connecticut. They also build acoustic basses and mandolins. In October, '04, Fender acquired Tacoma.

BM-6C Thunderhawk Baritone
2004-present. Single-cut acoustic baritone.

| 2004-2010 | | $900 | $1,100 |

C-1C/C-1CE Chief
1997-present. Cutaway flat-top with upper bass bout soundhole, solid cedar top, mahogany back and sides, rosewood 'board. Sides laminated until 2000, solid after, CE is acoustic/electric.

| 1997-2010 | | $350 | $400 |
| 1997-2010 | Fishman electronics | $375 | $425 |

DM Series
1997-2006. Dreadnought, solid spruce top, mahogany back and sides, satin finish, natural. Models include DM-8, -9, -10 and -14.

| 1997-2006 | | $300 | $550 |

1965 Supro Martinique
Zak Izbinsky

1959 Supro Ranchero

Tacoma P-1

*Takamine 2011 Collectors
(Limited Edition)*

MODEL YEAR	FEATURES	EXC. COND. LOW	HIGH

DR Series
1997-2006. Dreadnought, solid sitka spruce top, rosewood back and sides, natural. Models include DR-20 (non-cut, herringbone trim, abalone rosette), DR-20E (with on-board electronics), DR-8C (cutaway), and DR-38.

1997-2006		$400	$650

JK-50C4 Jumbo Koa
1997-2003. Jumbo cutaway, 17" lower bout, sitka spruce top, figured koa back and sides.

1997-2003		$750	$950

JR-14C Jumbo Rosewood
Late-1990s. Jumbo cutaway, 16 5/8" lower bout, gloss spruce top, satin rosewood body.

1998		$650	$800

P-1/P-2 Papoose
1995-present. Travel-size mini-flat-top, all solid wood, mahogany back and sides (P-1), with on-board electronics (P-1E) or solid rosewood (P-2), cedar top, natural satin finish.

1995-2000	P-2	$350	$450
1995-2010	P-1	$300	$400
1995-2010	P-1E	$325	$425

Parlor Series
1997-2003. Smaller 14 3/4" body, solid spruce top, various woods for back and sides.

1997-2003	PK-30 Koa	$600	$725
1997-2003	PK-40 Rosewood	$600	$725

PM Series
1997-2003. Full-size, standard soundhole.

1997-2003		$400	$650

Takamine
1962-present. Intermediate and professional grade, production, steel- and nylon-string, acoustic and acoustic/electric guitars. They also make basses. Takamine is named after a mountain near its factory in Sakashita, Japan. Mass Hirade joined Takamine in '68 and revamped the brand's designs and improved quality. In '75, Takamine began exporting to other countries, including U.S. distribution by Kaman Music (Ovation). In '78, Takamine introduced acoustic/electric guitars. They offered solidbody electrics and some archtops for '83-'84.

Acoustic Electric (Laminate)
1980-1990s. All laminate (plywood) construction, non-cut, standard features, pickup and preamp.

1980-1990s		$200	$400

Acoustic Electric (Solid Top)
1980-1990s. Solid wood top, sides and back can vary, cutaway, standard features, preamp and pickup.

1980-1990s		$400	$900

Acoustic Electric Cutaway (Laminate)
1980-1990s. All laminate (plywood) construction, cutaway, standard features, pickup and preamp.

1980-1990s		$200	$400

Classical (Solid Top)
1980-1990s. Solid wood (often cedar) top, classical, sides and back can vary.

1980-1990s		$400	$600

MODEL YEAR	FEATURES	EXC. COND. LOW	HIGH

Collectors (Limited Edition)
1988-present. Each year a different limited edition collector's guitar is issued. '97 - solid top, koa body, cutaway, natural finish, preamp and pickup. '98 - solid top, rosewood body, cutaway, natural finish, preamp and pickup. '99 - solid top, rosewood body, cutaway, natural finish, preamp and pickup. '00 - solid top, rosewood body, cutaway, natural finish, preamp and pickup. '01 - solid top, rosewood body, cutaway, natural finish, preamp and pickup.

1988-2010		$700	$1,100

Solidbody Electric
1983-1984. Various models.

1983-1984		$400	$900

Takeharu (by Suzuki)
Mid-1970s. Classical guitars offered by Suzuki as part of their internationally known teaching method (e.g. Violin Suzuki method), various sized instruments designed to eliminate the confusion of size that has been a problem for classroom guitar programs.

Taku Sakashta Guitars
1994-2010. Premium and presentation grade, production/custom, archtop, flat-top, 12-sting, and nylon-string guitars, built by luthier Taku Sakashta in Sebastopol, California. He died in February, 2010.

Tama
Ca. 1959-1967, 1974-1979. Hoshino's (Ibanez) brand of higher-end acoutic flat-tops made in Japan. Many of the brand's features would be transferred to Ibanez's Artwood acoustics.

Tamura
1970s. Made in Japan by Mitsura Tamura, the line includes intermediate grade solid wood classical guitars.

Tanara
2000s. Student-level models imported by Chesbro, inside label identifies model and country of origin.

Taylor
1974-present. Intermediate, professional, premium, and presentation grade, production/custom, steel- and nylon-string, acoustic, acoustic/electric, semi-hollow, and solidbody guitars built in El Cajon, California. They have also built basses. Founded by Bob Taylor, Steve Schemmer and Kurt Listug in Lemon Grove, California, the company was originally named the Westland Music Company, but was soon changed to Taylor (Bob designed the guitars and it fit on the logo). Taylor and Listug bought out Schemmer in '83. Bob Taylor was the first commercially successful guitar maker to harness CAD/CAM CNC technology for acoustic guitars and in '91 introduced the 410 Model, the

MODEL YEAR	FEATURES	EXC. COND. LOW	HIGH

first all-solid wood American-made guitar with a list price under $1,000. The plain-appointment model using CNC technology was a major innovation combining quality and price. They added semi-hollowbodies in '05 and solidbodies in '07.

110
2003-present. Solid spruce top, sapele laminated back and sides.

2003-2009	110 GB	$325	$400
2008-2010	110 CE	$450	$550

114
2007-present. Grand auditorium, solid sitka spruce top, sapele laminated back and sides.

2007-2010		$375	$450

210e/210ce
2005-present. Sapele back and sides, dreadnought acoustic/electric, c is cutaway version.

2005-2010		$575	$700

214
2004-present. Grand auditorium, solid sitka spruce top, Indian rosewood laminated back and sides.

2004-2010		$475	$600

310
1998-2006. Dreadnought-style solid spruce top, sapele-mahogany back and sides.

1998-2006		$600	$750

310ce
1998-present. 310 with Venetian cutaway, on-board electronics.

1998-2010		$800	$1,000
2004	310ce L30 30th Anniversary	$850	$1,050

312ce
1998-present. Grand concert Venetian cutaway, solid spruce top, sapele-mahogany back and sides, on-board electronics.

1998-2010		$850	$1,050

314
1998-2006. Mid-size grand auditorium-style, solid spruce top, sapele-mahogany back and sides.

1998-2006		$600	$750

314ce
1998-present. 314 with Venetian cutaway, on-board electronics.

1998-2010		$1,000	$1,225

314cek
2000. Limited edition 314 with flamed koa body.

2000		$1,000	$1,225

315ce
1998-present. Jumbo-style Venetian cutaway, solid spruce top, sapele-mahogany back and sides, on-board electronics.

1998-2010		$1,000	$1,225

355 12-String
1998-2006. Jumbo, solid spruce top, sapele-mahogany back and sides.

1998-2006		$1,100	$1,250

355ce 12-String
1998-present. 355 with cutaway, on-board electronics.

1998-2010		$1,100	$1,250

410
1991-2006. Dreadnought-style, solid spruce top, mahogany back and sides until '98, African ovangkol back and sides after '98.

1991-2006		$875	$1,000

410ce
1991-present. 410 with cutaway, on-board electronics.

1991-2010		$1,025	$1,275

412
1991-1998. Grand concert, solid spruce top, mahogany back and sides until '98, African ovangkol back and sides after '98.

1991-1998		$1,000	$1,250

412ce
1998-present. Cutaway electric version replaced the 412 in '98.

1998-2010		$1,000	$1,250

412K
1996. Koa version of grand concert 412.

1996		$1,000	$1,250

414
1998-2006. Grand auditorium, solid sitka spruce top, ovangkol back and sides, pearl dot inlays, natural.

1998-2006		$1,000	$1,250

414ce
1998-present. 414 with cutaway, on-board electronics.

1998-2010		$1,075	$1,325

414K
1997. Koa version of grand auditorium 414.

1997		$800	$1,000

414 L10
2005. Limited edition, rosewood sides and back, gloss spruce top, satin finish.

2005		$1,175	$1,450

414L 30th Anniversary
2004. 30th Anniversary inlays on ebony 'board.

2004		$1,275	$1,525

415
1998-2006. Jumbo, solid sitka spruce top, ovangkol back and sides, pearl dot inlays.

1998-2006		$900	$1,100

420
1990-1997. Dreadnought-style, sitka spruce top, Indian rosewood back and sides, natural.

1990-1997		$900	$1,100

422
1991-1998. Grand concert, solid koa construction, satin natural finish.

1991-1998	422K	$900	$1,100
1997	422R	$900	$1,100

450 12-String
1996-1997. Dreadnought, satin finish.

1996-1997		$900	$1,100

454ce
2007-present. Ovangkol 12-string grand auditorium.

2004-2010		$1,100	$1,375

455 12-String
2001-2006. Solid sitka spruce top, ovangkol back and sides, dot markers.

2001-2006		$1,100	$1,375

Taku Sakashta Karizma

1986 Taylor 422K

GUITARS

1987 Taylor 510

Emmitt Omar

Taylor 612ce

MODEL YEAR	FEATURES	EXC. COND. LOW	HIGH
455ce 12-String			
2001-present. 455 with cutaway, on-board electronics.			
2001-2010		$1,100	$1,375
455ce LTD 12-String			
2001. Limited edition.			
2001-2003		$1,275	$1,525
510			
1978-2006. Dreadnought, all solid wood, spruce top, mahogany back and sides.			
1978-1979		$1,150	$1,375
1980-2006		$1,050	$1,275
510 Limited			
2002. Limited edition.			
2002		$1,175	$1,400
510ce			
1978-present. 510 with cutaway, on-board electronics.			
1978-1979		$1,400	$1,650
1980-2010		$1,300	$1,550
512			
1978-2000. Grand concert, solid Engelmann spruce top, solid American mahogany back and sides, dot markers.			
1978-2000		$1,200	$1,425
512ce			
1978-present. 512 with cutaway, on-board electronics.			
1978-2010		$1,300	$1,500
512 Custom Limited Edition			
2005	All mahogany	$1,400	$1,700
512NG Nanci Griffith			
1996-1997. 512ce with sunburst finish.			
1996-1997		$1,700	$2,050
514			
1990-1998. Grand auditorium.			
1990-1998		$1,400	$1,675
514c			
1990-1998. Grand auditorium, Venetian cutaway, solid spruce or solid red cedar top, mahogany back and sides, no electronics, natural.			
1990-1998		$1,400	$1,675
514ce			
1998-present. 514c with on-board electronics.			
1998-2010		$1,500	$1,800
516ce			
2008-present. Solid red cedar top, mahoganyback and sides, on-board electronics.			
2008		$1,550	$1,850
555 12-String			
1978-2006. Jumbo, solid sitka spruce top, solid mahogany back and sides, higher-end appointments.			
1994-2006		$1,600	$1,900
555ce 12-String			
1994-2006. 555 with cutaway, on-board electronics.			
1994-2006		$1,600	$1,900
610			
1978-1998. Dreadnought, solid spruce top, solid maple back and sides, generally with amber stained finishes.			
1978-1998		$1,325	$1,575

MODEL YEAR	FEATURES	EXC. COND. LOW	HIGH
610ce			
1998-present. 610 with cutaway, on-board electronics.			
1998-2010		$1,400	$1,650
612			
1984-1998. Grand concert, solid spruce top, solid maple back and sides, generally with amber stained finishes.			
1984-1998		$1,325	$1,575
612ce			
1998-present. 612 with cutaway, on-board electronics.			
1998-2010		$1,400	$1,650
614			
1978-1998. Grand auditorium, solid spruce top, solid maple back and sides, generally with amber stained finishes.			
1978-1998		$1,725	$2,075
614ce			
1998-present. 614 with cutaway, on-board electronics.			
1998-2010		$1,800	$2,150
615			
1981-1998. Jumbo, spruce top, flamed maple back and sides, non-cut.			
1981-1998		$1,750	$2,150
615ce			
1981-present. Jumbo, 6-string.			
1981-2010		$1,825	$2,225
655 12-String			
1978-1991, 1996-2006. Solid spruce top, solid maple back and sides, generally with amber stained finishes.			
1978-2006		$1,500	$1,700
655ce 12-String			
1998-present. 655 with cutaway, on-board electronics.			
1998-2010		$1,675	$1,975
710			
1977-2006. Dreadnought-size, rosewood back and sides, spruce top.			
1977-2006		$1,550	$1,750
710BR			
1990s. 710 with Brazilian rosewood.			
1990s		$2,300	$2,800
710ce			
1998-present. 710 with cutaway, on-board electronics.			
1998-2010		$1,625	$1,825
710ce L30 Commemorative			
2004. 30th Anniversary Limited Edition, single-cut, Englemann spruce top, Indian rosewood body, on-board electronics, 30th Anniversary script logo on headstock.			
2004		$1,700	$2,100
712			
1984-2006. Grand concert small body, solid wood, non-cut, rosewood back and sides, spruce top, cedar soundboard.			
1984-2006		$1,400	$1,700
712ce			
2000-present. 712 with cutaway, on-board electronics.			
2000-2010		$1,475	$1,775

MODEL YEAR	FEATURES	EXC. COND. LOW	HIGH
714			
1996-2006. Grand auditorium, 15 7/8" lower bout, solid red cedar top, solid Indian rosewood back and sides.			
1996-2006		$1,475	$1,775
714ce			
1998-present. 714 with cutaway, on-board electronics.			
1998-2010		$1,550	$1,850
2004	714ce L1 Limited Edition	$1,650	$1,950
755 12-String			
1990-1998. Dreadnought-style, 12 strings, solid spruce top, rosewood back and sides, natural.			
1990-1998		$1,550	$1,850
810			
1975-2010. Classic original Taylor dreadnought design - early model.			
1975-2010		$1,450	$1,750
810c			
1993-1998. Single-cut version.			
1993-1998		$1,525	$1,825
810ce			
1996-present. 810 with cutaway, on-board electronics.			
1996-2010	Brazilian rosewood option	$2,800	$3,400
1996-2010	Indian rosewood	$1,600	$1,950
810 L30			
2004. 30th Anniversary.			
2004		$1,650	$2,000
812			
1993-2010. Rosewood back and sides, Englemann spruce top, cutaway, ce with on-board electronics.			
1993-1998	812c	$1,625	$2,000
1998-2010	812ce	$1,700	$2,100
814			
2005-2006. Grand auditorium, cutaway, rosewood back and sides, spruce top.			
1993-1998	814	$1,900	$2,300
1998-2006	814c	$1,900	$2,300
1998-2010	814ce	$1,900	$2,300
2000	814BE (Brazilian/ Englemann)	$2,800	$3,400
815			
1970s. Jumbo, solid sitka spruce top, Indian rosewood back and sides.			
1970s		$2,000	$2,400
815c			
1993-1998. Jumbo cutaway, no electronics, solid sitka spruce top, Indian rosewood back and sides.			
1993-1998		$2,000	$2,400
815c Brazilian Custom			
1997. High-end presentation model with Brazilian rosewood, single sharp cutaway.			
1997		$5,600	$7,000
815ce			
1998-present. 815c with on-board electronics.			
1998-2010		$2,075	$2,475
855 12-String			
1993-2006. Jumbo, solid sitka spruce top, rosewood back and sides, natural.			
1993-2006		$1,850	$2,300

MODEL YEAR	FEATURES	EXC. COND. LOW	HIGH
910			
1977-2010. Dreadnought, maple back and sides until change to Indian rosewood in '86, spruce top, wide abalone-style rosette.			
1977-1985	Maple	$1,900	$2,350
1986-2010	Indian rosewood	$2,800	$3,400
910ce			
1998-present. 910 with cutaway, on-board electronics.			
1998-2010		$1,975	$2,425
912c			
1993-2002. Grand concert, rosewood back and sides, abalone.			
1993-2002		$2,200	$2,700
914ce			
2002-present. 914c with on-board electronics.			
2002-2010		$2,400	$3,900
Baby			
1996-present. 3/4"-size dreadnought, solid spruce top, mahogany laminated back and sides until '99, sapele laminate after.			
1996-2010		$175	$225
Baby Mahogany (M)			
1998-present. Solid mahogany top version of Baby, mahogany laminated back and sides until '99, sapele laminate after.			
1998-2010		$175	$225
Baby Rosewood			
2000-2003. Laminated Indian rosewood back and sides version, solid sitka spruce top.			
2000-2003		$200	$250
Big Baby			
2000-present. 15/16"-size dreadnought, solid sitka spruce top, sapele-mahogany laminated back and sides, satin finish, gig bag.			
2000-2010		$200	$250
CPSM Chris Proctor Signature			
2001. Limited edition, 100 made.			
2001		$1,650	$1,950
CUJO-14 CST Walnut			
1995. Only 125 made.			
1995		$1,450	$1,800
DCSM Dan Crary Signature			
1986-2000. Dreadnought, Venetian cutaway, thin spruce top, Indian rosewood back and sides, Crary signature on headstock.			
1986-2000		$1,450	$1,800
DDAD Doyle Dykes Signature Anniversary			
2005. Sitka spruce top, Indian rosewood back and sides, soft cutaway, on-board transducer.			
2005		$2,400	$3,000
DDSM Doyle Dykes Signature			
2000-present. Grand auditorium cutaway acoustic/ electric, figured maple body.			
2000-2010		$2,400	$3,000
DMSM Dave Matthews Signature			
2010-present. Limited Edition based on 914ce, Taylor Expression pickup system.			
2010		$2,600	$3,200

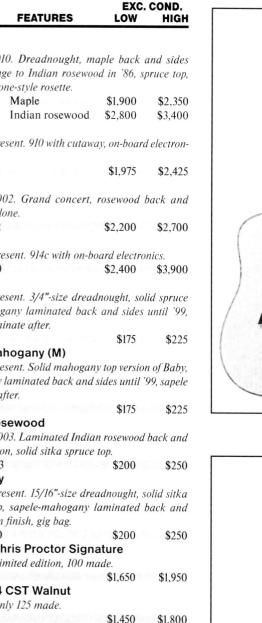

Taylor 910

Taylor Baby Mahogany

2010 Taylor NS-24
Emmitt Omar

Taylor T5 (S1)

MODEL YEAR	FEATURES	EXC. COND. LOW	HIGH
GA Series			
2007-present. Grand Auditorium Series.			
1995	GA-BE, Bob Taylor, 50 made	$3,800	$4,600
1995	GA-KC, Ltd. Ed., koa	$2,800	$3,400
1995	GA-WS, walnut/spruce	$2,400	$2,900
2007-2010	GA3, spruce/sapele	$775	$900
2007-2010	GA4, sitka/ovangkol	$850	$1,000
2007-2010	GA5, cedar/mahogany	$1,250	$1,550
2007-2010	GA6, spruce/ flamed maple	$1,250	$1,550
2007-2010	GA6-12, maple/sitka	$1,500	$1,850
2007-2010	GA7, cedar/rosewood	$1,250	$1,550
2007-2010	GA8, rosewood/sitka	$1,250	$1,550
2008-2010	GA-K-12, cedar/koa	$1,800	$2,200
GC Series			
2007-present. Grand Concert Series.			
2007-2010	GC3, spruce/sapele	$700	$875
2007-2010	GC4, spruce/ ovangkol	$800	$1,000
2007-2010	GC6, sitka/maple	$1,050	$1,300
2007-2010	GC7, cedar/ rosewood	$1,050	$1,300
K Series			
1983-present. Koa Series.			
1983-1992	K20	$1,850	$2,250
1983-2006	K10	$1,700	$2,100
1995-1998	K65, 12-string	$2,300	$2,800
1998-2000	K22	$2,000	$2,400
1998-2002	K14c	$1,725	$2,125
1998-2002	K20c	$1,900	$2,300
1998-2010	K14ce	$1,800	$2,200
2001-2006	K55, 12-string	$2,300	$2,800
2001-2010	K20ce	$2,000	$2,400
2003-2010	K22ce	$2,075	$2,475
2007-2010	K10ce	$1,775	$2,175
2007-2010	K54ce	$2,400	$3,000
LKSM-6/12 Leo Kottke			
1997-present. Jumbo 17" body, 6- or 12-string, rounded cutaway, sitka spruce top, mahogany back and sides, gloss finish, Leo Kottke signature.			
1997-2010	12-string	$1,500	$1,850
1997-2010	6-string	$1,500	$1,850
LTG Liberty Tree L.E.			
2002. Limited edition includes DVD and certificate which are important to instrument's value, solid wood grand concert body, high-end art and appointments. Around 400 made.			
2002		$4,400	$5,500
NS Series			
2002-present. Nylon Strung series, models include NS32ce (mahogany body), NS42ce and NS44 (ovangkol body), NS62ce and NS64ce (maple body) and NS74 (Indian rosewood). All models were cutaway electric (ce) by '04.			
2002-2006	NS42ce	$1,050	$1,300

MODEL YEAR	FEATURES	EXC. COND. LOW	HIGH
2002-2006	NS44/NS44ce	$1,050	$1,300
2002-2006	NS52ce	$1,150	$1,400
2002-2006	NS54ce	$1,250	$1,500
2002-2010	NS32ce	$900	$1,125
2002-2010	NS62ce	$1,400	$1,800
2002-2010	NS64ce	$1,450	$1,850
2002-2010	NS72ce	$1,750	$2,100
2002-2010	NS74/NS74ce	$1,750	$2,100
2004-2010	NS34ce	$1,050	$1,300
2010	NS24ce	$575	$725
Pre-Production Model			
1974. Early pre-production custom made (custom order), could be an instrument with the Taylor American Dream label, or may not have a logo or brand.			
1974		$3,000	$7,500
PS Series			
1996-present. Presentation Series, values vary depending on specs and appointments.			
1996	PS14BZ Special Edition	$4,200	$5,200
1996-2004	PS12c Grand Concert	$4,600	$5,700
1996-2006	PS15 Jumbo	$4,700	$5,800
1997	PS10	$3,800	$4,700
1998-2000	PS14c Special Edition	$4,700	$5,800
2003	PS Presentation Limited	$3,500	$4,400
Solidbody Classic			
2008-present. Single-cut ash body, pearl 'guard, maple neck, chrome hardware, 2 humbuckers or single-coils.			
2008-2010		$725	$900
Solidbody Standard			
2008-present. Single-cut sculpted body, figured ash top, Ivoroid binding, 2 exposed coil humbuckers.			
2008-2010		$1,025	$1,275
T3 Series			
2009. Semi-hollow thinline, single-cut.			
2009	T3/B9, flamed maple	$1,500	$1,850
T5 Series			
2005-present. Semi-hollow thinline body, sapele back and sides, spruce, maple, or koa tops, Custom models have gold hardware and Artist inlays, Standard is chrome with micro-dots.			
2005-2006	Custom 5M-C1, maple	$1,675	$2,050
2005-2010	Custom C, spruce top	$1,575	$1,925
2005-2010	Custom C1, flamed maple	$1,625	$2,025
2005-2010	Custom C2, koa top	$1,675	$2,100
2005-2010	Standard S, spruce top	$1,300	$1,600
2005-2010	Standard S1, maple top	$1,575	$1,925
2007-2010	Custom C2-12, 12-string	$1,900	$2,150

MODEL YEAR	FEATURES	EXC. COND. LOW	HIGH
TEG			
2007-2008. Single cut solidbody, 2 pickups.			
2007	Walnut Custom	$1,575	$1,925
2008	Koa Custom, flamed	$1,675	$2,100
W10			
1998-2006. Dreadnought, claro walnut back and sides, optional tops include sitka spruce, Western red cedar, or claro walnut.			
1998-2006		$1,625	$2,025
W12c			
1998-2000. Grand concert single cutaway, walnut back and sides, Western red cedar top.			
2001		$1,725	$2,125
W14ce			
2000-2006. Grand auditorium, claro walnut back and sides, red cedar top, on-board electronics.			
2000-2006		$1,775	$2,175
WHCM Windham Hill			
2003. Commemorative Model, D-size, spruce top, rosewood sides and back, fancy appointments with Windham Hill logo inlay.			
2003		$1,625	$2,025
XX-MC 20th Anniversary			
1994. Cedar, mahogany.			
1994		$2,075	$2,500
XX-RS 20th Anniversary			
1994. Grand auditorium 15 3/4" lower bout, spruce top, Indian rosewood back and sides.			
1994		$2,175	$2,600
XXV-RS 25th Anniversary			
1999-2000. Dreadnought-size, spruce top, sapele back and sides.			
1999-2000		$2,075	$2,500
XXX 30th Anniversary Series			
2004-2005. Various models and woods.			
2004-2005	XXX-BE, Brazilian rosewood	$3,200	$4,000
2004-2005	XXX-KE	$2,200	$2,750
2004-2005	XXX-MS, maple	$2,200	$2,750
2004-2005	XXX-RS, Indian rosewood	$2,200	$2,750
XXXV 35th Anniversary Series			
2009. Various models and woods.			
2009	XXXV-9, 9-string	$2,200	$2,750

Teisco

1946-1974, 1994-present. Founded in Tokyo, Japan by Hawaiian and Spanish guitarist Atswo Kaneko and electrical engineer Doryu Matsuda, the original company name was Aoi Onpa Kenkyujo; Teisco was the instrument name. Most imported into U.S. by Jack Westheimer beginning ca. '60 and Chicago's W.M.I. Corporation beginning around '64, some early ones for New York's Bugeleisen and Jacobson. Brands made by the company include Teisco, Teisco Del Rey, Kingston, World Teisco, Silvertone, Kent, Kimberly and Heit Deluxe.

In '56, the company's name was changed to Nippon Onpa Kogyo Co., Ltd., and in '64 the name changed again to Teisco Co., Ltd. In January '67, the company was purchased by Kawai. After '73,

the brand was converted to Kay in U.S.; Teisco went into hiatus in Japan until being revived in the early-'90s with plexiglass reproductions of the Spectrum 5 (not available in U.S.). Some older Teisco Del Rey stock continued to be sold in U.S. through the '70s.

Electric

		EXC. COND. LOW	HIGH
1966-1969	1 pickup	$100	$200
1966-1969	2 pickups	$125	$250
1966-1969	3 pickups	$250	$400
1966-1969	4 pickups or special finishes	$350	$500
1966-1969	Spectrum V	$450	$550
1968-1969	May Queen, black	$450	$550
1968-1969	May Queen, red	$500	$600

Tele-Star

1965-ca.1972. Imported from Japan by Tele-Star Musical Instrument Corporation of New York, New York. Primarily made by Kawai, many inspired by Burns designs, some in cool sparkle finishes. They also built basses.

Electric

		EXC. COND. LOW	HIGH
1966-1969	1, 2, or 3 pickups	$100	$300
1966-1969	4 pickups or special finishes	$300	$375
1966-1969	Amp-in-case	$225	$275
1969-1970	Double neck 6/4	$500	$625

Tempo

1950s-1970s. Solid and semi-hollow body electric and acoustic guitars, most likely imported by Merson Musical Products from Japan. They also offered basses and amps.

Tennessee

1970-1993, 1996-present. Luthier Mark Taylor builds his professional and premium grade, production/custom, acoustic guitars in Old Hickory, Tennessee. He also builds mandolins, banjos and the Tut Taylor brand of resophonic guitars. Mark and his father Robert "Tut" Taylor started making the Tennessee brand of acoustic and resophonic guitars, banjos, and mandolins in '71. In '77, Tut left the company and Mark continued on as Crafters of Tennessee. In '93, Mark and Greg Rich started building instruments as Rich and Taylor. In '96, Mark resumed production under the Tennessee brand.

Teuffel

1988-present. Luthier Ulrich Teuffel builds his production/custom, premium and presentation grade electric solidbody guitars in Neu-Ulm, Bavaria, Germany.

Texas

1959-ca. 1965. Line of aluminum neck electric solidbodies and basses made by France's Jacobacci company, which also built under its own brand. One, two, or three pickups.

1968 Teisco Vamper

Tele-Star

Timtone SH2

1983 Tokai TST-56

MODEL YEAR	FEATURES	EXC. COND. LOW	HIGH

Teye

2006-present. Luthier Teye Wijterp builds his premium and presentation grade, production/custom, solid and chambered body guitars in Austin, Texas. Some instruments are branded as Electric Gypsy guitars.

TheDon

Guitars made in Germany and imported into the U.S. by a guitar shop.

Thomas Rein

1972-present. Luthier Thomas Rein builds his premium grade, production/custom, classical guitars in St. Louis, Missouri.

Thompson Guitars

1980-present. Luthier Ted Thompson builds his professional and premium grade, production/custom, flat-top, 12-string, and nylon-string guitars in Vernon, British Columbia.

Thorell Fine Guitars

1994-present. Premium grade, custom/production, archtop, flattop and classical guitars built by luthier Ryan Thorell in Logan, Utah.

Thorn Custom Guitars

2000-present. Professional and premium grade, custom/production, solid and hollowbody electrics built by luthiers Bill Thorn and his sons Bill, Jr. and Ron in Glendale, California. They started Thorn Custom Inlay in the early '90s to do custom inlay work for other builders. In '00, they added their own line of guitars.

Threet Guitars

1990-present. Premium grade, production/custom, flat-tops built by luthier Judy Threet in Calgary, Alberta.

Tilton

1850s-late 1800s. Built by William B. Tilton, of New York City, New York. He was quite an innovator and held several guitar-related patents. He also built banjos.

Parlor

1850s-1860s. Parlor guitar with various woods.

MODEL YEAR	FEATURES	EXC. COND. LOW	HIGH
1850-1860s	Brazilian, fancy binding	$1,900	$2,400
1890s	Diagonal grain spruce top, Brazilian	$1,500	$1,900
1890s	Pearl trim, Brazilian	$2,800	$3,500
1890s	Standard grain spruce top, Brazilian	$900	$1,100

Tim Reede Custom Guitars

2004-present. Luthier Tim Reede builds his professional and premium grade, production/custom, archtop, flat top and electric guitars in Minneapolis, Minnesota.

Timeless Instruments

1980-present. Luthier David Freeman builds his professional, premium and presentation grade, custom, flattop, 12-string, nylon-string, and resonator guitars in Tugaske, Saskatchewan. He also builds mandolins and dulcimers.

Timm Guitars

1997-present. Professional grade, custom, flat-top, resonator and travel guitars built by luthier Jerry Timm in Auburn, Washington.

Timtone Custom Guitars

1993-2006. Luthier Tim Diebert built his premium grade, custom, solidbody, chambered-body and acoustic guitars in Grand Forks, British Columbia. He also built basses and lap steels.

Tippin Guitar Co.

1978-present. Professional, premium and presentation grade, production/custom, flat-top guitars built by luthier Bill Tippin in Marblehead, Massachusetts.

Tobias

1977-present. Known mainly for basses, Tobias did offer guitar models in the '80s. See Bass Section for more company info.

TogaMan GuitarViol

2003-present. Premium grade, production/custom, bow-playable solidbody guitars built by luthier Jonathan Wilson in Sylmar, California.

Tokai

1947-present. Japan's Tokai Company started out making a keyboard harmonica that was widely used in Japanese schools. In '65, they started producing acoustic guitars, followed shortly by electrics. In the late '60s, Tokai hooked up with Tommy Moore, a successful instrument merchandiser from Fort Worth, Texas, and by '70 they were producing private label and OEM guitars, sold in the U.S. under the brands of various importers. By the '70s, the Tokai name was being used on the instruments. Today Tokai continues to offer electrics, acoustics, and electric basses made in Japan and Korea.

ASD-403 Custom Edition

1980s. Classic offset double-cut solidbody, single-single-hum pickups, locking tremolo.

MODEL YEAR	FEATURES	EXC. COND. LOW	HIGH
1980s		$400	$500

AST-56

1980s. Classic offset double-cut solidbody style, 3 single-coils.

MODEL YEAR	FEATURES	EXC. COND. LOW	HIGH
1980s		$400	$500

MODEL YEAR	FEATURES	EXC. COND. LOW	HIGH

AST-62
Early-1980s. Classic offset double-cut solidbody style, rosewood slab board, 4-bolt neck plate with serial number, AST 62 model logo and Vintage Series logo on headstock.

1980s		$400	$500

ATE-52
1980s. Classic single-cut solidbody style, 2 single-coils.

1980s		$400	$500

ATE-67
1980s. Pink paisley.

1980s		$550	$650

CE-180W Cat's Eyes
Late-1970s-Early-1980s. D-style flat-top, made by Tokai Gakki, Cat's Eyes brand headstock logo, inside label indicates CE-180W model, Nyatoh sides and back.

1979-1980s		$200	$250

CE-250 Cat's Eyes
Late-1970s-Early-1980s. D-style flat-top.

1979-1980s		$200	$250

CE-300 Cat's Eyes
Late-1970s-Early-1980s. D-style flat-top, made by Tokai Gakki, Cat's Eyes brand headstock logo, inside label indicates CE-300 model, rosewood sides and back.

1979-1980s		$300	$375

CE-400 Cat's Eyes
Late-1970s-Early-1980s. D-style flat-top, made by Tokai Gakki, Cat's Eyes brand headstock logo, model CE-400 on neck block, rosewood sides and back.

1979-1980s		$450	$550

Flying V
1983		$350	$425

Goldstar Sound
1984. Replica that replaced the Springy Sound, new less litigiously pointy headstock shape.

1984		$325	$400

J-200N
1979-1980		$450	$550

Les Paul Reborn
1976-1985. LP replica with Gibson-style 'Tokai' headstock logo and Les Paul Reborn script logo instead of Les Paul Model, renamed Reborn Old in '82, becomes Love Rock in mid-'80s.

1976-1982	Les Paul Reborn	$500	$600
1982-1985	Reborn Old	$400	$500

Love Rock
1980s. Classic single-cut solidbody style, 2 humbuckers, figured tops at the high end.

1980s		$500	$600

SC Series
2000s	SC-1	$300	$375

Silver Star
1977-1984. Tokai's copy of the post-CBS large headstock model.

1977-1984		$300	$375

MODEL YEAR	FEATURES	EXC. COND. LOW	HIGH

Springy Sound
1977-1984. Replica, Tokai logo replaces spaghetti logo, Springy Sound in small block letters follows Tokai logo on headstock, original high-end nitro-finish.

1977-1979	With skunk stripe	$400	$500
1979-1984	No skunk stripe	$400	$500

Vintage Series Electric
1982. 'Tokai Electric Guitar' and 'Vintage Series' headstock logo, bolt-on neck, 1 or 2 humbucker pickups.

1982	1 pickup	$300	$375
1982	2 pickups	$350	$425

Vintage Series TST-'62
Early-1980s. Copy of vintage rosewood slab board, TST-'62 model and 'Vintage Series' headstock logo, 4-bolt neck plate with serial number, sunburst.

1980s		$400	$500

Tom Anderson Guitarworks
1984-present. Professional and premium grade, production/custom, solidbody, semi-solidbody and acoustic guitars built by luthier Tom Anderson in Newbury Park, California.

Atom
2008-present. Single-cut, flamed maple on mahogany.

2008-2010	CT Atom	$2,000	$2,400
2008-2010	Hollow Atom	$1,800	$2,200

Classic
1984-present. Double-cut solidbody, classic 3 pickup configuration, colors and appointments can vary.

1984-2010		$1,450	$1,675

Classic T
2006-present. Classic single-cut, 2 single-coil design.

2006-2010		$1,500	$1,725

Cobra
1993-present. Single-cut solid mahogany body with figured maple top.

1993-2010		$1,600	$1,825

Crowdster
2004-present. Acoustic/electric, Plus has added electric guitar pickup.

2004-2010	Crowdster Acoustic	$1,850	$2,150
2008-2010	Crowdster Plus	$1,900	$2,200

Drop Top
1992-present. Double-cut solidbody, single-single-hum pickups, various specs.

1992-2010		$1,900	$2,400

Hollow Classic
1996-2009. Ash double-cut with tone chambers, 3 pickups.

1996-2009		$1,700	$1,950

Hollow T
1995-2009. Semi-hollow, single-cut, hum-single-hum pickups.

1995-2009		$1,700	$1,950

TommyHawk
1993-2005. Acoustic travel guitars built by luthier Tom Barth in Succasunna, New Jersey. They also offered a full-scale acoustic/electric model. Barth died in '05.

2007 Tom Anderson Classic

2007 Tom Anderson Hollow T

1978 Travis Bean TB-1000 Standard

Traphagen Model OO

MODEL		EXC. COND.	
YEAR	FEATURES	LOW	HIGH

Toneline

1950s. Student-level private brand built by Chicago builders (Kay, Harmony). Typical '50s Stella brand specs like birch body with painted binding and rosette, pointed Toneline script logo on headstock.

Tonemaster

1960s. Guitars and basses, made in Italy by the Crucianelli Company, with typical '60s Italian sparkle plastic finish and push-button controls, bolt-on neck. Imported into the U.S. by The Imperial Accordion Company. They also offered guitar amps.

Rhythm Tone

1960-1963. Tonemaster headstock logo, Rhythm Tone logo on 'guard, single neck pickup, 3-in-line control knobs, bolt-on neck, black finish.

1960-1963		$750	$875

ToneSmith

1997-present. Luthier Kevin Smith builds his professional and premium grade, production/custom, semi-hollow body guitars in Rogers, Minnesota. He also builds basses. He previously built GLF brand guitars and built the line of Vox USA guitars from '98-'01.

Tony Nobles

1990-present. Professional and premium grade, custom, acoustic and electric guitars built by luthier Tony Nobles in Wimberley, Texas. Tony used to write a repair article for *Vintage Guitar* magazine.

Tony Vines Guitars

1989-present. Luthier Tony Vines builds his premium and presentation grade, custom/production, steel string guitars in Kingsport, Tennessee.

Torres (Antonio de Torres Jurado)

19th Century luthier most often associated with the initial development of the Classical Spanish guitar.

Tosca

1950s. Private economy brand made by Valco, possibly for a jobber, mail-order catalog or local department store.

Bolero 1123

1950s. Small three-quarter size electric similar to National (Valco) model 1123, single-cut, 1 neck pickup, guard mounted controls.

1950s		$450	$550

Toyota

1972-?. Imported from Japan by Hershman of New York, New York. At least 1 high-end acoustic designed by T. Kurosawa was ambitiously priced at $650.

MODEL		EXC. COND.	
YEAR	FEATURES	LOW	HIGH

Traphagen, Dake

1972-present. Luthier Dake Traphagen builds his premium grade, custom, nylon-string guitars in Bellingham, Washington.

Traugott Guitars

1991-present. Premium grade, production/custom, flat-top and acoustic/electric guitars built by luthier Jeff Traugott in Santa Cruz, California.

Traveler Guitar

1992-present. Intermediate grade, production, travel size electric, acoustic, classical and acoustic/electric guitars made in Redlands, California. They also make basses.

Travis Bean

1974-1979, 1999. Aluminum-necked solidbody electric guitars and basses. The company was founded by motorcycle and metal-sculpture enthusiast Travis Bean and guitar repairman Marc McElwee in Southern California; soon joined by Gary Kramer (see Kramer guitars). Kramer left Travis Bean in '75 and founded Kramer guitars with other partners. Guitar production began in mid-'76. The guitars featured carved aluminum necks with three-and-three heads with a T cutout in the center and wooden 'boards. Some necks had bare aluminum backs, some were painted black. A total of about 3,650 instruments were produced. Travis Bean guitar production was stopped in the summer of '79.

Serial numbers were stamped on headstock and were more-or-less consecutive. These can be dated using production records published by Bill Kaman in Vintage Guitar magazine. Original retail prices were $895 to $1195.

The company announced renewed production in '99 with updated versions of original designs and new models, but it evidently never got going.

TB-500

1975-1976. Aluminum neck, T-slotted headstock, double-cut, 2 single coils mounted in 'guard, 2 controls, dot markers, white.

1975-1976		$3,900	$4,800

TB-1000 Artist

1974-1979. Aluminum neck, T-slotted headstock, double-cut archtop, 2 humbuckers, 4 controls, block inlays.

1974-1979		$3,800	$4,700
1974-1979	Rare colors	$4,700	$5,800

TB-1000 Standard

1974-1979. Similar to TB-1000 Artist, but with dot inlays.

1974-1979		$3,600	$4,400

TB-3000 Wedge

1976-1979. Aluminum neck with T-slotted headstock, triangle-shaped body, 2 humbucking pickups, 4 controls, block markers on 'board.

1976-1979		$4,000	$5,000

MODEL		EXC. COND.	
YEAR	FEATURES	LOW	HIGH

Tregan Guitars

2007-present. Solidbody electrics including Bison-style sharp curved horns body style plus other less traditional styles, student and intermediate grade.

Tremblett Archtops

2006-present. Luthier Mark Tremblett builds his professional grade, custom, archtop guitars in Pouch Cove, Newfoundland.

Tremcaster

2008-present. Luthier John Mosconi, along with Robert Gelley and Jeff Russell, builds professional grade, production/custom, electric and acoustic guitars in Akron, Ohio.

Trenier

1998-present. Premium grade, production/custom, archtop guitars built by luthier Bryant Trenier in Seattle, Washington. From '02 to '04 he was located in Prague, Czech Republic.

Triggs

1992-present. Luthiers Jim Triggs and his son Ryan build their professional and premium grade, production/custom, archtop, flat-top, and solidbody guitars originally in Nashville Tennessee, and, since '98, in Kansas City, Kansas. They also build mandolins.

Acoustic/Electric Archtop

1992-present. Various archtop cutaway models.

1992-2009	Byrdland 17"	$2,200	$2,800
1992-2009	Excel 17"	$3,800	$4,800
1992-2009	Jazzmaster	$1,800	$2,300
1992-2009	New Yorker 18"	$4,800	$6,300
1992-2010	Stromberg		
	Master 400	$4,800	$6,300

Trinity River

2004-present. Located in Fort Worth, Texas, luthiers Marcus Lawyer and Ross McLeod import their production/custom, budget and intermediate grade, acoustic and resonator guitars from Asia. They also import basses, mandolins and banjos.

True North Guitars

1994-present. Luthier Dennis Scannell builds his premium grade, custom, flat-tops in Waterbury, Vermont.

True Tone

1960s. Guitars, basses and amps retailed by Western Auto, manufactured by Chicago guitar makers like Kay. The brand was most likely gone by '68.

Electric Archtop (K592 Kay)

1960s. Made by Kay and similar to their K592 double-cut thinline acoustic, 2 pickups, Bigsby tailpiece, burgundy red.

1960s		$500	$625

Fun Time

Early- to mid-1960s. Student 13" flat-top, painted 5-point 'guard, red sunburst finish.

1960s		$55	$75

Imperial Deluxe

Mid-1960s. Harmony-made (Rocket), 3 pickups, trapeze tailpiece, 6 control knobs, block markers, sunburst.

1960s		$700	$875

Jazz King (K573 Kay)

1960s. Kay's K573 Speed Demon, 3 pickups, thinline archtop electric with f-hole, eighth note art on 'guard, sunburst.

1960s		$550	$675

Rock 'n Roll Electric (K100 Kay)

1960s. Kay's K100, slab body, single pickup, but with a bright red multiple lacquer finish.

1960s		$225	$275

Solidbody (K300 Kay)

1960s. Made by Kay and similar to their K300, double-cut, dual pickups and vibrola arm, red.

1960s		$425	$525

Speed Master (K6533 Kay)

1960s. Made by Kay and similar to their K6533 full-body electric archtop Value Leader line, eighth note art 'guard, sunburst.

1960s		$300	$375

Western Spanish Auditorium

Early- to mid-1960s. 15" flat-top, laminate construction, celluloid 'guard, sunburst.

1960s		$125	$175

Tucker

2000-present. Founded by John N. "Jack" Tucker, John Morrall, and David Killingsworth, Tucker builds professional and premium grade, production/custom, albizzia wood solidbody guitars in Hanalei, Hawaii. They also build basses.

Tuscany Guitars

2008-present. Luthier Galeazzo Frudua in San Lazzaro di Savena, Italy, has designed a line of intermediate grade, production, classic model electric guitars, that is imported from Asia and finished in Italy.

Tut Taylor

Line of professional and premium grade, production/custom, resophonic guitars built by luthier Mark Taylor of Crafters of Tennessee in Old Hickory, Tennessee. Brand named for his father, dobro artist Tut Taylor. Taylor also builds the Tennessee line of guitars, mandolins and banjos and was part of Rich and Taylor guitars for '93-'96.

TV Jones

1993-present. Professional and premium grade, production/custom, hollow, chambered, and solid body guitars built by luthier Thomas Vincent Jones originally in California, now in Poulsbo, Washington. The instruments have either Jones or TV Jones inlaid on the headstock. He also builds

2009 Tremcaster SSH

TV Jones Spectra-Sonic

Valencia JF

Valley Arts Custom Pro

MODEL YEAR	FEATURES	EXC. COND. LOW	HIGH

U. A. C.

1920s. Instruments built by the Oscar Schmidt Co. and possibly others. Most likely a brand made for a distributor.

Unique Guitars

2003-ca. 2007. Professional and premium grade, production/custom, solidbody guitars built by luthier Joey Rico in California. He also built basses. Joey is the son of Bernie Rico, the founder of BC Rich guitars.

Univox

1964-1978. Univox started out as an amp line and added guitars around '68. Guitars were imported from Japan by the Merson Musical Supply Company, later Unicord, Westbury, New York. Many if not all supplied by Arai and Company (Aria, Aria Pro II), some made by Matsumoku. Univox Lucy ('69) first copy of lucite Ampeg Dan Armstrong. Generally mid-level copies of American designs.

Acoustic Flat-Top
1969-1978. Various models.

1970s		$175	$250

Bicentennial
1976. Offset double-cut, heavily carved body, brown stain, 3 humbucker-style pickups.

1976		$800	$1,000

Deep Body Electric
1960s-1970s. ES-175 style.

1960-1970s		$275	$475

Electric Solidbody
1970s. Includes Flying V, Mosrite and Hofner violin-guitar copies.

1960-1970s	Hi Flier	$450	$550
1960-1970s	Various models	$250	$450

Guitorgan FSB C-3000
1970s. Double-cut semi-hollow body, multiple controls, Guitorgan logo on headstock, footpedal.

1970s		$600	$750

Thin Line (Coily)

1960-1970s	12-string	$275	$475
1960-1970s	6-string	$275	$475

USA Custom Guitars

1999-present. Professional and premium grade, custom/production, solidbody electric guitars built in Tacoma, Washington. USA also does work for other luthiers.

Vaccaro

1997-2002. Founded by Henry Vaccaro, Sr., one of the founders of Kramer Guitars. They offered intermediate and professional grade, production/custom, aluminum-necked guitars designed by Vaccaro, former Kramer designer Phil Petillo, and Henry Vaccaro, Jr., which were made in Asbury Park, New Jersey. They also built basses.

MODEL YEAR	FEATURES	EXC. COND. LOW	HIGH

Val Dez

Early-1960s-early-1970s. Less expensive guitars built by Landola in Sweden or Finland; they also made the Espana brand.

Valco

1942-1968. Valco, of Chicago, was a big player in the guitar and amplifier business. Their products were private branded for other companies like National, Supro, Airline, Oahu, and Gretsch. In '42, National Dobro ceased operations and Victor Smith, Al Frost and Louis Dopyera bought the company and changed the name to Valco Manufacturing Company. Post-war production resumed in '46. Valco was purchased by treasurer Robert Engelhardt in '64. In '67, Valco bought Kay, but in '68 the new Valco/Kay company went out of business.

Valencia

1985-present. Budget grade, production, classical guitars imported by Rondo Music of Union, New Jersey.

Valley Arts

Ca. 1977-present. Professional and premium grade, production/custom, semi-hollow and solidbody guitars built in Nashville, Tennessee. They also make basses. Valley Arts originally was a Southern California music store owned by partners Al Carness and Mike McGuire where McGuire taught and did most of the repairs. Around '77, McGuire and Valley Arts started making custom instruments on a large scale. By '83, they opened a separate manufacturing facility to build the guitars. In '92 Samick acquired half of the company with McGuire staying on for a year as a consultant. Samick offered made-in-the-U.S. production and custom models under the Valley Arts name. In '02, Valley Arts became a division of Gibson Guitar Corp., which builds the guitars in Nashville. Founders Carness and McGuire are back with the company. They reintroduced the line in January, '03.

California Pro (U.S.-made)
1983-2002. Double-cut body, six-on-a-side tuners, single/single/hum pickups, 2 knobs and switch, various colors, serial number begins with CAL.

1983-1990		$600	$750
1990-1992	Pre-Samick	$450	$550
1993-1999	Samick owned	$325	$400

Custom Pro (U.S.-made)
1987-present. Solidbody, hard rock maple neck, maple 'board, Gotoh tuners, stationary bridge, ash or alder body, 3 EMG single-coil pickups, options include different 'board materials and widths, number of tremolos and types of pickups, offered in several colors.

1987-2010		$750	$900

Standard Pro (U.S.-made)
1990-1993. Double-cut body, six-on-a-side tuners, single/single/hum pickups, 2 knobs and switch, black opaque, serial number begins with VA.

1990-1993		$400	$500

MODEL		EXC. COND.	
YEAR	FEATURES	LOW	HIGH

Vantage

1977-present. Budget and intermediate grade, production, acoustic and electric guitars. They also build basses. Instruments from Japan from '77-'90 and from Korea from '90-present.

Vega

1880s-1980s, 1989-present. The name Vega means star and a star logo is often seen on the original Vega guitars. The original Boston-based company was purchased by C.F. Martin in '70 and used on imports. In '80, Martin sold the Vega trademark to Korea's Galaxy Trading Company. The Deering Banjo Company, in Spring Valley, California acquired the brand in '89 and uses it (and the star logo) on a line of banjos.

C Series Archtop

1930-1950s. Several different C-model numbers, mid-level archtops including carved solid tops with bookmatched figured maple backs, natural or sunburst.

1930s	Higher models (C-56)	$700	$900
1930s	Lower models	$500	$600
1940s		$500	$600
1950s	Cutaway	$550	$650

Duo-Tron Electric Archtop

1940s-1950s. Mid-level large body non-cut archtop, single pickup, block markers, natural or sunburst.

1940s		$900	$1,100
1950s		$900	$1,100

FT-90 Flat-Top

1960s. 15" body with narrow waist, dot markers, Vega logo, natural.

1960s		$325	$400

G-30

1960s. D-style with solid spruce top and solid mahogany sides and back, Vega logo with star on headstock, dot markers, natural finish.

1960s		$225	$300

O'Dell

1950s. Full body, single cut, acoustic-electric, 1 pickup, tailpiece controls.

1950s	Sunburst	$975	$1,200

Parlor Guitar

Early-1900s. Small parlor-sized instrument, Brazilian rosewood back and sides, styles vary, fancy appointments associated with higher-end models, including binding, purfling and inlays.

1900s	Mid-level	$725	$900
1910s	Higher-end	$1,600	$2,000

Profundo Flat-Top

1940s-1950s. Flat-top D-style body, spruce top, mahogany or rosewood back and sides.

1940-1950s	Mahogany	$1,350	$1,700
1940-1950s	Rosewood	$2,000	$2,500

Solidbody Electric (Import)

1970s-1980s. Solidbody copies of classic designs, Vega script logo on headstock, bolt-on necks.

1970s		$225	$300

Vega, Charles

1993-present. Luthier Charles Vega builds his premium, production/custom, nylon-string guitars in Baltimore, Maryland.

Veillette

1991-present. Luthiers Joe Veillette (of Veillette-Citron fame) and Martin Keith build their professional grade, production/custom, acoustic, acoustic/electric, electric 6- and 12-string and baritone guitars in Woodstock, New York. They also build basses and mandolins.

Veillette-Citron

1975-1983. Founded by Joe Veillette and Harvey Citron who met at the New York College School of Architecture in the late '60s. Joe took a guitar building course from Michael Gurian and by the Summer of '76, he and Harvey started producing neck-thru solidbody guitars and basses.

Veillette and Citron both are back building instruments.

Velázquez

1948-1972. Manuel Velázquez, New York, New York, gained a reputation as a fine repairman in the late 1940s. He opened his 3rd Avenue guitar building shop in the early 1950s. By the mid-1950s he was considered by some as being the finest American builder of classical guitars. Velázquez left New York in 1972 and moved to Puerto Rico. He continued building guitars for the Japanese market. He returned to the United States in 1982. By the 2000s he built instruments with this son and daughter.

Veleno

1967, 1970-1977, 2003-present. Premium and presentation grade, production/custom, all-aluminum electric solidbody guitars built by luthier John Veleno in St. Petersburg, Florida. First prototype in '67. Later production begins in late-'70 and lasts until '75 or '76. The guitars were chrome or gold-plated, with various anodized colors. The Traveler Guitar was the idea of B.B. King; only 10 were made. Two Ankh guitars were made for Todd Rundgren in '77. Only one bass was made. Approximately 185 instruments were made up to '77 and are sequentially numbered. In 2003, John Veleno reintroduced his brand.

Original (Aluminum Solidbody)

1973-1976. V-headstock, chrome and aluminum.

1973-1976		$6,500	$8,000

Traveler Guitar

1973-1976. Limited production of about a dozen instruments, drop-anchor-style metal body.

1973-1976		$8,000	$9,500

1960s Vega G-30

Veleno Original

Vengeance Guitars & Graphix Stiggy

Vinetto Legato

MODEL YEAR	FEATURES	EXC. COND. LOW	HIGH

Vengeance Guitars & Graphix

2002-present. Luthier Rick Stewart builds his professional and premium grade, custom/production, solidbody guitars in Arden, North Carolina. He also builds basses.

Ventura

1970s. Acoustic and electric guitars imported by C. Bruno Company, mainly copies of classic American models. They also offered basses.

Acoustic Flat-Top

1970s		$75	$350

Guitorgan

1970s. Based on MCI Guitorgan, converts standard electric guitar into a Guitorgan through the addition of electronic organ components, multiple switches, large Barney Kessel sharp-horned acoustic-electric style body.

1970s		$500	$600

Hollowbody Electric

1970s		$125	$550

Solidbody Electric

1970s		$125	$550

Verri

1992-present. Premium grade, production/custom, archtop guitars built by luthier Henry Verri in Little Falls, New York.

Versoul, LTD

1989-present. Premium grade, production/custom steel-string flat-top, acoustic/electric, nylon-string, resonator, solidbody, and baritone guitars built by luthier Kari Nieminen in Helsinki, Finland. He also builds basses and sitars.

Vicente Tatay

1894-late 1930s. Classical guitars built by luthier Vicente Tatay and his sons in Valencia, Spain.

Victor Baker Guitars

1998-present. Professional and premium grade, custom, carved archtop, flat-top and solidbody electric guitars built by luthier Victor Baker in Philadelphia, Pennsylvania.

Victor Guitars

2002-2008. Luthiers Edward Victor Dick and Greg German built their premium grade, production/custom, flat top guitars in Denver, Colorado.

Victoria

Ca. 1902-1920s. Brand name for New York distributor Buegeleisen & Jacobson. Instruments built by the Oscar Schmidt Co. and possibly others. Most likely a brand made for a distributor.

Vigier

2000s. Made in France by Patrice Vigier.

Viking Guitars

1998-present. Professional and premium grade, custom, solidbody guitars made in Las Vegas, Nevada by Ed Roman.

Vinetto

2003-present. Luthier Vince Cunetto builds his professional grade, production/custom, solid, chambered and semi-hollow body guitars in St. Louis, Missouri.

Vintage

Ca. 1993-present. Intermediate and professional grade, production, solidbody and semi-hollow acoustic and electro-acoustic guitars, imported from China, Korea and Vietnam by John Hornby Skewes & Co. in the U.K. They also offer basses and folk instruments.

Vintique

1990-present. Luthier Jay Monterose builds his premium grade, custom/production, electric guitars in Suffern, New York. Vintique also manufactures guitar hardware.

Virgin

2000s. Student economy imports from China.

Vivi-Tone

1933-ca. 1936. Founded in Kalamazoo, Michigan, by former Gibson designer Lloyd Loar, Walter Moon and Lewis Williams, Vivi-Tone built acoustic archtop guitars as well as some of the earliest electric solidbodies. They also built amps, basses and mandolins.

Guitar

1930s. Deep archtop-style body with F-holes on the backside and magnetic bridge pickup.

1930s	Rare model	$3,500	$4,400
1930s	Standard model, sunburst	$2,500	$3,000
1930s	Tenor, 4-string	$1,500	$1,900

Vox

1954-present. Name introduced by Jennings Musical Instruments (JMI) of England. First Vox products was a volume pedal, amplifiers were brought to the market in late '57 by Tom Jennings and Dick Denny. Guitars were introduced in '61, with an Echo Unit starting the Vox line of effects in '63.

Guitars and basses bearing the Vox name were offered from '61-'69 (made in England and Italy), '82-'85 (Japan), '85-'88 (Korea), '98-2001 (U.S.), and they introduced a limited edition U.S.-made teardrop guitar in '07 and the semi-hollow Virage guitars in '08. Vox products are currently distributed in the U.S. by Korg USA. Special thanks to Jim Rhoads of Rhoads Music in Elizabethtown, Pennsylvania, for help on production years of these models.

MODEL YEAR	FEATURES	EXC. COND. LOW	HIGH

Ace
Late 1960s. Offset double cut solidbody, 2 single-coils, Ace logo.

1967-1968		$650	$800

Apollo
1967-1968. Single sharp cutaway, 1 pickup, distortion, treble and bass booster, available in sunburst or cherry.

1967-1968		$600	$750

Bobcat
1963-1968. Double-cut semi-hollowbody style, block markers, 3 pickups, vibrato, 2 volume and 2 tone controls.

1963-1965	England	$900	$1,100
1966-1968	Italy	$700	$850

Bossman
1967-1968. Single rounded cutaway, 1 pickup, distortion, treble and bass booster, available in sunburst or cherry.

1967-1968		$500	$625

Bulldog
1966. Solidbody double-cut, 3 pickups.

1966		$750	$950

Delta
1967-1968. Solidbody, 2 pickups, distortion, treble and bass boosters, vibrato, 1 volume and 2 tone controls, available in white only.

1967-1968		$1,100	$1,350

Folk XII
1966-1969. Dreadnought 12-string flat-top, large 3-point 'guard, block markers, natural.

1966-1969		$325	$400

Guitar-Organ
1966. Standard Phantom with oscillators from a Continental organ installed inside. Plays either organ sounds, guitar sounds, or both. Weighs over 20 pounds.

1966		$1,100	$1,350

Harlem
1965-1967. Offset double-cut solidbody, 2 extended range pickups, sunburst or color option.

1965-1967		$550	$650

Hurricane
1965-1967. Double-cut solidbody, 2 pickups, spring action vibrato, sunburst or color option.

1965-1967		$450	$550

Mando Guitar
1966. Made in Italy, 12-string mandolin thing.

1966		$1,300	$1,600

Mark III
1998-2001. Teardrop reissue, made in U.S.A., 2 single-coils, fixed bridge or Bigsby. A limited was introduced in '08.

1998-2001		$850	$1,000

Mark III 50th Anniversary
2007. Only 100 made, teardrop body, 2 pickups, white finish.

2007		$800	$1,000

Mark III/Phantom Mark III
1963-1964. Teardrop body, 2 pickups, 2 controls, Marvin Bigsby, made in England, guitar version of Mark IV bass, while it is called a Phantom Mark III

it does not have a Phantom shape.

1963-1964		$2,600	$3,200

Mark IX
1965-1966. Solidbody teardrop-shaped, 9 strings, 3 pickups, vibrato, 1 volume and 2 tone controls.

1965-1966		$1,275	$1,450

Mark VI
1965-1967. Teardrop-shaped solidbody, 3 pickups, vibrato, 1 volume and 2 tone controls.

1964-1965	England, white, Brian Jones model	$3,500	$4,200
1965-1967	Italy, sunburst	$1,350	$1,700

Mark VI Reissue
1998-2001. Actually, this is a reissue of the original Phantom VI (Vox couldn't use that name due to trademark reasons), made in U.S.A.

1998-2001		$700	$875

Mark XII
1965-1967. Teardrop-shaped solidbody, 12 strings, 3 pickups, vibrato, 1 volume and 2 tone controls, sunburst. Reissued for '98-'01.

1965-1967		$1,300	$1,550

Meteor/Super Meteor
1965-1967. Solidbody double-cut, 1 pickup, Super Meteor with vibrato.

1965-1967	Meteor	$450	$550
1965-1967	Super Meteor	$500	$600

New Orleans
1966. Thin double-cut acoustic electric similar to ES-330, 2 pickups, a scaled down version of the 3-pickup Bobcat model.

1966		$675	$825

Phantom VI
1962-1967. Five-sided body, 6 strings, 3 pickups, vibrato, 1 volume and 2 tone controls.

1962-1964	English-made	$2,200	$2,600
1965-1967	Italian-made	$1,700	$2,100

Phantom XII
1964-1967. Five-sided body, 12 strings, 3 pickups, vibrato, 1 volume and 2 tone controls. There was also a stereo version with 3 offset pickups.

1964	English-made	$2,200	$2,600
1965-1967	Italian-made	$1,700	$2,100

Phantom XII Stereo
1966. Phantom shape, 3 special offset stereo pickups making 6 pickup conbinations, 3 separate pickup mode selectors, color option.

1966		$1,900	$2,400

Shadow
1965. Solidbody double-cut, 3 pickups, tremolo tailpiece, sunburst.

1965	English-made	$800	$1,000

Spitfire
1965-1967. Solidbody double-cut, 3 pickups, vibrato.

1965-1967		$450	$550

Starstream
1967-1968. Teardrop-shaped hollowbody, 2 pickups, distortion, treble and bass boosters, wah-wah, vibrato, 1 volume and 2 tone controls, 3-way pickup selector, available in cherry or sandburst.

1967-1968		$1,750	$2,200

1966 Vox Bobcat
Robbie Keene

Vox Phantom XII

2008 Vox Virage

Walden CD4041-CERT

MODEL YEAR	FEATURES	EXC. COND. LOW	HIGH
Starstream XII			
1967-1968. 12 string Starstream.			
1967-1968		$1,750	$2,200
Stroller			
1961-1966. Made in England, solidbody, single bridge pickup, Hurricane-style contoured body, dot markers, red.			
1961-1966		$375	$450
Student Prince			
1965-1967. Made in Italy, mahogany body thinline archtop electric, 2 knobs, dot markers.			
1965-1967		$325	$400
Super Ace			
1963-1965. Solidbody double-cut.			
1963-1965		$600	$725
Super Lynx			
1965-1967. Similar to Bobcat but with 2 pickups and no vibrola, double-cut, 2 pickups, adjustable truss rod, 2 bass and 2 volume controls.			
1965-1967		$700	$850
Super Lynx Deluxe			
1965-1967. Super Lynx with added vibrato tailpiece.			
1965-1967		$750	$900
Tempest XII			
1965-1967. Solidbody double-cut, 12 strings, 3 pickups.			
1965-1967		$700	$875
Thunder Jet			
1960s-style with single pickup and vibrato arm.			
1960s		$525	$650
Tornado			
1965-1967. Thinline archtop, single pickup, dot markers, sunburst.			
1965-1967		$400	$500
Typhoon			
1965-1967. Hollowbody single-cut, 2 pickups, 3-piece laminated neck.			
1965-1967		$450	$550
Ultrasonic			
1967-1968. Hollowbody double-cut, 2 pickups, distortion, treble and bass boosters, wah-wah, vibrato, 1 volume and 2 tone controls, 3-way pickup selector, available in sunburst or cherry.			
1967-1968	12-string	$1,100	$1,350
1967-1968	6-string	$1,500	$1,850
Viper			
1968. Double-cut, thinline archtop electric, built-in distortion.			
1968		$1,100	$1,350
Virage			
2008-present. Double- and single-cut semi-hollow bodies, 2 triple-coil pickups, made in Japan.			
2008-2010		$1,400	$1,700

W. J. Dyer

See listing under Dyer.

Wabash

1950s. Acoustic and electric guitars distributed by the David Wexler company and made by others, most likely Kay. They also offered lap steels and amps.

Walden Guitars

1996-present. Luthier Jonathan Lee of Portland, Oregon imports production, budget to professional grade, acoustic, acoustic-electric and classical guitars from Lilan, China.

Walker

1994-present. Premium and presentation grade, production/custom, flat-top and archtop guitars built by luthier Kim Walker in North Stonington, Connecticut.

Walker (Kramer)

1981. Kramer came up with idea to offer this brand to produce wood-neck guitars and basses; they didn't want to dilute the Kramer aluminum-neck market they had built up. The idea didn't last long, and few, if any, of these instruments were produced, but prototypes exist.

Wandre (Davoli)

Ca. 1956/57-1969. Solidbody and thinline hollowbody electric guitars and basses created by German-descended Italian motorcycle and guitar enthusiast, artist, and sculptor from Milan, Italy, Wandre Pioli. Brands include Wandre (pronounced Vahn-dray), Davoli, Framez, JMI, Noble, Dallas, Avalon, Avanti I and others. Until '60, they were built by Pioli himself; from '60-'63 built in Milan by Framez; '63-'65 built by Davoli; '66-'69 built in Pioli's own factory.

The guitars originally used Framez pickups, but from '63 on (or earlier) they used Davoli pickups. Mostly strange shapes characterized by neck-thru-tailpiece aluminum neck with plastic back and rosewood 'board. Often multi-color and sparkle finishes, using unusual materials like linoleum, fiberglass and laminates, metal bindings. Often the instruments will have numerous identifying names but usually somewhere there is a Wandre blob logo.

Distributed early on in the U.K. by Jennings Musical Industries, Ltd. (JMI) and in the U.S. by Don Noble and Company. Model B.B. dedicated to Brigitte Bardot. Among more exotic instruments were the minimalist Krundaal Bikini guitar with a built-in amplifier and attached speaker, and the pogo stick Swedenbass. These guitars are relatively rare and highly collectible. In '05, the brand was revived on a line of imported intermediate grade, production, solidbodies from Eastwood guitars.

MODEL YEAR	FEATURES	EXC. COND. LOW	HIGH
Electric			
1960s	Various models	$3,000	$6,000

Warren

2005-present. Luthier Don Warren builds his professional and premium grade, custom/production, solidbody electric guitars in Latham, New York.

MODEL YEAR	FEATURES	EXC. COND. LOW	HIGH

Warrior

1995-present. Professional, premium, and presentation grade, production/custom, acoustic and solidbody electric guitars built by luthier J.D. Lewis in Rossville, Georgia. Warrior also builds basses.

Washburn

1974-present. Budget, intermediate, professional, and premium grade, production/custom, acoustic and electric guitars made in the U.S., Japan, and Korea. They also make basses, amps, banjos and mandolins.

Originally a Lyon & Healy brand, the Washburn line was revived in '74, promoted by Beckman Musical Instruments. Beckman sold the rights to the Washburn name to Fretted Instruments, Inc. in '76. Guitars originally made in Japan and Korea, but production moved back to U.S. in '91. Currently Washburn is part of U.S. Music.

Washburn (Lyon & Healy)

1880s-ca.1949. Washburn was founded in Chicago as one of the lines for Lyon & Healy to promote high quality stringed instruments, ca. 1880s. The rights to manufacture Washburns were sold to J.R. Stewart Co. in '28, but rights to Washburn name were sold to Tonk Brothers of Chicago. In the Great Depression (about 1930), J.R. Stewart Co. was hit hard and declared bankruptcy. Tonk Brothers bought at auction all Stewart trade names, then sold them to Regal Musical Instrument Co. Regal built Washburns by the mid-'30s. The Tonk Brothers still licensed the name. These Washburn models lasted until ca. '49. In '74 the brand resurfaced.

Model 1897

1910. High-end appointments, plentiful pearl, 18 frets, slightly larger than parlor size, natural.

1910		$2,500	$3,100

Model 1915

1928. Brazilian rosewood back and sides.

1928		$1,800	$2,300

Model 5200 (Tonk Bros by Regal)

1934		$2,200	$2,700

Model 5249 Flat-Top

1940s. Vertical pearl inlay, Washburn logo and graphic, block markers, round soundhole, sunburst.

1940s		$3,800	$4,700

Model 5257 Solo

1930s. Jumbo size body, rosewood back and sides, natural.

1930s		$4,600	$5,700

Model 5265 Tenor

1920s. Pear-shaped mahogany body, 4-string tenor.

1920s		$500	$625

Parlor Guitar

Early-1900s. Lower-end, small 12"-13" body, plain appointments.

1900s		$375	$500

Style 188

1890s. Rosewood back and sides with full pearl 'board inlaid with contrasting colored pearl, pearl on edges and around soundhole.

1890s		$3,400	$4,300

Style A

1920s. Smaller body, rosewood back and sides, top stencil decoration, natural.

1920s		$2,600	$3,300

Washington

Washington was a brand manufactured by Kansas City, Missouri instrument wholesalers J.W. Jenkins & Sons. First introduced in 1895, the brand also offered mandolins.

Waterstone

2003-present. Intermediate and professional grade, production/custom, electric solid and semi-hollowbody and acoustic guitars imported from Korea by Waterstone Musical Instruments, LLC of Nashville, Tennessee. They also offer basses.

Watkins/WEM

1957-present. Watkins Electric Music (WEM) was founded by Charlie Watkins. Their first commercial product was the Watkins Dominator (wedge Gibson stereo amp shape) in '57. They made the Rapier line of guitars and basses from the beginning. Watkins offered guitars and basses up to '82. They currently build accordian amps.

Wayne

1998-present. Professional and premium grade, production/custom, solidbody guitars built by luthiers Wayne and Michael (son) Charvel in Paradise, California. They also build lap steels.

Webber

1988-present. Professional grade, production/custom flat-top guitars built by luthier David Webber in North Vancouver, British Columbia.

Weber

1996-present. Premium grade, production/custom, carved-top acoustic and resonator guitars built by luthier Bruce Weber and his Sound To Earth, Ltd. company, originally in Belgrade, Montana, and since '04, in Logan, Montana. They also build mandolins.

Webster

1940s. Archtop and acoustic guitars, most likely built by Kay or other mass builder.

Model 16C

1940s. Acoustic archtop.

1940s		$475	$600

Warren AR

Washburn WIDLXLITE

MODEL		EXC. COND.	
YEAR	FEATURES	LOW	HIGH

1930s Weissenborn

Weissenborn Style 1

Wechter

1984-present. Intermediate, professional and premium grade, production/custom, flat-top, 12-string, resonator and nylon-string guitars from luthier Abe Wechter in Paw Paw, Michigan. He also offers basses. The Elite line is built in Paw Paw, the others in Asia. Until '94 he built guitars on a custom basis. In '95, he set up a manufacturing facility in Paw Paw to produce his new line and in '00 he added the Asian guitars. In '04, he added resonators designed by Tim Scheerhorn. Wechter was associated with Gibson Kalamazoo from the mid-'70s to '84. He also offers the Maple Lake brand of acoustics.

Weissenborn

1910s-1937, present. Hermann Weissenborn was well-established as a violin and piano builder in Los Angeles by the early 1910s. Around '20, he added guitars, ukes and steels to his line. Most of his production was in the '20s and '30s until his death in '37. He made tenor, plectrum, parlor, and Spanish guitars, ukuleles, and mandolins, but is best remembered for his koa Hawaiian guitars that caught the popular wave of Hawaiian music. That music captivated America after being introduced to the masses at San Francisco's Panama Pacific International Exposition which was thrown in '15 to celebrate the opening of the Panama Canal and attended by more than 13 million people. He also made instruments for Kona and other brands. The majority of his instruments were most likely sold before the late 1920s. The Weissenborn brand has been revived on a line of reissue style guitars.

Spanish Acoustic

1920s. High-end Spanish set-up, rope binding, koa top, sides and back, limited production.

1920s		$3,200	$3,900

Style #1 Hawaiian

1920-1930s. Koa, no binding, 3 wood circle soundhole inlays.

1920s		$2,700	$3,300

Style #2 Hawaiian

1920-1930s. Koa, black celluloid body binding, white wood 'board binding, rope soundhole binding.

1920s		$3,000	$3,600

Style #2 Spanish

1920s. Spanish set-up, Style 2 features.

1920s		$3,500	$4,200

Style #3 Hawaiian

1920-1930s. Koa, rope binding on top, 'board, and soundhole.

1920s		$4,100	$5,100

Style #4 Hawaiian

1920-1930s. Koa, rope binding on body, 'board, headstock and soundhole.

1920s		$5,000	$6,000

Tenor

1920		$1,600	$1,800

MODEL		EXC. COND.	
YEAR	FEATURES	LOW	HIGH

Welker Custom

Professional and premium grade, production/custom, archtop and flat-top guitars built by luthier Fred Welker in Nashville, Tennessee.

Welson

1960s. Import copy models from accordion maker in Italy, copies range from Jazzmaster-style to ES-335-style, production was not large, Welson logo on the headstock, some sold in the U.S.A. by the Wurlitzer retail stores.

Electric

1960s	Copy models	$250	$500
1960s	Plastic cover, original design	$500	$850

Wendler

1999-present. Intermediate and professional grade, production/custom, solidbody, electro-acoustic guitars from luthier Dave Wendler of Ozark Instrument Building in Branson, Missouri. He also builds basses and amps. In '91, Wendler patented a pickup system that became the Taylor ES system.

Westbury-Unicord

1978-ca. 1983. Imported from Japan by Unicord of Westbury, New York. High quality original designs, generally with 2 humbuckers, some with varitone and glued-in necks. They also had basses.

Westone

1970s-1990, 1996-2001. Made by Matsumoku in Matsumoto, Japan and imported by St. Louis Music. Around '81, St. Louis Music purchased an interest in Matsumoku and began to make a transition from its own Electra brand to the Westone brand previously used by Matsumoku. In the beginning of '84, the brand became Electra-Westone with a phoenix bird head surrounded by circular wings and flames. By the end of '84 the Electra name was dropped, leaving only Westone and a squared-off bird with W-shaped wings logo. Electra, Electra-Westone and Westone instruments from this period are virtually identical except for the brand and logo treatment. Many of these guitars and basses were made in very limited runs and are relatively rare.

From '96 to '01, England's FCN Music offered Westone branded electric and acoustic guitars. The electrics were built in England and the acoustics came from Korea. Matsumoku-made guitars feature a serial number in which the first 1 or 2 digits represent the year of manufacture. Electra-Westone guitars should begin with either a 4 or 84.

Weymann

1864-1940s. H.A. Weymann & Sons was a musical instrument distributor located in Philadelphia that marketed various stringed instruments, but mainly known for banjos. Some guitar models made by Regal and Vega, but they also built their own instruments.

MODEL		EXC. COND.	
YEAR	FEATURES	LOW	HIGH

Acoustic
| 1930-1945 | Violin-shaped | $4,500 | $5,500 |

Jimmie Rodgers Signature Edition
| 1929 | | $6,400 | $8,000 |

Parlor
1904-ca. 1920. Small 14 5/8" body parlor-style, fancy pearl and abalone trim, fancy fretboard markers, natural.
| 1910 | | $2,800 | $3,500 |

Style 24
1920s. Mid-size body, 12-fret, slotted peghead, made by Vega for Weymann, mahogany sides and back, natural.
| 1920s | | $875 | $1,100 |

White Guitars and Woodley White Luthier

1992-present. Premium grade, custom, classical, acoustic and electric guitars, built by luthier Woodley White, first in Portland, Oregon and since 2008 in Naalehu, Hawaii.

Wicked

2004-present. Production/custom, intermediate and professional grade, semi-hollow and electric solidbody guitars built by luthier Nicholas Dijkman in Montreal, Quebec. He also builds basses.

Widman Custom Electrics

2008-present. Professional and premium grade, custom, electric guitars built in Arden, North Carolina by luthier John Widman.

Wilkanowski

Early-1930s-mid-1940s. W. Wilkanowski primarily built violins. He did make a few dozen guitars which were heavily influenced by violin design concepts and in fact look very similar to a large violin with a guitar neck.

Wilkat Guitars

1998-present. Professional grade, custom handmade, electric guitars built by luthier Bill Wilkat in Montreal, Quebec. He also builds basses.

Wilkins

1984-present. Custom guitars built by luthier Pat Wilkins in Van Nuys, California. Wilkins also does finish work for individuals and a variety of other builders.

William C. Stahl

See listing under Stahl.

William Hall and Son

William Hall and Son was a New York City based distributor offering guitars built by other luthiers in the mid to late 1800s.

William Jeffrey Jones

2006-present. Luthier William Jeffrey Jones builds his ornately carved, professional and premium grade, production/custom, solidbody and semi-hollow electric guitars in Neosho, Missouri.

Wilson

1960s-1970s. One of the brand names of guitars built in the 1960s for others by Egmond in Holland. Also a brand name used by England's Watkins WEM in the 1960s and '70s.

Wilson Brothers Guitars

2004-present. Intermediate and professional grade, production, imported electric and acoustic guitars. They also build basses. Founded by Ventures guitarist Don Wilson. VCM and VSP models made in Japan; VM electrics in Korea; VM acoustic in China.

Windsor

Ca. 1890s-ca. 1914. Brand used by Montgomery Ward for flat top guitars and mandolins made by various American manufacturers, including Lyon & Healy and, possibly, Harmony. Generally beginner-grade instruments.

Acoustic Flat-Top
| 1900s | | $200 | $250 |

Winston

Ca. 1963-1967. Imported from Japan by Buegeleisen and Jacobson of New York. Manufacturers unknown, but some are by Guyatone. Generally shorter scale beginner guitars. They also had basses.

Worland Guitars

1997-present. Professional grade, production/custom, flat-top, 12-string, and harp guitars built by luthier Jim Worland in Rockford, Illinois.

WRC Music International

1989-mid-1990s. Guitars by Wayne Richard Charvel, who was the original founder of Charvel Guitars. He now builds Wayne guitars with his son Michael.

Wright Guitar Technology

1993-present. Luthier Rossco Wright builds his unique intermediate and professional grade, production, travel/practice steel-string and nylon-string guitars in Eugene, Oregon. Basses were added in 2009.

Wurlitzer

Wurlitzer marketed a line of American-made guitars in the 1920s. They also offered American- and foreign-made guitars starting in '65. The American ones were built from '65-'66 by the Holman-Woodell guitar factory in Neodesha, Kansas. In '67, Wurlitzer switched to Italian-made Welson guitars.

Weissenborn Style 4

Worland Jumbo

XXL DC Model

Yamaha CG Series CG111S

MODEL YEAR	FEATURES	EXC. COND. LOW	HIGH

Model 2077 (Martin 0-K)
1920s. Made by Martin for Wurlitzer who had full-line music stores in most major cities. Size 0 with top, back and sides made from koa wood, limited production of about 28 instruments.

1922	Natural	$4,600	$5,600

Model 2090 (Martin 0-28)
1920s. Made by Martin for Wurlitzer who had full-line music stores in most major cities. Size 0 with appointments similar to a similar period Martin 0-28, limited production of about 11 instruments, Wurlitzer branded on the back of the headstock and on the inside back seam, Martin name also branded on inside seam.

1922	Natural	$6,400	$7,700

Wild One Stereo
1960s. Two pickups, various colors.

1967		$500	$625

Xaviere
Budget and intermediate grade, production, solid and semi-hollow body guitars from Guitar Fetish, which also has GFS pickups and effects.

Xotic Guitars
1996-present. Luthier Hiro Miura builds his professional grade, production/custom guitars in San Fernando, California. He also builds basses. The Xotic brand is also used on a line of guitar effects.

XOX Audio Tools
2007-present. U.S. debut in '08 of premium grade, production/custom, carbon fiber electric guitars built by luthier Peter Solomon in Europe.

Xtone
2003-present. Semi-hollow body electric, acoustic and acoustic/electric guitars from ESP. Originally branded Xtone on headstock, since '10 the instruments are marketed as a model series under LTD (ESP's other brand) and state such on the headstock.

XXL Guitars
2003-present. Luthier Marc Lupien builds his production/custom, professional grade, chambered electric guitars in Montreal, Quebec.

Yamaha
1946-present. Budget, intermediate, professional, and presentation grade, production/custom, acoustic, acoustic/electric, and electric guitars. They also build basses, amps, and effects. The Japanese instrument maker was founded in 1887. Began classical guitar production around 1946. Solidbody electric production began in '66; steel string acoustics debut sometime after that. They began to export guitars into the U.S. in '69. Production shifted from Japan to Taiwan (Yamaha's special-built plant) in the '80s, though some high-end guitars still made in Japan. Some Korean production began in '90s.

MODEL YEAR	FEATURES	EXC. COND. LOW	HIGH

Serialization patterns:
Serial numbers are coded as follows:
H = 1, I = 2, J = 3, etc., Z = 12
To use this pattern, you need to know the decade of production.
Serial numbers are ordered as follows:
Year/Month/Day/Factory Order
Example: NL 29159 represents a N=1987 year, L=5th month or May, 29=29th day (of May), 159=159th guitar made that day (the factory order). This guitar was the 159 guitar made on May 29, 1987.

AE Series
1966-present. Archtop models.

1966-2010	Lower-end	$200	$500
1966-2010	Mid-level	$500	$800

AE Series
1966-present. Archtop models.

1966-2010	Higher-end	$800	$1,100

AES Series
1990-present. Semi-hollowbody models.

1990-2010	Lower-end	$350	$500
1990-2010	Mid-level	$500	$800

AES Series
1990-present. Semi-hollowbody models.

1990-2010	Higher-end	$800	$1,100

APX Series
1987-present. Acoustic/electric, various features.

1987-2010	Lower-end	$200	$400
1987-2010	Mid-level	$400	$700

APX Series
1987-present. Acoustic/electric, various features.

1987-2010	Higher-end	$700	$1,000

CG Series
1984-present. Classical models.

1984-2010	Lower-end	$50	$200
1984-2010	Mid-level	$200	$300

CG Series
1984-present. Classical models.

1984-2010	Higher-end	$300	$400

DW Series
1999-2002. Dreadnought flat-top models, sunburst, solid spruce top, higher-end appointments like abalone rosette and top purfling.

1999-2002	Lower-end	$150	$300
1999-2002	Mid-level	$300	$375

DW Series
1999-2002. Dreadnought flat-top models, sunburst, solid spruce top, higher-end appointments like abalone rosette and top purfling.

1999-2002	Higher-end	$375	$450

EG Series
2000-2009. Electric solidbody.

2000-2009		$25	$125

Eterna Series
1983-1994. Folk style acoustics, there were 4 models.

1983-1994		$50	$325

MODEL YEAR	FEATURES	EXC. COND. LOW	HIGH

FG Series
1970s-present. Economy market flat-top models, laminated sides and back, a 12 suffix indicates 12-string, CE indicates on-board electronics, many models are D-style bodies.

1970-2010	Lower-end	$100	$200
1970-2010	Mid-level	$200	$300

FG Series
1970s-present. Economy market flat-top models, laminated sides and back, a 12 suffix indicates 12-string, CE indicates on-board electronics, many models are D-style bodies.

1970-2010	Higher-end	$300	$500
1970-2010	Highest-end	$500	$1,150

G Series
1981-2000. Classical models.

1981-2000		$50	$225

GC Series
1982-present. Classical models, '70s made in Japan, '80s made in Taiwan.

1982-2010	Lower-end	$450	$550
1982-2010	Mid-level	$550	$650

GC Series
1982-present. Classical models, '70s made in Japan, '80s made in Taiwan.

1982-2010	Higher-end	$650	$750

Image Custom
1988-1992. Electric double-cut, Brazilian rosewood 'board, maple top, 2 humbuckers, active circuitry, LED position markers, script Image logo on truss rod cover. The Image was called the MSG in the U.K.

1988-1992		$500	$625

L Series
1984-present. Custom hand-built flat-top models, solid wood.

1984-2010	Lower-end	$350	$600
1984-2010	Mid-level	$600	$800

L Series
1984-present. Custom hand-built flat-top models, solid wood.

1984-2010	Higher-end	$800	$1,000

PAC Pacifica Series
1989-present. Offset double-cut with longer horns, dot markers, large script Pacifica logo and small block Yamaha logo on headstock, various models.

1989-2010		$225	$650

RGX Series
1988-present. Bolt-on neck for the 600 series and neck-thru body designs for 1200 series, various models include 110 (1 hum), 211 (hum-single), 220 (2 hums), 312 (hum-single-single), 603 (3 singles), 612 (hum-single-single), 620 (2 hums), 1203S (3 singles), 1212S (hum-single-single), 1220S (2 hums).

1988-2010	Lower-end	$150	$250
1988-2010	Mid-level	$250	$350

RGX Series
1988-present. Bolt-on neck for the 600 series and neck-thru body designs for 1200 series, various models include 110 (1 hum), 211 (hum-single), 220 (2 hums), 312 (hum-single-single), 603 (3 singles), 612 (hum-single-single), 620 (2 hums), 1203S (3 singles), 1212S (hum-single-single), 1220S (2 hums).

1988-2010	Higher-end	$350	$600

RGZ Series
1989-1994. Double-cut solidbodies, various pickups.

1989-1994	Lower-end	$100	$250
1989-1994	Mid-level	$250	$350

RGZ Series
1989-1994. Double-cut solidbodies, various pickups.

1989-1994	Higher-end	$350	$600

SA Series
1966-1994. Super Axe series, full-size and thinline archtop models.

1966-1994	Lower-end	$450	$600
1966-1994	Mid-level	$600	$800

SA Series
1966-1994. Super Axe series, full-size and thinline archtop models.

1966-1994	Higher-end	$800	$1,000
1966-1994	Highest-end	$1,000	$1,400

SBG Series
1983-1992. Solidbody models, set necks, model name logo on truss rod cover.

1983-1992	Lower-end	$250	$500
1983-1992	Mid-level	$500	$1,000

SBG Series
1983-1992. Solidbody models, set necks, model name logo on truss rod cover.

1983-1992	Higher-end	$1,000	$1,500
1983-1992	Highest-end	$1,500	$2,000

SE Series
1986-1992. Solidbody electric models.

1986-1992	Lower-end	$100	$200
1986-1992	Mid-level	$200	$300

SE Series
1986-1992. Solidbody electric models.

1986-1992	Higher-end	$300	$400

SF Super Flighter Series

1980s		$600	$700

SG-3
1965-1966. Early double-cut solidbody with sharp horns, bolt neck, 3 hum-single pickup layout, large white guard, rotor controls, tremolo.

1965-1966		$850	$950

SG-5/SG-5A
1966-1971. Asymmetrical double-cut solidbody with extended lower horn, bolt neck, 2 pickups, chrome hardware.

1966-1971		$875	$975

SG-7/SG-7A
1966-1971. Like SG-5, but with gold hardware.

1966-1971		$975	$1,125

SG-20
1972-1973. Bolt-on neck, slab body, single-cut, 1 pickup.

1972-1973		$275	$375

1989 Yamaha Image Custom

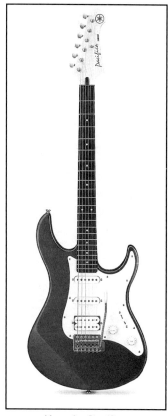

Yamaha Pacifica

Yanuziello Electric

Zanini Lyra

MODEL YEAR	FEATURES	EXC. COND. LOW	HIGH

SG-30/SG-30A

1973-1976. Slab katsura wood (30) or slab maple (30A) solidbody, bolt-on neck, 2 humbuckers, dot inlays.

| 1973-1976 | | $300 | $400 |

SG-35/SG-35A

1973-1976. Slab mahogany (35) or slab maple (35A) solidbody, bolt-on neck, 2 humbuckers, parallelogram inlays.

| 1973-1976 | | $350 | $450 |

SG-40

1972-1973. Bolt-on neck, carved body, single-cut.

| 1972-1973 | | $350 | $450 |

SG-45

1972-1976. Glued neck, single-cut, bound flat-top.

| 1972-1976 | | $400 | $500 |

SG-50

1974-1976. Slab katsura wood solidbody, glued neck, 2 humbuckers, dot inlays, large 'guard.

| 1974-1976 | | $400 | $500 |

SG-60

1972 only. Bolt-on neck, carved body, single-cut.

| 1972 | | $400 | $500 |

SG-60T

1973 only. SG-60 with large cast vibrato system.

| 1973 | | $400 | $500 |

SG-65

1972-1976. Glued neck, single-cut, bound flat-top.

| 1972-1976 | | $500 | $600 |

SG-70

1974-1976. Slab maple solidbody, glued neck, 2 humbuckers, dot inlays, large 'guard.

| 1974-1976 | | $500 | $600 |

SG-80

1972 only. Bolt-on neck, carved body, single-cut.

| 1972 | | $400 | $500 |

SG-80T

1973. SG-60 with large cast vibrato system.

| 1973 | | $450 | $550 |

SG-85

1972-1976. Glued neck, single-cut, bound flat-top.

| 1972-1976 | | $500 | $600 |

SG-90

1974-1976. Carved top mahogany solidbody, glued neck, elevated 'guard, bound top, dot inlays, chrome hardware.

| 1974-1976 | | $600 | $700 |

SG-175

1974-1976. Carved top mahogany solidbody, glued neck, elevated 'guard, abalone bound top, abalone split wing or pyramid inlays, gold hardware.

| 1974-1976 | | $700 | $800 |

SG-500

1976-1978. Carved unbound maple top, double pointed cutaways, glued neck, 2 exposed humbuckers, 3-ply bound headstock, bound neck with clay split wing inlays, chrome hardware. Reissued as the SBG-500 (800S in Japan) in '81.

| 1976-1978 | | $375 | $475 |

SG-700

1976-1978. Carved unbound maple top, double pointed cutaways, glued neck, 2 humbuckers, 3-ply bound headstock, bound neck with clay split wing inlays, chrome hardware.

| 1976-1978 | | $525 | $625 |

SG-700S

1999-2001. Set neck, mahogany body, 2 humbuckers with coil tap.

| 1999-2001 | | $525 | $625 |

SG-1000/SBG-1000

1976-1983 ('84 in Japan), 2007-present. Carved maple top, double pointed cutaways, glued neck, 2 humbuckers, 3-ply bound headstock, unbound body, bound neck with clay split wing inlays, gold hardware. Export model name changed to SBG-1000 in '80. SBG-1000 reissued in '07.

| 1976-1979 | SG-1000 | $800 | $1,000 |
| 1980-1983 | SBG-1000 | $800 | $1,000 |

SG-1500

1976-1979. Carved maple top, double pointed cutaways, laminated neck-thru-body neck, laminated mahogany body wings, 2 humbuckers, 5-ply bound headstock and body, bound neck with dot inlays, chrome hardware. Name used on Japan-only model in the '80s.

| 1976-1979 | | $750 | $900 |

SG-2000/SG-2000S

1976-1980 (1988 in Japan). Carved maple top, double pointed cutaways, laminated neck-thru-body neck, laminated mahogany body wings, 2 humbuckers, 5-ply bound headstock and body, bound neck with abalone split wing inlays, gold hardware. In '80, the model was changed to the SBG-2000 in the U.S., and the SG-2000S everywhere else except Japan (where it remained the SG-2000). Export model renamed SBG-2100 in '84.

| 1976-1980 | | $775 | $925 |

SG-2100S

1983. Similar to SG-2000 with upgrades such as the pickups.

| 1983 | | $900 | $1,100 |

SG-3000/SBG-3000/Custom Professional

1982-1992. SG-2000 upgrade with higher output pickups and abalone purfling on top.

| 1982-1992 | | $1,000 | $1,250 |

SGV-300

2000-2006. 1960s SG model features.

| 2000-2006 | | $300 | $400 |

SHB-400

1981-1985. Solidbody electric, set-in neck, 2 pickups.

| 1981-1985 | | $300 | $400 |

SJ-180

1983-1994. Student Jumbo, entry level Folk Series model, laminated top.

| 1983-1994 | | $100 | $125 |

SJ-400S

1983-1994. Student Jumbo Folk Series model, solid wood top.

| 1983-1994 | | $225 | $275 |

MODEL YEAR	FEATURES	EXC. COND. LOW	HIGH
SL Studio Lord Series			
1977-1981. LP-style copy models.			
1977-1981		$350	$450
SR SuperRivroller Series			
1977-1981. Strat copy models.			
1977-1981		$300	$400
SSC Series			
1983-1992. Solidbody electric models.			
1983-1992	SSC-400/SC-400	$275	$325
1983-1992	SSC-500	$250	$300
1983-1992	SSC-600/SC-600	$350	$425
Weddington Classic			
1989-1992. Electric solidbody, redesigned set-in neck/body joint for increased access to the higher frets.			
1989-1992		$475	$575

Yanuziello Stringed Instruments

1980-present. Production/custom resonator and Hawaiian guitars built by luthier Joseph Yanuziello, in Toronto, Ontario.

Yosco

1900-1930s. Lawrence L. Yosco was a New York City luthier building guitars, round back mandolins and banjos under his own brand and for others.

Zachary

1996-present. Luthier Alex Csiky builds his professional grade, production, solidbody electric guitars in Windsor, Ontario. He also builds basses.

Zanini

2007-present. Premium grade, production, electric guitars designed by Luca Zanini of Italy and built by luthier Alex Radovanovic in Switzerland.

Zeiler Guitars

1992-present. Custom flat-top, 12-string, and nylon-string guitars built by luthier Jamon Zeiler in Cincinnati, Ohio.

Zemaitis

1960-1999, 2004-present. Professional, premium, and presentation grade, custom/production, electric and acoustic guitars. Tony Zemaitis (born Antanus Casimere Zemaitis) began selling his guitars in 1960. He emphasized simple light-weight construction and was known for hand engraved metal front guitars. The metal front designs were originally engineered to reduce hum, but they became popular as functional art. Each hand-built guitar and bass was a unique instrument. Ron Wood was an early customer and his use of a Zemaitis created a demand for the custom-built guitars. Approximately 6 to 10 instruments were built each year. Tony retired in '99, and passed away in '02 at the age of 67. In '04, Japan's Kanda Shokai Corporation, with the endorsement of Tony Zemaitis, Jr., started building the guitars again. KSC builds the higher priced ones and licenses the lower priced

guitars to Greco.

Celebrity association with Zemaitis is not uncommon. Validated celebrity provenance may add 25% to 100% (or more) to a guitar's value. Tony Zemaitis also made so-called student model instruments for customers with average incomes. These had wood tops instead of metal or pearl. Some wood top instruments have been converted to non-Zemaitis metal tops, which are therefore not fully original Zemaitis instruments.

Acoustic Models

1965	12-string, 1st year	$15,000	$18,000
1970s	6-string	$9,500	$12,000
1980s	12-string, D-hole	$8,000	$10,000
1980s	12-string, heart-hole	$16,000	$20,000
1980s	6-string, D-hole	$8,000	$10,000
1980s	6-string, heart-hole	$15,000	$18,000

Electric Models

1980-1990s	Student model, wood top	$8,000	$10,000
1980s	Disc-front	$17,000	$21,000
1980s	Metal-front	$18,000	$22,000
1980s	Pearl-front	$21,000	$26,000
1994	"Black Pearl", very few made	$24,000	$29,000
1995	Disc-front 40th Anniversary	$19,000	$23,000

Zen-On

1946-ca.1968. Japanese manufacturer. By '67 using the Morales brand name. Not heavily imported into the U.S., if at all (see Morales).

Acoustic Hollowbody

1946-1968. Various models.

1950s		$175	$225

Electric Solidbody

1960s. Teisco-era and styling.

1960s		$175	$225

Zerberus

2002-present. Professional and premium grade, production/custom, electric guitars built in Speyer, Germany by luthier Frank Scheucher.

Zeta

1982-present. Zeta has made solid, semi-hollow and resonator guitars, many with electronic and MIDI options, in Oakland, California over the years, but currently only offer upright basses, amps and violins.

Ziegenfuss Guitars

2006-present. Luthier Stephen Ziegenfuss builds his professional and premium grade, custom, acoustic and solidbody electric guitars in Jackson, Michigan. He also builds basses.

1994 Zemaitis Pearl-Front

Zerberus Hydra II

Zimnicki Double Cutaway

MODEL YEAR	FEATURES	EXC. COND. LOW	HIGH

Zim-Gar

1960s. Imported from Japan by Gar-Zim Musical Instrument Corporation of Brooklyn, New York. Manufacturers unknown. Generally shorter scale beginner guitars.

Electric Solidbody

1960s		$175	$225

Zimnicki, Gary

1980-present. Luthier Gary Zimnicki builds his professional and premium grade, custom, flat-top, 12-string, nylon-string, and archtop guitars in Allen Park, Michigan.

Zion

1980-present. Professional and premium grade, production/custom, semi-hollow and solidbody guitars built by luthier Ken Hoover, originally in Greensboro, North Carolina, currently in Raleigh.

Classic

1989-present. Double-cut solidbody, six-on-a-side headstock, opaque finish, various pickup options, dot markers.

1989-2010	Custom quilted top	$550	$700
1989-2010	Opaque finish	$400	$500

Graphic

1980s-1994. Double-cut basswood body, custom airbrushed body design, bolt-on neck, Green Frost Marble finish.

1990		$700	$850

Radicaster

1987-present. Double-cut basswood body, graphic finish, bolt-on neck, various pickup configurations, marble/bowling ball finish.

1987-2010		$550	$700

The Fifty

1994-present. Single-cut ash solidbody, 2 single coils, bolt-on neck.

1994-2010	Custom figured top	$550	$700
1994-2010	Natural, plain top	$400	$550

Zolla

1979-present. Professional grade, production/custom, electric guitars built by luthier Bill Zolla in San Diego, California. Zolla also builds basses, necks and bodies.

Zon

1981-present. Currently luthier Joe Zon only offers basses, but he also built guitars from '85-'91. See Bass Section for more company info.

Zuni

1993-present. Premium grade, custom, solidbody electric guitars built by luthier Michael Blank in Alto Pass, Illinois and Amasa, Michigan.

ZZ Ryder

Solidbody electric guitars from Stenzler Musical Instruments of Ft. Worth, Texas. They also offer basses.

BASSES

MODEL YEAR	FEATURES	EXC. COND. LOW	HIGH

1983 Alembic Distillate
Paul J. Allen

Alembic Essence

A Basses

1976-2002. Luthier Albey Balgochian built his professional grade, solidbody basses in Waltham, Massachusetts. Sports the A logo on headstock.

Solidbody Bass

1976-2002		$1,200	$1,400

Acoustic

Ca. 1965-ca. 1987, 2001-2005, 2008-present. Mainly known for solidstate amps, the Acoustic Control Corp. of Los Angeles, did offer guitars and basses from around '69 to late '74. The brand was revived in '01 by Samick for a line of amps.

Black Widow Bass

1969-1970, 1972-1974. Around '69 Acoustic offered the AC600 Black Widow Bass (in both a fretted and fretless version) which featured an unique black equal double-cut body with German carve, an Ebonite 'board, 2 pickups, each with 1 row of adjustable polepieces, a zero fret, and a protective "spider design" pad on back. Also available was the AC650 short-scale. The '72-'74 version had the same body design, but had a rosewood 'board and only 1 pickup with 2 rows of adjustable pole pieces (the '72s had a different split-coil pickup with 4 pole pieces, 2 front and 2 back). Acoustic outsourced the production of the basses, possibly to Japan, but at least part of the final production was by Semie Moseley.

1969-1970		$1,000	$1,250
1972-1974		$900	$1,125

Aims

Ca. 1974-ca. 1976. Aims instruments, distributed by Randall Instruments in the mid-'70s, were copies of classic American guitar and bass models. Randall also offered a line of Aims amps during the same time.

Airline

1958-1968, 2004-present. Brand for Montgomery Ward. Built by Kay, Harmony and Valco. In '04, the brand was revived on a line of reissues from Eastwood guitars.

Electric Solidbody Bass

1958-1968	Various models	$300	$400

Pocket 3/4 Bass (Valco/National)

1962-1968. Airline brand of double-cut Pocket Bass, short-scale, 2 pickups, 1 acoustic bridge and 1 neck humbucker, sunburst and other colors.

1962-1968		$600	$750

Alamo

1947-1982. Founded by Charles Eilenberg, Milton Fink, and Southern Music, San Antonio, Texas. Distributed by Bruno & Sons.

Eldorado Bass (Model 2600)

1965-1966. Solidbody, 1 pickup, angular offset shape, double-cut.

1965-1966		$350	$425

Titan Bass

1963-1970. Hollowbody, 1 pickup, angular offset shape.

1963-1970		$350	$425

Alembic

1969-present. Professional, premium, and presentation grade, production/custom, 4-, 5-, and 6-string basses built in Santa Rosa, California. They also build guitars. Established in San Francisco as one of the first handmade bass builders. Alembic basses come with many options concerning woods (examples are maple, bubinga, walnut, vermilion, wenge, zebrawood), finishes, inlays, etc., all of which affect the values listed here. These dollar amounts should be used as a baseline guide to values for Alembic.

Anniversary Bass

1989. 20th Anniversary limited edition, walnut and vermillion with a walnut core, 5-piece body, 5-piece neck-thru, only 200 built.

1989		$2,200	$3,000

Custom Shop Built Bass

1969-present. Various one-off and/or custom built instruments. Each instrument should be evaluated individually. Prices are somewhat speculative due to the one-off custom characteristics and values can vary greatly.

1978	Dragon Doubleneck	$8,000	$10,000
2000	Stanley Clarke Custom	$4,500	$6,500
2004	Dragon 4-string, 4 made	$4,000	$5,000

Distillate Bass

1981-1991. One of Alembic's early lower-cost models, early ones with 1 pickup, 2 pickups by '82, exotic woods, active electronics.

1981-1991	Distillate 4	$2,000	$2,500
1981-1991	Distillate 5	$2,100	$2,600

Elan Bass

1985-1996. Available in 4-, 5-, 6- and 8-string models, 3-piece thru-body laminated maple neck, solid maple body, active electronics, solid brass hardware, offered in a variety of hardwood tops and custom finishes.

1985-1996	Elan 4	$1,600	$2,100
1985-1996	Elan 5	$1,700	$2,200

Epic Bass

1993-2009. Mahogany body with various tops, extra large pointed bass horn, maple/walnut veneer set-neck, available in 4-, 5-, and 6-string versions.

1993-1999	4-string	$1,400	$1,900
1993-1999	5-string	$1,500	$2,000
1993-1999	6-string	$1,600	$2,100
2000-2009	4-string	$1,400	$1,900
2000-2009	5-string	$1,500	$2,000
2000-2009	6-string	$1,600	$2,100

Essence Bass

1991-present. Mahogany body with various tops, extra large pointed bass horn, walnut/maple laminate neck-thru.

1991-1999	Essence 4	$1,500	$2,100
1991-1999	Essence 5	$1,600	$2,200
1991-1999	Essence 6	$1,700	$2,300
2000-2010	Essence 4	$1,500	$2,100
2000-2010	Essence 5	$1,600	$2,200
2000-2010	Essence 6	$1,700	$2,300

MODEL YEAR	FEATURES	EXC. COND. LOW	HIGH

Europa Bass
1992-present. Mahogany body with various tops,ebony 'board, available as 4-, 5-, and 6-string.

| 1992-2010 | 4- or 5-string | $2,800 | $3,800 |

Exploiter Bass
1980s. Figured maple solidbody 4-string, neck-thru, transparent finish.

| 1984-1988 | | $1,800 | $2,400 |

Persuader Bass
1983-1991. Offset double-cut solidbody, 4-string, neck-thru.

| 1983-1991 | | $1,400 | $1,900 |

Series I Bass
1971-present. Mahogany body with various tops, maple/purpleheart laminate neck-thru, active electronics, available in 3 scale lengths and with 4, 5 or 6 strings.

1971-1979	Medium- or long-scale	$4,500	$6,500
1971-1979	Short-scale	$4,500	$6,500
1980-1989	Medium- or long-scale	$4,000	$6,000
1980-1989	Short-scale	$4,000	$6,000
1990-2010	All scales, highly figured top	$4,000	$6,000

Series II Bass
1971-present. Generally custom-made option, each instrument valued on a case-by-case basis, guidance pricing only.

| 1971-2010 | | $5,000 | $7,000 |

Spoiler Bass
1981-1999. Solid mahogany body, maple neck-thru, 4 or 6 strings, active electronics, various high-end wood options.

1981-1986	6-string	$1,800	$2,400
1981-1989	4-string	$1,600	$2,200
1981-1989	5-string	$1,700	$2,300
1990-1999	4-string	$1,600	$2,200

Stanley Clarke Signature Standard Bass
1990-present. Neck-thru-body, active electronics, 24-fret ebony 'board, mahogany body with maple, bubinga, walnut, vermilion, or zebrawood top, 4-, 5-, and 6-string versions.

| 1990-2010 | All scales | $4,500 | $6,500 |

Alleva-Coppolo Basses and Guitars
1995-present. Luthier Jimmy Coppolo builds his professional and premium grade, custom/production, solidbody basses in Dallas, Texas for '95-'97, in New York City for '98-2008, and since in Upland, California. He also builds guitars.

Alternative Guitar and Amplifier Company
2006-present. Custom/production, intermediate grade, solidbody electric basses made in Piru, California, by luthiers Mal Stich and Sal Gonzales and imported from Korea under the Alternative Guitar and Amplifier Company and Mal n' Sal brands. They also build guitars.

MODEL YEAR	FEATURES	EXC. COND. LOW	HIGH

Alvarez
1965-present. Imported by St. Louis Music, they offered electric basses from '90 to '02 and acoustic basses in the mid-'90s.

Electric Bass (Mid-Level)
| 1990s | Hollowbody | $300 | $375 |
| 1990s | Solidbody | $300 | $375 |

American Showster
1986-2004. Established by Bill Meeker and David Haines, Bayville, New Jersey. They also made guitars.

AS-57-B Bass
1987-1997. Bass version of AS-57 with body styled like a '57 Chevy tail fin.

| 1987-1997 | | $1,650 | $1,900 |

Ampeg
1949-present. Ampeg was founded on a vision of an amplified bass peg, which evolved into the Baby Bass. Ampeg has sold basses on and off throughout its history. In '08 they got back into basses with the reissue of the Dan Armstrong Plexi Bass.

AEB-1 Bass
1966-1967. F-holes through the body, fretted, scroll headstock, pickup in body, sunburst. Reissued as the AEB-2 for '97-'99.

| 1966-1967 | | $2,500 | $3,200 |

ASB-1 Devil Bass
1966-1967. Long-horn body, fretted, triangular f-holes through the body, fireburst.

| 1966-1967 | | $3,300 | $4,000 |

AUB-1 Bass
1966-1967. Same as AEB-1, but fretless, sunburst. Reissued as the AUB-2 for '97-'99.

| 1966-1967 | | $2,500 | $3,200 |

AUSB-1 Devil Bass
1966-1967. Same as ASB-1 Devil Bass, but fretless.

| 1966-1967 | | $3,300 | $4,000 |

BB-4 Baby Bass
1962-1971. Electric upright slim-looking bass that is smaller than a cello, available in sunburst, white, red, black, and a few turquoise. Reissued as the ABB-1 Baby Bass for '97-'99.

| 1962-1971 | Solid color | $1,800 | $2,200 |
| 1962-1971 | Sunburst | $1,700 | $2,100 |

BB-5 Baby Bass
1964-1971. Five-string version.

| 1964-1971 | Sunburst | $1,900 | $2,300 |

Dan Armstrong Lucite Bass
1969-1971. Clear solid lucite body, did not have switchable pickups like the Lucite guitar.

| 1969-1971 | Clear | $2,400 | $2,900 |
| 1969-1971 | Smoke | $3,000 | $3,500 |

Dan Armstrong Lucite Reissue/ADA4 Bass
1998-2001, 2008-2009. Lucite body, Dan Armstrong Ampeg block lettering on 'guard. Reissue in '08 as the ADA4.

| 1998-2001 | | $700 | $800 |
| 2008-2009 | Reintroduced | $800 | $900 |

Alleva-Coppolo Standard 4

Ampeg AEB-1

1973 Ampeg Little Stud

Anderberg Francis

MODEL YEAR	FEATURES	EXC. COND. LOW	HIGH

GEB-101 Little Stud Bass
1973-1975. Import from Japan, offset double-cut solidbody, two-on-a-side tuners, 1 pickup.

| 1973-1975 | | $400 | $450 |

GEB-750 Big Stud Bass
1973-1975. Import from Japan, similar to Little Stud, but with 2 pickups.

| 1973-1975 | | $400 | $450 |

Anderberg
2002-present. Luthier Michael Anderberg builds his premium grade, production/custom, electric basses in Jacksonville, Florida. He also builds guitars.

Andreas
1995-present. Aluminium-necked, solidbody guitars and basses built by luthier Andreas Pichler in Dollach, Austria.

Angelica
1967-1975. Student and entry-level basses and guitars imported from Japan.

Electric Solidbody Bass
1970s. Japanese imports.

| 1970s | Various models | $175 | $200 |

Apollo
Ca. 1967-1972. Entry-level basses imported from Japan by St. Louis Music. They also had guitars and effects.

Electric Hollowbody Bass
1970s. Japanese imports.

| 1970s | | $225 | $275 |

Applause
1976-present. Intermediate grade, production, acoustic/electric basses. They also offer guitars, mandolins and ukes. Kaman Music's entry-level Ovation-styled brand. The instruments were made in the U.S. until around '82, when production was moved to Korea.

Arbor
1983-present. Budget grade, production, solidbody basses imported by Musicorp (MBT). They also offer guitars.

Electric Bass
1983-present. Various models.

| 1983-1999 | | $150 | $175 |
| 2000-2009 | | $100 | $125 |

Aria/Aria Pro II
1960-present. Budget and intermediate grade, production, acoustic, acoustic/electric, solidbody, hollowbody and upright basses. They also make guitars, mandolins, and banjos. Originally branded as Aria; renamed Aria Pro II in '75; both names used over the next several year; in '01, the Pro II part of the name was dropped altogether.

Electric Bass

| 1980s | Various models | $300 | $450 |

Aristides
2010-present. Premium grade, production/custom, solidbody electric basses built in the Netherlands using a material developed by Dutch engineer Aristides Poort. They also build guitars.

Armstrong, Rob
1971-present. Custom basses made in Coventry, England, by luthier Rob Armstrong. He also builds mandolins, flat-tops, and parlor guitars.

Artinger Custom Guitars
1997-present. Professional and premium grade, production/custom, basses built by luthier Matt Artinger in Emmaus, Pennsylvania. He also builds builds hollow, semi-hollow, and chambered solidbody guitars.

Asama
1970s-1980s. Japanese line of solidbody basses. They also offered guitars, effects, drum machines and other music products.

Atomic
2006-present. Luthiers Tim Mulqueeny and Harry Howard build their intermediate and professional grade, production/custom, basses in Peoria, Arizona. They also build guitars.

Audiovox
Ca. 1935-ca. 1950. Paul Tutmarc's Audiovox Manufacturing, of Seattle, Washington, was a pioneer in electric lap steels, basses, guitars and amps. Tutmarc is credited with inventing the electric bass guitar in '35, which his company started selling in the late '30s.

Austin
1999-present. Budget and intermediate grade, production, electric basses imported by St. Louis Music. They also offer guitars, amps, mandolins, ukes and banjos.

Austin Hatchet
Mid-1970s-mid-1980s. Trademark of distributor Targ and Dinner, Chicago, Illinois.

Hatchet Bass

| 1981 | Travel bass | $350 | $425 |

Avante
1997-2007. Shape cutaway acoustic bass designed by Joe Veillette and Michael Tobias originally offered by Alvarez. Later there was only a lower-priced baritone guitar offered by MusicYo.

Baldwin
1965-1970. The giant organ company got into guitars and basses in '65 when it bought Burns Guitars of England and sold those models in the U.S. under the Baldwin name.

BASSES

MODEL YEAR	FEATURES	EXC. COND. LOW	HIGH

Baby Bison Bass
1965-1970. Scroll head, 2 pickups, black, red or white finishes.

1965-1966		$775	$850
1966-1970	Model 560	$675	$750

Bison Bass
1965-1970. Scroll headstock, 3 pickups, black or white finishes.

1965-1966		$1,100	$1,400
1966-1970	Model 516	$1,000	$1,300

G.B. 66 Bass
1965-1966. Bass equivalent of G.B. 66 guitar, covered bridge tailpiece.

1965-1966		$700	$800

Jazz Split Sound Bass
1965-1970. Offset double-cut solidbody, 2 pickups, red sunburst.

1965-1966	Long-scale	$750	$950
1966-1970	Short-scale	$650	$825

Nu-Sonic Bass
1965-1966. Bass version of Nu-Sonic.

1965-1966		$625	$800

Shadows/Shadows Signature Bass
1965-1970. Named after Hank Marvin's backup band, solidbody, 3 slanted pickups, white finish.

1965-1966	Shadows	$1,100	$1,300
1966-1970	Shadows Signature	$1,000	$1,200

Vibraslim Bass
1965-1970. Thin body, scroll head, 2 pickups, sunburst.

1965-1966		$900	$1,100
1966-1970	Model 549	$800	$1,000

Barclay
1960s. Generally shorter-scale, student-level imports from Japan. They also made guitars.

Electric Solidbody Bass

1960s	Various models	$150	$225

Barrington
1988-1991. Budget to low-intermediate basses, see Guitars Section for company information.

Basone Guitars
1999-present. Professional grade, custom, solid and hollowbody electric basses built by Chris Basaraba in Vancouver, British Columbia. He also builds guitars.

Bass Collection
1985-1992. Mid-level imports from Japan, distributed by Meisel Music of Springfield, New Jersey. Sam Ash Music, New York, sold the remaining inventory from '92 to '94.

SB300 Series Bass
1985-1992. Offset double-cut, bolt neck, ash or alder body, models include 300, 301 (fretless) and 302 (5-string).

1985-1992		$325	$375

SB400/SB500 Series Bass
1985-1992. Offset double-cut, bolt neck, basswood body, active electronics, models include 401, 402 (fretless), 405 (5-string) and 501 (alder body).

1985-1992		$425	$500

BC Rich
1966-present. Budget, intermediate, and premium grade, production/custom, import and U.S.-made basses. They also offer guitars. Many BC Rich models came in a variety of colors. For example, in '88 they offered black, Competition Red, metallic red, GlitteRock White, Ultra Violet, and Thunder Blue. Also in '88, other custom colors, graphic features, paint-to-match headstocks, and special inlays were offered.

Bich Bass
1978-1998. Solidbody, neck-thru, 2 pickups.

1978-1979	USA	$1,450	$1,800
1980-1989		$1,200	$1,500
1989-1993	Class Axe era	$825	$1,025
1994-1998	2nd Rico-era	$775	$950

Bich Supreme 8-String Bass
Late-1970s-early-1980s.

1978-1982		$2,000	$2,500

Eagle Bass (U.S.A. Assembly)
1977-1996. Curved double-cut, solidbody, natural.

1977-1979		$1,675	$2,100
1980-1982		$1,525	$1,900

Gunslinger Bass
1987-1999. Inverted headstock, 1 humbucker.

1987-1989		$600	$700
1990-1999		$550	$650

Ironbird Bass
1984-1998. Kind of star-shaped, neck-thru, solidbody, 2 pickups, active electronics, diamond inlays.

1980s		$800	$1,000

Mockingbird Bass
1976-2009.

1976	USA, short-horn	$2,000	$2,500
1977-1978	USA, short-horn	$1,850	$2,300
1979-1983	USA, long-horn	$1,675	$2,100
1984-1989	End 1st Rico-era	$1,200	$1,400
1994-2009	New Rico-era	$1,200	$1,400

Mockingbird Heritage Classic Bass
2007-present. 4 string, neck-thru, quilted maple top, cloud inlay.

2007-2010		$300	$375

Nighthawk Bass
1979-ca.1980. Bolt-neck.

1978-1982		$575	$725

NJ Series Bass
1983-2006. Various mid-level import models include Beast, Eagle, Innovator, Mockingbird, Virgin and Warlock. Replaced by NT Series.

1983-1984	Early, Japan	$400	$700
1985-1986	Japan	$325	$500
1987-2006		$275	$375

Platinum Series Bass
1986-2006. Lower-priced import versions including Eagle, Mockingbird, Beast, Warlock.

1986-1999		$225	$325

Austin AU875

BC Rich Heritage Classic Mockingbird

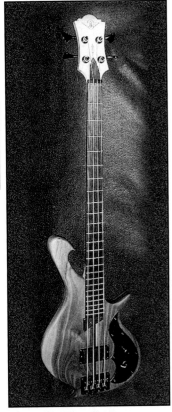

Birdsong Sadhana

Boulder Creek EBR1-TB4

MODEL YEAR	FEATURES	EXC. COND. LOW	HIGH

Seagull/Seagull II Bass
1973-1977. Solidbody, single cut to '75, double Seagull II after.

1973	Seagull	$2,800	$3,500
1974		$2,400	$3,000
1975		$2,325	$2,900
1976-1977	Seagull II	$2,150	$2,700

ST-III Bass
1987-1998. Available in bolt neck and non-bolt neck (1986 price at $999 & $1299 respectively), black hardware, P-Bass/J-Bass pickup configuration, 2 tone controls, 1 volume control, jumbo frets, ebony 'board.

1987-1989	Bolt-on	$550	$675
1987-1989	Neck-thru	$650	$800
1989-1993	Class Axe-era	$525	$650
1994-1998	New Rico-era	$525	$650

Warlock Bass (U.S.A.)
1981-present. Introduced in '81 along with the Warlock guitar, USA-made, standard bolt-on model, maple body and neck, rosewood 'board, 22/accyruzer jumbo frets, Badass II low profile bridge by '88.

1981-1989		$950	$1,200

Wave Bass

1983		$2,300	$2,700

Beltone
1950s-1960s. Japan's Teisco made a variety of brands for others, including the Beltone line of guitars, basses and amps. Italy's Welson guitars also marketed marble and glitter-finished guitars in the U.S. under this brand.

Benedict
1988-present. Founded by Roger Benedict. Professional and premium grade, production/custom, solidbody basses built by luthier Bill Hager in Cedar, Minnesota. They also build guitars.

Berkowitz Guitars
1995-present. Premium grade, custom/production, acoustic bass guitars built by luthier David D. Berkowitz in Washington, DC. He also builds guitars.

Bernie Rico Jr. Guitars
Professional and premium grade, production/custom, solidbody basses built by luthier Bernie Rico, Jr. in Hesperia, California. His father founded BC Rich guitars. He also makes guitars.

Birdsong Guitars
2001-present. Luthiers Scott Beckwith and Jamie Hornbuckle build their intermediate and professional grade, production/custom, solidbody basses in Wimberley, Texas. They also build guitars.

MODEL YEAR	FEATURES	EXC. COND. LOW	HIGH

Black Jack
1960s. Entry-level and mid-level imports from Japan. They also offered guitars.
Electric Solidbody Bass

1960s	Various models	$100	$175

Blade
1987-present. Intermediate and professional grade, production, solidbody basses from luthier Gary Levinson's Levinson Music Products Ltd. in Switzerland. He also builds guitars.

Blindworm Guitars
2008-present. Production/custom, premium and presentation grade, acoustic, electric and electric-acoustic basses built by luthiers Andrew J. Scott and Steven Sells in Colorado Springs, Colorado. They also build guitars and mandolins.

Bolin
1978-present. Professional and premium grade, production/custom, solidbody basses built by luthier John Bolin in Boise, Idaho. He also builds guitars.

Boulder Creek Guitars
2007-present. Imported, intermediate and professional grade, production, acoustic basses distributed by Morgan Hill Music of Morgan Hill, California. They also offer guitars and ukes.

Bradford
1960s. House brand of W.T. Grant department store, often imported. They also offered guitars.
Electric Solidbody Bass

1960s	Various models	$125	$175

Brawley Basses
Solidbody bass guitars designed by Keith Brawley and made in Korea. The company was headquartered in Temecula, California. They also made guitars.

Breedlove
1990-present. Founded by Larry Breedlove and Steve Henderson. Intermediate, professional and premium grade, production/custom, electric basses built in Tumalo, Oregon and imported. They also build guitars, laps, mandolins and ukes. In 2010 they became part of Bedell Guitars.

Brian Moore
1992-present. Brian Moore added basses in '97. Currently they offer professional grade, production, solidbody basses. They also build guitars and mandolins.

Brice
1985-present. Budget grade, production, electric and acoustic basses imported by Rondo Music of Union, New Jersey.

BASSES

MODEL YEAR	FEATURES	EXC. COND. LOW	HIGH

Brown's Guitar Factory

1982-present. Luthier John Brown builds his professional and premium grade, production/custom, 4-, 5-, and 6-string solid and chambered body basses in Inver Grove Heights, Minnesota. He also builds guitars.

BSX Bass

1990-present. Luthier Dino Fiumara builds his professional and premium grade, production/custom, acoustic, solidbody, semi-solid upright basses in Aliquippa, Pennsylvania.

Bunker

1961-present. Luthier Dave Bunker builds intermediate, professional, and premium grade, production/custom, basses in Port Angeles, Washington. He also builds guitars.

Burns

1960-1970, 1974-1983, 1992-present. Intermediate and professional grade, production, basses built in England and Korea. They also build guitars.

Nu-Sonic Bass
1964-1965, 2011-present. Offset double-cut solidbody, 2 pickups.

1964-1965		$725	$900

Scorpion Bass
Introduced 1979, 2003-2009. Double-cut scorpionlike solidbody.

2003-2009		$325	$375

Burns-Weill

1959. Jim Burns and Henry Weill teamed up to produce three solidbody electrics and three solidbody basses under this English brand.

Burrell

1984-2010. Luthier Leo Burrell built his professional grade, production/custom, acoustic and solidbody basses in Huntington, West Virginia. He also built guitars. He retired in '10.

Cameo

1960s-1970s. Japanese- and Korean-made electric basses. They also offered guitars.

Electric Bass

1960-1970s	EB-2 style	$300	$350

Campellone

1978-present. Archtop guitar builder Mark Campellone, of Greenville, Rhode Island, built basses in the '70s.

Canvas

2004-present. Budget and intermediate grade, production, solidbody basses made in China. They also offer guitars.

Carvin

1946-present. Intermediate and Professional grade, production/custom, acoustic and electric basses. They also build guitars and amps.

Casper Guitar Technologies

2009-present. Luthier Stephen Casper builds his production/custom, professional grade, solidbody electric basses in Leisure City, Florida. He also builds guitars.

Chandler

1984-present. Premium grade, production/custom, solidbody 12-string electric basses built by luthiers Paul and Adrian Chandler in Chico, California. They also build guitars, lap steels and effects.

Charles Shifflett Acoustic Guitars

1990-present. Luthier Charles Shifflett builds his premium grade, custom, acoustic basses in High River, Alberta. He also builds flat-top, classical, flamenco, resophonic, and harp guitars, and banjos.

Charvel

1976-present. U.S.-made from '78 to '85 and a combination of imports and U.S.-made post-'85. They also build guitars.

Pre-Pro Bass
1980-1981. Pre-mass production basses, made Nov. '80 to '81. Refer to Charvel guitar section for details.

1980-1981	All models	$2,100	$2,700

850 XL Bass
1988-1991. Four-string, neck-thru-body, active electronics.

1988-1991		$400	$500

CX-490 Bass
1991-1994. Double-cut, 4-string, bolt neck, red or white.

1991-1994		$200	$250

Eliminator Bass
1990-1991. Offset double-cut, active electronics, bolt neck.

1990-1991		$250	$300

Fusion Bass
1989-1991. 4- and 5-string models, active circuitry.

1989-1991	IV	$250	$300
1989-1991	V	$275	$325

Model 1 Bass
1986-1989. Double-cut, bolt neck, 1 pickup.

1986-1989		$250	$325

Model 2 Bass
1986-1989. Double-cut, bolt neck, 2 pickups.

1986-1989		$275	$350

Model 3 Bass
1986-1989. Neck-thru-body, 2 single-coil pickups, active circuitry, master volume, bass and treble knobs.

1986-1989		$275	$350

Model 4 Bass
1988-1989. Like Model 3, but with bolt neck.

1988-1989		$325	$400

Brown's Guitar Factory

Carvin SB4000

BASSES

Citron AE4

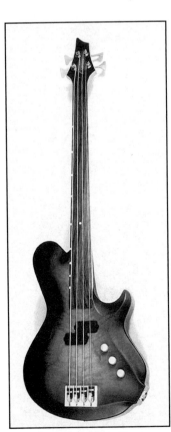

Conklin Custom Bass

MODEL YEAR	FEATURES	EXC. COND. LOW	HIGH
Model 5 Bass			
1986-1989. Double-cut, P/J pickups.			
1986-1989		$375	$450
San Dimas Serialized Plated Bass			
1981-1982. Soft headstock early models.			
1981-1982		$2,500	$3,000
SB-4 Bass			
1990s. Offset double cut solid, long bass horn, 2 pickups.			
1990s		$250	$300
Star Bass			
1980-1981. Unique 4-point solidbody, 1 pickup, considered by Charvel collectors to be Charvel's only original early design.			
1980-1981		$2,700	$3,400
Surfcaster Bass			
1991-1994. Semi-hollow, lipstick tube pickups.			
1991-1994		$875	$1,025

Cipher

1960s. Student market basses imported from Japan. They also made guitars.

Electric Solidbody Bass

1960s. Japanese imports.

1960s		$150	$200

Citron

1995-present. Luthier Harvey Citron (of Veillette-Citron fame) builds his professional and premium grade, production/custom basses in Woodstock, New York. He also builds solidbody guitars.

Clevinger

1982-present. Established by Martin Clevinger, Oakland, California. Mainly specializing in electric upright basses, but has offered bass guitars as well.

College Line

One of many Lyon & Healy brands, made during the era of extreme design experimentation.

Monster (Style 2089) Bass

Early-1900s. 22" lower bout, flat-top guitar/bass, natural.

1915		$2,700	$3,400

Conklin

1984-present. Intermediate, professional, and premium grade, production/custom basses from luthier Bill Conklin, of Springfield, Missouri. Conklin also offers guitars. Conklin instruments are made in the U.S. and overseas.

Conrad

Ca.1968-1978. Student and mid-level copy basses imported by David Wexler, Chicago, Illinois. They also offered guitars, mandolins and banjos.

Model 40096 Acoustical Slimline Bass

1970s. 2 pickups.

1970s		$250	$300

MODEL YEAR	FEATURES	EXC. COND. LOW	HIGH
Model 40177 Violin-Shaped Bass			
1970s. Scroll headstock, 2 pickups.			
1970s		$325	$375
Model 40224 Bumper Bass			
1970s. Ampeg Dan Armstrong lucite copy.			
1970s		$350	$400
Professional Bass			
1970s. Offset double-cut.			
1970s		$175	$225
Professional Bison Bass			
1970s. Solidbody, 2 pickups.			
1970s		$250	$300

Contessa

1960s. Acoustic, semi-hollow archtop, solidbody and bass guitars made in Germany. They also made banjos.

Coral

1967-1969. In '66 MCA bought Danelectro and in '67 introduced the Coral brand of guitars, basses and amps. The line included several solid and semi-solidbody basses.

Electric Solidbody Bass

1967-1969		$600	$750

Corey James Custom Guitars

2005-present. Professional and premium grade, production/custom solidbody basses built by luthier Corey James Moilanen in Davisburg, Michigan. He also builds guitars.

Cort

1973-present. North Brook, Illinois-based Cort offers intermediate and professional grade, production, acoustic and solidbody electric basses built in Korea. They also offer guitars.

CP Thornton Guitars

1985-present. Luthier Chuck Thornton builds solidbody guitars in Sumner, Maine. Up to '96 he also built basses.

Crafter

1986-present. Intermediate grade, production, solidbody basses made in Korea. They also build guitars and mandolins.

Creston

2004-present. Luthier Creston Lea builds professional grade, custom, electric basses in Burlington, Vermont. He also builds guitars.

Crestwood

1970s. Imported by La Playa Distributing Company of Detroit. Product line includes copies of the popular classical guitars, flat-tops, electric solidbodies and basses of the era.

MODEL YEAR	FEATURES	EXC. COND. LOW	HIGH

Electric Bass
1970s. Includes models 2048, 2049, 2079, 2090, 2092, 2093, and 2098.

1970s		$225	$300

Crimson Guitars
2005-present. Professional and premium grade, custom, solidbody basses built in Somerset, United Kingdom by luthiers Benjamin Crowe and Aki Atrill. They also build guitars.

Crook Custom Guitars
1997-present. Luthier Bill Crook builds his professional grade, custom, solidbody electric basses in Moundsville, West Virginia. He also builds guitars.

Crown
1960s. Violin-shaped hollowbody electrics, solidbody electric guitars and basses, possibly others. Imported from Japan.

Electric Solidbody Bass

1960s	Import	$150	$200

Cruzer
Intermediate grade, production, solidbody electric basses made by Korea's Crafter Guitars. They also build guitars, amps and effects.

CSR
1996-present. Luthiers Roger and Courtney Kitchens build their premium grade, production/custom, archtop and solidbody basses in Byron, Georgia. They also build guitars.

Cumpiano
1974-present. Professional and premium grade, custom steel-string and nylon-string guitars, and acoustic basses built by luthier William Cumpiano in Northampton, Massachusetts.

Curbow String Instruments
1994-present. Premium grade, production/custom, solidbody basses built by luthier Doug Somervell in Morganton, Georgia. They also offer a line of intermediate grade, production, Curbow basses made by Cort. Founded by Greg Curbow who passed away in '05. They also make guitars.

Custom
1980s. Line of solidbody guitars and basses introduced in the early-'80s by Charles Lawing and Chris Lovell, owners of Strings & Things in Memphis.

Custom Kraft
Late-1950s-1968. A house brand of St. Louis Music Supply, instruments built by Valco and others. They also offered guitars.

MODEL YEAR	FEATURES	EXC. COND. LOW	HIGH

Bone Buzzer Model 12178 Bass
Late 1960s. Symmetrical double-cut thin hollow body, lightning bolt f-holes, 4-on-a-side tuners, 2 pickups, sunburst or emerald sunburst.

1968		$475	$550

D'Agostino
1976-early 1990s. Import company established by Pat D'Agostino. Solidbodies imported from EKO Italy '77-'82, Japan '82-'84, and in Korea for '84 on. Overall, about 60% of guitars and basses were Japanese, 40% Korean.

Electric Solidbody Bass

1970s	Various models	$250	$300

Daion
1978-1984. Higher quality copy basses imported from Japan. Original designs introduced in '80s. They also had guitars.

Electric Bass

1978-1984	Higher-end	$500	$700
1978-1984	Lower-end	$300	$400

Daisy Rock
2001-present. Budget and intermediate grade, production, full-scale and 3/4 scale, solidbody, semi-hollow, and acoustic/electric basses. Founded by Tish Ciravolo as a Division of Schecter Guitars, initial offerings included daisy and heart-shaped electric guitars and basses.

Danelectro
1946-1969, 1997-present. Danelectro offered basses throughout most of its early history. In '96, the Evets Corporation, of San Clemente, California, introduced a line of Danelectro effects; amps, basses and guitars, many reissues of earlier instruments, soon followed. In early '03, Evets discontinued the guitar, bass and amp lines, but revived the guitar and bass line in '05. Danelectro also built the Coral brand instruments (see Coral).

Model 1444L Bass
Ca.1958-ca.1964. Masonite body, single-cut, 2 pickups, copper finish.

1958-1962		$650	$775
1963-1964		$650	$775

Model 3412 Shorthorn Bass
1958-ca.1966. Coke bottle headstock, 1 pickup, copper finish.

1958-1959		$900	$1,100
1960-1962		$825	$1,025
1963-1964		$750	$950
1965-1966		$600	$750

Model 3612 Shorthorn 6-String Bass
1958-ca.1966. Coke bottle headstock, 1 pickup, copper finish.

1958-1962		$1,400	$1,625
1963-1964		$1,200	$1,425
1965-1966		$1,100	$1,325

'58 Shorthorn
1997-2003. Reissues of classic Shorthorn bass.

1997-2003		$250	$300

Crafter USA BA400EQL

1960 Danelectro Model 3412 Shorthorn Bass

David J King Wesby II

1981 Dean ML

MODEL YEAR	FEATURES	EXC. COND. LOW	HIGH

Model 4423 Longhorn Bass
1958-ca.1966. Coke bottle headstock, 2 pickups, copper finish.

1958-1959		$1,750	$2,050
1960-1962		$1,650	$1,950
1963-1964		$1,550	$1,850
1965-1966		$1,450	$1,750

'58 Longhorn Reissue/Longhorn Pro Bass
1997-2010. Reissues of classic Longhorn bass.

1997-2010		$300	$400

UB-2 6-String Bass
1956-1959. Single-cut, 2 pickups.

1956-1959		$1,550	$1,850

Dave Maize Acoustic
1991-present. Luthier Dave Maize builds his premium grade, production/custom, acoustic basses in Cave Junction, Oregon. He also builds flat-tops.

David J King
1987-present. Production/custom, professional and premium grade, electric basses built by luthier David King first in Amherst, Massachusetts and since '92 in Portland, Oregon.

Dean
1976-present. Intermediate and professional grade, production, solidbody, hollowbody, acoustic, and acoustic/electric, basses made overseas. They also offer guitars, banjos, mandolins, and amps.

Baby ML Bass
1982-1986. Downsized version of ML.

1982-1986	Import	$250	$300

Mach V Bass
1985-1986. U.S.-made pointed solidbody, 2 pickups, rosewood 'board.

1985-1986	U.S.-made	$700	$800

ML Bass
1977-1986, 2001-2010. Futuristic body style, fork headstock.

1977-1983	U.S.-made	$1,200	$1,500
1984-1986	Korean import	$300	$350

Rhapsody Series (USA)
2001-2004. Scroll shaped offset double-cut, various models.

2001-2004	12-string	$250	$300
2001-2004	8-string	$225	$250
2001-2004	HFB fretless	$200	$225

Dean Markley
The string and pickup manufacturer offered a limited line of guitars and basses for a time in the late 1980s.

DeArmond
1999-2004. Electric basses based on Guild models and imported from Korea by Fender. They also offered guitars.

Electric Bass

1999	Jet Star, solidbody	$400	$500

MODEL YEAR	FEATURES	EXC. COND. LOW	HIGH
1999	Starfire, hollowbody	$500	$600
2001	Pilot Pro, solidbody	$250	$300

Decca
Mid-1960s. Solidbody basses imported from made in Japan by Teisco and imported by Decca Records, Decca headstock logo, student-level instruments. They also offered guitars and amps.

DeGennaro
2003-present. Professional and premium grade, custom/production, solidbody basses built by luthier William DeGennaro in Grand Rapids, Michigan. He also builds guitars and mandolins.

Delaney Guitars
2004-present. Professional grade, production/custom, electric basses built by luthier Mike Delaney in Atlanta, Georgia. He also builds guitars.

Delgado
1928-present. Premium and presentation grade, production/custom, classical acoustic basses built by Manuel A. Delgado in Nashville, Tennessee. He also builds, guitars, mandolins, ukuleles and banjos.

DeTemple
1995-present. Premium grade, production/custom, solidbody electric basses built by luthier Michael DeTemple in Sherman Oaks, California. He also builds guitars.

Dillion
1996-present. Dillion, of Cary, North Carolina, offers intermediate grade, production, acoustic/electric, hollow-body and solidbody basses made in Korea and Vietnam. They also have guitars.

Dillon
1975-present. Professional and premium grade, custom, acoustic basses built by luthier John Dillon in Taos, New Mexico. He also builds guitars.

Dingwall
1988-present. Luthier Sheldon Dingwall, Saskatoon, Saskatchewan, started out producing guitar bodies and necks, eventually offering complete guitars and basses. Currently Dingwall offers professional to premium grade, production/custom 4-, 5-, and 6-string basses featuring the Novax Fanned-Fret System.

DiPinto
1995-present. Intermediate and professional grade, production retro-vibe basses from luthier Chris DiPinto of Philadelphia, Pennsylvania. He also builds guitars. Until late '99, all instruments built in the U.S., since then built in Korea and the U.S.

MODEL		EXC. COND.	
YEAR	FEATURES	LOW	HIGH

Dodge

1996-present. Production, intermediate and professional grade, solidbody basses built by luthier Rick Dodge in Tallahassee, Florida. He also builds guitars.

Domino

Ca. 1967-1968. Imported from Japan by Maurice Lipsky Music of New York, mainly copies, but some original designs. They also offered guitars.

Electric Bass

1967-1968. Includes the Beatle Bass and Fireball Bass, a Vox Phantom IV copy.

1967-1968		$300	$375

Dorado

Ca. 1972-1973. Name used briefly by Baldwin/Gretsch on line of Japanese guitar and bass imports.

Electric Solidbody Bass

1970s	Import	$175	$300

Dragonfly

1994-present. Professional grade, production/custom, acoustic basses built by luthier Dan Richter in Roberts Creek, British Columbia. He also builds guitars and dulcitars.

Duesenberg

1995-present. Professional grade, production/custom, hollow and semi-hollow basses built by luthier Dieter Goelsdorf in Hannover, Germany. They also build guitars.

Dynacord

1950-present. The German Dynacord company makes audio and pro sound amps, as well as other electronic equipment. In 1966-'67 they offered solidbody guitars and basses from the Welson Company of Italy. They also had the Cora guitar and bass which is the center part of a guitar body with a tube frame in a guitar outline. They also offered tape echo machines.

Dynelectron

1960s-late 1970s. This Italian builder offered other bass models but is best known today for their almost exact copies of Danelectro Longhorns of the mid-'60s. They also made guitars.

Earthwood

1972-1985. Acoustic designs by Ernie Ball with input from George Fullerton. One of the first to offer acoustic basses.

Acoustic Bass

1972-1985. Big bodied acoustic bass alternative between Kay double bass and solidbody Fender bass.

1972-1985		$1,100	$1,400

MODEL		EXC. COND.	
YEAR	FEATURES	LOW	HIGH

Eastwood

1997-present. Budget and intermediate grade, production, imported solid and semi-hollowbody basses, many styled after 1960s models. They also offer guitars and mandolins.

EKO

1959-1985, 2000-present. Built by the Oliviero Pigini Company, Italy. Original importers included LoDuca Brothers, Milwaukee, Wisconsin. Since about 2000, production, acoustic and electric EKO basses are again available and made in Italy and China. They also make guitars and amps.

Barracuda Bass

1967-1978. Offset double-cut semi-hollow, 2 pickups.

1967-1978		$450	$550

Cobra II Bass

1967-ca.1969. Offset double-cut solidbody, 2 pickups.

1967-1969		$425	$475

Kadett Bass

1967-1978. Red or sunburst.

1967-1978		$450	$550

Model 995/2 Violin Bass

1966-ca.1969.

1966-1969		$500	$625

Model 1100/2 Bass

1961-1966. Jaguar-style plastic covered solidbody, 2 pickups, sparkle finish.

1961-1966		$550	$650

Rocket IV/Rokes Bass

1967-early-1970s. Rocket-shape design, solidbody, says Rokes on the headstock, the Rokes were a popular English band that endorsed EKO guitars. Marketed as the Rocket IV in the U.S. and as the Rokes in Europe. Often called the Rok. Sunburst, 1 pickup.

1967-1971		$625	$750

Electra

1971-1984. Imported basses from Japan by St. Louis Music. They also offered guitars.

Electric Solidbody Bass

1970s. Japanese imports, various models.

1970s		$350	$450

MPC Outlaw Bass

1970s. Has 2 separate modules that plug in for different effects, neck-thru-body.

1970s		$450	$550

Emperador

1966-1992. Student-level basses imported by Westheimer Musical Instruments. Early models appear to be made by either Teisco or Kawai; later models were made by Cort. They also had guitars.

Electric Solidbody Bass

1960s. Japanese imports, various models.

1960s	Beatle violin bass	$275	$350
1960s	Various models	$150	$175

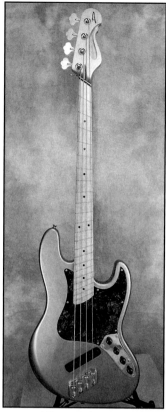

Dingwall Super J

Eastwood EEB-1

BASSES

1967 Epiphone Embassy

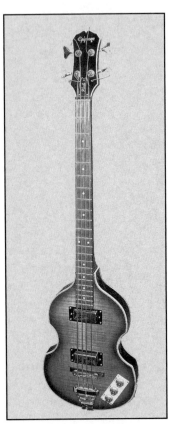

Epiphone Viola

Encore

Ca. 1986-present. Budget grade, production, solidbody basses imported from China and Vietnam by John Hornby Skewes & Co. in the U.K. They also offer guitars.

Hollowbody Bass
1960s. Copy model, greenburst.

Model Year	Features	Low	High
1960s		$250	$325

Engelhardt

Engelhardt specializes in student acoustic basses and cellos and is located in Elk Grove Village, Illinois.

Epiphone

1928-present. Epiphone didn't add basses until 1959, after Gibson acquired the brand. The Gibson Epiphones were American-made until '69, then all imports until into the '80s, when some models were again made in the U.S. Currently Epiphone offers intermediate and professional grade, production, acoustic and electric basses.

B-5 Acoustic Bass Viol
1950s. 3/4-size laminate construction.

1950s		$3,000	$3,500

EA/ET/ES Series (Japan)
1970-1979. Production of the Epiphone brand was moved to Japan in '70. Models included the EA (electric thinline) and ET (electric solidbody).

1970-1975	EA-260, EB-2	$300	$400
1970-1975	Solidbody, 1 pickup	$275	$375

EB-0 Bass
1998-present. SG body style, single pickup, bolt-on neck.

1998-2010		$200	$225

EB-1 Bass
1998-2000. Violin-shaped mahogany body, 1 pickup.

1998-2000		$225	$250

EB-3 Bass
1999-present. SG body style, 2 pickups.

1999-2010		$300	$375

EBM-4 Bass
1991-1998. Alder body, maple neck, split humbucker, white.

1991-1998		$200	$225

Elitist Series Bass
2003-2005. Higher-end appointments such as set-necks and USA pickups.

2003-2005	EB-3	$500	$550

Embassy Deluxe Bass
1963-1969. Solidbody, double-cut, 2 pickups, tune-o-matic bridge, cherry finish.

1963-1964		$2,300	$2,900
1965-1966		$1,900	$2,400
1967-1969		$1,800	$2,300

Explorer Korina Bass
2000-2001. Made in Korea, Gibson Explorer body style, genuine korina body, set neck, gold hardware.

2000-2001		$325	$400

Les Paul Special Bass
1997-present. LP Jr.-style slab body, single-cut, bolt neck, 2 humbuckers.

1997-2010		$200	$225

Newport Bass
1961-1970. Double-cut solidbody, 1 pickup (2 pickups optional until '63), 2-on-a-side tuners until '63, 4-on-a-side after that, cherry.

1961-1962		$1,900	$2,400
1963-1964		$1,800	$2,200
1965-1966		$1,400	$1,700
1965-1966	Custom color	$2,200	$2,700
1967-1969		$1,300	$1,600
1970		$900	$1,100

Rivoli Bass (1 Pickup)
1959-1961, 1964-1970. ES-335-style semi-hollowbody bass, 2-on-a-side tuners, 1 pickup (2 in '70), reissued in '94 as the Rivoli II.

1959		$3,100	$3,700
1960		$2,900	$3,500
1961		$2,400	$3,000
1964		$2,200	$2,700
1965		$1,700	$2,200
1966		$1,700	$2,200
1967-1969		$1,700	$2,200
1970		$1,400	$1,800

Rivoli Bass (2 Pickups)
1970 only. Double pickup Epiphone version of Gibson EB-2D.

1970	Sunburst	$2,100	$2,600

Rivoli II Reissue
1998. Made in Korea, set neck, blond.

1998		$550	$650

Thunderbird IV Bass
1997-present. Reverse-style mahogany body, 2 pickups, sunburst.

1997-2010		$250	$325

Viola Bass
1995-present. Beatle Bass 500/1 copy, sunburst.

1995-2010		$300	$375

ESP

1975-present. Intermediate, professional, and premium grade, production/custom, electric basses. Japan's ESP (Electric Sound Products) made inroads in the U.S. market with mainly copy styles in the early '80s, mixing in original designs over the years. In the '90s, ESP opened a California-based Custom Shop. They also build guitars.

B-1 Bass
1990s. Vague DC-style slab solidbody with bolt-on neck, ESP and B-1 on headstock.

1990s		$500	$600

Horizon Bass
1987-1993. Offset double-cut solidbody, 4- and 5-string versions, active electronics, 34" scale.

1987-1993	4-string	$500	$600

Essex (SX)

1985-present. Budget grade, production, electric basses imported by Rondo Music of Union, New Jersey. They also offer guitars.

Electric Solidbody Bass

1990s		$100	$125

MODEL		EXC. COND.	
YEAR	FEATURES	LOW	HIGH

Evergreen Mountain

1971-present. Professional grade, custom, acoustic basses built by luthier Jerry Nolte in Cove, Oregon. He also builds guitars and mandolins.

Exlusive

2008-present. Intermediate grade, production, electric basses, imported from Asia and finished in Italy by luthier Galeazzo Frudua. He also offers guitars.

Fano

1995-present. Luthier Dennis Fano builds professional grade, production/custom, solidbody electric basses in Fleetwood, Pennsylvania. He also builds guitars.

Farnell

1989-present. Luthier Al Farnell builds his professional grade, production, solidbody basses in Ontario, California. He also offers his intermediate grade, production, C Series which is imported from China. He also builds guitars.

Fat Cat Custom Guitars

2004-present. Luthier Scott Bond builds his intermediate to premium grade, production/custom, solidbody and chambered electric basses in Carpentersville, Illinois. He also builds guitars.

Fender

1946-present. Intermediate, professional, and premium grade, production/custom, electric and acoustic basses made in the U.S. and overseas. Leo Fender is the father of the electric bass. The introduction of his Precision Bass in late '51 changed forever how music was performed, recorded and heard. Leo followed with other popular models of basses that continue to make up a large part of Fender's production. Please note that all the variations of the Jazz and Precision Basses are grouped under those general headings.

A custom color is worth more than a standard color. The first Precision Bass standard color was blond but changed to sunburst in the late 1950s. The Jazz Bass standard color is sunburst. To understand a custom color, you need to know what the standard color is. Some custom colors are more rare than others. Below is a list of the custom colors offered in 1960 by Fender. They are sorted in ascending order with the most valuable color, Shell Pink, listed last. In the 1960 list, Black and Blond are the least valuable and Shell Pink is the most valuable. A Fiesta Red is typically worth 12% more than a Black or Blond. In the rare color group a Foam Green is normally worth 8% more than a Shoreline Gold. The two very rare colors are often worth 30% more than a Shoreline Gold. In our pricing information we will list the standard color, then the relative value of a common custom color, and then the value of a rare custom color. Remember that the amount

of fade also affects the price. These prices are for factory original custom colors with slight or no fade in excellent condition. Fade implies a lighter color, but with custom colors a faded example can also be much darker in color. Blue can fade to dark green. White can fade to deep yellow.

The Price Guide lists the standard color, plus the value of a Common Color and the value of a Rare Color. The list below defines which group a color falls into for 1960, and it is in ascending order so, for example, a Daphne Blue should be considered more valuable than a Lake Placid Blue, assuming they are in equal condition.

Common Color: Black, Blond, Olympic White, Lake Placid Blue, Dakota Red, Daphne Blue, Fiesta Red

Rare Color: Shoreline Gold, Inca Silver, Burgundy Mist, Sherwood Green, Sonic Blue, Foam Green

Rare (Very Rare) Color: Surf Green, Shell Pink

Ashbory Bass

2003-2006. Unique-shaped travel bass, Ashbory logo on body, Fender logo on back of headstock, previously sold under Fender's DeArmond brand.

2005-2006		$175	$200

Bass V

1965-1970. Five strings, double-cut, 1 pickup, dot inlay '65-'66, block inlay '66-'70. Please refer to the beginning of the Fender Bass Section for details on Fender color options.

1965	Common color	$3,000	$4,000
1965	Rare color	$4,000	$6,000
1965	Sunburst	$2,800	$3,500
1966-1967	Common color	$2,800	$3,500
1966-1967	Rare color	$3,500	$4,800
1966-1967	Sunburst, block inlay	$1,900	$2,400
1966-1967	Sunburst, dot inlay	$2,000	$2,500
1968-1970	Common color	$2,500	$3,200
1968-1970	Rare color	$3,200	$4,300
1968-1970	Sunburst	$1,700	$2,100

Bass VI

1961-1975. Six strings, Jazzmaster-like body, 3 pickups, dot inlay until '66, block inlay '66-'75. Reintroduced as Japanese-made Collectable model '95-'98. Please refer to the beginning of the Fender Bass Section for details on Fender color options.

1961-1962	Common color	$8,000	$10,000
1961-1962	Rare color	$10,000	$15,000
1961-1962	Sunburst	$6,000	$7,000
1963-1964	Common color	$7,000	$9,000
1963-1964	Rare color	$9,000	$13,500
1963-1964	Sunburst	$5,000	$6,000
1965	Common color	$6,000	$8,000
1965	Rare color	$8,000	$12,000
1965	Sunburst	$4,000	$5,000
1966	Common color	$4,500	$5,500
1966	Rare color	$5,500	$8,000
1966	Sunburst, block inlay	$3,200	$3,700
1966	Sunburst, dot inlay	$3,500	$4,000

1966 Fender Bass V

1965 Fender Bass VI
Steve Lee

1965 Fender Jazz Bass

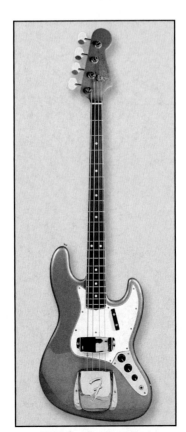

1966 Fender Jazz Bass

MODEL YEAR	FEATURES	EXC. COND. LOW	HIGH
1967-1969	Common color	$4,000	$5,000
1967-1969	Rare color	$5,000	$7,000
1967-1969	Sunburst	$3,000	$3,500
1970-1971	Common color	$3,500	$4,500
1970-1971	Rare color	$4,500	$6,000
1970-1971	Sunburst	$2,800	$3,300
1972-1974	Natural	$2,400	$2,700
1972-1974	Other custom colors	$3,500	$4,500
1972-1974	Sunburst	$2,700	$3,000
1972-1974	Walnut	$2,600	$2,900
1975	Natural	$1,900	$2,300
1975	Olympic White, black, blond	$2,400	$2,900
1975	Sunburst	$2,200	$2,700
1975	Walnut	$2,100	$2,600

Bass VI Reissue
1995-1998. Import, sunburst.

1995-1998		$1,350	$1,700

BG Series Bass
1995-present. Acoustic flat-top bass, single-cut, two-on-a-side tuners, Fishman on-board controls, black.

1995-2009	BG-29, black	$250	$325
1995-2009	BG-32, natural	$300	$350
1995-2010	BG-31, black	$250	$325

Bullet Bass (B30, B34, B40)
1982-1983. Alder body, 1 pickup, offered in short- and long-scale, red or walnut. U.S.-made, replaced by Japanese-made Squire Bullet Bass.

1982-1983		$450	$525

Bullet Deluxe Bass
1982-1983. Fender logo with Bullet Bass Deluxe on headstock, E-series serial number, small Telecaster-style headstock shape.

1982-1983		$475	$575

Coronado I Bass
1966-1970. Thinline, double-cut, 1 pickup, dot inlay, sunburst and cherry red were the standard colors, but custom colors could be ordered.

1966-1970	Cherry red, sunburst	$900	$1,100
1966-1970	Custom colors	$1,200	$1,450

Coronado II Bass
1967-1972. Two pickups, block inlay, sunburst and cherry red standard colors, but custom colors could be ordered. Only Antigua finish offered from '70 on.

1967-1969	Cherry red, sunburst	$1,200	$1,450
1967-1969	Custom colors	$1,400	$1,700
1967-1969	Wildwood option	$1,400	$1,700
1970-1972	Antigua only	$1,400	$1,700

Dimension Bass
2004-2006. Made in Mexico, 4- or 5-string, P and J pickups.

2004-2006		$400	$500

HM Bass
1989-1991. Japanese-made, 4 strings (IV) or 5 strings (V), basswood body, no 'guard, 3 Jazz Bass pickups, 5-way switch, master volume, master TBX, sunburst.

1989-1991	IV, 4-string	$325	$400
1989-1991	V, 5-string	$350	$425

MODEL YEAR	FEATURES	EXC. COND. LOW	HIGH

Jaguar Bass
2006-2010. Made in Japan, Jaguar Bass logo on headstock.

2006-2010		$600	$700

Jaguar Baritone Custom Bass
2007. Fender Jaguar Baritone Custom logo on headstock, 6-string.

2007		$800	$1,000

Jazz Bass
The following are variations of the Jazz Bass. The first four listings are for the main U.S.-made models. All others are listed alphabetically after that in the following order:

> Jazz Bass
> Standard Jazz Bass
> American Standard Jazz Bass
> American Series Jazz Bass
> American Series Jazz V Bass
> 50th Anniversary American Standard Jazz Bass
> '60 Jazz Bass (Custom Shop)
> '60s Jazz Bass (Japan)
> '62 Jazz Bass
> '64 Jazz Bass (Custom Shop)
> '75 Jazz Bass American Vintage Series
> Aerodyne Jazz Bass
> American Deluxe Jazz Bass
> American Deluxe Jazz V Bass
> American Deluxe FMT Jazz Bass
> Custom Classic Jazz Bass
> Deluxe Jazz Bass (Active)
> Deluxe Jazz Bass V (Active)
> Deluxe Power Jazz Bass
> Foto Flame Jazz Bass
> FSR Standard Special Edition Jazz Bass
> Geddy Lee Signature Jazz Bass
> Gold Jazz Bass
> Highway One Jazz Bass
> Jaco Pastorius Jazz Bass
> Jazz Plus Bass
> Jazz Plus V Bass
> Jazz Special Bass (Import)
> JP-90 Bass
> Marcus Miller Signature Jazz Bass
> Noel Redding Signature Jazz Bass
> Reggie Hamilton Jazz Bass
> Roscoe Beck Jazz IV/V Bass
> Standard Jazz Bass (Later Model)
> Standard Jazz Fretless Bass (Later Model)
> Standard Jazz V Bass (Later Model)
> Ventures Limited Edition Jazz Bass
> Victor Baily Jazz Bass

Jazz Bass
1960-1981. Two stack knobs '60-'62, 3 regular controls '62 on. Dot markers '60-'66, block markers from '66 on. Rosewood 'board standard, but maple available from '68 on. With the introduction of vintage reissue models in '81, Fender started calling the American-made version the Standard Jazz Bass. That became the American Standard Jazz Bass in '88 and

MODEL YEAR	FEATURES	EXC. COND. LOW	HIGH

then became the American Series Jazz Bass in 2000. Renamed back to the American Standard Jazz Bass in '08. Post '71 Jazz Bass values are affected more by condition than color or neck option. The Jazz Bass was fitted with a 3-bolt neck or bullet rod in late-'74. Prices assume a 3-bolt neck starting in '75. Please refer to the beginning of the Fender Bass Section for details on Fender color options.

MODEL YEAR	FEATURES	LOW	HIGH
1960	Common color	$24,000	$30,000
1960	Rare color	$30,000	$45,000
1960	Sunburst	$19,000	$24,000
1961-1962	Common color, stack knob	$24,000	$30,000
1961-1962	Rare color, stack knob	$30,000	$45,000
1961-1962	Sunburst, stack knob	$19,000	$24,000
1962	Common color, 3 knob, curved	$13,000	$17,000
1962	Common color, 3 knob, slab	$15,000	$19,000
1962	Rare color, 3 knob, curved	$17,000	$22,000
1962	Rare color, 3 knob, slab	$19,000	$25,000
1962	Sunburst, 3 knob, curved	$11,000	$14,000
1962	Sunburst, 3 knob, slab	$12,000	$15,000
1963-1964	Common color	$11,000	$14,000
1963-1964	Rare color	$14,000	$19,000
1963-1964	Sunburst	$8,000	$10,000
1965	Common color	$10,000	$12,000
1965	Rare color	$12,000	$15,000
1965	Sunburst	$6,500	$8,500
1966	Common color	$9,300	$11,300
1966	Rare color	$11,300	$15,000
1966	Sunburst, blocks	$5,800	$7,000
1966	Sunburst, dots	$6,000	$7,600
1967	Common color	$7,000	$8,500
1967	Rare color	$8,500	$11,000
1967	Sunburst	$5,500	$7,000
1968	Common color	$6,500	$8,000
1968	Rare color	$8,000	$10,500
1968	Sunburst	$4,700	$5,700
1969	Common color	$5,900	$7,500
1969	Rare color	$7,500	$9,400
1969	Sunburst	$4,100	$5,000
1970	Common color	$4,900	$6,500
1970	Rare color	$6,500	$8,400
1970	Sunburst	$3,400	$4,400
1971	Common color	$3,900	$5,500
1971	Rare color	$5,500	$7,400
1971	Sunburst	$3,000	$3,600
1972	Common color	$3,200	$4,500
1972	Sunburst	$2,700	$3,100
1973	Natural	$2,500	$2,900
1973	Other custom colors	$2,800	$3,700
1973	Sunburst	$2,700	$3,100
1973	Walnut	$2,500	$2,900

MODEL YEAR	FEATURES	LOW	HIGH
1974	Natural	$2,200	$2,700
1974	Other custom colors	$2,700	$3,600
1974	Sunburst, 3-bolt neck, late-'74	$2,100	$2,600
1974	Sunburst, 4-bolt neck	$2,600	$3,100
1974	Walnut	$2,000	$2,500
1975-1977	Black, blond, white, wine, 3-bolt neck	$2,600	$3,300
1975-1977	Natural, walnut, 3-bolt neck	$1,900	$2,300
1975-1977	Sunburst, 3-bolt neck	$2,000	$2,400
1978-1979	Antigua	$2,000	$2,500
1978-1979	Black, blond, white, wine	$1,900	$2,400
1978-1979	Natural	$1,600	$2,000
1978-1979	Sunburst, 3-bolt neck	$1,700	$2,100
1980	Antigua	$1,900	$2,400
1980	Black, white, wine	$1,800	$2,300
1980	Natural	$1,500	$1,900
1980	Sunburst, 3-bolt neck	$1,600	$2,000
1981	Black & Gold Collector's Edition	$1,400	$1,700
1981	Black, white, wine	$1,500	$1,900
1981	International colors	$1,500	$1,900
1981	Sunburst	$1,350	$1,650

Standard Jazz Bass

1981-1985. Replaced Jazz Bass ('60-'81) and replaced by the American Standard Jazz Bass in '88. Name now used on import version. Please refer to the beginning of the Fender Bass Section for details on Fender color options.

MODEL YEAR	FEATURES	LOW	HIGH
1981-1982	Black, white, wine	$1,400	$1,600
1981-1982	Rare colors	$1,600	$2,100
1982	Gold Edition, top jack	$1,800	$2,200
1982-1984	Top mounted input jack	$1,200	$1,500
1985	Japan import	$500	$600

American Standard Jazz Bass

1988-2000, 2008-present. Replaced Standard Jazz Bass ('81-'88) and replaced by the American Series Jazz Bass in '00, back to American Standard in Jan. '08.

MODEL YEAR	FEATURES	LOW	HIGH
1988-1989		$850	$1,050
1990-2000		$675	$850
2008-2010		$675	$850

American Series Jazz Bass

2000-2007. Replaces American Standard Jazz Bass. Renamed American Standard in '08.

MODEL YEAR	FEATURES	LOW	HIGH
2000-2007		$675	$850

American Series Jazz V Bass

2000-2007. 5-string version.

MODEL YEAR	FEATURES	LOW	HIGH
2000-2007		$725	$875

1967 Fender Jazz Bass

Fender American Standard Jazz Bass

Fender American Deluxe Jazz Bass

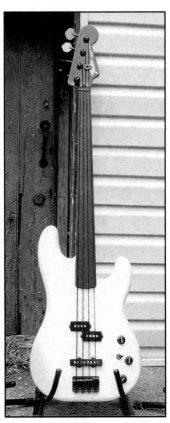

1987 Fender Jazz Special Bass

MODEL YEAR	FEATURES	EXC. COND. LOW	HIGH

50th Anniversary American Standard Jazz Bass
1996. Regular American Standard with gold hardware, 4- or 5-string, gold 50th Anniversary commemorative neck plate, rosewood 'board, sunburst.

1996	IV or V	$1,075	$1,300

'60 Jazz Bass (Custom Shop)
1997, 2000-present.

1997	Relic (Cunetto)	$1,900	$2,200
2000-2006	Closet		
	Classic option	$1,700	$1,900
2000-2010	N.O.S option	$1,600	$1,800
2000-2010	Relic option	$1,900	$2,100

'60s Jazz Bass (Import)
1994-1996, 2001-present. Classic series, '60s features, rosewood 'board, made in Japan first 2 years, Mexico after.

2001-2010		$600	$700

'62 Jazz Bass
1982-present. U.S.A.-made, American Vintage series, reissue of '62 Jazz Bass. Please refer to the beginning of the Fender Bass Section for details on Fender color options.

1982-1985	Standard colors	$2,500	$3,000
1986-1989		$1,200	$1,500
1990-1999		$1,200	$1,500
2000-2010		$1,075	$1,300

'64 Jazz Bass (Custom Shop)
1998-2009. Alder body, rosewood 'board, tortoise shell 'guard. From June '95 to June '99 Relic work was done outside of Fender by Vince Cunetto and included a certificate noting model and year built, an instrument without the certificate is worth less than the value shown.

1998-1999	Relic (Cunetto)	$1,900	$2,200
2000-2009	Closet		
	Classic option	$1,700	$1,900
2000-2009	N.O.S option	$1,600	$1,800
2000-2009	Relic option	$1,900	$2,100

'75 Jazz Bass American Vintage Series
1994-present. Maple neck with black block markers.

1994-2010		$1,100	$1,250

Aerodyne Jazz Bass
2003-present. Bound basswood body, P/J pickups, Deluxe Series.

2003-2010		$550	$675

American Deluxe Jazz Bass
1998-present. Made in the U.S.A., active electronics, alder or ash body. Alder body colors - sunburst or transparent red, ash body colors - white, blond, transparent teal green or transparent purple.

1998-1999		$850	$1,000
2000-2010		$850	$1,000

American Deluxe Jazz V Bass
1998-present. Five-string model, various colors.

1998-2010		$950	$1,100

American Deluxe FMT Jazz Bass
2001-2006. Flame maple top version (FMT), active EQ, dual J pickups.

2001-2006		$950	$1,100

MODEL YEAR	FEATURES	EXC. COND. LOW	HIGH

Custom Classic Jazz Bass
2001-2009. Custom Shop, slightly slimmer waist, deeper cutaways, maple or rosewood 'board, block inlays, 4 (IV) or 5-string (V).

2001-2009	IV	$1,100	$1,300
2001-2009	V	$1,150	$1,350

Deluxe Jazz Bass (Active)
1995-present. Made in Mexico, active electronics, various colors.

1995-2010		$350	$450

Deluxe Jazz Bass V (Active)
1995-present. Made in Mexico, various colors.

1995-2010		$375	$475

Deluxe Power Jazz Bass
2006. Part of Deluxe Series with Fishman piezo power bridge.

2006		$575	$700

Foto Flame Jazz Bass
1994-1996. Japanese import, alder and basswood body with Foto Flame figured wood image.

1994-1996		$450	$550

FSR Standard Special Edition Jazz Bass
2007-2009. Made in Mexico, Fender Special Edition logo on back of headstock, ash body with natural finish.

2007-2009		$325	$400

Geddy Lee Signature Jazz Bass
1998-present. Limited run import in '98, now part of Artist Series, black.

1998-2003		$500	$600
2004-2010		$500	$600

Gold Jazz Bass
1981-1984. Gold finish and gold-plated hardware.

1981-1984		$1,300	$1,600

Highway One Jazz Bass
2003-present. U.S.-made, alder body, satin lacquer finish.

2003-2010		$575	$650

Jaco Pastorius Jazz Bass
1999-2000. Artist Signature Series, standard production model made in Corona, '62 3-color sunburst body without pickup covers.

1999-2000	Fretless	$1,050	$1,300
1999-2000	Fretted	$1,000	$1,250

Jazz Plus Bass
1990-1994. Alder body, 2 Lace Sensors, active electronics, rotary circuit selector, master volume, balance, bass boost, bass cut, treble boost, treble cut, various colors.

1990-1994		$650	$800

Jazz Plus V Bass
1990-1994. Five-string version.

1990-1994		$675	$825

Jazz Special Bass (Import)
1984-1991. Japanese-made, Jazz/Precision hybrid, Precision-shaped basswood body, Jazz neck (fretless available), 2 P/J pickups, offered with active (Power) or passive electronics.

1984-1991		$275	$325

JP-90 Bass
1990-1994. Two P/J pickups, rosewood fretboard, poplar body, black or red.

1990-1994		$400	$500

*The **Vintage Guitar Price Guide** shows low to high values for items in all-original excellent condition, and, where applicable, with original case or cover.*

MODEL YEAR FEATURES	EXC. COND. LOW	HIGH

Marcus Miller Signature Jazz Bass
1998-present. Artist series.
| 1998-2004 Import | $600 | $725 |
| 2005-2010 U.S. Custom Shop | $1,100 | $1,400 |

Noel Redding Signature Jazz Bass
1997. Limited Edition import, artist signature on 'guard, sunburst, rosewood 'board.
| 1997 | $800 | $1,000 |

Reggie Hamilton Jazz Bass
2002-present. Artist series, alder body, C-profile neck, passive/active switch and pan control.
| 2002-2010 | $600 | $750 |

Roscoe Beck Jazz IV/V Bass
1997-2009. Artist series, 5-string version offered '97-'06 , 4-string '09.
| 1997-2009 5-string | $1,000 | $1,200 |
| 2004-2009 4-string | $950 | $1,150 |

Standard Jazz Bass (Later Model)
1988-present. Imported from various countries. Not to be confused with '81-'88 American-made model with the same name.
| 1988-2010 | $275 | $350 |

Standard Jazz Fretless Bass (Later Model)
1994-present. Fretless version.
| 1994-2010 | $275 | $350 |

Standard Jazz V Bass (Later Model)
1998-present. 5-string, import model.
| 1998-2010 | $300 | $375 |

Ventures Limited Edition Jazz Bass
1996. Made in Japan, part of Ventures guitar and bass set, dark purple.
| 1996 | $950 | $1,050 |

Victor Baily Jazz Bass
2002-present. Artist series, koa, rosewood and mahogany body, fretless with white fret markers.
| 2002-2010 | $1,200 | $1,400 |

MB Bass
1994-1995. Offset double cut, 1 P- and 1 J-style pickup, made in Japan.
| 1994-1995 Japan | $275 | $350 |

Musicmaster Bass
1970-1983. Shorter scale, solidbody, 1 pickup. various colors.
| 1970-1983 | $650 | $775 |

Mustang Bass
1966-1982. Shorter scale, solidbody, 1 pickup, offered in standard and competition colors, (competition colors refer to racing stripes on the body).
1966-1969	$1,500	$1,900
1970-1979	$1,300	$1,650
1978-1980 Antigua finish	$1,700	$2,000
1980-1982	$1,050	$1,150

Mustang Bass (Japan)
2002-present. Alder body, '60s features.
| 2002-2010 | $400 | $500 |

Performer Bass
1985-1986. Swinger-like body style, active electronics, various colors.
| 1985-1986 | $1,025 | $1,250 |

Precision Bass
The following are variations of the Precision Bass. The first four listings are for the main U.S.-made models. All others are listed alphabetically after that in the following order:

Precision Bass
Standard Precision Bass
American Standard Precision Bass
American Series Precision Bass
American Series Precision V Bass
40th Anniversary Precision Bass (Custom Shop)
50th Anniversary American Standard Precision Bass
50th Anniversary Precision Bass
'51 Precision Bass
'55 Precision Bass (Custom Shop)
'57 Precision Bass
'57 Precision Bass (Import)
'59 Precision Bass (Custom Shop)
60th Anniversary Precision Bass (Mexico)
'61 Precision Bass (Custom Shop)
'62 Precision Bass
'62 Precision Bass (Import)
Aerodyne Classic Precision Special Bass
American Deluxe Precision Bass
American Deluxe Precision V Bass
American Deluxe Zone/Zone Bass
Big Block Precision Bass
California Precision Bass Special
Deluxe Active P-Bass Special
Elite I Precision Bass
Elite II Precision Bass
Foto Flame Precision Bass
Gold Elite I Precision Bass
Gold Elite II Precision Bass
Highway One Precision Bass
Mark Hoppus Signature Precision Bass
Precision Bass Jr.
Precision Bass Lyte
Precision Special Bass (U.S.A.)
Precision Special Bass (Mexico)
Precision U.S. Deluxe/Plus Deluxe Bass
Precision U.S. Plus/Plus Bass
Prodigy/Prodigy Active Bass
Standard Precision Bass (Later Model)
Sting Precision Bass
Tony Franklin Precision Bass
Walnut Elite I Precision Bass
Walnut Elite II Precision Bass
Walnut Precision Special Bass

Precision Bass
1951-1981. Slab body until '54, 1-piece maple neck standard until '59, optional after '69, rosewood 'board standard '59 on (slab until mid-'62, curved after), blond finish standard until '54, sunburst standard after that (2-tone '54-'58, 3-tone after '58). Replaced by the Standard Precision Bass in '81-'85, then the American Standard Precision in '88-'00, and the American Series Precision Bass in '00-'08. Renamed American Standard again in '08. Unlike the Jazz and Telecaster Basses, the Precision

Fender Victor Bailey Jazz Bass

1955 Fender Precision

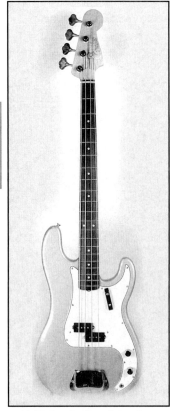

1962 Fender Precision Bass

1966 Fender Precision Bass

was never fitted with a 3-bolt neck or bullet rod. Please refer to the beginning of the Fender Bass Section for details on Fender color options.

MODEL YEAR	FEATURES	EXC. COND. LOW	HIGH
1951	Butterscotch blond, slab body	$16,000	$20,000
1952	Butterscotch blond, slab body	$14,000	$17,000
1953	Butterscotch blond, slab body	$13,000	$16,000
1954	Blond, slab body	$12,000	$15,000
1955	Blond, contour body	$11,000	$13,000
1956	Blond, contour body	$11,000	$13,000
1956	Sunburst	$9,500	$11,500
1957	Blond, standard guard	$11,000	$13,000
1957	Sunburst, anodized guard late '57	$9,500	$12,000
1957	Sunburst, white guard early '57	$8,500	$11,000
1958	Blond option	$9,100	$11,000
1958	Custom color	$15,000	$20,000
1958	Sunburst, anodized guard	$9,100	$11,000
1959	Blond	$9,100	$11,000
1959	Custom color	$15,000	$20,000
1959	Sunburst	$8,600	$10,600
1959	Sunburst, anodized guard	$9,100	$11,000
1960	Blond	$9,100	$11,000
1960	Custom color	$15,000	$20,000
1960	Sunburst	$8,200	$10,200
1961	Common color	$12,000	$15,000
1961	Rare color	$15,000	$20,000
1961	Sunburst	$7,500	$9,500
1962	Common color, curved	$9,000	$11,000
1962	Common color, slab	$9,300	$11,300
1962	Rare color, curved	$11,000	$17,000
1962	Rare color, slab	$11,300	$17,300
1962	Sunburst, curved	$7,000	$8,500
1962	Sunburst, slab	$7,300	$8,800
1963-1964	Common color	$8,000	$11,000
1963-1964	Rare color	$10,000	$15,000
1963-1964	Sunburst	$5,800	$7,000
1965	Common color	$6,500	$8,500
1965	Rare color	$8,500	$13,000
1965	Sunburst	$5,200	$6,100
1966	Common color	$5,500	$7,000
1966	Rare color	$7,000	$10,000
1966	Sunburst	$4,400	$5,200
1967	Common color	$5,000	$6,000
1967	Rare color	$6,000	$7,500
1967	Sunburst	$3,900	$4,900
1968	Common color	$4,500	$5,500
1968	Rare color	$5,500	$7,000
1968	Sunburst	$3,500	$4,500
1969	Common color	$4,000	$5,000
1969	Rare color	$5,000	$6,500

MODEL YEAR	FEATURES	EXC. COND. LOW	HIGH
1969	Sunburst	$3,000	$4,000
1970	Common color	$3,500	$4,500
1970	Rare color	$4,500	$5,500
1970	Sunburst	$2,500	$3,000
1971	Common color	$3,300	$4,300
1971	Rare color	$4,300	$5,300
1971	Sunburst	$2,300	$2,800
1972	Common color	$2,600	$4,300
1972	Sunburst	$2,100	$2,700
1973	Color option	$2,200	$3,400
1973	Natural	$2,000	$2,500
1973	Sunburst	$2,100	$2,700
1973	Walnut	$2,000	$2,500
1974	Color option	$2,100	$3,100
1974	Natural	$2,000	$2,500
1974	Sunburst	$2,100	$2,600
1974	Walnut	$2,000	$2,500
1975-1977	Black, blond, Olympic White, wine	$1,800	$2,250
1975-1977	Natural, walnut	$1,700	$2,100
1975-1977	Sunburst	$1,800	$2,250
1978-1979	Antigua	$1,950	$2,500
1978-1979	Black, blond, Olympic White, wine	$1,600	$2,000
1978-1979	Natural, walnut	$1,400	$1,700
1978-1979	Sunburst	$1,600	$2,000
1980	Antigua	$1,950	$2,500
1980	Black, Olympic White, wine	$1,550	$1,900
1980	Natural	$1,200	$1,500
1980	Sunburst	$1,400	$1,700
1981	Black & gold	$1,400	$1,700
1981	Black, Olympic White, wine	$1,500	$1,900
1981	International colors	$1,500	$1,900
1981	Sunburst	$1,350	$1,650

Standard Precision Bass

1981-1985. Replaces Precision Bass, various colors. Replaced by American Standard Precision '88-'00. The Standard name is used on import Precision model for '88-present.

1981-1984	Top mount jack	$1,200	$1,500
1985	Japan import	$475	$575

American Standard Precision Bass

1988-2000, 2008-present. Replaces Standard Precision Bass, replaced by American Series Precision in '00, back to American Standard in Jan. '08.

1988-1989	Blond, gold hardware	$900	$1,100
1988-1989	Various colors	$850	$1,050
1990-2000	Various colors	$675	$850
2008-2010		$675	$850

American Series Precision Bass

2000-2007. Replaces American Standard Precision Bass, various colors. Renamed American Standard in '08.

2000-2007		$675	$850

American Series Precision V Bass

2000-2007. 5-string version.

2000-2007		$750	$850

MODEL YEAR	FEATURES	EXC. COND. LOW	HIGH

40th Anniversary Precision Bass (Custom Shop)

1991. 400 made, quilted amber maple top, gold hardware.

| 1991 | | $1,400 | $1,600 |

50th Anniversary American Standard Precision Bass

1996. Regular American Standard with gold hardware, 4- or 5-string, gold 50th Anniversary commemorative neck plate, rosewood 'board, sunburst.

| 1996 | | $1,075 | $1,300 |

50th Anniversary Precision Bass

2001. Commemorative certificate with date and serial number, butterscotch finish, ash body, maple neck, black 'guard.

| 2001 | With certificate | $1,075 | $1,300 |

'51 Precision Bass

2003-2010. Import from Japan, does not include pickup or bridge covers as part of the package, blond or sunburst. Offered in Japan in the '90s.

| 1994 | Japan only | $600 | $700 |
| 2003-2010 | | $600 | $700 |

'55 Precision Bass (Custom Shop)

2003-2006. 1955 specs including oversized 'guard, 1-piece maple neck/fretboard, preproduction bridge and pickup covers, single-coil pickup. Offered in N.O.S., Closet Classic or highest-end Relic.

2003-2006	Closet Classic	$1,700	$1,900
2003-2006	N.O.S.	$1,600	$1,800
2003-2006	Relic	$1,900	$2,100

'57 Precision Bass

1982-present. U.S.-made reissue, American Vintage series, various colors.

1982-1989	Standard colors	$1,300	$1,400
1990-1999	Standard colors	$1,200	$1,300
2000-2010	Standard colors	$1,175	$1,300

'57 Precision Bass (Import)

1984-1986. Foreign-made, black.

| 1984-1986 | | $500 | $600 |

'59 Precision Bass (Custom Shop)

2003-2008. Custom Shop built with late-'59 specs, rosewood 'board.

2003-2008	Closet Classic	$1,700	$1,900
2003-2008	N.O.S.	$1,600	$1,800
2003-2008	Relic	$1,900	$2,100

60th Anniversary Precision Bass (Mexico)

2005. Made in Mexico, with 60th Anniversary gig bag.

| 2005 | | $275 | $325 |

'61 Precision Bass (Custom Shop)

2010.

2010	Closet Classic	$1,700	$1,900
2010	N.O.S.	$1,600	$1,800
2010	Relic	$1,900	$2,100

'62 Precision Bass

1982-present. U.S.-made reissue, American Vintage series, alder body. No production in '85.

1982-1984		$2,500	$3,000
1986-1989		$1,200	$1,500
1990-1999		$1,200	$1,500
2000-2010		$1,075	$1,300

'62 Precision Bass (Import)

1984-1986. Foreign-made, black.

| 1984-1986 | | $600 | $750 |

Aerodyne Classic Precision Special Bass

2006. Made in Japan, logo states Precision Bass and Aerodyne P Bass, radiused figured maple top, matching headstock, basswood body, P-J pickups, white 'guard.

| 2006 | | $550 | $675 |

American Deluxe Precision Bass

1998-2010. Made in U.S.A., active electronics, alder or ash body. Alder body colors - sunburst or transparent red. Ash body colors - white blond, transparent teal green or transparent purple.

| 1998-1999 | | $850 | $1,000 |
| 2000-2010 | | $850 | $1,000 |

American Deluxe Precision V Bass

1999-2004. 5-string version.

| 1999-2004 | | $950 | $1,100 |

American Deluxe Zone/Zone Bass

2003. Sleek lightweight offset double-cut body, active humbucker pickups, exotic tone woods.

| 2003 | | $950 | $1,150 |

Big Block Precision Bass

2005-2009. Pearloid block markers, black finish with matching headstock, 1 double Jazz Bass humbucker, bass and treble boost and cut controls.

| 2005-2009 | | $600 | $675 |

California Precision Bass Special

1997. California Series, assembled and finished in Mexico and California, P/J pickup configuration.

| 1997 | | $550 | $650 |

Deluxe Active P-Bass Special

1995-present. Made in Mexico, P/J pickups, Jazz Bass neck.

| 1995-2010 | | $350 | $450 |

Elite I Precision Bass

1983-1985. The Elite Series feature active electronics and noise-cancelling pickups, ash body, 1 pickup, various colors.

| 1983-1985 | | $850 | $1,050 |

Elite II Precision Bass

1983-1985. Ash body, 2 pickups, various colors.

| 1983-1985 | | $900 | $1,100 |

Foto Flame Precision Bass

1994-1996. Made in Japan, simulated woodgrain finish, natural or sunburst.

| 1994-1996 | | $450 | $550 |

Gold Elite I Precision Bass

1983-1985. The Elite Series feature active electronics and noise-cancelling pickups, gold-plated hardware version of the Elite Precision I, 1 pickup.

| 1983-1985 | | $1,300 | $1,600 |

Gold Elite II Precision Bass

1983-1985. Two pickup version.

| 1983-1985 | | $1,350 | $1,650 |

Highway One Precision Bass

2003-present. U.S.-made, alder body, satin lacquer finish.

| 2003-2010 | | $575 | $650 |

1971 Fender Precision
Robbie Keene

1983 Fender Elite II Precision

1982 Fender Precision Special Bass (U.S.A.)

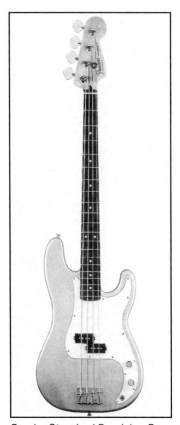

Fender Standard Precision Bass

MODEL YEAR	FEATURES	EXC. COND. LOW	HIGH

Mark Hoppus Signature Precision Bass
2001. Mark Hoppus engraved on neck plate.

| 2001 | | $525 | $625 |

Precision Bass Jr.
2004-2006. 3/4 size.

| 2004-2006 | | $250 | $300 |

Precision Bass Lyte
1992-2001. Japanese-made, smaller, lighter basswood body, 2 pickups, sunburst.

| 1992-2001 | | $350 | $450 |

Precision Special Bass (U.S.A.)
1980-1983. Gold hardware, matching headstock, active electronics.

| 1980-1983 | | $850 | $1,050 |

Precision Special Bass (Mexico)
1997-1998. 1 P- and 1 J-pickup. chrome hardware.

| 1997-1998 | | $275 | $325 |

Precision U.S. Deluxe/Plus Deluxe Bass
1991-1994. P-style bass with P-bass and Jazz bass pickups, concentric knobs, no 'guard models available, various colors.

| 1991-1994 | | $650 | $800 |

Precision U.S. Plus/Plus Bass
1989-1992. P-style bass with P- and J-bass pickup, model variations, black.

| 1989-1992 | | $675 | $825 |

Prodigy/Prodigy Active Bass
1992-1995. Poplar body, 1 J- and 1 P-style pickup, active.

| 1992-1995 | | $450 | $550 |

Standard Precision Bass (Later Model)
1987-present. Traditional style, import, currently made in Mexico. Not to be confused with '81-'85 American-made model with the same name.

| 1987-2010 | | $275 | $350 |

Sting Precision Bass
2001-present. Made in Japan, 2-tone sunburst, 1 single-coil, Sting's signature.

| 2001-2010 | | $575 | $700 |

Tony Franklin Precision Bass
2007-present. P and J pickups, 3-way selector, lacquer finish.

| 2007-2010 | | $1,000 | $1,250 |

Walnut Elite I Precision Bass
1983-1985. The Elite Series feature active electronics and noise-cancelling pickups. Walnut body, 1 pickup, rosewood 'board, natural.

| 1983-1985 | | $1,050 | $1,250 |

Walnut Elite II Precision Bass
1983-1985. Two-pickup version.

| 1983-1985 | | $1,150 | $1,350 |

Walnut Precision Special Bass
1980-1983. Precision Bass Special with a walnut body, natural.

| 1980-1983 | | $925 | $1,150 |

Squier Bronco Bass
2007. Squier Bronco logo on headstock, single coil plastic cover pickup, 3/4 body.

| 2007 | | $100 | $125 |

MODEL YEAR	FEATURES	EXC. COND. LOW	HIGH

Squier Bullet Bass
1980s. Japanese-made, Squier-branded, replaces Bullet Bass, black.

| 1980s | | $275 | $325 |

Squier Jazz Bass
1983-present. Jazz bass import, without cover plates, various colors.

1983-1984	1st logo	$350	$450
1985-1989	2nd logo	$300	$350
1990-1999		$125	$175
2000-2010		$85	$125

Squier Jazz Bass Affinity (China)
2000-present. Made in China.

| 2000s | | $60 | $100 |

Squier Precision Bass
1983-present.

1983-1984	1st logo	$350	$450
1985-1989	2nd logo	$300	$350
1990-1999		$125	$175
2000-2010		$75	$100

Squier Precision Bass Special
1999-present. Agathis body, P/J pickups.

| 1999-2010 | | $85 | $125 |

Squier Precision Bass V Special
2000-2008. 5-string version.

| 2000-2008 | | $85 | $125 |

Stu Hamm Urge Bass (U.S.A.)
1992-1999. Contoured Precision-style body with smaller wide treble cutaway, J and P pickups, 32" scale.

| 1992-1999 | | $900 | $1,100 |

Stu Hamm Urge II Bass (U.S.A.)
1999-2009. J and P pickups, 34" scale.

| 1999-2009 | | $1,100 | $1,300 |

Telecaster Bass
1968-1979. Slab solidbody, 1 pickup, fretless option '70, blond and custom colors available (Pink Paisley or Blue Floral '68-'69). Please refer to the beginning of the Fender Bass Section for details on Fender color options.

1968	Black, nitro	$3,600	$4,400
1968	Black, poly	$3,300	$4,000
1968	Blond, nitro	$3,300	$4,000
1968	Blond, poly	$2,900	$3,500
1968	Blue Floral, Paisley	$6,500	$7,900
1968	Lake Placid Blue	$5,800	$7,000
1968	Pink Paisley	$6,500	$7,900
1969	4-bolt, single-coil	$2,100	$2,500
1970	4-bolt, single-coil	$2,100	$2,500
1971	4-bolt, single-coil	$2,100	$2,500
1972	4-bolt, single-coil	$2,150	$2,500
1973-1974	3-bolt, humbucker	$1,700	$2,000
1973-1974	3-bolt, humbucker, rare color	$1,900	$2,250
1975-1976	3-bolt, humbucker	$1,650	$1,950
1977-1979	3-bolt, humbucker	$1,650	$1,950

Fernandes

1969-present. Intermediate and professional grade, production, solidbody basses. Established '69 in Tokyo. Early efforts were classical guitars, but they now offer a variety of guitars and basses.

MODEL YEAR	FEATURES	EXC. COND. LOW	HIGH

Fina

Production acoustic basses built at the Kwo Hsiao Music Wooden Factory in Huiyang City, Guang Dong, mainland China. They also build guitars.

First Act

1995-present. Budget and professional grade, production/custom, basses built in China and their Custom Shop in Boston. They also make guitars, violins, and other instruments.

Fleishman Instruments

1974-present. Premium and presentation grade, acoustic and solidbody basses made by luthier Harry Fleishman in Sebastopol, California. He also offers electric uprights, designed by him and built in China. Fleishman also designs basses for others and is the director of Luthiers School International. He also builds guitars.

Fodera

1983-present. Luthiers Vinnie Fodera and Joseph Lauricella build their professional and premium grade, production/custom, solidbody basses in Brooklyn, New York.

Higher-end Bass

1983-2010	4 strings	$3,500	$4,500
1983-2010	5, 6 strings	$4,000	$5,000

Mid-level Bass

1983-2010	4, 5, 6 strings	$1,000	$1,500

Framus

1946-1975, 1996-present. Professional and premium grade, production/custom, basses made in Germany. They also build guitars and amps.

Atlantic Model 5/140 Bass

1960s. Single-cut thinline with f-holes, 2 pickups, sunburst or blackrose.

1960s		$475	$575

Atlantic Model 5/143 Bass

1960s. Offset double-cut thinbody with f-holes, 2 pickups, 4-on-a-side keys.

1960s		$475	$575

Atlantic Model 5/144 Bass

1960s. Double-cut thinbody with f-holes, ES-335 body style, 2 pickups. Becomes Model J/144 in '70s.

1960s		$475	$575

Charavelle 4 Model 5/153 Bass

1960s. Double-cut thinline with f-holes, 335-style body, 2 pickups, sunburst, cherry red or Sunset.

1960s		$550	$675

De Luxe 4 Model 5/154 Bass

1960s. Double-cut thinline with sharp (acute) hornes and f-holes, 2 pickups, mute, sunburst or natural/ blond. 2nd most expensive in Framus bass lineup in the mid-'60s, although not as famous as the Stone/ Bill Wyman bass.

1960s		$575	$700

Electric Upright Bass

1950s. Full-scale neck, triangular body, black.

1958		$1,600	$2,000

MODEL YEAR	FEATURES	EXC. COND. LOW	HIGH

Star Series (Bill Wyman) Bass

1959-1968. Early flyer says, Bill Wyman of the Rolling Stones prefers the Star Bass. The model name was later changed to Framus Stone Bass. Single-cut semi-hollow body, 5/149 (1 pickup) and 5/150 (2 pickups), sunburst.

1959-1965	Model 5/150	$1,150	$1,400
1960s	Model 5/149	$850	$1,050

Strato De Luxe Star Model 5/165 Bass

Ca. 1964-ca. 1972. Offset double-cut solidbody, 2 pickups, sunburst. There was also a gold hardware version (5/165 gl) and a 6-string (5/166).

1960s		$475	$600

Strato Star Series Bass

Ca. 1963-ca. 1972. Double-cut solidbody, 5/156/50 (1 pickup) or 5/156/52 (2 pickups), beige, cherry or sunburst.

1960s	Model 5/156/50	$475	$575
1960s	Model 5/156/52	$525	$625

T.V. Star Bass

1960s. Offset double-cut thinbody with f-holes, 2 pickups, short-scale, sunburst or cherry red. Most expensive of the '60s Framus basses, although not as popular as the Bill Wyman 5/150 model.

1960s		$525	$650

Triumph Electric Upright Bass

1956-1960. Solidbody bean pole electric bass, small body, long neck, slotted viol peghead, gold or black.

1956-1960		$1,400	$1,800

Fresher

1973-1985. Japanese-made, mainly copies of popular brands and not imported into the U.S., but they do show up at guitar shows. They also made guitars.

Solidbody Electric Bass

1970s		$225	$300

Fret-King

2008-present. Professional and premium grade, production, solidbody and semi-hollow electric basses built by luthier Trev Wilkinson in the U.K. A line is also imported from Korea. He also builds guitars.

Fritz Brothers

1988-present. Luthier Roger Fritz builds his premium grade, production/custom, semi-hollow body basses in Mendocino, California. He also builds guitars.

Frudua Guitar Works

1988-present. Intermediate to premium grade, production/custom, electric basses built by luthier Galeazzo Frudua in Imola, Italy. He also builds guitars and amps.

Fury

1962-present. Founded by Glenn McDougall in Saskatoon, Saskatchewan, Fury currently offers production, solidbody basses. They also build guitars.

1968 Fender Telecaster Bass

Fodera Bass

G & L ASAT

1981 G&L L-1000

MODEL YEAR	FEATURES	EXC. COND. LOW	HIGH

Fylde

1973-present. Luthier Roger Bucknall builds his professional and premium grade, production/custom acoustic basses in Penrith, Cumbria, United Kingdom. He also builds guitars, mandolins, mandolas, bouzoukis, and citterns.

G & L

1980-present. Intermediate and professional grade, production/custom, electric basses made in the U.S. In '03, G & L introduced the Korean-made G & L Tribute Series. A Tribute logo is clearly identified on the headstock. They also build guitars.

ASAT Bass

1989-present. Single-cut, solidbody, active and passive modes, 2 humbuckers, various colors.

1989-1991	About 400 made	$875	$1,000
1992-2010		$825	$950

ASAT Commemorative Bass

1991-1992. About 150 made, 4-string ASAT commemorating Leo Fender's life.

1991-1992		$1,550	$1,800

ASAT Semi-Hollow Bass

2001-present. Semi-hollowbody style on ASAT bass.

2001-2010		$775	$900

Climax Bass

1992-1996. Single active humbucker MFD.

1992-1996		$650	$750

El Toro Bass

1983-1991. Double-cut, solidbody, 2 active, smaller, humbuckers, sunburst.

1983-1991		$875	$1,000

Interceptor Bass

1984-1991. Sharp pointed double-cut, solidbody, 2 active, smaller humbuckers, sunburst.

1984-1986		$800	$925
1987-1991	Body signature	$800	$925

JB-2 Bass

2001-present. Alder body, 2 Alnico V pickups.

2001-2010		$750	$850

L-1000 Bass

1980-1994, 2008. Offset double-cut, solidbody, 1 pickup, various colors. Limited run in '08.

1980-1985	Ash	$950	$1,100
1980-1985	Mahogany	$1,000	$1,200
1980-1985	Maple	$1,100	$1,300
1986-1998		$900	$1,000

L-1500 Bass

1997-present. Offset double-cut solidbody, 1 MFD humbucker.

1997-2010		$700	$800

L-1500 Custom Bass

1997 only.

1997		$725	$825

L-1505 Bass

1998-present. Five-string version, single MFD humbucker.

1998-2010		$725	$825

MODEL YEAR	FEATURES	EXC. COND. LOW	HIGH

L-2000 Bass

1980-present. Offset double-cut solidbody, 2 pickups, active electronics. Originally, the L-2000 was available with active (L-2000E) or passive (L-2000) electronics.

1980-1982		$1,000	$1,200
1983-1986		$875	$1,000
1987-1991	Leo signature	$850	$950
1992-2010		$800	$900

L-2000 C.L.F. Centennial

2009-2010. Swamp ash body, blonde, black hardware, planned run of 50, Certificate of Authenticity.

2009-2010	COA, CD	$1,600	$1,800
2009-2010	No COA or CD	$1,300	$1,500

L-2000 Custom Bass

1997. Ash top, wood-grain binding upgrade.

1997		$800	$900

L-2000 Fretless Bass

1980-1998. Fretless version.

1980-1982		$1,200	$1,400

L-2000(E) Bass

1980-1982. Offset double-cut, solidbody, 2 pickups, active electronics. Originally, the L-2000 was available with active (L-2000E) or passive (L-2000) electronics.

1980-1982		$1,000	$1,200

L-2500 Bass

1997-present. Five-string, dual MFD humbuckers, figured tops can vary.

1997-2010		$800	$925

L-2500 Custom Bass

1997. Ash top, wood-grain binding upgrade.

1997		$800	$925

L-5000 Bass

1988-1993. Offset double-cut, solidbody, G & L Z-shaped split-humbucker, 5 strings, approximately 400 made.

1988-1992		$750	$850

L-5500 Bass

1993-1997. Alder body, 5-string.

1993-1997		$700	$800

L-5500 Custom Bass

1997. Ash top, wood-grain binding upgrade.

1997		$700	$800

LB-100 Bass

1993-2000. Follow-up to earlier Legacy Bass.

1993-2000		$600	$700

Legacy Bass

1992-1993. Offset double-cut solidbody, 1 split-coil, renamed LB-100 in '93.

1992-1993		$700	$800

Lynx Bass

1984-1991. Offset double-cut, solidbody, 2 single-coils, black.

1984-1991		$800	$1,000

SB-1 Bass

1982-2000. Solidbody, maple neck, body and 'board, split-humbucker, 1 tone and 1 volume control.

1982-1989		$775	$900
1990-2000		$725	$850

MODEL YEAR	FEATURES	EXC. COND. LOW	HIGH

SB-2 Bass
1982-present. Maple neck with tilt adjustment, 1 split-coil humbucker and 1 single-coil.

1982-1989		$800	$900
1990-1999		$750	$850
2000-2010		$700	$800

G.L. Stiles
1960-1994. Built by Gilbert Lee Stiles primarily in the Miami, Florida area. He also built guitars.

Gadow Guitars
2002-present. Luthier Ryan Gadow builds his professional and premium grade, custom/production, solidbody basses in Durham, North Carolina. He also builds guitars.

Galveston
Budget and intermediate grade, production, imported acoustic, acoustic/electric and solidbody basses. They also offer guitars and mandolins.

Garage by Wicked
2004-2010. A line of basses imported from China by luthier Nicholas Dijkman (Wicked) of Montreal, Quebec.

Gibson
1890s (1902)-present. Professional grade, production, U.S.-made electric basses. Gibson got into the electric bass market with the introduction of their Gibson Electric Bass in '53 (that model was renamed the EB-1 in '58 and reintroduced under that name in '69). Many more bass models followed. Gibson's custom colors can greatly increase the value of older instruments. Custom colors offered from '63 to '69 are Cardinal Red, Ember Red, Frost Blue, Golden Mist Metallic, Heather Metallic, Inverness Green, Kerry Green, Pelham Blue Metallic, Polaris White, Silver Mist Metallic.

20/20 Bass
1987-1988. Designed by Ned Steinberger, slim-wedge Steinberger style solidbody, 2 humbucker pickups, 20/20 logo on headstock, Luna Silver or Ferrari Red finish.

1987-1988		$800	$1,000

Electric Bass (EB-1)
1953-1958. Introduced as Gibson Electric Bass in '53, but was called the EB-1 by Gibson in its last year of '58, thus, the whole line is commonly called the EB-1 by collectors, reissued in '69 as the EB-1 (see EB-1 listing), brown.

1953-1958		$5,000	$6,200

EB Bass
1970 only. Renamed from Melody Maker Bass, SG body, 1 humbucker pickup.

1970		$1,300	$1,600

EB-0 Bass
1959-1979. Double-cut slab body with banjo-type tuners in '59 and '60, double-cut SG-type body with conventional tuners from '61 on, 1 pickup. Faded custom colors are of less value.

1959-1960	Cherry, slab body	$3,700	$4,600
1961	Cherry, SG body	$1,900	$2,400
1962	Cherry	$1,900	$2,400
1963-1964	Cherry	$1,800	$2,200
1965	Cherry	$1,400	$1,800
1966	Cherry	$1,300	$1,600
1967	Cherry	$1,300	$1,600
1968	Black	$1,600	$2,000
1968	Burgundy Metallic	$1,800	$2,200
1968	Cherry	$1,300	$1,600
1968	Pelham Blue	$2,000	$2,400
1969	Cherry, slotted head	$950	$1,200
1969	Cherry, solid head	$1,200	$1,500
1969	Pelham Blue	$2,000	$2,400
1970-1971	Cherry, slotted head	$900	$1,100
1972-1974	Cherry, solid head	$900	$1,100
1975-1979	Cherry	$800	$1,000

EB-0 F Bass
1962-1965. EB-0 with added built-in fuzz, cherry.

1962		$1,900	$2,400
1963-1964		$1,900	$2,400
1965		$1,700	$2,100

EB-0 L Bass
1969-1979. 34.5 inch scale version of the EB-0, various colors.

1969		$900	$1,100
1970-1971		$900	$1,100
1972-1979		$900	$1,100

EB-1 Bass
1969-1972. The Gibson Electric Bass ('53-'58) is often also called the EB-1 (see Electric Bass). Violin-shaped mahogany body, 1 pickup, standard tuners.

1969-1972		$2,700	$3,300

EB-2 Bass
1958-1961, 1964-1972. ES-335-type semi-hollowbody, double-cut, 1 pickup, banjo tuners '58-'60 and conventional tuners '60 on.

1958	Sunburst, banjo tuners	$3,800	$4,700
1959	Natural, banjo tuners	$4,700	$5,800
1959	Sunburst, banjo tuners	$3,500	$4,300
1960	Sunburst, banjo tuners	$3,300	$4,100
1961	Sunburst, conventional tuners	$2,300	$2,900
1964	Sunburst	$2,200	$2,700
1965	Sunburst	$1,900	$2,400
1966	Cherry, sunburst	$1,700	$2,100
1967-1968	Cherry, sunburst	$1,700	$2,100
1967-1969	Sparkling Burgundy	$2,200	$2,700
1967-1969	Walnut	$1,300	$1,600
1969	Cherry, sunburst	$1,700	$2,100
1970-1972	Sunburst	$1,500	$1,800

1964 Gibson EB-0F

1969 Gibson EB-1

BASSES

BASSES

Gibson EB-3
Ron Puzzitiello

1961 Gibson EB-6

MODEL YEAR	FEATURES	EXC. COND. LOW	HIGH
EB-2 D Bass			
1966-1972. Two-pickup version of EB-2, cherry, sunburst, or walnut.			
1966	Cherry, sunburst	$2,200	$2,800
1967-1969	Cherry, sunburst	$2,200	$2,800
1967-1969	Sparkling Burgundy	$2,600	$3,200
1967-1969	Walnut	$1,800	$2,300
1970-1972	Cherry, sunburst	$2,000	$2,400
EB-3 Bass			
1961-1979. SG-style solidbody, 2 humbuckers, solid peghead '61-'68 and '72-'79, slotted peghead '69-'71, cherry to '71, various colors after.			
1961		$4,000	$5,000
1962		$3,800	$4,800
1963		$3,500	$4,500
1964		$3,500	$4,500
1965		$2,900	$3,600
1966		$2,300	$2,900
1967-1968		$2,300	$2,900
1969		$1,600	$2,300
1970-1971		$1,300	$1,600
1972-1974		$1,300	$1,600
1975-1979		$1,200	$1,500
EB-3 L Bass			
1969-1972. 34.5" scale version of EB-3, slotted headstock, EB-3L logo on truss rod cover, cherry, natural, or walnut.			
1969		$1,600	$2,000
1970-1971		$1,300	$1,600
1972		$1,300	$1,600
EB-4 L Bass			
1972-1979. SG-style, 1 humbucker, 34.5" scale, cherry or walnut.			
1972-1979		$1,100	$1,400
EB-6 Bass			
1960-1966. Introduced as semi-hollowbody 335-style 6-string with 1 humbucker, changed to SG-style with 2 pickups in '62.			
1960	Natural, 335-style	$7,500	$8,500
1960-1961	Sunburst, 335-style	$6,000	$7,000
1962-1964	Cherry, SG-style	$7,000	$8,000
1965-1966	Cherry, SG-style	$5,500	$6,500
EB-650 Bass			
1991-1993. Semi-acoustic single cut, maple neck, laminated maple body with center block, 2 TB Plus pickups.			
1991-1993		$900	$1,100
EB-750 Bass			
1991-1993. Like EB-650, but with Bartolini pickups and TCT active EQ.			
1991-1993		$1,000	$1,200
Explorer Bass			
1984-1987. Alder body, 3-piece maple neck, ebony 'board, dot inlays, 2 humbuckers, various colors.			
1984-1987	Standard finish	$1,100	$1,350
1985	Designer series graphics	$1,300	$1,650
Flying V Bass			
1981-1982 only. Solidbody, Flying V body.			
1981-1982	Blue stain or ebony	$2,900	$3,500
1981-1982	Silverburst	$3,100	$3,800

MODEL YEAR	FEATURES	EXC. COND. LOW	HIGH
Gibson IV Bass			
1986-1988. Mahogany body and neck, double-cut, 2 pickups, black chrome hardware, various colors.			
1986-1988		$500	$625
Gibson V Bass			
1986-1988. Double-cut, 5 strings, 2 pickups.			
1986-1988		$600	$650
Grabber Bass			
1974-1982. Double-cut solidbody, 1 pickup, bolt maple neck, maple 'board, various colors.			
1974-1982		$750	$950
Grabber III Bass (G-3)			
1975-1982. Double-cut solidbody, 3 pickups, bolt maple neck, maple 'board, nickel-plated hardware, various colors.			
1975-1982		$800	$1,000
L9-S Bass			
1973. Natural maple or cherry, renamed Ripper Bass in '74.			
1973		$775	$950
Les Paul Bass			
1970-1971. Single-cut solidbody, 2 pickups, walnut finish, renamed Les Paul Triumph Bass '71-'79.			
1970-1971		$1,750	$2,200
Les Paul Deluxe Plus LPB-2 Bass			
1991-1998. Upgraded Les Paul Special LPB-1 bass, with carved maple top, trapezoid inlays, TCT active eq and Bartolini pickups. Flame maple top Premium version offered '93-'98.			
1991-1998		$1,175	$1,450
Les Paul Money Bass			
2007-2008. Solidbody offset double-cut, 2 humbuckers, dot markers, figured maple top over mahogany body, 400 made.			
2007-2008		$850	$1,050
Les Paul Signature Bass			
1973-1979. Double-cut, semi-hollowbody, 1 pickup, sunburst or gold (gold only by '76). Name also used on LPB-3 bass in '90s.			
1973-1975	Sunburst	$2,500	$3,000
1973-1979	Gold	$2,500	$3,000
Les Paul Special LPB-1 Bass			
1991-1998. 2 TB-Plus pickups, ebony 'board, dots, slab mahogany body, active electronics, also available as 5-string.			
1991-1998		$700	$825
Les Paul Special V Bass			
1993-1996. Single-cut slab body, 5-string, 2 pickups, dot markers, black/ebony.			
1993-1996		$800	$1,000
Les Paul Standard Bass			
2005-2006		$1,200	$1,400
Les Paul Standard LPB-3 Bass			
1991-1995. Like Les Paul Deluxe LPB-2 Bass, but with TB Plus pickups. Flame maple top Premium version offered '93-'95.			
1993-1995	Flamed top	$875	$1,100
Les Paul Triumph Bass			
1971-1979. Renamed from Les Paul Bass.			
1971-1979	Various colors	$1,500	$1,800
1973-1974	Optional white	$1,600	$1,900

The *Vintage Guitar Price Guide* shows low to high values for items in all-original excellent condition, and, where applicable, with original case or cover.

MODEL YEAR	FEATURES	EXC. COND. LOW	HIGH
Melody Maker Bass			
1967-1970. SG body, 1 humbucker pickup.			
1967-1970		$1,300	$1,600
Nikki Sixx Blackbird (Thunderbird) Bass			
2000-2002, 2009-present. Thunderbird style, black finish and hardware, iron cross inlays.			
2000-2010		$1,300	$1,500
Q-80 Bass			
1986-1988. Victory Series body shape, 2 pickups, bolt neck, black chrome hardware, renamed Q-90 in '88.			
1986-1988		$400	$500
Q-90 Bass			
1988-1992. Renamed from Q-80, mahogany body, 2 active humbuckers, maple neck, ebony 'board.			
1988-1992		$400	$500
RD Artist Bass			
1977-1982. Double-cut solid maple body, laminated neck, 2 pickups, active electronics, string-thru-body, block inlays, various colors.			
1977-1982		$1,400	$1,700
RD Artist Custom Bass			
1977-1982. Custom option with bound top, low production, mild figure, sunburst.			
1977-1982		$1,300	$1,600
RD Standard Bass			
1977-1979. Double-cut, solid maple body, laminated neck, 2 pickups, regular electronics, string-thru-body, dot inlays, various colors.			
1977-1979		$1,100	$1,400
Ripper Bass			
1974-1982. Introduced as L-9 S Bass in '73, double-cut solidbody, glued neck, 2 pickups, string-thru-body, various colors.			
1974-1982		$1,250	$1,500
Ripper II Bass			
2009-present. Solid maple body, 34" scale, 2 pickups, natural nitrocellulose lacquer.			
2009-2010		$1,100	$1,300
SB Series Bass			
1971-1978. The early version, 1971, had oval pickups with wide metal surrounds, these were replaced mid-model with more traditional rectangular pickups with rectangular surrounds. This 2nd version can often fetch a bit more in the market. Various models include 300 (30" scale, 1 pickup), 350 (30" scale, 2 pickups), 400 (34" scale, 1 pickup), 450 (34" scale, 2 pickups). From '75 to '78 the 450 was special order only.			
1971-1973	SB-300	$725	$875
1971-1973	SB-400	$725	$875
1972-1974	SB-350	$725	$875
1972-1974	SB-450	$750	$925
1975-1978	SB-450 special order	$750	$925
SG Reissue/SG Standard Bass			
2005-present. Modern version of 1960s EB-3 bass, 2 pickups, '60s specs, mahogany body and neck, cherry or ebony, currently called the SG Standard.			
2005-2010		$800	$1,000
SG Supreme Bass			
2007-2008. Made in Nashville, SG body with AAA maple top, 2 pickups.			
2007-2008		$950	$1,200

MODEL YEAR	FEATURES	EXC. COND. LOW	HIGH
Thunderbird II Bass			
1963-1969. Reverse solidbody until '65, non-reverse solidbody '65-'69, 1 pickup, custom colors available, reintroduced with reverse body for '83-'84.			
1963	Sunburst, reverse	$7,100	$8,900
1964	Pelham Blue, reverse	$10,800	$13,200
1964	Sunburst, reverse	$5,700	$7,000
1965	Cardinal Red, non-reverse	$6,000	$7,500
1965	Inverness Green, non-reverse	$6,000	$7,500
1965	Sunburst, non-reverse	$3,200	$4,000
1965	Sunburst, reverse	$5,200	$6,500
1966	Cardinal Red, non-reverse	$5,900	$7,400
1966	Sunburst, non-reverse	$3,200	$4,000
1967	Cardinal Red, non-reverse	$5,800	$7,300
1967	Sunburst, non-reverse	$3,000	$3,800
1968	Cardinal Red, non-reverse	$5,800	$7,300
1968	Sunburst, non-reverse	$3,000	$3,800
1969	Sunburst, non-reverse	$3,000	$3,800
Thunderbird IV Bass			
1963-1969. Reverse solidbody until '64, non-reverse solidbody '65-'69, 2 pickups, custom colors available, reintroduced with reverse body for '86-present (see Thunderbird IV Bass Reissue).			
1963	Sunburst, reverse	$9,700	$12,000
1964	Frost Blue, reverse	$18,000	$22,000
1964	Pelham Blue, reverse	$18,000	$22,000
1964	Sunburst, reverse	$9,500	$11,800
1965	Cardinal Red, non-reverse	$11,000	$13,500
1965	Inverness Green, non-reverse	$11,000	$13,500
1965	Sunburst, reverse	$9,000	$11,300
1965-1966	Sunburst, non-reverse	$5,000	$6,200
1966	White, non-reverse	$8,500	$10,800
1967	Sunburst, non-reverse	$4,800	$6,000
1968	Sunburst, non-reverse	$4,800	$6,000
1969	Sunburst, non-reverse	$4,800	$6,000
Thunderbird IV Bass (Reissue)			
1987-present. Has reverse body and 2 pickups, sunburst.			
1987-1989		$1,225	$1,500
1990-2010		$1,125	$1,400
1991-2010	Rare color	$1,325	$1,600

1966 Gibson Thunderbird IV

Gibson Thunderbird IV Reissue

1983 Gibson Victory

Sean Sweeney

Gold Tone ABG-4

MODEL YEAR	FEATURES	EXC. COND. LOW	HIGH

Thunderbird IV Bass Zebra Wood Bass
2007. Guitar of the Week (week 11 of '07), limited run of 400, Zebrawood body.

2007		$1,900	$2,300

Thunderbird 76 Bass
1976 only. Reverse solidbody, 2 pickups, rosewood 'board, various colors.

1976		$2,600	$3,300

Thunderbird 79 Bass
1979 only. Reverse solidbody, 2 pickups, sunburst.

1979		$2,600	$3,300

Thunderbird Studio/IV Studio
2005-2007. 4- or 5-string versions.

2005-2007		$1,000	$1,200

Victory Artist Bass
1981-1985. Double-cut, solidbody, 2 humbuckers and active electronics, various colors.

1981-1985		$700	$875

Victory Custom Bass
1982-1984. Double-cut, solidbody, 2 humbuckers, passive electronics, limited production.

1982-1984		$700	$875

Victory Standard Bass
1981-1986. Double-cut, solidbody, 1 humbucker, active electronics, various colors.

1981-1986		$500	$600

GMP (Genuine Musical Products)
2010-present. Luthiers Dan Lawrence, Glen Matejzel and William Stempke build production/custom, professional and premium grade, electric basses in San Dimas, California. They also build guitars.

Godin
1987-present. Intermediate and professional grade, production, solidbody electric and acoustic/electric basses from luthier Robert Godin. They also build guitars and mandolins.

A Series Bass
1990s-present. Acoustic/electric, 5-string starts in '00.

1990s-2010	A-4	$375	$450
2000-2010	A-5 SA	$550	$650

Freeway A Series Bass
2005-present. Double-cut solidbodies, 4- or 5-string, passive or active.

2005-2010	Freeway A-4	$350	$450
2005-2001	Freeway A-5	$400	$500

Godlyke
2006-present. Professional and premium grade, production, solidbody basses from effects distributor Godlyke.

Gold Tone
1993-present. Intermediate grade, production/custom acoustic basses built by Wayne and Robyn Rogers in Titusville, Florida. They also offer guitars, lap steels, mandolins, ukuleles, banjos and banjitars.

Goya
1955-1996. Originally imports from Sweden, brand later used on Japanese and Korean imports. They also offered basses, mandolins and banjos.

Electric Solidbody Bass

1960s	Various models	$550	$675

Graf
See listing under Oskar Graf Guitars.

Granada
1970s-1980s. Japanese-made electric basses, most being copies of classic American models. They also offered guitars.

Greco
1960s-present. Currently owned by Kanda Shokai, of Japan, and offering solidbody basses. They also offer guitars. Early bass models were copies of popular brands, but by the '70s original designs appear.

Gretsch
1883-present. Intermediate and professional grade, production, solidbody, hollow body, and acoustic/electric basses. Gretsch came late to the electric bass game, introducing their first models in the early '60s.

Broadkaster Bass (7605/7606)
1975-1979. Double-cut solidbody, 1 pickup, bolt-on maple neck, natural (7605) or sunburst (7606).

1975-1979		$575	$700

Committee Bass (7629)
1977-1980. Double-cut walnut and maple solidbody, neck-thru, 1 pickup, natural.

1977-1980		$600	$750

G6072 Long Scale Hollow Body Bass
1998-2006. Reissue of the '68 double-cut hollowbody, 2 pickups, sunburst, gold hardware.

1998-2006		$1,000	$1,250

Model 6070/6072 Bass
1963-1971 (1972 for 6070). Country Gentleman thinline archtop double-cut body, fake f-holes, 1 pickup (6070) or 2 (6072), gold hardware.

1963-1964	6070, with endpin	$2,200	$2,700
1965-1972	6070, no endpin, 1 pickup	$1,600	$2,000
1968-1971	6072, 2 pickups	$1,300	$1,700

Model 6071/6073 Bass
1968-1971 (1972 for 6071). Single-cut hollowbody, fake f-holes, 1 pickup (6071) or 2 (6073), padded back, red mahogany.

1968-1971	6073, 2 pickups	$2,000	$2,400
1968-1972	6071, 1 pickup	$1,800	$2,200

Model 7615 Bass
1972-1975. Offset double-cut solidbody, slotted bass horn (monkey grip), large polished rosewood 'guard covering most of the body, 2 pickups, dot markers, brown mahogany finish. Only bass offered in Gretsch catalog for this era.

1972-1975		$750	$900

MODEL YEAR	FEATURES	EXC. COND. LOW	HIGH

TK 300 Bass (7626/7627)
1976-1981. Double-cut solidbody, 1 pickup, Autumn Red Stain or natural.

| 1976-1981 | | $550 | $675 |

Groove Tools
2002-2004. Korean-made, production, intermediate grade, solidbody basses that were offered by Conklin Guitars of Springfield, Missouri. They also had guitars.

Grosh
1993-present. Professional grade, production/custom, solidbody basses built by luthier Don Grosh in Santa Clarita, California. He also builds guitars.

Guild
1952-present. Guild added electric basses in the mid-'60s and offered them until '02.

Ashbory Bass
1986-1988, 2009. 18" scale, total length 30", fretless, silicone rubber strings, active electronics, low-impedance circuitry.

| 1986-1988 | | $375 | $475 |
| 2009 | Fender Guild reissue | $175 | $200 |

B-4 E Bass
1993-1999. Acoustic/electric single-cut flat-top, mahogany sides with arched mahogany back, multi-bound, gold hardware until '95, chrome after.

| 1993-1999 | | $550 | $675 |

B-30 E Bass
1987-1999. Single-cut flat-top acoustic/electric, mahogany sides, arched mahogany back, multi-bound, fretless optional.

| 1987-1999 | | $900 | $1,100 |

B-50 Acoustic Bass
1976-1987. Acoustic flat-top, mahogany sides with arched mahogany back, spruce top, multi-bound, renamed B-30 in '87.

| 1976-1987 | | $1,150 | $1,350 |

B-301/B-302 Bass
1976-1981. Double-cut solidbody, chrome-plated hardware. Models include B-301 (mahogany, 1 pickup), B-301 A (ash, 1 pickup), B-302 (mahogany, 2 pickups), B-302 A (ash, 2 pickups), and B-302 AF (ash, fretless).

1976-1981	B-301	$650	$825
1976-1981	B-302	$675	$850
1977-1981	B-301 A	$700	$875
1977-1981	B-302 A	$700	$825
1977-1981	B-302 AF	$700	$825

B-500 Acoustic Bass
1992-1993. Acoustic/electric flat-top, round soundhole, single-cut, solid spruce top, maple back and sides, dark stain, limited production.

| 1992-1993 | | $1,000 | $1,250 |

Jet Star Bass
1964-1970 (limited production '68-'70). Offset double-cut solidbody, short treble horn, 1 pickup, 2-on-a-side tuners '64-'66 and 4 in-line tuners '66-'70.

| 1964-1966 | 2-on-side tuners | $1,150 | $1,400 |
| 1966-1970 | 4-in-line tuners | $1,100 | $1,350 |

JS I/JS II Bass
1970-1977. Double-cut solidbody, 30" scale, 1 pickup (JS I or 1) or 2 (JS II or 2), mini-switch, selector switch, carved-top oak leaf design available for '72-'76. 34" long scale (LS) versions offered fretted and fretless for '74-'75.

| 1970-1975 | JS I | $1,000 | $1,250 |
| 1970-1977 | JS II | $1,100 | $1,350 |

M-85 I/M-85 II Bass (Semi-Hollow)
1967-1972. Single-cut semi-hollowbody, 1 pickup (M-85 I) or 2 (M-85 II).

| 1967-1972 | M-85 I | $1,575 | $2,000 |
| 1967-1972 | M-85 II | $1,750 | $2,200 |

M-85 I/M-85 II BluesBird Bass (Solidbody)
1972-1976. Single-cut solidbody archtop, Chesterfield headstock inlay, cherry mahogany, 1 humbucker pickup (I) or 2 (II).

| 1972-1973 | M-85 I | $1,575 | $2,000 |
| 1972-1976 | M-85 II | $1,750 | $2,200 |

MB-801 Bass
1981-1982. Double-cut solidbody, 1 pickup, dot inlays.

| 1981-1982 | | $600 | $725 |

SB-201/SB-202/SB-203 Bass
1982-1983. Double-cut solidbody, 1 split coil pickup (201), 1 split coil and 1 single coil (202), or 1 split coil and 2 single coils (203).

1982-1983	SB-201	$650	$775
1982-1983	SB-202	$700	$825
1983	SB-203	$750	$875

SB-502 E Bass
1984-1985. Double-cut solidbody, 2 pickups, active electronics.

| 1984-1985 | | $750 | $875 |

SB-601/SB-602/SB-602 V Pilot Bass
1983-1988. Offset double-cut solidbody, bolt-on neck, poplar body. Models include SB-601 (1 pickup), SB-602 (2 pickups or fretless) and SB-602 V (2 pickups, 5-string).

1983-1988	SB-601	$450	$550
1983-1988	SB-602	$475	$575
1983-1988	SB-602 V	$500	$600
1983-1988	SB-602, fretless	$500	$600
1983-1988	SB-605, 5-string	$550	$650

SB-608 Flying Star Motley Crue Bass
1984-1985. Pointy 4-point star body, 2 pickups, E version had EMG pickups.

| 1984-1985 | | $650 | $700 |

Starfire Bass
1965-1975. Double-cut semi-hollow thinbody, 1 pickup, mahogany neck, chrome-plated hardware, cherry or sunburst.

| 1965-1969 | Single-coil | $1,800 | $2,300 |
| 1970-1975 | Humbucker | $1,400 | $1,800 |

Starfire II Bass
1965-1978. Two-pickup version of Starfire Bass.

| 1965-1969 | 2 single-coils | $1,900 | $2,400 |
| 1970-1978 | 2 humbuckers | $1,500 | $1,900 |

Starfire II Reissue Bass
1998-2002. Reissue of 2 humbucker version.

| 1998-2002 | | $1,250 | $1,550 |

Greco Bass

1975 Guild Jet Star II

Halfling Bass

Hamer Velocity 5

X-701/X-702 Bass

1982-1984. Body with 4 sharp horns with extra long bass horn, 1 pickup (X-701) or 2 (X-702), various metallic finishes.

Year	Features	Low	High
1982-1984	X-701	$700	$875
1982-1984	X-702	$750	$925

Guitar Mill

2006-2011. Professional grade, production/custom, solidbody basses built by Mario Martin in Murfreesboro, Tennessee. He also builds guitars. In '11, he started branding his guitars as Mario Martin.

Guyatone

1933-present. Large Japanese maker which also produced instruments under the Marco Polo, Winston, Kingston, Kent, LaFayette, and Bradford brands.

GW Basses & Luthiery

2004-present. Professional and premium grade, production/custom, basses built by luthier Grandon Westlund in West Lafayette, Indiana.

Hagstrom

1921-1983, 2004-present. This Swedish guitar company first offered electric basses in '61.

8-String Bass

1967-1969. Double-cut solidbody, 2 pickups, various colors.

Year	Low	High
1967-1969	$1,150	$1,400

Coronado IV Bass

1963-1970. Offset double cut, Bi-Sonic pickups.

Year	Low	High
1963-1964	$1,100	$1,350
1965-1970	$1,050	$1,300

Kent Bass

1963-1964. 2 single-coils, 4 sliders.

Year	Low	High
1962-1966	$625	$725

Model I B/F-100 B Bass

1965-1973. Offset double-cut solidbody, 2 single-coils, 5 sliders, 30" scale.

Year	Low	High
1965-1970	$475	$625
1970-1973	$425	$575

Model II B/F-400 Bass

1965-1970. Like Model I, but with 30.75" scale, called F-400 in U.S., II B elsewhere.

Year	Low	High
1965-1970	$475	$625

Swede 2000 Bass (With Synth)

1977. Circuitry on this Swede bass connected to the Ampeg Patch 2000 pedal so bass would work with various synths.

Year	Low	High
1977	$925	$1,150

Swede Bass

1980-1981. Single-cut solidbody, block inlays, bolt neck, 2 humbuckers, 30.75" scale, cherry or black

Year	Low	High
1971-1976	$800	$975

Super Swede Bass

1980-1981. Like Swede, but with neck-thru body, 32" scale, sunburst, mahogany or black.

Year	Low	High
1980-1981	$925	$1,150

V-IN Bass/Concord Bass

1970s. Bass version of V-IN guitar, 335-style body, 2 pickups, sunburst.

Year	Low	High
1970s	$800	$975

Halfling Guitars and Basses

2003-present. Premium grade, production/custom, acoustic basses built by luthier Tom Ribbecke in Healdsburg, California. He also builds guitars.

Hallmark

1965-1967, 2004-present. Imported, intermediate grade, production, basses. Hallmark is located in Greenbelt, Maryland. They also make guitars. The brand was originally founded by Joe Hall in Arvin, California, in '65.

Hamer

1975-present. Intermediate and professional grade, production/custom, acoustic and electric basses made in the U.S. and imported. Founded in Arlington Heights, Illinois, by Paul Hamer and Jol Dantzig, Hamer was purchased by Kaman in '88. They also build guitars.

8-String Short-Scale Bass

1978-1993. Double cut solidbody, 1 or 2 pickups, 30.5" scale.

Year	Low	High
1978-1993	$1,450	$1,750

12-String Acoustic Bass

1985-2010. Semi-hollow, long scale, single cut, soundhole, 2 pickups. Import XT model added in the 2000s.

Year	Low	High
1985-2010	$1,500	$1,900

12-String Short-Scale Bass

1978-1996. Four sets of 3 strings - a fundamental and 2 tuned an octave higher, double cut maple and mahogany solidbody, 30.5" scale.

Year	Low	High
1978-1996	$1,500	$1,900

Blitz Bass

1982-1990. Explorer-style solidbody, 2 pickups, bolt-on neck.

Year	Features	Low	High
1982-1984	1st edition	$900	$1,150
1984-1990		$700	$800

Chaparral Bass

1986-1995, 2000-2008. Solidbody, 2 pickups, glued-in neck, later basses have bolt-on neck.

Year	Features	Low	High
1986-1987	Set-neck	$800	$950
1987-1995	Bolt-on neck	$700	$800

Chaparral 5-String Bass

1987-1995. Five strings, solidbody, 2 pickups, glued-in neck, later basses have 5-on-a-side reverse peghead.

Year	Low	High
1987-1995	$575	$700

Chaparral 12-String Bass

1992-present. Long 34" scale 12-string, offset double cut. Import XT model added in '01.

Year	Features	Low	High
1992-2010	USA	$1,500	$1,850
2000-2010	Import	$325	$400

Chaparral Max Bass

1986-1995. Chaparral Bass with figured maple body, glued-in neck and boomerang inlays.

Year	Low	High
1986-1995	$600	$725

MODEL YEAR	FEATURES	EXC. COND. LOW	HIGH

Cruise Bass
1982-1990, 1995-1999. J-style solidbody, 2 pickups, glued neck ('82-'90) or bolt-on neck ('95-'99), also available as a 5-string.

1982-1990	Set-neck	$575	$675
1995-1999	Bolt-on neck	$525	$625

Cruise 5 Bass
1982-1989. Five-string version, various colors.

1982-1989		$575	$675

FBIV Bass
1985-1987. Reverse Firebird shape, 1 P-Bass Slammer and 1 J-Bass Slammer pickup, mahogany body, rosewood 'board, dots.

1985-1987		$550	$650

Standard Bass
1975-1984, 2001. Explorer-style bound body with 2 humbuckers.

1975-1979	USA	$1,500	$1,850
1980-1984	USA	$1,050	$1,300
2001	Import	$325	$400

Velocity 5 Bass
2002-present. Offset double-cut, long bass horn, active, 1 humbucker.

2002-2010		$150	$175

Harmony
1892-1976, late 1970s-present. Harmony once was one of the biggest instrument makers in the world, making guitars and basses under their own brand and for others.

H Series Bass
Late-1980s-early-1990s. F-style solidbody copies, 1 or 2 pickups, all models begin H.

1980-1990s		$100	$125

H-22 Bass
1959-1972. Single-cut hollowbody, 2-on-a-side, 1 pickup.

1959-1972		$675	$825

H-27 Bass
1968-1972. Double-cut hollowbody, 4-on-a-side, 2 pickups.

1968-1972		$700	$850

Hartke
Hartke offered a line of wood and aluminum-necked basses from 2000 to '03.

Hayman
1970-1973. Solid and semi-hollow body guitars and basses developed by Jim Burns and Bob Pearson for Ivor Arbiter of the Dallas Arbiter Company and built by Shergold in England.

Heartfield
1989-1994. Distributed by Fender, imported from Japan. They also offered guitars.

Electric Bass
1989-1994. Double-cut solidbody, graphite reinforced neck, 2 single-coils, available in 4-, 5- and 6-string models.

1989-1994		$250	$325

Heit Deluxe
Ca. 1967-1970. Imported from Japan, many were made by Teisco. They also had guitars.

Hembry Guitars
2004-present. Luthier Scott Hembry builds professional grade, production/custom, solidbody electric basses in Shelton, Washington. He also builds guitars.

HenBev
2005-present. Luthier Scotty Bevilacqua builds his premium grade, production, basses in Oceanside, California. He also builds guitars.

Henman Guitars
2010-present. Premium grade, production/custom, solidbody and chambered electric basses built by luthier Rick Turner in Santa Cruz, California for owners Graham and Paris Henman. They also build guitars.

Heritage
1985-present. Mainly a builder of guitars, Kalamazoo, Michigan's Heritage has offered a few basses in the past.

HB-1 Bass
1987. P-style body, limited production, single-split pickup, 4-on-a-side tuners, figured maple body, bolt-on neck.

1987		$600	$675

Höfner
1887-present. Professional grade, production, basses. They also offer guitars and bowed instruments. Höfner basses, made famous in the U.S. by one Paul McCartney, are made in Germany.

Icon Series
2007-present. Chinese versions of classic Hofners.

2007-2010		$200	$270

Model 172 Series Bass
1968-1970. Offset double-cut, 6-on-a-side tuners, 2 pickups, 2 slide switches, dot markers, 172-S shaded sunburst, 172-R red vinyl covered body, 172-I vinyl covered with white top and black back.

1968-1970	172-I, white	$475	$575
1968-1970	172-R, red	$475	$575
1968-1970	172-S, sunburst	$500	$600

Model 182 Solid Bass
1962-1985. Offset double-cut solidbody, 2 pickups.

1960s		$400	$500

Model 185 Solid Bass
1962-ca. 1970. Classic offset double-cut solidbody, 2 double-coil pickups.

1962-1970		$425	$525

Model 500/1 Beatle Bass
1956-present. Semi-acoustic, bound body in violin shape, glued-in neck, 2 pickups, sunburst. Currently listed as 500/1 Vintage '58, '59, '62 and '63.

1956-1959	Right-handed or lefty	$4,500	$5,500

Hembry Thunder

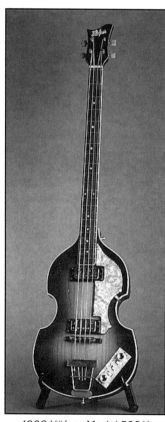

1966 Höfner Model 500/1

1970 Höfner Model 500/2

Ibanez SR-405

MODEL YEAR	FEATURES	EXC. COND. LOW	HIGH
1960-1961	Lefty, McCartney	$4,800	$5,800
1960-1961	Right-handed	$3,700	$4,500
1962-1963	Lefty	$3,500	$4,300
1962-1963	Right-handed	$2,700	$3,300
1964	Lefty	$3,500	$4,300
1964	Lefty, McCartney	$5,000	$6,000
1964	Right-handed	$2,600	$3,300
1964	Right-handed, McCartney	$3,800	$4,600
1965-1967	Lefty	$2,700	$3,400
1965-1967	Right-handed	$2,100	$2,600
1968-1969	Lefty	$2,200	$2,800
1968-1969	Right-handed	$1,600	$2,000
1970-1973	Lefty	$2,100	$2,700
1970-1973	Right-handed	$1,500	$1,900
1974-1979	Right-handed or lefty	$1,400	$1,700

'58 Model 500/1 Reissue
2008-present.

2008-2010		$1,300	$1,600

'62 Model 500/1 Beatle Bass Reissue
1990s-present.

1990s-2010		$900	$1,200

'63 Model 500/1 Beatle Bass Reissue
1994-2010. Right- or left-handed.

1994-2010		$1,300	$1,600

Model 500/1 1964-1984 Reissue Bass
1984. '1964-1984' neckplate notation.

1984		$1,500	$1,800

Model 500/1 50th Anniversary Bass
2006. Pickguard logo states '50th Anniversary Höfner Violin Bass 1956-2006', large red Höfner logo also on 'guard, 150 made.

2006		$2,800	$3,200

Model 500/1 Cavern Bass
2005. Limted run of 12, includes certificate.

2005		$1,550	$1,900

Model 500/1 Contemporary CS
2007-2008. Contemporary Series.

2007-2008		$500	$600

Model 500/2 Bass
1965-1970. Similar to the 500/1, but with 'club' body Höfner made for England's Selmer, sunburst. Club Bass has been reissued.

1965-1970		$1,200	$1,400

Model 500/3 Senator Bass
1962-1964. Single-cut thin body, f-holes, 1 511b pickup.

1962-1964	Sunburst	$1,200	$1,400

Model 500/5 Bass
1959-1979. Single-cut body with Beatle Bass-style pickups, sunburst.

1959		$2,600	$3,100
1960s		$2,300	$2,800

Model 500/6 Bass
Late-1960s. Introduced in '67, semi-acoustic, thinline, soft double-cut, 2 pickups, 4 control knobs, dot markers, sunburst.

1967		$1,300	$1,600

Model 500/8BZ / B500/8BZ
Late-1960s. Semi-acoustic, thinline, sharp double-cut, multiple-line position markers, built in flip-fuzz and bass boost, sunburst or natural.

1967	500/8BZ, sunburst	$1,400	$1,700
1967	B500/8BZ, natural	$1,500	$1,800

Model (G)5000/1 Super Beatle (G500/1) Bass
1968-present. Bound ebony 'board, gold-plated hardware, natural finish, the version with active circuit is called G500/1 Super Beatle, reissued in '94.

1968-1970s		$1,400	$1,700

President Bass
Made for England's Selmer, single-cut archtop, 2 pickups, sunburst.

1961-1962		$1,800	$2,200
1963-1965		$1,700	$2,100
1966-1967		$1,400	$1,800
1968-1969		$1,400	$1,700
1970-1972		$1,300	$1,600

Hohner
1857-present. Intermediate and professional grade, production, solidbody basses. Hohner has been offering basses at least since the early '70s. They also offer guitars, banjos, mandolins and ukuleles.

Hondo
1969-1987, 1991-2005. Budget grade, production, imported acoustic and electric solidbody basses. They also offered guitars, banjos and mandolins.

Electric Solidbody Bass

1970-1990s	Rare models	$250	$400
1970-1990s	Standard models	$75	$250

H 1181 Longhorn Bass
Ca. 1978-1980s. Copy of Danelectro Longhorn Bass, 1 split pickup.

1978-1980s		$350	$425

Hopf
1906-present. From the mid-'50s to the late-'70s, Hopf offered electric basses made in their own factory and by others. Hopf currently mainly offers classical guitars and mandolins.

Hoyer
1874-present. Intermediate grade, production, electric basses. They also build guitars.

Electric Bass

1960s		$400	$550

Hutchins
2006-present. Intermediate and professional grade, production, acoustic and electric basses imported from China, Germany and Korea, by Gary Hutchins in Sussex, U.K. He also offers guitars.

Ibanez
1932-present. Intermediate and professional grade, production, solidbody basses. They also have guitars, amps, and effects.

MODEL YEAR	FEATURES	EXC. COND. LOW	HIGH

AXB Axstar Series Bass
1986-1987. Various models.

1986-1987		$175	$450

BTB Series Bass
1999-present. Various models.

1999-2010		$200	$500

Challenger Bass
1977-1978. Offered as P-bass or J-bass style, and with ash body option.

1977-1978		$325	$400

DB Destroyer II X Series Bass
1984-1986. Futuristic-style body, P- and J-style pickups, dot markers, bolt neck.

1984-1986		$275	$475

DT Destroyer II Series Bass
1980-1985. Futuristic-style body.

1980-1985		$400	$600

ICB Iceman Bass
1994-1996, 2011-present. Iceman body, basswood (300) or mahogany (500) body. 300 reissued in '11.

1994-1996	ICB300	$300	$375
1994	ICB500, black	$600	$750

MC Musician Series Bass
1978-1988. Various models, solidbody, neck-thru.

1978-1988		$600	$1,200

Model 2030 Bass
1970-1973. First copy era bass, offset double-cut, sunburst.

1970-1973		$475	$600

Model 2353 Bass
1974-1976. Copy model, offset double-cut, 1 pickup, black.

1974-1976		$475	$600

Model 2364B Bass
1971-1973. Dan Armstrong see-thru Lucite copy with 2 mounted humbucker pickups, clear finish.

1971-1973		$700	$850

Model 2365 Bass
1974-1975. Copy model, Offset double-cut, rosewood 'board, pearloid block markers, sunburst.

1974-1975		$475	$600

Model 2366 B/2366 FLB Bass
1974-1975. Copy model, offset double-cut, 1 split-coil pickup, sunburst, FLB fretless model.

1974-1975		$475	$600

Model 2385 Bass
1974-1975. Copy model, offset double-cut, 1 pickup, ash natural finish.

1974-1975		$475	$600

Model 2388 B Bass
1974-1976. Ric 4001 copy.

1974-1976		$475	$600

Model 2452 Bass
1975. Ripper copy.

1975		$475	$600

Model 2459 B Destroyer Bass
1974-1977. Laminated ash body, copy of Korina Explorer-style.

1974-1977		$1,300	$1,700

Model 2537 DX Bass
1974-1975. Hofner Beatle copy.

1974-1975		$475	$600

PL Pro Line Series Bass
1986-1987. Offset double cut solidbody.

1986-1987		$250	$450

RB/RS Roadstar Series Bass
1983-1987. Solidbody basses, various models and colors.

1983-1987		$250	$500

Rocket Roll Bass
1974-1976. Korina solidbody, V-shape, natural.

1974-1976		$875	$1,075

S/SB Series Bass
1990-1992. Various ultra slim solidbody basses.

1990-1992		$200	$500

SR Sound Gear Series Bass
1987-present. Sleek, lightweight designs, active electronics, bolt necks. Model numbers higher than 1000 are usually arched-top, lower usually flat body.

1987-2010		$250	$550

ST-980 Studio Bass
1979-1980. Double cut, 8-string, bolt-on neck, walnut-maple-mahogany body.

1979-1980		$400	$500

Imperial
Ca.1963-ca.1970. Imported by the Imperial Accordion Company of Chicago, Illinois. Early guitars and basses made in Italy, but by ca. '66 Japanese-made.

Electric Solidbody Bass

1960s	Various models	$150	$250

Hollowbody Bass
1960s. Hollowbody with sharp double-cuts.

1960s		$200	$275

Infeld
2003-2005. Solidbody guitars and basses offered by string-maker Thomastik-Infeld of Vienna.

Italia
1999-present. Intermediate grade, production, solid and semi-solidbody basses designed by Trevor Wilkinson and made in Korea. They also build guitars.

J Backlund Design
2008-present. Professional and premium grade, production/custom, electric basses designed by J. Backlund and built in Chattanooga, Tennessee by luthier Bruce Bennett. He also builds guitars.

J.B. Player
1980s-present. Intermediate grade, production, imported, acoustic/electric and solidbody basses. They also offer guitars, banjos and mandolins.

J.T. Hargreaves Basses & Guitars
1995-present. Luthier Jay Hargreaves builds his premium grade, production/custom, acoustic basses, in Seattle, Washington. He also builds guitars.

Italia Maranello

J.T. Hargreaves Jayhawk

BASSES

Jackson C20 Concert

1965 Kay K5915 Pro Model

Jack Daniel's

2004-present. Solidbody electric bass built by Peavey for the Jack Daniel Distillery. They also offer a guitar model and amp.

Jackson

1980-present. Intermediate, professional, and premium grade, production, solidbody basses. They also offer guitars. Founded by Grover Jackson, who owned Charvel.

Concert C5P 5-String Bass (Import)
1998-2000. Bolt neck, dot inlay, chrome hardware.

		LOW	HIGH
1998-2000		$125	$150

Concert Custom Bass (U.S.A.)
1984-1995. Neck-thru Custom Shop bass.

1984-1989		$625	$725
1990-1995		$525	$625

Concert EX 4-String Bass (Import)
1992-1995. Bolt neck, dot inlay, black hardware.

1992-1995		$225	$300

Concert V 5-String Bass (Import)
1992-1995. Bound neck, shark tooth inlay.

1992-1995		$375	$450

Concert XL 4-String Bass (Import)
1992-1995. Bound neck, shark tooth inlay.

1992-1995		$275	$350

Kelly Pro Bass
1994-1995. Pointy-cut bouts, neck-thru solidbody, shark fin marker inlays.

1994-1995		$525	$625

Piezo Bass
1986. Four piezo electric bridge pickups, neck-thru, active EQ, shark tooth inlays. Student model has rosewood 'board, no binding. Custom Model has ebony 'board and neck and headstock binding.

1986		$375	$450

Soloist Bass
1996. Pointy headstock, 4-string.

1996		$600	$700

James Trussart

1980-present. Premium grade, custom/production, solid and semi-hollow body electric basses built by luthier James Trussart in Los Angeles California. He also builds guitars.

James Tyler

Early 1980s-present. Luthier James Tyler builds his professional and premium grade, custom/production, solidbody basses in Van Nuys, California. He also builds guitars.

Jay Turser

1997-present. Intermediate grade, production, imported semi-hollow and solidbody basses. They also offer guitars and amps.

Jerry Jones

1981-2011. Intermediate grade, production, semi-hollow body electric basses from luthier Jerry Jones, and built in Nashville, Tennessee. They also build guitars and sitars. Jones retired in 2011.

Neptune Longhorn 4 Bass
1988-2011. Based on Danelectro longhorn models, 4-string, 2 lipstick-tube pickups, 30" scale.

		LOW	HIGH
1988-2011		$475	$575

Neptune Longhorn 6 Bass
1988-2011. 6-string version.

1988-2011		$525	$625

Neptune Shorthorn 4/Shorthorn Bass
1990s. Danelectro inspired with Dano Coke bottle headstock, short horns like double cut U-2, 2 pickups, color options.

1990s		$500	$600

Jim Dyson

1972-present. Luthier Jim Dyson builds his intermediate, professional and premium grade, production/custom electric basses in Torquay, Southern Victoria, Australia. He also builds guitars and lap steels.

Johnson

Mid-1990s-present. Budget and intermediate grade, production, solidbody and acoustic basses imported by Music Link, Brisbane, California. They also offer guitars, amps, mandolins and effects.

Jon Kammerer Guitars

1997-present. Professional grade, custom/production, solidbody, chambered, acoustic, and acoustic/electric basses built by luthier Jon Kammerer in Keokuk, Iowa. He also builds guitars.

Juzek

Violin maker John Juzek was originally located in Prague, Czeckoslovakia, but moved to West Germany due to World War II. Prague instruments considered by most to be more valuable. Many German instruments were mass produced with laminate construction and some equate these German basses with the Kay laminate basses of the same era. Juzek still makes instruments.

JY Jeffrey Yong Guitars

2003-present. Luthier Jeffrey Yong builds professional and premium grade, production/custom, electric basses in Kuala Lumpur, Malaysia. He also builds guitars.

Kalamazoo

1933-1942, 1965-1970. Kalamazoo was a brand Gibson used on one of their budget lines. They also used the name on electric basses, guitars and amps from '65 to '67.

Electric Bass

		LOW	HIGH
1965-1970	Bolt-on neck	$375	$450

MODEL YEAR	FEATURES	EXC. COND. LOW	HIGH

Kapa

Ca. 1962-1970. Kapa was founded by Koob Veneman in Maryland and offered basses and guitars.

Electric Bass

1962-1970	Various models	$200	$500

Kawai

1927-present. Japanese instrument manufacturer Kawai started offering guitars under other brand names around '56. There were few imports carrying the Kawai brand until the late-'70s; best known for high quality basses. Kawai quit offering guitars and basses around 2002.

Electric Bass

1970-1980s	Various models	$200	$450

Kay

Ca. 1931-present. Currently, budget and intermediate grade, production, imported solidbody basses. They also make amps, guitars, banjos, mandolins, ukes, and violins. Kay introduced upright acoustic laminate basses and 3/4 viols in '38 and electric basses in '54.

C1 Concert String Bass

1938-1967. Standard (3/4) size student bass, laminated construction, spruce top, figured maple back and sides, shaded light brown.

1938-1949		$1,800	$2,200
1950-1959		$1,700	$2,100
1960-1967		$1,500	$1,800

K160 Electronic Bass

1955-1956. Same as K-162, but with plain white plastic trim.

1955-1956		$1,400	$1,800

K-162 Electronic Bass

1955-1956. Bass version of K-161Thin Twin "Jimmy Reed," single-cut, 1 tube-style pickup.

1955-1956		$1,400	$1,800

K-5965 Pro Bass

1954-1965. Single-cut, 1 pickup, named K-5965 Pro by 1961.

1954-1965		$1,400	$1,800

K5970 Jazz Special Electric Bass

1960-1964. Double-cut, pickup, Kelvinator headstock, black or blond.

1960-1964		$1,400	$1,700

M-1 (Maestro) String Bass

1952-late-1960s. Standard (3/4) size bass, laminated construction, spruce top and curly maple back and sides. Model M-3 is the Junior (1/4) size bass, Model M-1 B has a blond finish, other models include the S-51 B Chubby Jackson Five-String Bass and the S-9 Swingmaster.

1952-1959		$1,800	$2,200
1960-1967		$1,700	$2,100

M-5 (Maestro) String Bass

1957-late-1960s. Five strings.

1957-1967		$2,200	$2,700

Semi-hollowbody Bass

1954-1966. Single or double cut, 1 or 2 pickups.

1954-1966	1 pickup	$300	$375
1954-1966	2 pickups	$350	$450

Solidbody Bass

1965-1968. Single or double cut, 1 or 2 pickups.

1965-1968	1 pickup	$400	$550
1965-1968	2 pickups	$450	$600

KB

1989-present. Luthier Ken Bebensee builds his premium grade, custom, solidbody basses in North San Juan, California. He also builds guitars and mandolins.

Ken Smith

See listing under Smith.

Kent

1961-1969. Guitars and basses imported from Japan by Buegeleisen and Jacobson of New York, New York. Manufacturers unknown but many early instruments by Guyatone and Teisco.

Electric Bass

1962-1969. Import models include 628 Newport, 634 Basin Street, 629, and 635.

1961-1969	Common model	$125	$250
1961-1969	Rare model	$250	$325

Kimberly

Late-1960s-early-1970s. Private branded import made in the same Japanese factory as Teisco. They also made guitars.

Violin Bass

1960s		$325	$400

Kinal

1969-present. Luthier Michael Kinal builds and imports his production/custom, professional and premium grade, solidbody electric basses, in Vancouver, British Columbia. He also builds guitars.

Kingslight Guitars

1980-present. Luthier John Kingslight builds his premium grade, custom/production, acoustic basses in Portage, Michigan (in Taos, New Mexico for '80-'83). He also builds guitars.

Kingston

Ca. 1958-1967. Imported from Japan by Westheimer Importing Corp. of Chicago. Early examples by Guyatone and Teisco. They also offered guitars.

Electric Bass

1960s	Common model	$125	$250
1960s	Rare model	$250	$325

Klein Acoustic Guitars

1972-present. Luthiers Steve Klein and Steven Kauffman build their production/custom, premium and presentation grade acoustic basses in Sonoma, California. They also build guitars.

Klein Electric Guitars

1988-2007. Lorenzo German produced his professional grade, production/custom, basses in Linden, California. He also built guitars.

KB Sefano Roncarolo

Kingslight ABG

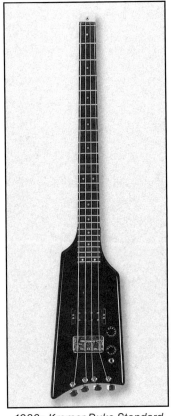

1980s Kramer Duke Standard

1978 Kramer DMZ-4000

K-Line Guitars

2005-present. Luthier Chris Kroenlein builds his professional grade, production/custom, basses in St. Louis, Missouri. He also builds guitars.

Klira

Founded in 1887 in Schoenbach, Germany, mainly making violins, but added guitars and basses in the 1950s. The instruments of the '50s and '60s were aimed at the budget market, but workmanship improved with the '70s models.

Electric Bass

MODEL YEAR	FEATURES	EXC. COND. LOW	HIGH
1960s	Beatle Bass copy	$525	$600
1960s	Common model	$300	$400
1960s	Rare model	$400	$500

Knutson Luthiery

1981-present. Professional and premium grade, custom, electric upright basses built by luthier John Knutson in Forestville, California. He also builds guitars, lap steels and mandolins.

Koll

1990-present. Professional and premium grade, custom/production, solidbody and chambered basses built by luthier Saul Koll, originally in Long Beach, California, and since '93, in Portland, Oregon. He also builds guitars.

Kona Guitar Company

2000-present. Located in Fort Worth, Texas, Kona imports budget and intermediate grade, production, electric basses. They also offer guitars, amps, mandolins and ukes.

Kramer

1976-1990, 1995-present. Budget grade, production, imported solidbody basses. They also offer guitars. Kramer's first guitars and basses featured aluminum necks with wooden inserts on back. Around '80 they started to switch to more economical wood necks and aluminum necks were last produced in '85. Gibson acquired the brand in '97.

250-B Special Bass

1977-1979. Offset double-cut, aluminum neck, Ebonol 'board, zero fret, 1 single-coil, natural.

1977-1979		$600	$700

350-B Standard Bass

1976-1979. Offset double-cut, aluminum neck, Ebonol 'board, tropical woods, 1 single-coil, dots. The 350 and 450 were Kramer's first basses.

1976-1979		$775	$900

450-B Deluxe Bass

1976-1980. As 350-B, but with 2 single-coils and blocks.

1976-1980		$825	$1,000

650-B Artist Bass

1977-1980. Double-cut, birdseye maple/burled walnut, aluminum neck, zero fret, mother-of-pearl crowns, 2 humbuckers.

1977-1980		$1,200	$1,400

Deluxe 8 Bass

1980. Multi-piece body, aluminum neck.

1980		$1,200	$1,500

DMB 2000 Bass

1979. Bolt-on aluminum neck, slot headstock.

1979		$600	$750

DMZ 4000 Bass

1978-1982. Bolt-on aluminum neck, slot headstock, double-cut solidbody, active EQ and dual-coil humbucking pickup, dot inlay.

1978-1981		$600	$750
1982	Bill Wyman-type	$700	$875

DMZ 4001 Bass

1979-1980. Aluminum neck, slot headstock, double-cut solidbody, 1 dual-coil humbucker pickup, dot inlay.

1979-1980		$550	$700

DMZ 5000 Bass

1979-1980. Double-cut solidbody, aluminum neck, slotted headstock, 2 pickups, crown inlays.

1979-1980		$750	$950

DMZ 6000B Bass

1979-1980. Double-cut, aluminum neck, slotted headstock, 2 pickups, crown inlays.

1979-1980		$775	$975

Duke Custom/Standard Bass

1981-1983. Headless, aluminum neck, 1 humbucker.

1981-1983		$300	$375

Duke Special Bass

1982-1985. Headless, aluminum neck, 2 pickups, with frets or fretless.

1982-1985		$350	$425

Ferrington KFB-1/KFB-2 Acoustic Bass

1987-1990. Acoustic/electric, bridge-mounted active pickup, tone and volume control, various colors. KFB-1 has binding and diamond dot inlays; the KFB-2 no binding and dot inlays. Danny Ferrington continued to offer the KFB-1 after Kramer closed in '90.

1987-1990		$275	$350

Focus 7000 Bass

1985-1987. Offset double-cut solidbody, P and double J pickups, Japanese-made.

1985-1987		$200	$250

Focus 8000 Bass

1985-1987. Offset double-cut solidbody, Japanese-made.

1985-1987		$225	$275

Focus K-77 Bass

1984. Offset double-cut solidbody, 1 pickup, Japanese-made.

1984		$225	$275

Focus K-88 Bass

1984. Two pickup Focus.

1984		$225	$275

Forum Series Bass

1987-1990. Japanese-made double-cut, 2 pickups, neck-thru (I & III) or bolt-neck (II & IV).

1987-1990	Forum I	$400	$500
1987-1990	Forum II	$325	$400
1987-1990	Forum III	$300	$350
1987-1990	Forum IV	$250	$300

BASSES

MODEL YEAR	FEATURES	EXC. COND. LOW	HIGH

Gene Simmons Axe Bass
1980-1981. Axe-shaped bass, slot headstock.

1980-1981		$2,500	$3,000

Hundred Series Bass
1988-1990. Import budget line, 7/8th solidbody.

1988-1990	710	$175	$225
1988-1990	720	$200	$250

Pacer Bass
1982-1984. Offset double-cut solidbody, red.

1982-1984		$525	$650

Pioneer Bass
1981-1986. First wood neck basses, offset double cut, JBX or PBX pickups, dots, '81-'84 models with soft headstocks, later '84 on with banana headstocks.

1981-1986	Double J, 2 JBX	$450	$550
1981-1986	Imperial, JBX & PBX	$425	$525
1981-1986	Special, 1 PBX	$400	$500
1982-1984	Carrera, JBX & PBX	$450	$550

Ripley Four-String Bass
1985-1987. Four-string version.

1985-1987		$700	$875

Ripley Five-String Bass
1984-1987. Offset double-cut, 5 strings, stereo, pan pots for each string, front and back pickups for each string, active circuitry.

1984-1987		$725	$900

Stagemaster Custom Bass (Import)
1982-1985, 1987-1990. First version had an aluminum neck (wood optional). Later version was neck-thru-body, bound neck, either active or passive pickups.

1982-1985	Imperial	$550	$650
1982-1985	Special	$500	$600
1982-1985	Standard	$550	$650

Stagemaster Deluxe Bass (U.S.A.)
1981. Made in USA, 8-string, metal neck.

1981		$850	$1,050

Striker 700 Bass
1985-1989. Offset double-cut, Korean-import, 1 pickup until '87, 2 after. Striker name was again used on a bass in '99.

1985-1987	1 pickup	$200	$250
1988-1989	2 pickups	$225	$275

Vanguard Bass
1981-1983. V-shaped body, Special (aluminum neck) or Standard (wood neck).

1981-1982	Special	$475	$575
1983-1984	Standard	$525	$625

XKB-10 (Wedge) Bass
1980-1981. Wedge-shaped body, aluminum neck.

1980-1981		$550	$700

XKB-20 Bass
1981. 2nd version, more traditional double cut body.

1981		$475	$550

XL Series Bass
1980-1981. Odd shaped double-cut solidbody, aluminum neck.

1980-1981	XL-9, 4-string	$700	$850
1981	XL-24, 4-string	$800	$1,000
1981	XL-8, 8-string	$900	$1,100

ZX Aero Star Series Bass (Import)
1986-1989. Various models include ZX-70 (offset double-cut solidbody, 1 pickup).

1986-1989		$150	$200

KSD
2003-present. Intermediate grade, production, imported bass line designed by Ken Smith (see Smith listing) and distributed by Brooklyn Gear.

Kubicki
1973-present. Professional and premium grade, production/custom, solidbody basses built by luthier Phil Kubicki in Santa Barbara, California. Kubicki began building acoustic guitars when he was 15. In '64 at age 19, he went to work with Roger Rossmeisl at Fender Musical Instrument's research and development department for acoustic guitars. Nine years later he moved to Santa Barbara, California, and established Philip Kubicki Technology, which is best known for its line of Factor basses and also builds acoustic guitars, custom electric guitars, bodies and necks, and mini-guitars and does custom work, repairs and restorations.

Ex Factor 4/Factor 4 Bass
1985-present. Solidbody, maple body, bolt-on maple neck, fretless available, 4 strings, 2 pickups, active electronics.

1980s		$750	$900

Ex Factor 5/Factor 5 Bass
1985-ca.1990. Solidbody, bolt-on maple neck, fretless available, 5 strings, 2 pickups, active electronics.

1980s		$800	$1,000

Kustom
1968-present. Founded by Bud Ross in Chanute, Kansas, and best known for the tuck-and-roll amps, Kustom also offered guitars and basses from '68 to '69.

Electric Hollowbody Bass

1968-1969	Various models	$800	$1,000

La Baye
1967. Short-lived brand out of Green Bay, Wisconsin and built by the Holman-Woodell factory in Neodesha, Kansas. There was also a guitar model.

Model 2x4 II Bass
1967. Very low production, dual pickups, long-scale, small rectangle solidbody, sometimes referred to as the Bass II.

1967		$1,100	$1,400

Model 2x4 Mini-Bass
1967. Short-scale, 1 pickup, small rectangle solidbody.

1967		$1,100	$1,400

Lado
1973-present. Founded by Joe Kovacic, Lado builds professional and premium grade, production/custom, solidbody basses in Lindsay, Ontario. Some model lines are branded J. K. Lado. They also build guitars.

1978 Kramer DMZ-4001

KSD 704

BASSES

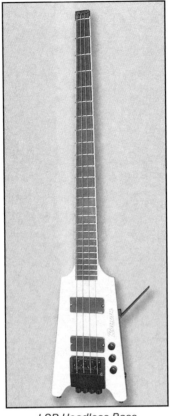

LSR Headless Bass

1965 Magnatone Hurricane X-10

Tom Roberts

MODEL YEAR	FEATURES	EXC. COND. LOW	HIGH

Lafayette

Ca. 1963-1967. Sold through Lafayette Electronics catalogs. Early Japanese-made guitars and basses from pre-copy era, generally shorter scale beginner instruments. Many made by Guyatone, some possibly by Teisco.

Lakland

1994-present. Professional and premium grade, production/custom, solid and hollowbody basses from luthier Dan Lakin in Chicago, Illinois. Lakland basses are built in the U.S. and overseas (Skyline series).

4 - 63 Classic Bass

1994-2002. Offset double-cut alder body, large bass horn, bolt neck.

1994-2002		$1,600	$2,100

4 - 63 Deluxe Bass

1994-2002. Like Classic but with figured maple top on ash body.

1994-2002		$1,800	$2,300

4 - 63 Standard Bass

1994-2002. Like Classic, but with swamp ash body.

1994-2002		$1,600	$2,100

4 - 94 Classic Bass

1994-present. Offset double-cut alder body with maple top, large bass horn, bolt neck. Series now called 44-94.

1994-2010		$1,600	$2,100

4 - 94 Deluxe Bass

1994-present. Like Classic but with flamed maple top on swamp ash body.

1994-2010		$1,800	$2,300

4 - 94 Standard Bass

1994-present. Like Classic, but with quilt maple top.

1994-2010		$1,600	$2,100

Joe Osborn Bass

1998-present. Classic offset double-cut, 4- or 5-string, alder or swamp ash body, 2 pickups, name changed to 44-60 (4-string) and 55-60 (5-string) in '09.

1998-2010		$1,900	$2,400

Larrivee

1968-present. Founded by Jean Larrivee in Toronto and currently located in Vancouver, British Columbia, Larrivee has offered several acoustic and a few electric basses over the years.

Leach

1980-present. Luthier Harvey Leach builds his premium grade, custom, acoustic basses in Cedar Ridge, California. He also builds guitars.

Lehtela

1993-present. Professional and premium grade, custom/production, solidbody basses built by luthier Ari Lehtela in Charlotte, North Carolina. He also builds guitars.

Linc Luthier

Professional and premium grade, custom/production, electric, acoustic and upright basses built by luther Linc Luthier in Upland, California. He also builds guitars and double-necks.

Lipe Guitars USA

1983-1989, 2000-present. Luthier Michael Lipe builds his custom, professional grade, basses in Sunvalley, California. He also builds guitars.

Lotus

Late-1970-2004. Electric basses imported originally by Midco International, and mose recently by Musicorp. They also made guitars, banjos and mandolins.

Lowrider Basses

2003-present. Professional grade, production/custom, solidbody basses made in Las Vegas, Nevada by Ed Roman.

LSR Headless Instruments

1988-present. Professional grade, production/custom, solidbody headless basses made in Las Vegas, Nevada by Ed Roman. They also make guitars.

LTD

1995-present. Intermediate grade, production, Korean-made solidbody basses offered by ESP. They also offer guitars.

Luna Guitars

2005-present. Budget to professional grade, production, acoustic and electric basses imported from Japan, Korea and China by Yvonne de Villiers in Tampa, Florida. She also imports guitars, amps and ukes.

Lyle

Ca. 1969-1980. Japanese guitars and basses imported by distributor L.D. Heater in Portland, Oregon.

Lyon by Washburn

1990s-present. Budget grade, production, basses sold by mass merchandisers such as Target. They also offer guitars.

Lyric

1996-present. Luthier John Southern builds his professional and premium grade, custom, basses in Tulsa, Oklahoma. He also builds guitars.

Magnatone

Ca. 1937-1971. Founded as Dickerson Brothers, known as Magna Electronics from '47. Produced instruments under own brand and for many others.

Hurricane X-10 Bass

1965-1966. Offset double cut solidbody, 1 single-coil, 4-on-a-side tuners, Magnatone logo on guard and headstock, Hurricane logo on headstock.

1965-1966		$700	$850

MODEL YEAR	FEATURES	EXC. COND. LOW	HIGH

Mako

1985-1989. Line of solidbody basses from Kaman (Ovation, Hamer). They also offered guitars and amps.

Electric Solidbody Bass

1985-1989	Student bass	$75	$225

Mal n' Sal

See listing for Alternative Guitar and Amplifier Company.

Malinoski

1986-present. Production/custom, professional and premium grade, solidbody electric basses built in Hyattsville, Maryland by luthier Peter Malinoski. He also builds guitars.

MalinoskiArt Guitars

1986-present. Professional and premium grade, production/custom, solidbody electric basses built by luthier Peter Malinoski in Hyattsville, Maryland. He also builds guitars.

Manne

1987-present. Luthier Andrea Ballarin builds his professional and premium grade, production/custom, semi-acoustic and electric basses in Italy. He also builds guitars.

Marco Polo

1960- ca.1964. One of the first inexpensive Japanese brands to be imported into the U.S., they also offered guitars.

Solidbody Bass

1960s	Various models	$75	$175

Mario Martin Guiars

2011-present. Professional grade, production/custom, solidbody basses built by Mario Martin in Murfreesboro, Tennessee. He also builds guitars. From 2006 to '11, he built under the Guitar Mill brand name.

Marleaux

1990-present. Luthier Gerald Marleaux builds his custom, premium grade, electric basses in Clausthal-Zellerfeld, Germany.

Marling

Ca. 1975. Budget line instruments marketed by EKO of Recanati, Italy; probably made by them, although possibly imported. They also had guitars.

Electric Solidbody Bass

Models include the E.495 (copy of LP), E.485 (copy of Tele), and the E.465 (Manta-style).

1970s		$125	$175

Martin

1833-present. Professional grade, production, acoustic basses made in the U.S. In 1978, Martin re-entered the electric market and introduced their solidbody EB-18 and EB-28 Basses. In the '80s they offered Stinger brand electric basses. By the late '80s, they started offering acoustic basses.

00C-16GTAE Bass

2006-present. Mahogany back and sides, Fishman electronics.

2006-2010		$800	$1,000

B-1/B-1E Acoustic Bass

2002-2006. Mahogany back and sides, E has Fishman electronics.

2002-2006		$900	$1,100

B-40 Acoustic Bass

1989-1996. Jumbo-size, spruce top and Indian rosewood back and sides, mahogany neck, ebony 'board, built-in pickup and volume and tone controls. The B-40B had a pickup.

1989-1996	B-40B	$1,300	$1,600
1989-1996	Without pickup	$1,100	$1,400

B-65 Acoustic Bass

1989-1993. Jumbo-size, spruce top, maple back and sides, mahogany neck, ebony 'board with 23 frets, built-in pickup and volume and tone controls, natural.

1989-1993		$1,200	$1,500

BC-15E Acoustic Bass

1999-2006. Single-cut, all mahogany, on-board electronics.

1999-2006		$750	$950

EB-18 Bass

1979-1982. Electric solidbody, neck-thru, 1 pickup, natural.

1979-1982		$900	$1,100

EB-28 Bass

1980-1982. Electric solidbody.

1980-1982		$1,000	$1,200

SBL-10 Bass

1980s. Stinger brand solidbody, maple neck, 1 split and 1 bar pickup.

1980s		$175	$225

Marvel

1950s-mid-1960s. Brand used for budget guitars and basses marketed by Peter Sorkin Company in New York, New York.

Electric Solidbody Bass

1950s	Various models	$150	$300

Max B

2000-present. Professional grade, production/custom, electric basses built by luthier Sebastien Sulser in Kirby, Vermont. He also builds guitars.

Messenger

1967-1968. Built by Musicraft, Inc., Messengers featured a neck-thru metal alloy neck. They also made guitars.

Bass

1967-1968. Metal alloy neck. Messenger mainly made guitars - they offered a bass, but it is unlikely many were built.

1967-1968		$2,000	$2,500

Martin 00C-16GTAE

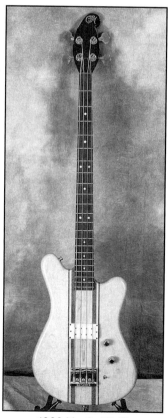

1982 Martin EB-18

Mollerup Orca

1966 Mosrite Ventures

MODEL YEAR	FEATURES	EXC. COND. LOW	HIGH

Messenger Upright

Made by Knutson Luthiery, see that listing.

Michael Kelly

2000-present. Intermediate grade, production, acoustic/electric basses imported by Elite Music Brands of Clearwater, Florida. They also offer mandolins and guitars.

Michael Tuttle

2003-present. Luthier Michael Tuttle builds his professional and premium grade, custom, solid and hollow body basses in Saugus, California. He also builds guitars.

Microfrets

1967-1975, 2004-2005. Professional grade, production, electric basses built in Myersville, Maryland. They also built guitars.

Husky Bass
1971-1974/75. Double-cut, 2 pickups, 2-on-a-side tuners.

1971-1975		$700	$900

Rendezvous Bass
1970. One pickup, orange sunburst.

1970		$775	$1,025

Signature Bass
1969-1975. Double-cut, 2 pickups, 2-on-a-side tuners.

1969-1975		$975	$1,275

Stage II Bass
1969-1975. Double-cut, 2 pickups, 2-on-a-side tuners.

1969-1975		$975	$1,275

Thundermaster Bass

1969		$975	$1,275

Mike Lull Custom Guitars

1995-present. Professional and premium grade, production/custom, basses built by luthier Mike Lull in Bellevue, Washington. He also builds guitars.

Mirabella

1997-present. Professional and premium grade, custom, basses built by luthier Cristian Mirabella in Babylon, New York. He also builds guitars, mandolins and ukes.

Mitre

1983-1985. Bolt-neck solidbody basses made in Aldenville (or East Longmeadow), Massachusetts. They also built guitars.

MJ Guitar Engineering

1993-present. Luthier Mark Johnson builds his professional grade, production/custom, chambered basses in Rohnert Park, California. He also builds guitars.

Modulus

1978-present. Founded by aerospace engineer Geoff Gould, Modulus currently offers professional and premium grade, production/custom, solidbody basses built in California. They also build guitars.

Bassstar SP-24 Active Bass
1981-ca. 1990. EMG J pickups, active bass and treble circuits.

1980s		$1,300	$1,600

Flea 4/Flea Signature Bass
1997-2003. Offset double-cut alder solidbody, also offered as 5-string.

1997-2003		$1,400	$1,700

Genesis Series Bass
1997-1998, 2003-present. Offset double-cut, 2 pickups, 4- or 5-string.

2003-2010	Various models	$1,000	$1,250

Quantum-4 Series Bass
1982-present. Offset double-cut, 2 pickups, 35" scale.

1982-2010		$1,400	$1,700

Quantum-5 Series Bass
1982-present. 5-String version.

1982-2010		$1,500	$1,800

Quantum-6 Series Bass
1982-present. 6-string version.

1982-2010		$1,600	$1,900

Vintage V Series Bass

2002	VJ-4	$1,500	$1,800

Mollerup Basses

1984-present. Luthier Laurence Mollerup builds his professional grade, custom/production, electric basses and electric double basses in Vancouver, British Columbia. He has also built guitars.

Monroe Guitars

2004-present. Professional grade, custom, solidbody electric basses built by Matt Handley in State Center, Iowa. He also builds guitars.

Moon (Japan)

1979-present. Professional grade, production/custom, basses made in Japan. They also build guitars.

Moonstone

1972-present. Luthier Steve Helgeson builds his premium grade, production/custom, acoustic and electric basses in Eureka, California. He also builds guitars.

Eclipse Deluxe Bass
1980-1984. Double-cut solidbody.

1980-1984		$1,600	$1,950

Exploder Bass
1980-1983. Figured wood body, Explorer-style neck-thru-body.

1980-1983		$1,600	$1,950

Vulcan Bass
1982-1984. Solidbody, flat top (Vulcan) or carved top (Vulcan II), maple body, gold hardware.

1982-1984		$1,600	$1,950

BASSES

MODEL YEAR	FEATURES	EXC. COND. LOW	HIGH

Morales

Ca.1967-1968. Guitars and basses made in Japan by Zen-On and not heavily imported into the U.S.

Electric Solidbody Bass

| 1967-1968 | Various models | $125 | $200 |

Morgan Monroe

1999-present. Intermediate grade, production, acoustic/electric basses made in Korea and distributed by SHS International of Indianapolis, Indiana. They also offer guitars, mandolins, banjos, and fiddles.

Mosrite

Semie Moseley's Mosrite offered various bass models throughout the many versions of the Mosrite company.

Brut Bass

Late-1960s. Assymetrical body with small cutaway on upper treble bout.

| 1960s | | $900 | $1,100 |

Celebrity Bass

1965-1969. ES-335-style semi-thick double-cut body with f-holes, 2 pickups.

1965-1966	Custom color	$1,000	$1,200
1965-1967	Sunburst	$900	$1,100
1968	Red	$800	$1,000
1969	Red	$750	$925
1969	Sunburst	$800	$1,000

Combo Bass

1966-1968. Hollowbody, 2 pickups.

| 1966-1968 | | $1,500 | $1,750 |

Joe Maphis Bass

1966-1969. Ventures-style body, hollow without f-holes, 2 pickups, natural.

| 1966-1969 | | $1,800 | $2,200 |

Ventures Bass

1965-1972. Two pickups.

1965	Various colors	$2,100	$2,600
1966	Various colors	$1,900	$2,400
1967-1968	Various colors	$1,700	$2,100
1969	Various colors	$1,600	$2,000
1970-1972	Various colors	$1,500	$1,900

V-II Bass

1973-1974. Ventures-style, 2 humbuckers, sunburst.

| 1973-1974 | | $1,800 | $2,200 |

Mouradian

1983-present. Professional and premium grade, production/custom, electric basses, built in Winchester, Massachusetts by luthiers Jim and Jon Mouradian. They also build guitars.

MTD

1994-present. Intermediate, professional, and premium grade, production/custom, electric basses built by luthier Michael Tobias (who founded Tobias Basses in '77) in Kingston, New York. Since '00, he also imports basses built in Korea to his specifications.

MODEL YEAR	FEATURES	EXC. COND. LOW	HIGH

Murph

1965-1967. Mid-level electric solidbody basses built by Pat Murphy in San Fernado, California. Murph logo on headstock. They also offered guitars and amps.

Solidbody Bass

| 1965-1967 | | $675 | $825 |

Music Man

1972-present. Intermediate and professional grade, production, electric basses. They also build guitars.

Bongo Bass

2003-present. Double cut solidbody, squared-off horns, 2 pickups, 4-, 5-, and 6-string.

| 2003-2010 | Bongo 4 | $750 | $900 |
| 2003-2010 | Bongo 5 | $800 | $950 |

Cutlass I/Cutlass II Bass

1982-1987. Ash body, graphite neck, string-thru-body.

1982-1984	CLF era Cutlass I	$1,500	$1,800
1982-1984	CLF era Cutlass II	$1,700	$2,000
1984-1987	Ernie Ball era Cutlass I	$1,200	$1,500
1984-1987	Ernie Ball era Cutlass II	$1,400	$1,700

S.U.B. Series Bass

2003-2007. Offset double-cut, 4- or 5-string, 1 humbucker.

| 2003-2007 | IV Bass | $475 | $575 |
| 2003-2007 | V Bass | $525 | $650 |

Sabre Bass

1978-ca.1991. Double-cut solidbody bass, 3-and-1 tuning keys, 2 humbucking pickups, on-board preamp, natural.

1978-1979	CLF era	$1,300	$1,600
1980-1984	CLF era	$1,100	$1,400
1984-1991	Ernie Ball era	$900	$1,100

Sterling Bass

1990-present. Rosewood, 1 pickup, EQ, pearl blue. In '05, additional pickup options available.

| 1990-2010 | | $750 | $950 |

StingRay Bass

1976-present. Offset double-cut solidbody, 1 pickup, 3-and-1 tuners, string-thru until '80, various colors. 5-string version first offered in '87. In '05, additional pickup options available.

1976-1979	CLF era	$2,000	$2,500
1980-1984	CLF era	$1,700	$2,100
1984-1989	Ernie Ball era	$1,100	$1,400
1990-2009		$850	$1,000
1990-2009	5-string	$900	$1,050

StingRay 20th Anniversary Bass

1992. 1400 made, flamed maple body.

| 1992 | | $1,600 | $1,850 |

StingRay Classic Bass

2010-present. Ash body, birds-eye or flame maple neck, 4- or 5-string.

| 2010 | | $1,200 | $1,450 |

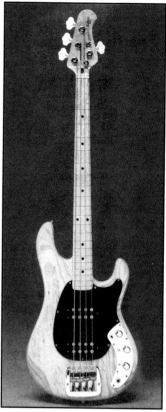

1979 Music Man Sabre Bass

Music Man StingRay

Musicvox Space Cadet

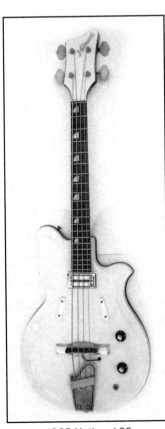

1965 National 85

MODEL YEAR	FEATURES	EXC. COND. LOW	HIGH

Musicvox

1996-2001, 2011-present. Intermediate grade, production, Korean-made retro-vibe guitars and basses from Matt Eichen of Cherry Hill, New Jersey.

Nady

1976-present. Wireless sound company Nady Systems offered guitars and basses with built-in wireless systems for 1985-'87. The neck-thru bass was made by Fernandes in Japan and was only available for about a year.

NashGuitars

2001-present. Luthier Bill Nash builds his professional grade, production/custom, solidbody basses in Olympia, Washington. He also builds guitars.

National

Ca. 1927-present. National offered electric basses in the '60s when Valco owned the brand.

Beatle (Violin) Bass
1970s. Strum & Drum era import, National script logo on headstock, 2 pickups, shaded brown finish.

1970		$400	$475

EG 700V-2HB German Style Bass
1970s. Strum & Drum era import, Beatle-style violin body, 2 humbuckers, bolt neck.

1970s		$425	$500

N-850 Bass
1967-1968. Semi-hollow double-cut, art deco f-holes, 2 pickups, block markers, bout control knobs, sunburst.

1967-1968		$600	$700

Val-Pro 85 Bass
1961-1962. Res-O-Glas body shaped like the U.S. map, 2 pickups, snow white, renamed National 85 in '63.

1961-1962		$1,000	$1,200

National Reso-Phonic

1988-present. Professional grade, production/custom, acoustic and acoustic/electric resonator basses built in San Luis Obispo, California. They also build guitars, mandolins and ukuleles.

Navarro Custom

1986-present. Luthier Mike Navarro builds his production/custom, professional and premium grade, electric basses in San Juan, Puerto Rico. He also builds guitars.

New York Bass Works

1989-present. Luthier David Segal builds his professional and premium grade, production/custom, electric basses in New York.

Noble

Ca. 1950-ca. 1969. Guitars and basses distributed by Don Noble and Company of Chicago. Made by other companies. They also offered amps.

Nordy (Nordstrand Guitars)

2003-present. Luthier Carey Nordstrand builds his production/custom, professional and premium grade, electric basses in Yucaipa, California. He also builds guitars.

Norma

Ca.1965-1970. Guitars and basses imported from Japan by Chicago's Strum and Drum.

Electric Solidbody Bass

1960s	Various models	$125	$250

Normandy Guitars

2008-present. Production, professional grade, aluminum archtop basses built in Salem, Oregon by Jim Normandy. He also builds guitars.

Northworthy

1987-present. Professional and premium grade, production/custom, acoustic and electric basses built by luthier Alan Marshall in Ashbourne, Derbyshire, England. He also builds guitars and mandolins.

Novax

1989-present. Luthier Ralph Novak builds his fanned-fret professional grade, production/custom, solidbody basses in San Leandro, California. He also builds guitars.

Noyce

1974-present. Production/custom, professional and premium grade, acoustic and electric basses, and semi-acoustic double bass built by luthier Ian Noyce in Ballarat, Victoria, Australia. He also builds guitars.

O'Hagan

1979-1983. Designed by Jerol O'Hagan in St. Louis Park, Minnesota. He also offered guitars.

Electric Solidbody Bass
1979-1983. Models include the Shark Bass, Night-Watch Bass, NightWatch Regular Bass, and the Twenty Two Bass.

1979-1983		$550	$700

Old Kraftsman

1930s-1960s. Brand used by the Spiegel Company. Guitars and basses made by other American manufacturers.

Electric Solidbody Bass

1950s	Various models	$300	$400

OLP (Officially Licensed Product)

2001-2009. Intermediate grade, production, imported basses based on models officially licensed from the original manufacturer. OLP logo on headstock. They also offered guitars.

BASSES

MODEL YEAR	FEATURES	EXC. COND. LOW	HIGH

Oncor Sound

1980-ca. 1981. This Salt Lake City-based company made both a guitar and a bass synthesizer.

Original Senn

2004-present. Production/custom, professional and premium grade, solidbody electric basses built in Nashville, Tennessee by luthier Jeff Senn. He also builds guitars.

Oscar Schmidt

1879-1938, 1979-present. Budget and intermediate grade, production, acoustic basses distributed by U.S. Music Corp. (Washburn, Randall, etc.). They also offer guitars, mandolins, banjos, ukuleles and the famous Oscar Schmidt autoharp.

Oskar Graf Guitars

1970-present. Luthier Oskar Graf builds his premium and presentation grade, custom, basses in Clarendon, Ontario. He also builds guitars and lutes.

Ovation

1966-present. Intermediate and professional grade, production, acoustic/electric basses. Ovation offered electric solidbody basses early on and added acoustic basses in the '90s. They also offer guitars and mandolins.

Celebrity Series Bass

1990s-2000s. Deep bowl back, cutaway, acoustic/electric.

1990-2000s		$300	$350

Magnum Series Bass

1974-1980. Magnum I is odd-shaped mahogany solidbody, 2 pickups, mono/stereo, mute, sunburst, red or natural. Magnum II is with battery-powered preamp and 3-band EQ. Magnum III and IV had a new offset double-cut body.

1974-1978	Magnum I	$900	$1,100
1974-1978	Magnum II	$1,000	$1,200
1978-1980	Magnum III	$900	$1,100
1978-1980	Magnum IV	$1,000	$1,200

Typhoon II/Typhoon III Bass

1968-1971. Ovation necks, but bodies and hardware were German imports. Semi-hollowbody, 2 pickups, red or sunburst. Typhoon II is 335-style and III is fretless.

1968-1971	Typhoon II	$950	$1,150
1968-1971	Typhoon III	$1,050	$1,250

Ultra Bass

1984. Korean solidbodies and necks assembled in U.S., offset double-cut with 1 pickup.

1984		$325	$400

Overture Guitars

2008-present. Professional to presentation grade, custom/production, solidbody basses built in Morton, Illinois by luthier Justin Hoffman. He also builds guitars.

PANaramic

1961-1963. Guitars and basses made in Italy by the Crucianelli accordion company and imported by PANaramic accordion. They also offered amps made by Magnatone.

Electric Bass

1961-1963. Double-cut solidbody or hollowbody, 2 pickups, dot markers, sunburst.

1961-1963	Hollowbody	$425	$525
1961-1963	Solidbody	$425	$525

Parker

1992-present. Premium grade, production/custom, solidbody electric basses. They also build guitars.

Fly Bass

2002-present. Offered in 4- and 5-string models.

2002-2010		$1,100	$1,350

Patrick Eggle Guitars

1991-present. Solidbody electric basses built in Birmingham, England. They also build guitars.

Paul Reed Smith

1985-present. PRS added basses in '86, but by '92 had dropped the models. In 2000 PRS started again offering professional and premium grade, production, solidbody electric basses. Bird inlays can add $100 or more to the values of PRS basses listed here.

Bass-4

1986-1992, 2007. Set neck, 3 single-coil pickups, hum-cancelling coil, active circuitry, 22-fret Brazilian rosewood 'board. Reintroduced (OEB Series) in 2000s.

1986-1987		$2,700	$3,300
1988-1992		$1,400	$1,700
2007		$1,400	$1,700

Bass-5

1986-1992. Five-string, set-neck, rosewood 'board, 3 single-coil pickups, active electronics. Options include custom colors, bird inlays, fretless 'board.

1986-1987		$2,800	$3,400
1988-1992		$1,500	$1,800

CE Bass-4

1986-1991. Solidbody, maple bolt neck, alder body, rosewood 'board, 4-string.

1986-1987		$1,300	$1,600
1988-1991		$1,000	$1,250

CE Bass-5

1986-1991. Five-string solidbody, maple bolt neck, alder body, rosewood 'board.

1986-1987		$1,400	$1,700
1988-1991		$1,100	$1,350

Curly Bass-4

1986-1992. Double-cut solidbody, curly maple top, set maple neck, Brazilian rosewood 'board (ebony on fretless), 3 single-coil and 1 hum-cancelling pickups, various grades of maple tops, moon inlays.

1986-1987		$2,300	$2,700
1988-1992		$2,000	$2,400

Parker Mojo

PRS Bass-4

BASSES

Peavey Millenium

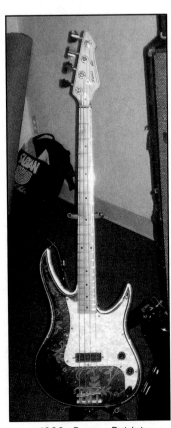

1980s Peavey Patriot

Sean Sweeney

MODEL YEAR	FEATURES	EXC. COND. LOW	HIGH

Curly Bass-5
1986-1992. Five-string version of Curly Bass-4.

| 1986-1987 | | $2,400 | $2,800 |
| 1988-1992 | | $2,100 | $2,500 |

Electric Bass
2000-2007. Bolt neck 4-string, offered in regular and maple top versions.

| 2000-2007 | Maple | $1,300 | $1,650 |
| 2000-2007 | Plain | $1,150 | $1,450 |

Peavey

1965-present. Intermediate and professional grade, production/custom, electric basses. They also build guitars and amps. Hartley Peavey's first products were guitar amps and he added guitars and basses to the mix in '78.

Axcelerator Bass
1994-1998. Offset double-cut, long thin horns, 2 humbuckers, stacked control knobs, bolt neck, dot markers.

| 1994-1998 | | $325 | $400 |

Cirrus Series Bass
1998-present. Offset double-cut, active electronics, in 4-, 5-, 6-string, and custom shop versions.

1998-2009	Cirrus 5	$700	$750
1998-2010	Cirrus 4	$675	$725
1998-2010	Cirrus 6	$725	$775

Dyna-Bass
1987-1993. Double-cut solidbody, active electronics, 3-band EQ, rosewood 'board, opaque finish.

| 1987-1993 | | $250 | $300 |

Dyna-Bass Limited
1987-1990. Neck-thru-body, ebony 'board, flamed maple neck/body construction, purple heart strips, mother-of-pearl inlays.

| 1987-1990 | | $450 | $550 |

Forum Bass
1994-1995. Double-cut solidbody, rosewood 'board, dot inlays, 2 humbuckers.

| 1994-1995 | | $250 | $300 |

Forum Plus Bass
1994. Forum Bass with added active electronics.

| 1994 | | $275 | $325 |

Foundation Bass
1984-2002. Double-cut solidbody, 2 pickups, maple neck.

| 1984-2002 | | $225 | $275 |

Foundation S Active Bass
1987-1991. Similar to Foundation S Bass with added active circuitry, provides low-impedance output, 2 pickups.

| 1987-1991 | | $250 | $300 |

Foundation S Bass
1986-1991. Two split-coil pickups, maple body, rosewood 'board, black hardware, black painted headstock.

| 1986-1991 | | $225 | $275 |

Fury Bass
1983-1999. Double-cut solidbody, rosewood 'board, 1 split-coil humbucker.

| 1983-1999 | | $175 | $200 |

MODEL YEAR	FEATURES	EXC. COND. LOW	HIGH

Fury Custom Bass
1986-1993. Fury Bass with black hardware and narrow neck.

| 1986-1993 | | $250 | $300 |

Fury VI Bass
2001-2003. 6-string, active electronics, quilt top.

| 2001-2003 | | $300 | $375 |

G-Bass V
1999-2002. Offset double-cut 5-string, humbucker, 3-band EQ.

| 1999-2002 | | $750 | $850 |

Grind Series Bass
2001-present. Offset double-cut, neck-thru, long bass horn, 2 pickups, 4-, 5-, or 6-string.

| 2001-2010 | Grind 4 | $200 | $250 |
| 2001-2010 | Grind 5, Grind 6 | $225 | $275 |

Milestone Series Bass
1994-present. Import offset double cut, Milestone I ('94) replaced by 1 P-style pickup II ('95-'01), split humbucker IV ('99-'04); 2 single-coil III ('99-present) now just called Milestone.

1994	Milestone I	$75	$100
1995-2001	Milestone II	$75	$100
1999-2004	Milestone IV	$100	$150
1999-2010	Milestone III, Milestone	$100	$150

Millenium Series Bass
2001-present. Offset double-cut, agathis bodies, maple tops, in 4- or 5-string.

| 2001-2010 | | $200 | $250 |

Patriot Bass
1984-1988. General J-Bass styling with larger thinner horns, 1 single-coil, maple neck.

| 1984-1988 | | $125 | $150 |

Patriot Custom Bass
1986-1988. Patriot with rosewood neck, matching headstock.

| 1986-1988 | | $175 | $250 |

RJ-IV Bass
1990-1993. Randy Jackson Signature model, neck-thru-body, 2 split-coil active pickups, ebony 'board, mother-of-pearl position markers.

| 1990-1993 | | $325 | $400 |

Rudy Sarzo Signature Bass
1989-1993. Double-cut solidbody, active EQ, ebony 'board, 2 pickups.

| 1989-1993 | | $500 | $600 |

T-20FL Bass
1983. Fretless double-cut solidbody, 1 pickup, also available as the fretted T-20 ('82-'83).

| 1983 | | $200 | $250 |

T-40/T-40FL Bass
1978-1987. Double-cut solidbody, 2 pickups. T-40FL is fretless.

| 1978-1987 | T-40 | $300 | $350 |
| 1978-1987 | T-40FL | $300 | $350 |

T-45 Bass
1982-1986. T-40 with 1 humbucking pickup, and a mid-frequency rolloff knob.

| 1982-1986 | | $300 | $350 |

MODEL YEAR	FEATURES	EXC. COND. LOW	HIGH
TL Series Bass			

1988-1998. Neck-thru-body, gold hardware, active humbuckers, EQ, flamed maple neck and body, 5-string (TL-Five) or 6 (TL-Six).

MODEL YEAR	FEATURES	EXC. COND. LOW	HIGH
1988-1998	TL-Five	$500	$600
1989-1998	TL-Six	$550	$650

Pedulla

1975-present. Professional and premium grade, production/custom, electric basses made in Rockland, Massachusetts. Founded by Michael Pedulla, Pedulla offers various upscale options which affect valuation so each instrument should be evaluated on a case-by-case basis. Unless specifically noted, the following listings have standard to mid-level features. High-end options are specifically noted; if not, these options will have a relatively higher value than those shown here.

Buzz-4/Buzz-5 Bass

1980-2008. Double-cut neck-thru solidbody, fretless, long-scale, maple neck and body wings, 2 pickups, preamp, some with other active electronics, various colors, 4-, 5-, 6-, 8-string versions.

1980-1999		$1,100	$1,450

Interceptor Bass

1980s. Double-cut, maple/walnut laminated neck-thru.

1980s		$925	$1,200

MVP Series Bass

1984-present. Fretted version of Buzz Bass, standard or flame top, 4-, 5-, 6-, 8-string versions, MVP II is bolt-on neck version.

1980s	MVP-6	$1,300	$1,575
1984-1990s	MVP-4 flame top	$1,200	$1,475
1984-1990s	MVP-4 standard top	$1,100	$1,375
1984-1990s	MVP-5	$1,200	$1,475
1990s	MVP II	$800	$1,025

Orsini Wurlitzer 4-String Bass

Mid-1970s. Body style similar to late-'50s Gibson double-cut slab body SG Special, neck-thru, 2 pickups, natural. Sold by Boston's Wurlitzer music store chain.

1970s		$1,250	$1,625

Quilt Limited Bass

Neck-thru-body with curly maple centerstrip, quilted maple body wings, 2 Bartolini pickups, available in fretted or fretless 4- and 5-string models.

1987		$1,250	$1,550

Rapture Series Bass

1995-present. Solidbody with extra long thin bass horn and extra short treble horn, 4- or 5-string, various colors.

1995-2010	Rapture 4	$1,100	$1,375
1995-2010	Rapture 5	$1,200	$1,475

Series II Bass

1987-1992. Bolt neck, rosewood 'board, mother-of-pearl dot inlays, Bartolini pickups.

1987-1992		$775	$950

Thunderbass Series Bass

1993-present. Solidbody with extra long thin bass horn and extra short treble horn, 4-, 5- or 6-string, standard features or triple A top.

1993-1999	4, AAA top	$1,400	$1,775
1993-1999	4, Standard	$1,150	$1,450
1993-1999	5, AAA top	$1,500	$1,875
1993-1999	5, Standard	$1,250	$1,550
1993-1999	6, AAA top	$1,600	$1,975
1993-1999	6, Standard	$1,350	$1,650
2000-2010	4, AAA top	$1,400	$1,775
2000-2010	5, AAA top	$1,500	$1,875
2000-2010	6, AAA top	$1,600	$1,975

Penco

Ca. 1974-1978. Generally high quality Japanese-made copies of classic American bass guitars. They also made guitars, mandolins and banjos.

Electric Bass

1974-1978	Various models	$150	$250

Pensa (Pensa-Suhr)

1982-present. Premium grade, production/custom, solidbody basses built in the U.S. They also build guitars.

Phantom Guitar Works

1992-present. Intermediate grade, production/custom, solid and hollowbody basses assembled in Clatskanie, Oregon. They also build guitars and the MandoGuitar.

Pieper

2005-present. Premium grade, production/custom, solidbody basses with interchangable necks built by luthier Robert Pieper in New Haven, Connecticut. He also builds guitars.

Premier

Ca.1938-ca.1975, 1990s-2010. Originally American-made instruments, but by the '60s imported parts were being used. 1990s instruments were Asian imports.

Bantam Bass

1950-1970. Small body, single-cut short-scale archtop electric, torch headstock inlay, sparkle 'guard, sunburst.

1950-1970		$475	$600

Electric Solidbody Bass

1960s	Various models	$325	$400

Prestige

Professional grade, production, acoustic and electric basses from Vancouver, British Columbia. They also offer guitars.

Rambler

2003-present. Custom, professional grade, electric travel basses built by luthier Russ Strobel in Boca Raton, Florida. He also builds guitars and offers a production, intermediate grade, travel bass built in Korea.

Rarebird Guitars

1978-present. Luthier Bruce Clay builds his professional grade, production/custom, basses originally in Arvada, Colorado, and currently in Woodstock, Georgia. He also builds guitars.

1991 Peavey RJ-IV

Pedulla Buzz 4

BASSES

1980 Rick Turner Model 1

1978 Rickenbacker 4001
(Bob "Willard" Henke)

Rat Fink

2002-present. Lace Music Products offered these intermediate grade, production, basses and guitars, featuring the artwork of Ed Big Daddy Roth until '05. They still offer amps.

Regal

Ca. 1884-1966, 1987-present. Early marketer and manufacturer of instruments, names has been revived on a line of intermediate grade, production, acoustic wood body resonator basses from Saga. They also build guitars.

Renaissance

1978-1980. Plexiglass solidbody electric guitars and basses made in Malvern, Pennsylvania.

Plexiglas Bass

1978-1980. Plexiglas bodies and active electronics, models include the DPB bass (double-cut, 1 pickup, '78-'79), SPB (single-cut, 2 pickups, '78-'79), T-100B (Bich-style, 1 pickup, '80), S-100B (double-cut, 1 pickup, '80), and the S-200B (double-cut, 2 pickups, '80).

1978-1980	$525	$650

Renaissance Guitars

1994-present. Professional grade, custom, acoustic and solidbody basses built by luthier Rick Turner in Santa Cruz, California. He also builds guitars and ukuleles.

Reverend

1996-present. Reverend built electric basses in Warren, Michigan, from '98 to '04. They continue to build guitars.

Rice Custom Guitars

1998-present. Professional and premium grade, solidbody, semi-hollow and hollowbody electric basses built by father and son luthiers, Richard and Christopher Rice in Arlington Heights, Illinois. They also build guitars.

Rick Turner

1979-1981, 1990-present. Rick Turner has a long career as a luthier, electronics designer and innovator. He also makes the Renaissance line of guitars in his shop in Santa Cruz, California. Turner estimates that during the three years his company was in business the first time around, only 25 to 30 basses were built, approximately half of which were shipped to Japan.

Rickenbacker

1931-present. Professional grade, production/custom, electric basses. They also build guitars. Rickenbacker introduced their first electric bass in '57 and has always been a strong player in the bass market.

Electric Upright Bass

1936. Cast aluminum neck and body, horseshoe pickup, extension pole.

1936	$4,000	$5,000

Model 1999 (Rose-Morris) Bass

1964-1967. Export made for English distributor Rose-Morris of London, built along the lines of the U.S. Model 4000 Bass but with small differences that are considered important in the vintage guitar market.

1964-1967	$4,300	$5,200

Model 2030 Hamburg Bass

1984-1997. Rounded double-cut, 2 pickups, active electronics.

1984-1989	$700	$900
1990-1997	$700	$900

Model 2030GF (Glenn Frey) Bass

1992-1995. Limited Edition, double-cut, 2 humbuckers, Jetglo finish.

1992-1995	$1,300	$1,600

Model 2050 El Dorado Bass

1984-1992. Gold hardware, 2 pickups, active.

1984-1992	$900	$1,100

Model 2060 El Dorado Bass

1992-1997. Gold hardware, 2 pickups, active, double-bound body.

1992-1997	$1,000	$1,250

Model 3000 Bass

1975-1984. Rounded double-cut, 30" scale, 1 pickup, brown sunburst.

1975-1984	$1,100	$1,350

Model 3001 Bass

1975-1984. Same as Model 3000 but with longer 33-1/2" scale, Wine Red.

1975-1984	$1,100	$1,350

Model 3261 (Rose-Morris Slim-Line) Bass

1967. Export model made for English distributor Rose-Morris, built along the lines of a U.S. equivalent Model 4005 Bass.

1967	$5,500	$6,500

Model 4000 Bass

1958-1985. Cresting wave body and headstock, 1 horseshoe pickup (changed to regular pickup in '64), neck-thru-body.

1958-1959	Plank style	$9,000	$11,000
1960	Plank style	$8,000	$10,000
1961-1962	Plank style	$6,000	$7,500
1963-1965		$6,000	$7,500
1966-1969		$4,000	$5,000
1970-1972		$2,500	$3,000
1973-1974		$2,000	$2,500
1975-1979		$2,000	$2,500
1980-1985		$1,500	$1,800

Model 4001 Bass

1961-1965, 1968-1986. Fancy version of 4000, 1 horseshoe magnet pickup (changed to regular pickup in '64) and 1 bar magnet pickup, triangle inlays, bound neck.

1961-1965	Fireglo	$6,400	$7,700
1963-1965	Mapleglo	$6,900	$8,300
1967-1969	Various colors	$4,300	$5,200
1970-1972	Various colors	$2,800	$3,500
1973-1979	Various colors	$2,300	$2,800
1980-1986	Various colors	$1,900	$2,300

MODEL YEAR	FEATURES	EXC. COND. LOW	HIGH

Model 4001 C64S Bass
2001-present. Recreation of Paul McCartney's 4001 featuring changes he made like a reshaped body and zero-fret 'board.

2001-2010		$1,800	$2,200

Model 4001 CS Bass
1991-1997. Chris Squire signature model.

1991-1997	With certificate	$2,800	$3,500

Model 4001 FL Bass
1968-1986. Fretless version of 4001 Bass, special order in '60s, various colors.

1968-1986		$2,000	$4,300

Model 4001 V63 Bass
1984-2000. Vintage '63 reissue of Model 4001S, horseshoe-magnet pickup, Mapleglo.

1984-2000		$2,200	$2,700

Model 4001S Bass
1964-1985. Same as Model 4000, but with 2 pickups, export model.

1980-1985		$1,500	$1,800

Model 4002 Bass
1967-1985. Cresting wave body and headstock, 2 humbuckers, black 'guard, checkerboard binding.

1980-1985		$3,200	$4,100

Model 4003 Bass
1979-present. Similar to Model 4001, split 'guard, deluxe features.

1979-1989		$1,500	$1,900
1990-1999		$1,500	$1,900
2000-2010		$1,400	$1,700

Model 4003 FL Bass
1979-present. Fretless version.

1979-2010		$1,400	$1,700

Model 4003S Bass
1986-2003. Standard feature version of 4003, 4 strings.

1986-1999		$1,500	$1,900
2000-2003		$1,400	$1,700

Model 4003S Redneck Bass
Late 1980s. Red body, 'board and headstock, black hardware.

1980s		$2,700	$3,200

Model 4003S Tuxedo Bass
1987. White body with black 'guard and hardware. 100 made.

1987		$2,700	$3,200

Model 4003S/5 Bass
1986-2003. 5-string 4003S.

1986-1999		$1,600	$2,000
2000-2003		$1,500	$1,900

Model 4003S/8 Bass
1986-2003. 8-string 4003S.

1986-1999		$3,000	$3,600
2000-2003		$2,900	$3,400

Model 4003S/SPC Blackstar Bass
1989. Black version, black finish, 'board, knobs, and hardware. Also offered as 5-string.

1989		$2,700	$3,200

Model 4004C Cheyenne/Cheyenne II Bass
1993-present. Cresting wave, maple neck-thru-body with walnut body and head wings, gold hardware, dot inlay. Replaced by maple top 4004Cii Cheyenne II in '00.

1993-2010		$1,300	$1,600

Model 4005 Bass
1965-1984. New style double-cut semi-hollowbody, 2 pickups, R tailpiece, cresting wave headstock.

1965-1969	Fireglo	$6,800	$8,500
1965-1969	Mapleglo	$8,000	$10,000
1970-1979	Various colors	$4,800	$6,000
1980-1984	Various colors	$4,500	$5,600

Model 4005 L (Lightshow) Bass
1970-1975. Model 4005 with translucent top with lights in body that lit up when played, needed external transformer.

1970-1971	1st edition	$9,000	$11,500
1972-1975	2nd edition	$11,000	$13,500

Model 4005 WB Bass
1966-1983. Old style Model 4005 with white-bound body.

1966		$7,000	$8,700
1967-1969		$7,000	$8,700
1970-1979		$5,300	$6,500
1980-1983		$4,800	$5,900

Model 4005-6 Bass
1965-1977. Model 4005 with 6 strings.

1965-1969		$7,500	$9,200
1970-1977		$5,800	$7,000

Model 4005-8 Bass
Late-1960s. Eight-string Model 4005.

1968-1969	Fireglo, Mapleglo	$9,000	$11,000

Model 4008 Bass
1975-1983. Eight-string, cresting wave body and headstock.

1975-1983		$1,700	$2,100

Model 4080 Doubleneck Bass
1975-1992. Bolt-on 6- and 4-string necks.

1975-1979	Jetglo, Mapleglo	$6,000	$7,000
1980-1992		$5,000	$6,000

Ritter Royal Instruments
Production/custom, solidbody basses built by luthier Jens Ritter in Wachenheim, Germany.

RKS
2003-present. Professional and premium grade, production/custom, solidbody basses designed by Ravi Sawhney and guitarist Dave Mason and built in Thousand Oaks, California. They also build guitars.

Rob Allen
1997-present. Professional grade, production/custom, lightweight basses made by luthier Robert Allen in Santa Barbara, California.

2005 Rickenbacker 4003

1979 Rickenbacker 4005

Rogue VB100

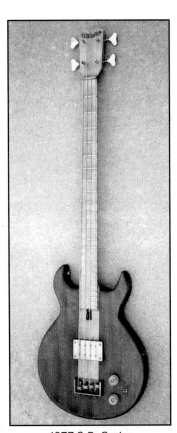

1977 S.D. Curlee

MODEL YEAR	FEATURES	EXC. COND. LOW	HIGH

Robin

1982-2010. Founded by David Wintz and located in Houston, Texas, Robin built basses until 1997. Most basses were Japanese-made until '87; American production began in '88. They aslo built guitars and also made Metropolitan ('96-'08) and Alamo ('00-'08) brand guitars.

Freedom Bass I

1984-1986. Offset double-cut, active treble and bass EQ controls, 1 pickup.

1984-1986		$525	$600

Freedom Bass I Passive

1986-1989. Non-active version of Freedom Bass, I humbucker. Passive dropped from name in '87.

1986-1989		$525	$600

Medley Bass

1984-1997. Offset deep cutaways, 2 pickups, reverse headstock until '89, then split headstock, back to reverse by '94. Japanese-made until '87, U.S. after.

1984-1987	Japan	$400	$500
1988-1997	USA	$650	$800

Ranger Bass

1984-1997. Vintage style body, dot markers, medium scale and 1 pickup from '84 to '88 and long scale with P-style and J-style pickup configuration from '89 to '97.

1984-1987	Japan	$400	$500
1988-1997	USA	$625	$775

Rock Bass

2002-present. Chinese-made, intermediate and professional grade, production, bolt neck solidbody basses from the makers of Warwick basses.

RockBeach Guitars

2005-present. Professional grade, custom, chambered body basses built by luthier Greg Bogoshian in Rochester, New York. He also builds guitars.

Rockit Guitar

2006-present. Luthier Rod MacKenzie builds his premium grade, custom, electric basses in Everett, Washington. He also builds guitars.

Rogue

2001-present. Budget grade, production, solidbody and acoustic/electric basses. They also offer guitars, lap steels, mandolins, banjos, and ukuleles.

Roland

Best known for keyboards, effects, and amps, Roland offered synthesizer-based guitars and basses from 1977 to '86.

GR-33B (G-88) Bass Guitar Synthesizer

Early-mid 1980s. Solidbody bass with synthesizer in the guitar case, G-88 deluxe bass.

1983-1985		$900	$1,050

Rolf Spuler

1981-present. Luthier Rolf Spuler builds custom, premium grade, solidbody basses in Gebenstorf, Switzerland. He also builds guitars.

MODEL YEAR	FEATURES	EXC. COND. LOW	HIGH

Roman & Blake Basses

1977-2003. Professional grade, production/custom, solidbody bass guitars made in Warren, Connecticut by Ed Roman.

Roman & Lipman Guitars

1989-2000. Production/custom, solidbody basses made in Danbury, Connecticut by Ed Roman. They also made guitars.

Roman USA Basses

2000-present. Professional grade, production/custom, solidbody basses made in Las Vegas, Nevada by Ed Roman.

Rono

1967-present. Luthier Ron Oates builds his professional and premium grade, production/custom, acoustic and solidbody basses in Boulder, Colorado. He also builds guitars and mandolins.

Roscoe Guitars

Early 1980s-present. Luthier Keith Roscoe builds his production/custom, professional and premium grade, solidbody electric basses in Greensboro, North Carolina.

S.D. Curlee

1975-1982. S.D. Curlee guitars and basses were made in Illinois; S.D. Curlee International instruments were made in Japan.

Electric Solidbody Bass

1970s	Various models	$350	$400

S101

2002-present. Budget and intermediate grade, production, solidbody basses imported from China. They also offer guitars, mandolins, and banjos.

Sadowsky

1980-present. Professional and premium grade, production/custom, solidbody basses built by luthier Roger Sadowsky in Brooklyn, New York. He also builds guitars. In '96, luthier Yoshi Kikuchi started building Sadowsky Tokyo instruments in Japan; those basses are now available in the U.S.

Samick

1958-2001, 2002-present. Budget, intermediate, and professional grade, production, imported acoustic and electric basses. They also offer guitars, mandolins, ukes and banjos.

Saturn

1960s-1970s. Imported, most likely from Japan, solid and semi-hollow body electric basses. Large S logo with Saturn name inside the S. Many sold through Eaton's in Canada. They also had guitars.

MODEL		EXC. COND.	
YEAR	FEATURES	LOW	HIGH

Schecter

1976-present. Intermediate and professional grade, production/custom, electric basses made in the U.S. and overseas. They also offer guitars. Schecter Custom Shop basses are made in Burbank, California and their Diamond Series is made in South Korea.

Scott French

2004-present. Luthier Scott French builds professional grade, custom, basses in Auburn, California. He also builds guitars.

Serenader

Mainly known for lap steels this Seattle, Washington brand also built a solidbody bass.

Serenghetti

Late-2007-present. Production/custom, professional and premium grade, neck-thru basses built in Ocala, Florida by luthier Ray Patterson. He also builds guitars.

Shergold

1968-1992. Founded by Jack Golder and Norman Houlder, Shergold originally made guitars for other brands. In '75, they started building guitars and basses under their own name. By '82, general guitar production was halted but custom orders were filled through '90. In '91, general production was again started but ended in '92 when Golder died.

Shifflett

1990-present. Luthier Charles Shifflett builds his premium grade, custom, acoustic basses in High River, Alberta. He also builds guitars and banjos.

Sigma

1970-2007. Budget and intermediate grade, production, import acoustic basses distributed by C.F. Martin Company. They also offered guitars, mandolins and banjos.

Silvertone

1941-ca.1970, present. Brand used by Sears. Instruments were U.S.-made and imported.
Hornet Bass
1950s-1960s. Fender-shape, 1 lipstick pickup.

1950-1960s		$500	$600

Model 1376L/1373L 6-String Bass
1956-1958. Short scale, 2 pickups.

1956-1958		$1,450	$1,750

Model 1444 Electric Bass
1959-1965. Bass version of 6-string electric guitar Model 1415 (bronze) and 1416 (black), 4-on-a-side replaces the prior year coke-bottle headstock, single pickup on single-cut U-1 style body, black finish.

1959-1965		$650	$800

MODEL		EXC. COND.	
YEAR	FEATURES	LOW	HIGH

Simmons

2002-present. Luthier David L. Simmons builds his professional grade, production/custom, 4- and 5-string basses in Hendersonville, North Carolina.

Singletouch

Luthier Mark Singleton builds his professional and premium grade, custom/production, solidbody basses in Phillips Ranch, California. He also builds guitars.

Sinister

2003. A short run of intermediate grade, solidbody basses built for Sinister Guitars by luthier Jon Kammerer.

Slammer

1999-present. Budget and intermediate grade, production, basses imported by Hamer. They also offer guitars.

Smith

1978-present. Professional and premium grade, production/custom, electric basses built by luthier Ken Smith in Perkasie, Pennsylvania. Earlier models had Ken Smith on the headstock, recent models have a large S logo. He also designs the imported KSD line of basses.
American-Made Bass

1978-2000	Various models	$2,000	$2,400

Custom VI Series Bass
1985-present. Six strings, double-cut, neck-thru-body.

1985-2010		$2,900	$3,400

Imported Bass

1990s	Various models	$550	$700

SMK Music Works

2002-present. Professional grade, production/custom, solidbody electric basses built by luthier Scott Kenerson in Waterford, Michigan. He also builds guitars.

Smooth Stone Guitars

2007-present. Professional and premium grade, production/custom electric and acoustic basses built by luthier R. Dale Humphries in Pocatello, Idaho. He also builds guitars.

Soundgear by Ibanez

1987-present. SDGR Soundgear by Ibanez headstock logo, intermediate grade, production, solidbody electric basses, made in Japan, Korea and Indonesia.

Spaltinstruments

2002-present. Professional and premium grade, production/custom, electric basses built in Los Angeles, California by luthier Michael Spalt. He also builds guitars.

Silvertone Model 373L 6-String Bass

1959 Silvertone Model 1444

2007 Spector NS230 30th Anniversary

Standel 400

MODEL YEAR	FEATURES	EXC. COND. LOW	HIGH

Specht Guitars

1991-present. Luthier Oliver Specht builds his premium grade, production/custom, basses in Vancouver, British Columbia. He also builds guitars.

Specimen Products

1984-present. Luthier Ian Schneller builds his professional and premium grade, production/custom, aluminum and wood body basses in Chicago, Illinois. He also builds guitars, ukes, amps and speaker cabs.

Spector/Stuart Spector Design

1975-1990 (Spector), 1991-1998 (SSD), 1998-present (Spector SSD). Imtermediate, professional, and premium grade, production/custom, basses made in the U.S., the Czech Republic, Korea, and China. Stuart Spector's first bass was the NS and the company quickly grew to the point where Kramer acquired it in '85. After Kramer went out of business in '90, Spector started building basses with the SSD logo (Stuart Spector Design). In '98 he recovered the Spector trademark.

Bob Series Bass

1996-1999. US-made, offset deep double-cut swamp ash or alder body, bolt neck, various colors, SSD logo on headstock, 4-string (Bob 4) or 5 (Bob 5).

1996-1999	Bob 4	$700	$900
1996-1999	Bob 5	$800	$1,000

NS Series Bass

1979-present. US-made, offset double-cut solidbody (X body optional), neck-thru, 1 pickup (NS-1, made into '80s) or 2 (NS-2).

1979-1984	NS-1	$1,300	$1,600
1979-1984	NS-2	$1,400	$1,700
1985-1990	NS-1, NS-2, Kramer era	$1,000	$1,200
1990-2010	SSD era	$1,100	$1,300

St. Blues

1980-1989, 2005-present. Intermediate and professional grade, production/custom, solidbody basses imported and set up in Memphis, Tennessee. They also build guitars.

St. Moritz

1960s. Japanese imports, generally shorter-scale, beginner basses. They also offered guitars.

Stambaugh

1995-present. Luthier Chris Stambaugh builds his professional grade, custom/production, solidbody basses in Stratham, New Hampshire. He also builds guitars.

Standel

1952-1974, 1997-present. Amp builder Bob Crooks offered instruments under his Standel brand name three different times during the '60s. See Guitar section for production details. See Amp section for more company information.

MODEL YEAR	FEATURES	EXC. COND. LOW	HIGH

Custom Deluxe Solidbody 401 Bass

1967-1968. Custom with higher appointments, various colors.

1967-1968		$800	$1,000

Custom Deluxe Thinbody 402 Bass

1967-1968. Custom with higher appointments, various colors.

1967-1968		$800	$1,000

Custom Solidbody 501 Bass

1967-1968. Solidbody, 1 pickup, various colors.

1967-1968		$550	$700

Custom Thinbody 502 Bass

1967-1968. Thin solidbody, 2 pickups, various colors.

1967-1968		$600	$750

Status Graphite

Professional and premium grade, production/custom, solid and semi-solid body basses built in Colchester, Essex, England. They also build guitars. Status was the first English company to produce a carbon fiber instrument.

Steinberger

1979-present. Steinberger offers budget and intermediate grade, production, electric basses. They also offer guitars.

Q-4 Bass

1990-1991. Composite neck, Double Bass system, headless with traditional-style maple body, low-impedance pickups.

1990-1991		$1,000	$1,200

Q-5 Bass

1990-1991. Five-string version of Q Bass.

1990-1991		$1,050	$1,250

XL-2 Bass

1984-1993. Rectangular composite body, 4-string, headless, 2 pickups.

1984-1989	Black	$1,800	$2,200
1990-1993	Red	$1,400	$1,800

XL-2GR Bass

1985-1990. Headless, Roland GR synthesizer controller.

1985-1990		$1,600	$2,000

XM-2 Bass

1986-1992. Headless, double-cut maple body, 4-string, 2 low-impedance pickups, optional fretted, lined fretless or unlined fretless, black, red or white.

1986-1992		$1,400	$1,800

XP-2 Spirit Bass

2003	Korea	$250	$300

Stevenson

1999-present. Luthier Ted Stevenson, of Lachine, Quebec, added professional grade, production/custom, basses to his product line in '05. He also builds guitars and amps.

Stewart Basses

2000-present. Luthier Fred Stewart builds his premium grade, custom/production, solidbody basses in Charlton, Maryland. He has also built guitars since '94.

BASSES

MODEL		EXC. COND.	
YEAR	FEATURES	LOW	HIGH

Stiehler

2005-present. Professional and premium grade, production/custom, acoustic and electric solidbody basses built by luthier Bob Stiehler in Wellington, Nevada. He also builds guitars.

Stinger

See Martin listing.

Stonetree Custom Guitars

1996-present. Luthier Scott Platts builds his professional and premium grade, custom/production, solidbody basses in Saratoga, Wyoming. He also builds guitars.

Strad-O-Lin

Ca.1920s-ca.1960s. The Strad-O-Lin mandolin company was operated by the Hominic brothers in New York. Around '57 Multivox/Premier bought the company and added the name to electric and acoustic guitars and basses. Premier also marketed student level guitars under the U.S. Strad brand.

Strobel Guitars

2003-present. Custom, professional grade, electric travel basses built by luthier Russ Strobel in Boca Raton, Florida. He also builds guitars.

Suhr Guitars

1997-present. In '03, luthier John Suhr added professional grade, production/custom, solidbody basses, to his instrument line built in Lake Elsinore, California. He also builds guitars.

Supersound

1952-1974. England's Alan Wootton worked with Jim Burns to produce a handful of solidbody guitars and basses bearing this name. The firm also built amps and effects.

Supro

1935-1968, 2004-present. Supro was a budget brand for the National Dobro Company. Supro offered only two bass models in the '60s. Amp builder Bruce Zinky revived the Supro name for a line of guitars and amps.

Pocket Bass

1960-1968. Double-cut, neck pickup and bridge mounted pickup, semi-hollow, short-scale, black.
| 1960-1968 | | $600 | $700 |

Taurus Bass

1967-1968. Asymmetrical double-cut, neck pickup and bridge mounted pickup.
| 1967-1968 | | $450 | $550 |

SX

See listing for Essex.

Tacoma

1995-present. Professional grade, production, acoustic basses produced in Tacoma, Washington. They also build acoustic guitars and mandolins.

Thunderchief CB10C/E4 Bass

1998-present. 17 3/4 flat-top, solid spruce top, solid mahogany back, laminated mahogany sides, rounded cutaway, bolt-on neck, natural satin finish, factory Fishman Prefix Plus pickup system (E4), dot markers.
| 1998-2010 | | $900 | $1,100 |

Takamine

1962-present. Intermediate, professional and premium grade, production, acoustic and acoustic/electric basses. They also make guitars. They offered solidbody electrics for '83-'84.

Taylor

1974-present. Professional and premium grade, production, acoustic basses built in El Cajon, California. They presently build guitars.

AB1 Bass

1996-2003. Acoustic/electric, sitka spruce top, imbuia walnut back and sides, designed for 'loose' woody sound.
| 1996-2003 | | $1,200 | $1,500 |

AB2 Bass

1996-2003. Acoustic/electric, all imbuia walnut body.
| 1996-2003 | | $1,200 | $1,500 |

AB3 Bass

1998-2003. Acoustic/electric, sitka spruce top, maple back and sides.
| 1998-2003 | | $1,200 | $1,500 |

Teisco

1946-1974, 1994-present. The Japanese Teisco line started offering basses in '60.

Electric Bass

1968-1969. EB-100 (1 pickup, white 'guard), EB-200 (solidbody), EB-200B (semi-hollowbody) and Violin bass.
1968-1969	EB-100	$75	$150
1968-1969	EB-200	$400	$500
1968-1969	EB-200 B	$250	$300
1968-1969	Violin	$400	$500

Tele-Star

1965-ca.1972. Guitars and basses imported from Japan by Tele-Star Musical Instrument Corporation of New York. Primarily made by Kawai, many inspired by Burns designs, some in cool sparkle finishes.

Electric Solidbody Bass

| 1960s | Various models | $150 | $200 |

Timtone Custom Guitars

1993-2006. Luthier Tim Diebert built his premium grade, custom, solidbody and chambered-body basses in Grand Forks, British Columbia. He also built guitars and lap steels.

Tobias

1977-present. Founded by Mike Tobias in Orlando, Florida. Moved to San Francisco for '80-'81, then to Costa Mesa, eventually ending up in Hollywood. In '90, he sold the company to Gibson

Steinberger XM-2

Tacoma Thunderchief

Traben Chaos Core 5

Tucker Paua

MODEL YEAR	FEATURES	EXC. COND. LOW	HIGH

which moved it to Burbank. The first Tobias made under Gibson ownership was serial number 1094. The instruments continued to be made by the pre-Gibson crew until '92, when the company was moved to Nashville. The last LA Tobias/Gibson serial number is 2044. Mike left the company in '92 and started a new business in '94 called MTD where he continues to make electric and acoustic basses. In '99, production of Tobias basses was moved overseas. In late '03, Gibson started again offering U.S.-made Tobias instruments; they are made in Conway, Arkansas, in the former Baldwin grand piano facility. Currently Tobias offers imported and U.S.-made, intermediate and professional grade, production, acoustic and electric basses.

Basic Bass
1984-1999. 30", 32", or 34" scale, neck-thru-body in alder, koa or walnut, 5-piece laminated neck.

1984-1999	Basic B-4	$1,600	$2,000
1984-1999	Basic B-5	$1,700	$2,100

Classic C-4 Bass
1978-1999. One or 2 pickups, active or passive electronics, 2-octave rosewood 'board, available in short-, medium-, and long-scale models.

1978-1999		$2,000	$2,500

Classic C-5 Bass
1985-1999. 30", 32" or 34" scale, alder, koa or walnut body, bookmatched top, ebony or phenolic 'board, hardwood neck.

1985-1999		$2,100	$2,600

Classic C-6 Bass
Ca. 1986-1999. Flamed maple and padauk neck, alder body, padauk top, ebony 'board, active electronics, 32" or 34" scale.

1986-1999		$2,200	$2,700

Growler GR-5 Bass
1996-1999. 5-string, offset double-cut, bolt neck, various colors.

1996-1999		$750	$925

Killer Bee Bass
1991-1999. Offset double-cut, swamp ash or lacewood body, various colors.

1991-1999	KB-4	$1,200	$1,500
1991-1999	KB-5	$1,300	$1,600

Model T Bass
1989-1991. Line of 4- and 5-string basses, 3-piece maple neck-thru-body, maple body halves, active treble and bass controls. Fretless available.

1989-1991		$1,150	$1,400

Signature S-4 Bass
1978-1999. Available in 4-, 5-, and 6-string models, chrome-plated milled brass bridge.

1978-1990	Tobias-Burbank	$2,800	$3,500
1990-1992	Gibson-Burbank	$2,200	$2,700

Standard ST-4 Bass
1992-1995. Japanese-made, 5-piece maple neck-thru, swamp ash body wings.

1992-1995		$1,050	$1,300

Toby Deluxe TD-4 Bass
1994-1996. Offset double-cut, bolt neck.

1994-1996		$550	$675

Toby Deluxe TD-5 Bass
1994-1996. 5-string version.

1994-1996		$575	$700

Toby Pro 5 Bass
1994-1996. Solidbody 5-string, Toby Pro logo on truss rod cover, neck-thru body.

1994-1996		$475	$600

Toby Pro 6 Bass
1994-1996. Solidbody 6-string, Toby Pro logo on truss rod cover, neck-thru body.

1994-1996		$575	$700

Tokai
1947-present. Tokai started making guitars and basses around '70 and by the end of that decade they were being imported into the U.S. Today Tokai offers electrics, acoustics, and electric basses made in Japan and Korea.

Vintage Bass Copies
1970s-1980s. Tokai offered near copies of classic U.S. basses.

1970-1980s		$375	$650

Tonemaster
1960s. Guitars and basses, imported from Italy, with typical '60s Italian sparkle plastic finish and push-button controls, bolt-on neck.

Electric Bass

1960s	Sparkle finish	$550	$650

ToneSmith
1997-present. Luthier Kevin Smith builds his professional and premium grade, production/custom, semi-hollow body basses in Rogers, Minnesota. He also builds guitars.

Traben
2004-present. Intermediate grade, production, solidbody basses imported by Elite Music Brands of Clearwater, Florida.

Traveler Guitar
1992-present. Intermediate grade, production, travel size electric basses made in Redlands, California. They also make guitars.

Travis Bean
1974-1979, 1999. The unique Travis Bean line included a couple of bass models. Travis Bean announced some new instruments in '99, but general production was not resumed.

TB-2000 Bass
Aluminum neck, T-slotted headstock, longer horned, double-cut body, 2 pickups, 4 controls, dot markers, various colors.

1970s		$3,600	$4,400

TB-4000 (Wedge Vee) Bass
1970s. Bass version of Bean's Wedge guitar, few made.

1970s		$4,000	$5,000

MODEL YEAR	FEATURES	EXC. COND. LOW	HIGH

Trinity River

2004-present. Intermediate grade, production/custom, acoustic basses imported from Asia by luthiers Marcus Lawyer and Ross McLeod in Fort Worth, Texas. They also import guitars, mandolins and banjos.

True Tone

1960s. Western Auto retailed this line of basses, guitars and amps which were manufactured by Chicago builders makers like Kay. The brand was most likely gone by '68.

Electric Bass

1960s		$225	$300

Tucker

2000-present. John N. Tucker builds professional and premium grade, production/custom, albizzia wood solidbody basses in Hanalei, Hawaii. He also builds guitars.

Unique Guitars

2003-ca. 2007. Professional and premium grade, production/custom, solidbody basses built by luthier Joey Rico in California. He also built guitars.

Univox

1964-1978. Univox started out as an amp line and added guitars and basses around '69. Guitars were imported from Japan by the Merson Musical Supply Company, later Unicord, Westbury, New York. Generally mid-level copies of American designs.

Badazz Bass

1971-ca. 1975. Based on the Guild S-100.

1971-1977		$400	$500

Bicentennial

1976. Carved eagle in body, matches Bicentennial guitar (see that listing), brown stain, maple 'board.

1976		$800	$1,000

Hi Flier Bass

1969-1977. Mosrite Ventures Bass copy, 2 pickups, rosewood 'board.

1969-1977		$450	$550

'Lectra (Model 1970F) Bass

1969-ca. 1973. Violin bass, walnut.

1969-1973		$425	$525

Model 3340 Semi-Hollow Bass

1970-1971. Copy of Gibson EB-0 semi-hollow bass.

1970-1971		$425	$525

Precisely Bass

1971-ca. 1975. Copy of Fender P-Bass.

1971-1975		$400	$500

Stereo Bass

1976-1977. Rickenbacker 4001 Bass copy, model U1975B.

1976-1977		$450	$550

Thin Line Bass

1968		$425	$525

Vaccaro

1997-2002. They offered intermediate and professional grade, production/custom, aluminum-necked basses built in Asbury Park, New Jersey. They also built guitars.

Valley Arts

Ca. 1977-present. Professional and premium grade, production/custom, solidbody basses built in Nashville, Tennessee. They also make guitars.

Vantage

1977-present. Intermediate grade, production, electric basses imported from Korea (from Japan until '90). They also offer guitars.

Vega

1903-1980s, 1989-present. The original Boston-based brand name was purchased by C.F. Martin in '70 and used on imports. Deering Banjo currently uses the name on a line of banjos.

Veillette

1991-present. Luthiers Joe Veillette and Martin Keith build their professional and premium grade, production/custom, electric basses in Woodstock, New York. They also build guitars and mandolins.

Veillette-Citron

1975-1983. Founded by Joe Veillette and Harvey Citron who met at the NY College School of Architecture in the late '60s. Joe took a guitar building course from Michael Gurian and by the Summer of '76, he and Harvey started producing neck-thru solidbody guitars and basses. Veillette and Citron both are back building instruments.

Vengeance Guitars & Graphix

2002-present. Luthier Rick Stewart builds his professional and premium grade, custom/production, solidbody basses in Arden, North Carolina. He also builds guitars.

Ventura

1970s. Import classic bass copies distributed by C. Bruno (Kaman). They also had guitars.

Vintage Bass Copies

1970s		$225	$550

Versoul, LTD

1989-present. Production/custom acoustic/electric and solidbody basses built by luthier Kari Nieminen in Helsinki, Finland. He also builds guitars and sitars.

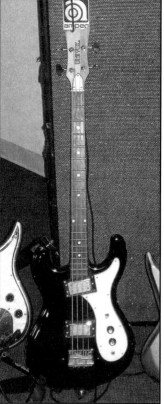

Early-1970s Univox Hi-Flier
Sean Sweeney

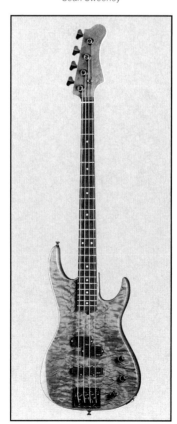

Valley Arts Custom Pro

BASSES

BASSES

1968 Vox Sidewinder IV (V272)

Wendler electroCoustic Bass

MODEL YEAR	FEATURES	EXC. COND. LOW	HIGH

Vintage

Ca. 1993-present. Intermediate and professional grade, production, solidbody and semi-hollow acoustic and electro-acoustic guitars, imported from China, Korea and Vietnam by John Hornby Skewes & Co. in the U.K. They also offer guitars and folk instruments.

Vox

1954-present. Guitars and basses bearing the Vox name were offered from 1961-'69 (made in England, Italy), '82-'85 (Japan), '85-'88 (Korea), '98-2001 (U.S.), with a limited edition teardrop bass offered in late '07. Special thanks to Jim Rhoads of Rhoads Music in Elizabethtown, Pennsylvania, for help on production years of these models.

Apollo IV Bass
1967-1969. Single-cut hollowbody, bolt maple neck, 1 pickup, on-board fuzz, booster, sunburst.

1967-1969		$750	$900

Astro IV Bass
1967-1969. Violin-copy bass, 2 pickups.

1967-1969		$775	$925

Clubman Bass
1961-1966. Double-cut 2-pickup solidbody, red.

1961-1966		$550	$700

Constellation IV Bass
1967-1968. Teardrop-shaped body, 2 pickups, 1 f-hole, 1 set of controls, treble, bass and distortion boosters.

1967-1968		$1,200	$1,400

Cougar Bass
1963-1967. Double-cut semi-hollow body, 2 f-holes, 2 pickups, 2 sets of controls, sunburst.

1963-1967		$1,000	$1,250

Delta IV Bass
1967-1968. Five-sided body, 2 pickups, 1 volume and 2 tone controls, distortion, treble and bass boosters.

1967-1968		$1,100	$1,350

Guitar-Organ Bass
1966. The 4-string bass version of the Guitar-Organ, Phantom-style body, white.

1966		$1,100	$1,350

Mark IV Bass
1963-1969. Teardrop-shaped body, 2 pickups, 1 set of controls, sunburst.

1963-1965	England, white	$2,500	$3,100
1965-1969	Italy, sunburst	$1,500	$1,900

Panther Bass
1967-1968. Double-cut solidbody, 1 slanted pickup, rosewood 'board, sunburst.

1967-1968		$500	$600

Phantom IV Bass
1963-1969. Five-sided body, 2 pickups, 1 set of controls.

1963-1964	England	$2,100	$2,600
1965-1969	Italy	$1,300	$1,700

Saturn IV Bass
1967-1968. Single-cut, 2 f-holes, 1 set of controls, 1 pickup.

1967-1968		$700	$850

Sidewinder IV Bass (V272)
1967-1968. Double-cut semi-hollow body, 2 f-holes, 2 pickups, 1 set of controls, treble, bass, and distortion boosters.

1967-1968		$1,200	$1,500

Stinger Bass
1968. Teardrop-shaped, boat oar headstock.

1968		$800	$1,000

Violin Bass
1966. Electro-acoustic bass with violin shaped body, 2 extended range pickups, sunburst.

1966		$800	$1,000

Wyman Bass
1966. Teardrop-shaped body, 2 pickups, 1 f-hole, 1 set of controls, sunburst.

1966		$1,200	$1,500

Wal

1976-present. Founded in England by luthier Ian Waller and his partner Peter Stevens, forming the company under the name Electric Wood in '78. Waller died in '88, Stevens enlists help of luthier Paul Herman, and in 2000s Stevens retires and Herman takes over. In the early years, the Mark designation was used generically. Newer contemporary models are named Mk1, Mk2 and Mk3. Prices shown will increase 5% with LED option, or 10% with rare top, but no value difference between fretted and fretless. MIDI electronics does not increase the value.

Custom (IV) Bass
1980s-1990s. 4-string, active, no guard, generally highly figured front and back.

1980	Mark I	$3,800	$4,700
1985	Mark II	$3,800	$4,700
1994	Mark III	$4,000	$5,000

Custom (V) Bass
1980s-1990s. 5-string, active, no guard, generally highly figured front and back.

1985	Mark II	$4,600	$5,700
1994	Mark III	$4,800	$5,900

Custom (VI) Bass
1990s. 6-string, active, no guard, generally highly figured front and back.

1994	Mark III	$5,000	$6,200

JG Bass
1976-1978. 4-string, passive with either tooled leather (34 made), or leather guard.

1976-1978	Non-tooled	$4,500	$5,600
1976-1978	Tooled	$5,500	$6,800

Pro (Mark I) Bass
1978. Passive, black guard.

1978		$2,300	$2,800

Walker (Kramer)

1981. Kramer came up with idea to offer this brand to produce wood-neck guitars and basses; they didn't want to dilute the Kramer aluminum-neck market they had built up. The idea didn't last long, and few, if any, of these were produced.

MODEL		EXC. COND.	
YEAR	FEATURES	LOW	HIGH

Wandre (Davoli)

Ca. 1956/57-1969. Italian-made guitars and basses.

Warrior

1995-present. Professional and premium grade, production/custom, solidbody basses built by luthier J.D. Lewis in Roseville, Georgia. He also builds guitars.

Warwick

1982-present. Professional and premium grade, production/custom, electric and acoustic basses made in Markneukirchen, Germany; founded by Hans Peter Wilfer, whose father started Framus guitars. They also build amps.

Washburn

1974-present. Intermediate and professional grade, production, acoustic and electric basses. Washburn instruments were mostly imports early on, U.S. production later, currently a combination of both. Washburn also offers guitars, banjos, mandolins, and amps.

Electric Bass

1980-2000s Various models	$200	$500

Waterstone

2002-present. Intermediate and professional grade, production/custom, solid and semi-hollowbody electric basses imported from Korea by Waterstone Musical Instruments, LLC of Nashville. They also offer guitars.

Watkins

1957-present. Watkins Electric Music (WEM) was founded by Charlie Watkins. Their first commercial product was the Watkins Dominator amp in '57. They made the Rapier line of guitars and basses from the beginning. Watkins offered guitars and basses up to '82.

Wechter

1984-present. Professional grade, production/custom acoustic basses built by luthier Abe Wechter in Paw Paw, Michigan. He also offers U.S-made and import guitars.

Welson

1960s. Italian-made copy model guitars and basses.

Electric Bass

1960s	Copy models	$250	$500

Wendler

1999-present. Luthier Dave Wendler, of Ozark Instrument Building, builds his intermediate and professional grade, production/custom, solidbody, electro-acoustic basses in Branson, Missouri. He also builds guitars.

Westbury-Unicord

1978-ca. 1983. Japanese guitars and basses imported by Unicord.

Westone

1970s-1990, 1996-2001. Guitars and basses originally imported from Japan by St. Louis Music. Name revived from '96 to '01, by England's FCN Music.

Wicked

2004-present. Luthier Nicholas Dijkman builds intermediate and professional grade, production/custom, electric solidbody basses in Montreal, Quebec. He also builds guitars.

Wilkat Guitars

1998-present. Luthier Bill Wilkat builds his professional grade, custom handmade, electric basses in Montreal, Quebec. He also builds guitars.

Wilson Brothers Guitars

2004-present. Production electric basses. They also build guitars. Founded by Ventures guitarist Don Wilson.

Winston

Ca. 1963-1967. Guitars and basses imported by Buegeleisen & Jacobson of New York.

Wright Guitar Technology

1993-present. Luthier Rossco Wright builds his unique professional grade, production, travel/practice acoustic bass in Eugene, Oregon. He also builds guitars.

Wurlitzer

1970s. Private branded by Pedulla for the Wurlitzer music store chain. Manufacturer and retailer were both based in Massachusetts. Refer to Pedulla listing.

Xotic Guitars

1996-present. Professional grade, production/custom basses built by luthier Hiro Miura in San Fernando, California. He also builds guitars. The Xotic brand is also used on a line of guitar effects.

Yamaha

1946-present. Budget, intermediate, professional and premium grade, production, electric basses. They also build guitars. Yamaha began producing solidbody instruments in '66.

Attitude Custom Bass

1990-1994. Part of the Sheehan Series, champagne sparkle.

1990-1994	$650	$800

Electric Bass

1960-present. Various models.

1960-1999	$100	$600

2001 Warwick Corvette Pro

1987 Westone Genesis

BASSES

Ziegenfuss Standard Series

Zon Sonus

MODEL YEAR	FEATURES	EXC. COND. LOW	HIGH

Zachary

1996-present. Professional grade, production, solidbody electric basses built by Luthier Alex Csiky in Windsor, Ontario. He also builds guitars.

Zemaitis

1960-1999, 2004-present. Tony Zemaitis began selling his guitars in '60 and he retired in '99. He emphasized simple lightweight construction and his instruments are known for hand engraved metal fronts. Each hand-built custom guitar or bass was a unique instrument. Approximately 10 custom guitars were built each year. In '04, Japan's Kanda Shokai, with the endorsement of Tony Zemaitis, Jr., started building the guitars again.

Electric Bass

MODEL YEAR	FEATURES	EXC. COND. LOW	HIGH
1970s	Heart hole (4 made)	$20,000	$24,000
1980s	1/2 metal & spruce	$10,000	$12,000
1980s	Metal-front 4-string	$13,000	$16,000

Zen-On

1946-ca.1968. Japanese-made. By '67 using the Morales brandname. Not heavily imported into the U.S., if at all (see Morales).

Electric Solidbody Bass

MODEL YEAR	FEATURES	EXC. COND. LOW	HIGH
1950s	Various models	$175	$250

Zeta

1982-present. Zeta has made professional and premium grade, acoustic and electric basses, many with electronic and MIDI options, in Oakland, California over the years. Currently they only offer upright basses, amps and violins.

Ziegenfuss Guitars

2006-present. Professional and premium grade, custom, solidbody electric basses built in Jackson, Michigan by luthier Stephen Ziegenfuss. He also builds guitars.

Zim-Gar

1960s. Japanese guitars and basses imported by Gar-Zim Musical Instrument Corporation of Brooklyn, New York.

Electric Solidbody Bass

MODEL YEAR	FEATURES	EXC. COND. LOW	HIGH
1960s	Various models	$175	$250

Zolla

1979-present. Professional grade, production/ custom, electric basses built by luthier Bill Zolla in San Diego, California. Zolla also builds guitars, necks and bodies.

Zon

1981-present. Luthier Joe Zon builds his professional and premium grade, production/custom, solidbody basses in Redwood City, California. Zon started the brand in Buffalo, New York and relocated to Redwood City in '87. He has also built guitars.

Legacy Elite VI Bass

1989-present. Six-string, 34" scale carbon-fiber neck, Bartolini pickups, ZP-2 active electronics.

MODEL YEAR	FEATURES	EXC. COND. LOW	HIGH
1990s		$1,000	$1,250

Scepter Bass

1984-1993. Offset body shape, 24 frets, 1 pickup, tremolo.

MODEL YEAR	FEATURES	EXC. COND. LOW	HIGH
1984-1993		$925	$1,125

Sonus Custom Bass

1990s-present. Offset swamp ash body, 2 pickups.

MODEL YEAR	FEATURES	EXC. COND. LOW	HIGH
1990s-2010		$1,350	$1,650

Zorko

Late-1950s-early-1962. Original maker of the Ampeg Baby Bass (see that listing), sold to Ampeg in 1962, Zorko logo on scroll.

Baby Bass

MODEL YEAR	FEATURES	EXC. COND. LOW	HIGH
1950s-1962		$1,700	$2,100

ZZ Ryder

Solidbody electric basses from Stenzler Musical Instruments of Ft. Worth, Texas. They also offer guitars.

AMPS

3rd Power British Dream 112

3 Monkeys Orangutan

2007 65Amps Soho

3 Monkeys Amps

2007-present. Intermediate and professional grade, production/custom, amps and cabinets built by Gred Howard in Raleigh, North Carolina.

3rd Power

Mid-2009-present. Professional grade, production/custom, guitar amps built in Franklin, Tennessee by Jamie Scott.

65amps

2004-present. Founded by Peter Stroud and Dan Boul, 65 builds tube guitar head and combo amps and speaker cabs in Valley Village, California.

Ace Tone

Late-1960-1970s. Made by Sakata Shokai Limited of Osaka, Japan, early importer of amps and effects pedals. Later became Roland/Boss.

B-9 Amp
Late-1960s-early-1970s. Solid-state bass amp head.

MODEL YEAR	FEATURES	EXC. COND. LOW	HIGH
1960-1970s		$100	$125

Mighty-5 Amp
Late-1960s-early-1970s. Tubes, 50-watt head.

1960-1970s		$75	$100

Solid A-5 Amp
1960s-1970s. Solidstate 2x12 combo with verticle cab, reverb and tremolo, black tolex, silver grille.

1960-1970s		$125	$150

Acoustic

Ca.1965-ca.1987, 2001-2005, 2008-present. The Acoustic Control Corp., of Los Angeles, California, was mostly known for solidstate amplifiers. Heads and cabinets were sold separately with their own model numbers, but were also combined (amp sets) and marketed under a different model number (for example, the 153 amp set was the 150b head with a 2x15" cabinet). The brand was revived by Samick in '01 for a line of amps. In '08 brand back again on line of amps sold through Guitar Center and Musician's Friend.

114 Amp
Ca.1977-mid-1980s. Solidstate, 50 watts, 2x10", reverb, master volume.

1978-1984		$175	$225

115 Amp
1977-1978. Solidstate, 1x12", 50 watts, reverb, master volume.

1977-1978		$175	$225

116 Bass Amp
1978-mid-1980s. Solidstate, 75 watts, 1x15", power boost switch.

1978-1984		$175	$225

120 Amp Head
1977-mid-1980s. Solidstate head, 125 watts.

1977-1984		$150	$175

123 Amp
1977-1984. 1x12" combo.

1977-1984		$150	$175

124 Amp
1977-mid-1980s. Solidstate, 4x10", 5-band EQ, 100 watts, master volume.

1977-1984		$200	$250

125 Amp
1977-mid-1980s. Solidstate, 2x12", 5-band EQ, 100 watts, master volume.

1977-1984		$200	$250

126 Bass Amp
1977-mid-1980s. Solidstate, 100 watts, 1x15", 5-band EQ.

1977-1984		$200	$250

134 Amp
1972-1976. Solidstate, 100-125 watts, 4x10" combo.

1972-1976		$200	$250

135 Amp
1972-1976. Solidstate, 125 watts, 2x12" combo, reverb, tremolo.

1972-1976		$200	$250

136 Amp
1972-1976. Solidstate, 125 watts, 1x15" combo.

1972-1976		$200	$250

140 Bass Head
1972-1976. Solidstate, 125 watts, 2 channels.

1972-1976		$150	$175

150 Amp Head
1960s-1976. Popular selling model, generally many available in the used market. Solidstate, 110 watts until '72, 125 watts after.

1968-1976		$150	$175

150b Bass Head
1960s-1971. Bass amp version of 150 head.

1968-1971		$150	$175

153 Bass Amp Set
1960s-1971. 150b head (bass version of 150) with 2x15" 466 cabinet, 110 watts.

1968-1971		$325	$400

165 Amp
1979-mid-1980s. All tube combo, switchable to 60 or 100 watts, brown tolex.

1979-1984		$250	$300

220 Bass Head
1977-1980s. Solidstate, 5-band EQ, either 125 or 160 watts, later models 170 or 200 watts, black tolex.

1977-1984		$175	$200

230 Amp Head
1977-1980s. Solidstate head, 125/160 watts, 5-band EQ.

1977-1984		$175	$200

260 Amp Head
1960s-1971. Solidstate, 275 watt, stereo/mono.

1968-1971		$300	$350

270 Amp Head
1970s. 400 watts.

1970s		$300	$350

320 Bass Head
1977-1980s. Solidstate, 5-band EQ, 160/300 watts, 2 switchable channels, black tolex.

1977-1984		$300	$350

MODEL		EXC. COND.	
YEAR	FEATURES	LOW	HIGH

360 Bass Head

1960s-1971. One of Acoustic's most popular models, 200 watts. By '72, the 360 is listed as a "preamp only."

1968-1971		$350	$425

370 Bass Head

1972-1977. Solidstate bass head, 365 watts early on, 275 later, Jaco Pastorius associated.

1972-1977	275 or 365 watt	$425	$525

402 Cabinet

1977-1980s. 2x15" bass cab, black tolex, black grille.

1977-1984		$175	$225

404 Cabinet

1970s. 6x10", Jaco Pastorius associated.

1970s		$350	$425

450 Amp Head

1974-1976. 170 watts, 5-band EQ, normal and bright inputs.

1974-1976		$250	$300

455 Amp Set

1974-1977. 170 watt 450 head with 4x12" cabinet, black.

1974-1977		$475	$575

470 Amp Head

1974-1977. 170 watt, dual channel.

1974-1977		$250	$300

AG15 Amp

2008-present. Small combo, 15 watts.

2008-2010		$45	$55

B100 Amp

2008-present. Classic style combo, 100 watts, 1x15.

2008-2010		$125	$175

B200 Amp

2009-present. 200 watts, 1x15 combo.

2009-2010		$200	$250

G20-110 Amp

1981-mid-1980s. Solidstate, 20 watts, 1x10". The G series was a lower-priced combo line.

1981-1985		$100	$125

G20-120 Amp

1981-mid-1980s. Solidstate, 20 watts, 1x12".

1981-1985		$100	$125

G60-112 Amp

1981-mid-1980s. Solidstate, 60 watts, 1x12".

1981-1985		$125	$150

G60-212 Amp

1981-mid-1980s. Solidstate, 60 watts, 2x12".

1981-1985		$150	$175

G60T-112 Amp

1981-1987. Tube, 60 watts, 1x12".

1981-1985		$250	$300

Tube 60 Amp

1986-1987. Combo, 60 watts, 1x12", spring reverb, bright switch, master volume control, effects loop.

1986-1987		$250	$300

ADA

1977-2002. ADA (Analog/Digital Associates) was located in Berkeley, California, and introduced its Flanger and Final Phase in '77. The company later moved to Oakland and made amplifiers, high-tech signal processors, and a reissue of its original Flanger.

Aguilar

1995-present. U.S.-made tube and solidstate amp heads, cabinets, and pre-amps from New York City, New York.

Aiken Amplification

2000-present. Tube amps, combos, and cabinets built by Randall Aiken originally in Buford, Georgia, and since '05 in Pensacola, Florida.

Aims

Ca. 1972-ca. 1976. Aims (American International Music Sales, Inc.) amps were distributed by Randall Instruments in the mid-'70s. They also offered guitars and basses.

Airline

Ca.1958-1968. Brand for Montgomery Ward, built by Danelectro, Valco and others.

Tube Amp 1x6" Speaker

1950-1960s		$200	$250

Tube Amp 1x8" Speaker

1950-1960s		$200	$250

Tube Amp 1x10" Speaker

1950-1960s		$225	$275

Tube Amp 1x12" Speaker

1950-1960s		$250	$300

Tube Amp Higher-End

1950-1960s		$500	$600

Tube Amp Highest-End

1950-1960s		$525	$650

Alamo

1947-1982. Founded by Charles Eilenberg, Milton Fink, and Southern Music, San Antonio, Texas, and distributed by Bruno and Sons. Alamo started producing amps in '49 and the amps were all-tube until '73; solidstate preamp and tube output from '73 to ca. '80; all solidstate for ca. '80 to '82.

Birch "A" Combo Amp

1949-1962. Birch wood cabinets with A-shaped grill cutout, 2 to 5 tubes. Models include the Embassy Amp 3, Jet Amp 4, Challenger Amp 2, Amp 5, and the Montclair.

1949-1962		$225	$300

Bass Tube Amp

1960-1972. Leatherette covered, all tube, 20 to 35 watts, 15" speakers, combo or piggyback, some with Lansing speaker option. Models include the Paragon Special, Paragon Bass, Piggyback Band, Piggyback Bass, Fury Bass, and Paragon Bass (piggyback).

1960-1972		$225	$300

Bass Solidstate Preamp-Tube Output Amp

1973-ca.1979. Solidstate preamp section with tube output section, 35 or 40 watts, 15" speakers, combo or piggyback. Models include the Paragon Bass, Paragon Bass Piggyback, Paragon Country Western Bass, Paragon Super Bass, and the Fury Bass.

1973-1979		$125	$150

ADA Viper

Aiken Sabre

'60s Alamo

Alamo Challenger

Alessandro Working Dog

Allen Old Flame

MODEL YEAR	FEATURES	EXC. COND. LOW	HIGH

Small Tube Amp

1960-1972. Leatherette covered, all tube, 3 to 10 watts, 6" to 10" speakers, some with tremolo. Models include the Jet, Embassy, Challenger, Capri, Fiesta, Dart, and Special.

| 1960-1972 | | $200 | $275 |

Mid-Power Tube Amp

1960-1970. Leatherette covered, all tube, 15 to 30 watts, 12" or 15" speakers, some with tremolo and reverb, some with Lansing speaker option. Models include Montclair, Paragon, Paragon Band, Titan, and Futura.

| 1960-1970 | | $325 | $425 |

Twin Speaker Tube Amp

1962-1972. Leatherette covered, all tube, up to 45 watts, 8", 10", 12" or 15" speaker configurations, some with tremolo and reverb, some with Lansing speaker option. Models include the Electra Twin Ten, Century Twin Ten, Futuramic Twin Eight, Galaxie Twin Twelve, Galaxie Twin Twelve Piggyback, Piggyback Super Band, Alamo Pro Reverb Piggyback, Futura, Galaxie Twin Ten, Twin-Ten, and Band Piggyback.

| 1962-1972 | | $300 | $600 |

Small Solidstate Preamp-Tube Output Amp

1973-ca.1979. Solidstate preamp section with tube output section, 3 to 12 watts, 5" to 12" speaker, some with reverb. Models include the Challenger, Capri, Special, Embassy, Dart, and Jet.

| 1973-1979 | | $125 | $150 |

Mid-Power Solidstate Preamp-Tube Output Amp

1973-ca.1979. Solidstate preamp section with tube output section, 25 watts, 12" speaker, with reverb and tremolo. Models include the Montclair.

| 1973-1979 | | $125 | $150 |

Twin Speaker Combo (Tube/Hybrid) Amp

1973-ca.1979. Solidstate preamp section with tube output section, 20 or 70 watts, 10", 12" and 15" speaker configurations, some with reverb and tremolo. Models include the 70-watt Paragon Super Reverb Piggybacks, the 45-watt Futura 2x12, and the 20-watt Twin-Ten.

| 1973-1979 | | $200 | $275 |

Solidstate Amp

Ca.1980-1982. All solidstate.

| 1980-1982 | | $25 | $50 |

Alden

Small budget grade solidstate guitar and bass amps from Muse, Inc. of China.

Alesis

1992-present. Alesis has a wide range of products for the music industry, including digital modeling guitar amps. They also offer guitar effects.

Alessandro

1998-present. Tube amps built by George Alessandro in Huntingdon Valley, Pennsylvania. Founded in '94 as the Hound Dog Corporation, in '98 the company name was changed to Alessandro. The

Redbone ('94) and the Bloodhound ('96) were the only models bearing the Hound Dog mark. Serial numbers are consecutive regardless of model (the earliest 20-30 did not have serial numbers). In '98 the company converted to exotic/high-end components and the name changed to Alessandro High-End Products. In '01, he added the Working Dog brand line of amps.

Allen Amplification

1998-present. Tube combo amps, heads and cabinets built by David Allen in Walton, Kentucky. He also offers the amps in kit form and produces replacement and upgrade transformers and a tube overdrive pedal.

Aloha

Late-1940s. Electric lap steel and amp Hawaiian outfits made for the Dallas-based Aloha.

Ampeg

1949-present. Ampeg was originally primarily known for their bass amps. In the eastern U.S., Ampeg was Fender's greatest challenger in the '60s and '70s bass amplifier market. Currently offering tube and solidstate heads, combos and speaker cabinets. They also build guitars.

Amp Covering Dates:

Wood veneer	1946-1949.
Smooth brown	1949-1952.
Dot tweed	1952-1954.
Tweed	1954-1955.
Rough gray	1957-1958.
Rough tan	1957-1958.
Cream	1957-1958.
Light blue	1958.
Navy blue	1958-1962.
Blue check	1962-1967.
Black pebble	1967.
Smooth black	1967-1980.
Rough black	1967-1985.

AC-12 Amp

1970. 20 watts, 1x12", accordion amp that was a market failure and dropped after 1 year.

| 1970 | | $325 | $375 |

B-2 Bass Amp

1994-2000. Solidstate, 200 watts, 1x15" combo or 4x8" combo, black vinyl, black grille, large A logo.

| 1994-2000 1x15" | | $450 | $500 |

B-2 R Bass Amp Head

1994-2005. 200 watts, rackmount, replaced by 450 watt B2RE.

| 1994-2005 | | $250 | $300 |

B-3 Amp

1995-2001. Solidstate head, 150 watts, 1x15".

| 1995-2001 | | $375 | $425 |

B-12 N Portaflex Amp

1961-1965. 25 watts, 2x12", 2 6L6 power tubes.

| 1961-1965 | | $1,100 | $1,375 |

MODEL YEAR	FEATURES	EXC. COND. LOW	HIGH

B-12 X/B-12 XT Portaflex Amp
1961-1969. Tube, 50 watts, 2x12", reverb, vibrato, 2x7027A power tubes.

| 1961-1969 | Style 1 | $900 | $1,100 |
| 1961-1969 | Style 2 | $1,100 | $1,375 |

B-15 N (NB, NC, NF) Portaflex Amp
1960-1970. Introduced as B-15 using 2 6L6 power tubes, B-15 N in '61, B-15 NB in '62, B-15 NC with rectifier tube in '64, B-15 NF with fixed-bias 2 6L6 power tubes and 30 watts in '67, 1x15".

1960-1965		$1,200	$1,500
1966-1970	1x15"	$1,000	$1,250
1967-1968	2x15"	$1,100	$1,375

B-15 R Portaflex Amp (Reissue)
1997-2007. Reissue of '65 Portaflex 1x15", blue check, 60/100 watts.

| 1997-2007 | | $900 | $1,100 |

B-15 S Portaflex Amp
1971-1977. 60 watts, 2x7027A power tubes, 1x12".

| 1971-1977 | | $900 | $1,100 |

B-18 N Portaflex Amp
1964-1969. Bass, 50 watts, 1x18".

| 1964-1965 | | $1,500 | $1,800 |
| 1966-1969 | | $1,300 | $1,500 |

B-25 Amp
1969 only. 55 watts, 2 7027A power tubes, 2x15", no reverb, guitar amp.

| 1969 | | $825 | $1,000 |

B-25 B Bass Amp
1969-1980. Bass amp, 55 watts, 2 7027A power tubes, 2x15".

| 1969-1980 | | $825 | $1,000 |

B-50 R Rocket Bass Amp (Reissue)
1996-2005. 50 watts, 1x12" combo, vintage-style blue check cover.

| 1996-2005 | | $300 | $400 |

B-100 R Rocket Bass Amp (Reissue)
1996-2005. Solidstate, 100 watts, 1x15" combo bass amp, vintage-style blue check cover.

| 1996-2005 | | $300 | $400 |

B-115 Amp
1973-1980. 120 watts, solidstate, 1x15" combo.

| 1973-1980 | | $300 | $375 |

B-410 Bass Amp
1973-1980. Solidstate, 120 watts, 4x10", black vinyl, black grille.

| 1973-1980 | | $350 | $425 |

BA Series Amp
2000-present. Solidstate bass combo amps, model number is speaker config.

| 2000-2010 | BA-112, 50w | $200 | $225 |
| 2000-2010 | BA-115, 100w | $200 | $225 |

BT-15 Amp
1966-1968. Ampeg introduced solidstate amps in '66, the same year as Fender. Solidstate, 50 watts, 1x15", generally used as a bass amp. The BT-15D has 2 1x15" cabinets. The BT-15C is a 2x15" column portaflex cabinet.

| 1966-1968 | | $300 | $375 |

BT-18 Amp
1966-1968. Solidstate, 50 watts, 1x18", generally used as a bass amp. The BT-18D has dual 1x18" cabinets. The BT-18C is a 2x18" column portaflex cabinet.

| 1966-1968 | | $300 | $375 |

ET-1 Echo Twin Amp
1961-1964. Tube, 30 watts, 1x12", stereo reverb.

| 1961-1964 | | $900 | $1,200 |

ET-2 Super Echo Twin Amp
1962-1964. Tube, 2x12", 30 watts, stereo reverb.

| 1962-1964 | | $1,100 | $1,300 |

G-12 Gemini I Amp
1964-1971. Tube, 1x12", 22 watts, reverb.

| 1964-1971 | | $500 | $625 |

G-15 Gemini II Amp
1965-1968. Tube, 30 watts, 1x15", reverb.

| 1965-1968 | | $525 | $650 |

G-18 Amp
1977-1980. Solidstate, 1 channel, 10 watts, 1x8", volume, treble, and bass controls.

| 1977-1980 | | $75 | $100 |

G-20 Gemini 20
1969-1970. Tubes, 35 watts, 2x10".

| 1969-1970 | | $600 | $750 |

G-110 Amp
1978-1980. Solidstate, 20 watts, 1x10", reverb, tremolo.

| 1978-1980 | | $125 | $150 |

G-115 Amp
1979-1980. Solidstate, 175 watts, 1x15" JBL, reverb and tremolo, designed for steel guitar.

| 1979-1980 | | $150 | $200 |

G-212 Amp
1973-1980. Solidstate, 120 watts, 2x12".

| 1973-1980 | | $175 | $225 |

GS-12 Rocket 2 Amp
1965-1968. This name replaced the Reverberocket 2 (II), 15 watts, 1x12".

| 1965-1968 | | $425 | $525 |

GS-12-R Reverberocket 2 Amp
1965-1969. Tube, 1x12", 18 watts, reverb. Called the Reverberocket II in '68 and '69, then Rocket II in '69.

| 1965-1969 | | $525 | $650 |

GS-15-R Gemini VI Amp
1966-1967. 30 watts, 1x15", single channel, considered to be "the accordion version" of the Gemini II.

| 1966-1967 | | $525 | $650 |

GT-10 Amp
1971-1980. Solidstate, 15 watts, 1x10", basic practice amp with reverb.

| 1971-1980 | | $125 | $150 |

GV-22 Gemini 22 Amp
1969-1972. Tube, 30 watts, 2x12".

| 1969-1972 | | $650 | $775 |

J-12 Jet Amp
1957-1964, 1967-1972. 20 watts, 1x12", 6V6GT power tubes. Second addition, also known as the Jet II, was like the J-12 D Jet but with 12AX7s.

1957-1958	Rough tan	$550	$700
1959	Blue	$575	$650
1960-1963	Blue	$450	$525
1967-1972	Model reappears	$350	$400

1965 Ampeg B-15-N

Ampeg B-50 R Rocket Bass Amp (reissue)

Ampeg G-15 Gemini II

Early 1960 Ampeg M-15 Big M

1966 Ampeg Rocket 2

(Rob Bernstein)

Ampeg Reverbojet 275

MODEL YEAR FEATURES	EXC. COND. LOW	HIGH
J-12 A Jet Amp		
1964. Jet Amp with 7591A power tubes.		
1964	$350	$425
J-12 D Jet Amp		
1966. Jet Amp with new solidstate rectifier.		
1966	$350	$425
J-12 R Reverbojet Amp		
1967-1970. 18 watts, 1x12" combo, single channel, tremolo and reverb.		
1967-1970	$300	$400
J-12 T Jet Amp		
1965, 2006-2008. J-12 A with revised preamp.		
1965	$350	$425
J-20 Jet Amp		
2007-2008. Tubes, 20 watts, 1x12.		
2007-2008	$375	$425
Jet II/J-12 T		
2007-2008. 15 watts, 1x12".		
2007-2008	$250	$275
M-12 Mercury Amp		
1957-1965. 15 watts, 2 channels, Rocket 1x12".		
1957-1959	$475	$550
1960-1965	$450	$525
M-15 Big M Amp		
1959-1965. 20 watts, 2x6L6 power, 1x15".		
1959	$550	$650
1960-1965	$525	$625
Model 815 Bassamp Amp		
1955. 15 watt combo, 1 channel.		
1955	$600	$750
Model 820 Bassamp Amp		
1956-1958. 20 watt combo, 1 channel.		
1956-1958	$600	$750
Model 822 Bassamp Amp		
1957-1958. 2 channel 820.		
1957-1958	$650	$800
Model 830 Bassamp Amp		
1956-1958. 30 watt combo.		
1956-1958	$675	$825
Model 835 Bassamp Amp		
1959-1961. 35 watt 1x15" combo, 2 channels.		
1959-1961	$700	$850
PB Series		
2002-2008. Portabass Series amps and speaker cabs.		
2002-2004 PB-122H Cab	$225	$250
2002-2008 PB-250 Head	$250	$300
R-12 B Rocket Amp		
1964. 12 watts, 1x12", follow-up to the R-12 Rocket.		
1964	$500	$625
R-12 R Reverberocket Amp		
1961-1963. Rocket with added on-board reverb.		
1961-1963	$625	$775
R-12 R Reverberocket Amp (Reissue)		
1996-2007. 50 watts, 2xEL34 power tubes, 1x12" (R-212R is 2x12").		
1996-2007	$350	$425
R-12 R-B Reverberocket Amp		
1964. 7591A power tubes replace R-12-R 6V6 power tubes.		
1964	$625	$775

MODEL YEAR FEATURES	EXC. COND. LOW	HIGH
R-12 Rocket Amp		
1957-1963. 12 watts, 1x12", 1 channel.		
1957-1963	$525	$650
R-12 R-T Reverberocket Amp		
1965. 7591A or 7868 power tubes, revised preamp.		
1965	$625	$775
R-15 R Superbreverb (Supereverb) Amp		
1963-1964. 1x15 combo, originally called Super-everb, but Fender had a problem with that name.		
1963-1964	$800	$975
R-212 R Reverberocket Combo 50 Amp (Reissue)		
1996-2007. 50 watts, 2x12", all tube reissue, vintage-style blue check cover, vintage-style grille.		
1996-1999	$450	$525
2000-2007	$450	$525
SB-12 Portaflex Amp		
1965-1971. 22 watts, 1x12", designed for use with Ampeg's Baby Bass, black.		
1965-1971	$675	$775
SBT Amp		
1969-1971. 120 watts, 1x15", bass version of SST Amp.		
1969-1971	$650	$750
SE-412 Cabinet		
1996-1999. 4x12" speakers.		
1996-1999	$300	$350
SJ-12 R/RT Super Jet Amp		
1996-2007. 50 watts, tube, 1x12", SJ-12 RT has tremolo added.		
1996-2007	$300	$350
SS-35 Amp		
1987-1992. Solidstate, 35 watts, 1x12", black vinyl, black grille, large A logo.		
1987-1992	$175	$200
SS-70 Amp		
1987-1990. Solidstate, 70 watts, 1x12".		
1987-1990	$225	$275
SS-70 C Amp		
1987-1992. Solidstate, 70 watts, 2x10", chorus, black vinyl.		
1987-1992	$250	$300
SS-140 C Amp		
1987-1992. Solidstate, 2x12 combo, chorus and reverb, large SS-140C logo on upper right front control panel.		
1987-1992	$275	$325
SS-150 Amp Head		
1987-1992. Solidstate, 150 watts.		
1987-1992	$275	$325
SVT Bass Amp Head		
1969-1985. 300 watt head only.		
1969 Stones World-Tour Assoc.	$1,800	$2,200
1970-1972	$1,600	$2,000
1973-1979	$1,300	$1,600
1980-1985	$1,200	$1,500
SVT Bass Cabinets		
1969-1985. Two 8x10" cabs only.		
1969	$1,300	$1,600
1970-1985	$1,200	$1,500

MODEL YEAR	FEATURES	EXC. COND. LOW	HIGH

SVT-II Bass Amp Head
1989-1994. Rackmount, 300 watts, tube.
1989-1994 $900 $1,050

SVT-2 Pro Bass Amp Head
1993-present. 300 watts, rackmount, tube preamp and power section, black metal.
1993-2010 $950 $1,100

SVT-III Bass Amp Head
1991-1994. Mosfet, 275/450 watts.
1991-1994 $650 $750

SVT-3 Pro Bass Amp Head
1993-present. Tube preamp and MOS-FET power section, 450 watts, rackmount, black metal.
1993-2010 $550 $625

SVT-4 Pro Bass Amp Head
1997-present. Rackmount, all tube preamp, MOS-FET power section yielding 1600 watts.
1997-2010 $800 $900

SVT-5 Pro Bass Amp Head
2002-2005. Rackmount, all tube preamp, MOS-FET power section yielding 1350 watts.
2002-2005 $800 $900

SVT-6 Pro Bass Amp Head
2005-2009. Rackmount, all tube preamp, MOS-FET power section yielding 1100 watts.
2005-2009 $550 $650

SVT-15 E Bass Cabinet
1994-present. Compact 1x15.
1994-2010 $250 $300

SVT-100 T Bass Combo Amp
1990-1992. Solidstate, ultra-compact bass combo, 100 watts, 2x8".
1990-1992 $375 $425

SVT-200 T Amp Head
1987 only. Solidstate, 200 watts to 8 ohms or 320 watts to 4 ohms.
1987 $325 $375

SVT-350 Amp Head
1995-2005. Solidstate head, 350 watts, graphic EQ.
1995-2005 $375 $425

SVT-400 Amp Head
1987-1997. Solidstate, 2 200 watt stereo amps, rack-mountable head with advanced (in '87) technology.
1987-1997 $375 $425

SVT-410 HE Bass Cabinet
1994-present. 4x10, horn/driver.
1994-2010 $400 $450

SVT-450 H Amp Head
2007-present. Solidstate head, 275/450 watts.
2007-2010 $450 $500

SVT-610 HLF Cabinet
2003-present. 6x10, horn/driver.
2003-2010 $475 $575

SVT-810 E Cabinet
1994-present. 8x10.
1994-2010 $625 $750

SVT-AV Anniversary Edition Amp
2001 $800 $925

SVT-CL Classic Bass Amp Head
1994-present. Tube, 300 watts.
1994-2010 $850 $950

V-2 Amp Cabinet
1971-1980. 4x12" cab, black tolex.
1971-1980 $400 $450

V-2 Amp Head
1971-1980. 60 watt tube head.
1971-1980   Head only $450 $525

V-4 B Bass Amp Head
1972-1980. Bass version of V-4 without reverb.
1972-1980   Head only $550 $625

V-4 Cabinet
1970s. Single 4x12" cabinet only.
1970-1980 $375 $425

V-7 SC Amp
1981-1985. Tube, 100 watts, 1x12", master volume, channel switching, reverb.
1981-1985 $525 $600

VH-70 Amp
1991-1992. 70 watts, 1x12" combo with channel switching.
1991-1992 $325 $375

VH-140 C Amp
1992-1995. Varying Harmonics (VH) with Chorus (C), two 70-watt channel stereo, 2x12".
1992-1995 $375 $425

VH-150 Amp Head
1991-1992. 150 watts, channel-switchable, reverb.
1991-1992 $300 $350

VL-502 Amp
1991-1995. 50 watts, channel-switchable, all tube.
1991-1995 $350 $400

VL-1001 Amp Head
1991-1993. 100 watts, non-switchable channels, all tube.
1991-1993 $325 $375

VL-1002 Amp Head
1991-1995. 100 watts, channel-switchable, all tube.
1991-1995 $350 $400

VT-22 Amp
1970-1980. 100 watt combo version of V-4, 2x12".
1970-1980 $700 $800

VT-40 Amp
1971-1980. 60 watt combo, 4x10".
1971-1980 $700 $800

VT-60 Amp Head
1989-1991. Tube head only, 6L6 power, 60 watts.
1989-1991 $350 $400

VT-60 Combo Amp
1989-1991. Tube, 6L6 power, 60 watts, 1x12".
1989-1991 $425 $500

VT-120 Amp Head
1989-1992. 120 watts, 6L6 tube head.
1989-1992 $350 $400

VT-120 Combo Amp
1989-1992. Tube, 6L6 power, 120 watts, 1x12", also offered as head only.
1989-1992 $425 $500

Anderson Amplifiers

1993-present. Tube amps and combos built by Jack Anderson in Gig Harbor, Washington.

Ampeg SVT-4 Pro

Anderson 20-45 Combo

Ampeg SVT-CL Classic Bass Amp Head

AMPS

Area 51 Model One

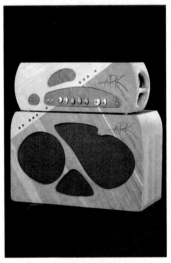

Ark Model A+

Bacino

MODEL YEAR	FEATURES	EXC. COND. LOW	HIGH

Andrews

2006-present. Professional grade, production/custom, amps and cabinets built by Jeff Andrews in Dunwoody, Georgia.

ARACOM Amplifiers

1997-present. Jeff Aragaki builds his tube amp heads, combos, and cabinets in Morgan Hill, California.

Area 51

2003-present. Guitar amps made in Newaygo, Michigan (made in Texas until early '06), by Dan Albrecht. They also build effects.

Aria/Aria Pro II

1960-present. The Japanese instrument builder offered a range of amps from around '79 to '89.

Ariatone

1962. Another private brand made by Magnatone, sold by private music and accordion studios.

Model 810
1962. 12 watts, 1x8, tremolo, brown cover.

1962		$325	$400

Ark

2005-present. Owners Matt Schellenberg and Bill Compeau build professional and premium grade, production/custom amps in Farmington Hills, Michigan (cabinet shop), with all wiring done in Windsor, Ontario.

Ashdown Amplification

1999-present. Founded in England by Mark Gooday after he spent several years with Trace Elliot, Ashdown offers amps, combos, and cabinets.

Audio Guild

1969 to 1971. Private brand by Magnatone at the end of their era.

Grand Prix
1969-1971. Tube combo 1x12, reverb and tremolo, dual channel, large 'Grand Prix' logo on upper front panel.

1969-1971		$375	$450

Ultraflex
1969-1971. All-tube, higher power combo, 2 speakers, reverb and tremolo.

1969-1971		$550	$650

Universal
1969-1971. Tube combo amp with reverb and tremolo, 'Universal' logo on front, 'Mfg. by Audio Guild' logo below tremolo control on front panel.

1969-1971		$375	$450

Audiovox

Ca.1935-ca.1950. Paul Tutmarc's Audiovox Manufacturing, of Seattle, Washington, was a pioneer in electric lap steels, basses, guitars and amps.

Auralux

2000-present. Founded by Mitchell Omori and David Salzmann, Auralux builds effects and tube amps in Highland Park, Illinois.

Austin

1999-present. Budget and intermediate grade, production, guitar and bass amps imported by St. Louis Music. They also offer guitars, basses, mandolins, ukes and banjos.

Bacino

2002-present. Tube combo amps, heads and cabinets built by Mike Bacino in Arlington Heights, Illinois.

Backline Engineering

2004-present. Gary Lee builds his tube amp heads in Camarillo, California. He also builds guitar effects.

Bad Cat Amplifier Company

1999-present. Founded in Corona, California by James and Debbie Heidrich, Bad Cat offers class A combo amps, heads, cabinets and effects. In '09 the company was moved to Anaheim.

Baer Amplification

2009-present. Professional grade, production, bass amps built in Palmdale, California by Roger Baer.

Baldwin

Piano maker Baldwin offered amplifiers from 1965 to '70. The amps were solidstate with organ-like pastel-colored pushbutton switches.

Exterminator Amp
1965-1970. Solidstate, 100 watts, 2x15"/2x12"/2x7", 4' vertical combo cabinet, reverb and tremolo, Supersound switch and slide controls.

1965-1970		$450	$525

Model B1 Bass Amp
1965-1970. Solidstate, 45 watts, 1x15"/1x12", 2 channels.

1965-1970		$225	$275

Model B2 Bass Amp
1965-1970. Solidstate, 35 watts, 1x15", 2 channels.

1965-1970		$200	$250

Model C1 Custom (Professional) Amp
1965-1970. Solidstate, 45 watts, 2x12", reverb and tremolo, Supersound switch and slide controls.

1965-1970		$300	$350

Model C2 Custom Amp
1965-1970. Solidstate, 40 watts, 2x12", reverb and tremolo.

1965-1970		$300	$350

Professional Deluxe
1965-1970. Supersound, 1x12.

1965-1970		$300	$350

MODEL		EXC. COND.	
YEAR	FEATURES	LOW	HIGH

Barcus-Berry
1964-present. Pickup maker Barcus-Berry offered a line of amps from '75 to '79.

Barth
1960s. Products of Paul Barth's Barth Musical Instrument Company. Barth was also a co-founder of Rickenbacker.

Studio Deluxe 958 Amp
1960s. Small practice combo amp.

1950-1960s		$300	$350

Basson
2001-present. Speaker cabinets for guitar, bass and PA made by Victor Basson in Carlsbad, California.

BC Audio
2009-present. Bruce Clement builds his production/custom, professional grade, tube amps in San Francisco, California.

Bedrock
1984-1997. Tube amp company founded by Brad Jeter and Ron Pinto in Nashua, New Hampshire. They produced 50 amps carrying the brand name Fred before changing the company name to Bedrock in '86. Around '88, Jay Abend joined the company, eventually becoming President. In '88, Evan Cantor joined the company as an amp designer. In '90, Jeter left Bedrock and, shortly after, Pinto and Abend moved the company to Farmington, Massachusetts. The company closed in '97.

Behringer
1989-present. Founded in Germany by Uli Behringer, offering a full line of professional audio products. In '98 they added tube, solidstate, and modeling amps. They also offer effects and guitars.

Beltone
1950s-1960s. Japan's Teisco made a variety of brands for others, including the Beltone line of amps. There were also guitars sold under this name made from a variety of builders.

BigDog Amps
2005-2007. Tube head and combo guitar and bass amps and speaker cabinets built in Galveston, Texas, by Steve Gaines.

Big M
1966-1967, 1975-1976. The Marshall name in Germany was owned by a trumpet maker, so Jim Marshall marketed his amps and cabs there under the Big M Made In England brand name until the issue was resolved. A decade later, in a failed attempt to lower speaker cabinets prices in the U.S., Marshall's American distributor built cabs, with Marshall's permission, on Long Island, mainly for sales with Marshall solidstate lead and bass heads

MODEL		EXC. COND.	
YEAR	FEATURES	LOW	HIGH

of the time, and labeled them Big M. They were loaded with cheaper Eminence speakers, instead of the usual Celestions.

Big M Cabinets
1975-1976. The M2412 with 4x12 for lead and the M2212F 2x12 bass cabs.

1975-1976	2x12	$325	$400
1975-1976	4x12	$700	$800

JTM-45 Amp Head
1966-1967. Branded Big M.

1966-1967		$5,500	$7,000

Blackstar Amplification
2007-present. Joel Richardson builds his intermediate and professional grade guitar amps and cabinets in Northampton, England. He also offers effects pedals.

Blankenship Amplification
2005-present. Roy Blankenship began building tube head and combo amps and cabinets in North Hollywood, California. He also built amps under the Point Blank brand. In '09 he moved his business to Houston, Texas.

Blue Tone Amplifiers
2002-present. Founded by Alex Cooper in Worcestershire, England, Blue Tone offers professional grade, production amps employing their virtual valve technology.

Bluetron
2004-present. Tube amp heads, combos, and speaker cabinets built by David Smith in Mt. Juliet, Tennessee.

Bogen
1932-present. Founded in New York City by David Bogen, this company has made a wide range of electronic products for consumers and industry including a few small guitar combo tube amps such as the GA-5 and GA-20 and tube PA equipment. The company name (David Bogen, New York) and model number are on the lower back panel. The '50s Bogen tube amps are well respected as tone-generating workhorses. In '56 he sold the company and it was moved to New Jersey, and they continue to offer pro audio PA gear.

Bogner
1988-present. Tube combos, amp heads, and speaker cabinets from builder Reinhold Bogner of North Hollywood, California.

Brand X
2004-2009. Small solidstate combo amps from Fender Musical Instruments Corporation.

Bronson
1930s-1950s. Private brand utilized by Detroit lap steel instruction George Bronson. These amps

BC Audio

Behringer VT30FX

Bogner Shiva
(Rob Bernstein)

Callaham EL34 Amp

Carr, Rambler
Rob Bernstein

Chicago Blues Box Kingston

MODEL YEAR	FEATURES	EXC. COND. LOW	HIGH

often sold with a matching lap steel and were made by other companies.

Lap Steel Amp

MODEL YEAR	FEATURES	EXC. COND. LOW	HIGH
1930-1950s	Melody King 1x10	$300	$375
1930-1950s	Pearloid	$200	$250

Bruno (Tony)
1995-present. Tube combos, amp heads, and speaker cabinets from builder Tony Bruno of Cairo, New York.

Budda
1995-present. Amps, combos, and cabinets originally built by Jeff Bober and Scott Sier in San Francisco, California. In '09, Budda was acquired by Peavey and they started building Budda products in their Meridian, Mississippi Custom Shop. They also produce effects pedals.

Burriss
2001-present. Bob Burriss builds custom and production guitar and bass tube amps, bass preamps and speaker cabinets in Lexington, Kentucky. He also builds effects.

Byers
2001-present. Tube combo amps built by Trevor Byers, a former Fender Custom Shop employee, in Corona, California. His initial focus was on small early-Fender era and K & F era models.

Cage
1998-present. Production/custom, professional grade, amp heads and cabinets built in Damascus, Maryland by Pete Cage.

California
2004-present. Student/budget level amps and guitar/amp packs, imported by Eleca International.

Callaham
1989-present. Custom tube amp heads built by Bill Callaham in Winchester, Virginia. He also builds solidbody electric guitars.

Campbell Sound
1999-present. Intermediate and professional grade, production/custom, guitar amps built by Walt Campbell in Roseville, California.

Carl Martin
1993-present. In '05, the Denmark-based guitar effects company added tube combo amps.

Carlsbro
1959-present. Guitar, bass, and keyboard combo amps, heads and cabinets from Carlsbro Electronics Limited of Nottingham, England. They also offer PA amps and speaker cabinets.

Carol-Ann Custom Amplifiers
2003-present. Premium grade, production/custom, tube guitar amps built by Alan Phillips in North Andover, Massachusetts.

Carr Amplifiers
1998-present. Steve Carr started producing amps in his Chapel Hill, North Carolina amp repair business in '98. The company is now located in Pittsboro, North Carolina, and makes tube combo amps, heads, and cabinets.

Carvin
1946-present. Founded in Los Angeles by Lowell C. Kiesel who sold guitars and amps under the Kiesel name until late-'49, when the Carvin brand was introduced. They added small tube amps to their product line in '47 and today offer a variety of models. They also build guitars and basses.

Caswell Amplification
2006-present. Programmable tube amp heads built by Tim Caswell in California.

Chicago Blues Box/Butler Custom Sound
2001-present. Tube combo amps built by Dan Butler of Butler Custom Sound originally in Elmhurst, and now in Lombard, Illinois.

Clark Amplification
1995-present. Tweed-era replica tube amplifiers from builder Mike Clark, of Cayce, South Carolina. He also makes effects.

Club Amplifiers
2005-present. Don Anderson builds intermediate to premium grade, custom, vacuum tube guitar amps and cabinets in Felton, California.

CMI
1976-1977. Amps made by Marshall for Cleartone Musical Instruments of Birmingham, England. Mainly PA amps, but two tube heads and one combo amp were offered.

CMI Electronics
Late-1960s-1970s. CMI branded amplifiers designed to replace the Gibson Kalamazoo-made amps that ceased production in '67 when Gibson moved the electronics lab to Chicago, Illinois.

Sabre Reverb 1 Amp
Late-1960s-early-1970s. Keyboard amp, 1x15" and side-mounted horn, utilized mid- to late-'60s cabinets and grilles, look similar to mid-late '60s Gibson black tolex and Epiphone gray amp series, black or gray tolex and silver grille.

MODEL YEAR	FEATURES	EXC. COND. LOW	HIGH
1970		$100	$150

MODEL YEAR	FEATURES	EXC. COND. LOW	HIGH

CMW Amps

2002-present. Chris Winsemius builds his premium grade, production/custom, guitar amps in The Netherlands.

Comins

1992-present. Archtop luthier Bill Comins, of Willow Grove, Pennsylvania, introduced a Comins combo amp, built in collaboration with George Alessandro, in '03.

Coral

1967-1969. In '66 MCA bought Danelectro and in '67 introduced the Coral brand of guitars, basses and amps. The amp line included tube, solidstate, and hybrid models ranging from small combo amps to the Kilowatt (1000 Watts of Peak Power!), a hybrid head available with two 8x12" cabinets.

Cornell/Plexi

Amps based on the '67 Marshall plexi chassis built by Denis Cornell in the United Kingdom. Large Plexi logo on front.

Cosmosound

Italy's Cosmosound made small amps with Leslie rotating drums in the late '60s and '70s. They also made effects pedals.

Crafter

1986-present. Giant Korean guitar and bass manufacturer Crafter also offered an acoustic guitar amp.

Crate

1979-present. Solidstate and tube amplifiers originally distributed by St. Louis Music. In '05 LOUD Technologies acquired SLM and the Crate brand.

Solidstate Amp
1970s-1990s. Various student to mid-level amps, up to 150 watts.

1970s		$50	$75
1980s		$50	$75
1990s		$50	$75

Vintage Club Series Amps
1994-2001. Various tube amps.

1994-1997	5310/VC-5310	$300	$325
1994-1999	20	$200	$225
1994-1999	30/VC-2110	$275	$300
1994-1999	30/VC-3112	$300	$325
1994-1999	50/VC-50	$275	$300
1994-1999	60/VC-60	$275	$300
1994-2001	5212/VC-5212	$300	$325

Cruise Audio Systems

1999-2003. Founded by Mark Altekruse, Cruise offered amps, combos, and cabinets built in Cuyahoga Falls, Ohio. It appears the company was out of business by '03.

Cruzer

Solidstate guitar amps built by Korea's Crafter Guitars. They also build guitars, basses and effects under that brand.

Custom Kraft

Late-1950s-1968. A house brand of St. Louis Music Supply, instruments built by others. They also offered basses and guitars.

Import Student Amp

1960s	1x6 or 1x8	$50	$75

Valco-Made Amp

1960s	1x12 or 1x15	$325	$375

Da Vinci

Late-1950s-early-1960s. Another one of several private brands (for example, Unique, Twilighter, Titano, etc.) that Magnatone made for teaching studios and accordion companies.

Model 250 Amp
1958-1962. Similar to Magnatone Model 250 with about 20 watts and 1x12".

1958-1962		$850	$1,000

Model 440A/D40 Custom
1964-1966. 1x12", reverb, vibrato.

1964-1966		$1,000	$1,200

Danelectro

1946-1969, 1997-present. Founded in Red Bank, New Jersey, by Nathan I. "Nate" or "Nat" Daniel. His first amps were made for Montgomery Ward in '47, and in '48 he began supplying Silvertone Amps for Sears. His own amps were distributed by Targ and Dinner as Danelectro and S.S. Maxwell brands. In '96, the Evets Corporation, of San Clemente, California, reintroduced the Danelectro brand on effects, amps, basses and guitars. In early '03, Evets discontinued the amp line, but still offers guitars, basses, and effects.

Cadet Amp
1955-1969. A longstanding model name, offered in different era cabinets and coverings but all using the standard 3-tube 1x6" format. Models 122 and 123 had 6 watts. 1x6", 3 tubes, 1 volume, 1 control, 2 inputs, 16x15x6" 'picture frame' cabinet with light-colored cover, dark grille.

1955-1959	1x6"	$200	$250
1960		$200	$250
1961		$200	$250
1962	Model 122	$200	$250
1963-1965	Model 123	$200	$250
1966	1x6"	$200	$250
1967-1969	1x6"	$200	$250

Challenger Amp
1950s. Compact combo amp, 5 tubes including 2x6L6, 2 channels, bass and treble control, 2 vibrato controls, golden-brown cover, tan woven cloverleaf-shaped grille.

1950s		$350	$425

CMW Amps Plexi Junior

Crate V100H

Cruise MQ4212

AMPS

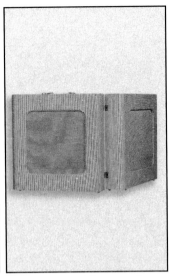

Danelectro Commando

Danelectro Maestro

Dean Bassola 40

MODEL YEAR	FEATURES	EXC. COND. LOW	HIGH

DM-10 Amp
1965-1967. Combo 'large knobs' cabinet, 10 watts, 1x8", 2 control vibrato, 2 inputs, 1 volume, 1 tone, dark vinyl with light grille, DM-10 logo next to script Danelectro logo right upper front.

1965-1967		$275	$350

DM-25 Amp
1965-1967. Stow-away piggyback, 25 watts, 1x12", reverb, vibrato, 4 inputs, 9 control knobs, dark vinyl cabinet with light grille, DM-25 logo next to script Danelectro logo below control knobs.

1965-1967		$550	$675

DS-50 Amp
1965-1969. 75 watts, 3x10" stow-away piggyback cabinet, reverb and tremolo, suitable for bass accordion.

1965-1969		$725	$875

DS-100 Amp
1967-1969. 150 watts, stow-away piggyback cabinet, 6x10" Jensens, reverb, tremolo, suitable for bass accordion, 36x22x12" cabinet weighs 79 lbs.

1965-1969		$825	$1,025

DTR-40
1965. Solidstate combo, 40 watts, 2x10", vibrato, DTR-40 logo under control knobs.

1965		$350	$425

Model 68 Special Amp
1950s. 20 watts, 1x12", light tweed-fabric cover, light grille, leather handle, script Danelectro plexi-plate logo.

1950s		$550	$675

Model 72 Centurion Amp (Series D)
1954-1957. 1x12" combo, blond tweed, rounded front D cabinet.

1954-1957		$550	$675

Model 89 Amp (Series D)
1954-1957. 1x15" combo, blond tweed, rounded front D cabinet.

1954-1957		$575	$700

Model 98 Twin 12 Amp (Series D)
1954-ca.1957. Blond tweed-style cover, brown control panel, 2x12", vibrato speed and strength, rounded front Series D.

1954-1957		$850	$1,050

Model 132 Corporal Amp
Early-1960s. 2x8", 4 tubes, 3 inputs, 4 control knobs, 19x15x7" picture frame cabinet in light-colored material with dark grille.

1962-1964		$450	$550

Model 142 Viscount Amp
Late-1950s. Combo amp, lower watts, 1x12", light cover, brown grille, vibrato.

1959		$550	$675

Model 143 Viscount Amp
1962-1964. 12 watts, 1x12", 6 tubes, 2 control vibrato, 1 volume, 1 tone, 'picture frame' narrow panel cabinet, light-colored cover with dark grille.

1962-1964		$425	$525

Model 217 Twin-Fifteen Amp
1960s. Combo amp, 60 watts, 2x15" Jensen C15P speakers, black cover, white-silver grille, 2 channels with tremolo.

1962-1964		$750	$900

Model 274 Centurion Amp
1961-1962. 15 watts, 1x12", 6 tubes, 2 channels with separate volume, treble, bass controls, Vibravox electronic vibrato, 4 inputs, 20x20x9 weighing 25 lbs., 'picture frame' cabinet with black cover and light grille.

1961-1962		$425	$525

Model 275 Centurion Amp
1963-1964. Reverb added in '63, 15 watts, 1x12", 7 tubes, Vibravox vibrato, 2 channels with separate volume, bass, treble, picture frame cabinet with black cover and light grille.

1963-1964		$550	$675

Model 291 Explorer Amp
1961-1964. 30 watts, 1x15", 7 tubes, 2 channels each with volume, bass, and treble controls, Vibravox vibrato, square picture frame cabinet, black cover and light grille.

1961-1964		$525	$650

Model 300 Twin-Twelve Amp
1962-1964. 30 watts, 2x12", reverb, 8 tubes, 2 channels with separate volume, bass, and treble, Vibravox vibrato, picture frame cabinet with black cover and light grille.

1962-1964		$750	$900

Model 354 Twin-Twelve (Series C) Amp
Early 1950s. Part of C Series product line, Twin 12" combo with diagonal speaker baffle holes, brown cover with light gold grille, Twin Twelve script logo on front as well as script Danelectro logo, diagonally mounted amp chassis, leather handle.

1950s		$850	$1,000

Dean
1976-present. Acoustic, electric, and bass amps made overseas. They also offer guitars, banjos, mandolins, and basses.

Dean Markley
The string and pickup manufacturer added a line of amps in 1983. Distributed by Kaman, they now offer combo guitar and bass amps and PA systems.

K Series Amps
1980s. All solidstate, various models include K-15 (10 watts, 1x6"), K-20/K-20X (10 to 20 watts, 1x8", master volume, overdrive switch), K-50 (25 watts, 1x10", master volume, reverb), K-75 (35 watts, 1x12", master volume, reverb), K-200B (compact 1x12 combo).

1980s	K-15, 20, 20X	$30	$35
1980s	K-200B	$100	$125
1980s	K-50	$35	$40
1980s	K-75	$55	$65

DeArmond
Pickup manufacturer DeArmond starting building tube guitar amps in 1950s. By '63, they were out of the amp business. They also made effects. Fender revived the name for a line of guitars in the late '90s.

R-5T Amp
1950s. Low power, 1 6V6, single speaker combo amp.

1950s		$1,300	$1,500

MODEL YEAR	FEATURES	EXC. COND. LOW	HIGH

R-15T Amp
1950s. Low to mid power, 2 6V6 power section, single speaker.

1950s		$1,500	$1,700

Decca
Mid-1960s. Small student-level amps made in Japan by Teisco and imported by Decca Records. They also offered guitars and a bass.

Demeter
1980-present. James Demeter founded the company as Innovative Audio and renamed it Demeter Amplification in '90. Originally located in Van Nuys, in '08 they moved to Templeton, California. First products were direct boxes and by '85, amps were added. Currently they build amp heads, combos, and cabinets. They also have pro audio gear and guitar effects.

Diaz
Early-1980s-2002. Cesar Diaz restored amps for many of rock's biggest names, often working with them to develop desired tones. Along the way he produced his own line of professional and premium grade, high-end custom amps and effects. Diaz died in '02; his family announced plans to resume production of effects in '04.

Dickerson
1937-1947. Dickerson was founded by the Dickerson brothers in 1937, primarily for electric lap steels and small amps. Instruments were also private branded for Cleveland's Oahu company, and for the Gourley brand. By '47, the company changed ownership and was renamed Magna Electronics (Magnatone).

Oasis Amp
1940s-1950s. Blue pearloid cover, 1x10", low wattage, Dickerson silk-screen logo on grille with Hawaiian background.

1940s		$225	$275

Dime Amplification
2011-present. Solidstate combo and head amps and cabinets from Dean Guitars, designed by Gary Sunda and Grady Champion.

Dinosaur
2004-present. Student/budget level amps and guitar/amp packs, imported by Eleca International. They also offer effects.

Divided By Thirteen
Mid-1990s-present. Fred Taccone builds his tube amp heads and cabinets in the Los Angeles, California area. He also builds effects.

Dr. Z
1988-present. Mike Zaite started producing his Dr. Z line of amps in the basement of the Music

Manor in Maple Heights, Ohio. The company is now located in its own larger facility in the same city. Dr. Z offers combo amps, heads and cabinets.

Drive
2000s-present. Budget grade, production, import solidstate amps. They also offer guitars.

DST Engineering
2002-present. Jeff Swanson and Bob Dettorre build their tube amp combos, heads and cabinets in Beverly, Massachusetts. They also build reverb units.

Duca Tone
The Duca Tone brand was distributed by Lo Duca Brothers, Milwaukee, Wisconsin, which also distributed EKO guitars in the U.S.

Tube Amp
1950s. 12 watts, 1x12".

1950s		$450	$550

Dumble
1963-present. Made by Howard Alexander Dumble, an early custom-order amp maker from California. Initial efforts were a few Mosrite amps for Semie Moseley. First shop was in '68 in Santa Cruz, California. Dumble amp values should be considered on a case-by-case basis. Early on, Dumble also modified other brands such as Fender and those Dumble-modified amps are also valuable, based on authenticated provenance.

Overdrive Special Amp and Cabinet
1970s-present. 100 watts, 1x12", known for durability, cabinets vary.

1970s-2000s		$30,000	$45,000

Dynamic Amps
2008-present. David Carambula builds production/custom, professional grade, combo amps, heads and cabinets in Kalamazoo, Michigan.

Earth Sound Research
1970s. Earth Sound was a product of ISC Audio of Farmingdale, New York, and offered a range of amps, cabinets and PA gear starting in the '70s. They also made Plush amps.

2000 G Half-Stack Amp
1970s. 100 watts plus cab.

1970s		$400	$475

Model G-1000 Amp Head
1970s	Reverb	$200	$225

Original 2000 Model 340 Amp
1970s. Black Tolex, 400-watt head and matching 2x15" cab.

1970s		$375	$450

Producer Model 440
1970s. 700-watt head and matching 2x15" cab.

1970s		$375	$450

Demeter TGA-2.1 Tube Guitar Amplifier

Dinosaur DG-200R

Dr. Z Maz 18

AMPS

Eden ENC112

Egnater Renegade

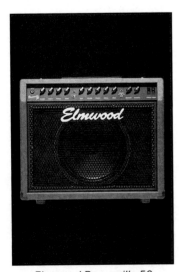

Elmwood Bonneville 50

MODEL YEAR	FEATURES	EXC. COND. LOW	HIGH

Revival Amp
1970s. 2x12" tweed twin copy, with similar back mounted control panel, tweed covering, but with solid-state preamp section and 4x6L6 power.

1970		$350	$400

Super Bass/B-2000 Amp
1970s. Tuck & roll black cover, 2 channels - super and normal, volume, bass, mid range, and treble tone controls, no reverb or tremolo.

1970s	Cabinet	$200	$225
1970s	Head only	$200	$250

Traveler Amp
1970s. Vertical cab solidstate combo amp, 50 watts, 2x12 offset, black tolex.

1977		$275	$300

EBS
1988-present. The EBS Sweden AB company builds professional grade, production bass amps and cabinets in Stockholm, Sweden. They also build effects.

Eden
1976-present. Founded by David Nordschow in Minnesota as a custom builder, Eden now offers a full line of amps, combos, and cabinets for the bassist, built in Mundelein, Illinois. In '02, the brand became a division of U.S. Music Corp (Washburn, Randall). They also produce the Nemesis brand of amps.

Egnater
1980-present. Production/custom, intermediate and professional grade, tube amps, combos, preamps and cabinets built in Berkley, Michigan by Bruce Egnater. He also imports some models.

EKO
1959-1985, 2000-present. In '67 EKO added amps to their product line, offering three piggyback and four combo amps, all with dark covering, dark grille, and the EKO logo. The amp line may have lasted into the early '70s. Since about 2000, EKO Asian-made, solidstate guitar and bass amps are again available. They also make basses and guitars.

Eleca
2004-present. Student level imported combo amps, Eleca logo on bottom of grille. They also offer guitars, effects and mandolins.

Electar
1996-2008. The Gibson owned Electar brand offered tube and solidstate amps, PA gear and wireless systems. Epiphone had a line of Electar amps in the 1930s.

Electro-Harmonix
1968-1981, 1996-present. Electro-Harmonix offered a few amps to go with its line of effects. See Effects section for more company information.

Freedom Brothers Amp
Introduced in 1977. Small AC/DC amp with 2x5 1/2" speakers. E-H has reissued the similar Freedom amp.

1977		$200	$225

Mike Matthews Dirt Road Special Amp
25 watts, 1x12" Celestion, built-in Small Stone phase shifter.

1977		$200	$225

Electromuse
1940s-1950s. Tube amps made by others, like Valco, and usually sold as a package with a lap steel. They also offered guitars.

Amps
Late-1940s. Vertical cabinet with metal handle, Electromuse stencil logo on front of cab.

1948-1949	Lower power	$175	$200

Electrosonic Amplifiers
2002-2010. Intermediate and professional grade, production/custom, tube amps built by Josh Corn in Boonville, Indiana. He also built effects.

Elk
Late-1960s. Japanese-made by Elk Gakki Co., Ltd. Many were copies of American designs. They also offered guitars and effects.

Custom EL 150L Amp
Late-1960s. Piggyback set, all-tube with head styled after very early Marshall and cab styled after large vertical Fender cab.

1968		$300	$350

Guitar Man EB 105 (Super Reverb) Amp
Late-1960s. All-tube, reverb, copy of blackface Super Reverb.

1968		$250	$300

Twin Amp 60/Twin Amp 50 EB202 Amps
Late-1960s. All-tube, reverb, copy of blackface Dual Showman set (head plus horizontal cab).

1968		$300	$350

Viking 100 VK 100 Amp
Late-1960s. Piggyback set, head styled after very early Marshall and cab styled after very large vertical Fender cab.

1968		$300	$350

Elmwood Amps
1998-present. Jan Alm builds his production/custom, professional and premium grade, guitar tube amps and cabinets in Tanumshede, Sweden.

Elpico
1960s. Made in Europe, PA tube amp heads sometimes used for guitar.

PA Power Tube Amp
1960s. Tubes, 20-watt, metal case, 3 channels, treble and bass control, 2 speaker outs on front panel, Elpico logo on front, small Mexican characterization logo on front.

1960s		$300	$350

AMPS

MODEL YEAR	FEATURES	EXC. COND. LOW	HIGH

Emery Sound

1997-present. Founded by Curt Emery in El Cerrito, California, Emery Sound specializes in custom-made low wattage tube amps.

Emmons

1970s-present. Owned by Lashley, Inc. of Burlington, North Carolina. Amps sold in conjunction with their steel guitars.

Epiphone

1928-present. Epiphone offered amps into the mid-'70s and reintroduced them in '91 with the EP series. Currently they offer tube and solidstate amps.

Century Amp
1939. Lap steel companion amp, 1x12" combo, lattice wood front with Electar insignia "E" logo.
| 1939 | | $400 | $500 |

Cornet Amp
1939. Lap steel companion amp, square shaped wood box, Electar insignia "E" logo.
| 1939 | | $325 | $400 |

E-30 B Amp
1972-1975. Solidstate model offered similarly to Gibson G-Series (not GA-Series), 30 watts, 2x10", 4 knobs.
| 1972-1975 | | $125 | $150 |

E-60 Amp
1972-1975. Solidstate, 30 watts, 1x10", volume and tone knobs.
| 1972-1975 | | $100 | $125 |

E-60 T Amp
1972-1975. E-60 with tremolo, volume, tone, and tremolo knobs.
| 1972-1975 | | $100 | $125 |

E-70 Amp
1971-1975. Solidstate, tremolo, 1x10", 3 knobs.
| 1971-1975 | | $100 | $125 |

E-1051 Amp
1970s. Tube practice amp, 1x10".
| 1970s | | $140 | $175 |

EA-12 RVT Futura Amp
1962-1967. Low- to mid-power, 4x8", '60s gray tolex, light grille.
| 1962-1967 | | $575 | $700 |

EA-14 RVT Ensign Amp
1965-1969. Gray tolex, silver-gray grille, 50 watts, 2x12", split C logo.
| 1965-1969 | | $525 | $650 |

EA-15 RVT Zephyr Amp
1961-1965. 14 or 20 watts, 1x15", gray tolex, light grille, split C logo on panel, tremolo and reverb, script Epiphone logo lower right grille.
| 1961-1965 | | $600 | $775 |

EA-16 RVT Regent Amp
1965-1969. 25 watts, 1x12", gray vinyl, gray grille, tremolo, reverb. Called the Lancer in first year.
| 1965-1969 | | $400 | $500 |

EA-22 RVT Mighty Mite Amp
1965-ca. 1966. 1x12", mid-level power, stereo, reverb, vibrato, old style rear mounted control panel.
| 1965-1966 | | $1,000 | $1,250 |

EA-26 RVT Electra Amp
1965-1969. Gray tolex, reverb, tremolo, footswitch, 1x12".
| 1965-1969 | | $400 | $500 |

EA-28 RVT Pathfinder Amp
Mid-1960s. Similar to Gibson's GA-19 RVT, medium power, 1x12, reverb and tremolo.
| 1964-1966 | | $400 | $500 |

EA-30 Triumph Amp
1959-1961. Low-power, limited production, 1x12, light colored cover, 3 knobs.
| 1959-1961 | | $800 | $1,000 |

EA-32 RVT Comet Amp
1965-1967. 1x10", tremolo, reverb.
| 1965-1967 | | $350 | $425 |

EA-33 RVT Galaxie Amp
1963-1964. Gray tolex, gray grille, 1x10".
| 1963-1964 | | $400 | $475 |

EA-35 Devon Amp
1961-1963. 1x10" until '62, 1x12" with tremolo in '63.
| 1961-1963 | | $450 | $525 |

EA-50 Pacemaker Amp
1961-1969. 1x8" until '62, 1x10" after. EA-50T with tremolo added in '63. Non-tremolo version dropped around '67.
1961-1962	1x8"	$375	$450
1963-1965	1x8"	$275	$325
1966	1x10"	$275	$325
1967-1969	1x10"	$225	$275

EA-300 RVT Embassy Amp
1965-1969. 90 watts, 2x12", gray vinyl, gray grille, tremolo, reverb.
| 1965-1969 | | $625 | $750 |

EA-500T Panorama Amp
1963-1967. 65 watts, head and large cabinet, tremolo, 1x15" and 1x10" until '64, 1x15" and 2x10" after.
| 1964-1967 | | $500 | $625 |

EA-600 RVT Maxima Amp
1966-1969. Solidstate Epiphone version of Gibson GSS-100, gray vinyl, gray grille, two 2x10" cabs and hi-fi stereo-style amp head.
| 1966-1969 | | $375 | $450 |

Electar Amp
1935-1939. All models have large "E" insignia logo on front, first model Electar in rectangular box with 1x8" speaker, 3 models introduced in '36 (Model C, Model M, and Super AC-DC), the Special AC-DC was introduced in '37, later models were 1x12" combos. Old Electar amps are rarely found in excellent working condition and prices shown are for those rare examples.
1935	Electar	$450	$550
1936-1939	Model C	$600	$750
1936-1939	Model M	$600	$750
1936-1939	Super AC-DC	$725	$900
1937-1939	Special AC-DC	$650	$775

Model 100
1960s. Made in Kalamazoo, label with serial number, Model 100 logo on small 10" speaker, blue cover, 3 tubes, 3 knobs.
| 1965 | | $250 | $275 |

Emery Sound Stagebaby

Epiphone Blues Custom

'60s Epiphone Pacemaker

AMPS

Esteban G-10

Evans Custom SE200

Fender Acoustasonic SFX II

MODEL YEAR	FEATURES	EXC. COND. LOW	HIGH

Zephyr Amp

1939-1957. Maple veneer cabinet, 30 watts with 2x6L6 power, 1x12" until '54, 1x15" after, made by Danelectro using their typical designs, Dano D-style blond covering, large split "E" logo on front, brown grille cloth, large block Zephyr logo on back panel.

| 1939-1953 | 1x12" | $600 | $750 |
| 1953-1957 | 1x15" | $575 | $675 |

Zephyr Dreadnaught Amp

1939. Similar to Zephyr amp but higher power and added microphone input.

| 1939 | | $650 | $800 |

Esteban

2005-2007. Imported brand from China, student budget level compact amps.

Evans Custom Amplifiers

1994-present. Professional grade, production, solidstate head and combo amps built by Scot Buffington in Burlington, North Carolina.

EVH

2007-present. Eddie Van Halen's line of professional and premium grade, production, tube amp heads and cabinets built by Fender. They also build guitars.

Evil Robot

2010-present. Produced by David Brass and Fretted Americana, made in the U.S.A., initial product produced in limited quantities is based on the '59 Tonemaster (Magnatone) Troubadour amp.

Excelsior

The Excelsior Company started offering accordions in 1924 and had a large factory in Italy by the late '40s. They started building guitars and amps around '62. By the early '70s they were out of the guitar business.

Americana Stereophonic High Fidelity Amp

Late 1960s. 50 watts, 1x15", 2x8", 2x3x9" ovals, 2xEL34 power, tube rectifier, large Excelsior logo and small Excelsior The House of Music logo, guitar and accordion inputs, stereo reverb and vibrato.

| 1968-1969 | | $750 | $900 |

Citation C-15 Amp

1962. Made by Sano, mid power with 2x6V6 power tubes, single speaker combo amp, large Citation by Excelsior logo on front panel.

| 1962 | | $500 | $600 |

Fargen

1999-present. Benjamin Fargen builds his professional and premium grade, production/custom, guitar and bass tube amps in Sacramento, California. He also builds guitar effects.

Fender

1946-present. Leo Fender developed many ground-breaking instruments, but Leo's primary passion was amplifiers, and of all his important contributions to musicians, none exceed those he made to the electric tube amplifier.

Tweed Fender amp circuits are highly valued because they defined the tones of rock and roll. Blackface models remained basically the same until mid-'67. Some silverface circuits remained the same as the blackface circuits, while others were changed in the name of reliability. Price Guide values are for all original, excellent condition amps. Small differences in an amp's condition can generate larger differences in selling prices. Non-original speakers will significantly reduce a pre-'68 amp's value. Reconed speakers will reduce the value, but a reconed speaker is preferable to a replacement speaker. Multi-speaker amps generally have matching speaker codes. Different speaker codes require explanation. Fender leather handles are often broken and replaced. A replacement handle drops the value of an amp. Grille cloths should have no tears and a single tear can drop the value of an amp. Each Tweed amp should be evaluated on a case-by-case basis, and it is not unusual for a Tweed amp to have a wide range of values. Alnico speaker replacement is more significant than ceramic speaker replacement. Fender converted to ceramic about '62. Speaker replacement is of less concern in post-'70 Fender amps.

From 1953 to '67, Fender stamped a two-letter date code on the paper tube chart glued inside the cabinet. The first letter was the year (C='53, D='54, etc.) with the second the month (A=January, etc.).

The speaker code found on the frame of an original speaker will identify the manufacturer, and the week and year that the speaker was assembled. The speaker code is typically six (sometimes seven) digits. The first three digits represent the Electronics Industries Association (E.I.A.) source code which identifies the manufacturer. For example, a speaker code 220402 indicates a Jensen speaker (220), made in '54 (4) during the second week (02) of that year. This sample speaker also has another code stamped on the frame. ST654 P15N C4964 indicates the model of the speaker, in this case it is a P15N 15" speaker. The sample speaker also had a code stamped on the speaker cone, 4965 1, which indicates the cone number. All of these codes help identify the originality of the speaker. The value ranges provided in the Guide are for amps with original speaker and original speaker cone.

Most Fender speakers from the '50s will be Jensens (code 220). By the late-'50s other suppliers were used. The supplier codes are: Oxford (465), C.T.S. (137), Utah (328). JBL speakers were first used in the late-'50s Vibrasonic, and then in the Showman series, but JBL did not normally have a E.I.A. source code. An amp's speaker code should be reconciled with other dating info when the amp's original status is being verified.

Piggyback amps from '68-'79 utilize rather heavy, bulky cabinets, which can be difficult and expensive to ship. Therefore a standalone amp head from this

MODEL YEAR	FEATURES	EXC. COND. LOW	HIGH

period is worth significantly more than a standalone cabinet.

General Production Eras:
Diagonal tweed era
Brown tolex era
Blackface era
Silverface era with raised Fender logo with underlining tail
Silverface era with raised Fender logo without underlining tail
Silverface era with raised Fender logo with small MADE IN USA designation

Nameplate and Logo Attribution:
Fender nameplate with city but without model name (tweed era)
Fender nameplate without city or model name (tweed era)
Fender nameplate with model name noted (tweed era)
Fender flat logo (brown era)
Fender script raised logo (blackface era)

30 Amp
1980-1981. Tube combo amp, 30 watts, 2x10" or 1x12".

1980-1981		$400	$500

75 Amp
1980-1982. Tube, 75 watts, offered as a 1x15" or 1x12" combo, or as head and 4x10" or 2x12" cab.

1980-1982		$450	$550

85 Amp
1988-1992. Solidstate, 85 watt 1x12" combo, black cover, silver grille.

1988-1992		$200	$225

800 Pro Bass Amp Head
2004-2008. Rack-mount, 800 watts, 5-band EQ.

2004-2008		$400	$475

Acoustasonic 30/30 DSP Amp
2000-present. Small combo, brown tolex, wheat grille. Upgrade model includes DSP (Digital Signal Processor) effects.

2000-2005	30	$150	$175
2000-2010	30 DSP	$275	$325

Acoustasonic Junior/Junior DSP Amp
1998-present. 2x40 watts, 2x8", Piezo horn.

1998-2010		$300	$375

Acoustasonic SFX/SFX II Amp
1998-present. SFX technology, 32 stereo digital presents, 2x80 watts, 1x10" and 1x8", Piezo horn.

1998-2010		$350	$425

AmpCan Amp
1997-2008. Cylindrical can-shaped battery powered portable amp.

1997-2008		$60	$75

Bandmaster Amp
1953-1974. Wide-panel 1x15" combo '53-'54, narrow-panel 3x10" combo '55-'60, tolex '60, brownface with 1x12" piggyback speaker cabinet '61, 2x12" '62, blackface '62-'67, silverface '68-'74.

The Fender tweed 4x10" Bassman and tweed 3x10" Bandmaster amps are highly sensitive to condition. Because there are so few that are truly excellent, the price

ranges listed may be misleading. Most Bassman amps are at best very good minus (VG-) because their tweed is so damaged and stained. It is also rare to find the original speakers, and if the frames are original, they have often been reconed. 4x10" Bassman and 3x10" Bandmasters that are excellent plus plus (Exc++) may have price ranges that are much higher than the values listed. It is estimated that 90% of the vintage 4x10" Bassman are really only VG or less. Because of the extreme condition factor for these tweed amps, the prices below include amps in very good (VG) condition. Therefore the condition for these listed amps is VG to Exc. Exc+ will be more than the values listed here. As per other high-end collectible, each amp should be taken on a case by case basis.

Fender piggyback amps include a head and separate cabinet. The prices shown are for a factory-original matching set. A factory-original set is worth 25% more than the combined value of a head and cabinet that were not originally sold together when new. Heads are worth more than cabinets. The value of a separate head is 40% of the value shown here, and the value of a separate cabinet is 35% of the value shown. In summary, the math is as follows: 40% head + 35% cabinet + 25% premium = 100% value of factory-original set.

1953-1954	Tweed, 1x15"	$3,500	$4,500
1955-1958	Tweed, 3x10"	$7,500	$9,500
1959-1960	Old style cab, pink-brown tolex	$8,000	$10,000
1959-1960	Tweed, 3x10"	$8,000	$10,000
1960	Brown tolex, 3x10"	$5,700	$6,900
1961	Rough white & oxblood, 1x12"	$2,200	$2,700
1961-1962	Rough white & oxblood, 2x12"	$2,200	$2,700
1963-1964	Smooth white & gold, 2x12"	$1,800	$2,250
1964-1967	Black tolex, 2x12"	$1,100	$1,325
1967-1968	Black, 2x12"	$900	$1,100
1967-1969	Silverface, 2x12"	$725	$900
1970-1974	Silverface, 2x12"	$725	$900

Bandmaster Reverb Amp
1968-1980. 45 watt silverface head with 2x12" cabinet.

1968-1972		$800	$1,000
1973-1980		$775	$950

Bantam Bass Amp
1969-1971. 50 watts, large unusual 1x10" Yamaha speaker.

1969-1971	Original speaker	$525	$625

Bassman Amp
1952-1971. Tweed TV front combo, 1x15" in '52, wide-panel '53-'54, narrow-panel and 4x10" '54-'60, tolex brownface with 1x12" in piggyback cabinet '61, 2x12" cabinet '61-'62, blackface '63-'67, silverface '67-'71, 2x15" cabinet '68-'71. Renamed the Bassman 50 in '72.

The Fender tweed 4x10" Bassman and tweed 3x10" Bandmaster amps are highly sensitive to condition. Because there are so few that are truly excellent, the price ranges listed may be misleading. Most Bassman amps are at best very good minus (VG-) because their

Late-'50s Fender Bandmaster

1958 Fender Bassman

1961 Fender Bassman

1963 Fender Bassman

Fender Bassman 100

1948 Fender Champion 800

tweed is so damaged and stained. It is also rare to find the original speakers, and if the frames are original, they have often been reconed. 4x10" Bassmans and 3x10" Bandmasters that are excellent plus plus (Exc++) may have price ranges that are much higher than the values listed. It is estimated that 90% of the vintage 4x10" Bassman are really only VG or less. Because of the extreme condition factor for these tweed amps, the prices below include amps in very good (VG) condition. Therefore the condition for these listed amps is VG to Exc. Exc+ will be more than the values listed here. As per other high-end collectibles, each amp should be taken on a case by case basis.

Fender piggyback amps include a head and separate cabinet. The prices shown are for a factory-original matching set. A factory-original set is worth 25% more than the combined value of a head and cabinet that were not originally sold together when new. Heads are worth more than cabinets. The value of a separate head is 40% of the value shown here, and the value of a separate cabinet is 35% of the value shown. In summary, the math is as follows: 40% head + 35% cabinet + 25% premium = 100% value of factory-original set.

MODEL YEAR	FEATURES	EXC. COND. LOW	HIGH
1952	TV front, 1x15"	$3,500	$4,500
1953-1954	Wide panel, 1x15"	$3,500	$4,500
1955-1957	Tweed, 4x10", 2 inputs	$7,000	$9,000
1957-1958	Tweed, 4x10", 4 inputs	$7,200	$9,200
1959-1960	Old style cab, pink-brown tolex	$7,500	$9,500
1959-1960	Tweed, 4x10", 4 inputs	$7,500	$9,500
1961	White 1x12", 6G6, tube rectifier	$2,400	$2,900
1962	Late '62, white 2x12	$2,300	$2,800
1962	White 1x12", 6G6A, s.s. rectifier	$2,300	$2,800
1963-1964	Smooth white 2x12", 6G6A/B	$2,100	$2,600
1964	Transition, black, white knobs	$1,650	$2,000
1965-1966	AA165/AB165, black knobs	$1,500	$1,800
1967-1969	Silverface, vertical 2x15"	$725	$900
1970-1971	Silverface, 2x15"	$725	$900

Bassman '59 Reissue Amp
1990-2004. Tube, 45 watts, 4x10", tweed covering.

1990-2004		$675	$850

Bassman LTD/'59 Limited Edition Amp
2004-2009. Limited edition with solid pine finger-jointed cabinet, tube rectifier, 45 watts, 4x10", vintage laquered tweed (for original look).

2004-2009		$800	$1,000

Bassman 10 Amp
1972-1982. 4x10" combo, silverface and 50 watts for '72-'80, blackface and 70 watts after.

1972-1980	50w	$450	$525
1981-1982	70w	$475	$550

MODEL YEAR	FEATURES	EXC. COND. LOW	HIGH
Bassman 20 Amp			
1982-1985. Tubes, 20 watts, 1x15".			
1982-1985		$325	$375
Bassman 25 Amp			
2000-2005. Wedge shape, 1x10", 25 watts, 3-band EQ.			
2000-2005		$85	$100
Bassman 50 Amp			
1972-1977. 50 watts, with 2x12" cab.			
1972-1977		$400	$475
Bassman 60 Amp			
1972-1976. 60 watts, 1x12".			
1972-1976		$425	$500
Bassman 60 Amp (later version)			
2000-2005. Solidstate, 60 watts, 1x12".			
2000-2005	Combo	$150	$175
Bassman 70 Amp			
1977-1979. 70 watts, 2x15" cab.			
1977-1979		$425	$500
Bassman 100 Amp			
1972-1977, 2000-2009. Tube, 100 watts, 4x12", name reused on solidstate combo amp.			
1972-1977	4x12"	$425	$500
2000-2009	1x15" combo	$200	$250
Bassman 135 Amp			
1978-1983. Tube, 135 watts, 4x10".			
1978-1983		$525	$650
Bassman 150 Combo Amp			
2005-2009. Solidstate 1x12" combo, 150 watts.			
2005-2009		$250	$300
Bassman 250 Combo Amp			
2006. 250 watts, 2x10".			
2006		$250	$300
Bassman 300 Pro Amp Head			
2002-present. All tube, 300 watts, black cover, black metal grille.			
2002-2010		$700	$825
Bassman 400 Amp			
2000-2004. Solidstate, 350 watts with 2x10" plus horn, combo, black cover, black metal grille.			
2000-2004	Combo	$300	$375
2000-2004	Head	$275	$325
Bassman Bassbreaker (Custom Shop) Amp			
1998-2003. Classic Bassman 4x10" configuration. Not offered by 2004 when the '59 Bassman LTD was introduced.			
1998-2003	2x12"	$750	$900
1998-2003	4x10"	$750	$900
Bassman Solidstate Amp			
1968-1971. Small head, piggyback cab. The whole late 1960s Solidstate series were unreliable and prone to overheating, more of a historical novelty than a musical instrument.			
1968-1971		$325	$400
B-Dec 30 Amp			
2006-2009. Bass version of the G-Dec, 30 watts, 1x10.			
2006-2009		$175	$200

MODEL YEAR	FEATURES	EXC. COND. LOW	HIGH
Blues Deluxe Amp			
1993-1996. All tube Tweed Series, 40 watts, 2 5881 output tubes, reverb, 1x12", tweed covering (blond tolex optional '95 only).			
1993-1996	Tweed	$400	$500
1995	Blond	$375	$475
Blues Deluxe Reissue Amp			
2006-present. All tube, tweed, 40 watts, reverb, 1x12".			
2006-2010		$400	$500
Blues DeVille Amp			
1993-1996. All tube Tweed Series, 60 watts, 4x10" (optional 2x12" in '94), reverb, high-gain channel, tweed cover (blond tolex optional '95 only).			
1993-1996	Tweed, 4x10"	$450	$550
1994-1996	Tweed, 2x12"	$450	$550
1995	Blond tolex, 4x10"	$425	$525
Blues DeVille Reissue Amp			
2006-present. 60 watts, 4x10, tweed.			
2006-2010		$475	$575
Blues Junior Amp (III)			
1995-pressent. All tube, 15 watts, 1x12", spring reverb, tweed in '95, black tolex with silver grille standard '96 on. Tweed available again '04-'05 and '08-present, blonde 2000-'09, brown '08, surf green '09.			
1995-2010	Black	$325	$375
2000-2009	Blonde, brown, surf green	$400	$450
2008-2010	NOS lacquer tweed	$450	$500
Blues Junior III Limited Amp			
2010. Exclusively sold at ProGuitarShop, 150 made, red tolex, wheat grille.			
2010		$450	$500
Blues Junior Woody Amp			
2002-2003. Custom Shop exotic hardwood version of Blues Jr.			
2002-2003		$500	$575
Bronco Amp			
1968-1974, 1993-2001. 1x 8" speaker, all tube, 5 watts until '72, 6 watts for '72-'74, ('90s issue is 15 watts), solidstate, tweed covering (blond tolex was optional for '95 only).			
1968-1974		$325	$375
1993-2001	15w, no reverb	$100	$125
Bullet/Bullet Reverb Amp			
1994-2005. Solidstate, 15 watts, 1x8", with or without reverb.			
1994-2005	With reverb	$40	$55
1994-2005	Without reverb	$40	$55
BXR Series Bass Amp			
1987-2000. Various models.			
1987-2000		$75	$200
Capricorn Amp			
1970-1972. Solidstate, 105 watts, 3x12".			
1970-1972		$350	$425
Champ Amp			
1953-1982. Renamed from the Champion 600. Tweed until '64, black tolex after, 3 watts in '53, 4 watts '54-'64, 5 watts '65-'71, 6 watts '72-'82, 1x6" until '57, 1x8" after.			
1953-1954	Wide panel, 1x6"	$1,075	$1,275

MODEL YEAR	FEATURES	EXC. COND. LOW	HIGH
1955-1956	Narrow panel, tweed, 1x6"	$1,200	$1,400
1956-1964	Narrow panel, tweed, 1x8"	$1,400	$1,750
1964	Old cab, black, 1x8", last F51	$900	$1,075
1964-1967	New cab, black tolex, 1x8", AA764	$450	$550
1968-1972	Silverface, 1x8"	$350	$425
1973-1982	Silverface, 1x8"	$325	$400
1981-1982	Blackface	$325	$400
Champ II Amp			
1982-1985. 18 watts, 1x10".			
1982-1985		$450	$550
Champ '57 Reissue Amp			
2009-present. Custom Series reissue with tweed and leather handle, handwired.			
2009-2010		$600	$700
Champ 12 Amp			
1986-1992. Tube, 12 watts, overdrive, reverb, 1x12".			
1986-1992	Black	$275	$375
1986-1992	Red, white, gray or snakeskin	$300	$350
Champ 25 SE Amp			
1992-1993. Hybrid solidstate and tube combo, 25 watts, 1x12".			
1992-1993		$200	$250
Champion 30/30 DSP Amp			
1999-2003. Small solidstate combo, 30 watts, 1x8", reverb.			
1999-2003		$75	$100
Champion 110 Amp			
1993-2000. Solidstate, 25 watts, 1x10", 2 channels, black tolex, silver grille.			
1993-2000		$100	$125
Champion 300 Amp			
2004-2007. 30 watt solidstate combo, Dyna-Touch Series, DSP effects.			
2004-2007		$100	$125
Champion 600 Amp			
1949-1953. Replaced the Champion 800, 3 watts, 1x6", 2-tone tolex, TV front. Replaced by the Champ.			
1949-1953		$950	$1,125
Champion 600 Amp (later version)			
2007-present. Small 5 watt combo.			
2007-2010		$100	$125
Champion 800 Amp			
1948. About 100 made, TV front, luggage tweed cover, 1x8, 3 tubes, becomes Champion 600 in '49.			
1948		$975	$1,150
Concert Amp			
1960-1965. Introduced with 40 watts and 4x10", brown tolex until '63, blackface '63-'65. In '62 white tolex was ordered by Webbs Music (CA) instead of the standard brown tolex. A wide range is noted for the rare white tolex, and each amp should be valued on a case-by-case basis. In '60, the very first brown tolex had a pink tint but only on the first year amps.			
1960	Brown (pink) tolex	$2,400	$2,900
1960	Brown (pink), tweed grille	$3,100	$3,800

Fender Blues Junior

1966 Fender Champ
David Green

Fender Champ (5E1)

Fender Concert (6G12)

1970s Fender Deluxe

1965 Fender Deluxe Reverb
(Rob Bernstein)

MODEL YEAR	FEATURES	EXC. COND. LOW	HIGH
1961-1963	Brown tolex	$2,300	$2,800
1962	White tolex (Webb Music)	$2,400	$2,900
1963-1965	Blackface	$1,900	$2,300

Concert (Pro Tube Series) Amp
1993-1995. Tube combo, 60 watts, 1x12, blackface.

1993-1995		$625	$725

Concert Reverb (Pro Tube Series) Amp
2002-2005. 4x10" combo, reverb, tremolo, overdrive.

2002-2005		$650	$725

Concert 112 Amp
1982-1985. Tube, 60 watts, 1x12", smaller Concert logo (not similar to '60s style logo).

1982-1985		$500	$600

Concert 210 Amp
1982-1985. Tube, 60 watts, 2x10".

1982-1985		$525	$650

Concert 410 Amp
1982-1985. Tube, 60 watts, 4x10".

1982-1985		$550	$675

Cyber Champ Amp
2004-2005. 65 watts, 1x12", Cyber features, 21 presets

2004-2005		$200	$250

Cyber Deluxe Amp
2002-2005. 65 watts, 1x12", Cyber features, 64 presets.

2002-2005		$300	$350

Cyber-Twin (SE) Amp
2001-present. Hybrid tube/solidstate modeling amp, 2x65 watts, 2x12".

2001-2003	Head only	$400	$500
2001-2010	Combo	$450	$550
2005-2010	2nd Edition SE	$475	$600

Deco-Tone (Custom Shop) Amp
2000. Art-deco styling, 165 made, all tube, 15 watts, 1x12", round speaker baffle opening, uses 6BQ5/ES84 power tubes.

2000		$875	$1,075

Deluxe Amp
1948-1981. Name changed from Model 26 ('46-'48). 10 watts (15 by '54 and 20 by '63), 1x12", TV front with tweed '48-'53, wide-panel '53-'55, narrow-panel '55-'60, brown tolex with brownface '61-'63, black tolex with blackface '63-'66.

1948-1952	Tweed, TV front	$2,200	$2,700
1953-1954	Wide panel	$2,500	$3,000
1955	Narrow panel, sm. Cab	$3,600	$4,400
1956-1960	Narrow panel, lg. cab	$3,500	$4,300
1961-1963	Brown tolex	$1,900	$2,300
1964-1966	Black tolex	$1,900	$2,300

Deluxe Reverb Amp
1963-1981. 1x12", 20 watts, blackface '63-'67, silverface '68-'80, blackface with silver grille option introduced in mid-'80. Replaced by Deluxe Reverb II. Reissued as Deluxe Reverb '65 Reissue.

1963-1967	Blackface	$2,150	$2,650
1967-1968	Silverface	$1,700	$2,100
1969-1970	Silverface	$1,500	$1,800

MODEL YEAR	FEATURES	EXC. COND. LOW	HIGH
1971-1972	Silverface	$1,250	$1,500
1973-1980	Silverface	$1,000	$1,250
1980-1981	Blackface	$1,000	$1,250

Deluxe Reverb Solidstate Amp
1966-1969. Part of Fender's early solidstate series.

1966-1969	.	$350	$425

Deluxe '57 Reissue Amp
2007-present. Custom Series reissue, handwired, tweed, 12 watts, 1x12".

2007-2010		$1,050	$1,250

Deluxe Reverb '65 Reissue Amp
1993-present. Blackface reissue, 22 watts, 1x12".

1993-1999	Blond (ltd. production)	$675	$775
1993-2010	Black tolex	$650	$750

Deluxe Reverb II Amp
1982-1986. Updated Deluxe Reverb with 2 6V6 power tubes, all tube preamp section, black tolex, blackface, 20 watts, 1x12".

1982-1986		$750	$900

Deluxe 85 Amp
1988-1993. Solidstate, 65 watts, 1x12", black tolex, silver grille, Red Knob Series.

1988-1993		$250	$300

Deluxe 90 Amp
1999-2003. Solidstate, 90 watts, 1x12" combo, DSP added in '02.

1999-2002		$200	$250
2002-2003	DSP option	$225	$275

Deluxe 112 Amp
1992-1995. Solidstate, 65 watts, 1x12", black tolex with silver grille.

1992-1995		$175	$225

Deluxe 112 Plus Amp
1995-2000. 90 watts, 1x12", channel switching.

1995-2000		$200	$250

Deluxe 900 Amp
2004-2006. Solidstate, 90 watts, 1x12" combo, DSP effects.

2004-2006		$225	$275

Dual Professional Amp
1994-2002. Custom Shop amp, all tube, point-to-point wiring, 100 watts, 2x12" Celestion Vintage 30s, fat switch, reverb, tremolo, white tolex, oxblood grille.

1994-2002		$1,250	$1,500

Dual Professional/Super Amp
1947. V-front, early-'47 small metal name tag "Fender/Dual Professional/Fullerton California" tacked on front of cab, 2x10 Jensen PM10-C each with transformer attached to speaker frame, tube chart on inside of cab, late-'47 renamed Super and new metal badge "Fender/Fullerton California".

1947		$5,300	$6,500

Dual Showman Amp
1962-1969. Called the Double Showman for the first year. White tolex (black available from '64), 2x15", 85 watts. Reintroduced '87-'94 as solidstate, 100 watts, optional speaker cabs.

Fender piggyback amps include a head and separate cabinet. The prices shown are for a factory-original matching set. A factory-original set is worth

MODEL YEAR	FEATURES	EXC. COND. LOW	HIGH

25% more than the combined value of a head and cabinet that were not originally sold together when new. Heads are worth more than cabinets. The value of a separate head is 40% of the value shown here, and the value of a separate cabinet is 35% of the value shown. In summary, the math is as follows: 40% head + 35% cabinet + 25% premium = 100% value of factory-original set.

1962	Rough blond & oxblood	$4,000	$5,000
1963	Smooth blond & wheat	$2,700	$3,300
1964-1967	Black tolex, horizontal cab	$2,100	$2,600
1968	Blackface, large vertical cab	$1,400	$1,700
1968-1969	Silverface	$1,000	$1,200

Dual Showman Reverb Amp
1968-1981. Black tolex with silver grille, silverface, 100 watts, 2x15".

1968-1972		$950	$1,150
1973-1981		$850	$1,050

Fender '57 Amp
2007. Only 300 made, limited edition combo, hand-wired, 1x12", retro styling.

2007		$1,350	$1,675

FM 212R Amp
2003-2007. 100 watts, 2x12" combo, solidstate, reverb

2003-2007		$175	$225

Frontman Series Amp
1997-present. Student combo amps, models include 15/15B/15G/15R (15 watts, 1x8"), 25R (25 watts, 1x10", reverb).

1997-2004	15DSP w/15 FX selections	$60	$95
1997-2006	65DSP	$100	$150
1997-2010	15/15B/15G/15R	$45	$55
1997-2010	25R	$60	$85
1997-2010	65R	$75	$125
2007-2010	212R	$150	$200

G-Dec Amp
2005-2009. Digital, amp and effects presets.

2005-2009	G-Dec (sm. model)	$125	$150
2006-2009	G-Dec 30 (lg. model)	$175	$200
2007-2008	G-Dec Exec, maple cab	$225	$275
2011	G-Dec Jr, Champ cab	$85	$100

H.O.T. Amp
1990-1996. Solidstate, 25 watts, 1x10", gray carpet cover (black by '92), black grille.

1990-1996		$75	$90

Harvard Solidstate Amp
1980-1983. Reintroduced from tube model, black tolex with blackface, 20 watts, 1x10".

1980-1983		$100	$125

Harvard Tube Amp
1956-1961. Tweed, 10 watts, 1x10", 2 knobs volume and roll-off tone, some were issued with 1x8". Reintroduced as a solidstate model in '80.

1956-1961		$1,800	$2,250

Harvard Reverb Amp
1981-1982. Solidstate, 20 watts, 1x10", reverb, replaced by Harvard Reverb II in '83.

1981-1982		$125	$150

Harvard Reverb II Amp
1983-1985. Solidstate, black tolex with blackface, 20 watts, 1x10", reverb.

1983-1985		$150	$175

Hot Rod Deluxe Amp
1996-present. Updated Blues Deluxe, tube, 40 watts, 1x12", black tolex. Various covering optional by '98, also a wood cab in 2003.

1996-2009	Blond tolex option	$375	$475
1996-2009	Brown option	$375	$475
1996-2010	Black tolex	$375	$475
1996-2010	Tweed option	$450	$550
2000s	Ltd. Ed. With case	$600	$800
2001-2006	Red tolex	$375	$475
2003	Wood cab	$600	$750

Hot Rod DeVille 212 Amp
1996-present. Updated Blues DeVille, tube, 60 watts, black tolex, 2x12".

1996-2000		$425	$525
2001-2010	Black tolex	$425	$525

Hot Rod DeVille 410 Amp
1996-present. Tube, 60 watts, black tolex, 4x10".

1996-2000		$425	$525
2001-2006	Ltd. Ed. brown tolex	$425	$525
2001-2010	Black tolex	$425	$525

J.A.M. Amp
1990-1996. Solidstate, 25 watts, 1x12", 4 preprogrammed sounds, gray carpet cover (black by '92).

1990-1996		$50	$75

Jazz King Amp
2005-2008. 140 watt solidstate 1x15" combo.

2005-2008		$425	$525

KXR Series Amp
1995-2002. Keyboard combo amps, 50 to 200 watts, solidstate, 1x12" or 15".

1998-2002		$75	$150

Libra Amp
1970-1972. Solidstate, 105 watts, 4x12" JBL speakers, black tolex.

1970-1972		$350	$425

London 185 Amp
1988-1992. Solidstate, 160 watts, black tolex.

1988-1992	Head only	$200	$225

London Reverb 112 Amp
1983-1985. Solidstate, 100 watts, black tolex, 1x12".

1983-1985		$300	$350

London Reverb 210 Amp
1983-1985. Solidstate, 100 watts, black tolex, 2x10".

1983-1985		$325	$375

London Reverb Amp Head
1983-1985. Solidstate head, 100 watts.

1983-1985		$225	$250

M-80 Amp
1989-1994. Solidstate, 90 watts, 1x12". The M-80 series were also offered as head only amp.

1989-1993		$175	$200

Fender Dual Showman

Fender G-Dec 30

Fender Harvard

AMPS

1959 Fender Princeton
(KC Cormack)

1971 Fender Princeton Reverb

1955 Fender Pro

MODEL YEAR	FEATURES	EXC. COND. LOW	HIGH
M-80 Bass Amp			
1991-1994. Solidstate, bass and keyboard amp, 160 watts, 1x15".			
1991-1994		$175	$200
M-80 Chorus Amp			
1990-1994. Solidstate, stereo chorus, 2 65-watt channels, 2x12", 90 watts.			
1990-1994		$250	$275
M-80 Pro Amp			
1992. Rackmount version of M-80, 90 watts.			
1992		$150	$175
Model 26 Amp			
1946-1947. Tube, 10 watts, 1x10", hardwood cabinet. Sometimes called Deluxe Model 26, renamed Deluxe in '48.			
1946-1947		$1,300	$1,600
Montreux Amp			
1983-1985. Solidstate, 100 watts, 1x12", black tolex with silver grille.			
1983-1985		$300	$350
Musicmaster Bass Amp			
1970-1983. Tube, 12 watts, 1x12", black tolex.			
1970-1972	Silverface	$350	$425
1973-1980	Silverface	$325	$400
1981-1983	Blackface	$325	$400
Mustang Series Amp			
2010-present. Mustang I thru V, modeling amp effects, small combo up to a half-stack.			
2010-2011	I, 20w, 1x8	$50	$75
2010-2011	II, 40w, 1x12	$150	$175
2011	III, 100w, 1x12	$175	$200
2011	IV, 150w, 2x12	$275	$325
2011	V, 150w, 4x12 cab	$325	$375
PA-100 Amp			
1970s. 100 watts.			
1970s		$300	$375
Performer 650 Amp			
1993-1995. Solidstate hybrid amp with single tube, 70 watts, 1x12".			
1993-1995		$225	$275
Performer 1000 Amp			
1993-1995. Solidstate hybrid amp with a single tube, 100 watts, 1x12".			
1993-1995		$250	$300
Princeton Amp			
1948-1979. Tube, 4.5 watts (12 watts by '61), 1x8" (1x10" by '61), tweed '48-'61, brown '61-'63, black with blackface '63-'69, silverface '69-'79.			
1948	Tweed, TV front	$1,200	$1,400
1949-1953	Tweed, TV front	$925	$1,100
1953-1954	Wide panel	$975	$1,125
1955-1956	Narrow panel, sm. Box	$1,300	$1,575
1956-1961	Narrow panel, lg. box	$1,300	$1,575
1961-1963	Brown, 6G2	$1,225	$1,475
1963-1964	Black, 6G2	$1,000	$1,250
1964-1966	Black, AA964, no grille logo	$1,000	$1,250
1966-1967	Black, AA964, raised grille logo	$1,000	$1,250

MODEL YEAR	FEATURES	EXC. COND. LOW	HIGH
1968-1969	Silverface, alum. grille trim	$675	$775
1969-1970	Silverface, no grille trim	$625	$725
1971-1979	Silverface, AB1270	$625	$725
1973-1975	Fender logo-tail	$625	$725
1975-1978	No Fender logo-tail	$625	$725
1978-1979	With boost pull-knob	$625	$725
Princeton Reverb Amp			
1964-1981. Tube, black tolex, blackface until '67, silverface after until blackface again in '80.			
1964-1967	Blackface	$1,600	$1,950
1968-1972	Silverface, Fender logo-tail	$925	$1,150
1973-1979	Silverface, no Fender logo-tail	$875	$1,100
1980-1981	Blackface	$875	$1,100
Princeton Reverb II Amp			
1982-1985. Tube amp, 20 watts, 1x12", black tolex, silver grille, distortion feature.			
1982-1985		$625	$750
Princeton Reverb '65 Reissue Amp			
2009-present. Vintage Reissue series.			
2009-2010		$525	$625
Princeton Chorus Amp			
1988-1996. Solidstate, 2x10", 2 channels at 25 watts each, black tolex. Replaced by Princeton Stereo Chorus in '96.			
1988-1996		$125	$175
Princeton 65 Amp			
1999-2003. Combo 1x2", reverb, blackface, DSP added in '02.			
1999-2001		$140	$170
2002-2003	With DSP	$145	$175
Princeton 112/112 Plus Amp			
1993-1997. Solidstate, 40 watts (112) or 60 watts (112 Plus), 1x12", black tolex.			
1993-1994	40 watt	$150	$175
1995-1997	60 watt	$150	$175
Princeton 650 Amp			
2004-2006. Solidstate 65 watt 1x12" combo, DSP effects, black tolex.			
2004-2006		$175	$225
Princeton Recording Amp			
2007-2009. Based on classic '65 Princeton Reverb, 15 watts, 1x10" combo, 2 on-board effects (overdrive/compression), 4-button footswitch, blackface cosmetics.			
2007-2009		$575	$700
Pro Amp			
1947-1965. Called Professional '46-'48. 15 watts (26 by '54 and 25 by '60), 1x15", tweed TV front '48-'53, wide-panel '53-'54, narrow-panel '55-'60, brown tolex and brownface '60-'63, black and blackface '63-'65.			
1947-1953	Tweed, TV front	$2,700	$3,200
1953-1954	Wide panel	$3,000	$3,600
1955	Narrow panel (old chassis)	$3,100	$3,900
1955-1959	Narrow panel (new chassis)	$3,300	$4,100

AMPS

MODEL YEAR	FEATURES	EXC. COND. LOW	HIGH
1960	Pink/brown, tweed-era cover	$2,800	$3,400
1961-1962	Brown tolex	$1,900	$2,400
1963-1965	Black tolex	$1,900	$2,400

Pro Reverb Amp

1965-1982. Tube, black tolex, 40 watts (45 watts by '72, 70 watts by '81), 2x12", blackface '65-'69 and '81-'83, silverface '69-'81.

1965-1967	Blackface	$1,700	$2,100
1968	Silverface	$1,400	$1,700
1969-1970		$1,300	$1,600
1971-1972		$1,200	$1,500
1973-1980	Silverface	$900	$1,125
1981-1982	Blackface	$900	$1,125

Pro Reverb Solidstate Amp

1967-1969. Fender's first attempt at solidstate design, the attempt was unsuccessful and many of these models will overheat and are known to be unreliable. 50 watts, 2x12", upright vertical combo cabinet.

1967-1969		$350	$425

Pro Reverb Reissue (Pro Series) Amp

2002-2005. 50 watts, 1x12", 2 modern designed channels - clean and high gain.

2002-2005		$575	$675

Pro 185 Amp

1989-1991. Solidstate, 160 watts, 2x12", black tolex.

1989-1991		$250	$300

Pro Junior Amp

1994-present. All tube, 2xEL84 tubes, 15 watts, 1x10" Alnico Blue speaker, tweed until '95, black tolex '96 on.

1994-1999	Tweed	$400	$475
1994-1999	White	$350	$425
2000-2010		$250	$325

Pro Junior 60th Anniversary Woody Amp

2006. Recreation of original Fender model (1946-2006), 15 watts, 1x10, wood cab.

2006		$500	$575

Pro Junior Masterbuilt Custom Shop Amp

Late 1990s. Transparent white-blond wood finish.

1990s		$500	$550

Prosonic Amp

1996-2001. Custom Shop combo, 60 watts, 2 channels, 3-way rectifier switch, 2x10" Celestion or separate cab with 4x12", tube reverb, black, red or green.

1996-2001		$625	$750

Prosonic Amp Head

1996-2001. Amp head only version.

1996-2001		$525	$625

Quad Reverb Amp

1971-1978. Black tolex, silverface, 4x12", tube, 100 watts. Large Fender combo amps built in the '70s are not often in excellent condition. Any grille stain or tear to the grille can mean an amp is not in excellent condition and can significantly reduce the values shown.

1971-1978		$800	$1,000

R.A.D. Amp

1990-1996. Solidstate, 20 watts, 1x8", gray carpet cover until '92, black after.

1990-1996		$55	$70

R.A.D. Bass Amp

1992-1994. 25 watts, 1x10", renamed BXR 25.

1992-1994		$55	$70

Roc-Pro 1000 Amp

1997-2001. Hybrid tube combo or head, 100 watts, 1x12", spring reverb, 1000 logo on front panel.

1997-2001	Combo	$200	$250
1997-2001	Half stack, head & cab	$375	$450

Rumble Bass Amp Head

1994-1998. Custom Shop tube amp, 300 watts.

1994-1998		$2,000	$2,400

Rumble Series Amp

2003-present. Solidstate bass amps, include Rumble 15 (15 watts, 1x8"), 25 (25 watts, 1x10"), 60 (60 watts, 1x12"), 100 (100 watts, 1x15" or 2x10"), and 150 (150 watts, 1x15").

2003-2009	Rumble 100	$100	$125
2003-2009	Rumble 25	$60	$70
2003-2009	Rumble 60	$70	$80
2003-2010	Rumble 15	$50	$60
2003-2010	Rumble 150	$125	$150

Scorpio Amp

1970-1972. Solidstate, 56 watts, 2x12", black tolex.

1970-1972		$275	$325

SFX Keyboard 200 Amp

1998-1999. Keyboard combo amp, digital effects, black tolex.

1998-1999		$225	$275

SFX Satellite Amp

1997-2001. Hybrid tube combo or head, 100 watts, 1x12", spring reverb.

1998-2000		$200	$250

Showman 12 Amp

1960-1966. Piggyback cabinet with 1x12", 85 watts, blond tolex (changed to black in '64), maroon grille '61-'63, gold grille '63-'64, silver grille '64-'67.

1960-1962	Rough blond & oxblood	$3,600	$4,400
1963-1964	Smooth blond & gold	$2,900	$3,500
1964-1966	Black	$1,900	$2,400

Showman 15 Amp

1960-1968. Piggyback cabinet with 1x15", 85 watts, blond tolex (changed to black in '64), maroon grille '61-'63, gold grille '63-'64, silver grille '64-'67.

1960-1962	Rough blond & oxblood	$3,600	$4,400
1963-1964	Smooth blond & gold	$2,900	$3,500
1964-1967	Blackface	$1,900	$2,400
1967-1968	Silverface	$1,000	$1,200

Showman 112 Amp

1983-1987. Solidstate, 2 channels, 200 watts, reverb, 4 button footswitch, 5-band EQ, effects loop, 1x12".

1983-1987		$400	$475

Showman 115 Amp

1983-1987. Solidstate, 1x15", 2 channels, reverb, EQ, effects loop, 200 watts, black tolex.

1983-1987		$425	$500

1956 Fender Pro

1966 Fender Pro Reverb
(Rob Bernstein)

Late '60s Fender Pro Reverb
Frank Salvato

1959 Fender Super Amp

1960 Fender Super Amp

1967 Fender Super Reverb

MODEL YEAR	FEATURES	EXC. COND. LOW	HIGH

Showman 210 Amp

1983-1987. Solidstate, 2 channels, reverb, EQ, effects loop, 2x10", 200 watts, black tolex.

| 1983-1987 | | $425 | $500 |

Showman 212 Amp

1983-1987. Solidstate, 2 channels, reverb, EQ, effects loop, 2x12", 200 watts, black tolex.

| 1983-1987 | | $475 | $575 |

Sidekick 10 Amp

1983-1985. Small solidstate Japanese or Mexican import, 10 watts, 1x8".

| 1983-1985 | | $40 | $60 |

Sidekick Bass 30 Amp

1983-1985. Combo, 30 watts, 1x12".

| 1983-1985 | | $50 | $70 |

Sidekick Reverb 15 Amp

1983-1985. Small solidstate import, reverb, 15 watts.

| 1983-1985 | | $60 | $75 |

Sidekick Reverb 20 Amp

1983-1985. Small solidstate Japanese or Mexican import, 20 watts, reverb, 1x10".

| 1983-1985 | | $70 | $80 |

Sidekick Reverb 30 Amp

1983-1985. Small solidstate Japanese or Mexican import, 30 watts, 1x12", reverb.

| 1983-1985 | | $80 | $90 |

Sidekick Reverb 65 Amp

1986-1988. Small solidstate Japanese or Mexican import, 65 watts, 1x12".

| 1986-1988 | | $90 | $100 |

Sidekick 100 Bass Amp Head

1986-1993. 100 watt bass head.

| 1986-1993 | | $70 | $90 |

Squire SKX Series Amp

1990-1992. Solidstate, 15 watts, 1x8", model 15R with reverb. Model 25R is 25 watts, 1x10, reverb.

1990-1992	15, non-reverb	$30	$35
1990-1992	15R, reverb	$35	$45
1990-1992	25R, reverb	$45	$55

Squire SP10 Amp

2003-present. 10 watt solidstate, usually sold as part of a Guitar Pack.

| 2003-2010 | | $25 | $30 |

Stage 100/Stage 1000 Amp

1999-2006. Solidstate, 1x12", combo or head only options, 100 watts, blackface. Head available until 2004.

1999-2004	Head only	$150	$200
1999-2006	Combo	$200	$250
1999-2006	Combo stack, 2 cabs	$275	$375

Stage 1600 DSP Amp

2004-2006. Solidstate, 160 watts, 2x12" combo, 16 digital effects (DSP).

| 2004-2006 | | $250 | $325 |

Stage Lead/Lead II Amp

1983-1985. Solidstate, 100 watts, 1x12", reverb, channel switching, black tolex. Stage Lead II has 2x12".

| 1983-1985 | 1x12" | $225 | $275 |
| 1983-1985 | 2x12" | $250 | $300 |

MODEL YEAR	FEATURES	EXC. COND. LOW	HIGH

Starcaster by Fender 15G Amp

2000s. Student economy pac amp, sold with a guitar, strap and stand, Starcaster by Fender logo. Sold in Costco and possibly other discounters.

| 2000s | | $25 | $35 |

Steel-King Amp

2004-2009. Designed for pedal steel, 200 watts, solidstate, 1x15".

| 2004-2009 | | $475 | $575 |

Studio 85 Amp

1988. Studio 85 logo on upper right front of grille, solidstate, 1x12" combo, 65 watts, red knobs.

| 1988 | | $175 | $225 |

Studio Bass Amp

1977-1980. Uses Super Twin design, tube, 200 watt combo, 5-band eq, 1x15".

| 1977-1980 | | $400 | $500 |

Studio Lead Amp

1983-1986. Solidstate, 50 watts, 1x12", black tolex.

| 1983-1986 | | $200 | $250 |

Super Amp

1947-1963, 1992-1997. Introduced as Dual Professional in 1946, renamed Super '47, 2x10" speakers, 20 watts (30 watts by '60 with 45 watts in '62), tweed TV front '47-'53, wide-panel '53-'54, narrow-panel '55-'60, brown tolex '60-'64. Reintroduced '92-'97 with 4x10", 60 watts, black tolex.

1947-1952	V-front	$5,000	$6,000
1953-1954	Tweed, wide panel	$4,400	$5,400
1955	Tweed, narrow panel, 6L6	$5,500	$6,600
1956-1957	Tweed, narrow panel, 5E4, 6V6	$5,000	$6,000
1957-1960	Tweed, narrow panel, 6L6	$6,000	$7,500
1960	Pink, tweed-era grille	$2,900	$3,600
1960	Pink/brown metal knobs	$3,200	$4,000
1960	Pink/brown reverse knobs	$3,200	$4,000
1960-1962	Brown, oxblood grille, 6G4	$2,300	$2,800
1962-1963	Brown, tan/ wheat grille, 6G4	$2,200	$2,700

Super (4x10") Amp

1992-1997. 60 watts, 4x10", black tolex, silver grille, blackface control panel.

| 1992-1997 | | $650 | $750 |

Super 60 Amp

1989-1993. Red Knob series, 1x12", 60 watts, earlier versions with red knobs, later models with black knobs, offered in optional covers such as red, white, gray or snakeskin.

| 1989-1993 | | $325 | $400 |

Super 112 Amp

1990-1993. Red Knob series, 1x12", 60 watts, earlier versions with red knobs, later models with black knobs, originally designed to replace the Super60 but the Super60 remained until '93.

| 1990-1993 | | $325 | $400 |

*The **Vintage Guitar Price Guide** shows low to high values for items in all-original excellent condition, and, where applicable, with original case or cover.*

MODEL YEAR	FEATURES	EXC. COND. LOW	HIGH

Super 210 Amp
1990-1993. Red Knob series, 2x10", 60 watts, earlier versions with red knobs, later models with black knobs.

1990-1993		$350	$425

Super Champ Amp
1982-1986. Black tolex, 18 watts, blackface, 1x10".

1982-1986		$750	$950

Super Champ Deluxe Amp
1982-1986. Solid oak cabinet, 18 watts, upgrade 10" Electro-Voice speaker, see-thru brown grille cloth.

1982-1986		$1,300	$1,600

Super Champ XD Amp
2008-present. Tube amp with extra preamp voicing, 1x10" combo, blackface cosmetics.

2008-2010		$200	$225

Super Reverb Amp
1963-1982. 4x10" speakers, blackface until '67 and '80-'82, silverface '68-'80. Large Fender combo amps built in the '70s are not often in excellent condition. Any grille stain or tear to the grille can mean an amp is not in excellent condition and can significantly reduce the values shown.

1963-1967	Blackface	$2,000	$2,500
1968	Silverface, AB763	$1,400	$1,700
1969-1970	Silverface	$1,300	$1,600
1970-1972	Silverface, AA270	$1,200	$1,500
1973-1980	Silverface, no MV	$1,100	$1,350
1981-1982	Blackface	$1,100	$1,350

Super Reverb Solidstate Amp
1967-1970. 50 watts, 4x10".

1967-1970		$400	$500

Super Reverb '65 Reissue Amp
2001-present. 45 watts, all tube, 4x10", blackface cosmetics.

2001-2010		$700	$825

Super Six Reverb Amp
1970-1979. Large combo amp based on the Twin Reverb chassis, 100 watts, 6x10", black tolex. Large Fender combo amps built in the '70s are not often in excellent condition. Any grille stain or tear to the grille can mean an amp is not in excellent condition and can significantly reduce the values shown.

1970-1979		$900	$1,100

Super Twin (Non-Reverb) Amp
1975-1976. 180 watts (6 6L6 power tubes), 2x12", distinctive dark grille.

1975-1976		$400	$500

Super Twin (Reverb) Amp
1976-1980. 180 watts (6 6L6 power tubes), 2x12", distinctive dark grille.

1976-1980		$450	$550

Super-Sonic Amp
2006-present. Pro Tube Series, all tube, various options, 1x12 combo or 2x12 piggyback, blond and oxblood.

2006-2010	1x12" combo, blackface	$675	$825
2006-2010	1x12" combo, blond/oxblood	$725	$875
2006-2010	2x12" piggyback, blond	$750	$900

Taurus Amp
1970-1972. Solidstate, 42 watts, 2x10" JBL, black tolex, silver grille, JBL badge.

1970-1972		$275	$350

Tonemaster Amp Set
1993-2002. Custom Shop, hand-wired head with Tonemaster 2x12" or 4x12" cabinet.

1993-2002	Blond & oxblood	$1,500	$1,750
1993-2002	Custom color red	$1,500	$1,750

Tremolux Amp
1955-1966. Tube, tweed, 1x12" '55-'60, white tolex with piggyback 1x10" cabinet '61-'62, 2x10" '62-'64, black tolex '64-'66.

1955-1960	Tweed, 1x12", narrow panel	$3,100	$3,800
1961	Rough white & oxblood, 1x10"	$2,000	$2,500
1961-1962	Rough white & oxblood, 2x10"	$2,000	$2,500
1962-1963	Rough white & wheat, 2x10"	$1,900	$2,300
1963-1964	Smooth white & gold, 2x10"	$1,800	$2,200
1964-1966	Black tolex, 2x10"	$1,600	$1,900

Twin Amp
1952-1963, 1996-2010. Tube, 2x12"; 15 watts, tweed wide-panel '52-'55; narrow-panel '55-'60; 50 watts '55-'57; 80 watts '58; brown tolex '60; white tolex '61-'63. Reintroduced in '96 with black tolex, spring reverb and output control for 100 watts or 25 watts.

1952-1954	Tweed, wide panel	$7,000	$8,500
1955-1957	Tweed, 50 watts	$8,000	$10,000
1958-1959	Tweed, 80 watts	$14,000	$17,000
1960	Brown tolex, 80 watts	$10,500	$12,500
1960-1962	Rough white & oxblood	$6,500	$8,000
1963	Smooth white & gold	$6,000	$7,500

Twin '57 Reissue Amp
2004-present. Custom Shop '57 tweed, low power dual rectifier model, 40 watts, 2x12", authentic tweed lacquering.

2004-2010		$1,200	$1,500

Twin Reverb Amp
1963-1982. Black tolex, 85 watts (changed to 135 watts in '81), 2x12", blackface '63-'67 and '81-'82, silverface '68-'81, blackface optional in '80-'81 and standard in '82. Large Fender combo amps built in the '70s are not often in excellent condition. Any grille stain or tear to the grille can mean an amp is not in excellent condition and can significantly reduce the values shown.

1963-1967	Blackface	$1,800	$2,300
1968-1972	Silverface, no master vol.	$1,100	$1,400
1973-1975	Silverface, master vol.	$900	$1,100
1976-1980	Silverface, push/pull	$900	$1,100
1980-1982	Blackface	$900	$1,100

Fender Super Reverb

Fender Twin Amp

Fender Twin Reverb '65 Reissue

Fender Vibroverb

1965 Fender Vibro Champ
Rob Bernstein

Fishman Loudbox Performer

MODEL YEAR	FEATURES	EXC. COND. LOW	HIGH
Twin Reverb Solidstate Amp			
1966-1969. 100 watts, 2x12", black tolex.			
1966-1969		$400	$500
Twin Reverb '65 Reissue Amp			
1992-present. Black tolex, 2x12", 85 watts.			
1992-2010	High or low output	$700	$875
Twin Reverb II Amp			
1983-1985. Black tolex, 2x12", 105 watts, channel switching, effects loop, blackface panel, silver grille.			
1983-1985		$800	$950
Twin "The Twin"/"Evil Twin" Amp			
1987-1992. 100 watts, 2x12", red knobs, most black tolex, but white, red and snakeskin covers offered.			
1987-1992		$650	$750
Two-Tone (Custom Shop) Amp			
2001-2003. Limited production, modern styling, slanted grille, 15 watts, 1x10" and 1x12", 2-tone blond cab, based on modified Blues Deluxe circuit, Two Tone on name plate.			
2001-2003		$750	$950
Ultimate Chorus DSP Amp			
1995-2001. Solidstate, 2x65 watts, 2x12", 32 built-in effect variations, blackface cosmetics.			
1995-2001		$250	$300
Ultra Chorus Amp			
1992-1994. Solidstate, 2x65 watts, 2x12", standard control panel with chorus.			
1992-1994		$250	$300
Vibrasonic Amp			
1959-1963. First amp to receive the new brown tolex and JBL, 1x15", 25 watts.			
1959-1963		$2,100	$2,600
Vibrasonic Custom Amp			
1995-1997. Custom Shop designed for steel guitar and guitar, blackface, 1x15", 100 watts.			
1995-1997		$625	$725
Vibrasonic Reverb Amp			
1972-1981. Black tolex, 100 watts, 1x15", silverface.			
1972-1981		$650	$775
Vibro-Champ Amp			
1964-1982. Black tolex, 4 watts, (5 watts '69-'71, 6 watts '72-'80), 1x8", blackface '64-'68 and '82, silverface '69-'81.			
1964-1967	Blackface, AA764	$600	$750
1968-1972	Silverface	$425	$475
1973-1981	Silverface	$400	$450
1982	Blackface	$400	$450
Vibro-Champ XD Amp			
2008-present. Made in China, 5 watts, 1x8.			
2008-2010		$125	$150
Vibro-King Amp			
1993-present. Custom Shop combo, blond tolex, 60 watts, 3x10", vintage reverb, tremolo, single channel, all tube.			
1993-2010		$1,400	$1,700
Vibro-King 212 Cabinet			
1993-present. Custom Shop extension cab, blond tolex, 2x12" Celestion GK80.			
1993-2010		$425	$525

MODEL YEAR	FEATURES	EXC. COND. LOW	HIGH
Vibrolux Amp			
1956-1964. Narrow-panel, 10 watts, tweed with 1x10" '56-'61, brown tolex and brownface with 1x12" and 30 watts '61-'62, black tolex and blackface '63-'64.			
1956-1961	Tweed, 1x10"	$2,400	$2,900
1961-1962	Brown tolex, 1x12", 2x6L6	$2,500	$3,000
1963-1964	Black tolex, 1x12"	$2,500	$3,000
Vibrolux Reverb Amp			
1964-1982. Black tolex, 2x10", blackface '64-'67 and '81-'82, silverface '70-'80. Reissued in '96 with blackface and 40 watts.			
1964-1967	Blackface	$2,700	$3,400
1968-1972	Silverface	$1,400	$1,700
1973-1982	Silverface or blackface	$1,200	$1,400
Vibrolux Reverb Solidstate Amp			
1967-1969. Fender CBS solidstate, 35 watts, 2x10", black tolex.			
1967-1969		$400	$500
Custom Vibrolux Reverb Amp			
1995-present. Part of Professional Series, Custom Shop designed, standard factory built, 40 watts, 2x10", tube, white knobs, blond Tolex and tan grill for '95 only, black Tolex, silver grille after. Does not say Custom on face plate.			
1995	Blond & tan	$650	$775
1996-2010	Black & silver	$650	$775
Vibroverb Amp			
1963-1964. Brown tolex with 35 watts, 2x10" and brownface '63, black tolex with 1x15" and blackface late '63-'64.			
1963	Brown tolex, 2x10"	$6,900	$8,300
1963-1964	Black tolex, 1x15"	$4,000	$4,700
Vibroverb '63 Reissue Amp			
1990-1995. Reissue of 1963 Vibroverb, 40 watts, 2x10", reverb, vibrato, brown tolex.			
1990-1995		$775	$925
Vibroverb '64 Custom Shop Amp			
2003-2008. Reissue of 1964 Vibroverb with 1x15" blackface specs.			
2003-2008		$1,700	$2,000
Yale Reverb Amp			
1983-1985. Solidstate, black tolex, 50 watts, 1x12", silverface.			
1983-1985		$225	$275

FireBelly Amps

2008-present. Production/custom, professional and premium grade, vintage tube amps built by Steven Cohen in Santa Monica, California.

Fishman

2003-present. Larry Fishman offers professional grade, production, amps that are designed and engineered in Andover, Massachusetts and assembled in China. They also build effects.

FJA Mods

2002-present. In 2007, Jerry Pinnelli began building his professional grade, production, guitar amps in Central Square, New York. He also builds effects.

| MODEL | | EXC. COND. | |
YEAR	FEATURES	LOW	HIGH

Flot-A-Tone

Ca.1946-early 1960s. Flot-A-Tone was located in Milwaukee, Wisconsin, and made a variety of tube guitar and accordion amps. Most were distrubuted by the Lo Duca Brothers.

Large Amp

1960s. Four speakers.

1960s		$550	$675

Small Amp

1960s. 1x8" speaker.

1960s		$275	$350

Fortune

1978-1979. Created by Jim Kelley just prior to branding Jim Kelley Amplifiers in 1980, Fortune Amplifiers logo on front panel, specifications and performance similar to early Jim Kelley amplifiers, difficult to find in original condition, professional grade, designed and manufactured by Active Guitar Electronics company.

Fox Amps

2007-present. Marc Vos builds professional grade, production/custom, guitar amps and cabinets in Budel, Netherlands.

Framus

1946-1977, 1996-present. Tube guitar amp heads, combos and cabinets made in Markneukirchen, Germany. They also build guitars, basses, mandolins and banjos. Begun as an acoustic instrument manufacturer, Framus added electrics in the mid-'50s. In the '60s, Framus instruments were imported into the U.S. by Philadelphia Music Company. The brand was revived in '96 by Hans Peter Wilfer, the president of Warwick, with production in Warwick's factory in Germany. Distributed in the U.S. by Dana B. Goods.

Fred

1984-1986. Before settling on the name Bedrock, company founders Brad Jeter and Ron Pinto produced 50 amps carrying the brand name Fred in Nashua, New Hampshire.

Frenzel

1952-present. Jim Frenzel built his first amp in '52 and began using his brand in '01. He offers intermediate and professional grade, production/custom, hand-wired, vintage tube, guitar and bass amps built in Mabank, Texas.

Frudua Guitar Works

1988-present. Intermediate grade, production, guitar and bass amps built by guitar luthier Galeazzo Frudua in Calusco d'Adda, Italy. He also builds guitars and basses.

Fryette

2009-present. Professional and premium grade amps, combos, and cabinets built by Steven M.

| MODEL | | EXC. COND. | |
YEAR	FEATURES	LOW	HIGH

Fryette, who also founded VHT amps. At the beginning of '09 AXL guitars acquired the VHT name to build their own product. Fryette continues to manufacture the VHT amp models under the Fryette brand in Burbank, California.

Fuchs Audio Technology

2000-present. Andy Fuchs started the company in '99 to rebuild and modify tube amps. In 2000 he started production of his own brand of amps, offering combos and heads from 10 to 150 watts. They also custom build audiophile and studio tube electronics. Originally located in Bloomfield, New Jersey, since '07 in Clifton, New Jersey.

Fulton-Webb

1997-present. Steve Fulton and Bill Webb build their tube amp heads, combos and cabinets in Austin, Texas.

Gabriel Sound Garage

2004-present. Gabriel Bucataru builds his tube amp heads and combos in Arlington Heights, Illinois.

Gallien Krueger

1969-present. Gallien-Krueger has offered a variety of bass and guitar amps, combos and cabinets and is located in San Jose, California.

Garcia

2004-present. Tube amp heads and speaker cabinets built by Matthew Garcia in Myrtle Beach, South Carolina. He also builds effects.

Garnet

Mid 1960s-1989. In the mid '60s, "Gar" Gillies started the Garnet Amplifier Company with his two sons, Russell and Garnet, after he started making PA systems in his Canadian radio and TV repair shop. The first PA from the new company was for Chad Allen & the Expressions (later known as The Guess Who). A wide variety of tube amps were offered and all were designed by Gar, Sr. The company also produced the all-tube effects The Herzog, H-zog, and two stand-alone reverb units designed by Gar in the late '60s and early '70s. The company closed in '89, due to financial reasons caused largely by a too rapid expansion. Gar repaired and designed custom amps up to his death in early 2007.

GDS Amplification

1998-present. Tube amps, combos and speaker cabinets from builder Graydon D. Stuckey of Fenton, Michigan. GDS also offers amp kits. In January, '09, GDS bought the assets of Guytron Amplification.

Genesis

Genesis was a 1980s line of student amps from Gibson.

Fryette Memphis

Gallien Krueger Fusion 550

Garcia 60-Watt Combo

AMPS

George Dennis Blue 60 Combo

1948 Gibson BR-9

David Stuckey

Gibson EH-150

MODEL YEAR	FEATURES	EXC. COND. LOW	HIGH
B40 Amp			
1984-late-1980s. Bass combo with 40 watts.			
1984-1989		$100	$125
G Series Amps			
1984-late-1980s. Small combo amps.			
1984-1989	G10, 10w	$50	$75
1984-1989	G25, 25w	$75	$100
1984-1989	G40R, 40w, reverb	$125	$150

Genz Benz

1984-present. Founded by Jeff and Cathy Genzler and located in Scottsdale, Arizona, the company offers guitar, bass, and PA amps and speaker cabinets. In late 2003, Genz Benz was acquired by Kaman (Ovation, Hamer, Takamine). On January 1, '08, Fender acquired Kaman Music Corporation and the Genz Benz brand.

George Dennis

1991-present. Founded by George Burgerstein, original products were a line of effects pedals. In '96 they added a line of tube amps. The company is located in Prague, Czech Republic.

Gerhart

2000-present. Production/custom, amps and cabinets from builder Gary Gerhart of West Hills, California. He also offers an amp in kit form.

Germino

2002-present. Intermediate to professional grade tube amps, combos and cabinets built by Greg Germino in Graham, North Carolina.

Gibson

1890s (1902)-present. Gibson has offered a variety of amps since the mid-'30s to the present under the Gibson brandname and others. The price ranges listed are for excellent condition, all original amps though tubes may be replaced without affecting value. Many Gibson amps have missing or broken logos. The prices listed are for amps with fully intact logos. A broken or missing logo can diminish the value of the amp. Amps with a changed handle, power cord, and especially a broken logo should be taken on a case-by-case basis. Vintage amplifiers are rarely found in original, excellent condition. Many vintage amps have notable wear and have a non-original speaker. The prices shown are for fully original (except tubes and caps) amplifiers that are pleasing clean, and contain no significant wear, blemishes, grille stains, or damage.

MODEL YEAR	FEATURES	EXC. COND. LOW	HIGH
Atlas IV Amp			
1963-1967. Piggyback head and cab, introduced with trapezoid shape, changed to rectangular cabs in '65-'66 with black cover, simple circuit with 4 knobs, no reverb or tremolo, mid-power with 2 6L6, 1x15".			
1963-1965	Brown	$500	$625
1966-1967	Black	$500	$625

MODEL YEAR	FEATURES	EXC. COND. LOW	HIGH
Atlas Medalist Amp			
1964-1967. Combo version with 1x15".			
1964-1967		$500	$625
B-40 Amp			
1972-1975. Solidstate, 40 watts, 1x12".			
1972-1975		$225	$275
BR-1 Amp			
1946-1948. 15 watts, 1x12" field-coil speaker, brown leatherette cover, rectangular metal grille with large G.			
1946-1948		$650	$800
BR-3 Amp			
1946. 12 watts, 1x12" Utah field-coil speaker (most BR models used Jensen speakers).			
1946		$650	$800
BR-4 Amp			
1946-1947. 14 watts, 1x12" Utah field-coil speaker (most BR models used Jensen speakers).			
1946-1947		$500	$600
BR-6 Amp			
1946-1954. 10 to 12 watts, 1x10", brown leatherette, speaker opening split by cross panel with G logo, bottom mounted chassis with single on-off volume pointer knob.			
1946-1947	Verticle cab	$400	$475
1948-1954	Horizontal cab	$400	$475
BR-9 Amp			
1948-1954. Cream leatherette, 10 watts, 1x8". Originally sold with the BR-9 lap steel. Renamed GA-9 in '54.			
1948-1954		$325	$400
Duo Metalist Amp			
1968-early 1970s. Upright vertical combo cab, tubes, faux wood grain panel, mid-power, 1x12".			
1968-1970s		$300	$375
EH-100 Amp			
1936-1942. Electric-Hawaiian companion amp, 1x10". AC/DC version called EH-110.			
1936-1942		$650	$800
EH-125 Amp			
1941-1942. 1x12", rounded shoulder cab, brown cover in '41 and dark green in '42, leather handle.			
1941-1942		$725	$900
EH-126 Amp			
1941. Experimental model, 6-volt variant of EH-125, about 5 made.			
1941		$800	$1,000
EH-135 Amp			
1941. Experimental model, alternating and direct current switchable, about 7 made.			
1941		$900	$1,100
EH-150 Amp			
1935-1942. Electric-Hawaiian companion amp, 1x12" ('35-'37) or 1x10" ('38-'42). AC/DC version called EH-160.			
1935	13 3/4" square cab	$1,400	$1,700
1936-1937	14 3/4" square cab	$1,400	$1,700
1937-1942	15 3/8" round cab	$1,400	$1,700
EH-185 Amp			
1939-1942. 1x12", tweed cover, black and orange vertical stripes, marketed as companion amp to the EH-185 Lap Steel. AC/DC version called EH-195.			
1939-1942		$1,600	$1,900

EH-195 Amp
1939-1942. EH-185 variant with vibrato.

MODEL YEAR	FEATURES	EXC. COND. LOW	HIGH
1939-1942		$1,600	$1,900

EH-250 Amp
1940. Upgraded natural maple cabinet using EH-185 chassis, only 2 made, evolved into EH-275.

1940		$1,700	$2,000

EH-275 Amp
1940-1942. Similar to EH-185 but with maple cab and celluloid binding, about 30 made.

1940-1942		$1,700	$2,000

Epoch Series
2000s. Solidstate student practice amps.

2000s	G-10	$20	$25

Falcon III F-3 Amp
Early 1970s. Solidstate, 1x12" combo, 65 watts, made in Chicago by CMI after Gibson ceased amp production in Kalamazoo ('67), black tolex, dark grille.

1970		$200	$250

Falcon Medalist (Hybrid) Amp
1967. Transitional tube 1x12" combo amp from GA-19 tube Falcon to the solidstate Falcon, Falcon logo and Gibson logo on front panel, brown control panel, dark cover and dark grille, vertical combo cabinet.

1967		$325	$400

Falcon Medalist (Solidstate) Amp
1968-1969. Solidstate combo, 15 watts, 1x12".

1968-1969		$300	$325

G-10 Amp
1972-1975. Solidstate, 10 watts, 1x10", no tremolo or reverb.

1972-1975		$70	$85

G-20 Amp
1972-1975. Solidstate with tremolo, 1x10", 10 watts.

1972-1975		$100	$125

G-25 Amp
1972-1975. 25 watts, 1x10".

1972-1975		$125	$150

G-35 Amp
1975. Solidstate, 30 watts, 1x12".

1975		$150	$175

G-40/G-40 R Amp
1972-1974. Solidstate with tremolo and reverb, 40 watts, 1x12" (G-40) and 2x10" (G-40 R).

1972-1974		$200	$225

G-50/G-50 A/G-50 B Amp
1972, 1975. Solidstate with tremolo and reverb, models G-50 and 50 A are 1x12", 40 watts, model 50 B is a bass 1x15", 50 watts.

1972-1975		$250	$275

G-55 Amp
1975. 50 watts, 1x12".

1975		$275	$300

G-60 Amp
1972-1973. Solidstate with tremolo and reverb, 1x15", 60 watts.

1972-1973		$300	$325

G-70 Amp
1972-1973. Solidstate with tremolo and reverb, 2x12", 60 watts.

1972-1973		$300	$325

G-80 Amp
1972-1973. Solidstate with tremolo and reverb, 4x10", 60 watts.

1972-1973		$350	$375

G-100 A/G-100 B Amp
1975. 100 watts, model 100 A is 2x12" and 100 B is 2x15".

1975		$350	$375

G-105 Amp
1974-1975. Solidstate, 100 watts, 2x12", reverb.

1974-1975		$350	$375

G-115 Amp
1975. 100 watts, 4x10".

1974-1975		$375	$400

GA-5 Les Paul Jr. Amp
1954-1957. Tan fabric cover (Mottled Brown by '57), 7" oval speaker, 4 watts. Renamed Skylark in '58.

1954		$500	$600
1955-1957		$500	$600

GA-5 Les Paul Jr. Amp (Reissue)
2004-2008. Class A, 5 watts, 1x8".

2004-2008		$275	$325

GA-5 Skylark Amp
1957-1968. Gold cover (brown by '63 and black by '66), 1x8" (1x10" from '64 on), 4.5 watts (10 watts from '64 on), tremolo. Often sold with the Skylark Lap Steel.

1957	Gold, 4.5w, 1x8"	$450	$550
1958-1959	Gold, 4.5w, 1x8"	$425	$525
1960	Gold, 4.5w, 1x8"	$400	$500
1961-1962	Gold, 4.5w, 1x8"	$375	$450
1963	Brown, 4.5w, 1x8"	$275	$325
1964	Brown, 10w, 1x10"	$275	$325
1965-1967	Black, 10w, 1x10"	$275	$325
1968	Skylark, last version	$225	$275

GA-5 T Skylark Amp
1960-1968. Tremolo, 4.5 watts early on, 10 later, gold covering and 1x8" until '63, brown '63-'64, black and 1x10" after.

1961-1962	Gold, 4.5w, 1x8"	$400	$500
1963	Brown, 4.5w, 1x8"	$325	$400
1964	Brown, 10w, 1x10"	$325	$400
1965-1967	Kalamazoo, black, 10w, 1x10"	$325	$400
1968	Norlin, vertical cab, 10w, 1x10, tubes	$225	$275

GA-5 W Amp
Late-1960s. Norlin-era, post-Kalamazoo production, 15 watts, small speaker, volume and tone controls.

1969		$75	$100

GA-6 Amp
1956-1959. Replaced the BR-6, 8 to 12 watts, 1x12", has Gibson 6 above the grille. Renamed GA-6 Lancer in '60.

1956-1959		$550	$675

GA-6 Lancer Amp
1960-1961. Renamed from GA-6, 1x12", tweed cover, 3 knobs, 14 watts.

1960-1961		$725	$900

GA-7 Les Paul TV Model Amp
1954-1956. Basic old style GA-5 with different graphics, 4 watts, small speaker.

1954-1956		$525	$650

Gibson EH-185

1957 Gibson GA-5 Les Paul Junior

Gibson GA-5 Skylark

AMPS

Gibson GA-15

Gibson GA-30

Gibson GA-40 Les Paul

MODEL YEAR	FEATURES	EXC. COND. LOW	HIGH
GA-8 Discoverer Amp			
1962-1964. Renamed from GA-8 Gibsonette, gold fabric cover, 1x12", 10 watts.			
1960-1963		$500	$600
GA-8 Gibsonette Amp			
1955-1962. Tan fabric cover (gold by '58), 1x10", 8 watts (9 watts by '58). See Gibsonette for 1952-'54. Name changed to GA-8 Discoverer in '62.			
1955	Gibsonette logo on front, square hole	$500	$600
1956-1957	Gibsonette l logo on front	$500	$600
1958-1959	Gibson logo on front	$500	$600
1960-1962	Gibson logo upper right front	$500	$600
GA-8 T Discoverer Amp			
1960-1966. Gold fabric cover, 1x10", 9 watts (tan cover, 1x12" and 15 watts by '63), tremolo.			
1960-1962	Tweed, 9w, 1x10"	$525	$650
1963-1964	Brown, 15w, 1x12"	$400	$500
1965-1966	Black, 15w, 1x12"	$350	$425
GA-9 Amp			
1954-1959. Renamed from BR-9, tan fabric cover, 8 watts, 1x10". Often sold with the BR-9 Lap Steel.			
1954-1957	Gibson 9 logo	$475	$575
1958-1959	Tweed, 6V6s	$475	$575
GA-14 Titan Amp			
1959-1961. About 15 watts using 2x6V6 power tubes, 1x10", tweed cover.			
1959-1961		$575	$675
GA-15 RV Goldtone Amp			
1999-2004. 15 watts, Class A, 1x12", spring reverb.			
1999-2004		$475	$575
GA-15 RVT Explorer Amp			
1965-1967. Tube, 1x10", tremolo, reverb, black vinyl.			
1965-1967		$350	$425
GA-17 RVT Scout Amp			
1963-1967. Low power, 1x12", reverb and tremolo.			
1963-1965	Brown	$450	$550
1966-1967	Black	$400	$475
GA-18 Explorer Amp			
1959. Tweed, tube, 14 watts, 1x10". Replaced in '60 by the GA-18 T Explorer.			
1959		$600	$725
GA-18 T Explorer Amp			
1960-1963. Tweed, 14 watts, 1x10", tremolo.			
1960-1962		$600	$725
1963		$450	$550
GA-19 RVT Falcon Amp			
1961-1967. One of Gibson's best selling amps. Initially tweed covered, followed by smooth brown, textured brown, and black. Each amp has a different tone. One 12" Jensen with deep-sounding reverb and tremolo.			
1961	Tweed, 6V6	$1,300	$1,600
1962	Tweed, 6V6	$1,200	$1,500
1962-1963	Smooth brown	$500	$625
1964	Textured brown	$500	$625
1965-1967	Black	$400	$500

MODEL YEAR	FEATURES	EXC. COND. LOW	HIGH
GA-20 Amp			
1950-1962. Brown leatherette (2-tone by '55 and tweed by '60), tube, 12 watts early, 14 watts later, 1x12". Renamed Crest in '60.			
1950	Brown, single G logo on front	$700	$825
1951-1954	Brown, single G logo on front	$700	$825
1955-1958	2-tone salt & maroon	$900	$1,100
1959	2-tone blue & blond	$925	$1,150
GA-20 Crest Amp			
1960-1961. Tweed, tube, 14 watts, 1x12".			
1960-1961		$925	$1,150
GA-20 RVT Amp			
2004-2007. 15 watts, 1x12", reverb, tremolo.			
2004-2007		$600	$725
GA-20 RVT Minuteman Amp			
1965-1967. Black, 14 watts, 1x12", tube, reverb, tremolo.			
1965-1967		$375	$475
GA-20 T Amp			
1956-1959. Tube, 16 watts, tremolo, 1x12", 2-tone. Renamed Ranger in '60.			
1956-1958	2-tone	$925	$1,150
1959	New 2-tone	$950	$1,175
GA-20 T Ranger Amp			
1960-1961. Tube, 16 watts, tremolo, 1x12", tweed.			
1960-1962	Tweed	$950	$1,175
GA-25 Amp			
1947-1948. Brown, 1x12" and 1x8", 15 watts. Replaced by GA-30 in '48.			
1947-1948		$775	$950
GA-25 RVT Hawk Amp			
1963-1968. Reverb, tremolo, 1x15".			
1963	Smooth brown	$575	$700
1964	Rough brown	$475	$575
1965-1967	Black	$450	$550
1968	Last version	$250	$300
GA-30 Amp			
1948-1961. Brown until '54, 2-tone after, tweed in '60, 1x12" and 1x8", 14 watts. Renamed Invader in '60.			
1948-1954	Brown	$750	$925
1955-1959	2-tone salt & maroon	$1,100	$1,300
1960-1961	Tweed	$1,100	$1,300
GA-30 RV Invader Amp			
1961. Tweed, 1x12" and 1x8", 14-16 watts, reverb but no tremolo.			
1961		$1,200	$1,500
GA-30 RVH Goldtone Amp Head			
1999-2004. 30 watts, Class A head, reverb.			
1999-2004		$600	$725
GA-30 RVS (Stereo) Goldtone Amp			
1999-2004. 15 watts per channel, Class A stereo, 2x12", reverb.			
1999-2004		$675	$800
GA-30 RVT Invader Amp			
1962-1967. Updated model with reverb and tremolo, dual speakers 1x12" and 1x8", first issue in tweed.			
1962	Tweed	$1,200	$1,500
1963	Smooth brown	$725	$900

MODEL YEAR	FEATURES	EXC. COND. LOW	HIGH
1964-1965	Rough brown	$625	$750
1966-1967	Black	$550	$675

GA-300 RVT Super 300 Amp
1962-1963. 60 watts, 2x12" combo, reverb, tremolo, smooth brown.

1962-1963		$2,000	$2,450

GA-35 RVT Lancer Amp
1966-1967. Black, 1x12", tremolo, reverb.

1966-1967		$525	$650

GA-40 Les Paul Amp
1952-1960. Introduced in conjunction with the Les Paul Model guitar, 1x12" Jensen speaker, 14 watts on early models and 16 watts later, recessed leather handle using spring mounting (the handle is easily broken and an unsimilar replacement handle is more common than not). Two-tone leatherette covering, '50s checkerboard grille ('52-early-'55), Les Paul script logo on front of the amp ('52-'55), plastic grille insert with LP monogram, gold Gibson logo above grille. Cosmetics changed dramatically in early/mid-'55. Renamed GA-40 T Les Paul in '60.

1952-1955	Brown 2-tone, LP grille	$1,500	$1,800
1955-1957	2-tone salt & maroon	$1,550	$1,850
1958-1959	2-tone blue & blond	$1,550	$1,850

GA-40 RVT Limited Edition Amp
2008-present. GA-40RVT Limited Edition logo on back left corner plate, 2-tone brown/tan, front control panel, 30/15 switchable watts.

2008-2010		$500	$575

GA-40 T Les Paul Amp
1960-1962. Renamed from GA-40 Les Paul, 1x12", 16 watts, tremolo. Renamed Mariner in '62-'67.

1960-1961	Tweed	$1,800	$2,200
1962	Smooth brown	$600	$750

GA-40 T Mariner Amp
1962-1967. 1x12" combo, 25 watts, tremolo.

1962-1963	Smooth brown	$600	$750
1964	Rough brown	$500	$625
1965-1967	Rough brown	$500	$625

GA-45 RVT Saturn Amp
1965-1967. 2x10", mid power, tremolo, reverb.

1965-1967		$525	$650

GA-50/GA-50 T Amp
1948-1955. Brown leatherette, 25 watts, 1x12" and 1x8", T had tremolo.

1948-1955	GA-50	$1,700	$2,100
1948-1955	GA-50 T	$1,750	$2,150

GA-55 RVT Ranger Amp
1965-1967. Black cover, 4x10", tremolo, reverb.

1965-1967		$550	$675

GA-55/GA-55 V Amp
1954-1958. 2x12", 20 watts, GA-55 V with vibrato.

1954-1958	GA-55	$1,900	$2,300
1954-1958	GA-55 V	$2,000	$2,500

GA-60 Hercules Amp
1962-1963. 25 watts, 1x15, no-frills 1-channel amp, no reverb, no tremolo.

1962-1963		$600	$725

GA-60 RV Goldtone Amp
1999-2004. 60 watts, A/B circuit, 2x12", spring reverb, earliest production in England.

1999-2004		$800	$975

GA-70 Country and Western Amp
1955-1958. 25 watts, 1x15", 2-tone, longhorn cattle western logo on front, advertised to have extra bright sound.

1955-1958		$2,000	$2,400

GA-75 Amp
1950-1955. Mottled Brown leatherette, 1x15", 25 watts.

1950-1955		$1,725	$2,125

GA-75 L Recording Amp
1964-1967. 1x15" Lansing speaker, no reverb or tremolo, 2 channels, dark cover, gray grille.

1964-1967		$525	$650

GA-75 Recording Amp
1964-1967. 2x10" speakers, no reverb or tremolo, 2 channels, dark cover, gray grille.

1964-1967		$525	$650

GA-77 Amp
1954-1961. 1x15" JBL, 25-30 watts, 2x6L6 power tubes, 2-tone covering, near top-of-the-line for the mid-'50s.

1954-1957	2-tone salt/maroon, leather handle	$1,700	$2,000
1958-1961	2-tone blue/blond, metal handle	$1,700	$2,000

GA-77 RET Vanguard Amp
1964-1967. Mid-power, 2x10", tremolo, reverb, echo.

1964	Rough brown	$625	$775
1965	Rough brown or black	$600	$750
1966-1967	Black	$575	$700

GA-77 RVTL Vanguard Amp
1962-1963. 50 watts, 1x15", Lansing speaker option (L), tremolo, reverb..

1962-1963	Smooth brown	$625	$775

GA-77 Vanguard Amp
1960-1961. 1x15" JBL, 25-30 watts, 2 6L6 power tubes, tweed cover, first use of Vanguard model name.

1960-1961		$1,700	$2,100

GA-78 Bell Stereo Amp
1960. Gibson-branded amp made by Bell, same as GA-79 series, Bell 30 logo on front, 30 watts, 2x10" wedge cab.

1960		$2,000	$2,400

GA-79 RV Amp
1960-1962. Stereo-reverb, 2x10", 30 watts.

1960-1961	Tweed	$2,300	$2,800
1962	Gray tolex	$2,200	$2,750

GA-79 RVT Multi-Stereo Amp
1961-1967. Introduced as GA-79 RVT, Multi-Stereo was added to name in '61. Stereo-reverb and tremolo, 2x10", tweed (black and brown also available), 30 watts.

1961	Tweed	$2,300	$2,800
1961-1962	Gray sparkle	$2,000	$2,500
1963-1964	Textured brown	$2,000	$2,500
1965-1967	Black	$2,000	$2,500

Gibson GA-40T Les Paul

1955 Gibson GA-55V

1961 Gibson GA-79 RV

AMPS

AMPS

*1962 Gibson GA-200
Rhythm King*

Gibson Hawk

Ginelle El Toro Pequeno

GA-80/GA-80 T/Vari-Tone Amp
1959-1961. 25 watts, 1x15", 2 channels, described as "6-in-1 amplifier with improved tremolo," 6 Vari-Tone pushbottons which give "six distinctively separate sounds," 7 tubes, tweed cover.

Model Year	Features	Low	High
1959-1961		$1,800	$2,200

GA-83 S Stereo-Vibe Amp
1959-1961. Interesting stereo amp with front baffle mounted 1x12" and 4x8" side-mounted speakers (2 on each side), 35 watts, Gibson logo on upper right corner of the grille, tweed cover, brown grille (late '50s Fender-style), 3 pointer knobs and 3 round knobs, 4 inputs.

1959-1961		$2,700	$3,200

GA-85 Bass Reflex Amp
1957-1958. Removable head, 25 watts, 1x12", very limited production.

1957-1958		$1,150	$1,400

GA-90 High Fidelity Amp
1953-1960. 25 watts, 6x8", 2 channels, advertised for guitar, bass, accordion, or hi-fi.

1953-1960		$1,500	$1,800

GA-95 RVT Apollo Amp
1965-1967. 90 watts, 2x12", black vinyl, black grille, tremolo, reverb.

1965-1967		$625	$750

GA-100 Bass Amp
1960-1963. 35 watts, 1x12" cabinet, for '60-'61 tweed and tripod included for separate head, for '62-'63 brown covering and Crestline Tuck-A-Way head.

1960-1961	Tweed	$1,000	$1,250
1962-1963	Smooth brown	$600	$725

GA-200 Rhythm King Amp
1957-1961. Introduced as GA-200, renamed Rhythm King in '60, 2-channel version of GA-400. Bass amp, 60 watts, 2x12".

1957-1959	2-tone	$2,100	$2,600
1960-1961	Tweed	$2,200	$2,750
1961	Smooth brown, no trem or reverb	$1,800	$2,250

GA-300 RVT Super 300 Amp
1962-1963. 60 watts, 2x12" combo, reverb, tremolo, smooth brown.

1962-1963		$2,000	$2,450

GA-400 Super 400 Amp
1956-1961. 60 watts, 2x12", 3 channels, same size as GA-200 cab, 1 more tube than GA-200.

1956-1959	2-tone	$2,200	$2,750
1960-1961	Tweed	$2,300	$2,800
1961	Smooth brown, no trem or reverb	$1,900	$2,300

GA-CB Custom-Built Amp
1949-1953. 25-30 watts, 1x15", the top model in Gibson's '51 line of amps, described as having sound quality found only in the finest public address broadcasting systems, about 47 made, this high-end amp was replaced by the GA-77 and a completely different GA-90.

1949-1953		$1,750	$2,150

Gibsonette Amp
1952-1954. Gibsonette logo on front, round hole. See GA-8 Gibsonette for later models.

1952-1954		$475	$575

GM Series
2008-2009. Imported solidstate student models.

2008-2009	GM-05, 5w	$10	$15

GSS-50 Amp
1966-1967. Solidstate, 50 watts, 2x10" combo, reverb and tremolo, black vinyl cover, silver grille, no grille logo.

1966-1967		$350	$425

GSS-100 Amp
1966-1967, 1970. Solidstate, 100 watts, two 24"x12" 2x10" sealed cabs, black vinyl cover, silver grille, 8 black knobs and 3 red knobs, slanted raised Gibson logo. Speakers prone to distortion. Reissued in '70 in 3 variations.

1966-1967		$375	$450

Lancer
1968-1969. CMI-Chicago produced, small combo, black upright cab, dark grille, post-McCarty era Gibson logo.

1968-1969		$50	$75

LP-1/LP-2 Amp Set
1970. Les Paul model, piggyback amp and cab set, LP-1 head and LP-2 4x12" plus 2 horns cab, large vertical speaker cabinet, rather small compact 190 watt solidstate amp head.

1970		$350	$425

Medalist 2/12 Amp
1968-1970. Vertical cabinet, 2x12", reverb and temolo.

1968-1970		$375	$450

Medalist 4/10 Amp
1968-1970. Vertical cabinet, 4x10", reverb and tremolo.

1968-1970		$400	$475

Mercury I Amp
1963-1965. Piggyback trapezoid-shaped head with 2x12" trapezoid cabinet, tremolo, brown.

1963-1965		$475	$575

Mercury II Amp
1963-1967. Mercury I with 1x15" and 1x10", initially trapezoid cabinets then changed to rectangular.

1963-1964	Brown trapezoid cabs	$550	$675
1965-1967	Black rectangular cabs	$475	$575

Plus-50 Amp
1966-1967. 50 watts, powered extension amplifier. Similar to GSS-100 cabinet of the same era, 2x10" cab, black vinyl cover, silver grille, slant Gibson logo.

1966-1967		$450	$550

Super Thor Bass Amp
1970-1974. Solidstate, part of the new G-Series (not GA-Series), 65 watts, 2x15", black tolex, black grille, upright vertical cab with front control, single channel.

1970-1974		$350	$425

Thor Bass Amp
1970-1974. Solidstate, smaller 2x10" 50 watt version of Super Thor.

1970-1974		$300	$375

MODEL		EXC. COND.	
YEAR	FEATURES	LOW	HIGH

Titan I Amp
1963-1965. Piggyback trapezoid-shaped head and 2x12" trapezoid-shaped cabinet, tremolo.

1963-1965		$475	$575

Titan III Amp
1963-1967. Piggyback trapezoid-shaped head and 1x15" + 2x10" trapezoid-shaped cabinet, tremolo.

1963-1964	Brown	$500	$625
1965-1967	Black	$500	$625

Titan Medalist Amp
1964-1967. Combo version of Titan Series with 1x15" and 1x10", tremolo only, no reverb, black.

1964-1967		$525	$650

Titan V Amp
1963-1967. Piggyback trapezoid-shaped tube head and 2x15" trapezoid-shaped cabinet, tremolo.

1963-1964	Brown	$525	$650
1965-1967	Black	$525	$650

TR-1000 T/TR-1000 RVT Starfire Amp
1962-1967. Solidstate, 1x12" combo, 40 watts, tremolo, RVT with reverb.

1962-1967		$275	$325

Ginelle
1996-present. Rick Emery builds his tube combo amps in West Berlin, New Jersey.

Giulietti
1962. Amps made by Magnatone for the Giulietti Accordion Company, New York. Models closely approximate the Magnatone equivalent and model numbers are often similar to the copied Magnatone model. Large Giulietti logo on upper front panel.

S-9 Amp (Magnatone 460)
1962. 35 watts, 2x12 plus 2 tweeters, true vibrato combo, black sparkle.

1962		$1,200	$1,400

Gnome Amplifiers
2008-present. Dan Munro builds professional grade, production, guitar amps and cabinets in Olympia, Washington. He also builds effects.

Gomez Amplification
2005-present. Tube combo amps built by Dario G. Gomez in Rancho Santa Margarita, California.

Goodsell
2004-present. Tube head and combo amps built by Richard Goodsell in Atlanta, Georgia.

Gorilla
1980s-present. Small solidstate entry-level amps, distributed by Pignose, Las Vegas, Nevada.

Compact Practice Student Amp
1980s-2009. Solidstate, 10 to 30 watts, compact design.

1980s		$35	$45
1990s		$35	$45
2000s		$35	$45

Goya
1955-1996. Goya was mainly known for acoustics, but offered a few amps in the '60s. The brand was purchased by Avnet/Guild in '66 and by Martin in the late '70s.

Grammatico Amps
2009-present. Production/custom, professional and premium grade, hand-wired, guitar and bass amps built by John Grammatico in Austin, Texas.

Green
1993-present. Amp model line made in England by Matamp (see that brand for listing), bright green covering, large Green logo on the front.

Greer Amplification
1999-present. Tube guitar amps and speaker cabinets built by Nick Greer in Athens, Georgia. He also builds effects.

Gregory
1950s-1960s. Private branded amps sold via music wholesalers, by late '60s solidstate models made by Harmony including the 007, C.I.A., Mark Six, Mark Eight, Saturn 80, most models were combo amps with Gregory logo.

Solidstate Amps

1960s		$125	$150

Gretsch
1883-present. In '05, Gretsch again starting offering amps after previously selling them from the 1950s to '73. Initially private branded for them by Valco (look for the Valco oval or rectangular serialized label on the back). Early-'50s amps were covered in the requisite tweed, but evolved into the Gretsch charcoal gray covering. The mid-'50s to early-'60s amps were part of the Electromatic group of amps. The mid-'50s to '62 amps often sported wrap-around and slanted grilles. In '62, the more traditional box style was introduced. In '66, the large amps went piggyback. Baldwin-Gretsch began to phase out amps effective '65, but solidstate amps continued being offered for a period of time. The '73 Gretsch product line only offered Sonax amps, made in Canada and Sho-Bud amps made in the U.S. In '05, they introduced a line of tube combo amps made in U.S. by Victoria Amp Company.

Artist Amp
1946. Early post-war Gretsch amp made before Valco began to make their amps. Appears to be made by Operadio Mfg. Co., St. Charles, Illinois. Low power small combo amp, Gretsch Artist script logo on grille, round speaker baffle hole.

1946		$200	$250

Broadkaster Mini Lead 50 Amp
Late 1960s. Solidstate compact verticle combo amp.

1969		$200	$300

Goodsell Custom 33

Grammatico Kingsville

Greer Cam 18

1964 Gretsch, Model 6161
(Paul Moser III)

1959 Gretsch Model 6169
Electromatic Twin Western

Gretsch Safari

MODEL YEAR	FEATURES	EXC. COND. LOW	HIGH

Electromatic Amp
1947-1949. Valco-made with era-typical Valco styling, Electromatic logo metal badge riveted on lower front of amp, 3 slat speaker baffle openings, leather handle, two-tone leatherette, 3 tubes with small speaker, single volume knob, on-off toggle switch.

1947-1949		$500	$575

Electromatic Artist Amp (6155)
1950s. Small compact amp, 2x6V6 power, 1x10", volume knob, tone knob, Electromatic logo on back panel.

1957-1958		$500	$575

Model 6150 Compact Amp
Late-1950s-1960s. Early amps in tweed, '60s amps in gray covering, no tremolo, single volume knob, no treble or bass knob, 1x8".

1950s	Brown tweed	$350	$400
1960s	Gray	$350	$400

Model 6151 Electromatic Std/Compact Tremolo Amp
Late-1940s-late-1960s. 1x8", various covers.

1940s		$425	$475
1950s		$425	$475
1960s		$425	$475

Model 6152 Compact Tremolo Reverb Amp
Ca.1964-late-1960s. Five watts, 11"x6" elliptical speaker early on, 1x12" later.

1964-1966	Elliptical speaker	$500	$625
1966-1969	Round speaker	$500	$625

Model 6153T White Princess Amp
1962. Compact combo, Princess logo front right, 6x9" oval speaker, higher priced than the typical small combo amp because it is relatively rare and associated with the White Princess guitar - making it valuable in a set, condition is very important, an amp with any issues will be worth much less.

1962		$800	$975

Model 6154 Super-Bass Amp
Early-1960s-mid-1960s. Gray covering, 2x12", 70 watts, tube.

1960s		$625	$775

Model 6156 Playboy Amp
Early-1950s-1966. Tube amp, 17 watts, 1x10" until '61 when converted to 1x12", tweed, then gray, then finally black covered.

1950s-1960	Tweed, 1x10"	$500	$625
1961-1962	Tweed, 1x12"	$500	$625
1963-1966	Black or gray, 1x12"	$600	$725

Model 6157 Super Bass (Piggyback) Amp
Mid-late-1960s. 35 watts, 2x15" cabinet, single channel.

1960s		$450	$550

Model 6159 Dual Bass Amp
Mid-late-1960s. 35 watts, tube, 2x12" cabinet, dual channel, black covering. Replaced by 6163 Chet Atkins Piggyback Amp.

1965		$625	$775

Model 6160 Chet Atkins Country Gentleman Amp
Early-late-1960s. Combo tube amp, 35 watts, 2x12" cabinet, 2 channels. Replaced by 6163 Chet Atkins Piggyback amp with tremolo but no reverb.

1960s		$600	$725

Model 6161 Dual Twin Tremolo Amp
Ca.1962-late-1960s. 19 watts (later 17 watts), 2x10" with 5" tweeter, tremolo.

1962-1967		$575	$700

Model 6161 Electromatic Twin Amp
Ca.1953-ca.1960. Gray Silverflake covering, two 11x6" speakers, 14 watts, tremolo, wraparound grille '55 and after.

1953-1960		$675	$825

Model 6162 Dual Twin Tremolo/Reverb Amp
Ca.1964-late-1960s. 17 watts, 2x10", reverb, tremolo. Vertical combo amp style introduced in '68.

1964-1967	Horizontal combo style	$625	$775
1968-1969	Vertical combo style	$450	$550

Model 6163 Chet Atkins (Piggyback) Amp
Mid-late-1960s. 70 watts, 1x12" and 1x15", black covering, tremolo, reverb.

1960s		$550	$650

Model 6163 Executive Amp
1959. 1x15, gray cover.

1959		$1,000	$1,250

Model 6164 Variety Amp
Early-mid-1960s. 35 watts, tube, 2x12".

1960s		$600	$725

Model 6165 Variety Plus Amp
Early-mid-1960s. Tube amp, 35 watts, 2x12", reverb and tremolo, separate controls for both channels.

1960s		$725	$875

Model 6166 Fury (Combo) Amp
Mid-1960s. Tube combo stereo amp, 70 watts, 2x12", separate controls for both channels, large metal handle, reverb.

1960s		$725	$875

Model 6169 Electromatic Twin Western Finish Amp
Ca.1953-ca.1960. Western finish, 14 watts, 2-11x6" speakers, tremolo, wraparound grill '55 and after.

1950s		$5,000	$6,000

Model 6169 Fury (Piggyback) Amp
Late-1960s. Tube amp, 70 watts, 2x12", separate controls for both channels.

1960s		$600	$700

Model 6170 Pro Bass Amp
1966-late-1960s. 25 or 35 watts, depending on model, 1x15", vertical cabinet style (vs. box cabinet).

1966-1969		$375	$450

Model 7154 Nashville Amp
Introduced in 1969. Solidstate combo amp, 4' tall, 75 watts, 2x15", reverb, tremolo, magic echo.

1970s		$425	$525

MODEL YEAR	FEATURES	EXC. COND. LOW	HIGH

Model 7155 Tornado PA System Amp
Introduced in 1969. Solidstate piggyback head and cab, 150 watts, 2 column speaker cabs, reverb, tremolo, magic echo.

1970s	2x2x15"	$425	$525
1970s	2x4x15"	$500	$625

Model 7517 Rogue Amp
1970s. Solidstate, 40 watts, 2x12", tall vertical cabinet, front control panel.

1970s		$225	$275

Model G6156 Playboy Amp
2005-2007. 15 watts, 1x12" combo amp with retro Gretsch styling, made by Victoria.

2005-2007		$950	$1,200

Model G6163 Executive Amp
2005-2007. Boutique quality made by Victoria for FMIC Gretsch, 20 watts, 1x15", cabinet Uses to the modern retro early '60s Supro Supreme modified-triangle front grille pattern, maroon baffle with white grille, tremolo and reverb.

2005-2007		$950	$1,200

Rex Royal Amp Model M-197-3V
1950s. Small student compact amp, low power, 1x8", Rex Royal logo on grille, Fred Gretsch logo on back panel, single on-off volume knob.

1951		$325	$400

Gries
2004-present. Dave Gries builds his intermediate and professional grade, production/custom, amps and cabinets in Mattapoisett, Massachusetts.

Groove Tubes
1979-present. Started by Aspen Pittman in his garage in Sylmar, California, Groove Tubes is now located in San Fernando. GT manufactures and distributes a full line of tubes. In '86 they added amp production and in '91 tube microphones. Aspen is also the author of the Tube Amp Book. The Groove Tubes brand was purchased by Fender in June, '08.

Guild
1952-present. Guild offered amps from the '60s into the '80s. Some of the early models were built by Hagstrom.

Double Twin Amp
1953-1955. 35 watts, 2x12" plus 2 tweeters, 2-tone leatherette covered cab.

1953-1955		$700	$850

G-1000 Stereo Amp
1992-1994. Stereo acoustic combo amp with cushioned seat on top, 4x6 and 1x10 speakers.

1990s		$575	$700

Master Amp
Ca. 1957- Ca. 1957. 2-tone tweed and leatherette combo, tremolo, Guild script logo and smaller block Master logo.

1950s		$400	$500

Maverick Amp
1960s. Dual speaker combo, verticle cab, tremolo, reverb, red/pink control panel, 2-tone black and silver grille.

1960s		$265	$325

MODEL YEAR	FEATURES	EXC. COND. LOW	HIGH

Model One Amp
Mid-1970s-1977. 30 watts, 1x12" vertical cab combo, reverb and tremolo.

1970s		$175	$200

Model Two Amp
Mid-1970s-1977. 50 watts, 2x10" vertical cab combo, reverb and tremolo.

1977-1978		$200	$250

Model Three Amp
Mid-1970s-1977. 60 watts, 1x15" vertical cab combo, for bass, organ and guitar.

1977-1978		$200	$250

Model Four Amp
Early-1980s. Six watts.

1980s		$100	$150

Model Five Amp
Early-1980s. 10 watts, 6.25" speaker.

1980s		$125	$150

Model Six Amp
Early-1980s. Same as Model Five but with reverb.

1980s		$160	$200

Model Seven Amp
Early-1980s. Small amp for guitar, bass and keyboard, 12 watts.

1980s		$180	$225

Model 50-J Amp
Early-1960s. 14 watts, 1x12", tremolo, blue/gray vinyl.

1962-1963		$225	$275

Model 66 Amp
1953-1955. 15 watts, 1x12", tremolo, 2-tone leatherette.

1953-1955		$250	$300

Model 66-J Amp
1962-1963. 20 watts, 1x12", tremolo, blue/gray vinyl.

1962-1963		$400	$500

Model 98-RT Amp
1962-1963. The only stand-alone reverb amp from Guild in the early '60s, 30 watts, 1x12", blue/gray vinyl.

1962-1963		$550	$675

Model 99 Amp
1953-1955. 20 watts, 1x12", tremolo, 2-tone leatherette.

1953-1955		$350	$425

Model 99-J Amp
Early-1960s. 30 watts, 1x12", tremolo, blue/gray vinyl.

1962-1963		$375	$450

Model 99-U Ultra Amp
Early-1960s. Piggyback 30-watt head with optional 1x12" or 1x15" cab, cab and head lock together, tremolo, blue/gray vinyl.

1962-1963		$400	$500

Model 100-J Amp
Early-1960s. 35 watts, 1x15", blue/gray vinyl.

1962-1963		$400	$500

Model 200-S Stereo Combo Amp
Early-1960s. 25 watts per channel, total 50 watts stereo, 2x12", tremolo, blue/gray vinyl, wheat grille.

1962-1963		$750	$900

Gretsch Model G6156 Playboy

Gries Minnow

1971 Guild Maverick

AMPS

Harmony H-200

Harmony Model H303A

Harry Joyce Custom 50

Model RC-30 Reverb Converter Amp

Early-1960s. Similar to Gibson GA-1 converter, attaches with 2 wires clipped to originating amp's speaker, 8 watts, 1x10", blue/gray vinyl.

Year	Features	Low	High
1962-1963		$400	$500

Superbird Amp

1968. Piggyback tube amp with 2x12 cab, 'Superbird By Guild' logo on front panel, Guild logo upper left corner of cab.

Year	Features	Low	High
1968		$500	$600

SuperStar Amp

Ca.1972-ca.1974. 50 watts, all tubes, 1x15" Jensen speakers, vertical combo, reverb, tremolo, black vinyl cover, 2-tone black/silver grille.

Year	Features	Low	High
1972-1974		$325	$400

Thunder 1 Amp

Introduced 1965. Combo with single speaker, no reverb, light tan cover, 2-tone tan grille.

Year	Features	Low	High
1965-1968	1x10"	$275	$325
1965-1968	1x12"	$300	$350

Thunder 1 (Model 11RVT)/T1 Amp

Introduced 1965. Combo with dual speakers and reverb, light tan cover, 2-tone tan grille.

Year	Features	Low	High
1965-1968		$425	$525

ThunderBass Amp

Introduced 1965. Piggyback combo, 2x15".

Year	Features	Low	High
1965-1972	100 watt	$450	$550
1965-1972	200 watt	$475	$575

ThunderBird Amp

1965-1972. 50 watts, tube, 2x12", reverb, tremolo, with or without TD-1 dolly, black vinyl, black/silver grille.

Year	Features	Low	High
1965-1972		$350	$425

ThunderStar Bass Amp

1965-1968. Piggyback bass tube head or combo, 50 watts.

Year	Features	Low	High
1965-1972	Full stack, 2x1x15"	$550	$675
1965-1972	Half stack, 1x1x15"	$450	$550

ThunderStar Guitar Amp

1965-1968. Combo, 50 watts, 1x12".

Year	Features	Low	High
1965-1972		$425	$525

Guyatone

1933-present. Started offering amps by at least the late '40s with their Guya lap steels. In '51 the Guyatone brand is first used on guitars and most likely amps. Guyatone also made the Marco Polo, Winston, Kingston, Kent, LaFayette and Bradford brands.

Guytron

1995-present. Tube amp heads and speaker cabinets built by Guy Hedrick in Columbiaville, Michigan. In January, '09, GDS Amplification bought the assets of Guytron Amplification.

Hagstrom

1921-1983. The Swedish guitar maker built a variety of tube and solidstate amps from ca. 1961 into the '70s. They also supplied amps to Guild.

Hanburt

1940-ca. 1950. Harvey M. Hansen built electric Hawaiian guitars in Seattle, Washington, some sold as a set with a small amp. The wooden amps have a large HB in the speaker cutout. He also built at least one mandolin.

Harmony

1892-1976, late-1970s-present. Harmony was one of the biggest producers of guitars, and offered amps as well. MBT International offered Harmony amps for 2000-'02.

H Series Amps

1940s-1960s. Harmony model numbers begin with H, such as H-304, all H series models shown are tube amps unless otherwise noted as solidstate.

Year	Features	Low	High
1940-1950s	H-190/H-191	$375	$450
1940-1950s	H-200	$375	$450
1950s	H-204, 18w, 1x12"	$375	$450
1960s	H-303A, 8w, 1x8"	$200	$250
1960s	H-304, low pwr, small spkr	$200	$250
1960s	H-305A, low pwr, small spkr	$200	$250
1960s	H-306A, combo 1x12"	$275	$350
1960s	H306C, piggyback 2x12"	$375	$450
1960s	H-400, 8w, 1x8", vol	$175	$225
1960s	H-400A, 8w, 1x8", vol/tone	$200	$250
1960s	H-410A, 10w, 1x10"	$350	$450
1960s	H-415, 20w, 2x12"	$575	$700
1960s	H-420, 20w, 1x12"	$375	$450
1960s	H-430, 30w, 2x12"	$575	$700
1960s	H-440, 2x12", trem & verb	$600	$725

Solidstate Amps

1970s. Dark covering, dark grille.

Year	Features	Low	High
1970s	Large amp	$125	$150
1970s	Small amp	$25	$30

Harry Joyce

1993-2000. Hand-wired British tube amps, combos, and cabinets from builder Harry Joyce. Joyce was contracted to build Hiwatt amps in England during the '60s and '70s. He died on January 11, 2002.

Hartke

1984-present. Guitar and bass amps, combos and cabinets made in the U.S. Founded by Larry Hartke, since the mid-'80s, Hartke has been distributed by Samson Technologies. Hartke also offered basses in the past.

Haynes

Haynes guitar amps were built by the Amplifier Corporation of America (ACA) of Westbury, New York. ACA also made an early distortion device powered by batteries. Unicord purchased

MODEL YEAR	FEATURES	EXC. COND. LOW	HIGH

the company in around 1964, and used the factory to produce its Univox line of amps, most likely discontinuing the Haynes brand at the same time.

Jazz King II Amp
1960s. Solidstate, stereo console-style, 2x12", Haynes logo upper left side.

1960s		$325	$375

Headstrong
2002-present. Tube combo amps built by Wayne Jones and Jessica Winterbottom, originally in Asheville, North Carolina, since '10 in Berkley, California. They also offer a range of replacement cabinets for vintage amps.

Henriksen JazzAmp
2006-present. Professional grade, production, solidstate amps voiced for jazz guitar built by Peter Henriksen in Golden, Colorado.

Heritage
2004-2008. Founded by Malcolm MacDonald and Lane Zastrow who was formerly involved with Holland amps. Located in the former Holland facility in Brentwood, Tennessee, they built tube combo and piggyback amps.

Hilgen
1960s. Mid-level amplifiers from Hilgen Manufacturing, Hillside, New Jersey. Dark tolex covering and swiggle-lined light color grille cloth. Examples have been found with original Jensen speakers.

Basso B-2501 Amp
1960s. 25 watts, 1x15" combo, swirl grille, Hilgen crest logo, compact size.

1965		$350	$400

Basso B-2502 Amp
1960s. 25 watts, 1x15" combo, swirl grille, Hilgen crest logo, large cab.

1965		$400	$475

Basso Grande B-2503 Amp
1960s. Brown sparkle cover, piggyback, 2x12".

1965		$500	$600

Basso Profondo B-2502 Amp
1965. Combo 1x15".

1965		$350	$400

Champion R-2523 Amp
Mid-1960s. Highest offering in their amp line, piggyback with 2x12" cab, tremolo, reverb, swirl grille cloth.

1965		$500	$600

Galaxie T-2513 Amp
1960s. 25 watts, 2x12" piggyback cab, tremolo.

1965		$500	$600

Metero T-2511 Amp
Mid-1960s. Compact 1x12" combo, tremolo.

1965		$375	$450

Pacesetter R-2521 Amp
Mid-1960s. 1x12" combo, tremolo, reverb, swirl grille cloth.

1965		$375	$450

MODEL YEAR	FEATURES	EXC. COND. LOW	HIGH

Star T-2512 Amp
1960s. 25 watts, 1x12" combo, tremolo.

1965		$375	$450

Troubadour T-1506 Amp
Mid-1960s. Small practice amp.

1965		$275	$325

Victor R-2522 Amp
Mid-1960s. 1x12" combo, larger cab, reverb, tremolo.

1965		$500	$600

HiWatt
Bass 100 Amp Head

1980s	100w, England	$1,000	$1,200

Bulldog SA112 Amp
1980s, 1994-present. 50 watts, combo, 1x12".

1980s		$1,000	$1,200
1990s		$800	$1,000

Bulldog SA112FL Amp
1980s-1990s. 100 watts, combo, 1x12".

1980s		$1,000	$1,200
1990s		$800	$1,000

Custom 100 Amp Head

2007	100w	$1,100	$1,375

DR-103 Custom 100 Amp Head
1970-late-1980s, 2005-present. Tube head, 100 watts, custom Hiwatt 100 logo on front.

1970-1980s		$2,300	$2,800
2005-2010 Reissue		$1,100	$1,350

DR-201 Hiwatt 200 Amp Head
1970s. 200-watt amp head, Hiwatt 200 logo on front.

1970s		$2,400	$2,700

DR-405 Hiwatt 400 Amp Head
1970s. 400-watt amp head.

1970s		$2,400	$2,900

DR-504 Custom 50 Amp Head
1970-late-1980s, 1995-1999. Tube head, 50 watts.

1970s		$1,300	$1,600

Lead 20 (SG-20) Amp Head
1980s. Tube amp head, 30 watts, black cover, rectangular HiWatt plate logo.

1980s		$450	$550

Lead 50R Combo Amp
1980s. Combo tube amp, 50 watts, 1x12", reverb, dark cover, dark grille, HiWatt rectangular plate logo.

1980s		$675	$825

OL-103 Lead 100 Amp Head

1982	100w, England	$1,100	$1,350

PW-50 Tube Amp
1989-1993. Stereo tube amp, 50 watts per channel.

1989-1993		$750	$900

S50L Amp Head
1989-1993. Lead guitar head, 50 watts, gain, master volume, EQ.

1989-1993		$650	$800

SA 112 Combo Amp

1970s	50w, 1x12"	$2,400	$2,900

SA 212 Combo Amp

1970s	50w, 2x12"	$2,600	$3,100

SA 412 Combo Amp

1970s	50w, 4x12"	$3,000	$3,700

Heritage Victory

1982 HiWatt Bulldog SA112

HiWatt DR-504 Custom 50

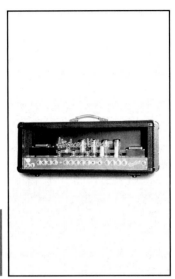

Hughes & Kettner Duotone

Ibanez MIMX65

Jackson JG-3

MODEL YEAR	FEATURES	EXC. COND. LOW	HIGH

SE 2150 Speaker Cabinet
1970s. Veritcal 2x15" cab.

1970s	2x15" vertical	$1,600	$2,000

SE 4122 (Lead) Speaker Cabinet
1971- mid-1980s. 4x12" Fane speakers, 300 watts.

1971-1980s		$1,600	$2,000

SE 4122 Speaker Cabinet

1970s	4x12", 1/2 stack	$1,600	$2,000

SE 4123 (Bass) Speaker Cabinet
1970s. Bass version of SE, often used with DR103 head, straight-front cab and stackable, black tolex with gray grille, Hiwatt logo plate in center of grille.

1970s		$1,600	$2,000

SE 4129 (Bass) Speaker Cabinet
1970s. SE series for bass, 4x12", often used with DR 201 head.

1970s		$1,700	$2,100

SE 4151 Speaker Cabinet
1970s. SE series with 4x15".

1970s		$1,800	$2,200

Hoagland
2008-present. Professional grade, production, guitar amps built by Dan Hoagland in Land O Lakes, Florida.

Hoffman
1993-present. Tube amps, combos, reverb units, and cabinets built by Doug Hoffman from 1993 to '99, in Sarasota, Florida. Hoffman no longer builds amps, concentrating on selling tube amp building supplies, and since 2001 has been located in Pisgah Forest, North Carolina.

Hoffmann
1983-present. Tube amp heads for guitar and other musical instruments built by Kim Hoffmann in Hawthorne, California.

Hohner
1857-present. Matthias Hohner, a clockmaker in Trossingen, Germany, founded Hohner in 1857, making harmonicas. Hohner has been offering guitars and amps at least since the early '70s.

Panther Series Amps
1980s. Smaller combo amps, master volume, gain, EQ.

1980s	P-12, 12w	$70	$85
1980s	P-20, 20w	$75	$90
1980s	P-25R, 25w	$75	$90
1980s	PBK-20 bass/ keyboard, 25w	$80	$100

Sound Producer Series Amps
1980s. Master volume, normal and overdrive, reverb, headphone jack.

1980s	BA 130 bass	$75	$90
1980s	SP 35	$80	$100
1980s	SP 55	$80	$100
1980s	SP 75	$100	$125

MODEL YEAR	FEATURES	EXC. COND. LOW	HIGH

Holland
1992-2004. Tube combo amps from builder Mike Holland, originally in Virginia Beach, Virginia, and since 2000 in Brentwood, Tennessee. In 2000, Holland took Lane Zastrow as a partner, forming L&M Amplifiers to build the Holland line. The company closed in '04.

Holmes
1970-late 1980s. Founded by Harrison Holmes. Holmes amplifiers were manufactured in Mississippi and their product line included guitar and bass amps, PA systems, and mixing boards. In the early '80s, Harrsion Holmes sold the company to On-Site Music which called the firm The Holmes Corp. Products manufactured by Harrison have an all-caps HOLMES logo and the serial number plate says The Holmes Company.

Performer PB-115 Bass Amp
60 watts, 1x15", black tolex.

1982		$100	$125

Pro Compact 210S Amp
60 watts, 2x10", 2 channels, active EQ, black tolex.

1982		$100	$125

Pro Compact 212S Amp
2x12" version of Pro.

1982		$125	$150

Rebel RB-112 Bass Amp
35 watts, 1x12", black tolex.

1982		$75	$100

Hondo
1969-1987, 1991-present. Hondo has offered imported amps over the years. 1990s models ranged from the H20 Practice Amp to the H160SRC with 160 watts (peak) and 2x10" speakers.

Amps
1970s-1990s. Various models.

1970-1990s	Mid-size	$40	$50
1970-1990s	Small	$20	$25

Hottie
2005-present. Jean-Claude Escudie and Mike Bernards build their budget and intermediate grade, production/custom, solid state "toaster" amps in Portland, Oregon. They also offer guitars.

Hound Dog
1994-1998. Founded by George Alessandro as the Hound Dog Corporation. Name was changed to Alessandro in 1998 (see that brand for more information).

Hughes & Kettner
1985-present. Hughes & Kettner offers a line of solidstate and tube guitar and bass amps, combos, cabinets and effects, all made in Germany.

Hurricane
1998-present. Tube guitar and harmonica combo amps built by Gary Drouin in Sarasota, Florida. Drouin started the company with harp master Rock Bottom, who died in September, 2001.

MODEL		EXC. COND.	
YEAR	FEATURES	LOW	HIGH

Hy Lo

1960s-1970s. Budget grade, small compact amps made in Japan, Hy Lo logo on grille.

Ibanez

1932-present. Ibanez added solidstate amps to their product line in '98. They also build guitars, basses and effects.

Idol

Late-1960s. Made in Japan. Dark tolex cover, dark grille, Hobby Series with large Idol logo on front.

Hobby Series Amps

1968	Hobby 10	$70	$85
1968	Hobby 100	$160	$200
1968	Hobby 20	$100	$125
1968	Hobby 45	$150	$185

Impact

1963-early 1970s. Based in London, England, tube amps made by Don Mackrill and Laurie Naiff for Pan Musical Instrument Company and their music stores. About a dozen different models of combos, piggyback half-stacks and PAs were offered.

Imperial

Ca.1963-ca.1970. The Imperial Accordion Company of Chicago, Illinois offered one or two imported small amps in the '60s.

Jack Daniel's

2004-present. Tube guitar amp built by Peavey for the Jack Daniel Distillery. They also offer guitars and a bass model.

Jackson

1980-present. The Jackson-Charvel Company offered budget to intermediate grade amps and cabinets in the late '80s and the '90s.

Jackson Ampworks

2001-present. Brad Jackson builds his tube amp heads and speaker cabinets in Bedford, Texas.

Jackson-Guldan

1920s-1960s. The Jackson-Guldan Violin Company, of Columbus, Ohio, offered lap steels and small tube amps early on. They also built acoustic guitars.

Jay Turser

1997-present. Smaller, inexpensive imported solidstate guitar and bass amps. They also offer basses and guitars.

JCA Circuits

1995-present. Tube guitar combo amps built by Jason C. Arthur in Pottstown, Pennsylvania.

MODEL		EXC. COND.	
YEAR	FEATURES	LOW	HIGH

Jennings

Late 1960s. Tom Jennings formed another company after resigning from Vox. Large block letter Jennings logo on front panel, Jennings Amplifier logo on back control plate with model number and serial number.

Jet City Amplification

2009-present. Budget to professional grade, production/custom, guitar amps and cabinets designed in Seattle, Washington by Doug White, Dan Gallagher, Michael Soldano and built in Asia.

Jim Kelley

1979-1985. Channel-switching tube amps, compact combos and heads, hardwood cabinets available, made by Jim Kelley at his Active Guitar Electronics in Tustin, California. He produced about 100 amps a year. In 1978 and early '79 he produced a few amps under the Fortune brand name for Fortune Guitars.

JMI (Jennings Musical Industries)

2004-present. Jennings built the Vox amps of the 1960s. They are back with tube amp heads and cabinets based on some of their classic models. They also offer effects.

Johnson

Mid-1990s-present. Line of solidstate amps imported by Music Link, Brisbane, California. Johnson also offers guitars, basses, mandolins and effects.

Johnson Amplification

1997-present. Intermediate and professional grade, production, modeling amps and effects designed by John Johnson, of Sandy, Utah. The company is part of Harman International. In 2002, they quit building amps, but continue the effects line.

JoMama

1994-present. Tube amps and combos under the JoMama and Kelemen brands built by Joe Kelemen in Santa Fe, New Mexico.

Juke

1989-present. Tube guitar and harmonica amps built by G.R. Croteau in Troy, New Hampshire. He also built the Warbler line of amps.

Kafel

2004-present. Jack Kafel builds his tube amp heads in Chicago, Illinois.

Kalamazoo

1933-1942, 1965-1970. Kalamazoo was a brand Gibson used on one of their budget lines. They used the name on amps from '65 to '67.

JCA Circuts GR 1.6

Johnson Barn Burner

Kafel S150 Head

Kalamazoo Model 4

Kay 703

KJL Companion

MODEL YEAR	FEATURES	EXC. COND. LOW	HIGH

Bass 30 Amp
Late 1960s-early 1970s. Tube combo, verticle cabinet, 2x10".

1970		$250	$300

Bass Amp
1965-1967. Enclosed back, 2x10", flip-out control panel, not a commonly found model as compared to numerous Model 1 and 2 student amps.

| 1965-1967 | | $200 | $250 |

KEA Amp
1948-1952. Small compact amp, round speaker baffle grille, slant Kalamazoo logo on front, oxblood leatherette.

| 1948-1952 | | $250 | $300 |

Lap Steel Amp
1940s. Kalamazoo logo on front lower right, low power with 1-6V6, round speaker grille opening, red/brown leatherette.

| 1940s | | $350 | $425 |

Model 1 Amp
1965-1967. No tremolo, 1x10", front control panel, black.

| 1965-1967 | | $175 | $200 |

Model 2 Amp
1965-1967. Same as Model 1 with tremolo, black.

| 1965-1967 | | $250 | $275 |

Model 3 Amp
Late 1960s-early 1970s. Made by CMI Electronics in Chicago, post Gibson Kalamazoo era, student compact solidstate combo, Kalamazoo 3 logo on front panel, Kalamazoo Model 3 logo on label on speaker magnet.

| 1960-1970s | | $80 | $100 |

Model 4 Amp
Late 1960s-early 1970s. Made by CMI Electronics in Chicago, post Gibson Kalamazoo era, student compact solidstate combo, 3 control knobs, tone, tremolo, volume, Kalamazoo 4 logo on front panel, Kalamazoo Model 4 logo on label on speaker magnet.

| 1960-1970s | | $100 | $125 |

Reverb 12 Amp
1965-1967. Black vinyl cover, 1x12", reverb, tremolo.

| 1965-1967 | | $350 | $425 |

Kay

Ca.1931-present. Kay originally offered amps up to around '68 when the brand changed hands. Currently they offer a couple small solidstate imported amps. They also make basses, guitars, banjos, mandolins, ukes, and violins.

K506 Vibrato 12" Amp
1960s. 12 watts, 1x12", swirl grille, metal handle.

| 1962 | | $325 | $400 |

K507 Twin Ten Special Amp
1960s. 20 watts, 2x10", swirl grille, metal handle.

| 1962 | | $350 | $425 |

K700 Series Amp
Introduced in 1965. Value Leader/Vanguard/Galazie models, transistorized amps promoted as eliminates tube-changing annoyance and reliable performance, combo amps with tapered cabinets, rear slant control panel, rich brown and tan vinyl cover, brown grille cloth.

MODEL YEAR	FEATURES	EXC. COND. LOW	HIGH
1965	700, 1x8"	$100	$125
1965	703, 1x8"	$100	$125
1965	704, 1x8"	$100	$125
1965	705, 1x10"	$110	$135
1965	706, 1x15"	$125	$150
1965	707, 1x12"	$125	$150
1965	708, 1x12"	$125	$150
1965	720 bass, 1x15"	$125	$150
1966	760, 1x12"	$125	$150

Model 703 Amp
1962-1964. Tube student amp, small speaker, 3 tubes, 1 volume, 1 tone, 2-tone white front with brown back cabinet, metal handle, model number noted on back panel, Kay logo and model number badge lower front right.

| 1962-1964 | | $175 | $200 |

Model 803 Amp
1962-1964. Student amp, 1x8", 3 tubes, 1 volume, 1 tone, metal handle, 14.75x11.75x6.75" cabinet with dark gray cover.

| 1962-1964 | | $150 | $175 |

Model 805 Amp
1965. Solidstate, 35 watts, 1x10", 4 control knobs, 2-tone cabinet.

| 1965 | | $100 | $125 |

Small Tube Amps

1940s	Wood cabinet	$275	$340
1950s	Various models	$275	$340
1960s	Models K503, K504, K505	$265	$330

Kelemen

1994-present. Tube amps and combos under the JoMama and Kelemen brands built by Joe Kelemen in Santa Fe, New Mexico.

Kendrick

1989-present. Founded by Gerald Weber in Austin, Texas and currently located in Kempfner, Texas. Mainly known for their intermediate to professional grade, tube amps, Kendrick also offers guitars, speakers, and effects. Weber has authored books and videos on tube amps.

Kent

Ca.1962-1969. Imported budget line of guitars and amps.

Guitar and Bass Amps
1960s. Various models.

1966	1475, 3 tubes, brown	$50	$60
1966	2198, 3 tubes, brown	$50	$60
1966	5999, 3 tubes, brown	$60	$75
1966	6104, piggyback, 12w	$100	$125
1969	6610, solidstate, small	$25	$30

Kiesel

See Carvin.

King Amplification

2005-present. Tube combo amps, head and cabinets built by Val King in San Jose, California.

MODEL		EXC. COND.	
YEAR	FEATURES	LOW	HIGH

Kingsley

1998-present. Production/custom, professional grade, tube amps and cabinets built by Simon Jarrett in Vancouver, British Columbia.

Kingston

1958-1967. Economy solidstate amps imported by Westheimer Importing, Chicago, Illinois.

Cat Amps
Mid-1960s. Solidstate Cat Series amps have dark vinyl, dark grilles.

1960s	P-1=3w, P-2=5w	$40	$50
1960s	P-3=8w, P-8=20w, both 1x8"	$45	$55

Cougar BA-21 Bass Piggyback Amp
Mid-1960s. Solidstate, 60 watts, 2x12" cab, dark vinyl, light silver grille.

1960s		$100	$120

Cougar PB-5 Bass Combo Amp
Mid-1960s. Solidstate, 15 watts, 1x8".

1960s		$45	$55

Lion 2000 Piggyback Amp
Mid-1960s. Solidstate, 90 watts, 2x12" cab.

1960s		$120	$150

Lion 3000 Piggyback Amp
Mid-1960s. Solidstate, 250 watts, 4x12" cab.

1960s		$145	$180

Lion AP-281 R Piggyback Amp
Mid-1960s. Solidstate, 30 watts, 2x8" cab, dark vinyl cover, light silver grille.

1960s		$70	$85

Lion AP-281 R10 Piggyback Amp
Mid-1960s. Solidstate, 30 watts, 2x10" cab.

1960s		$100	$120

Kitchen-Marshall

1965-1966. Private branded for Kitchen Music by Marshall, primarily PA units with block logos. Limited production.

JTM 45 MKII 45-Watt Amp Head
1965-1966. Private branded for Kitchen Music, JTM 45 Marshall with Kitchen logo plate, 45 watts.

1965-1966		$5,500	$7,000

Slant 4x12 1960 Cabinet
1965-1966. Slant front 4x12" 1960-style cab with gray bluesbreaker grille, very limited production.

1965-1966	Black on green vinyl	$3,500	$4,300

KJL

1995-present. Founded by Kenny Lannes, MSEE, a professor of Electrical Engineering at the University of New Orleans. KJL makes budget to intermediate grade, tube combo amps, heads and an ABY box.

KMD (Kaman)

1986-ca.1990. Distributed by Kaman (Ovation, Hamer, etc.) in the late '80s, KMD offered a variety of amps and effects.

Koch

All-tube combo amps, heads, effects and cabinets built in The Netherlands.

Komet

1999-present. Intermediate to professional grade, tube amp heads built in Baton Rouge, Louisanna, by Holger Notzel and Michael Kennedy with circuits designed by Ken Fischer of Trainwreck fame. They also build a power attenuator.

Kona

2001-present. Budget solidstate amps made in Asia. They also offer guitars, basses, mandolins and banjos.

Krank

1996-present. Founded by Tony Dow and offering tube amp heads, combos and speaker cabinets built in Tempe, Arizona. They also build effects. The company greatly upped its distribution in '03.

Kustom

1965-present. Kustom, a division of Hanser Holdings, offers guitar and bass combo amps and PA equipment. Founded by Bud Ross in Chanute, Kansas, who offered tuck-and-roll amps as early as '58, but began using the Kustom brand name in '65. From '69 to '75 Ross gradually sold interest in the company (in the late '70s, Ross introduced the line of Ross effects stomp boxes). The brand changed hands a few times, and by the mid-'80s it was no longer in use. In '89 Kustom was in bankruptcy court and was purchased by Hanser Holdings Incorporated of Cincinnati, Ohio (Davitt & Hanser) and by '94, they had a new line of amps available.

Prices are for excellent condition amps with no tears in the tuck-and-roll cover and no grille tears. A tear in the tuck-and-roll will reduce the value, sometimes significantly.

Kustom model identification can be frustrating as they used series numbers, catalog numbers (the numbers in the catalogs and price lists), and model numbers (the number often found next to the serial number on the amp's back panel). Most of the discussion that follows is by series number (100, 200, 300, etc.) and catalog number. Unfortunately, vintage amp dealers use the serial number and model number, so the best way is to cross-check speaker and amplifier attributes. Model numbers were used primarily for repair purposes and were found in the repair manuals. In many, but not all cases, the model number is the last digit of the catalog number; for example the catalog lists a 100 series Model 1-15J-1, where the last digit 1 signifies a Model 1 amplifier chassis which is a basic amp without reverb or tremolo. A Model 1-15J-2 signifies a Model 2 amp chassis that has reverb and tremolo. In this example, Kustom uses a different model number on the back of the amp head. For the 1-15J-2, the model number on the back panel of

KJL Dirty 30

Koch Studiotone 20-Watt

Komet 19

Early '70s Kustom Challenger

Kustom 36

Kustom Hustler

the amp head would be K100-2, indicating a series 100 (50 watts) amp with reverb and tremolo (amp chassis Model 2).

Model numbers relate to the amplifier's schematic and electronics, while catalog numbers describe the amp's relative power rating and speaker configuration.

Amp Chasis Model Numbers ('68-'72)

Model 1 Amp (basic)
Model 2 Amp with reverb
Model 3 Amp with Harmonic Clip and Boost
Model 4 Amp with reverb, tremolo, vibrato, Harmonic Clip and Selective Boost
Model 5 PA with reverb
Model 6 Amp (basic) with Selectone
Model 7 Amp with reverb, tremolo, vibrato, boost (different parts)
Model 8 Amp with reverb, tremolo, vibrato, boost (different parts)

Naugahyde Tuck-&-Roll 200 ('65-'67)

The very first Kustoms did not have the model series on the front control panel. The early logo stipulated Kustom by Ross, Inc. The name was then updated to Kustom Electronics, Inc. 1965-'67 amp heads have a high profile/tall "forehead" area (the area on top of the controls) and these have been nicknamed "Frankenstein models." The '65-'67 catalog numbers were often 4 or 5 digits, for example J695. The first digit represents the speaker type (J = Jensen, etc.), other examples are L995, L1195, L795RV, etc. Some '67 catalog numbers changed to 2 digits followed by 3 digits, like 4-D 140f, or 3-15C (3 CTS speakers), etc. Others sported 5 characters like 4-15J-1, where 4 = 4 speakers, 15 = 15" speakers, J = Jensen, and 1 = basic amp chassis with no effects. The fifth digit indicated amp chassis model number as described above.

Naugahyde Tuck-&-Roll 100/200/400 ('68-'71)

Starting in '68, the Kustom logo also included the model series. A K100, for example, would have 100 displayed below the Kustom name. The model series generally is twice the relative output wattage, for example, the 100 Series is a 50-watt amp. Keep in mind, solidstate ratings are often higher than tube-amp ratings, so use the ratings as relative measurements. Most '68-'70 Kustom catalog numbers are x-xxx-x, for example 1-15L-1. First digit represents the number of speakers, the 2nd and 3rd represent the speaker size, the fourth represents the speaker type (A = Altec Lansing, L = J.B.L., J = Jensen, C = C.T.S. Bass), the fifth digit represents the amp chassis number. The power units were interchangeable in production, so amps could have similar front-ends but different power units (more power and different effect options) and visa versa. Some '68 bass amp catalog numbers were 4 digits, for example 2-12C, meaning two 12" CTS speakers. Again, there were several different numbers used. Kustom also introduced the 200 and 400 amp series and the logo included the series number. The catalog numbers were similar to the 100 series, but they had a higher power rating of 100 equivalent watts (200 series), or 200 equivalent watts (400

series). Kustom U.S. Naugahyde (tuck-&-roll) covers came in 7 colors: black (the most common), Cascade (blue/green), silver (white-silver), gold (light gold), red, blue, and Charcoal (gray). The market historically shows color options fetching more. The market has not noticeably distinguished power and features options. Condition and color seem to be the most important. Gold and Cascade may be the rarest seen colors.

Naugahyde Tuck-&-Roll 150/250/300/500/600 (c.'71-c.'75)

The amp heads changed with a slightly slanted control panel and the Kustom logo moved to the right/upper-right portion of the front panel. They continued to be tuck-&-roll offered in the same variety of colors. The sales literature indicated a 150 series had 150 watts, 250 had 250 watts, etc.

Naugahyde Tuck-&-Roll SC (Self Contained) Series

Most SC combo amps were rated at 150 watts, with the 1-12SC listed at 50 watts. They were offered in 7 colors of tuck-and-roll. Again the model numbers indicate the features as follows: 4-10 SC is a 4 x 10", 2-10 SC is a 2x10", etc.

Super Sound Tuck-and-Roll Combo Series

The last tuck-and-roll combo amps with slightly smaller tucks. Amp control panel is noticeably smaller and the Kustom logo is in the right side of the control panel.

Black Vinyl ('75-c.'78)

By '75 ownership changes were complete and the colorful tuck-and-roll was dropped in favor of more traditional black vinyl. The products had a slant Kustom logo spelled-out and placed in a position on the grille similar to a Fender blackface baffle. Models included the I, II, III, and IV Lead amps. Heads with half- and full-stacks were available. Bass amps included the Kustom 1, Bass I, II, III, IV, and IV SRO.

Black Vinyl K logo ('78-'83)

This era is easily recognized by the prominent capital K logo.

Bass V Amp

1990s. Large Kustom Bass V logo upper right side of amp, 35 watts, 1x12", black vinyl.

MODEL YEAR	FEATURES	EXC. COND. LOW	HIGH
1990s		$80	$90

Challenger Combo Amp

1973-1975. 1x12" speaker.

1973-1975	Black	$250	$300
1973-1975	Color option	$375	$450

Hustler Combo Amp

1973-1975. Solidstate, 4x10", tremolo, tuck-and-roll.

1973-1975	Black	$275	$325
1973-1975	Color option	$400	$475

K25/K25 C-2 SC Amp

1960s. SC (self-contained) Series, small combo tuck-and-roll, 1x12", solidstate, reverb, black control panel.

1971-1973	Black	$250	$300
1971-1973	Color option	$375	$450

AMPS

MODEL YEAR	FEATURES	EXC. COND. LOW	HIGH

K50-2 SC Amp
1971-1973. Self-contained (SC) small combo tuck-and-roll, 1x12", reverb and tremolo.

| 1971-1973 | Black | $250 | $300 |
| 1971-1973 | Color option | $375 | $450 |

K100-1 1-15C Bass Amp Set
1968-1972. The K100-1 with 1-15C speaker option with matching 1x15" cab, black tuck-and-roll standard, but several sparkle colors offered, C.T.S. bass reflex speaker.

| 1968-1972 | Black | $250 | $300 |
| 1968-1972 | Color option | $425 | $525 |

K100-1 1-15L-1/1-15A-1/1-15J-1 Amp Set
1968-1972. K100-1 with matching 1x15" cab, black tuck-and-roll standard, but several colors offered, speaker options are JBL, Altec Lansing or Jensen.

| 1968-1972 | Black | $250 | $300 |
| 1968-1972 | Color option | $425 | $525 |

K100-1 1-D140F Bass Amp
1968-1972. K100-1 with matching 1x15" JBL D-140F cab, black tuck-and-roll standard, but several sparkle colors offered.

| 1968-1972 | Black | $250 | $300 |
| 1968-1972 | Color option | $425 | $525 |

K100-1 2-12C Bass Amp Set
1968-1972. K100-1 with matching 2x12" cab, black tuck-and-roll standard, but several sparkle colors offered, C.T.S. bass reflex speakers.

| 1968-1972 | Black | $300 | $350 |
| 1968-1972 | Color option | $475 | $575 |

K100-2 1-15L-2/1-15A-2/1-15J-2 Amp Set
1968-1972. K100-2 head and matching 1x15" cab, black tuck-and-roll standard, but several sparkle colors offered.

| 1968-1972 | Black | $250 | $300 |
| 1968-1972 | Color option | $425 | $525 |

K100-2 2-12A-2/2-12J-2 Amp Set
1968-1972. K100-2 head with matching 2x12" cab, black tuck-and-roll standard, but several sparkle colors offered.

| 1968-1972 | Black | $300 | $350 |
| 1968-1972 | Color option | $475 | $575 |

K100-6 SC Amp
1970-1972. Basic combo amp with selectone, no reverb.

| 1970-1972 | Black | $225 | $275 |

K100-7 SC Amp
1970-1972. Combo amp with reverb, tremolo, vibrato and boost.

| 1970-1972 | Black | $250 | $300 |
| 1970-1972 | Color option | $375 | $450 |

K100-8 SC Amp
1970-1972. Combo amp with reverb, tremolo, vibrato and boost.

| 1970-1972 | Black | $250 | $300 |
| 1970-1972 | Color option | $375 | $450 |

K100C-6 Combo Amp
1968-1970. Kustom 100 logo middle of the front control panel, 1x15" combo, selectone option.

| 1968-1970 | Black | $250 | $300 |
| 1968-1970 | Color option | $375 | $450 |

K100C-8 Combo Amp
1968-1970. Kustom 100 logo middle of the front control panel, 4x10" combo, reverb, tremolo, vibrato.

| 1968-1970 | Black | $350 | $425 |

K150-1 Amp Set
1972-1975. Piggyback, 150 watts, 2x12", no reverb, logo in upper right corner of amp head, tuck-and-roll, black or color option.

| 1972-1975 | Color option | $375 | $450 |

K150-2 Amp Set
1972-1975. K150 with added reverb and tremolo, piggyback, 2x12", tuck-and-roll, black or color option.

| 1972-1975 | Color option | $400 | $475 |

K150-5 PA Amp Set
1972-1975. PA head plus 2 PA cabs.

| 1972-1975 | | $325 | $400 |

K150/150C Combo Amp
1972-1975. Combo, 2x10".

| 1972-1975 | Black | $250 | $300 |

K200-1/K200B Bass Amp Set
1966-1972. K200 head with 2x15" cab.

1966-1967	Black	$300	$350
1966-1967	Color option	$475	$575
1968-1972	Black	$300	$350
1968-1972	Color option	$475	$575

K200-2 Reverb/Tremolo Amp Set
1966-1972. K200-2 head with 2x15" or 3x12" cab, available with JBL D-140F speakers, Altec Lansing (A) speakers, C.T.S. (C), or Jensen (J).

1966-1967	Black	$300	$350
1966-1967	Color option	$475	$575
1968-1972	Black	$300	$350
1968-1972	Color option	$475	$575

K250 Amp Set
1971-1975. K250 head with 2x15" cab, tuck-and-roll cover.

| 1971-1975 | Black | $325 | $400 |
| 1971-1975 | Color option | $500 | $600 |

K300 PA Amp and Speaker Set
1971-1975. Includes 302 PA, 303 PA, 304 PA, 305 PA, head and 2 cabs.

| 1971-1975 | Color option | $475 | $575 |

K400-2 Reverb/Tremolo Amp Set
1968-1972. 200 relative watts, reverb, tremolo, with 6x12" or 8x12" cab, available with JBL D-140F speakers, Altec Lansing (A), C.T.S. (C), or Jensen (J). The K400 was offered with no effects (suffix 1), with reverb and tremolo (suffix 2), with Harmonic Clipper & Boost (suffix 3), and Reverb/Trem/Clipper/Boost (suffix 4). The 400 heads came with a separate chrome amp head stand.

| 1968-1972 | Black | $325 | $400 |
| 1968-1972 | Color option | $500 | $600 |

KBA-10 Combo Amp
Late-1980s-1990s. Compact solidstate bass amp, 10 watts, 1x8".

| 1990s | | $25 | $75 |

KBA-20 Combo Amp
Late-1980s-early-1990s. KBA series were compact solidstate bass amps with built-in limiter, 20 watts, 1x8".

| 1989-1990 | | $25 | $75 |

'60s Kustom K25 C-2 SC

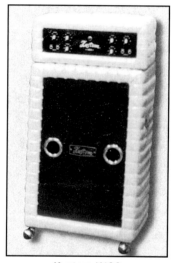
Kustom K100

Kustom K250-2-15

AMPS

Kustom K400-2

Lab Series K5

Laboga Caiman Series

MODEL YEAR	FEATURES	EXC. COND. LOW	HIGH
KBA-30 Combo Amp			
Late-1980s-early-1990s. 30 watts, 1x10".			
1989-1990		$25	$75
KBA-40 Combo Amp			
Late-1980s-early-1990s. 40 watts, 1x12".			
1989-1990		$50	$75
KBA-80 Combo Amp			
Late-1980s-early-1990s. 80 watts, 1x15".			
1989-1990		$75	$125
KBA-160 Combo Amp			
Late-1980s-early-1990s. Solidstate bass amp with built-in limiter, 160 watts, 1x15".			
1989-1990		$100	$125
KGA-10 VC Amp			
1999-2006. 10 watts, 1x6.5" speaker, switchable overdrive.			
1999-2006		$25	$50
KLA-15 Combo Amp			
Late-1980s-early-1990s. Solidstate, overdrive, 15 watts, 1x8".			
1989-1990		$50	$75
KLA-20 Amp			
Mid-1980s-late-1980s. 1x10", MOS-FET, gain, EQ, reverb, headphone jack.			
1986		$50	$75
KLA-25 Combo Amp			
Late-1980s-early-1990s. Solidstate, overdrive, reverb, 25 watts, 1x10".			
1989-1990		$50	$75
KLA-50 Combo Amp			
Late-1980s-early-1990s. Solidstate, overdrive, reverb, 50 watts, 1x12".			
1989-1990		$75	$100
KLA-75 Amp			
Mid-1980s-late-1980s. 75 watts, reverb, footswitching.			
1987		$100	$125
KLA-100 Combo Amp			
Late-1980s-early-1990s. Solidstate, reverb, 100-watt dual channel, 1x12".			
1989-1990		$100	$125
KLA-185 Combo Amp			
Late-1980s-early-1990s. Solidstate, reverb, 185-watt dual channel, 1x12".			
1989-1990		$125	$150
KPB-200 Bass Combo Amp			
1994-1997. 200 watts, 1x15".			
1994-1997		$200	$250
SC 1-12 SC Amp			
1971-1973 50 watts, 1x12" Jensen speaker.			
1971-1973	Black	$250	$300
1971-1973	Color option	$375	$450
SC 1-15 SC Amp			
1971-1973 150 watts, 1x15" C.T.S. speaker.			
1971-1973	Black	$250	$300
1971-1973	Color option	$375	$450
SC 1-15AB SC Amp			
1971-1973. 150 watts, 1x15" Altec Lansing speaker.			
1971-1973	Black	$250	$300
1971-1973	Color option	$375	$450

MODEL YEAR	FEATURES	EXC. COND. LOW	HIGH
SC 2-12A SC Amp			
1971-1973. 150 watts, 2x12" Altec Lansing speakers.			
1971-1973	Black	$275	$325
1971-1973	Color option	$400	$475
SC 2-12J SC Amp			
1971-1973. 150 watts, 2x12" Jensen speakers.			
1971-1973	Black	$275	$325
1971-1973	Color option	$400	$475
SC 4-10 SC Amp			
1971-1973. 150 watts, 4x10" Jensen speakers.			
1971-1973	Black	$275	$325
1971-1973	Color option	$400	$475

Lab Series

1977-1980s. Five models of Lab Series amps, ranging in price from $600 to $3,700, were introduced at the '77 NAMM show by Norlin (then owner of Gibson). Two more were added later. The '80s models were Lab Series 2 amps and had a Gibson logo on the upper-left front.

MODEL YEAR	FEATURES	EXC. COND. LOW	HIGH
B120 Amp			
Ca.1984. Bass combo, 120 watts, 2 channels, 1x15".			
1984		$150	$175
G120 R-10 Amp			
Ca.1984. Combo, 120 watts, 3-band EQ, channel switching, reverb, 4x10".			
1984		$300	$375
G120 R-12 Amp			
Ca.1984. Combo, 120 watts, 3-band EQ, channel switching, reverb, 2x12".			
1984		$300	$375
L2 Amp Head			
1977-1983. Head, 100 watts, black covering.			
1977-1983		$175	$200
L3 Amp			
1977-ca.1983. 60 watt 1x12" combo.			
1977-1983		$300	$375
L4 Amp Head			
1977-1983. Solidstate, 200 watts, black cover, dark grille, large L4 logo on front panel.			
1977-1983		$225	$275
L5 Amp			
1977-ca.1983. Solidstate, 100 watts, 2x12" piggyback.			
1977-1983		$500	$600
L7 Amp			
1977-1983. Solidstate, 100 watts, 4x10" piggyback.			
1977-1983		$500	$600
L11 Amp			
1977-1983. 200 watts, 8x12", piggyback.			
1977-1983		$500	$600

Laboga

1973-present. Adam Laboga builds intermediate and professional grade, production, tube guitar amps and cabinets in Wroclaw, Poland.

Lace Music Products

1979-present. Lace Music Products, which was founded by pickup innovator Don Lace Sr., added amplifiers in '96. They also offered amps under the Rat Fink and Mooneyes brands.

The *Vintage Guitar Price Guide* shows low to high values for items in all-original excellent condition, and, where applicable, with original case or cover.

MODEL		EXC. COND.	
YEAR	FEATURES	LOW	HIGH

Lafayette

Ca.1963-1967. Japanese-made guitars and amps sold through the Lafayette Electronics catalogs.

Tube Amp

1960s. Japanese-made tube, gray speckle 1x12" with art deco design or black 2x12".

1960s	Larger, 2 speakers	$175	$200
1960s	Small, 1 speaker	$125	$150

Landry

2008-present. Production, professional grade, amps and cabinets built by Bill Landry in St. Louis, Missouri.

Laney

1968-present. Founded by Lyndon Laney and Bob Thomas in Birmingham, England. Laney offered tube amps exclusively into the '80s. Currently they offer intermediate and professional grade, tube and solidstate amp heads and combos and cabinets.

100-Watt Amp Head

1968-1969. Similar to short head Plexi Marshall amp cab, large Laney with underlined "y" logo plate on upper left front corner, black vinyl cover, grayish grille.

1968-1969		$1,450	$1,700

Lectrolab

1950s-1960s. Budget house brand for music stores, made by Sound Projects Company of Cicero, Illinois. Similar to Valco, Oahu, and Danelectro student amps of the '50s, cabinets were generally made from inexpensive material. The Lectrolab logo can generally be found somewhere on the amp.

Tube Amp

1950-1960s	Larger	$275	$350
1950-1960s	Small	$200	$250

Legend

1978-1984. From Legend Musical Instruments of East Syracuse, New York, these amps featured cool wood cabinets. They offered heads, combos with a 1x12" or 2x12" configuration, and cabinets with 1x12", 2x12" or 4x12".

A-30 Amp

Late-1970s-early-1980s. Natural wood cabinet, Mesa-Boogie compact amp appearance.

1980s		$325	$400

A-60 Amp

Late-1970s-early-1980s. Mesa-Boogie appearance, wood cabinet and grille, transtube design dual tube preamp with solidstate power section.

1980s		$325	$400

Rock & Roll 50 Amp Set

1978-1983. Tube preamp section and solidstate power supply.

1978-1983	Half stack matching	$750	$950

Rock & Roll 50 Combo Amp

1978-1983. Mesa-Boogie-style wood compact combo, either 1x15" or 2x12" options, tube preamp section and solidstate power supply.

1978-1979	2x12" option	$375	$450
1978-1983	1x15" option	$375	$450

MODEL		EXC. COND.	
YEAR	FEATURES	LOW	HIGH

Super Lead 50 Amp

Late-1970s-early-1980s. Rock & Roll 50-watt model with added bass boost and reverb, 1x12", hybrid tube and solidstate.

1978-1983		$375	$450

Super Lead 100 Amp

Late-1970s-early-1980s. 100-watt version, 2x12".

1978-1983		$375	$450

Leslie

Most often seen with Hammond organs, the cool Leslie rotating speakers have been adopted by many guitarists. Many guitar effects have tried to duplicate their sound. And they are still making them.

16 Rotating Speaker Cabinet

1960s-1970s. 1x10" or 1x12" rotating speaker (requires an amp head), black vinyl cover, silver grille, Leslie 60 logo on grille.

1960s	1 cab	$650	$800
1970s	1 cab	$475	$600

60 M Rotating Speaker Cabinets

1960s-1970s. Two 1x10" rotating speaker cabs with 45-watt amp, black vinyl cover, light silver grille, Leslie logo upper left on grille.

1960-1970s	2 cabs	$650	$800

103 Amp

1960s. Two-speed.

1960s		$375	$450

118 Amp

1960s. 1x12" Altec speaker.

1960s		$375	$450

125 Amp

Late-1960s. All tube amp with 2-speed rotating 1x12" speaker.

1960s		$375	$450

145 Amp

1960s		$650	$800

Line 6

1996-present. Founded by Marcus Ryle and Michel Doidic and specializing in digital signal processing in both effects and amps. They also produce tube amps.

Little Lanilei

1997-present. Small hand-made, intermediate grade, production/custom, amps made by Songworks Systems & Products of San Juan Capistrano, California. In '09, owner Tom Pryzgoda changed Songworks to Mahaffay Amplifiers, and introduced amps under that name as well as continuing the Little Lanilei brand. They also build a reverb unit and a rotary effect.

Little Walter

2008-present. Phil Bradbury builds his professional grade, production, amp heads and cabinets in West End, North Carolina.

Landry LS100

AMPS

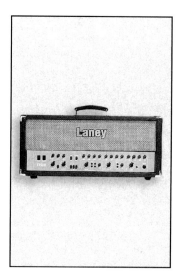

Laney TT 50H

Line 6 Vetta II

Louis Electric Ferrari

Mack Heatseeker HS-18

Magnatone Model 111

MODEL YEAR	FEATURES	EXC. COND. LOW	HIGH

London City

Late 1960s-early 1970s. Intermediate to professional grade amps and cabinets made in Netherlands, London City logo.

Louis Electric Amplifier Co.

1993-present. Founded by Louis Rosano in Bergenfield, New Jersey. Louis produces custom-built tweeds and various combo amps from 35 to 80 watts.

Luna Guitars

2005-present. Located in Tampa, Florida, Yvonne de Villiers imports her budget to professional grade, production, acoustic and electric guitars from Japan, Korea and China. She also imports guitars, basses and ukes.

Mack

2005-present. Made in Toronto, Ontario by builder Don Mackrill, the company offers intermediate and professional grade, production, tube amps.

Mad Professor

2002-present. Bjorn Juhl and Jukka Monkkonen build their premium grade, production/custom, tube amps in Tampere, Finland. They also offer effects pedals.

Maestro

Maestro amps are associated with Gibson and were included in the Gibson catalogs. For example, in the '62-'63 orange cover Gibson catalog, tweed Maestro amps were displayed in their own section. Tweed Maestro amps are very similar to Gibson tweed amps. Maestro amps were often associated with accordions in the early-'60s but the amps featured standard guitar inputs. Gibson also used the Maestro name on effects in the '60s and '70s and In 01, Gibson revived the name for a line of effects, banjos, and mandolins and added guitars and amps in '09.

The price ranges listed are for excellent condition, all original amps though tubes may be replaced without affecting value. The prices listed are for amps with fully intact logos. A broken or missing logo may diminish the value of the amp. Amps with a changed handle, power cord, and especially a broken logo, should be taken on a case-by-case basis.

Amp models in '58 include the Super Maestro and Maestro, in '60 the Stereo Maestro Accordion GA-87, Super Maestro Accordion GA-46 T, Standard Accordion GA-45 T, Viscount Accordion GA-16 T, in '62 the Reverb-Echo GA-1 RT, Reverb-Echo GA-2 RT, 30 Stereo Accordion Amp, Stereo Accordion GA-78 RV.

GA-1 RT Reverb-Echo Amp
1961. Tweed, 1x8".

1961		$725	$875

GA-2 RT Deluxe Reverb-Echo Amp
1961. Deluxe more powerful version of GA-1 RT, 1x12", tweed.

1961		$975	$1,200

GA-15 RV/Bell 15 RV Amp
1961. 15 watts, 1x12", gray sparkle.

1961		$725	$900

GA-16 T Viscount Amp
1959-1961. 14 watts, 1x10", white cab with brown grille.

1959-1961		$600	$725

GA-45 Maestro Amp
1955-1961. 14-16 watts, 4x8", 2-tone.

1955-1961		$925	$1,150

GA-45 RV Standard Amp
1961. 16 watts, 4x8", reverb.

1961		$1,100	$1,300

GA-45 T Standard Accordion Amp
1961. 16 watts, 4x8", tremolo.

1961		$925	$1,150

GA-46 T Super Maestro Accordion and Bass Amp
1957-1961. Based on the Gibson GA-200 and advertised to be designed especially for amplified accordions, 60 watts, 2x12", vibrato, 2-tone cover, large Maestro Super logo on top center of grille.

1957-1961		$2,000	$2,500

GA-78 Maestro Series Amps
1960-1961. Wedge stereo cab, 2x10", reverb and tremolo.

1960-1961	GA-78 RV Maestro 30	$2,000	$2,500
1960-1961	GA-78 RVS	$2,000	$2,500
1960-1961	GA-78 RVT	$2,000	$2,500

Magnatone

Ca.1937-1971. Magnatone made a huge variety of amps sold under their own name and under brands like Dickerson, Oahu (see separate listings), and Bronson. They also private branded amps for several accordion companies or accordion teaching studios. Brands used for them include Da Vinci, PAC - AMP, PANaramic, Titano, Tonemaster, Twilighter, and Unique (see separate listings for those brands).

Model 108 Varsity Amp
1948-1954. Gray pearloid cover, small student amp or lap steel companion amp.

1948-1954		$475	$550

Model 109 Melodier Amp
1950s. 10 watts, 2 speakers.

1950s		$550	$650

Model 110 Melodier Amp
1953-1954. 12 watts, 1x10", brown leatherette cover, light grille.

1953-1954		$525	$625

Model 111 Student Amp
1955-1959. 1x8", 2-3 watts, brown leatherette, brown grille.

1955-1959		$425	$500

MODEL YEAR	FEATURES	EXC. COND. LOW	HIGH

Model 112/113 Troubadour Amp
1955-1959. 18 watts, 1x12", brown leatherette, brown grille, slant back rear control panel.
1955-1959 $725 $875

Model 118 Amp
1960. Compact, tubes, low power, volume and tone knobs, brown tolex era, Model 118 logo on rear-mounted control panel.
1960 $350 $450

Model 120B Cougar Bass Amp
1967-1968. Initial Magnatone entry into the solid-state market, superseded by Brute Series in '68, 120 watts, 2x12" solidstate bass piggyback amp, naugahyde vinyl cover with polyester rosewood side panels.
1967-1968 $250 $300

Model 120R Sting Ray Reverb Bass Amp
1967-1968. Initial Magnatone entry into the solid-state market, superseded by Brute Series in '68, 150 watts, 4x10" solidstate combo amp, naugahyde vinyl cover with polyester rosewood side panels.
1967-1968 $250 $300

Model 130V Custom Amp
1969-1971. Solidstate 1x12" combo amp.
1969-1971 $175 $225

Model 150R Firestar Reverb Amp
1967-1968. Initial Magnatone entry into the solid-state market, superseded by Brute Series in '68, 120 watts, 2x12" solidstate combo amp, naugahyde vinyl cover with polyester rosewood side panels.
1967-1968 $250 $300

Model 180 Triplex Amp
Mid-to-late-1950s. Mid-level power using 2 6L6 power tubes, 1x15" and 1x8" speakers.
1950s $750 $900

Model 192-5-S Troubadour Amp
Early-1950s. 18 watts, 1x12" Jensen Concert speaker, brown alligator covering, lower back control panel, 3 chicken-head knobs, Magnatone script logo on front, Troubadour script logo on back control panel.
1950s $500 $600

Model 194 Lyric Amp
1947-mid-1950s. 1x12" speaker, old-style tweed vertical cab typical of '40s.
1940s $500 $600

Model 195 Melodier Amp
1951-1954. Vertical cab with 1x10" speaker, pearloid with flowing grille slats.
1951-1954 $500 $600

Model 196 Amp
1947-mid-1950s. 1x12", 5-10 watts, scroll grille design, snakeskin leatherette cover.
1940s $500 $600

Model 197-V Varsity Amp
1948-1952. Small compact student amp, 1x8", tubes, Varsity model logo and model number on back panel, old style layout with back bottom-mounted chasis, curved cross-bars on front baffle, brown lizard leatherette, leather handle.
1948-1952 $475 $575

Model 198 Varsity Amp
1948-1954. 1x8", tubes.
1948-1954 $475 $575

Model 199 Student Amp
1950s. About 6 to 10 watts, 1x8", snakeskin leatherette cover, metal handle, slant grille design.
1950s $475 $575

Model 210 Deluxe Student Amp
1958-1960. 5 watts, 1x8", vibrato, brown leatherette, V logo lower right front on grille.
1958-1960 $475 $575

Model 213 Troubadour Amp
1957-1958. 10 watts, 1x12", vibrato, brown leatherette cover, V logo lower right of grille.
1957-1958 $650 $800

Model 240 SV Magna-Chordion Amp
1967-1968. Initial Magnatone entry into the solid-state market, superseded by Brute Series in '68, 240 watts, 2x12" solidstate stereo accordion or organ amp, naugahyde vinyl cover, polyester rosewood side panels, input jacks suitable for guitar, reverb and vibrato, lateral combo cab, rear mounted controls.
1967-1968 $275 $350

Model 250 Professional Amp
1958-1960. 20 watts, 1x12", vibrato, brown leatherette with V logo lower right front of grille.
1958-1960 $1,000 $1,200

Model 260 Amp
1957-1958. 35 watts, 2x12", brown leatherette, vibrato, V logo lower right front corner of grille.
1957-1958 $1,400 $1,700

Model 262 Jupiter/Custom Pro Amp
1961-1963. 35 watts, 2x12", vibrato, brown leatherette.
1961-1963 $1,100 $1,300

Model 280/Custom 280 Amp
1957-1958. 50 watts, brown leatherette covering, brown-yellow tweed grille, 2x12" plus 2x5" speakers, double V logo.
1957-1958 $1,450 $1,750

Model 280A Amp
1958-1960. 50 watts, brown leatherette covering, brown-yellow tweed grille, 2x12" plus 2x5" speakers, V logo lower right front.
1958-1960 $1,400 $1,700

Model 410 Diana Amp
1961-1963. Five watts, 1x12", advertised as a 'studio' low power professional amp, brown leatherette cover, vibrato.
1961-1963 $550 $650

Model 412 Amp
1960s. Estey era compact student amp, low power, 1x8", tubes.
1960s $175 $225

Model 413 Centaur Amp
1961-1963. 18 watts, 1x12", brown leatherette cover, vibrato.
1961-1963 $850 $1,000

Model 415 Clio Bass Amp
1961-1963. 25 watts, 4x8", bass or accordion amp, brown leatherette cover.
1961-1963 $900 $1,100

Magnatone Model 112/113 Troubadour

Magnatone 280

Magnatone 401-A

AMPS

1962 Magnatone Custom 450

Magnatone 480 Venus

Mahaffay The Little Lanilei 3350LT

MODEL YEAR	FEATURES	EXC. COND. LOW	HIGH

Model 422 Amp
1966-1967. Low power 1x12", 3 inputs, black vinyl, light swirl grille.

| 1966-1967 | | $500 | $600 |

Model 432 Amp
Mid-1960s. Compact student model, wavey-squiggle art deco-style grille, black cover, vibrato and reverb.

| 1960s | | $525 | $625 |

Model 435 Athene Bass Amp
1961-1963. 55 watts, 4x10", piggyback head and cab, brown leatherette.

| 1961-1963 | | $1,250 | $1,500 |

Model 440 Mercury Amp
1961-1963. 18 watts, 1x12", vibrato, brown leatherette.

| 1961-1963 | | $1,000 | $1,200 |

Model 450 Juno/Twin Hi-Fi Amp
1961-1963. 25 watts, 1x12" and 1 oval 5"x7" speakers, reverb, vibrato, brown leatherette.

| 1961-1963 | | $1,350 | $1,600 |
| 1961-1963 | Extension cab only | $500 | $600 |

Model 460 Victory Amp
1961-1963. 35 watts, 2x12" and 2 oval 5"x7" speakers, early-'60s next to the top-of-the-line, reverb and vibrato, brown leatherette.

| 1961-1963 | | $1,400 | $1,650 |

Model 480 Venus Amp
1961-1963. 50 watts, 2x12" and 2 oval 5"x7" speakers, early-'60s top-of-the-line, reverb and stereo vibrato, brown leatherette.

| 1961-1963 | | $1,400 | $1,650 |

Model M6 Amp
1964 (not seen in '65 catalog). 25 watts, 1x12", black molded plastic suitcase amp.

| 1964 | | $525 | $625 |

Model M7 Bass Amp
1964-1966. 38 watts, 1x15" bass amp, black molded plastic suitcase amp.

| 1964-1966 | | $525 | $625 |

Model M8 Amp
1964-1966. 27 watts, 1x12", reverb and tremolo, black molded plastic suitcase amp.

| 1964-1966 | | $625 | $725 |

Model M9 Amp
1964-1966. 38 watts, 1x15", tremolo, no reverb, black molded plastic suitcase amp.

| 1964-1966 | | $600 | $700 |

Model M10/M10A Amp
1964-1966. 38 watts, 1x15", tone boost, tremolo, transistorized reverb section, black molded plastic suitcase amp.

| 1964-1966 | | $600 | $700 |

Model M12 Bass Amp
1964-1966. 80 watts, 1x15" or 2x12", mid-'60s top-of-the-line bass amp, black molded plastic suitcase amp.

| 1964-1966 | | $625 | $725 |

Model M14 Amp
1964-1966. Stereo, 75 watts, 2x12" plus 2 tweeters, stereo vibrato, no reverb, black molded plastic suitcase amp.

| 1964-1966 | | $750 | $900 |

Model M15 Amp
1964-1966. Stereo 75 watts, 2x12" plus 2 tweeters, stereo vibrato, transistorized reverb, black molded plastic suitcase amp.

| 1964-1966 | | $800 | $1,000 |

Model M27 Bad Boy Bass Amp
1968-1971. 150 watts, 2x15" (1 passive), reverb, vibrato, solidstate, vertical profile bass amp, part of Brute Series.

| 1968-1971 | | $250 | $300 |

Model M30 Fang Amp
1968-1971. 150 watts, 2x15" (1 passive), 1 exponential horn, solidstate, vibrato, reverb, vertical profile amp.

| 1968-1971 | | $250 | $300 |

Model M32 Big Henry Bass Amp
1968-1971. 300 watts, 2x15" solidstate vertical profile bass amp.

| 1968-1971 | | $250 | $300 |

Model M35 The Killer Amp
1968-1971. 300 watts, 2x15" and 2 horns, solidstate, vibrato, vertical profile amp.

| 1968-1971 | | $250 | $300 |

Model MP-1 (Magna Power I) Amp
1966-1967. 30 watts, 1x12", dark vinyl, light grille, Magnatone-Estey logo on upper right of grille.

| 1966-1967 | | $650 | $775 |

Model MP-3 (Magna-Power 3) Amp
1966-1967. Mid-power, 2x12", reverb, dark vinyl, light grille, Magnatone-Estey logo on upper right of grille.

| 1966-1967 | | $675 | $800 |

Model PS150 Amp
1968-1971. Powered slave speaker cabinets, 150 watts, 2x15" linkable cabinets.

| 1968-1971 | | $175 | $225 |

Model PS300 Amp
1968-1971. Powered slave speaker cabinets, 300 watts, 2x15" (1 passive) linkable cabinets.

| 1968-1971 | | $175 | $225 |

Small Pearloid Amp
1947-1955. Pearloid (MOTS) covered low- and mid-power amps generally associated with pearloid lap steel sets.

| 1947-1955 | Fancy grille | $375 | $475 |
| 1947-1955 | Plain grille | $225 | $300 |

Starlet Amp
1951-1952. Student model, 1x8", pearloid cover early, leatherette later, low power, single on-off volume control, Starlet logo on back panel, Magnatone logo plate upper left front of grille.

| 1951-1954 | Pearloid | $300 | $400 |
| 1955-1959 | Leatherette | $300 | $400 |

Starlite Model 401 Amp
Magnatone produced the mid-'60s Starlite amplifier line for the budget minded musician. Each Starlite model prominently notes the Magnatone name. The grilles show art deco wavy circles. Magnatone 1960-'63 standard amps offer models starting with 12" speakers. Starlite models offer 10" and below. Model 401 has 15 watts, 1x8" and 3 tubes.

| 1960s | | $275 | $325 |

AMPS

MODEL YEAR	FEATURES	EXC. COND. LOW	HIGH

Starlite Model 411 Amp
Mid-1960s. 15 watts, 1x8", 5 tubes, tremolo (not advertised as vibrato), art deco wavy grille.

1960s		$275	$325

Starlite Model 441A Bass Amp
Early-mid-1960s. Lower power with less than 25 watts, 1x15", tube amp.

1960s		$450	$550

Starlite Model Custom 421 Amp
Early-mid-1960s. Tube amp, 25 watts, 1x10".

1960s		$450	$550

Starlite Model Custom 431 Amp
Early-mid-1960s. Tube amp, 30 watts, 1x10", vibrato and reverb.

1960s		$500	$600

Mahaffay Amplifiers
2009-present. See Little Lanilei.

Mako
1985-1989. Line of solidstate amps from Kaman (Ovation, Hamer). They also offered guitars and basses.

Marlboro Sound Works
1970-1980s. Economy solidstate amps imported by Musical Instruments Corp., Syosset, New York. Initially, Marlboro targeted the economy compact amp market, but quickly added larger amps and PAs.

GA-2 Amp
1970s. 3 watts, 1x8".

1970s		$15	$20

GA-3 Amp
1970s. 3 watts, 1x8", tremolo.

1970s		$20	$30

GA-20B Amp
1970s. Bass/keyboard amp, 25 watts, 1x12".

1970s		$30	$70

GA-20R Amp
1970s. 25 watts, 1x12", tremolo, reverb.

1970s		$30	$70

GA-40R Amp
1970s. 30 watts, 1x12", tremolo, reverb.

1970s		$75	$125

Model 520B Amp
1970s. 25 watts, 1x15", bass/keyboard amp.

1970s		$75	$125

Model 560A Amp
1970s. 45 watts, 2x10".

1970s		$75	$125

Model 760A Amp
1970s. Guitar/bass/keyboard, 60 watts, 1x15".

1970s		$75	$125

Model 1200R Amp Head
1970s. 60 watts, reverb.

1970s		$75	$125

Model 1500B Bass Amp Head
1970s. 60 watts.

1970s		$75	$125

MODEL YEAR	FEATURES	EXC. COND. LOW	HIGH

Model 2000 Bass Amp Set
1970s. 1500B head and 1x12" cab.

1970s		$75	$125

Marshall
1962-present. Drummer Jim Marshall started building bass speaker and PA cabinets in his garage in 1960. He opened a retail drum shop for his students and others and soon added guitars and amps. When Ken Bran joined the business as service manager in '62, the two decided to build their own amps. By '63 they had expanded the shop to house a small manufacturing space and by late that year they were offering the amps to other retailers. Marshall also made amps under the Park, CMI, Narb, Big M, and Kitchen-Marshall brands. Marshall continues to be involved in the company.

Mark I, II, III and IVs are generally '60s and '70s and also are generally part of a larger series (for example JTM), or have a model number that is a more specific identifier. Describing an amp only as Mark II can be misleading. The most important identifier is the Model Number, which Marshall often called the Stock Number. To help avoid confusion we have added the Model number as often as possible. In addition, when appropriate, we have included the wattage, number of channels, master or no-master info in the title. This should help the reader more quickly find a specific amp. Check the model's description for such things as two inputs or four inputs, because this will help with identification. Vintage Marshall amps do not always have the Model/Stock number on the front or back panel, so the additional identifiers should help. The JMP logo on the front is common and really does not help with specific identification. For example, a JMP Mark II Super Lead 100 Watt description is less helpful than the actual model/stock number. Unfortunately, many people are not familiar with specific model/stock numbers. VG has tried to include as much information in the title as space will allow.

Marshall amps are sorted as follows:
AVT Series - new line for Marshall
Club and Country Series (Rose-Morris)-introduced in '78
JCM 800 Series - basically the '80s
JCM 900 Series - basically the '90s
JCM 2000 Series - basically the '00s
JTM Series
  Micro Stack Group
Model Number/Stock Number (no specific series, basically the '60s, '70s) - including Artist and Valvestate models (Valvestate refers to specific Model numbers in 8000 Series)
Silver Jubilee Series

35th Anniversary Marshall Limited Edition Set
1997. Limited Edition 1997 logo, includes matching Super Lead MKII 100-watt head, PB100 power brake and MKII 1960A slant cab, all in white covering.

1997		$2,600	$3,100

Mako MAK2

Marlboro Sound 560A

Marshall AVT-50

Marshall AVT-150

Marshall AVT-275

Marshall AVT 412B Cabinet

MODEL YEAR	FEATURES	EXC. COND. LOW	HIGH
AVT 20 Combo Amp			
2001-present. Solidstate, 20 watts, 12AX7 preamp tube, 1x10", Advanced Valvestate Technology (AVT) models have black covering and grille, and gold panel.			
2001-2010		$150	$200
AVT 50/50H Amp			
2001-present. Solidstate, 50 watts, head only or 1x12" combo.			
2001-2010	Combo	$225	$300
2001-2010	Head	$200	$250
AVT 100 Combo Amp			
2001-present. Solidstate, 100 watts, tube preamp, 1x12".			
2001-2010		$300	$400
AVT 150 Series Amp			
2001-present. Solidstate, additional features over AVT 100. Combo (100 watts, 1x12"), Half-Stack (150 watts, 4x12") and Head only (150 watts).			
2001-2010	Combo	$475	$575
2001-2010	Half-stack	$625	$750
2001-2010	Head	$375	$450
AVT 275 Combo Amp			
2001-2007. Solidstate DFX stereo, 75 watts per side, 2x12".			
2001-2007		$500	$600
AVT 412/412A Cabinet			
2001-2008. Slant half-stack 4x12" cab, 200-watt load, 25-watt Celestions.			
2001-2008		$275	$300
AVT 412B Cabinet			
2001-2008. Straight-front half-stack 4x12" cab, 200-watt load.			
2001-2008		$250	$300
Club and Country Model 4140 Amp			
1978-1982. Tubes, 100 watts, 2x12" combo, Rose-Morris era, designed for the country music market, hence the name, brown vinyl cover, straw grille.			
1978-1982		$800	$1,000
Club and Country Model 4145 Amp			
1978-1982. Tubes, 100 watts, 4x10" combo, Rose-Morris era, designed for the country music market, hence the name, brown vinyl, straw grille.			
1978-1982		$800	$1,000
Club and Country Model 4150 Bass Amp			
1978-1982. Tubes, 100 watts, 4x10" bass combo, Rose-Morris era, designed for the country music market, hence the name, brown vinyl cover, straw grille.			
1978-1982		$750	$925
JCM 600 Series			
1997-2000. All tube, 60 watt models with modern features, includes the JCM600 head, JCM601 1x12" combo and JCM602 2x12" combo.			
1997-2000	JCM602	$525	$650
JCM 800 Model 1959 Amp Head			
1981-1991. 100 watts.			
1981-1991		$800	$1,000
JCM 800 Model 1987 Amp Head			
1981-1991. 50 watts.			
1981-1991		$800	$1,000

MODEL YEAR	FEATURES	EXC. COND. LOW	HIGH
JCM 800 Model 1992 Bass Amp Head			
1981-1986. Active tone circuit.			
1981-1986		$800	$1,000
JCM 800 Model 2000 Amp Head			
1981-1982. 200 watts.			
1981-1982		$800	$1,000
JCM 800 Model 2001 Amp Head			
1981-1982. Bass head, 300 watts.			
1981-1982		$800	$1,000
JCM 800 Model 2004 Amp Head			
1981-1990. 50 watts, master.			
1981-1990		$800	$1,000
JCM 800 Model 2004S Amp Head			
1986-1987. 50 watts, short head.			
1986-1987		$800	$1,000
JCM 800 Model 2005 Amp			
1983-1990. 50 watts, split channel.			
1983-1990	Head only	$800	$1,000
JCM 800 Model 2005 Full Stack Amp			
1983-1990. 2005 head with 2 2x12 cabs.			
1983-1990		$1,500	$1,850
JCM 800 Model 2203 20th Anniversary Half Stack Amp			
1982. 20th Anniversary plate in lower right corner of matching 1960A cab, matching white tolex cover.			
1982		$1,700	$2,100
JCM 800 Model 2203 Amp Head			
1981-1990, 2002-2010. 100 watts, master volume, reissued '02 in Vintage Series.			
1981-1990		$1,050	$1,300
2002-2010	Reissue	$800	$1,000
JCM 800 Model 2203KK Kerry King Signature Amp			
2008-present. Kerry King Signature logo on front panel, Union Jack style logo in upper right corner of amp head, 100 watts, 3-band EQ.			
2008-2010		$1,050	$1,300
JCM 800 Model 2204 Amp Head			
1981-1990. 50 watts, 1 channel, 2 inputs, master volume, front panel says JCM 800 Lead Series, back panel says Master Model 50w Mk 2.			
1981-1990		$1,000	$1,250
JCM 800 Model 2204S Amp Head			
1986-1987. Short head, 50 watts.			
1986-1987		$1,000	$1,250
JCM 800 Model 2205 Amp			
1983-1990. 50 watts, split channel (1 clean and 1 distortion), switchable, both channels with reverb, front panel reads JCM 800 Lead Series.			
1980s	Half-stack, red tolex	$1,250	$1,550
1983-1990	Head	$850	$1,050
JCM 800 Model 2205 Limited Edition Full Stack Amp			
Late-1980s. 50-watt head, 1960A slant and 1960B straight front 4x12" cabs.			
1988	Red tolex	$1,550	$1,900
JCM 800 Model 2210 Amp Head			
1983-1990. 100 watts.			
1983-1990		$1,000	$1,250

MODEL YEAR	FEATURES	EXC. COND. LOW	HIGH

JCM 800 Model 4010 Combo Amp
1981-1990. 50 watts, 1x12", reverb, single channel master volume.

| 1981-1990 | | $1,000 | $1,250 |

JCM 800 Model 4103 Combo Amp
1981-1990. Lead combo amp, 100 watts, 2x12".

| 1981-1990 | | $1,000 | $1,250 |

JCM 800 Model 4104 Combo Amp
1980-1990. Tube lead amp, 50 watts, 2x12".

| 1980-1990 | Black | $1,000 | $1,250 |
| 1980-1990 | White option | $1,000 | $1,250 |

JCM 800 Model 4210 Combo Amp
1982-1990. 50 watts, 1x12" tube combo, split-channel, single input, master volume.

| 1982-1990 | | $775 | $975 |

JCM 800 Model 4211 Combo Amp
1983-1990. Lead combo amp, 100 watts, 2x12".

| 1983-1990 | | $825 | $1,025 |

JCM 800 Model 4212 Combo Amp
1983-1990. 2x12" combo.

| 1983-1990 | | $725 | $900 |

JCM 800 Model 5005 Combo Amp
1983-1990. Solidstate combo amp, 12 watts, master volume, 1x10".

| 1983-1990 | | $325 | $400 |

JCM 800 Model 5010 Combo Amp
1983-1990. Solidstate combo amp, 30 watts, master volume, 1x12".

| 1983-1990 | | $350 | $425 |

JCM 800 Model 5150 Combo Amp
1987-1991. Combo amp, 150 watts, specially designed 12" Celestion speaker, split channel design, separate clean and distortion channels, presence and effects-mix master controls.

| 1987-1991 | | $475 | $575 |

JCM 800 Model 5212 Combo Amp
1986-1991. 2x12" split channel reverb combo.

| 1986-1991 | | $500 | $600 |

JCM 800 Model 5213 Combo Amp
1986-1991. MOS-FET solidstate combo, 2x12", channel-switching, effects loop, direct output, remote footswitch.

| 1986-1991 | | $300 | $375 |

JCM 800 Model 5215 Combo Amp
1986-1991. MOS-FET solidstate, 1x15", Accutronics reverb, effects loop.

| 1986-1991 | | $300 | $375 |

JCM 900 Model 2100 Mark III Amp Head
1990-1993. FX loop, 100/50-watt selectable lead head.

| 1990-1993 | | $800 | $1,000 |

JCM 900 Model 2100 SL-X Amp Head
1992-1998. Hi-gain 100 watt head amp, additional 12AX7 preamp tube.

| 1992-1998 | | $575 | $725 |

JCM 900 Model 2500 SL-X Amp Head
1990-2000. 50 watt version of SL-X.

| 1992-1998 | | $575 | $725 |

JCM 900 Model 4100 Dual Reverb Amp
1990-present. 100/50 switchable head, JCM 900 on front panel, black with black front.

| 1990-2010 | Head & 4x10" cab | $1,000 | $1,200 |
| 1990-2010 | Head only | $550 | $700 |

JCM 900 Model 4101 Combo Amp
1990-2000. All tube, 100 watts, 1x12" combo.

| 1990-2000 | | $600 | $700 |

JCM 900 Model 4102 Combo Amp
1990-2000. Combo amp, 100/50 watts switchable, 2x12".

| 1990-2000 | | $650 | $750 |

JCM 900 Model 4500 Amp Head
1990-2000. All tube, 2 channels, 50/25 watts, EL34 powered, reverb, effects loop, compensated recording out, master volume, black.

| 1990-2000 | | $550 | $675 |

JCM 900 Model 4501 Dual Reverb Combo Amp
1990-2000. 50/25 switchable, 1x12".

| 1990-2000 | | $625 | $775 |

JCM 900 Model 4502 Combo Amp
1990-2000. 50/25 switchable, 2x12".

| 1990-2000 | | $650 | $800 |

JCM 2000 DSL Series Amp
1998-present. DSL is Dual Super Lead, 2 independent channels labelled classic and ultra, JCM 2000 and DSL logos both on front panel.

1998-2010	DSL100 head, 100w	$550	$650
1998-2010	DSL50 head, 50w	$550	$650
1999-2002	DSL201 combo, 20w, 1x12"	$400	$475
2000-2010	DSL401 combo, 40w, 1x12"	$550	$650
2006	DSL100 half-stack, 100w, w/1960A	$900	$1,100

JCM 2000 TSL Series Amp
1998-present. TSL is Triple Super Lead, 3 independent channels labelled clean, crunch and lead, 8 tubes, JCM 2000 and TSL logos both on front panel.

1998-2010	TSL100 head, 100w	$625	$775
1998-2010	TSL122 combo, 100w, 2x12"	$750	$925
1998-2010	TSL60 head, 60w	$625	$775
1998-2010	TSL602, 60w, 2x12	$625	$775
2000-2009	TSL1000 head, 100w	$750	$925

JCM Slash Signature Model 2555SL Amp Set
1996. Based on JCM 800 with higher gain, matching amp and cab set, JCM Slash Signature logo on front panel, single channel, Slash Signature 1960AV 4x12" slant cab, black.

| 1996 | Half-stack | $2,200 | $2,700 |
| 1996 | Head only | $1,700 | $2,100 |

JTM 30 Series Amp
1995-1997. Tube combo, reverb, 30 watts, effects loops, 5881 output sections, footswitchable high-gain modes. Available as 1x15", 1x12", 2x12" or 3x10" combo or as 4x10" half-stack.

1995-1997	Combo 1x12"	$350	$450
1995-1997	Combo 2x10"	$350	$450
1995-1997	Combo 2x12"	$450	$550
1995-1997	Combo 3x10"	$450	$550

JTM 45 Amp Head
1962-1964. Amp head, 45 watts. The original Marshall amp. Became the Model 1987 45-watt for '65-'66.

| 1962-1964 | | $9,000 | $11,000 |

Marshall Club and Country 4140

Marshall JCM 800 Model 2203KK Kerry King Signature

Marshall JCM 2000 DSL 401

AMPS

Marshall JTM 50 Model 1962 Bluesbreaker

Marshall MG15MSII

Marshall Model 1936

MODEL YEAR	FEATURES	EXC. COND. LOW	HIGH

JTM 45 Model 1961 MK IV 4x10 Combo Amp
1965-1966. 45 watts, 4x10", tremolo, JTM 45 MK IV on panel, Bluesbreaker association.

| 1965-1966 | | $8,500 | $10,500 |

JTM 45 Model 1962 MK IV 2x12 Combo Amp
1965-1966. 45 watts, 2x12", tremolo, JTM 45 MK IV on panel, Bluesbreaker association.

| 1965-1966 | | $8,800 | $10,800 |

JTM 45 Model 1987 Amp Head Reissue
1989-1999. Black/green tolex.

| 1988-1999 | | $675 | $825 |

JTM 45 Model 1987 Mark II Lead Amp Head
1965-1966. Replaced JTM 45 Amp ('62-'64), but was subsequently replaced by the Model 1987 50-watt Head during '66.

| 1965-1966 | | $6,000 | $7,000 |

JTM 45 Offset Limited Edition Amp Set Reissue
Introduced in 2000. Limited run of 300 units, old style cosmetics, 45-watt head and offset 2x12" cab, dark vinyl cover, light gray grille, rectangular logo plate on front of amp and cab, Limited Edition plate on rear of cab, serial number xxx of 300.

| 2000 | | $2,800 | $3,400 |

JTM45/100 Limited Edition
2005-present. 100 watt head and 2 4x12 cabs, 250 to be made.

| 2005-2010 | | $4,000 | $5,000 |

JTM 50 Model 1961 MK IV 4x10 Amp
1965-1972. 50 watts, 4x10", Bluesbreaker association, tremolo, JTM 50 MK IV on front panel to '68, plain front panel without model description '68-'72.

1966-1967		$7,000	$8,500
1968		$6,500	$8,000
1969		$5,000	$6,500
1970		$4,500	$5,500
1971-1972		$4,000	$5,000

JTM 50 Model 1962 Bluesbreaker Amp Reissue
1989-present. 50 watts, 2x12", Model 1962 reissue Bluesbreaker.

| 1989-1999 | | $900 | $1,100 |

JTM 50 Model 1962 MK IV 2x12 Amp
1966-1972. 50 watts, 2x12", tremolo, Bluesbreaker association, JTM 50 MK IV on front panel to '68, plain front panel without model description '68-'72.

1966-1967		$8,500	$10,000
1968		$8,000	$9,500
1969		$6,500	$8,000
1970		$7,000	$7,000
1971-1972		$5,000	$6,000

JTM 50 Model 1963 PA Amp Head
1965-1966. MK II PA head, block logo.

| 1965-1966 | | $3,800 | $4,600 |

JTM 60 Series Amp
1995-1997. Tube, 60 watts, 1x12", 1x15", 2x12" or 3x10" combo or as 4x10" half-stack.

1995-1997	Combo 1x12"	$500	$600
1995-1997	Combo 2x12"	$600	$750
1995-1997	Half-stack	$650	$800

JTM 310 Amp
1995-1997. JTM 30 with 2x10".

| 1995-1997 | | $525 | $625 |

JTM 612 Combo Amp
1995-1997. Tube combo amp, 60 watts, 1x12", EQ, reverb, effects loop.

| 1995-1997 | | $525 | $625 |

MG Series Amp
1999-present. Models include 15CD, 15RCD or CDR (solidstate, 15 watts, 1x8"), 15MS (15 watts, micro stack, 1x8" slant and 1x8" straight cabs), 15MSII, (in '02, 10" speakers), 100RCD (Valvestate Series, made in Korea, head, 100 watts), 50DFX (50 watts, 1x12), 100DFX (100 watts, combo), 250DFX (250 watts, combo), 100HDFX (100 watts).

1999-2004	MG15MS/15MSII	$175	$225
1999-2004	MG15MSZW, 15w, 2x1x10	$225	$275
1999-2010	MG15CD	$60	$70
2000-2002	MG100RCD	$275	$300
2000-2010	MG15RCD/CDR	$70	$80
2002-2009	MG100DFX	$250	$300
2002-2009	MG250DFX	$300	$350
2002-2009	MG50DFX	$275	$300
2006-2010	MG100HDFX Half-stack	$350	$450
2009-2010	MG10KK, 10w, 1x6	$50	$60

Micro Stack 3005 Amp
1986-1991. Solidstate head, 12 watts, 2 1x10" stackable cabs (one slant, one straight). Standard model is black, but was also offered in white, green, red, or the silver Silver Jubilee version with Jubilee 25/50 logo.

1986-1991	Black	$225	$300
1986-1991	Green or red	$300	$375
1986-1991	White	$325	$425
1987-1989	Silver Jubilee/silver	$375	$475

Mini-Stack 3210 MOS-FET Amp Head with 2x4x10"
1984-1991. Model 3210 MOS-FET head with 2 4x10" cabs, designed as affordable stack.

| 1984-1991 | | $350 | $425 |

Model 1710 Bass Cabinet
1990s. 1x15" speaker.

| 1990s | | $300 | $375 |

Model 1917 PA-20 Amp Head
1967-1973. PA head with 20 watts, but often used for guitar.

| 1967-1968 | Plexi panel | $3,200 | $4,000 |
| 1969-1973 | Aluminum panel | $2,800 | $3,500 |

Model 1930 Popular Combo Amp
1969-1973. 10 watts, 1x12", tremolo.

| 1969-1973 | | $2,300 | $2,800 |

Model 1933 Cabinet
1981-1991. 1x12" expension cab for JCM 800 Series amps.

| 1981-1991 | | $300 | $375 |

Model 1935/1935A/1935B Bass Cabinet
1967-1990s. Models 1935, 4x12" bass cab, black, A slant front, B straight front.

| 1967-1970 | 75w | $2,300 | $2,700 |

MODEL YEAR	FEATURES	EXC. COND. LOW	HIGH
1971-1972	Black, weave	$1,300	$1,600
1973-1975	Black, checkerboard	$1,000	$1,250
1976-1979	Black	$900	$1,100
1979-1983	260w	$575	$700
1983-1986	280w	$575	$700
1990s		$275	$350

Model 1936 2x12" Cabinet (JCM 800/900)
1981-present. 2x12" speakers, extension straight-front cab, black.

1981-1999		$300	$375

Model 1937 Bass Cabinet
1981-1986. 4x12", 140 watts.

1981-1986		$600	$750

Model 1958 18-Watt Lead Amp
1965-1968. 18 watts, 2x10" combo, Bluesbreaker cosmetics.

1965		$4,500	$5,500
1966		$4,500	$5,500
1967		$4,500	$5,500
1968		$4,500	$5,500

Model 1958 20-Watt Lead Amp
1968-1972. 20 watts, 2x10" combo, tremolo.

1968		$4,000	$5,000
1969		$4,000	$5,000
1970		$3,800	$4,500
1971-1972		$3,400	$4,000

Model 1959 Super Lead Amp
1966-1981. Two channels, 100 watts, 4 inputs, no master volume. Plexiglas control panels until mid-'69, aluminum after. See Model T1959 for tremolo version. Early custom color versions are rare and more valuable.

1966-1969	Black, plexi	$4,500	$5,500
1966-1969	Custom color, plexi	$7,000	$8,500
1969-1970	Black, aluminum	$3,600	$4,400
1969-1970	Custom color, aluminum	$4,700	$5,700
1971-1972	Black, hand-wired, small box	$1,800	$2,300
1971-1972	Custom color, hand-wired	$3,100	$3,800
1973-1975	Black, printed C.B., large box	$1,700	$2,100
1973-1975	Custom color, printed C.B.	$1,800	$2,200
1976-1979	Black	$1,200	$1,500
1976-1979	Custom color	$1,850	$2,250
1980-1981	Black	$1,150	$1,400
1980-1981	Custom color	$1,500	$1,850

Model T1959 Super Lead (Tremolo) Amp Head
1966-1973. Head amp, 100 watts, plexi until mid-'69, aluminum after. Tremolo version of the Model 1959 Amp.

1966-1969	Black, plexi	$4,900	$6,100
1966-1969	Custom color, plexi	$7,200	$8,900
1969-1970	Black, aluminum	$3,700	$4,500
1969-1970	Custom color, aluminum	$4,800	$5,900

1971-1973	Black, hand-wired, small box	$2,000	$2,500
1971-1973	Custom color, hand-wired	$3,200	$3,900

Model 1959 SLP Reissue Amp Head
1992-present. SLP refers to Super Lead Plexi.

1992-1999	Black vinyl	$850	$1,050
1992-1999	Purple vinyl	$1,100	$1,350
1992-1999	White limited edition	$1,050	$1,300
2000-2009	Black vinyl	$850	$1,050

Model 1959 SLP Reissue Amp Set
1992-present. 100 watt Super Lead head and matching 4x12" slant cab.

1992-1999	Purple, full-stack, 2x4x12"	$2,400	$2,900
1992-1999	Purple, half-stack, 1x4x12"	$1,800	$2,200

Model 1959HW Amp
2005-present. Hand-wired, 100 watts, 4x12" slant front 1960HW cab (1/2 stack).

2005-2010	Head & half-stack	$2,100	$2,600
2005-2010	Head only	$1,600	$1,900

Model 1959RR Ltd. Ed. Randy Rhoads Amp
2008-present. Randy Rhoads Tribute, full stack, 100 watts.

2008-2010		$2,300	$2,800

Model 1960 4x12 Speaker Cabinet
1964-1979. Both straight and slant front. The original Marshall 4x12" cab designed for compact size with 4x12" speakers. First issue in '64/'65 is 60-watt cab, from '65-'70 75 watts, from '70-'79 100 watts. After '79, model numbers contained an alpha suffix: A for slant front, B straight.

1966-1970	Black, weave	$2,500	$3,000
1966-1970	Custom color, weave	$3,500	$4,300
1971-1972	Black, weave	$1,400	$1,700
1971-1972	Custom color, weave	$1,900	$2,100
1973-1975	Black, checkerboard	$1,050	$1,250
1973-1975	Custom color, checkerboard	$1,700	$1,900
1976-1979	Black	$925	$1,100
1976-1979	Custom color	$1,600	$1,800

Model 1960A/1960B 4x12 Speaker Cabinet
1980-1983 (260 watts), '84-'86 (280 watts, JCM 800 era), '86-'90 (300 watts, JCM 800 era), '90-2000 (300 watts, JCM 900 era, stereo-mono switching). A for slant front, B straight.

1980-1983	Black	$550	$700
1980-1983	Custom color	$800	$1,000
1984-1986	Black	$450	$550
1984-1986	Custom color	$700	$850
1984-1986	Rare color	$900	$1,100
1986-1990	Black	$400	$500
1986-1990	Custom color	$650	$800
1986-1990	Rare color	$800	$1,000
2000-2007	Black	$375	$475

1976 Marshall Model 1959 Super Lead

Marshall Model 1959HW Stack

Marshall Model 1960A Slant Cab

AMPS

Marshall Model 1960TV 4X12 Cabinet

Marshall Model 1974x

Marshall Model 2060 Mercury

Model 1960AC Classic Speaker Cabinet
2005-2006. 4x12" Celestion G-12M-25 greenback speakers, black.

Year	Features	Low	High
2005-2006		$650	$800

Model 1960AHW 4x12 Slant Cabinet
2005-2008. Half stack slant front cab for HW series.

Year	Features	Low	High
2005-2008		$750	$950

Model 1960AV 4x12 Slant Cabinet
1990-present. JCM 900 updated, stereo/mono switching, AV slant, BV straight front.

Year	Features	Low	High
1990-1999	Black vinyl, black grille	$375	$475
1990-1999	Red vinyl, tan grille	$425	$525
2000-2010	Black	$375	$475

Model 1960AX/1960BX 4x12 Cabinet
1990-present. Cab for Model 1987X and 1959X reissue heads, AX slant, BX straight.

Year	Features	Low	High
1990-2010	AX	$650	$800
1990-2010	BX	$475	$600

Model 1960BV 4x12 Straight Cabinet
1990-present. JCM 900 updated, stereo/mono switching, AV slant, BV straight front.

Year	Features	Low	High
1990-1999	Black vinyl, black grille	$475	$600
1990-1999	Red vinyl, tan grille	$550	$650
2000-2010	Black	$475	$600

Model 1960TV 4x12 Slant Cabinet
1990-present. Extra tall for JTM 45, mono, 100 watts.

Year	Features	Low	High
1990-1999		$475	$600
2000-2010	Black	$475	$600

Model 1962 Bluesbreaker Combo Amp
1999-present. Similar to JTM 45 but with 2 reissue 'Greenback' 25-watt 2x12" speakers and addition of footswitchable tremolo effect.

Year	Features	Low	High
1999-2010		$1,000	$1,250

Model 1964 Lead/Bass 50-Watt Amp Head
1973-1976. Head with 50 watts, designed for lead or bass.

Year	Features	Low	High
1973-1976		$1,100	$1,300

Model 1965A/1965B Cabinet
1984-1991. 140 watt 4x10" slant front (A) or straight front (B) cab.

Year	Features	Low	High
1984-1991		$400	$500

Model 1966 Cabinet
1985-1991. 150 watt 2x12" cab.

Year	Features	Low	High
1985-1991		$325	$400

Model 1967 Major 200-Watt Amp Head
1968-1974. 200 watts, the original Marshall 200 Pig was not popular and revised into the 200 'Major'. The new Major 200 was similar to the other large amps and included 2 channels, 4 inputs, but a larger amp cab.

Year	Features	Low	High
1968		$3,200	$3,900
1969		$2,700	$3,200
1970		$2,500	$3,000
1971-1974		$1,500	$1,850

Model 1967 Pig 200-Watt Amp Head
1967-early-1968 only. Head with 200 watts. The control panel was short and stubby and nicknamed

the Pig, the 200-watt circuit was dissimilar (and unpopular) to the 50-watt and 100-watt circuits.

Year	Features	Low	High
1967-1968		$3,100	$3,500

Model 1968 100-Watt Super PA Amp Head
1966-1975. PA head with 100 watts, 2 sets of 4 inputs (identifies PA configuration), often used for guitar.

Year	Features	Low	High
1966-1969	Plexi	$3,200	$4,000
1969-1975	Aluminum	$2,800	$3,500

Model 1973 Amp
1965-1968. Tube combo, 18 watts, 2x12".

Year	Features	Low	High
1965		$8,000	$10,000
1966		$7,600	$9,400
1967		$6,200	$7,750
1968		$5,400	$6,700

Model 1973 JMP Lead/Bass 20 Amp
1973 only. Front panel: JMP, back panel: Lead & Bass 20, 20 watts, 1x12" straight front checkered grille cab, head and cab black vinyl.

Year	Features	Low	High
1973		$2,300	$2,800

Model 1974 Amp
1965-1968. Tube combo, 18 watts, 1x12".

Year	Features	Low	High
1965		$4,800	$6,000
1966		$4,800	$5,800
1967		$4,500	$5,500
1968		$4,000	$5,000

Model 1974X Amp
2004. Reissue of 18-watt, 1x12" combo.

Year	Features	Low	High
2004	1974CX ext. cab	$400	$475
2004	Combo amp	$1,300	$1,600

Model 1982 Cabinet
1970-1980. 100-watt, 4x12".

Year	Features	Low	High
1970-1980		$1,000	$1,250

Model 1986 50-Watt Bass Amp Head
1966-1981. Bass version of 1987, 50-watt.

Year	Features	Low	High
1966-1969	Black, plexi	$3,200	$4,000
1969-1970	Black, aluminum	$2,600	$3,300
1971-1972	Black, hand-wired, small box	$1,800	$2,300
1973-1975	Black, printed C.B., large box	$1,600	$2,000
1976-1979	Black	$1,100	$1,400
1980-1981	Black	$1,000	$1,300

Model 1987 50-Watt Amp Head
1966-1981. Head amp, 50 watts, plexiglas panel until mid-'69, aluminum panel after.

Year	Features	Low	High
1966-1969	Black, plexi	$3,700	$4,600
1966-1969	Custom color, plexi	$5,800	$7,200
1969-1970	Black, aluminum	$3,100	$3,850
1969-1970	Custom color, aluminum	$4,300	$5,350
1971-1972	Black, hand-wired, small box	$1,900	$2,375
1971-1972	Custom color, hand-wired	$3,000	$3,700
1973-1975	Black, printed C.B., large box	$1,700	$2,100
1973-1975	Custom color, printed C.B.	$1,900	$2,300
1976-1979	Black	$1,200	$1,500
1976-1979	Custom color	$1,800	$2,100

| MODEL | | EXC. COND. | |
YEAR	FEATURES	LOW	HIGH
1980-1981	Black	$1,100	$1,400
1980-1981	Custom color	$1,800	$2,100

Model 1987X Amp Head

1992-present. Vintage Series amp, all tube, 50 watts, 4 inputs, plexi.

1992-2009		$925	$1,075

Model 1992 Super Bass Amp Head

1966-1981. 100 watts, plexi panel until mid-'69 when replaced by aluminum front panel, 2 channels, 4 inputs.

1966-1969	Black, plexi	$3,500	$4,500
1966-1969	Custom color, plexi	$6,000	$7,500
1969-1970	Black, aluminum	$3,500	$4,300
1969-1970	Custom color, aluminum	$4,600	$5,600
1971-1972	Black, hand-wired, small box	$1,800	$2,300
1971-1972	Custom color, hand-wired	$3,100	$3,800
1973-1975	Black, printed C.B., large box	$1,700	$2,100
1973-1975	Custom color, printed C.B.	$1,900	$2,300
1976-1979	Black	$1,200	$1,500
1976-1979	Custom color	$1,900	$2,200
1980-1981	Black	$1,100	$1,400
1980-1981	Custom color	$1,500	$1,900

Model 1992LEM Lemmy Signature Super Bass Amp

2008-present. Lemmy Kilmister specs, matching 100-watt head with 4x12" and 4x15" stacked cabinets.

2008-2011	Full-stack	$4,300	$4,800

Model 2040 Artist 50-Watt Combo Amp

1971-1978. 50 watts, 2x12" Artist/Artiste combo model with a different (less popular?) circuit.

1971-1978		$2,000	$2,400

Model 2041 Artist Head/Cabinet Set

1971-1978. 50 watts, 2x12" half stack Artist/Artiste cab with a different (less popular?) circuit.

1971-1978		$2,000	$2,400

Model 2046 Specialist 25-Watt Combo Amp

1972-1973. 25 watts, 1x15" speaker, limited production due to design flaw (amp overheats).

1972-1973		$850	$1,000

Model 2060 Mercury Combo Amp

1972-1973. Combo amp, 5 watts, 1x12", available in red or orange covering.

1972-1973		$1,400	$1,700

Model 2061 20-Watt Lead/Bass Amp Head

1968-1973. Lead/bass head, 20 watts, plexi until '69, aluminum after. Reissued in '04 as the Model 2061X.

1968-1969	Black, plexi	$3,300	$3,900
1969-1973	Black, aluminum	$2,400	$3,000

Model 2061X 20-Watt Lead/Bass Amp Head Reissue

2004-present. Handwired Series, reissue of 2061 amp head, 20 watts.

2004-2010		$1,000	$1,250

Model 2078 Combo Amp

1973-1978. Solidstate, 100 watts, 4x12" combo, gold front panel, dark cover, gray grille.

1973-1978		$800	$1,000

Model 2103 100-Watt 1-Channel Master Combo Amp

1975-1981. One channel, 2 inputs, 100 watts, 2x12", first master volume design, combo version of 2203 head.

1975-1981		$1,200	$1,500

Model 2104 50-Watt 1-Channel Master Combo Amp

1975-1981. One channel, 2 inputs, 50 watts, 2x12", first master volume design, combo version of 2204 head.

1975-1981		$1,200	$1,500

Model 2144 Master Reverb Combo Amp

1978 only. Master volume similar to 2104 but with reverb and boost, 50 watts, 2x12".

1978		$1,550	$1,650

Model 2150 100-Watt 1x12 Combo Amp

1978. Tubes.

1978		$800	$1,000

Model 2159 100-Watt 2-Channel Combo Amp

1977-1981. 100 watts, 2 channels, 4 inputs, 2x12" combo version of Model 1959 Super Lead head.

1977-1981		$1,200	$1,500

Model 2200 100-Watt Lead Combo Amp

1977-1981. 100 watts, 2x12" combo, early solidstate, includes boost section, no reverb.

1977-1981		$800	$1,000

Model 2203 Lead Amp Head

1975-1981. Head amp, 100 watts, 2 inputs, first master volume model design, often seen with Mark II logo.

1975-1981	Black	$1,200	$1,450
1975-1981	Fawn Beige	$1,600	$1,800

Model 2203X JCM800 Reissue Amp Head

2002-2010. 100 watts

2002-2008		$1,000	$1,250

Model 2204 50-Watt Amp Head

1975-1981. Head only, 50 watts with master volume.

1975-1981		$1,200	$1,450

Model 2466 Amp Head

2007-present. Part of Vintage Modern series, 100 watts.

2007-2010		$775	$925

Model 3203 Artist Amp Head

1986-1991. Tube head version of earlier '84 Model 3210 MOS-FET, designed as affordable alternative, 30 watts, standard short cab, 2 inputs separated by 3 control knobs, Artist 3203 logo on front panel, black.

1986-1991		$375	$450

Model 3210 MOS-FET Amp Head

1984-1991. MOS-FET solidstate head, refer Mini-Stack listing for 3210 with 4x10" stacked cabinets. Early-'80s front panel: Lead 100 MOS-FET.

1984-1991		$250	$300

Marshall Model 2061X 20-Watt Lead

Marshall Model 2203X JCM 800 Reissue

Marshall Model 2466

Marshall MS-2

1946 Masco Map-15

Masco Sound System 100 watt

MODEL YEAR	FEATURES	EXC. COND. LOW	HIGH

Model 3310 100-Watt Lead Amp
1988-1991. Solidstate, 100 watts, lead head with channel switching and reverb.

1988-1991		$400	$475

Model 4001 Studio 15 Amp
1985-1992. 15 watts using 6V6 (only model to do this up to this time), 1x12" Celestion Vintage 30 speakers.

1985-1992		$550	$700

Model 4104 50-Watt Combo Amp
1981-1990. Combo version of 2204 amp, 20 watts, 1x10", master volume.

1981-1990		$1,200	$1,500

Model 4203 Artist 30 Combo Amp
1986-1991. 30-watt tube hybrid combo, 1x12", channel switching.

1986-1991		$425	$525

Model 5002 Combo Amp
1984-1991. Solidstate combo amp, 20 watts, 1x10", master volume.

1984-1991		$175	$200

Model 5005 Combo Amp
1984-1991. Solidstate, 12 watts, 1x10", practice amp with master volume, headphones and line-out.

1984-1991		$150	$175

Model 5302 Keyboard Amp
1984-1988. Solidstate, 20 watts, 1x10", marketed for keyboard application.

1984-1988		$150	$175

Model 5502 Bass Amp
1984-ca.1992. Solidstate bass combo amp, 20 watts, 1x10" Celestion.

1984-1992		$150	$175

Model 6100 30th Anniversary Amp
1992-1995. Matching head with 100/50/25 switchable watts and 4x12" cabinet (matching colors), first year was blue tolex.

1992	Half-stack	$1,300	$1,600
1992-1993	1x12" combo	$1,100	$1,400
1992-1995	Head only	$750	$900
1993-1995	Half-stack	$1,200	$1,400

Model 6101 Combo Amp
1992-1995. 1x12" combo, 100 watts.

1992-1995		$1,100	$1,300

Model 6101 LE Amp
1992-1995. Limited Edition, 1x12", 100/50/25 switchable watts, blue/purple cover.

1992-1995	Half-stack	$1,300	$1,600
1992-1995	Head only	$800	$1,000

Model 8008 Valvestate Rackmount Amp
1991-2001. Valvestate solidstate rack mount power amp with dual 40-watt channels.

1991-2001		$300	$375

Model 8010 Valvestate VS15 Combo Amp
1991-1997. Valvestate solidstate, 10 watts, 1x8", compact size, black vinyl, black grille.

1991-1997		$125	$150

Model 8040 Valvestate 40V Combo Amp
1991-1997. Valvestate solidstate with tube preamp, 40 watts, 1x12", compact size, black vinyl, black grille.

1991-1997		$275	$325

Model 8080 Valvestate 80V Combo Amp
1991-1997. Valvestate solidstate with tube 12AX7 preamp, 80 watts, 1x12", compact size, black vinyl, black grille.

1991-1997		$300	$350

Model 8100 100-Watt Valvestate VS100H Amp Head
1991-2001. Valvestate solidstate head, 100 watts.

1991-2001		$325	$375

Model 8200 200-Watt Valvestate Amp Head
1993-1998. Valvestate solidstate reverb head, 2x100-watt channels.

1993-1998		$375	$425

Model 8222 Valvestate Cabinet
1993-1998. 200 watts, 2x12 extention cab, designed for 8200 head.

1993-1998		$375	$425

Model 8240 Valvestate Stereo Chorus Amp
1992-1996. Valvestate, 80 watts (2x40 watts stereo), 2x12" combo, reverb, chorus.

1992-1996		$400	$450

Model 8280 2x80-Watt Valvestate Combo Amp
1993-1996. Valvestate solidstate, 2x80 watts, 2x12".

1993-1996		$450	$500

Model 8412 Valvestate Cabinet
1991-2001. 140 watts, 4x12 extention cab, designed for 8100 head.

1991-2001		$350	$425

MS-2/R/C Amp
1990-present. One watt, battery operated, miniature black half-stack amp and cab. Red MS-2R and checkered speaker grille and gold logo MS-2C added in '93.

1990-2010		$25	$30

MS-4 Amp
1998-present. Full-stack version of MS-2, black.

1998-2010		$45	$50

P.A. 20 Amp
1969-1970. Simple public address format with 2 channels each with volume and tone controls, front panel has JMP logo, rear panel has P.A. 20 logo, aluminum panel, 2 speaker outs.

1969-1970	Head only	$1,900	$2,300

Silver Jubilee Model 2550 50/25 (Tall) Amp Head
1987-1989. 50/25 switchable tall box head for full Jubilee stack.

1987-1989		$1,600	$1,900

Silver Jubilee Model 2551 4x12 Cabinet
1987-1989. Matching silver 4x12" cab for Jubilee 2550 head, various models.

1987-1989	2551A, slant, half-stack	$900	$1,100
1987-1989	2551AV, slant, half-stack	$900	$1,100
1987-1989	2551B, straight, full-stack	$900	$1,100
1987-1989	2551BV, Vintage 30	$925	$1,125

MODEL YEAR	FEATURES	EXC. COND. LOW	HIGH

Silver Jubilee Model 2553 (Short) 2556A (Mini)

1987-1989. Short box, 100/50 watt, two 2x12".

1987-1989		$2,500	$3,000

Silver Jubilee Model 2553 50/25 (Short) Amp Head

1987-1989. 50/25 switchable small box head for mini-short stack.

1987-1989		$1,400	$1,700

Silver Jubilee Model 2554 1x12 Combo Amp

1987-1989. 50/25 watts, 1x12" combo using 2550 chassis.

1987-1989		$1,800	$2,200

Silver Jubilee Model 2555 Amp Head

1987-1989. 100/50 version of 2550 head, cosmetic condition is exceptionally important on this model.

1987-1989		$2,000	$2,500

Silver Jubilee Model 2555 Amp with Full Stack

1987-1989. Silver vinyl covering, chrome control panel, 100/50 watts with 2 2551A 4x12" cabinets, cosmetic condition is exceptionally important on this model.

1987-1989		$4,000	$5,000

Silver Jubilee Model 2555 Amp with Half Stack

1987-1989. 100/50 watts, one 4x12", cosmetic condition is exceptionally important on this model.

1987-1989		$3,200	$4,000

Silver Jubilee Model 2556 4x12 Cabinet

1987-1989. Cab with 4x12" speakers, various models.

1987-1989	2556A, slant, half-stack	$525	$650
1987-1989	2556AV, slant, half-stack	$525	$675
1987-1989	2556B, straight, full-stack	$525	$675
1987-1989	2556BV, Vintage 30	$525	$675

Silver Jubilee Model 2558 2x12 Combo Amp

1987-1989. 50/25 watts, 2x12" combo using 2550 chassis.

1987-1989		$2,000	$2,500

Martin

Martin has dabbled in amps a few times, under both the Martin and Stinger brand names. The first batch were amps made by other introduced with their electric acoustics in 1959.

Model 112 Amp

1959-1960. Branded C.F. Martin inside label, made by Rowe-DeArmond, 1x12 combo, limited production, 2x6V6 power tubes, 2x12AX7 preamp tubes, with tube rectifier, 4 inputs, 3 control knobs.

1959-1960		$1,500	$1,700

SS140 Amp

1965		$600	$725

Stinger FX-1 Amp

1988-1990. 10 watts, EQ, switchable solidstate tube-synth circuit, line out and footswitch jacks.

1988		$125	$150

Stinger FX-1R Amp

1988-1990. Mini-stack amp, 2x10", 15 watts, dual-stage circuitry.

1989		$150	$175

Stinger FX-6B Amp

1989-1990. Combo bass amp, 60 watts, 1x15".

1989		$150	$175

Masco

1940s-1950s. The Mark Alan Sampson Company, Long Island, New York, produced a variety of electronic products including tube PA amps and small combo instrument amps. The PA heads are also popular with harp players.

Massie

1940s. Ray Massie worked in Leo Fender's repair shop in the 1940s and also built tube amps. He later worked at the Fender company.

Matamp

1966-present. Tube amps, combos and cabinets built in Huddersfield, England, bearing names like Red, Green, White, Black, and Blue. German-born Mat Mathias started building amps in England in '58 and designed his first Matamp in '66. From '69 to '73, Mathias also made Orange amps. In '89, Mathias died at age 66 and his family later sold the factory to Jeff Lewis.

1x15" Cabinet

1970s		$550	$650

GT-120 Amp Head

1971		$2,000	$2,500

GT-120 Green Stack Amp

1990s. 120 watt GT head with 4x12" straight front cab.

1993-1999		$1,450	$1,800

Matchless

1989-1999, 2001-present. Founded by Mark Sampson and Rick Perrotta in California. Circuits based on Vox AC-30 with special attention to transformers. A new Matchless company was reorganized in 2001 by Phil Jamison, former head of production for the original company.

Brave 40 112 Amp

1997-1999. 40 watts class A, 1x12", footswitchable between high and low inputs.

1997-1999		$1,300	$1,600

Brave 40 212 Amp

1997-1999. 2x12" version of Brave.

1997-1999		$1,500	$1,900

Chief Amp Head

1995-1999. 100 watts class A, head.

1995-1999		$2,500	$3,200

Chief 212 Amp

1995-1999. 100 watts class A, 2x12", reverb.

1995-1999		$2,500	$3,200

Massie Amp

Matamp 1224

Matchless Avalon 30

AMPS

Matchless Chieftan

Matchless DC-30

Matchless SC-30 Standard

MODEL YEAR	FEATURES	EXC. COND. LOW	HIGH
Chief 410 Amp			
1995-1999. 100 watts class A, 4x10", reverb.			
1995-1999		$2,500	$3,200
Chieftan Amp			
1995-1999. 40 watts class A head, reverb, chicken-head knobs.			
1995-1999	Head only	$1,500	$1,900
1995-1999	Matching head & cab	$2,200	$2,700
Chieftan 112 Amp			
1995-1999, 2001. 40 watts class A, 1x12", reverb.			
1995-1999		$2,000	$2,500
2001	Jamison era	$2,000	$2,500
Chieftan 210 Amp			
1995-1999. 40 watts class A, 2x10", reverb.			
1995-1999		$2,000	$2,500
Chieftan 212 Amp			
1995-1999, 2001. 40 watts class A, 2x12", reverb.			
1995-1999		$2,200	$2,800
2001	Jamison era	$2,200	$2,800
Chieftan 410 Amp			
1995-1999. 40 watts class A, 4x10", reverb.			
1995-1999		$2,200	$2,800
Clipper 15 112 Amp			
1998-1999. 15 watts, single channel, 1x12".			
1998-1999		$900	$1,100
Clipper 15 210 Amp			
1998-1999. 15 watts, single channel, 2x10".			
1998-1999		$900	$1,100
Clubman 35 Amp Head			
1993-1999. 35 watts class A head.			
1993-1999		$1,600	$2,000
DC-30 Standard Cabinet			
1991-1999. 30 watts, 2x12", with or without reverb.			
1991-1999	Non-reverb	$2,800	$3,400
1991-1999	With reverb	$2,900	$3,500
DC-30 Exotic Wood Cabinet Option			
1995-1999. 30 watts, 2x12", gold plating, limited production.			
1995-1999	Non-reverb	$4,000	$5,000
1995-1999	With reverb	$4,200	$5,200
EB115 Bass Cabinet			
1997-1999. 1x15" bass speaker cabinet.			
1997-1999		$325	$400
EB410 Bass Cabinet			
1997-1999. 4x10" bass speaker cabinet.			
1997-1999		$375	$450
ES/210 Cabinet			
1993-1999. 2x10" speaker cabinet.			
1993-1999		$375	$450
ES/410 Cabinet			
1993-1999. 4x10" speaker cabinet.			
1993-1999		$500	$600
ES/412 Cabinet			
1993-1999. 4x12" speaker cabinet.			
1993-1999		$525	$650
ES/1012 Cabinet			
1993-1999. 2x10" and 2x12" speaker cabinet.			
1993-1999		$525	$650

MODEL YEAR	FEATURES	EXC. COND. LOW	HIGH
ES/D Cabinet			
1993-1999. 2x12" speaker cabinet.			
1993-1999		$500	$600
ES/S Cabinet			
1991-1999. 1x12" speaker cabinet.			
1991-1999		$375	$450
HC-30 Amp Head			
1991-1999, 2003. The first model offered by Matchless, 30 watts class A head.			
1991-1999	Head only	$2,000	$2,500
2003	Jamison era	$2,000	$2,500
HC-85 Amp Head			
1992. Only 25 made, similar to HC-30 but more flexible using various tube substitutions.			
1992		$2,200	$2,700
Hurricane Amp Head			
1997. 15 watts class A head.			
1997		$1,100	$1,300
Hurricane 112 Amp			
1994-1997. 15 watts class A, 1x12".			
1994-1997		$1,200	$1,400
Hurricane 210 Amp			
1996-1997. 15 watts class A, 2x10".			
1996-1997		$1,200	$1,400
JJ-30 112 John Jorgensen Amp			
1997-1999. 30 watts, DC-30 chasis with reverb and tremolo, 1x12" Celestion 30, offered in white, blue, gray sparkle tolex or black.			
1997-1999		$3,500	$4,500
Lightning 15 Amp Head			
1997. 15 watts class A head.			
1997		$1,400	$1,700
Lightning 15 112 Amp			
1994-1999, 2001. 15 watts class A, 1x12".			
1994-1999	Non-reverb	$1,600	$2,000
1997-1999	Jamison era	$1,600	$2,000
2001	Jamison era	$1,600	$2,000
Lightning 15 210 Amp			
1996-1997, 2001-2006. 15 watts class A, 2x10".			
1996-1997	Non-reverb	$1,450	$1,750
1997	With reverb	$1,550	$1,850
2001-2006	Jamison era	$1,550	$1,850
Lightning 15 212 Amp			
1996-1997. 15 watts class A, 2x12".			
1996-1997	Non-reverb	$1,650	$2,000
1997	With reverb	$1,750	$2,100
Little Monster Amp			
2007-2009. 9 watts, offered as head, and 1x12" or 2x12" combo.			
2007-2009		$950	$1,200
Nighthawk Amp			
2003-present. 15 watts, offered as head, and 1x12" or 2x12" combo.			
2003-2010	1x12	$1,000	$1,250
SC-30 Standard Cabinet Amp			
1991-1999. 30 watts class A, 1x12".			
1991-1999	Non-reverb	$2,300	$2,900
1991-1999	With reverb	$2,400	$3,000
2001-2006	Jamison era	$2,200	$2,800

The *Vintage Guitar Price Guide* shows low to high values for items in all-original excellent condition, and, where applicable, with original case or cover.

MODEL YEAR	FEATURES	EXC. COND. LOW	HIGH

SC-30 Exotic Wood Cabinet Amp
1995-1999. 30 watts class A, 1x12", gold plating, limited production.

| 1995-1999 | Non-reverb | $3,800 | $4,700 |
| 1995-1999 | With reverb | $3,900 | $4,800 |

Skyliner Reverb 15 112 Amp
1998-1999. 15 watts, 2 channels, 1x12".

| 1998-1999 | | $800 | $1,000 |

Skyliner Reverb 15 210 Amp
1998-1999. 15 watts, 2 channels, 2x10".

| 1998-1999 | | $800 | $1,000 |

Spitfire 15 Amp Head
1997. 15 watts, head.

| 1997 | | $900 | $1,100 |

Spitfire 15 112 Amp
1994-1997. 15 watts, 1x12".

| 1994-1997 | | $1,200 | $1,500 |

Spitfire 15 210 Amp
1996-1997. 15 watts, 2x10".

| 1996-1997 | | $1,200 | $1,500 |

Starliner 40 212 Amp
1999. 40 watts, 2x12".

| 1999 | | $1,300 | $1,600 |

Superchief 120 Amp Head
1994-1999. 120 watts, class A head.

| 1994-1999 | | $1,800 | $2,200 |

TC-30 Standard Cabinet Amp
1991-1999. 30 watts, 2x10" class A, low production numbers makes value approximate with DC-30.

| 1991-1999 | Non-reverb | $2,200 | $2,800 |
| 1991-1999 | With reverb | $2,300 | $2,900 |

TC-30 Exotic Wood Cabinet Amp
1991-1999. 30 watts, 2x10" class A, limited production.

| 1991-1999 | Non-reverb | $2,800 | $3,400 |
| 1991-1999 | With reverb | $2,900 | $3,500 |

Thunderchief Bass Amp Head
1994-1999. 200 watts, class A bass head.

| 1994-1999 | | $1,600 | $2,000 |

Thunderman 100 Bass Combo Amp
1997-1998. 100 watts, 1x15" in portaflex-style flip-top cab.

| 1997-1998 | | $1,700 | $2,100 |

Tornado 15 112 Amp
1994-1995. Compact, 15 watts, 1x12", 2-tone covering, simple controls--volume, tone, tremolo speed, tremolo depth.

| 1994-1995 | | $750 | $950 |

Maven Peal
1999-present. Amps, combos and cabinets built by David Zimmerman in Plainfield, Vermont (the name stands for "expert sound"). Serial number format is by amp wattage and sequential build; for example, 15-watt amp 15-001, 30-watt 30-001, and 50-watt 50-001 with the 001 indicating the first amp built. S = Silver Series, no alpha = Gold Series.

Mega Amplifiers
Budget and intermediate grade, production, solidstate and tube amps from Guitar Jones, Inc. of Pomona, California.

Merlin
Rack mount bass heads built in Germany by Musician Sound Design. They also offer the MSD guitar effects.

Mesa-Boogie
1971-present. Founded by Randall Smith in San Francisco, California. Circuits styled on high-gain Fender-based chassis designs, ushering in the compact high-gain amp market. The following serial number information and specs courtesy of Mesa Engineering.

.50 Caliber/.50 Caliber+ Amp Head
Jan. 1987-Dec. 1988, 1992-1993. Serial numbers: SS3100 - SS11,499. Mesa Engineering calls it Caliber .50. Tube head amp, 50 watts, 5-band EQ, effects loop. Called the .50 Caliber Plus in '92 and '93.

| 1987-1988 | Caliber | $500 | $600 |
| 1992-1993 | Caliber+ | $500 | $600 |

.50 Caliber+ Combo Amp
Dec. 1988-Oct. 1993. Serial numbers FP11,550 - FP29,080. 50 watts, 1x12" combo amp.

| 1988-1993 | | $600 | $725 |

20/20 Amp
Jun. 1995-2010. Serial numbers: TT-01. 20-22 watts per channel.

| 1995-2010 | | $600 | $725 |

50/50 (Fifty/Fifty) Amp
May 1989-2001. Serial numbers: FF001-. 100 watts total power, 50 watts per channel, front panel reads Fifty/Fifty, contains 4 6L6 power tubes.

| 1989-2001 | | $600 | $725 |

395 Amp
Feb. 1991-Apr. 1992. Serial numbers: S2572 - S3237.

| 1991-1992 | | $700 | $850 |

Bass 400/Bass 400+ Amp Head
Aug. 1989-Aug. 1990. Serial numbers: B001-B1200. About 500 watts using 12 5881 power tubes. Replaced by 400+ Aug.1990-present, serial numbers: B1200- . Update change to 7-band EQ at serial number B1677.

| 1989-1990 | Bass 400 | $900 | $1,050 |
| 1990-1999 | Bass 400+ | $900 | $1,050 |

Big Block Series Amp
2004-present. Rackmount bass amps, models 750 and Titan V-12.

| 2004-2010 | 750 Bass Head, 750w | $950 | $1,150 |
| 2006-2010 | Titan V-12, 650-1200w | $950 | $1,150 |

Blue Angel Series Amp
Jun. 1994-2004. Serial numbers BA01-. Lower power 4x10" combo, blue cover.

| 1994-2004 | | $775 | $950 |

Buster Bass Amp Head
Dec. 1997-Jan. 2001. Serial numbers: BS-1-999. 200 watts via 6 6L6 power tubes.

| 1997-2001 | | $500 | $625 |

Buster Bass Combo Amp
1999-2001. 200 watts, 2x10", wedge cabinet, black vinyl, metal grille.

| 1999-2001 | | $525 | $650 |

Matchless Skyliner Reverb

Maven Peal Naked Zeeta 1->50

Mesa-Boogie Big Block 750

Mesa-Boogie Lone Star

Mesa-Boogie Mark 1

Mesa-Boogie Mark IV B Reissue

MODEL YEAR	FEATURES	EXC. COND. LOW	HIGH
Coliseum 300 Amp			
Oct. 1997-2000. Serial numbers: COL-01 - COL-132. 200 watts/channel, 12 6L6 power tubes, rack mount.			
1997-2000		$1,000	$1,250
D-180 Amp Head			
Jul. 1982-Dec. 1985. Serial numbers: D001-D681. All tube head amp, 200 watts, preamp, switchable.			
1982-1985		$775	$900
DC-3 Amp			
Sep. 1994-Jan. 1999. Serial numbers: DC3-001 - DC3-4523. 35 watts, 1x12".			
1994-1999	Combo 1x12"	$575	$700
1994-1999	Head only	$575	$700
DC-5 Amp			
Oct. 1993-Jan. 1999. Serial numbers: DC1024 - DC31,941. 50-watt head, 1x12" combo.			
1993-1999	Combo 1x12"	$750	$850
1993-1999	Head only	$750	$850
DC-10 Amp			
May 1996-Jan. 1999. Serial numbers: DCX-001 - DCX-999. Dirty/Clean (DC), 100 watts (6L6s), 2x12".			
1993-1996	Combo 2x12"	$850	$1,000
1996-1999	Head only	$700	$800
Express Series Amp			
2007-present. Compact combo or head tube amps with power switching.			
2007-2010	5:25, 1x10", 5-25w	$725	$875
2007-2010	5:50, 1x12", 5-50w	$775	$925
2008	5:25, short head	$575	$700
Extension Cabinet			
1990-present. Mesa-Boogie offered cabs as 'extension cabinets' which could be mixed and matched with amp heads, using different configurations with correct impedence, most other manufacturers considered an extension cab as an extra cab, but Mesa Engineering considered the extension cab to be the main cab (not an extra), grille could be metal or cloth.			
1990s	Verticle 2x12"	$350	$500
2000s	Horizontal 1x12"	$250	$400
2000s	Horizontal 2x12"	$350	$500
2000s	Slant 2x12"	$350	$425
2000s	Slant or straight 4x12"	$550	$675
2000s	Verticle 1x12"	$250	$400
2000s	Verticle 2x15"	$400	$500
2000s	Widebody 1x12"	$250	$325
F-30 Amp			
2002-Feb. 2007. Combo, 30 watts, 1x12".			
2002-2007		$575	$675
F-50 Amp			
2002-Feb. 2007. Combo, 50 watts, 1x12", AB 2 6L6 power.			
2002-2007		$675	$800
2002-2007	Head only	$600	$700
Formula Preamp			
Jul. 1998-2002. Serial numbers: F-01. Used 5 12AX7 tubes, 3 channels.			
1998-2002		$450	$550
Heartbreaker Amp Head			
1996-2001. Head only, 100 watts.			
1996-2001		$800	$950

MODEL YEAR	FEATURES	EXC. COND. LOW	HIGH
Heartbreaker Combo Amp			
Jun. 1996-2001. Serial numbers: HRT-01. 60 to 100 watts switchable, 2x12" combo, designed to switch-out 6L6s, EL34s or the lower powered 6V6s in the power section, switchable solidstate or tube rectifier.			
1996-2001		$925	$1,100
Lone Star Series Amp			
2004-present. Designed by founder Randall Smith and Doug West with focus on boutique-type amp. Class A (EL84) or AB (4 6L6) circuits, long or short head, 1x12" combo, 2x12" combo, and short head 4x10" cab, and long head 4x12" cab.			
2004-2010	1x12" combo	$1,200	$1,400
2004-2010	2x12" combo	$1,300	$1,600
2004-2010	4x10" combo, blue	$1,300	$1,600
2004-2010	Head, class A or AB	$1,025	$1,225
Lone Star Special Amp			
2005-present. Smaller lighter version using EL84 power tubes, 5/15/30 watts, long or short head amp or 1x12", 2x12" or 4x10" combo.			
2005-2010	1x12" combo	$1,200	$1,375
M-180 Amp			
Apr. 1982-Jan. 1986. Serial numbers: M001-M275.			
1982-1986		$575	$700
M-2000 Amp			
Jun. 1995-2003. Serial numbers: B2K-01.			
1995-2003		$750	$925
Mark I Amp Head			
1990. 60/100 watts, tweed cover.			
1990		$1,000	$1,200
Mark I Combo (Model A) Amp			
1971-1978. The original Boogie amp, not called the Mark I until the Mark II was issued, 60 or 100 watts, 1x12", Model A serial numbers: 1-2999, very early serial numbers 1-299 had 1x15".			
1971-1978	1x12" or 1x15"	$1,000	$1,200
Mark I Reissue Amp			
Nov. 1989-Sept. 2007. Serial numbers: H001- . 100 watts, 1x12", reissue features include figured maple cab and wicker grille.			
2000-2007	Hardwood cab	$1,450	$1,800
2000-2007	Standard cab	$800	$1,000
Mark II B Amp Head			
Head only.			
1981-1983		$650	$800
Mark II Combo Amp			
1978-1980. Late-'78 1x12", serial numbers: 3000-5574. Effective Aug.'80 1x15", serial numbers: 300-559 until Mark II B replaced.			
1978-1980	1x12" or 1x15"	$750	$900
Mark II B Combo Amp			
1980-1983. Effective Aug. '80 1x12" models, serial numbers 5575 - 110000. May '83 1x15" models, serial numbers 560 - 11000. The 300 series serial numbers K1 - K336.			
1981-1983	1x12" or 1x15", tolex	$750	$900
1981-1983	Custom hardwood cab	$1,450	$1,800

MODEL YEAR	FEATURES	EXC. COND. LOW	HIGH

Mark II C/Mark II C+ Amp

May 1983-Mar. 1985. Serial numbers 11001 - 14999 for 60 watts, 1x15", offered with optional white tolex cover. 300 series serial numbers after C+ are in the series K337 - K422.

1983-1985		$2,000	$2,300
1983-1985	White tolex	$2,000	$2,300
1985	Hardwood	$3,500	$4,200

Mark II C+ Amp Head

1983-1985. 60-watt head.

1983-1985	Hardwood	$3,500	$4,200
1983-1985	Standard	$1,700	$2,000

Mark III Amp Head

1985-1999. 100 watts, black vinyl.

1985-1990		$750	$850
1990-1999	Graphic EQ model	$1,000	$1,300

Mark III Combo Amp

Mar. 1985-Feb. 1999. Serial numbers: 15,000 - 28,384. 300 series serialization K500- . Graphic equalizer only Mark III since Aug.'90, 100 watts, 1x12" combo. Custom cover or exotic hardwood cab will bring more than standard vinyl cover cab.

1985-1990	Black	$850	$1,050
1985-1990	Custom color	$875	$1,100
1985-1999	Custom hardwood cab	$1,200	$1,500
1990-1999	Graphic EQ, hardwood cab	$1,375	$1,600
1990-1999	Graphic EQ, standard cab	$1,100	$1,350

Mark IV (Rack Mount) Amp Head

1990-May 2008. Rack mount version.

1990-2008		$1,100	$1,350

Mark IV Amp Head

1990-May 2008. Clean rhythm, crunch rhythm and lead modes, 85 watts, EQ, 3-spring reverb, dual effects loops, digital footswitching. Also available in custom hardwood cab with wicker grill.

1990-2008	Custom hardwood cab	$1,600	$1,900
1990-2008	Short head, tolex	$1,300	$1,600

Mark IV/Mark IV B Combo Amp

May 1990-May 2008. Changed to Model IV B Feb.'95, serial numbers: IV001. Clean rhythm, crunch rhythm and lead modes, 40 watts, EQ, 3-spring reverb, dual effects loops, digital footswitching.

1991-1999		$1,200	$1,450
1991-1999	Custom hardwood cab	$1,600	$1,900
2000-2008		$1,200	$1,450
2000-2008	Custom hardwood cab	$1,600	$1,900

Mark V Combo Amp

2010-present. 3 channels, 10/45/90 watts, 1x12, also offered as a head.

2010		$1,450	$1,650

Maverick Dual Rectifier Amp Head

1994-Feb. 2005. 35 watts, Dual Rectifier head, white/blond vinyl cover.

1994-2005		$750	$950

Maverick Dual Rectifier Combo Amp

1997-Feb. 2005. Dual channels, 4 EL84s, 35 watts, 1x12" or 2x12" combo amp, 5AR4 tube rectifier, cream vinyl covering. Serial number: MAV. Also available as head.

1997-2005	1x12"	$800	$1,000
1997-2005	2x12"	$825	$1,050

Maverick Dual Rectifier Half Stack Amp Set

Apr. 1994-2004. Serial numbers: MAV001-. 35 watts, Dual Rectifier head and half stack cab set.

1994-2004		$1,200	$1,500

M-Pulse 360 Amp

Jul. 2001-2005. Serial numbers: MP3-01- . Rack mount, silver panel.

2001-2003		$600	$725

M-Pulse 600 Amp

Apr. 2001-present. Serial numbers: MP6-01-. Rack mount bass with 600 watts, tube preamp.

2001-2010		$700	$850

Nomad 45 Amp Head

1999-Feb. 2005. 45 watts, dark vinyl cover, dark grille.

1999-2005		$550	$700

Nomad 45 Combo Amp

Jul. 1999-Feb. 2005. Serial numbers: NM45-01. 45 watts, 1x12, 2x12" or 4x10" combo, dark vinyl cover, dark grille.

1999-2005	1x12"	$600	$725
1999-2005	2x12"	$700	$850
1999-2005	4x10"	$700	$850

Nomad 55 Amp Head

1999-2004. 55 watt head only.

1999-2004		$550	$700

Nomad 55 Combo Amp

Jul. 1999-2004. Serial numbers: NM55-01. 55 watts, 1x12", 2x12" or 4x10" combo.

1999-2004	1x12"	$600	$725
1999-2004	2x12"	$700	$850

Nomad 100 Amp Head

Jul. 1999-Feb. 2005. 100 watts, black cover, black grille.

1999-2005		$700	$850

Nomad 100 Combo Amp

Jul. 1999-Feb. 2005. 100 watts, 1x12" or 2x12" combo, black cover, black grille.

1999-2005	1x12"	$725	$900
1999-2005	2x12"	$775	$950

Powerhouse Series Bass Cabinet

2004-present.

2004-2010	1x15", 400w	$450	$550
2004-2010	2x10", 600w	$500	$600
2004-2010	4x10", 600w	$550	$675

Princeton Boost Fender Conversion Amp

1970. Fender Princeton modified by Randall Smith, Boogie badge logo instead of the Fender blackface logo on upper left corner of the grille. About 300 amps were modified and were one of the early mods that became Mesa-Boogie.

1970		$2,100	$2,600

Mesa-Boogie M-Pulse 600

Mesa-Boogie Nomad 45

Mesa-Boogie Powerhouse Series Bass Cabinet

Mesa-Boogie Rect-O-Verb II Combo Amp

Mesa-Boogie Road King

Mesa-Boogie Roadster

MODEL YEAR	FEATURES	EXC. COND. LOW	HIGH

Quad Preamp
Sep. 1987-1992. Serial numbers: Q001-Q2857. Optional Quad with FU2-A footswitch Aug.'90-Jan.'92, serial numbers: Q2022 - Q2857.

1987-1992	Without footswitch	$475	$575
1990-1992	With footswitch	$575	$700

Recto Recording Preamp
2004-present. Rack mount preamp.

2004-2010		$700	$850

Rect-O-Verb Combo Amp
Dec. 1998-2001. Serial numbers R50- . 50 watts, 1x12", black vinyl cover, black grille.

1998-2001		$725	$900

Rect-O-Verb I Amp Head
Dec. 1998-2001. Serial numbers: R50-. 50 watts, head with 2 6L6 power tubes, upgraded Apr.'01 to II Series.

1998-2001		$700	$850

Rect-O-Verb II Amp Head
Apr. 2001-2010. Upgrade, serial number R5H-750.

2001-2010		$700	$875

Rect-O-Verb II Combo Amp
April 2001-2010. Upgrade R5H-750, 50 watts, AB, 2 6L6, spring reverb.

2001-2010		$800	$1,000

Rect-O-Verb/Recto Cabinet
1998-2001. Slant front 4x12" or 2x12" option cab, black cover, dark grille.

1998-2001	2x12" option	$325	$400
1998-2001	4x12" slant front	$500	$625

Road King Dual Rectifier Amp Head
2002-present. Tube head, various power tube selections based upon a chasis which uses 2 EL34s and 4 6L6, 2 5U4 dual rectifier tubes or silicon diode rectifiers, 50, 100 or 120 watts. Series II upgrades start in '06.

2002-2010		$1,600	$1,900
2006-2010	Series II	$1,600	$1,900

Road King Dual Rectifier Combo Amp
2002-present. 2x12" combo version, Series II upgrades start in '06.

2002-2005	Select watts	$1,750	$2,150
2006-2010	Series II	$1,750	$2,150

Roadster Dual Rectifier Amp
2006-present. 50/100 watts, head only or 1x12" or 2x12" combo.

2006-2010		$1,350	$1,550

Rocket 440 Amp
Mar. 1999-Aug. 2000. Serial numbers: R440-R44-1159. 45 watts, 4x10".

1999-2000		$675	$850

Satellite/Satellite 60 Amp
Aug. 1990-1999. Serial numbers: ST001-ST841. Uses either 6L6s for 100 watts or EL34s for 60 watts, dark vinyl, dark grille.

1990-1999		$450	$550

Solo 50 Rectifier Series I Amp Head
Nov. 1998-Apr. 2001. Serial numbers: R50. 50-watt head.

1998-2001		$750	$900

Solo 50 Rectifier Series II Amp Head
Apr. 2001-present. Upgrade, serial numbers: S50-S1709. Upgrades preamp section, head with 50 watts.

2001-2010		$750	$900

Solo Dual Rectifier Amp
1997-present. Triple Rectifier Solo logo on front panel, 3x5U4, 150 watts.

1997-2010		$900	$1,100

Solo Triple Rectifier Amp
1997-present. Triple Rectifier Solo logo on front panel, 3x5U4, 150 watts.

1997-2010		$1,150	$1,350

Son Of Boogie Amp
May 1982-Dec. 1985. Serial numbers: S100-S2390. 60 watts, 1x12", considered the first reissue of the original Mark I.

1982-1985		$550	$625

Stereo 290 (Simul 2-Ninety) Amp
Jun. 1992-present. Serial numbers: R0001- . Dual 90-watt stereo channels, rack mount.

1992-2010		$700	$850

Stereo 295 Amp
Mar. 1987-May 1991. Serial numbers: S001-S2673. Dual 95-watt class A/B stereo channels, rack mount. Selectable 30 watts Class A (EL34 power tubes) power.

1987-1991		$600	$750

Stilleto Ace Series Amp
2007-present.

2007-2010	1x12" combo	$1,000	$1,200
2007-2010	2x12" combo	$1,050	$1,275
2007-2010	Head only	$950	$1,150

Stilleto Series Amp Head
2004-present. Series includes the Deuce (50 or 100 watts, 4 EL-34s) and Trident (50 or 150 watts, 6 EL-34s).

2004-20010	Deuce\Trident	$1,100	$1,400

Strategy 400 Amp
Mar. 1987-May 1991. Serial numbers: S001-S2627. 400 to 500 watts, power amplifier with 12 6L6 power tubes.

1987-1991		$800	$950

Strategy 500 Amp
Jun. 1991-Apr. 1992. S2,552- . Rack mount, 500 watts, 4 6550 power tubes.

1991-1992		$850	$1,000

Studio .22/Studio .22+ Amp
Nov. 1985-1988. Serial numbers: SS000-SS11499, black vinyl, black grille, 22 watts, 1x12". Replaced by .22+ Dec. '88-Aug. '93. Serial numbers: FP11,500 - FP28,582. 22 watts.

1985-1988	.22	$500	$625
1988-1993	.22+	$500	$625

Studio Caliber DC-2 Amp
Apr. 1994-Jan. 1999. Serial numbers: DC2-01 - DC2-4247 (formerly called DC-2). 20 watts, 1x12" combo, dark vinyl, dark grille.

1994-1999		$425	$525

Studio Preamp
Aug. 1988-Dec. 1993. Serial numbers: SP000-SP7890. Tube preamp, EQ, reverb, effects loop.

1988-1993		$425	$525

MODEL		EXC. COND.	
YEAR	FEATURES	LOW	HIGH

Subway Reverb Rocket Amp
Jun. 1998-Aug. 2001. Serial numbers: RR1000-RR2461. 20 watts, 1x10".

1998-2001		$475	$600

Subway Rocket (Non-Reverb) Amp
Jan. 1996-Jul. 1998. Serial numbers: SR001-SR2825. No reverb, 20 watts, 1x10".

1996-1998		$475	$600

Subway/Subway Blues Amp
Sep. 1994-Aug. 2000. Serial numbers: SB001-SB2515. 20 watts, 1x10".

1994-2000		$450	$550

TransAtlantic TA-15 Amp Head
2010-present. Lunchbox-sized tube head, 2 channels, 5/15/25 watts.

2010		$675	$775

Trem-O-Verb Dual Rectifier Amp Head
Jun. 1993-Jan. 2001. 100-watt head version.

1993-2001		$825	$1,025
1993-2001	Rackmount version	$800	$1,000

Trem-O-Verb Dual Rectifier Cabinet
Late-1980s-early-1990s. Half stack 4x12" slant cab with open half back, or straight-front cab, 2x12" straight-front option, not strictly for this model, useable for any Boogie with matching output specs, often loaded with Celestion Vintage 30s, small weave grille (not see-thru crossing strips).

1988-1990s	2x12" straight	$525	$650
1988-1990s	4x12" slant or straight	$600	$750

Trem-O-Verb Dual Rectifier Combo Amp
Jun.1993-Jan.2001. Serial numbers: R- to about R-21210. 100 watts, 2x12" Celestion Vintage 30.

1993-2001		$1,000	$1,250

Trem-O-Verb Dual Rectifier Half Stack Amp
Jun.1993-Jan.2001. 100 watts, head with matching 4x12" slant cab.

1993-2001		$1,650	$2,100

Triaxis Preamp
Oct. 1991-present. Serial numbers:T0001-. 5 12AX7 tube preamp, rack mount.

1991-2010		$900	$1,100

Venture Bass (M-Pulse) Amp
2007-2009.

2007-2009		$600	$750

V-Twin Rackmount Amp
May 1995-Jun. 1998. Serial numbers: V2R-001 to V2R-2258.

1995-1998		$350	$425

WalkAbout M-Pulse Bass Amp Head
Sep. 2001-present. Serial numbers: WK-01-. Lightweight 13 pounds, 2 12AX7s + 300 MOS-FET.

2001-2010		$550	$650

Meteoro
1986-present. Guitar, bass, harp and keyboard combo amps, heads, and cabinets built in Brazil. They also build effects.

Metropoulos Amplification
2004-present. George Metropoulos builds his professional and premium grade amps in Flint, Michigan.

MG
2004-present. Tube combo guitar amps built by Marcelo Giangrande in São Paulo, Brazil. He also builds effects.

Mighty Moe Ampstraps
2007-present. Peter Bellak builds his guitar amp straps in Sacramento, California. He also offers an amp strap for ukulele.

Mission Amps
1996-present. Bruce Collins' Mission Amps, located in Arvada, Colorado, produces a line of custom-made combo amps, heads, and cabinets.

Mojave Amp Works
2002-present. Tube amp heads and speaker cabinets by Victor Mason in Apple Valley, California.

Montgomery Ward
Amps for this large retailer were sometimes branded as Montgomery Ward, but usually as Airline (see that listing).

Higher Power 1x12" Combo Amp
1950s. 1x12", about 2 6L6 power tubes, includes brown covered Maestro C Series with cloverleaf grille.

1950s		$400	$475

Lower Power 1x12" Combo Amp
1950s. 1x12" speaker, around 12 watts, includes Model 8439.

1950s		$325	$400

Mooneyes
Budget solid state amp line from Lace Music Products. They also offer amps under the Rat Fink and Lace brands. Lace has a Mooneyes guitar model line.

Morley
Late-1960s-present. The effects company offered an amp in the late '70s. See Effects section for more company information.

Bigfoot Amp
1979-ca.1981. Looks like Morley's '70s effects pedals, produced 25 watts and pedal controlled volume. Amp only, speakers were sold separately.

1979-1981		$150	$175

Mosrite
1968-1969. Mosrite jumped into the amp business during the last stages of the company history, the company was founded as a guitar company in 1954 and attained national fame in the '60s but by the time the company entered the amp business, the guitar boom began to fade, forcing the original Mosrite out of business in '69.

Mesa-Boogie Solo 50

AMPS

Mission Aurora Reverb

Mojave PeaceMaker

AMPS

1968 Mosrite 400 Fuzzrite
Dennis Carden

1981 Music Man 210 Sixty-Five
(KC Cormack)

1983 Music Man RD Fifty

MODEL YEAR	FEATURES	EXC. COND. LOW	HIGH
Model 400 Fuzzrite Amp			
1968-1969. Solidstate, 1x15 combo, black tolex with silver grille, reverb and tremolo.			
1968-1969		$625	$725
Model SS-550 The Gospel Amp			
1968. Solidstate, 1 speaker combo, 2 channels normal and tremolo, reverb, black tolex.			
1968		$550	$650

Mountain

Mountain builds a 9-volt amp in a wood cabinet. Originally built in California, then Nevada; currently being made in Vancouver, British Columbia.

Multivox

Ca.1946-ca.1984. Multivox was started as a subsidiary of Premier to manufacture amps, and later, effects. Generally student grade to low intermediate grade amps.

Murph

1965-1967. Amps marketed by Murph Guitars of San Fernado, California. At first they were custom-made tube amps, but most were later solidstate production models made by another manufacturer.

Music Man

1972-present. Music Man made amps from '73 to '83. The number preceding the amp model indicates the speaker configuration. The last number in model name usually referred to the watts. RD indicated Reverb Distortion. RP indicated Reverb Phase. Many models were available in head-only versions and as combos with various speaker combinations.

MODEL YEAR	FEATURES	EXC. COND. LOW	HIGH
Sixty Five Amp			
1973-1981. Head amp, 65 watts, reverb, tremolo.			
1973-1981		$450	$550
110 RD Fifty Amp			
1980-1983. 50 watts, 1x10", reverb, distortion.			
1980-1983		$550	$650
112 B Bass Amp			
1983. 50 watts, 1x12".			
1983		$550	$650
112 RD Fifty Amp			
1980-1983. 50 watts, 1x12", reverb, distortion.			
1980-1983		$550	$650
112 RD Sixty Five Amp			
1978-1983. 65 watts, 1x12", reverb, distortion.			
1978-1983		$550	$650
112 RD One Hundred Amp			
1978-1983. 100 watts, 1x12", reverb, distortion, EVM option for heavy duty 12" Electro-Voice speakers.			
1978-1983		$550	$650
1978-1983	EVM option	$550	$650
112 RP Sixty Five Amp			
1978-1983. 65 watts, 1x12", reverb, built-in phaser.			
1978-1983		$550	$650
112 RP One Hundred Amp			
1978-1983. Combo amp, 100 watts, 1x12", reverb, built-in phaser.			
1978-1983		$550	$650

MODEL YEAR	FEATURES	EXC. COND. LOW	HIGH
112 Sixty Five Amp			
1973-1981. Combo amp, 65 watts, 1x12", reverb, tremolo.			
1973-1977		$550	$650
1978-1981		$550	$650
115 Sixty Five Amp			
1973-1981. Combo amp, 65 watts, 1x15", reverb, tremolo.			
1973-1981		$550	$650
210 HD130 Amp			
1973-1981. 130 watts, 2x10", reverb, tremolo.			
1973-1981		$575	$675
210 Sixty Five Amp			
1973-1981. 65 watts, 2x10", reverb, tremolo.			
1973-1981		$575	$675
212 HD130 Amp			
1973-1981. 130 watts, 2x12", reverb, tremolo.			
1973-1981		$600	$700
212 Sixty Five Amp			
1973-1981. 65 watts, 2x12", reverb, tremolo.			
1973-1981		$600	$700
410 Sixty Five Amp			
1973-1981. 65 watts, 4x10", reverb, tremolo.			
1973-1981		$600	$700
410 Seventy Five Amp			
1982-1983. 75 watts, 4x10", reverb, tremolo.			
1982-1983		$600	$700
HD-130 Amp			
1973-1981. Head amp, 130 watts, reverb, tremolo.			
1973-1981	Head only	$500	$600
HD-150 Amp			
1973-1981. Head amp, 75/100 watts.			
1973-1981	Head only	$550	$650
RD Fifty Amp			
1980-1983. Head amp, 50 watts, reverb, distortion.			
1980-1983	Head only	$450	$550

Nady

1976-present. Wireless sound company Nady Systems started offering tube combo and amp heads in '06.

NARB

1973. Briefly made by Ken Bran and Jim Marshall, about 24 made, all were Marshall 100-watt tremolo half-stack, NARB logo on amp and cabinet.

MODEL YEAR	FEATURES	EXC. COND. LOW	HIGH
100 Watt Half-Stack			
1973. 100 watts, 4x12".			
1973		$3,300	$4,100

National

Ca.1927-present. National/Valco amps date back to the late-'30s. National introduced a modern group of amps about the same time they introduced their new Res-O-Glas space-age guitar models in '62. In '64, the amp line was partially redesigned and renamed. By '68, the Res-O-Glas models were gone and National introduced many large vertical and horizontal piggyback models which lasted until National's assets were assigned during bankruptcy in '69. The National name went to Chicago importer

MODEL		EXC. COND.	
YEAR	FEATURES	LOW	HIGH

Strum N' Drum. Initially, Strum N' Drum had one amp, the National GA 950 P Tremolo/Reverb piggyback.

Aztec Amp

1948-1953. Combo with 3 Rola 7x11" speakers using 3 speaker baffle openings, about 20 watts using 2x6L6 power tubes, Aztec logo on top chassis, 2-tone brown leatherette and tweed cover.

1948-1953		$750	$900

Bass 70/Bass 75 Amp

1962-1967. 35 watts (per channel), 2x12" (often Jensen) speakers, large control knobs, large National script logo on front control panel, Raven Black tolex with silver and white grille, designed for bass. New model name in '64 with nearly identical features but listed as total of 70 watts, in '62 called Bass 70 but renamed Bass 75 in '64.

1962-1963	Bass 70	$675	$825
1964-1967	Bass 75 N6475B	$675	$825

Chicago 51 Amp

1954. 1x10", 1x6V6, Chicago 51 logo name on control panel.

1954		$525	$625

Chicago 51 Aztec/Valco Amp

1948-1953. Low- to mid-power, 2x6L6, 3 oval Rola speakers, 3 baffle openings (1 for each speaker), tweed cover.

1948-1953		$750	$900

Chicagoan Model 1220 Amp

1948-1953		$750	$900

Dynamic 20 Amp

1962-1963. 17 watts, 2x8" (often Jensen) speakers, two large control knobs, large National script logo on front control panel, Raven Black tolex with silver and white grille, compact student-intermediate amp.

1962-1963		$575	$700

Glenwood 90 Amp

1962-1967. 35 watts, 2x12" (often Jensen) speakers, large control knobs, large National script logo on front control panel, reverb and tremolo, Raven Black tolex with silver and white grille, top of the line, becomes the nearly identical N6490TR in '64.

1962-1963		$1,100	$1,350
1964-1967	Model N6490TR	$1,000	$1,250

Glenwood Vibrato Amp

1964-1967. 70 watts, 2x12", vibrato and reverb.

1964-1967	Model N6499VR	$1,025	$1,150

Model 75 Amp

1940s. Vertical tweed combo cabinet, volume and tone knobs, 3 inputs.

1940s		$475	$575

Model 100 Amp

1940. Tube amp, 40 watts, 1x12".

1940		$500	$600

Model GA 950-P Tremolo/Reverb Piggyback Amp

1970s. Strum N' Drum/National model, solidstate, 50 watts, 2-channel 2x12" and 1x7" in 32" tall vertical cabinet, black.

1970s		$150	$250

Model N6800 - N6899 Piggyback Amps

1968-1969. National introduced a new line of tube amps in '68 and most of them were piggybacks. The N6895 was sized like a Fender piggyback Tremolux, the N6875 and N6878 bass amps were sized like a '68 Fender large cab piggyback with a 26" tall vertical cab, the N6898 and N6899 were the large piggyback guitar amps. These amps feature the standard Jensen speakers or the upgrade JBL speakers, the largest model was the N6800 for PA or guitar, which sported 3x70-watt channels and 2 column speakers using a bass 2x12" + 1x3" horn cab and a voice-guitar 4x10" + 1x3" horn cab.

1968-1969		$500	$600

Model N6816 (Model 16) Amp

1968-1969. Valco-made tube amp, 6 watts, 1x10" Jensen speaker, 17" vertical cab, tremolo, no reverb, black vinyl cover and Coppertone grille, National spelled out on front panel.

1968-1969		$375	$450

Model N6820 Thunderball Bass Amp

1968-1969. Valco-made tube amp, about 35 watts, 1x15" Jensen speaker, 19" vertical cab, black vinyl cover and Coppertone grille, National spelled out on front panel.

1968-1969		$425	$525

Model N6822 (Model 22) Amp

1968-1969. Valco-made, 6 watts tube (4 tubes) amp, 1x12" Jensen speaker, 19" vertical cab, tremolo and reverb, black vinyl cover and Coppertone grille, National spelled out on front panel.

1968-1969		$375	$450

National Dobro Amp

1930s. Sold by the National Dobro Corp. when the company was still in Los Angeles (they later moved to Chicago). National Dobro plate on rear back panel, suitcase style case that flips open to reveal the speaker and amp, National logo on outside of suitcase. The noted price is for an all-original amp in excellent condition (this would be a rare find), there are other 1930s models included in the price range below.

1930s	Early metal baffle	$500	$600
1930s	Later standard baffle	$400	$500
1930s	Suitcase style	$500	$600

Newport 40 Amp

1964-1967. 17 watts, 2x10", tremolo only.

1964-1967	Model N6440T	$650	$775

Newport 50 Amp

1964-1967. 17 watts, 2x10", tremolo and reverb.

1964-1967	Model N6450TR	$800	$1,000

Newport 97 Amp

1964-1967. 35 watts, 1x15", rear mounted chasis, tremolo.

1964-1967	Model N6497T	$625	$750

Sportman Amp

1950s	1x10"	$475	$575

Student Practice Amp

1970s. Strum N' Drum era, small solidstate, single control.

1970s		$25	$35

1950s National Valco

Nady GTA-1060

National Glenwood 90

AMPS

National Stagestar

Naylor Electra-Verb 60 Head

Nemesis NC-115

MODEL		EXC. COND.	
YEAR	FEATURES	LOW	HIGH

Studio 10 Amp
1962-1967. Five watts, 1x8", 3 tubes, 1 channel, 1 volume control, no tone control, no reverb or tremolo.

1962-1963		$375	$475
1964-1967	Model N6410	$375	$475

Tremo-Tone Model 1224 Amp
1956-1959. Small combo, tremolo, dual Rola oval 6x11" speakers, tweed, by Valco, National script logo, flying bird pattern on lower front grille.

1956-1959		$1,000	$1,250

Val-Pro 80 Amp
1962-1963. 35 watts, 2x12" (often Jensen) speakers, 8 tubes, large control knobs, tremolo, black cover with white and silver trim, replaced by Glenwood 90 in '64 with added reverb.

1962-1963		$1,000	$1,250

Val-Trem 40 Amp
1962-1963. 17 watts, 2x10" (often Jensen) speakers, large control knobs, large National script logo on front control panel, Val-Trem logo on back panel, Clear-Wave tremolo, Raven Black tolex with silver and white grille, open back combo amp, becomes Newport 40 in '64.

1962-1963		$800	$1,000

Val-Verb 60 Amp
1962-1963. 17 watts, 2x10" (often Jensen) speakers, large control knobs, large National script logo on front control panel, Val-Verb logo on back panel, reverb, no tremolo, Raven Black tolex with silver and white grille, open back combo amp.

1962-1963		$900	$1,100

Westwood 16 Amp
1964-1967. Five watts using 1 6V6 power, 2 12AX7 preamp, 1 5Y3GT rectifier, tremolo, 2x8", dark vinyl cover, silver grille.

1964-1967	Model N6416T	$525	$650

Westwood 22 Amp
1964-1967. 5 watts, 2x8", reverb and tremolo, 1 channel, 6 tubes.

1964-1967	Model N6422TR	$600	$750

Naylor Engineering
1994-present. Joe Naylor and Kyle Kurtz founded the company in East Pointe, Michigan, in the early '90s, selling J.F. Naylor speakers. In '94 they started producing amps. In '96, Naylor sold his interest in the business to Kurtz and left to form Reverend Guitars. In '99 David King bought the company and moved it to Los Angeles, California, then to Dallas, Texas. Currently Naylor builds tube amps, combos, speakers, and cabinets.

Nemesis
From the makers of Eden amps, Nemesis is a line of made-in-the-U.S., FET powered bass combos and extension cabinets. The brand is a division of U.S. Music Corp.

Newcomb
1950s. Newcomb Audio Products, Hollywood, California, Newcomb script logo on back panel

MODEL		EXC. COND.	
YEAR	FEATURES	LOW	HIGH

along with model number, they offered instrument amplifiers that could also be used as small PA.

Model G 12
1953. 1x12" (Rolla) combo amp, 2 controls (volume and tone), large metal handle, oxblood-brown leatherette.

1953		$175	$225

Nobels
1997-present. Effects manufacturer Nobels Electronics of Hamburg, Germany also offers a line of small practice and portable amps.

Noble
Ca. 1950-ca. 1969. From Don Noble and Company, of Chicago, Illinois, owned by Strum N' Drum by mid-'60s. They also offered guitars and amps.

Mid-Size Tube Amp
1950s. Low- to mid-power tube amp, Noble logo on front.

1950s		$600	$750

Norma
1965-1970. Economy line imported and distributed by Strum N' Drum, Wheeling (Chicago), Illinois. As noted in the National section, Strum N' Drum acquired the National brand in the '70s. Some early amps were tube, but the majority were solidstate.

GA-93 Amp
1969-1970. 6 watts, 1x6".

1969-1970		$50	$60

GA-97 T Amp
1969-1970. 13 watts, 1x8", tremolo.

1969-1970		$55	$65

GA-725 B Amp
1969-1970. Bass amp, 38 watts, 1x10".

1969-1970		$55	$65

GA-918 T Amp
1969-1970. 24 watts, 1x12", tremolo and reverb.

1969-1970		$65	$80

GA-930 P (Piggyback) Amp
1969-1970. 40 watts, 2x12", piggyback.

1969-1970		$75	$90

GA-6240 Amp
1969-1970. 50 watts.

1969-1970		$75	$90

GAP-2 Amp
1969-1970. 3 watts, 1x4".

1969-1970		$50	$60

Oahu
The Oahu Publishing Company and Honolulu Conservatory, based in Cleveland, Ohio, started with acoustic Hawaiian and Spanish guitars, selling large quantities in the 1930s. As electric models became popular, Oahu responded with guitar/amp sets. The brand has been revived on a line of U.S.-made tube amps.

MODEL YEAR	FEATURES	EXC. COND. LOW	HIGH

Combo Amp

1965. Small 1x10" combo, 1 6V6, 4 12AX7. 15Y3GT, white cover, light grille, Oahu script logo upper left grille.

1965		$500	$600

Mid-Size Amp

1940s-1950s. 1x10".

1940-1950s		$500	$600

Small Guitar/Lap Steel Amps

1940s-1950s. 1x8", various colors

1940-1950s		$375	$450

Oliver

Ca.1966-ca. 1978. The Oliver Sound Company, Westbury, New York, was founded by former Ampeg engineer, Jess Oliver, after he left Ampeg in '65. Tube amp designs were based upon Oliver's work at Ampeg. The Oliver Powerflex Amp is the best-known design, and featured an elevator platform that would lift the amp head out of the speaker cabinet.

Model B-120 Amp Head

1970s. B-120 logo on front panel, 35 watts, all tube head.

1970s		$350	$425

Model G-150R Combo Amp

1970s. Reverb, tremolo, 2 6L6 power tubes, 40 watts, 1x15", black tolex with black grille, silver control panel.

1970s		$500	$600

Model P-500 Combo Amp

1960s. All tube combo with 15" motorized amp chassis that rises out of tall lateral speaker cabinet as amp warms up.

1960s		$600	$725

Orbital Power Projector Amp

Late-1960s-early-1970s. Rotating speaker cabinet with horn, Leslie-like voice.

1970s		$600	$725

Sam Ash Oliver Amp Head

Late-1960s-early-1970s. Private branded for Sam Ash Music, about 30 watts using the extinct 7027A power tubes, Sam Ash script logo on front grille.

1960s		$250	$300

Omega

2009-present. James Price builds his premium grade, production/custom, amps in Moravian Falls, North Carolina.

Orange

1968-1981, 1995-present. Orange amps and PAs were made in England by Cliff Cooper and Matthew Mathias. The Orange-colored amps were well-built and were used by many notable guitarists. Since '95, Cliff Cooper is once again making Orange amplifiers in England, with the exception of the small Crush Practice Combo amps, which are made in Korea. '68-'70 amps made by Matamp in Huddersfield, classic designs started in '71 at Bexleyheath/London plant.

Model GRO-100 Graphic Overdrive Amp Head

1969-1971. Four EL34 power, only 2 pre-amp tubes, short-style head, model number on back panel.

1969-1971		$2,600	$3,200

Model OR-80 Amp

1971-1981. Half-stack head and cab, 80 watts, 4x12" straight-front cab with Orange crest on grille, orange vinyl and light orange grille.

1971-1975		$2,400	$3,000
1976-1981		$2,100	$2,700

Model OR-80 Combo Amp

1971-1981. About 80 watts, 2x12" combo.

1971-1975		$2,100	$2,600
1976-1981		$1,800	$2,300

Model OR-120 Graphic Amp

1972-1981. Half-stack head and cab, 120 watts, 4x12" straight front cab with Orange crest on grille, orange vinyl and light orange grille.

1972-1975		$2,900	$3,500
1976-1981		$2,000	$2,500

Model OR-200 212 Twin Amp

1970s. 120 watts, 2x12" combo, orange vinyl, dark grille, Orange crest on grille, reverb and vibrato, master volume.

1971-1975		$2,100	$2,600
1976-1981		$1,800	$2,300

Orepheus

Early 1960s. Private branded for Coast Wholesale Music Co., Orepheus logo on control panel along with model number.

Small Tube Amp

1960s. Student compact tube amps, some with 2 knobs, volume and tone.

1960s	Model 708	$300	$375

Orpheum

Late-1950s-1960s. Student to medium level amps from New York's Maurice Lipsky Music.

Small/Mid-Size Amps

Late-1950s-1960s. U.S.-made, 2 6V6 power tubes, Jensen P12R 12" speaker, light cover with gray swirl grille.

1959		$325	$400

Osborne Sound Laboratories

Late 1970s. Guitar amps built by Ralph Scaffidi and wife guitarist Mary Osborne in Bakersfield, California. They also offered guitars.

Ovation

1966-present. Kaman made few amps under the Ovation name. They offered a variety of amps under the KMD brand from '85 to around '94.

Little Dude Amp

1969-ca.1971. Solidstate combo, 100 watts, 1x15" and horn, matching slave unit also available.

1970s		$165	$200

Nobels SM-15 Streetman

*Ca. 1950 Oahu 230K
Tone Master*

Omega Amps

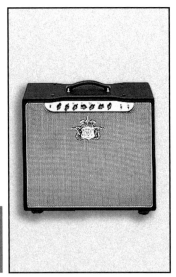

Overbuilt Napoleon

Palette 1X15 Combo

1970s Park 50-Watt Lead

MODEL YEAR	FEATURES	EXC. COND. LOW	HIGH

The Kat (Model 6012) Amp
1970s. Solidstate, 2x12" combo.

1970s		$165	$200

Overbuilt Amps
1999-2007. Tube amps and combos built by Richard Seccombe in West Hills, California. He nows works at Fender R&D.

PAC-AMP (Magnatone)
Late-1950s-early-1960s. Private branded by Magnatone, often for accordion studios.

Model 280-A Amp
1961-1963. About 50 watts, 2x12" + 2x5", brown leatherette, light brown grille, stereo vibrato, PAC-AMP nameplate logo.

1961-1963		$1,400	$1,700

Palette Amps
2003-present. Robert Wakeling builds his tube amp heads and combos and speaker cabinets in Stillwater, Oklahoma.

PANaramic (Magnatone)
1961-1963. Private branded equivalent of '61-'63 Magnatone brown leatherette series, large PANaramic logo. Many Magnatone private brands were associated with accordion companies or accordian teaching studios. PANaramic was a brand name of PANaramic accordion. They also made guitars.

Audio Guild Ultraflex Amp
1968. Vertical cabinet, pre-amp tubes, 1x12, 1x8.

1968		$550	$650

Model 260/262-style Amp
1961-1963. 35 watts, 2x12", gray vinyl and light grille, vibrato, large PANaramic logo.

1961-1963		$1,400	$1,700

Model 413-style Amp
1961-1963. 18 watts, 1x12", black leatherette cover, light silver grille, vibrato, large PANaramic logo.

1961-1963		$850	$1,000

Model 450-style Amp
1961-1963. 20 watts, 1x12", reverb and vibrato, reverb not generally included in an early-'60s 1x12" Magnatone amp, dark vinyl, dark cross-threaded grille, large PANaramic logo.

1961-1963		$1,350	$1,600

Model 1210 (250-style) Amp
1961-1963. 1x12" combo, 20 watts, 2.5 channels, true vibrato.

1961-1963		$1,000	$1,200

Paris
Master Series Amps
1960s. Compact solidstate combo, 1x12", slanted Paris logo front upper left side of grille, black tolex-style cover, silver grille (like Fender blackface), rear mounted slanted control panel.

1960s		$60	$75

MODEL YEAR	FEATURES	EXC. COND. LOW	HIGH

Park
1965-1982, 1992-2000. Park amps were made by Marshall from '65 to '82. Park logo on front with elongated P. In the '90s, Marshall revived the name for use on small solidstate amps imported from the Far East.

G Series Amp
1992-2000. Student compact amps, models include G-10 (10 watts, 1x8"), G-25R (25w, reverb), G-215R (15w, 2x8") and GB-25 (25w, 1x12" bass).

1990s	G-10	$40	$90
1990s	G-15R	$45	$100
1990s	G-215R	$80	$110
1990s	G-25R	$50	$100
1990s	GB-25	$45	$95

Lead 50 Combo Amp
1970s. 50 watts, 1x12".

1970s		$2,000	$2,500

Model 50 Amp Head
1967-1969. Plexi, 50 watts.

1967-1969		$4,000	$5,000

Model 75 Amp Head
1967-1971. Head amp, 50 watts, 2xKT88s, small-box plexi (later aluminum), black tolex.

1967-1969	Plexi	$4,000	$5,000
1969-1971	Aluminum	$3,100	$3,800

Model 75 1960 4x12 Slant Cabinet
Early 1970s. Similar to Marshall 1960 4x12" cab.

1970-1971		$1,750	$2,100

Model 1206 50-Watt Amp Head
1981-1982. 50 watts, based upon JCM 800 50-watt made at the same time period.

1981-1982		$850	$1,050

Model 1212 50-Watt 2x12 Combo
1970s. 50 watts, 2x12", reverb.

1970s		$1,700	$2,050

Model 1213 100-Watt Reverb Combo Amp
1970s. 100 watts, 2x12", reverb, dark vinyl, light grille.

1970s		$1,900	$2,300

Model 1228 50-Watt Lead Amp Head
1970s. 50 watts, based upon Marshall 50-watt made at the same time period.

1970s		$1,900	$2,400

Model 1231 Amp
1975. 20 watts, 1x12".

1975		$1,900	$2,400

Model 2046 25-Watt Combo Amp
1970s. 25 watts, 1x15", '70s era blue grille cloth, black tolex, large P Park logo upper center of grille.

1970s		$1,700	$2,100

Model 2203 100-Watt Amp Head

1970s		$1,900	$2,400

Paul Reed Smith
1985-present. In the late '80s, PRS offered two amp models. Only 350 amp units shipped. Includes HG-70 Head and HG-212 Combo. HG stands for Harmonic Generator, effectively a non-tube, solidstate amp. In '09, PRS introduced tube combo and head amps and cabinets designed by Doug Sewell.

AMPS

MODEL YEAR	FEATURES	EXC. COND. LOW	HIGH

4x12" Straight-Front Cabinet
1989. Straight-front 4x12" black vinyl cab with silver grille, PRS logo front lower right of grille.

1989		$500	$600

HG-70 Amp Head
1989-1990. 70 watts, reverb, effects loop, noise gate. Options include 150-watt circuitry and 4x12" straight and slant cabinets, gray-black.

1989		$500	$600

HG-212 Amp
1989-1990. Combo, 70 watts, 2x12", reverb, effects loop, noise gate. Options include 150-watt circuitry and 4x12" straight and slant cabinets, gray-black.

1989		$550	$675

Paul Ruby Amplifiers
2000-present. Professional grade, custom, tube amps built by Paul Ruby in Folsom, California.

Peavey
1965-present. Hartley Peavey's first products were guitar amps. He added guitars to the mix in '78. Headquartered in Meridan, Mississippi, Peavey continues to offer a huge variety of guitars, amps, and PAs. TransTube redesign of amps occurs in '95.

5150 212 Combo Amp
1995-2004. Combo version of 5150 head, 60 watts, 2x12", large 5150 logo on front panel, small Peavey logo on lower right of grille.

1995-2004		$525	$625

5150 EVH Head/Cabinet Amp Set
1995-2008. Half stack 5150 head and 4x12" cab, large 5150 logo on front of amp.

1995-2004	Cab only	$350	$425
1995-2004	Head & cab	$1,000	$1,250
1995-2008	Head only	$700	$825

5150 II Amp
2004. Has 5051 II logo on front, look for 'II' designation.

2004	Head & cab	$1,000	$1,250

6505 Series Amp
2008-present.

2008-2010	2x12" combo, 60w	$550	$750
2008-2010	6505+ head, 120w	$500	$700

Alphabass Amp
1988-1990. Rack mount all tube, 160 watts, EQ, includes 2x15" Black Widow or 2x12" Scorpion cabinet.

1988-1990		$250	$300

Artist Amp
Introduced in 1975 as 120 watts, 1x12", bright and normal channels, EQ, reverb, master volume.

1970s		$200	$225

Artist 110 Amp
1990s. TransTubes, 10 watts.

1990s		$100	$125

Artist 250 Amp
1990s. 100 watts, 1x12", solidstate preamp, 4 6L6 power tubes.

1990s		$175	$200

Artist VT Amp
1990s. Combo amp, 120 watts, 1x12".

1990s		$200	$250

Audition 20 Amp
1980s-1990s. 20 watts, single speaker combo.

1980-1990s		$40	$50

Audition 30 Amp
1980s-1990s. 30 watts, 1x12" combo amp, channel switching.

1980-1990s		$45	$55

Audition 110 Amp
1990s. 25 watts, 1x10" combo, 2 channels.

1990s		$55	$65

Audition Chorus Amp
1980s. 2x10-watt channels, 2x6", channel switching, post gain and normal gain controls.

1980s		$75	$100

Audition Plus Amp
1980s. Solidstate, 20 watts, 1x10".

1980s		$50	$65

Backstage Amp
1977-mid-1980s. Master gain control, 18 watts, 1x10", 3-band EQ. Name reused in 2000s on small 6.5" speaker, 10 watt amp.

1977-1984		$40	$50

Backstage 30 Amp
1980s. 30 watts, 1x8".

1980s		$40	$50

Backstage 110 Amp
Repackaged and revoiced in 1988, 65 watts, 1x10", Peavey SuperSat preamp circuitry, new power sections.

1980s		$50	$75

Backstage Chorus 208 Amp
1990s. 150 watts, 2x8", reverb, channel switching.

1990s		$100	$125

Backstage Plus Amp
1980s. 35 watts, 1x10" combo, reverb, saturation effect.

1980s		$55	$65

Bandit/65/75 Amp
1981-1989. 1x12" combo, originally 50 watts, upped to 65 watts in '85 and 75 in '87, renamed Bandit 112 in '90.

1981-1984	Bandit	$75	$100
1985-1986	Bandit 65	$75	$100
1987-1989	Bandit 75	$100	$125

Bandit 112/Bandit II 112 Amp
1990-2010. 80 watts (II is 100), 1x12", active EQ circuit for lead channel, active controls. TransTube in '95.

1990-1994		$125	$150
1994-2010	TransTube	$175	$200

Basic 40 Amp
1980s. 40 watts, 1x12".

1980s		$75	$100

Basic 60 Amp
1988-1995. Solidstate combo amp, 50-60 watts, 1x12", 4-band EQ, gain controls, black.

1988-1995		$125	$150

Basic 112 Bass Amp
1996-2006. 75 watts, 1x12" bass combo, 2000-era red border control panel.

1996-2006		$125	$150

PRS HG-212

Paul Ruby AX84 High Octane

Peavey 5150 2x12"

Peavey Classic 50/410

Peavey Envoy 110

Peavey Nashville 112

MODEL YEAR	FEATURES	EXC. COND. LOW	HIGH

Blazer 158 Amp
1995-2005. 15 watts, 1x8", clean and distortion, later called the TransTube Blazer III.

| 1995-2005 | | $65 | $80 |

Bluesman Amp
1992. Tweed, 1x12" or 1x15".

| 1992 | | $225 | $275 |

Bravo 112 Amp
1988-1994. All tube reverb, 25 watts, 1x12", 3-band EQ, 2 independent input channels.

| 1988-1994 | | $175 | $225 |

Butcher Amp Head
1985-1987, 2010-present. All tube head, 120 watts. Current version is all tube, 100 watts with half power switch

| 1985-1987 | | $325 | $400 |

Classic 20 Amp
1990s. Small tube amp with 2xEL84 power tubes, 1x10" narrow panel combo, tweed cover.

| 1990s | | $175 | $225 |

Classic 30 Amp
1994-present. Tweed combo, 30 watts, 1x12", EL84 tubes.

1994-2010	Narrow panel combo	$300	$375
2008-2010	Badge front	$275	$350
2008-2010	Head	$250	$325

Classic 50/212 Amp
1990-present. Combo, 50 watt, 2x12", 4 EL84s, 3 12AX7s, reverb, high-gain section.

| 1990-2010 | | $425 | $525 |

Classic 50/410 Amp
1990-present. Combo amp, 4x10", EL84 power, reverb, footswitchable high-gain mode.

| 1990-2010 | | $400 | $500 |

Classic 120 Amp
1988-ca.1990. Tube, 120 watts.

| 1988-1990 | | $325 | $400 |

DECA/750 Amp
1989-ca.1990. Digital, 2 channels, 350 watts per channel, distortion, reverb, exciter, pitch shift, multi-EQ.

| 1989-1990 | | $200 | $250 |

Decade Amp
1970s. Practice amp, 10 watts, 1x8", runs on 12 volt or AC.

| 1970s | | $30 | $35 |

Delta Blues Amp
1995-present. 30 watts, tube combo, 4 EL84 tubes, 1x15" or 2x8", tremolo, large-panel-style cab, blond tweed.

| 1995-2010 | | $400 | $475 |

Deuce Amp
1972-1980s. 120 watts, tube amp, 2x12" or 4x10".

| 1972-1980s | | $200 | $250 |

Deuce Amp Head
1972-1980s. Tube head, 120 watts.

| 1972-1980s | | $150 | $175 |

Ecoustic Series Amp
1996-present. Acoustic combo amps, 110 (1x12) and 112 (1x12, offered until '10) at 100 watts, digital effects (EFX, later E) added in '03. E20 and E208 added in '11.

| 2003-2010 | E110 | $125 | $150 |
| 1996-2010 | 112 | $125 | $150 |

MODEL YEAR	FEATURES	EXC. COND. LOW	HIGH

Encore 65 Amp
1983. Tube combo, 65 watts.

| 1983 | | $225 | $275 |

Envoy 110 Amp
1988-present. Solidstate, 40 watts, 1x10", Trans-Tubes.

| 1988-2010 | | $75 | $100 |

Heritage VTX Amp
1980s. 130 watts, 4 6L6s, solidstate preamp, 2x12" combo.

| 1980s | | $150 | $175 |

Jazz Classic Amp
1980s. Solidstate, 210 watts, 1x15", electronic channel switching, 6-spring reverb.

| 1980s | | $150 | $175 |

JSX (Joe Satriani) Amp
2004-2010. Joe Satriani signature, 120 watt tube head. Also offered were JSX 50 (50 watts, '09-'10), JSX 212 Combo ('05-'10) and 5-watt JSX Mini Colossal ('07-'10).

| 2004-2010 | 120 watt head | $500 | $525 |

KB Series Amp
1980s. Keyboard amp, 1x15", models include KB-100 (100 watts), and KB-300 (300 watts, with horn).

| 1980s | KB-100 | $150 | $175 |
| 1980s | KB-300 | $175 | $200 |

LTD Amp
1975-1980s. Solidstate, 200 watts, 1x12" Altec or 1x15" JBL.

| 1975-1982 | | $150 | $175 |

Mace Amp Head
1976-1980s. Tube, 180 watts.

| 1976-1980s | | $225 | $275 |

MegaBass Amp
1986-ca. 1992. Rack mount preamp/power amp, 200 watts per 2 channels, solidstate, EQ, effects loop, chorus.

| 1986-1992 | | $175 | $225 |

Microbass Amp
1988-2005. 20 watts, 1x8" practice amp, made in China.

| 1988-2005 | | $40 | $45 |

Minx 110 Bass Amp
1987-2005. Solidstate, 35 watts RMS, 1x10" heavy-duty speaker.

| 1987-2005 | | $85 | $105 |

Musician Amp Head
Introduced in 1965 as 120 watt head, upped to 210 watts in '72.

| 1965-1970s | | $125 | $150 |

Nashville 112 Steel Guitar Amp
2008-present. Compact size, 1x12", 80 watts.

| 2008 | | $375 | $450 |

Nashville 400 Steel Guitar Amp
1982- 2000. 210 watts, 1x15" solidstate steel guitar combo amp.

| 1982-2000 | | $375 | $450 |

Nashville 1000 Steel Guitar Amp
1998-2008. 1x15" speaker, solidstate steel guitar combo amp.

| 1998-2008 | | $375 | $450 |

The *Vintage Guitar Price Guide* shows low to high values for items in all-original excellent condition, and, where applicable, with original case or cover.

MODEL		EXC. COND.	
YEAR	FEATURES	LOW	HIGH

Pacer Amp
1974-1985. Master volume, 45 watts, 1x12", 3-band EQ.

1974-1985		$75	$100

ProBass 1000 Amp
1980s. Rack mount, effects loops, preamp, EQ, crossover, headphone output.

1980s		$125	$150

Rage/Rage 158 Amp
1988-2008. Compact practice amp, 15 watts, 1x8". 158 starts '95. Replaced by 25 watt Rage 258.

1988-2008		$25	$50

Reno 400 Amp
1980s. Solidstate, 200 watts, 1x15" with horn, 4-band EQ.

1980s		$125	$150

Renown 112 Amp
1989-1994. Crunch and lead SuperSat, 160 watts, 1x12", master volume, digital reverb, EQ.

1989-1994		$125	$150

Renown 212 Amp
1989-1994. Crunch and lead SuperSat, 160 watts, 2x12", master volume, digital reverb, EQ.

1989-1994		$150	$175

Renown 400 Amp
1980s. Combo, 200 watts, 2x12", channel switching, Hammond reverb, pre- and post-gain controls.

1980s		$200	$250

Revolution 112 Amp
1992-2002. 100 watts, 1x12" combo, black vinyl, black grille.

1992-2002		$175	$200

Session 400 Amp
1974-ca. 1999. 200 watts, 1x15 or early on as 2x12, steel amp, available in the smaller box LTD, offered as a head in '76, available in wedge-shaped enclosure in '88.

1974-1999		$275	$325

Session 500 Amp
1979-1980s. 250 watts, 1x15", steel amp.

1979-1985		$275	$325

Special 112 Amp
1980s. 160 watts, 1x12". In 1988, available in wedge-shaped enclosure.

1980s		$200	$250

Special 130 Amp
1980s. 1x12", 130 watts.

1980s		$200	$250

Special 212 Amp
1995-2005. 160 watts, 2x12, transtube, solidstate series.

1995-2005		$250	$300

Studio Pro 50 Amp
1980s. 50 watts, 1x12".

1980s		$115	$140

Studio Pro 112 Amp
1980s. Repackaged and revoiced in 1988. Solidstate, 65 watts, 1x12", Peavey SuperSat preamp circuitry, new power sections.

1980s		$125	$150

TKO Series Bass Amp
1978-present. Solidstate, 1x15, original TKO was 40 watts, followed by TKO 65 (65 watts) for '82-'87, TKO 75 for '88-'90, and TKO 80 for '91-'92. Renamed TKO 115 in '93 with 75, 80 or 100 watts until '09 when jumping to 400 watts.

1982-1987	TKO 65	$100	$125
1988-1990	TKO 75	$150	$175
1991-1992	TKO 80	$175	$200

TNT Series Bass Amp
1974-present. Solidstate, 1x15, original TNT was 45 watts, upped to 50 for '79-'81, followed by TNT 130 (130 watts) for '82-'87, TNT 150 for '88-'90, and TNT 160 for '91-'92. Renamed TNT 115 in '93 with 150, 160 or 200 watts until '09 when jumping to 600 watts.

1982-1987	TNT 130	$175	$225
1988-1990	TNT 150	$175	$225
1991-1990	TNT 160	$225	$275

Transchorus 210 Amp
1999-2000. 50 watts, 2x10 combo, stereo chorus, channel switching, reverb.

1999-2000		$225	$275

Triple XXX Series Amp
2001-2009. Made in USA.

2001-2009	Head, 120w	$550	$650
2001-2009	Super 40, 40w, 1x12	$400	$500

Triumph 60 Combo Amp
1980s. Tube head, effects loop, reverb, 60 watts, 1x12", multi-stage gain.

1980s		$150	$175

Triumph 120 Amp
1989-1990. Tube, 120 watts, 1x12", 3 gain blocks in preamp, low-level post-effects loop, built-in reverb.

1989-1990		$175	$200

Ultra 60 Amp Head
1991-1994. 60 watts, all tube, 2 6L6 power, black, black grille.

1991-1994		$225	$275

Ultra 112 Amp
1998-2002. 60 watts, 1x12", all tube, 2 6L6 power, black, black grille.

1998-2002		$250	$300

Ultra 212 Amp
1998-2002. 60 watts, 2x12".

1998-2002		$300	$350

Ultra 410 Amp
1998-2002. 60 watts, 4x10".

1998-2002		$300	$350

Ultra Plus 120 Amp Head
1998-2002. 120 watts, all tube.

1998-2002		$350	$400

Vegas 400 Amp
1980s. 210 watts, 1x15", some prefer as a steel guitar amp.

1980s		$325	$400

ValveKing Series Amp
2005-present. Tube head amp, combos and cabs.

2005-2010	100 w head	$250	$300

VTM Series Amp
1987-1993. Vintage Tube Modified series, head amps, 60 or 120 watts.

1987-1993	VTM-60	$275	$300

1978 Peavey TNT-100

AMPS

Peavey Special 112

Peavey Triple XXX Head

Peavey Vypyr Tube 60

Port City Dual Fifty

Randall R6-200 ES

MODEL YEAR	FEATURES	EXC. COND. LOW	HIGH

Vypyr Series Amp
2008-present. Modeling head amps and combos, 60 and 120 watt tube and 15, 30, 75 and 100 watt solidstate models.

| 2008-2010 | 15w, combo | $55 | $60 |

Wiggy 212 Amp
2001-2008. 100-watt head in mono (2x75-watt in stereo) with matching 2x12" cab, 2 EQ, 5-band sliders, rounded amp head.

| 2001-2008 | | $375 | $475 |

Penn
1994-present. Tube amps, combos, and cabinets built by Billy Penn, originally in Colts Neck, New Jersey, currently in Long Branch, New Jersey.

Pignose
1972-present. Made in Las Vegas, Nevada. Pignose Industries was started by people associated with the band Chicago, including guitarist Terry Kath, with help from designers Wayne Kimball and Richard Erlund. In '74, it was sold to Chicago's band accountant, who ran it until '82, when ownership passed to the company that made its sturdy, wood cabinets. They also offer guitars and effects.

7-100 Practice Amp
1972-present. The original Pignose, 7"x5"x3" battery-powered portable amplifier, 1x5".

| 1972-2010 | | $40 | $50 |

30/60 Amp
1978-ca.1987. Solidstate, 30 watts, 1x10", master volume.

| 1978-1987 | | $85 | $105 |

60R Studio Reverb Amp
Solidstate, 30 watts.

| 1980 | | $140 | $170 |

G40V Amp
2000s. Tubes, 1x10", 40 watts.

| 2000s | | $140 | $170 |

G60VR Amp
2000s. Tubes, 1x12", 60 watts.

| 2000s | | $145 | $175 |

Hog Amps
2000s. Battery powered, Hog 20 (20 watts, 6.5" speaker) and Hog 30 (30 watts, 8").

| 2000s | Hog 20 | $35 | $45 |
| 2000s | Hog 30 | $40 | $50 |

Plush
Late 1960s-early 1970s. Tuck and roll covered tube amps made by the same company that made Earth Sound Research amps in Farmingdale, New York.

Tube Amplifiers
Early 1970s. All tube heads and combos including the 450 Super 2x12" combo, 1000/P1000S head, and 1060S Royal Bass combo.

| 1971-1972 | | $325 | $400 |

Point Blank
2002-2004. Tube amps built by Roy Blankenship in Orlando, Florida before he started his Blankenship brand.

Polytone
1960s-present. Made in North Hollywood, California, Polytone offers compact combo amps, heads, and cabinets and a pickup system for acoustic bass.

Guitar or Bass Amps
1980s-1990s. Various models.

| 1980-1990s | | $325 | $400 |

Port City
2005-present. Daniel Klein builds his amp heads, combos, and cabinets in Rocky Point, North Carolina.

Premier
Ca.1938-ca.1975. Produced by Peter Sorkin Music Company in Manhattan. First radio-sized amplifiers introduced by '38. After World War II, established Multivox subsidiary to manufacture amplifiers ca.'46. By mid-'50s at least, the amps featured lyre grilles. Dark brown/light tan amp covering by '60. By '64 amps covered in brown woodgrain and light tan. Multivox amps were made until around '84.

B-160 Club Bass Amp
1963-1968. 15 to 20 watts, 1x12" Jensen speaker, '60s 2-tone brown styling, 6V6 tubes.

| 1963-1968 | | $375 | $450 |

Model 50 Amp
1940s-1960s. In '62 this was the entry-level student grade amp in their product line, 4 to 5 watts, 1x8" similar to Fender Champ circuit with more of a vertical suitcase-style cab.

| 1940-1960s | | $275 | $350 |

Model 71 Amp
1961-1962. Combo with 1x12" (woofer) and 2 small tweeters, 24 watts. '61 styling with circular speaker baffle protected with metal X frame, Premier logo on grille, 2 tweeter ports on upper baffle, 2-tone light tan and brown, large Premier 71 logo on back control panel, 8 tubes with tremolo. The '62 styling changed to baffle with a slight V at the top, Premier logo above grille and 2-tone cover.

| 1961 | Round baffle | $475 | $575 |
| 1962 | V-baffle | $475 | $575 |

Model 76 Amp
1950s. Suitcase latchable cabinet that opens out into 2 wedges, Premier 76 logo on amp control panel, 2-tone brown, lyre grille, 1x12".

| 1950s | | $475 | $575 |

Model 88 Multivox Amp
1962. Multi-purpose combo amp, organ-stop control panel, 1x15" woofer with 2 tweeters, vertical suitcase cab, 2-tone cover, classic circular speaker baffle with X brace, script Premier logo on grille, 10 tubes, top-of-the-line in '62 catalog.

| 1962 | | $475 | $575 |

Model 88N Amp
1950s-early-1960s. Rectangular suitcase cabinet, 2-tone tan and brown, Premier and lyre logo, 25 watts, 1x12".

| 1950s-1961 | | $475 | $575 |

MODEL YEAR	FEATURES	EXC. COND. LOW	HIGH

Model 100R Amp
1960s. Combo amp, 1x12", reverb and tremolo.

1960s		$475	$575

Model 110 Amp
1962. 12-watt 1x10 student combo, lyre grille logo, 2-tone cab.

1962		$375	$450

Model 120 Amp
1958-1963. 12-watt 1x12" combo, tremolo, 2-tone brown cab, large Premier script logo on front, Model 120 logo on control panel.

1958-1963		$575	$700

Model 200 Rhythm Bass Amp
1962. 1x15" combo bass amp.

1962		$400	$500

T-12 Twin-12 Amp
1958-1962. Early reverb amp with tremolo, 2x12", rectangular cabinet typical of twin 12 amps (Dano and Fender), brown cover.

1958-1962		$750	$900

T-8 Twin-8 Amp
1964-1966. 20 watts, 2x8", tremolo, reverb.

1964-1966		$525	$650

Pritchard Amps
2004-present. Professional grade, production/custom, single and two-channel amps and cabinets built by Eric Pritchard in Berkeley Springs, West Virginia.

Pyramid Car Audio
2008-present. Inexpensive student models, imported.

Quantum
1980s. Economy amps distributed by DME, Indianapolis, Indiana.

Q Terminator Economy Amps
1980s. Economy solidstate amps ranging from 12 to 25 watts and 1x6" to 1x12".

1980s		$20	$25

Quidley Guitar Amplifiers
2006-present. Intermediate and professional grade, production/custom, tube guitar amp heads, combos and cabinets built by Ed Quidley in Wilmington, North Carolina.

Quinn
2005-present. Professional and premium grade, production/custom, amps and cabinets built by Shadwell J. Damron III in Vancouver, Washington.

Randall
1960s-present. Randall Instruments was originally out of California and is now a division of U.S. Music Corp. They have offered a range of tube and solidstate combo amps, heads and cabinets over the years.

Guitar and Bass Amps
1980s-present. Mostly solidstate amps.

1980-2010	Intermediate-grade	$250	$300

MODEL YEAR	FEATURES	EXC. COND. LOW	HIGH
1980-2010	Student-grade	$100	$125
2001-2010	Intermediate-grade	$250	$300

Rastopdesigns
2002-present. Professional grade, custom amps built by Alexander Rastopchin in Long Island City, New York. He also builds effects.

Rat Fink
2002-present. Solidstate amp line from Lace Music Products. They also sold guitars and basses under this brand and offer amps under the Mooneyes and Lace brands.

Reason
2007-present. Professional grade, production/custom, amps and cabinets built by Obeid Khan and Anthony Bonadio in St. Louis, Missouri.

Red Bear
1994-1997. Tube amps designed by Sergei Novikov and built in St. Petersburg, Russia. Red Bear amps were distributed in the U.S. under a joint project between Gibson and Novik, Ltd. Novik stills builds amps under other brands.

MK 60 Lead Tube Amp
1994-1997. Head with 4x12" half stack, Red Bear logo on amp and cab.

1994-1997		$600	$750

MK 100 Full Stack
1994-1997. 100 watts, 2x4x12".

1994-1997		$775	$950

Red Iron Amps
2001-present. Paul Sanchez builds his tube amp heads in Lockhart, Texas.

Reeves Amplification
2002-present. Started by Bill Jansen, Reeves builds tube amps, combos, and cabinets in Cincinnati, Ohio, based on the classic British designs of Dan Reeves.

Reinhardt
2004-present. Bob Reinhardt builds his professional grade, production/custom, guitar and bass amps and cabinets in Lynchburg, Virginia. He also builds effects pedals.

Retro-King Amplifier Company
2004-present. Tube combo and head amps built by Chuck Dean in Marcellus, New York.

Reverend
1996-present. Joe Naylor started building amps under the Naylor brand in '94. In '96 he left Naylor to build guitars under the Reverend brand. From '01 to '05, Reverend offered tube amps, combos, and cabinets built in Warren, Michigan, that Naylor co-designed with Dennis Kager.

Reason SM25

Reeves Custom 18

Reinhardt Titan Combo
Rob Bernstein

AMPS

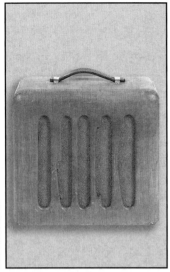

1937 Rickenbacker Model M-11

Rickenbacker Transonic

Rivera Fandango 2x12"

MODEL YEAR	FEATURES	EXC. COND. LOW	HIGH

Rex

1920s-1940s, 1950s-1960s. Name used on a line of beginner-grade guitars and amps sold through Fred Gretsch distributors. In the '50s and '60s, there were European-made electrics bearing the Rex brand. See Gretsch for listings.

Reynolds Valveart

1997-present. Professional and premium grade, production/custom, amps and cabinets built by Peter Reynolds in Windsor, Australia.

Rickenbacker

1931-present. Rickenbacker made amps from the beginning of the company up to the late '80s. Rickenbacker had many different models, from the small early models that were usually sold as a guitar/amp set, to the large, very cool, Transonic.

E-12 Amp
1963. 1x12" combo with tremolo depth and speed, volume, and on-off tone knobs.

1963		$375	$450

Electro-Student Amp
Late-1940s. Typical late-'40s vertical combo cabinet, 1x12" speaker, lower power using 5 tubes, bottom mounted chassis, dark gray leatherette cover.

1948-1949		$275	$350

Model B-9E Amp
1960s. 1x12" combo, 4 knobs, gray.

1960s		$400	$500

Model M-8 Amp
1950s-1960s. Gray, 1x8".

1950s		$400	$500
1960s		$350	$450

Model M-11 Amp
1950s. 12-15 watts, 1x12", 2x6V6 power. There was a different M-11 offered in the 1930s.

1959		$500	$600

Model M-12 Amp
1950s. 12-15 watts, 1x12", M-12 logo on back panel, brown leatherette. There was a different M-12 offered in the 1930s.

1950s		$550	$650

Model M-14A Amp
Late 1950s-early 1960s. 1x12 combo, mid-power 2x6V6, dual channel with vibrato, rough-brown tolex cover.

1962		$550	$650

Model M-15 Amp
1950s-Early 1960s. 1x15" combo, 35 watts, 2 x 6L6 power tubes, model name on top panel.

1950s-1960		$700	$850

Model M-30 EK-O-Sound Amp
1961. Recording echo chamber and amp in 1x12 combo format, 11 tubes, gray grille and cover, very limited production.

1961		$3,000	$3,800

Professional Model 200-A Amp
1930s. 15 watts, was sold with the Vibrola Spanish guitar.

1938		$400	$500

RB30 Amp
1986. Bass combo amp, 30 watts, tilted control panel, 1x12".

1986		$150	$175

RB60 Amp
1986. Bass combo amp, 60 watts, tilted control panel, 1x15".

1986		$200	$225

RB120 Amp
1986. Bass combo amp, 120 watts, tilted control panel, 1x15".

1986		$225	$275

Supersonic Model B-16 Amp
1960s. 4x10" speakers, gray cover.

1960s		$700	$850

Supersonic Model B-22 Amp Head
1960s. Tube head, gray cover.

1960s		$550	$675

TR7 Amp
1978-1982. Solidstate, 7 watts, 1x10", tremolo.

1978-1982		$100	$125

TR14 Amp
1978-ca.1982. Solidstate, 1x10", reverb, distortion.

1978-1982		$125	$150

TR25 Amp
1979-1982. Solidstate, 1x12" combo, reverb, tremolo, distortion.

1978-1982		$150	$175

TR35B Bass Amp
1978-ca.1982. Solidstate, mid-power, 1x15".

1978-1982		$175	$200

TR75G Amp
1978-ca.1982. 75 watts, 2x12", 2 channels.

1978-1982		$200	$225

TR75SG Amp
1978-ca.1983. 1x10" and 1x15" speakers.

1978-1982		$200	$225

TR100G Amp
1978-ca.1982. Solidstate, 100 watts with 4x12", 2 channels.

1978-1982		$250	$300

Transonic TS100 Amp
1967-1973. Trapezoid shaped 2x12" combo, solidstate, 100 watts, Rick-O-Select

1967-1973		$900	$1,100

Rivera

1985-present. Amp designer and builder Paul Rivera modded and designed amps for other companies before starting his own line in California. He offers heads, combos, and cabinets.

Chubster 40 Amp
2000-present. 40 watts, 1x12" combo, burgundy tolex, light grille.

2000-2010		$700	$900

Clubster 25 Amp
2005-present. 25 watts, 1x10", 6V6.

2005-2010		$600	$800

Clubster 45 Amp
2005-present. 45 watts, 1x12" combo.

2005-2010		$800	$1,000

MODEL YEAR	FEATURES	EXC. COND. LOW	HIGH

Fandango 112 Combo Amp
2001-present. 55 watts, 2xEL34, 1x12".

2001-2010		$800	$1,000

Fandango 212 Combo Amp
2001-present. 55 or 100 watts, 2x12" tube amp.

2001-2010		$900	$1,100

Jake Studio Combo Amp
1997. 55 watts, 1x12", reverb and effects loop.

1997		$800	$1,000

Knucklehead 55 Amp
1995-2002. 55 watts, head amp, replaced by reverb model.

1995-2002		$800	$1,000

Knucklehead 100 Amp
1995-2002. 100 watt head, head amp, replaced by reverb model.

1995-2002		$800	$1,000

Los Lobottom/Sub 1 Amp
1999-2004. 1x12" cabinet with 300-watt powered 12" subwoofer.

1999-2004		$450	$550

M-60 Amp Head
1990-2009. 60 watts.

1990-2009		$600	$800

M-60 112 Combo Amp
1989-2009. 60 watts, 1x12".

1989-2009		$700	$900

M-100 Amp Head
1990-2009. 100 watts.

1990-2009		$700	$900

M-100 212 Combo Amp
1990-2009. 100 watts, 2x12" combo.

1990-2009		$700	$900

Pubster 45 Amp
2005-present. 45 watts, 1x12".

2005-2010		$475	$575

Quiana Combo Amps
2000-present. Combo, 55 watts.

2000-2010	1x12"	$900	$1,100
2000-2010	2x12" or 4x10"	$1,000	$1,200

R-30 112 Combo Amp
1993-2007. 30 watts, 1x12", compact cab, black tolex cover, gray-black grille.

1993-2007		$700	$900

R-100 212 Combo Amp
1993-2007. 100 watts, 2x12".

1993-2007		$800	$1,000

Suprema R-55 112/115 Combo Amp
2000-present. Tube amp, 55 watts, 1x12" (still available) or 1x15" ('00-'01).

2000-2010	1x12" or 1x15"	$975	$1,200

TBR-1 Amp
1985-1999. First Rivera production model, rack mount, 60 watts.

1985-1999		$650	$800

Roccaforte Amps
1993-present. Tube amps, combos, and cabinets built by Doug Roccaforte in San Clemente, California.

Rocktron
1980s-present. Tube and solidstate amp heads, combos and cabinets. Rocktron is a division of GHS Strings and also offers stomp boxes and preamps.

Rodgers
1993-present. Custom tube amps and cabinets built by Larry Rodgers in Naples, Florida.

Rogue
2001-present. They offered student-level solid-state import (Korea) compact amps up to around '06. They also offer guitars, basses, lap steels, mandolins, banjos, ukuleles and effects.

Small Solidstate Amps
2001-2006. Various models.

2001-2006		$25	$140

Roland
Japan's Roland Corporation's products include amplifiers and keyboards and, under the Boss brand, effects.

Acoustic Chorus Series Amp
1995-present. Number in model indicates wattage (i.e. AC-60 = 60 watts).

1995-2009	AC-100, 1x12", 2x5"	$225	$275
1995-2010	AC-60, 2x6"	$225	$275
1995-2010	AC-90, 2x8"	$225	$275

Bolt 60 Amp
Early 1980s. Solidstate/tube, 1x12".

1980s		$225	$275

Cube Series Amp
1978-present. Number in model indicates wattage (i.e. Cube-15X = 15 watts).

1978-1982	100, 1x12"	$175	$200
1978-1982	20, 1x8"	$100	$125
1978-1983	40, 1x10"	$125	$150
1978-1983	60, 1x12"	$175	$200
1978-1983	60B, 1x12"	$175	$200
2000-2009	30 Bass, 1x10"	$125	$150
2000s	BC30	$125	$150
2006-2010	15X, 1x8"	$100	$125
2006-2010	20X, 1x8"	$100	$125
2006-2010	30X, 1x10"	$125	$150
2008-2010	80X, 1x12"	$175	$200

Jazz Chorus Series Amp
1975-present. Includes the JC-50 (50 watts, 1x12"), JC-55 (50 watts, 2x8"), JC-77 (80 watts, 2x10"), JC-90 (90 watts, 2x10") and JC-120 (120 watts, 2x12").

1975-2010	JC-120	$325	$375
1980s	JC-50	$250	$300
1987-1994	JC-55	$250	$300
1987-1994	JC-77	$275	$325
1990s	JC-90	$275	$325

Micro Cube
2000-present. Compact AC power or battery, 2 watts, 1x5".

2000-2010		$60	$70

Rivera Suprema R-55 112

Rocktron V50D

Roland AC-100

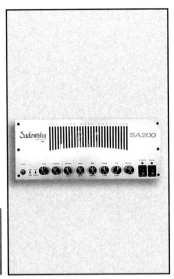

Sadowsky SA200

SamAmp VAC 40 Series

Satellite

MODEL YEAR	FEATURES	EXC. COND. LOW	HIGH

Spirit Series Amp
1982-late 1980s. Compact, model number indicates wattage.

1880s	Spirit 40A, combo	$100	$125
1980s	Spirit 30, 1x12	$100	$125

Studio Bass Amp
1979		$200	$225

VGA3 V-Guitar Amp
2003-2009. GK digital modeling amp, 50 watts, 1x12" combo.

2003-2009	$250	$275

VGA5 V-Guitar Amp
2001-2004. GK digital modeling amp, 65 watts, 1x12".

2001-2004	$275	$325

VGA7 V-Guitar Amp
2000-2009. 65 + 65 watts, 2x12", digital modeling with analog-style controls.

2000-2009	$300	$350

S.S. Maxwell
See info under Danelectro.

Sadowsky
1980-present. From '05 to '07, luthier Roger Sadowsky built a bass tube amp head in Brooklyn, New York. He also builds basses and guitars.

Sam Ash
1960s-1970s. Sam Ash Music was founded by a young Sam Ash (formerly Ashkynase - an Austro-Hungarian name) in 1924. Ash's first store was in Brooklyn, New York, and by '66 there were about four Ash stores. During this time Ash Music private branded their own amp line which was built by Jess Oliver of Oliver Amps and based upon Oliver's Ampeg designs.

Sam Ash Mark II Pro Combo Amp
1960s. 2x12" with reverb combo amp.

1960s	$325	$400

SamAmp
2004-present. Intermediate and professional grade, boutique amps built by Sam Timberlake in Vestavia Hills, Alabama.

Sano
1944-ca. 1970. Combo, heads and cabinets made in Irvington, New Jersey. Founded by Joseph Zon-Frilli, Louis Iorio, and Nick Sano, with initial offerings of accordion pickups, amplifiers, and all-electric accordions. Sano patented his accordion pickup in '44 and also developed a highly acclaimed stereophonic pickup accordion and matching amp. By '66 the Sano Corporation augmented their all-tube accordion amps with new solidstate circuitry models. In the mid-'60s they offered a new line of amps specifically designed for the guitar and bass market. Sano amps are generally low-gain, low power amplifiers. They also marketed reverb units and guitars.

Compact Combo Amp
1960s	160R, 15w, 1x12"	$225	$275
1960s	Sano-ette	$100	$125

Satellite Amplifiers
2004-present. Professional and premium grade, production/custom, tube amps, preamps and cabinets built by Adam Grimm in San Diego, California. He also builds effects.

Savage
1994-present. Tube combos, amp heads and cabinets built by Jeff Krumm at Savage Audio, in Savage, Minnesota.

Sceptre
1960s. Canadian-made. Sceptre script logo on upper left side of grille ('60s Fender-style and placement).

Signet Amp
1960s. Low power, 1x10", Class-A 6V6 power, Signet model name on front panel.

1960s	$150	$175

Schaller
1945-present. The German guitar accessory company's main products in the late '50s were tube amps and they had solid-state amps in the '60s.

Schertler
Made in Switzerland, model logo (e.g. David model) on front, intermediate to professional grade, modern designs for modern applications.

SDG Vintage
2003-present. Intermediate and professional grade, production/custom, tube amps, combos and heads built by Steven Gupta in Bristow, Virginia.

Selmer
1930s-1980s. The Selmer UK distributor offered mid- to high-level amps.

Constellation 14 Amp
1965. Single speaker combo, 14 watts, gray snakeskin tolex-type cover.

1965	$1,600	$2,000

Futurama Corvette Amp
1960s. Class A low power 1x8", volume and tone controls, plus amplitude and speed tremolo controls, large script Futurama logo on front of amp, Futurama Corvette and Selmer logo on top panel.

1960s	$500	$600

Mark 2 Treble and Bass Amp Head
1960s. About 30 watts (2xEL34s), requires power line transformer for U.S. use, large Selmer logo on grille.

1960s	$800	$900

MODEL YEAR	FEATURES	EXC. COND. LOW	HIGH

Truevoice Amp
1961. Truevoice and Selectortone logo on top-mounted chasis, 30-watt combo, 1x15 Goodmans speaker, 2xEL34 power tubes, tremolo, 6 push button Selectortone Automatic.

1961		$1,900	$2,300

Zodiac Twin 30 Amp
1964-1971. Combo amp, gray snakeskin tolex cover.

1964-1971		$2,200	$2,700

Sewell
1998-2008. Doug Sewell built his tube combo and head amps in Texas. He currently is the senior amp designer for Paul Reed Smith.

Seymour Duncan
Pickup maker Seymour Duncan, located in Santa Barbara, California, offered a line of amps from around 1984 to '95.

84-40/84-50 Amp
1989-1995. Tube combo, 2 switchable channels, 1x12", includes the 84-40 ('89-'91, 40 watts) and the 84-50 ('91-'95, 50 watts).

1989-1995	84-40 or 84-50	$225	$275

Bass 300 x 2 Amp
1986-1987. Solidstate, 2 channels (300 or 600 watts), EQ, contour boost switches, effects loop.

1986-1987		$225	$275

Bass 400 Amp
1986-1987. Solidstate, 400 watts, EQ, contour boost, balanced line output, effects loop.

1986-1987		$200	$250

Convertible Amp
1986-1995. 60-watt; dual-channel; effects loop; Accutronics spring reverb; 3-band EQ.

1986-1987	Head only	$250	$300
1988-1995	Combo	$300	$375

KTG-2075 Stereo Amp
1989-1993. Part of the King Tone Generator Series, 2 channels with 75 watts per channel.

1989-1993		$200	$225

SG Systems
1970s. A Division of the Chicago Musical Instrument Company (CMI), who also owned Gibson Guitars. Gibson outsourced amplifier production from Kalamazoo to CMI in '67 and CMI (Chicago) continued for a year or two with Gibson-branded amplifiers. In the early '70s CMI introduced the SG Systems brand of hybrid amplifiers, which had a tube power section and a solidstate preamp section. CMI was trying to stay modern with SG Systems by introducing futuristic features like the Notch Shift which would quickly switch between popular rock sounds and mellow jazz delivery. SG amps have a large SG logo on the front baffle and were built with metal corners. Amplifiers have similar power specs; for example, the models issued in '73 all were rated with 100-watt RMS with 200-watts peak music power, so models were based on different speaker configurations.

SG Series Amp
1973	SG-115, 1x15"	$275	$350
1973	SG-212, 2x12"	$300	$375
1973	SG-215 Bass, 2x15"	$300	$375
1973	SG-410, 4x10"	$300	$375
1973	SG-610, 6x10"	$325	$400
1973	SG-812 PA	$250	$300

Shaw
2008-present. Custom/production, intermediate and professional grade, guitar amp heads and cabinets built by Kevin Shaw in Lebanon, Tennessee.

Sherlock Amplifiers
1990-present. Dale Sherlock builds his intermediate to premium grade, production/custom, tube guitar amps and cabinets in Melbourne Victoria, Australia.

Sherwood
Late 1940s-early 1950s. Amps made by Danelectro for Montgomery Ward. There are also Sherwood guitars and lap steels made by Kay.

Sho-Bud
Introduced and manufactured by the Baldwin/Gretsch factory in 1970. Distributed by Kustom/Gretsch in the '80s. Models include D-15 Model 7838, S-15 Model 7836, Twin Tube Model 7834, and Twin Trans Model 7832.

D15 Sho-Bud Double Amp
Introduced in 1970. Solidstate, 100 watts. D-15 is 2 channels, S-15 is 1 channel, both with 1x15" JBL speaker.

1970s		$300	$375

S15 Sho-Bud Single Amp
Introduced in 1972. 100 watts, 1x15" JBL, solidstate single channel combo.

1970s		$250	$300

Sho-Bass Amp
Introduced in 1972. 100 watts, 1x15", solidstate combo, black grille, black vinyl cover.

1970s		$250	$300

Twin Trans Amp
Introduced in 1972. 100 watts, solidstate combo, 2x12", reverb, black vinyl cover, dark grille, Sho-Bud script logo front upper right.

1970s		$350	$450

Twin Tube Amp
Introduced in 1972. 100 watt tube combo, 4 6L6s, 2x12", reverb, black vinyl cover, dark grille.

1970s		$550	$650

Siegmund Guitars & Amplifiers
1993-present. Chris Siegmund builds his tube amp heads, combos and cabinets in Los Angeles, California. He founded the company in Seattle, moving it to Austin, Texas for '95-'97. He also builds effects pedals and guitars.

Schertler David

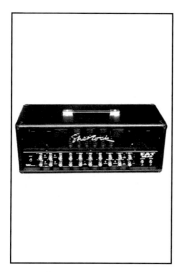
Sherlock Fat Head

Siegmund Diamond

Silvertone Model 1392

1959 Silvertone Model 1431

Mid-'60s Silvertone 1464
Dave McDermott

MODEL		EXC. COND.	
YEAR	FEATURES	LOW	HIGH

Silvertone

1941-ca.1970, present. Brand used by Sears. All Silvertone amps were supplied by American companies up to around '66.

Special thanks to Brian Conner for his assistance with Silvertone amplifier identification.

Model 1300 Amp
1948. Vertical combo cab, treble-clef logo on grille, 2-tone, 3 inputs, 2 controls.

1948		$375	$450

Model 1304 Amp
1949-1951. 18 watts, 1x12, 2x6L6 power tubes, 2-tone leatherette cover, round speaker baffle hole, volume, treble, bass and tremolo control knobs, becomes Model 1344.

1949-1951		$350	$450

Model 1330 Amp
1954-1957. Introduced in Sears Fall '54 catalog, 3 tubes (with rectifier), 1x6", wide-panel 13x13.75x7.5" cab in tan artificial leather, 9 lbs., replaced Model 1339 at the same price but with new wide-panel style, small Silvertone logo above the grille, replaced in '58 by Model 1390 Silvertone Meteor.

1954-1957		$175	$225

Model 1331 Amp
1954-1957. Made by Danelectro, 14 lbs., 1x8" student combo, 3 tubes (with rectifier), 1 volume, 1 tone, 2 inputs, tan tweed-effect cover with brown alligator trim, large-thread wheat-gold grille, brown metal control panel.

1954-1957		$200	$250

Model 1333 Amp
1954-1957. Made by Danelectro, 23 lbs., 1x12" combo, 2x6V6 power, 5 tubes (with rectifier), 2 volumes, 1 tone, 3 inputs, 2-control vibrato, tan tweed-effect cover with brown alligator trim, large-thread wheat-gold grille, brown metal control panel.

1954-1957		$375	$450

Model 1334 Amp
1954-1957. Made by Danelectro, 29 lbs., heavy-duty 1x12" combo, 6 tubes (with rectifier), 2 volumes, 2 tones, 3 inputs, 2-control vibrato, tan tweed-effect cover with brown alligator trim, large-thread wheat-gold grille, brown metal control panel.

1954-1957		$400	$475

Model 1335 Amp
1954-1957. Made by Danelectro, 99 lbs., heavy-duty 1x15" combo, 6 tubes (with rectifier), 2 volumes, 2 tones, 4 inputs, 2-control vibrato, tan tweed-effect cover with brown alligator trim, large-thread wheat-gold grille, brown metal control panel.

1954-1957		$500	$600

Model 1336 (Twin Twelve) Amp
1954-1957. Made by Danelectro, 26.75x17.5x9.25" cab, 45 lbs., 2x12" combo, 4x6L6 powe tubes, 3 volumes, 2 tones, 4 inputs, 2-control vibrato, tan tweed-effect cover with brown alligator trim, large-thread wheat-gold grille, brown metal control panel.

1954-1957		$575	$700

MODEL		EXC. COND.	
YEAR	FEATURES	LOW	HIGH

Model 1337 "Wide Range Eight Speaker" Amp
1956. Odd-looking suitcase cab that opens into 2 separate speaker baffles each containing 4x8" speakers, 2 preamps, 2 channels with separate controls for volume, bass and treble, 2-control vibrato, 42 lbs.

1956		$400	$500

Model 1339 Amp
Ca.1952-1954. Sears lowest-priced amp, 3 tubes (with rectifier), 1x6", 1 input, 1 knob, maroon artificial leather cover over 10.5x8x5" verticle cab, script Silvertone logo on low right grille, 7 lbs.

1952-1954		$175	$225

Model 1340 Amp
Ca.1952-1954. Sears second lowest-priced amp, 3 tubes (with rectifier), 1x6", 2 inputs, 1 knob, brown and white imitation leather cover over 15x12x8.5" verticle cab, script Silvertone logo on low right grille, 14 lbs.

1952-1954		$200	$250

Model 1342 Streamlined Amp
Ca.1952-1954. Sears third lowest-priced amp, 4 tubes (with rectifier), 1x12", 3 inputs, 2 knobs, green and beige imitation leather cover over 16x19x7.25" slanted-side cab, script Silvertone logo on low right grille, 23 lbs.

1952-1954		$325	$400

Model 1344 Amp
1950-1954. Retro-styled vertical 22.5x15.5x9.5" cab with round speaker baffle hole, 1x12" combo, first Silvertone built-in vibrato, 6 tubes (with rectifier), 3 inputs, 3 controls (treble, bass, volume) plus vibrato control, maroon imitation leather cover with sports-stripe around the bottom, 33 lbs., script Silvertone logo low right side of cab.

1950-1954		$350	$450

Model 1346 (Twin Twelve) Amp
Ca.1952-1954. Danelectro-made, brown control panel, 2x12", 4 6L6s, vibrato, leather handle, tan smooth leatherette cover, 2 speaker baffle openings.

1952-1954		$575	$700

Model 1390 Meteor Amp
1958-1959. Renamed from Model 1330, Meteor logo on front panel, 1x6" practice amp, 3 tubes (with rectifier), tan simulated leather cover, in '60 renamed Model 1430 (but no longer a Meteor).

1958-1959		$200	$225

Model 1391 Amp
1958-1959. Modern-style cab, 3 tubes (with rectifier), 5 watts, 1x8".

1958-1959		$275	$350

Model 1392 Amp
1958-1959. Modern-style cab, 6 tubes (with rectifier), 10 watts, 1x12", vibrato.

1958-1959		$350	$450

Model 1393 Amp
1958-1959. Modern-style cab, 7 tubes (with rectifier), 15 watts, heavy-duty 1x12", vibrato.

1958-1959		$375	$475

Model 1396 Two-Twelve Amp
1958-1959. Script Two-Twelve logo on lower left front and Silvertone logo on lower right front, 50 watts,

MODEL YEAR	FEATURES	EXC. COND. LOW	HIGH

2x12", 4x6L6 power tubes, 9 tubes (with rectifier), vibrato, 26.75x17.5x9.25" with gray and metallic fleck cover, white grille, 45 lbs.

1958-1959		$575	$700

Model 1420 Amp
1968. Tube-powered, 5 watts, 1x8" student combo.

| 1968 | | $150 | $175 |

Model 1421 Amp
1968. Tube-powered, 10 watts, 1x8" combo, covered in dark olive vinyl.

| 1968 | | $175 | $225 |

Model 1422 Amp
1968. Tube-powered, 40 watts, 1x12" combo, covered in dark olive vinyl.

| 1968 | | $325 | $400 |

Model 1423 Amp
1968. Solidstate, 125 watts, 2x12" cab, 55 lbs., dark olive.

| 1968 | | $350 | $425 |

Model 1425 Amp
1968. Solidstate, 200 watts, 6x10" cab, 86 lbs., dark olive.

| 1968 | | $350 | $425 |

Model 1426 Amp
1968. Solidstate, 250 watts, 6x15" cab, slide switches instead of control knobs, automatic E-tone for tuning, casters for 149 lb. head and cab.

| 1968 | | $350 | $425 |

Model 1428 Amp
1968. Solidstate, 60 watts, 1x15" cab, 36 lbs., dark olive.

| 1968 | | $300 | $350 |

Model 1430 Amp
1959-1966. Silvertone's lowest-price model, 3 tubes, 1x6", previously called Model 1390 Meteor, and prior to that named Model 1330, retro cab basically unchanged since first introduced in '54.

| 1959-1966 | | $200 | $225 |

Model 1431 Amp
1959-1961. 5 watts, 1x8", overhanging-top wraparound grille cab, 3 tubes (with rectifier), light gray cover with white grille.

| 1959-1961 | | $200 | $250 |

Model 1431 Bass Amp
1968. Solidstate, 200 watts, 6x12" cab, 91 lbs., dark olive.

| 1968 | | $450 | $550 |

Model 1432 Amp
1959-1961. 10 watts, 1x12", vibrato, overhanging-top wrap-around grille cab, 6 tubes (with rectifier), dark gray tweed-effect cover with white grille.

| 1959-1961 | | $275 | $350 |

Model 1433 Amp
1959-1961. 15 watts, 1x15", vibrato, overhanging-top wrap-around grille cab, 7 tubes (with rectifier), gray with metallic fleck cover with white grille.

| 1959-1961 | | $425 | $525 |

Model 1434 Twin Twelve Amp
1959-1961. 50 watts using 4x6L6 power, 2x12" combo, vibrato, 2 channels each with volume, bass and treble controls, black cover with gold-colored trim.

| 1959-1961 | | $575 | $700 |

Model 1459 Amp
1960s. Student tube amp, 3 watts, 1x8", black vinyl, square cab, 1 tone, 1 volume, 1 channel, 2 inputs.

| 1967-1968 | | $175 | $225 |

Model 1463 Bass Amp
1967-1968. Solidstate, 1x15", piggyback, 60 lbs., reverb, tremolo.

| 1967-1968 | | $300 | $350 |

Model 1464 Amp
1967-1968. Solidstate, 100 watts, 2x12", piggyback, 60 lbs., reverb, tremolo, gray vinyl cover.

| 1967-1968 | | $350 | $425 |

Model 1465 Amp
1966-1968. Solidstate, piggyback, 150 watts, 6x10", reverb, tremolo, gray vinyl cover, replaces Model 1485.

| 1966-1968 | | $450 | $550 |

Model 1466 Bass Amp
1966-1968. Solidstate, 150 watts, 6x10", gray vinyl cover.

| 1966-1968 | | $450 | $550 |

Model 1471 Amp
1961-1963. 5 watts, 1x8", 3 tubes, 1 volume, 1 tone, 2 inputs, black leathette cover with white grille.

| 1961-1963 | | $275 | $350 |

Model 1472 Amp
1960s. 10 watts, 2 6V6s provide mid-level power, 1x12", front controls mounted vertically on front right side, black cover with silver grille, large stationary handle, tremolo.

| 1961-1963 | | $375 | $450 |

Model 1473 Bass Amp
1961-1963. Designed for bass or accordion, 25 watts, 1x15" combo, 6 tubes (with rectifier), 2 channels, 4 inputs, 19x29x9" cab, 43 lbs., black leatherette with white grille.

| 1961-1963 | | $375 | $450 |

Model 1474 Twin Twelve Amp
1961-1963. Silvertone's first reverb amp, 50 watts, 4x6L6 power, 10 tubes (with rectifier), 2x12" combo, 2 control vibrato with dual remote footswitch, 2 channels each with bass, treble, and volume, 4 inputs, ground switch, standby switch, 19x29x9" combo cab, 54 lbs., black leatherette with silver grille.

| 1961-1963 | | $575 | $700 |

Model 1481 Amp
1963-1968. Compact student amp, 5 watts, 1x8", 3 tubes (with rectifier), volume and tone controls, gray leatherette cover with white grille, replaces Model 1471.

| 1963-1968 | | $275 | $350 |

Model 1482 Amp
1960s. 15 watts, 1x12", 6 tubes, control panel mounted on right side vertically, tremolo, gray leatherette.

| 1963-1968 | | $350 | $425 |

Model 1483 Bass Amp
1963-1966. 23 watts, 1x15" piggyback tube amp, gray tolex and gray grille.

| 1963-1966 | | $400 | $500 |

Silvertone Model 1471

Silvertone Model 1472

Silvertone Model 1474

*Smith Custom Amplifiers
Class A 10-Watt*

Snider Combo

Soldano Lucky 13

MODEL YEAR	FEATURES	EXC. COND. LOW	HIGH

Model 1484 Twin Twelve Amp
1963-1966. 60 watts, 2x12" piggyback tube amp, tremolo and reverb, gray cover with light grille.

1963-1966		$575	$700

Model 1485 Amp
1963-1965. 120 watts, 6x10" (Jensen C-10Q) piggyback, 10 tubes with 5 silicon rectifiers, 2 channels, reverb, tremolo, charcoal-gray tolex-style cover, white grille, replaced in '66 by solidstate Model 1465.

1963-1965		$750	$925

Model 4707 Organ Amp
1960s. Interesting '60s family room style cabinet with legs, 45-watt tube amp with vibrato, 1x12", front controls, could be used for organ, stereo, or record player turntable.

1960s		$350	$425

Simms-Watts
Late 1960s-1970s. Tube amp heads, combos, PA heads and cabinets made in London, England. Similar to Marshall and HiWatt offerings of the era.

Skip Simmons
1990-present. Custom and production tube combo amps built by Skip Simmons in Dixon, California.

Skrydstrup R&D
1997-present. Production/custom, premium grade, amps and cabinets built by Steen Skrydstrup in Denmark. He also builds effects.

Sligo Amps
2004-present. Intermediate and professional grade, production/custom, amps built by Steven Clark in Leesburg, Virginia.

SMF
Mid-1970s. Amp head and cabinets from Dallas Music Industries, Ltd., of Mahwah, New Jersey. Offered the Tour Series which featured a 150 watt head and 4x12" bottoms with metal speaker grilles and metal corners.

SMF (Sonic Machine Factory)
2002-present. Tube amps and cabinets designed by Mark Sampson (Matchless, Bad Cat, Star) and Rick Hamel (SIB effects) and built in California.

Smicz Amplification
Tube combos and extension cabinets built by Bob Smicz in Bristol, Connecticut.

Smith Custom Amplifiers
2002-present. All tube combo amps, heads and speaker cabinets built by Sam Smith in Montgomery, Alabama.

Smokey
1997-present. Mini amps often packaged in cigarette packs made by Bruce Zinky in Flagstaff, Arizona. He also builds Zinky amps and effects and has revived the Supro brand on a guitar and amp.

Snider
1999-present. Jeff Snider has been building various combo tube amps in San Diego, California, since '95. In '99 he started branding them with his last name.

Soldano
1987-present. Made in Seattle, Washington by amp builder Mike Soldano, the company offers a range of all-tube combo amps, heads and cabinets. They also offer a reverb unit.

Astroverb 16 Combo Amp
1997-present. Atomic with added reverb.

1997-2010		$550	$700

Atomic 16 Combo Amp
1996-2001. Combo, 20 watts, 1x12".

1996-2001		$500	$600

Decatone Combo Amp
1998-present. 2x12" 100-watt combo, rear mounted controls, still available as a head.

1998-2010	No footswitch	$1,500	$1,900
1998-2010	With Decatrol footswitch	$1,600	$2,000

HR 50/Hot Rod 50 Amp Head
1992-present. 50-watt single channel head.

1992-2010		$1,000	$1,200

HR 100/Hot Rod 100 Amp Head
1994-2001. 100-watt single channel head.

1994-2001		$1,000	$1,200

Lucky 13 Combo Amp
2000-present. 100 watts (50 also available), 2x12" combo.

2000-2010		$900	$1,100

Reverb-O-Sonic Combo Amp
1990s-present. 50 watts, 2 channels, 2x12" combo, reverb.

1990s-2010		$900	$1,100

SLO-100 Super Lead Overdrive 100-Watt Amp
1988-present. First production model, super lead overdrive, 100 watts, snakeskin cover head amp, 4x12" cabinet.

1988-1999	With cab	$2,400	$2,900
1988-2010	Head	$2,000	$2,500

Sommatone
1998-present. Jim Somma builds his tube combo and head amps and cabinets in Somerville, New Jersey.

Sonax
Introduced in 1972. Budget line of solidstate amps offered by Gretsch/Baldwin, made by Yorkville Sound (Traynor) in Toronto. Introduced with dark grille and dark cover.

MODEL YEAR	FEATURES	EXC. COND. LOW	HIGH

530-B Bass Amp
> *1970s. 30 watts, 1x12".*

1970s		$100	$125

550-B Bass Amp
> *1970s. 50 watts, 1x15".*

1970s		$125	$150

720-G Amp
> *1970s. Student amp, 20 watts, 2x8", reverb.*

1970s		$150	$200

730-G Amp
> *1970s. 30 watts, 2x10", reverb and tremolo.*

1970s		$250	$300

750-G Amp
> *1970s. 50 watts, 2x12", reverb and tremolo.*

1970s		$300	$375

770-G Amp
> *1970s. 75 watts, 4x10", reverb and tremolo.*

1970s		$325	$400

Songworks Systems

See listing under Little Lanilei.

Sonny Jr.

1996-present. Harmonica amplifiers built by harmonica player Sonny Jr. in conjunction with Cotton Amps in Tolland, Connecticut.

Sonola

Tube combo amps made for the Sonola Accordian company of Chicago in the 1950s and '60s, possibly built by Guild or Ampeg. There are also Sonola tube amp heads from the '70s made by MHB Amplifiers in Adelaide, South Australia.

Sound City

Made in England from the late-1960s to the late-'70s, the tube Sound City amps were Marshall-looking heads and separate cabinets. They were imported, for a time, into the U.S. by Gretsch.

50 PA Plus Amp
> *Late-1960s-late-1970s. Similar to 50 Plus but with 4 channels.*

1970s		$650	$800

50 Plus/50R Amp Head
> *Late-1960s-late-1970s. Amp head, labeled 50 Plus or 50 R.*

1960-1970s		$800	$1,000

120 Energizer Slave Unit Amp
> *1970s. 120-watt power amp only, no preamp, Energizer Slave Unit logo on front panel.*

1970s		$550	$675

120/120R Amp Head
> *Early-late-1970s. The 120-watt head replaced the late-1960s 100-watt model.*

1970s	120 no reverb	$900	$1,100
1970s	With reverb	$950	$1,150

200 Plus Amp Head

1970s		$950	$1,150

Concord Combo Amp
> *80 watts, 2x12" Fane speakers, cream, basketweave grille.*

1968		$950	$1,150

MODEL YEAR	FEATURES	EXC. COND. LOW	HIGH

L-80 Cabinet
> *1970s. 4x10" speaker cabinet.*

1970s		$500	$625

L-412 Cabinet
> *1970s. 4x12" speaker cabinet.*

1970s		$500	$625

X-60 Cabinet
> *1970s. 2x12" speaker cabinet.*

1970s		$600	$750

Sound Electronics

Sound Electronics Corporation introduced a line of amplifiers in 1965 that were manufactured in Long Island. Six models were initially offered, with solidstate rectifiers and tube preamp and power sections. Their catalog did not list power wattages but did list features and speaker configurations. The initial models had dark vinyl-style covers and sparkling silver grille cloth. The amps were combos with the large models having vertical cabinets, silver script Sound logo on upper left of grille. The larger models used JBL D120F and D130F speakers. Stand alone extension speakers were also available.

Various Model Amps
> *Mid-1960s. Includes X-101, X-101R, X-202 Bass/Organ, X-404 Bass and Organ, X-505R amps, hi-fi chassis often using 7868 power tubes.*

1960s		$375	$450

Southbay Ampworks

2002-present. Tube combo amps and speaker cabinets built by Jim Seavall in Rancho Palos Verdes, California. He also builds Scumback Speakers.

Sovtek

1992-1996. Sovtek amps were products of Mike Matthews of Electro-Harmonix fame and his New Sensor Corporation. The guitar and bass amps and cabinets were made in Russia.

Mig 30 Amp Head
> *1994-1996. Tube head, 30 watts.*

1994-1996		$375	$475

Mig 50 Amp Head
> *1992-1996. Tube head, 50 watts.*

1992-1996		$375	$475

Mig 60 Amp Head
> *1994-1996. Tube head, 60 watts, point-to-point wiring.*

1994-1996		$400	$500

Mig 100 Amp Head
> *1992-1996. Tube head, 100 watts.*

1992-1996		$425	$525

Mig 100B Amp Head
> *1996. Bass tube head, 100 watts.*

1996		$400	$500

Mig Cabinet

1994-1996	2x12"	$250	$300

Sommatone Roaring 40 2X12

Sonny Jr. Super Cruncher

Southbay Ampworks

AMPS

Speedster 25-Watt Deluxe

Standel 100 UL15

Stevenson GTA

| MODEL | | EXC. COND. | |
YEAR	FEATURES	LOW	HIGH

Space Tone

See Swart Amplifiers.

Specimen Products

1984-present. Luthier Ian Schneller added tube amps and speaker cabinets in '93. He also builds guitars, basses and ukes in Chicago, Illinois.

Speedster

1995-2000, 2003-present. Founded by Lynn Ellsworth, offering tube amps and combos designed by Bishop Cochran with looks inspired by dashboards of classic autos. In '03, Joe Valosay and Jevco International purchased the company and revived the brand with help from former owner Cory Wilds. Amps were originally built by Soldono, but are now built by Speedster in Gig Harbor, Washington. They also build effects pedals.

Splawn

2004-present. Production, professional grade, tube amps and cabinets built by Scott Splawn in Dallas, North Carolina.

St. George

1960s. There were Japanese guitars bearing this brand, but these amps may have been built in California.

Mid-Size Tube Amp
1965. Low power, 1x10" Jensen, 2 5065 and 2 12AX7 tubes.

1960s		$175	$225

Standel

1952-1974, 1997-present. Bob Crooks started custom building amps part time in '52, going into full time standard model production in '58 in Temple City, California. In '61 Standel started distributing guitars under their own brand and others. By late '63 or '64, Standel had introduced solidstate amps, two years before Fender and Ampeg introduced their solidstate models. In '67 Standel moved to a new, larger facility in El Monte, California. In '73 Chicago Musical Instruments (CMI), which owned Gibson at the time, bought the company and built amps in El Monte until '74. In '97 the Standel name was revived by Danny McKinney who, with the help of original Standel founder Bob Crooks and Frank Garlock (PR man for first Standel), set about building reissues of some of the early models in Ventura, California.

A-30 B Artist 30 Bass Amp
1964-early-1970s. Artist Series, the original Standel solidstate series, 80 watts, 2x15".

1964-1969		$325	$400

A-30 G Artist 30 Guitar Amp
1964-early-1970s. Artist Series, the original Standel solidstate series, 80 watts, 2x15".

1964-1974		$375	$450

A-48 G Artist 48 Guitar Amp
1964-early-1970s. Artist Series, the original Standel solidstate series, 80 watts, 4x12".

1964-1974		$450	$550

A-60 B Artist 60 Bass Amp
1964-early-1970s. Artist Series, the original Standel solidstate series, 160 watts, 4x15".

1964-1974		$450	$550

A-60 G Artist 60 Guitar Amp
1964-early-1970s. Artist Series, the original Standel solidstate series, 160 watts, 4x15".

1964-1974		$450	$550

A-96 G Artist 96 Guitar Amp
1964-early-1970s. Artist Series, the original Standel solidstate series, 160 watts, 8x12".

1964-1974		$500	$600

C-24 Custom 24 Amp
Late-1960s-1970s. Custom Slim Line Series, solidstate, 100 watts, 2x12", dark vinyl, dark grille.

1970s		$375	$450

I-30 B Imperial 30 Bass Amp
1964-early-1970s. Imperial Series, the original Standel solidstate series, 100 watts, 2x15".

1960s		$400	$500

I-30 G Imperial 30 Guitar Amp
1964-early-1970s. Imperial Series, the original Standel solidstate series, 100 watts, 2x15".

1960s		$450	$550

Model 10L8/15L12/25L15 Amp
1953-1958. Early custom made tube amps made by Bob Crooks in his garage, padded naugahyde cabinet with varying options and colors. There are a limited number of these amps, and brand knowledge is also limited, therefore there is a wide value range. Legend has it that the early Standel amps made Leo Fender re-think and introduce even more powerful amps.

1953-1958		$3,000	$3,700

S-10 Studio 10 Amp
Late-1960s-1970s. Studio Slim Line Series, solidstate, 30 watts, 1x10", dark vinyl, dark grille.

1970s		$275	$350

S-24 G Amp
1970s. Solidstate, 2x12.

1970s		$375	$450

S-50 Studio 50 Amp
Late-1963 or early-1964-late-1960s. Not listed in '69 Standel catalog, 60 watts, gray tolex, gray grille, piggyback.

1964		$375	$450

SM-60 Power Magnifier Amp
1970. Tall, verticle combo solidstate amp, 100 watts, 6x10".

1970		$325	$425

Star

2004-present. Tube amps, combos and speaker cabinets built by Mark Sampson in the Los Angeles, California area. Sampson has also been involved with Matchless, Bad Cat, and SMF amps.

Starcaster

See listing under Fender.

MODEL YEAR	FEATURES	EXC. COND. LOW	HIGH

Starlite

Starlite was a budget brand made and sold by Magnatone. See Magnatone for listings.

Stella Vee

1999-2005. Jason Lockwood built his combo amps, heads, and cabinets in Lexington, Kentucky.

Stephenson

1997-present. Mark Stephenson builds his intermediate to premium grade, production/custom, tube amps and cabinets in Regina, Saskatchewan 1997-'99, in Hope, British Columbia 2000-'06, and since in Parksville, British Columbia. He also offers effects.

Stevenson

1999-present. Luthier Ted Stevenson, of Lachine, Quebec, added amps to his product line in '05. He also builds basses and guitars.

Stimer

Brothers Yves and Jean Guen started building guitar pickups in France in 1946. By the late '40s they had added their Stimer line of amps to sell with the pickups. Early amp models were the M.6, M.10 and M.12 (6, 10 and 12 watts, respectively). An early user of Guen products was Django Reinhardt.

Stinger

Budget line imported by Martin.

Stramp

1970s. Stramp, of Hamburg, Germany, offered audio mixers, amps and compact powered speaker units, all in aluminum flight cases.

Solidstate Amp

1970s. Solidstate amp head in metal suitcase with separate Stramp logo cabinet.

1970s		$400	$500

Straub Amps

2003-present. Harry Straub builds his professional grade, production/custom, amps in St. Paul, Minnesota.

Suhr

1997-present. John Suhr builds his production/custom amps in Lake Elsinore, California. He also builds guitars and basses.

Sundown

1983-1988. Combo amps, heads and cabinets designed and built by Dennis Kager of Ampeg fame. By '88, he had sold out his interest in the company.

Sunn

1965-2002. Started in Oregon by brothers Conrad and Norm Sundhold (Norm was the bass player for the Kingsman). Sunn introduced powerful amps and extra heavy duty bottoms and was soon popular with many major rock acts. Norm sold his interest to Conrad in '69. Conrad sold the company to the Hartzell Corporation of Minnesota around '72. Fender Musical Instruments acquired the brand in '85 shortly after parting ways with CBS and used the brand until '89. They resurrected the brand again in '98, but quit offering the name in '02.

100S Amp and Cabinet Set

1967-1969. 250 watts, 1x15" JBL D130F and 1 LE 100S JBL Driver and Horn, piggyback, 5 tubes (with rectifier).

1967-1969		$1,125	$1,400

190L Amp and Cabinet Set

1970s. Solidstate, 80 watts, 2 speakers.

1970s		$500	$600

200S/215B Amp and Cabinet Set

1967-1969. 250 watts, 2x6550s, large verticle cab with 2x15" speakers.

1967-1969		$1,200	$1,450

601-L Cabinet

1980s. 6x10" plus 2 tweeters cab.

1980s		$350	$400

2000S Bass Amp Head

1968-1970s. 4x6550 power tubes, 120 watts.

1960s		$1,000	$1,250

Alpha 112 Amp

1980s. Solidstate, MOS-FET preamp section, 1x12" combo, reverb, overdrive, black.

1980s		$150	$200

Alpha 115 Amp

1980s. Solidstate, MOS-FET preamp section, 1x15", clean and overdrive.

1980s		$225	$250

Alpha 212 R Amp

1980s. Solidstate, MOS-FET preamp section, 2x12", reverb.

1980s		$250	$275

Beta Bass Amp

1978-1980s. Solidstate, 100 watts, large "beta bass" logo, 1x15" combo or head only.

1970s	Combo, 1x15"	$550	$650
1970s	Head	$500	$600

Beta Lead Amp

1978-1980s. Solidstate, 100 watts, as 2x12" or 4x10" combo or head only.

1970s	4x12" cab only	$350	$450
1970s	Combo, 2x12" or 4x10"	$600	$700
1970s	Head, 6x10" cab set	$650	$750

Coliseum 300 Bass Amp Head

1970s. Solidstate, Colisium-300 logo on front.

1970s		$375	$475

Coliseum Lead Amp Head

1970s. Solidstate, Coliseum Lead logo on front.

1970s		$425	$525

Coliseum Lead Full Stack Amp

1970s. Coliseum Lead logo on amp head, two 4x12" cabs.

1970s		$1,200	$1,500

Concert 215S Bass Amp Set

1970s. Solidstate head, 200 watts, Model 215S tall vertical cabinet with 2x12" Sunn label speakers, dark vinyl cover, silver sparkle grille.

1970s		$900	$1,100

Straub Twisted Triode

Suhr Badger
Rob Bernstein

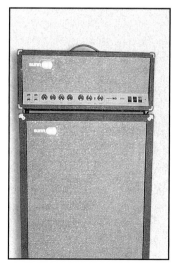

1969 Sunn 100S

AMPS

1967 Sunn Spectrum I

Supro Model 50

1950s Supro Comet

MODEL YEAR	FEATURES	EXC. COND. LOW	HIGH
Concert Bass Amp Head			
1970s. Solidstate, 200 watts.			
1970s		$450	$550
Concert Lead 610S Amp Set			
1970s. Solidstate, 200 watts, 6x10" piggyback, reverb and built-in distortion.			
1970s		$900	$1,100
Enforcer Amp			
1980s	Combo, 60/100w, 2x12"	$575	$700
1980s	Head, 100w	$500	$600
Fuse 200S Amp Head			
1970s. Sunn Fuse logo and model number on front panel, 140 watts.			
1970s		$500	$600
Model T Amp Head			
1970s. 100 watts.			
1970s		$1,500	$1,800
Model T Amp Reissue			
1990s. Reissue of '70s Model T, 100 watts, with 4x12" cab.			
1990s	Head	$900	$1,100
1990s	Head & cab	$1,200	$1,500
SB-160 Bass Amp			
1985. Combo, 60 watts.			
1985		$300	$375
SB-200 Amp			
1985. 200 watts, 1x15", 4-band EQ, master volume, compressor.			
1985		$325	$400
Sceptre Amp			
1968-1972. 60 watts, 6550 power tubes, tremolo, reverb.			
1968-1972	Head	$675	$800
1968-1972	Head & cab	$1,075	$1,300
Sentura Amp			
1967-1970s. Rectifier and power tubes, I and II versions.			
1967-1969	Head	$550	$650
1967-1969	I, 1x15" set	$900	$1,150
1967-1969	II, 2x15" set	$1,000	$1,200
SL 250 Amp			
1980s. 60 watts, 2x12" combo, SL 250 logo.			
1980s		$450	$550
SL 260 Amp			
1982-ca.1985. 60 watts, 2x12" combo with reverb, SL 260 logo.			
1982-1985		$450	$550
Solarus Amp			
1967-1970s. Tube amp (EL34s), 40 watts (upgraded to 60 watts in '69), 2x12", reverb, tremolo.			
1967-1970s	Combo	$550	$700
1967-1970s	Head only	$450	$550
Solo II Amp			
Early-1970s. Solo II logo on front panel, 120 watts, 2x12" combo, black tolex.			
1970s		$475	$550
Sonaro Amp Head			
Early-1970s. 60 watts, 2x6550s.			
1970s		$400	$500

MODEL YEAR	FEATURES	EXC. COND. LOW	HIGH
Sonic 1-40 Amp			
1967-1969. Tube head, 1x15" bass amp, 40 watts.			
1967-1969	Head	$525	$650
1967-1969	Head & cab	$700	$850
Sonic I Amp			
1967-1969. 125 watts, 1x15" JBL D130F in short cabinet, 5 tubes (with rectifier), piggyback, dark tolex.			
1967-1969		$600	$750
Sonic II Amp			
1967-1969. 250 watts, 2x15" JBL D130F in folding horn large cabinet, 5 tubes (with rectifier), piggyback, dark tolex.			
1967-1969		$900	$1,100
Sorado Amp and Cabinet			
1970s. 50 watts, tubes, 2x15" matching cab.			
1970s		$900	$1,100
Spectrum I Amp			
1967-1969. 125 watts, 1x15" JBL D130F large cabinet, 5 tubes (with rectifier), piggyback, dark tolex cover.			
1967-1969		$600	$750
Spectrum II Amp			
1967-1969. 250 watts, 2x12", piggyback, 5 tubes (with rectifier), Spectrum II logo on front panel.			
1967-1969	Head	$550	$650
1967-1969	Head & cab	$1,000	$1,200
SPL 7250 Amp			
Dual channels, 250 watts per channel, forced air cooling, switch-selectable peak compressor with LEDs.			
1989		$325	$400

Supersound

1952-1974. Founded by England's Alan Wootton, building custom amps and radios, the firm continued to build amps and effects into the early '60s. They also built guitars and basses.

Supertone

1914-1941. Supertone was a brand used by Sears for their musical instruments. In the '40s Sears started using the Silvertone name on those products. Amps were made by other companies.

Amp

1930s		$375	$450

Supro

1935-1968, 2004-present. Supro was a budget brand of the National Dobro Company, made by Valco in Chicago, Illinois. Amp builder Bruce Zinky revived the Supro name for a line of guitars and amps.

Accordion 1615T Amp

1957-1959. Compact combo, 1x15", 24 watts, 2x6L6 power, 5V4, 3x12AX7, 2 channels, tremolo, 3 control knobs, Accordion (model) logo upper left corner of grille, Supro logo lower right, Rhino-Hide gray with white sides.

1957-1959		$600	$725

Bantam Amp

1961-1966. Petite, 4 watts, 3 tubes, 1x 8" Jensen, gold weave Saran Wrap grille, Spanish Ivory fabric cover,

MODEL YEAR	FEATURES	EXC. COND. LOW	HIGH

red in '64, gray in '66. Also sold as matching set, for example in '64 with student-level red and white lap steel, add 65% to price for matching guitar and amp set.

1961-1963	1611S, Spanish ivory	$325	$400
1964-1965	S6411, red cover	$325	$400
1966	Gray cover	$325	$400

Bass Combo Amp
Early 1960s. 35 watts, 2x12", 2 channels (bass and standard), 7 tubes, tremolo, woven embossed black and white tolex that appears grey. The '61 model 1688T has a narrow panel body style somewhat similar to the Fender narrow panel cab style of the late '50s, in '62 the cab panel was removed and the 'no panel' style became the 1688TA model, the new cab was less expensive to build and Supro offered a price reduction on applicable models in '62.

| 1961 | 1688T, narrow panel | $650 | $800 |
| 1962-1963 | 1688TA, no panel | $650 | $800 |

Big Star Reverb S6451TR Amp
1964. 35 watts, 2x12", reverb and tremolo, 'no panel' cab.

| 1964 | | $900 | $1,100 |

Brentwood 1650T Amp
Mid-1950s. Advertised as Supro's "finest amplifier", model 1650T described as the "professional twin speaker luxury amplifier", 2 channels including high-gain, tremolo with speed control.

| 1956 | | $700 | $875 |

Combo Amp
1961-1964. 24 watts, 6 tubes, 1x15" Jensen, Rhino-Hide covering in black and white, light grille, tremolo.

| 1961 | 1696T, narrow panel | $600 | $725 |
| 1962-1963 | 1696TA, no panel | $600 | $725 |

Combo Tremolo S6497T Amp
1964. 35 watts, 1x15", standard 'no panel' cab, tremolo.

| 1964 | | $650 | $800 |

Comet 1610B Amp
1957-1959. Gray Rhino-Hide, 1x10".

| 1957-1959 | | $450 | $550 |

Comet 1610E Amp
Mid-1950s. Supro's only 1x10" amp from the mid-'50s, 3 input jacks, 2 control knobs, woven tweed and leatherette 2-tone covering.

| 1956 | | $450 | $550 |

Coronado Amp
1960-1963. 24 watts, 2x10", tremolo, 2 channels, 6 tubes, Supro logo upper right above grille, black and white mixed tolex appears gray, described as tremolo twin-speaker pro amp, '61 has 'narrow panel' body style, new body style in '62 becomes 1690TA model with grille only and no panel.

| 1960-1961 | 1690T, narrow panel | $650 | $800 |
| 1962-1963 | 1690TA, no panel | $650 | $800 |

Corsica Amp
Mid-1960s. Redesigned vertical combo amp, reverb, tremolo, blue control panel, black tolex, silver grille.

| 1965-1967 | | $450 | $575 |

Dual-Tone Amp
1961-1965. 17 watts, 6 tubes, 1x12" Jensen, organ tone tremolo, restyled in '64, Trinidad Blue vinyl fabric cover, light color grille.

1961	1624T, narrow panel	$550	$700
1962-1963	1624TA, no panel	$550	$700
1964-1965	S6424T, no panel	$550	$700

Galaxy Tremolo S6488 Amp
1965. 35 watts, 2x12" (often Jensen), 7 tubes, tremolo, multi-purpose for guitar, bass and accordion.

| 1965 | | $675 | $825 |

Galaxy Tremolo S6688 Amp
1966-1967. 35 watts, 2x12" (often Jensen), turquoise front control panel with Supro logo (not on grille), model name/number also on front control panel.

| 1966-1967 | | $625 | $775 |

Golden Holiday 1665T Amp
Mid-1950s. Supro's model for the 'semi-professional', 2 oval 11x6" speakers, 14 watts, 6 tubes, tremolo, 2 control knobs, black and tweed cover.

| 1956 | | $650 | $800 |

Model 24 Amp
1965. 18 watts, 1x12 combo, 2 channels each with bass and treble inputs, tremolo, Model 24 logo on top panel, Calypso Blue vinyl cover.

| 1965 | | $550 | $700 |

Reverb 1650R Amp
1963. 17 watts, 1x10", 'no panel' grille front style cab, reverb.

| 1963 | | $575 | $700 |

Royal Reverb 1650TR Amp
1963-1965. 17 watts, 15 tubes, 2x10" Jensens, catalog says "authentic tremolo and magic-reverberation."

| 1963-1965 | | $800 | $1,000 |

Special 1633E Amp
Mid-1950s. Supro's entry level student amp, 1x8", 3 tubes, large Supro stencil logo on grille, 2-tone red and white fabric cover, leather handle, available with matching Special Lap Steel covered in wine-maroon plastic.

| 1956 | | $300 | $400 |

Spectator 1614E Amp
Mid-1950s. 1x8", 3 tubes, 2 control knobs, white front with red and black body.

| 1956 | | $375 | $450 |

Sportsman S6689 Amp
1966. Piggyback, twin speakers.

| 1966 | | $775 | $950 |

Statesman S6699 Amp
1966. Piggyback with blue-green control panel, 4x6L6 power, horizontal 2x12" cab, reverb, tremolo, script Statesman logo with model number on upper left front of chasis.

| 1966 | | $650 | $800 |

Studio 1644E Amp
Mid-1950s. Supro's student model for teaching studios, 2 input jacks for student and instructor or guitar and lap steel guitar, 3 tubes, advertised for "true Hawaiian tone reproduction", covered in royal blue leatherette (in '56), available with a matching Studio Lap Steel covered in blue plastic.

| 1956-1957 | Blue leatherette | $375 | $450 |

Supro Golden Holiday

Supro Spectator

Supro Super

Supro Supreme Twin Speaker

1966 Supro Thunderbolt

SWR Goliath Junior III Cab

MODEL YEAR	FEATURES	EXC. COND. LOW	HIGH

Super 1606E Amp
Mid-1950s. Supro advertising states "with features important to women", oval 11x6" Rola speaker, 3 tubes, 1 control knob, 2 inputs, white (front) and grey sides, elliptical baffle soundhole with Supro logo, model number with E suffix common for '50s Supro's.

1956	White front & grey	$375	$450

Super Amp
1961-1963. 4.5 watts, 3 tubes, 1x8", 1606S has contrasting black and white covering with old narrow panel cab, in '63 new 1606B has 'no panel' style cab with lighter (gray) covering.

1961-1962	1606S	$350	$425
1963	1606B	$350	$425

Super Six S6406 Amp
1964-1965. Student practice amp, 4.5 watts, 1x8", blue vinyl cover.

1964-1965		$350	$425

Super Six S6606 Amp
1966. Updated version of student compact amp.

1966		$275	$325

Supreme Amp
1961-1963. 17 watts, 1x10", designed for use with Model 600 Reverb Accessory Unit, value shown does not include the Model 600 (see Effects Section for reverb unit). The initial 1600R model was designed with a triangle-like shaped soundhole, in '62 the more typical Supro no panel cab was introduced which Supro called the new slope front design.

1961	1600R	$500	$625
1962-1963	1600S, no panel	$500	$625

Supreme 17 S6400 Amp
1964-1965. 17 watts, 1x10", cab larger than prior models of this type.

1964-1965		$500	$625

Supreme Twin Speaker 1600E Amp
Mid-1950s. 2 oval 11x6" speakers, 5 tubes, 3 input jacks, 2 control knobs, grille logo states "Twin Speaker" but unlike most Supro amps of this era the Supro logo does not appear on the front.

1956		$500	$625

Thunderbolt S6420(B) Bass Amp
1964-1967. 35 watts, 1x15" Jensen, introduced in the '64 catalog as a no frills - no fancy extra circuits amp. Sometimes referred to as the "Jimmy Page amp" based on his use of this amp in his early career.

1964-1967		$775	$975

Thunderbolt S6920 Amp
1967-1968. Redesign circuit replaced S6420B, 35 watts, 1x12".

1967-1968		$400	$500

Tremo-Verb S6422TR Amp
1964-1965. Lower power using 4 12AX7s, 1 5Y3GT, and 1 6V6, 1x10", tremolo and reverb, Persian Red vinyl cover.

1964-1965		$700	$875

Trojan Tremolo Amp
1961-1966. 5 watts, 4 tubes, 1 11"x6" oval (generally Rolla) speaker, '61-'64 black and white fabric cover and Saran Wrap grille, '64-'66 new larger cab with vinyl cover and light grille.

1961	1616T, narrow panel	$400	$500

MODEL YEAR	FEATURES	EXC. COND. LOW	HIGH
1962-1963	1616TA, no panel	$400	$500
1964-1966	S6461,		
	blue vinyl cover	$400	$500

Vibra-Verb S6498VR Amp
1964-1965. Billed as Supro's finest amplifier, 2x35-watt channels, 1x15" and 1x10" Jensens, vibrato and reverb.

1964-1965		$1,000	$1,225

Swampdonkey
2006-present. Professional and premium grade, production/custom, guitar amp heads, combos and speaker cabinets built in Rural Rocky View, Alberta by Chris Czech.

Swanpro Amps
2004-present. Robert Swanson builds his tube combo and head amps and cabinets in Denver, Colorado.

Swart Amplifier Co. (Space Tone)
2003-present. Michael J. Swart builds tube combo and head amps and cabinets under the Swart and Space Tone brand names in Wilmington, North Carolina. He also builds effects.

SWR Sound
1984-present. Founded by Steve W. Rabe in '84, with an initial product focus on bass amplifiers. Fender Musical Instruments Corp. acquired SWR in June, 2003.

Baby Blue Studio Bass System
1990-2003. Combo, all tube preamp, 150 watts solidstate power amp, 2x8", 1x5" cone tweeter, gain, master volume, EQ, effects-blend.

1990-2003		$400	$500

Basic Black Amp
1992-1999. Solidstate, 100 watts, 1x12", basic black block logo on front, black tolex, black metal grille.

1992-1999		$350	$425

California Blonde Amp
2000s. Vertical upright combo, 100 watts, 1x12" plus high-end tweeters, blond cover, thin black metal grille.

2003		$400	$500

Goliath III Cabinet
1996-2008. Black tolex, black metal grille, includes the Goliath III Jr. (2x10") and the Goliath III (4x10").

1996-2008	2x10"	$250	$250
1996-2008	4x10"	$375	$425

Strawberry Blonde Amp
1998-present. 80 watts, 1x10" acoustic instrument amp.

1998-2010		$275	$325

Studio 220 Bass Amp
1988-1995. 220 watt solidstate head, tube preamp

1988-1995		$250	$300

MODEL YEAR	FEATURES	EXC. COND. LOW	HIGH

Workingman's Series Amp
1995-2004. Introduced in '95, replaced by Working-Pro in '05.

1995-2004	10, 200w, 2x10"	$200	$250
1995-2004	12, 100w, 1x12"	$200	$250
1995-2004	15 Bass, 1x15"	$225	$275

Symphony
1950s. Probably a brand from an teaching studio, large Symphony script red letter logo on front.

Small Tube Amp
1950s. Two guitar inputs, 1x6" speaker, alligator tweed suitcase.

1950s		$200	$250

Synaptic Amplification
2007-present. Intermediate to premium grade, production/custom, amps built in Brunswick, Maine by Steven O'Connor.

Takt
Late-1960s. Made in Japan, tube and solidstate models.

GA Series Amps
1968. GA-9 (2 inputs and 5 controls, 3 tubes), GA-10, GA-11, GA-12, GA-14, GA-15.

1968	GA-14/GA-15	$50	$75
1968	GA-9 thru GA-12	$25	$50

Talos
2004-present. Doug Weisbrod and Bill Thalmann build their tube amp heads, combo amps, and speaker cabinets in Springfield, Virginia. They started building and testing prototypes in '01.

Tech 21
1989-present. Long known for their SansAmp tube amplifier emulator, Tech 21 added solidstate combo amps, heads and cabinets in '96.

Teisco
1946-1974, 1994-present. Japanese brand first imported into the U.S. around '63. Teisco offered both tube and solidstate amps.

Checkmate CM-10 Amp
1960s. Tubes or solidstate, 10 watts.

1960s	Solidstate	$25	$50
1960s	Tubes	$150	$200

Checkmate CM-15 Amp
Late-1960s. Tubes, 15 watts.

1960s		$150	$200

Checkmate CM-16 Amp
1960s. Tubes or solidstate, 15 watts.

1960s	Solidstate	$40	$65
1960s	Tubes	$150	$200

Checkmate CM-17 Amp
1960s. Tubes, 1x10", reverb, tremolo.

1960s		$275	$325

Checkmate CM-20 Amp
Late-1960s. Tubes, 20 watts.

1960s		$275	$325

MODEL YEAR	FEATURES	EXC. COND. LOW	HIGH

Checkmate CM-25 Amp
Late-1960s. Tubes, 25 watts.

1960s		$275	$325

Checkmate CM-50 Amp
Late-1950s-early-1960s. Tubes, 2 6L6s, 50 watts, 2x12" open back, reverb, tremolo, piggyback, gray tolex cover, light gray grille.

1960s		$400	$500

Checkmate CM-60 Amp
Late-1960s. Tubes, 60 watts, piggyback amp and cab with wheels.

1960s		$200	$250

Checkmate CM-66 Amp
Late-1960s. Solidstate, dual speaker combo, Check Mate 66 logo on front panel.

1960s		$50	$75

Checkmate CM-88 Amp
1960s. Solidstate, 10 watts, 2x8".

1960s		$50	$75

Checkmate CM-100 Amp
Late-1960s. Tubes, 4x6L6 power, 100 watts, piggyback with Vox-style trolley stand.

1960s		$200	$250

King 1800 Amp
Late-1960s. Tubes, 180 watts, piggyback with 2 cabinets, large Teisco logo on cabinets, King logo on lower right side of one cabinet.

1960s		$350	$400

Teisco 8 Amp
Late-1960s. Solidstate, 5 watts.

1960s		$50	$75

Teisco 10 Amp
Late-1960s. Solidstate, 5 watts.

1960s		$50	$75

Teisco 88 Amp
Late-1960s. Solidstate, 8 watts.

1960s		$75	$100

Tempo
1950s-1970s. Tube (early on) and solidstate amps, most likely imported by Merson Musical Products from Japan. They also offered basses and guitars.

Model 39
1950s. Compact amp, verticle cab, tweed, 3 tubes, single control knob for on-off volume, 3 imputs.

1950s		$300	$350

Teneyck
1960s. Solidstate amp heads and speaker cabinets built by Bob Teneyck, who had previously done design work for Ampeg.

THD
1987-present. Tube amps and cabinets built in Seattle, Washington, founded by Andy Marshall.

The Valve
2000-present. Guitar luthier Galeazzo Frudua also builds a line of professional grade, production/custom, amps in San Lazzaro di Savena, Italy.

Synaptic Catalyst

Talos Basic

Tech 21 Bronzewood 60

TomasZewicZ TZZ-35212L

Tone King Galaxy

Top Hat Club Royale TC-R1

MODEL		EXC. COND.	
YEAR	FEATURES	LOW	HIGH

ThroBak Electronics

2004-present. Jonathan Gundry builds his tube combo guitar amps in Grand Rapids, Michigan. He also builds guitar effects and pickups.

Titano (Magnatone)

1961-1963. Private branded by Magnatone, often for an accordion company or accordion studio, uses standard guitar input jacks.

Model 262 R Custom Amp

1961-1963. 35 watts, 2x12" + 2x5", reverb and vibrato make this one of the top-of-the-line models, black vinyl, light silver grille.

| 1961-1963 | | $1,100 | $1,300 |

Model 313 Amp

1961-1963. Like Magnatone 213 Troubadour, 10 watts, 1x12" combo, vibrato, brown tolex, brownish grille.

| 1961-1963 | | $550 | $650 |

Model 415 Bass Amp

1961-1963. 25 watts, 4x8", bass or accordion amp, black cover, darkish grille.

| 1961-1963 | | $900 | $1,100 |

TomasZewicZ Amplifiers

2008-present. Intermediate and professional grade, production/custom, tube guitar amp heads and combos built by John Tomaszewicz in Coral Springs, Florida. He also builds effects.

Tombo

This Japanese harmonica manufacturer introduced a solidbody electric ukulele and a Silvertone-esque case with onboard amplifier in the mid-1960s.

Tone King

1993-present. Tube amps, combos, and cabinets built by Mark Bartel in Baltimore, Maryland. The company started in New York and moved to Baltimore in '94.

Tonemaster (Magnatone)

Late-1950s-early-1960s. Magnatone amps private branded for Imperial Accordion Company. Prominent block-style capital TONEMASTER logo on front panel, generally something nearly equal to Magnatone equivalent. This is just one of many private branded Magnatones. Covers range from brown to black leatherette and brown to light silver grilles. They also offered guitars.

Model 214 (V logo) Amp

1959-1960. Ten watts, 1x12", vibrato, brown leatherette, V logo lower right corner front, large TONEMASTER logo.

| 1959-1960 | | $650 | $800 |

Model 260 Amp

1961-1963. About 30 watts, 2x12", vibrato, brown leatherette and brown grille, large TONEMASTER logo on front.

| 1961-1963 | | $1,400 | $1,700 |

Model 261 Custom Amp

1961-1963. Tonemaster Custom 261 High Fidelity logo on back chasis panel, Tonemaster logo on front panel, 35 watts, 2x12" combo, 2 channels, vibrato.

| 1961-1963 | | $1,400 | $1,700 |

Model 380 Amp

1961-1963. 50 watts, 2x12" and 2 oval 5"x7" speakers, vibrato, no reverb.

| 1961-1963 | | $1,400 | $1,700 |

Model 381 Custom Amp

1961-1963. Tonemaster Custom 381 High Fidelity logo on back chasis panel, Tonemaster logo on front panel, 2x12", 1x5".

| 1961-1963 | | $1,400 | $1,700 |

Small Combo Amp

1950s-1960s. 1x8", tremolo, light tan.

| 1950-1960s | | $425 | $525 |

Tonic Amps

2003-present. Darin Ellingson builds professional and premium grade, production/custom, amps and cabinets in Redwood City, California.

Top Hat Amplification

1994-present. Mostly Class A guitar amps built by Brian Gerhard originally in La Habra, California, then in '05 in Fuquay-Varina, North Carolina, and since '09 in Apex, North Carolina. He also makes effects.

Ambassador 100 TH-A100 Amp Head

Jan.1999-present. 100 watts, Class AB, 4 6L6s, reverb, dark green vinyl cover, white chicken-head knobs.

| 1999-2010 | | $1,050 | $1,200 |

Ambassador T-35C 212 Amp

1999-present. 35 watts, 2x12" combo, reverb, master volume, blond cover, tweed-style fabric grille.

| 1999-2010 | | $1,050 | $1,200 |

Club Deluxe Amp

1998-2009. 20 watts, 6V6 power tubes, 1x12".

| 1998-2009 | | $1,050 | $1,200 |

Club Royale TC-R1 Amp

Jan.1998-present. Class A using EL84s, 20 watts, 1x12".

| 1998-2010 | | $725 | $850 |

Club Royale TC-R2 Amp

Jan.1999-present. Class A using EL84s, 20 watts, 2x12".

| 1999-2010 | | $1,100 | $1,300 |

Emplexador 50 TH-E50 Amp Head

Jan.1997-present. 50 watts, Class AB vint/high-gain head.

| 1997-2010 | | $1,250 | $1,500 |

King Royale Amp

1996-present. 35 watts, Class A using 4 EL84s, 2x12".

| 1996-2010 | | $1,150 | $1,400 |

Portly Cadet TC-PC Amp

Jan.1999-2004. Five watts, 6V6 power, 1x8", dark gray, light gray grille.

| 1999-2004 | | $475 | $575 |

MODEL YEAR	FEATURES	EXC. COND. LOW	HIGH

Prince Royale TC-PR Amp
Jan.2000-2002. Five watts using EL84 power, 1x8", deep red, light grille.

| 2000-2002 | | $475 | $575 |

Super Deluxe TC-SD2 Amp
Jan.2000-present. 30 watts, Class A, 7591 power tubes, 2x12".

| 2000-2010 | | $950 | $1,150 |

Torres Engineering

Founded by Dan Torres, the company builds tube amps, combos, cabinets and amp kits originally in San Mateo, California, then San Carlos and since '11 in Milton, Washington. Dan wrote monthly columns for *Vintage Guitar* magazine for many years and authored the book *Inside Tube Amps.*

Trace Elliot

1978-present. Founded in Essex, England. U.S. distribution picked up by Kaman (Ovation) in '88 which bought Trace Elliot in '92. In '98 Gibson acquired the brand and in early '02 closed the factory and moved what production was left to the U.S. In '05 Peavey bought the brand name, hiring back many of the old key people, and currently offers professional grade, production, tube and solidstate, acoustic guitar and bass amp heads, combos, and cabinets, with product built in England and the U.S.

Trainwreck

1983-2006. High-end tube guitar amp heads built by Ken Fischer in Colonia, New Jersey. Limited production, custom-made amps that are generally grouped by model. Models include the Rocket, Liverpool and Express, plus variations on those themes. Instead of using serial numbers, he gave each amp a woman's name. Due to illness, Fischer didn't make many amps after the mid '90s, but he continued to design amps for other builders. His total production is estimated at less than 100. Each amp's value should be evaluated on a case-by-case basis. Ken wrote many amp articles for *Vintage Guitar.* Fischer died in late 2006.

Custom Built Amp

| 1980s | High-end model | $20,000 | $25,000 |

Traynor

1963-present. Started by Pete Traynor and Jack Long in the back of Long & McQuade Music in Toronto, Canada where Traynor was a repairman. Currently offering tube and solidstate amp heads, combos and cabinets made by parent company Yorkville Sound, in Pickering, Ontario.

YBA1 Bass Master Amp Head
1963-1979. 45 watts, called Dynabass for 1963-'64, this was Pete Traynor's first amp design.

| 1963-1979 | | $425 | $525 |

YBA1A Mark II Bass Master Amp Head
1968-1976. Like YBA1, but with 90 watts and cooling fan.

| 1968-1976 | | $450 | $550 |

YBA3 Custom Special Bass Amp Set
1967-1972. Tube head with 130 watts and 8x10" large vertical matching cab, dark vinyl cover, light grille.

| 1967-1972 | | $675 | $825 |

YGA1 Amp Head
1966-1967. 45 watts guitar amp, tremolo.

| 1966-1967 | | $425 | $525 |

YGL3 Mark III Amp
1971-1979. All tube, 80 watts, 2x12" combo, reverb, tremolo.

| 1971-1979 | | $625 | $750 |

YGM3 Guitar Mate Reverb Amp
1969-1979. Tubes, 25 watts, 1x12", black tolex, gray grille until '74, black after.

| 1969-1979 | | $475 | $575 |

YRM1 Reverb Master Amp Head
1973-1979. 45 watt tube amp, reverb, tremolo.

| 1973-1979 | | $350 | $425 |

YRM1SC Reverb Master Amp
1973-1979. YRM1 as a 4x10" combo.

| 1973-1979 | | $400 | $500 |

YSR1 Custom Reverb Amp Head
1968-1973. 45 watt tube amp, reverb, tremolo.

| 1968-1973 | | $350 | $450 |

YVM Series PA Amp Head
1967-1980. Public address heads, models include tube YVM-1 Voice Master, and solidstate YVM-2 and 3 Voice Mate and YVM-4, all with 4 inputs.

1967-1972	1, tubes	$300	$350
1969-1975	2, solidstate	$100	$150
1970-1980	3, solidstate, reverb	$150	$175
1972-1977	4, solidstate, reverb	$175	$200

Trillium Amplifier Company

2007-present. Brothers Stephen and Scott Campbell build their professional and premium grade, production/custom tube amps in Indianapolis, Indiana.

Trinity Amps

2003-present. Stephen Cohrs builds his production/custom, professional grade, tube amps and cabinets in Toronto, Ontario.

True Tone

1960s. Guitars and amps retailed by Western Auto, manufactured by Chicago guitar makers like Kay.

Hi-Fi 4 (K503 Hot-Line Special) Amp
1960s. Similar to K503, 4 watts from 3 tubes, gray cabinet, gray grille, metal handle.

| 1960s | | $250 | $300 |

Vibrato 704 Amp
1960s. Solidstate, 10 watts, 1x8", white sides and gray back, gray grille.

| 1960s | | $250 | $300 |

Vibrato 706 Amp
1960s. Solidstate, 15 watts, 1x15", white sides and gray back, brown grille.

| 1960s | | $400 | $475 |

Torres Engineering Boogie Mite

1970 Traynor YBA1 Bass Master

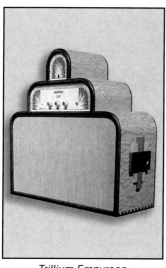

Trillium Empyrean

AMPS

Two-Rock Jet

Ugly Amps 18 Head

UltraSound DS4

MODEL YEAR	FEATURES	EXC. COND. LOW	HIGH

Tube Works

1987-2004. Founded by B.K. Butler in Denver, Tube Works became a division of Genz Benz Enclosures of Scottsdale, Arizona in 1997. Tube Works' first products were tube guitar effects and in '91 they added tube/solidstate amps, cabinets, and DI boxes to the product mix. In '04, Genz Benz dropped the brand.

Twilighter (Magnatone)

Late-1950s-early-1960s. Magnatone amps private branded for LoDuca Brothers. Prominent block-style capital TWILIGHTER logo on front panel, generally something nearly equal to Magnatone equivalent. This is just one of many private branded Magnatones. Covers range from brown to black leatherette, and brown to light silver grilles.

Model 213 Amp
1961-1963. About 20 watts, 1x12", vibrato, brown leatherette and brown grille.
1961-1963 $550 $700

Model 260R Amp
1961-1963. About 18 to 25 watts, 1x12", vibrato, brown leatherette cover.
1961-1963 $900 $1,100

Model 280A Amp
Late-1950s-early-1960s. About 35 watts, 2x12", vibrato, brown leatherette cover.
1961-1963 $1,000 $1,250

Two-Rock

1999-present. Tube guitar amp heads, combos and cabinets built by Joe Mloganoski and Bill Krinard (K&M Analog Designs) originally in Cotati, California, currently in Rohnert Park. They also build speakers.

Ugly Amps

2003-present. Steve O'Boyle builds his tube head and combo amps and cabinets in Burbank, California and Reading, Pennsylvania.

UltraSound

A division of UJC Electronics, UltraSound builds acoustically transparent amps, designed by Greg Farres for the acoustic guitarist, in Adel, Iowa.

Unique (Magnatone)

1961-1963. Private branded, typically for an accordion company or accordion studio, uses standard guitar input jacks.

Model 260R Amp
1961-1963. Based on Magnatone 260 Series amp, 35 watts, 2x12" but with reverb, black vinyl-style cover with distinctive black diamond-check pattern running through the top and sides.
1961-1963 $1,200 $1,500

Model 460 Amp
1961-1963. 35 watts, 2x12" and oval 5"x7" speakers, reverb and vibrato make it one of the top models, black vinyl, black grille.
1961-1963 $1,300 $1,600

Univox

1964-ca.1978. From '64 to early-'68, these were American-made tube amps with Jensen speakers. By '68, they were using Japanese components in American cabinets, still with Jensen speakers. Electronics were a combination of tube and transistors during this time; this type lasted until the mid-'70s. Around '71, Univox introduced a line of all solidstate amps, as well.

Model Tube Lead Amp
1960s. Tube amp, 2x10" or 2x12".
1965-1969 $600 $700

Model U45B Bass Amp
1965-1968. 1x12" combo tube bass amp, 10 watts.
1965-1968 $275 $325

Model U60A Amp
1965-1968. 1x12" tube combo.
1965-1968 $300 $350

Model U65R Amp
1965-1968. 20 watts, 1x12" tube combo.
1965-1968 $350 $450

Model U65RD Lead 65 Amp
1976-1978. Solidstate, 65 watts, reverb, 1x12" or 2x12" in a vertical cab.
1976-1978 $50 $75

Model U102 Amp
1965-1968. 1x12" tube combo.
1965-1968 $350 $450

Model U130B Bass Amp
1976-1978. Solidstate, 130 watts, 1x15".
1976-1978 $150 $200

Model U130L Lead Amp
1976-1978. Solidstate, 130 watts.
1976-1978 $150 $200

Model U155R Amp
1965-1968. 20 watts, 1x12" tube combo.
1965-1968 $450 $550

Model U202R Amp
1965-1968. 1x12" tube combo.
1965-1968 $450 $550

Model U305R Amp
1965-1968. 30 watts, 1x15" tube combo.
1965-1968 $550 $650

Model U1011 Lead Amp Head
1976-1978. Solidstate, 100 watts, reverb, tremolo.
1976-1978 $225 $275

Model U1061 Bass Amp Head
1976-1978. Solidstate.
1976-1978 $225 $275

Model U1220 Amp
1968-1971. Tubes or tube-hybrid, piggyback, 2x12".
1968-1971 $350 $450

Model U1246B Bass Amp Head
1976-1978. Solidstate, 60 watts.
1976-1978 $225 $275

Model U1246L Lead Amp Head
1976-1978. Solidstate.
1976-1978 $225 $275

AMPS

MODEL		EXC. COND.	
YEAR	FEATURES	LOW	HIGH

Valco

Valco, from Chicago, Illinois, was a big player in the guitar and amplifier business. Their products were private branded for other companies like National, Supro, Airline, Oahu, and Gretsch.

Valvetech

1997-present. Production/custom, professional grade, amps built by Rob Pierce in Ossian, Indiana.

Valvetrain Amplification

2005-present. Tube combos, amp heads, and speaker cabinets built by Rick Gessner in Sorrento, Florida. He also builds reverb units.

Vamp

1970s. Tube and solidstate amps and speaker cabinets built at Triumph Electronics in England.

Bass Master Amp Head

1970. 100 watts.

1970		$1,200	$1,500

VanAmps

1999-present. Tim Van Tassel builds professional, production/custom, amps and cabinets in Golden Valley, Minnesota. He also builds effects.

Vega

1903-present. The original Boston-based company was purchased by C.F. Martin in '70. In '80, the Vega trademark was sold to a Korean company.

A-49 Amp

1960s. Tubes, 6 watts, 1x8", tan cover.

1960s		$225	$275

Director Combo Amp

1950s. Small to mid-size tube amp, 2-tone cover, 2 volume and 1 tone controls, rear mounted control chassis similar to Fender or Gibson from the '50s.

1950s		$475	$575

Super Amp

Early 1950s. 1 6L6, 1x10", vertical combo amp typical of the era.

1950s		$450	$550

Vesta Fire

1980s. Japanese imports by Shiino Musical Instruments Corp.; later by Midco International. Mainly known for effects pedals.

Power Amps

1980s	PT-I	$125	$150
1980s	PT-II	$175	$200

Preamps

1980s	J-I, J-II	$75	$100

VHT

1989-present. Founded by Steven M. Fryette, VHT built amps, combos, and cabinets in Burbank, California. At the beginning of '09 AXL guitars acquired the VHT name and manufactures their own product under that brand. Fryette continues to build the VHT amp models under Fryette Amplification.

Vibe Amplification

2008-present. Intermediate grade, production, tube amps, imported from Asia by Lorenzo Brogi in Bologna, Italy.

Victor

Late-1960s. Made in Japan.

MA-25 Amp

Late-1960s. Student model, light cover, dark grille, solidstate, 6 controls, 2 inputs, script Victor logo.

1960s		$100	$125

Victoria

1994-present. Tube amps, combos, and reverb units built by Mark Baier in Naperville, Illinois.

Double Deluxe Amp

1994-present. 35 watts, 2x12".

1994-2010		$1,300	$1,600

Electro King Amp

2008-present. 1957 GA-40 type circuit, tubes, 15 watts, 1x12".

2008-2010		$1,500	$1,850

Model 518 Amp

1994-present. Tweed, 1x8".

1994-2010		$550	$700

Model 5112-T Amp

2001-present. 5 watts, 5F1 circuit, 1x12".

2001-2010		$700	$850

Model 20112 Amp

1994-present. 20 watts, 1x12", tweed.

1994-2010		$1,100	$1,400

Model 35210 Amp

1994-present. 35 watts, 2x10", tweed.

1994-2010		$1,125	$1,300

Model 35212-T Amp

1990s. 35 watts, 2x12".

1990s		$1,450	$1,800

Model 35310-T Amp

1994-present. 35 watts, 3x10".

1994-2010		$1,350	$1,600

Model 45115-T Amp

2008-2009.

2008-2009		$1,250	$1,500

Model 45410-T Amp

1994-present. 45 watts, 4x10" combo, tweed.

1994-2010		$1,350	$1,600

Model 50212-T Amp

2002-present. 50 watts, 2x12" combo.

2002-2010		$1,450	$1,800

Model 80212 Amp

1994-present. 80 watts, 2x12", tweed.

1994-2010		$1,450	$1,800

Regal Amp

2004-2006. Class A with 1 x 6L6, 15 watts, 1x15", brown tolex cover, rear mount controls.

2004-2006		$1,550	$1,750

Regal II Amp

2006-present. Class A, 35 watts, 1x15", tweed or vanilla tolex, rear mount controls.

2006-2010		$1,550	$1,750

Valvetrain 205 Tall Boy

VHT Standard 12

Victoria Regal

AMPS

Voodoo Witchdoctor Combo

Vox AC-4 TV Mini

Vox AC-15CC

Victoriette Amp

2001-present. 20 watts, 1x12" or 2x10", reverb, tremolo in '01.

2001-2010	2x10"	$1,300	$1,600

Victorilux Amp

2001-present. 35 watts, 2x12", 3x10" or 1x15", EL84s, reverb, tremolo.

2001-2010	3x10"	$1,300	$1,600

Vivi-Tone

1933-ca.1936. Founded in Kalamazoo, Michigan, by former Gibson designer Lloyd Loar and others, Vivi-Tone built small amps to accompany their early electric solidbody guitars. They possibly also built basses and mandolins.

V-M (Voice of Music) Corp.

1944-1977. Started out building record changers in Benton Harbor, Michigan. By the early '50s had added amplified phonographs, consoles, and tape recorders as well as OEM products for others. Their portable PA systems can be used for musical instruments. Products sport the VM logo.

Small Portable Amp

1950s. Standard phono input for instrument, phono and microphone controls, wood combo cabinet, 1x10" or 1x12" Jensen.

1950s		$275	$325

Voltmaster

Trapezoid-shaped combo amps and reverb units made in Plano, Texas, in the late 1990s.

Voodoo

1998-present. Tube amp heads and speaker cabinets built in Lansing, New York by Trace Davis, Anthony Cacciotti, and Mike Foster.

Vox

1954-present. Tom Jennings and Dick Denney combined forces in '57 to produce the first Vox amp, the 15-watt AC-15. The period between '57-'68 is considered to be the Vox heyday. Vox produced tube amps in England and also the U.S. from '64 to '65. English-made tube amps were standardized between '60 and '65. U.S.-made Vox amps in '66 were solidstate. In the mid-'60s, similar model names were sometimes used for tube and solidstate amps. In '93 Korg bought the Vox name and current products are built by Marshall. Those amps that originally came with a trolley are priced including the original trolley, and an amp without one will be worth less than the amount shown. Smaller amps were not originally equipped with a trolley.

4120 Bass Amp

1966-1967. Hybrid solidstate and tube bass amp.

1966-1967		$475	$575

7120 Guitar Amp

1966-1967. Hybrid solidstate and tube amp, 120 watts.

1966-1967		$500	$600

AC-4 Amp

1961-1965. Made in England, early Vox tube design, 3.5 watts, 1x8", tremolo.

1961-1965		$1,200	$1,500

AC-4TV Amp

2009-present. Tube, 4 watts, in 1x10 (AC-4TV8 is 1x8) combo or head amp with 1x12 cab, EL84 power tube, 12AX7 powered preamp. AC-4TVmini combo has 6.5 inch speaker.

2009-2010	TV, Combo	$150	$175
2009-2010	TVH, Head only	$125	$150
2009-2010	V112-TV 1x12 cab	$100	$125

AC-10 Amp

1958-1965. Made in England, 12 watts, 1x10", tremolo, this tube version not made in U.S. ('64-'65).

1958-1965		$2,200	$2,800

AC-10 Twin Amp

1962-1965. Made in England, also made in U.S. '64-'65, 12 watts (2xEL84s), 2x10".

1962-1965		$2,700	$3,300

AC-15 Amp

1958-1965. 15 watts, 1x12".

1958-1965		$3,400	$4,000

AC-15 Twin Amp

1962-1965. Tube, 2x12", 18 watts.

1962-1965	Black Tolex	$3,600	$4,200
1962-1965	Custom colors	$4,200	$5,200

AC-15 50th Anniversary

2007. 50th Anniversary 1957-2007 plaque on lower left front of grille, hand wired, white tolex.

2007		$625	$775

AC-15H1TV Amp

2008-2009. Part of Heritage Collection, limited edition, 200 made, hand wired, oiled mahogany cabinet.

2008-2009		$1,050	$1,300

AC-15TBX Amp

1996-2000. 15 watts, top boost, 1x12" Celestion (lower cost Eminence available).

1996-2000		$750	$900

AC-15CC Custom Classic Amp

2006-present. Made in China, 15 watts, 1x12" tube combo, master volume, reverb, tremolo, 2-button footswitch.

2006-2010		$375	$450

AC-30 Reissue Model Amps

1980s-1990s. Standard reissue and limited edtion models with identification plate on back of the amp. Models include the AC-30 Reissue and Reissue custom color (1980s-1990s), AC-30 25th Anniv. (1985-1986), AC-30 30th Anniv. (1991), AC-30 Collector Model (1990s, mahogany cabinet) and the AC-30HW Hand Wired (1990s).

1980s	Reissue	$1,200	$1,500
1985-1986	25th Anniv.	$1,300	$1,600
1990-2000s	Reissue	$1,100	$1,300
1990s	Collector Model	$1,800	$2,200
1990s	Custom colors	$1,400	$1,700
1990s	Hand wired	$1,800	$2,200
1991	30th Anniv.	$1,550	$1,850

MODEL YEAR	FEATURES	EXC. COND. LOW	HIGH

AC-30 Super Twin Amp Head
1962-1965. Made in England, 30-watt head.

1962-1963	Custom colors	$4,000	$5,000
1962-1965	Black, with footswitch	$2,800	$3,600

AC-30 Twin/AC-30 Twin Top Boost Amp
1960-1972. Made in England, 30-watt head, 36 watts 2x12", Top Boost includes additional treble and bass, custom colors available in '60-'63.

1960-1963	Custom colors	$4,500	$5,500
1960-1965		$3,900	$4,500
1966	Tube	$3,000	$3,800
1967-1972	Solidstate	$2,000	$2,500

AC-30BM Brian May Limited Edition Amp
2007. 30 watts, 2x12" combo.

2007		$1,600	$1,800

AC-30CC Custom Classic Amp
2006. Made in China, 30 watts, 2x12", tubes, 2-button footswitch.

2006		$700	$900

AC-50 Amp Head
1963-1975. Made in England, 50-watt head, U.S. production '64-'65 tube version is Westminster Bass, U.S. post-'66 is solidstate.

1963-1965		$1,700	$2,100

AC-100 MK I Amp
1964-1965. All tube 100-watt with 4x12 cab, due to reliability concerns it was transitioned to AC-100 Super De Luxe MK II in '65.

1964-1965		$4,400	$5,400

AC-100 Super De Luxe MK II Amp
1965. Solidstate 100-watt head with 4x12 cab on speaker trolley.

1965		$2,400	$3,000

Berkeley II V108 (Tube) Amp
1964-1966. U.S.-made tube amp, revised '66-'69 to U.S.-made solidstate model V1081, 18 watts, 2x10" piggyback.

1964-1966		$1,000	$1,250

Berkeley II V1081 (Solidstate) Amp
1966-1967. U.S.-made solidstate model V1081, 35 watts, 2x10" piggyback, includes trolley stand.

1966-1967		$700	$850

Berkeley III (Solidstate) Amp
1968. Berkeley III logo on top panel of amp.

1968		$800	$950

Buckingham Amp
1966-1968. Solidstate, 70 watts, 2x12" piggyback, includes trolley stand.

1966-1968		$850	$925

Cambridge 15 Amp
1999-2001. 15 watts, 1x8", tremolo.

1999-2001		$125	$150

Cambridge 30 Reverb Amp
1999-2002. 30 watts, 1x10", tremolo and reverb.

1999-2002		$175	$200

Cambridge 30 Reverb Twin 210 Amp
1999-2002. 30 watts hybrid circuit, 2x10", reverb.

1999-2002		$275	$325

Cambridge Reverb V103 (Tube) Amp
1966. U.S-made tube version, 18 watts, 1x10", a Pacemaker with reverb, superceded by solidstate Model V1031 by '67.

1966		$800	$1,000

Cambridge Reverb V1031 (Solidstate) Amp
1966-1967. Solidstate, 35 watts, 1x10", model V1031 replaced tube version V103.

1966-1967		$500	$600

Churchill PA V119 Amp Head and V1091 Cabinet Set
Late-1960s. PA head with multiple inputs and 2 column speakers.

1960s	Head & cabs	$750	$900
1960s	PA head only	$350	$400

Climax V-125/V-125 Lead Combo Amp
1970-1991. Solidstate, 125 watts, 2x12" combo, 5-band EQ, master volume.

1970-1991		$475	$575

Defiant Amp
1966-1970. Made in England, 50 watts, 2x12" + Midax horn cabinet.

1966-1970		$1,600	$1,950

Escort Amp
Late 1960s-1983. 2.5 watt battery-powered portable amp.

1968-1986		$375	$425

Essex V1042 Bass Amp
1966-1968. U.S.-made solidstate, 35 watts, 2x12".

1966-1968		$475	$575

Foundation Bass Amp
1966-1970. Tube in '66, solidstate after, 50 watts, 1x18", made in England only.

1966	Tubes	$1,500	$1,800
1967-1970	Solidstate	$600	$700

Kensington V1241 Bass Amp
1967-1968. U.S.-made solidstate bass amp, 22 watts, 1x15", G-tuner.

1967-1968		$550	$650

Pacemaker V102 (Tube) Amp
1966. U.S.-made tube amp, 18 watts, 1x10", replaced by solidstate Pacemaker model V1021.

1966		$800	$1,000

Pacemaker V1021 (Solidstate) Amp
1966-1968. U.S.-made solidstate amp, 35 watts, 1x10", replaced Pacemaker model V102.

1966-1968		$400	$500

Pathfinder V101 (Tube) Amp
1965-1966. U.S.-made tube amp, 4 watts, 1x18", '66-'69 became U.S.-made solidstate V1011.

1965-1966		$800	$950

Pathfinder V1011 (Solidstate) Amp
1966-1968. U.S.-made solidstate, 25 watts peak power, 1x8".

1966-1968		$350	$450

Pathfinder (Import) Amp
1998-present. Compact amps with 1960s cosmetics.

1998-2010	15, 15w, 1x8"	$60	$75
2002-2010	10, 10w, 6.5"	$50	$65

1960 Vox AC-30 Twin

Vox AC-30CC

Vox Pathfinder 10

Vox UL-730 Head

Washburn WA30

1962 Watkins Dominator V-Front

MODEL YEAR	FEATURES	EXC. COND. LOW	HIGH

Royal Guardsman V1131/V1132 Amp
1966-1967. U.S.-made solidstate, 50 watts piggyback, 2x12" + 1 horn, the model below the Super Beatle V1141/V1142.

1966-1967		$1,100	$1,350

Scorpion (Solidstate) Amp
1968. Solidstate, 60 watts, 4x10" Vox Oxford speaker.

1968		$550	$650

Super Beatle V1141/V1142 Amp
1966. U.S.-made 120 watt solidstate, 4x12" + 2 horns, with distortion pedal (V1141), or without (V1142).

1966		$3,000	$3,500

VBM1 Brian May Special Amp
2003-2005. Compact 10-watt, 1x6, also called VBM1 Brian May Recording Amp, white, Brian May logo on grille.

2003-2005		$100	$130

Viscount V1151/V1152 Amp
1966. U.S.-made solidstate, 70 watts, 2x12" combo.

1966		$650	$800

Westminster V118 Bass Amp
1966. Solidstate, 120 watts, 1x18".

1966		$600	$700

V-Series
See Crate.

Wabash
1950s. Private branded amps, made by others, distributed by the David Wexler company. They also offered lap steels and guitars.

Model 1158 Amp
1955. Danelectro-made, 1x15", 2x6L6 power tubes, tweed.

1955		$225	$275

Small Amp

1940s	3 tubes	$125	$150

Wallace Amplification
2000-present. Production/custom, professional grade, amps built by Brian Wallace in Livonia, Michigan. (Please note: Not affiliated with a 1970's amp company from the United Kingdom also called Wallace that has since gone out of business.)

Warbler
See listing under Juke amps.

Warwick
1982-present. Combos, amp heads and cabinets from Warwick Basses of Markneukirchen, Germany.

Washburn
1974-present. Imported guitar and bass amps. Washburn also offers guitars, banjos, mandolins, and basses.

MODEL YEAR	FEATURES	EXC. COND. LOW	HIGH

Watkins
1957-present. England's Watkins Electric Music (WEM) was founded by Charlie Watkins. Their first commercial product was the Watkins Dominator (wedge Gibson stereo amp shape) in '57, followed by the Copicat Echo in '58. They currently build accordion amps.

Clubman Amp
1960s. Small combo amp with typical Watkins styling, blue cover, white grille.

1960s		$525	$650

Dominator MK Series
1970s. Similar circuit to '50s tube amps except solidstate rectifier, 15 watts, different speaker used for different applications.

1970s	MK I, bass, 1x15	$375	$500
1970s	MK II, organ, 1x12	$375	$500
1970s	MK III, guitar, 1x12	$450	$650

Dominator V-Front Amp
Late-1950s-1960s, 2004. 18 watts, 2x10", wedge cabinet similar to Gibson GA-79 stereo amp, tortoise and light beige cab, light grille, requires 220V step-up transformer. Was again offered in '04.

1959-1962		$2,300	$2,800

Webcor
1940s-1950s. The Webster-Chicago Company built recording and audio equipment including portable amplifiers suitable for record turntables, PAs, or general utility. Low power with one or two small speakers.

Small Amp

1950s	1 or 2 speakers	$200	$250

West Laboratories
1965-1970s, 2005-present. Founded by David W. West in Flint, Michigan, moved to Lansing in '68. The '71 catalog included three tube and two solidstate amps, speaker cabinets, as well as Vocal Units and Mini Series combo amps. Amps were available as heads, piggyback half-stacks and full-stacks, with the exception of the combo Mini Series. The Fillmore tube amp head was the most popular model. West equipment has a West logo on the front and the cabinets also have a model number logo on the grille. David West reestablished his company in 2005, located in Okemos, Michigan, with models offered on a custom order basis, concentrating on lower power EL84 designs.

Avalon Amp Head
1971. 50 watts, 2 6CA7 output tubes.

1971		$550	$650

Fillmore Amp Head
1971. 200 watts, 4 KT88 output tubes.

1971		$2,100	$2,500

Grande Amp Head
1971. 100 watts, 2 KT88 output tubes.

1971		$850	$1,000

Mini IR Amp
1971. 50 watts, 1x12 tube combo with reverb, black tolex, large West logo and model name Mini IR on front panel.

1971		$750	$900

AMPS

MODEL YEAR	FEATURES	EXC. COND. LOW	HIGH

White

1955-1960. The White brand, named after plant manager Forrest White, was established by Fender to provide steel and small amp sets to teaching studios that were not Fender-authorized dealers. The amps were sold with the matching steel guitar. See Steel section for pricing.

White (Matamp)

See Matamp listing.

Winfield Amplification

2001-present. Intermediate and professional grade, production, vacuum tube amps built by Winfield N. Thomas in Greensboro, Vermont.

Wizard

1988-present. Professional and premium grade, production/custom, guitar and bass, amps and cabinets built by Rick St Pierre in Cornwall, Ontario.

Woodson

Early 1970s. Obscure builder from Bolivar, Missouri. Woodson logo on front panel and Woodson Model and Serial Number plate on back panel, solidstate circuit, student level pricing.

Working Dog

2001-present. Lower cost tube amps and combos built by Alessandro High-End Products (Alessandro, Hound Dog) in Huntingdon Valley, Pennsylvania.

Wright Amplification

2004-present. Aaron C. Wright builds his professional grade, production/custom, amps and cabinets in Lincoln, Nebraska.

Yamaha

1946-present. Yamaha started building amps in the '60s and offered a variety of guitar and bass amps over the years. The current models are solidstate bass amps. They also build guitars, basses, effects, sound gear and other instruments.

Budokan HY-10G II Amp
1987-1992. Portable, 10 watts, distortion control, EQ.

1987-1992		$75	$100

G50-112 Amp
1983-1992. 50 watts, 1x12".

| 1983-1992 | | $225 | $275 |

G100-112 Amp
1983-1992. 100 watts, 1x12" combo, black cover, striped grille.

| 1983-1992 | | $225 | $275 |

G100-212 Amp
1983-1992. 100, 2x12" combo, black cover, striped grille.

| 1983-1992 | | $275 | $325 |

JX30B Amp
1983-1992. Bass amp, 30 watts.

| 1983-1992 | | $175 | $200 |

TA-20 Amp
1968-1972. Upright wedge shape with controls facing upwards, solidstate.

| 1968-1972 | | $150 | $175 |

TA-25 Amp
1968-1972. Upright wedge shape with controls facing upwards, 40 watts, 1x12", solidstate, black or red cover.

| 1968-1972 | | $175 | $200 |

TA-30 Amp
1968-1972. Upright wedge shape, solidstate.

| 1968-1972 | | $200 | $250 |

TA-50 Amp
1971-1972. Solidstate combo, 80 watts, 2x12", includes built-in cart with wheels, black cover.

| 1971-1972 | | $225 | $275 |

TA-60 Amp
1968-1972. Upright wedge shape, solidstate, most expensive of wedge-shape amps.

| 1968-1972 | | $225 | $275 |

VR4000 Amp
1988-1992. 50-watt stereo, 2 channels, EQ, stereo chorus, reverb and dual effects loops.

| 1988-1992 | | $275 | $325 |

VR6000 Amp
1988-1992. 100-watt stereo, 2 channels which can also be combined, EQ, chorus, reverb and dual effects loops.

| 1988-1992 | | $375 | $425 |

VX-15 Amp
1988-1992. 15 watts.

| 1988-1992 | | $125 | $175 |

VX-65D Bass Amp
1984-1992. 80 watts, 2 speakers.

| 1984-1992 | | $175 | $200 |

YBA-65 Bass Amp
1972-1976. Solidstate combo, 60 watts, 1x15".

| 1972-1976 | | $175 | $200 |

YTA-25 Amp
1972-1976. Solidstate combo, 25 watts, 1x12".

| 1972-1976 | | $175 | $200 |

YTA-45 Amp
1972-1976. Solidstate combo, 45 watts, 1x12".

| 1972-1976 | | $175 | $200 |

YTA-95 Amp
1972-1976. Solidstate combo, 90 watts, 1x12".

| 1972-1976 | | $175 | $200 |

YTA-100 Amp
1972-1976. Solidstate piggyback, 100 watts, 2x12".

| 1972-1976 | | $225 | $275 |

YTA-110 Amp
1972-1976. Solidstate piggyback, 100 watts, 2x12" in extra large cab.

| 1972-1976 | | $225 | $275 |

YTA-200 Amp
1972-1976. Solidstate piggyback, 200 watts, 4x12".

| 1972-1976 | | $275 | $325 |

YTA-300 Amp
1972-1976. Solidstate piggyback, 200 watts, dual cabs with 2x12" and 4x12".

| 1972-1976 | | $425 | $450 |

West Laboratories Picofire

Wizard Vintage Classic 2x12" Combo

Yamaha VR4000

AMPS

Z.Vex Nano Head

MODEL YEAR	FEATURES	EXC. COND. LOW	HIGH

YTA-400 Amp
1972-1976. Solidstate piggyback, 200 watts, dual 4x12".

1972-1976		$425	$450

Z.Vex Amps
2002-present. Intermediate grade, production amps built by Zachary Vex in Minneapolis, Minnesota with some subassembly work done in Michigan. He also builds effects.

Zapp
Ca.1978-early-1980s. Zapp amps were distributed by Red Tree Music, Inc., of Mamaroneck, New York.

Z-10 Amp
1978-1980s. Small student amp, 8 watts.

1979-1982		$25	$75

MODEL YEAR	FEATURES	EXC. COND. LOW	HIGH

Z-50 Amp
1978-1980s. Small student amp, 10 watts, reverb, tremelo.

1978-1982		$50	$75

Zeta
1982-present. Solid state amps with MIDI options, made in Oakland, California. They also make upright basses and violins.

Zinky
1999-present. Tube head and combo amps and cabinets built by Bruce Zinky in Flagstaff, Arizona. He also builds the mini Smokey amps (since '97), effects, and has revived the Supro brand on a guitar and amp.

EFFECTS

ADA Flanger with control pedal
(Jim Schreck)

Aguilar DB 924

Akai Head Rush E2

MODEL YEAR	FEATURES	EXC. COND. LOW	HIGH

Ace-Tone

1968-1972. Effects from Ace Electronic Industry, which was a part of Sakata Shokai Limited of Osaka, Japan, and and also made organs, amps, etc. Their Ace-Tone effects line was available from '68-'72 and was the precedessor to Roland and Boss.

Fuzz Master FM-1
1968-1972. Distortion and overdrive.

1968-1972		$225	$275

Fuzz Master FM-3
1968-1972. Distortion and clean boost.

1968-1972		$350	$425

Wah Master WM-1
1968-1972. Filter wah.

1968-1972		$225	$275

Acoustyx

1977-1982. Made by the Highland Corporation of North Springfield, Vermont.

Image Synthesizer IS-1
1977-1982. Modulation effect.

1977-1982		$50	$60

Phase Five
1977-ca.1982. Used 6 C cell batteries!

1977-1982		$50	$60

ADA

1975-2002. ADA is an acronym for Analog/ Digital Associates. The company was located in Berkeley, California, and introduced its Flanger and Final Phase in '77. The company later moved to Oakland and made amplifiers, high-tech signal processors, and a reissue of its original Flanger.

Final Phase
1977-1979. Reissued in '97.

1977-1979		$375	$450

Flanger
1977-1983, 1996-2002. Reissued in '96.

1977-1979	With control pedal	$375	$450
1977-1979	Without control pedal	$325	$400
1980-1983		$225	$300
1996-2002		$75	$100

MP-1
1987-1995. Tube preamp with chorus and effects loop, MIDI.

1987-1995	With optional foot controller	$200	$250
1987-1995	Without optional foot controller	$150	$200

MP-2
Ca.1988-1995. Tube preamp with chorus, 9-band EQ and effects loop, MIDI.

1988-1995		$225	$275

Pitchtraq
1987. Programmable pitch transposer including octave shifts.

1987		$150	$200

Stereo Tapped Delay STD-1
Introduced in 1981.

1980s		$150	$200

MODEL YEAR	FEATURES	EXC. COND. LOW	HIGH

TFX4 Time Effects
Introduced in 1982, includes flanger, chorus, doubler, echo.

1980s		$150	$200

Aguilar

The New York, New York amp builder also offers a line of tube and solidstate pre-amps.

Akai

1984-present. In '99, Akai added guitar effects to their line of electronic samplers and sequencers for musicians.

Alamo

1947-1982. Founded by Charles Eilenberg, Milton Fink, and Southern Music, San Antonio, Texas. Distributed by Bruno & Sons. Mainly known for guitars and amps, Alamo did offer a reverb unit.

Reverb Unit
1965-ca.1979. Has a Hammond reverb system, balance and intensity controls. By '73 the unit had 3 controls - mixer, contour, and intensity.

1965-1970		$300	$375

Alesis

1992-present. Alesis has a wide range of products for the music industry, including digital processors and amps for guitars.

Allen Amplification

1998-present. David Allen's company, located in Richwood, Kentucky, mainly produces amps, but they also offer a tube overdrive pedal.

Altair Corp.

1977-1980s. Company was located in Ann Arbor, Michigan.

Power Attenuator PW-5
1977-1980. Goes between amp and speaker to dampen volume.

1977-1980		$90	$120

Amdek

Mid-1980s. Amdek offered many electronic products over the years, including drum machines and guitar effects. Most of these were sold in kit form so quality of construction can vary.

Delay Machine DMK-200
1983. Variable delay times.

1983		$85	$115

Octaver OCK-100
1983. Produces tone 1 or 2 octaves below the note played.

1983		$75	$100

Phaser PHK-100

1983		$75	$100

Ampeg

Ampeg entered the effects market in the late-1960s. Their offerings in the early-'60s were really

MODEL YEAR	FEATURES	EXC. COND. LOW	HIGH

amplifier-outboard reverb units similar to the ones offered by Gibson (GA-1). Ampeg offered a line of imported effects in '82-'83, known as the A-series (A-1 through A-9), and reintroduced effects to their product line in '05.

Analog Delay A-8
1982-1983. Made in Japan.

1982-1983		$75	$125

Chorus A-6
1982-1983. Made in Japan.

1982-1983		$50	$75

Compressor A-2
1982-1983. Made in Japan.

1982-1983		$50	$75

Distortion A-1
1982-1983. Made in Japan.

1982-1983		$50	$75

Echo Jet Reverb EJ-12
1963-1965. Outboard, alligator clip reverb unit with 12" speaker, 12 watts, technically a reverb unit. When used as a stand-alone amp, the reverb is off. Named EJ-12A in '65.

1963-1965		$500	$600

Echo Satellite ES-1
1961-1963. Outboard reverb unit with amplifier and speaker alligator clip.

1961-1963		$500	$600

Flanger A-5
1982-1983. Made in Japan.

1982-1983		$50	$75

Multi-Octaver A-7
1982-1983. Made in Japan.

1982-1983		$50	$100

Over Drive A-3
1982-1983. Made in Japan.

1982-1983		$50	$75

Parametric Equalizer A-9
1982-1983. Made in Japan.

1982-1983		$45	$70

Phaser A-4
1982-1983. Made in Japan.

1982-1983		$50	$75

Phazzer

1975-1977		$50	$75

Scrambler Fuzz
1969. Distortion pedal. Reissued in '05.

1969		$250	$300

Amplifier Corporation of America
Late '60s company that made amps for Univox and also marketed effects under their own name.

Amptweaker
2010-present. James Brown, an amp design engineer previously employed by Peavey and currently for Kustom amps, also designs and builds effects in Batavia, Ohio.

amukaT Gadgets
2006-present. Guitar effects built by Takuma Kanaiwa in New York, New York.

Analog Man
1994-present. Founded by Mike Piera in '94 with full-time production by 2000. Located in Danbury, Connecticut (until '07 in Bethel), producing chorus, compressor, fuzz, and boost pedals by '03. He wrote the book Analog Man's Guide To Vintage Effects.

Aphex Systems
1975-present. Founded in Massachusetts by Marvin Caesar and Curt Knoppel, to build their Aural Exciter and other pro sound gear. Currently located in Sun Valley, California, and building a variety of gear for the pro audio broadcast, pro music and home-recording markets.

Apollo
Ca.1967-1972. Imported from Japan by St. Louis Music, includes Fuzz Treble Boost Box, Crier Wa-Wa, Deluxe Fuzz. They also offered basses and guitars.

Crier Wa-Wa
Ca.1967-1972.

1967-1972		$125	$200

Fuzz/Deluxe Fuzz
Ca.1967-1972. Includes the Fuzz Treble Boost Box and the Deluxe Fuzz.

1967-1972		$125	$200

Surf Tornado Wah Wah
Ca.1967-1972.

1967-1972		$150	$225

Arbiter
Ivor Arbiter and Arbiter Music, London, began making the circular Fuzz Face stompbox in 1966. Other products included the Fuzz Wah and Fuzz Wah Face. In '68 the company went public as Arbiter and Western, later transitioning to Dallas-Arbiter. Refer to Dallas-Arbiter for listings.

Area 51
2003-present. Guitar effects made in Newaygo, Michigan (made in Texas until early '06), by Dan Albrecht. They also build amps.

Aria
1960-present. Aria provided a line of effects, made by Maxon, in the mid-'80s.

Analog Delay AD-10
1983-1985. Dual-stage stereo.

1983-1985		$65	$75

Chorus ACH-1
1986-1987. Stereo.

1986-1987		$40	$50

Chorus CH-10
1983-1985. Dual-stage stereo.

1983-1985		$40	$50

Chorus CH-5

1985-1987		$40	$50

Compressor CO-10

1983-1985		$40	$50

Amptweaker Tight Drive

amukaT Gadgets Optical Expression Device

Aphex Guitar Xciter

EFFECTS

Arteffect Bonnie Wah

Automagic British Steel BS-1

BBE Soul Vibe

MODEL YEAR	FEATURES	EXC. COND. LOW	HIGH
Digital Delay ADD-100			
1984-1986. Delay, flanging, chorus, doubling, hold.			
1984-1986		$65	$75
Digital Delay DD-X10			
1985-1987		$65	$75
Distortion DT-5			
1985-1987		$40	$50
Distortion DT-10			
1983-1985. Dual-stage.			
1983-1985		$40	$50
Flanger AFL-1			
1986. Stereo.			
1986		$50	$60
Flanger FL-10			
1983-1985. Dual-stage stereo.			
1983-1985		$50	$60
Flanger FL-5			
1985-1987		$50	$60
Metal Pedal MP-5			
1985-1987.			
1985-1987		$40	$50
Noise Gate NG-10			
1983-1985		$30	$40
Over Drive OD-10			
1983-1985. Dual-stage.			
1983-1985		$40	$50
Parametric Equalizer EQ-10			
1983-1985		$40	$50
Phase Shifter PS-10			
1983-1984. Dual-stage.			
1983-1984		$50	$60
Programmable Effects Pedal APE-1			
1984-1986. Compression, distortion, delay, chorus.			
1984-1986		$50	$60

Arion

1984-present. Arion offers a wide variety of budget imported effects.

Guitar and Bass Effects

1984-2010		$15	$45

Arteffect

2006-present. Tom Kochawi and Dan Orr build analog effects in Haifa and Natanya, Israel.

Asama

1970s-1980s. This Japanese company offered solidbody guitars with built-in effects as well as stand-alone units. They also offered basses, drum machines and other music products.

Astrotone

Late 1960s. By Universal Amp, which also made the Sam Ash Fuzzz Boxx.

Fuzz

1966. Introduced in '66, same as Sam Ash Fuzzz Boxx.

1966		$175	$275

ATD

Mid-1960s-early 1980s. Made by the All-Test Devices corporation of Long Beach, New York. In the mid-'60s, Richard Minz and an associate started making effects part-time, selling them through Manny's Music in New York. They formed All-Test and started making Maestro effects and transducer pickups for CMI, which owned Gibson at the time. By '75, All-Test was marketing effects under their own brand. All-Test is still making products for other industries, but by the early to mid-'80s they were no longer making products for the guitar.

PB-1 Power Booster

1976-ca.1980.

1979-1980		$50	$60

Volume Pedal EV-1

1979-ca.1980.

1979-1980		$30	$40

Wah-Wah/Volume Pedal WV-1

1979-ca.1981.

1979-1981		$50	$60

Audio Matrix

1979-1984. Effects built by B.K Butler in Escondido, California. He later designed the Tube Driver and founded Tube Works in 1987. He nows operates Butler Audio, making home and auto hybrid tube stereo amps.

Mini Boogee B81

1981. Four-stage, all-tube preamp, overdrive, distortion.

1981		$100	$135

Audioworks

1980s. Company was located in Niles, Illinois.

F.E.T. Distortion

1980s		$40	$55

Auralux

2000-present. Founded by Mitchell Omori and David Salzmann, Auralux builds effects and tube amps in Highland Park, Illinois.

Austone Electronics

1997-2009. Founded by Jon Bessent and Randy Larkin, Austone offers a range of stomp boxes, all made in Austin, Texas. Bessent died in '09.

Overdrive and Fuzz Pedals

1997-2009. Various overdrive and fuzz boxes.

1997-2009		$125	$175

Automagic

1998-present. Wah pedals and distortion boxes made in Germany by Musician Sound Design.

Avalanche

Late 1980s. Effects built by Brian Langer in Toronto, Ontario.

Brianizer

Late-1980s. Leslie effect, dual rotor, adjustable speed and rates.

1980s		$75	$90

Axe

1980s. Early '80s line of Japanese effects, possibly made by Maxon.

MODEL		EXC. COND.	
YEAR	FEATURES	LOW	HIGH

B & M

1970s. A private brand made by Sola/Colorsound for Barns and Mullens, a U.K. distributor.

Fuzz Unit

1970s. Long thin orange case, volume, sustain, tone knobs, on-off stomp switch.

1970s		$275	$325

Backline Engineering

2004-present. Guitar multi-effects built by Gary Lee in Camarillo, California. In '07, they added tube amps.

Bad Cat Amplifier Company

2000-present. Amp company Bad Cat, originally of Corona, California, also offers guitar effects. In '09 the company was moved to Anaheim.

Baldwin

1965-1970. The piano maker got into the guitar market when it acquired Burns of London in '65, and sold the guitars in the U.S. under the Baldwin name. They also marketed a couple of effects at the same time.

Banzai

2000-present. Effects built by Olaf Nobis in Berlin, Germany.

Bartolini

The pickup manufacturer offered a few effects from around 1982 to '87.

Tube-It

1982-ca.1987. Marshall tube amplification simulator with bass, treble, sustain controls.

1982-1987	Red case	$80	$90

Basic Systems' Side Effects

1980s. This company was located in Tulsa, Oklahoma.

Audio Delay

1986-ca.1987. Variable delay speeds.

1986-1987		$75	$100

Triple Fuzz

1986-ca.1987. Selectable distortion types.

1986-1987		$50	$60

BBE

1985-present. BBE, owner of G & L Guitars and located in California, manufactures rack-mount effects and added a new line of stomp boxes in '05.

Behringer

1989-present. The German professional audio products company added modeling effects in '01 and guitar stomp boxes in '05. They also offer guitars and amps.

Beigel Sound Lab

1980. Music product designer Mike Beigel helped form Musitronics Corp, where he made the Mu-

Tron III. In 1978 he started Beigel Sound Lab to provide product design in Warwick, New York, where in '80 he made 50 rack-mount Enveloped Controlled Filters under this brand name.

Bell Electrolabs

1970s. This English company offered a line of effects in the '70s.

Vibrato

1970s		$150	$200

Bennett Music Labs

Effects built in Chatanooga, Tennessee by Bruce Bennett.

Bigsby

Bigsby has been making volume and tone pedals since the 1950s. They currently offer a volume pedal.

Foot Volume and Tone Control

1950s		$125	$175

Binson

Late 1950s-1982. Binson, of Milan, Italy, made several models of the Echorec, using tubes or transistors. They also made units for Guild, Sound City and EKO.

Echorec

Ca.1960-1979. Four knob models with 12 echo selections, 1 head, complex multitap effects, settings for record level, playback and regeneration. Includes B1, B2, Echomaster1, T5 (has 6 knobs), T5E, and Baby. Used a magnetic disk instead of tape. Guild later offered the Guild Echorec by Binson which is a different stripped-down version.

1960s	Tube	$900	$1,100

Bixonic

1995-2007. The round silver distortion pedals were originally distributed by SoundBarrier Music, later by Godlyke, Inc.

Expandora EXP-2000

1995-2000. Analog distortion, round silver case, internal DIP switches.

1995-2000		$175	$200

Black Cat Pedals

1993-2007, 2009-present. Founded by Fred Bonte and located in Texas until late 2007 when production was discontinued. In '09, using Bonte's same designs, new owner Tom Hughes restarted production in Foxon, Connecticut.

Blackbox Music Electronics

2000-2009. Founded by Loren Stafford and located in Minneapolis, Minnesota, Blackbox offered a line of effects for guitar and bass. The Blackbox models are now made under the Ooh La La brand.

Blackout Effectors

2007-present. Kyle Tompkins began building effects pedals in Vancouver, British Columbia and now builds them in Asheville, North Carolina.

BBE Two Timer

EFFECTS

Behringer Vintage Tube Overdrive VT911

Blackout Effectors Dual Fix'd Fuzz & Musket Fuzz

Boomerang Wah
(Jim Schreck)

Boss Blues Driver BD-2

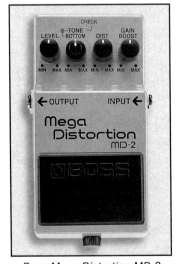

Boss Mega Distortion MD-2

Blackstar Amplification

2007-present. Guitar effects pedals built by Joel Richardson in Northampton, England. He also builds amps.

Blackstone Appliances

1999-present. Distortion effects crafted by Jon Blackstone in New York, New York.

Bon, Mfg

Bon was located in Escondido, California.

Tube Driver 204
1979-ca.1981.

MODEL YEAR	FEATURES	EXC. COND. LOW	HIGH
1979-1981		$100	$150

Boomerang

1995-present. Effects pedals built in Grapevine, Texas by Boomerang Musical Products, Ltd.

Boss

1976-present. Japan's Roland Corporation first launched effect pedals in '74. A year or two later the subsidiary company, Boss, debuted its own line. They were marketed concurrently at first but gradually Boss became reserved for effects and drum machines while the Roland name was used on amplifiers and keyboards. Boss still offers a wide line of pedals.

Acoustic Simulator AC-2
1997-2007. Four modes that emulate various acoustic tones.

1997-2007		$50	$60

Auto Wah AW-2

1991-1999		$40	$50

Bass Chorus CE-2B

1987-1995		$40	$50

Bass Equalizer GE-7B
1987-1995. Seven-band, name changed to GEB-7 in '95.

1987-1995		$40	$50

Bass Flanger BF-2B

1987-1994		$40	$50

Bass Limiter LM-2B

1990-1994		$35	$40

Bass Overdrive ODB-3
1994-present.

1994-2010		$40	$50

Blues Driver BD-2
1995-present.

1995-2010		$40	$50

Chorus Ensemble CE-1
1976-1984. Vibrato and chorus.

1976-1984		$145	$245

Chorus Ensemble CE-2

1979-1982		$45	$95

Chorus Ensemble CE-3

1982-1992		$45	$95

Chorus Ensemble CE-5
1991-present.

1991-2010		$45	$95

Compressor Sustainer CS-1

MODEL YEAR	FEATURES	EXC. COND. LOW	HIGH
1978-1982		$70	$95

Compressor Sustainer CS-2

1981-1986		$70	$95

Compressor Sustainer CS-3
1986-present.

1986-2010		$70	$95

Delay DM-2
1981-1984. Analog, hot pink case.

1981-1984		$170	$245

Delay DM-3

1984-1988		$145	$195

Digital Delay DD-2

1983-1986		$120	$170

Digital Delay DD-3
1986-present. Up to 800 ms of delay.

1986-1989		$120	$170
1990-2010		$95	$145

Digital Delay DD-5
1995-2005. Up to 2 seconds of delay.

1995-2005		$95	$145

Digital Delay DD-6
2003-2007. Up to 5 seconds of delay.

2003-2007		$55	$70

Digital Dimension C DC-2
1985-1989. Two chorus effects and tremolo.

1985-1989		$135	$145

Digital Metalizer MZ-2

1987-1992		$80	$90

Digital Reverb RV-2

1987-1990		$95	$145

Digital Reverb RV-5
2003-present. Dual imput and dual output, four control knobs, silver case.

2003-2010		$60	$95

Digital Reverb/Delay RV-3

1994-2004		$95	$120

Digital Sampler/Delay DSD-2

1985-1986		$120	$170

Digital Space-D DC-3/Digital Dimension DC-3
1988-1993. Originally called the Digital Space-D, later changed to Digital Dimension. Chorus with EQ.

1988-1993		$130	$180

Digital Stereo Reverb RV-70
1994-1995. Rack mount, MIDI control, reverb/delay, 199 presets.

1994-1995		$130	$180

Distortion DS-1
1978-1989, 1990s-present.

1978-1989		$50	$60
1990-1999		$30	$50
2000-2010		$20	$25

Dr. Rhythm DR-55
1979-1989. Drum machine.

1979-1989		$145	$195

Dual Over Drive SD-2

1993-1998		$45	$55

Dynamic Filter FT-2
1986-1988. Auto wah.

1986-1988		$70	$95

MODEL YEAR FEATURES	EXC. COND. LOW	HIGH
Dynamic Wah AW-3		
2000-present. Auto wah with humanizer, for guitar or bass.		
2000-2010	$50	$60
Enhancer EH-2		
1990-1998	$35	$45
Flanger BF-1		
1977-1980	$55	$70
Flanger BF-2		
1980-1989	$55	$70
1990-2005	$40	$55
Foot Wah FW-3		
1992-1996	$45	$55
Graphic Equalizer GE-6		
1978-1981. Six bands.		
1978-1981	$45	$70
Graphic Equalizer GE-7		
1981-present. Seven bands.		
1982-1989	$70	$95
1990-2010	$45	$65
Graphic Equalizer GE-10		
1976-1985. 10-band EQ for guitar or bass.		
1976-1985	$95	$120
Harmonist HR-2		
1994-1999. Pitch shifter.		
1994-1999	$70	$95
Heavy Metal HM-2		
1983-1991. Distortion.		
1983-1991	$30	$40
Hyper Fuzz FZ-2		
1993-1997	$45	$70
Hyper Metal HM-3		
1993-1998	$35	$45
Limiter LM-2		
1987-1992	$25	$35
Line Selector LS-2		
1991-present. Select between 2 effects loops.		
1991-2010 With adapter	$45	$70
Mega Distortion MD-2		
2003-present.		
2003-2010	$45	$55
Metal Zone MT-2		
1991-present. Distortion and 3-band EQ.		
1991-2010	$45	$70
Multi Effects ME-5		
1988-1991. Floor unit.		
1988-1991	$70	$120
Multi Effects ME-6		
1992-1997	$70	$120
Multi Effects ME-8		
1996-1997	$70	$120
Multi Effects ME-30		
1998-2002	$70	$120
Multi Effects ME-50		
2003-2009. Floor unit.		
2003-2009	$170	$195
Noise Gate NF-1		
1979-1988	$40	$50
Noise Suppressor NS-2		
1987-present.		
1987-2010	$40	$50

MODEL YEAR FEATURES	EXC. COND. LOW	HIGH
Octaver OC-2/Octave OC-2		
1982-2003. Originally called the Octaver.		
1982-2003	$55	$70
Overdrive OD-1		
1977-1979	$95	$170
1980-1985	$70	$145
Overdrive OD-3		
1997-present.		
1997-2010	$45	$70
Parametric Equalizer PQ-4		
1991-1997	$45	$70
Phaser PH-1		
1977-1981	$70	$95
Phaser PH-1R		
1982-1985. Resonance control added to PH-1.		
1982-1985	$70	$120
Pitch Sifter/Delay PS-2		
1987-1993	$95	$120
Reverb Box RX-100		
1981-mid-1980s.		
1981-1985	$70	$95
Rocker Distortion PD-1		
1980-mid-1980s. Variable pedal using magnetic field.		
1980-1985	$45	$70
Rocker Volume PV-1		
1981-mid-1980s.		
1980-1985	$45	$55
Rocker Wah PW-1		
1980-mid-1980s. Magnetic field variable pedal.		
1980-1985	$55	$65
Slow Gear SG-1		
1979-1982. Violin swell effect, automatically adjusts volume.		
1979-1982	$325	$375
Spectrum SP-1		
1977-1981. Single-band parametric EQ.		
1977-1981	$325	$375
Super Chorus CH-1		
1989-present.		
1989-2010	$45	$70
Super Distortion & Feedbacker DF-2		
1984-1994. Also labeled as the Super Feedbacker & Distortion.		
1984-1994	$95	$120
Super Over Drive SD-1		
1981-present.		
1981-1989	$45	$85
1990-2010	$30	$50
Super Phaser PH-2		
1984-1989	$45	$85
1990-2001	$30	$50
Super Shifter PS-5		
1999-present. Pitch shifter/harmonizer.		
1999-2010	$95	$120
Touch Wah TW-1/T Wah TW-1		
1978-1987. Auto wah, early models were labeled as Touch Wah.		
1978-1987	$95	$120
Tremolo TR-2		
1997-present.		
1997-2010	$65	$75

Boss Super Chorus CH-1

EFFECTS

Boss Reverb Box RX-100

Boss Tremolo TR-2

Boss Turbo Distortion DS-2

Budda Phatman

Burriss Boostier

MODEL YEAR	FEATURES	EXC. COND. LOW	HIGH
Tremolo/Pan PN-2			
1990-1995		$120	$145
Turbo Distortion DS-2			
1987-present.			
1987-2010		$70	$120
Turbo Overdrive OD-2			
1985-1994. Called OD-2R after '94, due to added remote on/off jack.			
1985-1994		$70	$120
Vibrato VB-2			
1982-1986. True pitch-changing vibrato, warm analog tone, 'rise time' control allows for slow attach, 4 knobs, aqua-blue case.			
1982-1986		$400	$450
Volume FV-50H			
1987-1997. High impedance, stereo volume pedal with inputs and outputs.			
1987-1997		$45	$55
Volume FV-50L			
1987-1997. Low impedance version of FV-50.			
1987-1997		$35	$45
Volume Pedal FV-100			
Late-1980s-1991. Guitar volume pedal.			
1987-1991		$35	$45

Browntone Electronics

2006-present. Foot pedal guitar effects built in Lincolnton, North Carolina by Tim Brown.

Bruno

1834-present. Music distributor Bruno and Sons had a line of Japanese-made effects in the early '70s.

Budda

1995-present. Wahs and distortion pedals originally built by Jeff Bober and Scott Sier in San Francisco, California. In '09, Budda was acquired by Peavey Electronics. They also build amps.

Build Your Own Clone

2005-present. Build it yourself kits based on vintage effects produced by Keith Vonderhulls in Othello, Washington. Assembled kits are offered by their Canadian distributor.

Burriss

2001-present. Guitar effects from Bob Burriss of Lexington, Kentucky. He also builds amps.

Carl Martin

1993-present. Line of effects from Søren Jongberg and East Sound Research of Denmark. In '06 they added their Chinese-made Vintage Series. They also build amps.

Carlsbro

1959-present. English amp company Carlsbro Electronics Limited offered a line of effects from '77 to '81.

Carrotron

Late-1970s-mid-1980s. Carrotron was out of California and offered a line of effects.

MODEL YEAR	FEATURES	EXC. COND. LOW	HIGH
Noise Fader C900B1			
1981-ca.1982.			
1980-1982		$50	$60
Preamp C821B			
1981-ca.1982.			
1981-1982		$55	$65

Carvin

1946-present. Carvin introduced its line of Ground Effects in '02 and discontinued them in '03.

Castle Instruments

Early 1980s. Castle was located in Madison, New Jersey, and made rack-mount and floor phaser units.

MODEL YEAR	FEATURES	EXC. COND. LOW	HIGH
Phaser III			
1980-1982. Offered mode switching for various levels of phase.			
1980-1982		$100	$175

Catalinbread

2003-present. Nicholas Harris founded Catalinbread Specialized Mechanisms of Music in Seattle, Washington, in '02 to do mods and in '03 added his own line of guitar effects.

Cat's Eye

2001-present. Dean Solorzano and Lisa Kroeker build their analog guitar effects in Oceanside, California.

Cause & Effect Pedals

2009-present. Guitar effects pedals built in Ontario, Canada by Mark Roberts and Brian Alexson.

Celmo

2008-present. The Celmo Sardine Can Compressor is made by Kezako Productions in Montcaret, France.

Chandler

1984-present. Located in California, Chandler Musical Instruments offers instruments, pickups, and pickguards, as well as effects.

MODEL YEAR	FEATURES	EXC. COND. LOW	HIGH
Digital Echo			
1992-2000. Rackmount, 1 second delay, stereo.			
1992-2000		$350	$450
Tube Driver			
1986-1991. Uses a 12AX7 tube. Not to be confused with the Tube Works Tube Driver.			
1980s	Large Box	$200	$325
1980s	Rackmount	$100	$150
1990s	Rackmount	$100	$150

Chapman

1970-present. From Emmett Chapman, maker of the Stick.

MODEL YEAR	FEATURES	EXC. COND. LOW	HIGH

Patch of Shades
1981, 1989. Wah, with pressure sensitive pad instead of pedal. 2 production runs.

1980s		$50	$75

Chicago Iron
1998-present. Faithful reproductions of classic effects built by Kurt Steir in Chicago, Illinois.

Chunk Systems
1996-present. Guitar and bass effects pedals built by Richard Cartwright in Sydney, Australia.

Clark
1960s. Built in Clark, New Jersey, same unit as the Orpheum Fuzz and the Mannys Music Fuzz.

SS-600 Fuzz
1960s. Chrome-plated, volume and tone knobs, toggle switch.

1960s		$150	$200

Clark Amplification
1995-present. Amplifier builder Mike Clark, of Cayce, South Carolina, offers a reverb unit and started building guitar effects as well, in '98.

ClinchFX
2006-present. Hand made pedals by Peter Clinch in Brisbane, Queensland, Australia.

Coffin
Case manufacturer Coffin Case added U.S.-made guitar effects pedals to their product line in 2006.

Colorsound
1967-2010. Colorsound effects were produced by England's Sola Sound, which was founded in '62 by former Vox associate Larry Macari and his brother Joe. The first product was a fuzzbox called the Tone Bender, designed by Gary Hurst and sold at Macari's Musical Exchange stores. The first readily available fuzz in Britain, it was an instant success. In '67, the Colorsound brand was launched. In the late-'60s, wah and fuzz-wah pedals were added, and by the end of the '70s, Colorsound offered 18 different effects, an amp, and accessories. Few early Colorsound products were imported into the U.S., so today they're scarce. Except for the Wah-Wah pedal, Colorsound's production stopped by the early '80s, but in '96 most of their early line was reissued by Dick Denny of Vox fame. Denny died in 2001. Afterwards, Anthony and Steve Macari build Colorsound effects in London. Mutronics offered a licensed rack mount combination of 4 classic Colorsound effects for a short time in the early 2000s.

Flanger

1970s		$110	$210

Fuzz Phazer
Introduced in 1973.

1970s		$160	$235

Jumbo Tonebender
1974-early 1980s. Replaced the Tonebender fuzz, with wider case and light blue lettering.

1974-1980s		$160	$260

Octivider
Introduced in 1973.

1970s		$160	$235

Overdriver
Introduced in 1972. Controls for drive, treble and bass.

1970s		$160	$235

Phazer
Introduced in 1973. Magenta/purple-pink case, slanted block Phazer logo on front.

1970s		$160	$235

Ring Modulator
Introduced in 1973. Purple case, Ring Modulator name with atom orbit slanted block logo on case.

1970s		$260	$285

Supa Tonebender Fuzz
1977-early 1980s. Sustain and volume knobs, tone control and toggle. Same white case as Jumbo Tonebender, but with new circuit.

1970s		$160	$235

Supa Wah-Swell
1970s. Supa Wah-Swell in slanted block letters on the end of the pedal, silver case.

1970s		$160	$235

Supaphase

1970s		$160	$235

Supasustain

1960s		$135	$210

Tremolo

1970s		$160	$210

Tremolo Reissue
1996-2009. Purple case.

1996-2009		$110	$135

Wah Fuzz Straight
Introduced in 1973. Aqua-blue case, Wah-Fuzz-Straight in capital block letters on end of wah pedal.

1970s		$185	$260

Wah Fuzz Swell
Introduced in 1973. Yellow case, block letter Wah Fuzz Swell logo on front, three control knobs and toggle.

1970s		$260	$360

Wah Swell
1970s. Light purple case, block letter Wah-Swell logo on front.

1970s		$235	$285

Wah Wah
1970s. Dark gray case, Wah-Wah in capital block letters on end of wah pedal.

1975		$310	$360

Wah Wah Reissue
1996-2005. Red case, large Colorsound letter logo and small Wah Wah lettering on end of pedal.

1996-2005		$85	$110

Wah Wah Supremo
1970s. Silver/chrome metal case, Wah-Wah Supremo in block letters on end of wah pedal.

1975		$435	$485

Catalinbread Teaser Stallion

Chandler Tube Driver
(Jim Schreck)

*Chunk Systems
Octavius Squeezer*

To get the most from this book, be sure to read "Using *The Guide*" in the introduction.

MODEL YEAR	FEATURES	EXC. COND. LOW	HIGH

Crazy Tube Circuits Splash

Crowther Audio Hot Cake

Cusack Music More Louder

Companion

1970s. Private branded by Shinei of Japan, which made effects for others as well.

Tape Echo

1960-1970		$350	$450

Wah Pedal

1970s		$125	$175

Conn

Ca.1968-ca.1978. Band instrument manufacturer and distributor Conn/Continental Music Company, of Elkhart, Indiana, imported guitars and effects from Japan.

Strobe ST-8 Tuner

Late-1960s. Brown case.

1968		$215	$225

Coopersonic

2006-present. Martin Cooper builds his guitar effects in Nottingham, UK.

Coron

1970s-1980s. Japanese-made effects, early ones close copies of MXR pedals.

Cosmosound

Italy's Cosmosound made small amps with Leslie drums and effects pedals in the late '60s and '70s. Cosmosound logo is on top of pedals.

Wah Fuzz CSE-3

1970s. Volume and distortion knobs, wah and distortion on-off buttons, silver case.

1970s		$275	$350

Crazy Tube Circuits

2004-present. Guitar effects designed and built by Chris Ntaifotis in Athens, Greece.

Creation Audio Labs

2005-present. Guitar and bass boost pedal and re-amplifying gear built in Nashville, Tennessee.

Crowther Audio

1976-present. Guitar effects built by Paul Crowther, who was the original drummer of the band Split Enz, in Auckland, New Zealand. His first effect was the Hot Cake.

Crybaby

See listing under Vox for early models, and Dunlop for recent versions.

CSL

Sola Sound made a line of effects for C. Summerfield Ltd., an English music company.

Cusack Music

2003-present. Effects built in Holland, Michigan by Jon Cusack.

MODEL YEAR	FEATURES	EXC. COND. LOW	HIGH

Dallas/Dallas Arbiter

Dallas Arbiter, Ltd. was based in London and it appeared in the late-1960s as a division of a Dallas group of companies headed by Ivor Arbiter. Early products identified with Dallas logo with the company noted as John E. Dallas & Sons Ltd., Dallas Building, Clifton Street, London, E.C.2. They also manufactured Sound City amplifiers and made Vox amps from '72 to '78. The Fuzz Face is still available from Jim Dunlop.

Fuzz Face

Introduced in 1966. The current reissue of the Dallas Arbiter Fuzz Face is distributed by Jim Dunlop USA.

1968-1969	Red	$900	$1,100
1970	Red	$900	$1,100
1970-1976	Blue	$800	$1,000
1977-1980	Blue	$700	$900
1981	Grey, reissue	$500	$600
1990-1999	Red, reissue	$100	$125
2000-2010	Red, reissue	$100	$125

Fuzz Wah Face

1970s	Black	$550	$650
1990s	Reissue copy	$65	$75

Rangemaster Treble Boost

1966		$2,000	$2,500

Sustain

1970s		$400	$500

Treble and Bass Face

1960s		$500	$600

Trem Face

Ca.1970-ca.1975. Reissued in '80s, round red case, depth and speed control knobs, Dallas-Arbiter England logo plate.

1970-1975		$500	$600

Wah Baby

1970s. Gray speckle case, Wah Baby logo caps and small letters on end of pedal.

1970s		$500	$600

Damage Control

2005-present. Guitar effects pedals and digital multi-effects built in Moorpark, California.

Dan Armstrong

1976-1981, 1991-present. In '76, Musitronics, based in Rosemont, New Jersey, introduced 6 inexpensive plug-in effects designed by Dan Armstrong. Perhaps under the influence of John D. MacDonald's Travis McGee novels, each effect name incorporated a color, like Purple Peaker. Shipping box labeled Dan Armstrong by Musitronics. They disappeared a few years later but were reissued by WD Products from '91 to '02 (See WD for those models). From '03 to '06, Vintage Tone Project offered the Dan Armstrong Orange Crusher. Since '06, a licensed line of Dan Armstrong effects that plug directly into the output of a guitar or bass (since '07 some also as stomp boxes) has been offered by Grafton Electronics of Grafton, Vermont. Dan Armstrong died in '04.

MODEL YEAR FEATURES	EXC. COND. LOW	HIGH

Blue Clipper

1976-1981. Fuzz, blue-green case.

1976-1981	$85	$100

Green Ringer

1976-1981. Ring Modulator/Fuzz, green case.

1976-1981	$85	$100

Orange Squeezer

1976-1981.

1976-1981	$85	$100

Purple Peaker

1976-1981. Frequency Booster, light purple case.

1976-1981	$85	$100

Red Ranger

1976-1981. Bass/Treble Booster, light red case.

1976-1981	$85	$100

Yellow Humper

1976-1981. Yellow case.

1976-1981	$85	$100

Danelectro

1946-1969, 1996-present. The Danelectro brand was revived in '96 with a line of effects pedals. They also offer the Wasabi line of effects. Prices do not include AC adapter, add $10 for the Zero-Hum adapter.

Chicken Salad Vibrato

2000-2009. Orange case.

2000-2009	$20	$25

Cool Cat Chorus

1996-present. Blue case.

1996-2010	$20	$25

Corned Beef Reverb

2000-2009. Blue-black case.

2000-2010	$15	$20

Daddy-O Overdrive

1996-2009. White case.

1996-2009	$30	$40

Dan Echo

1998-2009. Lavender case.

1998-2009	$40	$45

Fab Tone Distortion

1996-present. Red case.

1996-2010	$30	$40

Reverb Unit

1965	$200	$300

Davoli

1960s-1970. Davoli was an Italian pickup and guitar builder and is often associated with Wandre guitars.

TRD

1970s. Solidstate tremolo, reverb, distortion unit.

1970s	$175	$225

DDyna Music

2008-present. Dan Simon builds his guitar effects pedals in Bothell, Washington.

Dean Markley

The string and pickup manufacturer offered a line of effects from 1976 to the early-'90s.

Overlord Classic Overdrive Model III

1990-1991. Battery-powered version of Overlord pedal. Black case with red letters.

1990-1991	$40	$70

Overlord Classic Tube Overdrive

1988-1991. Uses a 12AX7A tube, AC powered.

1988-1991	$60	$80

Voice Box 50 (Watt Model)

1976-1979	$75	$125

Voice Box 100 (Watt Model)

1976-1979, 1982-ca.1985.

1976-1979	$75	$125

Voice Box 200 (Watt Model)

1976-1979	$75	$125

DeArmond

In 1947, DeArmond may have introduced the first actual signal-processing effect pedal, the Tremolo Control. They made a variety of effects into the '70s, but only one caught on - their classic volume pedal. DeArmond is primarily noted for pickups.

Pedal Phaser Model 1900

1974-ca.1979.

1974-1979	$75	$125

Square Wave Distortion Generator

1977-ca.1979.

1977-1979	$100	$150

Thunderbolt B166

1977-ca.1979. Five octave wah.

1977-1979	$50	$100

Tone/Volume Pedal 610

1978-ca.1979.

1978-1979	$75	$125

Tornado Phase Shifter

1977-ca.1979.

1977-1979	$100	$125

Tremolo Control Model 60A/60B

The Model 60 Tremolo Control dates from 1947 to the early-1950s. Model 60A dates from mid- to late-'50s. Model 60B, early-'60s.

1950s	60A	$300	$400
1960s	60B	$150	$300

Twister 1930

1980. Phase shifter.

1980	$100	$125

Volume Pedal Model 602

1960s	$40	$70

Volume Pedal Model 1602

1978-ca. 1980s.

1970s	$40	$60

Volume Pedal Model 1630

1978-1980s. Optoelectric.

1970s	$40	$60

Weeper Wah Model 1802

1970s. Weeper logo on foot pedal.

1970s	$100	$125

Death By Audio

2001-present. Oliver Ackermann builds production and custom guitar effects in Brooklyn, New York.

Dan Armstrong Purple Peaker

Damage Control Solid Metal

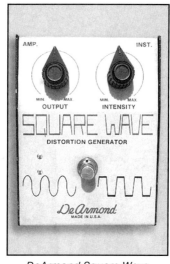

DeArmond Square Wave Distortion Generator

EFFECTS

MODEL YEAR	FEATURES	EXC. COND. LOW	HIGH

Demeter Compulator Pro

DigiTech Reverberator XP400

Digitech Whammy Pedal
(Jim Schreck)

DeltaLab Research

Late 1970s-early 1980s. DeltaLab, which was located in Chelmsford, Massachusetts, was an early builder of rackmount gear.

DL-2 Acousticomputer
1980s. Delay.

1980s		$75	$125

DL-4 Time Line
1980s. Delay.

1980s		$75	$125

DL-5
1980s. Various digital processing effects, blue case, rackmount.

1980s		$175	$225

DLB-1 Delay Control Pedal
1980s. Controls other DeltaLab pedals, chrome, Morley-looking pedal.

1980s		$50	$75

Electron I ADM/II ADM
1980s. Blue case, rackmount effects. Models include the Electron I ADM, and the Electron II ADM.

1980s	Electron I ADM	$50	$75
1980s	Electron II ADM	$75	$125

Demeter

1980-present. Amp builder James Demeter and company, located in Van Nuys, California, also build guitar effects.

Denio

Line of Japanese-made Boss lookalikes sold in Asia and Australia.

Devi Ever : Fx

2009-present. Devi Ever builds his guitar effects in Portland, Oregon. Prior to '09 he built the Effector 13 effects.

Diamond Pedals

2004-present. Designed by Michael Knappe and Tim Fifield, these effects are built in Bedford, Nova Scotia.

Diaz

Early 1980s-2002, 2004-present. Line of effects from the amp doctor Cesar Diaz. Diaz died in '02; in '04, his family announced plans to resume production.

DigiTech

The DigiTech/DOD company is in Utah and the effects are made in the U.S.A. The DigiTech name started as a line under the DOD brand in the early 1980s; later spinning off into its own brand. They also produce vocal products and studio processors and are now part of Harman International Industries.

Digital Delay and Sampler PDS 2000
1985-1991. 2 second delay.

1985-1991		$125	$175

Digital Delay PDS 1000
1985-ca.1989. One second delay.

1985-1989		$100	$150

Digital Delay PDS 2700 Double Play
1989-1991. Delay and chorus

1989-1991		$125	$175

Digital Stereo Chorus/Flanger PDS 1700

1986-1991		$100	$150

Echo Plus 8 Second Delay PDS 8000

1985-1991		$175	$200

Guitar Effects Processor RP 1
1992-1996. Floor unit, 150 presets.

1992-1996		$100	$150

Guitar Effects Processor RP 3
1998-2003. Floor unit.

1998-2003		$110	$150

Guitar Effects Processor RP 5
1994-1996. Floor unit, 80 presets.

1994-1996		$120	$175

Guitar Effects Processor RP 6
1996-1997. Floor unit.

1996-1997		$125	$200

Guitar Effects Processor RP 7
1996-1997. Floor unit.

1996-1997		$125	$175

Guitar Effects Processor RP 10
1994-1996. Floor unit, 200 presets.

1994-1996		$125	$175

Guitar Effects Processor RP 14D
1999. Floor unit with expression pedal, 1x12AX7 tube, 100 presets.

1999		$300	$350

Guitar Effects Processor RP 100

2000-2006		$100	$125

Guitar Effects Processor RP 200
2001-2006. 140 presets, drum machine, Expression pedal.

2001-2006		$100	$125

Hot Box PDS 2730
1989-1991. Delay and distortion

1989-1991		$100	$125

Modulator Pedal XP 200
1996-2002. Floor unit, 61 presets.

1996-2002		$100	$125

Multi Play PDS 20/20
1987-1991. Multi-function digital delay.

1987-1991		$125	$150

Pedalverb Digital Reverb Pedal PDS 3000

1987-1991		$100	$125

Programmable Distortion PDS 1550

1986-1991	Yellow case	$50	$75

Programmable Distortion PDS 1650

1989-1991	Red case	$50	$75

Rock Box PDS 2715
1989-1991. Chorus and distortion.

1989-1991		$50	$75

Two Second Digital Delay PDS 1002

1987-1991		$100	$125

Whammy Pedal Reissue
2000-present. Reissue version of classic WP-1 with added dive bomb and MIDI features.

2000-2010		$125	$150

MODEL YEAR	FEATURES	EXC. COND. LOW	HIGH
Whammy Pedal WP I			
1990-1993. Original Whammy Pedal, red case, reissued as WP IV in '00.			
1990-1993		$375	$475
Whammy Pedal WP II			
1994-1997. Can switch between 2 presets, black case.			
1994-1997		$200	$275

DiMarzio

The pickup maker offered a couple of effects in the late-1980s to the mid-'90s.

MODEL YEAR	FEATURES	EXC. COND. LOW	HIGH
Metal Pedal			
1987-1989		$50	$75
Very Metal Fuzz			
Ca.1989-1995. Distortion/overdrive pedal.			
1989-1995		$50	$75

Dino's

1995-present. A social co-op founded by Alessio Casati and Andy Bagnasco, in Albisola, Italy. It builds a line of boutique analog pedals as well as guitars.

Dinosaur

2004-present. Guitar effects pedals imported by Eleca International. They also offer amps.

Divided By Thirteen

Mid-1990s-present. Fred Taccone builds his stomp box guitar effects in the Los Angeles, California area. He also builds amps.

DNA Analogic

2006-present. Line of Japanese-built guitar effects distributed first by Godlyke and presently Pedals Plus+ Effects Warehouse.

DOD

DOD Electronics started in Salt Lake City, Utah in 1974. Today, they're a major effects manufacturer with dozens of pedals made in the U.S. They also market effects under the name DigiTech and are now part of Harman International Industries.

MODEL YEAR	FEATURES	EXC. COND. LOW	HIGH
6 Band Equalizer EQ601			
1977-1982		$45	$65
AB Box 270			
1978-1982		$25	$30
American Metal FX56			
1985-1991		$35	$45
Analog Delay 680			
1979-ca.1982.			
1979-1982		$120	$145
Attacker FX54			
1992-1994. Distortion and compressor.			
1992-1994		$35	$45
Bass Compressor FX82			
1987-ca.1989.			
1987-1989		$35	$45
Bass EQ FX42B			
1987-1996		$35	$45
Bass Grunge FX92			
1995-1996		$35	$45

MODEL YEAR	FEATURES	EXC. COND. LOW	HIGH
Bass Overdrive FX91			
1998-present.			
1998-2010		$35	$45
Bass Stereo Chorus Flanger FX72			
1987-1997		$45	$55
Bass Stereo Chorus FX62			
1987-1996		$45	$55
Bi-FET Preamp FX10			
1982-1996		$25	$35
Buzz Box FX33			
1994-1996. Grunge distortion.			
1994-1996		$40	$55
Chorus 690			
1980-ca.1982. Dual speed chorus.			
1980-1982		$70	$95
Classic Fuzz FX52			
1990-1997		$30	$40
Classic Tube FX53			
1990-1997		$40	$50
Compressor 280			
1978-ca.1982.			
1978-1982		$40	$50
Compressor FX80			
1982-1985		$40	$50
Compressor Sustainer FX80B			
1986-1996		$40	$50
Death Metal FX86			
1994-2009. Distortion.			
1994-2009		$30	$45
Delay FX90			
1984-ca.1987.			
1984-1987		$70	$95
Digital Delay DFX9			
1989-ca.1990.			
1989-1990		$60	$85
Digital Delay Sampler DFX94			
1995-1997		$70	$95
Distortion FX55			
1982-1986. Red case.			
1982-1986		$30	$40
Edge Pedal FX87			
1988-1989		$20	$40
Envelope Filter 440			
1981-ca.1982. Reissued in '95.			
1981-1982		$60	$70
Envelope Filter FX25			
1982-1997. Replaced by FX25B.			
1982-1997		$40	$60
Envelope Filter FX25B			
1981-present.			
1998-2010		$40	$60
Equalizer FX40			
1982-1986		$35	$50
Equalizer FX40B			
1987-2010. Eight bands for bass.			
1987-2010		$35	$50
Fet Preamp 210			
1981-ca.1982.			
1981-1982		$35	$50
Flanger 670			
1981-1982		$70	$95

DigiTech Guitar Effects Processor RP 100

Dino's Dynabox

DNA Bass Dragger

To get the most from this book, be sure to read "Using *The Guide*" in the introduction.

DOD Supra Distortion FX55

Dredge-Tone Overdrive

DST Fat Acid Overdrive

MODEL YEAR	FEATURES	EXC. COND. LOW	HIGH
Gate Loop FX30			
1980s		$25	$35
Graphic Equalizer EQ-610	*1980-ca.1982. Ten bands.*		
1980-1982		$45	$60
Graphic Equalizer EQ-660	*1980-ca.1982. Six bands.*		
1980-1982		$35	$50
Grunge FX69	*1993-2009. Distortion.*		
1993-2009		$30	$45
Hard Rock Distortion FX57	*1987-1994. With built-in delay.*		
1987-1994		$30	$45
Harmonic Enhancer FX85	*1986-ca.1989.*		
1986-1989		$30	$45
I. T. FX100	*1997. Intergrated Tube distortion, produces harmonics.*		
1997		$45	$55
IceBox FX64	*1996-2008. Chorus, high EQ.*		
1996-2008		$20	$30
Juice Box FX51			
1996-1997		$25	$35
Master Switch 225	*1988-ca.1989. A/B switch and loop selector.*		
1988-1989		$25	$35
Meat Box FX32			
1994-1996		$35	$45
Metal Maniac FX58			
1990-1996		$35	$45
Metal Triple Play Guitar Effects System TR3M			
1994		$35	$45
Metal X FX70			
1993-1996		$35	$45
Milk Box FX84	*1994-present. Compressor/expander.*		
1994-2010		$35	$45
Mini-Chorus 460	*1981-ca.1982.*		
1981-1982		$45	$70
Mixer 240	*1978-ca.1982.*		
1978-1982		$20	$30
Momentary Footswitch	*Introduced in 1987. Temporally engages other boxes.*		
1980s		$20	$30
Mystic Blues Overdrive FX102	*1998-present. Medium gain overdrive.*		
1998-2010		$20	$25
Noise Gate 230			
1978-1982		$25	$35
Noise Gate FX30	*1982-ca.1987.*		
1982-1987		$25	$35
Octoplus FX35	*1987-1996. Octaves.*		
1987-1996		$35	$40

MODEL YEAR	FEATURES	EXC. COND. LOW	HIGH
Overdrive Plus FX50B			
1986-1997		$30	$40
Overdrive Preamp 250	*1978-1982, 1995-present. Reissued in '95.*		
1978-1982		$100	$300
1995-2010		$25	$40
Overdrive Preamp FX50			
1982-1985		$30	$40
Performer Compressor Limiter 525			
1981-1984		$50	$55
Performer Delay 585			
1982-1985		$55	$70
Performer Distortion 555			
1981-1984		$35	$45
Performer Flanger 575			
1981-1985		$35	$45
Performer Phasor 595			
1981-1984		$40	$50
Performer Stereo Chorus 565	*1981-1985. FET switching.*		
1981-1985		$55	$70
Performer Wah Filter 545			
1981-1984		$45	$70
Phasor 201	*1981-ca.1982. Reissued in '95.*		
1981-1982		$65	$95
Phasor 401			
1978-1981		$65	$95
Phasor 490	*1980-ca.1982.*		
1980-1982		$65	$95
Phasor FX20			
1982-1985		$35	$45
Psychoacoustic Processor FX87			
1988-1989		$35	$45
Punkifier FX76			
1997		$35	$45
Resistance Mixer 240	*1978-ca.1982.*		
1978-1982		$25	$30
Silencer FX27	*1988-ca.1989. Noise reducer.*		
1988-1989		$30	$40
Stereo Chorus FX60			
1982-1986		$35	$45
Stereo Chorus FX65	*1986-1996. Light blue case.*		
1986-1996		$35	$45
Stereo Flanger FX70	*1982-ca.1985.*		
1982-1985		$35	$45
Stereo Flanger FX75	*1986-1987. Silver case with blue trim.*		
1986-1987		$40	$50
Stereo Flanger FX75B			
1987-1997		$40	$50
Stereo Phasor FX20B			
1986-1999		$40	$50
Stereo Turbo Chorus FX67			
1988-1991		$35	$45

The *Vintage Guitar Price Guide* shows low to high values for items in all-original excellent condition, and, where applicable, with original case or cover.

MODEL YEAR	FEATURES	EXC. COND. LOW	HIGH
Super American Metal FX56B			
1992-1996		$30	$40
Super Stereo Chorus FX68			
1992-1996		$35	$45
Supra Distortion FX55			
1986-present.			
1986-2010		$25	$35
Thrash Master FX59			
1990-1996		$25	$35
Votec Vocal Effects Processor and Mic Preamp			
1998-2001		$55	$60
Wah-Volume FX-17 (pedal)			
1987-2000		$40	$50

Dredge-Tone

Located in Berkeley, California, Dredge-Tone offers effects and electronic kits.

DST Engineering

2001-present. Jeff Swanson and Bob Dettorre build reverb units in Beverly, Massachusetts. They also build amps.

Dunlop

Jim Dunlop, USA offers the Crybaby, MXR (see MXR), Rockman, High Gain, Heil Sound (see Heil), Tremolo, Jimi Hendrix, Rotovibe, Uni-Vibe and Way Huge brand effects.

Crybaby Bass
1985-present. Bass wah.

1985-2010		$75	$100

Crybaby Multi-Wah 535/535Q
1995-present. Multi-range pedal with an external boost control.

1995-2010		$70	$90

Crybaby Wah-Wah GCB-95
1982-present. Dunlop began manufacturing the Crybaby in '82.

1982-1989		$55	$75
1990-1999		$45	$70
2000-2010		$40	$50

High Gain Volume + Boost Pedal

1983-1996		$35	$45

High Gain Volume Pedal GCB-80

1983-2010		$40	$50

Jimi Hendrix Fuzz JH-2 (Round)
1987-1993. Round face fuzz, JH-2S is the square box version.

1987-1993		$50	$75

Rotovibe JH-4S Standard
1989-1998. Standard is finished in bright red enamel with chrome top.

1989-1998		$125	$150

Tremolo Volume Plus TVP-1
1995-1998. Pedal.

1995-1998		$125	$140

Uni-Vibe UV-1
1995-present. Rotating speaker effect.

1995-1999		$175	$225
2000-2010		$175	$200

Durham Electronics

2001-present. Alan Durham builds his line of guitar effects in Austin, Texas.

Dynacord

1950-present. Dynacord is a German company that makes audio and pro sound amps, as well as other electronic equipment and is now owned by TELEX/EVI Audio (an U.S. company), which also owns the Electro-Voice brand. In the '60s they offered tape echo machines and guitars. In '94 a line of multi-effects processors were introduced under the Electro-Voice/Dynacord name, but by the following year they were just listed as Electro-Voice.

EchoCord
Introduced in 1959. Tape echo unit.

1959-1960s		$275	$350

Dyno

See Dytronics.

Dytronics

Mid-1970s-early 1980s. The Japanese Dytronics company made a chorus rackmount unit for electric piano called the Dyno My Piano with flying piano keys or a lightning bolt on the front. Another version was called the Tri-Stereo Chorus and a third, called the Songbird, had a bird's head on the front.

E Bow

See Heet Sound Products.

E.W.S. (Engineering Work Store)

2007-present. Guitar effects pedals built in Tokyo, Japan for Prosound Communications in Van Nuys, California.

EarthQuaker Devices

2006-present. Guitar effects pedals built by Jamie Stillman in Akron, Ohio.

EBS

1992-present. Bass and guitar effects built in Stockholm, Sweden by the EBS Sweden AB company. They also build bass amps.

Ecco Fonic

The Ecco Fonic was distributed by Fender in 1958-'59.

Echo Unit
1958-1959. Reverb unit.

1958-1959	With brown case	$900	$1,100

Echoplex

The Echoplex tape echo units were first sold under the Maestro brand. After Maestro dropped the Echoplex, it was marketed under the Market Electronics name from the late-'70s to the early-'80s. In the later '80s, Market Electronics was dropped from the ads and they were marketed

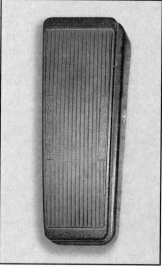
Crybaby Wah-Wah GCB-95

1987 Dunlop Jimi Hendrix JH-2
Jesse Isselbacher

EBS Valve Drive

EFFECTS

Eden Analog Detroit

Electra Metal 698HM

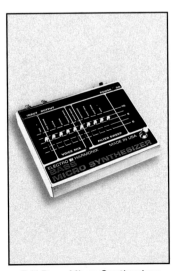

E-H Bass Micro-Synthesizer

MODEL YEAR	FEATURES	EXC. COND. LOW	HIGH

under the Echoplex brand. Both the Market and Echoplex brands are listed here; for earlier models see Maestro. In '94, Gibson's Oberheim division introduced a rackmount unit called the Echoplex. In '01, it was relabeled as Gibson.

Echoplex EP3
1984-ca. 1988. Solidstate version.

1984-1988		$350	$425

Echoplex EP4
1984-1991. Solidstate version.

1984-1991		$350	$425

Echoplex EP6T
1980-ca.1988. All-tube reissue of the EP2.

1980-1988		$400	$475

Eden Analog

2004-present. Guitar effects pedals built by Chris Sheppard and Robert Hafley in Pelham, Alabama.

Effector 13

2002-2008. Guitar effects built by Devi Ever in Minneapolis, Minnesota. Located in Austin, Texas until mid-'04. Name changed to Devi Ever : Fx in '09.

Effectrode

1996-present. Effects pedals built in Corvallis, Oregon by Phil Taylor.

EFX

1980s. Brand name of the Los Angeles-based EFX Center; they also offered a direct box and a powered pedal box/board.

Switch Box B287
1984. Dual effects loop selector.

1984		$25	$35

EKO

1959-1985, 2000-present. In the '60s and '70s EKO offered effects made by EME and JEN Elettronica, which also made Vox effects.

Eleca

2004-present. Guitar effects pedals imported by Eleca International. They also offer guitars, mandolins and amps.

Electra

1971-1984. Guitar brand imported by St. Louis Music, Electra offered a line of effects in the late '70s.

Chorus 504CH
Ca.1975-ca.1980.

1975-1980		$55	$75

Compressor 502C/602C
Ca.1975-ca.1980.

1975-1980		$45	$55

Distortion 500D
Ca.1976-ca.1980.

1976-1980		$55	$75

MODEL YEAR	FEATURES	EXC. COND. LOW	HIGH

Flanger (stereo) 605F
Ca.1975-ca.1980.

1975-1980		$55	$75

Fuzz Wah
Ca.1975-ca.1980.

1975-1980		$75	$125

Pedal Drive 515AC
Ca.1976-ca.1980. Overdrive.

1976-1980		$40	$50

Phaser Model 501P
Ca.1976-ca.1980.

1976-1980		$50	$60

Phaser Model 875
Ca.1975-ca.1980.

1975-1980		$50	$60

Roto Phase I
1975-ca.1980. Small pocket phaser.

1975-1980		$70	$85

Roto Phase II
1975-ca.1980. Pedal phasor.

1975-1980		$80	$95

Electro-Harmonix

1968-1984, 1996-present. Founded by Mike Matthews in New York City, the company initially produced small plug-in boosters such as the LPB-1. In '71, they unveiled the awe-inspiring Big Muff Pi fuzz and dozens of innovative pedals followed. After years of disputes, the nonunion E-H factory became the target of union organizers and a '81 union campaign, combining picketing and harrying of E-H employees, brought production to a halt. Matthews' financier then cut his funding, and in early '82, E.H. filed for bankruptcy. Later that year, Matthews was able to reopen and continue through '84. In '96, he again began producing reissues of many of his classic effects as well as new designs.

10 Band Graphic Equalizer
1977-1981. Includes footswitch.

1977-1981		$60	$70

16-Second Digital Delay
Early-1980s, 2004-2008. An updated version was reissued in '04.

1980s	With foot controller	$675	$825
1980s	Without foot controller	$500	$625
1990s		$325	$500
2004-2008		$275	$375

3 Phase Liner

1981		$50	$60

5X Junction Mixer

1977-1981		$30	$40

Attack Equalizer
1975-1981. Active EQ, a.k.a. "Knock Out."

1975-1981		$150	$200

Attack/Decay
1980-1981. Tape reverse simulator.

1980-1981		$200	$225

Bad Stone Phase Shifter
1975-1981.

1975-1981	Three knobs	$200	$250

MODEL YEAR	FEATURES	EXC. COND. LOW	HIGH
1975-1981	Two knobs, color switch	$175	$225

Bass Micro-Synthesizer
1981-1984, 1999-present. Analog synthesizer sounds.

1981-1984		$225	$300
1999-2010		$150	$175

Bassballs
1978-1984, 1998-present. Bass envelope filter/distortion.

1978-1984		$200	$225

Big Muff Pi
1971-1984. Sustain, floor unit, issued in 3 different looks, as described below.

1970s	Earlier black graphics, knobs in triangle pattern	$350	$425
1970s	Later red/ black graphics, 1/2" letters	$225	$425
1980s	Red/black graphics, logo in 1" letters	$150	$250

Big Muff Pi (reissue)
1996-present. Originally made in Russia, but currently both Russian- and U.S.-made versions are available.

1996-2010	Russian-made	$40	$45

Big Muff Sovtek
2000s. Big Muff Pi, Electro Harmonix, and Sovtek logos on an olive green case.

2000s		$125	$175

Black Finger Compressor Sustainer
1977, 2003-present. Original has 3 knobs in triangle pattern.

1977		$125	$225
2003-2010		$75	$100

Clap Track
1980-1984. Drum effect.

1980-1984		$40	$60

Clone Theory
1977-1981. Chorus effect, The Clone Theory logo.

1977-1981		$150	$175

Crash Pad
1980-1984. Percussion synth.

1980-1984		$40	$60

Crying Tone Pedal
1976-1978. Wah-wah.

1976-1978		$175	$225

Deluxe Big Muff Pi
1978-1981. Sustain, AC version of Big Muff Pi, includes a complete Soul Preacher unit.

1978-1981	Red graphics	$125	$200

Deluxe Electric Mistress Flanger
1977-1983, 1996-present. AC.

1977-1979		$150	$250
1980-1983		$125	$175

Deluxe Memory Man
1977-1983, 1996-present. Echo and delay, featured 4 knobs '77-'78, from '79-'83 it has 5 knobs and added vibrato and chorus.

1977-1978	Four knobs	$225	$300
1979-1983	Five knobs	$200	$275
1996-2010		$150	$165

MODEL YEAR	FEATURES	EXC. COND. LOW	HIGH

Deluxe Octave Multiplexer

1977-1981		$200	$250

Digital Delay/Chorus
1981-1984. With digital chorus.

1981-1984		$250	$300

Digital Rhythm Matrix DRM-15

1981-1984		$225	$250

Digital Rhythm Matrix DRM-16

1979-1983		$225	$250

Digital Rhythm Matrix DRM-32

1981-1984		$225	$250

Doctor Q Envelope Follower
1976-1983, 2001-present. For bass or guitar.

1976-1983		$150	$200
2001-2010		$30	$35

Domino Theory
1981. Sound sensitive light tube.

1981		$50	$100

Echo 600

1981		$175	$225

Echoflanger
1977-1982. Flange, slapback, chorus, filter.

1977-1982		$200	$250

Electric Mistress Flanger

1976-1984		$175	$275

Electronic Metronome

1978-1980		$25	$30

Frequency Analyzer
1977-1984, 2001-present. Ring modulator.

1977-1984		$200	$250

Full Double Tracking Effect
1978-1981. Doubling, slapback.

1978-1981		$100	$150

Fuzz Wah
Introduced around 1974.

1970s		$175	$225

Golden Throat

1977-1984		$300	$400

Golden Throat Deluxe
1977-1979. Deluxe has a built-in monitor amp.

1977-1979		$300	$400

Golden Throat II

1978-1981		$150	$225

Guitar Synthesizer
1981. Sold for $1,495 in May '81.

1981		$225	$300

Hog's Foot Bass Booster

1977-1980		$70	$90

Holy Grail
2002-present. Digital reverb.

2002-2010		$80	$90

Hot Foot
1977-1978. Rocker pedal turns knob of other E-H effects.

1977-1978	Gold case, red graphics	$75	$100

Hot Tubes
1978-1984, 2001-2007. Tube distortion.

1978-1984		$125	$200

Early 1970s E-H Big Muff Pi
Andrea Scarfone

EFFECTS

E-H Electric Mistress
(Jim Schreck)

E-H Frequency Analyzer

E-H Pulse Modulator

(Jim Schreck)

E-H Q-Tron

E-H Soul Preacher Nano

MODEL YEAR	FEATURES	EXC. COND. LOW	HIGH
Linear Power Booster LPB-1			
1968-1983.			
1976-1979		$55	$80
1980-1983		$45	$75
Linear Power Booster LPB-2			
Ca.1968-1983.			
1968-1983		$90	$100
Little Big Muff Pi			
1976-1980, 2006-present. Sustain, 1-knob floor unit.			
1976-1980		$150	$175
Memory Man/Stereo Memory Man			
1976-1984, 1999-present. Analog delay, newer version in stereo.			
1976-1979		$250	$300
1980-1984		$150	$250
Micro Synthesizer			
1978-1984, 1998-present. Mini keyboard phaser.			
1978-1979		$225	$250
1978-1984		$225	$250
1998-2010		$150	$170
Mini Q-Tron/Micro Q-Tron			
2002-present. Battery-operated smaller version of Q-Tron envelope follower, changed to identical effect in smaller box Micro in '06.			
2002-2010		$40	$45
Mini-Mixer			
1978-1981. Mini mic mixer, reissued in '01.			
1978-1981		$30	$40
MiniSynthesizer			
1981-1983. Mini keyboard with phaser.			
1981-1983		$300	$400
MiniSynthesizer With Echo			
1981. Mini keyboard with phaser.			
1981		$375	$500
Mole Bass Booster			
1968-1978.			
1968-1969		$60	$80
1970-1978		$40	$60
Muff Fuzz			
1976-1983. Fuzz and line boost, silver case with orange lettering.			
1976-1983		$85	$100
Muff Fuzz Crying Tone			
1977-1978. Fuzz, wah.			
1977-1978		$150	$250
Octave Multiplexer Floor Unit			
1976-1980			
1976-1980		$175	$275
Octave Multiplexer Pedal			
1976-1977, 2001-present.			
1976-1977		$150	$250
2001-2010		$40	$45
Panic Button			
1981. Siren sounds for drum.			
1981		$30	$40
Poly Chorus/Stereo Polychorus			
1981, 1999-present. Same as Echoflanger.			
1981		$175	$200
1999-2010		$125	$150
Polyphase			
1979-1981. With envelope.			
1979-1981		$175	$225

MODEL YEAR	FEATURES	EXC. COND. LOW	HIGH
Pulsar/Stereo Plusar			
2004-present. Variable wave form tremolo.			
2004-2010		$45	$55
Pulse Modulator			
Ca.1968 -ca.1972. Triple tremolo.			
1968-1969		$250	$325
1970-1972		$200	$250
Q-Tron			
1997-present. Envelope controlled filter.			
1997-2010		$125	$175
Q-Tron +			
1999-present. With added effects loop and Attack Response switch.			
1999-2010		$70	$80
Queen Triggered Wah			
1976-1978. Wah/Envelope Filter.			
1976-1978		$125	$150
Random Tone Generator RTG			
1981			
1981		$40	$60
Rhythm 12 (Rhythm Machine)			
1978			
1978		$75	$125
Rolling Thunder			
1980-1981. Percussion synth.			
1980-1981		$40	$50
Screaming Bird Treble Booster			
Ca.1968-1980. In-line unit.			
1968-1980		$75	$100
Screaming Tree Treble Booster			
1977-1981. Floor unit.			
1977-1981		$100	$150
Sequencer Drum			
1981. Drum effect.			
1981		$40	$50
Slapback Echo			
1977-1978. Stereo.			
1977-1978		$150	$200
Small Clone			
1983-1984, 1999-present. Analog chorus, depth and rate controls, purple face plate, white logo.			
1983-1984		$150	$200
1999-2010		$35	$40
Small Stone Phase Shifter			
1975-1984, 1996-present. Both Russian and U.S. reissues were made.			
1975-1979		$175	$225
1980-1984		$125	$175
Soul Preacher			
1977-1983, 2007-present. Compressor sustainer. Nano version for present.			
1977-1983		$100	$150
Space Drum/Super Space Drum			
1980-1981. Percussion synthesizer.			
1980-1981		$125	$175
Switch Blade			
1977-1983. A-B Box.			
1977-1983		$45	$55
Talking Pedal			
1977-1978. Creates vowel sounds.			
1977-1978		$350	$550

MODEL		EXC. COND.	
YEAR	FEATURES	LOW	HIGH

The Silencer
1976-1981. Noise elimination.
| 1976-1981 | | $60 | $80 |

The Wiggler
2002-present. All-tube modulator including pitch vibrato and volume tremolo.
| 2002-2010 | | $100 | $110 |

The Worm
2002-present. Wah/Phaser.
| 2002-2010 | | $55 | $65 |

Tube Zipper
2001-present. Tube (2x12AX7) envelope follower.
| 2001-2010 | | $100 | $120 |

Vocoder
1978-1981. Modulates voice with instrument.
| 1978-1981 | Rackmount | $425 | $525 |

Volume Pedal
| 1978-1981 | | $45 | $65 |

Y-Triggered Filter
| 1976-1977 | | $140 | $160 |

Zipper Envelope Follower
1976-1978. The Tube Zipper was introduced in '01.
| 1976-1978 | | $200 | $300 |

Electrosonic Amplifiers
2002-2010. Amp builder Josh Corn also offered a preamp pedal, built in Boonville, Indiana.

Elk
Late-1960s. Japanese company Elk Gakki Co., Ltd. mainly made guitars and amps, but did offer effects as well.

Elka
In the late '60s or early '70s, Italian organ and synthesizer company Elka-Orla (later just Elka) offered a few effects, likely made by JEN Elettronica (Vox, others).

EMMA Electronic
Line of guitar effects built in Denmark and distributed by Godlyke.
ReezaFRATzitz RF-1
2004-present. Overdrive and distortion, red case.
| 2004-2010 | | $80 | $95 |

Empress Effects
2005-present. Guitar effects pedals built by Steve Bragg and Jason Fee in Ottawa, Ontario.

EMS
1969-1979. Peter Zinnovieff's English synth company (Electronic Music Studios) also offered a guitar synthesizer. The company has reopened to work on original EMS gear.

eowave
2002-present. Effects built first in Paris and now in Burgundy, France by Marc Sirguy.

Epiphone
Epiphone pedals are labeled G.A.S Guitar Audio System and were offered from around 1988 to '91.
Pedals
Various models with years available.
1988-1989	Chorus EP-CH-70	$35	$45
1988-1989	Delay EP-DE-80	$45	$60
1988-1991	Compressor EP-CO-20	$35	$40
1988-1991	Distortion EP-DI-10	$35	$45
1988-1991	Flanger EP-FL-60	$40	$55
1988-1991	Overdrive EP-OD-30	$35	$45

Ernie Ball
Ernie Ball owned a music store in Tarzana, California, when he noticed the demand for a better selection of strings. The demand for his Slinky strings grew to the point where, in '67, he sold the store to concentrate on strings. He went on to produce the Earthwood brand of guitars and basses from '72-'85. In '84, Ball purchased the Music Man company.
Volume Pedals
1977-present.
| 1977-2010 | | $35 | $65 |

Euthymia Electronics
Line of guitar effects built by Erik Miller in Alameda, California.

Eventide
1971-present. This New Jersey electronics manufacturer has offered studio and rackmount effects since the late '70s. In '08 they added guitar effects pedals.

EXR
The EXR Corporation was located in Brighton, Michigan.
Projector
1983-ca.1984. Psychoacoustic enhancer pedal.
| 1983-1984 | | $65 | $75 |

Projector SP III
1983-ca.1984. Psychoacoustic enhancer pedal, volume pedal/sound boost.
| 1983-1984 | | $65 | $70 |

Farfisa
The organ company offered effects pedals in the 1960s. Their products were manufactured in Italy by the Italian Accordion Company and distributed by Chicago Musical Instruments.
Model VIP 345 Organ
Mid-1960s. Portable organ with Syntheslalom used in the rock and roll venue.
| 1960s | | $500 | $600 |

Repeater
| 1969 | | $100 | $150 |

Sferasound
1960s. Vibrato pedal for a Farfisa Organ but it works well with the guitar, gray case.
| 1960s | | $275 | $375 |

E-H Switch Blade

EFFECTS

Electrosonic Amplifiers EF86 Preamp

Eowave Ring O' Bug

Fender Fuzz-Wah

Fishman Jerry Douglas

Fishman Aura T01 Acoustic Imaging

MODEL YEAR	FEATURES	EXC. COND. LOW	HIGH

Wah/Volume
1969		$100	$150

Fargen
1999-present. Guitar effects built in Sacramento, California by Benjamin Fargen. He also builds amps.

Fender
Although Fender has flirted with effects since the 1950s (the volume/volume-tone pedal and the EccoFonic), it concentrated mainly on guitars and amps. Fender effects ranged from the sublime to the ridiculous, from the tube Reverb to the Dimension IV. Presently they offer a reverb unit and retro effects pedals.

'63 Tube Reverb
1994-present. Reissue spring/tube Reverb Units with various era cosmetics as listed below. Currently offered in brown or, since '09, in lacquered tweed.
1994	White (limited run)	$375	$425
1994-1997	Black or blonde	$350	$400
1994-1997	Tweed	$375	$425
1994-2008	Brown	$350	$400

Blender Fuzz
1968-1977, 2005-2010. Battery operated fuzz and sustain.
1968-1969		$350	$375
1970-1977		$275	$300

Contempo Organ
1967-1968. Portable organ, all solidstate, 61 keys including a 17-key bass section, catalog shows with red cover material.
1967-1968		$525	$550

Dimension IV
1968-1970. Multi-effects unit using an oil-filled drum.
1968-1970		$150	$200

Echo-Reverb
1966-1970. Solidstate, echo-reverb effect produced by rotating metal disk, black tolex, silver grille.
1966-1970		$300	$350

Electronic Echo Chamber
1962-1968. Solidstate tape echo, up to 400 ms of delay, rectangle box with 2 controls '62-'67, slanted front '67-'68.
1962-1968		$275	$325

Fuzz-Wah
1968-1984, 2007-present. Has Fuzz and Wah switches on sides of pedal '68-'73, has 3 switches above the pedal '74-'84. Current version has switches on sides.
1968-1973	Switches on side	$175	$225
1974-1984	Switches above	$150	$200

Phaser
1975-1977, 2007-present. AC powered, reissued in '07.
1975-1977		$125	$175

Reverb Unit
1961-1966, 1975-1978. Fender used a wide variety of tolex coverings in the early-'60s as the coverings matched those on the amps. Initially, Fender used rough blond tolex, then rough brown tolex, followed by smooth white or black tolex.
1961	Blond tolex, Oxblood grille	$950	$1,200
1961	Brown tolex	$725	$875
1962	Blond tolex, Oxblood grille	$950	$1,200
1962	Brown tolex, Wheat grille	$725	$875
1963	Brown tolex	$725	$875
1963	Rough blond tolex	$725	$875
1963	Smooth white tolex	$725	$875
1964	Black tolex	$725	$875
1964	Brown tolex, gold grille	$725	$875
1964	Smooth white tolex	$725	$875
1965-1966	Black tolex	$725	$875
1966	Solidstate, flat cabinet	$175	$225
1975-1978	Tube reverb reinstated	$500	$600

Reverb Unit Reissue
1990s-2000s. Optional covers in white (limited run), brown, black, blond or tweed.
1990-2000s	Various covers	$400	$500

Vibratone
1967-1972. Leslie-type speaker cabinet made specifically for the guitar, 2-speed motor.
1960s		$750	$850

Volume-Tone Foot Pedal
1954-1984, 2007-present.
1960s		$125	$175

Fishman
2003-present. Larry Fishman of Andover, Massachusetts offers a line of acoustic guitar effects pedals. He also builds amps.

FJA Mods
2002-present. Jerry Pinnelli builds amp effects and guitar pedals in Central Square, New York. In 2007 he also began building amps.

FlexiSound
FlexiSound products were made in Lancaster, Pennsylvania.

F. S. Clipper
1975-ca.1976. Distortion, plugged directly into guitar jack.
1975-1976		$55	$65

The Beefer
1975. Power booster, plugged directly into guitar jack.
1975		$40	$50

Flip
Line of tube effects by Guyatone and distributed in the U.S. by Godlyke Distributing.

Tube Echo (TD-X)
2004-present. Hybrid tube power delay pedal.
2004-2010		$90	$100

EFFECTS

MODEL YEAR	FEATURES	EXC. COND. LOW	HIGH

FM Acoustics

Made in Switzerland.

E-1 Pedal
1975. Volume, distortion, filter pedal.

1975		$70	$80

Foxx

Foxx pedals are readily identifiable by their fur-like covering. They slunk onto the scene in 1971 and were extinct by '78. Made by Hollywood's Ridinger Associates, their most notable product was the Tone Machine fuzz. Foxx-made pedals also have appeared under various brands such as G and G, Guild, Yamaha and Sears Roebuck, generally without fur. Since 2005, reissues of some of the classic Foxx pedals are being built in Provo, Utah.

Clean Machine
1974-1978		$250	$275

Down Machine
1971-1977. Bass wah.

1971-1977	Blue case	$250	$275

Foot Phaser
1975-1977, 2006-present.

1975-1977		$450	$650

Fuzz and Wa and Volume
1974-1978, 2006-present. Currently called Fuzz Wah Volume.

1974-1978		$300	$350

Guitar Synthesizer I
1975		$300	$350

O.D. Machine
1972-ca.1975.

1972-1975		$150	$200

Phase III
1975-1978		$100	$150

Tone Machine
1971-1978, 2005-present. Fuzz with Octave.

1971-1978		$375	$475

Wa and Volume
1971-1978		$200	$225

Wa Machine
1971-ca.1978.

1971-1978		$150	$200

Framptone

2000-present. Founded by Peter Frampton, Framptone offers hand-made guitar effects.

Frantone

1994-present. Effects and accessories hand built in New York City.

Fulltone

1991-present. Fulltone effects are based on some of the classic effects of the past. Fulltone was started in Los Angeles, California by Michael Fuller who says the company was born out of his love for Jimi Hendrix and fine vintage pedals.

Deja Vibe
1991-2002. UniVibe-type pedal, later models have a Vintage/Modern switch. Stereo version also available. Now offerered in Mini version.

1991-2004	Mono	$175	$200

Deja Vibe 2
1997-present. Like Deja Vibe but with built-in speed control. Stereo version also available.

1997-2010	Mono	$200	$225

Distortion Pro
2002-2008. Red case, volume and distortion knobs with four voicing controls.

2002-2008		$125	$150

Fat Boost
2001-2007. Clean boost, silver-sparkle case, volume and drive knobs.

2001-2007		$125	$135

Full-Drive 2
1995-present. Blue case, four control knobs.

1995-2010		$120	$145

Octafuzz
1996-present. Copy of the Tycobrahe Octavia.

1996-2010		$85	$100

Soul Bender
1994-2008. Volume, tone and dirt knobs.

1994-2008		$100	$125

Supa-Trem
1995-present. Black case, white Supa-Trem logo, rate and mix controls.

1995-2010		$100	$125

Tube Tape Echo TTE
2004-present. EchoPlex style using tape.

2004-2010		$725	$850

Furman Sound

1993-present. Located in Petaluma, California, Furman makes audio and video signal processors and AC power conditioning products for music and other markets.

LC-2 Limiter Compressor
1990s. Rackmount unit with a black suitcase and red knobs.

1990s		$40	$50

PQ3 Parametric EQ
1990s. Rackmount preamp and equalizer.

1998-1999		$110	$150

PQ6 Parametric Stereo
1990s		$135	$175

RV1 Reverb Rackmount
1990s		$110	$150

Fxdoctor

2003-present. Joshua Zalegowski originally built his effects in Amherst, Massachusetts, and in 2005 moved to Boston.

Fxengineering

2002-present. Production and custom guitar effects built by Montez Aldridge in Raleigh, North Carolina.

FJA Mods Fuzz Pedal

Framptone Amp Switcher

Fxdoctor Clean Boost

EFFECTS

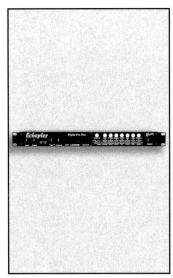

*Gibson Echoplex
Digital Pro Plus*

Gizmoaudio Sawmill

Guild Foxey Lady

(Jim Schreck)

MODEL YEAR	FEATURES	EXC. COND. LOW	HIGH

G2D
1999-present. David Manning and Grant Wills build their guitar effects pedals in Auckland, New Zealand.

Garcia
2004-present. Guitar effects built by Matthew Garcia in Myrtle Beach, South Carolina. He also builds amps.

Geek MacDaddy
See listing under The Original Geek.

George Dennis
1991-present. Founded by George Burgerstein, original products were a line of effects pedals. In '96 they added a line of tube amps. The company is located in Prague, Czech Republic.

Gibson
Gibson did offer a few effects bearing their own name, but most were sold under the Maestro name (see that listing).

Echoplex Digital Pro Plus
1994-2010. Rackmount unit with digital recording, sampling and digital delay. Labeled as just Echoplex until '01 when Gibson name added.

1994-2010		$575	$700

GA-3RV Reverb Unit
1964-1967. Small, compact, spring reverb unit, black tolex, gray grille.

1964-1967		$325	$400

GA-4RE Reverb-Echo Unit
1964-1967. Small, compact, lightweight accessory reverb-echo unit that produces complete reverberation and authentic echo, utilizes Gibson's "electronic memory" system for both reverb and echo, black tolex, gray grille.

1964-1967		$450	$550

Gig-FX
2004-present. Founder Jeff Purchon of Waltham, Massachusetts, imports guitar effects pedals built at his company-owned factory in Shenzhen, China.

Gizmoaudio
2009-present. Guitar effects built by Charles Luke in Cumming, Georgia.

Gnome Amplifiers
2008-present. Guitar effects pedals built by Dan Munro in Olympia, Washington. He also builds amps.

Godbout
Sold a variety of effects do-it-yourself kits in the 1970s. Difficult to value because quality depends on skills of builder.

Effects Kits

1970s		$20	$30

MODEL YEAR	FEATURES	EXC. COND. LOW	HIGH

Goodrich Sound
1970s-present. Originally located in Michigan, and currently in Dublin, Georgia, Goodrich currently offers volume pedals and a line boost.

Match Box Line Boost
Early-1980s-present. Small rectangular line buffer/driver.

1980s		$45	$55

Volume Pedal 6122
Late 1970s-1980s. Uses a potentiometer.

1970s		$45	$55

Volume Pedal 6400ST
Late 1970s-1980s. Stereo pedal, using photocells.

1970s		$45	$55

Volume Pedal 6402
Late 1970s-1980s. Uses photocell.

1970s		$45	$55

Greer Amplification
1999-present. Guitar stomp box effects built by Nick Greer in Athens, Georgia. He also builds amps.

Gretsch
Gretsch has offered a limited line of effects from time to time.

Controfuzz
Mid-1970s. Distortion.

1970s		$150	$225

Deluxe Reverb Unit Model 6149
1963-1969. Similar to Gibson's GA-1 introduced around the same time.

1963-1969		$400	$500

Expandafuzz
Mid-1970s. Distortion.

1970s		$150	$200

Reverb Unit Model 6144 Preamp Reverb
1963-1967. Approximately 17 watts, preamp functionality, no speaker.

1963-1967		$250	$350

Tremofect
Mid-1970s. Tremolo effect, 3-band EQ, speed, effect, bass, total, and treble knobs.

1970s		$225	$300

Guild
Guild marketed effects made by Binson, Electro-Harmonix, Foxx, WEM and Applied in the 1960s and '70s.

Copicat
1960s-1979. Echo.

1970s		$300	$400

DE-20 Auto-Rhythm Unit
1971-1974. 50 watt rhythm accompaniment unit. Included 20 rhythms and a separate instrument channel with its own volume control. 1x12" plus tweeter.

1971-1974		$200	$300

Echorec (by Binson)
Ca.1960-1979. This was different stripped-down version of the Binson Echorec.

1960s		$675	$825

EFFECTS

MODEL YEAR	FEATURES	EXC. COND. LOW	HIGH

Foxey Lady Fuzz
1968-1977. Distortion, sustain.

| 1968-1975 | 2 knobs, made by E-H | $200 | $250 |
| 1976-1977 | 3 knobs in row, same as Big Muff | $150 | $200 |

Fuzz Wah FW-3
1975-ca.1979. Distortion, volume, wah, made by Foxx.

| 1970s | | $150 | $175 |

HH Echo Unit
1976-ca.1979.

| 1970s | | $200 | $300 |

VW-1
1975-ca.1979. Volume, wah, made by Foxx.

| 1970s | | $200 | $250 |

Guyatone
1998-present. Imported stomp boxes, tape echo units and outboard reverb units distributed by Godlyke Distributing.

HAO
2000-present. Line of guitar effects built in Japan by J.E.S. International, distributed in the U.S. by Godlyke.

Harden Engineering
2006-present. Distortion/boost guitar effects pedals built by William Harden in Chicago, Illinois. He also builds guitars.

Heathkit
1960s. Unassembled kits sold through various retailers.

TA-28 Distortion Booster
1960s. Fuzz assembly kit, heavy '60s super fuzz, case-by-case quality depending on the builder.

| 1960s | | $140 | $150 |

Heavy Metal Products
Mid-1970s. From Alto Loma, California, products for the heavy metal guitarist.

Raunchbox Fuzz

| 1975-1976 | | $75 | $100 |

Switchbox
1975-1976. A/B box.

| 1975-1976 | | $25 | $35 |

Heet Sound Products
1974-present. The E Bow concept goes back to '67, but a hand-held model wasn't available until '74. Made in Los Angeles, California.

E Bow
1974-1979, 1985-1987, 1994-present. The Energy Bow, hand-held electro-magnetic string driver.

| 1974-1979 | | $50 | $60 |

E Bow for Pedal Steels
1979. Hand-held electro-magnetic string driver.

| 1979 | | $35 | $55 |

MODEL YEAR	FEATURES	EXC. COND. LOW	HIGH

Heil Sound
1960-present. Founded by Bob Heil, Marissa, Illinois. Created the talk box technology as popularized by Peter Frampton. In the '60s and '70s Heil was dedicated to innovative products for the music industry. In the late-'70s, innovative creations were more in the amateur radio market, and by the '90s Heil's focus was on the home theater market. The Heil Sound Talkbox was reissued by Jim Dunlop USA in '89.

Talk Box
1976-ca.1980, 1989-present. Reissued by Dunlop.

1976-1980		$100	$125
1989-1999		$75	$85
2000-2010		$70	$80

Hermida Audio
2003-present. Alfonso Hermida builds his guitar effects in Miramar, Florida.

High Gain
See listing under Dunlop.

Hohner
Hohner offered effects in the late-1970s.

Dirty Booster
1977-ca.1978. Distortion.

| 1977-1978 | | $55 | $65 |

Dirty Wah Wah'er
1977-ca.1978. Adds distortion.

| 1977-1978 | | $65 | $75 |

Fuzz Wah
1970s. Morley-like volume pedal with volume knob and fuzz knob, switch for soft or hard fuzz, gray box with black foot pedal.

| 1970s | | $65 | $75 |

Multi-Exciter
1977-ca.1978. Volume, wah, surf, tornado, siren.

| 1977-1978 | | $60 | $70 |

Tape Echo/Echo Plus
1970s. Black alligator suitcase.

| 1970s | | $200 | $300 |

Tri-Booster
1977-ca.1978. Distortion, sustain.

| 1977-1978 | | $55 | $65 |

Vari-Phaser
1977-ca.1978.

| 1977-1978 | | $55 | $65 |

Vol-Kicker Volume Pedal
1977-ca.1978.

| 1977-1978 | | $30 | $40 |

Wah-Wah'er
1977-ca.1978. Wah, volume.

| 1977-1978 | | $55 | $65 |

HomeBrew Electronics
2001-present. Stomp box effects hand made by Joel and Andrea Weaver in Glendale, Arizona.

HAO Rust Driver

Heet E Bow

HomeBrew Compressor Retro

EFFECTS

Ibanez Classic Phase PH-99

Ibanez Analog Delay AD9

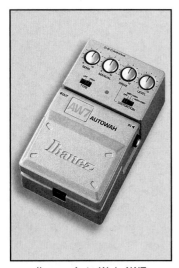

*Ibanez Auto Wah AW7
(Tone-Lok)*

MODEL YEAR	FEATURES	EXC. COND. LOW	HIGH

Hughes & Kettner

1985-present. Hughes & Kettner builds a line of tube-driven guitar effects made in Germany. They also build amps and cabinets.

Ibanez

Ibanez effects were introduced ca. 1974, and were manufactured by Japan's Maxon Electronics. Although results were mixed at first, a more uniform and modern product line, including the now legendary Tube Screamer, built Ibanez's reputation for quality. They continue to produce a wide range of effects.

60s Fuzz FZ5 (SoundTank)
1991-1992, 1996-1998. Fuzz with level, tone and distortion controls, black plastic case, green label.

1990s		$25	$30

7th Heaven SH7 (Tone-Lok)
2000-2004. Lo, high, drive and level controls, gray-silver case, blue-green label.

2000-2004		$20	$30

Acoustic Effects PT4
1993-1998. Acoustic guitar multi-effect with compressor/limiter, tone shaper, stereo chorus, digital reverb, with power supply.

1993-1998		$75	$100

Analog Delay AD9
1982-1984. 3 control analog delay, Hot Pink metal case.

1982-1984		$200	$275

Analog Delay AD80
1980-1981. Pink case.

1980-1981		$225	$300

Analog Delay AD99
1996-1998. Reissue, 3 control knobs and on/off switch, winged-hand logo, black case.

1996-1998		$125	$150

Analog Delay AD100 (Table Unit)
1981-1983. Stand-alone table/studio unit (not rack mount) with power cord.

1981-1983		$200	$250

Analog Delay 202 (Rack Mount)
1981-1983. Rack mount with delay, doubling, flanger, stereo chorus, dual inputs with tone and level.

1981-1983		$200	$250

Auto Filter AF9
1982-1984. Replaces AF201 model.

1982-1984		$150	$200

Auto Filter AF201
1981. Two min-max sliders, 3 mode toggle switches, orange metal case.

1981		$175	$200

Auto Wah AW5 (SoundTank)
1994-1999. Plastic case SoundTank series.

1994-1999		$30	$40

Auto Wah AW7 (Tone-Lok)
2000-2010. Silver case.

2000-2010		$20	$30

Bass Compressor BP10

1986-1991		$70	$80

MODEL YEAR	FEATURES	EXC. COND. LOW	HIGH

Bi-Mode Chorus BC9
1984. Dual channel for 2 independent speed and width settings.

1984		$75	$100

Chorus CS-505
1980-1981. Speed and depth controls, gray-blue case, stereo or mono input, battery or external power option.

1980-1981		$100	$125

Chorus Flanger CF7 (Tone-Lok)
1999-2010. Speed, depth, delay, regeneration controls, mode and crazy switches.

1999-2010		$35	$40

Classic Flange FL99
1997-1999. Analog reissue, silver metal case, winged-hand artwork, 4 controls, 2 footswitch buttons.

1997-1999		$90	$110

Classic Phase PH99
1995-1999. Analog reissue, silver metal case, winged-hand artwork, speed, depth, feedback, effect level controls, intense and bypass footswitches.

1995-1999		$90	$110

Compressor CP5 (SoundTank)

1991-1998		$20	$30

Compressor CP10

1986-1992		$75	$80

Compressor CP830

1975-1979		$100	$125

Compressor II CP835

1980-1981		$100	$125

Compressor Limiter CP9

1982-1984		$100	$125

Delay Champ CD10
1986-1989. Red case, 3 knobs.

1986-1989		$125	$150

Delay Echo DE7 (Tone-Lok)
1999-2010. Stereo delay/echo.

1999-2010		$40	$50

Delay Harmonizer DM1000
1983-1984. Rack mount, with chorus, 9 control knobs.

1983-1984		$175	$225

Delay III DDL20 Digital Delay
1988-1989. Filtering, doubling, slap back, echo S, echo M, echo L, Seafoam Green coloring on pedal.

1988-1989		$100	$125

Delay PDD1 (DPC Series)
1988-1989. Programmable Digital Delay (PDD) with display screen.

1988-1989		$125	$150

Digital Chorus DSC10
1990-1992. 3 control knobs and slider selection toggle.

1990-1992		$75	$100

Digital Delay DL5 (SoundTank)

1991-1998		$35	$45

Digital Delay DL10
1989-1992. Digital Delay made in Japan, blue case, 3 green control knobs, stompbox.

1989-1992		$100	$125

The *Vintage Guitar Price Guide* shows low to high values for items in all-original excellent condition, and, where applicable, with original case or cover.

MODEL YEAR	FEATURES	EXC. COND. LOW	HIGH

Distortion Charger DS10
1986-1989 $70 $90

Distortion DS7 (Tone-Lok)
2000-2010. Drive, tone, and level controls.
2000-2010 $40 $45

Echo Machine EM5 (SoundTank)
1996-1998. Simulates tape echo.
1996-1998 $45 $55

Fat Cat Distortion FC10
1987-1989. 3-knob pedal with distortion, tone, and level controls.
1987-1989 $50 $75

Flanger FFL5 (Master Series)
1984-1985. Speed, regeneration, width, D-time controls, battery or adapter option.
1984-1985 $70 $90

Flanger FL5 (SoundTank)
1991-1998 $25 $35

Flanger FL9
1982-1984. Yellow case.
1982-1984 $100 $150

Flanger FL301
1979-1982. Mini flanger, 3 knobs, called the FL-301 DX in late '81-'82.
1979-1982 $100 $125

Flanger FL305
1976-1979. Five knobs.
1976-1979 $100 $125

Flying Pan FP777
1976-1979. Auto pan/phase shifter, 4 control knobs, phase on/off button, pan on/off button, silver metal case with blue trim and Flying Pan winged-hand logo.
1976-1979 $575 $725

Flying Pan FP777 Reissue
2007   777 made $275 $350

Fuzz FZ7 (Tone-Lok)
2000-2010. Drive, tone and level controls, gray-silver case, blue-green FZ7 label.
2000-2010 $45 $50

Graphic Bass EQ BE10
1986-1992. Later labeled as the BEQ10.
1986-1992 $60 $80

Graphic EQ GE9
1982-1984. Six EQ sliders, 1 overall volume slider, turquoise blue case.
1982-1984 $60 $80

Graphic EQ GE10
1986-1992. Eight sliders.
1986-1992 $60 $80

Graphic Equalizer GE601 (808 Series)
1980-1981. 7-slider EQ, aqua blue metal case.
1980-1981 $75 $100

Guitar Multi-Processor PT5
1993-1997. Floor unit, programmable with 25 presets and 25 user presets, effects include distortion, chorus, flanger, etc, green case.
1993-1997 $100 $125

LA Metal LM7
1988-1989. Silver case.
1988-1989 $55 $65

LoFi LF7 (Tone-Lok)
2000-2010. Filter, 4 knobs.
2000-2010 $20 $30

Metal Charger MS10
1986-1992. Distortion, level, attack, punch and edge control knobs, green case.
1986-1992 $45 $55

Metal Screamer MSL
1985. 3 control knobs.
1985 $55 $65

Modern Fusion MF5 (SoundTank)
1990-1991. Level, tone and distortion controls.
1990-1991 $45 $50

Modulation Delay DM500
1983-1984. Rack mount.
1983-1984 $75 $100

Modulation Delay DM1000
1983-1984. Rack mount with delay, reverb, modulation.
1983-1984 $100 $125

Modulation Delay PDM1
1988-1989. Programmable Digital Modulation pedal.
1988-1989 $100 $125

Mostortion MT10
1990-1992. Mos-FET circuit distortion pedal, 5 control knobs, green case.
1990-1992 $50 $60

Multi-Effect PUE5/PUE5 Tube (Floor Unit)
1990-1993. Yellow version has tube, blue one does not. Also available in PUE5B bass version.
1990-1993   Tube $350 $450

Multi-Effect UE300 (Floor Unit)
1983-1984. Floor unit, 4 footswitches for super metal, digital delay, digital stereo chorus, and master power, 3 delay modes.
1983-1984 $275 $350

Multi-Effect UE300B (Floor Unit)
1983-1984. Floor unit for bass.
1983-1984 $275 $350

Multi-Effect UE400 (Rackmount)
1980-1984. Rack mount with foot switch.
1980-1984 $300 $375

Multi-Effect UE405 (Rackmount)
1981-1984. Rack mount with analog delay, parametric EQ, compressor/limiter, stereo chorus and loop.
1981-1984 $300 $375

Noise Buster NB10
1988-1989. Eliminates 60-cycle hum and other outside signals, metal case.
1988-1989 $70 $75

Overdrive OD850
1975-1979 $275 $400

Overdrive II OD855
1977-1979. Distortion, tone, and level controls, yellow/green case, large Overdrive II logo.
1977-1979 $300 $400

Pan Delay DPL10
1990-1992. Royal Blue case, 3 green control knobs.
1990-1992 $100 $125

Ibanez DS7 Distortion

Ibanez LA Metal

1978 Ibanez Flanger FL-303

EFFECTS

Ibanez Phaser PH7 (Tone-Lok)

Ibanez Tube King TK999

Ilitch Electronics Classic One Dyna Dist Overdrive

MODEL YEAR FEATURES	EXC. COND. LOW	HIGH
Parametric EQ PQ9		
1982-1984	$125	$175
Parametric EQ PQ401		
1981. 3 sliders, dial-in knob, light aqua blue case.		
1981	$125	$175
Phase Tone PT909		
1979-1982. Blue box, 3 knobs, early models with flat case (logo at bottom or later in the middle) or later wedge case.		
1979-1982	$140	$150
Phase Tone PT999		
1975-1979. Script logo, 1 knob, round footswitch, becomes PT-909.		
1975-1979	$125	$150
Phase Tone PT1000		
1974-1975. Morley-style pedal phase, light blue case, early model of Phase Tone.		
1974-1975	$200	$300
Phase Tone II PT707		
1976-1979. Blue box, 1 knob, script logo for first 2 years.		
1976-1979	$100	$130
Phaser PH5 (SoundTank)		
1991-1998	$20	$30
Phaser PH7 (Tone-Lok)		
1999-2010. Speed, depth, feedback and level controls.		
1999-2010	$35	$40
Phaser PT9		
1982-1984. Three control knobs, red case.		
1982-1984	$75	$100
Powerlead PL5 (SoundTank)		
1991-1998. Metal case '91, plastic case '91-'98.		
1991 Metal	$25	$40
1991-1998 Plastic	$15	$20
Renometer		
1976-1979. 5-band equalizer with preamp.		
1976-1979	$75	$100
Rotary Chorus RC99		
1996-1999. Black or silver cases available, requires power pack and does not use a battery.		
1996-1999 Black case	$100	$125
Session Man SS10		
1988-1989. Distortion, chorus.		
1988-1989	$70	$80
Session Man II SS20		
1988-1989. 4 controls plus toggle, light pink-purple case.		
1988-1989	$70	$80
Slam Punk SP5 (SoundTank)		
1996-1999	$35	$40
Smash Box SM7 (Tone-Lok)		
2000-2010.		
2000-2010	$30	$35
Sonic Distortion SD9		
1982-1984	$75	$100
Standard Fuzz (No. 59)		
1974-1979. Two buttons (fuzz on/off and tone change).		
1974-1979	$175	$200

MODEL YEAR FEATURES	EXC. COND. LOW	HIGH
Stereo Box ST800		
1975-1979. One input, 2 outputs for panning, small yellow case.		
1975-1979	$175	$225
Stereo Chorus CS9		
1982-1984	$75	$100
Stereo Chorus CSL (Master Series)		
1985-1986	$70	$90
Super Chorus CS5 (SoundTank)		
1991-1998	$20	$30
Super Metal SM9		
1984. Distortion.		
1984	$75	$95
Super Stereo Chorus SC10		
1986-1992	$75	$100
Super Tube Screamer ST9		
1984-1985. 4 knobs, light green metal case.		
1984-1985	$225	$300
Super Tube STL		
1985	$75	$95
Swell Flanger SF10		
1986-1992. Speed, regeneration, width and time controls, yellow case.		
1986-1992	$55	$100
Trashmetal TM5 (SoundTank)		
1990-1998. Tone and distortion pedal, 3 editions (1st edition, 2nd edition metal case, 2nd edition plastic case).		
1990-1998	$15	$20
Tremolo Pedal TL5 (SoundTank)		
1995-1998	$45	$95
Tube King TK999		
1994-1995. Has a 12AX7 tube and 3-band equalizer.		
1994-1995 Includes power pack	$150	$200
Tube King TK999US		
1996-1998. Has a 12AX7 tube and 3-band equalizer, does not have the noise switch of original TK999. Made in the U.S.		
1996-1998 Includes power pack	$150	$200
Tube Screamer Classic TS10		
1986-1993	$200	$225
Tube Screamer TS5 (SoundTank)		
1991-1998	$20	$25
Tube Screamer TS7 (Tone-Lok)		
1999-2010. 3 control knobs.		
1999-2010	$30	$35
Tube Screamer TS9		
1982-1984, 1993-present. Reissued in '93.		
1982-1984	$200	$300
1993-2010	$75	$125
Tube Screamer TS808		
1980-1982, 2004-present. Reissued in '04.		
1980-1982 Original	$250	$300
2004-2010 Reissue	$75	$100
Turbo Tube Screamer TS9DX		
1998-present. Tube Screamer circuit with added 3 settings for low-end.		
1998-2010	$70	$85
Twin Cam Chorus TC10		
1986-1989. Four control knobs, light blue case.		
1986-1989	$75	$100

EFFECTS

MODEL YEAR FEATURES	EXC. COND. LOW	HIGH
Virtual Amp VA3 (floor unit)		
1995-1998. Digital effects processor.		
1995-1998	$55	$75
VL10		
1987-1997. Stereo volume pedal.		
1987-1997	$50	$75
Wah Fuzz Standard (Model 58)		
1974-1981. Fuzz tone change toggle, fuzz on toggle, fuzz depth control, balance control, wah volume pedal with circular friction pads on footpedal.		
1974-1981	$225	$300
Wah WH10		
1988-1997	$50	$75

Ilitch Electronics

2003-present. Ilitch Chiliachki builds his effects in Camarillo, California.

Indy Guitarist

See listing under Wampler Pedals.

Intersound

1970s-1980s. Intersound, Inc. was located in Boulder, Colorado and was a division of Electro-Voice.

Reverb-Equalizer R100F

1977-1979. Reverb and 4-band EQ, fader.

1977-1979	$75	$100

J. Everman

2000-present. Analog guitar effects built by Justin J. Everman in Richardson, Texas.

Jack Deville Electronics

2008-present. Production/custom, guitar effects built in Portland, Oregon by Jack Deville.

Jacques

One-of-a-kind handmade stomp boxes and production models made in France.

JangleBox

2004-present. Stephen Lasko and Elizabeth Lasko build their guitar effects in Springfield, Virginia and Dracut, Massachusetts.

Jan-Mar Industries

Jan-Mar was located in Hillsdale, New Jersey.

The Talker

1976. 30 watts.

1976	$75	$125

The Talker Pro

1976. 75 watts.

1976	$100	$150

Jax

1960s-1970. Japanese imports made by Shinei.

Fuzz Master

1960s	$400	$500

Vibrachorus

1969. Variant of Univibe.

1969	$775	$950

MODEL YEAR FEATURES	EXC. COND. LOW	HIGH
Wah-Wah		
1960s	$400	$500

Jersey Girl

1991-present. Line of guitar effects pedals made in Japan. They also build guitars.

Jet Sounds LTD

1977. Jet was located in Jackson, Mississippi.

Hoze Talk Box

1977. Large wood box, 30 watts.

1977	$90	$125

Jetter Gear

2005-present. Brad Jeter builds his effects pedals in Marietta, Georgia.

JHD Audio

1974-1990. Hunt Dabney founded JHD in Costa Mesa, California, to provide effects that the user installed in their amp. Dabney is still involved in electronics and builds the BiasProbe tool for tubes.

SuperCube/SuperCube II

1974-late 1980s. Plug-in sustain mod for Fender amps with reverb, second version for amps after '78.

1974-1980s	$50	$75

Jimi Hendrix

See listing under Dunlop.

John Hornby Skewes & Co.

Mid-1960s-present. Large English distributor of musical products which has also made their own brands, or self-branded products from others, over the years.

Johnson

Mid-1990s-present. Budget line of effects imported by Music Link, Brisbane, California. Johnson also offers guitars, amps, mandolins and basses.

Johnson Amplification

1997-present. Modeling amps and effects designed by John Johnson, of Sandy, Utah. The company is part of Harman International. In '02, they quit building amps, but continue the effects line.

Jordan

1960s. Jordan effects were distributed by Sho-Bud of Nashville, Tennessee.

Boss Tone Fuzz

1968-1969. Tiny effect plugged into guitar's output jack.

1968-1969	$125	$175

Compressor J-700

1960s	$75	$100

Creator Volume Sustainer

1960s	$125	$175

Gig Wa-Wa Volume

1960s	$125	$150

Janglebox Compression/Sustain

Jax Fuzz

(Jim Schreck)

Jeeter Gear Gain Stage Purple

Keeley Compressor

Krank Distortus Maximus

Lehle D.Loop Signal Router

MODEL YEAR	FEATURES	EXC. COND. LOW	HIGH

Phaser
1960s. Black case, yellow knobs.

1960s	Black case	$125	$150

Kay
1931-present. Kay was once one of the largest instrument producers in the world, offering just about everything for the guitarist, including effects.

Effects Pedals
1970s. Includes the Wah, Graphic Equalizer GE-5000, Rhythmer, and Tremolo.

1970s		$50	$75

Keeley
2001-present. Line of guitar effects designed and built by Robert Keeley in Edmond, Oklahoma. Keeley Electronics also offers a range of custom modifications for other effects.

Kendrick
1989-present. Texas' Kendrick offers guitars, amps, and effects.

ABC Amp Switcher
1990s		$100	$140

Buffalo Pfuz
1990s		$70	$100

Model 1000 Reverb
1991-2003. Vintage style, 3 knobs: dwell, tone, and mix, brown cover, wheat grille with art deco shape.

1991-2003		$400	$450

Powerglide Attenuator
1998-present. Allows you to cut the output before it hits the amp's speakers, rack mount, metal cab.

1998-2010		$180	$200

Kent
1961-1969. This import guitar brand also offered a few effects.

Kern Engineering
Located in Kenosha, Wisconsin, Kern offers pre-amps and wah pedals.

Klon
1994-present. Originally located in Brookline, Massachusetts, and now located in Cambridge, Massachusetts, Klon was started by Bill Finnegan after working with two circuit design partners on the Centaur Professional Overdrive.

Centaur
2010-present. Smaller overdrive unit with burnished silver case.

2010		$700	$900

Centaur Professional Overdrive
1994-2009. Standard size with gold case. A smaller unit was introduced in '10.

1994-2009		$1,050	$1,300

KMD (Kaman)
1986-ca. 1990. Distributed by Kaman (Ovation, Hamer, etc.) in the late '80s.

MODEL YEAR	FEATURES	EXC. COND. LOW	HIGH

Effects Pedals
1986-1990	Analog Delay	$65	$90
1986-1990	Overdrive	$30	$45
1987-1990	Distortion	$30	$45
1987-1990	Flanger	$30	$50
1987-1990	Phaser	$30	$50
1987-1990	Stereo Chorus	$30	$50

Korg
Most of the Korg effects listed below are modular effects. The PME-40X Professional Modular Effects System holds four of them and allows the user to select several variations of effects. The modular effects cannot be used alone. This system was sold for a few years starting in 1983. Korg currently offers the Toneworks line of effects.

PEQ-1 Parametric EQ
1980s. Dial-in equalizer with gain knob, band-width knob, and frequency knob, black case.

1980s		$40	$50

PME-40X Modular Effects
1983-1986	KAD-301 Analog Delay	$60	$70
1983-1986	KCH-301 Stereo Chorus	$25	$35
1983-1986	KCO-101 Compressor	$45	$55
1983-1986	KDI-101 Distortion	$45	$55
1983-1986	KDL-301 Dynamic Echo	$90	$110
1983-1986	KFL-401 Stereo Flanger	$40	$50
1983-1986	KGE-201 Graphic EQ	$25	$35
1983-1986	KNG-101 Noise Gate	$25	$35
1983-1986	KOD-101 Over Drive	$45	$55
1983-1986	KPH-401 Phaser	$45	$55
1983-1986	OCT-1 Octaver	$70	$80

PME-40X Professional Modular Effects System
1983-ca.1986. Board holds up to 4 of the modular effects listed below.

1983-1986		$125	$150

SSD 3000 Digital Delay
1980s. Rack mount, SDD-3000 logo on top of unit.

1980s		$775	$925

KR Musical Products
2003-present. Kevin Randall presently builds his vintage style, guitar effects in White Marsh, Virginia. In 2009 he plans to move his business to the Tacoma, Washington area.

Krank
1996-present. Tempe, Arizona, amp builder Krank also builds effects pedals.

Laney
1968-present. Founded by Lyndon Laney and Bob Thomas in Birmingham, England, this amp builder also offered a reverb unit.

MODEL YEAR	FEATURES	EXC. COND. LOW	HIGH

Reverberation Unit
1968-1969. Sleek reverb unit, plexi-style front panel, black vinyl cover.

1968-1969		$300	$400

Lehle
2001-present. Loop switches from Burkhard Georg Lehle of Lehle Gitarrentechnik in Voerde, Germany.

D.Loop Signal Router

2004		$150	$175

Line 6
1996-present. Effects from Marcus Ryle and Michel Doidic who were product line designers prior to forming their own design company. A sixth company telephone line was added to their product design business to handle their own product line, thus Line 6. They also produce amps and guitars. All prices include Line 6 power pack if applicable.

DL-4 Delay Modeler
1999-present. Green case.

1999-2010		$175	$225

DM-4 Distortion Modeler
1999-present. Yellow case.

1999-2010		$100	$125

FM-4 Filter Modeler
2001-present. Purple case.

2001-2010		$175	$225

MM-4 Modulation Modeler
1999-present. Aqua blue case.

1999-2010		$150	$185

POD 2.0
2001-present. Updated version of the original Amp Modeler.

2001-2010		$150	$200

Little Lanilei
1997-present. Best known for their small hand-made amps, Songworks Systems & Products of San Juan Capistrano, California, also offers effects bearing the Little Lanilei name. In '09, owner Tom Pryzgoda changed Songworks to Mahaffay Amplifiers, and introduced amps under that name as well as continuing the Little Lanilei brand.

Lizard Leg Effects
2007-present. Steve Miller builds a line of effects pedals in Gonzales, Louisiana.

Lock & Rock
2003-present. Line of floor pedal guitar and microphone effects produced by Brannon Electronics, Inc. of Houston, Texas.

Loco Box
1982-1983. Loco Box was a brand of effects distributed by Aria Pro II for a short period starting in '82. It appears that Aria switched the effects to their own brand in '83.

Effects

1982-1983	Analog Delay AD-01	$35	$45
1982-1983	Chorus CH-01	$55	$65
1982-1983	Compressor CM-01	$35	$45
1982-1983	Distortion DS-01	$40	$55
1982-1983	Flanger FL-01	$35	$45
1982-1983	Graphic Equalizer GE-06	$25	$35
1982-1983	Overdrive OD-01	$40	$50
1982-1983	Phaser PH-01	$45	$55

Lovepedal
2000-present. Sean Michael builds his preamps and guitar stomp boxes in Detroit, Michigan.

Lovetone
1995-present. Hand-made analog effects from Oxfordshire, England.

Ludwig
For some reason, drum builder Ludwig offered a guitar synth in the 1970s.

Phase II Guitar Synth
1970-1971. Oversized synth, mushroom-shaped footswitches, vertical silver case.

1970-1971		$650	$800

M.B. Electronics
Made in San Francisco, California.

Ultra-Metal UM-10
1985. Distortion.

1985		$35	$40

Mad Professor
2002-present. Guitar effects pedals built by Bjorn Juhl and Jukka Monkkonen in Tampere, Finland. They also build amps.

Maestro
1950s-1970s, 2001-present. Maestro was a Gibson subsidiary; the name appeared on 1950s accordian amplifiers. The first Maestro effects were the Echoplex tape echo and the FZ-1 Fuzz-Tone, introduced in the early-'60s. Maestro products were manufactured by various entities such as Market Electronics, All-Test Devices, Lowrey and Moog Electronics. In the late-'60s and early-'70s, they unleashed a plethora of pedals; some were beautiful, others had great personality. The last Maestro effects were the Silver and Black MFZ series of the late-'70s. In 2001, Gibson revived the name for a line of effects, banjos and mandolins, adding guitars and amps in '09.

Bass Brassmaster BB-1
1971-ca.1974. Added brass to your bass.

1971-1974		$925	$1,075

Boomerang
Ca.1969-ca.1972. Wah pedal made by All-Test Devices.

1969-1972		$175	$200

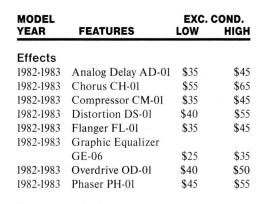

Lovepedal Meatball

Mad Professor Fire Red Fuzz

Maestro Boomerang

EFFECTS

Maestro Stage Phaser MPP-1
(Jim Schreck)

Maestro Theremin

Marshall Shred Master

EFFECTS

MODEL YEAR	FEATURES	EXC. COND. LOW	HIGH

Boomerang BG-2
1972-ca.1976. Wah pedal made by All-Test Devices.

1972-1976		$100	$125

Echoplex EM-1 Groupmaster
Ca.1970-ca.1977. Two input Echoplex, solidstate.

1970-1977	Without stand	$800	$1,000

Echoplex EP-1
1962/63-mid-1960s. Original model, smaller green box, tube, separate controls for echo volume and instrument volume, made by Market Electronics. Though not labeled as such, it is often referred to as the EP-1 by collectors.

1960s	Earlier small box	$900	$1,100

Echoplex EP-2
Mid-1960s-ca.1970. Larger green box than original, tube, single echo/instrument volume control, made by Market Electronics. Around '70, the EP-2 added a Sound-On-Sound feature.

1960s	Larger box	$900	$1,100

Echoplex EP-3
Ca.1970-1977. Solidstate, made by Market Electronics, black box.

1970-1977		$350	$425

Echoplex Groupmaster
Ca.1970-ca.1974. Two input Echoplex, solidstate.

1970-1977	With stand	$1,050	$1,300

Echoplex IV (EP-4)
1977-1978. Solidstate, last version introduced by Maestro. See brands Market Electronics and Echoplex for later models.

1977-1978		$375	$500

Echoplex Sireko ES-1
Ca.1971-mid-1970s. A budget version of the Echoplex, solidstate, made by Market.

1971-1975		$200	$300

Envelope Modifier ME-1
1971-ca.1976. Tape reverse/string simulator, made by All-Test.

1971-1976		$150	$225

Filter Sample and Hold FSH-1
1975-ca.1976.

1975-1976		$475	$700

Full Range Boost FRB-1
1971-ca.1975. Frequency boost with fuzz, made by All-Test.

1971-1975		$150	$200

Fuzz MFZ-1
1976-1979. Made by Moog.

1976-1979		$150	$200

Fuzz Phazzer FP-1

1971-1974		$200	$300

Fuzz Tone FZ-1
1962-1963. Brown, uses 2 AA batteries.

1962-1963		$250	$325

Fuzz Tone FZ-1A
1965-1967. Brown, uses 1 AA battery.

1965-1967		$250	$325

Fuzz Tone FZ-1A (reissue)

2001-2009		$65	$70

Fuzz Tone FZ-1B
Late-1960s- early-1970s. Black, uses 9-volt battery.

1970s		$150	$250

Fuzztain MFZT-1
1976-1978. Fuzz, sustain, made by Moog.

1976-1978		$200	$250

Mini-Phase Shifter MPS-2
1976. Volume, speed, slow and fast controls.

1976		$110	$125

Octave Box OB-1
1971-ca.1975. Made by All-Test Devices.

1971-1975		$225	$300

Parametric Filter MPF-1
1976-1978. Made by Moog.

1976-1978		$350	$450

Phase Shifter PS-1
1971-1975. With or without 3-button footswitch, made by Oberheim.

1971-1975	With footswitch	$275	$325
1971-1975	Without footswitch	$175	$225

Phase Shifter PS-1A

1976		$150	$250

Phase Shifter PS-1B

1970s		$150	$250

Phaser MP-1
1976-1978. Made by Moog.

1976-1978		$100	$120

Repeat Pedal RP-1

1970s		$200	$300

Rhythm King MRK-2
1971-ca.1974. Early drum machine.

1971-1974		$400	$500

Rhythm Queen MRQ-1
Early 1970s. Early rhythm machine.

1970s		$125	$150

Rhythm'n Sound G-2
Ca.1969-1970s. Multi-effect unit.

1969-1975		$475	$600

Ring Modulator RM-1

1971-1975	With MP-1 control pedal	$650	$700
1971-1975	Without control pedal	$550	$600

Rover Rotating Speaker
1971-ca.1973. Rotating Leslie effect that mounted on a large tripod.

1971-1973	RO-1 model	$1,150	$1,450

Sound System for Woodwinds W-1
1960s-1970s. Designed for clarinet or saxaphone input, gives a variety of synthesizer-type sounds with voices for various woodwinds, uses Barrel Joint and integrated microphone.

1960-1970s		$350	$400

Stage Phaser MPP-1
1976-1978. Had slow, fast and variable settings, made by Moog.

1976-1978		$175	$225

Super Fuzztone FZ-1S

1971-1975		$200	$300

Sustainer SS-2
1971-ca.1975. Made by All-Test Devices.

1971-1975		$100	$150

MODEL YEAR FEATURES	EXC. COND. LOW	HIGH

Theramin TH-1
1971-mid-1970s. Device with 2 antennae, made horror film sound effects. A reissue Theremin is available from Theremaniacs in Milwaukee, Wisconsin.

1971-1975	$825	$975

Wah-Wah/Volume WW-1
1970s. Wah-Wah Volume logo on end of pedal, green foot pad.

1971-1975	$150	$250

Magnatone
1937-1970s. Magnatone built very competitive amps from '57 to '66. In the early-'60s, they offered the RVB-1 Reverb Unit. The majority of Magnatone amps pre-'66 did not have on-board reverb.

Model RVB-1 Reverb Unit
1961-1966. Typical brown leatherette cover, square box-type cabinet. From '64-'66, battery operated, solidstate version of RVB-1, low flat cabinet.

1961-1963		$275	$400
1964-1966	Battery and solidstate	$200	$300

Mannys Music
Issued by the New York-based retailer.

Fuzz
1960s. Same unit as the Orpheum Fuzz and Clark Fuzz.

1960s	$225	$325

Market Electronics
Market, from Ohio, made the famous Echoplex line. See Maestro section for earlier models and Echoplex section for later versions.

Marshall
1962-present. The fuzz and wah boom of the '60s led many established manufacturers, like Marshall, to introduce variations on the theme. They got back into stomp boxes in '89 with the Gov'nor distortion, and currently produce several distortion/overdrive units.

Blues Breaker
1992-1999. Replaced by Blues Breaker II in 2000.

1992-1999	$100	$130

Blues Breaker II Overdrive
2000-present. Overdrive pedal, 4 knobs.

2000-2010	$50	$65

Drive Master
1992-1999	$70	$75

Guv'nor
1989-1991. Distortion, Guv'nor Plus introduced in '99.

1989-1991	$75	$100

Jackhammer
1999-present. Distortion pedal.

1999-2010	$55	$65

PB-100 Power Brake
1993-1995. Speaker attenuator for tube amps.

1993-1995	$190	$230

Shred Master
1992-1999	$75	$100

Supa Fuzz
Late-1960s. Made by Sola Sound (Colorsound).

1967	$600	$800

Supa Wah
Late-1960s. Made by Sola Sound (Colorsound).

1969	$300	$425

Vibratrem VT-1
1999-present. Vibrato and tremolo.

1999-2010	$75	$85

Matchless
1989-1999, 2001-present. Matchless amplifiers offered effects in the '90s.

AB Box
1990s. Split box for C-30 series amps (DC 30, SC 30, etc.)

1990s	$175	$300

Coolbox
1997-1999. Tube preamp pedal.

1997-1999	$275	$350

Dirtbox
1997-1999. Tube-driven overdrive pedal.

1997-1999	$225	$350

Echo Box
1997-1999. Limited production because of malfunctioning design which included cassette tape. Black case, 8 white chickenhead control knobs.

1990s	Original unreliable status	$300	$400
1990s	Updated working order	$700	$850

Hotbox/Hotbox II
1995-1999. Higher-end tube-driven preamp pedal.

1995-1999	$375	$425

Mix Box
1997-1999. 4-input tube mixer pedal.

1997-1999	$375	$425

Reverb RV-1
1993-1999. 5 controls, tube reverb tank.

1993-1999	Various colors	$1,400	$1,700

Split Box
1990s. Tube AB box.

1997	Standard AB	$275	$325

Tremolo/Vibrato TV-1
1993-1995. Tube unit.

1993-1995	$350	$400

Maxon
1970s-present. Maxon was the original manufacturer of the Ibanez line of effects. Currently offering retro '70s era stomp boxes distributed in the U.S. by Godlyke.

AD-9 Analog Delay
2001-present. Purple case.

2001-2010	$225	$275

CS-550 Stereo Chorus
2001-present. Light blue case.

2001-2010	$100	$130

DS-830 Distortion Master
2001-present. Light blue-green case.

2001-2010	$100	$125

Marshall Blues Breaker II Overdrive

Matchless Reverb RV-1

Maxon AD9 Pro

EFFECTS

Metal Pedals Demon Drive

Mica Wau-Wau SG-150
(Jim Schreck)

Moogerfooger MF-105 MuRF

MODEL YEAR	FEATURES	EXC. COND. LOW	HIGH

OD-820 Over Drive Pro
2001-present. Green case.

2001-2010		$140	$175

McQuackin FX Co.
1997-2010. Analog guitar effects hand made by Rich McCracken II in Augusta, Georgia. He also built them for three years while living in Nashville, Tennessee.

Mesa-Boogie
1971-present. Mesa added pre-amps in the mid '90s.

V-Twin Bottle Rocket
2000-2004		$100	$150

V-Twin Preamp Pedal
Dec. 1993-2004. Serial number series: V011-. 100 watts, all tube preamp, floor unit, silver case.

1993-1999		$225	$275
2000-2004	Updated bottom tone adj.	$275	$325

Metal Pedals
2006-present. Brothers Dave and Mike Pantaleone build their guitar effects in New Jersey.

Meteoro
1986-present. Guitar effects built in Brazil. They also build guitar and bass amps.

MG
2004-present. Guitar effects built by Marcelo Giangrande in São Paulo, Brazil. He also builds amps.

Mica
Early 1970s. These Japanese-made effects were also sold under the Bruno and Marlboro brand names.

Tone Fuzz
1970s. Silver case, black knobs.

1970s		$200	$250

Tone Surf Wah Siren
1970s. Wah pedal.

1970s		$150	$175

Wailer Fuzz
1970		$75	$100

Wau Wau Fuzz
1970s. Wau Wau Fuzz logo on end of pedal, black.

1970s		$150	$175

Moog/Moogerfooger
1964-present. Robert Moog, of synth fame, introduced his line of Moogerfooger analog effects in 1998. They also offer guitars.

Misc. Effects
2004-2010	MF-105 MuRF	$250	$275
2004-2010	Theremin	$250	$275

Moonrock
2002-present. Fuzz/distortion unit built by Glenn Wylie and distributed by Tonefrenzy.

MODEL YEAR	FEATURES	EXC. COND. LOW	HIGH

Morley
Late-1960s-present. Founded by brothers Raymond and Marvin Lubow, Morley has produced a wide variety of pedals and effects over the years, changing with the trends. In '89, the brothers sold the company to Accutronics (later changed to Sound Enhancements, Inc.) of Cary, Illinois.

ABY Switch Box
1981-ca.1985. Box.

1981-1985		$25	$35

Auto Wah PWA
1976-ca.1985.

1976-1985		$25	$35

Bad Horsie Steve Vai Signature Wah
1997-present.

1997-2010		$65	$70

Black Gold Stereo Volume BSV
1985-1991		$25	$35

Black Gold Stereo Volume Pan BSP
1985-1989		$30	$40

Black Gold Volume BVO
1985-1991		$25	$35

Black Gold Wah BWA
1985-1991		$30	$40

Black Gold Wah Volume BWV
1985-1989		$30	$40

Chrystal Chorus CCB
1996-1999. Stereo output.

1996-1999		$25	$30

Deluxe Distortion DDB
1981-1991. Box, no pedal.

1981-1991		$40	$60

Deluxe Flanger FLB
1981-1991. Box, no pedal.

1981-1991		$55	$65

Deluxe Phaser DFB
1981-1991. Box, no pedal.

1981-1991		$40	$60

Distortion One DIB
1981-1991. Box, no pedal.

1981-1991		$35	$45

Echo Chorus Vibrato ECV
1982-ca.1985.

1982-1985		$150	$225

Echo/Volume EVO-1
1974-ca.1982.

1974-1982		$150	$225

Electro-Pik-a-Wah PKW
1979-ca.1982.

1979-1982		$55	$65

Emerald Echo EEB
1996-1999. 300 millisecond delay.

1996-1999	Green case	$40	$50

Jerry Donahue JD-10
1995-1997. Multi-effect, distortion, overdrive.

1995-1997		$80	$90

Power Wah PWA/PWA II
1992-2006. Wah with boost. Changed to II in '98.

1992-2006		$40	$50

MODEL YEAR FEATURES	EXC. COND. LOW	HIGH
Power Wah PWO		
Ca.1969-1984, 2006-present. Reissued in '06.		
1969-1984	$60	$70
Power Wah/Boost PWB		
Introduced in 1973, doubles as a volume pedal.		
1970s	$70	$80
Power Wah/Fuzz PWF		
Ca.1969-ca.1984.		
1969-1984	$75	$125
Pro Compressor PCB		
1978-1984. Stomp box without pedal, compress-sustain knob and output knob.		
1978-1984	$45	$55
Pro Flanger PFL		
1978-1984	$100	$125
Pro Phaser PFA		
1975-1984	$100	$125
Rotating Sound Power Wah Model RWV		
1974-1982	$325	$375
Select-Effect Pedal SEL		
1980s. Lets you control up to 5 other pedals.		
1980s	$20	$30
Slimline Echo Volume 600		
1983-1985. 20 to 600 ms delay.		
1983-1985	$45	$55
Slimline Echo Volume SLEV		
1983-1985. 20 to 300 ms delay.		
1983-1985	$50	$60
Slimline Variable Taper Stereo Volume SLSV		
1982-1986	$70	$100
Slimline Variable Taper Volume SLVO		
1982-1986	$35	$50
Slimline Wah SLWA		
1982-1986. Battery operated electro-optical.		
1982-1986	$55	$75
Slimline Wah Volume SLWV		
1982-ca.1986. Battery operated electro-optical.		
1982-1986	$55	$75
Stereo Chorus Flanger CFL		
1980-ca. 1986. Box, no pedal.		
1980-1986	$60	$70
Stereo Chorus Vibrato SCV		
1980-1991. Box, no pedal.		
1980-1991	$80	$100
Stereo Volume CSV		
1980-ca. 1986. Box, no pedal.		
1980-1986	$30	$45
Volume Compressor VCO		
1979-1984	$30	$45
Volume Phaser PFV		
1977-1984. With volume pedal.		
1977-1984	$125	$150
Volume VOL		
1975-ca.1984.		
1975-1979	$30	$45
1980-1984	$25	$40
Volume XVO		
1985-1988	$25	$40
Volume/Boost VBO		
1974-1984	$50	$60

MODEL YEAR FEATURES	EXC. COND. LOW	HIGH
Wah Volume CWV		
1987-1991. Box, no pedal.		
1987-1991	$65	$80
Wah Volume XWV		
1985-ca.1989.		
1985-1989	$65	$80
Wah/Volume WVO		
1977-ca.1984.		
1977-1984	$80	$100

Mosferatu

Line of guitar effects pedals built by Hermida Audio Technology.

Mosrite

Semie Moseley's Mosrite company dipped into effects in the 1960s.

Fuzzrite
1960s. Sanner reissued the Fuzzrite in 1999.

1966	$175	$225

Multivox

New York-based Multivox offered a variety of effects in the 1970s and '80s.

Big Jam Effects
Multivox offered the Big Jam line of effects from 1980 to ca. '83.

YEAR	FEATURES	LOW	HIGH
1980-1983	6-Band EQ, Compressor, Phaser, Spit-Wah	$40	$50
1980-1983	Analog Echo/Reverb	$100	$125
1980-1983	Bi-Phase 2, Flanger, Jazz Flanger	$50	$60
1980-1983	Chorus	$45	$55
1980-1983	Distortion	$70	$80
1980-1983	Octave Box	$40	$55
1981-1983	Noise Gate, Parametric EQ	$35	$45
1981-1983	Space Driver, Delay	$60	$70
1982-1983	Volume Pedal	$30	$35

Full Rotor MX-2
1978-ca.1982. Leslie effect.

1978-1982	$300	$350

Little David LD-2
1970s. Rotary sound effector in mini Leslie-type case.

1970s	With pedal	$375	$450
1970s	Without pedal	$325	$375

Multi Echo MX-201
1970s. Tape echo unit, reverb.

1970s	$200	$250

Multi Echo MX-312
1970s. Tape echo unit, reverb.

1970s	$225	$300

Rhythm Ace FR6M
1970s. 27 basic rhythms.

1970s	$60	$80

Mu-tron

1972-ca.1981. Made by Musitronics (founded by Aaron Newman), Rosemont, New Jersey, these rugged and unique-sounding effects were a high point of the

1974 Morley RWV
Christopher Wright

Morley Volume Boost VBO

Mosferatu

Mu-Tron Octave Divider

Muza GP300

MXR Analog Delay

'70s. The Mu-Tron III appeared in '72 and more products followed, about 10 in all. Musitronics also made the U.S. models of the Dan Armstrong effects. In '78 ARP synthesizers bought Musitronics and sold Mutron products to around '81. A reissue of the Mu-Tron III was made available in '95 by NYC Music Products and distributed by Matthews and Ryan Musical Products.

III Envelope Filter
1972-ca.1981. Envelope Filter.

MODEL YEAR	FEATURES	EXC. COND. LOW	HIGH
1972-1981		$450	$550

Bi-Phase
1975-ca.1981.

1975-1981	With optical pedal option	$1,000	$1,250
1975-1981	With 2-button footswitch	$675	$850

C-100 OptiPot Control Pedal

1975-1981	Blue case	$550	$700

C-200 Volume-Wah

1970s		$300	$400

Flanger
1977-ca.1981.

1977-1981		$1,000	$1,250

Micro V
Ca.1975-ca.1977. Envelope Filter.

1970s		$200	$250

Octave Divider
1977-ca.1981.

1977-1981		$550	$700

Phasor
Ca.1974-ca.1976. Two knobs.

1974-1976		$200	$300

Phasor II
1976-ca.1981. Three knobs.

1976-1981		$225	$275

Muza
2006-present. Digital guitar effects made in China by Hong Kong's Medeli Electronics Co., Ltd. They also build digital drums.

MXR
1972-present. MXR Innovations launched its line of pedals in '72. Around '77, the Rochester, New York, company changed lettering on the effects from script to block, and added new models. MXR survived into the mid-'80s. In '87, production was picked up by Jim Dunlop. Reissues of block logo boxes can be differentiated from originals as they have an LED above the switch and the finish is slightly rough; the originals are smooth.

6 Band EQ
1975-1982. Equalizer.

1975-1979		$70	$85
1980-1982		$60	$70

6 Band EQ M-109 (Reissue)
1987-present. Reissued by Jim Dunlop.

1987-2010		$30	$40

10 Band EQ M-108
1975-1981, 2004-present. Graphic equalizer.

1975-1981	With AC power cord	$80	$100

MODEL YEAR	FEATURES	EXC. COND. LOW	HIGH

Analog Delay
1975-1981. Green case, power cord.

1975-1979	Earlier 2-jack model	$300	$325
1980-1981	Later 3-jack model	$150	$200

Blue Box
1972-ca.1978. Octave pedal, M-103.

1970s	Earlier script logo	$350	$400
1970s	Later block logo	$225	$250

Blue Box M-103 (Reissue)
1995-present. Reissued by Jim Dunlop. Produces 1 octave above or 2 octaves below.

1995-2010		$40	$45

Commande Effects
1981-1983. The Commande series featured plastic housings and electronic switching.

1981-1983	Overdrive	$40	$50
1981-1983	Phaser	$100	$110
1981-1983	Preamp	$40	$50
1981-1983	Stereo Chorus	$60	$70
1981-1983	Sustain	$60	$70
1981-1983	Time Delay	$70	$80
1982-1983	Stereo Flanger	$70	$80

Distortion +
1972-1982.

1970s	Earlier script logo	$185	$225
1970s	Later block logo	$85	$110
1980s	Block logo	$80	$95

Distortion + (Series 2000)

1983-1985		$60	$70

Distortion + M-104 (Reissue)
1987-present. Reissued by Jim Dunlop.

1987-1990		$55	$65
1991-2010		$45	$55

Distortion II

1981-1983	With AC power cord	$140	$150

Double Shot Distortion M-151
2003-2005. 2 channels.

2003-2005		$65	$75

Dyna Comp
1972-1982. Compressor.

1970s	Earlier script logo, battery	$175	$200
1970s	Later block logo, battery	$90	$120
1980s	Block logo, battery	$65	$80

Dyna Comp (Series 2000)

1982-1985		$65	$75

Dyna Comp M-102 (Reissue)
1987-present. Reissued by Jim Dunlop.

1987-2010		$35	$40

Envelope Filter

1976-1983		$125	$225

Flanger
1976-1983, 1997-present. Analog, reissued by Dunlop in '97.

1976-1979	AC power cord, 2 inputs	$175	$225
1980-1983	AC power cord	$100	$150
1997-2010	M-117R reissue	$60	$70

Flanger/Doubler

1979	Rack mount	$150	$175

MODEL YEAR	FEATURES	EXC. COND. LOW	HIGH

Limiter
1980-1982. AC, 4 knobs.

1980-1982	AC power cord	$125	$200

Loop Selector
1980-1982. A/B switch for 2 effects loops.

1980-1982		$50	$60

Micro Amp
1978-1983, 1995-present. Variable booster, white case, reissued in '95.

1978-1983		$75	$100
1995-2010	M-133 reissue	$40	$45

Micro Chorus
1980-1983. Yellow case.

1980-1983		$125	$175

Micro Flanger

1981-1982		$100	$150

Noise Gate Line Driver
1974-1983.

1970s	Script logo	$75	$125
1980s	Block logo	$75	$100

Omni
1980s. Rack unit with floor controller, compressor, 3-band EQ, distortion, delay, chorus/flanger.

1980s		$425	$475

Phase 45
Ca.1976-1982.

1970s	Script logo, battery	$125	$175
1980s	Block logo, battery	$75	$125

Phase 90
1972-1982.

1970s	Earlier script logo	$325	$400
1970s	Later block logo	$175	$275
1980s	Block logo	$150	$200

Phase 90 M-101 (Reissue)
1987-present. Reissued by Jim Dunlop.

1987-1989	Block logo	$60	$85
1990-2010	Block or script logo	$50	$75

Phase 100
1974-1982.

1970s	Earlier script logo	$250	$325
1970s	Later block logo, battery	$175	$275

Phaser (Series 2000)
1982-1985. Series 2000 introduced cost cutting die-cast cases.

1982-1985		$60	$85

Pitch Transposer

1980s		$400	$475

Power Converter

1980s		$45	$60

Smart Gate M-135
2002-present. Noise-gate, single control, battery powered.

2002-2010		$60	$70

Stereo Chorus
1978-1985. With AC power cord.

1978-1979		$175	$275
1980-1985		$150	$200

Stereo Chorus (Series 2000)
1983-1985. Series 2000 introduced cost cutting die-cast cases.

1983-1985		$55	$75

Stereo Flanger (Series 2000)
1983-1985. Series 2000 introduced cost cutting die-cast cases, black with blue lettering.

1983-1985		$60	$80

Super Comp M-132
2002-present. 3 knobs.

2002-2010		$40	$55

Nobels
1997-present. Effects pedals from Nobels Electronics of Hamburg, Germany. They also make amps.

ODR-1 Overdrive
1997-present.

1997-2010		$30	$40

TR-X Tremolo
1997-present. Tremolo effect using modern technology, purple case.

1997-2010		$30	$40

Nomad
Fuzz Wah
1960s. Import from Japan, similar looking to Morley pedal with depth and volume controls and fuzz switch, silver metal case and black foot pedal.

1960s		$75	$125

Olson
Olson Electronics was based in Akron, Ohio.

Reverberation Amplifier RA-844
1967. Solidstate, battery-operated, reverb unit, depth and volume controls, made in Japan.

1967		$100	$150

Ooh La La Manufacturing
2007-present. Hand-made guitar effects originally built in Chattanooga, Tennessee, and currently in St. Louis Park, Minnesota, including the models formerly offered under the Blackbox brand.

Ovation
Ovation ventured into the solidstate amp and effects market in the early '70s.

K-6001 Guitar Preamp
1970s. Preamp with reverb, boost, tremolo, fuzz, and a tuner, looks something like a Maestro effect from the '70s, reliability may be an issue.

1970s		$100	$125

PAIA
1967-present. Founded by John Paia Simonton in Edmond, Oklahoma, specializing in synthesizer and effects kits. PAIA did make a few complete products but they are better known for the various electronic kit projects they sold. Values on kit projects are difficult as it depends on the skills of the person who built it.

MXR GT-OD Custom Shop

EFFECTS

MXR '74 Vintage Phase 90

MXR Super Comp M-132

Peavey EDI

PedalDoctor FX Queen Bee

Pedalworx McFuzz

EFFECTS

MODEL YEAR	FEATURES	EXC. COND. LOW	HIGH
Roctave Divider 5760	*1970s. Kit to build analog octave divider.*		
1970s		$70	$85

Pan*Damn*ic

2007-present. Guitar effects pedals made by PLH Professional Audio in West Chester, Pennsylvania.

Park

1965-1982, 1992-2000. Sola/Colorsound made a couple of effects for Marshall and their sister brand, Park. In the '90s, Marshall revived the name for use on small solidstate amps.

Pax

1970s. Imported Maestro copies.

Fuzz Tone Copy			
1970s		$125	$150
Octave Box Copy	*1970s. Dual push-buttons (normal and octave), 2 knobs (octave volume and sensitivity), green and black case.*		
1970s		$125	$150

Pearl

Pearl, located in Nashville, Tennessee, and better known for drums, offered a line of guitar effects in the 1980s.

Analog Delay AD-08	*1983-1985. Four knobs.*		
1983-1985		$100	$150
Analog Delay AD-33	*1982-1984. Six knobs.*		
1982-1984		$175	$225
Chorus CH-02	*1981-1984. Four knobs.*		
1981-1984		$75	$100
Chorus Ensemble CE-22	*1982-1984. Stereo chorus with toggling between chorus and vibrato, 6 knobs.*		
1982-1984		$125	$175
Compressor CO-04			
1981-1984		$50	$75
Distortion DS-06			
1982-1986		$40	$60
Flanger FG-01	*1981-1986. Clock pulse generator, ultra-low frequency oscillator.*		
1981-1986		$75	$100
Graphic EQ GE-09			
1983-1985		$40	$55
Octaver OC-07			
1982-1986		$100	$250
Overdrive OD-05			
1981-1986		$75	$100
Parametric EQ PE-10			
1983-1984		$45	$60
Phaser PH-03	*1981-1984. Four knobs.*		
1981-1984		$75	$100

MODEL YEAR	FEATURES	EXC. COND. LOW	HIGH
Phaser PH-44	*1982-1984. Six knobs.*		
1982-1984		$150	$175
Stereo Chorus CH-22	*1982-1984. Blue case.*		
1982-1984		$75	$125
Thriller TH-20	*1984-1986. Exciter, 4 knobs, black case.*		
1984-1986		$175	$225

Peavey

1965-present. Peavey made stomp boxes from '87 to around '90. They offered rack mount gear after that.

Accelerator Overdrive AOD-2			
1980s		$30	$35
Biampable Bass Chorus BAC-2			
1980s		$30	$35
Companded Chorus CMC-1			
1980s		$25	$30
Compressor/Sustainer CSR-2			
1980s		$35	$40
Digital Delay DDL-3			
1980s		$30	$35
Digital Stereo Reverb SRP-16			
1980s		$50	$55
Dual Clock Stereo Chorus DSC-4			
1980s		$30	$35
Hotfoot Distortion HFD-2			
1980s		$25	$30

PedalDoctor FX

1996-present. Tim Creek builds his production and custom guitar effects in Nashville, Tennessee.

Pedalworx

2001-present. Bob McBroom and George Blekas build their guitar effects in Manorville, New York and Huntsville, Alabama. They also do modifications to wahs.

Pharaoh Amplifiers

1998-present. Builder Matt Farrow builds his effects in Raleigh, North Carolina.

Pignose

1972-present. Guitar stomp boxes offered by the amp builder in Las Vegas, Nevada. They also offer guitars.

Pigtronix

2003-present. Dave Koltai builds his custom guitar effects originally in Brooklyn, and currently in Yonkers, New York and also offers models built in China.

Plum Crazy FX

2005-present. Guitar effects built by Kaare Festovog in Apple Valley, Minnesota.

MODEL YEAR	FEATURES	EXC. COND. LOW	HIGH

Premier

Ca.1938-ca.1975, 1990-present. Premier offered a reverb unit in the '60s.

Reverb Unit
1961-late-1960s. Tube, footswitch, 2-tone brown.

1960s		$250	$300

Prescription Electronics

1994-present. Located in Portland, Oregon, Jack Brossart offers a variety of hand-made effects.

Dual-Tone
1998-2009. Overdrive and distortion.

1998-2009		$165	$175

Throb
1996-present. Tremolo.

1996-2010		$165	$175

Yardbox
1994-present. Patterned after the original Sola Sound Tonebender.

1994-2010		$90	$125

Pro Tone Pedals

2004-present. Guitar effects pedals built by Dennis Mollan in Dallas, Texas until early-2011, and presently in Summerville, South Carolina.

ProCo

1974-present. Located in Kalamazoo, Michigan and founded by Charlie Wicks, ProCo produces effects, cables and audio products.

Rat
1979-1987. Fuzztone, large box until '84. The second version was 1/3 smaller than original box. The small box version became the Rat 2. The current Vintage Rat is a reissue of the original large box.

1979-1984	Large box	$200	$250
1984-1987	Compact box	$100	$150

Rat 2
1987-present.

1987-1999		$50	$75
2000-2010		$40	$50

Turbo Rat
1989-present. Fuzztone with higher output gain, slope-front case.

1989-2010		$40	$50

Vintage Rat
1992-2005. Reissue of early-'80s Rat.

1992-2005		$40	$50

Pro-Sound

The effects listed here date from 1987, and were, most likely, around for a short time.

Chorus CR-1

1980s		$25	$40

Delay DL-1
1980s. Analog.

1980s		$35	$55

Distortion DS-1

1980s		$20	$35

Octaver OT-1

1980s		$25	$40

Power and Master Switch PMS-1

1980s		$15	$25

Super Overdrive SD-1

1980s		$20	$35

Providence

1996-present. Guitar effects pedals built in Japan for Pacifix Ltd. and distributed in the U.S. by Godlyke Distributing, Inc.

Radial Engineering

1994-present. Radial makes a variety of products in Port Coquitlam, British Columbia, including direct boxes, snakes, cables, splitters, and, since '99, the Tonebone line of guitar effects.

Rapco

The Jackson, Missouri based cable company offers a line of switch, connection and D.I. Boxes.

The Connection AB-100
1988-present. A/B box

1988-2010		$25	$35

Rastopdesigns

2002-present. Alexander Rastopchin builds his effects in Long Island City, New York. He also builds amps.

Real McCoy Custom

1993-present. Wahs and effects by Geoffrey Teese. His first wah was advertised as the Real McCoy, by Teese. He now offers his custom wah pedals under the Real McCoy Custom brand. He also used the Teese brand on a line of stomp boxes, starting in '96. The Teese stomp boxes are no longer being made. In '08 he moved to Coos Bay, Oregon.

Red Witch

2003-present. Analog guitar effects, designed by Ben Fulton, and made in Paekakariki, New Zealand.

Reinhardt

2004-present. Amp builder Bob Reinhardt of Lynchburg, Virginia also offers a line of effects pedals.

Retro FX Pedals

2006-present. Guitar effects pedals made in St. Louis, Missouri.

Retroman

2002-present. Joe Wolf builds his retro effects pedals in Janesville, Wisconsin.

Retro-Sonic

2002-present. Tim Larwill builds effects in Ottawa Ontario, Canada.

Pigtronix Keymaster

Pro Co '85 Rat Reissue

Retroman Dum-Box

EFFECTS

EFFECTS

Reverend Drivetrain II

Rocktek Metal Worker

Rocktron Vertigo Vibe

MODEL YEAR	FEATURES	EXC. COND. LOW	HIGH

Reverend
1996-present. Reverend offered its Drivetrain effects from '00 to '04. They also build guitars.

RGW Electronics
2003-present. Guitar effects built by Robbie Wallace in Lubbock, Texas.

Rockman
See listings under Scholz Research and Dunlop.

Rocktek
1986-2009. Imports formerly distributed by Matthews and Ryan of Brooklyn, New York; and later by D'Andrea USA.

Effects

1986-2009	Delay, Super Delay	$30	$40
1986-2009	Distortion, 6 Band EQ, Bass EQ, Chorus, Compressor	$15	$25
1986-2009	Overdrive, Flanger, Metal Worker, Phaser, Vibrator, Tremolo	$15	$20

Rocktron
1980s-present. Rocktron is a division of GHS Strings and offers a line of amps, controllers, stomp boxes, and preamps.

Austin Gold Overdrive
1997-present. Light overdrive.

1997-2010		$25	$35

Banshee Talk Box
1997-present. Includes power supply.

1997-2010		$65	$80

Hush Rack Mount
1980s-present.

2000-2010		$50	$100

Hush The Pedal
1996-present. Pedal version of rackmount Hush.

1996-2010		$25	$35

Rampage Distortion
1996-present. Sustain, high-gain and distortion.

1996-2010		$25	$35

Surf Tremolo

1997-2000		$60	$80

Tsunami Chorus
1996-2009. Battery or optional AC adapter.

1996-2009	Battery power	$40	$50
1996-2009	With power supply	$50	$60

Vertigo Vibe
2003-2006. Rotating Leslie speaker effect.

2003-2006	Battery power	$50	$60
2003-2006	With power supply	$60	$70

XDC
1980s. Rack mount stereo preamp, distortion.

1980s		$100	$150

Roger Linn Design
2001-present. Effects built in Berkeley, California by Roger Linn.

Roger Mayer Electronics
1964-present. Roger Mayer started making guitar effects in England in '64 for guitarists like Jimmy Page and Jeff Beck. He moved to the U.S. in '69 to start a company making studio gear and effects. Until about 1980, the effects were built one at a time in small numbers and not available to the general public. In the '80s he started producing larger quantities of pedals, introducing his rocket-shaped enclosure. He returned to England in '89.

Axis Fuzz
Early 1980s-present.

1987-2010		$125	$150

Classic Fuzz
1987-present. The Fuzz Face.

1987-2010		$175	$200

Metal Fuzz
Early 1980s-1994.

1987-1994		$125	$150

Mongoose Fuzz
Early 1980s-present.

1987-2010		$175	$200

Octavia
Early 1980s-present. Famous rocket-shaped box.

1981-2010		$150	$200

Voodoo-1
Ca.1990-present.

1990-2010		$175	$300

Rogue
2001-present. Budget imported guitar effects. They also offer guitars, basses, lap steels, mandolins, banjos, ukuleles and amps.

Roland
Japan's Roland Corporation first launched effect pedals in 1974; a year or two later the subsidiary company, Boss, debuted its own line. They were marketed concurrently at first, but gradually Boss became reserved for compact effects while the Roland name was used on amplifiers, keyboards, synths and larger processors.

Analog Synth SPV
1970s. Multi-effect synth, rack mount.

1970s		$750	$900

Bee Baa AF-100
1975-ca.1980. Fuzz and treble boost.

1975-1980		$350	$550

Bee Gee AF-60
1975-ca.1980. Sustain, distortion.

1975-1980		$75	$125

Double Beat AD-50
1975-ca.1980. Fuzz wah.

1975-1980		$175	$200

Expression Pedal EV-5

1970s		$50	$75

Expression Pedal EV-5 Reissue
2000. Black pedal, blue foot pad.

2000		$25	$30

MODEL YEAR	FEATURES	EXC. COND. LOW	HIGH

Guitar Synth Pedal GR-33 and Pickup GK-2A
2000-2005. Requires optional GK-2A pickup, blue case.

2000-2005		$475	$550

Human Rhythm Composer R-8
1980s. Drum machine, key pad entry.

1980s		$175	$250

Human Rhythm Composer R-8 MK II
2000s. Black case.

2000s		$300	$400

Jet Phaser AP-7
1975-ca.1978. Phase and distortion.

1975-1978		$225	$250

Phase Five AP-5
1975-ca.1978.

1975-1978		$200	$225

Phase II AP-2
1975-ca.1980. Brown case.

1975-1980		$125	$175

Space Echo Unit
1974-ca.1980. Tape echo and reverb, various models.

1970s	RE-101	$500	$600
1970s	RE-150	$550	$650
1970s	RE-201	$700	$900
1970s	RE-301	$750	$950
1970s	RE-501	$800	$1,000
1970s	SRE-555 Chorus Echo	$900	$1,100

Vocoder SVC-350
Late-1970s-1980s. Vocal synthesis (vocoder) for voice or guitar, rack mount version of VP-330.

1980		$550	$700

Vocoder VP-330 Plus
Late-1970s-1980s. Analog vocal synthesis (vocoder) for voice or guitar, includes 2 1/2 octaves keyboard.

1978-1982		$750	$900

Wah Beat AW-10
1975-ca.1980.

1975-1980		$100	$125

Rosac Electronics
1969-1970s. Founded by Ralph Scaffidi and former Mosrite engineer Ed Sanner with backing from Morris Rosenberg and Ben Sacco in Bakersfield, California. Made the Nu-Fuzz which was a clone of Mosrite's Fuzzrite and the Nu-Wah. Closed in mid- to late-'70s and Scaffidi went on the co-found Osborne Sound Laboratories.

Ross
Founded by Bud Ross, who also established Kustom, in Chanute, Kansas, in the 1970s. Ross produced primarily amplifiers. In about '78, they introduced a line of U.S.-made effects. Later production switched to Asia.

10 Band Graphic Equalizer

1970s		$80	$100

Compressor
1970s. Gray or black case.

1970s		$350	$400

MODEL YEAR	FEATURES	EXC. COND. LOW	HIGH

Distortion
1978-ca.1980. Brown.

1979-1980		$75	$125

Flanger
1977-ca.1980. Red.

1977-1980		$100	$150

Phase Distortion R1
1979. Purple.

1979		$100	$125

Phaser
1978-ca.1980. Orange.

1978-1980		$80	$100

Stereo Delay
1978-ca.1980.

1978-1980		$125	$175

Rotovibe
See listing under Dunlop.

S. Hawk Ltd
1970s. Various effect pedals, no model names on case, only company name and logo.

Hawk I Fuzz
1970s. Linear pre-amp, fuzz, headphone amp, 1 slider.

1970s		$100	$125

Hawk II Tonal Expander
1970s. EQ, treble booster, headphone amp, silver case, 3 sliders.

1970s		$300	$400

Sam Ash
1960s-1970s. Sam Ash Music was founded by a young Sam Ash (nee Askynase) in '24. Ash's first store was in Brooklyn, and was relocated in '44. By '66, there were about four Ash stores. During this time, Ash Music private branded their own amps and effects.

Fuzzz Boxx
1966-1967. Red, made by Universal Amplifier Company, same as Astrotone Fuzz.

1967		$200	$225

Volume Wah
1970s. Italian-made.

1970s		$175	$200

Sanner
1999. Reissue from Eddie Sanner, who was the engineer behind the 1960s Mosrite Fuzzrite, using the identical circuitry as the original. Issued as a limited edition.

Sano
1944-ca. 1970. Sano was a New Jersey-based accordion company that built their own amps and a reverb unit. They also imported guitars for a few years, starting in '66.

Satellite Amplifiers
2004-present. Analog effects pedals made in San Diego, California by amp builder Adam Grimm.

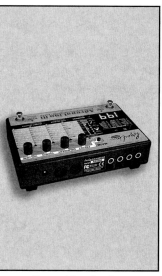
Roger Linn Design Adrenalinn III

Roger Mayer Electronics Octavia

Roland Bee Gee AF-60

EFFECTS

1970s Sekova 2011 Bass Booster
Bill Cherensky

*Seymour Duncan
Shape Shifter SFX-07*

*Siegmund Micro Tube
DoubleDrive*

MODEL YEAR	FEATURES	EXC. COND. LOW	HIGH

Schaller
1945-present. The German guitar accessories company offered guitar effects off and on since the '60s and currently has reissue versions of its volume pedal and tremolo.

Scholz Research
1982-1995. Started by Tom Scholz of the band Boston. In '95, Jim Dunlop picked up the Rockman line (see Dunlop).

Power Soak

1980s		$100	$160

Rockman

1980s		$70	$130

Rockman X100
1980s. Professional studio processor.

1980s		$100	$150

Soloist
1980s. Personal guitar processor.

1980s		$50	$80

Seamoon
1973-1977, 1997-2002. Seamoon made effects until '77, when Dave Tarnowski bought up the remaining inventory and started Analog Digital Associates (ADA). He reissued the brand in '97.

Fresh Fuzz
1975-1977. Recently reissued by ADA.

1975-1977		$150	$200

Funk Machine
1974-1977. Envelope filter. Recently reissued by ADA.

1974-1977		$175	$225

Studio Phase
1975-1977. Phase shifter.

1975-1977		$75	$125

Sekova
Mid-1960s-mid-1970s. Entry level instruments imported by the U.S. Musical Merchandise Corporation of New York.

Seymour Duncan
In late 2003, pickup maker Seymour Duncan, located in Santa Barbara, California, added a line of stomp box guitar effects.

Shinei
Japanese imports. Shinei also made effects for Univox and probably others.

Fuzz Wah

1970s		$400	$500

Resly (Repeat Time) Machine
1970s. Black case, 3 speeds.

1970s		$400	$500

Sho-Bud
1956-1980. This pedal steel company offered volume pedals as well.

Volume Pedal

1965		$90	$95

SIB
Effects pedals from Rick Hamel, who helped design SMF amps.

Siegmund Guitars & Amplifiers
1993-present. Los Angeles, California amp and guitar builder Chris Siegmund added effects to his product line in '99.

Skrydstrup R&D
1997-present. Effects pedals built by Steen Skrydstrup in Denmark. He also builds amps.

Skull Crusher
2009-present. Partners John Kasha and Shawn Crosby of Tone Box Effects, build their guitar effects in Simi Valley, California.

Snarling Dogs
1997-present. Started by Charlie Stringer of Stringer Industries, Warren, New Jersey in '97. Stringer died in May '99. The brand is now carried by D'Andrea USA.

Sobbat
1995-present. Line of effects from Kinko Music Company of Kyoto, Japan.

Sola/Colorsound
1962-2010. Sola was founded by London's Macari's Musical Exchange in '62. Sola made effects for Vox, Marshall, Park, and B & M and later under their own Colorsound brand. Refer to Colorsound for listings and more company info.

Soldano
1987-present. Seattle, Washington amp builder Soldano also builds a reverb unit.

Songbird
See Dytronics.

Sonic Edge
2010-present. Guitar and bass effects pedals built by Ben Fargen in Sacramento, California. He also builds the Fargen amps.

1975	Silver case, slider	$100	$125

Speedster
1995-2000, 2003-present. Amp builder Speedster added guitar effects pedals to their product line in '04, built in Gig Harbor, Washington.

StarTouch
2001-present. Tony Chostner builds production/custom, effects pedals in Salem, Oregon.

Stephenson
1997-present. Amp builder Mark Stephenson in Parksville, British Columbia also offers a line of guitar pedals.

EFFECTS

MODEL YEAR	FEATURES	EXC. COND. LOW	HIGH

Stinger

Stinger effects were distributed by the Martin Guitar Company from 1989 to '90.

Effects

1989-1990	CH-70 Stereo Chorus	$25	$55
1989-1990	CO-20 Compressor	$35	$55
1989-1990	DD-90 Digital Delay	$45	$65
1989-1990	DE-80 Analog Delay	$50	$70
1989-1990	DI-10 Distortion	$40	$65
1989-1990	FL-60 Flanger	$40	$65
1989-1990	OD-30 Overdrive	$40	$65
1989-1990	TS-5 Tube Stack	$45	$65

Studio Electronics

1989-present. Synth and midi developer Greg St. Regis' Studio Electronics added guitar pedal effects to their line in '03.

Subdecay Studios

2003-present. Brian Marshall builds his guitar effects in Woodinville, Washington.

Supersound

1952-1974. Founded by England's Alan Wootton, this firm built echo units in the 1960s. They also built amps, guitars and basses.

Supro

1935-1968. Supro offered a few reverb units in the '60s.

500 R Standard Reverb Unit

1962-1963. Outboard reverb unit.

1962-1963		$325	$375

600 Reverb Power Unit

1961. Independent reverb unit amp combination to be used with Supro Model 1600R amp or other amps, 3 tubes, 1x8" speaker.

1961		$725	$850

Swart Amplifier

2003-present. Effects pedals built by Michael J. Swart in Wilmington, North Carolina. He also builds amps.

Sweet Sound

1994-present. Line of effects from Bob Sweet, originally made in Trenton, Michigan, and then in Coral Springs, Florida. Bob died in 2008. Currently built by his brother Gerald.

Swell Pedal Company

1997-present. Mike Olienechak builds his line of tube pedals for guitar and bass in Nashville, Tennessee.

Systech (Systems & Technology in Music, Inc)

1975-late-1970s. Systech was located in Kalamazoo, Michigan.

Effects

1975-1979	Envelope & Repeater	$75	$125
1975-1979	Envelope Follower	$75	$125
1975-1979	Flanger	$75	$125
1975-1979	Harmonic Energizer	$150	$225
1975-1979	Overdrive Model 1300	$75	$125
1975-1979	Phase Shifter Model 1200	$75	$125

T.C. Electronics

1976-present. Brothers Kim and John Rishøj founded TC Electronic in Risskov, Denmark, and made guitar effects pedals for several years before moving into rack-mounted gear. Currently they offer a wide range of pro audio gear and rack and floor guitar effects.

Booster + Distortion

1980s		$325	$400

Dual Parametric Equalizer

1980s		$275	$350

Stereo Chorus/Flanger

Introduced in 1982, and reissued in '91.

1980s		$175	$225

Sustain + Equalizer

1980s		$225	$300

T.C. Jauernig Electronics

2004-present. Tim Jauernig, of Rothschild, Wisconsin, built effects for several years before launching his T.C. Jauernig brand in '04.

Tech 21

1989-present. Tech 21 builds their SansAmp and other effects in New York City. They also build amps.

Sansamp

1989-present. Offers a variety of tube amp tones.

1989	1st year	$125	$175
1990-2010		$100	$125

XXL Pedal

1995-2000, 2005-present. Distortion, fuzz.

1995-2000		$50	$75

Teese

Geoffrey Teese's first wah was advertised as the Real McCoy, by Teese. He now offers his custom wah pedals under the Real McCoy Custom brand. The Teese brand was used on his line of stomp boxes, starting in '96. The Teese stomp boxes are no longer being made.

The Original Geek

2009-present. Jeff Rubin began building guitar effects pedals in Los Angeles, California under the Geek MacDaddy brand in 2004. After a split with his business partner in '09 he began using The Original Geek brand.

Thomas Organ

The Thomas Organ Company was heavily involved with Vox from 1964 to '72, importing their instruments into the U.S. and designing and assembling products, including the wah-wah pedal. Both Thomas Organ and JMI, Vox's European distributor, wanted to offer the new effect. The problem was solved by labeling the Thomas Organ wah the

Speedster Turbo Charger

Stephenson Stage Hog

Sweet Sound Fillmore West Fuzz

EFFECTS

ThroBak stRange Master

ToadWorks John Bull

(TWA) Totally Wycked Audio Little Dipper

Crybaby. The Crybaby is now offered by Dunlop. Refer to Vox listing for Crybaby Stereo Fuzz Wah, Crybaby Wah, and Wah Wah.

ThroBak Electronics

2004-present. Jonathan Gundry builds his guitar effects in Grand Rapids, Michigan. He also builds guitar amps and pickups.

ToadWorks

2001-present. Guitar effects built in Spokane, Washington by Ryan Dunn and Doug Harrison.

TomasZewicZ or TZZ

2008-present. Guitar effects pedals built by John Tomaszewicz in Coral Springs, Florida, which he labels TZZ. He also builds amps.

Tone Box Effects

See listing for Skull Crusher.

Tonebone

See Radial Engineering listing.

ToneCandy

2007-present. Mike Marino builds his guitar effects pedals in Santa Rosa, California.

Top Gear

1960s-1970s. Top Gear was a London music store. Their effects were made by other manufacturers.

Rotator
1970s. Leslie effect.

1970s	$100	$175

Top Hat Amplification

1994-present. Originally in La Habra, California, then Fuquay-Varina, North Carolina, Brian Gerhard now builds his amps and effects in Apex, North Carolina.

Traynor

1963-present. Amp and PA builder Traynor also built two spring reverb units, one tube and one solidstate, in Canada from 1966-'72 and a 7-band EQ from '73-'78.

Tremolo

See listing under Dunlop.

T-Rex

2003-present. Made in Denmark and imported by European Musical Imports.

Tube Works

1987-2004. Founded by B.K. Butler (see Audio Matrix) in Denver, Colorado, Tube Works became a division of Genz Benz Enclosures of Scottsdale, Arizona in 1997 which dropped the brand in 2004. They also offered tube/solidstate amps, cabinets, and DI boxes.

Blue Tube
1989-2004. Overdrive bass driver with 12AX7A tube.

1989-2004	$100	$150

Real Tube
Ca.1987-2004. Overdrive with 12AX7A tube.

1987-1999	$100	$150

Tube Driver
1987-2004. With tube.

1987-2004 With tube	$100	$150

TWA (Totally Wycked Audio)

2009-present. Boutique analog effect pedals made in the U.S. and offered by Godlyke, Inc.

Tycobrahe

The Tycobrahe story was over almost before it began. Doing business in 1976-1977, they produced only three pedals and a direct box, one the fabled Octavia. The company, located in Hermosa Beach, California, made high-quality, original devices, but they didn't catch on. Now, they are very collectible.

Octavia
1976-1977. Octave doubler.

1976-1977	$1,100	$1,300

Parapedal
1976-1977. Wah.

1976-1977	$1,100	$1,300

Pedalflanger
1976-1977. Blue pedal-controlled flanger.

1976-1977	$1,100	$1,300

Uni-Vibe

See listings under Univox and Dunlop.

Univox

Univox was a brand owned by Merson (later Unicord), of Westbury, New York. It marketed guitars and amps, and added effects in the late-'60s. Most Univox effects were made by Shinei, of Japan. They vanished in about '81.

EC-80 A Echo
Early-1970s-ca.1977. Tape echo, sometimes shown as The Brat Echo Chamber.

1970s	$75	$100

EC-100 Echo
1970s. Tape, sound-on-sound.

1970s	$75	$150

Echo-Tech EM-200
1970s. Disc recording echo unit.

1970s	$130	$170

Micro 41 FCM41 4 channel mixer

1970s	$35	$50

Micro Fazer
1970s. Phase shifter.

1970s	$75	$100

Noise-Clamp EX110

1970s	$45	$55

Phaser PHZ1
1970s. AC powered.

1970s	$50	$75

MODEL YEAR	FEATURES	EXC. COND. LOW	HIGH

Pro Verb
1970s. Reverb (spring) unit, black tolex, slider controls for 2 inputs, 1 output plus remote output.
| 1970s | | $80 | $100 |

Square Wave SQ150
Introduced in 1976, distortion, orange case.
| 1970s | | $75 | $125 |

Super-Fuzz
1968-1973. Early transistor effect, made by Shinei.
| 1968-1973 | Gray box, normal bypass switch | $600 | $700 |
| 1968-1973 | Unicord, various colors, blue bypass pedal | $600 | $700 |

Uni-Comp
1970s. Compression limiter.
| 1970s | | $50 | $100 |

Uni-Drive
| 1970s | | $150 | $200 |

Uni-Fuzz
1960s. Fuzz tone in blue case, 2 black knobs and slider switch.
| 1960s | | $275 | $375 |

Uni-Tron 5
1975. A.k.a. Funky Filter, envelope filter.
| 1975 | | $200 | $525 |

Uni-Vibe
Introduced around 1969, with rotating speaker simulation, with pedal.
| 1960s | | $1,300 | $1,500 |
| 1970s | | $875 | $1,025 |

Uni-Wah Wah/Volume
| 1970s | | $100 | $125 |

VanAmps
1999-present. Amp builder Tim Van Tassel of Golden Valley, Minnesota, also offers a line of reverb effects pedals.

Vesta Fire
Ca.1981-ca.1988. Brand of Japan's Shiino Musical Instrument Corp.

Effects
1981-1988	Digital Chorus/ Flanger FLCH	$35	$50
1981-1988	Distortion DST	$35	$50
1981-1988	Flanger	$35	$50
1981-1988	Noise Gate	$25	$40
1981-1988	Stereo Chorus SCH	$35	$50

Vintage Tone Project
2003-present. Line of guitar effects made by Robert Rush and company originally in Lafayette, Colorado, and currently in Delmar, New York. They also built reissues of Dan Armstrong's '70s effects from '03 to '06.

VintageFX
2003-present. Effects based on vintage pedals from the '60s and '70s built by Dave Archer in Grand Island, New York.

Visual Sound
1995-present. Effects pedals designed by Bob Weil and R.G. Keen in Spring Hill, Tennessee and built in China.

VooDoo Lab
1994-present. Line of effects made by Digital Music Corp. in California.

Analog Chorus
1997-present.
| 1997-2010 | | $100 | $120 |

Bosstone
1994-1999. Based on '60s Jordan Electronics Fuzz.
| 1994-1999 | | $70 | $75 |

Microvibe
1996-present. UniVibe swirl effect.
| 1996-2010 | | $55 | $65 |

Overdrive
1994-2002. Based on '70s overdrive.
| 1994-2002 | | $55 | $65 |

Superfuzz
1999-present.
| 1999-2010 | | $75 | $90 |

Tremolo
1995-present.
| 1995-2010 | | $55 | $75 |

Vox
1954-present. The first Vox product was a volume pedal. Ca. '66, they released the Tone Bender, one of the classic fuzzboxes of all time. A year or so later, they delivered their greatest contribution to the effects world, the first wah-wah pedal. The American arm of Vox (then under Thomas Organ) succumbed in '72. In the U.K., the company was on-again/off-again.

Clyde McCoy Wah-Wah Pedal
Introduced in 1967, reissued in 2001-2008. Clyde's picture on bottom cover.
1967	Clyde's picture	$900	$1,100
1968	No picture	$700	$850
2001-2008	Model V-848	$150	$175

Crybaby Wah
Introduced in 1968. The Thomas Organ Company was heavily involved with Vox from '64 to '72, importing their instruments into the U.S. and designing and assembling products. One product developed in conjunction with Vox was the wah-wah pedal. Both Thomas Organ and JMI, Vox's European distributor, wanted to offer the new effect. The problem was solved by labeling the Thomas Organ wah the Crybaby. The original wahs were built by Jen in Italy, but Thomas later made them in their Chicago, Illinois and Sepulveda, California plants. Thomas Organ retained the marketing rights to Vox until '79, but was not very active with the brand after '72. The Crybaby brand is now offered by Dunlop.
| 1960s | Jen-made | $200 | $250 |
| 1970 | Sepulveda-made | $125 | $175 |

Univox Super-Fuzz
Jim Schreck

Visual Sound Comp 66

Voodoo Lab Tremolo

EFFECTS

EFFECTS

Vox V-847 Wah-Wah

Warmenfat Tube Preamp

*Way Huge Electronics
Fat Sandwich*

MODEL YEAR	FEATURES	EXC. COND. LOW	HIGH

Double Sound
1970s. Jen-made, Double Sound model name on bottom of pedal, double sound derived from fuzz and wah ability.
| 1970s | | $200 | $250 |

Flanger
| 1970s | | $200 | $250 |

King Wah
1970s. Chrome top, Italian-made.
| 1970s | | $200 | $250 |

Repeat Percussion
Late-1960s. Plug-in module with on-off switch and rate adjustment.
| 1968 | | $100 | $125 |

Stereo Fuzz Wah
Stereo Fuzz Wah
| 1970s | | $150 | $200 |

Tone Bender V-828
1966-1970s. Fuzz box, reissued as the V-829 in '93.
| 1966-1968 | Gray | $600 | $800 |
| 1969 | Black | $500 | $700 |

Tonelab Valvetronix
2003-present. Multi-effect modeling processor, 12AX7 tube preamp.
| 2003-2010 | | $400 | $425 |

V-807 Echo-Reverb Unit
1967. Solidstate, disc echo.
| 1967 | | $275 | $375 |

V-837 Echo Deluxe Tape Echo
1967. Solidstate, multiple heads.
| 1967 | | $350 | $450 |

V-846 Wah
1969-1970s. Chrome top, Italian-made.
| 1969 | Transitional Clyde McCoy | $500 | $650 |
| 1970s | | $300 | $400 |

V-847 Wah-Wah
1992-present. Reissue of the original V-846 Wah.
| 1992-2010 | | $65 | $80 |

Volume Pedal
Late 1960s. Reissued as the V850.
| 1960s | | $50 | $100 |

Wampler Pedals
2004-present. Brian Wampler began building effects under the brand Indy Guitarist in 2004, and changed the name to Wampler Pedals in 2007. They are built in Greenwood, Indiana.

MODEL YEAR	FEATURES	EXC. COND. LOW	HIGH

Warmenfat
2004-present. Pre-amps and guitar effects built in Sacramento, California, by Rainbow Electronics.

Wasabi
2003-2008. Line of guitar effect pedals from Danelectro.

Washburn
Washburn offered a line of effects from around 1983 to ca. '89.
Effects
1980s	Analog Delay AX:9	$30	$35
1980s	Flanger FX:4	$35	$40
1980s	Phaser PX:8	$40	$45
1980s	Stack in a Box SX:3	$30	$35

Watkins/WEM
1957-present. Watkins Electric Music (WEM) was founded by Charlie Watkins. Their first commercial product was the Watkins Dominator amp in '57, followed by the Copicat Echo in '58.
Copicat Tape Echo
1958-1970s, 1985-present. The Copicat has been reissued in various forms by Watkins.
| 1958-1970s | Solidstate | $325 | $400 |
| 1958-1970s | Tube | $800 | $1,000 |

Way Huge Electronics
1995-1998, 2008-present Way Huge offered a variety of stomp boxes, made in Sherman Oaks, California. Jim Dunlop revived the brand in '08.

WD Music
Since 1978, WD Music has offered a wide line of aftermarket products for guitar players. From '91 to '02, they offered a line of effects that were copies of the original Dan Armstrong color series (refer to Dan Armstrong listing).
Blue Clipper
1991-2002. Fuzz.
| 1991-2002 | | $30 | $45 |
Orange Squeezer
1991-2002. Signal compressor.
| 1991-2002 | Light Orange case | $40 | $50 |
Purple Peaker
1991-2002. Mini EQ.
| 1991-2002 | | $40 | $50 |

MODEL		EXC. COND.	
YEAR	FEATURES	LOW	HIGH

Westbury

1978-ca.1983. Brand imported by Unicord.

Tube Overdrive

1978-1983. 12AX7.

1978-1983	$150	$200

Whirlwind

1976-present. Effects from Michael Laiacona, who helped found MXR, originally made in Rochester, New York. Currently the company offers guitar effects, DI boxes and other music devices built in Greece, New York.

Commander

1980s. Boost and effects loop selector.

1980s	$75	$100

Wilson Effects

2007-present. Guitar effects built by Kevin Wilson in Guilford, Indiana.

WMD (William Mathewson Devices)

2008-present. William Mathewson builds his instrument effects in Denver, Colorado.

Wurlitzer

Wurlitzer offered the Fuzzer Buzzer in the 1960s, which was the same as the Clark Fuzz.

Xotic Effects

2001-present. Hand-wired effects made in Los Angeles, California, and distributed by Prosound Communications.

Yamaha

1946-present. Yamaha has offered effects since at least the early '80s. They also build guitars, basses, amps, and other musical instruments.

Analog Delay E1005

1980s. Free-standing, double-space rack mount-sized, short to long range delays, gray case.

1980s	$160	$180

MODEL		EXC. COND.	
YEAR	FEATURES	LOW	HIGH

Yubro

Yubro, of Bellaire, Texas, offered a line of nine effects in the mid- to late-'80s.

Analog Delay AD-800

300 ms.

1980s	$75	$125

Stereo Chorus CH-600

1980s	$50	$75

Z.Vex Effects

1995-present. Zachary Vex builds his effects in Minneapolis, Minnesota with some subassembly work done in Michigan. A few lower-cost versions of his most popular effects are also built in Taipei, Taiwan. In 2002 he also began building amps.

Zinky

1999-present. Guitar effects built by Bruce Zinky in Flagstaff, Arizona. He also builds amps and has revived the Supro brand on a guitar and amp.

Zoom

Effects line from Samson Technologies Corp. of Syosset, New York.

503 Amp Simulator

1998-2000	$25	$40

504 Acoustic Pedal

1997-2000. Compact multi-effects pedal, 24 effects, tuner, replaced by II version.

1997-2000	$25	$40

505 Guitar Pedal

1996-2000. Compact multi-effects pedal, 24 effects, tuner, replaced by II version.

1996-2000	$30	$40

506 Bass Pedal

1997-2000. Compact multi-effects bass pedal, 24 effects, tuner, black box, orange panel. Replaced by II version.

1997-2000	$35	$45

507 Reverb

1997-2000	$25	$40

1010 Player

1996-1999. Compact multi-effects pedal board, 16 distortions, 25 effects.

1996-1999	$40	$75

Wilson Effects Q-Wah

WMD Geiger Counter

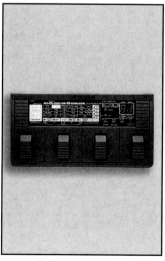

Zoom 1010 Player

STEELS & LAP STEELS

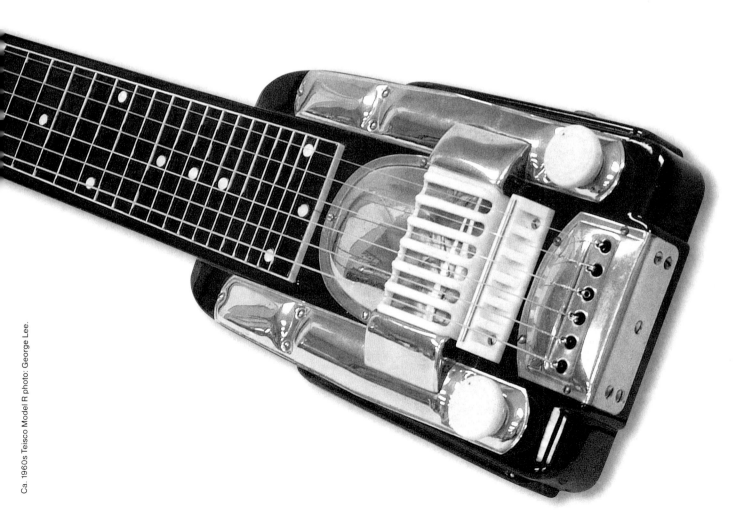

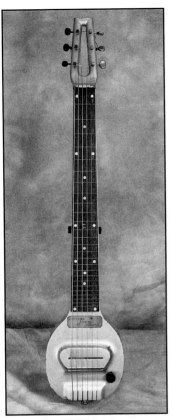

*Ca. 1935 Bronson
Singing Electric*

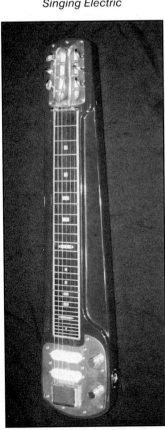

Aria

MODEL		EXC. COND.	
YEAR	FEATURES	LOW	HIGH

Airline
Ca. 1958-1968. Name used by Montgomery Ward for instruments built by Kay, Harmony and Valco.
Lap Steel

1960s	Res-O-Glas/plastic	$425	$525
1960s	Wood	$275	$325

Rocket 6-String Steel
1960s. Black and white, 3 legs, Valco-made.

1960s		$300	$375

Student 6 Steel

1950s	Black	$200	$225

Alamo
1947-1982. The first musical instruments built by Alamo, of San Antonio, Texas, were lap steel and amp combos with early models sold with small birch amps.
Hawaiian Lap Steels
1947-ca. 1967. Models include the '50s Challenger and Futuramic Dual Eight, the '50s and early-'60s Embassy (pear-shape) and Jet (triangular), the early-'60s Futuramic Eight and Futuramic Six, and the late-'60s Embassy (triangular Jet).

1950s		$200	$250

Alkire
1939-1950s. Founded by musician and teacher Eddie Alkire, with instruments like his E-Harp Steel built by Epiphone and maybe others (see Epiphone for values).

Aloha
1935-1960s. Private branded by Aloha Publishing and Musical Instruments Company, Chicago, Illinois. Made by others. There was also the Aloha Manufacturing Company of Honolulu which made musical instruments from around 1911 to the late '20s.

Alvarez
Ca. 1966-present. Imported by St. Louis Music from mid-'60s. They also offered guitars, banjos and mandolins.
Model 5010 Koa D Steel-String

1960s		$175	$225

Aria
1960-present. Aria offered Japanese-made steels and lap steels in the '60s.
Laps Steels

1960s		$200	$250

Asher
1982-present. Intermediate, professional and premium grade, production/custom, solidbody, semi-hollow body and acoustic lap steels built by luthier Bill Asher in Venice, California. He also builds guitars.

Audiovox
Ca. 1935-ca. 1950. Paul Tutmarc's Audiovox Manufacturing, of Seattle, Washington, was a pioneer in electric lap steels, basses, guitars and amps.
Lap Steel

1940s		$650	$800

Bel-Tone
1950s. Private brand made by Magnatone, Bel-Tone oval logo on headstock.
Lap Steel

1950s	Pearloid cover	$200	$250

Bigsby
1947-1965, 2002-present. All handmade by Paul Arthur Bigsby, in Downey, California. Bigsby was a pioneer in developing pedal steels and they were generally special order or custom-made and not mass produced. The original instruments were made until '65 and should be valued on a case-by-case basis. Models include the Single Neck pedal steel, Double 8 pedal steel, 8/10 Doubleneck pedal steel, Triple 8 pedal steel (all ca. '47-'65), and the '57-'58 Magnatone G-70 lap steel. A solidbody guitar and a pedal steel based upon the original Paul Bigsby designs were introduced January, 2002.
Triple 8-String Neck Steel
1947-1965. Bigsby steel were generally special order or custom-made and not mass produced. Instruments should be valued on a case-by-case basis.

1947-1959	Natural	$5,000	$6,000

Blue Star
1984-present. Intermediate grade, production/custom, lap steels built by luthier Bruce Herron in Fennville, Michigan. He also builds guitars, mandolins, dulcimers, and ukes.

Breedlove
1990-present. Founded by Larry Breedlove and Steve Henderson. Professional and premium grade, custom, Weissenborn-style lap steels made in Tumalo, Oregon. They also offer guitars, basses, mandolins and ukes. In 2010 they became part of Bedell Guitars.

Bronson
George Bronson was a steel guitar instructor in the Detroit area from the 1930s to the early '50s and sold instruments under his own brand. Most instruments and amps were made by Rickenbacker, Dickerson or Valco.
Leilani Lap Steel and Amp Set
1940s. Pearloid lap steel and small matching amp.

1940s		$350	$450

Melody King Model 52 Lap Steel
1950s. Brown bakelite body with 5 gold cavity covers on the top, made by Rickenbacker.

1950s		$775	$925

MODEL YEAR	FEATURES	EXC. COND. LOW	HIGH

Model B Style
1948-1952. Rickenbacker-made.

1948-1952		$875	$1,075

Singing Electric
1950s. Round body, Valco-made.

1950s		$275	$325

Streamliner Lap Steel
1950s. Guitar-shape body, single pickup, 1 control knob, red-orange pearloid cover, Bronson and Streamliner logo on headstock.

1950s		$200	$250

Carvin

1946-present. Founded by Lowell C. Kiesel who produced lapsteels under the Kiesel brand for 1947-'50. In late '49, he renamed the instrument line Carvin after sons Carson and Galvin. Until '77, they offered lap, console, and pedal steels with up to 4 necks.

Double 6 Steel With Legs

1960s		$700	$800

Double 8 Steel With Legs

1960s	Sunburst	$750	$850

Electric Hawaiian Lap Steel

1950s		$250	$300

Single 8 With Legs
1960s. Large block position markers, 1 pickup, 2 knobs, blond finish.

1960s		$525	$625

Chandler

1984-present. Intermediate grade, production/custom, solidbody Weissenborn-shaped electric lap steels built by luthiers Paul and Adrian Chandler in Chico, California. They also build guitars, basses and effects.

Coppock

1930s-1959. Lap and console steels built by luthier John Lee Coppock in the Los Angeles area and in Peshastin, Washington. Coppock played Hawaiian music professionally in the 1920s and '30s and had a music studio where he started building his brand of steels around 1932. He moved to Washington in '44.

Cromwell

1935-1939. Budget model brand built by Gibson and distributed by various mail-order businesses.

Lap Steel
1939. Charlie Christian bar pickup.

1939	Sunburst	$275	$350

Danelectro

1946-1969, 1997-present. Known mainly for guitars and amps, Danelectro did offer a few lap steels in the mid-'50s.

Lap Steel

1950s	Common model	$375	$475
1950s	Rare model	$475	$600

Deckly

1970s-1980s. Intermediate and professional grade pedal steel models, Deckly logo on front side of body.

Denley

1960s. Pedal steels built by Nigel Dennis and Gordon Huntley in England. They also made steels for Jim Burns' Ormston brand in the '60s.

Dickerson

1937-1948. Founded by the Dickerson brothers in '37, primarily for electric lap steels and small amps. Besides their own brand, Dickerson made instruments for Cleveland's Oahu Company, Varsity, Southern California Music, Bronson, Roland Ball, and Gourley. The lap steels were often sold with matching amps, both covered in pearloid mother-of-toilet-seat (MOTS). By '48, the company changed ownership and was renamed Magna Electronics (Magnatone).

Lap Steel
1950s. Gray pearloid.

1950s		$250	$300

Dobro

1929-1942, ca.1954-present. Dobro offered lap steels from '33 to '42. Gibson now owns the brand and recently offered a lap steel.

Hawaiiian Lap Steel

1933-1942		$400	$500
1984	'37 reissue	$575	$650

Lap Steel Guitar and Amp Set
1930s-1940s. Typical pearloid covered student 6-string lap steel and small matching amp (with 3 tubes and 1 control knob).

1933-1942		$525	$600

Metal Body Lap Steel
1936. All metal body, Dobro logo on body.

1936		$600	$750

Dwight

1950s. Private branded instruments made by National-Supro. Epiphone made a Dwight brand guitar in the '60s which was not related to the lap-steels.

Lap Steel
1950s. Pearloid, 6 strings.

1950s	Gray pearloid	$375	$475

Electro

1964-1975. The Electro line was manufactured by Electro String Instruments and distributed by Radio-Tel. The Electro logo appeared on the headstock rather than Rickenbacker. Refer to the Rickenbacker section for models.

Electromuse

1940s-1950s. Mainly offered lap steel and tube amp packages but they also offered acoustic and electric hollowbody guitars.

Asher Electro Hawaiian

1950s Coppock

STEELS & LAPS

Ellis Weissenborn

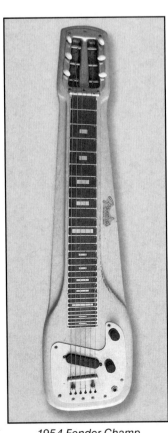

1954 Fender Champ
(Marco Parmiggiani)

MODEL YEAR	FEATURES	EXC. COND. LOW	HIGH
Lap Steel			
1940s		$225	$275

Ellis

2008-present. Professional and premium grade, production/custom, lap steel guitars built by Andrew Ellis in Perth, Western Australia. He also builds guitars.

Emmons

1970s-present. Professional and premium grade, production/custom, pedal steels built by Lashley, Inc. of Burlington, North Carolina.

Double 10 Steel			
1970-1982. Push/pull pedal steel.			
1970-1982		$2,600	$2,900
Lashley LeGrande III Steel			
2001-present. Double-neck, 8 pedals, 4 knee levers, 25th Anniversary.			
2001-2010		$2,200	$2,700
S-10 Pedal Steel			
1970-1982. Single 10-string neck pedal steel.			
1970-1982		$1,700	$2,100
Student, 3-Pedal Steel			
1970s. Single neck.			
1970s		$425	$525

English Electronics

1960s. Norman English had a teaching studio in Lansing, Michigan, where he gave guitar and steel lessons. He had his own private-branded instruments made by Valco in Chicago.

Tonemaster Lap Steel			
1960s. Cream pearloid, 6 strings, 3 legs, Valco-made.			
1960s		$325	$400
1960s	Stringtone pitch changer	$550	$675

Epiphone

1928-present. The then Epiphone Banjo Company was established in '28. Best known for its guitars, the company offered steels from '35 to '58 when Gibson purchased the brand.

Century Lap Steel			
1939-1957. Rocket-shaped maple body, 1 pickup, metal 'board, 6, 7 or 8 strings, black finish.			
1939-1957		$400	$500
Eddie Alkire E-Harp			
1939-1950s. 10-string, similar to Epiphone lap steel with Epi-style logo, offered in lap steel or console.			
1939-1950s		$600	$700
Electar Hawaiian Lap Steel			
1935-1937. Wood teardrop-shaped body, bakelite top, black, horseshoe pickup, 6 string.			
1935-1937		$400	$475
Electar Model M Hawaiian Lap Steel			
1936-1939. Metal top, stair-step body, art deco, black ('36-'37) or gray ('38-'39), 6, 7 or 8 strings.			
1936-1939		$700	$900

MODEL YEAR	FEATURES	EXC. COND. LOW	HIGH
Kent Hawaiian Lap Steel			
1949-1953. Guitar-shaped maple body, 6 strings, lower-end of Epiphone Hawaiian line, Electar script logo below bottom of fretboard.			
1949-1953		$300	$350
Solo Console Steel			
1939-1954. Maple with white mahogany laminated body, black binding, black metal 'board, 6, 7 or 8 strings.			
1939-1954		$525	$625
Triple-Neck Console Steel			
1954-1957. neck version of Solo, sunburst or natural finish.			
1954-1957		$1,150	$1,450
Zephyr Hawaiian Lap Steel			
1939-1957. Maple stair-step body, metal 'board, 6, 7 or 8 strings.			
1939-1949	Black, with white top	$575	$700
1950-1957	Sunburst	$550	$675

Fender

1946-present. Fender offered lap and pedal steels from '46 to '80. In 2005 they introduced a new lap steel model under their Folk Music series, which lasted until 2009.

400 Pedal Steel			
1958-1976. One 8-string neck with 4 to 10 pedals.			
1958-1964		$800	$1,000
1965-1976		$750	$950
800 Pedal Steel			
1964-1976. One 10-string neck, 6 to 10 pedals.			
1964-1976		$900	$1,100
1000 Pedal Steel			
1957-1976. Two 8-string necks, 8 or 10 pedals, sunburst or natural.			
1957-1976		$1,000	$1,200
2000 Pedal Steel			
1964-1976. Two 10-string necks, 10 or 11 pedals, sunburst.			
1964		$1,300	$1,600
1965-1976		$1,200	$1,500
Artist Dual 10 Pedal Steel			
1976-1981. Two 10-string necks, 8 pedals, 4 knee levers, black or mahogany.			
1976-1981		$700	$900
Champ Lap Steel			
1955-1980. Replaced Champion Lap Steel, tan.			
1955-1959		$550	$700
1960-1969		$550	$700
1970-1980		$500	$650
Champion Lap Steel			
1949-1955. Covered in what collectors call mother-of-toilet-seat (MOTS) finish, also known as pearloid. Replaced by Champ Lap Steel.			
1949-1955	Tan	$775	$925
1949-1955	White or yellow pearloid	$775	$925
Deluxe 6/Stringmaster Single Steel			
1950-1981. Renamed from the Deluxe, 6 strings, 3 legs.			
1950-1969	Blond or walnut	$900	$1,000
1970-1981	Black or white	$800	$900

STEELS & LAPS

MODEL YEAR	FEATURES	EXC. COND. LOW	HIGH
Deluxe 8/Stringmaster Single Steel			

1950-1981. Renamed from the Deluxe, 8 strings, 3 legs.

MODEL YEAR	FEATURES	EXC. COND. LOW	HIGH
1950-1969	Blond or walnut	$950	$1,100
1970-1981	Black or white	$850	$1,000

Deluxe Steel

1949-1950. Strings-thru-pickup, Roman numeral markers, became the Deluxe 6 or Deluxe 8 Lap Steel in '50.

1946	Wax	$950	$1,150
1947-1950	Blond or walnut	$950	$1,150

Dual 6 Professional Steel

1950-1981. Two 6-string necks, 3 legs optional, blond or walnut.

1952-1981		$850	$1,000

Dual 8 Professional Steel

1946-1957. Two 8-string necks, 3 legs optional, blond or walnut.

1946-1957		$1,000	$1,250

FS-52 Lap Steel

2008-2009. Two-piece ash body, 22.5" scale, chrome hardware, white blonde gloss finish.

2008-2009		$250	$275

K & F Steel

1945-1946. Made by Doc Kauffman and Leo Fender, strings-thru-pickup.

1945-1946	Black	$1,600	$2,000

Organ Button Steel

1946-1947	Wax	$800	$1,000

Princeton Steel

1946-1948. Strings-thru-pickup, Roman numeral markers.

1946-1948	Wax	$850	$950

Stringmaster Steel (Two-Neck)

1953-1981. The Stringmaster came in 3 versions, having 2, 3 or 4 8-string necks (6-string necks optional).

1953-1954	Blond, 26" scale	$1,700	$2,000
1953-1954	Walnut, 26" scale	$1,500	$1,900
1955-1959	Blond, 24.5" scale	$1,700	$2,000
1955-1959	Walnut, 24.5" scale	$1,500	$1,900
1960-1969	Blond	$1,500	$1,900
1960-1969	Walnut	$1,300	$1,600
1970-1981	Blond or walnut	$1,200	$1,500

Stringmaster Steel (Three-Neck)

1953-1981.

1953-1954	Blond, 26" scale	$2,200	$2,600
1953-1954	Walnut, 26" scale	$1,900	$2,300
1955-1959	Blond, 24.5" scale	$2,200	$2,600
1955-1959	Walnut, 24.5" scale	$1,900	$2,300
1960-1969	Blond	$1,900	$2,300
1960-1969	Walnut	$1,700	$2,100
1970-1981	Blond or walnut	$1,600	$2,000

Stringmaster Steel (Four-Neck)

1953-1968.

1953-1954	Blond, 26" scale	$2,300	$2,700
1953-1954	Walnut, 26" scale	$2,000	$2,400
1955-1959	Blond, 24.5" scale	$2,300	$2,700
1955-1959	Walnut, 24.5" scale	$2,000	$2,400
1960-1968	Blond	$2,000	$2,400
1960-1968	Walnut	$1,800	$2,200

MODEL YEAR	FEATURES	EXC. COND. LOW	HIGH
Studio Deluxe Lap Steel			

1956-1981. One pickup, 3 legs.

1956-1981	Blond	$800	$900

Framus

1946-1977, 1996-present. Imported into the U.S. by Philadelphia Music Company in the '60s. The brand was revived in '96 by Hans Peter Wilfer, the president of Warwick.

Deluxe Table Steel 0/7

1970s	White	$325	$400

Student Hawaiian Model 0/4

1970s	Red	$150	$175

G.L. Stiles

1960-1994. Gilbert Lee Stiles made a variety of instruments, mainly in the Miami, Florida area.

Doubleneck Pedal Steel

1970s		$475	$550

Gibson

1890s (1902)-present. Gibson offered steels from '35-'68.

BR-3 Lap Steel

1946-1947. Guitar-shaped body, script Gibson logo, 1 P-90, 2 control knobs, 2-tone sunburst over mahogany body. Replaced by BR-4 in '47.

1946-1947		$600	$700

BR-4 Lap Steel

1947. Guitar-shaped of solid mahogany, round neck, 1 pickup, varied binding.

1947	Sunburst	$600	$750

BR-6 Lap Steel

1947-1960. Guitar-shaped solid mahogany body, square neck (round by '48).

1947-1960		$475	$575

BR-9 Lap Steel

1947-1959. Solidbody, 1 pickup, tan.

1947-1949	Non-adj. poles	$400	$500
1950-1959	Adj. poles	$475	$575

Century 6 Lap Steel

1948-1968. Solid maple body, 6 strings, 1 pickup, silver 'board.

1948-1968		$550	$650

Century 10 Lap Steel

1948-1955. Solid maple body, 10 strings, 1 pickup, silver 'board.

1948-1955	Black	$575	$675

Console Grand Steel

1938-1942, 1948-1967. Hollowbody, 2 necks, triple-bound body, standard 7- and 8-string combination until '42, double 8-string necks standard for '48 and after, by '61 becomes CG-620.

1938-1942		$1,200	$1,500
1961-1967	CG-620	$1,200	$1,500

Console Steel (C-530)

1956-1966. Replaced Consolette during '56-'57, double 8-string necks, 4 legs optional.

1956-1966	With legs	$1,200	$1,400

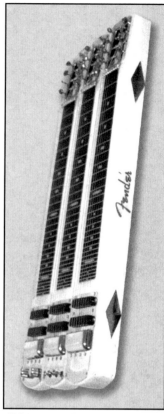

1961 Fender Stringmaster Steel (Three-Neck)

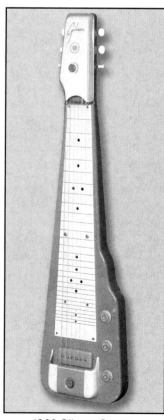

1960 Gibson Century

STEELS & LAPS

1950s Gibson Royaltone Lap Steel

Gold Tone LS-6 Lap

STEELS & LAPS

MODEL YEAR	FEATURES	EXC. COND. LOW	HIGH
Consolette Table Steel			
1952-1957. Rectangular korina body, 2 8-string necks, 4 legs, replaced by maple-body Console after '56.			
1952-1957		$900	$1,100
EH-100 Lap Steel			
1936-1949. Hollow guitar-shaped body, bound top, 6 or 7 strings.			
1936-1939		$800	$1,000
1940-1949		$700	$900
EH-125 Lap Steel			
1939-1942. Hollow guitar-shaped mahogany body, single-bound body, metal 'board, sunburst.			
1939-1942		$850	$1,100
EH-150 Doubleneck Electric Hawaiian Steel			
1937-1939. Doubleneck EH-150 with 7- and 8-string necks.			
1937-1939		$2,600	$3,100
EH-150 Lap Steel			
1936-1943. Hollow guitar-shaped body, 6 to 10 strings available, bound body.			
1936	1st offering metal body	$2,600	$3,000
1937-1939	Sunburst	$900	$1,150
1940-1943	Sunburst	$850	$1,100
EH-185 Lap Steel			
1939-1942. Hollow guitar-shaped curly maple body, triple-bound body, 6, 7, 8 or 10 strings.			
1939-1942	Sunburst	$1,600	$1,900
EH-500 Skylark Deluxe Lap Steel			
1958-1959. Like Skylark, but with dot markers.			
1958-1959		$800	$1,000
EH-500 Skylark Lap Steel			
1956-1968. Solid korina body, 8-string available by '58, block markers with numbers.			
1956-1968	Natural	$600	$700
EH-620 Steel			
1955-1967. Eight strings, 6 pedals.			
1955-1967	Natural	$900	$1,100
EH-630 Electraharp Steel			
1941-1967. Eight strings, 8 pedals (4 in '49-'67). Called just EH-630 from '56-'67.			
1941-1967	Sunburst	$1,000	$1,200
EH-820 Steel			
1960-1966. Two necks, 8 pedals, Vari-Tone selector.			
1960-1966	Cherry	$1,100	$1,400
Royaltone Lap Steel			
1950-1952, 1956-1957. Volume and tone knobs on treble side of pickup, Gibson silk-screen logo, brown pickup bridge cover.			
1950-1952	Symmetrical body	$550	$700
1956-1957	Guitar-shaped body	$450	$600
Ultratone Lap Steel			
1946-1959. Solid maple body, plastic 'board, 6 strings.			
1940s	White	$800	$1,000
1950s	Dark blue or Seal Brown	$700	$900

Gilet Guitars

1976-present. Production/custom, premium grade, lap steels built in Botany, Sydney, New South Wales, Australia by luthier Gerard Gilet. He also builds guitars.

Gold Tone

1993-present. Wayne and Robyn Rogers build their intermediate grade, production/custom lap steels in Titusville, Florida. They also build guitars, basses, mandolins, ukuleles, banjos and banjitars.

Gourley

See Dickerson listing.

Gretsch

1883-present. Gretsch offered a variety of steels from 1940-'63. Gretsch actually only made 1 model; the rest were built by Valco. Currently they offer 2 lap steel models.

MODEL YEAR	FEATURES	EXC. COND. LOW	HIGH
Electromatic (5700/5715) Lap Steel			
2005-present. Made in China, designed like the original Jet Mainliner (6147) steel, tobacco sunburst (5700) or black sparkle (5715).			
2005-2010		$150	$175
Electromatic Console (6158) Twin Neck Steel			
1949-1955. Two 6-string necks with six-on-a-side tuners, Electromatic script logo on end cover plates, 3 knobs, metal control panels and knobs, pearloid covered.			
1949-1955		$600	$750
Electromatic Hawaiian Lap Steel			
1940-1942. Guitar shaped mahogany body, wooden pickup cover.			
1940-1942		$700	$900
Electromatic Standard (6156) Lap Steel			
1949-1955. Brown pearloid.			
1949-1955		$350	$450
Electromatic Student (6152) Lap Steel			
1949-1955. Square bottom, brown pearloid, pearloid cover.			
1949-1955		$250	$350
Jet Mainliner (6147) Steel			
1955-1963. Single-neck version of Jet Twin.			
1955-1963		$500	$600
Jet Twin Console (6148) Steel			
1955-1963. Valco-made, 2 6-string necks, six-on-a-side tuners, Jet Black.			
1955-1963		$850	$950

Guyatone

1933-present. Large Japanese maker. Brands also include Marco Polo, Winston, Kingston, Kent, LaFayette and Bradford. They offered lap steels under various brands from the '30s to the '60s.

MODEL YEAR	FEATURES	EXC. COND. LOW	HIGH
Lap Steels			
1960s		$250	$300
Table Steels			
1960s. Three legs, 2 pickups.			
1960s		$400	$500

*The **Vintage Guitar Price Guide** shows low to high values for items in all-original excellent condition, and, where applicable, with original case or cover.*

MODEL YEAR	FEATURES	EXC. COND. LOW	HIGH

Hanburt

1940-ca. 1950. Harvey M. Hansen built his electric Hawaiian guitars in Seattle, Washington that were sold through his wife's music instruction studio. His designs were influenced by Seattle's Audiovox guitars. He also built amps and at least one mandolin.

Harlin Brothers

1930s-1960s. Harlin Brothers, of Indianapolis, Indiana, were one of the early designers of pedal steel applications. Prices can vary because some instruments have a reputation of being hard to keep in tune.

Multi-Kord Pedal Steel

1950s	Single neck	$525	$625

Harmony

1982-1976, late 1970s-present. Founded by Wilhelm Schultz and purchased by Sears in 1916. The company evolved into the largest producer of stringed instruments in the U.S. in the '30s. They offered electric lap steels by '36.

Lap Steels

1936-1959	Various models	$275	$350
1960s	Painted body	$275	$350
1960s	Pearloid body	$275	$350

Hilo

1920s-1930s. Weissenborn-style guitars most likely made by New Jersey's Oscar Schmitt Company, Hilo orange label inside back.

Hawaiian Steel Guitar

1930s. Guitar shaped body, round sound hole, acoustic steel.

1930s		$1,400	$1,700

Hollingworth Guitars

1995-present. Premium grade, production/custom, lap steels built by luthier Graham Hollingworth in Mermaid Beach, Gold Coast, Queensland, Australia. He also builds guitars.

Jackson-Guldan

1920s-1960s. The Jackson-Guldan Violin Company, of Columbus, Ohio, offered lap steels and small tube amps early on. They also built acoustic guitars.

Jim Dyson

1972-present. Production/custom, intermediate, professional and premium grade lap steels built in Torquay, Southern Victoria, Australia by luthier Jim Dyson. He also builds guitars and basses.

K & F (Kaufman & Fender)

See listing under Fender.

Kalamazoo

1933-1942, 1946-1947, 1965-1970. Budget brand produced by Gibson in Kalamazoo, Michigan. They offered lap steels in the '30s and '40s.

MODEL YEAR	FEATURES	EXC. COND. LOW	HIGH

Lap Steel

1938-1942, 1946-1947.

1938-1942		$400	$500
1946-1947		$300	$400

Kamico

Late-1940s. Private branded by Kay for student lap steel market, Kamico logo on lap steels and amplifiers. They also made guitars.

Lap Steel and Amp Set

1948. Symmetrical 6-string lap steel with small, single-knob 1x8" amp, both with matching sunburst finish.

1948		$275	$350

Kay

Ca. 1931-present. Huge Chicago manufacturer Kay offered steels from '36 to '60 under their own brand and others.

Lap Steel

1940s		$300	$350
1950s		$300	$350
1960s		$300	$350

Lap Steel With Matching Amp

1940s	Dark mahogany	$450	$550
1950s	Green	$450	$550

Kiesel

1946-1949. Founded by Lowell Kiesel as L.C. Kiesel Co., Los Angeles, California, but renamed Carvin in '49. Kiesel logo on the headstock.

Bakelite Lap Steel

1946. Small guitar-shaped bakelite body, 1 pickup, 2 knobs, diamond markers.

1946		$325	$400

Knutson Luthiery

1981-present. Professional grade, custom, electric lap steels built by luthier John Knutson in Forestville, California. He also builds guitars, basses and mandolins.

Lapdancer

2001-present. Intermediate and professional grade, custom/production, lap steels built by luthier Loni Specter in West Hills, California.

Lockola

1950s. Private brand lap and amp sets made by Valco for Lockola of Salt Lake City, Utah.

Lap Steel

1950s	Pearloid	$300	$350

Maestro

A budget brand made by Gibson.

Lap Steel

1940s-1950s. Pearloid, 1 pickup, 6 strings.

1940s		$275	$325
1950s		$275	$325

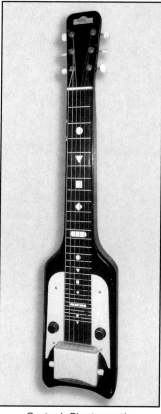

Gretsch Electromatic

Jim Dyson Pro

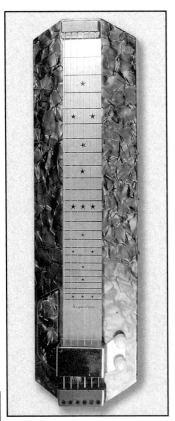

Magnatone (Pearloid)

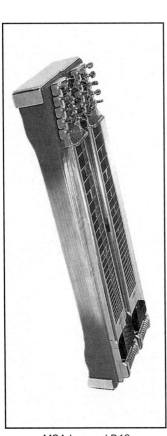

MSA Legend D10

MODEL YEAR	FEATURES	EXC. COND. LOW	HIGH

Magnatone

Ca. 1937-1971. Magnatone offered lap steels from '37 to '58. Besides their own brand, they also produced models under the Dickerson, Oahu, Gourley, and Natural Music Guild brands.

Lyric Doubleneck Lap Steel

Ca.1951-1958. Model G-1745-D-W, 8 strings per neck, hardwood body, 3 legs included.

1951-1958		$900	$1,100

Maestro Tripleneck Steel

Ca.1951-1958. Model G-2495-W-W, maple and walnut, 8 strings per neck, legs.

1951-1958		$1,000	$1,250

Pearloid (MOTS) Lap Steel

1950s. These were often sold with a matching amp; price here is for lap steel only.

1950s	Common	$225	$275
1950s	Less common	$375	$450

Pearloid Steel Guitar

1950s. Six-string non-pedal steel, 3 legs, 2 knobs, 8 push buttons, star position markers, pearloid cover, Magnatone script logo at lower end of fretboard.

1950s		$450	$575

Marvel

1950-mid 1960s. Budget brand marketed by the Peter Sorkin Company of New York.

Electric Hawaiian Lap Steel

1950s		$150	$200

Mastertone

Late 1920s-early 1940s. Mastertone was a budget brand made by Gibson and was used on lap steel, Hawaiian and archtop guitars.

Special Lap Steel

1940s	Brown crinkle	$500	$600

May Bell

See listing under Slingerland.

McKinney

1950s. Private branded for McKinney Guitars by Supro, blue McKinney Guitar logo on headstock.

Lap Steel

1950s. Similar to Supro Comet.

1950s	White pearloid	$300	$375

Melobar

1967-present. Designed by Walt Smith, of Smith Family Music, Melobar instruments feature a guitar body with a tilted neck, allowing the guitarist to play lap steel standing up. The instrument was developed and first made in Ed and Rudy Dopyera's Dobro factory. Most were available in 6-, 8-, or 10-string versions. Ted Smith took over operations from his father. Ted retired in late 2002. Production ceased in '06, pending a sale of the company, but resumed in '07 under new owners Jim and Carrie Frost.

6-String Electric Steel

1990s. Solidbody cutaway body shape, portable Melobar-style.

1990s		$600	$700

10-String Electric Steel

1970s. Double-cut guitar-shaped body, portable Melobar-style. Similar model currently offered as the Skreemr.

1970s		$600	$750

Skreemr Electric Steel

Early 1990s-2006. The classic Melobar in a V (Skreemr SK2000) or double-cut (Skreemr) version, available in 6-, 8- and 10-string versions.

1990s-2006		$600	$750

V-10 Power-Slide Guitar

1982-early 1990s. Solidbody, V-shaped body, tilted neck, 10 strings (6- or 8-string models were available). Similar model now called the Skreemr SK2000.

1982-1990s		$650	$800

X-10 Power-Slide Guitar

1981-early 1990s. Solidbody, futuristic body shape, tilted neck, 10 strings (6- or 8-string models were available). Called the Power-Slide One in early literature.

1981-1990s		$650	$800

MSA

1963-1983, 2001-present. Professional and premium grade, production/custom, pedal and lap steel guitars built in Dallas, Texas by Maurice Anderson. The company was dissolved in '83, and reorganized in '01.

National

Ca. 1927-present. Founded in Los Angeles as the National String Instrument Corporation in '27, the brand has gone through many ownership changes over the years. National offered lap steels from '35 to '68.

Chicagoan Lap Steel

1948-1961. Gray pearloid, metal hand rest.

1948-1961		$325	$375

Console (Dual 8) Steel

1939-1942. Two 8-string necks, parallelogram markers, black top with white sides.

1939-1942		$750	$950

Dynamic Lap Steel

1941-1968. New Yorker-style body, 6 strings, 3 detachable screw-in legs added by '56.

1941-1965	Lap	$375	$475
1956-1968	With legs	$475	$600

Electric Hawaiian Lap Steel

1935-1937. Cast aluminum round body, 1 pickup, square neck, 6 or 7 strings.

1935-1937		$600	$700

Grand Console Steel

1947-1968. 2 or 3 8-string necks, Totem Pole 'board markers, black and white, came with or without legs, National's answer to Fender Stringmaster Series.

1947-1959	Double neck	$750	$900
1947-1959	Triple neck	$900	$1,100
1960-1968	Double neck	$700	$850

STEELS & LAPS

MODEL YEAR	FEATURES	EXC. COND. LOW	HIGH

New Yorker Lap Steel

1939-1967. Introduced as Electric Hawaiian model in '35, square end body with stair-step sides, 7 or 8 strings, black and white finish.

1939-1949		$800	$1,000
1950-1959		$700	$850
1960-1967		$600	$700

Princess Lap Steel

1942-1947. Strings-thru-pickup, parallelogram markers, white pearloid.

1942-1947		$300	$375

Rocket One Ten Lap Steel

1955-1958. Rocket-shaped, black and white finish.

1955-1958		$300	$375

Studio 76 N476 Lap Steel

1964. Easy to recognize half and half stair-step design on fretboard, 3-on-a-side tuners with open-book shaped headstock, 1 pickup, 2 control knobs, onyx black pearloid body with soft shoulders.

1964		$350	$425

Trailblazer Steel

1948-1950. Square end, numbered markers, black.

1948-1950		$300	$375

Triplex 1088 Chord Changer Lap Steel

1944-1958. Maple and walnut body, 2 knobs, natural.

1944-1958		$375	$450

Nioma

Regal and others (maybe Dickerson?) made instruments for this brand, most likely for a guitar studio or distributor.

Lap Steel

1930s	Pearloid	$200	$250

Oahu

1926-1985. The Oahu Publishing Company and Honolulu Conservatory, based in Cleveland, published a very popular guitar study course. They sold instruments to go with the lessons, starting with acoustic Hawaiian and Spanish guitars, selling large quantities in the '30s. As electric models became popular, Oahu responded with guitar-amp sets. Lap steel and matching amp sets were generally the same color; for example, yellow guitar and yellow amp, or white pearloid guitar and white amp. These sets were originally sold to students who would take private or group lessons. The instruments were made by Oahu, Valco, Harmony, Dickerson, and Rickenbacker and were offered into the '50s and '60s.

Dianna Lap Steel

1950s. Oahu and Diana logos on headstock, Oahu logo on fretboard, fancy bridge, pleasant unusual sunburst finish.

1950s		$350	$400

Hawaiiian Lap Steel

1930s	Sunburst, student-grade	$225	$300
1930s	Tonemaster with decal art	$250	$325
1930s-40s	Rare style, higher-end	$500	$600
1930s-40s	Rare style, student-grade	$225	$300
1940s	Pearloid, Supro-made	$225	$300
1950s	Pearloid or painted	$225	$300
1950s	Tonemaster	$225	$300

Iolana

1950-1951, Late-1950s. Gold hardware, 2 6-string necks. Early model is lap steel, later version a console.

1950-1951	Lap	$450	$550
1950s	Console	$675	$825

K-71 Acoustic Lap Steel

1930s. Flat top, round sound hole, decals on lower bouts.

1930s		$325	$400

Lap Steel/Amp Set

See also Lap Steel Oahu Amp listing in the Guide's amp section.

1930s-40s	Sunburst, mahogany	$400	$475

Triplex 1088 Chord Changer Lap Steel

1948. Oahu-branded National 6-string lap steel guitar with "tuning change mechanism", Oahu logo on peghead.

1948		$400	$500

Ormston

1966-1968. Pedal steels built in England by Denley and marketed by James Ormston Burns between his stints with Burns London, which was bought by America's Baldwin Company in '65, and the Dallas Arbiter Hayman brand.

Premier

Ca.1938-ca.1975, 1990s-present. Premier made a variety of instruments, including lap steels, under several brands.

Recording King

Ca. 1930-1943. Brand used by Montgomery Ward for instruments made by Gibson, Regal, Kay, and Gretsch.

Electric Hawaiian Lap Steel

1930s		$400	$450

Roy Smeck Model AB104 Steel

1938-1941. Pear-shaped body, 1 pickup.

1938-1941		$500	$600

Regal

Ca. 1884-1954. Regal offered their own brand and made instruments for distributors and mass-merchandisers. The company sold out to Harmony in '54.

Electric Hawaiian Lap Steel

1940s		$175	$225

Octophone Steel

1930s		$350	$400

Reso-phonic Steel

1930s. Dobro-style resonator and spider assembly, round neck, adjustable nut.

1930s		$750	$850

1950s National Reso-Phonic 1133

Recording King Roy Smeck

STEELS & LAPS

Rickenbacker Seven-String

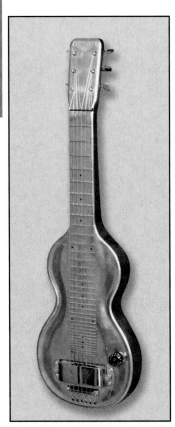

*Ca. 1938 Rickenbacker 100/NS
Silver Hawaiian*

MODEL		EXC. COND.	
YEAR	FEATURES	LOW	HIGH

Rickenbacker
1931-present. Rickenbacker produced steels from '32 to '70.

Acadamy Lap Steel
1946-1947. Bakelite student model, horseshoe pickup, replaced by the Ace.

1946-1947		$375	$450

Ace Lap Steel
1948-1953. Bakelite body, 1 pickup.

1948-1953		$375	$450

Console 518 Triple Neck Steel
1955-1970. 22.5" scale, 3 8-string necks.

1955-1970		$1,600	$2,100

Console 758 Triple Neck Steel
1957-1970. 25" scale, 3 8-string necks.

1957-1970		$1,600	$2,100

CW Steel
1957-1970. Single neck on wood body, several neck options, 3 attachable legs.

1957-1970		$700	$800

DC-16 Steel
1950-1952. Metal, double 8-string necks.

1950-1952		$800	$1,000

Electro Lap Steel
1940s, 1960s. Large Rickenbacker logo and smaller Electro logo on headstock ('40s), then on side ('60s).

1940s		$1,000	$1,250
1960s	Electro logo side	$800	$1,000

Electro Doubleneck Steel
1940-1953. Two bakelite 8-string necks.

1940-1953		$1,200	$1,500

Electro Tripleneck Steel
1940-1953. Three bakelite 8-string necks.

1940-1953		$1,500	$1,800

Electro EH-3 Lap Steel
1970s. 6-string neck, legs.

1971		$500	$600

JB (Jerry Bird) Model Steel
1961-1970. Single neck on large wood body, 6-, 7-, 8-, or 10-string neck, 3 attachable legs, Jerry Bird Model logo on top plate.

1961-1970		$700	$825

Model 59 Lap Steel
1937-1943. Sheet steel body, baked-enamel light-colored crinkle finish, 1 pickup.

1937-1943		$600	$750

Model 100 Lap Steel
1956-1970. Wood body, 6 strings, block markers, light or silver gray finish.

1956-1970		$525	$650

Model 102 Lap Steel
1960s. Wood body, 6 strings, slot head, block markers, natural finish.

1960		$500	$600

Model A-22 Frying Pan Steel
1932-1936. Originally called the Electro-Hawaiian Guitar, small round body lap steel, offered as 6- or 7-string, 22.5" scale (the A-25 25" scale also available).

1932-1936		$3,000	$3,700

Model B Steel
1935-1955. Bakelite body and neck, 1 pickup, strings-thru-body, decorative metal plates, 6 or 8 strings, black.

1935-1955	6-string	$1,100	$1,300
1935-1955	8-string	$1,200	$1,400

Model B-10 Steel
1935-1955. Model B with slot head and 12 strings.

1935-1955		$1,000	$1,250

Model BD Steel
1949-1970. Bakelite body, 6 strings, deluxe version of Model B, black.

1949-1960		$700	$800

Model CW-6 Steel
1957-1961. Wood body, grille cloth on front, 6 strings, 3 legs, renamed JB (Jerry Byrd) model in '61.

1957-1961	Walnut	$700	$800

Model DW Steel
1955-1961. Wood body, double 6- or 8-string necks, optional 3 legs.

1955-1961		$900	$1,000

Model G Lap Steel
Ca.1948-1957. Chrome-plated ornate version of Silver Hawaiian, gold hardware and trim, 6 or 8 strings.

1948-1957		$700	$800

Model S/NS (New Style) Steel
1946-early-1950s. Sheet steel body, 1 pickup, gray, gray sparkle or grayburst, also available as a doubleneck.

1946-1949		$800	$900

Model SD Steel
1949-1953. Deluxe NS, sheet steel body, 6, 7 or 8 strings, Copper Crinkle finish.

1949-1953		$650	$750

Model SW
1956-1962. Straight body style, 6 or 8 strings, block markers, dark or blond finish.

1956-1962	8 strings	$1,000	$1,250
1956-1962	8 strings with legs	$1,400	$1,600

Silver Hawaiiian Lap Steel
1937-1943. Chrome-plated sheet steel body, 1 horseshoe pickup, 6 strings.

1937-1943		$1,200	$1,500

Rogue
2001-present. Budget grade, production, lap steels. They also offer guitars, basses, mandolins, banjos, and ukuleles.

Roland Ball
See Dickerson listing.

Serenader
Built by the Bud-Electro Manufacturing Company which was founded in Seattle, Washington in the late 1940s by Paul "Bud" Tutmarc, Jr., whose father built Audiovox instruments. He built mainly lap steels but also offered a solidbody bass.

MODEL		EXC. COND.	
YEAR	FEATURES	LOW	HIGH

Sherwood

Late 1940s-early 1950s. Lap steel guitars made for Montgomery Ward made by Chicago manufacturers such as Kay. They also had archtop guitars and amps under that brand.

Deluxe Lap Steel

1950s. Symmetrical body, bar pickup, volume and tone controls, wood body, sunburst, relatively ornate headstock with script Sherwood logo, vertical Deluxe logo, and lightning bolt art.

1950s		$150	$200

Sho-Bud

1956-1981. Founded by Shot Jackson in Nashville. Distributed by Gretsch. They also had guitar models. Baldwin bought the company and closed the factory in '81.

Crossover Twin Neck Steel

1967-1971. Sho-Bud Baldwin double neck, Sho-Bud logo.

1967-1971		$1,700	$2,100

Maverick Pedal Steel

Ca. 1970-1981. Beginner model, burl elm cover, 3 pedals.

1970-1981		$550	$650

Pro I

1970-1981. Three pedals, natural.

1970-1975	Round front	$1,500	$1,800
1976-1981	Square front	$1,600	$1,900

Pro II

1973-1981. Birdseye maple, double 10-string necks, natural.

1973-1975	Round front	$1,600	$1,900
1976-1981	Square front	$1,700	$2,000

Pro III

1975-1981. Metal necks.

1975	Round front	$1,700	$2,000
1976-1981	Square front	$1,800	$2,100

Super Pro

1977-1980. Doubleneck 10 strings, 8 floor pedals, 6 knee levers, Jet Black.

1977-1980		$2,100	$2,500

Sierra

1960-present. Originally designed and built by Chuck Wright in California and Oregon until '74, then by Don Christensen in Gresham and Portland, Oregon. In 2003, Ed W. Littlefield Jr. took ownership, with professional and premium grade, production, lap and pedal steel guitars built by luthers Tom Baker and Rob Girdis in Molalla, Oregon. Girdis died in '09. There is an unrelated Sierra brand of guitars.

Silvertone

1940-1970. Brand name for instruments sold by Sears.

Amp-In-Case Lap Steel

Early 1940s. Lap steel and amp set, amp cabinet doubles as lap case with the lap stored above the amp, amp is in a long vertical cabinet with brown tweed cover-

ing, manufacturer appears to be the same as used by Gibson in the late '30s, low to mid power, 1x10" speaker.

1941-1942		$650	$800

Six-String Lap Steel

1940s	Valco-made	$275	$350
1950s	Pearloid	$300	$400
1950s	Standard finish	$250	$325
1960s		$250	$325

Slingerland

1916-present. Offered by Slingerland Banjos and Drums. They also sold the May Bell brand. Instruments were made by others and sold by Slingerland in the '30s and '40s.

May Bell Lap Steel

1930s. Guitar-shaped lap steel with May Bell logo. This brand also had '30s Hawaiian and Spanish guitars.

1930s		$250	$300

Songster Lap Steel

1930s. Slingerland logo headstock, Songster logo near nut, guitar-shaped body, sunburst maple top, some with figured maple back, 1 pickup, 2 bakelite brown knobs, dot markers.

1930s		$750	$900

SPG

2006-2009. Intermediate grade, custom, solid-body lapsteels originally built by luthier Rick Welch in Farmingdale, Maine and Hanson, Massachusetts; more recently by luthier Eric C. Brown in Farmingdale, Maine.

Stella

Ca. 1899-1974, 2000s. Stella was a brand of the Oscar Schmidt Company. Harmony acquired the brand in '39. The Stella brand was reintroduced in the 2000s by MBT International.

Electric Hawaiian Lap Steel

1937		$550	$675

Supertone

1914-1941. Brand name for Sears which was replaced by Silvertone. Instruments made by Harmony and others.

Electric Hawaiian Lap Steel

1930s	Various models	$250	$300

Supro

1935-1968, 2004-present. Budget brand of the National Dobro Company. Amp builder Bruce Zinky revived the Supro name for a guitar and amp model.

Airline

1952-1962. Asymmetrical body with straight left side and contoured right (treble) side, black pearloid with small white pearloid on right (treble) side, 2 knobs, available with optional set of 3 legs, later versions available with 6 or 8 strings, described in catalog as "Supro's finest". Renamed Jet Airliner in '64.

1952-1962	6-string	$475	$600
1952-1962	8-string	$525	$625
1952-1962	With optional legs	$575	$700

Sierra SL-8

Silvertone

STEELS & LAPS

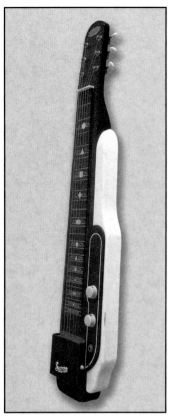

1960s Supro Comet
(Marco Parmiggiani)

Ca. 1960s Teisco Model R
George Lee

MODEL YEAR	FEATURES	EXC. COND. LOW	HIGH
Clipper Lap Steel			
1941-1943. One pickup, bound rosewood 'board, dot inlay, brown pearloid.			
1941-1943		$325	$400
Comet Lap Steel			
1947-1966. One pickup, attached cord, painted-on 'board, pearloid.			
1947-1949	Gray pearloid	$375	$450
1950-1966	White pearloid	$375	$450
Comet Steel (With Legs)			
1950s-1960s. Three-leg 6-string steel version of the lap steel, 2 knobs, Supro logo on cover plate, 1 pickup.			
1960s	Black & white	$475	$600
Console 8 Steel			
1958-1960. Eight strings, 3 legs, black and white.			
1958-1960		$500	$625
Irene Lap Steel			
1940s. Complete ivory pearloid cover including headstock, fretboard and body, Roman numeral markers, 1 pickup, 2 control knobs, hard-wired output cord.			
1940s		$350	$450
Jet Airliner			
1964-1968. Renamed from Airline, described in catalog as "Supro's finest", 1 pickup, totem pole markings, 6 or 8 strings, pearloid, National-made.			
1964-1968	6-string	$475	$600
1964-1968	8-string	$525	$625
1964-1968	With optional legs	$575	$700
Professional Steel			
1950s. Light brown pearloid.			
1950s		$325	$400
Special Steel			
1955-1962. Pearloid lap steel, student model, large script Special logo near pickup on early models, red until '57, white after.			
1955-1957	Red pearloid	$275	$325
1957-1962	White pearloid	$275	$325

MODEL YEAR	FEATURES	EXC. COND. LOW	HIGH
Spectator Steel			
1952-1954. Wood body, 1 pickup, painted-on 'board, natural.			
1952-1954		$200	$250
Student De Luxe Lap Steel			
1952-1955. One pickup, pearloid, large script Student De Luxe logo located near pickup, replaced by Special in '55.			
1952-1955	Black & white, or red pearloid	$300	$350
1952-1955	Natural or white paint	$250	$300
Studio			
1955-1964. Symmetrical body, 2 knobs, priced in original catalog below the Comet, but above the Special, issued in '55 with blue plastic covered body.			
1955-1964		$300	$375
Supreme Lap Steel			
1947-1960. One pickup, painted-on 'board, brown pearloid until ca.'55, then red until ca.'58, Tulip Yellow after that.			
1947-1960		$400	$500
Supro 60 Lap Steel and Amp-in-Case			
Late 1930s-early '40s. Supro 60 logo near the single volume knob, long horizontal guitar case which houses a small tube amp and speaker, the case cover folds out to allow ventilation for the tubes, white pearloid, black amp case, the amp was made by National Dobro of Chicago.			
1939-1941		$550	$700
Twin Lap Steel			
1948-1955. Two 6-string necks, pearloid covering, renamed Console Steel in '55.			
1948-1955		$550	$700

STEELS & LAPS

MODEL YEAR	FEATURES	EXC. COND. LOW	HIGH

Teisco

1946-1974. The Japanese guitar-maker offered many steel models from '55 to around '67. Models offered '55-'61: EG-7L, -K, -R, -NT, -Z, -A, -S, -P, -8L, -NW, and -M. During '61-'67: EG-TW, -O, -U, -L, -6N, -8N, -DB, -DB2, -DT, H-39, H-905, TRH-1, Harp-8 and H-850.

Hawaiian Lap Steel

1955-1967		$225	$275

Timtone Custom Guitars

1993-2006. Luthier Tim Diebert built his professional grade, custom, lap steel guitars in Grand Forks, British Columbia. He also built guitars and basses.

True Tone

1960s. Brand name sold by Western Auto (hey, everybody was in the guitar biz back then). Probably made by Kay or Harmony.

Lap Steel

1960s. Guitar-shaped, single-cut, 1 pickup.

1960s		$225	$275

Varsity

See Dickerson listing.

Vega

1880s-present. The original Boston-based company was purchased by C.F. Martin in '70. In '80, the Vega trademark was sold to a Korean company. The company was one of the first to enter the electric market by offering products in '36 and offered lap steels into the early '60s. The Deering Banjo Company acquired the brand in '89 and uses it on a line of banjos.

DG-DB Steel

1950s. Two necks, 8 strings.

1950s		$575	$700

Odell Lap Steel

1950s. White pearloid.

1950s		$300	$375

Other Lap Steels

1930s		$300	$375
1940s	Art deco-style	$375	$450

Wabash

1950s. Lap steels distributed by the David Wexler company and made by others. They also offered guitars and amps.

Lap Steel (Hawaiian Scene Tailpiece)

1950s. Natural, 12 frets.

1950s		$225	$275

Wayne

1998-present. Luthiers Wayne and Michael Charvel, of Paradise, California, added intermediate grade, production, lap steel guitars to their line in '04. They also build guitars.

White

1955-1960. The White brand, named after plant manager Forrest White, was established by Fender to provide steel and small amp sets to teaching studios that were not Fender-authorized dealers. A standard guitar was planned, but never produced.

6-String Steel

1955-1956. White finish, block markers, 2 knobs, 3 legs. The 6 String Steel was usually sold with the matching white amp Model 80. Possibly only 1 batch of these was made by Fender in October/November '55.

1955-1956		$800	$1,000

Matching Steel and Amp Set

1955-1956		$1,600	$2,000

1930s Vega Lap Steel

Wayne Lap Steel

STEELS & LAPS

MANDOLINS

Applause MAE148

MODEL YEAR	FEATURES	EXC. COND. LOW	HIGH

Airline

Ca. 1958-1968. Brand for Montgomery Ward. Instruments were built by Kay, Harmony and Valco.

Electric Mandolin (Kay K390)

Early-1960s. In '62 the K390 was advertised as the Kay Professional Electric Mandolin. Venetian shape with sunburst spruce top, curly maple back and sides, tube-style pickup, white 'guard, rope-style celluloid binding.

1962		$375	$450

Mandolin (Lower-End)

1960s. Acoustic, plainer features.

1960s		$200	$250

Allen

1982-present. Premium grade, production resonators, steel-string flat-tops, and mandolins built by Luthier Randy Allen, Colfax, California.

Alvarez

C.1966-present. An import brand for St. Louis Music, Alvarez currently offers intermediate grade, production, mandolins. They also offer guitars, lap steels and banjos.

Model A Mandolin

Classic F-style mandolin features, round soundhole or f-holes. Models include the A700 and A910.

1970s		$400	$500

American Conservatory (Lyon & Healy)

Late-1800s-early-1900s. Mainly catalog sales of guitars and mandolins from the Chicago maker. Marketed as a less expensive alternative to the Lyon & Healy Washburn product line.

Arched Back Mandolin

1910s. Flat back with a mild arch, standard appointments, nothing fancy.

1910s		$325	$400

Bowl Back Mandolin

1917. Bowl back style, 14 ribs, Brazilian.

1917		$225	$275

Bowl Back Mandolin Style G2603

Early-1900s. Bowl back-style, 28 rosewood ribs (generally more ribs and use of rosewood ribs versus mahogany indicates higher quality), color corded soundhole and edge inlay, inlaid tortoise shell celluloid guard plate underneath strings and below the soundhole, bent top, butterfly headstock inlay.

1917		$400	$500

Bowl Back Mandolin Style G2604

Early-1900s. Bowl back-style, 42 rosewood ribs (generally more ribs indicated higher quality), extra fancy color corded soundhole and edge inlay around, extra fancy inlaid tortoise shell celluloid guard plate underneath strings and below the soundhole, bent top, butterfly headstock inlay.

1917		$500	$600

Alvarez A100

Andersen Stringed Instruments

1978-present. Luthier Steve Andersen builds his premium grade, production/custom mandolins in Seattle, Washington. He also builds guitars.

Andy Powers Musical Instrument Co.

1996-present. Luthier Andy Powers, builds his premium grade, custom, mandolins in Oceanside, California. He also builds guitars and ukes.

Apitius

1976-present. Luthier Oliver Apitius builds his premium and presentation grade, production/custom, mandolins in Shelburne, Ontario.

Applause

1994-present. Applause currently offers intermediate grade, production, mandolins. Kaman Music's entry-level Ovation-styled import brand added mandolins in '94.

Mandolin

1990s		$175	$200

Aria/Aria Pro II

1960-present. Intermediate grade, production, acoustic and electric mandolins from Aria/Aria Pro II, which added Japanese and Korean mandolins to their line in '76.

AM200 Mandolin

1994-present. Pear-shaped A body, plywood.

1994-2010		$150	$200

AM400 Mandolin

1994-present. F-style, plywood.

1994-2010		$250	$300

AM600 Mandolin

1994-2008. F-style, solid wood.

1994-2008		$300	$350

PM750 Mandolin

1976-ca. 1982. F-style Loar copy, maple plywood body, sunburst.

1976-1982		$400	$450

Armstrong, Rob

1971-present. Custom mandolins made in Coventry, England, by luthier Rob Armstrong. He also builds basses, flat-tops, and parlor guitars.

Atkin Guitars

1993-present. Luthier Alister Atkin builds his production/custom mandolins in Canterbury, England. He also builds flat-top guitars.

Austin

1999-present. Budget and intermediate grade, production, mandolins imported by St. Louis Music. They also offer guitars, basses, amps, ukes and banjos.

MANDOLINS

MODEL		EXC. COND.	
YEAR	FEATURES	LOW	HIGH

Bacon & Day

Established in 1921 by David Day and Paul Bacon, primarily known for fine quality tenor and plectrum banjos in the '20s and '30s.

Mandolin Banjo Orchestra
1920s. Mandolin neck and banjo body with open back, headstock with Bacon logo.

1920s		$350	$400

Senorita Banjo Mandolin

1930s		$700	$850

Silverbell #1 Banjo Mandolin
1920s. Fancy appointments, closed-back resonator.

1920s		$900	$1,100

Bauer (George)

1894-1911. Luthier George Bauer built guitars and mandolins in Philadelphia, Pennsylvania. He also built instruments with Samuel S. Stewart (S.S. Stewart).

Acme Professional Bowl Mandolin
1890s. Bowl back, 29 ribs, Brazilian.

1890s	Fancy	$475	$600
1890s	Mid-level	$275	$350
1890s	Plain	$200	$250

Beltona

1990-present. Production metal body resonator mandolins made in New Zealand by Steve Evans and Bill Johnson. They also build guitars and ukes.

Beltone

1920s-1930s. Acoustic and resonator mandolins and banjo-mandolins made by others for New York City distributor Perlberg & Halpin. Martin did make a small number of instruments for Beltone, but most were student-grade models most likely made by one of the big Chicago builders. They also made guitars.

Resonator Mandolin
1930s. F-hole top, banjo-style resonator back.

1930s		$300	$375

Bertoncini Stringed Instruments

1995-present. Luthier Dave Bertoncini mainly builds flat-top guitars in Olympia, Washington, but has also built mandolins.

Bigsby

Ca. 1947-present. Guitar builder Paul Arthur Bigsby also built 6 electric mandolins.

Blindworm Guitars

2008-present. Premium and presentation grade, production/custom, acoustic and electric mandolins built in Colorado Springs, Colorado by luthiers Andrew J. Scott and Steven Sells. They also build guitars and basses.

Blue Star

1984-present. Luthier Bruce Herron builds his intermediate grade, production/custom, electric solidbody mandolins in Fennville, Michigan. He also builds guitars, lap steels, dulcimers, and ukes.

Bohmann

1878-ca.1926. Established by Czechoslavakian-born Joseph Bohmann in Chicago, Illinois.

Fancy Bowl Mandolin
1890-1900. Spruce top, marquetry trimmed, inlay, pearl.

1890-1900	Fancy	$1,200	$1,500
1890-1900	Mid-level	$450	$550
1890-1900	Plain	$300	$400

Brandt

Early 1900s. John Brandt started making mandolin-family instruments in Chicago, Illinois around 1898.

Mandola
1900s. Spruce top, rosewood body, scroll headstock, pearl and abalone fretboard binding.

1900		$1,075	$1,300

Presentation Mandolin
1900s. Spruce top, tortoise shell-bound.

1900s		$775	$950

Breedlove

1990-present. Founded by Larry Breedlove and Steve Henderson. Professional and premium grade, production/custom, mandolins made in Tumalo, Oregon. They also produce guitars, basses, laps and ukes. In 2010 they were acquired by Bedell Guitars.

Alpine Master Class Mandolin
2000s. O-style body, spruce/maple.

2000s		$1,775	$2,200

K-5 Mandolin
1990s. Asymmetric carved top, maple body.

1990s		$1,500	$1,800

Olympic Mandolin
1990s. Solid spruce top, teardrop-shaped, oval soundhole, highly flamed maple back, sunburst.

1990s		$1,150	$1,425

Quartz OF/OO Mandolin
2000s. Basic A-style body with f-holes.

2000s		$825	$975

Brian Moore

1992-present. Brian Moore offers premium grade, production/custom, semi-hollow electric mandolins. They also build guitars and basses.

Bruno and Sons

1834-present. Established in 1834 by Charles Bruno, primarily as a distributor, Bruno and Sons marketed a variety of brands, including their own. In the '60s or '70s, a Japanese-made solidbody electric mandolin was sold under the Bruno name.

Banjo Mandolin
1920s. Open back, 10" model.

1920s		$275	$325

Beltona Koru

Bertoncini F5M

MANDOLINS

Dean Bluegrass F-Style

Dudenbostel A5a

MODEL YEAR	FEATURES	EXC. COND. LOW	HIGH

Bowl Back Mandolin
1890s-1920s. Brazilian rosewood, spruce, rosewood ribs.

| 1920s | | $275 | $325 |

Calace
1825-present. Nicola Calace started The Calace Liuteria lute-making workshop in 1825 on the island of Procida, which is near Naples. The business is now in Naples and still in the family.

Lyre/Harp-Style Mandolin
Late-1800s-early-1900s. Lyre/harp-style, 8 strings, round soundhole, slightly bent top. Condition is important for these older instruments and the price noted is for a fully functional, original or pro-restored example.

| 1900 | | $1,100 | $1,350 |

Carvin
1946-present. Carvin offered solidbody electric mandolins from around '56 to the late '60s, when they switched to a traditional pear-shaped electric/acoustic.

MB Mandolin
1956-1968. Solidbody, 1 pickup, single-cut Les Paul shape until '64, double-cut Jazzmaster/Strat shape after. Models include the #1-MB and the #2-MB, with different pickups.

| 1950s | | $800 | $1,000 |

Clifford
Clifford mandolins were manufactured by Kansas City, Missouri instrument wholesalers J.W. Jenkins & Sons. First introduced in 1895, the brand also offered guitars.

Collings
1986-present. Professional and premium grade, production/custom, mandolins built in Austin, Texas. Collings added mandolins to their line in '99. They also build guitars and ukuleles.

MF Mandolin
1999-present. F-style, carved top and back.

| 1999-2010 | | $2,900 | $3,500 |

MF-5 Deluxe Mandolin
2005. Limited production, varnish finish, hand engraved nickel tailpiece unique to each instrument.

| 2005 | | $11,500 | $14,000 |

MF-5V Mandolin
2007. Carved Adirondack spruce top, highly flamed maple body.

| 2007 | | $6,000 | $7,000 |

MT Mandolin
1999-present. A-style, 2 f-holes, carved top and back, matte finish, tortoise-bound top.

| 1999-2010 | | $1,700 | $1,925 |

MT-2 Mandolin
1999-present. MT with high gloss finish, ivoroid body, neck and headstock binding.

| 1999-2010 | | $2,200 | $2,500 |

MT-2V Mandolin
Like MT-2, but with oil-based varnish finish and ivoroid-bound ebony 'guard.

| 2008-2010 | | $3,000 | $3,500 |

Comins
1992-present. Luthier Bill Comins builds premium and presentation grade, custom mandolins in Willow Grove, Pennsylvania. He also builds guitars and offers an amp.

Conrad
Ca. 1968-1977. Imported from Japan by David Wexler and Company, Chicago, Illinois. Mid- to better-quality copy guitars, mandolins and banjos.

Crafter
1986-present. Korea-based Crafter builds intermediate grade, production, mandolins. They also build guitars and basses.

Crestwood
1970s. Copy models imported by La Playa Distributing Company of Detroit.

Mandolin
1970s. Includes models 3039 (electric A-style), 3041 (bowl back-style, flower 'guard), 3043 (bowl back-style, plain 'guard), 71820 (A-style), and 71821 (F-style).

| 1970s | | $150 | $175 |

Cromwell
1935-1939. Private branded instruments made by Gibson at their Parsons Street factory in Kalamazoo, Michigan. Distributed by a variety of mail order companies such as Continental, Grossman, and Richter & Phillips.

GM-2 Mandolin
1935-1939. Spruce top, mahogany back and sides, similar to KM-11.

| 1935-1939 | | $500 | $600 |

GM-4 Mandolin
1935-1939. Style A, f-holes, solid wood arched top, mahogany back and sides, block capital letter Cromwell headstock logo, dot markers, elevated 'guard, sunburst.

| 1935-1939 | | $600 | $800 |

Dan Kellaway
1976-present. Luthier Dan Kellaway builds his production/custom, premium grade, mandolins in Singleton NSW, Australia. He also builds guitars.

D'Angelico
1932-1964. Handcrafted by John D'Angelico. Models include Excel, Teardrop, and Scroll. Appointments can vary from standard to higher-end so each mandolin should be evaluated on a case-by-case basis.

Mandolin
1932-1949. Various models and appointments.

| 1932-1949 High-end appointments | | $17,000 | $20,000 |

MODEL YEAR	FEATURES	EXC. COND. LOW	HIGH
1932-1949	Plain styling, lower range	$2,600	$3,200
1932-1949	Plain, non-elevated pickguard	$10,000	$12,500

D'Aquisto

1965-1995. James D'Aquisto apprenticed under D'Angelico. He started his own production in '65.

Mandolin

1970s. Various models and appointments.

1970s	Only 3 made	$23,000	$28,000

Dean

1976-present. Intermediate grade, production, acoustic and acoustic/electric mandolins made overseas. They also offer guitars, banjos, basses, and amps.

Dearstone

1993-present. Luthier Ray Dearstone builds his professional and premium grade, custom, mandolin-family instruments in Blountville, Tennessee. He also builds guitars and violins.

DeCava Guitars

1983-present. Premium grade, production/custom, mandolins built by luthier Jim DeCava in Stratford, Connecticut. He also builds guitars, ukes, and banjos.

DeGennaro

2003-present. Professional and premium grade, custom/production, acoustic and electric mandolins built by luthier William DeGennaro in Grand Rapids, Michigan. He also builds guitars and basses.

Delgado

1928-present. Luthier Manuel A. Delgado builds premium grade, custom, classical mandolins in Nashville, Tennessee. He also builds guitars, basses, ukuleles and banjos.

DeLucia, Vincenzo

1910s-1920s. Luthier Vincenzo DeLucia built mandolins in Philadelphia, Pennsylvania.

Mandolin

Early-1900s. High quality material, rosewood body, fine ornamentation.

1910s		$900	$1,100

Dennis Hill Guitars

1991-present. Premium grade, production/custom, mandolins built by luthier Dennis Hill in Panama City, Florida. He has also built dulcimers, guitars, and violins.

Ditson

Mandolins made for the Oliver Ditson Company of Boston, an instrument dealer and music publisher. Turn of the century and early-1900s models were bowl back-style with the Ditson label. The '20s Ditson Style A flat back mandolins were made by

Martin. Models were also made by Lyon & Healy of Boston, often with a Ditson Empire label.

Mandola

1920. Bowl back.

1920		$875	$1,050

Style A Mandolin

1920s. Style A flat back made by Martin, mahogany sides and back, plain ornamentation.

1920s		$750	$925

Victory Mandolin

1890s. Brazilian rib bowl back with fancy inlays.

1890s		$650	$800

Dobro

1929-1942, 1954-present. Dobro offered mandolins throughout their early era and from the '60s to the mid-'90s.

Mandolin

1930s-1960s. Resonator on wood body.

1930s		$800	$1,000
1940s		$800	$1,000
1960s		$800	$1,000

Dudenbostel

1989-present. Luthier Lynn Dudenbostel builds his limited production, premium and presentation grade, custom, mandolins in Knoxville, Tennessee. He started with guitars and added mandolins in '96.

F-5 Mandolin

1996-2005. Loar-style, about 30 made.

1996-2005		$20,000	$25,000

Duff Mandolins and Guitars

1980s-present. Handcrafted by luthier Paul Duff in Palmyra, Western Australia.

F-5 (Loar) Mandolin

1999	Adirondack	$5,000	$6,000

Dyer

1902-1939. House brand for the W. J. Dyer store in St. Paul, Minnesota. The Larson brothers of Chicago built mandolin family instruments for the store from around 1906 to 1920. Other companies also built instruments for them.

Eastman

1992-present. Intermediate and professional grade, production, mandolins built in China. Eastman added mandolins in '04. They also build guitars, violins, and cellos.

Eastwood

1997-present. Intermediate grade, production, solidbody electric mandolins. They also offer basses and guitars.

EKO

1961-1985, 2000-present. The Italian-made EKOs were imported by LoDuca Brothers of Milwaukee. The brand was revived around 2000, but does not currently include mandolins.

Eastman 915

Eastwood Mandocaster

MANDOLINS

1967 Fender Electric Mandolin

Fender Octave FMO-66

MODEL YEAR	FEATURES	EXC. COND. LOW	HIGH

Baritone Mandolin
1960s. Baritone mandolin with ornate inlays.

| 1960s | | $350 | $425 |

Octave Mandolin
1960s. Octave mandolin with ornate inlays.

| 1960s | | $350 | $425 |

Eleca
2004-present. Student/budget level, production, acoustic and electric mandolins, imported by Eleca International. They also offer guitars, amps and effects.

Epiphone
1928-present. Intermediate grade, production, acoustic mandolins. Epiphone has offered several mandolin-family models over the years. Those from the '30s to the '60s were U.S.-made, the later models imported.

Adelphi Mandolin
1932-1948. A-style body, maple back and sides, f-holes, single-bound top and back.

| 1945-1946 | | $1,100 | $1,300 |

Mandobird VIII Mandolin
2004-present. Reverse Firebird-style body with mandolin neck, electric, various colors.

| 2004-2010 | | $120 | $130 |

MM50 Mandolin
1998-present. Import F-style with The Epiphone logo.

| 1998-2010 | | $400 | $450 |

Strand Mandolin
1932-1958. Walnut back and sides, f-holes, multi-bound, sunburst.

| 1944-1947 | | $900 | $1,100 |

Venetian Electric Mandolin
1961-1970. Gibson-made, pear-shaped body, 4 pole P-90 'dog-ear' mounted pickup, volume and tone knobs, dot markers, sunburst finish.

| 1961-1964 | | $1,400 | $1,750 |
| 1965-1970 | | $1,200 | $1,500 |

Zephyr Mandolin
1939-1958. A-style, electric, f-holes, maple body, 1 pickup, slotted block inlay.

| 1950s | | $525 | $650 |

Esquire
1930s. Student level instruments with painted Esquire logo and painted wood grain.

Mandolin
1930s. Laminate A-style wood body, sunburst.

| 1930s | | $225 | $275 |

Euphonon
1930-1944. Euphonon was a brand of the Larson Brothers of Chicago, introduced so Larson could compete in the guitar market with the new larger body 14-fret guitar models. Production also included mandolins, and most models were A-style, with teardrop body and flat backs.

Everett Guitars
1977-present. Luthier Kent Everett, of Atlanta, Georgia, mainly builds guitars, but has also built mandolins.

Evergreen Mountain
1971-present. Professional grade, custom, mandolins built by luthier Jerry Nolte in Cove, Oregon. He also builds guitars and basses.

Fairbanks
1875-1904. Primarily known for banjos, Fairbanks also offered mandolins.

Fairbuilt Guitar Co.
2000-present. Professional grade, custom/production, mandolins built by luthiers Martin Fair and Stuart Orser in Loudoun County, Virginia. They also build guitars and banjos.

Falk
1989-present. Luthier Dave Falk builds professional and premium grade, production/custom mandolins, in Amarillo, Texas. He also builds guitars and dulcimers.

Fender
1946-present. Intermediate grade, production, acoustic and acoustic/electric mandolins. Fender also offered an electric mandolin for 20 years.

FM-62SCE
2001-2007. Solid top, double-cut body.

| 2001-2007 | | $400 | $500 |

Mandolin
1956-1976. Electric solidbody, often referred to as the Mandocaster by collectors.

1956-1957	Blond	$2,500	$3,100
1958-1959	Sunburst	$2,100	$2,600
1960-1961	Sunburst	$2,100	$2,600
1962-1963	Sunburst	$2,100	$2,600
1964-1965	Sunburst	$2,100	$2,600
1966-1970	Sunburst	$2,000	$2,500
1971-1976	Sunburst	$1,900	$2,300

Fine Resophonic
1988-present. Professional grade, production/custom, wood and metal-bodied resophonic mandolins built by luthiers Mike Lewis and Pierre Avocat in Vitry Sur Seine, France. They also build guitars and ukes.

Flatiron
1977-2003, 2006-present. Gibson purchased Flatiron in 1987. Production was in Bozeman, Montana until the end of '96, when Gibson closed the Flatiron mandolin workshop and moved mandolin assembly to Nashville, Tennessee. General production tapered off after the move and Flatirons were available on a special order basis for a time. Currently they offer intermediate grade, production mandolins.

MODEL YEAR	FEATURES	EXC. COND. LOW	HIGH

A-2 Mandolin
1977-1987 Early, no truss rod, f-holes $2,800 $3,200
A-5 Mandolin
Teardrop shape, f-holes, figured maple body and neck, carved spruce top, X-bracing, unbound ebony 'board, nickel hardware, fleur-de-lis headstock inlay.
1987-1994 Gibson Montana $1,500 $1,800
A-5 Artist Mandolin
A-5 with highly figured maple body and neck, bound ebony headstock, gold hardware, fern headstock inlay.
1996-2003 Gibson Montana $2,000 $2,400
A-5 1 Mandolin
Carved top and back, bound body, dot inlays, The Flatiron headstock inlay.
1983-1985 Pre-Gibson $2,700 $3,200
A-5 2 Mandolin
Carved top and back, bound body, neck, headstock and pickguard, dot inlays, modified fern headstock inlay.
1983-1985 Pre-Gibson $3,200 $4,000
A-5 Junior Mandolin
As A-5 but with tone bar bracing, mahogany neck, The Flatiron headstock inlay.
1996-2003 Gibson Montana $1,100 $1,350
Cadet Mandolin
1990s. Flat-top, teardrop body, spruce top, maple body, rosewood 'board, nickel hardware.
1990-1996 $550 $700
F-2 Mandolin
1977-1987 Early, no truss rod $5,000 $6,000
F-5 Mandolin
F-style body, f-holes, flamed maple body and neck, carved spruce top, tone bar bracing, bound ebony 'board and headstock, nickel hardware, flower pot headstock inlay, cherry finish.
1987-1990 Gibson Montana $2,800 $3,500
F-5 Artist Mandolin
F-5 but with X-braces, bound ebony 'board, gold hardware, fern headstock inlay, and sunburst.
1984-1985 Pre-Gibson $4,600 $5,400
1987-1990 Gibson Montana $3,700 $4,300
1994-1995 $3,600 $4,200
Festival A Mandolin
Like Performer A, but with cherry finish and no body binding.
1988-1995 $1,300 $1,600
Festival F Mandolin
Like Performer F, but with no headstock or back body binding.
1988-1995 $2,000 $2,500
Model 1 Mandolin
Oval shape, spruce top, maple body, rosewood 'board, walnut headstock veneer.
1977-1987 Pre-Gibson $550 $675
1988-1995 Gibson Montana $500 $625
Model 1 Mandola
Model 1 features.
1977-1987 Pre-Gibson $700 $900
1983-1995 Gibson Montana $500 $625

Model 2 Mandolin
Like Model 1, but with curly maple (MC) or birdseye maple (MB) back and sides, ebony 'board, rosewood headstock veneer.
1977-1987 Pre-Gibson $600 $700
1977-1995 Flamed koa back & sides $700 $800
1988-1995 Gibson Montana $500 $600
Model 2 Mandola
Model 2 features, birdseye maple (MB) or curly maple (MC) body.
1977-1987 Pre-Gibson $650 $750
1988-1995 Gibson Montana $700 $850
Model 3 Octave Mandolin
Model 2 features, birdseye maple (MB) or curly maple (MC) body.
1977-1987 Pre-Gibson $800 $1,000
1988-1995 Gibson Montana $700 $900
Performer A Mandolin
Teardrop body, tone bar braced, maple back & sides, mahogany neck, ebony board, decal headstock, nickel hardware, top binding, sunburst top.
1990-1995 $1,500 $1,800
Performer F Mandolin
F shape, tone bar braced, maple back & sides and neck, ebony board, fern/banner headstock inlay, nickel hardware, top and back of body and headstock bound, sunburst top.
1990-1995 $2,200 $2,700

Fletcher Brock Stringed Instruments
1992-present. Custom mandolin-family instruments made by luthier Fletcher Brock originally in Ketchum, Idaho, and currently in Seattle, Washington. He also builds guitars.

Framus
1946-1977, 1996-present. Founded in Erlangen, Germany by Fred Wilfer. In the '60s, Framus instruments were imported into the U.S. by Philadelphia Music Company. They offered acoustic and electric mandolins. The brand was revived in '96.
12-String Mandolin
1960s $325 $400

Freshwater
1992-present. Luthier Dave Freshwater and family build mandolin family instruments in Beauly, Inverness, Scotland. They also build bouzoukis, dulcimers and harps.
Mandolin/Mandolin Family
2000s. Lateral Freshwater logo on headstock.
2000s $250 $350

Furch
See listing for Stonebridge.

Fylde
1973-present. Luthier Roger Bucknall builds his intermediate and professional, production/custom

Fine Resophonic Mandolin

Fletcher Brock F5

MANDOLINS

1916 Gibson A

Tim Fleck

1914 Gibson A-1

mandolins and mandolas in Penrith, Cumbria, United Kingdom. He also builds guitars and basses, bouzoukis, and citterns.

G.L. Stiles

1960-1994. Built by Gilbert Lee Stiles in Florida. He also built acoustics, soldibodies, basses, steels, and banjos.

Galiano/A. Galiano

New Yorkers Antonio Cerrito and Raphael Ciani offered instruments built by them and others under the Galiano brand during the early 1900s.

Mandolin

Bowl back, some fancy appointments.

YEAR	FEATURES	LOW	HIGH
1920s		$325	$400

Galveston

Budget and intermediate grade, production, imported mandolins. They also offer basses and guitars.

Gaylord

1940s. Private brand made by Harmony, painted Gaylord logo on headstock.

Artistic A Mandolin

YEAR	FEATURES	LOW	HIGH
1940s	Painted logo	$150	$175

Giannini

1900-present. Acoustic mandolins built in Salto, SP, Brazil near Sao Paolo. They also build guitars, violas, and cavaquinhos.

Gibson

1890s (1902)-present. Orville Gibson created the violin-based mandolin body-style that replaced the bowl back-type. Currently Gibson offers professional, premium and presentation grade, production/custom, mandolins.

Special Designations:

Snakehead headstock: 1922-1927 with production possible for a few months plus or minus.

Lloyd Loar era: Mid-1922-late 1924 with production possible for a few months plus or minus.

A Mandolin (Orville Gibson)

MODEL YEAR	FEATURES	LOW	HIGH
1899	Orville label	$20,000	$24,000

A Mandolin

1902-1933. Oval soundhole, snakehead headstock '22-27, Loar era mid-'22-late-'24.

YEAR	FEATURES	LOW	HIGH
1902-1909	Orange	$1,200	$1,500
1910-1918	Orange	$1,600	$2,000
1918-1921	Brown	$1,600	$2,000
1922-1924	Loar era	$2,300	$2,800
1925-1933		$1,600	$2,100

A-0 Mandolin

1927-1933. Replaces A Jr., oval soundhole, dot inlay, brown finish.

YEAR	FEATURES	LOW	HIGH
1927-1933		$1,600	$2,000

A-00 Mandolin

1933-1943. Oval soundhole, dot inlay, carved bound top.

YEAR	FEATURES	LOW	HIGH
1933-1943	Sunburst	$1,600	$2,000

A-1 Mandolin

1902-1918, 1922-1927, 1933-1943. Snakehead headstock '23-'27.

MODEL YEAR	FEATURES	LOW	HIGH
1902-1909	Orange	$1,200	$1,500
1910-1918	Orange	$1,600	$2,000
1922-1924	Loar era	$3,200	$4,000
1925-1927	Black	$2,400	$3,000
1927	Not snaked	$2,100	$2,600
1927	Snaked	$2,300	$2,800
1932	Re-introduced, oval	$2,100	$2,600
1933-1943	Sunburst, f-holes	$1,450	$1,800

A-2/A-2Z Mandolin

1902-1908, 1918-1922. A-2Z '22-'27. Renamed A-2 '27-'28. Snakehead headstock '23-'27. Lloyd Loar era mid-'22-late-'24.

YEAR	FEATURES	LOW	HIGH
1902-1908	Orange	$1,600	$2,000
1918-1921	Brown	$1,700	$2,000
1922-1924	Loar Era	$3,300	$4,100
1923-1924	Loar era, extra binding	$5,000	$6,000
1925-1928		$2,500	$3,100

A-3 Mandolin

1902-1922. Oval soundhole, single-bound body, dot inlay.

YEAR	FEATURES	LOW	HIGH
1902-1917	Orange	$1,900	$2,300
1918-1922	Ivory	$2,100	$2,600

A-4 Mandolin

1902-1935. Oval soundhole, single-bound body, dot inlay, snakehead '23-'27.

YEAR	FEATURES	LOW	HIGH
1902-1917	Various colors	$2,100	$2,400
1918-1921	Dark mahogany	$2,400	$2,800
1922-1924	Loar era	$5,000	$6,000
1925-1935	Various colors	$2,700	$3,400

A-5 Mandolin

1957-1979. Oval soundhole, maple back and sides, dot inlay, scroll headstock, sunburst. Name now used on extended neck version.

YEAR	FEATURES	LOW	HIGH
1957-1964		$2,500	$3,000
1965-1969		$2,200	$2,700
1970-1979		$1,300	$1,600

A-5G Mandolin

1988-1996. Less ornate version of the A-5 L, abalone fleur-de-lis headstock inlay.

YEAR	FEATURES	LOW	HIGH
1988-1996		$1,600	$1,800

A-5L/A-5 Mandolin

1988-present. Extended neck, raised 'board, flowerpot headstock inlay, curly maple and spruce, sunburst, based on custom-made 1923 Loar A-5. L has been dropped from name.

YEAR	FEATURES	LOW	HIGH
1988-1999		$2,200	$2,500

A-9 Mandolin

2002-present. Spruce top, maple back and sides, black bound top, satin brown finish.

YEAR	FEATURES	LOW	HIGH
2002-2010		$1,000	$1,250

A-12 Mandolin

1970-1979. F-holes, long neck, dot inlay, fleur-de-lis inlay, sunburst.

YEAR	FEATURES	LOW	HIGH
1970-1979		$1,400	$1,700

MODEL YEAR	FEATURES	EXC. COND. LOW	HIGH

A-40 Mandolin
1948-1970. F-holes, bound top, dot inlay, natural or sunburst.

1948-1949		$1,100	$1,350
1950-1964		$1,000	$1,250
1965-1970		$900	$1,100

A-50 Mandolin
1933-1971. A-style oval bound body, f-holes, sunburst.

1933-1941	Larger 11.25" body	$1,500	$1,800
1942-1949	Smaller 10" body	$1,500	$1,800
1950-1959		$1,300	$1,500
1960-1965		$1,200	$1,400
1966-1971		$1,000	$1,200

A-75 Mandolin
1934-1936. F-holes, raised fingerboard, bound top and back.

1934-1936		$2,200	$2,700

A-C Century Mandolin
1935-1937. Flat back, bound body, oval soundhole, sunburst.

1935-1937		$2,800	$3,200

A-Junior Mandolin
1920-1927. The Junior was the entry level mandolin for Gibson, but like most entry level Gibsons (re: Les Paul Junior), they were an excellent product. Oval soundhole, dot markers, plain tuner buttons. Becomes A-0 in '27.

1920-1927	Sheraton Brown	$1,600	$2,000

AN-Custom (Army-Navy) Mandolin
Mid-1990s. Made in Bozeman, Montana, round teardrop shape, flat spruce top, flat maple back, maple rims, Gibson script logo on headstock.

1995		$1,200	$1,500

Army and Navy Special Style DY/Army-Navy Mandolin
1918-1922. Lower-end, flat top and back, round soundhole, no logo, round label with model name, brown stain. Reintroduced as Army-Navy (AN Custom) '88-'96.

1918-1922		$775	$950

Bill Monroe Model F Mandolin
1992-1995. Limited run of 200, sunburst.

1992-1995		$9,000	$11,000

C-1 Mandolin
1932. Flat top, mahogany back and sides, oval soundhole, natural, painted on 'guard, a '32 version of the Army and Navy Special. This model was private branded for Kel Kroydon in the early-'30s.

1932		$675	$825

D "The Alrite" Mandolin
1917. Lower-end model, round body style, round soundhole, The Alrite on inside label, fancy colored wood on top binding and around center hole.

1917		$1,000	$1,250

Doyle Lawson F Mandolin
2003-present. F-5 style, carved spruce top, figured maple sides and back, sunburst finish.

2003-2004		$4,800	$6,100

EM-100/EM-125 Mandolin
1938-1943. Initially called EM-100, renamed EM-125 in '41-'43. Style A (pear-shape) archtop body, 1 blade pickup, 2 knobs on either side of bridge, dot markers, tortoise 'guard, sunburst.

1938-1940	EM-100	$1,500	$1,900
1941-1943	EM-125	$1,400	$1,750

EM-150 Mandolin
1936-1971. Electric, A-00 body, 1 Charlie Christian pickup early on, 1 P-90 later, bound body, sunburst.

1936-1940	Charlie Christian pickup	$2,100	$2,600
1941-1949	Rectangular pickup	$1,400	$1,700
1949-1965	P-90 pickup	$1,400	$1,700
1966-1971	P-90 pickup	$1,300	$1,600

EM-200/Florentine Mandolin
1954-1971. Electric solidbody, 1 pickup, gold-plated hardware, 2 control knobs, dot markers, sunburst. Called the EM-200 in '60 and '61.

1954-1960	Florentine	$2,500	$3,000
1960-1961	Renamed EM-200	$2,400	$2,900
1962-1971	Renamed Florentine	$2,300	$2,800

F Mandolin
1900-1903. 1900 model has O.H. Gibson Kalamazoo label, 3-point unbound body, early Gibson F-style, historically important design, inlaid star and crescent headstock. 1903 model is 3-point F-style, bound top rope-style, fancy inlay below-the-string guard, inlaid star and crescent headstock, large dot markers, black finish. Early F-style mandolin ornamentation can vary and values will vary accordingly.

1900	1900, signed by Orville	$5,000	$30,000
1900	1900, unsigned	$5,000	$25,000
1901-1902		$3,000	$17,000
1903		$3,000	$14,000

F-2 Mandolin
1902-1934. Oval soundhole, pearl inlay, star and crescent inlay on peghead.

1902-1909	3-point	$3,700	$4,500
1910-1917	2-point	$3,300	$4,100
1918-1921	2-point	$4,200	$5,200
1922-1924	Loar era	$6,200	$7,500
1925-1934		$4,200	$5,200

F-3 Mandolin
1902-1908. Three-point body, oval soundhole, scroll peghead, pearl inlayed 'guard, limited production model, black top with red back and sides.

1902-1908		$4,100	$4,800

F-4 Mandolin
1902-1943. Oval soundhole, rope pattern binding, various colors.

1902-1909	3-point	$4,600	$5,600
1910-1917	2-point	$5,000	$6,000
1918-1921	2-point	$5,700	$7,000
1922-1924	Loar era	$8,500	$10,500
1925-1943		$5,700	$7,000

F-5 Mandolin
1922-1943; 1949-1980. F-holes, triple-bound body and 'guard. The '20s Lloyd Loar era F-5s are extremely valuable. Reintroduced in '49 with single-bound body, redesigned in '70. The Loar era F-5 market is very specialized to the point that individual

1936 Gibson A-75

Ca. 1910 Gibson F-4

MANDOLINS

*Gibson F-5 Master Model
(Distressed)*

Gibson F-5L

MANDOLINS

instrument valuations can vary based upon the actual sound of the particular instrument. Valuations should be considered on a case-by-case basis.

MODEL YEAR	FEATURES	EXC. COND. LOW	HIGH
1922	Loar no virzi	$170,000	$190,000
1923	Loar July 9, 1923 side bound	$180,000	$210,000
1923	Loar non-side bound	$170,000	$190,000
1924	Loar with virzi	$140,000	$170,000
1924	Loar Mar. 31 specific	$160,000	$190,000
1924	Loar no virzi	$140,000	$170,000
1924	Late-1924 (unsigned)	$115,000	$135,000
1925-1928	Fern, Master Model	$80,000	$85,000
1928-1929	Fern, not Master Model	$65,000	$75,000
1930-1931	Fern peghead inlay	$55,000	$60,000
1932-1935	Fern peghead inlay	$50,000	$55,000
1936-1940	Fern (limited production)	$35,000	$45,000
1940-1943	Fleur-de-lis peghead inlay	$30,000	$35,000
1949	Flower pot, mahogany neck	$12,000	$15,000
1950-1953	Flower pot, maple neck	$9,000	$10,500
1954	Flower pot peghead inlay	$8,500	$10,000
1955-1956	Flower pot peghead inlay	$8,000	$9,500
1957-1959	Flower pot peghead inlay	$6,500	$8,000
1960-1965		$5,500	$6,500
1966-1969	Sunburst	$4,700	$5,300
1970-1980	Sunburst	$3,200	$3,900

F-5 Custom Mandolin

1993		$7,000	$8,800

F-5 Master Model Mandolin

2003-present. F-holes, triple-bound body and guard, red spruce top, maple back and sides, flowerpot inlay.

2003-2004	Derrington signed	$9,500	$12,000
2003-2009	F-5 Distressed	$11,200	$14,000
2003-2010		$8,800	$11,000
2003-2010	Ricky Skaggs Distressed	$11,200	$14,000

F-5G/F-5G Deluxe Mandolin

1997-present. Two-point style F, Deluxe has a slightly wider neck profile.

1997-2009		$2,900	$3,400

F-5L Mandolin

1978-present. Reissue of Loar F-5, gold hardware, fern headstock inlay (flowerpot inlay with silver hardware also offered for '88-'91), sunburst.

1978-1984	Kalamazoo-made	$4,600	$5,200
1984-1999		$5,000	$6,200
2000-2010		$5,000	$6,200

F-5V Mandolin

1990s. Based on Lloyd Loar's original F-5s of 1922-24, varnish Cremona Brown sunburst finish.

1990s		$6,500	$7,700

F-5X Mandolin

1996. F-5 Fern model, X-braced.

1996		$4,500	$5,500

Bella Voce F-5 Mandolin

1989. Custom Shop master-built model, high-end materials and construction, engraved tailpiece with Bella Voce F-5, sunburst.

1989		$8,100	$9,700

Sam Bush Signature F-5 Mandolin

2000-present. Artist Series model, carved spruce top, gold hardware, built at Opry Mill plant in Nashville.

2000-2010		$5,300	$6,100

Wayne Benson Signature F-5 Mandolin

2003-2006. Limited edition of 50, solid spruce top, figured maple back, sides and neck, gold hardware, vintage red satin.

2003-2006		$4,800	$5,700

F-7 Mandolin

1934-1940. F-holes, single-bound body, neck and 'guard, fleur-de-lis peghead inlay, sunburst.

1934-1937		$10,000	$12,500

F-9 Mandolin

2002-present. F-5 style, carved spruce top, no inlays, black bound body.

2002-2010		$1,800	$2,200

F-10 Mandolin

1934-1936. Slight upgrade of the '34 F-7 with extended 'board and upgraded inlay, black finish.

1934-1936		$12,000	$15,000

F-12 Mandolin

1934-1937, 1948-1980. F-holes, bound body and neck, scroll inlay, raised 'board until '37, 'board flush with top '48-on, sunburst.

1934-1937		$12,000	$15,000
1948-1959		$4,000	$4,900
1960-1964		$3,200	$4,000
1965-1969		$2,900	$3,600
1970-1980		$2,700	$3,100

H-1 Mandola

1902-1936. Has same features as A-1 mandolin, but without snakehead headstock.

1902-1908	Orange	$1,800	$2,200
1918-1921	Brown	$2,000	$2,400
1922-1924	Loar era	$2,600	$3,200
1925-1928		$2,100	$2,600

H-1E Mandola

Late-1930s. Limited number built, electric with built-in adjustable bar pickup, sunburst.

1938		$3,800	$4,700

H-2 Mandola

1902-1922. Has same features as A-4 mandolin.

1902-1917	Various colors	$2,800	$3,200
1918-1921	Dark Mahogany	$3,200	$3,700

H-4 Mandola

1910-1940. Same features as F-4 mandolin.

1910-1921		$4,000	$5,000
1922-1924	Loar era	$6,500	$8,000

MODEL		EXC. COND.	
YEAR	FEATURES	LOW	HIGH
1925-1940		$5,000	$6,300

H-5 Mandola

1923-1929 (available by special order 1929-1936), 1990-1991. Same features as the high-end F-5 Mandolin. This is a very specialized market and instruments should be evaluated on a case-by-case basis.

1923-1924	Loar era	$75,000	$85,000
1928-1929	Fern, not		
	Master Model	$37,000	$45,000
1990-1991	Limited		
	production	$5,000	$6,000

K-1 Mandocello

1902-1943. Same features as H-1 mandola, off & on production, special order available.

1902-1908	Orange	$2,900	$3,600
1918-1921	Brown	$3,200	$4,000
1922-1924	Loar era	$3,900	$4,800
1925-1943		$2,700	$3,400

K-2 Mandocello

1902-1922. Same features as A-4 mandolin.

1902-1917	Black or red		
	mahogany	$3,400	$4,200
1918-1922		$3,800	$4,700

K-4 Mandocello

1912-1929 (offered as special order post-1929). Same features as F-4 mandolin, sunburst.

1912-1921		$6,700	$8,300
1922-1924	Loar era	$12,000	$15,000
1925-1929		$7,000	$8,500

M-6 (Octave Guitar)

2002-2006. A-style mandolin body, short-scale 6-string guitar neck.

2002-2006		$1,300	$1,600

MB-1 Mandolin Banjo

1922-1923, 1925-1937.

1922-1923		$850	$1,050
1925-1937		$850	$1,050

MB-2 Mandolin Banjo

1920-1923, 1926-1937.

1920-1923		$1,100	$1,300
1926-1937		$1,100	$1,300

MB-3 Mandolin Banjo

1923-1939.

1923-1939		$1,300	$1,500

MB-4 Mandolin Banjo

1923-1932. Fleur-de-lis inlay.

1923-1932		$1,200	$1,400

MB-11 Mandolin Banjo

1931-1942.

1931-1942		$2,400	$3,000

MB-Junior Mandolin Banjo

1924-1925. Open back, budget level.

1924-1925		$750	$900

SPF-5 Mandolin

1938. F-style, single bar pickup with volume and tone controls, very limited production, natural.

1938		$25,000	$30,000

Style J Mando Bass

1912-1930 (special order post-1930). A-style body, 4 strings, round soundhole, bound top, dot inlay.

1912-1930		$4,500	$5,500

MODEL		EXC. COND.	
YEAR	FEATURES	LOW	HIGH

Style TL-1 Tenor Lute Mandolin

1924-1926. 4-string, A body, tenor banjo scale.

1924-1926		$2,000	$2,500

Gilchrist

1978-present. Premium and presentation grade, custom, mandolins made by luthier Steve Gilchrist of Warrnambool, Australia. Custom ordered but were also initially distributed through Gruhn Guitars, Nashville, Tennessee and then exclusively by Carmel Music Company. Designs are based upon Gibson mandolins built between 1910 and '25.

Mandola

1999. Classical styling.

1999		$17,000	$20,000

Model 5 Mandolin

1978-present. Based on the Gibson '22-'24 Loar-era F-5 mandolin, Gilchrist slant logo, spruce top, flamed maple back, sides, and neck, ebony 'board, multiple binding, sunburst.

1978-1995		$19,000	$21,000
1996-2010		$20,000	$23,000

Givens

1962-1992. Luthier R. L. (Bob) Givens hand-crafted about 800 mandolins and another 700 in a production shop.

A Mandolin

1962-1975. Early production A-style.

1962-1975		$2,400	$2,900

A-3 Mandolin

Mid-1970s-mid-1980s. Distinguished by use of decal (the only model with Givens decal).

1975-1988		$2,200	$2,700

A-4 Mandolin

1988-1993. No 'board binding, simple block-like multiple-line RL Givens inlay, nicer maple.

1988-1993		$1,900	$2,300

A-5 Mandolin

1988-1993. Bound 'board, pearl headstock inlay.

1988-1993		$2,100	$2,600

A-6 (Torch) Mandolin

1988-1992. Torch inlay (the only A model with this), gold hardware, snowflake markers.

1988-1992		$3,200	$3,900

A-6 Custom Mandolin

1991-1992. Elaborate customized A-6 model.

1991-1992		$4,000	$5,000

F-5 (Fern) Mandolin

1973-1985. Givens' own version with fern ornamentation.

1973-1985		$4,500	$5,500

F-5 (Loar) Mandolin

1962-1972. Givens' own version based upon the Loar model F-5.

1962-1972		$4,500	$5,500

F-5 (Torch) Mandolin

1988-1992. Givens F-5 with torch inlay (the only F model with this).

1988-1992		$7,500	$9,000

Gilchrist Standard Model 5

Gold Tone GM-110

MANDOLINS

1960s Harmony Monterey

Heiden F Artist

MODEL YEAR	FEATURES	EXC. COND. LOW	HIGH

F-5 (Wheat Straw) Mandolin
1986-1988. Givens F-5-style with wheat straw ornamentation.

1986-1988		$6,000	$7,500

Godin
1987-present. Intermediate grade, production, acoustic/electric mandolins from luthier Robert Godin. They also build basses and guitars.

A-8 Mandolin
2000-present. Single-cut chambered body, acoustic/ electric.

2000-2010		$425	$525

Gold Tone
1993-present. Intermediate grade, production/ custom mandolins built by Wayne and Robyn Rogers in Titusville, Florida. They also offer guitars, basses, lap steels, ukuleles, banjos and banjitars.

Goodman Guitars
1975-present. Premium grade, custom/production, mandolins built by luthier Brad Goodman in Brewster, New York. He also builds guitars.

Goya
1955-1996. Originally made in Sweden, by the late '70s from Japan, then from Korea.

Mandolin

1960s	Japan/Korea	$175	$200
1960s	Sweden built	$300	$350
1970s	Sweden built	$275	$325

Gretsch
1883-present. Gretsch started offering mandolins by the early 1900s. Currently Gretsch does not offer mandolins.

New Yorker Mandolin
Late 1940s-late 1950s. Teardrop shape, f-holes, arched top and back, spruce top, maple back, sides, and neck, rosewood 'board.

1950s		$600	$750

GTR
1974-1978. GTR (for George Gruhn, Tut Taylor, Randy Wood) was the original name for Gruhn Guitars in Nashville, Tennessee (it was changed in '76). GTR imported mandolins and banjos from Japan. An A-style (similar to a current Gibson A-5 L) and an F-style (similar to mid- to late-'20s F-5 with fern pattern) were offered. The instruments were made at the Moridaira factory in Matsumoto, Japan by factory foreman Sadamasa Tokaida. Quality was relatively high but quantities were limited.

A-Style Mandolin
1974-1978. A5-L copy with GTR logo on headstock.

1974-1978		$1,100	$1,400

F-Style Mandolin
1974-1978. F-5 Fern copy with slant GTR logo on headstock, sunburst, handmade in Japan.

1974-1978		$1,800	$2,300

MODEL YEAR	FEATURES	EXC. COND. LOW	HIGH

Guitar Company of America
1971-present. Luthier Dixie Michell builds professional grade, production mandolins in Tulsa, Oklahoma. She also builds guitars.

Haight
1989-present. Luthier Norman Haight builds his production/custom, premium and presentation grade, acoustic mandolins in Scottsdale, Arizona. He also builds guitars.

Harmony
1982-1976, late 1970s-present. Founded by Wilhelm Schultz in 1892, and purchased by Sears in 1916. The company evolved into one of the largest producers of stringed instruments in the U.S. in the '30s.

Baroque H35/H835 Electric Mandolin
Late 1960s-early 1970s. Electric version of Baroque H425 with single pickup and two controls.

1969-1970	H35	$300	$375
1971-1976	H835	$300	$375

Baroque H425/H8025 Mandolin
F-style arched body, extreme bass bout pointy horn, close grained spruce top, sunburst.

1969-1970	H425	$250	$300
1971-1976	H8025	$250	$300

Lute H331/H8031 Mandolin
1960s-1970s. A-style, flat top and back, student level.

1960s	H331	$125	$150
1970s	H8031	$125	$150

Monterey H410/H417/H8017 Mandolin
1950s-1970s. A-style arched body with f-holes, sunburst.

1950-1970s	All models	$125	$150

Heiden Stringed Instruments
1974-present. Luthier Michael Heiden builds his premium grade, production/custom mandolins in Chilliwack, British Columbia. He also builds guitars.

Heritage
1985-present. Started by former Gibson employees in Gibson's Kalamazoo, Michigan plant, Heritage offered mandolins for a number of years.

H-5 Mandolin
1986-1990s. F-style scroll body, f-holes.

1986-1990s		$2,900	$3,500

Hofner
1887-present. Hofner has offered a wide variety of instruments, including mandolins, over the years. They currently again offer mandolins.

Model 545/E545 Mandolin
1960s. Pear-shaped A-style with catseye f-holes, block-style markers, engraved headstock, Genuine Hofner Original and Made in Germany on back of headstock, transparent brown.

1968-1969	545 (acoustic)	$325	$375

MANDOLINS

MODEL			EXC. COND.	
YEAR	FEATURES		LOW	HIGH

1968-1969   E545
       (acoustic-electric) $400 $475

Hohner
1857-present. Intermediate grade, production, acoustic and acoustic/electric mandolins. They also offer guitars, basses, banjos and ukuleles.

Holst
1984-present. Premium grade, custom, mandolins built in Creswell, Oregon by luthier Stephen Holst. He also builds guitars.

Hondo
1969-1987, 1991-2005. Budget grade, production, imported mandolins. They also offered banjos, basses and guitars. Hondo also offered mandolins from around '74 to '87.

Mandolin
1974-1987. Hondo offered F-style, A-style, and bowl back mandolin models.

1970s	Acoustic	$75	$125
1970s	Acoustic-electric	$125	$175
1970s	Style F	$175	$225

Hopf
1906-present. Professional grade, production/custom, mandolins made in Germany. They also make basses, guitars and flutes.

Howe-Orme
1897-ca. 1910. Elias Howe patented a guitar-shaped mandolin on November 14, 1893 and later partnered with George Orme to build a variety of mandolin family instruments and guitars in Boston.

Mandola
1897-early-1900s. Guitar body-style with narrow waist, not the common mandolin F- or S-style body, pressed (not carved) spruce top, mahogany back and sides, flat-top guitar-type trapeze bridge, decalomania near bridge.
1890s $1,400 $1,600

Mandolinetto
1890s. Guitar body, mandolin neck and tuning, 'guard below oval soundhole, slightly arched top, Brazilian rosewood sides and back, dot/diamond/oval markers.
1890s $1,700 $2,000

Ianuario Mandolins
1990-present. Professional and premium grade, custom, mandolins built by luthier R. Anthony Ianuario in Jefferson, Georgia. He also builds banjos and violins.

Ibanez
1932-present. Ibanez offered mandolins from '65 to '83. In '04 they again added mandolins to the product line.

Model 511 Mandolin
1974-1979 $250 $300

Model 513 Mandolin
1974-1979. A-5 copy with double cutaways, oval sound hole, dot markers, sunburst.
1974-1979 $275 $350

Model 514 Mandolin
1974-1979. Arched back, spruce, rosewood, dot inlays, sunburst.
1974-1979 $275 $350

Model 522 Mandolin
1974-1978. Symmetrical double point.
1974-1978 $325 $400

Model 524 Artist Mandolin
1974-1978. F-5 Loar copy, solid wood carved top and solid wood carved top and solid wood back, sunburst.
1974-1978 $750 $875

Model 526 (electric) Mandolin
1974-1978. A-style body, single pickup, two control knobs, sunburst.
1974-1978 $325 $400

Model 529 Artist Mandolin
1982-1983. F-5 Loar era copy, solid wood carved top and solid wood spruce top and solid maple sides and back, sunburst.
1982-1983 $950 $1,150

Imperial
1890-1922. Imperial mandolins were made by the William A. Cole Company of Boston, Massachusetts.

Bowl Back Mandolin
1890s $225 $275

J.B. Player
1980s-present. Budget grade, production, imported mandolins. They also offer basses, banjos and guitars.

J.L. Smith
2008-present. Intermediate grade, custom, mandolins built in Myrtle Beach, South Carolina by luthier John L. Smith.

J.R. Zeidler Guitars
1977-2002. Luthier John Zeidler built premium grade, custom, mandolins in Wallingford, Pennsylvania. He also built guitars.

John Le Voi Guitars
1970-present. Production/custom, mandolin family instruments built by luthier John Le Voi in Lincolnshire, United Kingdom. He also builds guitars.

Johnson
Mid-1990s-present. Budget and intermediate grade, production, mandolins imported by Music Link, Brisbane, California. Johnson also offers guitars, amps, basses and effects.

MA Series A-Style Mandolins
Mid-1990s-present. Import, A-style copy. Several levels offered; the range shown is for all value levels.
1990s-2010 $75 $100

J.B. Player Florentine Style

J.L. Smith Electric 4-String

MANDOLINS

Johnson MF100 Savannah

Kentucky KM-9000

| MODEL | | EXC. COND. | |
YEAR	FEATURES	LOW	HIGH

MF Series F-Style Mandolins

Mid-1990s-2006. Import, F-style copy. Several levels offered; the range shown is for all value levels.

| 1990s-2006 | | $150 | $175 |

K & S

1992-1998. Mandolins and mandolas distributed by George Katechis and Marc Silber and handmade in Paracho, Mexico. They also offered guitars and ukes.

Kalamazoo

1933-1942, 1946-1947, 1965-1970. Budget brand produced by Gibson in Kalamazoo, Michigan. They offered mandolins until '42.

Kalamazoo/Oriole A-Style Mandolin

1930s. Kalamazoo and Oriole on the headstock, KM/A-style.

| 1930s | | $650 | $800 |

KM-11 Mandolin

1935-1941. Gibson-made, A-style, flat top and back, round soundhole, dot inlay, sunburst.

| 1935-1941 | | $450 | $575 |

KM-12N Mandolin

1935-1941. A-style with f-holes, spruce top, flamed maple sides and back, bound top and bottom, natural finish.

| 1935-1941 | | $450 | $575 |

KM-21 Mandolin

1936-1940. Gibson-made, A-style, f-holes, arched bound spruce top and mahogany back, sunburst.

| 1936-1940 | | $675 | $800 |

KM-22 Mandolin

1939-1942. Same as KM-21 with bound top and back.

| 1939-1942 | | $725 | $850 |

KMB Mandolin/Banjo

1930s. Banjo-mandolin with resonator.

| 1930s | | $400 | $500 |

Kay

1931-present. Located in Chicago, Illinois, the Kay company made an incredible amount of instruments under a variety of brands, including the Kay name. From the beginning, Kay offered several types of electric and acoustic mandolins. In '69, the factory closed, marking the end of American-made Kays. The brand survives today on imported instruments.

K68/K465 Concert Mandolin

1952-1968. Pear-shape, close-grain spruce top, genuine mahogany back and sides, natural. Renamed the K465 in '66. Kay also offered a Venetian-style mandolin called the K68 in '37-'42.

| 1952-1968 | | $200 | $250 |

K73 Mandolin

1939-1952. Solid spruce top, maple back and sides, A-style body, f-holes, cherry sunburst.

| 1939-1952 | | $200 | $250 |

K390/K395 Professional Electric Mandolin

1960-1968. Modified Venetian-style archtop, 1 pickup, f-hole, spruce top, curly maple back and sides, sunburst finish. Renamed K395 in '66.

| 1960-1968 | | $400 | $500 |

K494/K495 Electric Mandolin

1960-1968. A-style archtop, single metal-covered (no poles) pickup, volume and tone control knobs, sunburst. The K494 was originally about 60% of the price of the K390 model (see above) in '65. Renamed K495 in '66.

| 1960-1968 | | $350 | $425 |

Kay Kraft

1931-1937. First brand name of the newly formed Kay Company. Brand replaced by Kay in '37.

Mandola

| 1937 | | $675 | $825 |

Mandolin

1931-1937. Kay Kraft offered Venetian- and teardrop-shaped mandolins.

| 1931-1937 | | $350 | $425 |

KB

1989-present. Luthier Ken Bebensee builds his premium grade, production/custom, mandolins in North San Juan, California. He also builds guitars and basses.

Kel Kroydon (by Gibson)

1930-1933. Private branded budget level instruments made by Gibson. They also had guitars and banjos.

KK-20 (Style C-1) Mandolin

1930-1933. Flat top, near oval-shaped body, oval soundhole, natural finish, dark finish mahogany back and sides.

| 1930-1933 | | $675 | $825 |

Kent

1961-1969. Japanese-made instruments. Kent offered teardrop, A style, and bowlback acoustic mandolins up to '68.

Acoustic Mandolin

1961-1968. Kent offered teardrop, A-style, and bowlback acoustic mandolins up to '68.

| 1961-1968 | | $125 | $150 |

Electric Mandolin

1964-1969. Available from '64-'66 as a solidbody electric (in left- and right-hand models) and from '67-'69 an electric hollowbody Venetian-style with f-holes (they called it violin-shaped).

| 1964-1969 | | $225 | $275 |

Kentucky (Saga M.I.)

1977-present. Brand name of Saga Musical Instruments currently offering budget, intermediate, and professional grade, production, A- and F-style mandolins. Early models made in Japan, then Korea, currently made in China.

MANDOLINS

MODEL YEAR	FEATURES	EXC. COND. LOW	HIGH
KM Series Mandolin			
2000s	KM-140 A-style	$75	$100
2000s	KM-150 A-style	$160	$185
1980s	KM-180 A-style	$250	$300
1990s	KM-200S A-style	$300	$375
1990s	KM-250S A-style	$475	$575
2000s	KM-380S	$200	$250
1990s	KM-500S A-style	$500	$600
1990s	KM-620 F-style	$500	$600
2000s	KM-620 F-style	$300	$375
2000s	KM-630 F-style	$350	$400
1980s	KM-650 F-style	$500	$600
1990s	KM-675	$350	$425
2000s	KM-675	$400	$500
1980s	KM-700 F-style	$500	$600
2000s	KM-700 F-style	$350	$400
1980s	KM-800 F-style	$500	$600
2000s	KM-800 F-style	$350	$400
1998-2009	KM-850 F-style	$1,000	$1,200
1980-2000s	KM-1000 F-style	$1,000	$1,200

Kimble

2000-present. Luthier Will Kimble builds his premium grade, custom/production, mandolins, mandocellos, and mandolas in Cincinnati, Ohio.

Kingston

Ca. 1958-1967. Mandolins imported from Japan by Jack Westheimer and Westheimer Importing Corporation of Chicago, Illinois. They also offered guitars and basses.

Acoustic Mandolin

1960s		$150	$175

EM1 Electric Mandolin

1964-1967. Double-cut solidbody electric, 15.75" scale, 1 pickup.

1960s		$175	$200

Knutsen

1890s-1920s. Luthier Chris J. Knutsen of Tacoma/Seattle, Washington.

Harp Mandolin

1910s. Harp mandolin with tunable upper bass bout with 4 drone strings, and standard mandolin neck. The mandolin version of a harp guitar.

1910s		$4,000	$5,000

Knutson Luthiery

1981-present. Professional and premium grade, custom, acoustic and electric mandolins built by luthier John Knutson in Forestville, California. He also builds guitars, basses and lap steels.

Kona

2001-present. Budget grade, production, acoustic mandolins made in Asia. They also offer guitars, basses, banjos and amps.

La Scala

Ca. 1920s-1930s. A brand of the Oscar Schmidt Company of New Jersey, used on guitars, banjos,

and mandolins. These were often the fanciest of the Schmidt instruments.

Lakeside (Lyon & Healy)

1890-early-1900s. Mainly catalog sales of guitars and mandolins from the Chicago maker. Marketed as a less expensive alternative to the Lyon & Healy Washburn product line.

Style G2016 12-String Mandolin

1890-early-1900s. 12-string, 18 mahogany ribs with white inlay between, celluloid guard plate, advertised as "an inexpensive instrument, possessing a good tone, correct scale, and durable construction."

1890-1910		$300	$375

Lakewood

1986-present. Luthier Martin Seeliger built his professional grade, production/custom, mandolins in Giessen, Germany up to '07. He continues to build guitars.

Larson Brothers

1900-1944. Luthiers Carl and August Larson built and marketed instruments under a variety of brands including Stetson, Maurer, Prairie State, Euphonon, Dyer, Stahl and others, but never under the Larson name.

Laurie Williams Guitars

1983-present. Luthier Laurie Williams builds his premium grade, custom/production, acoustic mandolins on the North Island of New Zealand. He also builds guitars.

Levin

1900-1973. Acoustic mandolins built in Sweden. Levin was best known for their classical guitars, which they also built for other brands, most notably Goya. They also built ukes.

Lewis

1981-present. Luthier Michael Lewis builds his premium and presentation grade, custom/production, mandolin family instruments in Grass Valley, California. He also builds guitars.

Loar (The)

2005-present. Intermediate and professional grade, production, imported mandolins designed by Greg Rich for The Music Link, which also has Johnson and other brands of instruments.

Lotus

Late-1970s-2004. Acoustic mandolins imported by Musicorp. They also offered banjos and guitars.

Lyle

Ca. 1969-1980. Instruments imported by distributor L.D. Heater of Portland, Oregon. Generally Japanese-made copies of American designs. They also had basses and guitars.

Knutsen Harp-Mandolin

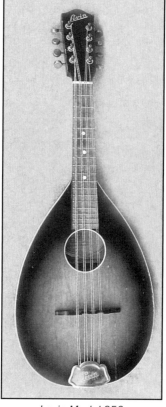

Levin Model 350

MANDOLINS

Mann Two Point Carved Back

1931 Martin Style B

MANDOLINS

MODEL YEAR	FEATURES	EXC. COND. LOW	EXC. COND. HIGH

TM-200 Mandolin
1970s	A-style	$125	$150

Lyon & Healy
1964-ca. 1945. Lyon & Healy was a large musical instrument builder and marketer, and produced under many different brands.

Style A Mandocello
1910-1920s. Scroll peghead, symmetrical 2-point body, natural.
1910s		$4,000	$5,000
1920s		$4,000	$5,000

Style A Professional Mandolin
1918-1920s. Violin scroll peghead, natural.
1918-1920s		$3,000	$4,000

Style B Mandolin
1920. Maple back and sides, 2-point body, natural.
1920		$1,300	$1,800

Style C Mandolin
1920s. Like Style A teardrop Gibson body style, oval soundhole, carved spruce top, carved maple back, natural.
1920s		$1,500	$1,900

Lyra
1920s-1930s. Private brand made by Regal, Lyra name plate on headstock.

Style A (Scroll) Mandolin
1920s-1930s. Scroll on upper bass bout.
1925-1935		$400	$500

Maccaferri
1923-1990. Mario Maccaferri made a variety of instruments over his career. He produced award-winning models in Italy and France until he fled to the U.S. due to WW II. He applied the new plastic to a highly successful line of instruments after the war. A mandolin was about the only stringed instument they didn't offer in plastic. His Europe-era instruments are very rare.

Mandolins/Mandolas made by Maccaferri 1928-ca. '31: No. 1 Mandolone, No. 2 Mandoloncello, No. 3 Mandola Baritono, No. 4 Mandola Tenore, No. 5 Mandola Soprano, No. 6 Mandolino, No. 7 Quartino.

Mann Mandolins
2002-present. Luthier Jonathan Mann builds his professional grade, production/custom, acoustic and electric mandolins in Joelton, Tennessee.

Manuel & Patterson
1993-present. Professional and premium grade, production/custom, carved top mandolins built by luthiers Joe Manuel and Phil Patterson in Abita Springs, Louisiana. They also build guitars.

Martin
1833-present. Martin got into the mandolin market in 1895 starting with the typical bowl back designs. By 1914, Gibson's hot selling, innovative, violin-based mandolin pushed Martin into a flat back, bent top hybrid design. By '29, Martin offered a carved top and carved back mandolin. Most models were discontinued in '41, partially because of World War II. Production resumed and standard models are offered up to 1993. From '94 to '02 mandolins are available on a custom order basis only.

Martin offered a Backpacker mandolin up to '06.

Backpacker Mandolin
1999-2006. Bell-shaped body.
1999-2006		$200	$250

Style 0 Mandolin
1905-1925. Bowl back-style, 18 rosewood ribs, solid peghead.
1905-1925		$725	$900

Style 00 Mandolin
1908-1925. Bowl back-style, 9 rosewood ribs (14 ribs by '24), solid peghead.
1908-1925		$600	$750

Style 000 Mandolin
1914 only. Bowl back, solid peghead, dot inlay, 9 mahogany ribs.
1914		$500	$625

Style 1 Mandolin
1898-1924. Bowl back, German silver tuners, 18 ribs.
1898-1924		$750	$925

Style 2 Mandolin
1898-1924. Bowl back, 26 rosewood ribs, higher appointments than Style 1.
1898-1924		$950	$1,150

Style 2-15 Mandolin
1936-1964. Carved spruce top, maple back and sides, f-hole, single-bound back, solid headstock.
1936-1964		$1,300	$1,500

Style 2-20 Mandolin
1936-1941. Carved spruce triple-bound top and bound maple back and sides, f-hole, dot inlay.
1936-1942		$2,300	$2,800

Style 2-30 Mandolin
1937-1941. Carved spruce top and maple back and sides, multi-bound, f-holes, diamond and square inlays.
1937-1941		$2,800	$3,300

Style 4 Mandolin
1898-1921. Bowl back, 34 rosewood ribs.
1907		$1,750	$2,200

Style 5 Mandolin
1898-1920. Bowl back, vine inlay, abalone top trim.
1898-1899		$1,850	$2,300
1900-1909		$1,850	$2,300
1910-1920		$1,850	$2,300

Style 6 Mandolin
1898-1921. Bowl back, top bound with ivory and abalone, vine or snowflake inlay.
1898-1921		$1,950	$2,400

Style 20 Mandolin
1929-1942. Symmetrical 2-point body, carved top and back with oval soundhole, dot markers.
1929-1942		$1,100	$1,350

MODEL YEAR	FEATURES	EXC. COND. LOW	HIGH

Style 20S Mandolin
1949-1957. 30 made, special ordered for Carlos DeFilipis, decorative point on each side of body, oval sound hole, carved spruce top, carved curly maple back.

1949-1957		$1,750	$2,200

Style A Mandolin
1914-1995. Flat back, oval soundhole, dot inlay, solid headstock.

1914-1919		$775	$950
1920-1939		$775	$950
1940-1949		$775	$950
1950-1959		$750	$900
1960-1969		$750	$900
1970-1995		$650	$800

Style AA Mandola
1915-1931, 1935, 1941. Mandola version of Style A mandolin.

1915-1941		$1,600	$2,000

Style AK Mandolin
1920-1937. Koa wood version of Style A, flat back.

1920-1937		$1,100	$1,300

Style B Mandolin
1914-1946, 1981-1987. Flat back with bent top, spruce top and rosewood back and sides, herringbone back stripe, multi-bound.

1914-1919		$1,100	$1,350
1920-1939		$1,150	$1,400
1940-1946		$1,100	$1,300
1981-1987		$850	$1,050

Style BB Mandola
1917-1921, 1932-1939. Brazilian rosewood, herringbone trim, features like Style B mandolin. This is the only Mandola offered.

1917-1921		$2,000	$2,500

Style C Mandolin
1914-1934. Flat back.

1914-1919		$2,300	$2,800
1920-1934		$2,400	$3,000

Style D Mandolin
1914-1916. Flat back.

1914-1916		$3,600	$4,500

Style E Mandolin
1915-1937. Flat back, rosewood back and sides, bent spruce top, Style 45 snowflake fretboard inlay and other high-end appointments. Highest model cataloged.

1915-1919		$5,000	$6,500
1920-1937		$6,500	$7,500

Maurer
Late 1880s-1944. Started by Robert Maurer in Chicago, and continued by Carl and August Larson after 1900. Earlier models were bowl-backs with flat-backs being offered by 1912. Models ranged from plain to presentation-style. Maurer Mandolins from the 1930s include Style 30 Flat Model, Style 40, Octave Mandola Style 45, Mandocello Style 50, and Mandola Tenor.

May Flower
Ca. 1901-1910. H. J. Flower's Chicago-based May Flower Music Company offered bowl back mandolins that he may or may not have built. There were also May Flower harp guitars built by others.

Bowl Back Mandolin
1901-1910. Mid-level bowl back-style with 19 rosewood ribs and mid-level appointments.

1901-1910		$875	$1,100

Menzenhauer & Schmidt
1894-1904. Founded by Frederick Menzenhauer and Oscar Schmidt International. Menzenhauer created the guitar-zither in the U.S. He had several patents including one issued in September 1899 for a mandolin-guitar-zither. Control of operations quickly went to Oscar Schmidt.

12-String Mandolin
1890s. Bowl back mandolin with 3 strings per course that were tuned in octaves, designed during an experimental era for mandolin-related instruments, 13 rosewood ribs, spruce top, inlays.

1890s		$250	$300

Michael Collins Guitars
2002-present. Luthier Michael Collins builds his professional and premium grade, production/custom, mandolins in Keswick, Ontario. He also builds guitars.

Michael Kelly
2000-present. Intermediate and professional grade, production, imported, acoustic and acoustic/electric mandolins. They also offer guitars and basses.

Michael Lewis Instruments
1992-present. Luthier Michael Lewis builds his premium grade, custom, mandolins in Grass Valley, California. He also builds guitars.

Mid-Missouri/The Big Muddy Mandolin Company
1995-present. Intermediate grade, production, acoustic and electric mandolins and mandolas built by luthier Michael Dulak in Columbia, Missouri. In late '06, they changed their name to The Big Muddy Mandolin Company.

M Series Mandolin
1995-present. Teardrop A-style body, solid spruce top, solid maple, mahogany or rosewood back and sides.

1995-1999	M-0	$225	$300
1995-1999	M-1	$275	$350
1995-2010	M-15 Mandola	$550	$700
1995-2010	M-2	$325	$400
1995-2010	M-3	$375	$450
1995-2010	M-4	$425	$525

1920 Martin Style C

Michael Kelly Legacy Elegante

MANDOLINS

Oscar Schmidt F Style

*Morgan Monroe MDM-1
Distressed*

MODEL YEAR	FEATURES	EXC. COND. LOW	HIGH

Mirabella

1997-present. Professional and premium grade, custom, mandolins built by luthier Cristian Mirabella in Babylon, New York. He also builds guitars, basses and ukes.

Mix

2007-present. Carbon fiber mandolins built by Peter Mix, Will Kimball, and Matt Durham of New Millennium Acoustic Design (NewMAD) in Waterville, Vermont.

Monteleone

1971-present. Primarily a guitar maker, luthier John Monteleone also builds presentation grade, custom, mandolins in West Islip, New York.

Grand Artist Mandola

1979-present. 15 7/8" scale until '90, then 17".

1990-1995		$20,000	$24,000

Grand Artist Mandolin

1977-present. Style F body, spruce top, curly maple back and sides, dot markers, currently offered in a Standard and Deluxe model.

1977-1989		$21,000	$25,000
1990-2010		$21,000	$25,000

Radio Flyer Mandolin

1996-present. Style F body, currently offered in a Standard and Deluxe model.

1996-2010		$25,000	$30,000

Style B Mandolin

1982-1990s. Long A body style with long f-holes, flamed curly maple back and sides, elongated fretboard over body, sunburst.

1982-1990		$15,000	$18,000

Moon (Scotland)

1979-present. Intermediate and professional grade, production/custom, acoustics and acoustic/electric mandolins and mandolas built by luthier Jimmy Moon in Glasgow, Scotland. They also build guitars.

Morales

Ca.1967-1968. Japanese-made, not heavily imported into the U.S.

Electric Mandolin

1967-1968		$275	$350

Morgan Monroe

1999-present. Intermediate and professional grade, production, acoustic mandolins made in Korea and distributed by SHS International of Indianapolis, Indiana. They also offer guitars, basses, banjos, and fiddles.

Morris

1967-present. Imported by Moridaira of Japan, Morris offered copy-era mandolins during the 1970s, including the popular F-5 style copy. They also build guitars.

Mozzani

Late-1800s-early-1900s. Founder Luigi Mozzani was an Italian (Bologna) master luthier and renowned composer and musician. There are original Mozzani-built mandolins and also factory-built instruments made later at various workshops.

Mandolin

1920s. Factory-built bowl back model.

1920s		$300	$375

Original Bowl Back Mandolin

Late-1800s-early-1900s. Handcrafted by Luigi Mozzani, about 24 ribs, soundhole ornamentation, snowflake-like markers.

1904		$1,100	$1,350

Muiderman Guitars

1997-present. Custom, premium grade, mandolins built by luthier Kevin Muiderman currently in Grand Forks, North Dakota, and previously in Beverly Hill, Michigan, 1997-2001, and Neenah, Wisconsin, '01-'07. He also builds guitars.

National

Ca.1927-present. The National brand has gone through many ownership changes and offered resonator mandolins from around 1927 to '41.

Style O Mandolin

1931-early-1940s. Metal body with Hawaiian scenes, single-cone resonator.

1930s		$2,600	$3,200

Style 1 Mandolin

1928-1936. Plain metal body, tri-cone resonator.

1928-1936	Single cone	$2,100	$2,600
1928-1936	Tricone version	$3,200	$4,000

Style 2 Mandolin

1928-1936. Metal body with rose engraving, tri-cone resonator.

1928-1936	Single cone	$4,000	$5,000
1928-1936	Tricone version	$5,600	$7,000

Style 3 Mandolin

1930s	Single cone	$5,000	$6,200
1930s	Tricone version	$5,600	$7,000

Style 97 Mandolin

1936-1940. Metal body, tri-cone resonator.

1936-1940		$5,500	$6,800

Triolian Mandolin

1928-1940. Metal body with palm trees, single-cone resonator.

1928-1940	Single cone	$2,400	$2,900

National Reso-Phonic

1988-present. Successors to the National name, with the designs and patented amplifying resonator assemblies of the original National models, they offer professional grade, production, mandolins from their shop in San Luis Obispo, California. They also build guitars, basses and ukuleles.

MANDOLINS

MODEL YEAR	FEATURES	EXC. COND. LOW	HIGH

Northworthy

1987-present. Professional and premium grade, production/custom, mandolin-family instruments built by luthier Alan Marshall in Ashbourne, Derbyshire, England. He also builds guitars.

Nouveau (Gibson)

1986-1989. Mandolin bodies and necks made in Japan, assembled and finished in U.S. Became Nouveau (by Epiphone) in '88 and the brand was discontinued in '89. They also made guitars.

C7 Mandolin

1986-1987. F-style, white wood body and neck.

1986-1987		$1,700	$2,100

Nugget

1970s-present. Luthier Mike Kemnitzer builds his premium grade mandolins in Central Lake, Michigan.

Nyberg Instruments

1993-present. Professional grade, custom, mandolins and mandolas built by luthier Lawrence Nyberg in Hornby Island, British Columbia. He also builds guitars, bouzoukis and citterns.

O'Dell, Doug

See listing under Old Town.

Old Hickory

2005-present. Budget grade, production, imported F- and A-style acoustic mandolins from Musician's Wholesale America, Nashville, Tennessee. They also offer banjos.

Style A Mandolin

2005-present.

2005-2010	AC-100 mid-level	$65	$80
2005-2010	FC-100 highest level	$125	$150
2005-2010	M-1 lowest level	$40	$50

Old Kraftsman

1930s-1960s. Brand name used by the Siegel Company on instruments made by Kay and others (even Gibson). Quality was mixed, but some better-grade instruments were offered.

Mandolin

1950s		$275	$325

Old Town

1974-2007. Luthier Doug O'Dell built his professional and premium grade, production/custom acoustic and electric mandolins in Ohio.

EM-10 Electric Mandolin

1980s-2006. Double-cut, flamed maple top, 1 pickup, 2 control knobs.

1980s-2006		$1,600	$2,000

Old Wave

1990-present. Luthier Bill Bussmann builds his professional and premium grade, production/custom, mandolins and mandolas in Caballo, New Mexico. He has also built guitars and basses.

Orpheum

1897-1942, 1944-early 1970s, 2001-2006. Intermediate grade, production, mandolins. They also offered guitars. An old brand often associated with banjos, 1930s branded guitars sold by Bruno and Sons. 1950s branded guitars and mandolins sold by Maurice Lipsky Music, New York, New York. The brand was revived for '01 to '06 by Tacoma Guitars.

Electric Mandolin Model 730 E

1950s. Private branded for Maurice Lipsky. Cataloged as a student model designed for ensemble playing. A-style body, single neck bar pickup, 2 side-mounted knobs, spruce top, maple back and sides, dot markers, sunburst.

1950s		$525	$650

Model No. 1 Mandolin-Banjo

1915		$650	$800

Model No. 2 Mandolin-Banjo

1920s. Mandolin neck on small banjo body, fancy headstock and fretboard inlay, carved heel.

1920s		$700	$850

Oscar Schmidt

1879-ca. 1939, 1979-present. Currently offering budget and intermediate grade, production, mandolins. They also offer guitars, basses, banjos, ukuleles and the famous Oscar Schmidt autoharp. The original Schmidt company offered innovative mandolin designs during the 1900-'30 mandolin boom.

Mandolin Harp Style B

1890s. More zither-autoharp than mandolin, flat autoharp body with soundhole.

1890s		$150	$175

Sovereign Mandolin

1920s. Bowl back, bent top, rope-style binding, mahogany ribs, dot inlay, plain headstock, natural.

1920s	Fancy appointments	$600	$750
1920s	Standard appointments	$225	$275

Ovation

1966-present. Known for innovative fiberglass-backed bowl back acoustic and acoustic/electric guitars, Ovation added mandolins in '94 and currently offers intermediate and professional grade, production, mandolins and mandocellos. They also offer guitars and basses.

MSC148 (Celebrity) Mandolin

1994-present. Single-cut, small Ovation body, Ovation headstock, red sunburst.

1994-2010		$300	$400

P. W. Crump Company

1975-present. Luthier Phil Crump builds his custom mandolin-family instruments in Arcata, California. He also builds guitars.

Paris Swing

2005-2008. Intermediate grade, production, imported acoustic mandolins from The Music Link, which also offers instruments under Johnson and other brands.

Ovation MSC148 (Celebrity)

Paris Swing John Jorgenson

MANDOLINS

Ratliff R-5

RedLine Traveler

MODEL		EXC. COND.	
YEAR	FEATURES	LOW	HIGH

Penco

Ca. 1974-1978. Japanese-made copies of classic American mandolins. They also made guitars, basses and banjos.

Phantom Guitar Works

1992-present. Intermediate grade, production, solidbody MandoGuitars assembled in Clatskanie, Oregon. They also build guitars and basses.

Phoenix

1990-present. Premium grade, production/custom, mandolins built by luthier Rolfe Gerhardt (formerly builder of Unicorn Mandolins in the '70s) in South Thomaston, Maine. Gerhardt's Phoenix company specializes in a 2-point Style A (double-cut) body style.

Premier

Ca.1938-ca.1975, 1990s-2010. Brand produced by Peter Sorkin Music Company in New York City. Around '57 the company acquired Strad-O-Lin and many of their mandolins were offered under that brand. By '75, the Premier brand went into hiatus. By the '90s, the Premier brand re-appears on Asian-made solidbody guitars and basses.

Ramsey

1990s. Built by luthier John Ramsey of Colorado Springs, Colorado.

Randy Wood Guitars

1968-present. Premium and presentation grade, custom/production, mandolins, mandolas, and mandocellos built by luthier Randy Woods in Bloomingdale, Georgia. He also builds guitars.

Ratliff

1982-present. Professional and premium grade, production/custom, mandolin family instruments built by luthier Audey Ratliff in Church Hill, Tennessee.

R Series Mandolin

1990s-present. R-5 is an F-style mando, R-4 is round-hole version of 5.

1995-2010	R-5	$2,000	$2,250
1996	R-4	$1,800	$2,000

Silver Eagle Mandolin

1998. A style.

1998		$1,200	$1,600

Recording King

1929-1943. Montgomery Ward house brand. Suppliers include Gibson, Kay, Regal, and Gretsch. Brand name revived by The Music Link in '05.

Mandolin

1929-1940. Gibson-made, A-style body, sunburst.

1930s		$500	$625

Red Diamond

Early 1980s-present. Luthier Don MacRostie builds his premium grade, production/custom, mandolins in Athens, Ohio.

RedLine Acoustics and RedLine Resophonics

2007-present. Luthiers Steve Smith, Jason Denton, Christian McAdams and Ryan Futch build their intermediate to premium grade, production, flat-top and carved A-style mandolins in Hendersonville, Tennessee. They also build guitars.

Regal

Ca.1884-1954. Large Chicago-based manufacturer which made their own brand name and others for distributors and mass merchandisers. Absorbed by the Harmony Company in 1955.

Bicentennial 76 Mandolin

1976. A-style body, flat back, oval soundhole, Bicentennial 76 logo on headstock, '76 logo on 'guard, white body, red peghead, blue stars on front and back.

1976		$350	$425

Mandolin

1920s	Flat-Top A-style	$375	$475
1930s	Standard, sunburst	$375	$475
1930s	Ultra Grand Deluxe	$800	$1,000

Octophone Mandolin

1920s. Octave mandolin, long body with double points, round soundhole.

1920s		$750	$925

Resonator Mandolin

1950s		$450	$550

Rickenbacker

1931-present. Rickenbacker had the Electro Mandolin in the late '30s and introduced 4-, 5- and 8-string electric models in 1958 and currently offers one model.

Model 5002V58

1997-present. 8 strings, maple front, walnut back, rosewood 'board.

1997-2010		$1,100	$1,400

Rigel

1990-2006. Professional and premium grade, production/custom mandolins and mandolas built by luthier Pete Langdell in Hyde Park, Vermont.

A-Plus Series Mandolin

1990s-2006. A-style body, carved spruce top, maple back and sides, dot markers.

1990-2006	F-holes	$1,150	$1,400
1990s	Oval soundhole	$1,050	$1,300

Classic S Mandolin

2000s. Double cutaway, f-holes.

2000s		$1,575	$1,900

Model G-110 Mandolin

1990-2006. Maple neck, back and sides, red spruce top, f-holes, sunburst.

1990-2006		$1,900	$2,300

MODEL YEAR	FEATURES	EXC. COND. LOW	HIGH

Roberts

1980s. Built by luthier Jay Roberts of California.

Tiny Moore Jazz 5 Mandolin

1980s. Based on Bigsby design of the early-1950s as used by Tiny Moore, five-string electric, sunburst.

| 1985 | | $1,550 | $1,925 |

Rogue

2001-present. Budget grade, production, imported mandolins. They also offer guitars, basses, ukes, and banjos.

Rono

1967-present. Luthier Ron Oates builds his professional grade, production/custom, electric mandolins in Boulder, Colorado. He also builds basses and guitars.

Ryder

1992-present. Luthier Steve Ryder builds his professional and premium grade, production/custom solid and semi-hollowbody electric mandolins, mandola and octave mandolins in South Portland, Maine.

S. S. Stewart

1878-1904. S.S. Stewart of Philadelphia was primarily known for banjos. Legend has it that Stewart was one of the first to demonstrate the mass production assembly of stringed instruments.

Mandolin Banjo

Early-1900s. Mandolin neck and a very small open back banjo body, star inlay in headstock.

| 1900s | | $375 | $450 |

S101

2002-present. Budget and intermediate grade, production, mandolins imported from China. They also offer guitars, basses, and banjos.

Samick

1958-2001, 2002-present. Budget and intermediate grade, production, imported acoustic and acoustic/electric mandolins. They also offer guitars, basses, ukes and banjos.

Sammo

1920s. Labels in these instruments state they were made by the Osborne Mfg. Co. with an address of Masonic Temple, Chicago, Illinois. High quality and often with a high degree of ornamentation. They also made ukes and guitars.

Sawchyn

1972-present. Intermediate and professional grade, production/custom, mandolins built by luthier Peter Sawchyn in Regina, Saskatchewan. He also builds flat-top and flamenco guitars.

Sekova

Mid-1960s-mid-1970s. Entry level, imported by the U.S. Musical Merchandise.

Electric Mandolin

1960s-1970s. Kay-Kraft-style hollowbody with f-holes, 1 pickup and Sekova logo on the headstock.

| 1965-1970s | | $275 | $325 |

Sigma

1970-2007. Budget and intermediate grade, production, import mandolins distributed by C.F. Martin Company. They also offered guitars, basses and banjos.

SM6 Mandolin

1970s-2007. Made in Korea.

| 1980s | | $250 | $300 |

Silvertone

1941-ca.1970. Brand name used by Sears on their musical instruments.

Mandolin

1941-ca.1970. Arched top and back, sunburst.

| 1940s | | $200 | $225 |
| 1950s | | $175 | $200 |

Smart Musical Instruments

1986-present. Premium and presentation grade, custom, mandolin family instruments built by luthier A. Lawrence Smart in McCall, Idaho. He also builds guitars.

Smith, Lawrence K.

1989-present. Luthier Lawrence Smith builds his premium grade, production/custom, mandolins in Australia. He also builds guitars.

Sovereign

Ca. 1899-ca. 1938. Sovereign was originally a brand of the Oscar Schmidt company of New Jersey. In the late '30s, Harmony purchased several trade names from the Schmidt Company, including Sovereign. Sovereign then ceased as a brand, but Harmony continued using it on a model line of Harmony guitars.

Mandolin

1920s. Old-style bent top.

| 1920s | | $275 | $325 |

Stahl

The William C. Stahl music publishing company claimed their instruments were made in Milwaukee, Wisconsin, in the early-1900s, but the Larson Brothers of Chicago built mandolin family instruments for them. Models included Style 4 (22 ribs) to Style 12 Presentation Artist Special. The more expensive models were generally 44-rib construction.

Stanley Mandolins

2003-present. Luthier Chris Stanley builds his premium grade, production/custom, A-style and F-style mandolins in Rhinelander, Wisconsin.

1976 Regal Bicentennial

Roberts Tiny Moore J5

MANDOLINS

MODEL YEAR	FEATURES	EXC. COND. LOW	HIGH

Stiver F Model

Stonebridge MF22SF

Stathopoulo
1903-1916. Original design instruments, some patented, by Epiphone company founder A. Stathopoulo.

A-Style Mandolin

1903-1916. A-style with higher-end appointments, bent-style spruce top, figured maple back and sides.

1912		$850	$1,100

Stefan Sobell Musical Instruments
1982-present. Luthier Stefan Sobell builds his premium grade, production/custom, mandolins in Hetham, Northumberland, England. He also builds guitars, citterns and bouzoukis.

Stella
Ca. 1899-1974, 2000s. Stella was a brand of the Oscar Schmidt Company which was an early contributor to innovative mandolin designs and participated in the 1900-'30 mandolin boom. Pre-World War II Stella instruments were low-mid to mid-level instruments. In '39, Harmony purchased the Stella name and '50s and '60s Stella instruments were student grade, low-end instruments. The Stella brand was reintroduced for a period in the 2000s by MBT International.

Banjo-Mandolin

1920s. One of several innovative designs that attempted to create a new market, 8-string mandolin neck with a banjo body, Stella logo normally impressed on the banjo rim or the side of the neck.

1920s		$200	$225

Bowl Back Mandolin

1920s. Typical bowl back, bent top-style mandolin with models decalomania, about 10 (wide) maple ribs, dot markers.

1920s		$150	$175

Pear-Shape Mandolin

1940s-1960s. Harmony-made lower-end mandolins, pear-shaped (Style A) flat back, oval soundhole.

1940s	Natural	$175	$200
1950s		$175	$200
1960s	Sunburst	$175	$200

Stelling
1974-present. Mainly known for banjos, Stelling also builds premium grade, production/custom mandolins in Afton, Virginia.

Sterling
Early-1900s. Distributed by wholesalers The Davitt & Hanser Music Co.

Stetson
1884-ca. 1924. Stetson was another house brand of the W. J. Dyer store in St. Paul, Minnesota. Starting around 1904, the Larson brothers built a few student grade Stetson mandolins under this brand.

Stiver
1971-present. Premium grade, custom/production, mandolins built by luthier Louis Stiver in Polk, Pennsylvania.

F-5 Mandolin

1982		$3,500	$4,000

Stonebridge
1981-present. Luthier Frantisek Furch builds his production/custom, professional and premium grade, acoustic mandolins in the Czech Republic. He also builds guitars.

Strad-O-Lin
Ca.1920s-ca.1960s. The Strad-O-Lin company was operated by the Hominic brothers in New York, primarily making mandolins for wholesalers. In the late '50s, Multivox/Premier bought the company and used the name on mandolins and guitars.

Baldwin Electric Mandolin

1950s. A-Style, single pickup, tone and volume knobs, spruce top, maple back and sides, Baldwin logo on headstock.

1950s	Natural	$400	$500

Junior A Mandolin

1950s. A-Style, Stradolin Jr. logo on headstock, dot markers.

1950s	Sunburst	$250	$300

Stromberg-Voisinet
1921-ca.1932. Marketed Stromberg (not to be confused with Charles Stromberg of Boston) and Kay Kraft brands, plus instruments of other distributors and retailers. Became the Kay Musical Instrument Company. By the mid-'20s, the company was making many better Montgomery Ward guitars, banjos and mandolins, often with lots of pearloid. The last Stromberg acoustic instruments were seen in '32.

Summit
1990-present. Professional and premium grade, production/custom mandolins built by luthier Paul Schneider in Hartsville, Tennessee. He was originally located in Mulvane, Kansas.

Superior
1987-present. Intermediate grade, production/custom mandolin-family instruments made in Mexico for George Katechis Montalvo of Berkeley Musical Instrument Exchange. They also offer guitars.

Supertone
1914-1941. Brand used by Sears before they switched to Silvertone. Instruments made by other companies.

Mandolin

Spruce top, mahogany back and sides, some with decalomania vine pattern on top.

1920s		$200	$250
1930s	With vine pattern	$200	$250

MANDOLINS

MODEL YEAR	FEATURES	EXC. COND. LOW	HIGH

Supro

1935-1968, 2004-present. Budget line from the National Dobro Company. Amp builder Bruce Zinky revived the Supro name for a guitar and amp model.

T30 Electric Mandolin

1950s		$500	$625

T.H. Davis

1976-present. Premium grade, custom, mandolins built by luthier Ted Davis in Loudon, Tennessee. He also builds guitars.

Tacoma

1995-present. Tacoma offered intermediate, professional and premium grade, production, electric and acoustic mandolins up to '06. They also build guitars and basses.

M Series Mandolin

1999-2006. Solid spruce top, typical Tacoma body-style with upper bass bout soundhole, E (i.e. M-1E) indicates acoustic/electric.

1999-2004	M2, rosewood	$350	$425
1999-2006	M1, mahogany	$275	$350
1999-2006	M1E, mahogany	$300	$375
1999-2006	M3/M3E, maple	$475	$600

Tennessee

1970-1993, 1996-present. Luthier Mark Taylor builds his professional and premium grade, production/custom, mandolins in Old Hickory, Tennessee. He also builds guitars, banjos and the Tut Taylor brand of resophonic guitars.

Timeless Instruments

1980-present. Luthier David Freeman builds his intermediate grade, mandolins in Tugaske, Saskatchewan. He also builds guitars and dulcimers.

Triggs

1992-present. Luthiers Jim Triggs and his son Ryan build their professional and premium grade, production/custom, mandolins in Kansas City, Kansas. They also build guitars. They were located in Nashville, Tennessee until '98.

Trinity River

2004-present. Production/custom, budget and intermediate grade, mandolins imported from Asia by luthiers Marcus Lawyer and Ross McLeod in Fort Worth, Texas. They also import guitars, basses and banjos.

Unicorn

1970s-late 1980s. Luthier Rolfe Gerhardt (currently luthier for Phoenix Mandolins) founded Unicorn in the mid-'70s. Gerhardt built 149 mandolins before selling Unicorn to Dave Sinko in '80. Sinko closed Unicorn in the late-'80s.

MODEL YEAR	FEATURES	EXC. COND. LOW	HIGH

Vega

1880s-present. The original Boston-based company was purchased by C.F. Martin in '70. Vega means star and a star logo is often seen on the original Vega instruments. In '80, the Vega trademark was sold to a Korean company. The Deering Banjo Company, in Spring Valley, California acquired the brand in '89 and uses it (and the star logo) on a line of banjos.

Lansing Special Bowl Mandolin

1890s. Spruce top, abalone, vine inlay.

1890s		$375	$450

Little Wonder Mandolin Banjo

1920s. Maple neck, resonator.

1920s		$375	$450

Mando Bass Mandolin

1910s-1920s. Large upright bass-sized instrument with bass tuners, body-style similar to dual-point A-style, scroll headstock.

1910-1920s		$2,800	$3,500

Mandolin Cittern

1910s. 10-string (five double strings tuned in 5ths), vague A-style with oval soundhole and cylinder back, natural.

1910s		$1,800	$2,200

Style 202 Lute Mandolin

Early-1900s. Basic A-style with small horns, natural spruce top, mahogany sides and cylinder back, dot markers.

1910s		$1,300	$1,600

Style 205 Cylinder Back Mandolin

1910s-1920s. Rounded tube cylinder shape runs the length of the back.

1910s		$1,700	$2,100
1920s		$1,400	$1,700

Style A Mandolin

1910s		$500	$600

Style F Mandolin

1910s. Scroll upper bass bout, oval soundhole, Vega and torch inlay in headstock.

1910s		$700	$900

Style K Mandolin Banjo

1910-1930s		$300	$400

Style L Banjo Mandolin/Whyte Laydie

1910s-1920s. Open back banjo body and mandolin 8-string neck.

1910-1920s		$1,200	$1,500

Super Deluxe Mandolin

1910s	Sunburst	$700	$850

Tubaphone Style X Mandolin Banjo

1923		$700	$850

Veillette

1991-present. Luthiers Joe Veillette and Martin Keith build their professional grade, production/custom, mandolins in Woodstock, New York. They also build basses and guitars.

Vinaccia

Italian-made by Pasquale Vinaccia, luthier.

Tacoma M-1

1921 Vega Style L Whyte Laydie Mandolin-Banjo

MANDOLINS

Washburn M1S

MODEL YEAR	FEATURES	EXC. COND. LOW	HIGH

Bowl Back Mandolin
High-end appointments and 'guard, 30 rosewood ribs.

1900-1920s		$1,700	$2,100

Vivi-Tone
1933-ca. 1936. Lloyd Loar's pioneering guitar company also built early electric mandolins and mandocellos in Kalamazoo, Michigan.

Electric Mandocello
1933-1935. Traditonal guitar-arch body, Vivi-Tone silkscreen logo on headstock.

1933-1935		$4,500	$5,500

Electric Mandola
1933-1935. Traditonal European teardrop/pear-shaped top, Vivi-Tone silkscreen logo on headstock.

1933-1935		$3,700	$4,500

Electric Mandolin
1933-1935. Vivi-Tone silkscreen logo on headstock.

1933-1935		$3,200	$4,000

Waldo
1891- early 1900s. Mandolin family instruments built in Saginaw, Michigan.

Bowl Back Mandolin
1890s. Alternating rosewood and maple ribs, some with script Waldo logo on pickguard.

1890s		$150	$175

Ward
Depression era private brand made by Gibson's Kalamazoo factory.

Style A Mandolin
1930s. Style A body with round soundhole and flat top and back, dot markers, mahogany back and sides, silkscreened Ward logo.

1935	Sunburst	$250	$300

Washburn (Lyon & Healy)
1880s-ca.1949. Washburn was founded in Chicago as one of the lines for Lyon & Healy to promote high quality stringed instruments, ca. 1880s. The rights to Washburn were sold to Regal which built Washburns by the mid-'30s until until ca. '49. In '74 the brand resurfaced.

Bowl Back Mandolin
1890s-1900s. Lyon and Healy sold a wide variety of bowl back mandolins, Brazilian ribs with fancy inlays and bindings.

1890s	Fancy inlays & bindings	$700	$800
1890s	Plain appointments	$350	$400
1900s	Fancy inlays & bindings	$700	$800
1900s	Plain appointments	$350	$400
1900s	Standard appointments	$450	$550

Style A Mandolin
1920s. Brazilian rosewood.

1920s		$800	$1,000

Style E Mandolin
1915-1923. Brazilian rosewood.

1915-1923		$1,000	$1,200

Washburn (Post 1974)
1974-present. Currently, Washburn offers imported intermediate and professional grade, production, mandolins.

Mandolin/Mandolin Family
1974-present.

1974-2010		$300	$375

Washington
Washington mandolins were manufactured by Kansas City, Missouri instrument wholesalers J.W. Jenkins & Sons. First introduced in 1895, the brand also offered guitars.

Weber
1996-present. Intermediate, professional, and premium grade, production/custom, mandolins, mandolas, and mandocellos. Many former Flatiron employees, including Bruce Weber, formed Sound To Earth, Ltd., to build Weber instruments when Gibson moved Flatiron from Bozeman, Montana, to Nashville. Originally in Belgrade, Montana, and since '04, in Logan, Montana. They also build guitars.

MANDOLINS

MODEL		EXC. COND.	
YEAR	FEATURES	LOW	HIGH

Aspen #1 Mandolin
1997-present. Teardrop A-style, solid spruce top, maple sides and back, mahogany neck.
| 1997-2010 | | $650 | $800 |

Aspen #2 Mandolin
1997-present. Like #1, but with maple neck.
| 1997-2010 | | $750 | $900 |

Beartooth Mandolin
1997-2009. Teardrop A-style, solid spruce top, curly maple sides, back, and neck.
| 1997-2010 | | $1,600 | $1,900 |

Bitterroot Mandolin
2005-present. F-style.
| 2005-2010 | | $1,700 | $2,100 |

Custom Vintage Mandolin
2007-present.
| 2007-2010 | A-style | $1,800 | $2,400 |
| 2007-2010 | F-style | $3,400 | $4,100 |

Fern Mandolin
1997-present. F-style, top of the product line.
| 1997-2010 | | $3,900 | $4,500 |

Gallatin Mandolin
1999-present.
| 1999-2010 | A-style | $1,000 | $1,200 |
| 1999-2010 | F-style | $1,400 | $1,600 |

Octar Mandolin
2008. Octave mando, 15" archtop body.
| 2008 | | $2,000 | $2,300 |

Sweet Pea Mandolin
2009-present. Flat-style.
| 2009-2010 | | $250 | $275 |

Y2K Mandolin
2000. Celtic-style teardrop body, satin natural finish.
| 2000 | | $700 | $800 |

Yellowstone Mandolin
1997-present. A-style and F-style available, solid spruce top, curly maple sides, back, and neck, sunburst.
| 1997-2010 | A-style | $1,200 | $1,500 |
| 1997-2010 | F-style | $2,200 | $2,600 |

Weymann
1864-1940s. H.A. Weymann & Sons was a musical instrument distributor located in Philadelphia. They also built their own instruments.

Keystone State Banjo Mandolin
1910s. Maple rim and back, ebony fretboard.
| 1910s | | $300 | $375 |

Mandolin Banjo
1920s. Mandolin neck on a open banjo body.
| 1920s | Various models | $350 | $425 |

Mando-Lute
1920s. Lute-style body, spruce top, flamed maple sides and back, rope binding, deluxe rosette, natural.
| 1920s | Various models | $475 | $575 |

Wurlitzer
The old Wurlitzer company would have been considered a mega-store by today's standards. They sold a wide variety of instruments, gave music lessons, and operated manufacturing facilities.

Mandolin
| 1920s | Koa | $375 | $525 |

Mandolin Banjo
1900s. Mandolin neck on open back banjo body, plain-style.
| 1900s | | $225 | $275 |

Yosco
1900-1930s. Lawrence L. Yosco was a New York City luthier building guitars, round back mandolins and banjos under his own brand and for others.

Zeta
1982-present. Zeta has made professional grade, acoustic/electric mandolins in Oakland, California over the years, but currently only offer upright basses, amps and violins.

Weber Absaroka

MANDOLINS

UKULELES

Chances are if you give any thought to the ukulele at all, you likely regard it as that tiny novelty instrument responsible for background music in SpongeBob Squarepants cartoons and minivan commercials. Yet through three waves of popularity since its invention in 1889, the uke has had such binges of WILD interest that demand frequently outstripped supply – they literally couldn't be made fast enough. And as with the guitar that nudged the uke aside, manufacturers looked from the start for ways to fuel sales with variety in size, shape, and ornamentation.

The first ukuleles, crafted by settlers to the Hawaiian Islands, were the literal copies of tiny, guitar-shaped, Portuguese machete de bragas settlers had carried with them on the long journey. Just like the machete, they were around 21 inches long from body-bottom to headstock-tip, and around 6 inches across. The only difference, really, was that the ukulele was now made exclusively out of Hawaiian koa wood, which the islands were practically crawling with. This was the genius of the ukulele: an old form in a new material. The taro patch fiddle was likely the first departure from the original four-stringed uke design. The Laverne & Shirley to the ukulele's Happy Days, this spin-off sported a slightly wider neck, longer scale, and beefier body, all to support the demands of eight gut strings in double courses. What Hawaiian root farming – or violins, for that matter – had to do with eight-stringed ukes is anybody's guess, but the scene was set for more variations.

Back on the mainland a curious public introduced to Hawaiian music through events like Chicago's Colombian Exhibition of 1893 and San Francisco's Pan Pacific of 1915 was eager to start strumming. And seeing gold in them thar ukes, America's instrument makers geared up. Preeminent guitar maker C.F. Martin & Co. entered the fray around 1916 with a line of the smallest ukes (which we now call soprano), originally offered in degrees of ornamentation from plain to mildly fancy. The Martin uke was an immediate success, and within a few years the company became the first stateside maker to exploit the ukulele's full potential for expansion.

At 7 ½ inches wide, the eight-stringed taro patch was a natural to join the Martin line, followed quickly by a four-stringed version – essentially half a taro patch – which Martin dubbed a concert sized uke. A still larger tenor uke soon appeared, with a body around 9 inches across. And before you could say King Kamehameha, Martin was offering three different sizes, in two different species of wood, and in five degrees of ornamentation. You do the math, a LOT of choices already.

The remainder of ukulele design evolution paralleled that of the guitar, and for the very same reasons. The desire to be heard above the din of louder instruments is essential to all musicians, and this was solved by modifying both size and voice. Larger, deeper uke bodies increased volume, or as with the taro patch, stringing was reconsidered to modify timbre. Both approaches were applied to the tiple, a miniature guitar of South American ancestry. Its tenor-sized body and ten steel strings made it loud and jangly and ensured that it sounded neither like uke or taro patch. The final major development came as a concession to playability. If you're a guitar player who's dabbled in uke, you may have noticed that any attempt to "play up the neck" of a soprano uke is met with an absence of any real neck to play up. Something of a problem from the start, this was remedied in the 1950s first by design of a tenor with a 14 fret neck, followed by the introduction of the long-necked, large-bodied baritone ukulele. Seemingly an oxymoron, like jumbo shrimp, the baritone – at 11 inches wide – was as large as the uke dared go.

And that's about the size of it. Many types, one big happy ukulele family. From smallest to largest: soprano, concert, tenor, and baritone. Ukes have four strings, taro patch fiddles have eight; tiples have ten. With few exceptions, geared tuners were for steel-strung instruments, pegs were for nylon. Some ukes were made out of koa wood, some birch, but most were mahogany. If you can't tell, it's mahogany.

Now go buy a uke, and pick the size that's just right for you.

R.J. Klimpert

| MODEL | | EXC. COND. | |
YEAR	FEATURES	LOW	HIGH

Aero Uke

1920s. Never branded, but almost certainly produced by Chicago's Stromberg-Voisenet Company, the precursor of Kay, the Aero Uke is an instrument quite unlike any other. With its spruce-capped body resembling an old-timey airplane wing and a neck and headstock that approximate a plane's fuselage, this clever '20s offering cashed in on the Lindbergh craze (like the Harmony Johnny Marvin model with its airplane-shaped bridge), and must have been a big hit at parties.

Aero Ukulele
Airplane body.

1927	Black deco on wing	$2,000	$2,500
1927	Gold deco on wing	$2,200	$2,800

Aloha

1935-1960s. The Aloha brand turns up on numerous vastly different ukes. In fact, the variety of features exhibited by Aloha ukuleles leads the modern observer to believe that the ukes that bear this headstock decal were made by as many as a dozen different manufacturers, each with access to the same logo. Many were undoubtedly Island-made, with all koa bodies and some with fancy rope binding; others bear unmistakable mainland traits. Some of these have a more traditional look and are stamped Akai inside the soundhole, while still others, strongly resembling mainland C.F. Martins in design, typically sport a decal of the Sam F. Chang curio shop on the reverse of the headstock.

Akai Soprano Ukulele
Koa construction.

1930s		$450	$550

Soprano Ukulele
Koa body, plain.

1950s		$550	$650

Andy Powers Musical Instrument Co.

1996-present. Luthier Andy Powers, builds his professional grade, custom, ukuleles in Oceanside, California. He also builds guitars and mandolins.

Applause

1976-present. Kaman Music's entry-level Ovation-styled import brand. Applause currently offers budget and intermediate grade, production, soprano and tenor ukuleles.

Austin

1999-present. Budget and intermediate grade, production, ukuleles imported by St. Louis Music. They also offer guitars, basses, amps, mandolins and banjos.

Bear Creek Guitars

1995-present. Intermediate and professional grade ukuleles built by luthier Bill Hardin in Kula, Hawaii. He also builds guitars.

MODEL		EXC. COND.	
YEAR	FEATURES	LOW	HIGH

Beltona

1990-present. Production metal body resonator ukuleles made in New Zealand by Steve Evans and Bill Johnson. They also build guitars and mandolins.

Beneteau

1974-present. Professional grade, custom, ukuleles built by luthier Marc Beneteau in St. Thomas, Ontario. He also builds guitars.

Bertoncini Stringed Instruments

1995-present. Luthier Dave Bertoncini mainly builds flat-top guitars in Olympia, Washington, but has also built ukuleles and mandolins.

Blackbird

2006-present. At the 2010 NAMM Show, luthier Joe Luttwak introduced the first ever carbon fiber ukulele, built in San Francisco, California. He also builds guitars.

Blue Star

1984-present. Intermediate grade, production/custom, acoustic and electric ukuleles built by luthier Bruce Herron in Fennville, Michigan. He also builds guitars, mandolins, dulcimers and lap steels.

Boulder Creek

2007-present. Imported, intermediate and professional grade, production, acoustic ukuleles distributed by Morgan Hill Music of Morgan Hill, California. They also offer guitars and basses.

Breedlove

1990-present. Founded by Larry Breedlove and Steve Henderson. Professional and premium grade, production/custom, ukuleles made in Tumalo, Oregon. They also build guitars, basses, laps and mandolins.

Bruno

1834-present. This New York distributor certainly subcontracted all of its ukulele production to other manufacturers, and as a result you'd be hard pressed to find two identical Bruno ukes.

Soprano Ukulele

1920s	Koa, rope soundhole	$350	$450
1930s	Koa, rope bound body	$550	$650

Chantus

1984-present. Professional grade, production/custom, ukuleles built in Austin, Texas, by luthier William King. He also builds guitars.

Char

1985-present. Luthier Kerry Char builds his professional grade, custom, ukuleles in Portland, Oregon. He also builds guitars and harpguitars.

Collings

1986-present. The Austin, Texas, based guitar builder added ukuleles in the summer of '09.

DeCava Guitars

1983-present. Professional grade, production/custom, ukuleles built by luthier Jim DeCava in Stratford, Connecticut. He also builds guitars, banjos, and mandolins.

Del Vecchio Dimonaco

With a design patterned after the pioneering work of Dobro and National, this Brazilian company produced a full line of resonator instruments, all constructed of native Brazilian rosewood, from the 1950s onward.

Resonator Ukulele

Brazilian rosewood.

1950s		$900	$1,200

Delgado

1928-present. Custom, premium grade, classical ukuleles built by luthier Manuel A. Delgado in Nashville, Tennessee. He also builds guitars, basses, mandolins and banjos.

Ditson

1916-1930. Don't be fooled. While some of the ukes that were commissioned by this East Coast music publisher and chain store were actually manufactured by C.F. Martin, Martin was by no means the sole supplier. The Martin-made instruments often bear a Martin brand as well as a Ditson one, or, barring that, at least demonstrate an overall similarity to the rest of the ukes in the regular Martin line, both inside and out. The most telling and desirable feature of these Martin-made Ditsons is a dreadnaught-style wide waisted body design.

Soprano Ukulele

1922	as Martin Style 1 K	$2,250	$2,500
1922	as Martin Style 1 M	$1,250	$1,600
1922	as Martin Style 2 K	$2,500	$3,000
1922	as Martin Style 2 M	$1,600	$1,750
1922	as Martin Style 3 K	$3,500	$4,000
1922	as Martin Style 3 M	$3,000	$3,500
1922	as Martin Style 5 K	$10,000	$13,000
1922	as Martin Style O	$1,250	$1,600

Dobro

1929-1942, ca. 1954-present. The ukulele version of the popular amplifying resonator instruments first produced in California, the Dobro uke was offered in 2 sizes (soprano and tenor), 2 styles (f-holes and screen holes), and 2 colors (brown and black). Models with Dobro headstock decals are often outwardly indistinguishable from others bearing either a Regal badge or no logo at all, but a peek inside often reveals the presence of a sound well in the belly of the former, making them the more desirable of the two.

Blackbird Super OM

Blue Star Baritone Konablaster

Char Spalted Koa Concert

UKULELES

Fine Resophonic Model 3

Gibson TU-1

Gold Tone GU-100

MODEL YEAR	FEATURES	EXC. COND. LOW	HIGH

Resonator Ukulele
Wood body.

1930s	F-holes, Regal-made	$200	$400
1930s	Screen holes	$750	$900
1935	Tenor, cyclops screen	$1,100	$1,500

Douglas Ching
1976-present. Luthier Douglas J. Ching builds his professional grade, production/custom, ukuleles currently in Chester, Virginia, and previously in Hawaii ('76-'89) and Michigan ('90-'93). He also builds guitars, lutes and violins.

Earnest Kaai
Hawaiian Earnest Kaai was many things (teacher, songbook publisher, importer/exporter) during the early part of the 20th century, but ukulele manufacturer was certainly one job that he couldn't add to his resume. Still, scads of ukes proudly bear his name, in a variety of different styles and variations. Even more puzzling is the fact that while some appear to actually have been island-made, an equal number bear the telltale signs of mainland manufacture. Some Kaai labeled ukes may have been made by the Larson Brothers of Chicago.

Soprano Ukulele
Koa body.

1925	No binding, decal on headstock	$400	$500
1930	No binding, rope inlaid soundhole	$500	$600
1935	Pearl inlaid top & soundhole	$1,250	$1,600
1935	Rope binding on top/back only	$400	$600

Epiphone
Ca. 1873-present. Epiphone made banjo ukes in the 1920s and '30s and recently got back into the market with koa and mahogany models.

Favilla
1890-1973. The small New York City family-owned factory that produced primarily guitars also managed to offer some surprisingly high quality ukes, the best of which rival Martin and Gibson for craftsmanship and tone. As a result, Favilla ukuleles are a real value for the money.

Baritone Ukulele

1950s	Plain mahogany	$300	$500

Soprano Ukulele

1950s	Mahogany, triple bound	$500	$650
1950s	Plain mahogany	$500	$650
1950s	Teardrop-shaped, birch	$300	$500
1950s	Teardrop-shaped, stained blue	$300	$500

MODEL YEAR	FEATURES	EXC. COND. LOW	HIGH

Fender
Fender offered Regal-made ukuleles in the 1960s, including the R-275 Baritone Ukulele. In '09 they again started offering ukes. Starting in '09 Fender offered 3 budget and intermediate grade, production tenor ukes.

Fin-der
1950s. The pitch of this short-lived plastic ukulele was apparently the ease of learning, since the included instructional brochure helped you to "find" your chords with the added help of rainbow color-coded nylon strings.

Diamond Head Ukulele
Styrene plastic, in original box.

1950s		$100	$150

Fine Resophonic
1988-present. Intermediate and professional grade, production/custom, wood and metal-bodied resophonic ukuleles built by luthiers Mike Lewis and Pierre Avocat in Vitry Sur Seine, France. They also build guitars and mandolins.

Flamingo
1950s. If swanky designs hot-foil stamped into the surface of these '50s swirly injection molded polystyrene ukes didn't grab you, certainly the built-in functional pitch pipe across the top of the headstock would. And I ask you, who can resist a ukulele with a built-in tuner?

Soprano Ukulele

1955	Brown top, white 'board	$100	$150
1955	White top, brown 'board	$100	$150

Gibson
1890s (1902)-present. A relative late-comer to the uke market, Gibson didn't get a line off the ground until 1927, fully nine years after Martin had already been in production. Even then they only produced three soprano styles and one tenor version. Worse still, they never made any ukes in koa, sticking to the easier-to-obtain mahogany.

Nonetheless, Gibson ukuleles exhibit more unintentional variety than any other major maker, with enough construction, inlay, binding, and cosmetic variations to keep collectors buzzing for many a year to come. In general, the earliest examples feature a Gibson logo in script, later shortened to just Gibson. Post-war examples adopted the more square-ish logo of the rest of the Gibson line, and, at some point in the late '50s, began sporting ink-stamped serial numbers on the back of the headstock like their guitar and mandolin brethren.

ETU 1 Ukulele
Electric tenor, unbound body, square black pickup, 88 made.

1949		$3,500	$5,000

MODEL YEAR	FEATURES	EXC. COND. LOW	HIGH

ETU 3 Ukulele
Electric tenor, triple bound body, rectangle pickup, rare.

1953		$5,000	$8,000

TU-1 Ukulele
Tenor, called the TU until 1 added in 1949, mahogany body, sunburst finish.

1930s		$1,000	$1,300

Uke-1 Ukulele
Soprano, plain mahogany body.

1927		$850	$1,000
1966	Red SG guitar-like finish	$650	$850

Uke-2 Ukulele
Soprano, mahogany body.

1934	Triple bound	$800	$1,000

Uke-3 Ukulele
Soprano, dark finish.

1933	Diamonds & squares inlay	$1,250	$1,500
1935	Diamond inlay, short 'board	$1,250	$1,500
1935	Rare curved designs inlay	$2,500	$3,000

Gold Tone
1993-present. Wayne and Robyn Rogers build their intermediate grade, production/custom ukuleles in Titusville, Florida. They also offer guitars, basses, lap steels, mandolins, banjos and banjitars.

Graziano
1969-present. Luthier Tony Graziano has been building ukuleles almost exclusively since '95 in his Santa Cruz shop. Like many, he sees the uke as the instrument of the new millennium, and his entirely handmade, custom orders can be had in a variety of shapes, sizes, and woods.

Gretsch
1883-present. The first (and most desirable) ukuleles by this New York manufacturer were actually stamped with the name Gretsch American or with interior brass nameplates. Subsequent pieces, largely inexpensive laminate-bodied catalog offerings, are distinguished by small round Gretsch headstock decals, and a lack of any kerfed linings inside the bodies.

Plain Soprano Ukulele
Natural mahogany body, no binding.

1950s		$150	$200

Round Ukulele
Round body, blue to green sunburst.

1940		$150	$200

Soprano Ukulele

1940s	Koa, fancy 'board inlay	$750	$900
1940s	Mahogany, fancy 'board inlay	$750	$900
1940s	Unbound, engraved rose peghead	$800	$1,100

1950s	Darker finish, dark binding border	$250	$350

Guild
1952-present. By rights this fine East Coast shop should have produced a full line of ukes to complement its impressive flat and carved-top guitar offerings. Alas, a lone baritone model was all that they could manage. And it's a darned shame, too.

B-11 Baritone Ukulele
1963-1976. Mahogany body, rosewood 'board.

1960s		$800	$1,100

Harmony
1892-1976, late 1970s-present. This manufacturer surely produced more ukuleles than all other makers put together. Their extensive line ran the gamut from artist endorsed models and ukes in unusual shapes and materials, to inexpensive but flashy creations adorned with eye-catching decals and silk screening. The earliest examples have a small paper label on the back of the headstock, and a branded logo inside the body. This was replaced by a succession of logo decals applied to the front of the headstock, first gold and black, later green, white, and black. By the '60s Harmony had become so synonymous with ukulele production that they were known around their Chicago locale as simply "the ukulele factory," as in, "Ma couldn't come to the bar-b-que on-a-counta she got a job at the ukulele factory."

Baritone Ukulele
Bound mahogany body.

1960s		$200	$300

Concert Ukulele
Mahogany body, bound, concert-sized.

1935		$200	$300

Harold Teen Ukulele
Carl Ed cartoon decals on front.

1930	Gray-blue	$350	$500
1930	Red	$350	$500
1930	Yellow	$450	$600

Johnny Marvin Tenor Ukulele
Sports an airplane bridge.

1930s	Flamed koa	$750	$1,000
1930s	Sunburst mahogany	$400	$500

Roy Smeck Concert Ukulele
Concert-sized, sunburst spruce top.

1935		$400	$500

Roy Smeck Ukulele
Mahogany body.

1955	Plastic 'board	$100	$150
1955	Wood 'board	$250	$350

Roy Smeck Vita Ukulele
Pear-shaped body, seal-shaped f-holes.

1926		$400	$500

Tiple Ukulele
Multicolored binding, 10 steel strings.

1935		$400	$600

Graziano Concert

1954 Harmony Baritone

1955 Harmony Roy Smeck
(Steve Bauman)

UKULELES

Hilo Baritone

1940s Kamaka Pineapple

1960 Kamaka Soprano

UKULELES

MODEL YEAR	FEATURES	EXC. COND. LOW	HIGH
Ukulele			
1930	Koa, unbound	$200	$300
1935	Plain mahogany, unbound	$150	$250

Hilo Bay Ukuleles

2003-present. Intermediate grade, production, tenor ukuleles made in Cebu City, Philippines for Hilo Guitars and Ukuleles of Hilo, Hawaii.

Hohner

1857-present. They currently offer budget grade, tenor, baritone, standard, pineapple, and concert ukuleles. They also have guitars, basses, banjos, and mandolins.

Johnson

Mid-1990s-present. Budget ukuleles imported by Music Link of Brisbane, California. They also offer guitars, amps, mandolins and effects. Most notable of the Johnson ukes are the National metal-bodied uke copies, which come surprisingly close to the look and feel of the originals, at an unfathomably low price.

K & S

1992-1998. Ukes distributed by George Katechis and Marc Silber and handmade in Paracho, Mexico. They also offered guitars. In '98, Silber started marketing the ukes under the Marc Silber Guitar Company brand and Katechis continued to offer instruments under the Casa Montalvo brand. The Mexican-made 'Frisco Uke' takes its inspiration from the inimitable '20s Roy Smeck Vita Uke (see Harmony), but with none of the whimsy of the original.

Kala

2005-present. Mike Upton's Petaluma, California company offers budget and intermediate grade, production, ukuleles.

Kamaka

Part of the second wave of ukulele builders on the Hawaiian islands (after Nunes, Dias, and Santos) Kamaka distinguished itself first with ukes of extremely high quality, subsequently with the most enduring non-guitar-derived designs, the Pineapple Uke, patented in 1928. Kamaka is the only maker which has been in continuous production for nearly a hundred years, offering Hawaiian-made products from native woods in virtually every size and ornamentation. In the early '70s, Kamaka began rubber stamping the full date of manufacture on the end of the neck block of each uke, visible right through the sound hole. Now don't you wish that every manufacturer did that?

Concert Ukulele
Koa body, extended rosewood 'board.

1975		$500	$750

MODEL YEAR	FEATURES	EXC. COND. LOW	HIGH
Lili'u Ukulele			
Concert-sized koa body.			
1965	8 strings	$700	$850
1985	6 strings	$700	$850
Pineapple Ukulele			
1928	Pearl inlay on top and/or 'board	$3,000	$4,000
1928	Pineapple art painted onto top or back	$2,500	$3,000
1930	Monkeypod wood, plain, unbound	$1,500	$1,850
1930	Rope bound top only, koa	$2,500	$3,000
1935	Rope bound soundhole only	$1,300	$1,500
1960	Koa, unbound, 2 Ks logo	$700	$900
1970	Koa, extended rosewood 'board	$600	$750
Soprano Ukulele			
Traditional uke shape, plain koa body.			
1920		$500	$600
Tenor Ukulele			
Koa body, extended rosewood 'board.			
1955		$500	$750

Kanile'a Ukulele

1998-present. Joseph and Kristen Souza build their intermediate, professional and premium grade, production/custom, ukuleles in Kaneohe, Hawaii.

Kay

1931-present. Kay offered banjo ukuleles in the 1920s and again in the late '50s; they offered ukuleles from '66-'68 and currently offer budget grade, production, imported ukuleles. They also make amps, guitars, banjos, mandolins, basses, and violins.

Kent

1961-1969. Large, student quality ukes of laminated construction were offered by this Japanese concern throughout the '60s.

Baritone Ukulele
Mahogany body, bound top, bound back.

1960s		$100	$150

Knutsen

1890s-1920s. While Christopher Knutsen was the inventor of flat-topped harp instruments featuring an integral sound chamber on the bass side of the body, he almost certainly left the manufacturing to others. Striking in both concept and design, Knutsen products nonetheless suffer from compromised construction techniques.

Harp Taro Patch Ukulele
Koa body, large horn chamber, 8 strings, unbound.

1915		$3,000	$3,500

MODEL YEAR	FEATURES	EXC. COND. LOW	HIGH

Harp Ukulele
Koa body, large horn chamber.

1915	Bound	$2,500	$3,000
1915	Unbound	$1,500	$2,000

Kumalae

Along with Kamaka, Kumalae was also of the second wave of Hawaiian uke makers. Jonah Kumalae's company quickly snagged the prestigious Gold Award at the Pan Pacific Exhibition in 1915, and the headstock decals and paper labels aren't about to let you forget it, either. Many assume that these all date from exactly that year, when in fact Kumalaes were offered right up through the late 1930s.

Soprano Ukulele
Figured koa body.

1919	Bound top/back/ 'board	$750	$900
1920	Rope bound top/back	$650	$800
1927	As 1919 but with fiddle-shaped peghead	$1,500	$2,000
1930	Unbound body	$650	$800
1933	Rope bound soundhole only	$650	$800

Tenor Ukulele
Koa body, unbound top and back.

1930		$1,000	$1,250

Lanikai

2000-present. Line of budget and intermediate grade, production, koa or nato wood, acoustic and acoustic/electric, ukuleles distributed by Hohner.

Larrivee

1968-present. This mainstream guitar manufacturer has an on-again off-again relationship with the ukulele, having occasionally produced some superb examples in various sizes, woods and degrees of ornamentation. They introduced three ukulele models in '00. They also build guitars.

Le Domino

This line of striking ukuleles turned the popularity of domino playing into a clever visual motif, displaying not only tumbling dominos on their soundboards and around their soundholes, but 'board markers represented in decal domino denominations (3, 5, 7, 10, 12, etc.). The ukuleles were, in fact, produced by at least two different companies - Stewart and Regal - but you can scarcely tell them apart.

Concert Ukukele
Concert size, black-finish, white bound, dominos.

1932		$1,250	$1,500

Soprano Ukukele
Domino decals.

1930	Black finish, white bound	$500	$750
1940	Natural finish, unbound	$150	$250

Leonardo Nunes

Leonardo was the son of Manuel, the self professed inventor of the ukulele. Whether actually the originator or not, Dad was certainly on the ship that brought the inventor to the islands in 1879. Leonardo, instead of joining up and making it Manuel & Son, set out on his own to produce ukes that are virtually indistinguishable from Pop's. All constructed entirely of koa, some exhibit considerable figure and rope binding finery, making them as highly desirable to collectors as Manuel's.

Radio Tenor Ukulele
Koa body, bound top, back and neck.

1935		$1,250	$1,500

Soprano Ukulele
Figured koa body.

1919	Bound top/back/ 'board	$750	$1,000
1920	Rope bound top/back	$750	$1,000
1927	Bound body/ 'board/head	$1,250	$1,500
1930	Unbound	$650	$800
1933	Rope bound soundhole only	$650	$800

Taro Patch Fiddle
Koa body, unbound top and back.

1930		$1,250	$1,500

Tenor Ukulele
Koa body, unbound top and back.

1930		$1,000	$1,200

Levin

1900-1973. Ukuleles built in Sweden. Levin was best known for their classical guitars, which they also built for other brands, most notably Goya. They also built mandolins.

Loprinzi

1972-present. Intermediate and professional grade, production/custom, ukuleles built in Clearwater, Florida. They also build guitars.

Luna Guitars

2005-present. Budget and intermediate grade, production, ukes imported from Japan, Korea and China by Yvonne de Villiers in Tampa, Florida. She also imports guitars, basses and amps.

Lyon & Healy

1880s-ca.1949. During different periods several different makers constructed ukes bearing this stamp – often with an additional Washburn tag as well. After initial production by Lyon & Healy, instrument manufacture then apparently bounced between Regal, Stewart, and Tonk Brothers all within a span of only a few short years. Adding to the confusion, ukes surface from time to time bearing no maker's mark that can be reasonably attributed to Lyon & Healy. Suffice it to say that the best of these ukes, those displaying the highest

1970 Kamaka Tenor

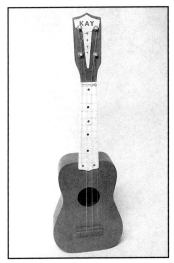
Kay

Loprinzi MRS

UKULELES

1953 Maccaferri Islander

(Steve Bauman)

Magic Fluke Surf

Martin Style O

degrees of quality and ornamentation, rival Gibson and Martin for collectability and tone and beauty.

Bell-Shaped Ukulele
Mahogany body.

MODEL YEAR	FEATURES	EXC. COND. LOW	HIGH
1927		$2,000	$2,500

Camp Ukulele
Round nissa wood body, black binding.

1935		$250	$350

Concert Ukulele
Mahogany body, bound top and back.

1930		$1,500	$2,200

Shrine Ukulele
Triangular body.

1927	Koa, abalone binding	$3,000	$4,000
1930	Mahogany, green binding	$1,750	$2,000
1933	Koa, green binding	$2,500	$3,000

Soprano Ukulele (Koa)

1927	Bound top, pearl rosette	$3,000	$3,500
1934	Bound top/back	$1,000	$1,250
1935	Pearl bound top/back	$7,500	$10,000

Soprano Ukulele (Mahogany)

1930	Unbound	$750	$1,000
1932	Bound top/back	$750	$1,000

Tenor Ukulele
Mahogany body, bound top and back.

1933		$1,500	$2,200

Maccaferri

1923-1990. Between the time he designed the Selmer guitar that became instantly synonymous with Django's gypsy jazz and his invention of the plastic clothespin, guitar design genius and manufacturing impresario Mario Maccaferri created a line of stringed instruments revolutionary for their complete plastic construction. The ukuleles were by far the greatest success, and most bore the tiny Maccaferri coat of arms on their tiny headstock.

Baritone Ukulele
Polystyrene cutaway body.

1959		$100	$150

Islander Ukulele
Polystyrene plastic body, crest in peghead.

1953		$100	$150

Playtune Ukulele
Polystyrene body.

1956		$100	$150

TV Pal Deluxe Ukulele
Extended 'board.

1960		$100	$150

TV Pal Ukulele
Polystyrene plastic body.

1955		$100	$150

Magic Fluke Company

1999-present. Budget grade, production, ukuleles made in New Hartford, Connecticut. With a clever design, exceptional quality, dozens of catchy fin-

ishes, and surprisingly affordable prices, it's little wonder that these little wonders have caught on. Riding – if not almost single-handedly driving – the coming third wave of uke popularity (the '20s and '50s were the first and second), Dale and Phyllis Webb of the Magic Fluke, along with Phyllis' brother, author Jumpin' Jim Beloff, are downright ukulele evangelists. The Fluke is the first new uke that you're not afraid to let the kids monkey with.

Mainland Ukes

2008-present. Mike Hater imports parts built in China to set-up his budget and intermediate grade, production/custom, solid wood ukes and banjo-ukes in Nashville, Indiana.

Manuel Nunes

The self-professed father of the ukulele was at least one of the first makers to produce them in any quantity. Beginning after 1879, when he and the first boat load of Portuguese settlers landed in Hawaii, until at least the 1930s, Manuel and his son Leonardo (see Leonardo Nunes section) produced some of the most beautiful and superbly crafted ukes offered by any Island maker.

Soprano Ukulele
Koa body.

MODEL YEAR	FEATURES	EXC. COND. LOW	HIGH
1919	Figured koa, bound top/back/'board	$1,500	$2,000
1920	Rope bound top/back	$750	$1,000
1927	Bound body/'board/head	$1,500	$2,000
1930	Unbound	$500	$750
1933	Rope bound soundhole only	$750	$1,000

Taro Patch Fiddle
Koa body.

1930	Rope bound top/back	$3,000	$3,500
1930	Unbound top/back	$1,750	$2,500

Tenor Ukulele
Koa body, unbound top and back.

1930		$1,000	$1,500

Marc Silber Guitar Company

1998-present. Mexican-made ukes from designer Marc Silber of Berkley, California. He also offers guitars. His Frisco Uke takes its inspiration from the inimitable Roy Smeck Vita Uke (see Harmony), but without the whimsy of the original.

Martin

1833-present. The C.F. Martin Company knew they wanted in on the uke craze, and toyed with some prototypes as early as 1907 or so, but didn't get around to actually getting serious until '16. The first of these were characterized by rather more primitive craftsmanship (by stringent Martin standards), bar frets, and an impressed logo in the back of the headstock. By '20, koa became available as a pricey option, and by the early '30s, regular frets and the

MODEL YEAR	FEATURES	EXC. COND. LOW	HIGH

familiar Martin headstock decal had prevailed. Martin single-handedly created the archetype of the mainland uke and the standard by which all competitors are measured.

Martin has recently re-entered the ukulele market with its budget Mexican-made model S-0, the Backpacker Uke, as well as a limited edition of the ornate, and pricey, 5K, 5M and 3K ukes.

Style 0 Ukulele
Unbound mahogany body.

1920	Wood pegs	$600	$750
1953	Patent pegs	$600	$750

Style 1 Ukulele
Mahogany body.

1940	Rosewood bound top only	$600	$750
1950	Tortoise bound top only	$600	$750
1960s	Tortoise bound top only	$600	$750

Style 1-C Concert Ukulele
Concert-sized mahogany body, bound top.

1950		$1,250	$1,500

Style 1-T Tenor Ukulele
Tenor-sized mahogany body, bound top only.

1940		$1,200	$1,700

Style 1-K Ukulele
Koa body, rosewood bound top.

1922	Wood pegs	$1,500	$2,000
1939	Patent pegs	$1,500	$2,000

Style 1-C K Concert Ukulele
Concert-sized koa body, bound top.

1950		$2,500	$3,500

Style 1 Taro Patch Ukulele
Mahogany body, 8 strings, rosewood bound.

1933		$1,200	$1,750

Style 1-K Taro Patch Ukulele
Style 1 with koa wood body.

1940		$1,500	$2,500

Style 2 Ukulele
Mahogany body, ivoroid bound top and back.

1922		$1,000	$1,250
1935		$1,000	$1,250
1961		$1,000	$1,200

Style 2-K Ukulele
Figured koa body, bound top and back.

1923		$2,200	$2,500
1939	Patent pegs	$2,200	$2,500

Style 2-C K Concert Ukulele
Same specs as 2-K, but in concert size.

1922		$5,000	$6,000

Style 2 Taro Patch Ukulele
Mahogany body, 8 strings, ivoroid bound.

1931		$1,500	$2,000

Style 2-K Taro Patch Ukulele
Style 2 with koa wood body.

1937		$1,700	$2,500

Style 3 Ukulele
Mahogany body.

1925	Kite inlay in headstock	$2,500	$3,000

1940	B/W lines in ebony 'board	$2,500	$3,000
1950	Extended 'board, dots	$2,500	$3,000

Style 3-K Ukulele
Figured koa body.

1924	Bow-tie 'board inlay	$3,500	$5,000
1932	B/W lines, diamonds, squares	$3,500	$5,000
1940	B/W lines and dot inlay	$3,500	$5,000

Style 3-C K Concert Ukulele
Same specs as 3-K, but in concert size.

1930		$10,000	$12,500

Style 3-T K Tenor Ukulele
Same specs as 3-K, but in tenor size.

1930		$9,000	$13,000

Style 3 Taro Patch Ukulele
Mahogany body, 8 strings, multiple bound.

1941		$2,500	$3,500

Style 3-K Taro Patch Ukulele
Style 3 with koa wood body.

1929		$3,500	$5,000

Style 5-K Ukulele
Highly figured koa body, all pearl trimmed.

1926		$7,500	$10,000

Style 5-C K Concert Ukulele
Same specs as 5-K, but in concert size.

1925		$10,000	$13,000

Style 5-T K Tenor Ukulele
Same specs as 5-K, but in tenor size.

1930		$12,500	$15,000

Style 5-M Ukulele
1941 only. Same as 5K, but mahogany body, extremely rare.

1941		$20,000	$30,000

Style 51 Baritone Ukulele
Mahogany body, bound top and back.

1966		$1,000	$1,500

Style T-15 Tiple Ukulele
Mahogany body, 10 metal strings, unbound.

1971		$800	$1,000

Style T-17 Tiple Ukulele
Mahogany body, 10 strings, unbound top and back.

1940		$1,000	$1,250

Style T-18 Tiple Ukulele
Mahogany body, 10 strings, spruce top.

1925		$1,000	$1,250

Style T-28 Tiple Ukulele
Rosewood body, 10 strings, bound top and back.

1950		$2,500	$3,500

Maurer

The Larson brothers of Maurer & Co., Chicago, built a few ukes and at least one taro patch under this brand from 1915 into the 1930s. Their small tops and backs are built-under-tension in the Larson tradition. A few of them have surfaced with the Hawaiian teacher/player's Earnest Kaai label and were probably sold through Stahl's Milwaukee store.

Martin Style 1-K

Martin Style 3-C K Concert

1947 Martin T-28 Tiple

UKULELES

1928 National Style 1

Oscar Schmidt

Pegasus Curly Koa Concert

MODEL YEAR	FEATURES	EXC. COND. LOW	HIGH

Michael Cone

1968-present. Luthier Michael Cone builds his professional and premium grade, production/custom, ukuleles in Kihei Maui, Hawaii. He also builds guitars.

Michael Dunn Guitars

1968-present. Luthier Michael Dunn builds a Knutsen-style harp uke in New Westminster, British Columbia. He also builds guitars.

Mirabella

1997-present. Professional grade, custom ukuleles built by luthier Cristian Mirabella in Babylon, New York. He also builds guitars, basses and mandolins.

National

Ca. 1927-present. To capitalize on the success of their amplifying guitars, the Dopyera brothers introduced metal-bodied ukuleles and mandolins as well. Large, heavy, and ungainly by today's standards, these early offerings nonetheless have their charms. Their subsequent switch to a smaller body shape produced an elegant and sweet-sounding resonator uke that soon became much sought after.

Style O Ukulele
Metal body, soprano size, sandblasted scenes.

1931		$2,500	$3,000

Style 1 Ukulele
Nickel body.

1928	Tenor, 6" resonator	$1,250	$3,000
1933	Soprano	$1,250	$3,000

Style 2 Ukulele
Nickel body, engraved roses.

1928	Tenor	$2,000	$3,000
1931	Soprano	$2,000	$3,000

Style 3 Ukulele
Nickel body, lilies-of-the-valley.

1929	Tenor	$3,500	$4,000
1933	Soprano	$3,500	$4,000

Triolian Ukulele

1928	Tenor, sunburst painted body	$1,000	$2,000
1930	Soprano, sunburst painted body	$1,000	$2,000
1934	Soprano, wood-grained metal body	$1,000	$2,000

National Reso-Phonic

1988-present. Successors to the National name, with the designs and patented amplifying resonator assemblies of the original National models, they offer professional grade, production, single cone ukuleles from their shop in San Luis Obispo, California. They also build guitars, basses and mandolins.

Oscar Schmidt

1879-1938, 1979-present. The same New Jersey outfit responsible for Leadbelly's 12-string guitar offered ukes as well during the same period. Many of these were odd amalgams of materials, often combining koa, mahogany, and spruce in the same instrument. Since 1979, when the name was acquired by the U.S. Music Corp. (Washburn, Randall, etc.), they have offered a line of budget grade, production, Asian-made ukes. They also offer guitars, basses, mandolins, and banjos.

Soprano Ukulele
Spruce top, bound mahogany body.

1930		$250	$300

Pegasus Guitars and Ukuleles

1977-present. Professional grade, custom, ukulele family instruments built by luthier Bob Gleason in Kurtistown, Hawaii, who also builds steel-string guitars.

Polk-a-lay-lee

1960s. These inexplicably shaped oddities were produced by Petersen Products of Chicago ca. the mid-'60s, and anecdotal Midwestern lore has it that their intent was to be offered as giveaways for the Polk Brothers, a local appliance chain. This may be how they ended up, although the gargantuan original packaging makes no reference to any such promotion. The box does call out what the optional colors were.

Many have noted the striking resemblance to the similarly named wares of the Swaggerty company (see Swaggerty) of California, who also offered brightly colored plywood-bodied ukes in comically oversized incarnations, but who was copying whom has yet to be determined.

Ukulele
Long boat oar body, uke scale, brown, natural, red, or black.

1965	Brown or natural	$250	$400
1965	Red or black	$250	$400

Recording King (TML)

2005-present. The Music Link added budget grade, production, stenciled ukuleles designed by Greg Rich. They also have banjos and guitars.

Regal

Ca. 1884-1966, 1987-present. Like the other large 1930s Chicago makers, Harmony and Lyon & Healy, the good ukes are very, very good, and the cheap ukes are very, very cheap. Unlike its pals, however, Regal seems to have produced more ukuleles in imaginative themes, striking color schemes, and in more degrees of fancy trim, making them the quintessential wall-hangers. And lucky for you, there's a vintage Regal uke to suit every décor.

Carson Robison Ukulele
Top sports painted signature, cowboy scene.

1935		$500	$750

Jungle Ukulele
Birch body, covered in leopard skin fabric.

1950		$750	$1,000

UKULELES

MODEL YEAR	FEATURES	EXC. COND. LOW	HIGH
Resonator Ukulele	*Black body, f-holes, see Dobro uke.*		
1934		$200	$400
Soprano Ukulele (Birch)	*Birch body.*		
1931	Brown sunburst	$250	$300
1931	Nautical themes, various colors	$100	$200
1945	Painted body, victory themes	$800	$1,000
Soprano Ukulele (Koa)	*Koa body, multicolored rope bound top.*		
1930		$350	$500
Soprano Ukulele (Mahogany)	*Mahogany body.*		
1930	Multiple bound top	$500	$800
1935	Spruce top, inlays	$300	$500
1940	Extended 'board	$250	$300
Tiple Ukulele			
1930	Birch body stained dark, black binding	$350	$500
1935	Spruce top, mahogany, fancy binding	$350	$500
Wendall Hall Red Head Ukulele	*Koa body, celebrity decal on headstock.*		
1935		$500	$750

Renaissance Guitars

1994-present. In '05 luthier Rick Turner added a line of acoustic and acoustic/electric ukuleles built in Santa Cruz, California. He also builds guitars and basses.

Rogue

2001-present. Budget grade, production, imported ukuleles. They also offer guitars, basses, lap steels, mandolins, banjos, effects and amps.

S. S. Stewart

Not much is known about the ukuleles of this Philadelphia firm, except that they were most certainly sub-contracted from another maker or makers.

Soprano Ukulele
Mahogany body, bound top and back.

1927		$150	$300

Samick

1958-2001, 2002-present. Budget grade, production, imported ukuleles. They also offer guitars, basses, mandolins and banjos.

Sammo

Flashy internal paper labels trumpet that these ukes (mandolins and guitars, too) were products of the Osborne Mfg. Co. Masonic Temple, Chicago-Illinois and what the heck any of that means is still open to modern speculation. Your guess is as good as mine. Still, the high quality and often opulent degree of ornamentation that the instruments exhibit, coupled with even the vaguest implication that they were made by guys wearing fezzes and/ or men who ride around in tiny cars at parades is all the reason we need to buy every one we see.

Soprano Ukulele

1925	Bound koa, fancy headstock shape	$500	$750
1925	Figured maple, 5-ply top, back binding	$350	$500
1925	Unbound koa, fancy headstock shape	$400	$600

Santa Cruz

1976-present. Professional grade, production, ukuleles from luthier Richard Hoover in Santa Cruz, California. They also build guitars.

Silvertone

1941-ca. 1970, present. Silvertone was the house brand of Sears & Roebuck and most (if not all) of its ukes were manufactured for them by Harmony.

Soprano Ukulele
Mahogany body, Harmony-made.

1950	Sunburst	$150	$300
1950	Unbound	$150	$300
1955	Bound	$150	$300
1960	Green	$150	$300

Slingerland

Slingerland started marketing ukes around 1916. Banjo ukuleles bearing this brand (see Slingerland Banjo uke section below) were certainly made by the popular drum company (banjos being little more than drums with necks, after all). Slingerland standard ukuleles, on the other hand, bear an uncanny resemblance to the work of the Oscar Schmidt company.

Soprano Ukulele
Koa body, rope bound top and soundhole.

1920		$350	$500

Specimen Products

1984-present. Luthier Ian Schneller builds his professional grade, production/custom, ukuleles in Chicago, Illinois. He also builds guitars, basses, amps and speaker cabs. Schneller has built some of the most offbeat, endearing - and high quality - custom ukuleles available.

Sterling

The miniscule reference buried deep within the headstock decal to a T.B. Co. can only mean that the Sterling ukulele somehow fits into the mind-numbing Tonk Bros./Lyon & Healy/Regal/S.S. Stewart manufacturing puzzle. Nonetheless, the brand must have been reserved for the cream of the crop, since the Sterling ukes that surface tend to be of the drop-dead-gorgeous variety.

Rogue Hawaiian Soprano

Samick UK70

Sammo

UKULELES

Supertone Soprano

Supertone Cheerleader

Weissenborn Soprano

UKULELES

MODEL YEAR	FEATURES	EXC. COND. LOW	HIGH

Soprano Ukulele
Flamed koa, multiple fancy binding all over.

1935		$1,500	$2,500

Stetson

Popular misconception – to say nothing of wishful thinking and greed – has it that all instruments labeled with the Stetson brand were the work of the Larson Brothers of Chicago. While a few Stetson guitars and a very few mandolins may be genuine Larson product, the ukuleles surely were made elsewhere.

Soprano Ukulele
Mahogany body, single bound top and back.

1930		$250	$300

Supertone

1914-1940s. For whatever reason, Supertone was the name attached to Sears' musical instruments before the line became Silvertone (see above). These, too, were all Harmony-made.

Soprano Ukulele (Koa)
Koa body, Harmony-made.

1935	Rope bound	$350	$500
1943	Unbound	$350	$500

Soprano Ukulele (Mahogany)
Mahogany body, Harmony-made.

1930	Unbound	$200	$300
1940	Bound	$200	$300

Swaggerty

Not enough is known of this West Coast company, except that their product line of unusually shaped 4-stringed novelty instruments oddly mirrors those made by Petersen Products in Chicago at the same time (see Polk-a-lay-lee). The two companies even seem to have shared plastic parts, such as 'boards and tuners. Go figure.

Kook-a-Lay-Lee Ukulele
Green plywood body, twin necks.

1965		$250	$500

Singing Treholipee
Orange plywood body, long horn.

1965		$250	$500

Surf-a-Lay-Lee Ukulele
Plywood body, long horn, green, yellow, or orange.

1965		$200	$400

Tabu

The Tabu brand on either the back of a ukulele's headstock or inside its soundhole was never an indication of its original maker. Rather, it was intended to assure the purchaser that the uke was, indeed of bona fide Hawaiian origin. So rampant was the practice of mainland makers claiming Island manufacture of their wares that in the late 'teens Hawaii launched a campaign to set the record straight, and – lucky for you – a nifty little brand was the result. The Tabu mark actually was used to mark the ukes of several different makers.

MODEL YEAR	FEATURES	EXC. COND. LOW	HIGH

Soprano Ukulele
Figured koa body.

1915	Rope bound	$750	$1,000
1915	Unbound	$500	$650

Tombo

This venerable Japanese harmonica manufacturer jumped on two bandwagons at once with its mid-Sixties introduction of a solid body electric ukulele. The Tombo Ukulet shares a tenor scale length and single coil pickup with Gibson's ETU electric tenor ukes, but the Tombo's thin, solidbody design is decidedly more Fender than jumping flea. Completing the imitation-is-the-sincerest-form-of-flattery theme is a snazzy Silvertone-esque case with onboard amplifier.

Ukulet
Solid body, amp-in-case, red sunburst or white finish.

1967	Red sunburst	$750	$1,000
1968	White	$1,350	$1,500

Turturro

Unlike manufacturers like Regal and Harmony who were content to produce novelty ukes by merely spray painting or applying decals with eye-catching motifs, New York manufacturer Nicola Turturro issued novelty ukuleles from his own patented designs. The most well-known is the Turnover Uke, a playable two-sided contraption strung as a 4-string uke on one side, and an 8-string mandolin on the other.

Concert Ukulele
Concert size, plain mahogany body.

1930		$400	$600

Peanut Ukulele
Ribbed peanut shaped body.

1928		$750	$900

Turnover Ukulele
Two-sided uke and mandolin.

1926		$750	$900

Vega

Famous for their banjos, the Vega name was applied to a sole baritone uke, tied with the endorsement of 1950s TV crooner Arthur Godfrey.

Arthur Godfrey Baritone Ukulele
Mahogany body, unbound.

1955		$350	$500

Washburn

See Lyon & Healy.

Weissenborn

1910s-1937. The mainland maker famous for their hollow-necked Hawaiian guitars was responsible for several uke offerings over the course of its 20-or-so-year run. Like their 6-stringed big brothers, they were the closest thing to Island design and detail to come from the mainland.

MODEL YEAR	FEATURES	EXC. COND. LOW	HIGH

Soprano Ukulele
Figured koa body.

| 1920 | Rope bound | $1,500 | $2,000 |
| 1920 | Unbound | $1,000 | $1,500 |

Weymann

Renowned for fine tenor banjos, Weyman affixed their name to a full line of soprano ukes of varying degrees of decoration, quite certainly none of which were made under the same roof as the banjos. Most were C.F. Martin knock-offs.

Soprano Ukulele

| 1925 | Mahogany, unbound | $750 | $1,000 |
| 1930 | Koa, fancy pearl vine 'board inlay | $1,000 | $1,250 |

Wm. Smith Co.

1920s. Like Ditson, the Wm. Smith Co. was a company for which C.F. Martin moonlighted without getting much outward credit. The South American cousin of the uke, the tiple, with its 10 metal strings and tenor uke sized body, was first produced exclusively for Smith by Martin starting around 1920, before being assumed into the regular Martin line with appropriate Martin branding.

Tiple Ukulele
Mahogany body, spruce top, ebony bridge.

| 1920 | | $1,000 | $1,250 |

Banjo Ukuleles
Bacon

This legendary Connecticut banjo maker just couldn't resist the temptation to extend their line with uke versions of their popular banjos. As with Gibson, Ludwig, Slingerland, and Weyman, the banjo ukuleles tended to mimic the already proven construction techniques and decorative motifs of their regular banjo counterparts. In materials, finish, and hardware, most banjo ukes share many more similarities with full sized banjos than differences. The banjo ukes were simply included as smaller, plainer, variations of banjos, much as concert, tenor, and baritone options fleshed out standard ukulele lines.

Banjo Ukulele
Walnut rim, fancy 'board inlays.

| 1927 | | $1,250 | $1,500 |

Silver Bell Banjo Ukulele
Engraved pearloid 'board and headstock.

| 1927 | | $1,750 | $2,500 |

Dixie

With chrome plated all-metal design, there's only one word for these banjo ukes - shiny. Their bodies, necks, and frets are die cast together in zinc (think Hot Wheels cars and screen door handles), the Dixie must have made the perfect indestructible instrument for Junior's birthday back in the 1960s. Similar to one made by Werko.

MODEL YEAR	FEATURES	EXC. COND. LOW	HIGH

Banjo Ukulele
One-piece, all-metal construction.

| 1960 | | $150 | $250 |

Gibson
BU-1 Banjo Ukulele
Small 6" head, flat panel resonator.

| 1928 | | $300 | $400 |

BU-2 Banjo Ukulele
8" head, dot inlay.

| 1930 | | $400 | $600 |

BU-3 Banjo Ukulele
8" head, diamond and square inlay.

| 1935 | | $1,250 | $1,500 |

BU-4 Banjo Ukulele
8" head, resonator and flange.

| 1932 | | $1,500 | $2,000 |

BU-5 Banjo Ukulele
8" head, resonator and flange, gold parts.

| 1937 | | $3,000 | $4,000 |

Le Domino
Banjo Ukulele
Resonator, decorated as Le Domino uke.

| 1933 | | $350 | $500 |

Ludwig

The Ludwig was then, and is today, the Cadillac of banjo ukes. British banjo uke icon George Formby's preference for Ludwig continues assuring their desirability, while the fact that they were available in only a couple of models, for a few short years, and in relatively small production numbers only adds to the mystique.

Banjo Ukulele
Flange with crown holes.

1927	Gold-plated parts	$4,000	$5,000
1928	Nickel-plated parts	$3,500	$4,000
1930	Ivoroid headstock overlay w/ art deco detail	$4,000	$5,000

Wendell Hall Professional Banjo Ukulele
Walnut resonator, flange with oval holes.

| 1927 | | $2,500 | $3,000 |

Lyon & Healy
Banjo Ukulele
Walnut neck and resonator, fancy pearl inlay.

| 1935 | | $1,000 | $1,250 |

Paramount

1920s-1942, Late 1940s. The William L. Lange Company began selling Paramount banjos, guitar banjos and mandolin banjos in the early 1920s. Gretsch picked up the Paramount name and used it on guitars for a time in the late '40s.

Banner Blue Banjo Ukulele
Brass hearts 'board inlay, walnut neck.

| 1933 | | $750 | $1,000 |

1920 Wm. Smith Co. Tiple

Ludwig Banjo Uke

Richter Banjo Uke

UKULELES

Werko Banjo Uke

MODEL YEAR	FEATURES	EXC. COND. LOW	HIGH

Regal
Banjo Ukulele
Mahogany rim, resonator, fancy rope bound.

| 1933 | | $300 | $500 |

Richter
Allegedly, this Chicago company bought the already-made guitars, ukes, and mandolins of other manufacturers, painted and decorated them to their liking and resold them. True or not, they certainly were cranked out in a bevy of swanky colors.

Banjo Ukulele
Chrome-plated body, 2 f-holes in back.

| 1930 | | $150 | $300 |
| 1930 | Entire body/neck painted | $150 | $300 |

Slingerland
May Bell Banjo Ukulele
Walnut resonator with multicolored rope.

| 1935 | | $150 | $300 |

MODEL YEAR	FEATURES	EXC. COND. LOW	HIGH

Werko
These Chicago-made banjo ukuleles had construction similar to the Dixie brand, and except for the addition of a swank layer of blue sparkle drum binding on the rim, you would be hard pressed to tell them apart.

Banjo Ukulele
Chrome-plated metal body and neck.

| 1960 | | $200 | $300 |

Weymann
Banjo Ukulele
Maple rim, open back, ebony 'board.

| 1926 | | $1,000 | $1,250 |

UKULELES

BANJOS

1920 Paramount Style F Plectrum, 1961 Vega Vox III Plectrum, 1929 Gibson TB-6 Tenor,
and 1940s Gretsch Bacon & Day Serenader Silver Bell Tenor photos: Elderly Instuments.

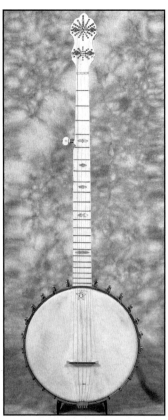

1924 Bacon & Day

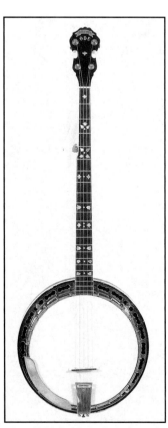

Ca. 1976 Baldwin Ode Style C

MODEL YEAR	FEATURES	EXC. COND. LOW	HIGH

Banjo collectors, hobbyists, and dealers often think nothing of changing the neck on a banjo; a banjo may have a true vintage neck or a new replacement neck. So, our all original parts concept that applies to the rest of this Price Guide doesn't always apply to vintage banjos.

The banjo market operates somewhat differently than many of the other markets that are covered in the Guide. The prices shown are guidance prices only and each instrument should be evaluated on a case by case basis.

Acme

1893-early 1900s. Banjos made for Sears by S.S. Stewart, and later George Bauer, both of Philadelphia.

The Pearl

1908. Open back, 5-string, pearl fretboard.

1908		$975	$1,200

Alvarez

Ca. 1966-present. An import brand for St. Louis Music, Alvarez currently offers intermediate grade, production, banjos. They also offer guitars, lap steels and mandolins.

Austin

1999-present. Budget and intermediate grade, production, banjos imported by St. Louis Music. They also offer guitars, basses, amps and mandolins.

Bacon & Day

1921-1967. David Day left Vega to join up with Fred Bacon in '21. Gretsch purchased Bacon & Day in '40, and ran the Bacon line until '67.

Blue Bell

1922-1939	Tenor	$1,000	$1,250

Blue Ribbon 17

1933-1939	Tenor	$500	$600

Ne Plus Ultra

1920s	#5, tenor	$7,000	$9,000
1920s	#6, tenor	$9,000	$11,000
1920s	#7, tenor	$14,000	$16,000
1920s	#8, tenor	$21,000	$26,000
1920s	#9, tenor	$21,000	$26,000
1930s	Tenor	$9,000	$11,000
1950s	Tenor	$2,500	$3,000
1960s	Tenor	$2,300	$2,800

Senorita

1930s	Plectrum, pearloid, resonator	$800	$1,000
1950s	4-string	$600	$750

Silver Bell Series

1920-1930s	#1, 5-string	$3,200	$3,900
1920s	#2, tenor	$1,800	$2,200
1920s	#3, tenor	$2,300	$2,800
1920s	#5, 5-string	$4,300	$5,300
1920s	Montana #3, tenor	$2,800	$3,400
1922-1939	#1, tenor/plectrum	$1,400	$1,700
1933-1939	Montana #1, tenor	$1,800	$2,200

MODEL YEAR	FEATURES	EXC. COND. LOW	HIGH
1933-1939	Montana #3, plectrum	$3,400	$4,100
1933-1939	Symphonie #1, tenor	$2,500	$3,100

Sultana #1

1933-1939	Tenor	$1,800	$2,200

Super

1920-1923	Tenor, non-carved neck	$900	$1,100
1927	5-string, carved neck	$2,800	$3,500
1927	5-string, non-carved neck	$2,500	$3,100

Baldwin

1966-1976. Baldwin was one of the largest piano retailers in the Midwest and in 1965, they got into the guitar market. In '66 they bought the ODE Banjo company. From '66 to '71 the banjos were labeled as Baldwin; after that ODE was added below the Baldwin banner. In '76 Gretsch took over ODE production.

Ode Style C

1968	Bluegrass, 5-string	$1,600	$2,000

Barratt

1890s. Made by George Barratt in Brooklyn, New York.

5-String

1890s	Victorian era	$375	$450

Benary and Sons

1890-1899. Manufactured by the James H. Buckbee Co. for music instrument wholesaler Robert Benary.

Celebrated Benary

1890-1899. 5-string, open back, plain appointments.

1890-1899		$600	$750

Bishline

1985-present. Professional and premium grade, production/custom, banjos built by luthier Robert Bishline in Tulsa, Oklahoma.

Boucher

1830s-1850s. William Boucher's operation in Baltimore is considered to be one of the very first banjo-shops. Boucher and the Civil War era banjos are rare. The price range listed is informational guidance pricing only. The wide range reflects conservative opinions. 150 year old banjos should be evaluated per their own merits.

Double Tack

1840s		$10,000	$13,000

Single Tack

1840s		$13,000	$17,000

Bruno and Sons

1834-present. Established by Charles Bruno, primarily as a distributor, Bruno and Sons marketed a variety of brands, including their own.

MODEL YEAR	FEATURES	EXC. COND. LOW	HIGH
Royal Artist Tenor			
1920s	Figured Resonator	$650	$775

Buckbee

1863-1897. James H. Buckbee Co. of New York was the city's largest builder. The company did considerable private branding for companies such as Benery, Dobson, and Farland.

5-String

1890-1897. 5-string, open back, plain appointments.

1890-1897	Higher-end models	$1,300	$1,600
1890-1897	Lower-end models	$650	$800

Charles Shifflett Acoustic Guitars

1990-present. Luthier Charles Shifflett builds his premium grade, custom, banjos in High River, Alberta. He also builds guitars and basses.

Cole

1890-1919. W.A. Cole, after leaving Fairbanks & Cole, started his own line in 1890. He died in 1909 but the company continued until 1919. He also made guitars.

Eclipse

1890-1919	Flower inlays, dots	$2,100	$2,600
1890-1919	Man-in-the-moon inlays	$2,500	$3,000

DeCava Guitars

1983-present. Premium grade, production/custom, banjos built by luthier Jim DeCava in Stratford, Connecticut. He also builds guitars, ukes, and mandolins.

Deering

1975-present. Greg and Janet Deering build their banjos in Spring Valley, California. In 1978 they introduced their Basic and Intermediate banjos. They also offer banjos under the Vega and Goodtime brands.

Delgado

1928-present. Premium grade, custom, classical banjos built by luthier Manuel A. Delgado in Nashville, Tennessee. He also builds guitars, basses, mandolins and ukuleles.

Ditson

1916-1930. The Oliver Ditson Company of Boston offered a variety of musical instruments.

Tenor

1920. 4-string, resonator with typical appointments.

1920		$550	$675

Dobson, George

1870-1890. Marketed by George C. Dobson of Boston, Massachusetts. Brothers Henry, George, and Edgar Dobson were banjo teachers and performers. They designed banjos that were built for them by manufactures such as Buckbee of New York.

MODEL YEAR	FEATURES	EXC. COND. LOW	HIGH
Matchless			
1880s	5-string	$600	$800

Epiphone

1873-present. Epiphone introduced banjos in the early 1920s, if not sooner, offering them up to WW II. After Gibson bought the company in '57, they reintroduced banjos to the line, which they still offer.

EB-44 Campus

1960s. Long neck, folk-era 5-string banjo.

1960s		$750	$950

EB-99 5-String

1970s	Higher-end, import	$575	$725

Electar (Electric)

1930s	Tenor	$900	$1,100

Recording A

Ca. 1925-ca. 1935. Epiphone Recording logo on headstock, flamed maple neck and resonator, fancy pearl inlay markers.

1920s	Tenor	$1,375	$1,700

Recording B

Ca. 1925-ca. 1935.

1930s	Tenor	$1,900	$2,300

Recording Concert C Special

1930s. Tenor, maple body, fancy appointments, resonator.

1930s		$2,700	$3,500

TB-100

Mid 1960s.

1960s	Tenor	$750	$950

Fairbanks/A.C. Fairbanks

1875-1904. From 1875 to 1880, A. C. Fairbanks built his own designs in Boston. In 1880, W. A. Cole joined the company, starting Fairbanks & Cole, but left in 1890 to start his own line. The company went by Fairbanks Co. until it was purchased by Vega in 1904. The banjos were then branded Vega Fairbanks (see Vega listings) until 1919.

Acme (F & C)

1880-1890. 5-string, open back, fancy markers.

1880-1890		$800	$1,000

Electric 5-String Series

1890s	F & C	$3,300	$4,100
1890s	Imperial	$2,400	$2,900
1890s	No. 3	$3,500	$4,300
1890s	No. 6	$6,600	$8,200

Electric Banjeaurine

1890s	5-string	$2,500	$3,100

Regent

1900-1904	5-string	$2,900	$3,600

Senator No. 1/Fairbanks 3

1900-1904	5-string	$1,100	$1,400

Special #0

1890-1904		$850	$1,050

Special #2

1890-1904	5-string	$900	$1,200

Special #4

1900-1904	5-string	$1,200	$1,500

Henry C. Dobson 1867 Patent Model

Fairbanks & Cole (Acme)

BANJOS

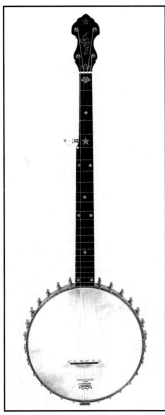

1903 Fairbanks Whyte Laydie No. 2

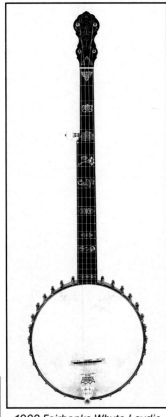

1902 Fairbanks Whyte Laydie No. 7

BANJOS

MODEL YEAR	FEATURES	EXC. COND. LOW	HIGH
Whyte Laydie #2			
1901-1904	5-string	$3,600	$4,500
Whyte Laydie #7			
1901	1st year	$8,000	$10,000
1902-1904		$7,000	$9,000

Farland

Ca. 1890-1920s. Buckbee and others made instruments for New York banjo teacher and performer A. A. Farland.

MODEL YEAR	FEATURES	EXC. COND. LOW	HIGH
Concert Grand			
1900-1920	5-string	$1,000	$1,200
Grand Artist No. 2			
1890s-1910. Ornate floral markers, open back, 5-string.			
1890-1910		$1,900	$2,300

Fender

1946-present. Fender added banjos to their product mix in the late 1960s, and continues to offer them.

MODEL YEAR	FEATURES	EXC. COND. LOW	HIGH
Allegro			
Late 1960s-1970s.			
1960s	Tenor or 5-string	$825	$975
Artist			
1960-1970s	5-string	$1,375	$1,650
FB-58			
1999-present. Import from Korea, style and design similar to '60s-'70s Fender banjos.			
1999-2010	5-string	$450	$550
Leo Deluxe			
1980-1988. Fancy inlay, Japanese-made.			
1980s		$750	$925

Framus

1946-1977, 1996-present. The new Framus company, located in Markneukirchen, Germany, continues to offer banjos.

MODEL YEAR	FEATURES	EXC. COND. LOW	HIGH
5-String Model			
1960s		$250	$300

Gibson

1890s (1902)-present. Gibson started making banjos in 1918, and continues to manufacture them. Vega and Gibson were the only major manufacturing companies that offered banjos in their product catalog in the '50s.

RB prefix = regular banjo (5-string)
TB prefix = tenor banjo (4-string, tenor tuning)
PB prefix = plectrum banjo (4-string, plectrum tuning)

The prices shown are guidance prices only and each instrument should be evaluated on a case by case basis.

MODEL YEAR	FEATURES	EXC. COND. LOW	HIGH
All American			
1930-1937. Tenor banjo, fancy appointments, historic art, gold hardware.			
1930-1937		$33,000	$42,000
Bella Voce			
1927-1931. Tenor banjo, fancy appointments, flower-pattern art, gold hardware.			
1927-1931		$24,000	$31,000

MODEL YEAR	FEATURES	EXC. COND. LOW	HIGH
Earl Scruggs Standard			
1984-present. 5-string, high-end appointments, Standard added to model name in '92.			
1980s		$2,700	$3,300
1990-1999		$2,700	$3,300
2000-2010		$2,700	$3,300
ETB Electric Tenor			
1938-1941. Electric Tenor Banjo, Charlie Christian pickup.			
1934-1941		$2,400	$3,000
Flint Hill Special			
2005-2006. Earl Scruggs style, 5-string.			
2005-2006		$3,900	$4,600
Florentine Plectrum			
1925-1930	2 piece flange	$16,000	$20,000
Florentine Tenor			
1927-1937. High-end appointments, gold hardware.			
1927-1935	40 hole	$15,000	$19,000
Granada FE			
2004. Flying eagle inlay.			
2004		$3,900	$4,600
Granada RB			
1925-1939. 5-string banjo with either a 2 piece flange (1925-1930), or a 1 piece flange (1933-1939).			
1925-1926	Ball bearing	$22,000	$28,000
1927-1930	40 hole arched	$31,000	$39,000
1933-1939	Flat head tone ring	$185,000	$220,000
Granada RB Pot and Reneck			
1933-1939. Original pot and replacement neck.			
1933-1939	Flat head tone ring	$48,000	$57,000
Granada TB			
1925-1939. Tenor banjo with either a 2 piece flange (1925-1930), or a 1 piece flange (1933-1939).			
1925-1926	Ball bearing	$10,000	$12,000
1927-1930	40 hole arched	$15,000	$18,000
1933-1939	Flat head tone ring	$114,000	$136,000
PB-1			
1926-1930s. PB stands for Plectrum Banjo.			
1920s		$1,000	$1,200
PB-3			
1923-1937. Laminated maple resonator Mastertone model, plectrum neck and tuning.			
1925-1927		$2,400	$2,900
PB-4			
1925-1940. Plectrum with either a 2 piece flange ('25-'32), or 1 piece ('33-'40).			
1925-1927	Ball bearing tone ring	$2,500	$3,000
1928-1932	Archtop	$3,100	$3,900
1933-1940	Archtop	$9,000	$11,000
1933-1940	Flat head tone ring	$55,000	$70,000
PB-100			
1948-1979. Plectrum with either a 1 piece flange ('48-'68), or 2 piece ('69-'79).			
1969-1979		$850	$1,050

MODEL YEAR	FEATURES	EXC. COND. LOW	HIGH

RB Jr.
1924-1925. 5-string, budget line, open back.

1924-1925		$1,175	$1,425

RB-00
1932-1942. Maple resonator, 1 piece flange.

1932-1939		$3,100	$3,900

RB-1
1922-1940.

1930-1932	1 piece flange	$3,700	$4,400
1933-1939	Diamond flange	$3,700	$4,400

RB-1 Reissue
1990-1993. Fleur-de-lis, brass tone ring.

1990-1993		$1,600	$2,000

RB-2

1933-1939		$5,000	$6,000

RB-3
1923-1937. Reissued in 1988.

1927-1928	5-string	$16,000	$20,000

RB-3 Reissue
1988-present. Currently called the RB-3 Wreath.

1988-1999		$2,400	$2,800
2000-2010		$2,400	$2,800

RB-4
1922-1937. 5-string with either a 2 piece flange ('25-'31), or 1 piece ('33-'37). Trap or non-trap door on earlier models ('22-'24).

1922-1924	Trap or non-trap door	$2,700	$3,300
1925-1931	Archtop, resonator	$16,000	$20,000
1933-1937	Archtop	$35,000	$45,000
1933-1937	Flat head tone ring	$90,000	$110,000

RB-4/R-4/Retro 4
1991-2008. Flying eagle inlay, multi-bound.

1991-2008		$3,000	$3,500

RB-6
1927-1937. 5-string banjo with fancy appointments.

1927-1933	Archtop	$20,000	$25,000

RB-11
1931-1942. Pearloid covered fingerboard, headstock and resonator.

1931-1942		$5,000	$7,000

RB-75 J.D. Crowe
1997-2006. Based on Crowe's instrument.

1997-2006		$3,200	$3,700

RB-100
1948-1979. Maple resonator.

1948-1965		$1,400	$1,700
1966-1979		$1,200	$1,500

RB-150
1948-1959. Laminated mahogany resonator, bow tie inlay.

1948-1959		$1,800	$2,200

RB-170
1960-1973. 5-string, no resonator, dot markers, decal logo, multi-ply maple rim.

1960-1973		$1,000	$1,200

RB-175
1962-1973. 2000s. Open back, long neck typical of banjos of the 1960s. Models include the RB-175, RB-175 Long Neck, RB-175 Folk.

1962	RB-175	$1,000	$1,250
1962-1964	Long Neck	$1,000	$1,250
1965-1969	Folk	$1,000	$1,250
1970-1973	RB-175	$900	$1,200

RB-250
1954-present. Mahogany, 2 piece flange until '88, 1 after.

1954-1965		$2,500	$3,000
1966-1969	Flat head tone ring	$2,200	$2,700
1970-1979	Mastertone	$1,800	$2,200
1980-1989	Mastertone	$1,800	$2,200
1990-1999		$2,000	$2,400
2002-2010	Reissue	$2,000	$2,400

RB-800
1964-1971, 1979-1986. Maple resonator, 1 piece flange until '69, 2 after.

1964-1986		$2,300	$2,700

TB
1918-1923. Renamed TB-4.

1918-1923		$1,500	$1,800

TB-00
1932-1942. Maple resonator, 1 piece flange.

1932-1942		$1,800	$2,300

TB-1
1922-1939. Tenor banjo with a 1 piece flange.

1922-1924	Trap door	$700	$850
1925	No resonator	$500	$600
1926	Maple resonator, shoe-plate	$800	$1,000
1933-1939	Simple hoop tone ring	$2,500	$3,000

TB-2
1920-1937.

1922-1928	Wavy flange	$800	$950
1933-1937	Pearloid board	$2,800	$3,500

TB-3
1925-1939. Tenor banjo with either a 2 piece flange (1925-1931), or a 1 piece flange (1933-1939).

1925-1926	Ball-bearing tone ring	$2,400	$2,800
1927-1931	40 or no hole ring	$3,200	$3,700
1933-1939	40 or no hole ring	$8,500	$10,500
1933-1939	Flat head tone ring	$55,000	$70,000
1933-1939	Wreath, archtop	$10,700	$13,300

TB-4
1923-1937. Dot inlay.

1923-1924	Trap door	$1,000	$1,200
1925-1926	Ball-bearing tone ring	$2,400	$2,800
1927-1931	40 or no hole ring	$3,200	$3,700
1933-1937	40 or no hole ring	$8,500	$10,500

TB-5
1923-1929.

1923-1924	Trap door	$1,500	$1,800
1927-1929	40 or no hole ring	$9,000	$11,000

Gibson PB-4

1929 Gibson RB-3 Archtop

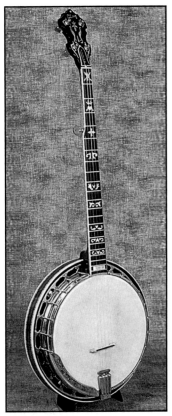

1964 Gibson RB-800

Gold Tone OB-300

MODEL YEAR	FEATURES	EXC. COND. LOW	HIGH
TB-6			
1927-1940.			
1927-1939	40 or no hole ring	$11,000	$13,000
1933-1939	Flat head tone ring	$30,000	$40,000
TB-11			
1931-1942. Pearloid covered fingerboard, headstock and resonator.			
1931-1942		$2,500	$3,000
TB-12			
1937-1939. Produced in limited quantities, 1 piece flange, flat head tone ring, double bound walnut resonator, price levels include both original and conversion instruments, conversions with original flat head tone rings are somewhat common in the vintage banjo market.			
1937	Top tension pot assembly	$50,000	$65,000
TB-18			
1937. Rare model.			
1937	Flat head top tension	$65,000	$80,000
TB-100			
1948-1979.			
1963-1967		$850	$1,050
TB-250			
1954-1996.			
1954-1965		$2,000	$2,500
1966-1969	Mastertone	$1,500	$1,800
1970s	Mastertone	$2,500	$3,000
Trujo Plectrum			
1928-1934		$2,500	$3,300

Gold Tone

1993-present. Professional and premium grade, production/custom banjos and banjitars built by Wayne and Robyn Rogers in Titusville, Florida. They also offer guitars, basses, lap steels, mandolins and ukuleles.

Gretsch

1883-present. Gretsch offered banjos in the '20s and again in the '50s and '60s.

Broadkaster

1920s-1939. Tenor or 5-string banjo with pearloid head and board.

1920s	Tenor	$300	$400
1932-1939	5-string	$975	$1,150
1932-1939	Tenor	$300	$400

Model 6536 Folk

1960s. Open-back, 5-string, long-neck style.

1964		$400	$500

New Yorker

1930s-1960s. New Yorker logo on headstock, 5-string or tenor.

1930-1960s		$250	$350

Orchestella

1925-1929. Tenor or 5-string banjo with gold engravings.

1925-1929	5-string	$2,000	$2,500
1925-1929	Tenor	$500	$650

MODEL YEAR	FEATURES	EXC. COND. LOW	HIGH
Tenor Short-Scale			
1925-1929	Plain styling	$200	$300
1950s	Plain styling	$200	$300

GTR

1974-1978. GTR (for George Gruhn, Tut Taylor, Randy Wood) was the original name for Gruhn Guitars in Nashville, and they imported mandolins and banjos from Japan.

5-String Copy

1974-1978		$875	$1,000

Harmony

1892-1976, late 1970s-present. Huge, Chicago-based manufacturer of fretted instruments, mainly budget models under the Harmony name or for many other American brands and mass marketers.

Electro

1950s. Electric banjo, wood body, 1 pickup.

1950s	5-string	$600	$700

Holiday Folk

1960s. Long neck, 5-string.

1960s		$200	$250

Roy Smeck Student Tenor

1963		$200	$250

Sovereign Tenor

1960s		$200	$250

Hohner

1857-present. They currently offer budget grade, open back, resonator style or travel size banjos. They also have guitars, basses, mandolins and ukuleles.

Hondo

1969-1987, 1991-2005. Budget grade, production, imported banjos. They also offered guitars, basses and mandolins.

Howard

Howard is a brand name of Cincinnati's Wurlitzer Co. used in the 1920s on banjos built by The Fred Gretsch Manufacturing Co. The brand name was also appeared on guitars in the mid-'30s by Epiphone.

Tenor

1920s	Open back	$200	$250
1920s	Resonator	$450	$550

Huber

1999-present. Premium grade, production, 5-string banjos built by luthier Steve Huber in Hendersonville, Tennessee.

Ianuario Mandolins

1990-present. Professional and premium grade, custom, banjos built by Luthier R. Anthony Ianuario in Jefferson, Georgia. He also builds mandolins and violins.

MODEL YEAR	FEATURES	EXC. COND. LOW	HIGH

Ibanez

1932-present. Ibanez introduced their Artist line of banjos in 1978 in a deal with Earl Scruggs, but they were dropped by '84.

Model 591
1978-1984. Flat head, 5-string copy.

1978-1984		$1,000	$1,100

J.B. Player

1980s-present. Budget grade, production, imported banjos. They also offer basses, mandolins and guitars.

John Wesley

Introduced in 1895 by Kansas City, Missouri instrument wholesalers J.W. Jenkins & Sons, founded by cello builder John Wesley Jenkins. May have been built by Jenkins until circa 1905, but work was later contracted out to others.

Kalamazoo

1933-1942, 1965-1970. Budget brand built by Gibson. Made flat-tops, solidbodies, mandolins, lap steels, banjos and amps.

Banjo

1935-1940	KPB, plectrum	$400	$500
1935-1941	KRB, 5-string	$600	$900

Kay

Ca. 1931 (1890)-present. Kay was a huge manufacturer and built instruments under their name and for a large number of other retailers, jobbers, and brand names.

Silva
1950s. Top of the line 5-string, Silva verticle logo along with Kay logo on headstock, block markers.

1950s		$700	$800

Student Tenor

1950s		$175	$200

Kel Kroydon

1930-1933. Private branded budget level instruments made by Gibson. They also had guitars and banjos. The name has been revived on a line of banjos by Tom Mirisola and made in Nashville.

Banjo

1930-1933	Conversion	$3,600	$4,400
1930-1933	Tenor	$3,000	$3,700

Keystone State

1920s. Brand of banjos built by Weymann.

Style 2
1920s. Tenor, resonator, fancy appointments.

1920s		$850	$1,050

Kona

2001-present. Budget grade, production, banjos made in Asia. They also offer guitars, basses and amps.

Lange

1920s-1942, Late 1940s. The William L. Lange Company began selling Paramount banjos, guitar banjos and mandolin banjos in the early 1920s. Gretsch picked up the Paramount name and used it on acoustics and electrics for a time in the late '40s. See Paramount for more listings.

Tourraine Deluxe

1920s	Tenor	$700	$900

Leedy

1889-1930. Founded in Indianapolis by U. G. Leedy, the company started making banjos in 1924. Leedy was bought out by C. G. Conn in '30.

Olympian

1930	Tenor	$600	$700

Solotone

1924-1930	Tenor	$1,000	$1,300

Ludwig

The Ludwig Drum Company was founded in 1909. They saw a good business opportunity and entered the banjo market in '21. When demand for banjos tanked in the '30s, Ludwig dropped the line and concentrated on its core business.

Bellevue
1920s. Tenor, closed-back banjo with fancy appointments.

1920s		$800	$950

Big Chief
1930. Carved and engraved plectrum banjo.

1930		$7,000	$8,000

Capitol

1920s		$600	$800

Columbia

1920s	Tenor, student-level	$350	$450

Commodore
1930s. Tenor or plectrum, with gold hardware and fancy appointments.

1930s	Tenor, Ambassador	$1,200	$1,600
1932	Plectrum	$1,500	$2,000

Deluxe
1930s. Engraved tenor, with gold hardware.

1930s		$2,500	$3,000

Dixie

1930s	Tenor	$300	$400

Kenmore Plectrum

1920s	Open back	$600	$750

Kingston

1924-1930	Tenor	$400	$500

Standard Art Tenor
1924-1930. Tenor banjo with fancy appointments.

1924-1930		$2,500	$3,000

The Ace
1920s. Tenor banjo, resonator and nickel appointments.

1920s		$1,000	$1,200

Kel Kroyden Conversion

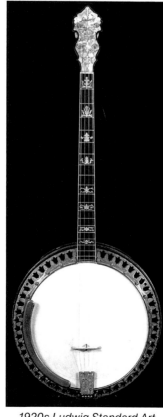

1920s Ludwig Standard Art Tenor Banjo

BANJOS

MODEL YEAR	FEATURES	EXC. COND. LOW	HIGH

Paramount Aristrocrat Special

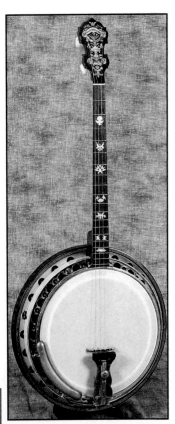

1933 Paramount Super

Luscomb

1888-1898. John F. Luscomb was a well-known banjo player who designed a line of instruments for Thompson & Odell of Boston.

5-String

1890s	Open back	$700	$850

Matao

1970s. High quality builder from Japan. Matao logo on headstock.

Bluegrass

1970s	5-string	$275	$350

Mitchell (P.J.)

1850s. Early gut 5-string banjo maker from New York City.

Gut 5-String

1850s		$4,000	$4,800

Morgan Monroe

1999-present. Intermediate and professional grade, production, banjos made in Korea and distributed by SHS International of Indianapolis, Indiana. They also offer guitars, basses, mandolins, and fiddles.

Morrison

Ca. 1870-ca. 1915. Marketed by New Yorker James Morrison, made by Morrison or possibly others like Buckbee. After 1875, his instruments sported the patented Morrison tone ring.

5-String

1885-1890		$600	$800

ODE/Muse

1961-1980. Founded by Charles Ogsbury in Boulder, Colorado, purchased by Baldwin in '66 and moved to Nashville. Until '71 the banjos were branded as Baldwin; afterwards as Baldwin ODE. Gretsch took over production in '76. Muse was a retail store brand of banjos produced by ODE from '61 to '66. In '71, Ogsbury started the OME Banjo Company in Colorado.

Model C

1976-1980. 5-string banjo, resonator and fancy markers.

1976-1980		$1,350	$1,650

Model D

1970s-1980. 5-string banjo, resonator and gold engravings.

1970s		$1,700	$2,100

Old Hickory

2005-present. Budget grade, production, imported banjos from Musician's Wholesale America, Nashville, Tennessee. They also offer mandolins.

Orpheum

1897-1922. Lange and Rettberg purchased the J.H. Buckbee banjo factory in 1897 and started making banjos under the Orpheum label. William Lange took control in 1922 and changed the name to Paramount.

Model #2

1920-1922	5-string	$1,500	$2,000
1920-1922	Tenor	$800	$1,000

Model #3

1910s	5-string	$2,200	$2,800
1910s	Tenor	$1,100	$1,300

Oscar Schmidt

1879-ca. 1939, 1979-present. Currently offering budget and intermediate grade, production, banjos. They also offer guitars, basses, mandolins, ukuleles and the famous Oscar Schmidt autoharp.

Paramount

1921-1935. William Lange and his Paramount company are generally accredited with commercializing the first modern flange and resonator in 1921.

Aristocrat

1921-1935	Plectrum	$1,900	$2,300
1921-1935	Tenor	$1,600	$2,000

Aristocrat Special

1921-1935. Plectrum or tenor with fancy appoinments.

1921-1935	Plectrum	$2,600	$3,100
1921-1935	Tenor	$2,200	$2,600

Artists Supreme

1930s. High-end appointments, 19-fret tenor, engraved gold-plated hardware.

1930s	Tenor	$4,900	$5,900

Junior

1921-1935	Plectrum	$800	$1,000
1921-1935	Tenor	$700	$900

Leader

1921-1935	Plectrum	$1,200	$1,450
1921-1935	Tenor	$1,100	$1,350

Style 1

1921-1935	Plectrum	$775	$925
1921-1935	Tenor	$650	$800

Style 2

1921-1935. Tenor banjo, resonator and plain appointments.

1921-1935		$600	$750

Style A

1921-1935. Models include the Style A Tenor, Plectrum, and the 5-string (with resonator and fancy appointments).

1921-1935	5-string	$2,300	$2,700
1921-1935	Plectrum	$1,000	$1,200
1921-1935	Tenor	$800	$1,000

Style B

1921-1935. Models include the Style B Tenor, and the Plectrum (with resonator and fancy appointments).

1921-1935	Plectrum	$1,100	$1,300
1921-1935	Tenor	$900	$1,100

The *Vintage Guitar Price Guide* shows low to high values for items in all-original excellent condition, and, where applicable, with original case or cover.

MODEL YEAR	FEATURES	EXC. COND. LOW	HIGH

Style C
1921-1935. Models include the Style C Tenor, Plectrum, and the 5-string (with resonator and fancy appointments).

1921-1935	5-string	$3,800	$4,700
1921-1935	Plectrum	$1,700	$2,000
1921-1935	Tenor	$1,500	$1,800

Style D
1921-1935	Plectrum	$2,100	$2,600
1921-1935	Tenor	$2,000	$2,500

Style E
1921-1935	Plectrum	$2,700	$3,400
1921-1935	Tenor	$2,500	$3,200

Style F
1921-1935	Plectrum	$3,000	$3,500
1921-1935	Tenor	$2,800	$3,200

Super/Super Paramount
1921-1935	Plectrum	$3,700	$4,400
1921-1935	Tenor	$3,400	$4,100

Trooper
1921-1935	Plectrum	$650	$800
1921-1935	Tenor	$550	$700

Penco
Ca. 1974-1978. Japanese-made banjos imported into Philadelphia. They also offered guitars, basses and mandolins.

Deluxe Tenor
1970s	Japan	$200	$250

Recording King
1929-1932, 1936-1941. Brand name used by Montgomery Ward for instruments made by various American manufacturers, including Kay, Gibson and Gretsch.

Studio King Tenor
1929-1932	40 hole archtop, Gibson	$4,000	$5,000

Recording King (TML)
2005-present. Intermediate and professional grade, production, banjos imported by The Music Link, which also offers Johnson and other brand instruments. They also have guitars and ukes.

Regal
Ca. 1884-1966, 1987-present. Mass manufacturer Regal made brands for others as well as marketing its own brand. In '87 the Regal name was revived by Saga.

Bicentennial '76
1976. Part of a series of Regal instruments with Bicentennial model logo on headstock (similar to the '76 Regal guitar model), blue finish on neck and headstock, large '76 on banjo head, American-Eagle USA art on back of resonator. Another style with red finish neck and fife and drum art on back of the resonator.

1976	5-string	$375	$425

Rogue
2001-present. Budget grade, production, imported banjos. They also offer guitars, basses, lap steels, mandolins, and ukuleles.

S.S. Stewart
1878-1904. S.S. Stewart of Philadelphia is considered to be one of the most important and prolific banjo manufacturers of the late 19th century. It's estimated that approximately 25,000 banjos were made by this company. The brand name was used on guitars into the 1960s.

20th Century
1890s		$1,000	$1,200

American Princess
1890s. 5-string, 10" rim.

1890s		$900	$1,100

Banjeaurine
1890. 5-string banjo, 10" head with an open back.

1890	Plain appointments	$850	$1,100

Champion
1895. Open back, 5-string.

1895	Plain appointments	$900	$1,100

Orchestra
1890s. 5-string, various styles.

1890s		$1,100	$1,300

Piccolo
1880s. 5-string, 7" rim.

1880s	Plain appointments	$1,000	$1,200

Special Thoroughbred
1890s-1900s. Open back, 5-string, carved heel.

1890-1900s	Plain appointments	$1,300	$1,600

Universal Favorite
1892. 11" head.

1892	Plain appointments	$700	$900

S101
2002-present. Budget and intermediate grade, production, banjos imported from China. They also offer guitars, basses, and mandolins.

Samick
1958-2001, 2002-present. Budget and intermediate grade, production, imported banjos. They also offer guitars, basses, ukes and mandolins.

Shifflett
1990-present. Luthier Charles Shifflett builds his premium grade, custom, banjos in High River, Alberta. He also guitars and basses.

Silvertone
1941-ca. 1970, present. Brand of Sears instruments which replaced their Supertone brand in '41. Currently, Samick offers a line of amps under the Silvertone name.

5-String Copy
1960s		$200	$350

Recording King RK-R60A

Ca. 1890 Stewart No. 2 Universal Favorite

BANJOS

Samick Gregg Bennett SB 1

Stelling Crusader

Slingerland

Late-1920s-mid-1940s. The parent company was Slingerland Banjo and Drums, Chicago, Illinois. The company offered other stringed instruments into the '40s. Slingerland Drums is now owned by Gibson.

MODEL YEAR	FEATURES	EXC. COND. LOW	HIGH
Deluxe			
1920s	Tenor, higher-end	$1,300	$1,700
May Bell			
1920-1930s	Various styles	$600	$1,200
Student/Economy			
1930s		$250	$400

Stelling

1974-present. Founded by Geoff Stelling, building premium and presentation grade, production/custom banjos in Afton, Virginia. They also build mandolins.

Studio King

1930s. Banjos made by Gibson, most likely for a mail-order house or a jobber.

MODEL YEAR	FEATURES	EXC. COND. LOW	HIGH
Studio King			
1933-1937	Original 5-string	$2,500	$3,000
1933-1937	Tenor	$1,000	$1,200

Superb

1920s. Private brand made by House of Stathopoulo, Inc., the company name of Epiphone from 1917 to 1928. The brand was also used on banjo ukuleles.

MODEL YEAR	FEATURES	EXC. COND. LOW	HIGH
Tenor			
1920s		$400	$500

Supertone

1914-1941. Brand used by Sears, Roebuck and Company for instruments made by various American manufacturers, including its own Harmony subsidiary Harmony. In '40, Sears began making a transition to the Silvertone brand.

MODEL YEAR	FEATURES	EXC. COND. LOW	HIGH
Prairie Wonder			
1925. 5-string, open back banjo.			
1925		$450	$550

Tennessee

1970-1993, 1996-present. Luthier Mark Taylor builds his professional and premium grade, production/custom, banjos in Old Hickory, Tennessee. He also builds guitars, mandolins and the Tut Taylor brand of resophonic guitars.

Thompson & Odell

1875-1898. Boston instrument importers Thompson & Odell started building banjos in the 1880s. They sold the company to Vega in 1898.

MODEL YEAR	FEATURES	EXC. COND. LOW	HIGH
Artist			
1880s	Various models	$775	$1,100

Tilton

1850s-late 1800s. Built by William B. Tilton, of New York City. He was quite an innovator and held several instrument-related patents. He also built guitars.

Toneking

1927. Private brand of the NY Band Instruments Company, Toneking logo on headstock.

MODEL YEAR	FEATURES	EXC. COND. LOW	HIGH
Tenor			
1927		$325	$400

Trinity River

2004-present. Luthiers Marcus Lawyer and Ross McLeod from Fort Worth, Texas import their intermediate grade, production/custom, banjos from Asia. They also import guitars, basses and mandolins.

Univox

1964-1978. Instruments imported from Japan by the Merson Musical Supply Company, later Unicord, Westbury, New York.

MODEL YEAR	FEATURES	EXC. COND. LOW	HIGH
Tenor			
1970s	Import	$200	$225

Van Eps

1920s. Designed by virtuoso banjo artist Fred Van Eps and sold through Lyon & Healy.

MODEL YEAR	FEATURES	EXC. COND. LOW	HIGH
Recording			
1920s	5-string	$1,000	$1,300

Vega

1880s-1980s, 1989-present. Vega of Boston got into the banjo business in 1904 when it purchased Fairbanks. Vega and Gibson were the only major manufacturing companies that offered banjos in their product catalog in the 1950s. The Deering Banjo Company acquired the brand in '89 and uses it on a line of banjos.

MODEL YEAR	FEATURES	EXC. COND. LOW	HIGH
Artist Professional #9			
1923-1929	Tenor	$2,000	$2,500
Earl Scruggs STII			
1969	5-string, resonator	$1,500	$1,700
Folk Ranger FR-5			
1960s	5-string, open back	$600	$700
Folk Wonder			
1960s	5-string	$700	$800
Folklore SS-5			
1966. 5-string, open back, long neck folk banjo.			
1966		$1,150	$1,350
Imperial Electric			
1921	5-string	$2,000	$2,500
Lady's Banjo			
1913		$800	$1,000
Little Wonder			
1920s	Guitar banjo	$900	$1,200
1920s	Plectrum	$600	$750
1920s	Tenor	$500	$650
1930s	Tenor	$500	$650
1950s	5-string	$900	$1,200

BANJOS

The *Vintage Guitar Price Guide* shows low to high values for items in all-original excellent condition, and, where applicable, with original case or cover.

MODEL YEAR	FEATURES	EXC. COND. LOW	HIGH

Pete Seeger
1958-1966. 5-string, long neck banjo.

1958-1964	Folk era	$3,000	$4,000
1965-1966		$2,400	$3,000

Professional
1960. 5-string banjo with a Tubaphone tone ring.

1960	Pro II, slits	$1,300	$1,600
1960	Professional, holes	$1,400	$1,700

Ranger
1960s. Standard appointments, dot markers.

1966	5-string	$500	$600

Regent
1920s. 5-string banjo with an open back and dot markers.

1920s		$1,600	$2,000

Style M
1920s. Tenor banjo, models include the Style M and the Style M Tubaphone.

1920s	With Tubaphone TR	$1,000	$1,300

Style N

1910-1920s		$400	$500

Style X #9
1926. Tenor banjo with fancy appointments.

1926		$1,900	$2,400

Tubaphone #3

1910-1919		$3,700	$4,700
1918-1929	5-string	$3,200	$3,900
1923-1929	Plectrum	$1,200	$1,500

Tubaphone #9

1929	5-string	$7,600	$9,300

Tubaphone Deluxe
1920s. Higher-end appointments, carved heel, Deluxe logo on tailpiece.

1923	5-string	$10,000	$12,500

V.I.P. Tenor
1970s. 4-string, open back, fancy engraved pearl markers, on-board electronics.

1970		$1,500	$1,800

V-45
1970. Plectrum banjo, flat head tone ring, fancy appointments.

1970s		$2,700	$3,100

Vegaphone De-Luxe

1929	Plectrum	$2,800	$3,200

Vegaphone Professional

1920s	Plectrum	$1,200	$1,500
1930s	Tenor	$1,000	$1,300
1960s	5-string	$900	$1,000

Vegavox I Tenor
1930s-1962. Vox-style deep resonator, alternating block/dot markers.

1930s		$1,800	$2,100
1956-1962		$1,500	$1,800

Vegavox IV
1956-1962. IV logo on truss rod cover, high-end appointments, 4-string plectrum neck.

1956-1962	Plectrum or tenor	$3,300	$4,200

Whyte Laydie #2

1923-1928	5-string	$3,200	$3,900

Whyte Laydie #7

1905	5-string	$8,500	$10,500
1909		$8,000	$9,500
1921		$8,000	$9,500

Whyte Laydie Style R
1920-1930s. Tenor banjo with closed back.

1920-1930s		$1,000	$1,200

Wonder Tenor
1973. Made by C.F. Martin (brand owner in the '70s), closed back resonator style.

1973		$525	$650

Washburn (Lyon & Healy)

1880s-ca.1949. Washburn was the brand name of Lyon & Healy of Chicago. They made banjos from 1880-1929.

5-String

1896	Old 1890s style	$850	$1,050

Irene

1920s	5-string	$700	$850

Washburn (Post 1974)

1974-present. Currently, Washburn offers imported intermediate and professional grade, production, banjos.

Weymann

1864-1940s. The Weymann company was founded in 1864 and got seriously into the banjo manufacturing business in 1917. They manufactured banjos until around 1930.

Plectrum

1924-1928	Style A	$650	$850

Tenor

1924-1928	Style #1	$1,300	$1,600
1924-1928	Style #2	$1,400	$1,700
1924-1928	Style #4	$2,600	$3,200
1924-1928	Style #50	$475	$575
1924-1928	Style #6	$3,900	$4,800
1924-1928	Style A, low pro model	$650	$800

Wilson Brothers

1915-1928. Brand name, possibly made by Lyon & Healy, for the Wilson Brothers Manufacturing Company, of Chicago, which was better known as a builder of drums.

Tenor

1920s	Resonator	$350	$450

Yosco

1900-1930s. Lawrence L. Yosco was a New York City luthier building guitars, round back mandolins and banjos under his own brand and for others.

Style 3

1920s	Tenor	$900	$1,200

Vega Little Wonder

1927 Vega Vegaphone De-Luxe

BANJOS

BIBLIOGRAPHY

60 Years of Fender, by Tony Bacon, 2010, Backbeat Books.

50 Years of Gretsch Electrics, by Tony Bacon, 2005, Backbeat Books.

Acoustic Guitars and Other Fretted Instruments, A Photographic History, by George Gruhn and Walter Carter, 1993, GPI Books.

Acoustic Guitar magazine, various issues, String Letter Publishing.

Acquired of the Angels, by Paul William Schmidt, 1998, Scarecrow Press.

American Basses, by Jim Roberts, 2003, Backbeat Books.

American Guitars, An Illustrated History, by Tom Wheeler, 1992, Harper Collins.

American's Instrument, The Banjo in the Nineteenth Century, by Philip F. Gura and James F. Bollman, 1999, University of North Carolina Press.

Ampeg - The Story Behind The Sound, by Gregg Hopkins and Bill Moore, 1999, Hal Leonard Publishing.

Analog Man's Guide to Vintage Effects, by Tom Hughes, 2004, Musicians Only Publishing.

The Boss Book, 2001, Hal Leonard Publishing.

The Burns Book, by Paul Day, 1990, PP Publishing and The Bold Strummer.

The Classical Guitar Book, by Tony Bacon, et al., 2002, Balafon Books.

The Complete History of Rickenbacker Guitars, by Richard R. Smith, 1987, Centerstream.

Cowboy Guitars, by Steve Evans andRon Middlebrook, 2002, Centerstream.

The Custom Guitar Shop and Wayne Richard Charvel, by Frank W/m Green, 1999, Working Musician Publications.

Electric Guitars and Basses, A Photographic History, by George Gruhn and Walter Carter, 1994, GPI Books.

Elektro-Gitarren Made in Germany, by Norbert Schnepel and Helmuth Lemme (German, with English translation), 1987, Musik-Verlag Schnepel-Lemme oHG.

Epiphone: The Complete History, by Walter Carter, 1995, Hal Leonard publishing.

Epiphone: The House of Stathopoulo, by Jim Fisch & L.B. Fred, 1996, Amsco Publications.

The Fender Amp Book, by John Morrish, 1995, Balafon Books and GPI Books.

Fender Amps: The First Fifty Years, by John Teagle and John Sprung, 1995, Hal Leonard Publishing.

The Fender Bass, by Klaus Blasquiz, 1990, Mediapresse.

The Fender Bass, An Illustrated History, by J.W. Black and Albert Molinaro, 2001, Hal Leonard Publishing.

Fender Bible, by Dave Hunter and Paul Day, 2007, Jawbone.

Fender: The Sound Heard 'Round the World, by Richard R. Smith, 1995, Garfish Publishing.

The Fender Stratocaster, by Andre Duchossoir, 1988, Mediapresse.

The Fender Telecaster, by Andre Duchossoir, 1991, Hal Leonard Publishing.

Framus Vintage, Edited by Hans-Peter Wilfer, 2009, Framus.

G&L: Leo's Legacy, by Paul Bechtoldt, 1994, Woof Associates.

Gibson Amplifiers, 1933-2008, by Wallace Marx Jr., 2009, Blue Book Publications.

Gibson Bible, by Dave Hunter and Walter Carter, 2008, Jawbone.

Gibson Electrics, The Classic Years, by A. R. Duchossoir, 1994, Hal Leonard Publishing.

Gibson's Fabulous Flat-Top Guitars, by Eldon Whitford, David Vinopal, and Dan Erlewine, 1994, GPI Books.

Gibson Guitars: 100 Years of An American Icon, by Walter Carter, 1994, W. Quay Hays.

Gibson Guitars: Ted McCarty's Golden Era: 1948-1966, by Gil Hembree, 2007, Hal Leonard Publishing Corporation.

The Gibson Super 400, Art of the Fine Guitar, by Thomas A. Van Hoose, 1991, GPI Books.

Gibson Shipping Totals 1948-1979, 1992, J.T.G.

The Gretsch Book, by Tony Bacon & Paul Day, 1996, Balafon Books and GPI Books.

Gruhn's Guide to Vintage Guitars, 3rd Edition, by George Gruhn and Walter Carter, 2010, Backbeat Books.

The Guild Guitar Book: The Company and the Instruments 1952-1977, by Hans Moust, 1995, GuitArchives Publications.

Guitar Identification: Fender-Gibson-Gretsch-Martin, by Andre Duchossoir, 1983, Hal Leonard Publishing Corporation.

Guitar Player magazine, various issues, Miller Freeman.

Guitar Stories, Vol. I, by Michael Wright, 1994, Vintage Guitar Books.

Guitar Stories, Vol. II, by Michael Wright, 2000, Vintage Guitar Books.

Guitar World magazine, various issues, Harris Publications.

The Guitars of the Fred Gretsch Company, by Jay Scott, 1992, Centerstream.

Guitars From Neptune, A Definitive Journey Into Danelectro-Mania, by Paul Bechtoldt, 1995, Backporch Publications.

Guitar Graphics, Vol. 1 (Japanese), 1994, Rittor Music Mooks.

The History and Artistry of National Resonator Instruments, by Bob Brozman, 1993, Centerstream.

The History of Marshall, by Michael Doyle, 1993, Hal Leonard Publishing.

The History of the Ovation Guitar, by Walter Carter, 1996, Hal Leonard publishing.

The History of Yamaha Guitars, by Mark Kasulen & Matt Blackett, 2006, Hal Leonard Corporation.

Ibanez, the Untold Story, by Paul Specht, Michael Wright, and Jim Donahue, 2005, Hoshino (U.S.A.) Inc.

The Larson's Creations, Guitars & Mandolins, by Robert Carl Hartman, 2007, Centerstream.

Martin Guitars, A History, by Mike Longworth, 1988, 4 Maples Press.

Martin Guitars, A Technical Reference, by Richard Johnston and Dick Boak, 2009, Hal Leonard Corporation.

Martin Guitars: An Illustrated Celebration of America's Premier Guitarmaker, by Jim Washburn & Richard Johnston, 1997, Rodale Press, Inc.

Musicial Merchandise Review magazine, various issues, Symphony Publishing.

The Music Trades magazine, various issues, Music Trades Corporation.

The Official Vintage Guitar Magazine Price Guide, all editions.

The Peavey Revolution, by Ken Achard, 2005, Backbeat Books.

The PRS Guitar Book, by Dave Burrluck, 1999, Outline Press, London.

The Rickenbacker Book, by Tony Bacon & Paul Day, 1994, Balafon Books and GFI Books.

Six Decades of the Fender Telecaster, by Tony Bacon, 2005, Backbeat Books.

Spann's Guide to Gibson 1902-1941, by Joesph E. Spann, 2011, Centerstream.

Stompbox, by Art Thompson, 1997, Miller Freeman Books.

The Tube Amp Book, 4th Edition, by Aspen Pittman, 1993, Groove Tubes.

The Ultimate Guitar Book, by Tony Bacon and Paul Day, 1991, Alfred A. Knopf.

Vintage Guitar magazine, various issues, Vintage Guitar, Inc.

VG Classics magazine, various issues, Vintage Guitar, Inc.

Vox Amplifiers, The JMI Years, by Jim Elyea, 2009, The History For Hire Press.

The Vox Story, A Complete History of the Legend, by David Peterson and Dick Denney, 1993, The Bold Strummer, Ltd.

Washburn: Over One Hundred Years of Fine Stringed Instruments, by John Teagle, 1996, Amsco Publications.

Various manufacturer catalogs, literature, and web sites.

DEALER DIRECTORY A GEOGRAPHICAL GUIDE

AUSTRALIA
Guitar Emporium
Darren Garth
155 Victoria Avenue
Albert Park, Victoria,
Australia, 3206
Phone 61.3.9696.8032
emporium@ozemail.
com.au
guitaremporium.com.au

CANADA
Capsule Music
Mark or Peter Kesper
921 Queen St. W.
Toronto, Ontario M6J
1G5
Phone: 416-203-0202
contact@capsulemusic.
com
capsulemusic.com

Folkway Music
Mark Stutman
163 Suffolk Street West
Guelph, Ontario N1H 2J7
Phone: 519-763-5524
info@folkwaymusic.com
folkwaymusic.com

Surfside Music
Robbie Keene
1645-140th St.
Unit 103
Surey, BC
V4A-4H1
Phone: 778-294-1088
gtrman@shaw.ca
surfsidemusic.com

The Twelfth Fret Inc.
Grant MacNeill/Chris
Bennett
2132 Danforth Avenue
Toronto, Ont., Canada
M4C 1J9
Phone: 416-423-2132
Repairs: 416-423-1554
sales@12fret.com
12fret.com

ENGLAND
Ampaholics
Authentic British Vintage
and Rare Guitar products
to inspire
Musicians and Collectors
Paul Goodhand-Tait
P.O. Box 542
Surrey, GU1 12F, England
Phone: +44-1483-825102
ampaholics@aol.com
ampaholics.org.uk

ITALY
Real Vintage
Nino Fazio
via Manzoni, 13
98057 Milazzo ME, Italy
Phone: +39-090-40646
realvintage@realvintage.it
realvintage.it

UNITED STATES
Arkansas
Blue Moon Music, Inc.
Les Haynie and Tim
Greene
3107 North College Ave.
Fayetteville, AR 72703-
2609
Phone: 479-521-8163
blumnmus@aol.com

California
Alva's Music
Dave Levine
1417 W. 8th St.
San Pedro, CA 90732
Phone: 800-403-3447
dave@alvas.com
alvasmusic.com

Buffalo Bros. Guitars
Bob Page
4901 El Camino Real
Carlsbad, CA 92008
Phone: 760-434-4567
Fax: 760-434-4347
bb_info@buffalobrosgui-
tars.com
buffalobrosguitars.com

Burst Brothers
Drew Berlin or Dave
Belzer
Mailing address:
13351-D Riverside Dr.
#502
Sherman Oaks, CA 91423
Phone: 310-325-4111
info@burstbrothers.com
burstbrothers.com

**California Vintage
Guitar and Amps**
5244 Van Nuys Blvd.
Sherman Oaks, CA 91401
Phone: 818-789-8884
sales@californiavintage-
guitarandamp.com
californiavintageguitaran-
damp.com

**Eric Schoenberg
Guitars**
Eric Schoenberg

106 Main Street
Tiburon, CA 94920
Phone: 415-789-0846
eric@om28. com
om28.com

Freedom Guitar, Inc.
Dewey L. Bowen
6334 El Cajon Boulevard
San Diego, CA 92115
Phone: 800-831-5569
Fax: 619-265-1414
info@freedomguitar.com
freedomguitar.com

Fretted Americana
23901 Calabasas Rd., Ste
2024
Calabasas, CA 91302
Phone: 818-222-4113
Fax: 818-222-6173
vgm@frettedamericana.
com
frettedamericana.com

**Gryphon Stringed
Instruments**
Richard Johnston
211 Lambert Ave.
Palo Alto, CA 94306
Phone: 650-493-2131
VintageInstruments@
gryphonstrings.com
gryphonstrings.com

Guitar Archeology
Mick and Kelly Flynn
13919 101st Pl NE
Kirkland, WA 98034
Phone: 20-999-6339
appraisals@guitararcheol-
ogy.com
guitararcheology.com

Guitar Center (CA)
7425 Sunset Boulevard
Hollywood, CA 90046
Phone: 323-874-2302
        323-874-1060
Fax: 323-969-9783
vintageguitars.net

Guitar Heaven (CA)
Frank Benna
1934 Oak Park Blvd.
Pleasant Hill, CA 94523-
4602
Phone: 925-938-5750
guitarheaven@sbcglobal.
net
guitarheaven.com

**Players Vintage
Instruments**
P.O. Box 445
Inverness, CA 94937-0445
Phone: 415-669-1107
Fax: 415-669-1102
info@vintageinstruments.
com
vintageinstruments.com

Sylvan Music
Al Markasky
1521 Mission St.
Santa Cruz, CA 95060
Phone: 831-427-1917
info@sylvanmusic.com
sylvanmusic.com

TrueTone Music
Ken Daniels
714 Santa Monica Blvd.
Santa Monica, CA 90401
Phone: 310-393-8232
        310-260-1415
sales@truetonemusic.com
truetonemusic.com

Virtual Vintage Guitars
Jason C. Allen
Phone: 949-635-9797
sales@virtualvintagegui-
tars.com
virtualvintageguitars.com

Colorado
**The Colorado Music
Exchange**
Ed Johnson
303 E. Pikes Peak Ave.
Colorado Springs, CO
80903
Phone: 719-578-0883
        866-578-0883
comusicexchange.com

Connecticut
AcousticMusic.Org
Brian Wolfe & Leonard
Wyeth
1238 Boston Post Rd
Guilford, CT 06437
Phone: 203-458-2525
brian@acousticmusic.org
acousticmusic.org

Florida
Andy's Guitars
Andy Eder
1208 North Monroe
Street
Tallahassee, FL 32303
Phone: 850-224-9944
Fax: 850-224-5381

info@andysguitars.com
andysguitars.com

Crescent City Music
Allen Glenn
111 North Summit Street
Crescent City, FL 32112
Phone/Fax: 386-698-2873
Phone: 386-698-2874
Cell: 386-559-0133
ccag@windstream.net
crescentcitymusic.biz

Jerry's Lefty Guitars
Jerry Welch
2401 Bern Creek Loop
Sarasota, FL 34240
Phone: 941-504-2634
jerry@jerrysleftyguitars.
com
jerrysleftyguitars.com

**Kummer's Vintage
Instruments**
Timm Kummer
Phone: 954-752-6063
prewar99@aol.com
kummersvintage.com

Legends Music, Inc.
Kent Sonenberg
Tampa, FL
Phone: 813-476-1396
ksonenbl@tampabay.
rr.com

Stevie B's
Joe Payne
30111 US Highway 19 N.
Clearwater, FL 33761
Phone: 727-785-9106
steviebs@verizon.net
steviebs.com

Georgia
**Atlanta Premier
Guitars**
Tommy Allen
875 Flat Shoals Road SE
#150
Conyers, GA 30094
Phone: 770-324-3031
atlpremierguitar@bell-
south.net
atlantapremierguitars.com

Atlanta Vintage Guitars
Greg Henderson
Phone: 707-324-3031
atlantavintage@bellsouth.
net
atlantavintageguitars.com

Blue Sky Guitars
Robbie Cantrell
730 E. Main
Canton, GA 30114
Phone: 404-556-8858
          770-479-9086
blueskyguitars@aol.com
blueskyguitars.com

Hawaii
Coconut Grove Music
Frank Kam
418 Kuulei Road, #105
Kailua, HI 96734
Phone: 808-262-9977
cgmusic@Hawaiiantel.biz
coconutgrovemusic.com

Illinois
Chicago Music Exchange
David Kalt
3316 N. Lincoln Ave.
Chicago, IL 60657
Phone: 773-525-7775
Fax: 773-477-2775
info@chicagomusicexchange.com
CME6.com

Guitar Works Ltd
Steve or Terry
709 Main Street
Evanston, IL 60202
Phone: 847-475-0855
Fax: 847-475-0715
guitarworksltd@aol.com
guitarworksltd.com

International Vintage Guitar
Collectors Association
Eddie Stambaugh
Springfield, IL
Phone: 217-787-7767
ivgca.com

Make 'n Music
Contact: Teddy
1455 W. Hubbard St.
Chicago, IL 60622
Phone: 312-455-1970
info@makenmusic.com
makenmusic.com

Music Gallery
Frank
2558 Greenbay Road
Highland Park, IL 60035
Phone: 847-432-6350 /
847-432-8883
MusicGlry@aol.com
musicgalleryinc.com

RWK Guitars
P.O. Box 1068
Highland Park, IL 60035
Phone: 847-432-4308

Bob@RWKGuitars.com
RWKGuitars.com

Third Coast Guitar
Chris Eudy
159 N. Racine Ave.
Chicago, IL 60607
Phone: 312-275-0095
thirdcoastguitar@ameri-tech.net
thirdcoastguitar.com

Indiana
Roadworthy Guitar and Amp
David Baas
Bloomington, IN
Phone: 812-824-1280
roadworthyguitars@gmail.com
roadworthyguitars.com

Kansas
Mass Street Music, Inc.
1347 Massachusetts St.
Lawrence, KS 66044-3431
Phone: 800-747-9980
sales@massstreetmusic.com
massstreetmusic.com
facebook.com/massstreet-music
twitter.com/massstreet-music

Kentucky
Guitar Emporium
1610 Bardstown Road
Louisville, KY 40205
Phone 502-459-4153
Fax: 502-454-3661
info@guitar-emporium.com
guitar-emporium.com

Maryland
Gypsyguitars.com
Jacques Mazzoleni
13113 Manor Rd.
Glen Arm, MD 21057
Phone: 410-817-9181
Fax: 410-817-9180
jacques@gypsyguitars.com
gypsyguitars.com

Nationwide Guitars, Inc.
Bruce Rickard
P.O. Box 2334
Columbia, MD 21045
Phone: 410-489-4074
nationwideguitars@comcast.net
nationwideguitars.com

Southworth Guitars
Gil Southworth
Phone/Fax: 703-759-4433
southworthguitar@aol.com
southworthguitars.com

Massachusetts
Bay State Vintage Guitars
Craig D. Jones
295 Huntington Avenue,
Room 304
Boston, MA 02115
Phone: 617-267-6077
baystateguitars@aol.com

Luthier's Co-op
Steven Baer
108 Cottage St.
Easthampton, MA 01027
Phone: 413-527-6627
info@luthiers-coop.com
luthiers-coop.com

Michigan
Elderly Instruments
Stan Werbin
1100 North Washington
P.O. Box 14210 -VGF
Lansing, MI 48901
Phone: 517-372-7890
Fax: 517-372-5155
elderly@elderly.com
elderly.com

Huber & Breese Music
33540 Groesbeck Highway
Fraser, MI 48026
Phone: 586-294-3950
Fax: 586-294-7616
info@huberbreese.com
huberbreese.com

Lakeshore Guitars
Rich Baranowski
Troy, MI
Phone: 248-879-7474
richbaronow@aol.com
lakeshoreguitars.com

Minnesota
EddieVegas.com
Ed Matthews
Duluth, MN
Phone: 218-879-3796
e.matthews@mchsi.com
eddievegas.com

Willie's American Guitars
254 Cleveland Avenue South
St. Paul, MN 55105
Phone: 651-699-1913
Fax: 651-690-1766
info@williesguitars.com
williesguitars.com

Missouri
Fly By Night Music
Dave Crocker
103 South Washington
Neosho, MO 64850-1816
Phone: 417-451-5110
Show number: 800-356-3347
crocker@joplin.com
texasguitarshows.com

Hazard Ware Inc./ Killer Vintage
Dave Hinson
P.O. Box 190561
St. Louis, MO 63119
Phone: 314-647-7795
          800-646-7795
Fax: 314-781-3240
killervintage.com

Nevada
AJ's Music In Las Vegas
Contact: Peter Trauth
2031 W. Sunset Rd.
Henderson, NV 89014-2120
Phone: 702-436-9300
Fax: 702-457-8764
ajsmusic@earthlink.net
ajsmusic.com

Cowtown Guitars
Jesse Amaroso
2797 South Maryland Parkway, Ste. 14
Las Vegas, NV 89109
Phone: 702-866-2600
Fax: 702-866-2520
cowtownguitars.com

New Hampshire
John Mann's Guitar Vault
Manchester, NH
Phone: 603-488-1912
sales@GuitarVaultUSA.com

Retro Music
Jeff Firestone
38 Washington Street
Keene, NH 03431
Phone/Fax: 603-357-9732
retromusic@myfairpoint.net
retroguitar.com

New Jersey
Kebo's Bassworks
Kevin 'KeBo' Borden and 'Dr. Ben' Sopranzetti
info@kebosbassworks.com
kebosbassworks.com

Lark Street Music
479 Cedar Lane

Teaneck, NJ 07666
Phone: 201-287-1959
Larkstreet@gmail.com
larkstreet.com

New Jersey Guitar & Bass Center
Jay Jacus
995 Amboy Avenue
Edison, NJ 08837
Phone: 732-225-4444
Fax: 732-225-4404
NJGtrBass@aol.com
newjerseyguitarandbass-center.com

Pick of the Ricks
Chris Clayton
121 Holly St.
Lindenwold, NJ 08021
Phone: 856-782-7300
sales@pickofthericks.com
pickofthericks.com

New Mexico
Rumble Seat Music "South West"
4011 Central Ave - Historic Rt. 66
Albuquerque, NM

New York
Babar's Vintage Guitars
Sam Mento
9 Mansion St.---
Coxsackie, NY 12051
Phone: 518-731-9014
          518-731-5499
crLme118@msn.com
babarsguitars.com

Bernunzio Uptown Music
John or Julie Bernunzio
122 East Ave.
Rochester, NY 14604
Phone: 585-473-6140
Fax: 585-442-1142
info@bernunzio.com
bernunzio.com

Imperial Guitar and Soundworks
Bill Imperial
99 Route 17K
Newburgh, NY 12550
Phone: 845-567-0111
igs55@aol.com
imperialguitar.com

Laurence Wexer Ltd.
Larry Wexer
251 East 32nd Street #11F
New York, NY 10016
Phone: 212-532-2994
lwexer@gmail.com
wexerguitars.com

Mandolin Brothers, Ltd.
629 Forest Avenue
Staten Island, NY 10310
Phone: 718-981-3226/8585
Fax: 718-816-4416
mandolin@mandoweb.com
mandoweb.com

Michael's Music
Michael Barnett
29 West Sunrise Highway
Freeport, NY 11520
Phone: 516-379-4111
Fax: 516-379-3058
michaelsmusic@optonline.net
michaelsmusic.com

Rivington Guitars
Howie Statland
73 E. 4th St.
New York, NY 10003
Phone: 212-505-5313
rivingtoninfo@gmail.com
rivingtonguitars.com

Rothman's Guitars
Ron Rothman
54180 Main Rd.
Southhold, NY 11971-0878
info@rothguitar.com
rothguitar.com

Rudy's Music
Rudy Pensa
169 West 48th Street
New York, NY 10036
Phone: 212-391-1699
info@rudysmusic.com
rudysmusic.com

Rumble Seat Music
Eliot Michael
121 West State St.
Ithaca, NY 14850
Phone: 607-277-9236
Fax: 607-277-4593
rumble@rumbleseatmusic.com
rumbleseatmusic.com

Sam Ash
Sammy Ash
Phone: 516-686-4104
sam.ash@samashmusic.com

Sam Ash
Mike Rock
Phone: 516-435-8653
mike.rock@samashmusic.com

We Buy Guitars
David Davidson
705A Bedford Ave.

Bellmore, NY 11710
Phone: 516-221-0563
Fax: 516-221-0856
webuyguitars1@aol.com
webuyguitars.net

We Buy Guitars
Richie Friedman
705A Bedford Ave.
Bellmore, NY 11710
Phone: 516-221-0563
Fax: 516-221-0856
webuyguitars@aol.com
webuyguitars.net

We Buy Guitars
Tom Dubas
705A Bedford Ave.
Bellmore, NY 11710
Phone: 516-221-0563
Fax: 516-221-0856
webuyguitars2@aol.com
webuyguitars.net

North Carolina
Bee-3 Vintage
Gary Burnette
PO Box 19509
Asheville, NC 28815
Phone: 828-298-2197
bee3vintage@hotmail.com
bee3vintage.com

Coleman Music
Chip Coleman
1021 S. Main St.
China Grove, NC 28023-2335
Phone: 704-857-5705
OR120@aol.com
colemanmusic.com

Legato Guitars
Bill Fender
8209-A 142 Market St.
Wilmington, NC 28411
Phone: 910-616-3458
By Appointment Only
legatoguitars@ec.rr.com
legatoguitars.com

Wilson's Vintage Guitars
Joe Wilson
5700 Ste. L W. Market St.
Greensboro, NC 27409
Phone: 336-314-7875
wvg1962@gmail.com
info@wilsonsvintageguitars.com
wilsonsvintageguitars.com

North Dakota
Nightlife Music
Rick or Jory Berge
1235 S. 12th St.

Bismarck, ND 58504
Phone: 701-222-0202
sales@nightlifemusic.com
nightlifemusic.com

Ohio
DHR Music
Dale Rabiner
9466 Montgomery Rd.
Cincinnati, OH 45242
Phone: 513-260-8260
      513-272-8004
dhrmusic@hotmail.com
dhrmusic.com

Fretware Guitars
Dave Hussong
400 South Main
Franklin, OH 45005
Phone: 937-743-1151
Fax: 937-743-9987
fretwaregtrs@yahoo.com
fretwareguitars.com

Gary's Classic Guitars
Gary Dick
Cincinnati, OH
Phone: 513-891-0555
Fax: 513-891-9444
garysclssc@aol.com
garysguitars.com

Mike's Music
Mike Reeder
2615 Vine Street
Cincinnati, OH 45219
Phone: 513-281-4900
Fax: 513-281-4968
mikesmusicohio.com

Oklahoma
Strings West
Larry Briggs
P.O. Box 999
20 E. Main Street
Sperry, OK 74073
Phone: 800-525-7273
Fax: 918-288-2888
larryb@stringswest.com
stringswest.com

Oregon
McKenzie River Music
Bob November
455 West 11th
Eugene, OR 97401
Phone: 541-343-9482
Fax: 541-465-9060
bob@mrmgtr.com
www.McKenzieRiverMusic.com

Pennsylvania
Guitar-Villa – Retro Music
Four miles from Martin Guitar factory - stop by
John Slog

216A Nazareth Pike
Bethlehem, PA 18020
Phone: 610-746-9200
qtown2@nni.com
www.guitar-villa.com

Guitar-Villa - Retro Music
John Slog
30 S. West End Blvd.
Quakertown, PA 18951
Phone: 215-536-5800
qtown2@nni.com
guitar-villa.com

Guitar Gallery
Vic DaPra
575 McClelland Rd.
Canonsbury, PA 15317
Phone: 724-746-9686
guitarg@verizon.net

Jim's Guitars, Inc.
Jim Singleton
2331 East Market St.
STE A
York, PA 17402
Tel: 866-787-2865
Fax: 410-744-0010
sunburst549@aol.com.
jimsguitars.com

Stevie B's Total Guitar
Stevie Burgess
890 Scalp Ave.
Johnstown, PA 15904
(inside Value-It Dept. Store)
Phone: 814-525-5132
totalgtr@aol.com
steviebs.com

West Chester Music
310 South High Street
West Chester, PA 19382
Phone: 610-436-8641
westchestermusic@hotmail.com
westchestermusicstore.com

York Music Shop
2331 East Market St.
STE A
York, PA 17402
Tel: 866-787-2865
Fax: 410-744-0010
jimsguitars@comcast.net
yorkmusicshop.com

Tennessee
Gruhn Guitars
George Gruhn
400 Broadway
Nashville, TN 37203
Phone: 615-256-2033
Fax: 615-255-2021
gruhn@gruhn.com

gruhn.com

Pickers Exchange (The)
Chris Stephens
4316 Ringgold Rd
East Ridge, TN 37412
(a suburb of Chatanooga)
Phone: 423*629*1661
pickersexchange@comcast.net
pickersexchange.com

Rick's Guitar Room
Rick Mikel
6415 Hixson Pike Ste B
Hixson, TN 37343
Phone: 423-842-9930
ricksguitarroom@bellsouth.net
ricksguitarroom.com

Texas
California World Guitar Shows
Larry Briggs
Phone: 800-525-7273
Fax: 918-288-2888
larryb@stringswest.com
texasguitarshows.com

Charley's Guitar Shop
Clay and Sheila Powers
2720 Royal Ln. Ste.100
Dallas, TX 75229-4727
Phone: 972-243-4187
Fax: 972-243-5193
shop@charleysguitar.com
charleysguitar.com

Chicago/Austin Guitar Show
Dave Crocker
Phone: 800-356-3347
Fax: 817-473-1089
crocker@joplin.com
texasguitarshows.com

Eugene's Guitars Plus
Eugene Robertson
2010 South Buckner Boulevard
Dallas, TX 75217-1823
Phone: 214-391-8677
pluspawnguitars@yahoo.com
texasguitarshows.com

Hill Country Guitars
Dwain Cornelius
110 Old Kyle Rd.
Wimberley, TX 78676-9701
Phone: 512-847-8677
Fax: 512-847-8699
info@hillcountryguitars.com
hillcountryguitars.com

Southpaw Guitars
Jimmy
5813 Bellaire Blvd.
Houston, TX 77081
Phone: 713-667-5791
Fax: 713-667-4091
info@southpawguitars.
com
www.southpawguitars.
com

Texas Amigos Guitar Shows
Arlington Guitar Show
(The 4 Amigos)
Contact: John or Ruth
Brinkmann
Phone: 800-473-6059
Fax: 817-473-1089
texasguitarshows.com

Van Hoose Vintage Instruments
Thomas Van Hoose
2722 Raintree Drive
Carrollton, TX 75006
Phone: (days) 972-250-2919 or (eves) 972-418-4863
Fax: 972-250-3644
tv0109@flash.net
vanhoosevintage.com

Waco Vintage Instruments
John Brinkman
1275 North Main Street,
Ste #4
Mansfield, TX 76063
Phone: 817-473-9144
Guitar Show Phone: 888-473-6059

Utah
Intermountain Guitar and Banjo
Leonard or Kennard
712 East 100 South
Salt Lake City, UT 84102
Phone: 801-322-4682
Fax: 801-355-4023
guitarandbanjo@earth-link.com
guitarandbanjo.com

Virginia
Action Music
7 miles south of Washington DC
Matt Baker
212-B N. West Street
Falls Church, VA 22046
Phone: 703-534-4801
action.music@comcast.
net
actionguitar.com

Callaham Guitars
Bill Callaham
217 Park Center Dr.
Winchester, VA 22603
Phone: 540-678-4043
Fax: 540-678-8779
callaham@callahamgui-tars.com
callahamguitars.com

Vintage Sound
Bill Holter
P.O. Box 11711
Alexandria, VA 22312
Phone: 703-914-2126
bhvsound@vintagesound.
com
vintagesound.com

Washington
Emerald City Guitars
Jay Boone
83 South Washington in
Pioneer Square
Seattle, WA 98104
Phone: 206-382-0231
jayboone@emeraldcity-guitar.com

Guitarville
Vallis Kolbeck
19258 15th Ave. North
East

Seattle, WA 98155-2315
Phone: 206-363-8188
Fax: 206-363-0478
sales@guitarville.com
guitarville.com

Mark's Guitar Shop
Nate Corning
918 W. Garland
Spokane, WA 99205
Phone: 866-219-8500
        509-325-8353
sales@marksguitarshop.
com
marksguitarshop.com

Wisconsin
Bizarre Guitars
Brian Goff
3601 Sunset Drive
Shorewood Hills, WI
53705
Phone: 608-235-3561
bdgoff@sbcglobal.net
bizarre-guitars.com

Cream City Music
Joe Gallenberger
12505 W. Bluemound Rd.
Brookfield, WI 53005-8026
Phone: 414-481-3430
joeg@warpdrivemusic.

com
warpdrivemusic.com

Dave's Guitar Shop
Dave Rogers
1227 South 3rd Street
La Crosse, WI 54601
Phone: 608-785-7704
Fax: 608-785-7703
davesgtr@aol.com
davesguitar.com

Gretschworld
Joe Gallenberger
12505 W. Bluemound Rd.
Brookfield, WI 53005-8026
Phone: 800-800-0087
joeg@warpdrivemusic.
com
gretschworld.com

Top Shelf Guitar Shop
2358 S. Kinnickinnic Ave.
Milwaukee, WI 53207
Phone: 414-481-8677
topshelfguitars@sbc-global.net
topshelfguitarshop.com

MANUFACTURER DIRECTORY

Aero Instrument Pickups
16 Years of manufacturing standard & cusom pickups. The best sound for the best value.
2798 Kaumana Dr.
Hilo, HI 96720
Phone: 808-969-6774
aeroinstrument.com

Alleva Coppolo Guitars
Jimmy Coppolo
1245 W. 9th St.
Upland, CA 91786
Phone: 909-981-9019
jimmy@allevacoppolo.cm
allevacoppolo.com

Analog Man Guitar Effects
Mike Piera
Route 6
Bethel, CT 06801
Phone: 203-778-6658
AnalogMike@aol.com
analogman.com

Callaham Guitars
Bill Callaham
217 Park Center Dr.
Winchester, VA 22603
Phone: 540-678-4043
Fax: 540-678-8779
callaham@callahamgui-tars.com
callahamguitars.com

Campbell American Guitars
Dean Campbell
PO Box 460
Westwood, MA 02090
Phone: 401-335-3101
Fax: 508-785-3577
sales@campbellamerican.com
campbellamerican.com

Carr Amplifiers
Steve Carr
433 West Salisbury St.
Pittsboro, NC 27312
Phone: 919-545-0747
Fax: 919-545-0739
info@carramps.com
carramps.com

Chandler Musical Instruments
Paul or Adrian
236A W. East Ave., Box 213
Chico, CA 95926-7236
Phone: 530-899-1503
info@chandlerguitars.
com
chandlerguitars.com
pickguards.us

Cimarron Guitars
John Walsh
Phone: 970-626-4464
cimgit@cimarronguitars.
com
cimarronguitars.com

Demeter Amplification
James Demeter
6990 Kingsbury Rd.
Templeton, CA 93465
Phone: 805-461-4100
Fax: 805-267-4079
sales@demeteramps.com
demeteramps.com

Duelin Guitars
Don Scheib
Phone: 818-288-3943
donscheib@yahoo.com
www.duelinguitars.com

Durham Electronics
Alan Durham
Austin, TX USA
Phone: 512-581-0663
sales@durhamelectronics.
com
durhamelectronics.com

Eric Schoenberg Guitars
Eric Schoenberg
106 Main Street
Tiburon, CA 94920
Phone: 415-789-0846
eric@om28.com
om28.com

Fuchs Audio Technology
Annette Fuchs
407 Getty Ave.
Clifton, NJ 07015

Phone: 973-772-4420
sales@fuchsaudio.com
fuchsaudio.com

Goodsell Electric Instrument Co., LLC
Richard Goodsell
781 Wheeler St. Studio 8
Atlanta, GA 30318
678-488-8176
richardgoodsell@bell-south.net
superseventeen.com

Graph Tech Guitar Labs
Product Lines: TUSQ,
TUSQ XL, Black TUSQ
XL, String Saver, Reso-Max, ghost, Nubone
James Markus
Phone: 800-388-7011 ext. 30
        604-940-5353 ext. 30
        604-940-4961
sales@graphtech.com
graphtech.com

Guitar Kits USA
Res-O-Glas Guitar Bodies & Fiberglass Guitar Kits
info@guitarkitsusa.com
guitarkitsusa.com

J. Backlund Designs
Bruce Bennett or Kevin Maxfield
100 Cherokee Blvd., Ste. 123
Chattanooga, TN 37405

Phone: 423-643-4999
423-316-4628
sales@jbacklund.com
jbacklund.com

Little Walter Tube Amps
Phil Bradbury
489 Mclendon Hills Dr.
West End, NC 27376
Phone: 910-315-2445
phil@littlewaltertube-amps.com

littlewaltertubeamps.com

Magnetic Components/Classic Tone Transformers
Schiller Park, IL
ClassicTone.net

Mercury Magnetics
Paul Patronette
Chatsworth, CA
Phone: 818-998-7791
Fax: 818-998-7835

paul@mercurymagnetics.com
mercurymagnetics.com

Strobel Guitars
Boca Raton, FL
Phone: 561-488-5698
strobelguitars.com

Trem King Fixed Bridge Vibrato
Fabulous Fixed Bridge Vibratos

Toll Free: 866-324-6300
info@tremking.com
tremking.com

Victoria Amplifiers
Mark Baier
Phone: 630-820-6400
sambisbee@sbcglobal.net
victoriaamp.com

TECH/REPAIR

CANADA
SD Custom Guitar Works
Atelier de Lutherie SD
6610 Blvd des-Galeries-D'Anjou (Ste. 102)
Montreal (Anjou), Quebec
Phone 514-543-3888
info@MontrealCustom-Guitars.com
MontrealCustomGuitars.com

UNITED STATES
California
A & D Music Incorporated
Since 1978
Rebecca Apodaca
Certified Appraisals & Restorations

22322 Colonna
Laguna Hills, CA 92653
Phone: 949-768-7110
admusic@cox.net
admusic.net

National Guitar Repair
Restoration of all fine resonator instruments,
Nationals & Dobros a speciality
Marc Schoenberger
Phone: 805-481-8532
805-471-5905
Luthier17@aol.com
nationalguitarrepair.com

Skip Simmons Amplifier Repair
Skip Simmons
8707 Robben Rd.
Dixon, CA 95620

707-678-5705
skip@skipsimmonsamps.com
skipsimmonsamps.com

Soest Guitar Shop
Steve Soest
760 North Main Street Suite D
Orange, CA 92868
Phone: 714-538-0272
Fax: 714-532-4763
soestguitar@earthlink.net

Iowa
AM Guitar Repair
Alan Morrison
2212 E. 12th St. Ste. 228
Davenport, IA 52803
Phone: 563-370-6810
amguitars@mchsi.com
amguitarrepair.com

guitarupgradesonline.com

New York
The Guitar Specialist, Inc.
Doug Proper
307 Route 22
Goldens Bridge, NY 10526
Phone: 914-401-9052
info@guitarspecialist.com
guitarspecialist.com

Ohio
Lay's Guitar Restoration
Since 1962
Dan Shinn
974 Kenmore Blvd.
Akron, OH 44314
Phone: 330-848-1392

Fax: 330-848-3727
laysguitar.com

Oklahoma
MandoAiki
Ed Cunliff
3433 Baird Dr.
Edmond, OK 73013
Phone: 405-341-2926
mandoaiki@yahoo.com
mandoaiki.com

Virginia
Fret Not Guitar Repair Inc.
Marguerite Pastella, owner
Newport News, VA 23608
Phone: 757-874-0086
guitarfixer@cox.net
fretnot.com

FOR DISPLAY OR DEALER DIRECTORY ADVERTISING INFO CONTACT JAMES AT ADSALES@VGUITAR.COM OR 1-800-1197.

INDEX

Bold Page numbers indicate first listing

3 Monkeys Amps	**364**
3rd Power	**364**
17th Street Guitars	**2**
65Amps	**364**
A Basses	**310**
A Fuller Sound	**2**
Abel	**2**
Abilene	**2**
Abyss	**2**
Ace-Tone	**364**
Effects	460
Acme	**2**
Banjos	560
Acoustic	**2**
Amps	364-365
Bass	310
Acoustyx	**460**
ADA	**365**
Effects	460
Aero Uke	**546**
Agile	**2**
Aguilar	**365**
Effects	460
Aiken Amplification	**465**
Aims	**2**
Amps	365
Bass	310
Airline	**2**
Amps	365
Bass	310
Mandolins	520
Lap/Steels	506
Akai	**460**
Alamo	**3**
Amps	365-366
Bass	310
Effects	460
Lap/Steels	506
Alamo Guitars	**3**
Alan Carruth	**3**
Albanus	**3**
Alberico, Fabrizio	**3**
Alden Amps	**366**
Alden Guitars	**3**
Alembic	**3**
Bass	310-311
Alesis	**366**
Effects	460
Alessandro	**366**
Alfieri Guitars	**3**
Alhambra	**3**
Alkire	**506**
Allen Amplification	**366**
Effects	460
Allen Guitars	**3**
Mandolins	520
Alleva-Coppolo	**3**
Bass	311
Aloha	**3**
Amps	366
Lap/Steels	506
Ukuleles	546
Alosa	**4**
Alpha	**4**
Alray	**4**
Altair Corp.	**460**
Alternative Guitar & Amp Co	**4**
Bass	310
AlumiSonic	**4**
Alvarez	**4**
Banjos	560
Bass	310
Lap/Steels	506
Mandolins	520
Alvarez Yairi	**4**
Alvarez, Juan	**4**
Amdek	**460**
American Acoustech	**4**

American Archtop	**4**
American Conservatory	**4**
Mandolins	520
American Showster	**5**
Bass	310
Ampeg	**5**
Amps	366-369
Bass	311-312
Effects	460-461
Amplifier Corp. of America	**461**
Amptweaker	**461**
amukaT Gadgets	**461**
Analog Man	**461**
Anderberg	**5**
Bass	312
Andersen	**5**
Mandolins	520
Anderson Amps	**369**
Andreas	**6**
Bass	312
Andrews	**370**
Andy Powers Instruments	**6**
Mandolins	520
Ukuleles	546
Angelica	**6**
Bass	312
Angus	**6**
Antares	**6**
Antique Acoustics	**6**
Antonio Hermosa	**6**
Antonio Lorca	**6**
Aphex Systems	**461**
Apitius	**520**
Apollo	**6**
Bass	312
Effects	461
Applause	**6**
Bass	312
Mandolins	520
Ukuleles	546
Applegate	**6**
APS Custom	**5**
Aracom Amplifiers	**370**
Arbiter	**461**
Arbor	**6**
Bass	312
Arch Kraft	**6**
Area 51	**370**
Effects	461
Aria Diamond	**6**
Aria/Aria Pro II	**7**
Amps	370
Bass	312
Effects	461-462
Lap/Steels	506
Mandolins	520
Ariatone	**370**
Arion	**462**
Aristides	**7**
Bass	312
Ark Amps	**370**
ARK - New Era Guitars	**7**
Armstrong, Rob	**7**
Bass	312
Mandolins	520
Arpeggio Korina	**7**
Art & Lutherie	**7**
Arteffect	**462**
Artesano	**7**
Artinger Custom Guitars	**7**
Bass	312
Artur Lang	**8**
Asama	**8**
Bass	312
Effects	462
Ashborn	**8**
Ashdown Amps	**370**
Asher	**8**

Lap/Steels	506
Ashland	**8**
Astro	**8**
Astrotone	**462**
Asturias	**8**
ATD	**462**
Atkin Guitars	**8**
Mandolins	520
Atlas	**8**
Atomic	**8**
Bass	312
Audio Guild	**370**
Audio Matrix	**462**
Audiovox	**8**
Amps	370
Bass	312
Lap/Steels	506
Audioworks	**462**
Auralux	**370**
Effects	462
Austin	**8**
Amps	370
Banjos	560
Bass	312
Mandolins	520
Ukuleles	546
Austin Hatchet	**8**
Bass	312
Austone Electronics	**462**
Automagic	**462**
Avalanche	**462**
Avalon	**8**
Avalon (Ireland)	**8**
Avante	**8**
Bass	312
Avanti	**8**
Avar	**9**
Axe	**462**
Aztec	**9**
b3 Guitars	**9**
B & M	**463**
Babicz	**9**
Bacino	**370**
Backline Engineering	**370**
Effects	463
Bacon	**557**
Bacon & Day	**9**
Banjos	560
Mandolins	521
Baden	**9**
Bad Cat	**370**
Effects	463
Baer	**370**
Baker U.S.A.	**9**
Baldwin	**9**
Amps	370
Banjos	560
Bass	312-313
Effects	463
Ballurio	**10**
Baltimore	**10**
Banzai	**463**
Baranik Guitars	**10**
Barclay	**10**
Bass	313
Barcus-Berry	**10**
Amps	371
Barratt	**560**
Barrington	**10**
Bass	313
Bartell of California	**10**
Barth	**11**
Amps	371
Bartolini	**11**
Effects	463
Bashkin Guitars	**11**
Basic Systems	**463**
Basone Guitars	**11**

Bass	313
Bass Collection	**313**
Basson	**371**
Bauer (George)	**11**
Mandolins	521
Baxendale & Baxendale	**11**
Bay State	**11**
Bazzolo Guitarworks	**11**
BBE	**463**
BC Audio	**371**
BC Kingston	**11**
BC Rich	**11-14**
Bass	313-314
Bear Creek Guitars	**14**
Ukuleles	546
Beardsell Guitars	**14**
Beaulieu	**14**
Beauregard	**14**
Bedell Guitars	**14**
Bedrock	**371**
Behringer	**15**
Amps	371
Effects	463
Beigel Sound Lab.	**463**
Bell Electrolabs	**463**
Beltona	**15**
Mandolins	521
Ukuleles	546
Bel-Tone	**506**
Beltone	**15**
Mandolins	521
Beltone (Import)	**15**
Amps	371
Bass	314
Benary and Sons	**560**
Benedetto	**15**
Benedetto (FMIC)	**15**
Benedict	**15**
Bass	314
Beneteau	**15**
Ukuleles	547
Bennett Music Labs	**15**
Effects	463
Bently	**16**
Berkowitz Guitars	**16**
Bass	314
Bernie Rico Jr.	**16**
Bass	314
Bertoncini	**16**
Mandolins	521
Ukuleles	547
Beyond The Trees	**16**
BigDog Amps	**371**
Big Lou Guitar	**16**
Big M	**371**
Big Tex Guitars	**16**
Bigsby	**16**
Effects	463
Mandolins	521
Lap/Steels	506
Bil Mitchell Guitars	**16**
Bilt Guitars	**16**
Binson	**463**
Birdsong Guitars	**16**
Bass	314
Bischoff Guitars	**16**
Bishline	**16**
Banjos	560
Bixonic	**463**
Black Cat Pedals	**463**
Black Jack	**16**
Bass	314
Blackbird	**16**
Ukuleles	547
Blackbox Music	**463**
Blackout Effectors	**463**
Blackshear, Tom	**17**
Blackstar Amplification	**371**

Bold Page numbers indicate first listing

Effects 464
Blackstone Appliances 464
Blade 17
Bass 314
Blanchard Guitars 17
Blankenship Amplification 371
Blindworm Guitars 17
Bass 314
Mandolins 521
Blount 17
Blue Star 17
Mandolins 521
Lap/Steels 506
Ukuleles 547
Blue Tone Amps 371
Bluebird 17
Blueridge 17
Bluesouth 17
Bluetron 371
Boaz Elkayam 17
Boedigheimer Instruments 17
Bogen 371
Bogner 371
Bohmann 17
Mandolins 521
Bolin 18
Bass 314
Bon, Mfg 464
Bolt 18
Bond 18
Boomerang 464
Borges Guitars 18
Boss 464-466
Boucher 560
Boulder Creek 18
Bass 314
Ukuleles 547
Bourgeois 18-19
Bown Guitars 19
Bozo 19
Bradford 19
Bass 314
Bradley 19
Brand X 371
Brandt 521
Brawley Basses 19
Bass 314
Brazen 19
Breedlove 19-20
Bass 314
Laps/Steels 506
Mandolins 521
Ukuleles 547
Brentwood 20
Brian May Guitar Company 20
Brian Moore 20-21
Bass 314
Mandolins 521
Brian Stone Guitars 21
Brice 314
Bridgecraft 314
Briggs 21
Broman 21
Bronson 21
Amps 371-372
Lap/Steels 506-507
Brook Guitars 21
Brown's Guitar Factory 21
Bass 315
Browntone Electronics 466
Bruné, R. E. 21
Bruno (Tony) 372
Bruno and Sons 21
Banjos 560-561
Effects 466
Mandolins 521-522
Ukuleles 547
BSX Bass 315
Buckbee 561
Budda 32
Effects 466
Buddy Blaze 21
Build Your Own Clone 466
Bunker 21
Bass 315
Burly Guitars 21
Burns 21-22
Bass 315
Burnside 22
Burns-Weill 22
Bass 315
Burny 22
Burrell 22
Bass 315
Burriss 372
Effects 466
Burrell 22
Burton Guitars 22
Buscarino Guitars 22
Byers Amplifiers 372
Byers, Gregory 23
Byrd 23
C. Fox 23
CA (Composite Acoustics) 23
Cage 372
Calace 522
Califone 23
California 372
Callaham 23
Amps 372
Camelli 23
Cameo 23
Bass 315
Campbell American 23
Campbell Sound 372
Campellone 23
Bass 315
Canvas 23
Bass 315
Carbonaro 23
Carl Martin 372
Effects 466
Carl Fischer 23
Carlos 23
Carlsbro 372
Effects 466
Carol-Ann Custom Amps 372
Carr Amplifiers 372
Carrotron 466
Carvin 23-24
Amps 372
Bass 315
Effects 466
Lap/Steels 507
Mandolins 522
Casa Montalvo 24
Casio 24
Casper Guitar Technologies 24
Bass 315
Castle Instruments 466
Caswell Amplification 372
Catalinbread 466
Cat's Eye 466
Cat's Eyes 24
Cause & Effect Pedals 466
Celmo 466
Champion 24
Chandler 24
Bass 315
Effects 466
Lap/Steels 507
Chantus 24
Ukuleles 547
Chapin 24
Chapman 24
Effects 466-467
Char 24
Ukuleles 547
Charis Acoustic 24
Charles Fox Guitars 25
Charles Shifflett 25
Banjos 561
Bass 315
Charvel 25-27
Bass 315-316
Chicago Blues Box 372
Chicago Iron 467
Chiquita 27
Chris George 27
Christopher Carrington 24
Chrysalis Guitars 27
Chunk Systems 467
Cimar/Cimar by Ibanez 27
Cimarron 27
Cipher 27
Bass 316
Citron 27
Bass 316
Clark 467
Clark Amplification 372
Effects 467
Clevinger 316
Clifford 27
Mandolins 522
ClinchFX 467
Clovis 28
Club Amplifiers 372
CMI 372
CMI Electronics 372
CMW Amps 372
Coffin 467
Cole 28
Banjos 561
Coleman Guitars 28
College Line 316
Collings 28-29
Mandolins 522
Ukuleles 547
Colorsound 467
Columbia 29
Comins 29
Amps 372
Mandolins 522
Commander 29
Companion 468
Concertone 29
Conklin 30
Bass 316
Conn 30
Effects 468
Connor, Stephan 30
Conrad 30
Bass 316
Mandolins 522
Contessa 30
Bass 316
Contreras *See Manuel Contreras*
Coopersonic 468
Coppock 507
Coral 30
Amps 372
Bass 316
Córdoba 30
Cordova 31
Corey James 31
Bass 316
Coriani, Paolo 31
Cornell/Plexi 372
Coron 468
Cort 31
Bass 316
CP Thornton Guitars 31
Basses 316
Cosmosound 372
Effects 468
Crafter 31
Amps 373
Bass 316
Mandolins 522
Crafters of Tennessee 31
See Tennessee
Cranium 31
Crate 373
Crazy Tube Circuits 468
Creation Audio Labs 468
Crescent Moon 31
Creston 31
Bass 316
Crestwood 31
Bass 316-317
Mandolins 522
Crimson Guitars 31
Bass 317
Cromwell 31
Lap/Steels 507
Mandolins 522
Cromwell (Guild) 31
Crook Custom Guitars 31
Bass 31
Crossley 31
Crown 32
Bass 317
Crowther Audio 468
Crucianelli 32
Cruise Audio 373
Cruzer 32
Amps 373
Bass 317
Crybaby 468
CSL 468
CSR 21
Bass 317
Cumpiano 21
Bass 317
Curbow String Instruments 32
Bass 317
Cusack Music 468
Custom 32
Bass 317
Custom Kraft 32
Amps 373
Bass 317
D.J. Hodson 32
Daddy Mojo String Instr. 32
D'Agostino 32
Bass 317
Daily Guitars 32
Daion 32
Bass 317
Daisy Rock 33
Bass 317
Dallas Arbiter 468
Damage Control 468
D'Ambrosio 33
Dan Armstrong 33
Effects 468-469
Dan Kellaway 33
Mandolins 522
Da Vinci 373
Danelectro 33-35
Amps 373-374
Bass 317-318
Effects 469
Lap/Steels 507
D'Angelico 34-36
Mandolins 522-523
D'Angelico (Lewis) 36
D'Angelico Guitars of America 36
D'Angelico II 36
Daniel Friederich 36
D'Aquisto 36
Mandolins 523
D'Aquisto (Aria) 37
Dauphin 37
Dave King Acoustics 37
Dave Maize Guitars 37
Bass 318
David J. King 318
David Rubio 37
David Thomas McNaught 37
Davis, J. Thomas 37
Davoli *See Wandre*
Effects 469
DBZ 37
DDyna Music 469
de Jonge, Sergei 37
De Paule 37
Dean 37-39
Amps 374
Bass 318
Mandolins 523
Dean Markley 39
Amps 374
Bass 318
Effects 469
DeArmond 39
Amps 374-375
Bass 318
Effects 469
Dearstone 39
Mandolins 523
Death By Audio 469
Decar 39
DeCava Guitars 39
Banjos 561
Mandolins 523
Ukuleles 547
Decca 39

Bold Page numbers indicate first listing

  - Amps 375
  - Bass 318
- Deckly 507
- Deering 561
- Defil 39
- DeGennaro 39
  - Bass 318
  - Mandolins 523
- Del Pilar Guitars 39
- Del Vecchio Dinamico 39
  - Ukuleles 547
- Delaney 39
  - Bass 318
- Delgado 39
  - Banjos 561
  - Bass 318
  - Mandolins 523
  - Ukuleles 547
- Delirium Custom Guitars 40
- Dell' Arte 40
- Delta Guitars 40
- DeltaLab Research 470
- DeLucia, Vincenzo 523
- Demeter 375
  - Effects 470
- Denio 470
- Denley 507
- Dennis Hill Guitars 40
  - Mandolins 523
- Desmond Guitars 40
- DeTemple 40
  - Bass 318
- Devi Ever : Fx 470
- DeVoe Guitars 40
- Diamond 40
- Diamond Pedals 470
- Diaz 375
  - Effects 470
- Dick, Edward Victor 40
- Dickerson 40
  - Amps 375
  - Lap/Steels 507
- DigiTech 470-471
- Dillion 40
  - Bass 318
- Dillon 40
  - Bass 318
- Dime Amplification 375
- DiMarzio 471
- Dingwall 318
- Dino's Guitars 40
  - Effects 471
- Dinosaur 375
  - Effects 471
- DiPinto 40
  - Bass 318
- Ditson 40-41
  - Banjos 561
  - Mandolins 523
  - Ukuleles 547
- Divided By Thirteen 375
  - Effects 471
- Dixie 557
- D'Leco Guitars 41
- DM Darling Guitars 41
- DNA Analogic 471
- Dobro 41-43
  - Lap/Steels 507
  - Mandolins 523
  - Ukuleles 547-548
- Dobson, George 561
- DOD 471-473
- Dodge 43
  - Bass 319
- Doitsch 43
- Domino 43-44
  - Bass 319
- Dommenget 44
- Don Musser Guitars 44
- Doolin Guitars 44
- Dorado 44
  - Bass 319
- Douglas Ching 44
  - Ukuleles 548
- D'Pergo Custom 44
- Dr. Z Amps 375
- Dragge Guitars 44
- Dragonfly Guitars 44
  - Bass 319
- Dredge-Tone 473
- Drive 44
  - Amps 375
- DST Engineering 375
  - Effects 473
- DTM 44
- Duca Tone 375
- Dudenbostel 523
- Duelin Guitars 44
- Duesenberg 44
  - Bass 319
- Duff 523
- Dumble 375
- Dunlop 473
- Dunwell Guitars 44
- Dupont 44
- Durham Electronics 473
- Dwight 44
  - Lap/Steels 507
- Dyer 44-45
  - Mandolins 523
- Dynacord 45
  - Bass 319
  - Effects 473
- Dynamic Amps 375
- Dynelectron 45
  - Bass 319
- Dyno/Dytronics 473
- E L Welker 45
- Earnest Kaai 548
- Earth Sound Research 375-376
- EarthQuaker Devices 473
- Earthwood 45
  - Bass 319
- Eastman 45
  - Mandolins 523
- Eastwood 45
  - Bass 319
  - Mandolins 523
- Eaton, William 45
- EBow *See Heet Sound*
- E.W.S. 473
- EBS 376
  - Effects 473
- Ecco Fonic 473
- Echoplex 473-474
- Ed Claxton Guitars 45
- Eden 376
- Eden Analog 474
- Eduardo Duran Ferrer 45
- Edward Klein 45
- EER Custom 45
- Effector 13 474
- Effectrode 474
- EFX 474
- Egmond 45
- Egnater 376
- Ehlers 45-46
- Eichelbaum Guitars 46
- EKO 46-47
  - Amps 376
  - Bass 319
  - Effects 474
  - Mandolins 523-524
- El Degas 47
- Eleca 47
  - Amps 376
  - Effects 474
  - Mandolins 524
- Electar *See Epiphone*
  - Amps 376
- Electra 47-48
  - Bass 319
  - Effects 474
- Electric Gypsy *See Teye*
- Electro 48
  - Lap/Steels 507
- Electro-Harmonix 376
  - Effects 474-477
- Electromuse 48
  - Amps 376
  - Lap/Steels 507-508
- Electrosonic Amplifiers 376
  - Effects 477
- Elferink 48
- Elite 48
- Elk 48
  - Amps 376
  - Effects 477
- Elka 477
- Elliott Guitars 48
- Ellis 48
  - Lap/Steels 508
- Elli-Sound 48
- Ellsberry Archtop Guitars 48
- Elmwood Amps 376
- Elpico 376
- Emery Sound 377
- EMMA Electronic 477
- Emmons 377
  - Lap/Steels 508
- Emperador 48
  - Bass 319
- Empress Effects 477
- Empire 48
- EMS 477
- Encore 48
  - Bass 320
- Engel Guitars 48
- Engelhardt 320
- English Electronics 48
  - Lap/Steels 508
- Eowave 477
- Epi 48
- Epiphone 48-59
  - Amps 377-378
  - Banjos 561
  - Bass 320
  - Effects 477
  - Lap/Steels 508
  - Mandolins 524
  - Ukuleles 548
- Epoch 59
- Equator Instruments 59
- Erlewine 59
- Ernie Ball 477
- ESP 59-60
  - Bass 320
- Espana 60
- Esquire 524
- Essex (SX) 60
  - Bass 320
- Este 60
- Esteban 60
  - Amps 378
- EtaVonni 60
- Euphonon 60
  - Mandolins 524
- Euthymia Electronics 477
- Evans Custom Amplifiers 378
- Eventide 477
- Everett Guitars 61
  - Mandolins 524
- Evergreen Mountain 61
  - Bass 321
  - Mandolins 524
- Everly Guitars 61
- EVH 61
  - Amps 378
- Evil Robot 378
- Excelsior 61
  - Amps 378
- Exlusive 61
  - Bass 321
- EXR 477
- F.S. Clipper 478
- Fairbanks 524
  - Banjo 561-562
- Fairbuilt Guitar Co. 61
  - Mandolins 524
- Falk 61
  - Mandolins 524
- Fano 61
  - Bass 321
- Farfisa 477-478
- Fargen 378
  - Effects 478
- Farland 562
- Farnell 61
  - Bass 321
- Fat Cat Custom Guitars 61
  - Bass 321
- Favilla 61
  - Ukuleles 548
- Fender
  - Guitars 61-89
    - *Strats* *70-81*
    - *Teles* *82-88*
  - Amps 378-388
  - Banjos 562
  - Bass 321-328
    - *Jazz Bass* *322-324*
    - *Precision* *325-328*
  - Effects 478
  - Lap/Steels 508-509
  - Mandolins 524
  - Ukuleles 548
- Fenton-Weill *See Burns-Weill*
- Fernandes 89
  - Bass 328
- Fina 89
  - Bass 329
- Finck, David 89
- Fin-der 548
- Fine Resophonic 89
  - Mandolins 524
  - Ukuleles 548
- FireBelly Amps 388
- First Act 89
  - Bass 329
- Firth Pond & Co. 89
- Fishman 388
  - Effects 478
- FJA Mods 388
  - Effects 478
- Flamingo 548
- Flammang Guitars 89
- Flatiron 524-525
- Flaxwood 89
- Fleishman 89
  - Bass 329
- Fletcher Brock 89
  - Mandolins 525
- FlexiSound 478
- Flip 478
- Flot-A-Tone 389
- Flowers Guitars 89
- Floyd Rose 89
- FM Acoustics 479
- Fodera 329
- Foggy Mountain 89
- Fontanilla 89
- Fortune 389
- Fouilleul 90
- Fox or Rocking F 90
- Fox Amps 389
- Foxx 90
  - Effects 479
- Frame Works 90
- Framptone 479
- Framus 90-91
  - Amps 389
  - Banjos 562
  - Bass 329
  - Lap/Steels 509
  - Mandolins 525
- Frantone 479
- Fraulini 91
- Fred 389
- FreeNote 91
- Frenzel 389
- Fresher 91
  - Bass 329
- Freshwater 525
- Fret-King 91
  - Bass 329
- Fritz Brothers 91
  - Bass 329
- Froggy Bottom 91
- Frudua Guitar Works 91
  - Amps 389
  - Bass 329
- Fryette 389
- Fuchs Audio 389
- Fukuoka Instruments 91
- Fulltone 479
- Fulton-Webb 389
- Furch *see Stonebridge*
- Furman Sound 479

Bold Page numbers indicate first listing

Furnace Mountain 91
Fury 91
Bass 329
Futurama 91
Fxdoctor 479
Fxengineering 479
Fylde Guitars 91
Bass 330
Mandolins 525-526
G2D 480
G & L 92-94
Bass 330-331
G.L. Stiles 94
Bass 331
Lap/Steels 509
Mandolins 526
Gabriel Sound Garage 389
Gabriel's Guitar Workshop 94
Gadotti Guitars 95
Gadow Guitars 95
Bass 331
Gagnon 95
Galanti 95
Galiano 95
Mandolins 526
Gallagher 95
Gallagher, Kevin 95
Gallien Krueger 389
Gallotone 95
Galloup Guitars 95
Galveston 95
Bass 331
Mandolins 526
Gamble & O'Toole 96
Ganz Guitars 96
Garage by Wicked 331
Garcia (guitars) 96
Garcia (amps) 389
Effects 480
Garnet 389
Garrison 96
Gary Kramer 96
Gauge Guitars 96
Gaylord 526
GDS Amplification 389
Geek MacDaddy *See Original Geek*
Gemelli 96
Gemunder 96
Genesis 389-390
Genz Benz 390
George *see Chris George*
George Dennis 390
Effects 480
Gerhart 390
German Guitars 96
Germino 390
Giannini 96
Mandolins 526
Gibson
Guitars 96-143
ESs *101-107*
Les Pauls *120-132*
SGs *135-139*
Amps 390-395
Banjos 562-564
Bass 331-334
Effects 480
Lap/Steels 509-510
Mandolins 526-529
Ukuleles 548-549
Banjo Ukuleles 557
Giffin 143
Gig-FX 480
Gigliotti 143
Gila Eban Guitars 143
Gilbert Guitars 143
Gilchrist 529
Gilet Guitars 143
Lap/Steels 510
Ginelle 395
Girl Brand Guitars 143
Gitane 143
Gittler 143-144
Giulietti 395
Givens 529-530
Gizmoaudio 480
Glendale 144
GLF 144
Glick Guitars 144
Global 144
GMP 144
Bass 334
GMW 144
Gnome Amplifiers 395
Effects 480
Godbout 480
Godin 144-145
Bass 334
Mandolins 530
Godlyke 334
Gold Tone 145
Banjos 564
Bass 334
Lap/Steels 510
Mandolins 530
Ukuleles 549
Goldbug Guitars 145
Golden Hawaiian 145
Goldentone 145
Goldon 145
Gomez Amplification 395
Goodall 145
Goodman Guitars 145
Mandolins 530
Goodrich Sound 480
Goodsell 395
Gordon-Smith 145
Gorilla 395
Gourley *See Dickerson*
Gower 145-146
Goya 146
Amps 395
Bass 334
Mandolins 530
Graf *see Oskar Graf*
Grammer 146
Grammatico Amps 395
Granada 146
Bass 334
Granata Guitars 146
Graveel 146
Graziano 146
Ukuleles 549
Grazioso 146
GRD 146
Great Divide Guitars 146
Greco 146-147
Bass 334
Green 395
Green, Aaron 147
Greene & Campbell 147
Greene, Jeffrey 147
Greenfield Guitars 147
Greer Amplification 395
Effects 480
Gregory 395
Gretsch 147-155
Amps 395-397
Banjos 564
Bass 334-335
Effects 480
Lap/Steels 510
Mandolins 530
Ukuleles 549
Greven 155
Gries 397
Griffin Instruments 155
Grimes Guitars 155
Grinnell 155
Groehsl 155
Groove Tools 155
Bass 335
Groove Tubes 397
Grosh, Don 155
Bass 335
Gruen Acoustic Guitars 155
Gruggett 155
GTR 530
Banjos 564
Guernsey Guitars 156
Guild 156-165
Amps 397-398
Bass 335-336
Effects 480-481
Ukuleles 549
Guillermo Roberto 165
Guitar Company of America 165
Mandolins 530
Guitar Mill 166
Bass 336
Gurian 166
Guyatone 166
Amps 398
Bass 336
Effects 481
Lap/Steels 510
Guytron 398
GW Basses & Luthiery 336
Hagenlocher, Henner 166
Hagstrom 166-167
Amps 398
Bass 336
Hahn 167
Haight 167
Mandolins 530
Halfling Guitars & Basses 167
Bass 336
Hallmark 167
Bass 336
Hamblin Guitars 167
Hamer 167-170
Bass 336-337
Hanburt 398
Lap/Steels 511
Hanson 170
HAO 481
Harden Engineering 170
Effects 481
Harlin Brothers 511
Harmony 170-172
Amps 398
Banjos 564
Bass 337
Lap/Steels 511
Mandolins 530
Ukuleles 549-550
Harptone 172
Harrison Guitars 173
Harry Joyce 398
Hartke 337
Amps 398
Harwood 173
Hascal Haile 173
Hauver Guitar 173
Hayes Guitars 173
Hayman 173
Bass 337
Haynes 173
Haynes (ACA) 398-399
Headstrong 399
Heartfield 173
Bass 337
Heathkit 481
Heavy Metal Products 481
Heet Sound 481
Heiden 173
Mandolins 530
Heil Sound 481
Heit Deluxe 173
Bass 337
Hembry Guitars 173
Bass 337
Hemken, Michael 173
HenBev 173
Bass 337
Henman Guitars 173
Bass 337
Henriksen JazzAmp 399
Heritage 173-175
Bass 337
Mandolins 530
Heritage Amps 399
Hermann Hauser 175
Hermann Hauser II 175
Hermann Hauser III 175
Hermida Audio 481
Hess 175
Hewett Guitars 175
High Gain *See Dunlop*
Hilgen 399
Hill Guitar Company 175
Hilo 511
Hilo Bay Ukuleles 550
Hirade Classical 175
HiWatt 399-400
HML Guitars 175
Hoagland 400
Hoffman (Amps) 400
Hoffman Guitars 176
Hoffmann 400
Hofner 176-17
Bass 337-338
Mandolins 530-531
Hohner 177-178
Amps 400
Banjos 564
Bass 338
Effects 481
Mandolins 531
Ukuleles 550
Holiday 178
Holland 400
Hollenbeck Guitars 178
Hollingsworth Guitars 178
Lap/Steels 510
Holman 178
Holmes 400
Holst 178
Mandolins 531
HomeBrew Electronics 481
Hondo 178-179
Amps 400
Banjos 564
Bass 338
Mandolins 531
Hopf 179
Bass 338
Mandolins 531
Hopkins 179
Horabe 179
Hottie 179
Amps 400
Hound Dog 400
House Guitars 179
Howard 564
Howe-Orme 179
Mandolins 531
Hoyer 179
Bass 338
Huber 564
Huerga 179
Hughes & Kettner 400
Effects 482
Humming Bird 179
Humphrey, Thomas 180
Hurricane 400
Huss and Dalton 180
Hutchins 180
Bass 338
Hy Lo 401
Ian A. Guitars 180
Ian Anderson Guitars 180
Ianuario Mandolins 531
banjos 564
Ibanez 180-187
Amps 401
Banjos 565
Bass 338-339
Effects 482-485
Mandolins 531
Ibanez, Salvador 187
Idol 401
Ignacio Fleta 187
Ignacio Rozas 187
Ilitch Electronics 485
Illusion Guitars 187
Impact 401
Imperial 187
Amps 401
Bass 339
Mandolins 531
Imperal (Japan) 187
Indy Guitarist *See Wampler Pedals*
Infeld 187
Bass 339
Infinox 187
Interdonati 187
Intersound 485

Bold Page numbers indicate first listing

Italia 187
   Bass.................................... 339
J. Backlund Design..................... 187
   Bass.................................... 339
J Burda Guitars 187
J. Everman 485
J. Frog Guitars 187
J.B. Player 187
   Banjos 565
   Bass.................................... 339
   Mandolins 531
J.L. Smith 531
J.R. Zeidler 187
   Mandolins 531
J.S. Bogdanovich 187
J.T. Hargreaves 187
   Bass.................................... 339
Jack Daniel's 188
   Amps 401
   Bass.................................... 340
Jack Deville Electronics 485
Jackson 188-189
   Amps 401
   Bass.................................... 340
Jackson Ampworks 401
Jackson-Guldan 189
   Amps 401
   Lap/Steels 511
Jacobacci 190
Jacques 485
Jamboree 190
James Einolf Guitars 190
James R. Baker 190
James Trussart 190
   Bass.................................... 340
James Tyler 190
   Bass.................................... 340
JangleBox 485
Jan-Mar Industries 485
Janofsky Guitars 190
Jaros 190
Jasmine 190
Jason Z. Schroeder Guitars....... 190
Jax 485
Jay Turser 190
   Amps 401
   Bass.................................... 340
JCA Circuits 401
JD Bluesville 190
Jeff Traugott 190
Jennings.................................. 401
Jeremy Locke Guitars 190
Jeronimo Pena Fernandez 190
Jerry Jones 190-191
   Bass.................................... 340
Jersey Girl 191
   Effects 485
JET 191
Jet City Amplification 401
Jet Sounds LTD 485
Jetter Gear 485
Jewel 191
JG Guitars 191
JHD Audio 485
Jim Dyson 191
   Bass.................................... 340
   Lap Steel 511
Jim Kelly 401
Jim Redgate Guitars 191
Jimi Hendrix .... See Dunlop
JMI (Jennings).......................... 401
John Hornby Skewes & Co........ 485
John Le Voi Guitars 191
   Mandolins 531
John Page Guitars 191
John Price Guitars 191
John Wesley 565
Johnson 191
   Amps 401
   Bass.................................... 340
   Effects 485
   Mandolins 531-532
   Ukuleles 550
Johnson Amplification 401
   Effects 485
JoMama 401
Jon Kammerer 191

Bass.................................... 340
Jones .... See TV Jones
Jordan 191
Jordan (Sho-Bud)............... 485-486
Jose Oribe 191
Jose Ramirez .... See Ramirez, Jose
Juke 401
Juzek 340
JY Jeffrey Yong Guitars.............. 191
   Bass.................................... 340
K & F .... See Fender
K & S 191
   Mandolins 532
   Ukuleles 550
Kafel 401
Kakos, Stephen 191
Kala 550
Kalamazoo 191-192
   Amps 401-402
   Banjos 565
   Bass.................................... 340
   Lap/Steels 511
   Mandolins 532
Kamaka 550
Kamico 192
   Lap/Steels 511
Kanile'a Ukulele....................... 550
Kapa 192
   Bass.................................... 341
Karol 192
Kasha 192
Kathy Wingert Guitars 192
Kawai 192
   Bass.................................... 341
Kay 193-195
   Amps 402
   Banjos 565
   Bass.................................... 341
   Effects 486
   Lap/Steels 511
   Mandolins 532
   Ukuleles 550
Kay Kraft 195
   Mandolins 532
KB 195
   Bass.................................... 341
   Mandolins 532
Keeley 486
Kel Kroyden 195
   Bass.................................... 565
   Mandolins 532
Kelemen 402
Keller Custom Guitars 195
Keller Guitars 195
Kelly Guitars 195
Ken Smith .... See Smith
Ken Franklin 195
Kendrick 195
   Amps 402
   Effects 486
Kent 195-196
   Amps 402
   Bass.................................... 341
   Effects 486
   Mandolins 532
   Ukuleles 550
Kentucky 532-533
Kern Engineering 486
Kevin Ryan Guitars 196
Keystone State 565
Kiesel .... See Carvin
   Lap/Steels 511
Kimberly 196
   Bass.................................... 341
Kimble.................................... 533
Kinal 196
   Bass.................................... 341
King Amplification 402
Kingsley 196
   Amps 403
Kingslight Guitars 196
   Bass.................................... 341
Kingston 196
   Amps 403
   Bass.................................... 341
   Mandolins 533
Kinscherff Guitars 196

Kitchen-Marshall 403
Kleartone 196
KJL 403
Klein Acoustic Guitars 196
   Bass.................................... 341
Klein Electric Guitars 196
   Bass.................................... 341
K-Line Guitars 196
   Bass.................................... 342
Klira 196
   Bass.................................... 342
Klon 486
KMD (Kaman) 403
   Effects 486
Knox 196
Knutsen 196-197
   Mandolins 533
   Ukuleles 550-551
Knutson Luthiery 197
   Bass.................................... 342
   Lap/Steels 511
   Mandolins 533
Koch 403
Kohno 197
Koll 197
   Bass.................................... 342
Komet 403
Kona 197
   Amps 403
   Banjos 565
   Bass.................................... 342
   Mandolins 533
Kona Guitar Company................ 197
Koontz 197
Kopp String Instruments 197
Kopy Kat 197
Korg 486
KR Musical Products 486
Kragenbrink 197
Kramer............................ 197-200
   Bass..............................342-343
Kramer-Harrison, Wm 201
Krank 403
   Effects 486
KSD 343
KSM 201
Kubicki 201
   Bass.................................... 343
Kumalae 551
Kustom 201
   Amps 403-406
   Bass.................................... 343
Kwasnycia Guitars 201
Kyle, Doug 201
L Benito 201
La Baye 201
   Bass.................................... 343
La Mancha 201
La Patrie 201
La Scala 201
   Mandolins 533
Lab Series 406
Laboga 406
Lace Music Products 201
   Amps 406
Lacey Guitars 201
Lado 201
   Bass.................................... 343
Lafayette 201
   Amps 407
   Bass.................................... 344
Laguna 201
Lakeside 201
   Mandolins 533
Lakewood 202
   Mandolins 533
Lakland 344
Landry.................................... 407
Laney 407
   Effects 486-487
Langdon Guitars 202
Lange 565
Langejans Guitars.................... 202
Lanikai 551
Lapdancer 511
Larrivee 202-203
   Bass.................................... 344

Ukuleles 551
Larson Brothers 203
   Mandolins 533
Laskin 203
Laurie Williams Guitars 203
   Mandolins 533
Le Domino 551
   Banjo Ukuleles 557
Leach Guitars 203
   Bass.................................... 344
Lectrolab 407
Leedy 565
Legend 407
Lehle 487
Lehmann Stringed Instrs........... 203
Lehtela 203
   Bass.................................... 344
Lentz 203
Leonardo Nunes 551
Les Stansell Guitars 203
Leslie 407
Levin 203
   Mandolins 533
   Ukuleles 551
Levy-Page Special 203
Lewis 203
   Mandolins 533
Linc Luthier 203
   Bass.................................... 344
Lindberg 203
Lindert 204
Line 6 204
   Amps 407
   Effects 487
Lion 204
Lipe Guitars USA 204
   Bass.................................... 344
Liscombe 204
Little Lanilei 407
   Effects 487
Little Walter 407
Lizard Leg Effects 487
Loar 204
Loar (The) 533
Lock & Rock 487
Lockola 511
Loco Box 487
Lollar 204
London City 408
Lopez, Abel Garcia 204
Loprinzi 204
   Ukuleles 551
Lord 204
Lotus 204
   Bass.................................... 344
   Mandolins 533
Louis Electric........................... 408
Louis Panormo 204
Lovepedal 487
Lovetone 487
Lowden 204
Lowrider Basses 344
LSL Instruments 204
LSR Headless 204
   Bass.................................... 344
LTD 204
   Bass.................................... 344
Lucas Custom Instruments 204
Lucas, A. J. 204
Ludwig 487
   Banjos 565
   Banjo Ukuleles 557
Luis Feu de Mesquita 205
Luna Guitars............................ 205
   Amps 408
   Bass.................................... 344
   Ukuleles 551
Luscomb 566
Lyle 205
   Bass.................................... 344
   Mandolins 533-534
Lyon & Healy 205
   Mandolins 533
   Ukuleles 551-552
   Banjo Ukuleles 557
Lyon by Washburn 205
   Bass.................................... 344